Religion, Hateful Expression and Violence

Morten Bergsmo and Kishan Manocha
(editors)

2023
Torkel Opsahl Academic EPublisher
Brussels

Editors of this volume:

Morten Bergsmo is the Director of the Centre for International Law Research and Policy (CILRAP). **Kishan Manocha** is Head, Tolerance and Non-Discrimination Department, Office for Democratic Institutions and Human Rights, Organization for Security and Co-operation in Europe.

Front cover: *Segment of the painting 'St. Yves Administering Justice' by Maestro di Sant'Ivo (1405–1410), the original of which can be seen in Galleria dell'Accademia in Florence (one block from where the project-conference took place). St. Yves (1253–1303), patron saint of lawyers, turns his attention to the poor and victimized. Similarly, religious leaders should protect victims of hate speech by their members or in the name of their community.*

Back cover: *Detail of the ancient* pietra serena *frame of the entrance to the CILRAP Bottega in Via San Gallo in Florence. Diametrically opposed to hateful expression (the topic of this book), the hand-carved surface is a loving expression of the meticulous work of the stone mason. The modest* pietra serena *stone has been quarried from hills outside Florence for centuries. All volumes in this Publication Series display a picture of publicly accessible ground (or frame that leads to the ground) on the back cover. Photograph: © CILRAP 2022.*

ISBNs: 978-82-8348-141-9 (print) and 978-82-8348-142-6 (e-book).

Dedicated to minority victims of hate speech in the name of religion.

PREFACE BY THE EDITORS

Hate speech is both a symptom and cause of deeper societal challenges. Hateful expression, particularly incitement to violence, online and offline, has negative effects on society as a whole and not just on those who are targeted, impacting relationships between individuals, communities and governing institutions. Because of its whole-of-society effects, everyone has a stake in working to counter hate speech. This includes religious leaders and other actors who are in a position to contribute to tackling hate speech, mitigating its impact, as well as addressing hate speech stemming from within their communities.

The focus of this anthology is hate speech perpetrated by religious actors or in the name of religion. Regrettably, such hate speech has grown in severity, leading to tragic occurrences of violence and acts of terrorism, having become a challenge of concern to the international community as a whole. The anthology offers in-depth case studies of religion-based or -related hate speech; discussions of relevant international law, philosophical and religious normative frameworks; expert analyses of factors motivating hate speech in the name of religion; and 250 pages of analysis of measures available to assist religious actors, particularly religious leaders, to reduce or prevent hate speech.

We would first of all like to thank our fellow authors for their remarkable chapters and tireless efforts. The book speaks for itself. We also place on record our gratitude to Antonio Angotti, Gabriel Bichet, Medha Damojipurapu, Rohit Gupta, Fadi Khalil, Lee Wai Chun and Mansi Srivastava of the Torkel Opsahl Academic EPublisher for their professional copy-editing.

Morten Bergsmo
Director, Centre for International Law Research and Policy

Kishan Manocha
Head, Tolerance and Non-Discrimination Department,
Office for Democratic Institutions and Human Rights,
Organization for Security and Co-operation in Europe

FOREWORD BY H.E. AMBASSADOR JOHAN VIBE

I feel honoured to have been invited by the two editors of this volume to write a foreword, and to the Centre for International Law Research and Policy (CILRAP) to open the conference on the same topic in Florence on 8–9 April 2022 in front of an eminent group of justices, religious leaders, civil society representatives, and legal and political scholars, including the third Prosecutor of the International Criminal Court, Mr. Karim A.A. Khan KC. The Court is an institution that Norway has supported since the outset and worked closely with in several peace processes. I had the pleasure of interacting with its second Prosecutor, Mrs. Fatou Bensouda, back in 2017 when I was involved in the follow up of the Colombian peace accords and the task of implementing the advanced transitional justice system which they prescribed, a first for a State Party to the Rome Statute.

Bringing together practitioners and scholars is key to achieving one of the goals of this research project, namely to provide religious leaders with common-sense tools that can help them to better prevent hate speech. It is important that the format of the project involves eminent representatives from various religious and cultural backgrounds to ensure that its findings are universal and well-embedded in the practices, needs and interests that religious leaders consider when they exercise influence. The venue of the project's conference, Florence, with its history, art and global perspective reaching back centuries, has also been fitting for the topic discussed in this anthology.

I cannot offer this foreword without referring to the immediate threat presented by the Russian invasion of Ukraine and the daily violations of international law that we are witnessing. At the time of writing, a number of actors are gathering evidence of committed war crimes. Religion certainly has a role in this conflict. Some religious actors are even justifying the war as a kind of metaphysical or spiritual cleansing, as discussed in several chapters of this book. The David Kennedy quote referenced by Morten Bergsmo in his excellent Chapter 1 below captures what we are facing: "imperial ambitions emboldened by religion, or ideology, straining against the leash of an agnostic territorial limit – that's evil". Let me however, emphasize that in a situation where the war in Ukraine absorbs most of the attention in Europe – and we refocus on the immediate security needs in our neighbourhood – we should not lose sight of conflicts, atrocities and humanitarian needs in other parts of the world.

Norway supports the research project that has led to this anthology for a number of reasons. First, under international law, countries are required to prohibit any advocacy of national, racial or religious hatred that constitutes incitement to discrimination, hostility or violence. This is an important starting point.

Secondly, hate speech counteracts an inclusive public discourse based on tolerance and mutual respect. The spread of hate speech – amplified by digital and social media – is of particular concern to Norway. Anti-democratic forces are gaining ground and spreading anti-Semitism, anti-Gypsyism and Islámophobia. We need to fight disinformation and hate speech, including on social media platforms.

Thirdly, the United Nations is at the centre of global efforts to establish and uphold norms against hate speech, and Norway wishes to support the United Nations' work both at home and on the global scene.

Fourthly, in the last decade, Norwegian efforts to fight hate speech in our own society have been systematized and embedded in a national strategy and action plans. It has also become an integral part of our foreign policy strategy promoting the freedom of expression. Indeed, addressing hate speech does not mean limiting freedom of expression. To prevent and combat hate speech, intercultural dialogue and education are vital to increase tolerance and awareness around the impact of hate speech.

Fifthly, Norway has, over the years supported international normative efforts aimed at preventing and alleviating humanitarian suffering. Let me just mention the processes to ban land mines and cluster munitions. Unfortunately, the suffering of civilian populations in conflict is on the rise. The number of refugees and displaced persons is higher than ever. Universal or widely respected international norms are being disregarded. Some of the violence at the origin of this suffering is rooted in religious hatred. In a more polarized world, strengthening international norms is not an easy task. Multilateralism is challenged. Many claim that it would not be possible today to agree on the normative framework established in the aftermath of the two world wars. Let us hope that the gruesome images from the wars in Ukraine and other parts of the world will give a new impetus to strengthen humanitarian norms and human rights. Religious leaders will have an important role to play.

Sixthly, Norway has acted as a facilitator in a number of peace processes, from the Middle East to Sri Lanka, from Sudan to Colombia, to mention a few. The results have not always been as we had hoped. Some have characterized the Norwegian efforts as naïve. However, we strongly believe in the need to promote spaces for political negotiation and dialogue as important tools to prevent and solve conflicts. Again, in this area, religious leaders have an important function, not least by addressing hateful expressions.

The aim of this anthology includes contributing knowledge on, and further research and analysis of, the Rabat Plan of Action, the Beirut Declaration, and the 18 Beirut Commitments. Part V of the anthology discusses supplementary tools and approaches that may assist religious leaders to prevent or reduce hate speech from within their communities. This is a novel, multi-disciplinary inquiry, guided by what we know about the practice of religion-based hate speech as exemplified in Part II, and by the relevant international law standards presented in Part III. I am also pleased to see that Part IV discusses in detail factors that may motivate religion-based hate speech. Developing a better understanding of these factors is important, as has also been underlined by the Norwegian Prime Minister, Mr. Jonas Gahr Støre.

By seeking to focus on advocacy of religious hatred that amounts to incitement to *violence*, the anthology zooms in on the most serious forms of religion-based hate speech, that which leads to violence and, in some extreme situations, contributes to armed conflicts. The project does not, however, suggest that incitement to *discrimination* or *hostility* is not deserving attention. The forms of incitement to discrimination that we see also in Europe is equally of serious concern to nations and regions. My own country, Norway, has seen how racial-religious hatred can lead to incitement to discrimination and violence, and even to mass-killings.

H.E. Johan Vibe
Ambassador of Norway to Italy

FOREWORD BY H.E. CARDINAL CHARLES M. BO

I thank the contributors to this anthology for coming together in these times when hope is difficult, when clarity of vision seems so clouded. The intention of the editors – to understand religion both as a precursor to hate speech and as essential to the response to hate speech – is important and timely, and I am glad that you have chosen to include Myanmar in your considerations.

I would like to first dwell a little on peace. Peace is always possible. Peace is not merely the absence of war. It is a positive force, derived, as St. Thomas Aquinas makes clear, from an inner state first of all: "A heart is not at peace for as long as it has not what it wants or, having what it wants, there remains still something it wants and which he cannot have at the same time". This hunger to possess, to own, to control and to demean – these are the opposites of peace.

Thereafter, Aquinas offers a view of peace that, at first sight, can seem quite arid. Does it belong, he asks, to the virtue of love? Of course it does, peace being, in his understanding, that wish to fulfil our neighbour's will as if it were ours. But, and this is important, St. Thomas also ascribes peace to the work of justice. Here, he learns from the prophets of the Hebrew Scriptures, with their strong sense that there can be no peace for a chosen people while they live unjustly with each other.

Ubi caritas et amor, Deus ibi est – where charity and love are found, there is God – is an antiphon from Holy Thursday. So we may say, by extension, *ubi caritas et justicia, ibi pacis erit*: where love and justice are found, there is peace.

Pope St. John XXIII spoke about this in his 1963 encyclical on peace, *Pacem in Terris*. He talked there of the fundamental building blocks of peace, of which the first and most important is that each individual person, irrespective of race or religion, history or future, is equal in value to all other people. Grace has made each of us, as the encyclical says, sons and friends of God. Peace begins with this radical equality of one person to another, of all of us to each.

From this essential equality in the eyes of God flows our rights and the reciprocity of rights between one person and another. This creates what Pope St. John speaks of as "an attitude of responsibility". He extends this later in the document from individuals to states:

> All over the world, people are either the citizens of an independent State, or are shortly to become so; nor is any nation nowadays content to submit to foreign domination.

Not "content to submit to foreign domination" – how relevant that is today.

Hate speech is best thought of as radical absence of peace. Narratives of hatred are peddled by paranoid forces in the world, creating a culture of death. Hate speech is the verbal 'nuclear' attack against innocent people. Genocides happen along with toxic hate speech. I use here what I judge to be a practical definition of hate speech, which I offer to you not as an academic well-versed in such things, but because my country Myanmar has lived with and still lives with the practical fact of hatred, while I preach a gospel of love.

For me, hate speech is simply that language meant to persuade one group of people to learn to hate another group, a hatred so deep that it permits violence.

Such language, in and of itself, can have little impact. Much of it is rooted in fear. But in Myanmar, hate speech found a pernicious cocktail of elements that magnified it, and is magnifying it still, with terrible results.

The first element in that combination that served to magnify hate speech in my country was the sudden acquisition of the means of communication. The Internet and smartphones came to Myamar later than in many parts of the world, and they came suddenly. We underwent a remarkable technological change from a time when a SIM card in Myanmar could cost 1,000 USD, to a time after 2013 when it cost just a single dollar. Suddenly, everyone was connected, and in that suddenness, that radical new belonging to each other, came both extraordinary opportunity and significant risk.

I do not want to blame technology, but I do want the readers, in particular serious academics and policy-makers, to understand the depth of change brought to my country by the smartphone. In a culture of memorisation, of learning from authority, the smartphone did not simply subvert those traditions. It made use of them. The smartphone became, in some sense, the new authority. Facebook, in particular, seemed to offer us the world. We read it and we believed all that it showed us.

This was in part as well because some leading religious figures took well and quickly to this new medium. This is important, I think, to understand the power that some religious leaders can exercise when they use online forms of speech.

Facebook was, in particular, the means by which some whose voices mattered chose to spread messages that demeaned and diminished people of the Islámic faith. This is not unique to Myanmar, as this anthology elaborates in some detail. For us, it had the most tragic and awful consequences in the violence perpetrated against the Rohingya Muslim community of Myanmar.

I have described this elsewhere as a new wound opened up in my country. I strongly urged the government not to allow speech promoting hatred. I argued then, and still believe now, that it corrupted a deep Burmese tradition of compassion.

The people of my country, and of all countries have a moral obligation to protect and promote the dignity of all human beings. To demonize others is to live in unpeace. It has a name drawn from the Hebrew Scriptures, scapegoating. It quickly leads to the denial of rights, political and human. In the case of the Rohingya, it lead religious leaders and other extremists to propose that they had no right even to exist in Myanmar.

Compassion and mercy are the two eyes of my nation. They allow for a vision of peace and dignity. We are a long way now from this. What then is the way forward? Myanmar has seen the pernicious and lasting impact of hate speech, which others in this anthology analyse in detail. I know what harm it has done to Myanmar, and will do to the minds and hearts of many people, if we do not find ways to address hate speech.

Silence is not a solution. We have the right and duty to speak of what we know and love. What then must we do? In the moral and personal sphere, first of all, we must learn to imagine ourselves as the other, as the stranger whom we might not know, not trust, not like. The humanity of the other is the core insight of so much of our Sacred Scriptures. We must learn to love the stranger.

This is hard. I do not pretend otherwise. It is a moral exercise that undoes the pernicious effects of histories of one group's greatness over another. I am not saying that my own religion has always got this right. But we can start to do so by looking at ourselves, as the *Book of Exodus*, 22:21, reminds us: "Do not wrong or oppress the stranger, for you yourselves were once strangers in the land of Egypt".

From that instinct, to look into oneself, it is not so far to the Gospel of Matthew, where to feed the hungry, to give water to the thirsty, to welcome the stranger, is to do so to Christ himself: "Insofar as you did this to the least of these brothers of mine, you did it also to me" (Matthew, 25:40).

People of faith need to go still further. The story of the Bible is that God has bestowed his love on the few, the weak, the vulnerable. On Christmas Eve in 2021, violence claimed the lives of some 30 innocent people in my country, burnt to death in our Kayah State, locked into their vehicles. On that same night, in the Roman Province of Judaea, the grace and glory and hope of God became incarnated in a vulnerable child. This was not the loud, abrasive voice of hatred, screaming for attention. It was the whispered voice that Samuel heard in the Temple, that Mary heard and to which she gave her yes.

How do we amplify the role of faith in speaking out for peace? An interconnected world, ironically fragmented in hatred. How to bring peace in this digitally toxic environment? Christ remains the answer. Christ's verses subvert even the Mosaic laws of 'eye for an eye' into 'love your enemies' and 'pray for those who persecute you'. This is a very dull order, but as Gandhi said succinctly, 'an eye for an eye makes the whole world blind'. Yes, there is a mutuality involved in the survival of the human race. The invisible Covid-19 virus taught us a visceral lesson: stand together or sink together. There is a new world, it is possible: Isaiah spoke of this when he talked about swords becoming plowshares. That is the dream of the *Book of Revelation*: a new earth and a new heaven, where there will be no more tears. Returning to Jesus, and to his teachings of compassion to all, forgiveness 77 times, showing the other cheek and thus winning over the enemy; the human evolution is astonishing, the digital evolution is staggering, but the moral evolution is on a slippery rock.

This is the challenge: it is this world evolving morally, in compassion, in humanity. There is a long road to traverse for all of us. I call upon men and women of faith, of goodwill, to take up the challenge: a moral rearmament of humanity. Peace is possible; peace is the only way.

H.E. Cardinal Charles Maung Bo
Cardinal Priest of Sant'Irenei a Centocelle,
Archbishop of Yangon

FOREWORD BY VINCENZO BUONOMO

I

The different and qualified outlooks expressed by the contributions of the authors who have given consistency to this volume highlight that between religion, hateful expression and violence there can be no relationship, but only a real antagonism, indeed a mutual exclusion.

Religious choice, belief, is a way in which the person manifests a free capacity to rise from human events, to rediscover his roots and give meaning to his existence. The human freedom to believe manifests itself as an immediate and personal condition, also expressed by the diversity of religions and beliefs. It is composed in the necessary relationship with others, avoiding the self-referentiality and indifference that are the two most evident temptations of our age – a relationship to which truth and justice belong, as prerequisites for respect for those who are part of the same community of faith, of other faiths or are non-believers.

These are some of the reasons that allow us to indicate how the religious choice also constitutes part of a doctrinal, juridical and institutional humus that implies the action of religious institutions, governments and inter-governmental organizations (from the United Nations ('UN') to regional or group organizations) on religious issues and the human right of freedom of religion or belief. An action from which an essential element arises: the choice of faith is a fascinating concept in which freedom, spirituality and mystery come together; but it is also a process in continuous evolution, leading us today to no longer consider faith as a *religious event* and *institutional reality*, intrinsically joint. In fact, religion is increasingly presented as an activity of religious structures and their leaders (in the form of diffusion of religion, religious precepts and doctrines, proselytism) towards which not only States pay attention (for example, State religion, State atheism, old and new forms of interference in the activities of religious experience), but also inter-governmental institutions (for example, the UN or the Organization for Security and Co-operation in Europe ('OSCE')) or institutions with a particular orientation such as the Organisation of Islamic Cooperation or the King Abdullah bin Abdulaziz International Centre for Interreligious and Intercultural Dialogue.

In other cases, religion is considered as a component of the believer's private sphere, reducing its public dimension, as if to preserve the life of States and the relations they establish in the wider community of peoples from visions of which religions are bearers. This image confirms that religious choice and practice or freedom of religion, in all its articulations, is, for people or communities, an identity factor, but cannot be a vehicle of violence or an instrument to create hate and conflict within a nation or with repercussions even on a global level. Rather, the religious sphere is a reality that can promote a true dialogue or the place in which to realize collaboration between different components and opposing visions. In this regard, we find a very effective synthesis in the words of Pope Francis when he states: "while promoting the fundamental freedom to profess one's belief, an intrinsic requirement of the very fulfillment of man, it also ensures that religion is not exploited and risks, by admitting violence and terrorism, denying itself" (*Address at the Founder's Memorial in Abu Dhabi*, 4 February 2019). This is today's problem of legal systems: the inability to prevent and supervise. Veiled indifference towards the religious element as part of the realization of the person can recompose their contradictions, and consequent contrasts.

II

The question of violence, hatred and intolerance – and more broadly of conflict – can never be an authentic viewpoint of the religious element. Indeed, it involves only a negative consideration of religion and believers. This is explained, for example, by the reference to the conflict between freedom of religion and freedom of expression that emerges in the *Strategy and Plan of Action on Hate Speech* adopted by the UN – a Plan designed primarily to prevent the use of the religious element "in speech, writing or behavior, that attacks or uses pejorative or discriminatory language with reference to a person or a group on the basis of who they are, in other words, based on their religion".

More broadly, multilateral action since 2001 has set as its aim the prevention of intolerance and discrimination on religious grounds, considered to be the source of forms of violence or hatred. In this perspective, the objective is to protect believers and religious communities from potential forms of violence, hatred and limitation of freedom that has led international organizations such as the UN and the OSCE to indicate Islámophobia, anti-Semitism and Christianophobia as ideologies and attitudes to be prevented and overcome. However, experience tells us that this is not enough. Indeed, the approach risks projecting only a negative consideration of the religious phenomenon, to the point of seeing it as the cause of conflicts.

This is demonstrated in some cases by the will to preserve religious freedom (or even religious expression alone) solely by preventing discrimination, leaving aside that necessary 'positive' approach aimed at promoting the contents of a choice of faith and the consequent fundamental right to religious freedom. Reading this positive dimension means understanding that the decision and the will to believe affect not only the moment of choice, belonging, worship or profession of faith. It also affects the lifestyle of the believer and therefore the commitment of individuals and groups in the great challenges that our societies present every day. For this reason, principles, doctrines, rites and operational elements of a 'community of believers' can have a direct impact on social life, without any opposition between 'being a believer' and 'being a citizen'. However, if the choice of believing is also a lifestyle of the believer, the religious element cannot be reduced to ritual or to paths of spirituality.

The need to prevent footsteps of hatred, violence and intolerance requires us to overcome the separation between being a citizen and being a believer, between political commitment and the religious dimension of the person. To exclude from the public dimension the vision that the believer has about the social life, the role of institutions, the principles that govern our societies, means applying the criteria of exclusion and discrimination to many people. However, this can never turn into partisan views, perhaps imposed. The contribution of believers, in fact, can contribute to building a healthier and more inclusive society, thus contributing towards eliminating the violations of fundamental rights, the various forms of violence and marginalization, and the language of hatred and, in that way, prevent actual (armed) conflicts.

III

An exclusively negative approach highlighted by reference to hatred, violence or defamation of a religion risks neglecting how education for dialogue and the different performances of dialogue are the way to go. Dialogue is one of the prerequisites guaranteeing an 'orderly' daily coexistence, at every level. It should not be looked upon as a mere objective, distant and unattainable.

On this basis, it is possible to create forms of limitations that guarantee effective proportionality. There is no need for norms that are incompatible with international standards on human rights, which result in the denial of the 'positive' content of the right to religious freedom. Otherwise, being a believer risks losing its correct value and its effective meaning, transforming faith into an exclusively functional element – thus forgetting that the believer lives a fundamental relationship both with his community of faith and with the civil society to which he belongs. Along these lines, there is also a conception of religious freedom that is correct and consistent with international human rights law: that is, as the right of every person to profess his own religion, according to the dictates of his conscience, in both individual and community form – a right whose exercise must remain protected from any coercion that may intervene from the outside or considers itself entitled to do so arbitrarily. This is a freedom that must be protected by identifying the existence of 'duties' and 'rights' that legal regulation is called to order and guarantee within the limits ordinarily set by international human rights law, summarized in the expressions of *security*, *public order*, *health*, *morals* and the rights of others (see Article 18(3) of the International Covenant on Civil and Political Rights).

It is desirable that this publication, with the numerous and authoritative interventions it contains, will serve as a tool for disseminating and fostering a formation that excludes violence, hatred or other behaviours that cannot have any connection with the religious element. Only in this way can dialogue, based on shared principles, become an instrument of government supported by the strength of fraternity. In this perspective, it will be possible not only to guarantee peace, development and human rights, but also above all to rediscover the authentic meaning and effect of religious freedom.

Vincenzo Buonomo
President,
Full Professor of International Law and Organization,
Pontifical Lateran University

FOREWORD BY CLAUS KREß

It was with great pleasure that I chaired the opening session of the conference 'Religion, Hateful Expression and Violence' convened in Florence on 8–9 April 2022, by the Centre for International Law Research and Policy (CILRAP) together with several institutional partners. On that occasion, I thanked at the outset most warmly Morten Bergsmo and CILRAP for having organized and conceptualized the conference at which chapters in this anthology were first presented.

The Faculties of Law of the Universities of Delhi and Haifa, the Centre of Evidence of Criminal Justice Studies at Northumbria Law School, the Observatory of International Humanitarian Law of the University of Buenos Aires Law School, Parliamentarians for Global Action, the Coalition for International Criminal Justice and the Norwegian Ministry of Foreign Affairs are among the institutional partners in this project. I wish to extend my warm thanks to those fine institutions for having helped to make the project and anthology possible.

It is always a blessing to be in the magnificent city of Florence, where the project-conference took place. As Morten Bergsmo writes in Chapter 1, "it is not difficult to savour the beauty of religion as rose petals when surrounded by the arts and architecture of Florence". To this observation, one might add a reminder of Pico della Mirandola, the eminent philosopher of the Renaissance. Not only because of his well-known speech about human dignity, but perhaps even more so because of his study, as a Christian thinker, of Jewish writings and traditions, and for his attempt to bring to light an accordance between all religious teachings, at the level of their fundamental tenets, with a view to contributing to world peace.

The Salone Brunelleschi, the conference venue in Florence, adds a rose petal of non-religious origin to the scene. It constitutes the centre of the Ospedale degli Innocenti, the Hospital of the Innocents or Foundlings, a complex which was built by the local guild of silk workers to protect the most vulnerable children from the oppression of strangers after the death of their parents.

Already when the idea of this anthology was born, nobody could seriously doubt, I would argue, that to keep in check the thorns of the rose of religion constitutes a world-order challenge of formidable importance. Since 24 February 2022, it must be added with sadness, that challenge has acquired an additional layer of urgency. How much one would have hoped for the leadership of the Russian Orthodox Church to get in the way of Russia's aggressive course of action. But instead, its leaders have lent their voices to Russia's President in his disgraceful attempt to portray his war of aggression against Ukraine as a kind of sacred mission to restore a Greater Russia of Russian Orthodox belief. This detestable abuse of religion for violent purposes constitutes the culmination of a year-long religious persecution in occupied Crimea and in the occupied Donetsk and Luhansk regions in Ukraine. Being a Christian myself, I cannot pass over these facts in silence.

Chapter 1 reminds us of two pillars of the international legal edifice which are central to the theme of the anthology, as elucidated in several of its chapters. Briefly, there is, first, the international human right of religion. In that context, Bergsmo makes an interesting reference to the writings of the late Judge Weeramantry. In his view, the authority and legitimacy of international law could benefit from allowing itself to be inspired by a broad convergence of revered religious texts in their aspiration for peace. In a sense, this is reminiscent of the great Florentine Pico della Mirandola.

The second pillar of the international legal edifice is the statement in Article 20, paragraph 2, of the International Covenant on Civil and Political Rights, that "any advocacy of religious hatred that constitutes incitement to discrimination, hostility or violence shall be prohibited by law". It is this statement that refers to the core of the endeavours of the authors in this anthology, not only those who discuss the international law framework in Part III.

The seven chapters of Part II present a number of case studies of relevant hate speech in the name of faith or religion, in India, Myanmar and the former Yugoslavia. In Part IV, authors offer more abstract reflections about motivational factors behind such occurrences. Such an understanding of the phenomenon is crucial in order to develop counter-strategies and concrete tools to reduce hate speech. Here again, certain important pillars are already in place. Chapter 1 refers prominently to the 2012 Rabat Plan of Action, the 2017 Beirut Declaration, and the ensuing 18 Commitments on Faith for Rights formulated by faith-based leaders. These documents are discussed by several authors in the anthology, notably Kishan Manocha in Chapter 23.

Part V aims further in at least two important respects. It asks, first, what can be done by religious leaders beyond the 18 Commitments. And, perhaps most innovatively, it discusses what can be done in cases where the relationship between religious leaders and the international human rights community is strained. As Chapter 1 provides: "This anthology will hopefully spur further efforts to develop a supplementary rationale for religious leaders to act that does not, at the same time, require them to accept a long list of international human rights instruments".

Taken together, this constitutes an extraordinarily ambitious intellectual undertaking. The anthology has become an extremely rich conversation through the contributions of leading thinkers from around the globe.

Claus Kreß
Professor,
University of Cologne

Foreword by Eli Salzberger and Fania Oz-Salzberger

Hate is a perennial human tendency and hate speech has always been with us, though seldom penalized before modern times. Hate speech is public speech that expresses hate or encourages violence towards a person or group based on their race, religion, nationhood, sex, sexual orientation or similar categorizations. Hate speech has always been a major cause or auxiliary for physical violence. Today, it is aided and proliferated by modern factors, including our justifiable enshrining of freedom of speech and freedom of religion as two of the most protected human rights. Another recent and enormous factor is the rise of digital technology that democratizes (or popularizes, and in worse cases ochlocratizes) public speech, enabling its fast and broad transmission, and encouraging formerly marginalized speakers and contents. In consequence, alongside many valuable changes in global public discourse, the potential and actual effects of hate speech on physical violence have increased significantly.

A considerable part of hate speech can be termed 'religious hate speech' or 'hate speech in the name of religion'. Why is religious hate speech a hypersensitive topic in the current age? Part of the answer, as explored in this volume, has to do with disagreements between numerous well-meaning people on whether any essential part of a religious belief system, its scriptures and practices, can at all be deemed hate speech, and if so, whether it is so deemed in a (merely) ethical or legally binding sense. There is an open argument, also in the present volume, on whether some kinds of hate speech are 'intrinsic' to certain religions or merely *attachable* to them from the outside, with more or less ease. While hate of specific human groups is not necessarily part of any belief system, some hate speech can be found in scriptures – or in several significant interpretations, past and present – of the major religions, where it is ascribed to God or to his immediate envoys, often as a command for believers to follow. In our opinion, the point is not whether such hate speech is 'intrinsic' to the great religions – alas, it sometimes is – but whether these religions can be practised without it. On the latter, our answer is yes.

For example, in the Hebrew Bible, God commands the annihilation of the people of Amalek, and one of the Israelite/Jewish commands of memorization is: "Remember what Amalek did to you" and subsequently, "leave no trace of it" (*Deuteronomy*, 15:17–19; note, however, the possible contradiction between 'remembrance' and 'leaving no trace'). Nevertheless, rabbinic traditions have voided this command by stating that the people of Amalek no longer exist, therefore its annihilation is not a practical religious injunction. By contrast, extremist Jewish interpretations in the present era attempt to see some of the Jews' modern enemies as Amalek, metaphorically or realistically, thus opening the way to generalized hatred of, say, all Germans or all Arabs. This interpretation allows hate speech under the auspices of religion, but it is deeply controversial and remains a minority opinion among Jewish believers. Similarly, Christianity and Islám include in their scriptures religious hate speech, culminating in actual violence. Think of Jesus' unusual aggression against the Temple's traders and financiers, which gave rise to medieval anti-Semitism and anti-commercial sentiments (in the same chapter of Matthew, 25, Jesus also uncharacteristically kills-by-speech a fig tree on which he found no fruit). However, believers and religious leaders and teachers can – and many of them do – opt out of violence-inducing aspects of their creed. Such statements and instances may be intrinsic to religion, but they are not a necessary condition for its practice. *They are not attached to religion from the outside, but they are detachable from within.* These observations provide special importance to the last section of this book concerning internal measures to reduce hate speech available to religious leaders.

The last point makes this whole volume so important and timely. It attests to the importance of deliberating and portraying the boundaries between 'acceptable' religious hate speech and one that is unacceptable, unethical or immoral; and further between unethical religious hate speech and that which is illegal (see Figure 1). Such distinctions between illegality, immorality and the unacceptable are complicated and controversial. Their complexity should support the assertion that religious hate speech has to be addressed by a multiplicity of means, legal as well as extra-legal (Figure 1), most of which are represented in designated chapters of this book.

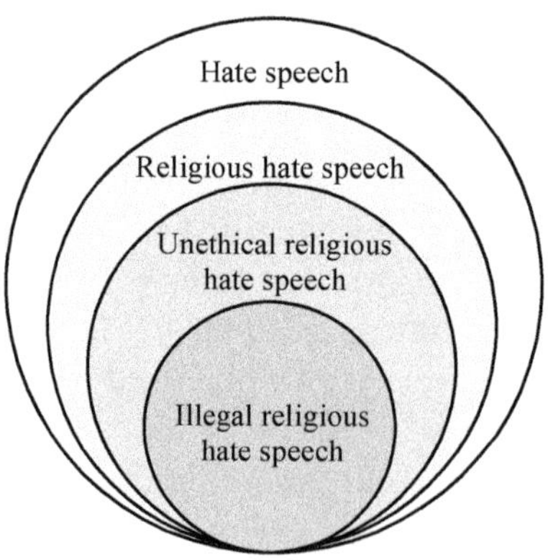

Hard law:	International criminal law State criminal law > State liability in international law
Soft law:	State public law Private law
Extra-legal measures:	Ethical rules Inter-governmental organizations Local regulation and community self-regulation Non-governmental organizations

Figure 1: Measures to fight religious hate speech.

Criminalizing the harshest, most violence-inducing forms of religious hate speech seem to us a necessity. Certain kinds of religious hate speech must be addressed by international criminal law, perhaps the most severe available legal measure. Other segments of religious hate speech belong outside the realm of international criminal law, but nevertheless have to be criminalized by state criminal law. This is indeed required by norms of public international law. However, one can conclude that both international and national criminal law have so far failed to address effectively even the most severe religious hate speech, and this is particularly true in liberal democracies that place freedom of speech and freedom of religion on the pedestal of superior rights. For instance, the use of direct quotes from the sacred scriptures' original texts makes prosecution and conviction very difficult. This leaves an important space for state public and private law as means to combat religious hate speech. A second edition of this volume could explore these directions further. For example, we could further explore the mitigation of religious hate speech through the administrative law doctrine of reasonableness or through torts and defamation in private law.

Soft law and extra-legal measures should act as complementary to hard law measures, or, in less severe cases, as supplementary. Such measures extend from professional, public office and business ethical codes, as well as local regulation and community self-government, on the state level, to inter-governmental organizations and non-governmental organizations' deliberations, declarations and decisions, on the international level. Religious hate speech can be sanctioned or denounced, for example, by a profession's disciplinary tribunal or by an international declaration, whenever criminal prosecution is not likely to materialize. When reading the varied chapters of this volume one can conclude that in contrast to, and perhaps as the result of, the fact that hard law has rarely been successfully applied, the utilization of soft- or extra-legal measures are far more present in our era.

We therefore hope that such alternatives are not a poor substitute or mere lip service to the cause, but can be viewed as a declaration of intent or as a warning and as part of an evolutionary process in which the fence between legal and illegal is shifting according to actual developments, pending the employment of harsher measures in light of the growing religious hate speech and ensuing physical violence we are witnessing in recent years.

Eli Salzberger
Professor and former Dean, University of Haifa Faculty of Law

Fania Oz-Salzberger
Professor Emerita of History at the University of Haifa Faculty of Law and the Haifa Center for German and European Studies

Foreword by David Donat-Cattin

The anthology *Religion, Hateful Expression and Violence* addresses a topic that must be at the centre of attention and engagement of States, relevant organs and actors within States (including religious communities and their leaders), civil society organizations, academics and researchers, practitioners (including judges and prosecutors), as well as the international community as a whole. Within the framework of pluralistic and democratic systems, this topic is of special importance and relevance for all those who are directly elected by the people, the members of parliaments.[1] In fact, the rights to freedom of thought, religion and belief, as well as the rights to freedom of expression and assembly are key components of the fabric of civil and political rights, as defined in the International Covenant on Civil and Political Rights, without the respect of which there cannot be any durable, long-standing form of democratic governance.

A peace-centred conception of international relations and international law – the latter may be defined as the glue of international relations – entails the respect for universal human rights under the rule of law, at least within the normative frameworks provided by the Charter of the United Nations, the Universal Declaration of Human Rights and relevant treaties. Universally accepted human rights include the right to freedom of religion or belief, in respect of the most serious violations of which there must be accountability and enforcement of relevant norms, including the principle of individual (criminal) responsibility to address the most serious breaches of this fundamental right. Hatred and violence are not only means utilized to negate these rights. They are also invoked and abused by certain religious leaders in order to bring about destruction of other religions or beliefs. Therefore, the fight against impunity for gross human rights abuses that are perpetrated in the name of a purported 'vision' of religion corresponding to a violent-extremist ideology is an imperative that must be recognized by the international community as a whole. It should not be confused with,

---

1 Parliamentarians for Global Action ('PGA') co-operates with the International Panel of Parliamentarians for Freedom of Religion or Belief ('IPPFoRB'), which is "a network of parliamentarians and legislators from around the world committed to combatting religious persecution and advancing freedom of religion or belief", as stated by former German Chancellor Angela Merkel. The PGA's 2022–23 President, Ms. Kasthuri Patto (Member of Parliament ('MP'), Malaysia), is also part of the Board of the IPPFoRB, co-founded by former Minister of Culture of Norway, Mr. Abid Raja (a PGA member when he was an MP, addressing, *inter alia*, the 2017 PGA Milan Forum for Parliamentary Action in Preventing Violent Extremism and Mass Atrocities).

and diluted by, other policy-goals such as counter-terrorism or stabilization in post-conflict situations. Academic researchers and various types of practitioners have a paramount responsibility to analyse how *distorted versions of religious beliefs* are used by certain leaders, including religious leaders, to pursue hatred, incitement to violence and discrimination, and to justify various forms of persecution, which may rise to the gravity threshold of crimes against humanity.

Persecution is probably the most common type of crimes against humanity perpetrated to curb freedom of religion as a way to discriminate against individuals on the basis of their belief. In light of its widespread commission especially within oppressive or totalitarian regimes (which made some members of the Arab League seek to restrict its scope at the Rome Diplomatic Conference on the International Criminal Court ('ICC') in 1998), the crime of persecution is the *only* crime against humanity subjected to retrogression during the negotiating process that led to the adoption of the ICC Statute. Under its Article 7(1)(h), persecution is punishable as a crime against humanity only when committed *in connection with* other crimes falling under the ICC jurisdiction.

This is the case in a situation of massive and systematic attack directed against a civilian population primarily targeted on 'religious' grounds before the ICC, namely, the situation of Muslims in northern Rakhine in Myanmar (known as 'Rohingyas') who, in my view, have been the victims of the crime against humanity of deportation (into Bangladesh, a State Party to the ICC Statute), accompanied by persecution. Article 7(2)(g) offers the following definition: "'Persecution' means the intentional and severe deprivation of fundamental rights contrary to international law by reason of the identity of the group or collectivity". Therefore, notwithstanding the retrogressive language in Article 7(1)(h), the ICC Office of the Prosecutor has, at the time of writing, taken significant steps in an extremely grave case of religion-based persecution against members of a minority. This illustrates once more the relevance and importance of this anthology and the project conference in Florence, which was inaugurated by the third ICC Prosecutor, Mr. Karim A.A. Khan KC.

In 2021, we saw a self-described religious group, the Taliban,[2] tragically return to power in Afghanistan after 20 years, reinstating a *de facto* totalitarian

---

[2] The official name that the Taliban forces used during their negotiations with the United States' government is "the Islamic Emirate of Afghanistan", see "Agreement for Bringing Peace to Afghanistan between the Islamic Emirate of Afghanistan which is not recognized by the United States ('US') as a state and is known as the Taliban and the United States of America", signed in Doha on 29 February 2020 (https://www.legal-tools.org/doc/icrns9/). On 15 August 2021, the Taliban reinstated an unconstitutional *de facto* government for Afghanistan in violation of this US–Taliban understanding, which was designed to prepare the way for a peace agreement between the Taliban rebels and the Afghan government (that was never concluded). The Taliban seized power by use of military force as a consequence of the withdrawal of foreign troops and the collapse of the central government (including its armed forces).

regime purportedly justified by a religious ideology. One year later, the international community does not appear to have properly analysed the causes of its failures in Afghanistan with a view to learning lessons for future interventions in conflict-situations characterized by the most serious crimes of international concern.[3] Curiously, a prevailing view among some opinion-makers has been that the Taliban 'just' wants to apply '*Sharí'ah* Law'.[4] Yet, throughout 2021, analysts and leaders from various Muslim-majority countries – including prominent legal scholars such as Professor Mohamed Elewa Badar, a contributor to this anthology – assessed the Taliban's law as a distorted, false representation of a religious belief, largely corresponding to tribal rules, running counter to many precepts and norms of what could be understood as '*Sharí'ah* Law' (which may vary in light of interpretations and relevant historical and geographic contexts). There should be no doubt that the propaganda machinery of the Taliban regime is based on hateful expression and violence inspired by an extremist religious sect, which also builds on tribal and ethnic identities and divisions.

While the connection between religion, hate speech and violence is evident in respect of mass atrocities committed in Myanmar against religious and ethnic minorities and those committed in Afghanistan against civilians who do not align with Taliban's rule, the link between widespread and systematic violence and hateful expression within the framework of the war of aggression in and against Ukraine appears to primarily derive from a nationalist and imperialist vision held by the Russian President: the Russian Federation is a 'superpower' that asserts its domination over its neighbours that are not even recognized as genuinely independent States by the Russian leader.[5] There is, however, also a religious-identity element that should not be underestimated, namely, the role played by Patriarch Kirill of the Russian Orthodox Church, as elaborated by Professor Svein Mønnesland's important chapter in this anthology. The Patriarch's concern is not only those Ukrainians who are not in favour of submitting themselves and their church(es) to the authority of Moscow, but also against those in the western world who are seen as sponsors of immoral models of family-life and society-at-large.[6] As documented as early as March 2022 (by a

---

3 See Parliamentarians for Global Action, "One Year After the Return of the Taliban's Dictatorial Regime: No More Empty Words, Afghanistan Needs Action Now! – The International Community Seems Not to Have Learned from Its Mistakes", 15 August 2022 (available on its web site).

4 Cf. Andrew Jeong, Jennifer Hassan and Sarah Pulliam Bailey, "The Taliban Says It Will Rule Under Sharia Law. What Does That Mean?", *The Washington Post*, 19 August 2021.

5 See Vladimir Putin, "On the Historical Unity of Russians and Ukrainians", *Kremlin*, 12 July 2021 (https://www.legal-tools.org/doc/tt382m/) and his answers to the media (https://www.legal-tools.org/doc/dumkzp/).

6 See, for example, Janine di Giovanni, "The Real Reason the Russian Orthodox Church's Leader Supports Putin's War: Homophobia Is at the Heart of Patriarch Kirill's Endorsement",

coalition of 81 Ukrainian non-governmental organizations working under the umbrella of the EuroMaidan SoS Coalition), the war in Ukraine and the illegal occupation of areas of the Donbas region and Crimea (which started in 2014) have been characterized by attacks against religious objects, churches and priests protected by international humanitarian law.[7] Such attacks may be qualified as war crimes or crimes against humanity, which are crimes that fall within the jurisdiction of the ICC.

These policy and legal observations on situations as diverse as the ones in Myanmar, Afghanistan and Ukraine illustrate the fundamental need for the in-depth reflection and study of the inter-connections between religion, hateful expression and violence offered by this very timely and useful anthology. It will be my pleasure to bring the findings of this project to the attention of concerned policy-makers, parliamentarians, officials of international and national institutions, as well as representatives of civil society organizations and academic institutions.

Dr. David Donat-Cattin
Former Secretary-General,
Parliamentarians for Global Action
CILRAP Research Fellow

Foreign Policy, 26 April 2022. See also, Andrzej Szabaciuk, "Patriarch Kirill's Holy War", in *IES Commentaries*, 23 March 2022, No. 573 (75/2022), which discusses how Patriarch Kirill has been "accused of propagating 'religious nationalism'".

7 See Center for Civil Liberties, "Appeal of Euromaidan SOS and the Religious Freedom Roundtable in Ukraine Regarding the Attack on Religious Freedom During the Armed Aggression of the Russian Federation Against Ukraine", 16 March 2022 (https://www.legal-tools.org/doc/vyym22/). The first crime against humanity highlighted in this document is persecution, which appears to be the favourite instrument of 'inhumanity' to attack freedom of religion in most conflicts and situations of mass-crime.

TABLE OF CONTENTS

Section C:
Alleged Hate Speech in the Name of Christianity: The Situation in the Balkans

Part III: Overarching Normative Frameworks

Section D: The International Law Framework

Section E:
Theological and Philosophical Frameworks

Part V: Measures Available to Prevent or Reduce Hateful Expression in Religious Communities

Section F: External Measures

PART I:
A DELICATE BALANCING OF VALUES

1

On the Problem of Hateful Expression in the Name of Religion

Morten Bergsmo*

1.1. Religion as Opium of the Masses, Not Just the Few

In 1843, Karl Marx wrote that religion "is the *opium* of the people",[1] an expression that has become widely known since the 1930s with the spread of Marxism.[2] His idea was that practical functions of religion in society[3] are similar to the function of opium in a sick person, reducing suffering and providing pleasant illusions that may give hope. Three years earlier, Heinrich Heine had expressed it more poetically: "Welcome be a religion that pours into the bitter chalice of the suffering human species some sweet, soporific drops of spiritual opium, some drops of love, hope and faith".[4] It is an evocative metaphor, long before the disheartening "U.S. Opioid Epidemic" which has become an opium of the

* **Morten Bergsmo** is the Director of the Centre for International Law Research and Policy (CILRAP). For relevant biographical information, see https://www.cilrap.org/bergsmo/. See also the film, Morten Bergsmo, "Statements During the Florence Conference on Religion, Hateful Expression and Violence", CILRAP Film, Florence, 8–9 April 2022 (https://www.cilrap.org/cilrap-film/220408-09-bergsmo/). The author thanks Song Tianying, Nora Helene Bergsmo and Rohit Gupta for comments.

1 The expression was included in the introduction to Marx' posthumously published *Critique of Hegel's Philosophy of Right* (criticizing Hegel's *Elements of the Philosophy of Right* (1820)). The original German words are "Die Religion [...] ist das Opium des Volkes", appearing in this context: "*Religious* suffering is, at one and the same time, the *expression* of real suffering and a *protest* against real suffering. Religion is the sigh of the oppressed creature, the heart of a heartless world, and the soul of soulless conditions. It is the *opium* of the people", see Karl Marx, *Critique of Hegel's Philosophy of Right*, 1844, edited by Joseph O'Malley, Annette Jolin, translated by Joseph O'Malley, Cambridge University Press, 1970, Introduction. A few sentences earlier, Marx wrote: "Religion is, indeed, the self-consciousness and self-esteem of man who has either not yet won through to himself, or has already lost himself again".

2 The sentence was included in a journal of limited circulation in 1844, but did not reach a broad audience in the 1800s.

3 He wrote that religion is the "enthusiasm" of the world, "its moral sanction, its solemn complement, and its universal basis of consolation and justification", see Marx, 1844, *supra* note 1.

4 Heinrich Heine, *Ludwig Börne – A Memorial*, 1840, Camden House, 2006, p. 95.

masses in a very tragic sense.[5] Marx' social criticism that religion can nourish values that consolidate power-relations in a society still remains valid.[6] Hate speech in the name of religion – the theme of this multi-disciplinary volume – can also be instrumentalized by actors whose principal interest is to wield or seek social or economic power.

Marx' description of religion was not only inspired by the vivid imagery of the poet Heine. More radical critique – and expectation – of religion stirred among Germans in the early 1840s. In his 1841 *The Essence of Christianity*, Ludwig A. von Feuerbach, a leading Young Hegelian,[7] proposed that "faith in God is only faith in the abstract nature of man" or "the faith of man in the infinitude and truth of his own nature".[8] He wrote that the "subjective human being

---

5 The term is used on the web site of the United States Department of Health and Human Services, noting that 10.1 million Americans "misused prescription opioids" in 2019. The Department declared a public health emergency in 2017 (hhs.gov site, 19 March 2022). Incidentally, opioid use in the Islamic Republic of Iran, a so-called theocracy, is very high: "the third national study of rapid assessment of substance abuse and drug dependence in Iran, estimated the number of opium and other opiate users about 1,100,000 to 1,200,000 people" (the two other studies referred to showing considerably higher numbers), see Ahmad Ali Noorbala *et al.*, "Evaluation of Drug and Alcohol Abuse in People Aged 15 Years and Older in Iran", in *Iranian Journal of Public Health*, 2020, vol. 49, no. 10, pp. 1940–1946.

6 The unveiling of masked power has been pursued as an inquiry by other CILRAP projects, see Morten Bergsmo, Mark Klamberg, Kjersti Lohne and Christopher B. Mahoney (eds.), *Power in International Criminal Justice*, Torkel Opsahl Academic EPublisher, Brussels, 2020, 884 pp. (https://www.toaep.org/ps-pdf/28-power).

7 Feuerbach, "perhaps the best known of the Left Hegelian philosophers", is singled out here because of the influence of his book on secularism since the mid-1800s: "His critique of religion *The Essence of Christianity* (1841) almost instantaneously turned him into a figure of great renown. The book became the centre of controversy among an inquisitive and religiously aware German public", see Howard Williams, "Ludwig Feuerbach's Critique of Religion and the End of Moral Philosophy", in Douglas Moggach (ed.), *The New Hegelians: Politics and Philosophy in the Hegelian School*, Cambridge University Press, 2006, p. 50. Williams points out that Feuerbach "remarkably presents his philosophy of religion in the 1840s as though it were the first to take seriously the apparent ethical, social, and anthropological limitations of the Christian religion. […] He regards himself as taking on the established church and its various priests almost single-handedly and exceptionally", understating the influence of Hegel and Kant on his work (p. 51). Exploring the Hegelian background to Feuerbach's thought falls outside the scope of this chapter. For a sympathetic reading, see the discussion in Hans Küng, *Does God Exist?*, translated by Edward Quinn, Doubleday & Company, New York, 1980, pp. 129–216. Küng acknowledges that "Hegel is undoubtedly the most difficult among the notoriously difficult German philosophers" (p. 129). As CILRAP continues its work on religion and international law, we will hopefully revisit this interesting topic.

8 Ludwig Andreas von Feuerbach (1804–1872), *The Essence of Christianity*, 1841 (2nd ed., 1843), translated by George Eliot, Dover Publications, Mineola, 2008, p. 152. It is "necessary to man to have a definite conception of God, and since he is man he can form no other than a human conception of him" (p. 13); "Religion is the dream of the human mind" (p. xii); "I

in his absolute freedom and unlimitedness" is the "Divine Being".[9] His book critically dissects more than 15 dogmas in Christian theology (as he knew them),[10] as for him "the illusions of theology"[11] or "the web of contradictions and delusions called theology"[12] is the problem.[13] Feeding dogmas,[14] 'faith' is

---

accept the Christ of religion, but I show that this superhuman being is nothing else than a product and reflex of the supernatural human mind" (p. xiv); "The Son lays hold on the heart, because the true Father of the Divine Son is the human heart, and the Son himself nothing else than the divine heart, *i.e.*, the human heart become objective to itself as a Divine Being" (pp. 58–59).

9 *Ibid.*, p. 152. Elsewhere in the book: "the object of any subject is nothing else than the subject's own nature taken objectively" (p. 10); "the qualities of God are nothing else than the essential qualities of man himself" (p. 16); "The divine being is nothing else than the human being, or, rather, the human nature purified, freed from the limits of the individual man, made objective – *i.e.*, contemplated and revered as another, a distinct being. All the attributes of the divine nature are, therefore, attributes of the human nature" (p. 12); "God, as a metaphysical being, is the intelligence satisfied in itself, or rather, conversely, the intelligence, satisfied in itself, thinking itself as the absolute being, is God as a metaphysical being" (p. 32).

10 Part I ("The True of Anthropological Essence of Religion") of Feuerbach's book is based entirely on this critique of dogmas, at the end of which he concludes: "We have reduced the supermundane, supernatural, and superhuman nature of God to the elements of human nature as its fundamental elements. Our process of analysis has brought us again to the position which we set out. The beginning, middle and end of religion is MAN" (*ibid.*, p. 152). Hans Küng wrote that Feuerbach's "atheistic critique of religion formed an unprecedented threat to any kind of belief in God and thus to the whole of Christian theology at its roots, a threat that is not to be minimized even today"; and that for "the first time in the history of humanity, we are faced with a fully considered, absolutely determined, unreservedly professed and – this, too, is important – *planned atheism, kept up to the very end*", in Küng, 1980, pp. 210, 211, see *supra* note 7.

11 *Ibid.*, p. xi.

12 *Ibid.*, p. ix.

13 The "secret of theology is anthropology" (*ibid.*, p. 221); "when this projected image of human nature is made an object of reflection, of theology, it becomes an inexhaustible mine of falsehoods, illusions, contradictions, and sophisms" (p. 176).

14 "It is in the history of dogma and speculation as in the history of states. World-old usages, laws, and institutions continue to drag out their existence long after they have lost their true meaning" (*ibid.*, p. 98).

attacked with equal singularity – in contrast with 'love',[15] 'unity'[16] and 'prayer'[17] which Feuerbach refers to less stridently. His insightful statements on contemplation, concentration and prayer temper his book,[18] while leaving us with questions about his polemics.[19]

---

15 See, for example, *ibid.*, p. 211: "Faith is the opposite of love". "Faith necessarily passes into hatred, hatred into persecution, where the power of faith meets with no contradiction, where it does not find itself in collision with a power foreign to faith, the power of love, of humanity, of the sense of justice" (p. 213); a "love which is limited by faith is an untrue love. Love knows no law but itself; it is divine through itself; it needs not the sanction of faith; it is its own basis" (p. 217, footnote omitted). But his understanding of love is consistent with his anthropocentric view: "God is love: that is, feeling is the God of man, nay, God absolutely, the Absolute Being. God is the nature of human feeling, unlimited, pure feeling, made objective" (p. 101).

16 Feuerbach refers to 'unity of the species' and 'mankind', see, for example: "Love is the universal law of intelligence and Nature; – it is nothing else than the realisation of the unity of the species through the medium of moral sentiment" (*ibid.*, p. 218), and: "Love can only be founded on the unity of the species, the unity of intelligence – on the nature of mankind" (p. 219).

17 Spiritual exercises – prayer prominently among them – constitute an important lens through which we can understand how religion functions. When Feuerbach discusses prayer, he seems to pause his "contest" (which he concedes "advances [...] impetuously" (*ibid.*, p. x)): "The ultimate essence of religion is revealed by the simplest act of religion – prayer [...]. [...] the prayer pregnant with sorrow, the prayer of disconsolate love, the prayer which expresses the power of the heart that crushes man to the ground, the prayer which begins in despair and ends in rapture" (p. 102). He writes that Sebastian Frank von Wörd's (1499–1543) saying "God is an unutterable sigh, lying in the depths of the heart" is the "most remarkable, the profoundest, truest expression of Christian mysticism" (p. 102). But then Feuerbach seems to reduce the analysis to 'needs-based prayer' – "Thus what is prayer but the wish of the heart expressed with confidence in its fulfilment?" and "in prayer, man speaks undisguisedly of that which weighs upon him" – while he does not reduce it all the way to mere dependency ("It is an extremely superficial view of prayer to regard it as an expression of the sense of dependence.") (pp. 102–103).

18 Feuerbach writes: "Contemplation and worship are not essentially distinguished. That which I contemplate I humble myself before, I consecrate to it my noblest possession, my heart, my intelligence, as an offering" (*ibid.*, p. 97); and concentration "is more than a condition; prayer is itself concentration, – the dismissal of all distracting ideas, of all disturbing influences from without, retirement within oneself, in order to have relation only with one's own being" (p. 103).

19 Feuerbach starts to capture aspects of the process of prayer, but quickly reinstates the needs-based framework in that only "a trusting, open, hearty, fervent prayer *is said to help*", and then doubles down by repeating that "this help lies *in the prayer itself*" (*ibid.*, italics added). What about prayer that furthers clarity or focus of mind? Or detachment? And prayer giving energy to the values or virtues that we have adopted and integrated? Or generating determination or resoluteness (rather than optativity)? Or processing aspects of our own relational conduct – forgiving ourselves – in order to move forward? A preoccupation with what you pray *to* – combined, in Feuerbach's case, with a contest against dogmas associated with such

Claiming both that his work is made in "the utmost clearness, simplicity, and definiteness" and that it "can be appreciated and fully understood only by the scholar",[20] Feuerbach confidently asserts that his fundamental ideas "will one day become the common property of mankind".[21] Indeed, his monograph has wielded remarkable influence during the past 180 years, including on Marx, Darwin, Freud and Engels and the movements and fields of study they inspired.[22] Engels wrote: "To get any idea of all this, one must himself have experienced for oneself the liberating effect of the book. Enthusiasm was universal; for the time being we were all Feuerbachians".[23]

Four decades after Feuerbach insisted that faith in God is faith in the nature of man and Marx associated religion with sickness, Friedrich W. Nietzsche took a further step by adopting the metaphor of death. "God is dead! God remains dead! And we have killed him!",[24] says Nietzsche's madman who, like

externality – may undermine a fuller appreciation of the actual processes of prayer in the lives of people around the world (and not only in a particular segment of the denomination placed under critical scrutiny – for Feuerbach, Christianity), including its vital function as positive self-programming. If his recognition that in "prayer man turns to the Omnipotence of Goodness" is immediately tied down by the pointed caveat "which simply means, that in prayer man adores his own heart, regards his own feelings as absolute", the potency of "Goodness" is simply diluted (p. 105). This reduction would seem to be deliberate given Feuerbach's preceding observation that the "omnipotence of Goodness, which, for the sake of the salvation of man, makes the impossible possible" (p. 104). Also, how could genuinely-experienced "feelings" possibly be somehow inferior? Do not most human beings live a significant portion of their lives in or with one or the other feeling? Feuerbach's contest against Christian dogmas becomes itself dogmatic.

20 He refers to the "ignorant and indiscriminating multitude" (*ibid.*, p. xii), while approvingly mentioning "the philosopher, the man of science, the free objective thinker in general" (p. 115).

21 *Ibid.*, Preface to the Second Edition, p. xv.

22 Hans Küng observed, in 1978: "In fact, it was only with Feuerbach and Marx and later – supported by atheistic natural scientists – with Nietzsche and Freud that atheism became a Weltanschauung, threatening belief in God and Christianity at their roots, penetrating all classes of the population and finally reaching global dimensions beyond the frontiers of Europe. Modern man's self-understanding thus came to be atheistically determined to a considerable degree. Not only the political mass movements of National Socialism in Germany and of Communism in the Soviet Union, in Eastern Europe and China were and are atheistically oriented", 1980 (German original in 1978), p. 189, see *supra* note 7. He also noted that "[e]ven today – it is scarcely necessary to stress the fact – Feuerbach is anything but passé" (p. 204).

23 Friedrich Engels (1820–1895), "Ludwig Feuerbach und der Ausgang der klassischen deutschen Philosophie", 1888, in *Marx-Engels-Werke*, vol. 21, Berlin, 1962, p. 272.

24 Friedrich W. Nietzsche, *The Gay Science*, 1882, translated by Josefine Nauckhoff, Cambridge University Press, 2001, p. 120. The quotation continues: "How can we console ourselves, the murderers of all murderers! The holiest and the mightiest thing the world has ever possessed has bled to death under our knives: who will wipe this blood from us? With what water could we clean ourselves?".

Nizámí's Majnún nearly seven centuries earlier,[25] is on a search beyond social conventions. His eyes piercing those around him, he asks questions which may still be gaining in importance: "How were we able to drink up the sea? Who gave us the sponge to wipe away the entire horizon? What were we doing when we unchained this earth from its sun? Where is it moving to now? Where are we moving to? Away from all suns? Are we not continually falling?".[26] These words by Nietzsche exhilarate open minds, just as much as his proposition that 'God is dead!' still echoes in repetitive speech around the world.

The metaphors used by Heine, Marx and Nietzsche have become commonplace, but they may not feel so apt when we consider angry hate speech in the name of religion, especially when the hateful expressions trigger violence or armed conflict, which is our main concern in this anthology. Far from opiate docility, such virulent speech begs the question of whether we are witnessing the death knells of denominations that find themselves unable to reign in abuse in their name. It has become such a concern around the world that David J. Luban's eloquent and thought-provoking Chapter 2 (which follows immediately after this introductory chapter) is called "Bloodthirsty Religion? An Inquiry into the Religious Sources of Hateful and Violent Speech".

From the vantage point of a city like Florence – where the project-conference of this volume took place[27] and from where I am writing this chapter – a less strident metaphor for religion may be that of a thorny rose. It is not difficult to savour the beauty of religion as rose petals when surrounded by the arts and architecture of Florence. Indeed, Feuerbach seems to ignore the role played by religion in the visual art of Florence in the fourteenth, fifteenth and sixteenth centuries, when he claims that Christians cannot "deck themselves in the arts […] as products of Christianity" or "reckon the treasures and riches, the arts and sciences of this world as part of Christianity. In all these points, [the Christians of older times] rather conceded the pre-eminence to the ancient heathens, the Greeks and Romans", as if the Italian Renaissance had not happened.[28] That aside, it is all too easy to observe the thorns of religion in the hateful expressions

---

25 Nizámí Ganjaví, *The Story of Layla and Majnun*, 1188, translated by Dr. Rudolf Gelpke, Omega Publications, New York, 1997. Active in twelfth-century Iran, Nizámí is widely considered one of the greatest poets in Persian literature. For a discussion of Nizámí's 'majnún' and its later iterations, see Michael W. Dols, *Majnún: The Madman in Medieval Islamic Society*, Clarendon Press, Oxford, 1992, pp. 320–339.

26 Nietzsche, 2001, see *supra* note 24.

27 The conference 'Religion, Hateful Expression and Violence' took place in Florence on 8–9 April 2022. The concept note, programme, films and podcasts of conference presentations, relevant publications and other information can be freely accessed at https://www.cilrap.org/events/220408-09-florence/.

28 Feuerbach, 2008, p. 237, see *supra* note 8.

(be they words or symbolic conduct of legitimation) by religious actors or in the name of religion, especially where such expressions have contributed to the kind of violence that we have seen in, for example, the former Yugoslavia or Myanmar. It is this thorn in the side of public order, security or peace in several countries – religion-based or -related hate speech – that we direct our attention to in the present book.

1.2. Religion 'Resurrected' as an International Human Right

Rather than solemnly burying God, 66 years after Nietzsche's madman pronounced God dead, nations of the world raised a normative shield by declaring that "everyone has the right to freedom of [...] religion", including "freedom to change his religion or belief, and freedom, either alone or in community with others and in public or private, to manifest his religion or belief in teaching, practice, worship and observance".[29] Article 18 of the 1948 Universal Declaration of Human Rights ('UDHR') recognized freedom of religion as a central value of the post-World War II international legal order. The right was cemented in Article 18 of the 1966 International Covenant on Civil and Political Rights ('ICCPR').[30] As a matter of fact, "freedom of every person to worship God in his own way – everywhere in the world" was one of the four freedoms to which President Roosevelt, in 1941, committed the post-World War II order.[31] A

---

[29] Universal Declaration of Human Rights, 10 December 1948 (https://www.legal-tools.org/doc/de5d83/).

[30] Paragraph 1 of which is restated here for convenience:

> Everyone shall have the right to freedom of thought, conscience and religion. This right shall include freedom to have or to adopt a religion or belief of his choice, and freedom, either individually or in community with others and in public or private, to manifest his religion or belief in worship, observance, practice and teaching.

See International Covenant on Civil and Political Rights, 19 December 1966, which has 173 States Parties at the time of writing (https://www.legal-tools.org/doc/2838f3/).

[31] Franklin D. Roosevelt, "The State of the Union Address to Congress", 6 January 1941, pp. 9–10 (https://www.legal-tools.org/doc/0ao7w5/):

> In the future days, which we seek to make secure, we look forward to a world founded upon four essential human freedoms.
>
> The first is freedom of speech and expression – everywhere in the world.
>
> The second is freedom of every person to worship God in his own way – everywhere in the world.
>
> The third is freedom from want – which, translated into world terms, means economic understandings which will secure to every nation a healthy peacetime life for its inhabitants – everywhere in the world.
>
> The fourth is freedom from fear – which, translated into world terms, means a world-wide reduction of armaments to such a point and in such a thorough fashion that no nation will be in a position to commit an act of physical aggression against any neighbor – anywhere in the world.

century after Feuerbach sought to make man the measure of all normativity, Roosevelt pledged that the American nation had placed its destiny in the hands and heads and hearts of Americans, and "its faith in freedom *under the guidance of God*. Freedom means the supremacy of human rights everywhere".[32]

Freedom of religion became a cornerstone of the emerging discipline of international human rights law, just as foundational as the freedom of expression in Article 19 of the Universal Declaration[33] (as further refined by Article 19(2) of the ICCPR).[34] Both freedoms originated in the domestic laws of several states[35] and the writings of some philosophers,[36] as developed in detail by

---

> That is no vision of a distant millennium. It is a definite basis for a kind of world attainable in our own time and generation. That kind of world is the very antithesis of the so-called new order of tyranny which the dictators seek to create with the crash of a bomb.
>
> To that new order we oppose the greater conception – the moral order. A good society is able to face schemes of world domination and foreign revolutions alike without fear.

32 *Ibid.*, p. 10 (italics added).

33 UDHR, *supra* note 29, Article 19: "Everyone has the right to freedom of opinion and expression; this right includes freedom to hold opinions without interference and to seek, receive and impart information and ideas through any media and regardless of frontiers".

34 ICCPR, *supra* note 30, Article 19(2) separated out the freedom to hold opinions and specified the media of expression: "Everyone shall have the right to freedom of expression; this right shall include freedom to seek, receive and impart information and ideas of all kinds, regardless of frontiers, either orally, in writing or in print, in the form of art, or through any other media of his choice".

35 Among these countries are Denmark, France, the United Kingdom and the United States. See Frede Castberg's classical work *Freedom of Speech in the West: A Comparative Study of Public Law in France, the United States and Germany*, Oslo University Press, 1960. The constitutional, philosophical and political discourse on these freedoms and their limitations is naturally richer in some of these countries than in the international society. Although the main normative framework of the present anthology is international law (as it is probably the only common global value system that we have), it nevertheless draws on the wealth of insights and considerations from the domestic level, as discussed, for example, in Jeremy Waldron's *The Harm in Hate Speech*, Harvard University Press, 2012. Some actors question whether international law provides coherent regulation on questions relevant to hate speech and the related fundamental freedoms. Toby Mendel seeks to answer such basic queries in his text "Does International Law Provide for Consistent Rules on Hate Speech?", in Michael Herz and Peter Molnar (eds.), *The Content and Context of Hate Speech: Rethinking Regulation and Responses*, Cambridge University Press, 2012, pp. 417–429.

36 Waldron (2012, pp. 207–233, see *supra* note 35) discusses how the idea of freedom of religion was integral to philosophers of the Enlightenment period, including John Locke's writings on toleration. Some passages by Locke remain highly relevant to our project: "all men, whether private persons or magistrates (if any such there be in his church), [should] diligently endeavour to ally and temper all that heat and unreasonable averseness of mind which either any man's fiery zeal for his own sect or the craft of others has kindled against dissenters"; "how happy and how great would be the fruit, both in Church and State, if the pulpits everywhere sounded with this doctrine of peace and toleration" (see John Locke, *A Letter Concerning Toleration*, edited by Patrick Romanell, Bobbs Merrill, Indianapolis, 1955, p. 28).

Matthias Neuner in Chapter 11 below. Both freedoms were included in Roosevelt's 1941 address.

The ICCPR specifies law-prescribed limitations or restrictions to the two freedoms, necessary to protect common (public order, health and morals) and specific interests.[37] Article 20(2) of the Covenant recognizes that the freedoms of religion and expression in association can pose particular societal risks: "Any advocacy of […] religious hatred that constitutes incitement to discrimination, hostility or violence shall be prohibited by law".[38] If we look to the ordinary meaning of its wording[39] and the negotiation history,[40] the core of the provision

---

37 Article 18(3) (freedom of religion) also provides limitations on the grounds of public safety and the fundamental rights and freedoms of others; and Article 19(3) (freedom of expression) does so on the grounds of the rights or reputations of others and national security.

38 Jeroen Temperman traces the origins of Article 20(2), discusses its implementation in domestic law, and proposes an understanding of the elements of the conduct to be prohibited by States Parties. He suggests that its drafters "adjudicated an abstract clash of fundamental rights and settled on an a priori balance. Accordingly, protection against violence and discrimination triumphed over absolute free speech. The *travaux préparatoires* pertaining to this article are a narrative of fear", see Jeroen Temperman, *Religious Hatred and International Law: The Prohibition of Incitement to Violence or Discrimination*, Cambridge University Press, 2018, p. 369. He argues that a 'necessity test' integral to Article 20(2) "requires that incitement only result in criminal punishment if it was likely that harm would shortly – imminently – befall the speech act's target group. In order to make that determination we need, first of all, knowledge of the speech act's overall societal context. In particular, we need to establish the position of the target group in terms of its vulnerability, as evidenced by, for instance, recorded hate crimes and discrimination monitors. Further, we need to establish the speech act's directly surrounding circumstances, such as the position, role and status of the speaker, the extent or reach of the speech, the composition of his or her audience, and suchlike. This information, together with the speech act's content (possibly containing e.g. fighting words, or acts of stereotyping or dehumanization) and its tone (possibly being inflammable) as well as the speaker's intent, will provide a fuller picture of the risk emanating from the hateful speech" (p. 372).

39 "[T]he text of Article 20(2) ICCPR itself – in addition to the drafters' views, subsequent state practice and the opinion of the UN Human Rights Committee – suggests that the Covenant's incitement provision is mandatory. This means that State parties, unless they have made a reservation to the opposite effect, are required to enact legislation prohibiting any advocacy of hatred that constitutes incitement to discrimination, hostility or violence", see *ibid.*, p. 369.

40 See Manfred Nowak, *U.N. Covenant on Civil and Political Rights: CCPR Commentary*, N.P. Engel Publisher, Kehl, 1993 (the early edition closer to the process), p. 366: "What the delegates in the HR Comm and the GA had in mind was to combat the horrors of fascism, racism and National Socialism at their roots, i.e., to prevent the public incitement of racial hatred and violence within a State or against other States and peoples"; Mona Elbahtimy, *The Right to Protection from Incitement to Hatred: An Unsettled Right*, Cambridge University Press, 2021, p. 182: "States belonging to the Western bloc resisted the very inclusion of the Article [20] in the ICCPR on the basis that it did not fall under the Covenant's substantive scope. They conceived of the ICCPR as an instrument that should set forth only individual rights of a negative

enjoins upon ICCPR States Parties to statutorily prohibit expressions of religious hatred that amount to incitement to violence, also when committed by non-state, religious actors.[41] Some States Parties do not recognize that they have an obligation to adopt legislation under the provision.[42] Other actors – prominently among them Mona Elbahtimy (see her Chapter 12 below) – have argued that there should be a human right to protection from incitement to hatred as the flip side of the obligation to prohibit incitement.[43]

---

nature, entailing the non-interference of states. Western states perceived Article 20 to impose unwarranted restrictions on freedom of expression, rather than setting forth a human right. Thus, they sought, during the negotiations, to narrow the scope of the Article's prohibitions as much as possible".

41 UN Human Rights Committee, General Comment No. 11: 'Prohibition of propaganda for war and inciting national, racial or religious hatred (Article 20)', 29 July 1983 (https://www.legal-tools.org/doc/43dd60/): "For article 20 to become fully effective there ought to be a law making it clear that propaganda and advocacy as described therein are contrary to public policy and providing for an appropriate sanction in case of violation".

42 Only a few Western states entered an express reservation, while a number of states have incitement laws that largely correspond to Article 20(2). In its first reservation to the Covenant, the United States observed that "article 20 does not authorize or require legislation or other action by the United States that would restrict the right of free speech and association protected by the Constitution and laws of the United States". Upon ratification, the United Kingdom interpreted "article 20 consistently with the rights conferred by articles 19 and 21 of the Covenant and having legislated in matters of practical concern in the interests of public order (*ordre public*) reserve the right not to introduce any further legislation". Australia also reserved the right "not to introduce any further legislative provision on these matters". The quotations are taken from the United Nations Treaty Collection's web page for the ICCPR (status as at 29 June 2023).

43 Mona Elbahtimy discusses the case for such a human right in detail in her monograph *The Right to Protection from Incitement to Hatred: An Unsettled Right*, 2021, see *supra* note 40: "While the original negotiations on the codification of the norm prohibiting incitement to hatred led, eventually, to the adoption of Article 20(2) of the ICCPR on the basis of a fragile international agreement, more recent negotiations on remodelling the norm ultimately reached an impasse. The standard-setting attempts at the UN, led by Islámic states, generated a dynamic of evolution, but this dynamic has failed to transform into actual normative evolution" (p. 183). See also Temperman, 2018, p. 370, *supra* note 38: "the Human Rights Committee has gradually derived from that standard a right to be free from or protected against incitement. For the time being that 'right' does not live the life of autonomous right that can be invoked by applicants against their state. It is mostly construed as a 'right of others', thus as a limiting factor with respect to the freedom of expression. Future case law may upgrade this right to a full-fledged legal entitlement, providing legal standing in cases in which State parties to the Covenant are alleged to have failed to uphold the protection offered by this standard". Elbahtimy argues that the attention should turn to "making Article 20(2) more practicable for states through the provision of guidance to prosecutorial and judicial authorities about the sound application of national incitement legislation" (pp. 186–187). Elbahtimy's monograph is valuable also as a study of challenges and imbalances in international human rights law-making.

Article 20(2) of the ICCPR goes to the core of the present anthology, which concerns the problem of *public advocacy of religious hatred (by religious actors or in the name of religion) that constitutes incitement to violence*, especially in situations where such violence has occurred or is likely to occur as a consequence of the advocacy or incitement.[44]

Beyond the fundamental freedoms of religion and expression and the treaty-obligation to prohibit incitement to violence, the sister-discipline of international criminal law also provides international law classifications that may apply to religious incitement to violence, as discussed in detail in Chapter 11

---

44 The anthology is not focused on advocacy of 'national' or 'racial' – as opposed to 'religious' – hatred. In particular, the project has focussed on situations where the perpetrators of hate speech (a) act in the name of religion and (b) target members of other religious communities with their hate speech. For a discussion on the relationship between advocacy of racial and religious hatred and free speech in the context of statutory regulation in England and Wales, see Peter Cumper, "Inciting Religious Hatred: Balancing Free Speech and Religious Sensibilities in a Multi-Faith Society", in Nazila Ghanea, Alan Stephens and Raphael Walden (eds.), *Does God Believe in Human Rights? Essays on Religion and Human Rights*, Martinus Nijhoff, Leiden, 2007, pp. 233–258.

Incitement to 'discrimination' or 'hostility' have not been excluded from the project, but have been treated as less important for our purposes than incitement to 'violence' pursuant to the expression of religious hatred. We have tried to focus on situations where religion-based or -related hate speech leads to – or has significant potential to lead to – actual violence, not only discrimination or hostility. In the words of Elbahtimy: "The prohibition of hate advocacy that constitutes clear and unambiguous incitement to immediate violence or illegal acts is the aspect of the norm that enjoys most transnational resonance, since it easily crosses cultural and ideological boundaries. However, legal regulation of hate advocacy that falls short of incitement to violence but creates a social climate conducive to hostility and discrimination does not enjoy the same universal resonance", see Elbahtimy, 2021, p. 186, see *supra* note 40.

Richard Moon describes the fine line between hate speech and incitement to violence: "Hate speech creates a risk of harm when it plays to an audience's fears and resentments and builds on their existing prejudices", and the concern is that "individuals, or small groups who are already inclined to bigoted thinking may be encouraged or emboldened to take extreme action against the targeted group's members" (see Richard Moon, *Putting Faith in Hate: When Religion is the Source or Target of Hate Speech*, Cambridge University Press, 2018, p. 149). Waldron explains how "[h]ate speech undermines this public good [the "sense of security in the space we all inhabit", "inclusiveness"], or it makes the task of sustaining it much more difficult than it would otherwise be. It does this not only by intimating discrimination and violence, but by reawakening living nightmares of what this society was like – or what other societies have been like – in the past. In doing so, it creates something like an environmental threat to social peace, a sort of slow-acting poison, accumulating here and there, word by word, so that eventually it becomes harder and less natural for even the good-hearted members of the society to play their part in maintaining this public good" (Waldron, 2012, p. 4, see *supra* note 35).

below. They include the modes of liability of incitement,[45] instigation[46] and ordering,[47] and the crime against humanity of persecution.[48]

Chapter 3 below by Justice Dorit Beinisch – "Drawing the Line Between the Preservation of Freedom of Religious Expression and the Fight Against Hate Speech and Incitement to Terrorism and Violence: The Perspective of a Judge and a Prosecutor" – discusses the difficult balancing of interests underlying the freedoms of religion and expression and prohibitions against hate speech and incitement to violence.

Part III of the anthology gives an overview of the international law framework sketched in the preceding paragraphs (in Section D), as well as some overarching normative frameworks of philosophy and religion (Section E).[49] In addition to the chapters by Neuner and Elbahtimy, Section D also includes Chapter 13 by Ioana Cismas which discusses the relevancy of international law framework to religious leaders. The four chapters in Section E are organized chronologically: "In the Name of Belief: Religious (In)tolerance, Hate Speech and Justice in Classical Greek and Roman Sources" (Chapter 14 by Emiliano J. Buis); "Hate Speech: A Christian Perspective and a Reflection on Myanmar" (Chapter 15 by Michael Marett-Crosby); "Incitement to Religious Hatred: An Examination of the Approaches of Extremists to Islámic *Sharí'ah*" (Chapter 16 by Adel Maged), and "Broader Normative Bases for Religious Leaders to Prevent Hate Speech" (Chapter 17 by Gunnar M. Ekeløve-Slydal, which includes an incisive analysis of Søren Kierkegaard). Possible future editions of this book should be expanded to include perspectives from more philosophical and religious traditions than what we have managed in this first edition.

1.3. Religion and International Law After the International Recognition of Freedom of Religion

Let us for a moment return to the broader context, as the project of which this anthology forms part is open to more general reflections on the relationship between international law and religion. International law's post-World War II shielding of freedom of religion – as pledged by Roosevelt in his paradigmatic speech – does not mean that the professional class of international lawyers perceived it as more than surviving in the twentieth century "as a set of 'principles'

---

45 See Gregory S. Gordon, *Atrocity Speech Law: Foundation, Fragmentation, Fruition*, Oxford University Press, 2017, pp. 136–166, 185–217 and 273–306.

46 *Ibid.*, pp. 174–178, 242–250 and 341–344.

47 *Ibid.*, pp. 178–181, 250–252 and 345–346.

48 *Ibid.*, pp. 166–173, 220–242 and 308–341.

49 With a few additions and exceptions, the book follows the structure of the project's conference programme, pursuant to the overall intellectual design of the project.

guiding the practice of institutions".[50] In the words of David Kennedy, they viewed religion as "private where the law is public. Religion is what we had before we had law. Religion is the domain of irrationality and charismatic authority, law the realm of reason and the bureaucratic. International law understands its birth as a flooding forth from the darkness of religious strife, antidote to the passions of faith, on guard against their re-emergence as ideology".[51] The end of the Cold War changed this, in Kennedy's view, allowing international lawyers "to come out [...] for a global law purged of ideological commitment but committed to liberal virtue. After ideology, all the censors can relax. Including, it seems, the secular separation from religion".[52] In all "the clamor for God and law we can feel, faintly, the slight weightlessness of a pendulum reversing its course",[53] "not to confront, but to confirm, less to confound, than to comfort".[54]

Others may see the community of international lawyers as more diverse and global than the constituency at the centre of Kennedy's analysis. The late Judge Christopher G. Weeramantry of the International Court of Justice, for example, recognized that "revered texts which command the respect and allegiance of over four billion of the world's population [...] converge in their teachings on the central question of peace. It is time therefore that international law delved deeper into this primary source of moral inspiration of the bulk of the world's population, thereby reinforcing its own authority to light up the path towards global peace".[55] Unless international law is brought "closer to the hearts and minds of the people of the entire world community", he warned us, with some persuasion, that "international law will achieve only a fraction of its

---

50 David Kennedy, "Losing Faith in the Secular: Law, Religion, and the Culture of International Governance", in Mark W. Janis and Carolyn Evans (eds.), *Religion and International Law*, Martinus Nijhoff, The Hague, 2004, p. 313.

51 *Ibid.* Kennedy captures the concern with acerbic talent: "imperial ambitions emboldened by religion, or ideology, straining against the leash of an agnostic territorial limit – that's evil". See the discussion on Christian Orthodox churches in the context of the conflict in Ukraine in Chapter 9 below by Svein Mønnesland.

52 *Ibid.*, p. 315.

53 *Ibid.*, p. 312.

54 *Ibid.*, p. 318. He suggests that we "normally return to religion less to question than to confirm our eclecticism, less as a displacement of secularism than as a continuation of its will to power. Like most interdisciplinary gestures, the move of law to politics, of politics to law, of both to religion, seeks across the border for reasons to celebrate the most central commitments of our own disciplinary domain".

55 Christopher G. Weeramantry, *Universalising International Law*, Martinus Nijhoff Publishers, Leiden, 2004, p. 368 (footnote omitted). See its Chapter 12 ('Religious Perspectives on Peace'), pp. 368–389.

potential".[56] Leaders of the Third World Approaches to International Law-movement, such as Antony Anghie, have pointed out how Judge Weeramantry sought "to develop an international law in which the developing world might recognize itself and pursue its own aspirations as a part of the global community. The legitimacy of international law depends crucially on these factors".[57] Weeramantry was conscious of the ways in which "law 'properly so called' was only one aspect of a much broader system of norms which regulated human action and had meaning and legitimacy for the people to whom they were applied", as he had become "acquainted with the ways in which four religions – Hinduism, Islam, Buddhism, and Christianity – shaped the laws he was called upon to administer".[58] Weeramantry's acceptance and use of a variety of sources (including religious texts that "command the respect and allegiance" of half of humankind), as supported by Anghie, may perhaps reflect Philip Allott's vision that international law – "the law of international society, the true law of a true society" – is made, "like all other law, through the total social process of international society, in which we all participate, the people of the world and all our subordinate societies, including the state-societies".[59]

Whether leaning in the direction of Kennedy's skinning analysis of Western-led discourse or Weeramantry's inclusive approach, there seems to be widespread recognition that developments since September 2001 have "taught us that respectful, thoughtful dialogue between people from different backgrounds and different religious beliefs is essential if humanity is to have a shared future. International law seeks to develop a legal framework that emphasizes our common humanity and dignity. If international law is to achieve this aim, then international lawyers can no longer afford to ignore the importance that religion plays for many individuals and in many societies".[60] The present anthology touches briefly on the *positive* side of this in Part III and elsewhere in more general discussions of the broader context of the relationship between religion and international law.

Ioana Cismas makes a distinction between three "clusters of topics" that have attracted the attention of legal scholars: (1) "church-state relations, the principle of state neutrality and secularism, including in relation to the display

---

56 *Ibid.*, in the dedication of the book.

57 Anthony Anghie, "C.G. Weeramantry at the International Court of Justice", in *Leiden Journal of International Law*, 2001, vol. 14, no. 4, pp. 845–846.

58 *Ibid.*, p. 833.

59 Philip Allott, *The Health of Nations: Society and Law beyond the State*, Cambridge University Press, 2002, p. 420.

60 Mark W. Janis and Carolyn Evans, "Introduction to the Paperback Edition", in *id.* (eds.), 2004, see *supra* note 50.

of religious symbols and the wearing of religious dress in public"; (2) the "relationship between law and religion(s) through a historical, theoretical, doctrinal, or empirical lens", including the contribution of religion to the development of international law (such as international human rights or humanitarian law) and the influence of law on religion; and (3) the "protection that international instruments and national legislation provide to freedom of religion, the prohibition of religious discrimination, and parental rights concerning the religious education of their children". To this, she proposes a further cluster: (4) the "agency of religious actors in interpreting religion. It reaches beyond freedom of religion to address a wider array of rights of religious actors, and beyond the incompatibility of religion with law to address the obligations of religious actors under international law". Directly relevant to the present project, Cismas offers a "new narrative that seeks to ensure the compliance of religious actors with international law".[61]

The discourse may in due course be further expanded to include considerations of (5) the complementarity of international law and religion as tools for the betterment of humankind, as recent works by authors such as Ronald Dworkin,[62] Anthony T. Kronman,[63] Roberto M. Unger[64] and Christopher G. Weeramantry[65] reach a certain level of eupepsia.

Kronman's latest book, for example, beautifully recounts how scientific inquiry, the pursuit of social justice, and love "are what remain of the idea of eternity and our desire to reach it" as we "set goals that we can neither avoid nor fully achieve, yet are able to approach, in an endless time, to an ever-increasing degree".[66] "In the broadest sense, the idea of God, in all its variant forms, *is* the idea of eternity",[67] the former Yale Law School Dean writes, quoting Kant's reference to a "remarkable predisposition of our nature, noticeable to every human being, never to be capable of being satisfied by what is temporal".[68] Kronman

---

61 See Ioana Cismas, *Religious Actors and International Law*, Oxford University Press, 2014, pp. 6–9.

62 See Ronald Dworkin, *Religion without God*, Harvard University Press, 2013.

63 See Anthony T. Kronman, *Confessions of a Born-Again Pagan*, Yale University Press, 2016.

64 See Roberto M. Unger, *The Religion of the Future*, Harvard University Press, 2014.

65 See Weeramantry, 2004, *supra* note 55.

66 See Anthony T. Kronman, *After Disbelief: On Disenchantment, Disappointment, Eternity, and Joy*, Yale University Press, New Haven, 2022, p. 44.

67 *Ibid.*, p. 17.

68 Immanuel Kant, *Kritik der reinen Vernunft* (Critique of Pure Reason), 1787, Vorrede (Foreword to the Second Edition), p. B XXXII, Suhrkamp, Frankfurt am Main, 1956, Werkausgabe, Bd. 3, p. 34: "die jedem Menschen bemerkliche Anlage seiner Natur, durch das Zeitliche (als zu den Anlagen seiner ganzen Bestimmung unzulänglich) nie zufrieden gestellt werden zu können".

argues that we "need some idea of what Aristotle calls 'the eternal and divine' to explain the meaning of those unattainable goals that give human life its peculiar drama, and to account for the fact that we can move closer to them without ever being able to overcome the gap completely".[69] The "fashionable belief that we can [dispense] with the idea of God altogether [...] engenders a false picture of the human condition", so we "need the right idea of God to understand who we are. And we can find our way to it by reason alone": the "world is inherently and infinitely divine".[70] Kronman did not even feel a need to include an index entry for Feuerbach in his 1,161-page *Confessions of a Born-Again Pagan*.

1.4. Religion as a Source of Incitement to Violence: Understanding the Words and Motivations

Our focus, however, is on a more *negative* dimension: the expression of religion-based or -related hatred in ways that amount to incitement to violence which can place the "respectful, thoughtful dialogue" of Evans and Janis under serious strain. Hate speech in the name of religion that triggers acts of terrorism or other forms of violence has become a challenge of concern to the international community as a whole. As Prosecutor Karim A.A. Khan KC remarked during the 2022 project-conference: "We see attacks in churches and temples. We see violence of expression being common currency, so what seems to identify or define us is our differences, not the common ground of our shared humanity".[71] He further underlined the seriousness of the situation in this clear manner:

> Those that purport to speak with religious authority, that use it, that contort it, that pervert it to justify hatred and division, they should not be given an extra margin because of a fear that somehow, they are religious or that they are godly. The simple reality by any metric, whatever the label – Hindu or Buddhist or Sikh or Muslim or whatever – anybody who tries to justify suicide bombing or killing or rape or violence against children, that is the antithesis of godliness, is it not? There is another word for it – it is devilish behaviour. And, at least it would be criminal behaviour under the constant yardstick of the law that we are seeking to apply.[72]

Sound attempts to address this grave challenge should be properly informed (a) of the real threat rather than assumptions or a theory about religious hate speech, and (b) by an attempt to understand the main factors that motivate such hate speech. To this end, Part II of the anthology includes three case studies

69 Kronman, 2022, p. 19, see *supra* note 66.

70 *Ibid.*, p. 20.

71 Karim A.A. Khan KC, "Statement on Hate Speech in the Name of Religion", 8 April 2022, CILRAP Film, Florence, at 03:21 ff. (https://www.cilrap.org/cilrap-film/220408-khan/).

72 *Ibid.*, at 35:33 ff.

of relevant hate speech: in Myanmar,[73] a country that has been in the intense focus of international justice actors in recent years; in India,[74] a country with

[73] See Burma Monitor (Research and Monitoring), Progressive Voice, International Human Rights Clinic at Harvard Law School and other civil society organizations, "Hate Speech Ignited: Understanding Hate Speech in Myanmar", 2020, 111 pp. (https://www.legal-tools.org/doc/6128hf/); ARTICLE 19, "Myanmar Briefing Paper: Countering 'Hate Speech'", 2020, 7 pp. (https://www.legal-tools.org/doc/4028dl/); Office of the President, Republic of the Union of Myanmar, Prevention of Incitement to Hatred and Violence (or) Prevention of Proliferation of Hate Speech, Directive No. 3/2020, 20 April 2020 (https://www.legal-tools.org/doc/mqiq91/); United States District Court for the District of Columbia, *The Republic of the Gambia v. The Facebook*, Facebook's Objections to the Magistrate Judge's Order Granting in Part and Denying in Part the Gambia's Section 1782 Application on September 22, 2021, 13 October 2021, 1:20-mc-00036-JEB-ZMF (https://www.legal-tools.org/doc/91cszf/); "Union Gov't Instructs Yangon Authorities to Prosecute Firebrand Monk", *The Irrawaddy*, 31 May 2019 (https://www.legal-tools.org/doc/78b78b/); "Mandalay Govt Asks Local Buddhist Authority to Keep Monks Away from Rallies", *The Irrawaddy*, 31 May 2019 (https://www.legal-tools.org/doc/07562a/); Khin Moh Moh Lwin, "Trials of far-right extremists Wirathu and Hla Swe to be conducted online", *Myanmar Now*, 13 January 2021 (https://www.legal-tools.org/doc/sin3w4/); "Junta drops charges against hate-preaching monk Wirathu", *Myanmar Now*, 6 September 2021 (https://www.legal-tools.org/doc/bty6wk/); Noel M. Morada, "Hate Speech and Incitement in Myanmar before and after the February 2021 Coup", in *Global Responsibility to Protect*, 2023, vol. 15, pp. 107–134; Amnesty International, "The Social Atrocity: Meta and the Right to Remedy for the Rohingya", 2022; Laurie Kim, "Tech Accountability in Face of Genocide: Gambia v. Facebook", in *Emory International Law Review*, 2022, vol. 36, no. 1, pp. 165–199; Claire Thomas, Mihaela Cojocaru and Noah Rosenberg, "The Hate Speech Crisis: Ways to Start Fixing It", Minority Rights International Group, May 2022; United States Department of State, "Burma 2021 International Religious Freedom Report", 2 June 2022; Arthur Klark and Gabriela Sagun, "Misinformation, Hate Speech and Ethno-Religious Tensions in Myanmar", in *United States Institute of Peace*, 27 April 2023 (available on its web site). See also Iselin Frydenlund, "The Birth of Buddhist Politics of Religious Freedom in Myanmar", in *Journal of Religious and Political Practice*, 2018, vol. 4, no. 1, pp. 107–121 and "Buddhist Islamophobia: Actors, Tropes, Contexts", in Asbjørn Dyrendal, David G. Robertson and Egil Asprem (eds.), *Handbook of Conspiracy Theory and Contemporary Religion*, Brill, Leiden, 2018, pp. 279–302.

[74] See Centre for Study of Society and Secularism, "The Covid Pandemic: A Report on the Scapegoating of Minorities in India", 2021 (https://www.legal-tools.org/doc/z2lhsu/); Maya Mirchandani, Dhananjay Sahai and Ojasvi Goel, "Encouraging Counter-Speech by Mapping the Contours of Hate Speech on Facebook in India", Observer Research Foundation, 2018 (https://www.legal-tools.org/doc/9q35bs/); Law Commission of India, "267th Report on Hate Speech in India", 2017 (https://www.legal-tools.org/doc/l6puhr/); Global Action Against Mass Atrocity Crimes (GAAMAC), "Preventing Hate Speech, Incitement, and Discrimination: Lessons in Promoting Tolerance and Respect for Diversity in the Asia Pacific", 2021, pp. 160–195 (https://www.legal-tools.org/doc/9ak28w/); Madan B. Lokur and Medha Damojipurapu, "Navigating the Meaning of Hate Speech and Sedition in India", Policy Brief Series No. 138 (2022), Torkel Opsahl Academic EPublisher, Brussels, 2022 (https://www.toaep.org/pbs-pdf/138-lokur-damojipurapu/); Constitutional Conduct Group, "Uncertain Justice: A Citizens' Committee Report on the North East Delhi Violence", 18 October 2022 (https://www.legal-

exceptional human resources and great potential for self-examination (although some Indian international lawyers seem reluctant to address religion-related hate speech in India); and the former Yugoslavia,[75] where the incidents occurred in the 1990s but communities still suffer lingering consequences of the advocacy of religious hatred and incitement to violence. These case studies seek to establish the exact words used or symbolic acts undertaken, their cultural connotations, and other aspects of the domestic context relevant to understanding the alleged hate speech.

Section A ("Alleged Hate Speech in the Name of Buddhism: Myanmar Perspectives") contains two detailed discussions by leading Burmese actors, one Buddhist, the other Muslim: "Mapping Some Controversial Public Utterances in Myanmar 2015–2020" (Chapter 4 by U Kyaw Tin) and "Alleged Hate Speech by Buddhists: A Myanmar Muslim's Perspective" (Chapter 5 by U Aye Lwin). Section B ("Alleged Hate Speech in the Name of Hinduism: The Situation in India") offers three comprehensive chapters by five prominent Indian jurists: "Reflections on Freedom of Expression, Hate Speech and Sedition in India" (Chapter 6 by Justice Madan B. Lokur and Shruti Narayan), "Patterns and Risks

---

tools.org/doc/whh08c/); Piyush Ghasiya and Kazutoshi Sasahara, "Rapid Sharing of Islamophobic Hate on Facebook: The Case of the Tablighi Jamaat Controversy", in *Social Media + Society*, 2022, vol. 8, no. 4, pp. 209–245; Cecilia Jacob and Mujeeb Kanth, "'Kill Two Million of Them': Institutionalised Hate Speech, Impunity and 21st Century Atrocities in India", in *Global Responsibility to Protect*, 2023, vol. 15, no. 2–3, pp. 1–14; and United States Commission on International Religious Freedom, "Annual Report, 2023", April 2023, pp. 24–25.

[75] See Milorad Tomanić, *The Serbian Orthodox Church During Times of War and the Wars Within It*, Krug, Belgrade, 2001; Svein Mønnesland, *National Symbols in Multinational States: The Yugoslav Case*, Sypress Forlag, Oslo, 2013, pp. 257–274; Majda Halilović and Nejra Veljan, "Exploring Ethno-Nationalist Extremism in Bosnia and Herzegovina", Atlantic Initiative, Sarajevo, 2021 (https://www.legal-tools.org/doc/1vlxhv/); Hikmet Karčić and Sead Turčalo (eds.), *Bosnian Genocide Denial and Triumphalism: Origins, Impact and Prevention*, Faculty of Political Science, University of Sarajevo, 2021, 185 pp. (https://www.legal-tools.org/doc/x1xcmh/); Sead Turčalo and Hikmet Karčić, "The Far Right in Bosnia and Herzegovina: Historical Revisionism and Genocide Denial", 31 August 2021, 25 pp. (https://www.legal-tools.org/doc/3l0ofs/); Aida Trepanić, "Bosnia Upholds Serb Chetniks' Hate Speech Convictions", in *Balkan Insight*, 20 December 2022 (available on its web site); "Izvestiteljka UN pozvala vlast u Srbiji da ispita i kazni zastrašivanja", *Radio Slobodna Evropa*, 5 June 2023; United States Department of State, "Bosnia And Herzegovina 2022 Human Rights Report", 2023; United States Department of State, "Serbia 2022 Human Rights Report", 2023. See also Gordon, 2017, pp. 41–46, *supra* note 45. For some explanatory background on the Eastern Orthodox world (of which the Serbian, Russian and Ukrainian Orthodox churches form part), see Meic Pearse, "Looking West, but Walking East: The Dilemma of Orthodoxy in a Modernising World", in Aleksandra Djurić Milovanović and Radmila Radić (eds.), *Orthodox Christian Renewal Movements in Eastern Europe*, Palgrave Macmillan, Cham, 2017, pp. 1–10.

in Contemporary Religion-Based Hate Speech in India" (Chapter 7 by Medha Damojipurapu), and "Religion-Based Hate Speech or Free Speech: Indian Courts in a Quandary" (Chapter 8 by Usha Tandon and Harleen Kaur). Section C considers hate speech in the name of Christianity, focusing on the situation in the West Balkans: "Religious Leaders and Nationalist Propaganda: The Serbian Orthodox Church" (Chapter 9 by Svein Mønnesland) and "Religion and Ethno-Nationalist Extremism in Bosnia and Herzegovina" (Chapter 10 by Majda Halilović).

These case studies provide sobering analyses of the scale of the challenges with which we are confronted and illustrate some commonalities across different denominations and countries. They amount to more than 360 pages of information, insights and sources, and could, in fact, have constituted a book in its own right. I have worked on the former Yugoslavia since the early 1990s, India since 2010, and Myanmar since 2018, so the selection of the three cases was pursuant to some deliberation. I have nevertheless benefitted greatly from reading and re-reading the thoroughly-researched chapters in Part II.

Part IV of the book explores several motivational factors behind relevant hateful expressions in the name of religion (including personality and situational factors,[76] colonial prejudice and discrimination, socio-political factors, and religious themes), and how hate speech contributes to atrocity-inducing environments through social influence. In this first edition, it includes five chapters: "Motivations for Terrorism: Personality Factors, Situational Factors and Hateful Incitement" (Chapter 18 by Ariel Merari), "Hate Speech on Social Media Platforms: Evidence from the Victims' and the Perpetrators' Perspectives" (Chapter 19 by Laura Dellagiacoma), "Colonial Prejudice and Discrimination Predicating Post-Colonial Hate Speech" (Chapter 20 by Jacques P. Leider), "Exploiting Social Influence: Embedded Human Agency and Perversion of Religion" (Chapter 21 by Song Tianying), and "The Use of Religious Themes to Islámize European Anti-Semitism and Motivate Hateful Expression in the Hamas Covenant" (Chapter 22 by Eliyahu Stern). Luban's Chapter 2 is also relevant to Part IV, and both the chapters by Leider and E. Stern shed significant light on the case-study approach of Part II.[77] As a matter of fact, hate speech against Jews in the Middle East should probably have been our fourth case study.

---

76 See Ariel Merari, *Driven to Death: Psychological and Social Aspects of Suicide Terrorism*, Oxford University Press, 2010.

77 As do Chapter 15 below by Michael Marett-Crosby ("Hate Speech: A Christian Perspective and a Reflection on Myanmar") and the film of the conference-presentation by U Kyaw Yin Hlaing ("Socio-Political Factors That Can Motivate Hate Speech", CILRAP Film, Ithaca, 9 April 2022 (https://www.cilrap.org/cilrap-film/220409-kyaw/)).

1.5. Measures Available to Prevent or Reduce Hateful Expression in the Name of Religion

Parts II, III (with Chapter 3) and IV of the anthology provide, respectively, factual, normative and explanatory foundation and context to Part V on "Measures Available to Prevent or Reduce Hateful Expression in Religious Communities", the book's main reservoir of policy information and ideas. Part V zooms in on measures external (Section F) and internal (Section G) to religious communities. Section F includes four chapters: Chapter 23 by my co-editor Kishan Manocha – "Relevant Activities and Recommendations of Intergovernmental Organizations on the Role of Religious Actors to Reduce Hate Speech, Including in Their Own Contexts or Communities" – gives a comprehensive overview of the topic, based on many years of work in this field. While substantively important for Part V, some may wish to read his chapter early in the interaction with the book (and the knowledge-base that it represents). Chapters 24 ("The Law as a Tool Against Hate Speech in Religious Contexts: Some Theoretical Comments in View of the Israeli Experience", by Gilad Noam) and 25 ("Elements of the Local Osaka Ordinance that May Be Relevant to Community Self-Regulation", by Ochi Megumi) concern national legislation[78] and local regulation, respectively. It is fortunate that the book can draw on these insightful analyses of the complex real-life situation in Israel and the innovative work of the city of Osaka. Chapter 26 offers a comprehensive non-governmental discussion of the efficacy of multilateral and bilateral measures: "A Non-Governmental Perspective on the Relative Effectiveness of Multilateral and Bilateral Measures to Combat Hate Speech: An Analysis of Tools Deployed in Response to Religious Hate Speech

[78] Temperman makes the following observations on the core external measure of domestic legislation in relation to ICCPR Article 20(2):

> [A] large number of national incitement laws do not neatly transpose Article 20(2) of the ICCPR. The most worrying shortcoming can be perceived in those laws that ban 'hate speech' or 'incitement to hatred'. The ICCPR prohibits a highly qualified offence of advocacy of hatred that constitutes incitement to concrete contingent harms, notably 'incitement to violence' and 'incitement to discrimination'. Those 'hate speech' offences fall short of that, thus critically broadening the actus reus of the speech offence. The effect is that citizens are liable to be prosecuted for speech that should not be combated under international standards. […] State parties to the ICCPR would do well to ensure that incitement laws and/or juris-prudence contain a strong focus on criminal intent. From Article 20(2) ICCPR a triple intent requirement can be distilled. First, this provision requires that the intent to 'advocate', that is to publicly disseminate hatred, be proven. Second, intent to target a group based on religion (or other traits such as ethnicity) must be proven. Third, in order to be convicted of incitement, a specific or oblique 'intent to incite' must be proven.

See Temperman, 2018, p. 372, *supra* note 38.

in Iran", by Bani Dugal. This chapter amounts to a very grave case study and reality check.

Section G contains five chapters on *internal* measures that may be available to religious leaders or actors within their communities: "How Should Responsible Religious Leaders React to Hate Speech in Their Community?" (Chapter 27 by Mohamed Elewa Badar and Rana Moustafa Essawy), "Religion as a Legal Resource: Religious or Belief Leaders and the Countering of 'Hateful Speech'" (Chapter 28 by Nazila Ghanea), "The Role of Al-Ázhár Ash-Sharíf in Combating Extremism and Hate Speech in Light of International Instruments" (Chapter 29 by Adel Maged), "Reflections on the Potential of Social Media to Assist Religious Actors Who Seek to Prevent or Reduce Hate Speech" (Chapter 30 by Peter J. Stern), and "Translational and Terminological Sensitizing of Muslim Religious Leaders of Al-Ázhár in the Combat Against Hate Speech" (Chapter 31 by Fathi M.A. Ahmed). These chapters go to the heart of this anthology and the research project it forms part of.

Although Part V offers more than 250 pages of analysis, it does not seek to advance a blueprint or agreed list of recommendations. Rather, it provides an overview of the state of our knowledge on existing public measures (international, domestic and local) and reflections on their potential and limitations, including a civil society perspective on their relative effectiveness; on formal and informal sanctions or means of disapproval available within religious communities (even if they are dormant or underutilized), with an emphasis on new ideas; on how education within religion and belief communities may function more effectively as prevention; on the potential of centralized doctrinal or religious-studies bodies within religious communities (such as the traditional Al-Ázhár Ash-Sharíf in Cairo) to play a more decisive role; on how social media can be used to assist religious actors who seek to prevent or reduce hate speech in the name of their own community; and on how religious leaders may benefit from translational and terminological sensitizing.

Formal sanctions within religious communities may include excommunication, withdrawal of voting rights within the community or referral of the matter to the secular police for criminal investigation. Excommunication or exclusion is a very strong sanction which may not be available in all religious communities. Interestingly, Locke acknowledged the function of excommunication, but argued that persons excommunicated should be afforded dignity: "no church is bound, by the duty of toleration, to retain any such person in her bosom as, after admonition, continues obstinately to offend against the laws of the society [which Waldron says "means the church's own laws of faith and worship"]. [...] nevertheless, in all such cases care is to be taken that the sentence of excommunication, and the execution thereof, carry with it no rough usage of word or action whereby the ejected person may any wise be damnified in body or estate".[79] Waldron adds: "this strongly suggests that Locke favours limits on what may be said about excommunicates, as well as on what may be done to them".[80]

Part V identifies a variety of 'informal sanctions' that may be available to religious leaders to express disapproval of hate speech by their members or in the name of their community. Such sanctions may include denial of access to some devotional gatherings or to certain locations of worship; inability to serve on boards or in other capacities in humanitarian or educational institutions of the community; inability to lead prayer or other forms of communal worship; denial of right to make financial contributions to (certain) funds of the community; suspension of access to some religious leaders or mass-media; suspension of the right to undertake pilgrimage; and dedicated information to other members of the community about the disapproved conduct of incitement to violence (naming and shaming). The informal sanctions approach concerns an area of great practical potential. The chapters of Section G are therefore of particular importance.

The list of measures discussed in Part V does not pretend to be exhaustive. It reflects the expertise brought together in the first edition of this book. And it serves as a basis for the development of further recommendations or policy input, additional to what is already articulated above, in Sections 1.6. and 1.7. below, and by other authors in the book. In addressing how religious leaders can be helped to better prevent or reduce hate speech by their members or in the name of their community, it is necessary to draw on a diverse background of expertise, not limited to lawyers.[81]

1.6. Implementation Efforts: The Rabat Plan of Action, Beirut Declaration, and 18 Commitments

The book takes cognizance of important efforts of the international community in this area, including the 'Rabat Plan of Action on the prohibition of advocacy of national, racial or religious hatred that constitutes incitement to

---

79 See Locke, 1955, p. 23, *supra* note 36.

80 See Waldron, 2012, p. 212, see *supra* note 35.

81 While jurists may enjoy some relevant methodological strengths – such as capacity for normative analysis, assessment of contributions towards the realization of violence, the role of sanctions, and strategies of prevention – the book cover shows the image of *St. Ivo Administering Justice* (the original of which is located in Florence, one block from where the project-conference took place) as a reminder of the importance of considering the interests of those most vulnerable in normative subsumption. As international law is a system of law as well as of action, it is important that lawyers participate in considerations of how to give full effect to ICCPR Article 20(2) (rather than considering that a non-legal question), see Jürgen Habermas, *Between Facts and Norms*, The MIT Press, Cambridge, 1996, pp. 79–80.

discrimination, hostility or violence' ('Rabat Plan'),[82] which contains some conclusions and recommendations adopted by a group of experts in Rabat on 5 October 2012 (based on four regional expert workshops organized by the United Nations ('UN') Office of the High Commissioner for Human Rights ('OHCHR') in 2011). The Plan concludes that "international human rights standards on the prohibition of incitement to national, racial or religious hatred still need to be integrated into domestic legislation and policies in many parts of the world. This explains both the objective difficulty and political sensitivity of defining this concept in a manner that respects the freedom of expression".[83] It develops conclusions and recommendations in clusters of legislation,[84] judicial infrastructure[85] and policy, and observes that anti-incitement policies adopted by states are "too general, not systematically followed up, lacking focus and deprived of proper impact assessments".[86] The policy recommendations are all addressed to states, the UN, media, political parties or civil society groups. There is not a single recommendation addressed to religious leaders or communities specifically, but one of the conclusions calls on political and religious leaders to (a) "refrain from using messages of intolerance or expressions which may incite violence, hostility or discrimination"; (b) speak "out firmly and promptly against intolerance, discriminatory stereotyping and instances of hate speech"; and (c) make "clear that violence can never be tolerated as a response to incitement to hatred".[87] Conclusion (a) simply provides that religious leaders should not themselves do what ICCPR Article 20(2) obliges States Parties to prohibit. Conclusions (b) and (c) offer the minimalist guidance that religious leaders should speak out against both hate speech and violent responses to it. A realistic description is therefore that the Rabat Plan concerns what we describe as

[82] Office of the High Commissioner for Human Rights, Rabat Plan of Action on the Prohibition of Advocacy of National, Racial or Religious Hatred that Constitutes Incitement to Discrimination, Hostility or Violence, UN Doc. A/HRC/22/17/Add.4, 5 October 2012 (https://www.legal-tools.org/doc/jh1be1/). Chapter 23 below by Kishan Manocha gives a comprehensive overview of this and other inter-governmental initiatives and activities.

[83] *Ibid.*, para. 60.

[84] It recommends that "States should ensure that the three-part test – legality, proportionality and necessity – for restrictions to freedom of expression also applies to cases of incitement to hatred", see *ibid.*, para. 22.

[85] It proposes a "a six-part threshold test […] for expressions considered as criminal offences" (relating to context; speaker; intent; content and form; extent of the speech act; likelihood, including imminence), and recommends that "[c]riminal sanctions related to unlawful forms of expression should be seen as last resort measures to be applied only in strictly justifiable situations", see *ibid.*, paras. 29 and 34.

[86] *Ibid.*, para. 11.

[87] *Ibid.*, para. 36. Hereinafter the 'Rabat conclusions'.

'*external* measures' in this anthology, including legislation against incitement and its enforcement by courts. In this sense, it largely takes a 'statist' approach.

Five years after the Rabat Plan, the OHCHR facilitated the adoption of a Beirut Declaration on the role of religions in promoting human rights by "faith-based and civil society actors working in the field of human rights and gathered in Beirut" in March 2017.[88] In encouraging terms, the Declaration refers to Rabat conclusions (a)–(c) discussed above as "three specific core responsibilities of religious leaders".[89] The faith-based actors commit to assume responsibilities and "support each other for their implementation through" the Declaration "on the basis of the thresholds articulated by the Rabat Plan", recognizing that "[w]ar starts in the minds and is cultivated by a reasoning fuelled by often hidden advocacy of hatred",[90] and that this "includes incitement to hatred by some religious leaders in the name of religion. Due to the speaker's position, context, content and extent of sermons, such statements by religious leaders may be likely to meet the threshold of incitement to hatred".[91] Beyond the Rabat conclusions, the Beirut Declaration adds one new normative measure for religious leaders: (d) "Remedial *advocacy to reconciliation* is equally a duty, including for religious leaders, particularly when hatred is advocated in the name of religions or beliefs".[92]

While the eloquent Declaration does not add much in terms of tools that can help religious leaders to better prevent or reduce hate speech in the name of their religious community, the faith-based leaders formulated '18 Commitments on "Faith for Rights"'.[93] In this text, they affirm their commitment to "universal norms and standards" expressed by a series of international human rights documents, "also sacred and inalienable entitlements according to religious teachings".[94] They see the "present declaration on 'Faith for Rights' as a common minimum standard for believers".[95] They restate Rabat conclusion (b) by pledging "to publicly denounce all instances of advocacy of hatred that incites to violence, discrimination or hostility, including those that lead to atrocity crimes.

---

88 Office of the High Commissioner for Human Rights, "Beirut Declaration Enhances Role of Religions in Promoting Human Rights", 29 March 2017 ('Beirut Declaration Enhances Role of Religions in Promoting Human Rights') (https://www.legal-tools.org/doc/acp88f/).

89 *Ibid.*, para. 22 (emphasis omitted).

90 *Ibid.*, para. 20.

91 *Ibid.*, para. 21 (emphasis omitted).

92 *Ibid.*

93 See Office of the High Commissioner for Human Rights, 18 Commitments on "Faith for Rights", 29 March 2017 ('18 Commitments on "Faith for Rights"') (https://www.legal-tools.org/doc/qp9nv2/).

94 See, for example, *ibid.*, Commitment I where this language is quoted from.

95 *Ibid.*, Commitment II.

We bear a direct responsibility to denounce such advocacy, particularly when it is conducted in the name of religion or belief".[96] Other commitments detail the restatement of Rabat conclusion (b)[97] and restate conclusion (a).[98]

But so far, the 18 Commitments do not really go beyond the minimalist conclusions regarding the role of religious leaders in the Rabat Plan, with three exceptions: a pledge to use technological tools more creatively and consistently (relevant to Chapter 30 below by Peter J. Stern);[99] a commitment to "leverage the spiritual and moral weight of religions and beliefs", touching on religion's central function and criterion for legitimacy;[100] and commitments that touch on the role of education (discussed in Chapter 28 by Nazila Ghanea).[101] The commitments on education do, however, leave a number of questions unanswered,[102] which illustrates some of the limitations of the Rabat Plan, the Beirut Declaration and the 18 Commitments. However, the 18 Commitments document expressly recognizes the need to develop "sustained partnerships with specialized academic institutions so as to promote interdisciplinary research on specific questions related to faith and rights and to benefit from their outcomes that could feed into the programs and tools of our coalition on Faith for Rights".[103] The present anthology responds to this recognition and seeks to contribute multi-disciplinary research-insights, *inter alia*, on how religious leaders can prevent or reduce hate speech *beyond* the minimum requirements that they should not

---

96 *Ibid.*, Commitment VII.

97 See *ibid.*, Commitments VIII and IX.

98 See *ibid.*, Commitments IX, X and XII.

99 See *ibid.*, Commitment XVIII: "We pledge to use technological means more creatively and consistently in order to disseminate this declaration and subsequent Faith for Rights messages to enhance cohesive societies enriched by diversity, including in the area of religions and beliefs".

100 See *ibid.*, Commitment XVI: "We commit to leverage the spiritual and moral weight of religions and beliefs with the aim of strengthening the protection of universal human rights and developing preventative strategies that we adapt to our local contexts, benefitting from the potential support of relevant United Nations entities".

101 See *ibid.*, Commitments XII, XIII and XVIII *i.f.*

102 Some of the questions that are relevant when we seek to strengthen the use of education within religious communities to prevent and reduce hate speech in the name of faith include the following: How can religious leaders be motivated or influenced to make better use of the tool of education? Should naming and shaming be used to expose glaring failures? What about telling positive stories of successful use of education to combat hate speech in religious contexts? Why are some religious communities (for example, the Catholic Church) seemingly doing better than several other denominations in terms of preventing religion-based or -related hate speech from within their own ranks? What is the role of individual leadership among religious leaders? Can technology be used in new ways to further relevant educational goals within religious communities? What about the film medium?

103 See 18 Commitments on "Faith for Rights", Commitment XVII, *supra* note 93.

themselves engage in hate speech (Rabat conclusion (a)), how they should speak out against both hate speech and violence in response to incitement to hatred (Rabat conclusions (b) and (c)), and how they should advocate reconciliation (point (d) taken from the Beirut Declaration).

In real life, the Beirut Declaration and 18 Commitments face a more fundamental limitation, as also discussed in Chapter 28. The term 'Faith for Rights' signals that "[f]aith and rights should be mutually reinforcing spheres. Individual and communal expression of religions or beliefs thrive and flourish in environments where human rights, based on the equal worth of all individuals, are protected. Similarly, human rights can benefit from deeply rooted ethical and spiritual foundations provided by religions or beliefs".[104] There are good reasons why the OHCHR aligned 'faith' and 'human rights' in this manner. It should be well received by religious leaders around the world. The problem is that religious actors who have engaged in some of the most notorious hate speech in recent years have, at best, a very strained relationship with the international human rights community. As pointed out in the project concept note leading to this anthology,[105] the link between 'faith' and 'human rights' reinforces the need to supplement the Beirut framework with analysis of *common-sense tools which help religious leaders to prevent hate speech and which are well-embedded in the practices, needs and interests*[106] *that religious leaders consider when they exercise influence*.[107] This was echoed by Prosecutor Khan KC at the project-conference.[108] This anthology will hopefully spur further efforts to develop a

104 18 Commitments on "Faith for Rights", para. 1, *supra* note 93.

105 For the text of the project concept note, see *supra* note 27.

106 One of the self-interests that may be shared by religious leaders around the world is concern that their community not be shamed by the conduct of a few extremist members who practice hate speech in the name of their faith. The risk of loss of reputation, standing and future prospects should be disconcerting to religious leaders of some denominations. It may be recalled that it was a thinker from the Middle East who remarked in 1912 that "if religion should prove to be the cause of enmity and hatred instead of love, its absence is preferable to its existence", see 'Abdu'l-Bahá 'Abbás, *The Promulgation of Universal Peace*, Bahá'í Publishing Trust, Wilmette, 1982, p. 315.

107 Religious leaders have power. In the words of the Beirut Declaration, they "exercise a heightened degree of influence over the hearts and minds of their followers at all times", see Beirut Declaration Enhances Role of Religions in Promoting Human Rights, para. 19, *supra* note 88. "When hateful views are expressed by an individual who claims to speak with religious authority, we may be concerned about the undue influence of such speech on an audience of believers. The hateful character and irrational appeal of such speech may be even greater when the religious audience believes that it is engaged in a struggle against the forces of evil", see Moon, 2018, p. 151, *supra* note 44.

108 Karim A.A. Khan KC, at 24:23 ff., see *supra* note 71: "When one talks about the Rome Statute or the Universal Declaration of Human Rights or the International Convention on Civil and

supplementary rationale for religious leaders to act that does not, at the same time, require them to accept a long list of international human rights instruments.

1.7. Further Ongoing Efforts and Some Concluding Remarks

There are other noteworthy contributions by inter-governmental and international non-governmental actors, three of which are mentioned here. Chapters 23 and 28 below contain more detailed discussion of these and other efforts. The United Nations Development Programme ('UNDP') has analysed socio-economic and other contextual factors relevant to the prevention of violent extremism, which also includes conduct amounting to hate speech. In a report from 2016, the UNDP observes that "[v]iolent extremism is the product of historical, political, economic and social circumstances, including the impact of regional and global power politics. Growing horizontal inequalities are one of the consistently cited drivers of violent extremism".[109] The report proposes "[w]orking with faith-based organizations and religious leaders to counter the abuse of religion by violent extremists" as one of eleven "interlinked building blocks for a theory of change explaining how development can help prevent violent extremism".[110]

In May 2019, the UN Secretary-General announced the 'United Nations Strategy and Plan of Action on Hate Speech', which expresses several key commitments by the UN with the aim "to give the United Nations the room and the resources to address hate speech".[111] The Strategy is about 'hate speech' construed as "any kind of communication in speech, writing or behaviour, that attacks or uses pejorative or discriminatory language with reference to a person or a group on the basis of who they are, in other words, based on their religion, ethnicity, nationality, race, colour, descent, gender or other identity factor".[112] The document concerns expression "that does not reach the threshold of incitement" to violence, and is therefore "not something that international law

---

Political Rights of 1966 or the Geneva Conventions, they will say: 'Well, this is not our dish, it is not to our palate. We repudiate it as somehow ungodly or concoction of somebody else'. […] Instead of trying to force-feed somebody, try to present an argument from their own value system". And at 24:09 ff.: "Sometimes the antidote to hatred from people that are preaching a religion is to unmask or disrobe them, and find out the truth of the religion and present it".

109 United Nations Development Programme, "Preventing Violent Extremism through Promoting Inclusive Development, Tolerance and Respect for Diversity: A Development Response to Addressing Radicalization and Violent Extremism", 2016, p. 4 (https://www.legal-tools.org/doc/guylbf/).

110 *Ibid.*, p. 5.

111 United Nations Secretary-General, "United Nations Strategy and Plan of Action on Hate Speech", May 2019, p. 2 (https://www.legal-tools.org/doc/5rrb5b/).

112 *Ibid.*

requires States to prohibit".[113] Its only reference to religious actors is the very broad commitment that the UN "should promote intercultural, interfaith and intrareligious dialogue and mutual understanding", and the inclusion of "religious and other civil society actors" among those who can take "meaningful action against hate speech".[114]

The November 2021 meeting of the Global Action Against Mass Atrocity Crimes (GAAMAC)[115] focused on national efforts against hate speech. The outcome document on "national prevention mechanisms and policies"[116] offers an important insight regarding prejudice: "hate speech builds on the existence of all forms of prejudice and maximizes their reach. It may incite certain behaviors against constructed figures of the other – who may become an enemy – and incitement may generate a 'license to kill' this despised person who is no longer considered an equal human being".[117] The outcome document does not specifically deal with the role of religious leaders or communities.[118] It adopts a broad approach (especially on "massive education programs") and links GAAMAC's contribution to democracy-promotion.[119]

---

[113] *Ibid.*

[114] *Ibid.*, pp. 4–5. It is encouraging when the Strategy calls for: "coordinated data collection and research, including of root causes, drivers and conditions conducive to hate speech"; that the "UN should support a new generation of digital citizens, empowered to recognize, reject and stand up to hate speech"; and that the UN, when convening key actors, should seek to "reframe problems in ways that make solutions more attainable" (pp. 3–4).

[115] GAAMAC describes itself as a "convener" and "community of commitment composed of states, civil society and academic institutions that pledges to prevent atrocities by establishing or strengthening national prevention mechanisms and policies", see Global Action Against Mass Atrocity Crimes (GAAMAC), "Strengthening National Efforts to Address Hate Speech, Discrimination, and Prevent Incitement: Outcome Document of the Fourth Global Meeting (GAAMAC IV)", 15–18 November 2021, p. 1 (https://www.legal-tools.org/doc/pi26u1/).

[116] The document observes: "These national prevention approaches will allow each society to design and implement locally grounded and tailor-made initiatives, policies and laws that enjoy legitimacy and credibility, generate trust and empower a culture and practice of democracy", see *ibid.*, p. 3.

[117] *Ibid.*

[118] Its only discussion of religious actors is the generic reference on page 6 to inter-religious dialogue and that religious leaders should "engage more actively on it": "Successful prevention and tackling of hate and discrimination against religious minorities happens when different religions, via religious leaders, come together and interreligious dialogue is initiated. There was broad consensus among participants that national prevention mechanisms should stress further the huge potential for the prevention of mass atrocities that lies within interreligious dialogue, thus calling for religious leaders to engage more actively on it, recognizing the great difference that religious leadership can make for the prevention agenda".

[119] The outcome document claims that "[s]uccessful prevention ["of hate speech, discrimination, and incitement"] can happen only through democratic public policies" (p. 3). This factual

As with the Beirut Declaration and 18 Commitments, the UNDP report, the UN Strategy, and the GAAMAC outcome document all take a human-rights based approach, for sound reasons. As discussed above, this may reduce their impact among actors who advocate religious hatred amounting to incitement to violence insofar as many of them do not accept the international human rights framework in the first place. This reinforces the need for clear-eyed, realistic analysis of the role of religious leaders, a topic that is not adequately addressed by the UN or GAAMAC documents discussed. International organizations and their member states should consider how their efforts in this area can become more incisive and effective.

If religious leaders fail to contain and reduce hateful expression in the name of their communities, they not only betray the trust which pious, reasonable believers have placed in them, but they weaken the ability of the norms and ideals which their teachings promote to have beneficial societal impact. They risk making a mockery of the spiritual exercises at the core of their faith, the tools offered to the believers for their self-improvement. As stated in Section 1.1. above, even Feuerbach held that the "ultimate essence of religion is revealed by the simplest act of religion – prayer".[120] Is prayer no longer an effective tool within the denominations that are notoriously plagued by hateful expression by their members or in the name of their community? If religious leaders do not use the formal and informal means of sanctioning or disapproval at their disposal to self-regulate – in new and innovative ways if necessary – they may end up feeding the flames of Feuerbach's view of religion, as discussed at the outset of this chapter, even within their own ranks.

It can be assumed that governments will take further measures to protect their societies against hateful expression and violence in the name of religion, including through legislation, local regulation and thematic prosecution (before domestic as well as international criminal jurisdictions). They should also consider how they can assist religious leaders to play a more effective preventive role.

---

proposition should not conceal the fact that well-established and large democracies such as India face serious challenges with hate speech as clearly illustrated by Section B of the present anthology. See also Amy Kazmin, "India Needs a Reckoning with its Growing Culture of Hate", *Financial Times*, 7 October 2021.

[120] Feuerbach, 2008, p. 102, see *supra* note 8.

2

Bloodthirsty Religion? An Inquiry into the Religious Sources of Hateful and Violent Speech

David Luban*

The title of this chapter is no doubt provocative, but I do not mean to provoke, because my answer to the title question is 'no': hate and violence are not intrinsic to religion. But understanding *why* might not be comforting: I will argue that it *is* intrinsic to some of the world's major religions that they can easily be recruited to the cause of hate and violence. Obviously, the mechanism of recruitment is speech – specifically, inflammatory speech by religious teachers and preachers that justifies violence in God's name. The question for legislators and policy-makers is where to draw the line between freedom of speech and religious expression and incitement to violence – or, one might say, between religious insight and religious incitement. That is not my question in this chapter; my aim is to investigate whether hatred is intrinsic to religion.

2.1. Hitchens' Provocation

Let me begin with a genuine provocation, by a writer who was trying his damnedest to provoke: the late journalist and polemicist Christopher Hitchens. Fifteen years ago, Hitchens wrote a flame-throwing book called *God Is Not Great*, subtitled *How Religion Poisons Everything*.[1] As you might guess from the title, it is not a good book; but it has its moments. Hitchens recalls one of his many public debates about religion, in which his opponent (a religious

---

* **David Luban** is Distinguished University Professor and Professor of Law and Philosophy at Georgetown University. Since 2013, he has also served as Class of 1965 Distinguished Chair in Ethics at the U.S. Naval Academy's Stockdale Center for Ethical Leadership. His research interests centre on moral and legal responsibility in organizational settings, including law firms, government and the military. His books include *Lawyers and Justice: An Ethical Study* (1988), *Legal Modernism* (1994), *Legal Ethics and Human Dignity* (2007), and *Torture, Power, and Law* (2014). He holds a B.A. from the University of Chicago, and M.A., M.Phil. and Ph.D. degrees in Philosophy from Yale University. This chapter originated as a keynote address at the CILRAP conference on 'Religion, Hateful Expression and Violence', CILRAP Film,Salone Brunelleschi, Ospedale degli Innocenti, Florence, 8–9 April 2022 (https://www.cilrap.org/cilrap-film/220408-luban/).

1 Christopher Hitchens, *God Is Not Great: How Religion Poisons Everything*, Atlantic Books, London, 2007.

broadcaster) challenged him: if Hitchens was alone at night in an unfamiliar city and saw a group of men walking toward him, would he not feel safer if he knew they were coming from a prayer meeting?

The reply was vintage Hitchens: he had had that experience in Belfast, Beirut, Bombay, Belgrade, Bethlehem and Baghdad – and in each of these cities he would feel *less* safe if knew the men were coming from a prayer meeting. He added that these are merely cities that start with the letter 'B'.[2]

Hitchens was writing at a time when a group of writers called the 'New Atheists' were first making headlines in the United Kingdom and United States with their all-out broadsides against religion. Along with Hitchens, the first-generation New Atheists included the biologist Richard Dawkins,[3] the philosopher Daniel Dennett,[4] the gadfly public intellectual Sam Harris,[5] and a few less well-known academic writers.[6] Their views were not identical, but one of their signature themes was that far from religion being the basis of morality, some of the greatest *im*moralities come from religion, both historically and now. A wealth of obvious examples bears this out: the history of religion is inseparable from the history of religious persecution and religious war. In the rueful words of Donniel Hartman (himself a rabbi, not a New Atheist):

> As these [monotheistic] religions entered the world stage, alongside their charge to love God and love humanity, they began to wage war with those who preceded or followed them. Wherever monotheism developed, it was accompanied by the belief that the one God could be truly represented or correctly understood by only one faith community. Love of God, or more accurately being loved by God, was perceived to be a zero-sum game.[7]

---

2 *Ibid.*, p. 18.

3 Richard Dawkins, *The God Delusion*, Mariner Books, Boston, 2011.

4 Daniel C. Dennett, *Breaking the Spell: Religion as a Natural Phenomenon*, Penguin Books USA, New York, 2007.

5 Sam Harris, *The End of Faith: Religion, Terror, and the Future of Reason*, W.W. Norton, New York, 2005; *Letter to a Christian Nation*, Vintage, New York, 2006.

Some, but not all, of the New Atheists mentioned here (and others I do not mention) have drifted over the years into alliance with the political far right. See Èmile P. Torres, "Godless grifters: How the New Atheists merged with the far right", *Salon*, 5 June 2021 (available on its web site). Even if true, I do not suggest that New Atheism is intrinsically right-wing, and by no means have all the New Atheists made such alliances.

6 These include some of the writers in Louise M. Antony (ed.), *Philosophers Without Gods: Meditations on Atheism and the Secular Life*, Oxford University Press, 2007; especially germane is Jonathan E. Adler's "Faith and Fanaticism" in *ibid.*, pp. 266–85.

7 Donniel Hartman, *Putting God Second: How to Save Religion from Itself*, Beacon Press, Boston, 2016, p. 3.

Hartman seems to attribute religious violence to monotheists, whose belief in one supreme god necessarily crowds all other gods out of the picture; but as the case of modern Hinduism in India shows, polytheism provides just as fertile a ground for religious hate speech and violence.

Even so, the sanguinary history of religions does not prove that violence is intrinsic to religion. Whether it is, is our question. Answering that question calls for analysis, not invective.

2.2. External and Internal Perspectives

Let us distinguish two points of view for examining religion, which I will call 'external' and 'internal'. The internal point of view is that of the believer and the theologian – people who discuss religion in religious terms. The external point of view is what we might call a scientific discussion of why religions come to exist, why they persist over time, and what social functions they perform: the sociology, anthropology, economics, and psychology of religion.

The New Atheists clearly adopt the external point of view, for polemical purposes in their critique of religion. But not all externalists (as we might call commentators on religion who adopt the external view) are critics of religion. Indeed, around the same time as the New Atheists, a spate of scientific books about religion appeared on the market that were by no means unsympathetic. The cognitive scientist and anthropologist Pascal Boyer explained how mental capabilities that evolve among language-using social animals – human beings, in other words – lend themselves to certain kinds of beliefs in supernatural powers; he analyses these structures in considerable depth.[8] The evolutionary biologist David Sloan Wilson showed how religions evolve the way that organisms do; groups themselves can engage in evolutionary competition in which the social glue of religion confers a selective advantage to religious communities over other groups. Religious self-sacrifice (of resources, time or life itself) might not enhance the reproductive fitness of individual group members, but it can improve the average survivability of the group, and in that indirect way it improves each member's *ex ante* odds of surviving to the age of procreation.[9]

Daniel Dennett, one of the New Atheists, offers a less benign Darwinian story: religious doctrines and symbols are 'selfish memes' that use human beings to propagate themselves, by no means to the advantage of their human hosts. His explanation draws on Dawkins's 'selfish gene' theory, according to which the biological unit of variation and selection is the gene rather than the

8 Pascal Boyer, *Religion Explained: The Evolutionary Origins of Religious Thought*, Basic Books, New York, 2001.

9 David Sloan Wilson, *In God's Cathedral: Evolution, Religion, and the Nature of Society*, University of Chicago Press, 2002, Chapter 1; the argument rehearsed here is on pp. 12–14.

individual. Dawkins used the theory to explain cultural as well as biological evolution. Genes are transgenerational carriers of biological information; in a culture, the transgenerational carriers of information are not genes, but rather specially vivid and memorable symbols and practices: *memes* (the word Dawkins coined, which has itself become a meme).[10] Religions are rich in memes – symbols, rituals, prayers, texts, sacred places, temples and cathedrals, martyrologies. The fact that people will martyr themselves for the Cross or Crescent is good for the Cross and Crescent even though it is bad for the martyrs.[11]

These are just a sample of external theories. What external theories have in common is that all of them are *naturalistic*: they explain religion as a natural social and biological phenomenon. They tell us why religions would exist even if gods, spirits and other supernatural entities do not. Some theories are *functionalist*: from Durkheim on, it is a familiar strategy to explain the persistence of religion by showing that it performs useful social functions. The newer work adds on the more complex and subtle view that religion is an accidental by-product of functional capacities (in the terminology of evolutionary theory: religion is a *spandrel*).[12] Either way, their explanations of religion neither posit nor require supernatural entities. That is what makes them external to religion itself.

2.3. The External Point of View

It does not follow that an external theorist must be an atheist. Explaining how religions can come into being and thrive even if their doctrines are false does

---

10 Richard Dawkins, *The Selfish Gene*, 4th ed., Oxford University Press, 2016; Kate Distin, *The Selfish Meme*, Cambridge University Press, 2004. Of course, calling genes or memes 'selfish' does not attribute thoughts or intentions to them. It simply means that those which survive over time are those that outcompete their rivals in the struggle for existence; and traits that are adaptive for the gene or meme will prevail heedless of the welfare of their hosts.

11 Dennett, 2007, pp. 69–85, see *supra* note 4.

12 For example, Scott Atran, *In Gods We Trust: The Evolutionary Landscape of Religion*, Oxford University Press, 2002. The spandrel concept originates with the great evolutionary biologists Stephen Jay Gould and Richard Lewontin. The term comes from architecture, where it refers to the empty space between the incurved tops of two adjacent arches. Skilled designers make the spandrels into decorative elements, but in engineering and geometric terms they are merely by-products – leftover spaces between the arches. The arches themselves are functional (they help support the building) but the spandrels are not. By analogy, Gould and Lewontin argued that some features of plant and animal morphology and behaviour confer no selective advantage to the organism, but rather are accidental by-products of traits that do confer a selective advantage. Gould and Lewontin introduced the concept to argue that evolutionary theory does not need to find a selective advantage for every observed trait of a living being. Stephen Jay Gould and Richard C. Lewontin, "The Spandrels of San Marco and the Panglossian Paradigm: A Critique of the Adaptationist Programme", in *Proceedings of the Royal Society B: Biological Sciences*, 1979, vol. 205, no. 1161, pp. 581–98.

not make the doctrines false. The question of truth is logically independent. It is important to see exactly why, because the point is easy to overlook.

Consider an analogy with mathematics. There are biological explanations of why we have mathematics. Our brains must be structured in a certain way to think mathematically, and evolutionary theory plus brain biology plus cognitive science can supply the details of how the brain got that way (figuratively: how the brain learned to count). Even the most abstract modern mathematics traces back to elementary human activities like counting, measuring, estimating, grouping and shaping – functional activities in every human society.[13] The history and sociology of mathematics can help explain why a mathematical idea becomes prominent at a specific time and place – for example, why modern conceptions of infinity arose from religious and mystical commitments among Russian mathematicians at Moscow State University in the early twentieth century.[14]

What do these external explanations have to tell us about the truth of mathematical propositions? Absolutely nothing. For truth, what you need is not explanations of why people do mathematics. For truth, you need mathematics. A 'selfish meme' theorist like Dennett might respond that 'being true' is a gimmick that selfish theorems use to propagate themselves among mathematicians; by the same reasoning, 'being beautiful' is the gimmick that Beethoven's late string quartets use to stay in the repertory. Obviously, such absurdity misses the whole point. So too with religion. A naturalistic theory of why we hold religious beliefs tells us nothing about their truth.

Of course, naturalistic explanations can lend themselves to atheism: if you can explain belief in God without positing the existence of God, then why complicate matters? As Laplace supposedly said, we have no need of that hypothesis. My point is that the external view is entirely available to religious believers. Religiously devout scientists will simply add that the sociology and biology of religion leave something out: the truth of religious beliefs. That pushes us toward the internal point of view.

---

13 On this point, see Saunders Mac Lane, "Mathematical Models: A Sketch for the Philosophy of Mathematics", in *American Mathematical Monthly*, 1981, vol. 88, no. 7, pp. 463–64. Mac Lane lists ten basic human activities which give rise to all the principal branches of higher mathematics.

14 This fascinating, almost unbelievable, episode is the subject of Loren Graham and John-Michel Kantor, *Naming Infinity: A True Story of Religious Mysticism and Mathematical Creativity*, Harvard University Press, Cambridge, 2009.

2.4. The Internal Point of View

The internal point begins with religious experience, what Rudolf Otto called the *numinous* – the idea of the holy, or, better put, the encounter with the holy.[15] For those who have experienced the numinous, it is hard to take the naturalist challenge seriously. I do not mean that religious believers are free from doubt – in fact, moments of doubting God (including doubts of God's existence) are constitutive of religious experience, a fact that theologians understand quite well. I mean only that from the internal point of view the external challenges to religious beliefs are a little bit silly, mere debater's points set against the *mysterium tremendum*. Holiness cannot be argued away, not even by very clever people. The unanswerable answer will be what the Voice in the Whirlwind says to Job: "Where were you when I founded earth?" (Job 38:4).

Viewed from inside, religion is, in addition, an ultimate source of meaning for billions of people. At times we experience meaning through fear and trembling. At other times, it is the ineffable sense expressed by the fourteenth century mystic Julian of Norwich: that even in a world where sin is everywhere, "all shall be well, and all shall be well and all manner of thing shall be well".[16] To externalists, these powerful religious emotions are phenomena to investigate; to believers, they are traces of the sacred.

2.5. Why Do Religions So Often Inspire Hate and Violence?

If all manner of thing shall be well, why should religion inspire hate and violence? One answer is: 'religion' does not; only some religions do. Anthropologist Pascal Boyer reminds us that supernaturalism takes myriad forms. In many African religions, the world was created by a god, but the creator-god is so remote that people take little interest in him and do not build rituals around the creator. What they care about is the ancestors and other spirits who need to be dealt with on a daily basis. Some cultures' gods are completely local: a sacred mountain, an ebony tree that eavesdrops on human conversations.[17] The sacred mountain has immense powers, but it has no interest in launching wars against other sacred mountains.[18] In some cultures, the spirits are a little stupid, and careful people can outwit them.[19] Not all religions have 'doctrines', and not all

---

15 Rudolf Otto, *The Idea of the Holy: An Inquiry into the Non-Rational Factor in the Idea of the Divine and Its Relation to the Rational*, published originally in German in 1917.

16 Famously quoted in T.S. Eliot, "Little Gidding", in *Four Quartets*, 1942:
Sin is behovely, but
All shall be well, and
All manner of thing shall be well.

17 Boyer, 2001, p. 69, see *supra* note 8.

18 *Ibid.*, p. 141.

19 *Ibid.*, pp. 7–8.

gods legislate moral rules. Think of Greek mythology. Hermes does not tell mortals who they can and cannot sleep with, and he does not say 'Thou shalt not steal'. Hermes is, after all, the patron god of thieves.

So our question must be refined. Why do what are today the world's major religions so often inspire hate and violence? Let me be more specific: why do some conservative strands of the major religions condemn blasphemy and apostasy, feminism and homosexuality with such fervour? I single these out because blasphemers, feminists, and LGBTQI people are familiar targets of religious hate speech and violence, a point to which I return at the end of this chapter.

The internal answer is that God hates blasphemy and homosexuality; and God sets the proper roles of men and women, commanding women to subordinate themselves to men.[20] We know this from sacred texts and from rulings by revered religious authorities. It is trivially easy to find hateful texts in holy books and clerical interpretations of them – a few minutes on the Internet will give you all the citations you need to support the case for hate.[21]

Now there is an obvious liberal rejoinder to this answer, also situated within the internal point of view: religious extremists are misreading the texts. Hateful sacred texts should not be interpreted literally, and it is the duty of religious leaders to combat hateful interpretations that "manifestly conflict with universal human rights norms and standards" (here, I am directly quoting the Eighth Commitment of the 'Faith for Rights' principles endorsed in the Beirut Declaration).[22]

In fact, there is a long and venerable tradition of anti-literalism in interpreting sacred texts, which buttresses the progressive rejoinder. Judaism's greatest philosopher, Moses Maimonides (the Rambam), argued elaborately that the Torah must be interpreted non-literally.[23] He was no outlier in his time: the Muslim theologians of the Fátimid dynasty also favoured figurative or allegorical interpretation; and across the Mediterranean, St. Thomas Aquinas endorsed

---

20 Blasphemy: Leviticus 24:16; Mark 3:29, King James Version. Homosexuality: Genesis 9:20–27, 19:1–11, Leviticus 18:22, 20:13, Babylonian Talmud Sanhedrin 54a, 1 Corinthians 6:9–10, 1 Timothy 1:10, Romans 1:26–27. Subordination of women: 1 Corinthians 11:3, 14:34–5; Ephesians 5:22–24; Colossians 3:18; 1 Timothy 2:11–12; 1 Peter 3:1.

21 In the time of Louis IX, egged on by Pope Clement IV, the punishment for blasphemy was mutilating the tongues and lips of blasphemers. The Pope's anti-blasphemy epistle is quoted in Robert Chazan, "The Condemnation of the Talmud Reconsidered (1239–1248)", in *Proceedings of the American Academy of Jewish Research*, 1988, vol. 55, p. 28.

22 Beirut Declaration on Faith for Rights, 29 March 2017, p. 30 (https://www.legal-tools.org/doc/k178m1/).

23 Moses Maimonides, *Guide of the Perplexed*, Shlomo Pines (trans.), vol. 1, University of Chicago Press, Chicago, 1974, chap. 56, pp. 130–31; chap. 57, pp. 132–33; chap. 59, pp. 139–40.

Maimonides' 'negative theology'.[24] Arguably it is scriptural hyper-literalism that is a modern invention, almost the antithesis of the historical tradition.[25] Indeed many scholars have argued that contemporary fundamentalisms are not in the least traditional – they are a modern phenomenon, an imaginary return to an imagined past.[26]

Notably, non-fundamentalist scholars and clerics have written libraries of progressive interpretations of their faiths' sacred texts. It is just as easy to pick out anti-hate sacred writings as hateful ones; the 'Faith for Rights' principles endorsed in the Beirut Declaration quote 30 of them. One of the major scholarly enterprises of the human rights movement has been anchoring international human rights within the religious traditions.

2.6. Us versus Them

Yet the fundamentalists remain unmoved by these efforts, and it is worth considering why. One reason is that non-literal interpretation seems to deny the inerrancy of the Word of God and his prophets. If the Bible commands that "with a male you shall not lie as one lies with a woman" because "it is an abomination" (Leviticus 18:22–23), then please do not say that the Bible does not really mean what it says.

A related answer is that non-literalism seems too fancy compared with reading the words on the page. Progressive interpretations can seem like pale sophisms by clever elites trying to pull a fast one on the faithful. Fundamentalists know very well that even the Devil can quote Scripture.

Then the question becomes: why do fundamentalists think that progressive, human rights-oriented clergy and theologians are the Devil? Here, I think, the answer is distressingly simple: they feel in their bones that the progressive theologians are not 'one of us'; and the Us versus Them distinction is what really matters. They sense that a human rights scholar writing feminist interpretations of 'Islám in his comfortable office at a Western university has exiled himself

---

24 Thomas Aquinas, *Summa Theologiae*, First Part, preamble to question 3; see Isaac Franck, "Maimonides and Aquinas on Man's Knowledge of God: A Twentieth-Century Perspective", in *Review of Metaphysics*, 1985, vol. 38, pp. 591–615. On the Fatimid theologians, see Joel L. Kraemer, *Maimonides: The Life and World of One of Civilization's Greatest Minds*, Doubleday, New York, 2008, pp. 153–57.

25 Moshe Halbertal has deeply analysed the many non-literal interpretive strategies the rabbis used over the centuries to adapt sacred laws to the real-world conditions of Jewish communities in the Diaspora. Moshe Halbertal, *People of the Book: Canon, Meaning, and Authority*, Harvard University Press, Cambridge, 1997. The same is true in Islám and Christianity. As Halbertal argues, a closed canon requires open interpretation.

26 As Michael Walzer puts it, conservative religion in its militant and ideological forms is "modern even in its anti-modernism". Michael Walzer, *The Paradox of Liberation: Secular Revolutions and Religious Counterrevolutions*, Yale University Press, New Haven, 2015, p. 28.

from Us, and joined with Them – and that discredits his interpretation. In just the same way, messianic Jews know that Talmudic interpretations by Rabbis for Human Rights come from Them, not Us.

The Us-versus-Them diagnosis takes us out of the internal view, because the distinction is at bottom political, not theological.[27] Us-versus-Them is the hallmark of a coalition trying to defend its boundaries against perceived threats. That is an external explanation, and I think it is correct; in the remainder of this chapter, I want to expand on it.

2.7. Generalized Norm-Making, Martyrdom and Proximity to Attractive Alternatives

To begin with, we should ask what kind of religions are especially vulnerable to this phenomenon. I suggest they are religions that share three characteristics:

First and most important, their God or gods are *generalized norm-makers*: they dictate entire ways of life, so that a threat to the religion is a threat to the way of life, and vice-versa. The gods of Greek mythology did not seem to engage in generalized norm-making; they had other pastimes. To be sure, they required sacrifice, propitiation and elaborate ritual practices – but they did not regulate every aspect of life. The religions I am concerned with do. Notably, they ferociously regulate sexual morality, and insist on the hierarchies of men and women.

Second, the sacredness of God is worth dying for. That is not true in all religions. To my knowledge, the Greek gods did not require mortals to martyr themselves for the faith. This does not mean the Greek gods could be trifled with. Offending Apollo and Artemis could bring a plague onto your city or force you to sacrifice your own daughter.[28] But these were punishments, not martyrdoms. (Although Antigone tells Creon she will die for the sake of the unwritten, immovable laws of the gods,[29] her true motive seems to be feelings for her brother, and she is not a reliable reporter of Greek religion.[30]) Martyrdom

27 It is very close to Carl Schmitt's friend/enemy distinction that he argues is "the concept of the political" in the eponymous book. However, when I assert that the distinction is externalist, I am oversimplifying, because the Us/Them distinction can be found in sacred texts, read internally. See, for example, Donniel Hartman, *The Boundaries of Judaism*, Continuum Books, New York, 2007.

28 I am referring to the myths of Oedipus and Iphigenia, as dramatized by Aeschylus, Euripides and Sophocles.

29 Sophocles, *Antigone*, lines 454–55.

30 Antigone tells Ismene that she will never betray her brother (line 45), and that she will lie with him, loved one with loved one, in the tomb that later she calls her bridal chamber (lines 73, 891). Bernard Williams acutely writes that Antigone is in love with her brother's death and with her own "ready and massive self-assertion". Bernard Williams, *Shame and Necessity*, University of California Press, Berkely, 1993, p. 86.

matters. If I am willing to die for my faith, I will attribute nearly infinite objective value to it, and then I will see nothing wrong with killing for my faith.[31]

Third, the religious community rubs elbows with people from other communities. That creates a perpetual threat of defection from the community, at relatively low cost.[32] Defection poses a mortal threat to the religious community. The other ways of life become something more than interesting alternatives – they become, or get perceived, as a deadly menace because of their allure. That includes not only foreign cultures, but also sexual minorities and their temptingly transgressive practices; and women challenging traditional hierarchies may well embolden other women to follow their example. All these alternatives are threats to the way of life – not because they are trying to attack the way of life, but because they offer alternatives that might be too enticing.

Notice that this is a radically different explanation of intercommunal hatred than the standard one. The standard one is that we find other ways of life too repulsive. The defection theory is that we find them too attractive, and we 'other' them because they are competing for our allegiance, or that of our children.

Here, I am borrowing an idea from Pascal Boyer, who writes:

> Fundamentalism is neither religion in excess nor politics in disguise. It is an attempt to preserve a particular kind of hierarchy based on coalition, when this is threatened by the perception of cheap and therefore likely defection.[33]

Nothing illustrates the defection theory better than the passages in the Hebrew Bible in which the God of Israel warns that he is a jealous god. The prophets amplify the point with powerful metaphors likening idolatry to sexual infidelity.[34] There were many Canaanite religions competing for the allegiance of the Children of Israel, and the allure of Baal and the Golden Calf was powerful.

The example illustrates that it also helps if the religious texts themselves contain the ingredients for hatred of those who defect from the way of life or tempt members to defect. Texts from antiquity can be counted on to provide fodder for modern-day hatred.

One crucial corollary of this model is that religiously-based violence will always present itself in the guise of self-defence – not only defence of our faith,

---

31 Moshe Halbertal, *On Sacrifice*, Princeton University Press, 2012, pp. 69–70.

32 I draw some of this analysis from Boyer, 2001, see *supra* note 8.

33 *Ibid.*, p. 296.

34 Exodus 20:5 and 30:14. On the sexual imagery in the prophets, see the powerful analysis of Moshe Halbertal and Avishai Margalit, *Idolatry*, Harvard University Press, Cambridge, 1992, pp. 11–20, citing Exodus 34:15–16, Hosea 1:2, 14–15; Ezekiel 16:15–34; Jeremiah 2:18–20.

but defence of our way of life. Members of the community call it the 'traditional' way of life. But, as I remarked above, that is an illusion: it is a modern fantasy of a traditional way of life that may never have existed. Imaginary or not, though, it explains why to many people religious violence is justified violence. It is not that God commands it. It is that violence in self-defence against deadly threats is justified.

A second corollary, though, is that this is not because 'religion poisons everything', Christopher Hitchens's accusation. For one thing, I am conjecturing that only religions with these three characteristics (generalized norm-making, martyrdom, and proximity to attractive alternatives) can be easily commandeered into violence. The main point is that it is not, or not primarily, about the religion – it is about maintaining a coalition that identifies the religion with a way of life.

2.8. Religious Hatred as a Rationalization or By-Product

That takes us to the next question. If it is the coalition that drives the violence, and the religion defines the coalition, in what sense is religion *responsible* for violence? In other words, how much blood do religions have on their hands? For New Atheists like Hitchens, the answer seems obvious: oceans of blood have been spilled in the name of religion. Religion causes hate and violence. Religion is bloodthirsty. I will argue that this view is wrong.

There are two ways of understanding the 'Bloodthirsty Religion' thesis that religion is responsible for violence carried out in its name. These correspond roughly to two notions of causation in the law, and my argument is that both fail.

The first reads the claim as but-for causation: but for religion, human life would be far less violent and cruel. That claim seems at best dubious. People kill each other over issues of money and power, honour and sex, Us and Them, and there is no reason to suppose that without religion the killing would diminish. Money and power, honour and sex, Us and Them will always be with us.

Even what we think of as wars of religion have complex causes. All parties in the English civil war used religious language to describe why they were fighting, but historians identify, and argue over, multiple causes of the war: class conflicts,[35] the financial demands of the Stuarts, the waning power of the rural aristocracy, national conflicts among English, Scots and Irish, or even a fortuitous combination of small tensions.[36] Does the but-for claim mean that a

[35] For example, the destruction and destitution of the peasantry by deforestation, enclosure and famine.

[36] The diagnosis that religious sects in the English Civil War were simply using the language of religion to wage class conflict originates in Marx: "Cromwell and the English people had borrowed from the Old Testament the speech, emotions, and illusions for their bourgeois

kingdom identical to the seventeenth century British Isles in every way except that its people held uniform religious beliefs or no religious beliefs would not have had a civil war? If so, the claim demands evidence that the other causes would be insufficient to tip over into mass violence. I see no such evidence. The other causes are weighty – so why think they would not have been enough?

Similar issues of multiple causation appear in the Balkan wars of the 1990s. To be sure, Croatia is Catholic, Serbia is Orthodox, and Bosnia is half Muslim. Some commentators thought that religious animosity played a tangible role; but ethnicity played a far larger role than religion in the Serb-Croat conflict, as did ethno-political grievances left over from World War II. So did the identity crisis of Yugoslav socialism, and the Croats' evident desire to abandon socialism and turn West, as the Slovenes did. Hitchens recalls a joke he heard in Croatia. A man is stopped at a roadblock. He responds that he is an atheist, but his captor presses on: "Croat atheist or Serb atheist?". In Belfast, it was "Protestant atheist or Catholic atheist?".[37] To Hitchens, the joke proves that 'religion poisons everything', but in fact it proves the opposite: the captors care which tribe you belong to, not which confession you embrace. The Irish troubles had to do with patterns of economic subordination as much as with religious differences that largely track the class structure of Northern Ireland. Christian peasants hated Jews for religious reasons, but also because European monarchs employed the Jews as tax farmers. Overdetermined hatred, not pure religious hatred, seems to be the historical rule rather than the exception.[38]

Test cases in which religion was not the issue in mass violence are not hard to find, and they weaken the Bloodthirsty Religion thesis. Thus, for

---

revolution. When the real goal had been achieved and the bourgeois transformation of English society had been accomplished, Locke supplanted Habakkuk", see Karl Marx, "The Eighteenth Brumaire of Louis Napoleon", *Die Revolution*, 1852. It has been most strongly associated with the historian Christopher Hill, *The World Turned Upside Down: Radical Ideas During the English Revolution*, Viking Adult, New York, 1972. The fortuitous combination of small tensions view originated in the "revisionist revolt" in Civil War historiography pioneered by Conrad Russell. See Conrad Russell, *The Causes of the English Civil War*, Clarendon Press, Oxford, 1990; Peter Gaunt (ed.), *The English Civil War: The Essential Readings*, Blackwell, Oxford, 1991; and especially the chapter by Mary Fulbrook, "The English Revolution and the Revisionist Revolt", in *ibid.*, pp. 59–78.

[37] Hitchens, 2007, pp. 18, 20, see *supra* note 1. I have heard an expert describe the Balkan wars as religious wars by people who are not religious.

[38] Conrad Russell cites an incident in which an armed crowd defended the organs at Norwich cathedral against puritans: "what they were defending was, at one and the same time, a religion, a way of life, and a corporate identity. This incident, and what it symbolizes, are somewhere near the epitome of Royalism"; Russell, 1990, p. 22, see *supra* note 36; see also *ibid.*, pp. 58–59, where Russell points out that the division of parties by religion does not mean they were fighting over religion.

example, religious differences between Hutus and Tutsis played no role in the Rwanda genocide (because both groups are largely Catholic). In Darfur, all the warring parties were Muslim, and the group bases of the conflict seem to be self-identified 'Arab' pastoralists pitted against 'black' farmers.[39]

But perhaps the Bloodthirsty Religion thesis is not about but-for causation. A proponent may argue that, even if violence is overdetermined, the fact that its perpetrators sincerely offer religious reasons for smiting the infidels makes religion causally responsible in a more direct and proximate way. If religion provides the psychologically motivating reason for a misdeed, religion is the cause even if the perpetrators would have done the same thing for different motives if religion were not an issue.

But this is not true in cases of overdetermined causation. For example, an individual may engage in violence against gays in part because of his visceral revulsion to gay sex (or more likely because of his visceral *attraction* to gay sex, causing gay panic); in part because gays seem threatening to traditional gender roles; and in part because of religious teachings that are anti-gay hate speech. What if the religious hatred is simply a cloak for hatred on other grounds? Or perhaps the secular grounds of hatred triggered the religious hatred? In other words, the perpetrators' homophobia could be driving their reading of the Bible rather than the other way around. In these cases, the religious motive for hate crime is effect, not cause. Religion is not the cause, even if the religious reason was the only occurrent thought going through the perpetrator's mind as he stalked the victim.

These two scenarios – religious hatred as a rationalization for hatred on other grounds, and religious hatred as a by-product of other grounds – strike me as better analogues of historical cases like the English wars of religion. They also seem like a better description of contemporary militant Islámism, which seamlessly succeeded secular ideologies such as pan-Arabism and secular

[39] Apart from these long-standing tensions, the conflict pitted the central government against rebels, with the government sponsoring 'Arab' militias as their agents; on this understanding, group-based hatred is at most a contributing or INUS cause of the genocide. 'INUS' is an acronym for 'insufficient but necessary part of an unnecessary but sufficient condition'. Consider a simple example of whether striking a match caused it to ignite. Striking the match was in this case a necessary condition for it to ignite, but it was not a sufficient condition: if the match had been wet, or there was no oxygen, striking the match would not light it. Striking the match under the right conditions is sufficient to light it, but it is not necessary, because there are other ways of lighting a match. Thus striking the match is an insufficient but necessary part of an unnecessary but sufficient condition for the match to ignite. Match-striking is an INUS cause of ignition. Religious convictions are at best an INUS cause of violence in many cases, and in Darfur group-based hatred was at best an INUS cause of genocide.

socialist nationalisms. All seem like by-products of the same set of historical and political grievances against colonialism and Western modern culture.

One confirmation comes from studies by the political scientists Robert Pape and James Feldman, who for years maintained a comprehensive database of suicide bombings. One of their findings was that suicide bombing need not correlate with religious extremism: secular insurrections have used the tactic too. They found a stronger correlation with the perception (justified or not) that one's homeland has been occupied by foreigners. Sometimes this grievance cloaks itself in religious garb; other times it does not.[40]

2.9. Religion as a Schelling Point

As an alternative to the Bloodthirsty Religion thesis, I propose a simple game-theoretic account of group polarization.[41] One of the abiding puzzles of group violence like the Balkan wars or the Sunní–Shí'ah conflict in Iraq in the wake of the United States invasion is why people who coexisted for many years could rapidly polarize along group lines and begin murdering their neighbours.

The obvious factor in both cases is that a strong centralized government collapsed, leaving behind a struggle over resources and jobs – in effect, an artificially induced state of nature.[42] Individuals in a state of nature will find it essential to form defensive coalitions: strength lies in numbers. And small coalitions will find it expedient to join larger coalitions. Even people with no personal desire to slaughter their neighbours can experience intense pressure to join a warring faction, which otherwise may simply treat them as a traitor and an enemy. "I really don't hate Muslims", a murderous paramilitary explained during the Balkan wars, "but because of the situation I want to kill them all".[43] In just the same way, a Rwandan Hutu explained his participation in the genocide thus: "If you stayed at home, you risked being labelled an accomplice and suffering death yourself".[44]

---

[40] Robert A. Pape and James K. Feldman, *Cutting the Fuse: The Explosion of Global Suicide Terrorism and How to Stop It*, University of Chicago Press, 2012.

[41] I draw on Russell Hardin, *One for All: The Logic of Group Conflict*, Princeton University Press, 1995, p. 142. I have elaborated a bit (not much) on Hardin's model.

[42] Moreover, both states were socialist, with large public sectors that provided a great many jobs, all of which now seemed up for grabs for whoever had the muscle to seize them.

[43] Quoted in Hardin, 1995, p. 148, see *supra* note 41.

[44] Mahmoud Mamdani, *When Victims Become Killers: Colonialism, Nativism, and Genocide in Rwanda*, Princeton University Press, 2001, pp. 203–05. In addition to the Hobbesian logic of the intergroup conflict, those most committed to violence within each group always have an interest in recruiting others to enhance impunity by spreading complicity as broadly as possible. Notoriously, warlords who kidnap or otherwise recruit child soldiers sometimes compel them to commit atrocities – for example, by killing another new recruit – as a rite of passage.

But why do coalitions form along specifically religious lines of fracture? Nobel Prize-winning economist Thomas Schelling explained that the rational way to co-ordinate with others is to organize around a salient characteristic, even if it has no special significance other than its salience.[45] Salience makes it a probable answer to the question 'what coalition are those I wish to co-ordinate with most likely to join, given that they are asking the same question about which coalition I will join?'. The structure of the game is that:

1) it has multiple equilibria;
2) every equilibrium is better than failure to co-ordinate; but
3) none will be achieved unless other players find the same equilibrium point.

Schelling's solution is that the most salient equilibrium will do the trick, provided that the players are astute enough to ask the right question: not 'which equilibrium is most salient *to me* (or preferred by me)?', nor even 'which equilibrium is best?', but 'which is most salient to most actors who are asking the same question because they too want to converge with as many players as possible?'.

For example, suppose you and your friends are in Florence, and have agreed to meet at 10 in the morning – but you forgot to say where. The obvious answer for each of you is to go to the Duomo plaza, because it is the most famous landmark in the city. It is the place that your friends are most likely to guess you will go, because they know you are trying to guess where they will go. For convenience, let us call the most salient equilibrium the 'Schelling point' (Schelling modestly calls it the focal point.) Nothing *a priori* dictates the Schelling point. In the Florence example, the Schelling point does not have to be the Duomo plaza. It might be the trattoria where you and your friends spent an especially memorable evening the last time you visited Florence together. What makes it the Schelling point is your confidence that your friends asking, 'what's the most likely meeting point we will all think of, knowing we are all asking this question?' will choose the trattoria.

When it comes to joining a coalition, the Schelling point may be clan or tribe or race or class; here too, nothing *a priori* dictates which salient characteristic will turn out to be the Schelling point. However, once a dominant coalition forms, its defining characteristic – its calling card – will become the Schelling point, simply because dominance automatically makes it the most salient equilibrium by elevating its prominence, power and the protection it can offer its members.

[45] Thomas C. Schelling, *The Strategy of Conflict*, Harvard University Press, Cambridge 1960, pp. 54–58.

That is where religion comes in. Religion is an obvious Schelling point because of its salience for so many people – and whenever religious confession is the obvious Schelling point, the society will fracture along lines of religion, even if most people were not fanatically devout before the crack-up. But, supposing the underlying state-of-nature remains the same, if religion were taken off the table some other Schelling point would substitute – perhaps nationality, perhaps race, or political party, or clan, or shared historical grievance. Any calling card will do, provided it is more salient than the other candidates.

This model can be readily extended beyond cases where a government collapses. Powerful governments can artificially induce group-against-group structures that force individuals to take sides. And charismatic leaders can use their own bully pulpit to lend salience to a calling card like 'Aryan' or 'the faithful'.

I cannot prove that this model of religious polarization is the best one. It is obviously an external rather than internal explanation. If something along these lines is roughly correct, however, the result undermines any claim of causation that aims to prove that religion intrinsically causes violence.

2.10. Three Implications

Let me conclude briefly with a few implications of this analysis for the project of tempering religious hatred and violence.

The first implication is that religious hate speech is most likely to motivate violence when the society is fracturing for other reasons. Hate speech is odious for many obvious reasons, and cloaking it in the robes of religion makes it worse, not better, by raising the stakes to divine levels – or, as I prefer to think, by dragging God or the gods into the gutter. But in an otherwise stable and pacific society, religious hate speech is less likely to translate into violence. The legal effort to balance freedom of speech and religion against the requirement of the International Covenant on Civil and Political Rights that states prohibit incitements of "discrimination, hostility or violence"[46] should take that into account.

The second implication is the converse of the first: social fracturing – an economic or social state of nature – is likely to generate religious hate speech. Thus, states aiming to diminish religious hate speech must address it not only directly, but also by addressing the secular causes of social fracture.

One such cause is improved economic and educational opportunities for women, which not only threatens male power, but also might induce women to defect from patriarchal society into 'modernity'. The resurgence of Taliban rule

[46] International Covenant on Civil and Political Rights, 19 December 1966, Article 20(2) (https://www.legal-tools.org/doc/2838f3/).

in Afghanistan is perhaps the most publicized recent example, but the backlash against feminism goes on everywhere in the world where women's equality has gained a toehold. The backlash puts on a religious cloak when the traditional religious way of life rests on gender hierarchy, as it does in all traditionalist religions. The obsessions of traditionalist religions with sexual morality and female modesty are strong evidence of how central gender hierarchy is. In the world's major religions, there is plentiful scriptural backing for anti-feminism, and (as noted earlier) that means that to many of the faithful, women's advancement violates the divinely-sanctioned order of things.

For those trying to bind up social fracture to reduce violence, one temptation is to give in and concede to religious demands for protection of gender hierarchy. The temptation must be resisted. Reducing women's rights and opportunities is not the way to address social fracture. Religious leaders must insist that the way to win a competition against an alternative way of life is to make your own more attractive, not to destroy the competitor.

Third, the issue of religious hate speech and violence is in the hands of religious leaders as well as states, as recognized by the Beirut Declaration on Faith for Rights. Ambitious or opportunistic religious leaders will always be tempted to make their religion the most salient feature in the political landscape for self-aggrandizing purposes, and political hate speech is their instrument of choice. They will wrap themselves in the mantle of free speech and free exercise of religion, even as they denounce the free speech of their critics as blasphemy, and secular values as persecution of the faithful. Perhaps it is unrealistic to expect them to dial it back at cost to their own power and relevance. Faith leaders who wish to advance human rights must instead do everything they can to quarantine a charismatic hatemonger behind a *cordon sanitaire* – and, of course, do everything they can to win over potential defectors by creating religious practices that link the power and beauty of faith with the power and beauty of human dignity and the rights that enhance it.

3

Drawing the Line Between the Preservation of Freedom of Religious Expression and the Fight Against Hate Speech and Incitement to Terrorism and Violence: The Perspective of a Judge and a Prosecutor

Justice Dorit Beinisch[*]

3.1. Introduction

Religious leaders and legal practitioners alike know that words have immense power. Words have the power to bring us together, and words have the power to tear us apart. It is with that in mind that we begin the discussion that follows, on freedom of expression and its relationship to religious expression.

Many international legal instruments and documents – the Rabat Plan of Action as a prime example – emphasize that as a matter of fundamental principle, limitation of speech *must* remain the exception, and not the rule.[1] Yet, democracies must balance the protection of freedom of expression, as a cornerstone of democratic principles and ideals, against the basic necessity of protecting their people and the democratic regime itself. And today, when speech can spread like wildfire on social media and in other forms, those dangers take on greater urgency. When speech is uttered in a religious setting, in spaces where religious communities gather, and when the power of the word is coupled with the power

---

* Justice **Dorit Beinisch** is President (Ret.) of the Supreme Court of Israel. She received her LL.B. and LL.M. (summa cum laude) from the Hebrew University of Jerusalem. In 1989, she was appointed the State Attorney of Israel; in 1995, she was appointed Justice of the Supreme Court, becoming its first woman President in 2006. Over the course of her career in public service, Justice Beinisch paid special emphasis to the fight against racism and ideological extremism, as well as the need to combat government corruption. This chapter is a written version of oral remarks delivered at the CILRAP conference on Religion, Hateful Expression and Violence in Florence on 8 April 2022 (https://www.cilrap.org/cilrap-film/220408-beinisch/). They have been edited for clarity, style and length.

1 "Rabat Plan of Action on the prohibition of advocacy of national, racial or religious hatred that constitutes incitement to discrimination, hostility or violence", 5 October 2012 in Report of the United Nations High Commissioner for Human Rights on the Expert Workshops on the Prohibition of Incitement to National, Racial or Religious Hatred, UN Doc. A/HRC/22/17/Add.4, 11 January 2013, para. 18 (https://www.legal-tools.org/doc/oymwge/).

of the Almighty, the dangers can be even more pronounced. At the same time, one's right to religious freedom, much like one's right to freedom of expression, is rightfully considered one of the bedrocks of individual liberties, such that a democracy must do its utmost to protect one's ability to freely exercise one's religion.

The State of Israel, as a relatively young and highly-polarized country with multiple cleavage-lines, must be especially sensitive to both of these ideals: it can ill-afford to infringe upon freedom of speech, with the attendant risk that the minority and disenfranchised populations' speech will be unduly infringed upon; and yet it can ill-afford to take the risk that free speech will lead to increased racism, violence and terrorism in our midst.

In this short chapter, which is primarily a reflection of the lessons learned throughout the course of my career,[2] I will describe the ways in which Israel attempts to find its balance between protecting free speech and fighting against racism, violence and terror. I will, in particular, focus in on two of the most salient forms of speech limitation in the Israeli legal system: criminal prosecution of *individuals* for incitement to racism, violence and terrorism, and the authority to disqualify *Parliamentary lists and candidates* who espouse racist views as representatives of the public. Through the prism of these two legal orders, and their historical development over the years, we will explore some of the dilemmas involving freedom of expression and religious extremism in Israel, and note the political and social events that affected both its legislation and jurisprudence. While this chapter sets out a single country's method of grappling with this topic, similar dilemmas can be seen in other countries and in the international arena.

3.2. Freedom of Speech and Incitement: The Early Years

From its inception, Israel's Supreme Court developed a robust jurisprudence on freedom of expression.[3] Israel did not have a written Constitution from which to draw constitutional principles. Nonetheless, in one of its earliest and oft-cited decisions, the Court ruled that the Government's suspension of a Hebrew newspaper, Kol Ha'am, and its Arabic-language counterpart was an unconstitutional restriction on free expression, based on the rights and values set out in Israel's

---

2 These remarks are mainly influenced by my years in the prosecution (beginning in 1967), and in particular as the State Attorney of Israel (from 1989 to 1995), where I represented the State of Israel in major cases before the Supreme Court, and in which position I was responsible for setting out state policy for the prosecution of incitement offenses; and then as a Justice in Israel's Supreme Court (from 1995 to 2012).

3 See, for example, Adam Shinar, "Freedom of Expression in Israel: Origins, Evolution, Revolution and Regression", in Aharon Barak, Barak Medina and Yaniv Roznai (eds.), *Oxford Handbook on the Israeli Constitution*, Oxford University Press (forthcoming).

Declaration of Independence.[4] The judicial integrity and fearless independence of the Justices in this case is one to emulate, for this was in the early 1950s – only a few years after Israel's creation, when the wounds from the War of Independence were still fresh, and security fears high.

Even in this most seminal of cases, however, the Court made it clear that incitement that could result in injury was not protected under the right to free speech. The legal test developed to ascertain whether speech could be limited was the test of 'near certainty', or 'imminent likelihood' that it would endanger the public safety. This high standard for limiting speech became the golden standard in Israel, at least as regards administrative action that limits free speech.

In the criminal sphere, in those years, incitement was primarily dealt with via two criminal provisions handed down to the Israeli system from British common law, a legal remnant of when the British ruled the region. The first – the Prevention of Terrorism Ordinance, prohibited incitement to violence and support for a terrorist organization.[5] The second – Israel's Penal Code ('Penal Code'), included the prohibition on what was called "sedition", which was defined not only as "the creation of discontent or resentment among Israeli residents" but also "the promotion of conflict and enmity between different parts of the population". In addition, Israel legislated the Law Against Genocide in 1950, which included a criminal prohibition on incitement to genocide.[6]

Jurisprudence over the next few decades on freedom of speech in general, and criminal incitement in particular, was limited, and neither the Courts nor the Knesset (Israel's parliament) devoted much attention to the question at hand. When I was in the prosecution, in the 1970s and 1980s, we focused our energy mainly on prosecuting crimes of physical acts of violence, while speech acts were often left unprosecuted. When those actions also were set against a background of hate speech of extreme ideology and hatred between sectors, the

---

4 Israeli High Court of Justice, *Kol Ha'am Co., Ltd. v. Minister of the Interior*, Judgment, 16 October 1953, H.C.J. 73/53, 87/53 (https://www.legal-tools.org/doc/2tr275/).

5 See Daphne Barak-Erez and David Scharia, "Freedom of Speech, Support for Terrorism, and the Challenge of Global Constitutional Law", in *Harvard National Security Journal*, 2011, vol. 2, pp. 1-30; Daphne Barak-Erez, "Israel's Anti-terrorism Law: Past, Present and Future", in Victor V. Ramraj, Michael Hor, Kent Roach and George Williams (eds.), *Global Anti-Terrorism Law and Policy*, 2nd. ed., Cambridge University Press, 2012, p. 597.

6 Interestingly, though the Jewish people's experience in the Holocaust must have impacted the will to legislate this law, the explanatory notes for the bill do not reference the Jewish people's experience as victims of genocide, but instead reference the desire to join the United Nations Convention on the Prevention and Punishment of the Crime of Genocide, 9 December 1948 (https://www.legal-tools.org/doc/498c38/), as the rationale for the bill (Israel, Prevention and Punishment of the Genocide Crime Act, 29 March 1950 (https://www.legal-tools.org/doc/ad0958/)).

prosecution took a particularly hard line – for instance, in stamping out Jewish violence and revenge actions against Arab terror, such as in the case of the 25 members of a Jewish underground terrorist cell whom we prosecuted, who had murdered and maimed a number of Arab victims in the early 1980s, and plotted, among other things, to blow up the mosque on Jerusalem's Dome of the Rock.

Around those same years, in July 1984, a prominent right-wing rabbi, Rabbi Meir Kahana, was elected to the Knesset (with 1.2 per cent of the vote) as the candidate for the extremist Kach party, which openly advocated racism and violence against the Arab population in Israel.

The fact that Kahana's party passed the electoral threshold was a jarring moment for many in Israel, and was a catalyst for change in Israeli policy regarding extremist speech. Within a year, the Government brought to the Knesset two legislative proposals on the same day[7] that were subsequently adopted into Israeli law and shape our legal framework to this very day. One focused on the criminal prosecution of *individuals* for incitement to racism, and the other set out the powers to disqualify *Parliamentary lists and candidates* who espouse racist views as representatives of the public.

3.3. Criminal Provisions on Incitement: Historical Trajectory

Israel has three main types of incitement crimes today: incitement to racism, incitement to violence, and incitement to terror.[8] The core of the crimes of incitement to terror was, as I noted, on the books from the early years. But it was Kahana's election that directly led to the adoption of Article 144B to the Penal Code, which prohibits any publication with an *intent of inciting racism* based on skin colour, racial or ethnic-national identity: what may be termed in some legal systems, 'hate speech'.[9] With the addition of this new offence, Israel explicitly made it clear that racism has no place in public discourse, nor does it have value that warrants legal protection.

---

[7] The proposals were brought on the same day (17 May 1985) – the two amendments were passed at different times (the Basic-Law was amended on 7 August 1985; the Penal Code was amended on 13 August 1986) (https://www.legal-tools.org/doc/7rzdt7/), see Israel, Basic-Law: The Knesset (5718-1958), 12 February 1958 ('Basic-Law: The Knesset') (https://www.legal-tools.org/doc/tt9mvj/); Israel, Penal Law 5737, 4 August 1977 ('Penal Code') (https://www.legal-tools.org/doc/93000f/).

[8] This is in addition to the crime of incitement to genocide, which was codified in Israel's legislation in 1950, Prevention and Punishment of the Genocide Crime Act, Article 3(2), see *supra* note 6.

[9] Racism is defined as "persecution, humiliation, demeaning, displaying animosity, hostility, violence or strife toward a population group or parts of such a group, all on the basis of skin color or membership in a racial or ethnic-national grouping", Penal Code, Article 144A, see *supra* note 7.

As the Knesset members themselves repeatedly remarked, on the legal level, the provisions already in place in Israeli law regarding sedition[10] could have in practice been wielded against racist speech; their motivation in adding a new provision on incitement to racism was primarily 'educational'.[11] The members of Knesset understood the importance of naming and labelling the phenomenon of racist speech in order to combat it – even if the criminal offense would not be frequently used as a basis for indictment, as indeed it has not been.[12]

The offense itself is quite broad: no imminent threat is required, and there is no requirement that an external event occur, just intent.[13] It was feared, however, that such a broad criminal offense of incitement could excessively infringe upon freedom of speech. As a result, a political compromise was reached to mitigate its effects (and as is often the case when compromise is the guiding force in legislation, the result was perhaps a less-than coherent criminal offence):

1) First, prosecution under the offence of incitement to racism requires the approval of the Attorney General, which allows him or her to supervise and direct the exercise of the prosecution's discretion – and also has the effect of limiting the use of the offense.
2) Second, the prosecution is required to prove, beyond a reasonable doubt, that the *intent* of the speaker was to incite racism – and not simply that the speech was itself racist. This too has the effect of limiting the cases in which the prosecution can bring charges.
3) Third, as a last-minute compromise, a somewhat opaque limitation on the offense was inserted in Article144C(b) of the Penal Code, which sets out that:

10 That is, the explanation of crime of sedition.

11 This reflects the principle of 'fair labelling', in Professor Ashworth's terms, which serves the condemnatory function of the criminal law, and helps hold perpetrators to account in both domestic and international law; see Talita de Souza Dias, "Recharacterisation of Crimes and the Principle of Fair Labelling in International Criminal Law", in *International Criminal Law Review*, 2018, vol. 18, no. 5, pp. 788–821.

12 Israel, Protocols of Knesset Plenary, 5 August 1996.

13 This is in some ways reminiscent of the *mens rea* standard that emerged in the International Criminal Tribunals for the former Yugoslavia and Rwanda ('ICTY' and 'ICTR', respectively) in their incitement jurisprudence, a jurisprudence has been described as "muddled" by Gregory S. Gordon. Some sort of intent standard certainly emerged there (see Gregory S. Gordon, *Atrocity Speech Law*, Oxford University Press, 2017, pp. 176–177), but since incitement in the international arena is only punishable when the object of the incitement is itself a crime, it is hard to draw comparisons with the Israeli offense of incitement to racism.

> Publication of a quotation from religious writings and prayer books or observance of a rite, shall not be an offence as long as it was not done with the purpose of inciting to racism.

While this addition does not substantively add anything to the requirement for intent, and merely reiterates that fact[14] – this clause served to remind the prosecution that, particularly in the context of religious expression, the criminal law should be wielded judiciously.[15]

Thus, the state of affairs at the end of the 1980s and the early 1990s was mixed: far-reaching legislation that accurately labelled and condemned racism was passed, to combat incitement on the personal and on the communal level. But for many reasons, including the desire to protect freedom of speech, all seemed to agree that the new legislation was going to be used only in extreme circumstances.[16]

On a personal level, it was in these early days that one of the dilemmas inherent in prosecuting incitement cases crystallized in my mind. During the years in which I served as a public prosecutor, I saw first-hand the limitations of the criminal law in combatting negative social phenomenon such as racist speech. A criminal prosecution based solely on a speech act may demonstrate to the public that the state and its organs take such dangerous speech quite seriously; seriously enough to bring down the full force of the criminal law. However, the law is a limited tool for effecting change in society. In fact, a trial runs the risk of being counter-productive from a social perspective. A trial may give the accused a public, state-sanctioned, platform from which to broadcast his or her noxious views. This is especially true when the accused is a public figure, or a religious leader, who is transformed by the trial into a victim of the State.[17] Even

---

14 This was, however, a matter of dispute before the courts, wherein J. Tal seemed to indicate that the addition should be seen as presumption of sorts (Supreme Court of Israel, *Rabbi Edo Elba v. The State of Israel*, 50 (5) PD 221 [1996], CrimA 2831/95, para. 4 ('Elba case') (https://www.legal-tools.org/doc/jmspn9/)), and J. Rubinstein in a later case clarifying that it should not be seen as such (Israeli High Court of Justice, *Movement to Strengthen Tolerance in Religious Education et. al. v. Attorney General*, 9 December 2015, H.C.J. 2684/12 (https://www.legal-tools.org/doc/8xn5hw/)).

15 See also Itai Weschler-Be'er, Amir Fuchs and Mordechai Kremnitzer, *The Crimes of Incitement to Racism and Violence: A Rethinking*, Israel Democracy Institute, 2019 (in Hebrew).

16 See David Kretzmer, "Racial Incitement in Israel", in *Israel Yearbook on Human Rights*, 1992, vol. 22, pp. 250–251, for other instances of Court's reluctance in those years to limit free speech. For some recent statistics on the use of this article, see the report on incitement of the Israeli Religious Action Center, "The Enforcement Policy of the Offences of Incitement to Racism and Violence in Israel", 2022 (in Hebrew; an English summary is available at https://www.legal-tools.org/doc/9uf6ea/).

17 David Kretzmer, "Freedom of Speech and Racism", in *Cardozo Law Review*, 1986–1987, vol. 8, p. 510.

when a conviction is achieved, the punishment meted out by the Courts for an offense that is solely speech-based will be quite light; that must be weighed against the 'opportunity' that the trial grants the defendants to further spread their ideology.

This was perhaps one of the reasons that the legal establishment did not prosecute the growing incitement that Israel witnessed during the lead up to and aftermath of the Oslo Accords, in the early 1990s. Some of this incitement was encouraged by, or at least condoned by, religious leaders, primarily those associated with the settler movement. The police on the ground respected the demonstrators' freedom of speech, and rarely investigated incidents of incitement; prosecutors were likewise wary of bringing charges even when the cases reached their desks, and so – prosecutions were few and far between. It is always difficult to know where to draw the line between legitimate political protest and illegitimate, dangerous, incitement.

Unfortunately, the political protests and mass demonstrations in Israel soon devolved into dangerous incitement with tragic consequences. In 1995, Israel's Prime Minister Yitzhak Rabin was assassinated by a right-wing religious extremist, and the dangers of extremist speech were once again thrust into the spotlight. This moment was a national trauma, and in a way, served as a wake-up call, much as Kahana's election to the Knesset did a decade previously.

These watershed moments often cause the legal establishment to use the law as best it can to combat new challenges. By that point, I was serving on Israel's Supreme Court, and while criminal prosecutions began to rise in the lower courts in those years following the Rabin assassination, only a few cases made their way to the highest Court. The court's jurisprudence on incitement was not particularly straightforward: the Court was trying to find its footing in those years, with the various justices sometimes pulling towards freedom of speech, sometimes towards restricting it, depending on the circumstances of the case and the varying viewpoints of the judges.

In three seminal cases, the Supreme Court attempted to clarify the boundaries of the prohibition on incitement to racism and violence. Understanding the grave importance of the topic, the cases were heard before an extended bench (generally the Israeli Supreme Court sits in panels of three, but in these important cases the Court expanded the panel).

In one high-profile case, a rabbi named Elba had written an article in the aftermath of a terrible massacre perpetrated by the religious extremist Baruch Goldstein, expounding upon the religious precepts that, in his view, allow for killing those who are not Jewish in wartime.[18] The Court convicted him under

[18] Elba case, para. 4, *supra* note 14.

the incitement to racism provision noted earlier, making it clear that such speech can have no place in our public discourse. In another case, the Jabarin case, a newspaper columnist praised attacks against Israeli soldiers, and the Court took a narrow view of the extant criminal prohibitions on incitement in the Prevention of Terror Ordinance, acquitting him.[19] In the third case, Benjamin Kahane (the son of the political figure I mentioned previously) had called for the bombing of Arab villages in retaliation for terrorist attacks against Jews. Despite legal difficulties in applying the statute on incitement to terrorism and sedition, the Court interpreted the statute broadly, and convicted him.[20]

In these cases, the Court had to find a balance between free speech and freedom of religion, and to locate where criminal incitement fits within those two. When and where is speech no longer legitimate? When should speech be criminalized on the basis of the speaker's intent alone, and when is an external outcome, or even a possibility of an outcome, required for a speech act to be considered criminal?

The Court found these questions increasingly difficult to answer, and the jurisprudence at this time was perhaps based more on the circumstances of each case than on a purely theoretical answer to the questions at hand. The forum of the speech, the relative importance of the speaker in the community, and the severity of the speech all played their part.[21] These tests, I should note, are quite similar to those developed recently within the international community. The Rabat test, for instance, with which I opened this chapter, emphasizes, among other considerations, the *context* of the speech act, such that we must be cognizant of the social and political context prevalent at the time the speech was made and disseminated, and consider the speaker's position or status in the society, specifically the context of the audience to whom the speech is directed. It was in a similar vein, that the Israeli Court's jurisprudence in those years was highly context-driven.

As the years passed, and racism and terrorism continued to rear their ugly head again and again, Israel continued to try and find the right balance between free speech and protection against incitement. The spread of terrorism worldwide highlighted for us in Israel, as for the world as a whole, the need to use all

---

[19] Israeli High Court of Justice, *State of Israel v. Jabarin*, Judgment, 27 November 2000, CrimFH 8613/96, 54(5) PD 193 (https://www.legal-tools.org/doc/91ejdy/).

[20] Israeli Court of Criminal Appeals, *State of Israel v. Benjamin Kahane*, Judgment, 27 November 2000, CrimFH 1789/98, 54(5) PD 145 (https://www.legal-tools.org/doc/c6mz7q/).

[21] See also J. Handel in Israeli Court of Criminal Appeals, *State of Israel et. al. v. Michael Ben Horin*, Judgment, 26 December 2011, CrimA 2533/10, para. 7 ('*State of Israel et. al. v. Michael Ben Horin*') (https://www.legal-tools.org/doc/m82y31/).

the tools at our disposal, including criminal law, not only against actions but also against words of incitement.

In the new millennium, this political climate, along with the Court's jurisprudence, again led to legislative reform. The global terror attacks of 2001, and the domestic terror attacks in the form of the Second Palestinian Intifada raging in Israel, again focused the legal establishment's attention on crimes of incitement.

The Knesset also reacted to the political climate and the Court's jurisprudence by legislating a new criminal offense in 2002, the crime of incitement to violence and terror, which carried with it a maximum penalty of five years imprisonment.[22] Under the new offense, the crime of incitement to violence and terror was broadened, as it was made clear that violent speech could be criminalized when connected to acts committed by individuals, and not just in the context of terrorist organizations. However, the prosecution is required to prove that the circumstances of the publication were such that there was a 'substantial likelihood' that an act of violence or terror would result (unlike the offense of incitement to racism, where no such condition is required).[23] This, in contrast to the higher threshold often required in administrative matters when infringing upon freedom of speech as set out in the Kol Ha'am case which I referred to previously: the likelihood of an *imminent* result.

More recently, in 2016, in the context of Israel's new Counterterrorism Law, which updated and consolidated the legal provisions related to counterterrorism, the offense of incitement to terror was removed from its place in the Penal Code and transferred to the new legislation. The glorification of a terrorist act, or the encouragement to commit such an act, remained prohibited, once again with the threshold being that there was a 'substantial likelihood' that an act of terror would result. But the threshold for prosecution was lowered: in line with criminal legislation in other countries that prohibit direct provocation to terror, a direct call to commit an act of terror was now prohibited (with a maximum penalty of five years) – irrespective of its likelihood of occurring.

Thus, the trifecta of criminal incitement provisions was completed: incitement to racism, incitement to violence, and incitement to terror. While constantly being calibrated, the Courts and the Legislature seemed to have found a balance that they could both stand behind in terms of criminal prosecution for incitement: while in other realms, the law may require imminent harm in order

---

22 The new offence replaced Section 4 of the Prevention of Terrorism Ordinance No. 33 of 5708, 23 September 1948 with Section 144D2 of the Penal Code, see *supra* note 7.

23 On the other hand, the *mens rea* of this offense is lower in contrast to the prohibition on racial incitement, where no special intent is required.

to limit speech, when it comes to incitement to violence, terrorism and racism, the bar is lowered.

This fragile balance seems to be in line with legislation around the world, particularly in the European context. Unlike in the American tradition, where the right to free speech has become, to a large extent, an absolute right, Israel's legislation and jurisprudence has shifted to resemble more closely the European and the Canadian traditions. The Israeli legal system does not speak in absolutes, but rather is concerned with 'balancing'. In a world of balancing, we may at times infringe upon the right to free speech, in order to protect other rights. In that regard, Israel's legislation also echoes the principles in the relevant articles of the International Covenant on Civil and Political Rights ('ICCPR') and the International Convention on the Elimination of All Forms of Racial Discrimination ('CERD'), conventions that Israel is party to. Article 20(2) of the ICCPR requires States to "prohibit" certain forms of speech which are intended to sow hatred, namely "any advocacy of national, racial or religious hatred that constitutes incitement to discrimination, hostility or violence" (CERD's Article 4(a) contains a similar provision, but is more detailed).[24] As is the case in most countries, the language of the Israeli legislation differs from that of the international conventions, but all try to find the balance between the sometimes-contradicting wish to protect freedom of speech, while also protecting people from discrimination, violence and terror.[25]

Throughout the decades, against the backgrounds of tensions which are ever-present in our society, the fear of terrorism and violence in Israel was palpable. The result was also an increasingly racist and violent discourse, in what seemed like a never-ending cycle. As a justice of a Supreme Court since 1996, it is in this context that I wrote, in the case of a combined criminal appeal of those convicted of praising racist violence:

> Due to the importance of the protected value [that of protecting the public from terror and violence], the Legislature explicitly provided that the required threshold for the danger occurring is that of

[24] ICCPR, 19 December 1966, Article 20(2) (https://www.legal-tools.org/doc/2838f3/); CERD, 21 December 1965, Article 4(a) (https://www.legal-tools.org/doc/43a925/). In international criminal law, the crime of incitement is also part of the discourse, but it is usually connected to the crime of genocide, whether directly (as in the International Criminal Court ('ICC') Statute, as a form of criminal liability (Rome Statute of the ICC, 17 July 1998, Article 25(3)(e) (https://www.legal-tools.org/doc/7b9af9/)) or as an independent crime, as was the case in ICTY and ICTR).

[25] See, for example, the analysis of major trends in national legislation in Europe, Louis-Léon Christians, "Expert workshop on the prohibition of incitement to national, racial or religious hatred", Study for the Workshop on Europe, 9–10 February 2011, Vienna (https://www.legal-tools.org/doc/1gf6sm/).

> 'substantial likelihood'. This is in contrast with other restrictions on freedom of speech, where a higher threshold is required, that of 'imminent likelihood'. On this matter I can only reiterate my position… that in light of the severity of the danger resulting from racist publications and incitement to terror, these offenses necessitate a lower threshold of probability, given the nature and intensity of the danger.[26]

That danger has only intensified, it seems, since those words were written.

3.4. Disqualifying Knesset Candidates for Incitement

Criminal legislation, of course, is not the only effective tool against racist speech. The manifestations of racism, in Israel and worldwide, are part of a wider social illness, and thus require a broad social response. Racism must be uprooted first and foremost by educating the public to democratic values, human dignity and equality. Criminal law can serve an important function in this battle, but it can only do so much.[27]

Therefore, alongside the development of the criminal law on incitement, the Israeli system also developed a constitutional mechanism for disqualifying Knesset lists and candidates who espouse racist views. Together, *these two legal regimes aimed to confront head-on the type of racist speech that Kahane and others espoused*, one by holding individuals who promulgate racist ideas criminally liable, and the second by barring those ideas from establishing a foothold inside the corridors of Knesset. As a result of the election of the racist and violent Kahanist party to the Knesset, the Israeli legislature saw the need to counter the very legitimacy of those political candidates.

In fact, the Central Elections Committee ('Elections Committee') had attempted to disqualify Kahane's party in the early 1980s, but absent legislation that explicitly authorized it to do so, the Supreme Court overturned its decision, noting that the fundamental right to be elected and to vote for one's representation could not be denied without explicit legislative authority.[28] In direct response to the Court's overturning the Elections Committee's decision, the Knesset added Article 7A to the 'Basic-Law: The Knesset' which established clearly

26 *State of Israel et. al. v. Michael Ben Horin*, see *supra* note 21.

27 See, for example, Raphael Cohen-Almagor, "Is Law Appropriate to Regulate Hateful and Racist Speech? The Israeli Experience", in *Israel Studies Review*, 2012, vol. 27, no. 2, pp. 41–64.

28 Israeli Court of Election Appeals, *Moshe Neiman et al. v. Chairman of the Central Elections Committee for the Eleventh Knesset*, Judgment, 15 May 1985, EA 2/84, 3/84, SC 39(2) 225 (https://www.legal-tools.org/doc/0zl93u/).

that a candidate list would be disqualified if it, among other things, "incites to racism".[29]

This addition to the Basic-Law in 1985 allowed for the banning of political parties, and at a later point, the law was again amended to allow for the disqualification of individual political candidates as well. As is immediately evident, the impact of such disqualifications is far-reaching. A party list or a candidate that is disqualified has had the right to free speech impinged upon, along with its right to be elected. The rights of its constituents to political representation, to have their political choices impact policy and decision-making at the highest level – have also been infringed.

On the other side of the scale lies the argument that a democracy has a right to defend itself against those who undermine the democratic order from within. The limits of this type of democratic self-preservation, or 'defensive democracy', have been thoroughly debated worldwide, most recently in the German context, one of a handful of countries that similarly allow for the disqualification of political parties.[30] Despite its dangers, one can understand the rationale of banning those who espouse anti-democratic, abhorrent racist views from using the very platform of democracy, its parliament, to broadcast them.[31]

As for its practical use, Article 7A (as it stands today), authorizes the Elections Committee to disqualify a list or candidate if its goals or actions include one of the following: (i) negation of the existence of the State of Israel as a Jewish and democratic State; (ii) incitement to racism; (iii) support for armed struggle by a hostile state or by a terrorist organization against the State of Israel. The Elections Committee is made up primarily of political representatives and its composition reflects the political make-up of the outgoing Knesset, and so, a check on its power, the Supreme Court has the authority to review its decisions.[32] All three potential conditions for disqualification are of the same ilk: they are seen as actions or goals that strike at the very core of the State, and as such, those who support them should not even be granted a 'seat at the table'. I would

---

29 Basic-Law: The Knesset, Article 7A, *supra* note 7 (https://www.legal-tools.org/doc/tt9mvj/).

30 See, for example, James Hogan, "Analyzing the Risk Thresholds for Banning Political Parties After NPD II", in *German Law Journal*, 2022, vol. 23, no. 1, pp. 97–116 (and see literature review there); Yigal Mersel, "The Dissolution of Political Parties: The Problem of Internal Democracy", in *International Journal of Constitutional Law*, 2006, vol. 4, pp. 84 ff. See also European Commission for Democracy Through Law, "Guidelines on Political Party Regulations", 2nd ed., 14 December 2020, CDL-AD(2020)032.

31 See for instance, J. Ben-Porat (minority) in High Court of Justice, *Miari v. Knesset Chair*, 41 PD (4) 169, H.C.J. 620/85.

32 For detailed explanation, see the backgrounder prepared by Dana Blander, "Disqualification of Electoral Lists and Candidates by the Central Elections Committee", *The Israel Democracy Institute*, 4 March 2021 (https://www.legal-tools.org/doc/346grc/).

note that for incitement to racism to be listed as antithetical to one of the core values of the state is in and of itself a powerful statement about the place of anti-racism in Israel. In practice, the only disqualifications that occurred to date, after the legislation was passed, were based on this ground of incitement to racism.

Ultimately, Kahane's party and its splinter party were banned in the lead-up to the 1988 elections and the 1992 elections. The Knesset and the Court both expressed their disapproval of the party's racist ideology, and delineated the contours of legitimate speech in the political arena. Their violent rhetoric should have no place in parliamentary discourse. Highlighting the need to protect democracy itself from racist speech, I wrote in a 2003 judgement:

> As a general rule, in order to defend the basic values of our system, we will give more weight to a decision that allows a candidate to run in the elections, as opposed to a decision that disqualifies a candidate. We do so when we wish to strengthen the right to vote and to be elected, in order to allow for the realization of the political "marketplace of ideas". On the other hand, when on the other side of the scale, opposite the basic right to be elected, stands the value of preventing "race-based" incitement [...]. this balance shifts, and the internal contradiction is weakened [...]. [It is my opinion that] racist theories have no standing in the competing marketplace of ideas in democratic proceedings, and therefore should not be considered a contender in the free marketplace of ideas, within the framework of democratic values that should be balanced, even before we determine the question of the infringement of the right to be elected. We have already said that any country that has "blocking" provisions that deny the right to engage in the political process, does so on the basis of its own history, its national heritage and the need to defend itself against potential dangers lurking within its own system. The heritage of the Jewish people requires us to not recognize racist ideology as legitimated.[33]

These words, written in 2003, are to my mind as true today as they were twenty years go. Unfortunately, in today's world, when social networks have immense power, our legal institutions are once again confronted with new challenges that necessitate rethinking our delicate balance once again.

The jury is still out as to whether this tool has the ability to prevent racist speech from infiltrating politics. Banning political parties comes with a host of problems, practical and ideological. Political speech in Israel is generally quite intense, and at times has continued to include racist speech from which we

33 Supreme Court of Israel, *Central Elections Committee v. Ahmed Tibi*, Judgment, 7 January 2003, Election Confirmation 11280/02, para. 5 (https://www.legal-tools.org/doc/kgp49b/).

certainly must recoil. Despite all of our best efforts, racist elements are still to be found among our parliamentarians, and in the public at large. Nonetheless, no other party or candidate was banned until quite recently, and the Israeli Knesset is home to broad representation from the widest spectrum of Israeli society, including nationalist Israeli-Palestinian members, members of the Islamic Movement in Israel, Jewish left-wing members, socialist and communist members, ultra-Orthodox members, centre-right Jewish members, and extreme right-wing Jewish religious representatives. The jurisprudence of the Court was very clear: Article 7A was to be interpreted as narrowly as possible, and the right to representation – and by extension the right to freedom of speech – was to be given as broad protection as possible.

Recently, however, there has been a shift, and in the run-up to the elections for the 21st and 22nd Knesset, three right-wing Jewish religious extremists were disqualified for inciting to racism (their parties and other similarly inclined candidates were not disqualified). Perhaps not surprisingly, those who were disqualified this time around have their ideological roots in the Kahanist parties of the 1980s. That being said, there have been a number of attempts by the Elections Committee to disqualify other parties and representatives, particularly those from the Arab parties and the Jewish left, that were rejected by the Supreme Court. As radical racist parties continue to gain a foothold in Israeli politics and elsewhere, we will have to continue examining the use of the power to disqualify candidates and political parties.

3.5. Conclusion

Over the years since I began my legal career, much has changed, including the explosion of the use of social media and disinformation, with wars being waged on TikTok, Twitter and Facebook alongside the disastrous wars in the 'real' world. Perhaps, though, some of what we are seeing is simply a return of the old fractures, in new forms and with new technologies. We are witnessing democratic backsliding even in established democracies, the return of strongmen and the continued rise of populism and fragmentism.

The use of religious rhetoric to couch political agendas is also not a new phenomenon. The leaders of the extremist movements may be grounded in religion, but they wish to impact politics: the *form* of the speech may be religious, but the content is political. Religion and politics cannot be neatly divided.

In this chapter, I touched upon only a few of the ways in which the state attempts to counter such extremist rhetoric, but it is not an exhaustive list. In Israel, for instance, on the criminal level, racist motives can also be relevant as an aggravating factor that can turn any crime into a 'hate crime', with a maximum penalty that doubles the 'regular' penalty.[34] Unfortunately, these types of racist crimes are becoming quite frequent and particularly violent throughout the world, most visibly in the United States, but in Europe as well. In addition, we have seen a proliferation of administrative tools to try to fight those trends, for instance the use of disciplinary actions against state employees who incite, when appropriate.

More prominently, perhaps, social media poses new challenges: ISIS's ability to harness the power of social platforms, particularly through religious incitement, to lure young recruits from Europe and elsewhere, is only one of many appalling examples. Israel is attempting, as are many other counties, to find an appropriate system for regulating social media platforms, for racist and dangerous speech proliferates on the internet, and, as we have all been witness to, has tragic consequences in the 'real world'. I personally headed a committee that recently pushed to revamp the legislation relevant to election campaigns, to meet the needs of the new era, in an effort to limit the use of racist and violent messaging around political campaigns, particularly online. Some of these reforms, I am happy to report, were recently passed in the Knesset.[35]

One must wield these tools carefully, of course, and one cannot underestimate the danger inherent in limiting free speech. When taken to the extreme, state control of speech carries with it its own risks, stifling dissent and even worse: denying the populace the very knowledge of the state's activities. So in our attempt to protect democracy, we must take care not to undermine its very foundations, foundations based on personal liberties and on freedom of expression. But we must also say loudly and clearly that racism, violence and terror have no place in our society. I do believe that the law will play a part in eradicating the evils of racism, violence and terror – but perhaps only in a supporting role: in order to alter a discourse that has become increasingly violent and shallow, the social atmosphere itself must become the target of change.

In my years in public service, I have come to better understand the limits of the law in impacting social behaviours, particularly when the law is faced with speech acts unaccompanied by physical harm at the moment of speech. 'Peaceful' protests, however filled they may be with racism and hate – and especially those spurred on by religious extremist ideologies – are no match for the criminal justice system, with its oft-delayed verdicts and relatively light sentences; extremist political candidates will similarly take their chances with being disqualified, for the threat is distant and its fulfilment is rare. Incitement to

---

34 Article 144f of the Penal Code (with a maximum penalty of ten years), see *supra* note 7.

35 The final legislation can be accessed on the ICC Legal Tools Database, see Israel, Law on Elections to the Twenty-fifth Knesset (Special Provisions and Legislative Amendments), 30 June 2022 (https://www.legal-tools.org/doc/q3dqdp/).

racism and violence, it seems, will not be bested by legal threats, but by courageous leadership against harmful rhetorical, and above all – by education.

To conclude, I hope to have conveyed a taste of what I, as a judge in Israel's highest court and as a prosecutor, have grappled with throughout my professional career – dilemmas involving the limitations of free speech in a democratic society in general, and limitations on hate speech in particular. Our goal is clear: to root out racism, incitement and violence in our midst whilst protecting the value of free speech in general, and religious discourse in particular. I pray that we are successful.

PART II: EXAMPLES OF HATEFUL EXPRESSION IN RELIGIOUS CONTEXTS

SECTION A: ALLEGED HATE SPEECH IN THE NAME OF BUDDHISM: MYANMAR PERSPECTIVES

4

Mapping Some Controversial Public Utterances in Myanmar 2015–2020

Kyaw Tin*

4.1. Introduction

On 1 February 2021, the military in Myanmar overthrew the democratically elected government bringing to an end another brief chapter of democracy in the country's history. These five years, from 2015 to 2020, were characterized by democratic freedoms but also simmering inter-communal tensions, unresolved ethnic conflicts, rising Buddhist nationalism, and intense rivalry between the civilian government and the military.

This chapter looks at how these factors manifested in controversial speech during parliamentary debates, public speech by the Commander-in-Chief, and a sermon by an influential monk. In August 2017, after attacks by armed Rohingya militants on security posts, the military responded with force resulting in killings and mass displacement of Rohingya. The three instances of controversial speech examined in this chapter were uttered just before, and during these events. With ongoing legal proceedings at the International Court of Justice ('ICJ'), International Criminal Court ('ICC') and other fora, it is foreseeable that these three instances of speech will be subject to scrutiny in court.

In the first section, the key events between the years 2015–2020 are listed to guide the reader on the relatedness between key events and controversial speech. This is followed by the section on the anatomy of hate speech that includes the legal framework on the classification of controversial speech,

* **Kyaw Tin** currently works with the Myanmar civil society on access to justice, federalism and constitutional law issues. Previously, he served as legal consultant to the civilian government in Nay Pyi Taw (2019–2020) and as legal counsel to the Myanmar government chief negotiator during negotiations with ethnic armed organizations (2013–2016). He has practiced law with Patton Boggs LLP, Washington, D.C. (2009-2013), and clerked with Justice Alex J. Martinez, Colorado Supreme Court Denver (2008-2009). He received a Juris Doctorate from the University of Colorado Law School, a Masters in Electrical Engineering with a focus on Communication Networks from Cornell University, and a Bachelors (with Honours) in Electrical and Electronic Engineering from the University of Sheffield. He worked for a Goldman Sachs company as a Senior Software Engineer (1995-2006). He is a native of Myanmar and a United States citizen. For an audio-visual recording of his statement to CILRAP's conference in Florence in April 2022 on the topic of this chapter, please see https://www.cilrap.org/cilrap-film/220409-kyaw/.

classification of speech and the Myanmar language, and metaphors. Next, three instances of controversial speech are examined using the legal framework. The first instance of controversial speech were statements made in the Parliament Pyidaungsu Hluttaw (Assembly of the Union) just prior to the outbreak of violence in northern Rakhine State, followed by a speech delivered by the Commander-in-Chief and a sermon by one of Myanmar's most revered monks. The institutional role of hate speech in Myanmar will also be examined. Finally, the last section posits that the coup has caused a shift in public opinion towards ethnic and religious minorities that may be a harbinger of a more tolerant society.

4.2. Key Events in Myanmar between 2015–2020

On 8 November 2015, general elections were held and the National League for Democracy ('NLD') was declared the winner.[1] On 30 March 2016, the NLD took office, the first civilian government to do so in 53 years.

In October 2016, Myanmar state media reported that insurgents had attacked guard posts along the border with Bangladesh killing nine officers.[2] In the ensuing crackdown, at least 86 people were killed, villages burned and 30,000 displaced.[3]

On 10 August 2017, the Arakan National Party ('ANP') met with the Commander-in-Chief to ask for designating 'No-Bengali' zones and increased security in Rakhine State's Maungdaw township.[4] The ANP delegation said the ruling party NLD and the army have different views on the Rakhine issue.[5] A battalion was deployed to northern Rakhine State on 11 August 2017, one day after ANP's meeting with the Commander-in-Chief.[6]

- Between 16–24 August 2017, the motion to deploy security forces to northern Rakhine State was debated in the Amyotha Hluttaw (House of Nationalities) and Pyithu Hluttaw (House of Representatives) chambers of Parliament, the Pyidaungsu Hluttaw.[7]

---

1 "Myanmar's 2015 Landmark Elections Explained", *BBC News*, 3 December 2015.

2 "Myanmar Says Nine Police Killed by Insurgents on Bangladesh Border", *The Guardian*, 10 October 2016.

3 Mohammad N. Islam, "More Rohingyas Flee to Bangladesh as Violence Spreads in Myanmar", *Reuters*, 23 November 2016.

4 Htet N. Zaw, "ANP Asks Army Chief to Segregate Ethnic Communities in Maungdaw", *Irrawaddy*, 10 August 2017.

5 Nyan H. Lynn, "Tatmadaw Meets ANP Ahead of Hluttaw Debate", *Frontier*, 11 August 2017: "We learned that the Tatmadaw has a decisive attitude towards increasing security forces so as to ensure that national sovereignty is not damaged, or territory lost".

6 "Myanmar Deploys More Troops to Restive Rohingya Area", *AFP*, 12 August 2017.

7 See motion of Daw Khin Saw Wai (Arakan National Party), Rathedaung constituency, 46th-day Pyithu Hluttaw Parliamentary Record, 5th Regular Session of the Second Pyithu Hluttaw,

- On 23 August 2017, the Advisory Commission chaired by former United Nations ('UN') Secretary-General Kofi Annan submitted its final report to national authorities.[8]
- On 25 August 2017, Arakan Rohingya Salvation Army ('ARSA') attacked security posts in northern Rakhine State, killing 12 members of the security forces.[9]
- Between 25–29 August 2017, military 'clearance operations' in northern Rakhine State led to killings and displacement of Rohingyas.[10]
- On 5 September 2017, 'clearance operations' ended, according to the government.[11] Rohingya continued to flee to Bangladesh.
- On 8 November 2020, general elections were held and the NLD was declared winner. On 1 February 2021, the military staged a coup, hours before the new parliament was to sit for the first time since the elections.[12] President U Win Myint and State Counsellor Daw Aung San Suu Kyi along with thousands of civilians are currently under detention. The National Unity Government ('NUG'), a coalition of NLD and ethnic minorities has been formed to resist the coup.

4.3. Anatomy of Hate Speech

4.3.1. Legal Framework for Classification of Controversial Speech

With legal proceedings at the ICJ, ICC and other jurisdictions in connection with the Rohingyas in Rakhine State, it is expected that controversial speech will come under scrutiny. Although there is generally no definition of hate speech under international law, the contours of unlawful speech have developed

---

The Republic of the Union of Myanmar, 18 August 2017, p. 56 ('46th-day Parliamentary Record, 18 August 2017') (https://www.legal-tools.org/doc/8eutxc/). See also motion of U Khin Maung Latt (ANP MP), Rakhine State constituency (2), 44th-day Amyotha Hluttaw Parliamentary Record, 5th Regular Session, The Republic of the Union of Myanmar, 16 August 2017, p. 42 ('44th-day Parliamentary Record, 16 August 2017') (https://www.legal-tools.org/doc/1udad8/).

8 "Advisory Commission on Rakhine State: Final Report", *Kofi Annan Foundation*, 24 August 2017.

9 "Myanmar: What Sparked Latest Violence in Rakhine?", *BBC News*, 19 September 2017.

10 UN Human Rights Council, Report of the Detailed Findings of the Independent International Fact-Finding Mission on Myanmar, UN Doc. A/HRC/39/CRP.2, 17 September 2018, pp. 178–205 ('2018 IIFFMM Report') (https://www.legal-tools.org/doc/0c0c69/) (most serious incidents occurred from 25–29 August 2017).

11 "Speech Delivered by Her Excellency Daw Aung San Suu Kyi, State Counsellor of the Republic of the Union of Myanmar on Government's Efforts with Regard to National Reconciliation and Peace", *Network Myanmar*, 19 September 2017.

12 "Myanmar Military Seizes Power, Detains Elected Leader Aung San Suu Kyi", *Reuters*, 1 February 2016.

through the Convention on the Prevention and Punishment of the Crime of Genocide ('Genocide Convention'), the Rome Statute of the ICC ('Rome Statute'), and jurisprudence from the various international tribunals. The statutory crimes are set forth in the Genocide Convention and the Rome Statute, direct and public incitement to commit genocide, and the Rome Statute and jurisprudence further criminalize instigation and persecution, as discussed in Chapter 11 below. Despite differences in the elements of the different classes of speech, the commonalities are to inquire into the linguistic analysis, context and purpose of the speech.

4.3.1.1. Definition of Hate Speech

Although there is no international standard definition of hate speech, generally the threshold level of hate speech involves the denigration of persons on the basis of their ethnic identity, religion or other group membership.[13] There is also no international consensus on criminalizing hate speech as can be seen from the significant number of States having entered reservations with respect to the application of provisions in Article 4 of the International Convention on the Elimination of all Forms of Racial Discrimination ('ICERD') and Article 20 of the International Covenant on Civil and Political Rights ('ICCPR') that require signatory States to prohibit certain forms of hate speech in their domestic laws.[14]

4.3.1.2. Unlawful Speech Under Myanmar Law

Myanmar does not have an anti-hate speech law, but the Myanmar Penal Code, which is based on the Indian Penal Code of 1860, criminalizes certain speech involving 'outraging the religious feelings' and incitement. These laws have been criticized for targeting critics and persons seen to be critical of Buddhism.

The relevant articles of the Myanmar Penal Code are:

Article 295A[15] provides:

---

13 See, for example, International Criminal Tribunal for Rwanda ('ICTR'), *Prosecutor v. Nahimana, Barayagwiza and Ngeze*, Trial Chamber I, Judgement and Sentence, 3 December 2003, ICTR-99-52-T ('Nahimana Trial Judgement') (https://www.legal-tools.org/doc/45b8b6/).

14 Committee on the Elimination of Racial Discrimination, Declarations, Reservations, Withdrawals of Reservations, Objections to Reservations and Declarations Relating to the ICERD: Note by the Secretary-General, UN Doc. CERD/C/60/Rev. 4, 16 May 2001 (https://www.legal-tools.org/doc/w2jreg/). See also International Criminal Tribunal for the Former Yugoslavia ('ICTY'), *Prosecutor v. Šešelj*, Trial Chamber III, Concurring Opinion of Presiding Judge Jean-Claude Antonetti attached to the Judgement, 31 March 2016, IT-03-67-T, p. 205 (https://www.legal-tools.org/doc/711bb3/).

15 Myanmar, Penal Code, MMR-1861-L-61342, 1 May 1861, Article 295A ('Myanmar Penal Code') (https://www.legal-tools.org/doc/1a6e18/).

> Whoever, with deliberate and malicious intention of outraging the religious feelings of any class of persons by words, either spoken or written, or by visible representations, insults or attempts to insult the religion or the religious beliefs of that class, shall be punished with imprisonment of either description for a term which may extend to two years, or with fine, or with both.

Article 505(c)[16] provides:

> Whoever makes, publishes or circulates any statement, rumour or report, […]
>
> (c) with intent to incite, or which is likely to incite, any class or community of persons to commit any offence against any other class or community,
>
> shall be punished with imprisonment which may extend to two years, or with fine, or with both.

4.3.1.3. Unlawful Speech under International Law

Unlawful speech under international law may be categorized as crimes against humanity (persecution), instigation, and direct and public incitement to commit genocide. Decisions at the International Military Tribunal at Nuremberg ('IMT'), the ICTY and the ICTR allow for the delineation of the different categories based on the elements of each crime informed by the linguistic content, context and purpose of the speech. Jurisprudence at these tribunals has classified propaganda that creates a general climate of war, historical research, dissemination of news and information and public accountability of government authorities as permissible speech, even though the speech contained ethnic or racial hate content since the purpose of the speech conveyed "historical information, political analysis, or advocacy of an ethnic consciousness".[17]

4.3.1.4. Crimes against Humanity (Persecution)

According to decisions at the international tribunals and under the Rome Statute, to determine if an utterance constitutes crimes against humanity (persecution), the prosecutor must: (i) prove those elements required for all crimes against humanity under the Rome Statute; (ii) find a gross or blatant denial of a fundamental right reaching the same gravity as the other acts prohibited under Article 5 of the Rome Statute; and (iii) establish discriminatory grounds.[18] Although the

---

16 *Ibid.*, Article 505(c).

17 Nahimana Trial Judgement, paras. 1000–1006, 1019, see *supra* note 13.

18 Rome Statute, 17 July 1998, Article 5 (http://www.legal-tools.org/doc/7b9af9/). See ICTR, *Prosecutor v. Ruggiu*, Trial Chamber I, Judgement and Sentence, 1 June 2000, ICTR-97-32-I, para. 21 ('Ruggiu Judgement') (https://www.legal-tools.org/doc/486d43/) (citing ICTY, *Prosecutor v. Kupreškić et al.*, Trial Chamber, Judgement, 14 January 2000, IT-95-16-T (https://www.legal-tools.org/doc/5c6a53/)).

latest case on crimes against humanity (persecution) appears to require a link to violence, even an indirect link may suffice if statements had the effect of "poison" injected into the minds of the listeners to commit violence.[19]

4.3.1.5. Instigating Crimes through Hate Speech

Article 25(3)(b) of the Rome Statute states that "a person shall be criminally responsible […] if that person […] [o]rders, solicits or induces the commission of such a crime which in fact occurs or is attempted". To establish instigation as a mode of criminal liability, the prosecution must prove that the defendant verbally encouraged or ordered a third party to commit one of the Rome Statute's core crimes (that is, crimes against humanity, war crimes or genocide) and the third party then committed the crime.[20] The instigation must be a factor substantially contributing to the conduct of another person committing a crime.[21]

4.3.1.6. Direct and Public Incitement to Commit Genocide

An inquiry into the direct incitement would need to take into account: (i) linguistic content, (ii) context, (iii) audience and (iv) intent.[22] If the discourse remains ambiguous, even when considered in its context, it cannot constitute direct incitement to commit genocide. The ICTR Appeals Chamber also required specifically urging another individual to take immediate criminal action, rather than merely making a vague or indirect suggestion. It would be necessary to conduct a case-by-case factual inquiry to determine "whether the persons for whom the message was intended immediately grasped the implication thereof".[23] The ICC has instructed that intent can be inferred from the circumstances. Thus, for example, genocidal intent of a particular act can be inferred from (i) the systematic perpetration of other culpable acts against the group; (ii)

19 See Mechanism for International Criminal Tribunals, *Prosecutor v. Šešelj*, Appeals Chamber, Judgement, 11 April 2018, MICT-16-99-A, para. 164 ('Šešelj Appeals Judgement') (https://www.legal-tools.org/doc/96ea58/), for causality requirement. See also IMT, *Prosecutor v. Hermann Wilhelm Goring et al.*, Judgment, 1 October 1946 (https://www.legal-tools.org/doc/f41e8b/), reprinted in *Trial of the Major War Criminals Before the International Military Tribunal, Nuremberg, 14 November 1945–1 October 1946, vol. 22: Official Documents, IMT, Nuremberg*, 1947, pp. 501–502 ('Streicher Judgement') (https://www.legal-tools.org/doc/844f64/); *id.*, pp. 525–526.

20 See, for example, Gregory S. Gordon, "Speech Along the Atrocity Spectrum", in *Georgia Journal of International and Comparative Law*, 2014, vol. 42, p. 425.

21 ICTY, *Prosecutor v. Kordić et al.*, Appeals Chamber, Judgement, 17 December 2004, IT-95-14/2-A, para. 27 (https://www.legal-tools.org/doc/738211/).

22 ICTR, *Prosecutor v. Nahimana et al.*, Appeals Chamber, Judgement, 28 November 2007, ICTR-99-52-A, para. 677 ('Nahimana Appeals Judgement') (https://www.legal-tools.org/doc/4ad5eb/).

23 ICTR, *Prosecutor v. Akayesu*, Trial Chamber, Judgement, 2 September 1998, ICTR-96-4-T, para. 558 ('Akayesu Trial Judgement') (https://www.legal-tools.org/doc/b8d7bd/).

the scale of any atrocities that are committed and their general nature in a region or a country; or (iii) the fact that victims are deliberately and systematically targeted on account of their membership in a particular group while the members of other groups are left alone. Moreover, the ICC emphasized that a speech given in the context of a genocidal environment will have a heightened impact, and for this reason the circumstances under which a statement is made can be an indicator of the speaker's intent. Direct and public incitement to commit genocide is an inchoate crime and is punishable even where the incitement fails to produce the result expected by the perpetrator, that is, even if no genocide actually follows.[24]

4.3.1.7. Common Elements in Speech Analytical Framework

The jurisprudence of international tribunals informs that a determination of whether a statement is permissible or unlawful must inquire into the (i) linguistic analysis, (ii) context and (iii) purpose of the speaker.[25] The linguistic analysis addresses any translation issues and the cultural and historical meaning of key terms. The circumstances, including the influence of the speaker on the listeners, place and time contexts of the statement, are indicators of the impact statements have on perpetrators of atrocity crimes. Finally, the purpose inquiry allows for an assessment of the speaker's intent and whether the statement is for a lawful purpose. This paper will examine some instances of controversial speech by applying these overarching criteria to classify the speech.

4.4. Classifying Speech and the Myanmar Language

Any study of speech faces challenges with the intricacies of language. Controversial speech may be spoken in lengthy speeches, religious sermons or bureaucratic documents making the differentiation between permissible and unlawful speech harder. The Myanmar language as often used by officials is euphemistic and sprinkled with metaphors posing challenges to translators.[26] Religious text, for instance in the case of Buddhist text requires the translator to be familiar with Pali, the language of the teachings in Theravada Buddhism.

---

[24] Nahimana Appeals Judgement, paras. 678, 720, 766, see *supra* note 22.

[25] Nahimana Trial Judgement, see *supra* note 13. See also Gregory S. Gordon, "From Incitement to Indictment? Prosecuting Iran's President for Advocating Israel's Destruction and Piecing Together Incitement Law's Emerging Analytical Framework", in *Journal of Criminal Law and Criminology*, 2008, vol. 98, no. 3, p. 874.

[26] Kim Guise, "Translating and Interpreting the Nuremberg Trials", *The National WWII Musuem*, 30 November 2020: "Among the many challenges faced by interpreters and translators at Nuremberg included words themselves, Nazi language, unique to the Third Reich, were euphemistic and intentionally obfuscating".

The Myanmar word 'kalar' is the one word most associated with hate speech in Myanmar but does not always have a negative connotation. 'Kalar' is now commonly considered a derogatory term for people of Indian origin although it has been used variously to mean "a native of India, but also misapplied to English and other Western who have come from India to Burma".[27] The word 'kalar' is also linked to food and items of Indian or foreign origin. For example, the word for chair is 'kalar-thaing', lentil beans are called 'kala-bae' and a type of chili known for its extraordinary heat is called 'kala-awe thee'. People may also refer to India as 'kala-byi' ('the country of the kalars'). Legacies of colonial era anti-Indian and anti-Muslim sentiments led to "enduring linguistic patronizing classification of the 'Kalas' by the Burmese language".[28] After years of 'Burmanization' processes, by initially military governments and now nationalist groups, Burmese old-age 'indophobic' sentiments have turned towards more 'Islámophobic' tendencies, now explicitly targeting the Muslim communities of Indian origin.[29]

Almost as deplored as 'kalar' is the word 'Bengali' which has become synonymous with the discrimination against the Rohingya. The use of 'Bengali' or 'Rohingya' to identify the Muslims in northern Rakhine State is highly contested.[30] The government including the military, and many ordinary Myanmar people refer to the Muslims in northern Rakhine as 'Bengali'. To the Muslims living in northern Rakhine State, who identify as Rohingya, the use of the term 'Bengali' perpetuates the narrative that they are interlopers from Bangladesh.

Facebook's experience addressing hate speech on its platform exemplifies the challenges of the Myanmar language. Myanmar was considered one of the Internet's last outposts. Although people enthusiastically adopted social media, the Myanmar script was neglected by major internet companies. The first Myanmar font, Zawgyi, was developed by Myanmar developers, and it quickly gained traction. Unfortunately, Zawgyi does not conform to encoding

---

27 Henry Yule, Arthur C. Burnell and William Crooke, *Hobson-Jobson: A Glossary of Colloquial Anglo-Indian Words and Phrases, and of Kindred Terms, Etymological, Historical, Geographical and Discursive*, John Murray, London, 1903, p. 495. See also "Challenging Entrenched Racism in Myanmar: Don't Call Me 'Kalar'", *Progressive Voice*, 18 June 2020.

28 Renaud Egreteau, "Burmese Indians in Contemporary Burma: Heritage, Influence, and Perceptions since 1988", in *Asian Ethnicity*, 2011, vol. 12, no. 1, pp. 33–54. See also Nyi N. Kyaw, "Islamophobia in Buddhist Myanmar: The 969 Movement and Anti-Muslim Violence", in Melissa Crouch (ed.), *Islam and the State in Myanmar: Muslim-Buddhist Relations and the Politics of Belonging*, Oxford University Press, 2016, pp. 183–210.

29 Egreteau, 2011, *ibid.*

30 See, for example, Jacques P. Leider, "Rohingya: The History of a Muslim Identity in Myanmar", in David Ludden (ed.), *Oxford Research Encyclopedia of Asian History*, Oxford University Press, 2018, p. 11. See also Anthony Ware and Costas Laoutides, *Myanmar's 'Rohingya Conflict'*, C. Hurst & Co. Publishers Ltd., 2018, pp. 90–92.

standards.[31] Disadvantages of text written in the Zawgyi font are incompatibility with machine learning, optical character recognition and text searching processes.[32] A Unicode version was developed in 2019 but the take up was slow.[33]

Facebook admitted that the slow rollout of the Unicode font affected its moderation since Facebook's moderating technology relies on the technologies. In 2018, Facebook engineers taught words such as 'kalar' and slang words for 'Rohingya' to its automated systems, and while it has blocked hate speech, the subtleties of the language may cause false positive characterization of speech.[34]

4.4.1. Metaphors

Like many languages, the Myanmar language is filled with fables and metaphors. Many of these metaphors are influenced by Buddhism, but some have been adopted cross-culturally.

In neighboring India which is experiencing religion-based hate speech, terms with the suffix 'jihád', which has a negative association with Muslim violence, are used to build a narrative of purported conspiracy on the part of Indian Muslims against Hindus.[35] William A. Schabas has observed that those who incite mass atrocity crimes often "speak in euphemisms".[36] Cases at international tribunals have also hinged on the meanings of expressions such as "go to work" or "Nyabarongo River" as expressions to incitement.[37] It is unsurprising the Myanmar language's metaphoric analogies are associated with hateful expressions.

Prior to the mass displacement and violence in Rakhine State, one metaphorical tale that gained notoriety was of the camel, or 'kalar-oak' in the

---

31 Juan Cebu, "Unified Under One Font System as Myanmar Prepares to Migrate from Zawgyi to Unicode", *Rising Voices*, 7 September 2019 (Zawgyi makes use of the visual typing and encoding method as one would write it on paper, rather than using logical linguistics and computer encoding conventions of Unicode).

32 Han-Teng Liao, "Encoding for Access: How Zawgyi Success Impedes Full Participation in Digital Myanmar", in *ACM SIGCAS Competers and Society*, 2017, vol. 46, no. 7, pp. 18–24.

33 Cebu, 7 September 2019, see *supra* note 31.

34 Aung K. Myat, "Facebook is Banning the Derogatory Word, Kalar, but not in the Way You Expect", *Medium*, 27 May 2017. See also Sam McNeil and Victoria Milko, "Hate Speech in Myanmar Continues to Thrive on Facebook", *AP News*, 17 November 2021.

35 Medha Damojipurapu, "Language, Themes and Responses to Hate Speech in India", Policy Brief Series No. 132 (2022), Torkel Opsahl Academic EPublisher ('TOAEP'), Brussels, 2022 (https://www.toaep.org/pbs-pdf/132-damojipurapu/).

36 William A. Schabas, "Mugesera v. Minister of Citizenship and Immigration", in *American Journal of International Law*, 1999, vol. 93, no. 2, p. 530 (speaking of incitement to genocide).

37 See also Ruggiu Judgement, *supra* note 18. See also, Supreme Court of Canada, *Mugesera v. Canada (Minister of Citizenship and Immigration)*, Judgment, 20 June 2005, [2005] 2 S.C.R. 100 ('*Mugesera v. Canada*'). The Court found that the reference to the 'Nyabarongo River' meant that Mugesera was suggesting that Tutsi corpses be sent back to Ethiopia.

Myanmar language, and his owner's tent. This is a common English term, sometimes known as the Camel's Nose, that dates from mid-nineteenth century, and is widely understood to describe what happens when a small, seemingly innocuous act leads to larger and unwanted actions.[38] The tale made a cross-cultural leap to the Myanmar language. In his 1962 book *Burmese Law Tales the Legal Element in Burmese Folklore*, the noted Burmese academic on Burmese folk tales, Htin Aung, uses "Aesop's tale of the camel" to discuss fables and metaphorical tales and does not mention any Myanmar derivatives of the tale.[39]

Camels are not native to Myanmar, and as with many words for items and food that were introduced to the country by outsiders, contains the word 'kalar'. The Myanmar-English Dictionary published by the Ministry of Education states that the Myanmar word for camel 'kalar-oak' is derived from the Pali word 'kular' and defines it as native of the Indian subcontinent or of foreign origin.[40] The use of the word 'kalar' to refer to people is considered offensive and has been used as a derogatory term for Muslims.[41] The second part of the term, 'oak', means group or collection.

The camel metaphorical tale was mentioned during fiery parliamentary debates to plead for the deployment of more security forces to northern Rakhine State in August 2017, prior to the violence and mass displacement of the Rohingyas. A Rakhine politician stated:

> the Bengali terrorist have a grand plan to wrest control of the state, land grab and set up their own sovereign state. This has become an issue of sovereignty because their plan is just like in the Arab tale where the camel evicts the tent's owner to completely take over.[42]

An earlier reference to the metaphor in the context of Rohingyas appeared in a 2011 paper where the author, writing in English, stated: "when we were young, our elderly people told us a fable about an Arab and an ungrateful

---

38 Geoffrey Nunberg, *Going Nucular: Language, Politics, and Culture in Confrontational Times*, PublicAffairs, New York, 2009, p. 118 ("letting the camel's nose into the tent").

39 Htin Aung, *Burmese Law Tales The Legal Element in Burmese Folk-lore*, Oxford University Press, 1962.

40 See Union of Myanmar, Ministry of Education, *Myanmar-English Dictionary*, Department of the Myanmar Language Commission, Ministry of Education, Union of Myanmar, Rangoon, 1998 ('Myanmar-English Dictionary') (defines 'kalar' as native of the Indian subcontinent. It owes its origins to the Pali word 'kula').

41 Egreteau, 2011, see *supra* note 28.

42 49th-day Parliamentary Record· 5th Regular Session of the Second Pyithu Hluttaw, The Republic of the Union of Myanmar, 23 August 2017 (sic.) ('49th-day Parliamentary Record, 23 August 2017') (https://www.legal-tools.org/doc/f9u4g9/) (author's translation).

camel".[43] Without making references to 'kalar-oak', the author asked rhetorically: "Maybe, this fable is the predicted warning for the Arakanese (Rakhaings) against the Chittagonian Bengalis, 'the Guest who want to kick out the Host from his own House!'".[44]

The 2018 report of the Independent International Fact-Finding Mission on Myanmar ('IIFFMM') called the camel's tale "a Myanmar parable [...] [that] implies that, if a few 'kalar' are let into the country, they will slowly take over and will force the original inhabitants out". According to the report, "this parable was explained in detail in connection with the issue of the Rohingya in Rakhine State" during a conference hosted by the military in September 2017.[45]

Another metaphor mentioned in the context of Rohingyas and Rakhine State is 'western gate' (*anouttagha* in the Myanmar language), a term to describe Rakhine State as the frontline against Islámic threats and potential flood of Muslims who might come in from overpopulated Bangladesh.[46] The Association for Protection of Race and Religion (known by its Burmese-language acronym, Ma Ba Tha), politicians and the military have used the term.[47] In December 2021, an editorial in the military-run newspaper described Rakhine State as "a great fortress guarding the western gate of the nation".[48]

During campaigning for the 2020 elections, Buddhist nationalism and identity politics manifested in metaphors that sought to bolster a party's nationalistic credentials or to smear the dominant party, the NLD.[49] A metaphor frequently invoked was "protect race, language, religion" (အမျိုး၊ ဘာသာ၊ သာသနာ), a term associated with the Buddhist nationalist organization Ma Ba Tha and understood to have discriminatory intent and to be targeted at Muslims.[50] The Ma

---

43 Khin M. Saw, "Islamization of Burma Through Chittagonian Bengalis as 'Rohingya Refugees'", September 2011.

44 *Ibid.*

45 2018 IIFFMM Report, 17 September 2018, p. 325, see *supra* note 10.

46 Anthony Ware, "The Muslim 'Rohingya' and Myanmar's Upcoming Election", *International Affairs*, 25 September 2015.

47 Htoo Thant, "NSDC Meeting May Be Called if Violence in Rakhine Worsens", *Myanmar Times*, 30 August 2017.

48 See Ronan Lee, "Extreme Speech in Myanmar: The Role of State Media in the Rohingya Forced Migration Crisis", *Myanmar Digital News*, 15 December 2021.

49 See Juan Cebu, "Myanmar Candidates and Parties Turn to Religious Nationalism Ahead of Elections", *Global Voices*, 6 November 2020.

50 International Crisis Group, "Buddhism and State Power in Myanmar", Asia Report No. 290, 5 September 2017.

Ba Tha had also lobbied for the enactment of the four Race and Religion Laws in 2015.[51]

A common refrain from opponents of the NLD, the incumbent party, was that the party supported Muslim causes at the expense of Buddhists. The NLD was labeled the "religion-destroying party" (သာသနာဖျက်ပါတီ) for various allegations including permitting the building of mosques, fielding Muslim candidates, and attempting to amend Section 59(f) of the Constitution of the Republic of the Union of Myanmar of 2008 ('2008 Constitution'), a move strongly opposed by the military and pro-military Union Solidarity and Development Party.[52]

4.5. Controversial Speech

With international court proceedings focusing on whether international crimes were committed in Rakhine State in 2017, this section assesses the legality of three instances of controversial speech made during this time period. The jurisprudence that has emerged from the IMT proceedings at Nuremberg, the ICTY and the ICTR as described above provide a framework to attempt classification of the controversial speech. The first instance of controversial speech is statements made by members of Parliament ('MPs') just before the violence and mass displacement of Rohingyas in August 2017. The second instance is a speech given by the Commander-in-Chief on 1 September 2017 that has gained notoriety for the utterances of 'unfinished job' and 'clearance operations'. Finally, the third instance is a 30 October 2017 sermon by an influential monk at a military training school where he appears to justify the killing of non-Buddhists.

4.5.1. Statements by Members of Parliament and Military Representatives

Prior to the violence and mass displacement of Rohingyas from northern Rakhine State in 2017, politicians from an ethnic Rakhine party, the ANP, lobbied for increased security in northern Rakhine State after the killings of seven villagers and heightened inter-communal tensions. The party's initial attempts were not successful. Its calls to debate conflict-related proposals in Parliament

---

[51] In May and August 2015, the four Race and Religion Laws (The Population Control Law, The Buddhist Women's Special Marriage Law, The Religious Conversion Law, The Monogamy Law) were enacted (Buddhist Women Special Marriage Law, No. 50/2015, 26 August 2015 (https://www.legal-tools.org/doc/d5c459/); Law Concerning Religious Conversion, No. 48/2015, 26 August 2015 (https://www.legal-tools.org/doc/961029/)).

[52] Section 59(f) of the 2008 Constitution, 29 May 2008 (https://www.legal-tools.org/doc/ea9567/) prohibits, *inter alia*, anyone married to a foreigner from the presidency. This provision was used to bar Daw Aung San Suu Kyi from becoming president. See Sithu A. Myint, "Is Constitutional Reform a Journey to Nowhere?", *Frontier Myanmar*, 4 March 2020. See also Nyan H. Lynn, "USDP Vows to Block Any Charter Changes on 59(f)", *Frontier Myanmar*, 16 March 2018.

were also rebuffed. On 10 August 2017, party representatives met with the Commander-in-Chief to ask for designating 'No-Bengali' zones and increased security in Rakhine State's Maungdaw township.[53]

There are indications that the ANP adopted its messaging to align with the military's fears and anti-Muslim prejudices. In its meetings with the Commander-in-Chief, party officials called for segregation and invoked fears of losing national sovereignty while praising the military as the sole guarantor of security. In Parliament, the language took on even more extreme tones.

On 16 and 18 August 2017, politicians from the ANP submitted motions in the Amyotha Hluttaw (House of Nationalities or 'Upper House') and the Pyithu Hluttaw (House of Representatives) to "urge the Union government to act against the terrorists operating in Maungdaw, Buthidaung and Rathedaung townships under the anti-terrorism law".[54] The debates continued until 23 August 2017.

4.5.1.1. Linguistic Analysis

Since the debates were conducted in the Myanmar language, a court may be confronted with deciding on their meaning, including in the historical context, and how the words were understood by the audience.[55] In these debates, MPs and military parliamentary representatives invoked historical memories in their pleas for military action to deal with the "Bengali terrorists".[56] The historical memories recalled in these statements may be put into three categories.

First, that the attacks by 'Bengali terrorists' were a grand plan akin to Muslim attempts between 1946–1951 to assert political control over northern Rakhine State either through incorporation with Pakistan or creation of an independent state in northern Rakhine State. One Rakhine politician compared the 'grand plan' to the camel tale:

> the Bengali terrorist have a grand plan to wrest control of the state, land grab and set up their own sovereign state. This has become an issue of sovereignty because their plan is just like in the Arab tale where the camel evicts the tent's owner to completely take over.[57]

---

53 Zaw, 10 August 2017, see *supra* note 4.

54 See motion of Daw Khin Saw Wai (ANP), Rathedaung constituency, 46th-day Parliamentary Record, 18 August 2017, p. 56, see *supra* note 7. See also motion of U Khin Maung Latt MP (ANP), Rakhine State constituency (2), 44th-day Parliamentary Record, 16 August 2017, p. 42, see *supra* note 7 (author's translation).

55 See, for example, Akayesu Trial Judgement, see *supra* note 23.

56 49th-day Parliamentary Record, 23 August 2017, see *supra* note 42.

57 U U Hla Saw (ANP), Mrauk-U constituency, 49th-day Parliamentary Record, 23 August 2017, see *supra* note 42 (author's translation).

Another MP from the same ethnic Rakhine party echoing the narrative referred to his state as the 'Western Gate':

> In Rakhine, Bengalis comprise one million out of a total population of three million. Terrorist acts have occurred before in 1942, 1988, 1994, 2012, 2016 and 2017, and it is well known that thousands of ethnic nationals have lost their lives guarding the Western Gate. These terrorist acts are being committed not because of the desire for citizenship, human rights, or freedom of movement but to grab land by creating a foothold in the three townships by destroying government administration, killing people that work with the government and committing acts of terror.[58]

Second, that 'Rohingya' is a 'fake' term for Bengali immigrants who arrived either during the colonial period or more recently through illegal means. Furthermore, the representatives spoke of their alarm from the threat of Islámization. A veteran Rakhine politician emphasized his point by accusing the Rohingyas of coming in through a "dog hole":

> They refused to accept the citizenship verification opportunity given to them but instead created the fake term "Rohingya" and are trying to come in through a dog hole.[59]

He compared alleged illegal immigration, high birth rates and Islámization of northern Rakhine as a "Bengali cancer":

> Our country suffers from many ethnic conflicts but these Bengali terrorist acts are different. Bengalis are neither ethnic nationals nor citizens. Their objective is to grab land and create an Islamic state to merge with the neighboring country.[60]
>
> The Bengali cancer has spread because of the inability to address it with the right medicine at the right time.[61]

An MP from an ethnic party asserted:

> polygamous marriage has led to a population explosion such that in Maungdaw township, Bengalis make up over 90% of the population, instead of the saying "if you do not control the kalar, Rakhines will turn black", it should be "if you do not control the

---

58 U Myint Naing (ANP), Rakhine State constituency, 44th-day Parliamentary Record, 16 August 2017, p. 42, see *supra* note 7 (author's translation).

59 U Pe Than (ANP), Myebon constituency, 46th-day Parliamentary Record, 18 August 2017, p. 52, see *supra* note 7 (author's translation).

60 *Ibid.*

61 *Ibid.*

> kalar, Rakhines have to flee", and it is clear the Bengalis wish to take a piece of Myanmar territory as theirs.[62]

Three, several representatives compared the situation in northern Rakhine State in August 2017 to 1942 when, according to some accounts, Muslims killed thousands of Rakhine villagers, burned their villages and took over the area.[63] An MP from an ethnic Rakhine party remarked:

> In 1942, as a result of the violence and burning by Bengali Muslims, in Maungdaw township, 129 Rakhine villages were burnt, and 98 were not rebuilt; in Buthidaung township, 217 villages were burnt, and 116 were not rebuilt. Not only did the Bengalis move into the villages that were destroyed but they have been building new villages almost daily.[64]

A military representative stated:

> since 1942, Bengali terrorists have been terrorizing local ethnic nationals. Therefore, the government must designate the Bengalis as terrorists so action can be taken against them in accordance with the anti-terrorism law.[65]

Finally, the representatives of an ethnic Rakhine party appealed for the deployment of security forces to respond to "Bengali terrorism":

> I urge effectively fighting terrorism through military means. Military affairs are the responsibility of the Defense Services, so I expect them to carry out their responsibilities. As the nation is trying to achieve internal peace, we must be united to effectively respond to the dangers of Bengali terrorism.[66]
>
> Terrorism may be contained if we deploy more security forces and increase security. I urge the government to make careful and patient efforts to impose law and order and to bring administrative structures to the Bengali villages. Only then will ethnic

---

[62] U Khun Maung Thaung (Pa-O National Organisation), Pinlaung constituency, 49th-day Parliamentary Record, 23 August 2017, p. 49, see *supra* note 42 (author's translation).

[63] See Leider, 2018, p. 6, see *supra* note 30 (these events, which were never thoroughly investigated, led to diverging stories of injustice and victimhood and fueled bitterness).

[64] U Aung T. Shwe (ANP), MP Buthidaung constituency, 49th-day Parliamentary Record, 23 August 2017, p. 47, see *supra* note 42 (author's translation).

[65] Colonel Tun M. Swe, Tatmadaw representative, 50th-day Parliamentary Record, 5th Regular Session of the Second Pyithu Hluttaw, The Republic of the Union of Myanmar, 24 August 2017, p. 58 ('50th-day Parliamentary Record, 24 August 2017') (https://www.legal-tools.org/doc/kdw3vw/) (author's translation).

[66] UU Hla Saw (ANP), Mrauk-U constituency, 49th-day Parliamentary Record, 23 August 2017, p. 58, see *supra* note 42 (author's translation).

> nationals sustain their lives in the area and there will be less violence and peace.[67]

Instead of explicit calls for violence, many civilian parliamentarians noted that force may be needed to restore law and order but they also cautioned the military to act with restraint, perhaps recalling the violence that the military was accused of committing against the Rohingyas in 2016:

> There will be times when Defense Services will have no choice but to enter Bengali villages, and will have to do so with full force. These situations are not sustainable.[68]

> The military response is a short-term strategy, and will not address the root causes of the problem. Military operations are likely to take place in civilian areas since the terrorists are using these areas as a shield. Therefore, I seriously urge conducting military operations in accordance with the Geneva Convention.[69]

4.5.1.2. Purpose

The statements were likely intended to accomplish three objectives. First, the Rakhine politicians shared a real concern by Rakhine ethnic leaders about the deteriorating security situation in northern Rakhine State. Furthermore, against the backdrop of an increasingly nationalistic environment in Rakhine State, to appeal to Rakhine society that their interests were being protected. Second, to sway the mostly hesitant MPs, weary of past military abuses, that an immediate robust military response was needed. Third, to legitimize the deployment of military units after prior discussions with the Commander-in-Chief. Finally, it is important to note that despite the incendiary language, the parliamentarians' statements were intended not explicitly as a call for violence, but for the deployment of security forces to restore law and order and administrative mechanisms.

4.5.1.3. Context

Prior to the parliamentary debates held from 16–24 August 2017, there were reports of increasing attacks by militants on security forces, local administrators and villagers, and discoveries of arm caches. On 10 August 2017, after meeting with the Commander-in-Chief, the representatives of the ANP mentioned that "the ruling party National League for Democracy (NLD) and the army have different views on the Rakhine issue" and further stated that the NLD-dominated

---

67 U Myint Naing (ANP), Rakhine State constituency (5), 44th-day Parliamentary Record, 16 August 2017, p. 42, see *supra* note 7 (author's translation).

68 *Ibid.*

69 Daw Pyone Kathy Naing (NLD), Kalaw constituency, 50th-day Parliamentary Record, 24 August 2017, p. 59, see *supra* note 65 (author's translation).

Parliament had refused a proposal to debate the issue.[70] However, on the same day as the meeting, the Upper House agreed to debate a proposal tabled by an MP from the ANP party.[71]

Parliamentary debates are aired on television and published in the Myanmar language. Participants in these debates would have included both elected members and military representatives appointed by the Commander-in-Chief, since, under the military-drafted 2008 Constitution, a quarter of the parliamentary seats are allocated to military representatives.

The military responded quickly to the ANP's outreach. Troops were deployed to northern Rakhine State on 11 August 2017, one day after ANP's meeting with the Commander-in-Chief.[72] As described in Section 4.5.2., the narratives shared in Parliament were echoed by the military in justifying their 'clearance operations' in Rakhine State.

4.5.1.4. Classification of the Parliamentary Statements

4.5.1.4.1. Are the Statements Permissible or Protected Speech?

A court's analysis of the legality of the statements may first have to determine if the statements are permissible or protected speech. The 2008 Myanmar Constitution and the laws of many countries grant immunity from prosecution for statements made within the scope of an MP's official duties, in particular with respect to parliamentary debates.[73] However, no immunity is conferred under the Genocide Convention and the Rome Statute for officials and MPs although international courts have yet to rule on whether Article 27 of the Rome Statute applies to officials from non-States Parties.[74] Although jurisprudence suggests

---

70 See Zaw, 10 August 2017, *supra* note 4. See also Win K.K. Latt and Min T. Aung, "Rakhine Lawmakers Meet With Myanmar's Military Chief to Discuss Security Crisis", *Radio Free Asia*, 10 August 2017.

71 *Ibid.*

72 Wa Lone, "Myanmar sends hundreds of troops to Rakhine as tension rises: sources", *Reuters*, 11 August 2017.

73 See 2008 Constitution, Section 92(a), *supra* note 52. See Constitution of the United States of America, 1787, Article I, Section 6, Clause 1 (https://www.legal-tools.org/doc/bc3d56/); Directorate-General for Internal Policies, Policy Department C, "Parliamentary Immunities in a European Context", 2015, p. 12 (recognizes the absolute freedom of parliamentary debates as a constitutional tradition present in all contracting states, and accepts it as a legitimate and proportionate limitation of the rights arising from Article 6 of the European Convention on Human Rights, 4 November 1950 (https://www.legal-tools.org/doc/8267cb/)).

74 See Convention on the Prevention and Punishment of the Crime of Genocide, 9 December 1948, Article IV (http://www.legal-tools.org/ doc/498c38/); see also Rome Statute, Article 27, see *supra* note 18; David P. Stewart, "Official Immunity Under the Rome Statute: The Path from Principle to Practice is Seldom Straight", in *Just Security*, 10 April 2018 (available on its web site).

that immunity will not always be granted to MPs, it is likely that the courts will give greater latitude to inflammatory statements made in parliament or other political statements.[75] For instance, during the trial of Šešelj, the ICTY considered speeches made by the defendant in the Serbian Parliament as "expression[s] of an alternative political programme" despite the speeches being "barely disguised calls for expulsion".[76] The ICTR has also determined that political analysis, although interspersed with hateful comments, was permissible speech. These determinations were case-by-case analyses based on the facts of each case. Therefore, should a court be asked to determine if the parliamentarians' statements are unlawful or instead fall under a permissible category, it is possible that the court will nonetheless proceed with a factual assessment of individual statements by applying the legal framework described previously.

4.5.1.4.2. Direct and Public Incitement to Commit Genocide

If charges were brought under this crime, a court's inquiry will likely centre on whether hateful language referring to Rohingyas as 'cancer', 'right medicine', 'dog hole' and denial of the existence of 'Rohingya' spoken in Parliament constitute direct incitement to genocide. In the ICTR cases, the Tribunal found that terms such as "cockroaches", and equating Tutsis to dogs, when uttered together with "exterminate", established incitement to genocide.[77] Unlike in the ICTR cases where words like 'exterminate' unequivocally called for killing of the Tutsis, the court here will have to be persuaded that, despite the absence of similar words, the parliamentarians' statements nevertheless unambiguously urged the audience to take immediate steps in the commission of genocidal acts against the Rohingyas. Witness testimony, for instance, from military representatives in Parliament, could be persuasive. There are also mitigating factors, such as, despite the utterances of incendiary language, none of the parliamentarians' explicitly urged violence but moderated their comments with calls for the deployment of security forces to restore law and order and administrative mechanisms.

4.5.1.4.3. Crimes against Humanity (Persecution)

The crux of any inquiry into crimes against humanity (persecution) is whether discriminatory words that led to violations of fundamental rights were spoken as "part of a widespread or systematic attack directed against any civilian population", the speakers had "knowledge of the attack" and the attacks were pursuant to "a State or organizational policy".[78] Proving the existence of a policy will require prosecutors to submit evidence such as military orders linking

---

75 See, for example, Šešelj Appeals Judgement, para. 132, see *supra* note 19.

76 *Ibid.*

77 Nahimana Trial Judgement, para. 396, see *supra* note 13.

78 Rome Statute, Article 7, see *supra* note 18.

statements such as 'unfinished job' or 'clearance operations' to an organized plan to attack the Rohingyas as examined in the next section. Widespread violence against the Rohingyas was reported on 24 August 2017, eight days after the start of the parliamentary debates, so the additional burden is on the prosecution to prove that the MPs responsible for the discriminatory speech knew about these attacks at the time of their statements. To show the violation of Rohingyas' fundamental rights, the prosecution may present statements such as 'cancer', 'right medicine', the military entering 'Bengali villages with full force' and 'there is no Rohingya ethnic nationality in Myanmar'. However, a further requirement is to show that the discriminatory statements had a "specific impact" on violence, so the link between the statements and subsequent killings, forcible displacement and other violent acts must be shown.[79]

4.5.1.4.4. Instigation

To prove criminal responsibility for instigation, the prosecution must prove that the statements substantially contributed to the conduct of another person committing a crime under the jurisdiction of the court. Testimony from witnesses could prove the impact of the statements on, for instance, military representatives present at the debates. Courts have found that the influence of the speaker on the perpetrators and the causal and temporal link between the statements and the crimes, such as, here, the time period between the statements and 'clearance operations', are indicators of substantial contribution.[80] The militant attacks that took place in the intervening period between the time of the statements and the beginning of the military's response may also be a factor in the assessment of the linkages.

4.5.2. Speech by the Commander-in-Chief

An English translation of a speech delivered by the Commander-in-Chief Senior General Min Aung Hlaing on 1 September 2017 was widely reported for the apparent utterances of the words 'unfinished job' and 'clearance operation' in reference to the situation in Rakhine State.[81] The IIFFMM contended that there was an "explicit link" between these words and the 2017 "clearance operations" in Rakhine State, and the Commander-in-Chief's stated vision to finish "the

---

79 See Šešelj Appeals Judgement, para. 132, *supra* note 19.

80 *Ibid.*, para. 154.

81 See Senior General Min Aung Hlaing, "Entire Government Institution and People Must Defend the Country with Strong Participation", 2 September 2017 ('Sr. Gen. Hlaing September 2017 Speech'). See also the speech in Myanmar language, Senior General Min Aung Hlaing, "နိုင်ငံ့ဝန်ထမ်းအဖွဲ့အစည်းအားလုံး၊ ပြည်သူအားလုံးက မျိုးချစ်စိတ်အပြည့်အဝဖြင့် ဝိုင်းဝန်းကာကွယ်", 2 September 2017.

unfinished job" of solving "the long-standing Bengali problem" suggested "a level of preplanning and design".[82]

The Commander-in-Chief delivered the speech at a donor meeting to benefit:

> security personnel and state service personnel who risked their lives while shouldering national defense and security duties and ethnic natives who fled their homes due to brutal attacks of ARSA extremist Bengali terrorists.[83]

Also in the audience were senior commanders including the Deputy Commander-in-Chief, Chief of General Staff, chiefs of the Air Force and Navy and other senior officers. Below are excerpts from the English translation of the speech, which was published in both the Myanmar language and in English on the Commander-in-Chief's website and Facebook page.

The Commander-in-Chief explained that the "root cause" of the attacks on security posts during August 2017 was that:

> The extremist Bengali terrorists blamed religious persecution for their retaliatory attacks. The Senior General said Myanmar ensures freedom of religion. Christians represent six percent of the population and Islam four percent. They have been living peacefully in the country since years ago. There were Muslims but there was no problem. But the situation in Buthidaung and Maungtaw regions is different. Bengalis from those regions were taken into the country as manpower from Bengal region during the colonial era. Their population increased through various means, and later they attacked the local ethnics.[84]

Next, the Commander-in-Chief utters the words 'unfinished job' that have now brought notoriety to this speech. He first equates the 2017 attacks with the 1942 Alethankyaw crises when he states that Bengalis slaughtered 20,000 ethnic Rakhine people and took over their land. He adds that "absolutely, our country has no Rohingya race":

> During the Alethankyaw crisis in 1942, over 20,000 ethnic Rakhine people were slaughtered. Bengalis after murdering ethnic Rakhine people seized their land and villages and lived there. There is no oppression or intimidation against Bengalis in Rakhine region. The only measure security forces are taking is to ensure everything is within the framework of the law. The root cause of the recent crisis is the well-planned terrorist acts that came

82 See 2018 IIFFMM Report, 17 September 2018, para. 1336, see *supra* note 10.

83 Sr. Gen. Hlaing September 2017 Speech, 2 September 2017, see *supra* note 81.

84 *Ibid.*

> together with the denial of legal verification while ignoring the 1982 Citizenship Law. The act of using religion as a tool to make instigation and violent attacks is totally unacceptable. People living in Myanmar must obey its laws. The Bengali problem was a long-standing one which has become an unfinished job despite the efforts of the previous governments to solve it. The government in office is taking great care in solving the problem.
>
> As regards the term Bengali, the Senior General said as the Bengalis in Rakhine State came from Bengal region during Myanmar was under British colonial rule, they have been termed Bengalis throughout the successive eras. It is known that in India people living in Bengal are also called Bengalis. The Bengalis calling themselves Rohingya has become a national cause. So we openly declare that "absolutely, our country has no Rohingya race."[85]

The Commander-in-Chief then stresses that the military's 'clearance operations' were required for national defense and that the "the situation of 1942 and territorial loss are unacceptable":

> The Tatmadaw sent military units there to conduct area clearance operations after giving the information to the government […] Without the Tatmadaw involvement, the situation could worsen. The situation of 1942 and territorial loss are unacceptable. The Tatmadaw will do its best to perform national defense duties.[86]

4.5.2.1. Linguistic Analysis

The concern of a court assessing speech is how it was understood by the intended audience.[87] The English translations of key terms – 'unfinished job' and 'clearance operations' – have been contested during hearings at the ICJ. The day after the Commander-in-Chief delivered his speech in the Myanmar language, an English translation was posted by 'Admin' on his Facebook page and personal web page. The probative value of the English version may be limited since the intended audience comprises Myanmar language speakers. In previous cases, linguistic and historical experts were asked to give their opinions and witnesses testimonies were heard as to their understanding of the statements.[88]

85 *Ibid.*

86 *Ibid.*

87 Nahimana Appeals Judgement, para. 701, see *supra* note 22 (the Appeals Chamber agrees that the culture, including the nuances of the Kinyarwanda language, should be considered in determining what constitutes direct and public incitement to commit genocide in Rwanda. For this reason, it may be helpful to examine how a speech was understood by its intended audience in order to determine its true message).

88 See, for example, Akayesu Trial Judgement, *supra* note 23.

4.5.2.1.1. The Translation and Connotation of 'Unfinished Job'

As quoted above, the English translation as it appears on the Facebook page and the Commander-in-Chief's web site is:

> The Bengali problem was a long-standing one which has become an unfinished job despite the efforts of the previous governments to solve it. The government in office is taking great care in solving the problem.

The translation of the original Myanmar words 'မပြီးပြတ်ခဲ့ ကြောင်း' (*ma pyi pyat khat kyaung*) to 'unfinished job' could be disputed. The Myanmar word for 'job', 'အလုပ်', is not mentioned anywhere in the same sentence.[89] Additionally, the inclusion of the word 'solve' later in the sentence suggests 'unresolved' is a more correct translation.

The inquiry into connotation will likely focus on the context in which the term appears in the speech. The sentence could be read in the context of the entire paragraph where there are two possible issues or 'Bengali problems' whose resolution remain 'unresolved' – the issues of 'terrorist acts' and verification under the framework of the Burma Citizenship Act of 1982. Notably, the Commander-in-Chief does not appear to distinguish between 'Bengalis' and those he accuses of committing 'terrorist acts'.

A connotation asserted, *inter alia*, by the IIFFMM and The Gambia imply that the term, read in conjunction with 'clearance operations', is similar to phrases such as 'go to work' or 'finish off' that have been found to be code words to commit genocide in Rwanda.[90] Although the words uttered in Rwanda convey immediate actions, the terms 'unresolved' or 'solving the problem', even considered together with 'clearance operations', do not appear to urge another individual to take immediate criminal action without additional evidence such as witness testimonies.

4.5.2.1.2. The Connotations of 'Clearance Operations'

The intended audience's understanding of the term 'clearance operations' is another issue a court will likely face. The dispute over the meaning of 'clearance operations' has played out already during hearings on provisional measures at

89 See Myanmar-English Dictionary, 1998, *supra* note 40.

90 See, for example, ICJ, *Application of the Convention on the Prevention and Punishment of the Crime of Genocide (The Gambia v. Myanmar)*, Application Instituting Proceedings and Request for Provisional Measures, 11 November 2019, G.L. No. 178, paras. 70–71 ('*The Gambia v. Myanmar*') (https://www.legal-tools.org/doc/69p376/).

the ICJ, being mentioned 30 times by The Gambia[91] and Myanmar's explanation of the term.[92]

One meaning advocated by the IIFFMM and The Gambia is that 'clearance operations' "suggests a level of preplanning and design on the part of the Tatmadaw leadership" to "target and terrorise the entire Rohingya population".[93] When spoken in conjunction with 'unfinished job', the assertion is that the Commander-in-Chief had genocidal intent against the Rohingyas.[94] Myanmar's lawyers disputed these assertions and contended that the meaning of the term had been distorted:

> As early as the 1950s, this term has been used during military operations against the Burma Communist Party in Bago Range. Since then, the military has used this expression in counter-insurgency and counter-terrorism operations after attacks by insurgents or terrorists. In the Myanmar language, nae myay shin lin yeh literally means "clearing of locality" meaning to clear an area of insurgents or terrorists.[95]

The Myanmar legal team's assertion that the term is a Myanmar military term to describe anti-insurgency operations appears to be supported by a reference to 'clearance operations' in the IIFFMM report in connection with military operations against a non-Muslim ethnic group army in Shan state.[96] The IIFFMM describes these operations, as it did with the ones in Rakhine State, as making no distinction between civilians and fighters.[97] This suggests that military 'clearance operations' may have caused civilian casualties, but the commission of atrocity crimes cannot be inferred from the use of the term alone.

The term 'clearance operation' is used in other militaries to describe the clearing of obstacles. For example, the United States ('US') Department of Defense defines 'clearing operation' as "to clear or neutralize all mines and

---

[91] See, for example, *The Gambia v. Myanmar*, Verbatim record 2019/18, 10 December 2019, p. 59, see *supra* note 90 (https://www.legal-tools.org/doc/39si5p/):

> "clearance operation" which is Myanmar's own Orwellian term for the targeted killing of Rohingya, burning of their homes and villages, and especially brutal and depraved acts of sexual violence against women and girls the very kinds of atrocities the Genocide Convention was intended to prevent.

[92] See *The Gambia v. Myanmar*, Verbatim record 2019/19, 11 December 2019, see *supra* note 90 (https://www.legal-tools.org/doc/yfx6vt/).

[93] 2018 IIFFMM Report, 17 September 2018, paras. 751–752, see *supra* note 10. See *The Gambia v. Myanmar*, Application Instituting Proceedings and Request for Provisional Measures, 11 November 2019, paras. 6 and 71, *supra* note 90.

[94] *Ibid.*, paras. 85, 71.

[95] *Ibid.*, para. 86.

[96] 2018 IIFFMM Report, 2018, para. 284, see *supra* note 10.

[97] *Ibid.*, para. 285.

obstacles from a route or area".[98] There have also been some instances where the term 'clearing operation' has been used in connection with clearing an area of enemy combatants.

Not surprising for disputed translations and meanings of the terms, it is uncertain how these terms would be understood by the intended audience. The opinions of linguistic and even military experts may be called upon to assist the trier of fact on the connotations of 'clearance operations' and whether 'unfinished job' is the correct translation.

4.5.2.2. Context

The court will next have to examine the context in which the speech was delivered. A speech given in the context of a genocidal environment will have a heightened impact, and, for this reason, the circumstances under which a statement is made can be an indicator of the speaker's intent.[99]

The setting for the 1 September 2017 speech was a donor event with a mixture of civilians and senior military officials in the audience. If the impressions on Facebook and the web site are included, the potential audience of the speech is in the millions. At the time of the speech, most incidents of killings against the Rohingyas had ended, although the clearance operations did not end until 5 September 2017.[100] The displacement of Rohingyas to Bangladesh was, however, gathering pace, with 14,500 people arriving daily in September.[101]

As the supreme commander in the armed forces, the Commander-in-Chief likely knew about the actions of his troops including any commission of crimes. It must also be noted that the Commander-in-Chief had been asked by Rakhine politicians to deploy troops in northern Rakhine State. In some of these meetings, the politicians had told the Commander-in-Chief the same narratives that he repeated in the speech.

4.5.2.3. Purpose of the Speech

The purpose of the speech at first impression appears to be to address corporate donors who donated to security forces and government staff involved in operations and civilians displaced during the violence in August 2017. It is unlikely the Commander-in-Chief would use this setting to issue military orders to his troops. But the speech covered a wide range of grievances and repeated

[98] US Department of Defense, *DOD Dictionary of Military and Associated Terms*, November 2021.

[99] *Mugesera v. Canada*, see *supra* note 37.

[100] 2018 IIFFMM Report, 2018, paras. 178–205, see *supra* note 10 (most serious incidents occurred from 25–29 August 2017).

[101] Assessment Capabilities Project, "Rohingya Crisis: Situation Analysis November 2017", 22 November 2017.

narratives about past inter-communal conflicts between the Muslims and Rakhines in northern Rakhine State may have an additional purpose as a policy-setting statement, to be shared with the Myanmar public and the world. This was the Commander-in-Chief's first public statement on the recent violence and how the military was responding. It should be noted that the speech in many ways mirror the statements made by Rakhine politicians in the Parliament. Other evidence that this speech reflects policy is that the Commander-in-Chief's subsequent comments to the Under Secretary-General for Political Affairs of the UN[102] and the US Secretary of State Rex Tillerson[103] on the events of August 2017 mostly repeated the points in this speech. The audience included not only the donors, but also senior commanders who were likely already familiar with the policies set forth in their superior's speech.

4.5.2.4. Classification of the Commander-in-Chief's Speech

After the linguistic analysis and inquiries into context and purpose, a court will next have to weigh all the evidence, testimonies and expert opinions to decide on the classification of the Commander-in-Chief's statements.

4.5.2.4.1. Is the Speech Permissible Speech?

As discussed above, no immunity exists for the Commander-in-Chief under either the Genocide Convention or Rome Statute for atrocity crimes. At an initial glance, the threshold level of hate speech which generally involves the denigration of persons on the basis of their ethnic identity or other group membership appears to be met. The number of times the terms 'Bengali' and 'Rohingya' appear in the speech leave little doubt as to the identity of the targeted group. A court may also find that the words express hatred against the Rohingya by denying their existence as a distinct group or associating them as terrorists. But not all hate expressions are unlawful under international law. A court will have to continue its inquiry into whether the speech falls under one of the unlawful categories.

4.5.2.4.2. Direct and Public Incitement to Commit Genocide

As an initial matter, the court may quickly dispense with the public element since this is met based on the public setting and dissemination of the speech on social media and web site. The court may have a harder time addressing the direct element, the *actus reus* of the crime. The main issue will likely be whether after consideration of all the facts, especially the meaning of the terms described

---

[102] "Crisis in Rakhine State Can Be Solved Only Through Comprehensive Knowledge of the Historical Facts", *Senior General Min Aung Hlaing*, 16 October 2017.

[103] "Conspirators of Terrorist Attacks and Families Flee to Bangladesh", *Senior General Min Aung Hlaing*, 15 November 2017.

above, the speech meets the legal standard for a call to "take immediate action" in the commission of genocide with specificity rather than vague or indirect suggestion.[104] Comparisons will be made between the expressions 'unfinished job', 'clearance operations' and utterances made during the Rwanda genocide such as 'go to work' or 'Nyabarongo River' that were found by the courts to be euphemisms to incite the commission of genocide, since these words were understood by the listeners to go kill the Tutsis.[105]

As mentioned above, the Commander-in-Chief's statements at first blush alone do not appear to call for immediate action to commit genocidal acts or issuing any military orders. Courts have also considered the circumstances, time and place of utterances to assess whether certain words have particular significance to the listener.[106] In some cases, a genocidal environment can give heightened meaning to words.[107] By the time the speech was delivered, most of the killings had ceased, and the government announced the end of the 'clearance operations' on 5 September 2017, five days after the speech.[108] Given the need to determine the effect of the statements on the audience within the circumstances at the time, expert and witness testimonies will be critical as part of the court's inquires.

4.5.2.4.3. Crimes against Humanity (Persecution)

The court tasked with determining whether the speech constitutes a crime against humanity will inquire: (i) if these acts were part of a widespread or systematic attack on the civilian Rohingya population and pursuant to a policy or plan; and (ii) whether the speech violated the fundamental rights of the Rohingyas. The court may find that the statement 'clearance operations' is understood as a term used by the military to plan an attack on the Rohingyas in northern Rakhine State in violation of their fundamental rights.[109] The crux of the court's inquiry will be a question of what actual impact the speech had on the discrimination, that is, the causal link between the speech and the discriminatory acts

---

[104] Nahimana Appeals Judgement, paras. 701, 703, 711, 715, see *supra* note 22. The ICTR Appeals Chamber also required specifically urging another individual to take immediate criminal action, rather than merely making a vague or indirect suggestion.

[105] Schabas, 1999, p. 530, see *supra* note 36 (speaking of incitement to genocide). See also Ruggiu Judgement, *supra* note 18; *Mugesera v. Canada, supra* note 37 (the Court found that the reference to the 'Nyabarongo River' meant that Mugesera was suggesting that Tutsi corpses be sent back to Ethiopia).

[106] Akayesu Trial Judgement, para. 361, see *supra* note 23 (the Tribunal found that in the context of the time, place and circumstances of Akayesu's speech, Inkotanyi was tantamount to Tutsi).

[107] *Mugesera v. Canada*, para. 89, see *supra* note 37.

[108] See 2018 IIFFMM Report, 2018, see *supra* note 10.

[109] See, for example, Šešelj Appeals Judgement, para. 163, see *supra* note 19.

must be established.[110] At the time of the speech, Rohingya villages were reportedly burned and the movement of Rohingyas into Bangladesh continued and may have even increased.[111] Furthermore, as elaborated by the IMT, even without a showing of a causal link to the acts, the court may examine if the speech had the effect of injecting 'poison' into the minds of the military for the acts that followed.[112]

The 'substantial impact' of the speech on the violence must also be affirmatively answered beyond a reasonable doubt for a conviction of instigation as a mode of liability. Again, the meaning of the terms will be challenged as to whether the intended audience understood them as encouragement or orders to commit atrocity crimes. Witness testimonies as to the speech's effect may be determinative.

4.5.3. A Sermon by a Senior Buddhist Monk

The hate speech emanating from ultra-nationalist Buddhist monk organization Ma Ba Tha[113] and the monk-led 969 movement has been widely discussed. But a 30 October 2017 sermon by a monk so revered that he was once sought out by former President of the US Barack Obama led to rare criticism of the senior monk (Sitagu Sayadaw) for his sermon's message, interpreted by some as justifying violence against non-Buddhists.[114] Whereas other high-profile persons mentioned in this chapter targeted the 'Bengalis' in their speech, the monk did not explicitly mention 'Bengalis', Muslims or the violence in Rakhine State. But what the monk's remarks appear to do is to suggest that violence is justified against non-believers in order to protect Buddhism. Coming so soon after the Rakhine events, it is unavoidable to infer that the monk's sermon was related. The linguistic content, context and intent are examined below.

4.5.3.1. Linguistic Analysis

The Sayadaw's sermon quotes from a passage in the Mahavamsa, the fifth century C.E. Sri Lankan chronicle. In its home country, the passage has been adopted by Sinhalese nationalists as a source of encouragement for conflict with

110 See, for example, *ibid.*, para. 164 (the Appeals Chamber referred to violence against the Croats following Šešelj's speech).

111 Human Rights Watch, "Burma: 40 Rohingya Villages Burned Since October", 17 December 2017.

112 See Streicher Judgement, *supra* note 19. See also Nahimana Trial Judgement, para. 1073, *supra* note 13.

113 'The Organization for the Protection of Race and Religion in Myanmar' also known as the Ma Ba Tha.

114 Paul Fuller, "Sitagu Sayadaw and justifiable Evils in Buddhism", *New Mandala*, 13 November, 2017.

non-Buddhists.[115] The passage describes a visit of eight Arahants (those with supernatural powers) to comfort King Dutthagamani who is suffering from remorse after waging a war that killed millions.[116] Several translations of the text have been presented. The IIFFMM's translation is as follows:

> There were about five hundred thousand non-religious and evil soldiers, who died in the war. Because of that, the King was not able to sleep at night, since, in Buddhism, killing humans is one of the worst sins. The eight monks who knew about this, told the King "Don't worry, your Highness. Not a single one of those you killed was Buddhist. They didn't follow the Buddhist teachings and therefore they did not know what was good or bad. Not knowing good or bad is the nature of animals. Out of over five hundred thousand you killed, only one and a half were worth to be humans. Therefore, it is a small sin and does not deserve your worry.[117]

Paul Fuller, an academic in Buddhist studies, submits that the sermon and the original text do not directly mention 'Buddhists' and 'non-Buddhists'.[118] The discrepancy between the IIFFMM's and Paul Fuller's translations may be because the Sayadaw delivered two sermons quoting from the Mahavamsa chronicle. The sermon delivered at the military school does not mention 'Buddhists' and 'non-Buddhists'.[119] The other sermon delivered at an unknown place and date mentions 'non-Buddhists'.[120]

The nineteenth century orientalist Wilhelm Geiger's translation of the chronicle used the word 'unbelievers' to describe the King's victims. Paul Fuller's translation, incorporating Geiger's work is:

> From this deed arises no hindrance in thy way to heaven. Only one and a half human beings have been slain here by thee, O lord of men. The one had come unto the (three) refuges, the other had taken on himself the five precepts. Unbelievers [they have "wrong-views", micchādiṭṭhi] and men of evil life were the rest, not more to be esteemed than beasts. But as for thee, thou wilt bring glory

115 Tisaranee Gunasekera, "Betraying Buddhism and Undermining Sri Lanka", *Colombo Telegraph*, 26 January 2014.

116 Fuller, 2017, see *supra* note 114.

117 2018 IIFFMM Report, 2018, para. 1328, see *supra* note 10.

118 *Ibid.*, p. 109.

119 "Lord Buddha Participated in Battle Killing Said Burmese Monk Sitagu 2", *Thang Laka*, 30 October 2017 (available on *YouTube*).

120 "Top Myanmar Buddhist Monk Sitagu Seyadaw Said Non-Muslim Aren't Human so Killing Them is Justified.", *Sadeck Khan*, 3 November 2017 (available on *YouTube*).

> to the doctrine of the Buddha in manifold ways; therefore cast away care from thy heart, O ruler of men![121]

The sermon's core message to combat troops that killing non-believers is justified is troubling in light of Myanmar's other conflicts involving non-Buddhist ethnic groups. Although, the IIFFMM described the sermon as "apparently absolving the military of any guilt or culpability for killing Rohingya", the sermon did not single out a particular ethnic group.[122] But Myanmar has sizable populations of Christians, Muslims, Hindus and other non-Buddhists, and ongoing bloody conflicts between the military and many Christian ethnic groups. The spokesperson for one ethnic army fighting the military, the Ta'ang National Liberation Army, warned that the sermon could inflame the civil war.[123] Many monks also spoke out against the sermon for contradicting the teachings of Buddha of compassion and tolerance.[124]

4.5.3.2. Context

Sitagu Sayadaw is a revered monk who is known for establishing a network of international Buddhist academies and for his philanthropic work. He was reportedly associated with the Ma Ba Tha, although he distanced himself from the organization in 2015.[125] The Sayadaw is close to the Commander-in-Chief and, after the coup in 2021, reportedly called the Commander-in-Chief 'king' or head of state of great generosity and wisdom.[126]

The sermon was delivered at an army combat forces training school on 30 October 2017 during the violence and displacement of Rohingyas in Rakhine State and was transmitted live to 250,000 viewers.[127] Photographs from the event showed hundreds of uniformed military personnel, including officers in the audience.

---

121 See Wilhelm Geiger, *The Mahavamsa*, Oxford University Press, 1912, p. 54, para. 47. See also, Fuller, 2017, *supra* note 114.

122 2018 IIFFMM Report, 2018, para. 1424, see *supra* note 10.

123 "Controversy over Sitagu Sayadaw's Sermon to Military Servicemen", 13 November 2017 ('Controversy over Sitagu Sayadaw's Sermon to Military Servicemen') (available on *YouTube* as of April 2022).

124 *Ibid.*

125 Aung K. Min, "Ma Ba Tha Meet to Resolve Questions over Sitagu Sayadaw Role", *Myanmar Times*, 16 June 2015.

126 "Monk Praises Myanmar Junta Chief for Honoring Prominent Nationalist", *The Irrawaddy*, 21 March 2022.

127 "Free Medical Treatment Conducted in Than Daung Gyi", *Myanmar Digital News*, 19 June 2019.

4.5.3.3. Purpose of the Sermon

The purpose of the sermon to military officers may be inferred from the Sayadaw's remarks at the beginning of the sermon, where he declared: "the King and people must unite, the Tatmadaw and Sangha must unite like a chair with four legs. If one leg goes, you cannot sit on the chair. It is important that all four legs are united".[128] One implication of this statement is that the Sayadaw believed there were divisions between the four entities, the 'four legs', and his visit was to show unity with the troops. The statement also reflects Buddhism's special place in Myanmar's politics.

4.5.3.4. Classification of the Sermon

The sermon illustrates the struggle in drawing the line between freedom of expression and religious speech that is considered to be hateful, in this case of other religions or non-believers. While unlikely to be enforced in this case under the present circumstances, Myanmar's Penal Code criminalizes "outraging the religious feelings of any class of persons".[129] As with political speech, religious speech is also afforded protections under freedom of expression. In Canada, one of the defenses in its hate speech laws is "in good faith, the person expressed or attempted to establish by an argument an opinion on a religious subject or an opinion based on a belief in a religious text".[130] Similarly, the United Kingdom Racial and Religious Hatred Act of 2006 permits "discussion, criticism or expressions of antipathy, dislike, ridicule, insult or abuse of particular religious or beliefs or practices".[131] Arguably, the sermon could fall under one of more of these permitted acts.

Even if the sermon falls under free speech, there are many other reasons why it is so fraught. First, the implication of condoning violence to defend Buddhism is likely to run counter to the beliefs of many adherents.[132] Second, the dehumanizing of 'unbelievers' is troubling because most of the military's conflicts are against religious minorities. Some ethnic leaders criticized the sermon as potentially inflaming the civil war.[133] Third, the sermon's message that killing is excusable emboldens the impunity of the military, especially coming so soon

---

[128] Mratt K. Thu, "Tatmadaw, Sangha and Government Must Work Together, Sitagu Sayadaw Says in Sermon to Officers", *Frontier Myanmar*, 1 November 2017.

[129] Myanmar Penal Code, 1861, Section 295A, see *supra* note 15.

[130] Canada, Criminal Code, R.S.C., 1985, Chapter C-46, Section 319(3)(b) (https://www.legal-tools.org/doc/6b8729/).

[131] United Kingdom, Racial and Religious Hatred Act, 2006, para. 29J (https://www.legal-tools.org/doc/acwj7h/).

[132] Controversy over Sitagu Sayadaw's Sermon to Military Servicemen, see *supra* note 123 (comments by monk).

[133] *Ibid.* (comments by TNLA spokesperson).

after the violence in Rakhine State. Finally, that this sermon was delivered at all by a senior monk seen to be influential with the military that portrays itself as the 'ultimate spiritual guardian' is concerning for the kind of moral and spiritual guidance its soldiers are receiving.[134] Despite the troubling implications of the sermon, there is no clear indication that the Sayadaw's statements could be considered incitement to commit violence or other unlawful acts against a specific group. The term 'unbelievers' is vague. At one point, the Sayadaw absolved himself from the message of the passage, reminding his audience, "I'm not saying that, monks from Sri Lanka said that".[135] Given the legal protections granted to religious speech, the sermon would be protected as free speech despite the hateful message of justifying violence against non-believers including possibly the Rohingyas.

4.5.4. Institutional Role in the Propagation of Hate Speech

The question of state and institutional involvement in the propagation of hate speech may be under scrutiny in the various legal proceedings.[136] Media reports and investigations have alleged the military's involvement in operating online hate speech campaigns targeting Muslims and the NLD. The New York Times ('NYT') headlining its story as *A Genocide Incited on Facebook, With Posts From Myanmar's Military* wrote that, according to sources including former military officials, the military had recruited as many as 700 military personnel located near Nay Pyi Taw to carry out a systematic campaign that targeted the country's mostly Muslim Rohingya minority group.[137] As part of the campaign, Facebook pages seemingly devoted to entertainment were set up but then were used as channels to spread hateful content. In 2017, the military's intelligence arm spread rumors on Facebook to both Muslim and Buddhist groups that an attack from the other side was imminent.

Facebook confirmed the media reports and announced that the company was taking down inauthentic accounts linked to the military. Between August and December 2018, Facebook removed the accounts of the Commander-in-Chief, at least 438 pages, 17 Facebook groups, 145 Facebook accounts and 15 Instagram accounts for links to the Myanmar military.[138]

---

[134] Hannah Beech, "Myanmar's Monks, Leaders of Past Protests, Are Divided Over the Coup", *The New York Times*, 28 August 2021.

[135] *Frontier Myanmar*, 1 November 2017, see *supra* note 128.

[136] For example, before the ICJ, the ICC, in The Gambia's request for subpoena or class action lawsuits.

[137] Paul Mozur, "A Genocide Incited on Facebook, with Posts From Myanmar's Military", *The New York Times*, 15 October 2018.

[138] "Removing Myanmar Military Officials From Facebook", *Meta*, 28 August 2018.

Central to Facebook's analysis for labeling an account as inauthentic involves determining whether an account is fake. According to its reports, Facebook asserts that the removed accounts misrepresented themselves as independent entertainment, beauty and informational pages but were in fact "linked to the Myanmar military".[139]

Facebook has not revealed how it verifies the link between the military and hate speech on its platforms. The NYT relied on statements of former military officials, researchers and civilian officials in the country. Recent accounts from military defectors appear to corroborate military involvement in organizing co-ordinated campaigns against opponents on social media.[140]

According to the NYT article and other sources, Facebook uses human monitors located in other countries, artificial intelligence and third-party reporting to detect inauthentic behavior.[141] Facebook also relies on local non-governmental organizations for information since it has said that it has no plans to open an office in Myanmar.[142]

The NYT article mentions that some of their sources used digital fingerprinting (in technical terms such as internet protocol (IP) address, browser settings, and cookies). On 5 May 2020, the Atlantic Council, a Facebook partner, in its analysis of alleged accounts with "links to members of the Myanmar Police Force" used the CrowdTangle tool which tracks publicly available posts.[143] The Atlantic Council in its analysis of accounts allegedly linked to the Myanmar Police found "little open-source evidence conclusively link[ing] these assets to the Myanmar military" or "little evidence of coordinated activity in the assets".[144] Atlantic Council suggested Facebook likely "relied on back-end information not available to open-source researchers".

The Gambia's legal team believes Facebook's internal records into military links could be critical in its case at the ICJ. In June 2020, The Gambia

139 *Ibid.*

140 "Myanmar Military Asks Soldiers to Create Fake Profiles and Spread Misinformation on Facebook, Twitter: Report", *IndiaToday*, 3 November 2021.

141 Myanmar technology Phandeeyar is a third party that has reported content to Facebook. See also Phandeeyar *et al.*, "Open Letter to Mark Zuckerberg", 5 April 2018; "Update on Myanmar", *Meta*, 15 August 2018; Rafael Frankel, "How Facebook Is Preparing for Myanmar's 2020 Election", *Meta*, 28 August 2018. See also, Michelle Quinn, "Q&A: Facebook Describes How It Detects 'Inauthentic Behavior'", *Voa News*, 26 October 2018.

142 John Russel, "Facebook Still Isn't Taking Myanmar Seriously", *TechCrunch*, 6 Novemebr 2018.

143 Chris Miles, "About Us", CrowdTangle (available on its web site).

144 Atlantic Council, Digital Forensic Research Lab, "Inauthentic Anti-Rohingya Facebook Assets in Myanmar Removed", *Medium*, 6 May 2020.

initiated a discovery request seeking information about these linkages and records of military accounts from Facebook.[145]

Evidence of institutionalized campaign to spread controversial speech could impute liability under international law not only to the State but also to individuals. The Genocide Convention imposes a duty on a contracting party not to commit acts enumerated in Article III, including direct and public incitement to commit genocide, through the actions of their organs or persons or groups whose acts are attributable to them.[146] Article 28 of the Rome Statute provides for the responsibility of commanders and other superiors for the criminal acts of force under his control and subordinates.[147] For the first time, the ICJ may be asked to determine whether online speech, specifically social media communications, meet the threshold for genocide.

4.6. A Glimmer of Hope?

Following the coup, and the ensuing resistance to it, a shift in public opinion towards ethnic and religious minorities appears to be underway. People from all backgrounds took part in nationwide protests against the coup, and some signs held up by protestors voiced solidarity with the Rohingyas for their treatment by the military.[148] Online discourses openly refer to the Muslims in Rakhine State as 'Rohingya'.

The NUG, formed with elected parliamentarians ousted by the coup, has promised fundamental rights, including citizenship for the Rohingyas, and accountability for the violence committed against them.[149] The NUG uses the term 'Rohingya', and has appointed a Rohingya representative to the body. Online inter-communal and inter-faith dialogues are organized monthly.

A more drastic change is taking place in northern Rakhine State. Since the coup, the Arakan Army ('AA') has reportedly taken administrative control

---

145 US District Court for the State of Columbia, *The Gambia v. Facebook*, Application pursuant to 28 U.S.C. §1782, 8 June 2020, Civil Action No. 20-mc-00036-JEB-ZMF. See also Poppy McPherson, "Facebook Shares Data on Myanmar with United Nations Investigators", *Reuters*, 25 August 2020.

146 ICJ, *Case Concerning the Application of the Convention on the Prevention and Punishment of the Crime of Genocide (Bosnia and Herzegovina v. Serbia and Montenegro)*, Judgment, 26 February 2007, p. 119 (http://www.legal-tools.org/doc/5fcd00/):

> The Contracting Parties are bound by the obligation under the Convention not to commit, through their organs or persons or groups whose conduct is attributable to them, genocide and the other acts enumerated in Article III. Thus, if an organ of the State, or a person or group whose acts are legally attributable to the State, commits any of the acts proscribed by Article III of the Convention, the international responsibility of that State is incurred.

147 Rome Statute, see *supra* note 18.

148 Tweet from handle @TheRohingyaPost, 28 February 2021 (available on Twitter).

149 NUG, "Policy Position on the Rohingya in Rakhine State", 3 June 2021.

of over 60 per cent of the area where the violence of 2017 occurred. In its bid to gain recognition and legitimacy, the AA has made statements about inclusivity and equal rights for all, including the Rohingyas, but has so far declined to use the term 'Rohingya' to identify the Muslims in the area.[150] The AA, whose ranks now include the same parliamentary representatives that made incendiary remarks in Parliament just before the violence of 2017, has also welcomed the cases brought against the military at the ICJ and ICC.[151]

Whether these are flickering signs of a more inclusive and tolerant society remains to be seen. The military, in contrast, has continued to spread conspiracy theories about Muslim involvement in the anti-coup resistance, and, in some cases, disseminate leaflets alleging the Organisation of Islamic Cooperation's support of anti-military forces. State-owned media continues to refer to "Bengalis" and the "Western Gate".[152] But with rising awareness, strong anti-military sentiments throughout the country, with even Bamar areas under attack by military 'clearance operations', and changing political complexion in Rakhine State, it is difficult to imagine that the widespread proliferation of hate speech in 2017 could happen again.

4.7. Conclusion

The period 2015–2020 in Myanmar will likely be remembered for the violence against the Rohingyas, Buddhist nationalism, and the failed relationship between the civilian government and the military. As described in this chapter, these factors played a role in the controversial speech that were uttered by members of the highest strata of Myanmar society: parliamentary representatives, the Commander-in-Chief and a senior Buddhist monk. This chapter has examined the legality of these statements to the extent afforded by the available information, based on the framework derived from the Genocide Convention, the Rome Statute and jurisprudence of the various international tribunals. While there are grounds for criminal responsibility for the statements, more detailed inquiries with input from linguistic experts and witness testimonies will be needed.

However, judicial processes alone may not prevent hate-based violence or speech in the future. As observers have noted, if local fears, prejudices and grievances, especially in the context of contested historical narratives, remain

---

150 Bertil Lintner, "Rebel Yell: Arakan Army Leader Speaks to Asia Times", *Asia Times*, 18 January 2022.

151 See Jacques P. Leider, "The Arakan Army, Rakhine State and the Promise of Arakan's Independence", Policy Brief No. 128 (2022), TOAEP, Brussels, 2022 (https://www.toaep.org/pbs-pdf/128-leider/).

152 "Honour Ethnics in Rakhine State Safeguarding Western Border of the Nation", *Myanmar Digital News*, 15 December 2021.

uninvestigated, a poisonous legacy will live on.[153] The coup has triggered changing public perceptions of ethnic minorities, and, in Rakhine State, we see tentative steps towards recognition of shared histories providing some encouragement for the future.

[153] Jacques P. Leider, "Territorial Dispossession and Persecution in North Arakan (Rakhine), 1942–43", Policy Brief Series No. 101 (2020), TOAEP, Brussels, 2020 (https://www.toaep.org/pbs-pdf/101-leider/). See also Ware and Laoutides, 2018, p. 212, see *supra* note 30 (the stalemate of historical narratives cannot be ignored).

5

Alleged Hate Speech by Buddhists: A Myanmar Muslim's Perspective

U Aye Lwin*

5.1. Introduction

This chapter explores the origins and evolution of alleged hate speech by Buddhists against Muslims in Myanmar, with the sincere hope of conveying the subject in a way that is fair and just. The Holy *Qur'án* is very explicit when it refers to fairness and justice:

> O you who believe, be upright and fulfil your duties to God and bear true witness with Justice. Do not allow your hatred for others to incite you to turn away from Justice. Be just, that bring closer to true piety. Fear God, God is cognizant of what you do.[1]
>
> O you who believe, be a maintainer of Justice [conduct yourself with justice] and bear true witness before God, even though it be against yourselves, your parents, or your kin. Be they rich or poor, God knows better about them both. So do not be led by passion [follow not your low desires], lest you deviate [swerve from the truth]. And if you distort or turn away from truth, God is cognizant of all your actions [aware of what you do].[2]

It is crucial to understand that in the original teachings of Lord Buddha, just like in those of the enlightened leaders of all major religions, there is

* **Al-Haj Khalifah U Aye Lwin** is the Chief Convener of the Islamic Centre of Myanmar; Chairman, Scholarship Program Implementation Committee, Islamic Development Bank Counterpart Organization, Myanmar; Khalifa, Spiritual Guide of the Qadariya Aliyah Ṣúfí Order, Myanmar; and Founder and Core Member, Religions for Peace, Myanmar. He was formerly a member of the Advisory Commission on Rakhine State, chaired by late Mr. Kofi Annan. For an audio-visual recording of his statement to CILRAP's conference in Florence in April 2022 on the topic of this chapter, please see https://www.cilrap.org/cilrap-film/220408-aye-lwin/. See also U Aye Lwin, "Myanmar: Buddhist Ultra-Nationalism, Anti-Muslim Sentiment, and a Pathway to Reconciliation", Policy Brief Series No. 137 (2022), Torkel Opsahl Academic EPublisher, Brussels, 2022 (https://www.toaep.org/pbs-pdf/137-aye/).

1 The *Qur'án*, 5:8. Unless otherwise indicated, the translations of the Holy *Qur'án* used in this chapter are provided by the author.

2 The *Qur'án*, 4:135. Similar instructions can be found in other verses of the Holy *Qur'án*, such as 6:152 and 4:105.

absolutely no place for hate. According to Buddhism, in reality (or in essence) there are only two aggregate components in a human being, that is, *Nama* (mind) and *Rupa* (physical body). There are no such things as men, women, individuals, persons, creatures, deities and beings.[3] Therefore, there is zero tolerance for discrimination and hatred in Buddhism *per se*, intrinsically.

The following teachings of Lord Buddha lend further support to the above-mentioned statements:

> Whether Perfect Ones (Buddhas) appear in the world, or whether Perfect Ones do not appear in the world, it still remains a firm condition, an immutable fact and fixed law: that all formations are impermanent (*anicca*), that all formations are subject to suffering (*dukkha*); that everything is without a Self (*an-attaa*).[4]

In Pali:

> Sabbe sankhaaraa aniccaa, sabbe sankhaaraa dukkhaa, sabbe dhammaa anattaa.

The word *Sankra* (formations), here, comprises all things that are conditioned or 'formed' (*Sankhata Dhamma*), that is, all possible physical and mental constituents of existence.

In another sermon, Lord Buddha made a similar statement:

> A corporeal phenomenon, a feeling, a perception, a mental formation, a consciousness, which is permanent and persistent, eternal and not subject to change, such a thing the wise man in this world do not recognize, and I also say that there is no such thing.[5]

Another relevant citation is from the *Sutta*, one of the 'three baskets' of Buddhist scriptures ('*Tipiṭaka*'):

> The *Samsara* [cycle of life and dead] is so long that there is no being in these infinite universes that you are not related to. You are either wife or husband, brother or sister, father or mother, son or daughter, of each other [you are all but one family] in one life cycle or the other in these thirty-one planes of existence of *Samsara* [cycle of life and dead].[6]

Nevertheless, we should bear in mind that, no matter how much good may be contained in the original doctrines of the religions, the correct interpretations and actual implementation of these precepts are what truly reflects the mindset,

---

3 *Abidama*, one of the baskets of *Tipiṭaka* (three spiritual baskets of Buddhism).

4 *Anguttara-Nikaaya*, III, 134 (here, the Roman number refers to the main division into Parts, or *Nipaatas*, and the second number refers to the *Sutta*).

5 *Samyutta-Nikaaya*, XXII, 94 (here, the Roman number refers to the main division into Kindred Groups, or *Samyutta*, and the second number refers to the *Sutta*).

6 Theravada Pali Canon (*Anamataka Thanyoke Deasana*), author's translation.

attitude and behaviour of their followers. It is indeed a time-tested fact that there are 'black sheep' in every community, who do not abide by the true teachings of their religions and even act against the noble doctrines of their own faith. To add to this, politicians, and particularly dictators, often tend to politicize religion and manipulate it unscrupulously for their own agendas, which are usually hidden. A fair assessment should clearly differentiate between the true believers of a religion and its so-called 'followers'. As we analyse, in search of truth, the alleged hate speech by Buddhists in Myanmar against Muslims, we should be cautious of this distinction.

I will begin this analysis by highlighting a remark made by American journalist Hannah Beech in her cover story "The Face of Buddhist Terror", in the 2013 July issue of the *Time* magazine:

> It's a faith famous for its pacifism and tolerance. But in several of Asia's Buddhist-majority nations, monks are inciting bigotry and violence – mostly against Muslims.[7]

She also described the growing tensions:

> Buddhist blood is boiling in Burma, also known as Myanmar – and plenty of Muslim blood is being spilled. Over the past year, Buddhist mobs have targeted members of the minority faith. The authorities say scores of Muslims have been killed; international human-rights workers put the number in the hundreds.[8]

The article continued:

> The communal bloodshed then spread to central Burma, where Wirathu lives and preaches his virulent sermons. The radical monk sees Muslims, who make up at least 5% of Burma's estimated 60 million people, as a threat to the country and its culture. "[Muslims] are breeding so fast and they are stealing our women, raping them," he tells me. "They would like to occupy our country, but I won't let them. We must keep Myanmar Buddhist."[9]

Hanna Beech branded the radical Buddhist monk from Mandalay as "the Buddhist monk who has taken the title 'the Burmese bin Laden'".[10] She described the sermon by Ashin Wirathu, Burmese Buddhist monk and the leader of the 969 Movement in Myanmar, as a "message [which] crackles with hate":

> "Now is not the time for calm," the 46-year-old monk intones, as he spends 90 minutes describing the many ways in which he

---

7 Hannah Beech, "The Face of Buddhist Terror", *Time*, 1 July 2013.

8 *Ibid.*

9 *Ibid.*

10 *Ibid.*

> detests the minority Muslims in this Buddhist-majority land. "Now is the time to rise up, to make your blood boil."[11]

Osama bin Laden, founder of the Islámic militant organization Al-Qaeda, and Wirathu are classic examples of the 'black sheep' that, as argued above, regrettably exist in all religious communities.

5.2. A Brief Account of the History and Origin of Buddhism in Myanmar

This section seeks to understand the origin and evolution of religion, hateful expression and violence in the context of Myanmar by briefly studying the history and origin of Buddhism in Myanmar. The information regarding this analysis can be traced back to two sources: the traditional beliefs of the native people and historical research.

5.2.1. Traditional Beliefs of the Native People of Myanmar

The traditional beliefs of the native people comprise of an amalgamation of mythologies, legends, folklore, customs and beliefs in a culture passed down – mostly orally, but sometimes in written form – from generation to generation. Some of these legends are found in stone inscriptions inside religious edifices. According to these tales, based largely on pagoda chronicles, Buddhism reached Burma right after the enlightenment of Lord Buddha. It is a popular belief that, more than 2,500 years ago, two Burmese merchants met Lord Buddha under the Bo Tree, or the Bodhi Fig Tree ('tree of awakening'), located in Bodh Gaya, Bihar, in India, and received the Holy Hairs of Lord Buddha. These relics have been enshrined in the Shwedagon Pagoda situated in Yangon (Rangoon).[12] Most historians disagree with this notion simply because the Bamar as a race emerged only in the eleventh century AD, during the reign of Anawrahta, founder of the Pagan Dynasty.[13] Khin Maung Saw, in his book *Behind the Mask: The Truth Behind the Name Rohingya*, wrote that:

> The Burmese (Myanmar) traditionally believed that they were the descendants of the four superior gods, the 'Brahmas' who came down to the earth from the abode of 'Brahmas'. Two of whom became women and the other two became men and settled in the

[11] *Ibid.*

[12] This belief is popularly known as the 'Shwedagon Pagoda Chronicle' and relates to the Shwedagon Pagoda in Yangon. A reference of the same can be found on the United Nations Educational, Scientific and Cultural Organization's web site.

[13] "Keynote Address by Al Haj U Aye Lwin, Chief Convenor for the Islamic Centre of Myanmar", Myanmar Update 2019, Australian National University, Canberra, 15 March 2019 ('Keynote Address by Al Haj U Aye Lwin').

> basin of the Irrawaddy River. Because of that traditional belief, they called themselves Bama in colloquial, the corruption of Brahma.[14]

He further states that,

> Burmese, Mons, Khmers, Laotians, and Thais believe that they came from India instead of Tibet or China, and they are the descendants of the Sakya Sakis, from which Gautama Buddha came. The main reason is that all of them are Buddhists and everybody, especially the kings, wanted to claim to be related to Lord Buddha. If Lord Buddha were a Chinese instead of an Indian, their traditional beliefs would have been changed to the other way round.[15]

According to Khin Maung Saw,

> [t]he Burmese traditionally believe that the Pyus, the Kamyams, and the Saks were the first Tibeto-Burmese ethnic groups who migrated to the country which is now Burma. Traditional historians like Thakin Kodaw Hmaing, U Pho Kyar, Deedok U Ba Cho, and so on, believed that the Pyus were the forefathers of the Burmese, the Kamyams were the ancestors of the Arakanese (Rakhaing) and the Chins are descendants of the Saks (Thak).[16]

However, according to Burmese historian Dr. Than Tun, the supposed two merchants from Burma were, in fact, from the region of Orissa in India, citing Indian historians to support his view.[17] He emphatically mentioned that Lord Buddha had not travelled beyond India. Regardless, the wider Burmese consensus accepted without argument the legends about Lord Buddha's visit to Burma.[18]

5.2.2. Historical Research

The second source is scientific historical research done by competent historians. According to these findings, no religion originated in Myanmar; however, all the major religions of the world have flourished in the nation. After Animism, Hinduism was the first major religion to reach Myanmar. Then, Mahayana (one of the main existing branches of Buddhism) and some sects of Tantric Buddhism

---

14 Khin Maung Saw, *Behind the Mask: The Truth Behind the Name "Rohingya"*, Yangon, 2016, p. 12.

15 *Ibid.* (sic.).

16 *Ibid.*, p. 13.

17 Than Tun, "History of Buddhism", doctoral dissertation, University of London, 1956, p. 200, of the 'revised and enlarged' version, lists, in its bibliography, Asoka Kumar Rath, "Buddhist Remains in the Cuttack District of Orrisa", in *Journal of the Andhra Historical Research Society*, 1961–1962, vol. 27, p. 155.

18 Than Tun, *Khit Haung Myanmar Yazawin*, Innwa Publishing House, Yangon, 1964.

became firmly rooted in the land. After hearing about Theravada Buddhism, King Anawrahta of the Pagan dynasty waged war against King Manuha of the Mon Kingdom in Thaton and captured the city along with the Theravada Buddhist scriptures, the *Tipiṭaka*.[19]

The advent of Buddhism in Myanmar is attributed to missionaries sent by Asoka, the third emperor of the Mauryan Empire in India, in the third century BC. According to the Sinhalese chronicle, the *Mahāvaṃsa*, the origin of Buddhism in Myanmar can be attributed to the mission of two monks, Sona and Uttara, who in the third century BC came to Suvarnabhumi[20] (Mon Kingdom), usually identified with Thaton, on the Gulf of Mottama. This episode is disputed by some modern scholars. However, it cannot be denied that Buddhism was already flourishing in Myanmar in the first century AD, as attested to by archaeological evidence at Beikthano, a city of great significance in the Pyu era (before the emergence of the Bamar race), 145 kilometres southeast of Bagan.[21] Buddhism was also an invigorating influence of Thayekhittaya (Sri Ksetra), one of the ancient Pyu capitals, near modern Pyay Myo, 255 kilometres south of Bagan, where a developed civilization such as the Pyu flourished from the fifth to the ninth century AD.[22]

By the end of the Pyu period, the major Animists (the *Nats*) had been subordinated to Theravada Buddhism, which became the religion of choice among the lowland rice farmers. Theravada Buddhism remains the predominant religion in Burma to the present day.

The Tibeto-Burman speaking Pyu are believed to have entered the Irrawaddy Valley from present day Yunnan in the second century BC, and to have founded city states throughout the Valley.[23] The Pyu were the earliest inhabitants of Burma of whom records are extant. By the fourth century AD, many in the Irrawaddy Valley had converted to Buddhism. Archaeological findings also indicate a widespread presence of Tantric Buddhism, Mahayana Buddhism and Hinduism in this region.[24] Avalokiteshvara (Lawkanatha, called '*Lawka Nat*' in Burmese), Tara, Manusi Buddha, Vais'ravan and Hayagriva, all prominent deities in Mahayana Buddhism, were very much part of the Pyu (and later, the

[19] Keynote Address by Al Haj U Aye Lwin, 2019, see *supra* note 13.

[20] The Mahāvaṃsa, Chapter XII, p. 94.

[21] Kyaw Myo Satt, "Buddhist Religion in the Pyu Period with the Reference to Archaeological Evidence", Asia Research Centre, Yangon University, 2015, pp. 2 ff.

[22] Stephen A. Murphy and Win Kyaing, "The Pyu: An Ancient Civilisation of Upper Myanmar", in Stephen A. Murphy *et al.* (eds.), *Cities and Kings: Ancient Treasures from Myanmar*, Asian Civilisations Museum, Singapore, 2016, pp. 22 ff.

[23] Elizabeth H. Moore, *Early Landscapes of Myanmar*, River Books, Bangkok, p. 236.

[24] Michael Aung-Thwin, *The Mists of Rāmañña: The Legend that was Lower Burma*, University of Hawai'i Press, Honolulu, 2005, pp. 31–34.

Pagan) iconography scene. Various Hindu Brahman iconography ranging from the Hindu Trinity (Brahama, Vishnu and Shiva) to Garuda and Lakshmi have been found, especially in lower Burma. Non-Theravada practices such as ceremonial cattle sacrifice and alcohol consumption were mainstays of the Pyu life.[25]

It is pertinent to note at this juncture that there are scholars, such as Than Tun, who dispute the episode of Anawrahta, or Aniruddha, founder of Pagan dynasty in the eleventh century A.D., seeking the Theravada *Tipiṭaka* (scriptures) at Thaton. In his thesis, submitted to the Faculty of Arts of the University of London in 1956, he wrote:

> The conquest of Thaton in 1057 by Aniruddha resulted, it is said, in the introduction of pure *Theravada* Buddhism into Upper Burma. But unfortunately there is no known contemporary evidence in support of this famous episode. All the information we have about this event is from various chronicles which are far from reliable for the period under consideration. This is what Professor G.H. Luce said on the subject:
>
>> Already these accounts cancel themselves out: Aniruddha goes seeking Tipitaka now at Thaton, now at the Khmer capital Angkor. He receives an insolent refusal now at Thaton, now at Angkor. […] Hero, scene and villain are alike lost in folktale and history sub-merged in the myth.[26]

According to Than Tun:

> It is more than possible that Buddhism has been known to the early Burman even before the 11th century. They may have been influenced in their civilization and religion by the Pyu because as late as A.D 1112–13 a Pagan prince called *Rajakumar*, the beloved son of *Thiluin Man* (1084–1113) used Pyu as one of the four languages to record a dedication that he made on behalf of his dying father. Their first capital Srikestra, four miles to the east of Prome, was probably built in A.D. 638 and it seems that they moved to Halingyi near Shwebo in about the middle of the 8th century when the Karens came. The Pyu kingdom was ultimately destroyed in A.D. 832.[27]
>
> It is important to discover what sort of religion the Burmans practised in the early part of Pagan Dynasty which has been

---

[25] Victor B. Lieberman, *Strange Parallels: Southeast Asia in Global Context, c. 800–1830, volume 1, Integration on the Mainland*, Cambridge University Press, 2003, pp. 116–117.

[26] Than Tun, "History of Buddhism in Burma A.D. 1000-1300", in *Journal of the Burma Research Society*, 1978, vol. 61, nos. 1–2, p. 51.

[27] *Ibid.*, p. 52.

> labelled the Mon period (1057–1113) as most of the inscriptions attributed to this era are in the Mon language. In the Great Shwezigon inscription of *Thiluin Man* (1084–1113) we have the eulogy of the king who shall rule Pagan after A.B. 1630 (A.D 1086). According to it the principal religion then practised was Buddhism. But there are references to other religions as well. Sri Tribhuvanadityadhammaraja (i.e. *Thiluin Man*) the Buddhist King is considered as a reincarnation of Vishnu. Evidently there is a good deal of Brahmanism in the Buddhism that they practised.[28]

As such, Than Tun is of the view that there is no contemporary evidence in support of this account and that the sources of such information are unreliable and that the accounts are contradictory.

5.2.3. The History and Origin of Buddhism in the Mindset of Buddhist Ultra-Nationalists in Myanmar

I briefly and critically elaborated on the origins of Buddhism in Myanmar with a view to analysing the mindset of close-minded Buddhist ultra-nationalists, who are primarily responsible for hate speech against Muslims in Myanmar. Buddhist ultra-nationalists believe, contrary to historical research, that they belong to the superior race related to Lord Buddha, known as '*Thargi Twe*' (blood relations of Lord Buddha). They believe that Lord Buddha favoured them as the 'chosen race' by accepting two Bamar merchants as his foremost disciples. Buddhist ultra-nationalists also believe that Bamars belong to the race of Gautam Buddha ('*Satkya Thargi*'), apparently drawing on the *Hmannan Yazawin* (the 'Glass Palace Chronicle'), the first official chronicle of the Konbaung dynasty of Burma. They also claim that Lord Buddha visited Burma occasionally during his lifetime.

With due respect to the sincere, pious and good-faith Burmese Buddhist majority, it is historically verified that the missions undertaken by Lord Buddha did not extend beyond the borders of present-day India. The farthest that Lord Buddha travelled to spread his teachings was around the shores of the Ganges and the Yamuna rivers in India.

According to Donald Eugene Smith:

> Relatively little is known about religion in Burma before the eleventh century A.D. An indigenous animism – the worship of *nat* spirits – coexisted and coalesced with various religions of Indian origin, including several Hindu sects and both Theravada and Mahayana Buddhism. Indian cultural influence became especially strong in the Mon Kingdom at Thahton, situated on the coast, and it was probably the Mon connection with the great Theravada

[28] *Ibid.*, p. 54.

> Buddhist center at Conjeeveran, in south India, which resulted in predominance of that faith at Thaton.[29]

Regardless of the origins of Buddhism in Myanmar, after the British colonized Myanmar and placed it under India as a province, some nationalist Bamar leaders believed that, in order to liberate and emancipate the Burmese from the yoke of colonial imperialism, there was a need to get rid of what they termed 'slave mentality'. The resistance groups that emerged right after the annexation of Myanmar following the third Anglo-Burmese war in 1885 eventually mobilized the Buddhist majority with the slogan that the race of Lord Buddha should not become slave of non-Buddhist heathens. Thus, they referred to themselves as *Thakhins* (masters)[30] and called the British *Kala Phyu* (White Indian) and the Indians *Kala Mae* (Black Indian). The word '*Kala*' literally means 'alien', and was used in a positive sense before; but as xenophobic, racist tensions gained strength in the region, it was distorted and used to connote a negative, abusive and derogatory meaning, akin to the word 'Nigger' for African-Americans.[31]

This mentality unfortunately appeared to take hold of some politically-minded monks and laypersons in the fight for independence in Myanmar. However, we should bear in mind that there were a number of Buddhist nationalists who were very tolerant and, as true Buddhists, welcomed and celebrated people belonging to other religious backgrounds, as illustrated in this chapter.[32]

The sad reality is that there still exist some ultra-nationalist Buddhists in present Myanmar society, as the next section of this chapter will discuss. A research officer from the Myanmar Ministry of Religious Affairs, U Hla Thein Htut, wrote a book titled 'Buddha Thee Myanmar Lu-Myo' ('Buddha Is From the Myanmar Race'). Bokalay Ashin Pandeeta, a prominent Buddhist monk, published a book in 2018 titled 'Doe Paya Thee Kala Ma Hoke Myanmar Pyit Thee' ('Our Lord Is Not Indian but a Burman'). Similar writings flooded print and social media in Myanmar. These are textbook examples of attempts to distort and contradict the teachings of Lord Buddha, which contain no tolerance for discrimination or racism. An International Crisis Group report titled 'Buddhism and State Power in Myanmar', released in September 2017, portrayed the scenario at that time as follows:

---

29 Donald Eugene Smith, *Religion and Politics in Burma*, Princeton University Press, 2015, p. 12.

30 Niklas Foxeus, "The Buddha Was a Devoted Nationalist: Buddhist Nationalism, Ressentiment, and Defending Buddhism in Myanmar", in *Religion*, 2019, vol. 49, no. 4, pp. 666–667.

31 Michał Lubina, "Overshadowed by Kala: India-Burma Relations", in *Politeja*, 2016, vol. 1, no. 40, pp. 435–454.

32 See discussions in Section 5.1. above.

> there is a widespread nationalist perception that they [National League for Democracy ('NLD')] have a generally Western liberal outlook that privileges minority rights and diversity (including religious diversity) over protection of the Buddhist faith – notwithstanding the fact that many minorities feel that the government is not taking account of their concerns.[33]

Inter-communal tensions and outbreaks of violence linked to hate speech and nationalists' provocations in Myanmar are a matter of grave concern at the time of writing. The Association for the Protection of Race and Religion (commonly referred to by the acronym 'Ma Ba Tha') – a prominent nationalist organization made up of monks, nuns and laypeople with the purported purpose of the protection of race (Bamar), religion (Theravada Buddhism) and language (Burmese) – is a notable example of organizations engaged in espousing anti-Muslim views and inciting and condoning violence in the name of protecting religion. In the context of tense inter-communal relations, there is a real risk that these actions contribute to major communal violence. It has been rightly pointed out that "the biggest threat may not be the Ma Ba Tha itself, but the dynamics which it has created and individuals it has empowered who may be beyond its control".[34]

5.3. Buddhist Nationalism in Myanmar

5.3.1. The Rise of Buddhist Nationalism in Myanmar

The recent resurgence of Buddhist nationalism in Myanmar was spearheaded, in part, by the 969 Movement, which first became prominent in the southern city of Mawlamyaing in 2011. The designation '969' is a numerological shorthand for the special attributes of Lord Buddha and his teachings, and a riposte to the number '786', a folk Islámic representation of *Bassmalah*,[35] long used by Muslims in Myanmar and elsewhere to identify Ḥalal restaurants and Muslim-owned shops. The 969 Movement, which is a loose association of monks that preaches intolerance and urges a boycott of Muslim businesses, was widely believed to be linked to a wave of violence against the Muslim minority in Myanmar in 2012 and 2013. It appears that considerable pent-up frustration and anger brewed under the years of authoritarianism are now being directed towards Muslims by populist political forces veiled behind religious respectability and moral authority.

[33] International Crisis Group, "Buddhism and State Power in Myanmar", Asia Report No. 290, 5 September 2017, Executive Summary, p. i ('Buddhism and State Power in Myanmar').

[34] *Ibid.*, p. ii.

[35] The *Bassmalah* is an Islámic phrase which means 'In the name of God, the Most Gracious, the Most Merciful'.

Anti-Indian and anti-Muslim violence are not new in Myanmar. This kind of violence is rooted in the country's colonial history and demographics, and the rise of Burman nationalism in that context. Deadly violence has erupted regularly in different parts of the country over the decades. However, the rise of authoritarian influence and the greater availability of modern communication in present times means that there is a much greater risk of violence.[36]

Indians have become targets of the growing Burmese nationalist movement. The lyrics of a popular song from the 1930s stated that Indians were "exploiting our economic resources and seizing our women, we are in danger of racial extinction".[37] Such allegations are strikingly similar to the terms in which present-day nationalist agendas are framed.[38] During the aforementioned period, the Doebama Asiayone ('We Burman' Movement) emerged as the main pro-independence political organization, with the principle of 'Burma for the Burmans' and the slogan "let him who desires peace prepare for war".[39]

Although the 969 Movement is new, it is repeating old prejudice. A British colonial inquiry into anti-Indian riots in Yangon in 1938 noted that "one of the major sources of anxiety in the minds of a great number of Burmese was the question of the marriage of their womenfolk with foreigners in general and with Indians in particular".[40]

The Burmese government estimates that Muslims constitute some four per cent of the country's population.[41] However, Muslim leaders believe that Muslims make up nearly 10 per cent of the population.[42] There has been no official census in Burma since it gained independence from Great Britain in 1948. Apart from Arakan (current day Rakhine State), the western Burmese state that borders Bangladesh and is home to Muslim Rohingyas, Burma's Muslims live predominantly in urban areas throughout the country. According to a senior Muslim leader in Rangoon, most Muslims are indistinguishable in appearance and behaviour from the country's Buddhists: they dress the same, wear *longyi*, speak Burmese and understand Burmese culture and history.[43]

---

36 International Crisis Group, "The Dark Side of Transition: Violence against Muslims in Myanmar", Asia Report No. 251, 1 October 2013, Executive Summary, p. i.

37 Khin Yi, *The Dobama Movement in Burma (1930-1938)*, Cornell University Press, Ithaca, 1988, p. 96.

38 *Ibid.*

39 *Ibid.*

40 Burma Riot Inquiry Committee, *Interim Report*, Govt. Printing and Stationery, Rangoon, 1939.

41 Minority Rights Group International, "World Directory of Minorities and Indigenous Peoples – Myanmar/Burma: Muslims and Rohingya", October 2017.

42 "Crackdown on Burmese Muslims", *Human Rights Watch*, 18 July 2002, p. 3 (https://www.legal-tools.org/doc/f9n0v8/).

43 *Ibid.*

In fact, Islám reached Myanmar more than 1,000 years ago, in the seventh century AD. When the first Burmese dynasty, the Pagan, was founded in the eleventh century AD by King Anawrahta, Muslims were firmly integrated as citizens and were part and parcel of Burmese society. Some Muslims were serving the King as loyal subjects and not as foreign mercenaries. While Myanmar kings used to hire foreign experts to serve in their court, Muslims were performing their duties as natives of the country. This historical fact is supported by Pagan stone inscriptions.[44]

From the time of the Pagan dynasty, there is evidence of religion being manipulated by individuals in bad faith as part of their schemes and power struggles. To mention a few examples, during the reign of King Anawratha, founder of the Pagan dynasty, two Muslim heroes were murdered due to the illicit planning of officials. The heroes were accused of religious bigotry when they refused to lay two bricks at a pagoda built by the King, a part of the royal ceremonial rituals. Distorted reports of the incident were transmitted to the King by mischievous palace officials with the intention of inciting his anger. The King thus ordered the palace officials to teach the two Muslim heroes a lesson, but the officials used this opportunity to kill them instead. Legend has it that when the King learnt about the fate of these beloved heroes, he allotted a place for them to live and rule as spirits. This spirit shrine is located in upper Myanmar and is known as Taungbyone. Every year since the eleventh century AD, great traditional festivals are celebrated in the shrines, worshiping the spirits (known as *Nat* in Myanmar). The two Muslims *Nats* are popularly known as Min Gyi and Min Galay.[45]

Another incident pertains to four Ṣúfí scholar saints during the reign of the prominent Buddhist King U Aung Zay Ya (Alaungphaya), founder of the royal city of Shwebo. Due to the pious acts of the Ṣúfí saints and the admiration and reverence shown to them by the King, ultra-nationalists Buddhists ministers

44 Keynote Address by Al Haj U Aye Lwin, 2019, see *supra* note 13; "Sasana yaung war Tun Pyaung Say Poe" (For the Sasana to be Illuminated), Ministry of Defense of Myanmar, Directorate of Resettlement, March 1997; Toe Hla, *Myay paw Myay out kyaut sar mhat tan myar ka pyaw thaw shay haung Myanmar naing nghan daw thamine* (The Ancient History of Myanmar Told by Stone Inscriptions, Both Underground and Above), U Khin Maung Than Than Sarpe, Yangon, September 2004; Moshe Yegar, *The Muslims of Burma: A Study of a Minority Group*, Harassowitz, Wiesbaden, 1972; Shwe Bo U Ba Oo, *Myanmar Muslim doe ee a htoke pat tii* (Biographies of Myanmar Muslims), 2nd ed., U Ba Oo, 1992; Lt. Colonel Ba Shin, *Coming of Islam to Burma Down to 1700 A.D.*, Azad Bhavan, New Delhi, 1961; Aung Moe, "Moslems in Burma", *Working People's Daily* (now, *The Global New Light of Myanmar*), 9 May 1978.

45 Paper presented by Tin Hlaing (Professor, International Buddhist University) at the Inter-Faith Dialogue Conference, Yogyakarta, Indonesia, 6–7 December 2004; Yegar, 1972, see *supra* note 44.

in the Palace, encouraged by the instigation of the Manipuri court astrologers (known as *Pone Nas*), conspired against the four saints. The saints were accused of anti-Buddhist schemes and forced to eat pork to prove their innocence. When the four saints refused, they were slaughtered. After the conspiracy was discovered by the King, he buried the four saints according to Islámic rites and a mausoleum was built, housing the saints' tombs. Moreover, the King donated funds for the construction of four gilded mosques around Shwebo and Myay Du in their honour.[46]

Another incident of extreme violence triggered by religious fanaticism occurred during the reign of King Bodawpaya (U Wyine) of the Konebaung dynasty in the seventeenth century AD. The efficiency and loyalty of the Myanmar Muslims throughout Myanmar's history have been recognized by successive Myanmar Buddhist kings and a majority of the fellow subjects (primarily Burmese Buddhists) living under these kings. The role of Myanmar Muslims in the state-building endeavour during the Konebaung dynasty was exceptional. During this period, there were Myanmar Muslim intellectuals, officials, traders and religious personalities who had won the hearts and minds of the Burmese kings and the tolerant Burmese Buddhists. Such amicable and harmonious relations among the diverse people of plural Myanmar society have been viewed as the genesis of the decline of Buddhist dominance in Myanmar by certain Buddhist ultra-nationalists. Their beliefs and mindset are very similar to those of present-day Buddhist ultra-nationalists. Eventually, these Buddhist extremists managed to affect influential court officials and poison the mind of King Bodawpaya with fabricated stories. Consequently, the King issued a royal decree to restrict Muslim religious activity in Myanmar. The gates of mosques around the capital were barred with thorny bamboo sticks, since there was no barbed wire fence at that time. During that period, a Burmese Ṣúfí scholar saint, U Nu (Muḥammad Qásim), who was a classmate of the King, wrote a supplication and submitted it to the King, clarifying the misconceptions regarding Islám and portraying the true image of the religion. This supplication is fortunately still available in book form. After realizing the actual teachings of Islám and having met Abbid Shah Husseinee, a Mogul prince who became a wandering dervish (a Ṣúfí saint) who walked to the Burmese capital Ava from Delhi in India, and having witnessed his sublime character and wisdom, the King revoked his royal

46 Stone inscription erected in front of the Shwebon Yadana Mingala Palace, Shwebo; Keynote Address by Al Haj U Aye Lwin, 2019, see *supra* note 13.

decree which persecuted and discriminated against his Burmese Muslim subjects.[47]

5.3.2. The Rise and Fall of the Ma Ba Tha

Over the last few decades, religion has continued to be manipulated and used for political gains. The military has been stirring up ultra-nationalist sentiments among Burmese Buddhists since the 1962 coup by projecting Islám as the main threat to Buddhism. Following the 1962 coup, military dictator Ne Win covertly and overtly manipulated religion and used it as a political tool. From 1988 onwards, military tyrants, with the intention of diverting the attention of the population, stirred anti-Muslim and anti-non-Buddhist sentiments among the majority Burmese Buddhists. Present-day events in Myanmar are a reflection of Ne Win's legacy. Although Ne Win himself met with a disgraceful downfall at the hands of his own protégés, his mentality is firmly implanted and embedded in the present-day junta leaders. That is why they are infamously referred to as "old wines in new bottles".[48]

The Union Solidarity and Development Party ('USDP'), backed by the military, won the 2010 elections in Myanmar, which had been boycotted by the NLD party. The reason for the boycott was the hasty adoption of the Constitution of the Republic of the Union of Myanmar in 2008 as well as the election commission's election law, which the NLD believed to not guarantee human rights and democracy. When other factors that led to the USDP's victory in the 2010 elections (such as the lack of interest and the related lack of participation of the majority of the voters as well as the absence of respectable rivals) became apparent, the USDP realized that it did not actually have the support of the people. As a result, the USDP followed a strategy of instigating hatred against the Rohingyas in Rakhine State, and other non-Rohingya Muslims in different parts of the country.

Renewed nationalism arose around 2012, when the rape of a young Buddhist woman in Rakhine State spurred an outbreak of communal violence in the region.[49] Since the 2012 conflicts, about 200 people have been killed, countless more have been injured and more than 70,000 people have been rendered homeless. The rise of nationalism in Myanmar also spurred conflicts across 14

---

47 "Tha Daw Oo Tin Hlwa Kyan (Supplication to the King)", 3rd ed., Islamic Council of the Union of Myanmar, July 2012; see also the stone inscriptions in front of the Tombs of Abbid Shah Husseinee and Ṣúfí scholar Saint U Nu (Muḥammad Qásim).

48 Htet Myet Min Tun, "Beware of False Peace in Myanmar", in *Fulcrum*, 1 June 2022; "Burma's Power Play", *The Irrawaddy*, 1997, vol. 5, no. 7.

49 "Four Killed as Rohingya Muslims Riot in Myanmar: Government", *Reuters*, 9 June 2012.

different cities. A wave of violence in 2013 left 43 people dead, 86 injured and more than 1,300 buildings destroyed.[50]

Later on, efforts were made by former President Thein Sein's USDP party, in collaboration with its stooges and other ultra-nationalists, to salvage its ultimate downfall. For example, certain compromises[51] were made during the 2012 by-elections, as a result of which Daw Aung San Suu Kyi was released from house arrest and the NLD, led by her, was allowed to contest. The NLD won nearly all the vacant seats, and the Rakhine crisis was systematically created by the ultra-nationalists, making it seem like a spontaneous racial and religious conflict. Radical extremists were used, making the hijacking of religion more prominent. The notion of the need to protect the race and religion was formulated to counter globalization and the liberal ideology of freedom of worship and multiculturalism.

The Ma Ba Tha allied itself with the USDP (led by then-President Thein Sein) for the 2015 elections, campaigning against Aung San Suu Kyi's NLD. The USDP's election slogan was 'protection of race (Bamar) and religion (Buddhism)'. Ultra-nationalist Buddhist monks allied with the USDP proclaimed that if the NLD won the elections, Myanmar would become an 'Islámic State'.[52] The USDP enacted four 'Protection of Race and Religion' laws in May and August 2015, in the lead-up to the November 2015 elections.[53]

These laws, branded as four 'black laws' by Cardinal Charles Bo,[54] are: (i) the Population Control Law (May 2015), (ii) the Buddhist Women's Special Marriage Law (August 2015), (iii) the Religious Conversion Law (August 2015), and (iv) the Monogamy Law (August 2015). The laws drew considerable international attention as they appeared to have a discriminatory intent and were targeted at Muslims, potentially violating not only Myanmar's constitutional provisions on religious freedom and non-discrimination, but also its treaty obligations under various international human rights conventions.[55]

---

50 Mon Mon Myat, "Buddhist Morality in Myanmar: Religious Nationalism and Solidarity after the Coup", Berkley Center for Religion, Peace & World Affairs, 15 March 2021.

51 Tin Maung Maung Tha, "Myanmar's 2012 By-Elections: The Return of NLD", in *Southeast Asian Affairs*, 2013, pp. 204 ff.

52 Anealla Safdar and Phil Rees, "Myanmar's 'Muslim-free' Election", *Al Jazeera*, 29 October 2015.

53 Buddhism and State Power in Myanmar, 2017, pp. 11–12, see *supra* note 33.

54 Also see H.E. Cardinal Charles M. Bo's statement on the occasion of the Florence conference on 'Religion, Hateful Expression and Violence': "Some Thoughts on Hate Speech in Myanmar", Centre for International Law Research and Policy (CILRAP) Film, 8 April 2022, Yangon (https://www.cilrap.org/cilrap-film/220408-cardinal-bo/).

55 *Ibid.*

However, the NLD's landslide victory in the 2015 elections signified that abuse of religion was rejected by most of the Burmese voters, a Buddhist majority. Despite their defeat in the 2015 elections, the military-backed USDP pursued a strategy of politicizing religion. Attacks on Muslim places of worship and religious schools, as well as disturbances to religious ceremonies, occurred more frequently than ever. The NLD government found itself in a tight position: the quasi-civilian government, which did not have much control on the general administration department and the security personnel, could not effectively stop the violence. The NLD government also had to be mindful of not appearing to favour the Muslim population of Myanmar, so as not to give credence to such allegations made by radical Buddhist nationalists during the campaigns for the 2015 elections. Furthermore, the NLD government was trying its best not to jeopardize the reconciliation process with Myanmar's military, which was, without a doubt, very crucial for the democratization process at that time. Daw Aung San Suu Kyi had to make sacrifices in choosing this amicable path, hoping that the military would understand the norms of a civilized culture of peace. At the moment, however, she has become a victim of her own choice. Her diplomatic and tactful policy in countering the military dictatorship earned her the anger of many Myanmar Muslims, including among the Rohingyas, for not publicly denouncing the military's atrocities.

Whatever the case may be, it was the NLD Minister of Religious Affairs, ex-general and USDP Member of Parliament during President Thein Sein's time (who was jailed by the junta after the 2021 coup) who dealt a crushing blow to the Ma Ba Tha in 2018–2019. It is ironic that the former Chief Minister of the Yangon region, U Pyo Min Thein, is now a prosecution witness testifying against Daw Aung San Suu Kyi in the bribery case brought against her by the junta, who first initiated the banning of the Ma Ba Tha.[56] Due to this onslaught, the military-backed ultra-nationalists revived the post-independence Buddhist nationalist organization called the Young Myanmar Buddhist Association ('YMBA'). After the 2021 coup, the YMBA conferred the highest religious title on Senior General Min Aung Hlaing, Commander-in-Chief of the Tatmadaw and Chairman of the State Administration Council (which governs Myanmar at the time of writing), and appointed him as its honorary supreme patron.

It can be assumed that most junta leaders are trained in psychological warfare as they employ multiple schemes in order to manipulate religion. Lately, their tactic has been to manoeuvre the concept of inter-faith harmony. During the 2020 election campaign, for example, Senior General Min Aung Hlaing went around different non-Buddhist religious places of worship, including those of

[56] "NLD's Ex-Yangon Chief Let Off With Fine After Testifying Against Daw Aung San Suu Kyi", *The Irrawaddy*, 22 February 2023.

Muslims, and made donations in cash and kind under the pretext of Covid-19 assistance. Right after the coup, he reformed the state-organized Interfaith Friendship Organization, which was originally formed by former President Thein Sein in 2011, consisting of USDP supporters from Buddhist, Christian, Hindu and Muslim organizations, and replaced the entire set up with his own cronies. Recently, during the trial pertaining to the alleged genocide against the Rohingya at the International Court of Justice ('ICJ'), Senior General Hlaing commanded his stooges from the Interfaith Friendship Organization to condemn The Gambia for suing Myanmar and termed the Rohingya as "terrorist religious extremists".[57]

At the same time, the junta has resuscitated the Ma Ba Tha and employs them in their fight against democratic forces. They seem to have embarked on a 'scorched earth' campaign in the region with the help of Pyu Saw Htee (pro-junta militias), but residents also say that hard-line monks from the Ma Ba Tha have added to the junta's military arsenal. On 15 March 2022, Radio Free Asia also reported ties between hard-line monks and pro-junta militias in Myanmar's Sagaing region, helping form the groups and even receiving weapon training. The televised news showed video footage of monks bearing arms, marching along with the pro-junta militias and later preaching to the villagers inside a monastery with automatic weapons hanging on their shoulders. The video footage also showed the monks undergoing target shooting training.[58]

5.4. The Muslim Population of Myanmar

5.4.1. Evidence of Historical Presence of Muslims in Myanmar

The old Kingdom of Arakan was bounded in the north by India, in the south and west by the Bay of Bengal and in the east by the high, inaccessible Yoma mountains. In the north and west, Arakan had a common boundary with Bengal in the Naf River, which is still the borderline between Bangladesh and Myanmar.[59]

Geopolitical science shows that borders are porous as well as elastic, swinging and changing depending upon which side is more powerful at a given historical time. Which means that demarcation lines or borders are, in fact, man-made. Occasionally, these man-made borders divide the same racial groups into two separate components of two different sovereign nations. For instance, the house of the headman of Longwa village, Mon, Nagaland, located on the India-

57 Republic of the Union of Myanmar, "Statement of Interfaith Friendship Organization (Central)", *The Global New Light of Myanmar*, 27 February 2022, p. 2.

58 Radio Free Asia, "Nationalist monks participate in closing ceremonies for military training in Myanmar's Sagaing", 15 March 2022 (available on YouTube).

59 Abdul Karim, *The Rohingyas: A Short Account of Their History and Culture*, Arakan Historical Society, Bangladesh, 2000, p. 1.

Myanmar border, happened to fall within the territories of both countries. The dining room is on the Burmese side and bedroom on the Indian side. The owner jokingly said: "I sleep in India and eat in Myanmar".[60] Therefore, ethnic races from Myanmar can be found living as natives of neighbouring countries as well.

Khin Maung Saw, in his book *Behind the Mask: The Truth Behind the Name Rohingya*, wrote that:

> As mentioned in the previous chapter, in 1978 and 1991, Burmese government, without considering the changes in geopolitics of the powers, chased out those Bangladeshi settlers who named themselves 'Rohingyas' and because of the pressure from the Powers the so-called Rohingyas were allowed to return after a bilateral agreement between the Burmese and Bangladeshi governments.
>
> It is the nature of people living at the borders. For example:
>
> (1). There are Karens & Shans in Burma. These peoples are also in Thailand.
>
> (2). There are Kachins & Shans in Burma. These peoples can be found also in China.
>
> (3). Nagas & Chins can be found in Burma. There are Nagas & Chins also in India.
>
> (4). Rakhaings & Saks inhabit in Burma. These peoples live also in Bangladesh and in India.
>
> However, is it not very strange or ridiculous that the so-called 'Rohingyas' exists only in Burma but not in Bangladesh and in India?[61]

It seems unlikely that Khin Maung Saw, a former lecturer in Burma studies at Humboldt University in Berlin and a former 'Scholar in Residence' at Ohio University in Athens, never came across the following historical evidence:

> Along the borders of Myanmar where mountain barriers do not hinder movement of population, minority groups are found on either side of the boundary. A small ethnic group named Young who lives in northern Thailand, Laos and northern Vietnam can be found in Kyaington of southern Shan State. The Kokant Chinese group is found east of the Thanlwin river Kokant Township. In northern Rakhine State close to the border with Bengladesh at

---

60 Al-Haj Khalifah U Aye Lwin, "Caring for Our Common Future by Preventing and Transforming Conflicts", presented at Religions for Peace, 10th World Assembly, Asia Regional Consultation, 4–7 March 2019. On the story about Longwa village, see "'Sleeping in India and Eating in Myanmar': Nagaland Minister Shares Video of Unique Village", *APB News*, 12 January 2023.

61 Khing Maung Saw, "Email to the British Prime Minister", 30 January 2018 (available on Network Myanmar's web site); see also Saw, 2016, pp. 97–98, see *supra* note 14.

> Butheedaung and Maungdaw townships are where the Rohinggas and Chittaganians [sic.] live. These minority ethnic groups had settled in the border regions since early days.[62]

The Myanmar Encyclopaedia, published by the Myanmar Translation Association, talks about the Mayu frontier area in Rakhine State in the following terms:

> There are nearly four to five hundred thousand population in May Yu frontier area. Most of the inhabitants are engaged in agriculture and fishery professions. The majority seventy five percent of the population consist of Rohingya race. Ethnic races such as Rakhine, Dai Net, Myo and Khmee also reside in that region. Rohingyas profess Islamic faith.[63]

According to Charles Paton, the Sub-Commissioner of Arakan, the population figures in Arakan (1826) were as follows: 60,000 'Maghs' (Rakhine Buddhists), 30,000 Muslims and 10,000 Burmese:[64]

> So on the date of the conquest of Arakan by the English, there had already been living 30 thousand Muslims and these 30 thousand Muslims were living there from before, now their descendants and successors have increased by leaps and bounds.[65]

During the reign of King Min Saw Mon, at the beginning of the Mrauk-U dynasty's reign over Arakan, ambassadors from Islámic countries stationed in the capital built a number of mosques and invited Islámic religious scholars from Persia, Arabia and India to propagate and spread Islám.[66] As a result, quite a number of natives converted to Islám. This phenomenon was noticed by a young monk named Saya Mya War. This young monk reported to the King and the minister at the court about the Islámic missionary activities taking place as a result of which persons were converting to Islám. At the request of the King, Saya Mya War, with the assistance of his master Shin Muni, wrote a book called 'Shwe Byine Dhamma Thet Kyan' to counter Islámization.[67]

---

62 The text is from a first-year textbook for history students, "Geography of Myanmar", No. Geog-1004, Department of Higher Education, Ministry of Education, Yangon University of Distance Education, Yangon, 2012.

63 *Myanmar Encyclopaedia*, Burma Translation Society, Printing and Publishing Department Ministry of Information, 2015, p. 90.

64 Charles Paton, "A Short Report on Arakan", 26 April 1826; A.C. Banerjee, *The Eastern Frontier of British India: 1784–1826*, 2nd ed., A. Mukherjee and Co., Calcutta, 1946, p. 351.

65 Karim, 2000, p. 108, see *supra* note 59.

66 Sayar Gyi U Tha Thun Aung, *Rakhine Yar Za Win Daw Gyi* (Royal History of Rakhine), Sittwe, 1927. The Mrauk-U dynasty, established by Min Saw Mon, begun its reign over Arakan in 1430 AD.

67 *Ibid.*

The presence of Muslims in ancient Rakhine was vividly described in the famous chronicle 'Dhanya Waddy Sit Kyaung (Dhanya Waddy Campaign)', written by highly-revered Rakhine monk Kawi Tha Ra Be The Re Waya, who held the title of 'Guru of the King'.[68] Another historian monk Dyanya Waddy Sayadaw U Nyana wrote, in his *Rakhine Yar Za Win* (Rakhine History), about Rakhine nationals' conversion to Islám.[69] Similar accounts of Rakhine Buddhists embracing Islám in olden days were reported by Rakhine scholars such as U Hla Htun Phyu as well.[70] Rakhine historian San Shwe Bu was quoted by Maurice Collis when he wrote about Muslims in Rakhine before the emergence of Kaman Muslims, who are accepted as a sub-ethnic race of Rakhine.[71]

The exact number of Muslim prisoners of war in Mrauk-U, which amounts to 47,500, was mentioned in a 2008 book which won the Sarpay Beikman literary award.[72] The same historical fact was mentioned in *Rakhine Yar Za Win Thit* (New Rakhine History) by Yan Byar Taung Kaung Sayardaw, a monk.[73]

These facts were further supported by Francois Bernier's record and Father Delaunoite's Catholic Encyclopaedia.[74] A point to note is that these Muslim prisoners of war, who later became residents of Mrauk-U and are considered the ancestors of the Rohingya, were present in the region from 1621 to 1624, more than 30 years before Mirza Shah Shuja', the second son of Mughal Emperor Mirza Shahab-ud-Dín Baig Muḥammad Khán Khurrám (or Shah Jáhán) took refuge in 1660 along with his archers, who were later recognized as the ethnic Kaman race of Rakhine.

Rakhine historian Sara Nga Mei wrote an account of the Arakanese chronicle in 1826 which more or less confirmed the accounts of other nationalist Rakhine historians, according to whom Muslims had been residing in Rakhine

68 *Dhanya Waddy Sit Kyaung (Dhanya Waddy Campaign)*, Parabaik MS, no. 732, National Library, Yangon.

69 Dyanya Waddy Sayadaw U Nyana, *Rakhine Yar Za Win* (Rakhine History), vol. 2, pp. 161–162.

70 Kyi Ngwe Sakar Ye Lu Pyaw, *Kyi Ngwe Debate*, U Hla Htun Phyu Pyinnya Beikman Press, Yangon, 1981, pp. 47–48.

71 Maurice S. Collis and San Shwe Bu, "Arakan's Place in the Civilization of the Bay: A Study of Coinage and Foreign Relations", in *Journal of the Burma Research Society*, 1925, vol. 15, pp. 41–42.

72 Maung Moe Yan (Major Myo Thant), *Kissa Pa Na Dee Mha Dyanya Waddy Thoe* (From the Kissa Pa Na Dee to the Dyanya Waddy Dynasty), Sarpay Beikmam Press, Yangon, 2010.

73 Yan Byar Taung Kaung Sayardaw, *Rakhine Yar Za Win Thit* (New Rakhine History), vol. 4, Hantha waddy Press, Mandalay, 1931, pp. 350, 352, 353.

74 Godfrey Eric Harvey, *Outline of Burmese History*, Orient Longman, Bombay, 1947, p. 94.

since the early days.[75] For instance, R.B. Smart, the Deputy Commissioner of the Akyab District, wrote that in the ninth century AD several ships were wrecked on Ramree Island and their Muslim crews moved into the villages in Arakan.[76] Nationalist Rakhine historian Dr. Aye Chan, who happened to be a staunch opponent of the Rohingya cause, stated that:

> However, I do not mean there was no Muslim community in Arakan before the state was absorbed into British India. Some Bengali retinues of King Saw Mun (r. 1430-1433) who regained the throne with the military aid from Sultanate of Bengal were allowed to settled [sic.] down in the suburban area of Mrauk-U, the new royal capital. They were the earliest Muslim settlers who do not seem to count many. There had been a minor Muslim presence mostly made up of Muslim mercenaries, itinerant merchants from Persia and Golkonda and some Bengali captives of the Arakanese and Portuguese pirates sold into slavery. The descendants of those people can be found in the vicinity of Royal capital Mrauk-U and Kyauktaw Township.[77]

When Aye Chan wrote that "[t]hey were the earliest Muslim settlers who do not seem to count to many", he failed to mention that there were 30,000 Muslims, amounting to half the size of the Maghs' (Arakan/Rakhine Buddhist) population in Arakan when the British occupied lower Burma in 1824.[78] The aforementioned number did not include the Muslim refugees who, along with the Arakan Buddhists, crossed over to Bengal after the invasion of Burmese forces in 1784. After the conquest of Arakan, Burmese troops took a large number of prisoners of war, including Muslims, along with the Mahamuni Buddha Statue, to Mandalay.[79] Muslims from Arakan who were taken as prisoners of war built a mosque named 'Shwe Phone Shine', which still exists today near the Mahamuni Pagoda in Mandalay, and has been maintained by the descendants of Muslims from Arakan. These figures were not reported in Paton's report. Otherwise, the number of Muslims would have exceeded 30,000.

In one of his research papers, Aye Chan wrote that:

---

75 Sara Nga Mei, *Rakhine Razawin* (Rakhine History), 1826, s. 1–5 (preserved in palm leaf in the Oriental and India Office Collection, British Library, Acc-3465(a)).

76 R.B. Smart, "Akyab District: Volume A", *Burma Gazetteer*, Government Printing and Stationery, Rangoon, 1957, p. 87.

77 Aye Chan, "Who Are the Rohingya", Kanda University of International Studies, Ciba City, Japan. See also an article in the annex of Khine Mya War's book written in rebut to "The Union of Burma and Ethnic Rohingyas", entitled *Critique on the Fake History of So-Called Rohingyas Under the Guise of Human Rights With Intention of Bengali Expansionism*, p. 269.

78 Paton, 1826, see *supra* note 64.

79 Xu Khin Maung Saw, "The Maha Muni Image and Its Rough Path", in *Original Buddhas* ('The Maha Muni Image and Its Rough Path') (available on its web site).

> The Muslims in the Arakan State can be divided into four different groups, namely the Chittagonian Bengalis in the Mayu Frontier; the descendents [sic.] of the Muslim Community of Arakan in the Mrauk-U period (1430-1784), presently living in the Mrauk-U and Kyauktaw townships; the decendents [sic.] of Muslim mercenaries in Ramree Island known to the Arakanese as Kaman; and the Muslims from the Myedu area of Central Burma, left behind by the Burmese invaders in Sandoway District after the conquest of Arakan in 1784.[80]

The Burma Citizenship Act of 1982 granted citizenship to all individuals who could trace their family residency to Burma prior to 1823. As per this law, three categories of citizenship were created, and, under the first category, several ethnically Burmese and non-Burmese communities present in Myanmar prior to 1823 were declared eligible for full citizenship. However, several Muslim communities, including the Rohingya, who were given citizenship status in the post-independence period, were excluded, rendering them stateless.[81]

It is interesting to note that, with reference to the 1931 census of Burma conducted by the British Administration in India, Derek Tonkin, former British Ambassador to Thailand, Vietnam and Laos, stated that:

> One group which particularly attracted my attention in British records was what the 1901 Census described as the 'Arakan Muhammadans'. By the 1931 Census, now described as 'Arakan Mohamedans', their numbers totalled 51,615 compared to 252,152 'Chittagonians' and 65,211 'Bengalis', in addition to 'Arakan Kamans' and 'Myedus [Muslims]' also resident in Arakan.
>
> The 'Arakan Mohamedans' comprised 26,153 males and 25,462 females, an even balance between the sexes as you would expect in a long-standing permanent community [...].[82]

Financial Secretary James Baxter's 'Report on Indian Immigration', released in 1940, clearly mentioned that:

> [t]here is little objection to assuming that all the Hindus were Indian but it is not so true to assume that all the Mohamedans were Indian. There was an Arakanese Muslim community settled so

80 Aye Chan, "The Development of a Muslim Enclave in Arakan (Rakhine) State of Burma (Myanmar)", in *SOAS Bulletin of Burma Research*, 2005, vol. 3, no. 2, p. 397.

81 Moshe Yegar, *Between Integration and Secession: The Muslim Communities of the Southern Philippines, Southern Thailand, and Western Burma/Myanmar*, Lexington Books, Lanham, Maryland, 2002.

82 Derek Tonkin, "The 'Rohingya' Identity – British Experience in Arakan 1826–1948", 9 April 2014 (available on Network Myanmar's web site).

> long in Akyab District that it had for all intents and purposes to be regarded as an indigenous race.[83]

The 1901 British census described some Muslims in the Arakan/Rakhine region as "Arakan Muhammadans" who had been "fetched from Arakan" as prisoners when the kingdom of Arakan fell to Burmese forces in 1785.[84]

Khin Maung Saw wrote that:

> The Muslims like Myey Du, Kaman and the descendants of Bengali slaves have been living in Arakan during the Mrauk-U period, they could be called the 'Muslims in Arakan'. For centuries to now, these 'Muslims in Arakan' lived and live peacefully with Burmese and Arakanese, who are Buddhists.[85]

The British Burma Gazetteer, published in 1879, further stated:

> About 788 A. D. Maha-taing Tsandaya ascended the throne, founded a new city on the site of the old Rama-waddee and died after a reign of 22 years. In his reign several ships were wrecked on Ramree Island and the crews, said to have been Mahomedans, were sent to Arakan Proper and settled in villages.[86]

After the Burmese conquest of Arakan in 1785, King Bodawpayar (U Wyne) appointed U Nu (Muḥammad Qásim) as the Governor of Rammawaddy, which covered the entire region of Arakan/Rakhine at that time. Another Ṣúfí saint who was a nephew of Mughal Emperor Muḥiyy al-Dín Muḥammad, or Aurangzeb, was appointed as the *Qází* (Chief of Islamic Justices) of King Bodawpayar's kingdom, which included the conquered region of Arakan/Rakhine. Anecdotes regarding these two Ṣúfí saints have been mentioned from a different historical perspective earlier in this chapter.[87]

Khin Maung Saw, in his book 'Behind the Mask', also stated:

> There is a narration that the Arakanese king Min Saw Mun (Man Saw Mwan) had to take refuge in Bengal because of Burmese invasion and he regained the Arakanese throne with the help of the

[83] James Baxter (Commissioner of Inquiry, Government of Burma), "Report on Indian Immigration", 12 October 1940, p. 4.

[84] C.C. Lowis (Census Superintendent) (ed.), *Census of India, 1901: Burma*, vol. 12, The Superintendent of Government Printing, Burma, 1901, para. 157, cited in Tonkin, 2014, see *supra* note 82.

[85] Saw, 2016, p. 39, see *supra* note 14.

[86] Horace R. Spearman, *The British Burma Gazetteer*, vol. 2, 1879, Government Press, Rangoon, p. 7.

[87] U Tin (Pagan Commissioner), *Myanmar Min Aoke Choke Pone Sar Tan Nint Bodaw Payar Ei Yaza Thet Khaw A Maint Taw Than Gyi* (Myanmar King Administrative System Paper and the Royal Degree Ordinance of King Bodawpaya), Part 4, Department of Culture, Directorate of Culture Centre, Government Press, 1973, p. 176.

> Sultan of Gaur. There were some Muslim soldiers to protect Min Saw Mun (Man Saw Mwan) and the Muslim settlement started in Arakan.[88]

Although the above-mentioned statement could be found in the Arakanese chronicles with slightly different versions, Bengali historians Habbibullah[89] and Serajuddin[90] have noted that Bengali sources mentioned nothing about Arakanese King Min Saw Mun's refuge in their land.

In the footnotes of *Behind the Mask: The Truth behind the Name Rohingya*, Khin Maung Saw also wrote that:

> Both Jacques Leider and Aye Chan have a new hypothesis. They doubt the story of King Narameik Hla's exile in Gaur because the Bengali source was completely silent about the king of neighbouring country who took refuge in Bengal.[91]

Aye Chan, who tried to refute the historical fact of Arakanese King Min Saw Mun taking refuge in Bengal by his 'hypothesis', contradicted himself by admitting that:

> some Bengali retinues of King Saw Mun (r. 1430-1433) who regained the throne with the military aid from Sultanate of Bangal were allowed to settled [sic.] down in the suburban area of Mrauk U, the new royal capital.[92]

The above-mentioned Bengali historians Habbibulah and Serajuddin might have been misinterpreted by Dr. Jacques P. Leider, or the statement of the latter, as a conscious historian, was distorted by Khin Maung Saw and Aye Chan, who jumped to their own conclusions. It is indeed a historical fact that the Sultan of Bengal, Jalal-ud-Dín Muḥammad Shah, reinstated the Arakanese King Min Saw Mun to his throne.[93]

According to Dr. Abdul Karim,

---

88 Saw, 2016, p. 26, see *supra* note 14.

89 Abu Mohammed Habbibullah, "Arakan in the Pre-Mughal, History of Bengal", in *Journal of the Royal Asiatic Society of Bengal*, 1945, vol. 11, no. 1, p. 34.

90 Alamgir M. Serajuddin, "Muslim Influence in Arakan and Muslim Names of the Arakanese Kings: A Reassessment", in *Asiatic Society of Bangladesh*, 1986, vol. 31, no. 1, p. 20.

91 Saw, 2016, p. 27, see *supra* note 14, also referring to Jacques P. Leider, "These Buddhist Kings with Muslim Names – Discussion of Muslim Influence in the Mrauk U Period", in Pierre Pichard and François Robinne (eds.), *Etudes birmanes en hommage à Denise Bernot*, École française d'Extrême-Orient, Paris, 1988, p. 198.

92 See *supra* note 77.

93 Anthony Ware and Costas Laoutides, "The Rohingya 'Origin' Narrative", in *id.*, *Myanmar's 'Rohingya' Conflict*, Oxford University Press, 2018, p. 82.

> [w]e do not know what were the points of agreement between the two kings, and in the absence of any written record it will not probably be possible to have any idea in the future also.[94]

Therefore, although the points of agreement between the two kings and the knowledge about the administration in Arakan in the fifteenth-sixteenth century were not recorded, there is no dispute about the fact that King Min Saw Mun sought refuge in Bengal and that he was restored to his throne by the Sultan of Bengal, Jalal-ud-Dín Muḥammad Shah.

Karim further wrote:

> Though we have no knowledge about the administration in Arakan in the 15th – 16th century, we find that not only soldiers and members of the subordinate staff but also the ministers and judges came from the Muslim community. The seventeenth century Bengali Muslim poets give in their writings an impression that the capital city of Roshang (Mrohaung or Mrauk-U) thronged with the Muslim population, so that the Muslim ministers-maintained courts, i.e., religious, social and cultural assemblies of their own. Then in the third category came the Muslim artisan and craftsmen, the officers and men connected with the mint and other state establishments. Last but not the least came the traders and businessmen in the hitherto terra incognita abounding in agricultural and natural resources.[95]

Aye Chan and Jacques P. Leider refuted the story of King Min Saw Mun's exile in the Bengali Royal city of Gaur. They stated that Bengali literature is completely silent about the King of the neighbouring country who took refuge in Bengal. On the contrary, however, abundant authentic accounts have reported on King Min Saw Mun and the Islámic influence on the Mrauk-U dynasty. Even Christian missionaries like Fray Sebastien Manrique admitted that the Arakanese King's preceptor was a Muslim. Manrique reported an account of a holy man who was a *Ḥajj*, one who had visited the holy city of Maccah and Madínah, but was acknowledged to be a saint by the King and his Magh subjects.[96] There are a few Bengali sources which refer to the start of the Mrauk-U dynasty from King Min Saw Mun.[97]

---

94 Karim, 2000, p. 32, see *supra* note 59.

95 *Ibid.*, p. 42.

96 Fray Sebastien Manrique, *Travels of Fray Sebastien Manrique 1629-1643: A Translation of the Itinerario de Las Missiones Orientales*, vol. 1, translated by C. Eckford Luard and H. Hosten, Hakluyt Society, London, 1926, p. 352.

97 A.P. Phayre, "On the History of Arakan", in *Journal of the Asiatic Society of Bengal*, 1844, vol. 13, no. 145, pp. 44–46; Karim, 2000, see *supra* note 59; Muhammad Ali Chowdhory (Professor of History, University of Chittagong), *Bangal-Arakan Relations*, Firma KLM,

Even Aye Chan and Jacques P. Leider, who refute the fact about King Min Saw Mun's exile, should not ignore the works of Bengali poets Syed Alaol and Daulat Kazi. Their poetry in Bengali literature speaks clearly about the Mrauk-U dynasty and the migration of Muslims in Arakan throughout history. Muslim influence during that time could be seen in great measure as they occupied government offices, posts of ministers and judges and other subordinate posts. The biographies of three prime ministers, three defense ministers and two ministers were well recorded by Syed Alaol and Daulat Kazi and other writers serving in the courts of Mrauk-U. For example, *Shariatnamah*, written by poet Náṣrulláh Khundkár, the seventh descendant of Burhán-ud-Dín, in 1749 (or 1755), concerned the first Lashkar Wazir (Defense or War Minister) of Arakan. Therefore, it may be inferred that Burhán-ud-Dín was alive around the last half of the sixteenth century.[98]

Likewise, poet Daulat Kazi wrote in his book *Lor Chandrani O Sati Moyna* about Ashraf Khan, the Lashkar Wazir (Defense Minister) of King Thiri Thudhamma, who ruled Arakan from 1622 to 1638.[99] Ashraf Khan was not only a minister but also a Ṣúfí of the Chistiya order. Due to his adherence to the principle of non-discrimination and his tolerant spirit, he was well-liked by the people of Arakan and the royal family. Daulat wrote that the Queen regarded Ashraf Khan as 'better than a prince', while the King considered him his son and therefore made him a great minister. Ashraf Khan not only constructed mosques, but also built other facilities such as water tanks for the benefit of the entire public. This historical figure was so prominent that even the Christian missionary Fray Sebastien Manrique acknowledged that Minister Ashraf Khan led the Muslim contingent of the army in the coronation procession of King Thiri Thudhamma in 1635.[100]

The historical accounts of the three Muslim prime ministers of the Arakan kings in the seventeenth century – Magan Thakur, Sayyid Musa and Nabaraj Majlis – were also mentioned in Syed Alaol's poetry.[101] There are several other Bengal-sourced records referencing Muslims in the history of Mrauk-U, despite Aye Chan and Jacques P. Leider's view.[102]

Kolkata, 2004, p. 2; Ramesh Chandra Majumdar, *Hindu Colonies in the Far East*, General Printers and Publishers, Calcutta, 1944, p. 202.

98 Aman Ullah, "The Growth of Muslim Nobility in the Medieval Court of Arakan", in *The Rohingya Post*, 4 April 2019 (available on its web site).

99 Daulat Kazi, *Lor Chandrani O Sati Moyna*, Sahitya Samsad, 1995.

100 Karim, 2000, p. 58, see *supra* note 59.

101 Karim, 2000, p. 59–72, see *supra* note 59.

102 Abdul Karim and Muhammad Enamul Hoque, *Arakan Rajsobhay Bangla Sahitya*, Som Publishing, Calcutta, 1935; *Sahitya Patrika*, Winter, 1957; Ahmad Sharif, *Alaol Birachita*

Thus, it may be considered that all the unbroken living traditions, civilization, chronicles and literature of Rakhine unanimously and vividly report about King Min Saw Mun's exile in Bengal. A nostalgic eulogy of King Min Saw Mun's exile in Bengal still holds a highly regarded position in Rakhine classical literature. It would be hard to imagine that such a classic is based on a false account.

Another pertinent fact to consider is the strong impact and influence of Islámic culture in Rakhine courts and monarchies. Starting from King Min Saw Mun (1430–1433) until Thiri Thudhamma (1622–1638), successive Rakhine kings had taken on Muslim titles. They minted coins with Arabic Islámic inscriptions.

Aye Chan advances the hypothesis that Min Saw Mun fled to southeast Bengal (present day Phalaungsheik and Panwah), where the Rakhine people were the majority, and that reconquering Arakan was not difficult because, according to both Arakanese and Burmese chronicles, Nawrahta and Shwe Pyi Chan Tha (the son-in-law and the daughter of King Mingaung of Ava) could have ruled largest city in the vicinity.[103] If this hypothesis is correct, then King Min Saw Mun would owe nothing to the Bengal Sultan. Thus, this hypothesis can be deemed weak, as it provides no explanation for the long-standing presence of Muslims in large numbers and for the enormous influence of Islámic culture on the Mrauk-U dynasty founded by the King. According to Abdul Karim, the reason could have been as follows:

> At the present stage of our knowledge, we know for certain that a Sultan of Bengal, Jalal-ud-din Muhammad Shah reinstated an Arakanese king Min Saw-Mun (Narameikhla) to his throne. This must have been done through an agreement between the two kings; otherwise the Bengal Sultan would not have incurred such a huge expenditure for fitting an army.[104]

Karim further elaborated that:

> the Arakanese kings did something more, they accepted Muslim names and inscribed these names in Arabic characters. There is no evidence that the Arakanese kings gave up their Buddhist religion and accepted Islam. So the reason for accepting Muslim names and inscription in Arabic, should be sought elsewhere.
>
> With the restoration of Min Saw-Mun to his throne, a big contingent of Muslims entered into Arakan. The contingent

Sikandarnama, Dhaka, 1977; Ahmed Sharif, *Bangali O Bangla Sahitya*, Naya Udyog, 2014; Abdul Karim, "Alaoler Atma Kahini", in *Monthly Muhammadi*, 1950, vol. 22, no. 1.

103 Saw, 2016, p. 27, see *supra* note 14.

104 Karim, 2000, p. 41, see *supra* note 59.

> included the army, not one army but two, of which the members of the first expeditionary force spread over the country and mixed with the people. The second army also must have been a big one, because they had to fight against both Arakanese and the first contingent of Bengal army. Next, the contingent included the administrators, officers and intellectual persons.[105]

5.4.2. Lord Buddha's Rakhine Visit and the Rakhine Claim

Let us consider the legend of Lord Buddha's visit to Rakhine, the creation of the Mahamuni Statue and the Rakhine claim of being related to the Saki race of Lord Buddha. The people of Rakhine are concerned about preserving their pure race. Lord Buddha denounced racism and preached that man is composed of impermanent mind and matter only. When his father reminded him of his Saki lineage, he simply replied: "You and your race may claim descent from kings; my descent is from the Buddhas of old".[106]

Modern Rakhine scholars such as Khin Maung Saw observed that "[t]he Rakhine (Arakanese) traditionally believe that they are descendants of the 'Sakya Sakis' the race from which Lord Buddha came".[107] Most historians and anthropologists, however, believe that they belong to the Tibeto-Burmese group.

Khin Maung Saw then assumed that "some of the Arakanese nowadays are the descendants of the hybrids of the Tibeto-Burmese and Indo-Aryan races after the migration of Mongolian tribes". He continued: "because […] some Arakanese do really have Indo-Mongoloid features and appearances in contrast to the Burmese who have pure features of a Mongolian race".[108]

Regarding the Mahamuni image, Khin Maung Saw was of the view that "[a]ccording to the legend of Maha Muni image, Arakan was already a Buddhist Kingdom during the time of Lord Buddha".[109] This was because, according to the same legend, as touched upon earlier in this chapter, Lord Buddha, accompanied by 500 disciples, visited Arakan on the invitation of King Sanda Thuriya (Chandra Suriya). The legend stated that the Lord Buddha and King Sanda Thuriya were once, in a past life, cow herds and close friends, so fond of each other

---

105 *Ibid.*, pp. 41–42, see *supra* note 59.

106 Bhimrao Ramji Ambedkar, *The Buddha and His Dhamma*, Siddharth Books, Delhi, 2006, Book II, Part IV ('Call from Home'), Section 1 ('Suddhodana and the Last Look'), para. 22.

107 See Khin Maung Saw, "Rakhaing or Rakhine or Arakanese?", unpublished manuscript, citing U Aung Tha Oo, *A Short History of Arakan (in Burmese)*, Mya Yadana Press, Rangoon, 1954, p. 8.

108 See *ibid.*, citing Maurice S. Collis and San Shwe Bu, "Arakan's Place in the Civilization of the Bay", in *Journal of Burma Research Society*, 50th Anniversary Publications no. 2, Rangoon, 1960, p. 488.

109 Khin Maung Saw, "On the Evolution of Rohingya Problems in Rakhine State of Burma", unpublished manuscript, Berlin, 2005, p. 24.

that when one had to travel, he would leave in his place his depiction as a statue or image. Therefore, the King requested Lord Buddha to leave his statue when the latter had to go back to India, and the statue was cast around 563 AD.[110]

U San Shwe Bu, on the other hand, wrote that King Thuriya ascended the throne of Arakan in 146 AD, 600 years after the *parinirvana* (nirvana after death) of Lord Buddha. In contrast to the legend, he stated that the statue was cast in the second century AD.[111]

Whether the Mahamuni image was made around 563 AD, or in the second century AD as U San Shwe Bu pointed out, is not within the scope of this chapter. However, we have to consider that sometimes traditional beliefs, myths and legends are found to be true in modern historical research and survey; but, in some cases, myths or legends and the real historical account are different.[112]

Compared to Khin Maung Saw, modern Arakanese writer Tun Myint (Myan Aung) has made a major breakthrough by tactfully and diplomatically citing eminent Buddhist scholars such as Dr. Bhimrao Ramji Ambedkar and other local Buddhist scholars. He gives sound evidence, historically, scientifically and logically, to refute the legend and myth of the Burmese and Rakhine claim that they belong to the Saki race and the myth of the Mahamuni statue, subtly establishing the fact that Lord Buddha has not visited Burma at all.[113]

5.5. The Rohingya Crisis

5.5.1. Crimes Against the Rohingya Population

Much has been written about the plight of the minority Muslim Rohingya group and about them living in Myanmar for thousands of years. Crimes alleged to have been committed by the Burmese military against the Rohingya have been brought on trial before various international courts and tribunals such as the ICJ and the International Criminal Court ('ICC'). The United States government has stated that the atrocities committed against the Rohingya amount to genocide.[114] In fact, the United States Commission on International Religious Freedom ('USCIRF') had designated Burma as a 'Country of Particular Concern' ('CPC') in 1999, and has continued to do so year after year, most recently in its 2022

[110] The Maha Muni Image and its Rough Path, see *supra* note 79.

[111] *Ibid.*

[112] Saw, 2016, pp. 23–24, see *supra* note 14.

[113] Tun Myint (Myan Aung), *Rakhine Myanmar Nhit Khit Pyaing Kabar* (Rakhine Myanmar and Contemporary World), Shu Taing Yin Press, March 2014.

[114] US Department of State, Bureau of Democracy, Human Rights, and Labor, "Genocide, Crimes Against Humanity and Ethnic Cleansing of Rohingya in Burma" (available on the US Department of State's web site).

Annual Report.[115] Among the key findings of 2021 Annual Report, the USCIRF states:

> In 2020, religious freedom conditions in Burma remained poor. The government continued to commit widespread and egregious religious freedom violations, particularly against Rohingya Muslims. Denial of basic citizenship rights and systematic discrimination based on ethnic-religious affiliation severely restricted the freedom of religious or belief of minority communities.[116]

In its recommendations to the United States government, the USCIRF mentioned, *inter alia*, that Burma is "engaging in systematic, ongoing, and egregious violations of religious freedom, as defined by the International Religious Freedom Act (IRFA)".[117]

In August 2017, the Advisory Commission on Rakhine State (chaired by late Kofi Annan) issued its final report titled 'Towards a Peaceful, Fair and Prosperous Future for the People of Rakhine: Final Report of the Advisory Commission on Rakhine State'. In the report, Rakhine State was portrayed as having a long and proud history, but as facing a developmental, human rights and security crisis. The report clearly mentioned that "the question should not be whether Rakhines and Muslims will live together, but rather how they will live together. Reintegration, not segregation, is the best path to long-term stability and development in Rakhine State".[118] The report, with its 88 recommendations, was lauded by fair and democratic-minded groups both locally and internationally, as well as by the Rohingya community and sober and pragmatic Rakhines. However, the report was criticized from the very beginning by ultra-nationalists, including members of the military. The present junta leaders have objected to the findings and recommendations of the report, accusing it of having "flaws and shortcomings".[119]

5.5.2. The Historical Context of the Rohingya of Burma

This section attempts to sum up the Rohingya crisis, offering some sources and observations to consider.

Firstly, contrary to the propaganda spread by successive military dictators in Myanmar, most scholars of Rakhine history, including modern scholars

---

[115] USCIRF, "Annual Report, 2022", April 2022, pp. 14–15.

[116] *Ibid.*

[117] *Ibid.*

[118] "Final Report of the Advisory Commission on Rakhine State: Towards a Peaceful, Fair and Prosperous Future for the People of Rakhine", August 2017, pp. 10–11 (https://www.legal-tools.org/doc/c76b63/).

[119] Moe Myint, "Analysis: The Rohingya Crisis and Kofi Annan's Legacy", *The Irrawaddy*, 24 August 2018 (available on its web site).

such as Jacques P. Leider, Pamela Gutman, Rick Hizman, Khin Maung Aye and Aye Chan, express the view that the term 'Rohingya' was not a new word coined by Bengali activists such as Muḥammad Ṭáhir Ba Tha in 1950, with the motive of creating a new ethnic race based on religion in order to Islámize the country. Scholars, however, agree that it is a Bengali word to identify the people living in Rohan (Rakhine). In the Bengali language, 'ja' means people. Therefore, whoever lives in Rohan is known as 'Rohinja'. According to a linguistic survey conducted by a Scottish surgeon, Dr. Francis Buchanan, in 1799, "there were Muslims who have been settled in Arakan, and who called themselves 'Rohingya or natives of Arakan'".[120] However, some opponents of the Rohingya cause like Khin Maung Saw tried to explain that:

> One can understand that term in Buchanan in two ways: either the people used the word as a 'name' or as 'place of origins'. My opinion is that they used it as a place of origins. Meaning 'We come from Arakan' which was basically correct. (and NOT: 'We are a Rooinga/Rosswan ethnic group'). They may not have used the word as an ethnonym to refer to themselves as a separate ethnic group.[121]

Jacques P. Leider, in an interview with the Irrawaddy magazine on 9 July 2012, is ascribed the following words:

> When you argue we are Muslims and we have been living in Rakhine for several generations, nobody can deny it. For me, Rohingya is the term, which is an old word that has been claimed as above all as a political label after the independence of Myanmar.[122]

Leider also stated that the term 'Rohingya' was used already in 1936 in the name of the Rohingya Jam'iyyat al-'Ulama', the first Muslim association of Arakan.[123]

Khin Maung Saw mentioned in his book *Behind the Mask: The Truth Behind the Name Rohingya* that veteran journalist Kyemon U Thaung, with the pen name Aungbala, told him that the Red Flag Communists invented the name 'Rohingya', which has some connection with Arakanese history, for the 'Mujahid Rebels' at the end of the 1940s while they were fighting together against U Nu's government. He also quoted Dr. Shwe Lu Maung's (alias Nawaz Khan)

---

[120] Francis Buchanan, "A Comparative Vocabulary of Some of the Languages Spoken in the Burma Empire", in *Asiatic Researches*, 1799, vol. 5, pp. 219–240, reprinted in *SOAS Bulletin of Burma Research*, vol. 1, no. 1, 2003.

[121] Khin Maung Saw, "Analysis of Francis Buchanan's 'Rooingas' and 'Rossawns'", unpublished manuscript, 2013, p. 2.

[122] Jacques P. Leider, "History Behind Arakan State Conflict", *The Irrawaddy*, 9 July 2012.

[123] Jacques P. Leider, "'Rohingya': A Historical and Linguistic Note", *Network Myanmar*, 26 August 2012, p. 1.

article "The Curse of Historical Rivalries in Arakan State of Burma", and wrote about Rakhine communist Bogri Kra Hla Aung, Chairman Kyaw Zan Rhee, and other members' recognition of the Rohingyas.[124]

While accepting that the term 'Rohingya' was not a new invention of the Bengali Muslims in the 1950s, Aye Chan insisted that the word denotes only Rakhine Buddhists and not the Muslims of Rakhine. Nevertheless, he did not deny the presence of Muslims in Rakhine before the British annexation in 1824.[125] Moshe Yegar, who served as a diplomat at the Embassy of Israel in Rangoon during the early 1960s, wrote:

> The rebels [Muslims] claimed that the Rohingya were natives of Arakan, indigenous to the region. They [that is, the Rohingya] were offspring of Muslims who had settled there hundreds of years earlier and despite similarities in religion, language and ethnicity differed from the population in the adjacent Chittagong region. It was simply propaganda on the part of Arakan Buddhist extremists that had attempted to identify them with Muslim of Pakistan [indicating the part that is now Bangladesh].[126]

Researchers like Jasmin Chia argued that Rohingya could not be regarded as an ethnic group because it "display[s] huge diversity of ethnic origins and social backgrounds, and, as Leider argues, the existence of a 'single identity' is difficult to pinpoint".[127]

The frequent Swedish commentator on Myanmar affairs, Bertil Lintner, chose to put it in these common-sensical terms:

> The first Muslims on the Arakan coast were Moorish, Arab and Persian traders who arrived between the ninth and the fifteenth centuries. Some of them stayed and married local women. Their offspring became the forefathers of yet another hybrid race, which much later was to become known as the Rohingya.[128]

Maung Tha Hla asserted that the term 'Magh' applies to the descendants of Rakhines who married Bengali women when parts of Bengal were under the wing of Rakhine. They are Buddhist and their dialect is Chittagonian.[129] This is indeed a reasonable assumption. If this is the case, there could be cases of

---

[124] Saw, 2016, pp. 93–94, see *supra* note 14.

[125] Aye Chan, "The Development of a Muslim Enclave in Arakan (Rakhine) State of Burma (Myanmar)", in *SOAS Bulletin of Burma Research*, 2005, vol. 3, no. 2, pp. 396–420.

[126] Yegar, 2002, p. 39, see *supra* note 81.

[127] Jasmine Chia, "The Truth About Myanmar's Rohingya Issue", *The Diplomat*, 5 March 2016.

[128] Bertil Lintner, *Burma in Revolt: Opium and Insurgency Since 1948*, Silkworm Books, Chiang Mai, 1999, p. 45.

[129] Maung Tha Hla, *The Rakhaing*, Buddhist Rakhaing Cultural Association, New York, 2004, p. 18.

Chittagonian Bengali Muslims marrying Rakhine Buddhist women as well. Chittagonian Rakhines who profess Islám as their faith are still in existence today.

Anthropology, demography, history, biology, genetics, morphology and related modern sciences are proving that races emerge out of racial mixture. There is no such thing as 'pure race' or 'mixed race'. The same has also been demonstrated by modern-day DNA tests. Modern geography also tells us that borders all over the world are man-made and, as mentioned above, porous and elastic. Bengali Rakhine borders throughout history swung and changed depending upon which side was more powerful. Muslims and Rakhine communities were, from time to time, living under the same king in the same territory and country. Thus, it does not seem acceptable that these two communities were divided by watertight compartments and segregated walls confining them in one place, and that there cannot be cases of racial mixture between them.

Muslims who have been living in Rakhine for centuries and called themselves Rohingya trace their lineage to diverse ethnic origins and social backgrounds, and have never tied their origin to a single identity. They claim that they are descendants and mixtures of Arab, Persian, Indian, Bengali and Rakhine. This racial mixture resulted in the emergence of the 'Rohingya' race. They also state that they have their own dialect which is different from Bengali and Hindi. They quote historians like Dr. Dagon (born Htay Myaing), a literary award recipient, and U Pyin Nyar Zaw Ta (monk scholar with the pen name Kopinya-Amarapura) in support of their contentions. The 300 words of the Vissali dialect (Ancient Arakan era) were described in Dr. Dagon's book *Yazawin dare Ma Pone-naa*. He concluded that 80 per cent of the dialect in the age of Vissali comprised of words which have been used by native inhabitants (whose faith is Islám) in Rakhine State today. These words were from the *Saigasu Phya Parabike* (palm leaf inscription). This fact was also pointed out by prominent Buddhist scholar monk U Pyinyar Zaw Ta of the Taung Thaman Taung Lay Lone monastery in Amarapura Township, Mandalay.[130]

More historical evidence that the Rohingya cite to prove their distinct dialect comes from Francis Buchanan's research. He wrote:

> I shall now add three dialects, spoken in the *Burma Empire*, but evidently derived from the language of *Hindu* nation.

[130] Dr. Dagon (Htay Myaing), *Yazawin dare Ma Pone-naa* ('Pone-naa' Mentioned in History), Sar Pae Beikman Press, pp. 172–180.

> The first is that spoken by the *Mohammedan*, who have long settled in *Arakan*, and who called themselves *Rooinga*, or natives of *Arakan*.[131]

A very significant but seldom highlighted point is the fact that there are Muslims living in Rakhine apart from the Kamans, who do not identify as Rohingyas; some consider themselves as Arakanese Muslims. A veteran Rakhine politician, Bonpauk Tha Kyaw, wrote about one such person – Sultan Mahmud – who was a minister in the past independent democratic government of Burma. Bonpauk Tha Kyaw portrayed people like Sultan Mahmud as follows:

> They usually taught their children and all Muslims there to know the gratitude of Arakan State of Burma and its people because they, ie. Bengalis could come to work and settle in this Buddhist country and some of them became rich. Hence, this country and its people became their benefactors and they should not betray their benefactors, as the way they were taught in Koran. They taught all Muslims there to learn the native language and culture, to behave like the natives, so that they would be assimilated with the natives except in the religion.[132]

This was Bonpauk Tha Kyaw's view, with which not all fair-minded, unbiased, qualified historians of Rakhine would agree. However, the statements regarding the assimilation of Muslims in Rakhine society would be accepted by all.

There are indeed Bengali descendants who have been living in Rakhine for centuries, who have assimilated with Rakhine society, but still identify as Bengalis. Even in Yangon, one will find grand mosques built by them. The most famous one is located right next to the historical Sule Pagoda, named 'Bengali Sunni Jameh Mosque'. Another grand mosque near the secretariat building in Yangon is called 'Arakati Mosque'. The trustees of the mosque must be able to link their genealogy with their forefathers in Bengal and identify their clan names. Those Muslims from Rakhine still recognize their origins from Bengal and are proud to be called Bengali, but they have also integrated with Rakhine/Myanmar culture and serve the country and its people.

There are also records of some native Rakhines converting to Islám in the early Mrauk-U period.[133] There were also inter-marriages between Rakhines and Muslims, and their offspring regard themselves as Arakanese/Rakhine Muslims

---

[131] Buchanan, 2003, p. 55, see *supra* note 120.

[132] Bonpauk Tha Kyaw, *The Rohingyas, The Danger for the Union of Burma*, Sittwe, 1992, p. 2.

[133] Collis and Bu, 1960, p. 493, see *supra* note 108; U Aung Tha Oo, *History of Arakan*, Mya Yadanar Press, Yangon, 1954, p. 132; Pandeeta U Tha Htun Aung, *Rakhine Yar Za Win Taw Gyi* (Royal History of Rakhine), Rakhine Press, Sittwe, 1962, p. 74.

rather than Kaman. There were many objections of this usage by Rakhine ultranationalists. In spite of that, Rakhine Muslims managed to form a political party, without using the name 'Rakine Muslim', in the 1990s general election. They did not consider themselves to be Bengalis, Kamans or Rohingyas. At the time, I was serving as Vice-President in a Myanmar Muslim political party named 'Free People League of Burma' ('FPL'), whose President was Daw Khin Khin Sein, daughter of martyr U Razak. The party was later abolished by the military junta after the 1990 election, citing what I consider to be fabricated reasons. During the election campaign in 1990, I met with the leaders of the above-mentioned political party of Rakhine Muslims and had a chance to discuss their vision and principles.

No matter what labels these Muslims may use, they have been living alongside Rakhines in the region for hundreds of years. Even if one accepts the narrative of the military junta for the sake of argument, and the suggestion that the Muslims are descendants of farmers from the neighbouring country and that later, during the British colonial period, there was an influx of illegal immigrants into Rakhine, it cannot be denied that Muslims have been residing in Rakhine since 1824. But this narrative of the military junta is false.

Unprejudiced and unbiased history testify that these Muslims, regardless of labels used, have served Myanmar, not only in the Rakhine region, but throughout the country, loyally and dutifully. They held high positions in military, administrative, educational, medical and various other fields and perform their obligations with good track records. They have been elected to various posts in Myanmar: starting from the British colonial era in 1936, the pre-independent era in 1947; the short-lived parliamentary-democracy era in 1951, 1956 and 1961; the so-called socialist era after the first coup (1962) in 1974 and 1978; and after the second coup (1988) in 1990 and 2010. The military-backed USDP, which later stripped them of their temporary identification cards and remaining voting rights,[134] made Rakhine Muslims stand under their party umbrella in 2010. The disenfranchisement of Rakhine Muslims is now an evident reality. Muslims in Rakhine have been oppressed and persecuted for several years. They are one of the largest stateless groups on Earth. They were driven out of their birthplace, their villages were burned, and Muslim women were sexually assaulted. But it is only in recent times that the rest of the world has become aware of their plight. Myanmar's junta now needs to answer a case of genocide before the ICJ.

Some Muslims in Rakhine State feel that they cannot successfully strive for their basic human rights through lawful and peaceful means. Therefore, they

[134] Minority Rights Group International, 2017, see *supra* note 41.

resort to armed struggle. The group known as the Arakan Rohingya Salvation Army ('ARSA'), an armed group active in the Rakhine area, underwent some sort of training by Al-Qaeda. However, this should not lead to the hasty conclusion that the Rohingyas have been radicalized by the terrorists and extremist Salafists. Most of the Muslims in Rakhine State follow the guidance of imáms who graduated from the Deoband Darul-Uloom in India (a seminary where the Sunní Deobandi Islámic Movement began). They are influenced by the Tablighi Jamaat movement, also originating from India, which has a certain inclination towards Ṣúfísm. Therefore, even though a few misguided Rohingyas regrettably underwent training by terrorist groups such as Al-Qaeda, there is a slim chance that they would have been theologically indoctrinated by extremist Salafis and radicalized.

The opponents of the Rohingya cause may differ widely on other issues, but when it comes to recognizing Rohingyas as an ethnic group, they stand united in their views. Anti-Muslim rhetoric are conveyed through press and social media by proxies of the junta (such as the USDP and its allied parties) and Rakhine ultra-nationalists who oppose the military on other issues, echoing the same stereotypes. The following are common allegations:[135]

- Non-Kaman Muslims in Rakhine are descendants of seasonal labourers who had crossed the border to work on fertile Rakhine lands and stayed back in Rakhine State during the British administration;
- Bangladesh, a country that is smaller in size than Myanmar and suffering from poverty and uncontrolled population growth, needs land for its citizens to live and work. With the blessing of the authorities, Bengalis sneaked into Rakhine and obtained some sort of identification cards by bribing corrupt Myanmar officials and thereafter settled permanently on Rakhine land without any hindrance;
- facts such as the granting of legal status to the Rohingya by civilian politicians (starting with Prime Minister U Nu), references to them in the Myanmar Encyclopaedia and educational textbooks prescribed by state universities, and the granting of rights to broadcast in the Rohingya language on the Burma Broadcasting Station under the Burma Ministry of Information, have been brought about by unpatriotic and selfish politicians with the political motive to win votes. Mention is not made of Thein Sein's USDP nominating Rohingyas (without letting them use the name) to stand in the 2010 election under their party umbrella, nor to the Muslim Members of Parliament in Ne Win's socialist era (1974–1988).

135 Khin Maung Saw, "Islamization of Burma through Chittagonian Bengalis as 'Rohingya Refugees'", unpublished manuscript, 2011, pp. 5 ff., quoted in Saw, 2016, see *supra* note 14.

As for the first allegation, there is some partial truth to it. However, it fails to acknowledge the reality which is the presence of not only Kaman but also non-Kaman Muslims before the British colonial period.[136] As for the second allegation, the poverty levels and the population of Bangladesh are data that could be transparently monitored and verified from reliable sources including United Nations agencies. In fact, most would argue that Bangladesh is more technologically advanced and financially sound than Myanmar. Indeed, the lands in the Rakhine border area are fertile, but so are the lands across the border in Bangladesh. Since national borders all over the world are, by nature, porous, there are possibilities of human traffic along both sides of the border. However, it is hard for some of us to believe that corrupt officials at the border of Rakhine State would hurt the national interest of Myanmar by accepting bribes to allow passage, less so since most immigration officers in Rakhine State are natives to the region. Besides, with the Burma Citizenship Act of 1982 (which, in my view, is drawn up to suppress Muslims), illegal immigrants would find it increasingly difficult to escape scrutiny. Furthermore, Muslims living in Rakhine State, including Rohingyas, are concerned with illegal migrants from neighbouring countries, making it less likely that they would harbour or support illegal immigration.

The third allegation is unlikely to be accepted by political scientists or qualified historians. In fact, it was not just civilian politicians, but the military itself that once recognized the identity of Rohingyas. Brigadier Aung Gyi, after his downfall and detention, formed a political party during the 1990 elections. In his party bulletin, he wrote in detail about how the military at that time had recognized Rohingyas. Military dictator Ne Win, of Burmese-Chinese descent, who tried to hide his true lineage by disguising himself as a staunch Burmese Buddhist nationalist, used to hypocritically harp on a xenophobic rhetoric. His socialist party under the one-party system (1974–1988) allotted seats for Muslims in the Buthidaung and Maungdaw constituencies in Rakhine. In fact, one of the most blatant acts of political hypocrisy was committed by Thein Sein's USDP when it nominated the Rohingya in Rakhine State under its umbrella in order to win votes from the Muslims in the 2010 elections. As mentioned, however, in the 2015 elections the USDP stripped the aforementioned Rohingyas (who had contested elections under the USDP umbrella) of their temporary identification cards and remaining voting rights, when they switched their political stance for the election campaign. Interestingly, these facts are never mentioned by the opponents of the Rohingya cause in their arguments against the existence of the Rohingya as a distinct ethnic group.

136 Melyn McKay, *The Religious Landscape in Myanmar's Rakhine State*, United States Institute of Peace, no. 149, August 2019, pp. 3 ff.

Those interested in researching the truth about the Rohingya crisis should therefore impartially analyse the sincerity and veracity of the version of facts presented by both the proponents of the Rohingya cause as well as its critics before forming an opinion.

By the time of writing, the main part of the population of Myanmar empathizes with the plight of Rohingyas, even more so given the fact that the whole country is under oppressive rule of the military. The population is witnessing the same fate that Rohingyas and other ethnic groups have faced since Burma gained independence in 1948. The Rohingya crisis has shown how dictators can manipulate religion to pursue their ends, and should be regarded as a lesson to identify the need to find ways to prevent or reduce such manipulation.

5.5.3. The Present Condition of Rohingyas

On 1 February 2021, the Myanmar military staged an attempted coup alleging voting fraud and other irregularities in the November 2020 general elections. They detained lawfully- and democratically-elected officials, including President U Win Myint, State Counsellor Daw Aung San Suu Kyi, certain Members of Parliament and others, and charged them under various offences based on what seems to be fabricated facts.

Mon Mon Myat, a writer and journalist, commented:

> There is only one positive thing about the recent coup, which is that people clearly see the real culprit behind all racial and religious conflicts. The violent acts of the Myanmar military against civilians and other minority ethnic groups are even more visible in the recent arbitrary crackdown nationwide.[137]

She continued:

> Solidarity among anti-coup protesters is becoming stronger than religious nationalism. The ultimate and common goal of anti-coup protesters across the nation is to end the military dictatorship.[138]

She also gave some advice on religion and peace-building in Myanmar. According to her,

> [t]he Buddhist tradition, part of our culture's background and history, carries a distinctive account of justice and practical rationality. The influence of Buddhist traditions in Myanmar's moral conduct is crucial. Moral courage and virtue, fearlessness, and justice are shared by both Buddhist and liberal traditions. [...] Only when our

---

[137] Mon Mon Myat, "Buddhist Morality in Myanmar: Religious Nationalism and Solidarity After the Coup", *Berkeley Forum*, 15 March 2021 (available on the Berkeley Center for Religion, Peace and World Affairs' web site).

[138] *Ibid.*

> religious traditions can contribute three elements – courage, justice, and dignity to the society –can the peacebuilding process in Myanmar begin.[139]

The following is a quotation from the statement issued by civil society organizations, including Progressive Voice Myanmar, on 29 March 2022:

> The same military that committed genocide against the Rohingya are committing massacres, airstrikes, extrajudicial killings, arbitrary mass arrests, sexual and gender-based violence, violence against children and mass displacement following its attempted coup – an attempt that failed, largely due to courageous and united resistance from the people of Myanmar in defense of their democracy.
>
> At the 49th Session of the UN Human Rights Council, the UN High Commissioner for Human Rights, stated that systematic abuses by the military junta may amount to war crimes and crimes against humanity, including deliberately targeting civilians with airstrikes and burning people alive. The impunity enjoyed by the Myanmar military must end and this can only be achieved through swift and rigorous justice and accountability.[140]

5.6. The Way Forward

The role of religious leaders is particularly crucial in finding a way out of the dilemmas and predicaments facing Myanmar. I believe the people of Myanmar, regardless of religious affiliations, possess the spirit of tolerance. Unfortunately, successive military dictators have systematically exploited the religiosity of the Burmese people for their hidden agendas.

This phenomenon continued even during the rule of the NLD government from 2015 to 2020. Even now, at the time of writing, public service training institutes in Myanmar have discriminatory, nationalist and racist lessons camouflaged under the guise of patriotism and nation-building. One dental surgeon even exposed the racist lessons being taught during the course of his lectures. This went viral on social media and the public began to realize how attempts are being made to brainwash and indoctrinate the budding leaders of the nation.[141] Worse still, primary-school textbooks contained language expressing prejudice

139 *Ibid.*

140 "Civil Society Organizations Welcome US Determination of Genocide Against Rohingya", *Progressive Voice Myanmar*, 29 March 2022.

141 Swe Win, "Zee Pine Gyi nei Phaung Gyi Mhar Lay Htan Nay Saei Wada Mhaing Sit Sin Yay Myar" (Propaganda Storm Still Going Strong in Zee Pin Gyi and Phaung Gyi), *Myanmar Now*, 25 December 2018.

against mixed-blood persons. This information instantly went viral on social media, shocking the whole nation.[142]

In 2017, when a local non-governmental organization published a series of civic education textbooks that promoted religious literacy and included information on the basic tenets of four major faiths (including Buddhism), it prompted a nationalist outcry with claims that it was an attempt at 'Islámization' and "religious colonialism in the name of education", followed by demands that children should only be taught about Buddhism.[143]

Unfortunately, even among religious leaders, there are pseudo-inter-faith peacemakers. For example, one monk, Dr. Ashin Thaw Bartha (a Sayadaw of the International Buddhist Education Center) wrote a book about his visit to The Hague to observe Daw Aung San Suu Kyi's defense at the ICJ hearing. In this book, he deliberately made factual errors with the intention of discrediting Muslims, such as alleging that the Rohingya (according to him 'Bangalis') who came to Burma during the British colonial period were money-lenders who charged exorbitant interest rates from Burmese or Rakhine farmers.[144] However, it is widely known that taking usury is prohibited in Islám, as the Holy *Qur'án* states:

> Those who devour usury shall not rise again except as he rises, whom Satan of the touch prostrates; that is because they say, 'Trafficking (trade) is like usury.' God has permitted trafficking, and forbidden usury. Whosoever receives an admonition from his Lord and gives over, he shall have his past gains, and his affair is committed to God; but whosoever reverts — those are the inhabitants of the Fire, therein dwelling forever.[145]
>
> God blots out usury, but freewill offerings He augments with interest. God loves not any guilty ingrate.[146]
>
> Allah destroys interest and gives increase for charities. And Allah does not like every sinning disbeliever.[147]
>
> O you who believe, keep your duty to Allah and relinquish what remains (due) from usury, if you are believer.[148]

142 So Myat Mon, "Civics Education in Primary Schools Is a Lesson in Discrimination", *Frontier Myanmar*, 5 February 2019.

143 Tin Htet Paing, "Nationalists Oppose NGO's Curriculum for Including Religious Education", *The Irrawaddy*, 7 March 2017.

144 Ashin Thaw Bartha, *Hman Yar Ko Thit Sar So Myee ICJ Si* (I Will Vow To Tell the Truth in the ICJ), 2020, p. 69.

145 The *Qur'án*, 2:275.

146 *Ibid.*, 2:276.

147 *Ibid.*, 2:277.

148 *Ibid.*, 2:278.

> And if you do not, then be informed of a war [against you] from Allah and His Messenger. But if you repent, you may have your principal - [thus] you do no wrong, nor are you wronged.[149]

Ashin Thaw Bartha also alleged that Muslims endorsed and condoned terrorism,[150] despite himself purportedly being an inter-faith peacemaker attempting to forge harmony between religions and having obtained a peace award in Stockholm. In fact, he is a trained disciple of a controversial but prominent Buddhist monk, Ashin Nyanissara, the Sitagu Sayadaw, just like Wirathu. The Sitagu Sayadaw, who was one of the founders of the Ma Ba Tha and often instigated hatred, shocked the world when he praised the assassination of a famous Muslim lawyer and NLD legal adviser, U Ko Ni, during his sermon to military personnel in 2018.[151] He quoted Dutta Ghamani (a national hero of Ceylon) and his killing of the Tamils to justify the murder, which was indeed wholly against Buddhism and a heinous crime by any standard. The Sayadaw has also praised the coup leader, Senior General Min Aung Hlaing, as a great statesman possessing enormous faith and intellect.

Nevertheless, there are numerous sincere and peace-loving Buddhist monks in Myanmar who do not agree with the politicizing of religion. Religions for Peace, Myanmar ('RfP-M') has approached genuine spiritual Buddhist leaders and has sought their wisdom and leadership, just like it did with other interfaith leaders. RfP-M has managed to hold three fora with the hope and aspiration of finding a way for national reconciliation and peace in Myanmar. The aim was to create a space for all stakeholders to express their views. As is clear from its name, the paradigm is absolutely faith-based. At the third forum, President U Win Myint, State Counsellor Daw Aung San Suu Kyi, and Senior General Min Aung Hlaing were in attendance.

The people of Myanmar have not given up the idea of resolving the conflict peacefully. However, under the present circumstances, the majority of them are bitterly hurt, especially the younger generation. Their peaceful protests have been brutally crushed and political scientists have opined that the country could become a 'failed state'.[152] Under the prevailing circumstances, all that can be done is to advocate for an education for peace and to instil awareness of peace, love and justice, while providing humanitarian aid to victims of religious hatred

---

149 *Ibid.*, 2:279.

150 Bartha, 2020, p. 69, see *supra* note 144.

151 Mikael Gravers, "Nationalist Monks Provide Spiritual Support to Myanmar's Brutal Generals", in *Asia Portal*, 21 April 2022.

152 Joshua Kurlantzick, "Post-Coup Myanmar Could Become a Failed State", in *Council on Foreign Relations*, 19 April 2021; David I. Steinberg, "Myanmar: Failed state or failed nation?", in *Frontier Myanmar*, 11 April 2021.

and violence and involving religious leaders. What is important is enhancing both intra- and inter-faith education. People are afraid of things they do not know, and the individuals who have hijacked religious sentiments in bad faith wish to perpetuate this ignorance. By imbibing fear in the minds of the people, I suppose they believe that they can implement their hidden agendas more easily. This is probably why, whenever there are attempts to impart inter- and intra-faith education, those who seek to manipulate religion as a political tool oppose them vehemently.

5.6.1. Facts to Ponder to Achieve Freedom from Fear of Alleged Islámization

It is clear that the military dictators of Myanmar deploy negative narratives regarding Islám to embed Islámophobia in the minds of the Burmese Buddhist majority.

This can easily be found in the works of anti-Muslim elements since the dawn of Islám; however, things worsened during the Crusades. Even in William Shakespeare's (1564–1616) play 'Romeo and Juliet', Juliet's beauty was symbolized as 'Mehmet'. According to the old version of the Oxford English Dictionary, 'Mehmet' means an idol, a statue. The root-word was traced back to the notion that Muslims make golden statues of Muḥammad and worship him.[153] We should bear in mind that these were classic examples of how far the world had been misled by Western literature, which was the most influential source of information in that era.

Another sad reality is that there was a time when scholars with prejudice and bias against Islám were entrusted with the task of compiling the Encyclopaedia of Islám. One of them was an author who wrote that "Djihad" (*Jihád*) denotes: "The spread of Islām by arms is a religious duty upon Muslims in general".[154] Klein, in *The Religion of Islam*, makes a similar statement:

> *Jihad* – the fighting against unbelievers with the object of either winning them over to Islam, or subduing and exterminating them in case they refuse to become Muslims, and the causing of Islam to spread and triumph over all religions is considered a sacred duty of the Muslim nation.[155]

---

[153] Ahmed A. Galwash, *The Religion of Islam: A Standard Book*, Misr S.A.E., 1958.

[154] Duncan B. MacDonald, "Djihād", in M. Thomas Houtsma, T.W. Arnold, R. Basset and R. Hartmann (eds.), *Encyclopaedia of Islam*, 1st ed., Brill Online, 1913–1936.

[155] Frederick Augustus Klein, *The Religion of Islam*, London, 1906, quoted Maulana Muhammad Ali, *The Religion of Islam*, Motilal Banarsidass Publishers Pvt. Ltd. and Ahmadiyyah Anjuman Ishā'at Islām (Lahore), Delhi, 1994, Chapter 5 ("Jihad"), p. 405.

The above examples are just the tip of the iceberg when it comes to the Islámophobia prevalent in this day and age. I will now attempt to present some relevant facts regarding Islám with a view to clarifying some misconceptions, thus paving the way to mitigate the fear of Islámization.

There is no formal concept of conversion in Islám.[156] Islám, as I understand it, does not use force, marriage, or economic domination as a means to fatten its flock. Muslims are urged to invite others to the 'way of Truth' with wisdom and fair preaching.[157] It is then the right of the person who has been invited to accept or reject.[158] The invitation to the way of Truth must be conducted with convincing proof, love, kindness, mercy, sympathy, empathy, cordiality, respect, intellect and politeness. The Holy Prophet Muḥammad and all the Great Prophets were sent to warn and bear good news and glad tidings to mankind. However, even they had no right to make people accept the truth without their own free conviction.[159]

In fact, it is reported that the Holy Prophet felt very sad when he learned that those who had forsaken the truth would encounter failure in this world and the next one, due to their misdeed. The Almighty, with His infinite wisdom, knew about the Holy Prophet's beloved plight and sent the following message to him:

> [O Prophet] And whoever has disbelieved, let not his disbelief grieve you. To Us is their return, and We will inform them of what

---

[156] Kim Knott, "Islam: Conversion", Centre For Research and Evidence on Security Threats (CREST), 23 January 2017, p. 2:

> Islam does not formally recognise the idea of conversion, but focuses instead on the concepts of submission (aslama) and reversion. According to Islamic teaching, all people are born Muslim: as such, it is not possible for someone to 'convert' to Islam, but is instead a question of 'reverting' to one's true identity and submitting fully to Allah.

[157] Maulana Muhammad Ali, *The Holy Qur'an with English Translation and Commentary*, 2010, 16:125:

> Call to the way of your Lord with wisdom and goodly exhortation, and argue with them in the best manner. Surely your Lord knows best him who strays from His path, and He knows best those who go aright.

[158] The *Qur'án*, 31:23, 18:29:

> And whoever disbelieves, do not let his disbelief grieve you. To Us is their return, then We shall inform them of what they did. Surely Allah is Knower of what they did. Surely Allah is Knower of what is in the hearts.
>
> The Truth is from your Lord; so whoever wishes, let him believe, and whoever wishes, let him disbelieve.

[159] The *Qur'án, inter alia*, 3:19, 5:92–99, 13:40, 16:35, 16:18, 24:54, 29:18, 36:17, 42:48, 50:45 and 64:12.

> they did [the truth of their deeds]. For Allah knows well all that is in [Men's] hearts.[160]

Again, in another verse, the Holy Prophet was informed:

> If it had been thy Lord's Will, they would all have believed, all who are on earth! Will thou then compel mankind against their will, to believe?[161]

Messages such as the following can be abundantly found in the Holy *Qur'án*:

> And if Lord had so willed. He could surely have made mankind one Ummah [the collective community of Islamic people], but they will not cease to disagree.[162]

It is a common misconception with some non-Muslims that Islám would not have millions of adherents all over the world if it had not been spread by use of force. The same argument was made regarding the flourishing of Islám in India. However, the above-mentioned facts, referenced in the Holy *Qur'án*, the *Sunnah* and the teachings of Islám, were acknowledged by the foremost leaders of India's national liberation movement. For example, the political and spiritual leader of the Indian Independence Movement, Mahatma Gandhi (1869–1948) said:

> I wanted to know the best of the life of one (Muhammad) who holds today an undisputed sway over the hearts of millions of mankind. I became more than ever convinced that it was not the sword that won a place for Islam in those days in the scheme of life. It was the rigid simplicity, the utter self-effacement of the Prophet the scrupulous regard for pledges, his intense devotion to his friends and followers, his intrepidity, his fearlessness, his absolute trust in God and in his own mission. Those and not the sword carried everything before them and surmounted every obstacle. When I closed the second volume (of the Prophet's biography), I was sorry that there was not more for me to read of that great life.[163]

Famous Indian philosopher and poet Sarojini Naidu has also said:

> It was the first religion that preached and practised democracy, for in the mosque when [from] the minaret [the call to prayer] is sounded and the worshippers are gathered together, the democracy of Islam is embodied five times a day when the peasant and the king kneel side by side and proclaim, 'God alone is great.'

[160] *Ibid.*, 31:23.

[161] *Ibid.*, 10:99.

[162] *Ibid.*, 11:118.

[163] Mahatma Gandhi, in *Young India*, Lahore, 16 September 1924.

> I have been struck over and over again by this indivisible unity of Islam that makes a man instinctively a brother.[164]

The views of the one of the most eminent Indian Prime Ministers, Jawaharlal Nehru, are also note-worthy:

> Like the founders of some other religions, Mohammad was a rebel against many of the existing social customs. The religion he preached, by its simplicity and directness and its flavour of democracy and equality, appealed to the masses in the neighbouring countries who had been ground down long enough by autocratic kings and equally autocratic and domineering priests.[165]

Additionally, Swami Vivekananda (1863–1902), the eminent representative and disciple of Ramakrishna Paramahansa, who was one of the luminous masters of Hindu Dharma, wrote:

> Practical Advaitism (non-duality), which looks upon and behaves to all mankind as one's own soul, was never developed among the Hindus universally.[166]
>
> I am firmly persuaded that without the help of practical Islam, theories of Vedantism, however fine and wonderful they may be, are entirely valueless to the vast mass of mankind.
>
> For our own motherland, a junction of the two systems, Hinduism and Islam – Vedanta brain and Islam body – is the only hope.

Regarding the 'forces' at the Prophet's disposal, and thus the actual capacity to force conversions, Reverend Bosworth Smith noted that:

> [The Holy Prophet Muhammad was] [h]ead of the state as well as the Church, he was Caesar and Pope in one; but he was Pope without the Pope's pretensions, and Caesar without the legions of Caesar. Without a standing army, without a bodyguard, without a palace, without a fixed revenue [...].[167]

Lastly, historian Karam Tej Singh Sarao, with regard to the British role in adding to Islámophobia, stated that:

> Communalization and distortion of Indian history began with the administrator-historians of the British Raj many of whom had a hidden agenda. In order to legitimize their colonial rule and to win

164 Verinder Grover and Ranjana Arora (eds.), *Great Women of Modern India: Sarojini Naidu*, Deep & Deep Publications, New Delhi, 1993, pp. 51–56.

165 Jawaharlal Nehru, *Glimpses of World History*, Penguin Books, 2004, Chapter 49, p. 145.

166 *The Complete Works of Swami Vivekananda*, vol. 6, Advaita Ashrama, Kolkata, 1992, pp. 415–416.

167 R. Bosworth Smith, *Mohammed and Mohammedanism: Lectures Delivered at the Royal Institution of Great Britain in February and March 1874*, Smith, Elder & Co., London, 1874, p. 235.

> the allegiance of the Indians, they tried to show that their policies were more humane than the previous "Muslim" rulers. Working with such an agenda as a guideline, temples in ruins were shown as having been demolished by Muslim fanatics and missing treasures or statues as either having been looted by Muslim raiders or as having been hidden by the Hindus and Buddhists for fear of Muslim raids. Even when a Muslim ruler gave permission for the repair of a temple, it was explained away as having been earlier destroyed by Muslim armies. Confusing military policy with religious policy and brushing aside economic or geopolitical motives, this kind of vulgar historiography propagated the view that all invasions by Muslim armies were motivated by the goal of propagating Islam and converting the Indian *kafirs* by the sword. Thus, conquest was equated with conversion and any later uprising was shown as an attempt to get rid of Islam. In this way, many colonial historians of the nineteenth century and many aficionados of such a communal history in present-day India, place in one box all the Arabs, Turks, and Mughals and put the label of "Islamic invaders" on this box. Such an *ad hominem* approach totally ignores the fact that these invaders were individual political entities, who not only differed from each other in many ways but were also often at war with each other. Moreover, it is often completely overlooked that "both Hindu and Muslim states fought among themselves as much as they did against one another."[168]

In the same breath, we may consider the findings of historians from other parts of the world. The noted historian De Lacy O'Leary wrote in his book *Islam at The Cross Roads: A Brief Survey of the Present Position and Problems of the World of Islam*:

> History makes it clear, however, that the legend of fanatical Muslims sweeping through the world and forcing Islam at the point of the sword upon conquered races is one of the most fantastically absurd myths that historians have ever repeated.[169]

The description of Johan Elverskog, Associate Professor of Religious Studies at Southern Methodist University in Texas, in *Buddhism and Islam on the Silk Road* reads:

> In the contemporary world the meeting of Buddhism and Islam is most often imagined as one of violent confrontation. Indeed, the Taliban's destruction of the Bamiyan Buddhas in 2001 seemed not

168 Karam Tej Singh Sarao, *The Decline of Buddhism in India: A Fresh Perspective*, Munshiram Manoharlal Publishers, New Delhi, 2012, pp. 151–152.

169 De Lacy Evans O'Leary, *Islam at the Cross Roads: A Brief Survey of the Present Position and Problems of the World of Islam*, 1st ed., Routledge, London, 2017, p. 14.

> only to reenact the infamous Muslim destruction of Nalanda monastery in the thirteenth century but also to reaffirm the stereotypes of Buddhism as a peaceful, rational philosophy and Islam as an inherently violent and irrational religion. But if Buddhist-Muslim history was simply repeated instances of Muslim militants attacking representations of the Buddha, how had the Bamiyan Buddha statues survived thirteen hundred years of Muslim rule?[170]

In his book, Elverskog, after conducting in-depth historical research, disprove the false story of the Nalanda University being attacked by Muslim soldiers in 1202:

> The Buddhist monastery of Nalanda was founded in northeast India in the early fifth century. Over time it became the premier institution of higher learning in Asia and, much like leading universities today, Nalanda had a world-renowned faculty working on the cutting edge of the theoretical sciences and a student body drawn from across the Buddhist world. This prestige also brought with it ample gifts from the rich and powerful. Not only had local rulers in northeast India bequeathed entire villages to help finance the running of Nalanda, but the king of Sumatra had also offered villages for the monastery's endowment, and a special fund had been created to support students specifically from China. At its peak Nalanda had an extensive faculty teaching a diverse student body of about three thousand on a beautiful campus composed of numerous cloisters with lofty spires that "resembled the snowy peaks of Mount Sumeru." Then suddenly the serenity of this Buddhist institution was shattered. In the fall of 1202, Muslim soldiers on horses rode in and hacked down teachers and students where they stood. The once majestic buildings were left in ruins. The savagery was so great it signalled the end of the Dharma in India.
>
> This powerful story has been told countless times. Today it is ubiquitous, being found in everything from scholarly monographs to travel brochures. Indeed, by its sheer pervasiveness, this one episode has in many ways come to encapsulate and symbolize the entire thirteen-hundred-year history of Buddhist-Muslim interaction. And on account of this, whenever the topic of Buddhism and Islam is ever mentioned it almost invariably revolves around the Muslim destruction of the Dharma.
>
> This is problematic for many reasons, not the least being that the story of Nalanda is not true. For example, not only did local Buddhist rulers make deals with the new Muslim overlords and thus stay in power, but Nalanda also continued as a functioning

[170] See the description to Johan Elverskog, *Buddhism and Islam on the Silk Road*, University of Pennsylvania Press, Philadelphia, 2011.

> institution of Buddhist education well into the thirteenth century. One Indian master, for example, was trained and ordained at Nalanda before he travelled to the court of Khubilai Khan. We also know that Chinese monks continued to travel to India and obtain Buddhist texts in the late fourteenth century. Indeed, contrary to the standard idea promoted by the above story that Nalanda's destruction signalled the death of Buddhism, the fact is that the Dharma survived in India at least until the seventeenth century. Or, in other words, Buddhists and Muslims lived together on the Asian subcontinent for almost a thousand years. […].
>
> The British, for example, used the same claims of Muslim barbarity and misrule in order to justify the introduction of their supposedly more humane and rational form of colonial rule.[171]

Much else that is commonly said about Islám is incorrect. Numerous scholars have shown that early Muslim rulers were notably tolerant and there was little tension among the diverse religious groups under their rule.[172]

The above-mentioned scholarly and academic research findings are backed by the following verse from the Holy *Qur'án* which entrusted Muslims with the noble task of protecting the places of worship belonging to different religions:

> And if Allah did not repel the aggression of some people by means of others, cloisters and churches and synagogues and Mosques, wherein the name of Allah is much invoked, would surely be destroyed.[173]

Having presented the above facts, readers should also be aware that the Muslim rule in India was not as uncontroversial as some Muslim sympathizers might think. Although the common view of the Muslim rule in India is one of violence and persecution, this was refuted by fair-minded, unbiased scholars who conducted research in the matter. However, there was evidence of atrocities committed by Muslim invaders. But those plunders should not be seen as part of the Muslims' religious policy. We should bear in mind that those Muslim warlords were just practising the political ideology of the era, that is, imperialism. In that period in history, the whole world was under the influence of expansionism, colonialism, feudalism and other dictatorial systems. Muslims during those ages were not fighting because of religious ideals; rather, their motives were more economic or geopolitical.

---

171 Elverskog, 2011, pp. 1–2, see *supra* note 170.

172 *Ibid.*, pp. 1, 2 and 48.

173 The *Qur'án*, 22:40.

Islám prohibits compulsion in religion and permission is given to fight only for protection and defence purposes. Indeed, aggression is against the teachings of Islám:

> And fight in the way of Allah those who fight you but transgress not the limits. Truly, Allah likes not the transgressors.[174]
>
> Let there be no compulsion in religion. Truth stands out clear from error.[175]
>
> Perhaps Allah will make friendship between you and those you hold as enemies. And Allah has power [over all things] and Allah is Oft-Forgiving, Most Merciful. Allah does not forbid you to deal justly and kindly with those who fought not against you on account of religion nor drove you out of your homes. Verily, Allah loves those who are just.[176]
>
> They are those who have been expelled from their homes in defiance of right [for no cause] except that they say, Our Lord is Allah.[177]
>
> But if the enemy inclines towards peace, do thou [also] incline towards peace, and trust in Allah.[178]

As per one saying of the Holy Prophet Muḥammad, the entire creation is viewed as one family. Allah loves the one who serves the family the most. In another saying, the Holy Prophet asks us to:

> Have mercy on the creatures of the earth and Allah Almighty from the heaven will shower Mercy on you.[179]

Many other sayings of the Holy Prophet prohibit violence, hatred, grudges, lack of kindness, selfishness and other evil thoughts and deeds. These are just a few ordinances prescribed in Islám regarding values such as love, peace, justice, kindness, non-aggression, selflessness, tolerance and peaceful co-existence. Nevertheless, we should bear in mind that no matter how good the teachings of each religion are, if followers do not implement the teachings in their thoughts and deeds, there will be no results. In fact, there are those namesake followers of religion who actually commit acts that are the exact opposite of what their religion teaches. There are such 'black sheep' in every community and Islám is not an exception.

---

174 *Ibid.*, 2:190.

175 *Ibid.*, 2:256.

176 *Ibid.*, 60:7–8.

177 *Ibid.*, 22:39–40.

178 *Ibid.*, 8:61.

179 Sunann at-Tirmidhí, *Ṣáḥíḥ*, Book 27, *ḥadíth* 30.

After the blessed leadership of the rightly guided successors, the *Khulafa'ar-Ráshidín* (the four Caliphs who led the Muslim community following the death of the Prophet Muḥammad), starting from Hazrat Abu Bakr (573–634 AD) and concluding with Hazrat Ali (599–661 AD), the system of *Ummah* being led by the people's representative, or the 'Khalifah', came to an end as predicted by the Holy Prophet. The reign of sultans who were despotic imperial kings dominated the Islámic world.

Undoubtedly, there were a few righteous kings like Hárún al-Ráshíd (766–809 AD) and Ṣáláḥuddín (Saladin) (1137–1193 AD) who had done great service to the civilized world. Some others also waged expansionist wars, just like contemporary imperialists. However, the colonial wars fought by the Muslim kings were not driven by religion; as stated above, there is no compulsion in religion. Furthermore, the ratio of the religious denomination in India, at the very least, should clear up the misconception that a near eon under Muslim rule has suppressed all religions and Islámized the entire region. The statistics vividly show that 88 per cent of Indians are non-Muslims and that the Muslims consist of less than 10 per cent of the total Indian population.[180]

5.6.2. Myths about Islámic Marriages and Religious Conversions

Islám is often accused of converting non-Muslims through polygamous marriages. This is among the most common propaganda spread by Islámophobic actors around the world. To dispel these misconceptions, one must consider the true nature of marriage as enshrined in Islám.

5.6.2.1. The Concept of Marriage in Islám

Islám is a way of life and a guide to action to attain sublime peace in this life and in the afterlife. Its teachings contain guidance for life before and after death. It acknowledges the importance of the physical mundane world and the significance of the higher spiritual realm. Matter, mind, soul and spirit are the creation of the Almighty given to man, who is the 'best of His creatures', to utilize them in performing the task of beautifying the two worlds, as His representative. Therefore, the secret doctrine of Islám relates not only to the spiritual growth of man but also to the growth of the community, or rather humanity, as a whole. The scope of Islám is very wide and covers the whole field of relations of man to man, as well as that of man to his or her Creator. The object of the laws relating to this part of human life is to teach man his or her duties and obligations to others, and to show him or her how to lead a happy life in this world in his or her relations with others.

---

180 Al-Haj Khalifah U Aye Lwin, *Brief History of Emperor Saint Bahadur Shah Zafar*, Colour Zone Press, November 2019.

The most important of the restrictive regulations of Islám are those relating to marriage, a basic institution of human civilization. The Arabic word for marriage is '*Nikāḥ*', which originally means merging or uniting. Marriage in Islám is a sacred contract which every Muslim must enter into, unless there are special reasons as to why he or she should not. Thus, in the Holy *Qur'án*, it is written:

> And marry those among you who are single and those who are fit among your male slaves and your female slaves; if they are needy, Allah will make them free from want out of His grace;[181]
>
> And Allah is Ample-giving, Knowing. And let those who do not find a match keep chaste until Allah makes them free from want out of His Grace.[182]

In another verse, marriages are given the same importance as blood-relationships:

> He it is Who has created man from water, then He made for him blood-relationship and marriage-relationship.[183]

Tradition also lays stress upon living in a married state. The Holy Prophet is reported to have said to those who talked of fasting in the day-time and insisted on staying awake during the night, praying to God and keeping away from marriage:

> I keep a fast and I break it, I pray and I sleep, and I am married, so whoever inclines to any other way than my Sunnah, he is not of me.[184]

Another saying of the Holy Prophet lays stress upon marriage:

> O assembly of young people! Whoever of you has the means to support a wife, he should get married, for this [that is, marriage] is the best means of keeping the looks cast down and guarding the chastity; and he who has not the means, let him keep fast, for this will act as castration.[185]

181 Merely being poor is not sufficient excuse for not marrying because the needy are told that if they marry, Allah will make them free from want out of His Grace. The Holy Prophet is reported to have performed the marriage of a man who did not possess so much as a ring of iron, see al-Bukhári, *Sahih*, Book 67, *ḥadíth* 16 (unless otherwise indicated, the translations of *ḥadíth* used in this chapter are provided by the author).

182 The *Qur'án*, 24:32, 24:33.

183 The *Qur'án*, 25:54.

184 Al-Bukhári, *Sahih*, Book 67, *ḥadíth* 1.

185 Al-Bukhári, *Sahih*, Book 67, *ḥadíth* 2.

Celibacy (*tabattul*) was expressly forbidden by the Prophet.[186] According to one *ḥadíṯẖ*:

> The man who marries perfects half of his religion.[187]

Another says:

> Matrimonial alliances increase friendship more than anything else.[188]

5.6.2.2. Marriage as the Union of Two Natures Which Are One in Their Essence

The Holy *Qur'án* repeatedly speaks of the two mates, man and woman, as being created from each other:

> O people, keep your duty to your Lord, Who created you from a single being and created its mate of the same [kind] and spread from these two many men and women.[189]
>
> He it is who created you from a single soul and of the same did He make his mate that he might find comfort in her.[190]

Both these verses are generally understood as referring to the creation of the first man and the first woman,[191] but that they signify the relation of man to woman in general is clear from other verses:

> And Allah has made wives for you from among yourselves, and has given you sons and daughters from your wives.[192]
>
> And of His Sign is this, that He created mates for you from yourselves, that you may find quiet of mind in them.[193]

And thus, a Makkah revelation of the middle period notes:

---

186 Al-Bukẖári, *Sahih*, Book 67, *ḥadíṯẖ* 8.

187 Al-Ṭabaráni, Al-Mu'jam al-'Awsaṭ, *ḥadíṯẖ* 922 (as translated in Syed Najis Mahmood, "Changing Patterns of Muslim Family in India with Special Reference to the Marriage and Divorce: A Review of the Literature", Master's dissertation, Department of Sociology and Social Work, Aligarh Muslim University, 2010, p. 38, referring to "MM.13: I-III" (on file with the author)).

188 *Ibid.*

189 The *Qur'án*, 4:1.

190 *Ibid.*, 7:189.

191 Nowhere in the Holy *Qur'án* or in evidence of any reliable tradition is there any mention of the woman being created from the rib of man or of Eve being created from the rib of Adam. The allegation made is that God created all men from a single being (*nafsin waḥidatin*) and created the *zaúj* (mate) of that being from the same single being. The word '*Wahidah*' as well as the personal pronoun '*Ha*', used twice, are all in the feminine gender, and three renderings are possible: the male being created from the female, the female being created from the male or both being created from the same essence.

192 The *Qur'án*, 16:72.

193 *Ibid.*, 30:21.

> The Originator of heavens and the earth; He has made for you pairs from among yourselves [...] multiplying you thereby.[194]

Thus, marriage is, according to Holy *Qur'án*, the union of two souls which are one in their essence.

5.6.2.3. The Multiplication of the Human Race, Society and Marriage: Love and Service

It will be noted that, in the above verses, the multiplication of the human race is mentioned as one of the objects of marriage. But it may be said that the multiplication of the race can be brought about without marriage, as with other animal species; that is to say, without uniting one man with one woman for their whole life. However, the institution of marriage is also responsible to a very great extent for the development of those feelings of love and service which are the pride of humanity today, the building blocks of society. The mutual love of husband and wife – a love based not on momentary passion but lifelong connection – and the consequent parental love for offspring leads to a very high development of the feeling of love for mankind as such, and thus to the disinterested service of humanity. This love is described as a sign of God in the Holy *Qur'án*:

> And of His Signs is this, that He has created for you pairs among yourselves that you may find quiet of mind in them, and He put between you love and compassion.[195]

The home or the family are, in fact, the first training grounds of love and service. Here, man finds real pleasure in the service of humanity, and the sense of service is thus gradually developed and broadened. It is, in fact, a training ground for every kind of morality, for it is in the home that a person learns to have a sense of his own obligations and responsibilities, to have respect for others' rights, and, above all, to have a real pleasure in suffering for the sake of others. The Holy Prophet is reported to have said:

> The best of you is he who treats his wife best.[196]

5.6.2.4. 'Marry Only One'

As a rule, Islám only recognizes the union of one man and one woman as a valid form of marriage. Under exceptional circumstances, men may marry more than one woman, but women are not allowed to take more than one husband (however, she can re-marry after the death of the first husband or after a legal and lawful divorce).

---

194 *Ibid.*, 42:11.

195 *Ibid.*, 30:21.

196 Sunann Ibn Majah (translation by the author), 9:50.

Thus, in the first place, it must be borne in mind that polygamy is allowed in Islám only as an exception. It is expressly so stated in the Holy *Qur'án*:

> And if you fear that you cannot do justice to orphans, marry such women as seem good to you, two or three of four; but if you fear that you will not do justice (between them), then marry only one […].[197]

This is the only passage in the Holy *Qur'án* that speaks of polygamy, and it will be seen that the Holy *Qur'án* does not enjoin polygamy, it only allows it conditionally and as a remedy for many of the evils of civilization.[198] These conditions relate more to the welfare of society than to the needs of the individual.

A consideration of the historical circumstances of the time when this part of the *Suráh* of the Holy *Qur'án* was revealed corroborates this conclusion – that is, after the Battle of Uhud, a time when the Muslims were compelled to carry on an incessant war. During this time, most breadwinners were forced to fight in wars, and many had been lost in unequal battles that were being fought by small Muslim bands against overwhelming force. Women had lost their husbands, as young children had lost their fathers, and these widows and orphans had to be provided for. It was under these circumstances that the fourth chapter was revealed, allowing the taking of more wives than one, so that the widows and orphans may find a shelter. If one fears, conveys the revelation, that he will not be able to do justice to orphans, marry women up to four, but only with a condition that he is just to all of them. The term 'women' here refers to the mothers of orphans, which is made clear in Holy *Qur'án*, 4:127.

The war had decimated the male population and the number of women exceeded that of men. This excess, if not provided with a home, would have led to moral depravity, which is the greatest danger to a civilization based on morality such as the Islámic one. The rationale is that while monogamy is undoubtedly a just rule of life under normal conditions, when abnormal conditions are brought about by the excess of females over males, monogamy fails, and that it is only through a regulated polygamy that this difficulty can be solved.

The Holy *Qur'án* is probably the only religious book, on the face of this Earth, that contains the phrase "marry only one". In none of the other religious scriptures, whether it be the Vedas, the Ramayana, the Bhagavad Gita, the Talmud or the Bible, does one find an unconditional and clear rejection of polygamy, and religious discourse offers divergent interpretations. In fact, it was only later that the Hindu Marriage Act (1955), passed by the Parliament of India and the pronouncements of the Christian churches restricted the number of wives to one

197 The *Qur'án*, 4:3.

198 Ali, 1994, pp. 475–476, see *supra* note 155.

for Hindus and Christians respectively.[199] Before the Holy *Qur'án* was revealed, there was no upper limit for polygamy and many men had scores of wives, some even hundreds. The Holy *Qur'án* introduced the restriction of up to four wives. Furthermore, the Holy *Qur'án* specifically prescribes that he who weds more than one woman may do so only on the condition that he deals justly with them:

> Ye are never able to be fair and just as between women, even if it is your ardent desire. But turn not away [from a woman] altogether, so as to leave her [as it were] hanging [in the air]. If ye come to a friendly understanding, and practice self-restraint, Allah is Oft-Forgiving, Most Merciful.[200]

While one may be able to provide four houses, four cloths, four vehicles and any other kind of four material things to his four wives, he will never be able to divide his love in four equal portions and provide them to his wives. Even the One who created mankind and the entire infinite physical universes and boundless spiritual realms had very precisely mentioned that:

> Ye are never able to be fair and just as between women [...].[201]

How then can a created person be able to meet this strict criterion and condition when the Creator said he cannot explicitly? Therefore, polygamy must be accepted as an exception, and not as a rule. Many are under the misconception that it is compulsory for a Muslim man to have more than one wife. On the contrary, it cannot be said that a Muslim who has two, three or four wives is a better Muslim than a Muslim who has only one wife.[202]

5.6.2.5. Islám Did Not Initiate Polygamy

It may also be noted that Islám did not introduce polygamy. Among all Eastern nations of antiquity, polygamy was a recognized institution. Among the Hindus, polygamy prevailed from the earliest times. There was, as among the ancient Babylonians, Assyrians and Persians, no restriction as to the number of wives a man might have. Although Greece and Rome were not polygamous societies, concubinage was the norm.[203] In fact, according to David Murray, an anthropologist, polygamy has historically been more common than monogamy.[204]

---

199 Stephanie Kramer, "Polygamy is Rare around the World and mostly Confined to a Few Regions", Pew Research Centre, 7 December 2020 (available on its web site).

200 The *Qur'án*, 4:129.

201 *Ibid.*

202 Dr. Zakir Naik, "International Da'wah Training Program".

203 Charles G. Herbermann, *The Catholic Encyclopedia: An International Work of Reference on the Constitution, Doctrine, Discipline, and History of the Catholic Church*, Catholic Way Publishing, 2014.

204 Cheryl Wetzstein, "Traditionalists Fear Same-Sex Unions Legitimize Polygamy", *The Washington Times*, 13 December 2000.

Even though the clear permissibility of polygamy in Islám is apparent, its actual practice is quite rare in many Muslim societies. Some researchers estimate no more than two per cent of married Muslim men practice polygamy.[205] Perhaps, it could be estimated that the percentage of polygamous marriages and extramarital affairs throughout Muslim nations is lower than the extramarital affairs of Western nations, combined; if so, then men in Muslim countries would be regarded as more strictly 'monogamous' than their counterparts in Western countries.[206]

Many of the countries that permit polygamy have Muslim majorities, and the practice is rare in many of them. Fewer than one per cent of Muslim men live with more than one spouse in Afghanistan, Pakistan, Iran and Egypt.[207] The report of the Committee of Status of Women in India, published in 1974, mentions that the percentage of polygamous marriages between 1951 and 1961 was 5.06 per cent among the Hindus and only 4.31 per cent among the Muslims.[208] According to the Indian legal system, only Muslim men are permitted to have more than one wife. Clearly, however, despite it being illegal, more Hindus have multiple wives than Muslims since, according to the 1971 Census of India, there were approximately 450 million Hindus but only 60 million Muslims residing in India at the time.[209]

5.6.2.6. Polygamy and the Practice of a Mundane Right Livelihood in Buddhism

According to Buddhism, in order to attain the final goal of *Nirvana*, one must renounce all worldly things, including marriage. Those who are pursuing the 'supra-mundane path' (*Lokkuttara Samma-ajva*) must practice celibacy and enter monkhood. Those who cannot follow this path can have a married life and pursue a 'mundane right livelihood' (*Lokiya-Samma-ajiva*) until they are ready to turn away from the world.

In Buddhism, right livelihood is of two kinds:

> 1. When the noble disciple, avoiding wrong living, gets his livelihood by a right way of living: this is called 'Mundane Right

---

[205] Jumah Al-Kholy, "Taaddud al-Zawjaat Wa Hikamatuhu fi Islam" (Multiple Marriages in Islám and Its Wisdom), in *Journal of the Islamic University of Medina*, 2006, vol. 46, pp. 222–231.

[206] Robert T. Michael, John H. Gagnon, Edward O. Laumann and Gina Kolata, *Sex in America*, Little, Brown and Co., Boston, 1994, p. 105.

[207] Kramer, 2020, see *supra* note 199.

[208] Committee of Status of Women in India, "Towards Equality: Report of the Committee on the Status of Women in India", Department of Social Welfare, Government of India, New Delhi, 1974, pp. 66–67.

[209] A. Chandra Shekhar (Registrar General and Census Commissioner of India), *Census of India, 1971: Religion*, Registrar General and Census Commissioner of India, 1972, p. iii.

> Livelihood' (lokiya-sammaa-aajiva), which yields worldly fruits and brings good results.
>
> 2. But the avoidance of wrong livelihood, the abstaining, desisting, refraining therefrom – the mind being holy, being turned away from the world, and conjoined with the path, the holy path being pursued – this is called the 'Supermundane Right Livelihood' (lokuttara-sammaa-aajiva), which is not of the world. but is supermundane, and conjoined with the path.[210]

Therefore, a Buddhist can have a family life as a layperson before renouncing the world to pursue the holy path to attain *Nirvana*. Lord Buddha has given some advice to the laypersons pertaining to leading a life of right livelihood and right action. For example:

> 3. He avoids unlawful sexual intercourse, and abstains from it. He has no intercourse with such persons as are still under the protection of father, mother, brother, sister or relatives, nor with married women, nor female convicts, nor lastly, with betrothed girls.
>
> This is called Right Action.[211]
>
> Now, Right Action, I tell you, is of two kinds:
>
> 1. Abstaining from killing, from stealing, and from unlawful sexual intercourse: this is called the 'Mundane Right Action' (lokiya-sammaa-kammanta) which yields worldly fruits and brings good results.[212]

Some guidelines to social dealing in mundane worldly life can be found in the *Mangala-Sutta* of Lord Buddha, but there are no specific instructions regarding monogamy or polygamy. In fact, Lord Buddha focused the code of conduct only for the monks and that was clearly stipulated in *Vina-Sutta*.

Therefore, Buddhists followed the customary law prevailing in each country regarding marriage. As far as Myanmar is concerned, as mentioned above, the so-called Protection of Race and Religion laws enacted in May and August 2015 include the Buddhist Women's Special Marriage Law (August 2015) and the Monogamy Law (August 2015).[213]

According to the age-old Burmese Buddhist custom in Myanmar, the would-be bride and bridegroom, after staying together, are supposed to hang their clothes on the same clothesline rope and, having done so, the public would

[210] *Majjhima-Nikaaya*, 117 (here, the number refers to the *Sutta*); Nyanatiloka Mahathera, *The Word of the Buddha: An Outline of the Teachings of the Buddha in the Words of the Pali Canon*, Buddhist Publication Society Inc., Kandy, Sri Lanka, 2001, p. 58.

[211] *Anguttara-Nikaaya, X, 176.*

[212] *Majjhima-Nikaaya*, 117.

[213] See discussions in Section 5.3.2. above.

acknowledge them as legally and lawfully-wedded husband and wife. Furthermore, there is no limit on how many wives a man can take. Throughout the history of Myanmar, not only rulers but also their subjects have practiced polygamy. The common saying among the traditional Burmese is, 'if the tree is good [big and strong] ten thousand birds can take shelter in it', denoting that a number of women (wives) can seek shelter and rely on a single manly and able husband. Another such saying is clearer and more precise: 'One thousand wives and concubines depend on one good dutiful husband' ('York kyar kaung maung ma ta taung').

Late U Kyaw Lwin, Director General of the Ministry of Religious Affairs, Myanmar stated that:

> Our ancestors of the past who were staunch Buddhist Bamars have been honest, loyal, steadfast, dutifully firm, courageous, valiant and patriotic. They uphold the nationalist spirit. Taking good example from the future, would be Buddha and do good deeds to accumulate merits in the future lives. In order to prosper and flourish the next coming generation they married more than one wife and practice polygamy while taking good care of them according to the auspicious noble precept of Mingalar doctrine. Thus, they endeavoured to increase the Buddhist population. Due to their right conduct in present Myanmar, Buddhists happened to be the majority. We are now enjoying the fruits of their righteous deeds and owed obligation and gratitude to them.[214]

According to some reports, most of the cases registered under the Buddhist Women's Special Marriage Law and the Monogamy Law have been by Buddhist men and women against other Buddhist men and women.[215]

During my tenure as a commissioner in the Advisory Commission on Rakhine State (the Annan Commission), I had interviewed Rohingyas living in Myanmar and some of those who had taken refuge inside the Cox's Bazaar camps. During my interviews, I found that very few Rohingyas had more than one wife. While conducting inter-faith dialogue with non-Muslim participants, I also conducted a survey as to whether the participants were aware of anyone from the Muslim community who had more than one wife, given that Muslims in Myanmar live in close proximity with members of other faiths and that mosques exist in nearly every town and village in the country. The answer was usually in the negative.

---

214 U Kyaw Lwin, in *Theik Pan Abidhamma Magazine*, vol. 2, June 1991, p. 134 (on file with the author).

215 Melissa Crouch, "Promiscuity, Polygyny, and the Power of Revenge: The Past and Future of Burmese Buddhist Law in Myanmar", in *Asian Journal of Law and Society*, 2016, vol. 3, p. 87.

Thus, the accusation against Muslims that they are spreading Islám by engaging in polygamy seems entirely baseless. Of course, there are a few Muslims who are polygamous; however, the number of such Muslims is not large enough to serve the purpose of proselytization. As demonstrated, such polygamous practices are also not unique to Islám, and, at its core, Islám rejects forced conversions of non-believers.

It is necessary to address such kinds of stereotyping and negative messaging about Islám, as well as any other religion. Failure to do so, as evidenced by the role of xenophobia in the situation of Burmese Muslims in Myanmar, can lead to a breakdown of communal and social harmony. Preventing inter-faith conflict may prove much easier than remedying its effects.

5.7. Conclusion

This chapter sought to understand the origins and evolution of hate speech on grounds of religion in the context of Myanmar, by providing an overview of relevant historical developments since the time of the Kingdom of Arakan and touching on more recent examples of hateful expression. In this analysis, the attempts by malicious actors to spread hate among religious communities have been discussed and criticized. The rise of Buddhist nationalism in Myanmar has unfortunately provided a wide range of examples of hateful expression in the religious context.

The process of mitigating hate speech, particularly when it can lead to violent radicalization, surely warrants a multidisciplinary approach, but any solution should grant religious sentiment due priority, and include humanitarian assistance while imparting intra- and inter-faith education.

SECTION B: ALLEGED HATE SPEECH IN THE NAME OF HINDUISM: THE SITUATION IN INDIA

6

Reflections on Freedom of Expression, Hate Speech and Sedition in India

Madan B. Lokur and Shruti Narayan*

6.1. Introduction

This chapter assesses the jurisprudence of India's free speech laws and how they have been weaponized, with the establishment permitting hateful, provocative, and incendiary speech while simultaneously targeting dissent and criticism. An inconsistent application of law has weakened the rule of law and is, thereby, weakening respect for the judiciary. This has encouraged polarization and intolerance and emboldened religious extremism. An analysis of Indian law and judgments and their application to several recent incidents of alleged hate speech confirms that religious majoritarianism threatens the safety of minorities, and has a chilling effect on the free speech rights of other members of civil society, particularly journalists.

Sedition, a colonial law used to target dissent against the British empire in India, is also being misused frequently to the point of being abused, thereby intimidating citizens and stifling free speech.

6.2. The Constitution of India and Legislation on Speech and Hatred

The Constitution of India ('Constitution') protects speech and expression as a fundamental and inalienable right. The right is not absolute and the Constitution enables the Indian Parliament to enact a law placing reasonable restrictions on this fundamental right. The reasonable restrictions must be in the interest of the sovereignty and integrity of India, the security of the State, friendly relations

---

* Hon'ble Justice (Retd.) **Madan B. Lokur** has been a judge of the Supreme Court of India (2012–2018). He was educated at the Modern School, New Delhi; in Allahabad for the Indian School Certificate examination; History (Hons.) from St. Stephen's College, Delhi University; and obtained a law degree from the Faculty of Law of Delhi University. He was enrolled at the Bar in 1977 and practised in the Supreme Court of India and at the Delhi High Court. He is presently a Judge in the Supreme Court of Fiji and is actively involved in human rights issues in India. **Shruti Narayan** is a lawyer based in New Delhi, India. She holds an LL.M. from Columbia Law School and an LL.B. and B.A. in political science from the University of Delhi. Her areas of interest are constitutional and criminal law. For an audio-visual recording of Justice Lokur's statement to CILRAP's conference in Florence in April 2022 on the topic of this anthology, please see https://www.cilrap.org/cilrap-film/220408-lokur/.

with foreign States, public order, decency or morality, or in relation to contempt of court, defamation or incitement to an offence.[1]

These limited constitutional restrictions have enabled statutory law in India to penalize what is often described in the context of religion or caste or ethnicity as 'hate speech'. Section 153A of the India:Penal Code, 1860 ('IPC') makes it an offence to promote "enmity between different groups on grounds of religion, race, place of birth" and so on by words, either spoken or written or by signs or by visible representation, or promote "disharmony or feelings of enmity, hatred or ill-will between different religious, racial [...] groups or castes or communities". 'Speech' therefore has been given an extended meaning and includes communication through methods other than verbal communication. There are analogous provisions of law elsewhere in the IPC[2] and in other statutes, such as the Protection of Civil Rights Act, 1955 which penalizes hateful speech against 'lower caste' groups[3] and the Scheduled Castes and the Scheduled Tribes (Prevention of Atrocities) Act, 1989 which criminalizes, *inter alia*, the act of promoting "feelings of enmity, hatred or ill-will against members of the Scheduled Castes or the Scheduled Tribes", either by speech or by signs or by visible representation.[4]

But those accused of alleged hate speech claim constitutional protection under the guise of freedom of speech and expression, and this is where the courts face a dilemma. The accused claim that their alleged hate speech does not fall within the prohibition of public order or incitement to an offence – it is merely an expression of an opinion and therefore constitutionally permitted. They draw attention to the fact that courts in India have always protected and, whenever necessary, expanded the meaning of free speech which has been held to include, *inter alia*, freedom of the press[5] and the right to criticize government policies.[6] The courts, therefore, encounter difficulties in finding a right balance in

1 Constitution of India, 26 January 1950, Article 19 (https://www.legal-tools.org/doc/9ov6kt/).

2 IPC, 6 October 1860, Sections 153B, 295A, 298, 505(1) and 505(2) (https://www.legal-tools.org/doc/6a8f6b/).

3 India, The Protection of Civil Rights Act 1955, 8 May 1955, Section 7(1)(c) (https://www.legal-tools.org/doc/kcg70x/).

4 India, The Scheduled Castes and the Scheduled Tribes (Prevention of Atrocities) Act 1989, 11 September 1989, Section 3(1)(u) (https://www.legal-tools.org/doc/57dcde/).

5 Supreme Court of India, *Sakal Papers Ltd. v. Union of India*, Judgment, 25 September 1961, Writ Petitions No. 331/1960 and No. 67–68/1961, AIR 1962 SC 305 (https://www.legal-tools.org/doc/mvlgup/); Supreme Court of India, *Bennett Coleman and Co. v. Union of India*, Judgment, 30 October 1972, Writ Petitions Nos. 334/1971 and 175, 186 and 264/1972, (1972) 2 SCC 788 (https://www.legal-tools.org/doc/ca6ys4/).

6 Supreme Court of India, *S. Rangarajan v. P. Jagjivan Ram*, Judgment, 30 March 1989, Judgment, Civil Appeal Nos. 1668–1669/1988, (1989) 2 SCC 574 ('*Rangarajan*') (https://www.legal-tools.org/doc/io5jdm/).

applying criminal law to restrict alleged hate speech, particularly in the absence of a working and manageable definition of hate speech. In fact, the Karnataka High Court declined to pass any order regarding the description of Muslims participating in a Tablighi Jamaat event as "super spreaders" of the Covid-19 virus. The primary reason given by the High Court was that since hate speech had no "precise legislative" definition, it would not be appropriate to analyse the speeches made by politicians and reports by the news media to determine whether they amounted to hate speech or not.[7]

On the other hand, the Madras High Court did not find it necessary to define hate speech, but held that the Constitution does not permit hate speech, which "create[s] discord amongst the various ethnic and religious communities […] [and] disrespects another citizen on grounds of religion, race, […] caste".[8]

In the absence of a definition of hate speech, High Courts may continue to provide differing interpretations of hate speech, leading to uncertainty in the legal position. Consequently, it has become more than necessary for the Indian Parliament to legislatively define 'hate speech' (to the extent possible), incorporating views expressed by the Supreme Court of India and international bodies. No doubt the task is difficult but not impossible. Unfortunately, the Indian Parliament has not attempted any definition and indeed as the primary legislative body, it has neglected to do so. In the absence of any clarity on what constitutes hate speech and how it should be balanced with the right to free speech and expression, the Supreme Court of India and other Indian courts have been unable to formulate an unambiguous and comprehensive response to cases involving allegations of hate speech.[9] With courts being unable to find the right balance, the law enforcement authorities are having a field day, so to speak. They arbitrarily use their discretion to arrest those whose views are unpalatable, but take no action against those whose verbal speech or non-verbal communications are demeaning and inflammatory, particularly in the context of religion.

Here, it is necessary to enter a caveat and state quite clearly that hate speech is not the sole domain of so-called right-wing Hindu organizations or individuals. Others too have been accused of employing hate speech for their

---

7 High Court of Karnataka, *Campaign Against Hate Speech, an Unregistered Organisation and Ors. v. State of Karnataka and Others*, Judgment, 13 May 2020, Writ Petition No. 6749/2020 (GM-RES/PIL) (https://www.legal-tools.org/doc/0dwlye/).

8 High Court of Madras, *G. Thirumurugan Gandhi v. State and Others*, Judgment, 9 July 2019, Crl. OP No. 30026/2018, 2019 (3) MLJ (Crl.) 397 (https://www.legal-tools.org/doc/2kzy30/).

9 Supreme Court of India, *Pravasi Bhalai Sangathan v. Union of India*, Judgment, 12 March 2014, Writ Petition No.157/2013, (2014) 11 SCC 477, para. 25 (https://www.legal-tools.org/doc/6drbwq/): "25. It is desirable to put reasonable prohibition on unwarranted actions but there may arise difficulty in confining the prohibition to some manageable standard and in doing so, it may encompass all sorts of speeches which needs to be avoided".

ends, but the difference is two-fold. Hate speech by right-wing Hindu groups and individuals attract greater attention and provide traction simply because they belong to the majority community and therefore address a larger audience. They also appear to have the tacit consent of the establishment to indulge in hate speech, if not by overt action, then certainly by the silence or absence of condemnation by religious or political leaders.

6.3. Understanding Hate Speech: A Definitional Overview

On occasion, the Supreme Court has appreciated the necessity for a constitutionally acceptable definition of hate speech. While doing so, it has adverted to Article 20(2) of the International Covenant on Civil and Political Rights, 1966 ('ICCPR') which provides that advocacy of national, racial or religious hatred that constitutes incitement to discrimination, hostility or violence shall be prohibited by law. Similarly, reference has been made to Articles 4 and 6 of the International Convention on the Elimination of All Forms of Racial Discrimination, 1965 which prohibit racial discrimination and mandate member States to make a law prohibiting racial discrimination through a suitable framework of law.

The Supreme Court of India has also referred to the 267th report of the Law Commission of India ('Law Commission') which draws attention to Recommendation No. R(97)20 of the Committee of Ministers of the Council of Europe on 'Hate Speech'.[10] The Recommendation defines hate speech with reference to its essence, that is, a hostile attitude based on identity factors. The Appendix to the Recommendation states that:

> [T]he term "hate speech" shall be understood as covering all forms of expression which spread, incite, promote or justify racial hatred, xenophobia, anti-Semitism or other forms of hatred based on intolerance, including: intolerance expressed by aggressive nationalism and ethnocentrism, discrimination and hostility against minorities, migrants and people of immigrant origin.

These views, internationally accepted, are in sync with the scheme of the Indian Constitution and statutory law that penalize incitement to an offence or promotion of hatred. This is also pithily expressed in the United Nations ('UN') Strategy and Plan of Action on Hate Speech ('Strategy') launched in May 2019.[11] The Strategy acknowledges that there is "no international legal definition of hate speech, and the characterization of what is 'hateful' is controversial

[10] Council of Europe, "Recommendation No. R(97)20 of the Committee of Ministers to Member States on 'Hate Speech'", 30 October 1997 (https://www.legal-tools.org/doc/rx2ckd/).

[11] UN Secretary-General, "United Nations Strategy and Plan of Action on Hate Speech", 31 May 2019 (https://www.legal-tools.org/doc/5rrb5b/).

and disputed." The Strategy seeks to understand hate speech as "any kind of communication […] that attacks or uses pejorative or discriminatory language with reference to a person or a group on the basis of who they are, in other words, based on […] [an] identity factor". The Strategy notes that international law seeks to punish speech which incites certain harmful activities associated with identity-based intolerance for communities – like discrimination or violence. The Strategy states that:

> Incitement is a very dangerous form of speech, because it explicitly and deliberately aims at triggering discrimination, hostility and violence, which may also lead to or include terrorism or atrocity crimes. Hate speech that does not reach the threshold of incitement is not something that international law requires States to prohibit. It is important to underline that even when not prohibited, hate speech may be harmful.

Clearly, drafting a precise legal provision to comprehensively cover speech which spreads 'hate' and divisiveness is undoubtedly problematic. But, as is evident, adequate guidance is available to tackle the vice of hate speech falling outside constitutional boundaries.

From this discussion, two propositions can be culled out which make for a meaningful discourse on defining hate speech. First, it is clear that alleged hate speech amounting to 'incitement to an offence' is constitutionally prohibited in India. The alleged hate speech may be verbal or non-verbal. The incitement need not result in commission of an offence or physical violence or public disorder.

The second proposition is equally significant and here the Indian Supreme Court draws upon two decisions of the Canadian Supreme Court (discussed later) which suggest that the impact of hate speech goes beyond the immediate action which it may or may not incite. Indeed, a non-violent response such as discrimination or loss of self-esteem is an equally important element of hate speech, violating the human right to equality and dignity and must be prohibited. It has a lasting and undesirable psychological impact on the target group (or individual). Proactive measures, therefore, need to be taken to reaffirm societal commitment to equality and dignity along with punishing the act of hate speech.

Experience shows that alleged hate speech in India includes elements of implied references and inferences that can be drawn by the audience, depending upon the context and the situation in which the speech is made. There have been instances of caustic, derogatory and demeaning utterances amounting to incitement to hate and to vilify a community or group without any call to commit an offence or to violence. Such instances were witnessed in January and February 2020 during a peaceful agitation against the Indian Citizenship (Amendment) Act, 2019 ('CAA') by a large number of women belonging to the Muslim community. Similarly, the target community that is vilified may not necessarily be identified, except inferentially, although the purpose, intended effect, and identification can be nuanced from the content of the alleged hate speech which again becomes clear from the context and situation. A more recent instance of this is a call to those who wear a *hijáb* to leave India and settle down in a country that permits the wearing of a *hijáb*. It is not difficult to identify the unstated religious community but there is also no call to commit an offence or violence.

6.3.1. The Supreme Court of India and Hate Speech

In the context of hate speech and religion, it must be emphasized that India is a secular State with a secular Constitution that protects and upholds the right to freedom of religion and expression or propagation of that religion.[12] The State has no official religion and respects all religions. Members of all religious groups are considered equal for the purposes of their activities.

The existing legal framework provides authority to the State to prevent hateful speech, even without specifically criminalizing hate speech. For example, in 2004 the Supreme Court dealt with a situation in *State of Karnataka v. Praveen Bhai Thogadia*[13] where the State, acting proactively, restrained Thogadia, a political leader associated with a right-wing Hindu religious group, from participating in any gathering within a certain district for about two weeks. Thogadia was scheduled to address a gathering in which several religious leaders were likely participants. The State's reasoning was that the atmosphere in the district was "communally sensitive", and Thogadia had recently made an "inflammatory speech which incited communal feelings" and the prognosis was that he would likely disturb communal harmony in the district. On these premises, the Supreme Court upheld the restriction on Thogadia's entry to the district. Importantly, the Court noted that while the decision of the local authorities might involve "an element of subjectivity", a person's "[p]ast conduct […] may certainly provide sufficient material or basis for the action contemplated on a reasonable expectation of possible turn of events, which may need to be avoided in public interest". The Court held that although this was a restriction on the freedom of speech, it was justified since public order was threatened by speech which in fact threatened secularism. The Court importantly recognized the positive obligations of the State to protect secularism, stating that:

> Persons belonging to different religions live throughout the length and breadth of the country. Each person whatever be his religion

---

[12] Constitution, Article 25, see *supra* note 1.

[13] Supreme Court of India, *State of Karnataka v. Praveen Bhai Thogadia*, Judgment, 31 March 2004, Criminal Appeal No. 401/2004, (2004) 4 SCC 684 (https://www.legal-tools.org/doc/qpmao9/).

> must get an assurance from the State that he has the protection of law freely to profess, practice and propagate his religion and freedom of conscience. Otherwise, the rule of law will become replaced by individual perceptions of one's own presumptuous good social order.

Quite evidently, while free speech must be protected, public order must not be threatened and inflammatory or incendiary speech must not be allowed as it could lead to incitement to an offence, particularly in a communally sensitive area.

Taking a cue from this and in an effort to deal with hate speech particularly in a communally sensitive atmosphere, the Indian Ministry of Home Affairs issued 'Guidelines on Communal Harmony, 2008'.[14] These Guidelines lay down preventive and administrative measures since preventing a communal riot is far more important than containing it. Importantly, the Guidelines provide that:

> Channels of communications also need to be established with leaders of all communities, and strict action should be taken against anyone inflaming passions and stoking communal tension by intemperate and inflammatory speeches/utterances.

The Guidelines also provide for relief and rehabilitation to victims of communal disturbances. Implementation of these Guidelines is quite another matter.

6.3.2. Application of International Norms and Expanding Hate Speech Jurisprudence

International views on hate speech have been taken note of and recognized by the Supreme Court in its subsequent decision in *Pravasi Bhalai Sangathan v. Union of India* ('*Pravasi Bhalai Sangathan*').[15] This public interest litigation sought action against politicians making hate speeches or otherwise demeaning remarks along religion, caste, region and ethnic lines. It was contended that the existing law is not sufficient to deal with the menace of hate speech. The Court rejected this submission and held that there were already "sufficient and effective" remedies for prosecution of hate speech, and that the "root of the problem is not the absence of laws but rather a lack of their effective execution". The Court declined to issue any guidelines to supplement the existing law, and expressed concern about defining hate speech and "confining the prohibition to a manageable standard". Notwithstanding this, the Court gave a working definition of hate speech based on a review of domestic and foreign law, including

[14] Ministry of Home Affairs, Government of India, "Guidelines on Communal Harmony", 23 June 2008 (https://www.legal-tools.org/doc/ra3g6q/).

[15] *Pravasi Bhalai Sangathan*, see *supra* note 9.

Canadian law. The judgment helpfully summarized important issues relating to the prosecution of hate speech.

The Supreme Court described hate speech as:

> an effort to marginalise individuals based on their membership in a group. Using expression that exposes the group to hatred, hate speech seeks to delegitimise group members in the eyes of the majority, reducing their social standing and acceptance within society. Hate speech, therefore, rises beyond causing distress to individual group members. It can have a societal impact [...]. Hate speech also impacts a protected group's ability to respond to the substantive ideas under debate, thereby placing a serious barrier to their full participation in our democracy.[16]

This description recognizes the psychological harm to an individual's self-worth or self-esteem and provides a helpful platform for building strong civil rights protections against hate speech. It also recognizes that hateful speech is a distinct wrong from the "later, broad attacks" which include physical violence.

The Supreme Court referred to the judgment in *Canada (Human Rights Commission) v. Taylor*,[17] in which the Canadian Supreme Court had occasion to consider the effect of anti-Semitic speech and the nature of speech that could be punished – not just speech inciting violence, but also speech that affects individual self-worth. The Court adopted a human rights perspective and noted that:

> individuals subjected to racial or religious hatred may suffer substantial psychological distress, the damaging consequences including a loss of self-esteem, feelings of anger and outrage and strong pressure to renounce cultural differences that mark them as distinct. This intensely painful reaction undoubtedly detracts from an individual's ability to, in the words of Section 2 of the [Canadian Human Rights] Act, "make for himself or herself the life that he or she is able and wishes to have".

The Canadian Supreme Court's decision in *Saskatchewan (Human Rights Commission) v. Whatcott ('Saskatchewan')*,[18] in which the Court gave a possible approach to interpret 'hatred' used in statutory provisions, has also been relied upon by the Indian Supreme Court. As per *Saskatchewan*, the first aspect is to

---

16 *Ibid.*, para. 7.

17 Supreme Court of Canada, *Canada (Human Rights Commission) v. Taylor*, Judgment, 13 December 1990, Case No. 20462, [1990] 3 SCR 892 (https://www.legal-tools.org/doc/375794/).

18 Supreme Court of Canada, *Saskatchewan (Human Rights Commission) v. Whatcott*, Judgment, 27 February 2013, Case No. 33676, [2013] 1 SCR 467 (https://www.legal-tools.org/doc/ojtnu8/).

apply hate speech prohibitions objectively using the test of a reasonable person. The second aspect is to interpret the words 'hatred' or 'hatred or contempt' as:

> extreme manifestations of the emotion described by the words "detestation" and "vilification". This approach filters out expression which, while repugnant and offensive, does not incite the level of abhorrence, delegitimization and rejection that risks causing discrimination or other harmful effects.

The third aspect is to determine the likely impact of the hate speech on the targeted person or group.

In a significant observation, the Supreme Court of India noted that hate speech "lays the groundwork for later, broad attacks on vulnerable [persons] that can range from discrimination, to ostracism, segregation, deportation, violence and, in the most extreme cases, to genocide".[19] As will be seen later, hate speech has gone through the range from discrimination to violence and a call for ethnic cleansing and perhaps genocide.

6.3.3. Understanding Hate Speech Through *Pravasi Bhalai Sangathan*

While the Supreme Court gave a progressive and liberal interpretation to alleged hate speech and its possible impact in *Pravasi Bhalai Sangathan*, at least one proposition adumbrated requires discussion. The Court referred to the definition of hate speech in Black's Law Dictionary, which states: "Speech that carries no meaning other than the expression of hatred for some group, such as a particular race, especially in circumstances in which the communication is likely to provoke violence".[20] In some situations, this definition may be inadequate for the purpose of effectively countering all hateful speech, because the reference to violence undermines the recognized harms hate speech causes to the human right to individual dignity, to equality, and against discrimination, which was also recognized by the Court.

The Court also referred to the offence of 'sedition', a colonial hangover, while discussing the existing legal provisions to deal with hate speech. Sedition is defined in Section 124A of the IPC as bringing or attempting to "bring into hatred or contempt […] towards the Government established by law" by words, either spoken or written, or by signs, or by visible representation, or otherwise. Quite clearly, sedition is an act against the State, and the incorporation of the word 'hatred' in the law would not bring it within the meaning of 'hate speech' as understood judicially.

---

19 *Pravasi Bhalai Sanghatan*, para. 7, see *supra* note 9.

20 Bryan A. Garner (ed.), *Black's Law Dictionary*, 9th ed., West Publishing, 2009, p. 1529, "Hate Speech".

The Court's reference to sedition seems to have unwittingly provided an occasion for the police to allege sedition in cases related to alleged hate speech. Thereby, the exposition of law by the Supreme Court is distorted by the law enforcement agencies, cynically confirming the view expressed that the "root of the problem is not the absence of laws but rather a lack of their effective execution".[21]

The Supreme Court concluded the discussion in the judgment by requesting the Law Commission, which was already studying the powers of the Election Commission of India ('Election Commission') to take action with regards to politicians engaging in hate speech, to include in its consideration the broader issues of hate speech and "if it deems proper, [to define] the expression "hate speech" and make recommendations to the Parliament to strengthen the Election Commission to curb the menace of "hate speeches" irrespective of whenever made".[22]

6.3.4. The 267th Report of the Law Commission of India

The twenty-first Law Commission was constituted in 2015. Ironically, the judge who authored the judgment in *Pravasi Bhalai Sangathan* was appointed the Chair of the Law Commission after he retired from judicial office. In deference to the request of the Supreme Court, the Law Commission prepared Report No. 267 in March 2017 on the subject of Hate Speech ('Report') and examined the issues referred to it by the Supreme Court in *Pravasi Bhalai Sangathan*. The Report refers to the centrality of individual rights in a democracy, and recognizes that:

> In a plural democracy, there is always a conflict between different narratives and interpretation of what constitutes public interest. Democracy thrives on disagreements provided they do not cross the boundaries of civil discourse. Critical and dissenting voices are important for a vibrant society. However, care must be taken to prevent public discourse from becoming a tool to promote speech inimical to public order.[23]

The Law Commission notes that in international law, incitement to violence and to discrimination is recognized as a ground for interfering with freedom of expression. In considering the ingredients of hate speech, the Law Commission observed that incitement to violence cannot be a determinative factor or the "sole test" for identifying hate speech, because:

---

21 *Pravasi Bhalai Sangathan*, para. 27, see *supra* note 9.

22 *Ibid.*, para. 28, fn. 6.

23 Law Commission, 267th Report on Hate Speech in India, 23 March 2017, para. 1.6 (https://www.legal-tools.org/doc/l6puhr/).

> Even speech that does not incite violence has the potential of marginalising a certain section of the society or individual. [False and offensive ideas] need not always incite violence but they might perpetuate the discriminatory attitudes prevalent in the society. Thus, incitement to discrimination is also a significant factor that contributes to the identification of hate speech.[24]

The Law Commission also acknowledges that hate speech can provoke "acts of terrorism, genocides, ethnic cleansing" and that "[i]ndisputably, offensive speech has real and devastating effects on people's lives and risks their health and safety. It is harmful and divisive for communities and hampers social progress."[25]

The Law Commission's review of the judicial decisions dealing with cases reveals that courts have had to repeatedly explain the very high standard that must be met before the provisions of law can be applied to successfully prosecute a case of hate speech. For example, the Supreme Court has clarified that for the offences of Sections 153A[26] and 505(2)[27] of the IPC to be invoked, two groups must be involved because the substance of the offences is not simply hurting the feelings of one community but promoting hatred between different groups.[28] This presumes that the effect of hateful speech in the context of these offences is not realized if two separate communities are not mentioned in the speech, whereas in practice, political rhetoric can make implicit references which vilify or degrade one community in the eyes of the other, without having to name either community.

In closing, the Law Commission concludes in its Report that there is "no water tight compartment to deal with the various acts relating to hate speech which generally overlap".[29] The Law Commission proposes that new provisions of law be introduced to deal with hate speech. The suggested draft Criminal Law (Amendment) Bill of 2017 proposes the insertion of two new offences that criminalize simply the act of expressing hate and causing not incitement to violence necessarily but an impact on the intended target. This is an important

---

24 *Ibid.*, para. 6.2.

25 *Ibid.*, para. 6.5.

26 IPC, Section 153A, see *supra* note 2: "Promoting enmity between different groups on ground of religion, race, place of birth, residence, language, etc., and doing acts prejudicial to maintenance of harmony".

27 *Ibid.*, Section 505(2): "505. Statements conducing to public mischief. – (2) Statements creating or promoting enmity, hatred or ill-will between classes".

28 Supreme Court of India, *Bilal Ahmed Kaloo v. State of Andhra Pradesh*, Judgment, 6 August 1997, Criminal Appeal No. 81/1997, (1997) 7 SCC 431 (https://www.legal-tools.org/doc/n4aknu/).

29 Report, para. 6.30, see *supra* note 23.

progression in Indian law, away from requiring the act to have incited public disorder, violence, or some other breach of law. There is sufficient acknowledgement in Indian understanding of the law of the harmful nature of hate speech and the potential adverse impact it can have on a person's dignity, equal status, and physical safety. Despite this, the Parliament has not acted on the Law Commission's recommendations.

The decision in *Pravasi Bhalai Sangathan* and the Law Commission's report make it quite clear that violence or the possibility of violence is not an essential element of hate speech. Discrimination, ostracism, hostility, loss of self-worth or self-esteem and other forms of non-violent psychological impact are factors that make up hate speech. In the authors' opinion, this is as good a starting point as any for defining hate speech.

6.4. Contemporary Developments in Law: Missed Opportunities

In *Jafar Imam Naqvi v. Election Commission of India*,[30] the issue of political hate speech re-entered the discourse of the Supreme Court during the 2014 parliamentary elections. In this case, the petitioner sought, *inter alia*, that the Election Commission should be directed to derecognize political parties resorting to "illegal" activities, referring to speeches stoking religious tensions. The Supreme Court's judgment ignored the specific plea made by the petitioner, and instead mainly focused on reasons why it should not enter the legislative field and issue "guidelines". Despite the clear danger that hate speech presents, the Court essentially abandoned the issue as one that should only be dealt with *post facto*, stating that:

> The matter of handling hate speeches could be a matter of adjudication in an appropriate legal forum and may also have some impact in an election dispute raised under the Representation of People Act, 1951. Therefore, to entertain a petition as a public interest litigation and to give directions would be inappropriate.[31]

The Court unfortunately missed an opportunity to lay down the limits of hate speech which gets aggravated during electioneering.

The Supreme Court's most recent judgment considering the issue of hate speech is *Amish Devgan v. Union of India* ('*Amish Devgan*').[32] Devgan, a television journalist, faced criminal charges under various provisions of the IPC. The charges were filed after he referred to a saint in Islám as an "invader,

---

30 Supreme Court of India, *Jafar Imam Naqvi v. Election Commission of India*, Judgment, 15 May 2014, Writ Petition (Civil) 429/2014, (2014) 15 SCC 420 (https://www.legal-tools.org/doc/7oun1u/).

31 *Ibid.*, para. 10.

32 Supreme Court of India, *Amish Devgan v. Union of India*, Judgment, 7 December 2020, Writ Petition (Criminal) 160/2020, (2021) 1 SCC 1 (https://www.legal-tools.org/doc/lrh6yj/).

terrorist and robber who had come to India to convert its population to Islam", during a TV programme hosted by him. The Court refused to quash the criminal cases, which is an affirmation of the adequacy of existing criminal law to recognize hate speech, even if made accidentally or in error, as was claimed by Devgan. In its rather lengthy judgment, the Court embarked on a comprehensive review of Indian and foreign decisions on hate speech while referring to some helpful academic articles.

The Court referred to the guaranteed right to equality in Article 14 of the Constitution and its various facets, including the right to dignity. The Indian Constitution prescribes not just rights but also duties, including the duty of citizens to promote harmony and fraternity, which the Court noted must transcend "religious [...] diversities". The Court distinguished between dignity which can be protected by criminalizing hate speech and a broader or more individualistic concept of dignity, which is protected by defamation law. In the former context, the Court held dignity as meaning "a person's basic entitlement as a member of a society in good standing, his status as a social equal, and as bearer of human rights and constitutional entitlements". The Court accorded dignity great importance, as being linked to the "unity and integrity of the nation" and held that divisiveness and alienation affects not only the dignity of the target group but also the pluralism and diversity of the country.

In discussing various subjective factors necessitating evaluation for deciding whether speech is punishable as hate speech, the Court referred to academic articles on the subject, including an essay titled 'Defining Hate Speech'[33] which deals with hate speech in various jurisdictions. The Supreme Court broadly accepted that the content of a speech must be coupled with the intent of the speaker to incite or cause harm. The Court also referred to an article which outlined the three elements of hate speech – content, intent, and harm or impact.[34] The problem, in the authors' opinion, is the unsatisfactory manner in which the Court dealt with the harm or impact that hate speech might have.

On the content aspect, the Court accepted an earlier view that "the effect of the words must be judged from the standards of reasonable, strong-minded, firm and courageous men, and not those of weak and vacillating minds, nor of

33 Andrew F. Sellars, "Defining Hate Speech", in *Berkman Klein Center for Internet & Society at Harvard University*, 2016, Research Publication No. 2016–20.

34 Alice E. Marwick, and Ross Miller, "Online Harassment, Defamation, and Hateful Speech: A Primer of the Legal Landscape", *Fordham Center on Law and Information Policy Report*, 2014.

those who scent danger in every hostile point of view".[35] On the intent aspect, the Court accepted the view that:

> The intent-based element of 'hate speech' requires the speaker's message to intend only to promote hatred, violence or resentment against a particular class or group without communicating any legitimate message. This requires subjective intent on the part of the speaker to target the group or person associated with the class/group.[36]

The Supreme Court also cited various definitions not previously considered by it or by the Law Commission. One of the definitions views hate speech as a racial insult intended to demean a group,[37] while another explains it as expression intended to "vilify, humiliate or incite hatred" against a target.[38]

The Court also affirmed that the freedom of speech may not be arbitrarily restrained by hate speech laws. The Court opined that there is a 'good faith' defence available where a speaker displays prudence and caution with his or her expression or content; and that there is also a 'legitimate purpose' defence available where the speech has some clear purpose other than just spreading hatred or intent. This is a corollary to the definition of hate speech in Black's Law Dictionary, which views hate speech as speech with no redeeming purpose other than spreading hatred. The Court held that the "legitimate purpose" defence is particularly applicable in cases of any publication having a genuine public interest purpose.

6.4.1. Hate Speech and Fair Criticism of Government

In *Amish Devgan*, the Court sought to clarify the law on restraining free speech by holding that speech which threatens the security of the State is not the same as speech prohibited by other provisions of the IPC. Even within the context of speech relating to government and public administration, the Court reaffirmed that the right to "favour or criticise" government policies is within the right to free speech, and such "political speech" does not constitute hate speech.

In the present context, this is an important distinction which needs to be understood by the police. The misuse of these provisions of law to target people making political comments is illustrated in the case of *Patricia Mukhim v. State*

---

35 Supreme Court of India, *Ramesh v. Union of India*, Judgment, 16 February 1988, Writ Petition (Civil) No. 107/1988, (1988) 1 SCC 668 (https://www.legal-tools.org/doc/bweb1s/).

36 *Amish Devgan*, para. 48, see *supra* note 32.

37 Richard Delgado, "Words that Wound: A Tort Action for Racial Insults, Epithets, and Name-Calling", in *Harvard Civil Rights-Civil Liberties Law Review*, 1982, vol. 17, p. 133.

38 Kenneth D. Ward, "Free Speech and the Development of Liberal Virtues: An Examination of the Controversies Involving Flag Burning and Hate Speech", in *University of Miami Law Review*, 1998, vol. 52, no. 3 p. 733.

of Meghalaya.[39] This case was decided by the Supreme Court on 25 March, 2021, just over three months after the passage of the judgment in *Amish Devgan*. Mukhim is a journalist in the north-eastern State of Meghalaya, where conflicts sometimes occur between tribal and non-tribal communities. In July 2020, Mukhim wrote a Facebook post criticizing the "apathy" of the State government functionaries in not taking any action in relation to an incident where certain persons attacked non-tribals. She was charged in a criminal case accusing her of promoting enmity between groups on grounds of religion and race as well as promoting hatred or ill-will.

The Supreme Court quashed the criminal case against Mukhim. In its judgment, it held that the Facebook post was an attempt to "highlight the discrimination against non-tribals in the State of Meghalaya" and in fact "pleads for equality of non-tribals in the State of Meghalaya". There was no discernible intent to promote hatred of any community. The Court went on to note that within India's multi-cultural society, where citizens enjoy the right to free movement within the country, there is potential for conflict which cannot be ignored. The Court held that:

> The fervent plea made by the Appellant for protection of non-tribals living in the State of Meghalaya and for their equality cannot, by any stretch of imagination, be categorized as hate speech. It was a call for justice – for action according to law, which every citizen has a right to expect and articulate. Disapprobation of governmental inaction cannot be branded as an attempt to promote hatred between different communities.[40]

6.4.2. Does the Impact of Hate Speech Need to Be 'Violent'?

The Supreme Court in *Pravasi Bhalai Sangathan* had already held that the impact of hate speech may include a non-violent psychological impact. This was reiterated by the Law Commission. However, in *Amish Devgan*, the Court noted that speech which goes beyond political criticism and "defames, stigmatizes and insults the targeted group provoking violence or psychosocial hatred" is not protected free speech.[41] The Court elaborated that speech reflecting "hate which tends to vilify, humiliate and incite hatred *or* violence against the target group upon identity of the group"[42] can be punished. In doing so, the Court appears to be veering towards the view that hate speech must extend to incitement to violence, if not violence itself. It was observed that in the absence of actual violence

---

39 Supreme Court of India, *Patricia Mukhim v. State of Meghalaya*, Judgment, 25 March 2021, Criminal Appeal No. 141 of 2021, 2021 SCC 258 (https://www.legal-tools.org/doc/sbc4ep/).

40 *Ibid.*, para. 15.

41 *Amish Devgan*, para. 50, see *supra* note 32.

42 *Ibid.*, para. 55.

or public disorder "something more than words, in the form of 'clear and present danger' or 'imminent lawless action', either by the maker or by others at the maker's instigation is required".[43]

The 'clear and present danger' and the 'imminent lawless action' tests are two distinct tests in US constitutional law, but have been equated by the Indian Supreme Court.[44] These expressions are employed in the context of public disorder or violence and not simply in the context of promoting feelings of hatred. This equation of the two distinct tests by the Indian Supreme Court has made it simple for the Court to decline any answer to the question as to whether, for example, economic boycott of a particular community falls within the meaning of 'clear and present danger' or 'imminent lawless action' in the context of public disorder. The Supreme Court did not elaborate on how the 'clear and present danger' and the 'imminent lawless action' tests may be applied to evaluate whether a given speech would promote feelings of hatred against a particular community without extending to physical harm. The Court merely accepted an earlier view that to criminalize speech, it is necessary to establish a proximate nexus with clear and present danger or imminent lawless action and public disorder or violence. The Court appears to recognize this problem but does not provide any satisfactory conclusion, holding:

> Having interpreted the relevant provisions, we are conscious of the fact that we have given primacy to the precept of 'interest of public order' and by relying upon 'imminent lawless action' principle, not given due weightage to the long-term impact of 'hate' speech as a propaganda on both the targeted and non-targeted groups. This is not to undermine the concept of dignity, which is the fundamental foundation on the basis of which the citizens must interact between themselves and with the State. [...]. Further, a 'hate speech' meeting the criteria of 'clear and present danger' or 'imminent lawless action' would necessarily have long term negative effect. Lastly, we are dealing with penal or criminal action and, therefore, have

---

43 *Ibid.*, para. 58.

44 Supreme Court of India, *Shreya Singhal v. Union of India*, Judgment, 24 March 2015, Writ Petition (Criminal) No. 167/2012, (2015) 5 SCC 1, para. 37 (https://www.legal-tools.org/doc/gvk8zj/). Earlier in *Rangarajan*, the Supreme Court held:

> Our commitment of freedom of expression demands that it cannot be suppressed unless the situations created by allowing the freedom are pressing and the community interest is endangered. The anticipated danger should not be remote, conjectural or far-fetched. It should have proximate and direct nexus with the expression. The expression of thought should be intrinsically dangerous to the public interest. In other words, the expression should be inseparably locked up with the action contemplated like the equivalent of a "spark in a powder keg".

> to balance the right to express and speak with retaliatory criminal proceedings. We have to also prevent abuse and check misuse.[45]

In the authors' opinion, the Supreme Court has taken a step back from its pronouncement in *Pravasi Bhalai Sangathan* and the recommendation of the Law Commission. Incitement to a non-violent reaction to hate speech is as much an offence as any. For example, an economic boycott of members of a minority community amounts to discriminatory treatment with an intent to humiliate and is, therefore, punishable under the existing legal provisions. Such an action is a direct manifestation of feelings of hate. While the Court in *Amish Devgan* does not expressly state as much, its silence is likely to be taken as an indication that only incitement to violence or a likelihood of violence will matter for prosecution under the law. Such an interpretation would go against the hate speech jurisprudence somewhat ambiguously elucidated in the decision in *Amish Devgan* itself. To avoid any doubt as to understanding speech as hate speech, it may be preferable to introduce specific provisions making hate speech an offence as proposed by the Law Commission in its Report regardless of the harm or impact on society or a community or an individual.

The Supreme Court in *Pravasi Bhalai Sangathan* pointed out that the existing legal provisions could be used to prosecute and punish hate speech when it occurred. In *Amish Devgan*, the Court refused to quash the criminal case against the journalist accused of making a hate speech. It appears that the judiciary approved the use of existing law to prosecute hate speech. However, upon examining some major contemporary incidents of divisive and hateful speech, it appears that the police are not always proactive in investigating, let alone prosecuting, such incidents.

6.5. Contemporary Incidents of Hate Speech, Its Weaponization[46]

Generally speaking, religion-based social organizations have been accused of recruiting and training young children and youth to further 'Hindu' social ideals for decades, but related groups are more militant, advocating discrimination and sometimes violent means to achieve their purposes. In 2014, a leader of the Vishwa Hindu Parishad, a Hindu right-wing organization, gave a speech in the Indian State of Gujarat urging Hindus not to allow Muslims to buy property in "Hindu localities".[47] The speech was not well received, and was condemned by

45 *Amish Devgan*, para. 69, see *supra* note 32.

46 These instances have been analysed in greater detail in Chapter 7 below by Ms. Medha Damojipurapu.

47 Rahi Gaikwad and Vinay Kumar, "Togadia's 'Hate Speech' Video under EC Scanner", *The Hindu*, 21 April 2014.

other right-wing leaders.[48] But recent incidents have been more explicit and less apologetic. There has also been a surge of hate crimes against religious minorities accompanying the increase in hate speech.

6.5.1. Background to the Present Circumstances

Perhaps the first hate crime in the recent past was the lynching of Mohammed Akhlaq (Ikhlaq) who was murdered by a frenzied mob on the suspicion of consuming and storing cow meat in his home in the Indian State of Uttar Pradesh on 28 September 2015.[49] It is worth mentioning immediately that a cow is sacred to Hindus and is the equivalent of a 'mother' to many. In another incident of a hate crime, in June 2017 Alimuddin was lynched on the suspicion that he was transporting beef in his vehicle. The vehicle was later set on fire. A year later, in July 2018, the accused were convicted of lynching and sentenced to imprisonment for life but were granted bail by the appellate court, pending a decision on their appeal. On being released from confinement, they were garlanded with flowers by a Minister of the Government of India.[50] These are just a couple of instances of hate crimes committed by mobs on members of a religious minority in India. According to a February 2019 report by Human Rights Watch ('HRW'), at least 44 murders were committed (and many injured) between May 2015 and December 2018 in religion-based attacks.[51] Most attackers were Hindu 'cow vigilantes' who made it their business to enforce a ban on consumption, use or sale of beef.[52] This is not to suggest that incidents of lynching have occurred only in the recent past. There has been cow-related lynching since 2010, but it is estimated that 98 per cent of these incidents have taken place since 2014.[53]

The year 2014 is significant since the elections to the Indian Parliament that year resulted in the Bharatiya Janata Party ('BJP') assuming the responsibility of governance in India at the federal level. Since then, hate crimes and hate speech against minorities have been on the rise.[54] The National Crime

---

48 Rohit Bhan and Abhinav Bhatt, "Narendra Modi Raps VHP's Pravin Togadia for Alleged Hate Speech: 10 Developments", *NDTV*, 22 April 2014.

49 Aishwarya S. Iyer, "Dadri Lynching Trial Begins: How Akhlaq's Kin Waited for 5 Years", *The Quint*, 26 March 2021.

50 "Union Minister Jayant Sinha Garlands 8 Convicted for Ramgarh Mob Lynching", *India Today*, 6 July 2018.

51 "India: Vigilante 'Cow Protection' Groups Attack Minorities", *HRW*, 18 February 2019 (https://www.legal-tools.org/doc/3xy1e1/).

52 Lauren Frayer, "'This Is It. I'm Going to Die': India's Minorities Are Targeted in Lynchings", *NPR*, 21 August 2019.

53 Harsh Mander, "Lynching, the Scourge of New India", *The Hindu*, 15 October 2019.

54 Bharath Kancharla, "Data: More Than a Four-Fold Increase in the Number of Cases Registered for 'Hate Speech' Between 2015 & 2020", *Factly*, 31 December 2021; Rana Ayyub,

Records Bureau, which is the government's record-keeper, reported that incidents of communal violence increased 41 per cent in just three years from 2014–2017. The incidents were highest in States where the elected government in place was the same as at the national or federal level.[55] From individuals lynched over suspicion of carrying beef to full-scale riots, religious nationalism in India is reaching dangerous new heights and garnering international attention.[56]

6.5.2. Discrimination in Law: The Citizenship (Amendment) Act

In the more recent past, the spurt in hatred against religious minorities and rampant use of hate speech can be traced back to December 2019, when the Indian government introduced an amendment to India's citizenship law. The Citizenship (Amendment) Bill (later an Act of Parliament – the CAA) became highly contentious, leading to nation-wide protests and a historic show of popular opposition across the country to the government's policy. The government's strategy to counter these protests was seemingly based on exploiting religious fault lines, leading to deadly riots in February 2020 in the capital city of Delhi and years of imprisonment of many student activists and others.

Essentially, the CAA provides that migrants from certain religious groups – Hindus, Sikhs, Buddhists, Jains, Parsis (Zoroastrians) or Christians – from Afghanistan, Bangladesh or Pakistan who entered India before a certain date would not be treated as 'illegal migrants' even if they had not entered India lawfully, and would be eligible for citizenship despite their unlawful entry into India. Muslim migrants, similarly situated, would not be eligible for citizenship.

The CAA therefore appeared to discriminate against Muslim migrants, and gave rise to a record 144 writ petitions filed in the Supreme Court

"What a Rising Tide of Violence Against Muslims in India Says About Modi's Second Term", *Time*, 28 June 2019; Harsh Mander, "New Hate Crime Tracker in India Finds Victims are Predominantly Muslims, Perpetrators Hindus", *Scroll*, 13 November 2018; Radha Kumar, "Rising Incidents of Hate Crimes Point to the Growing Power of the Lumpen", *The Hindu*, 10 July 2019.

55 Mukesh Ranjan, "Communal Violence Cases Up 41 percent in 3 Years: NCRB", *The Tribune*, 27 July 2017.

56 Sabah Gurmat, "'India Must Pass a Law that Specifically Outlaws Genocide, and Provide for Ways to Implement that Law', says Founder of Genocide Watch, Gregory H. Stanton", *The Leaflet*, 23 January 2022; Amom M. Singh, "The BJP and the Rise of Communal Violence", *South Asian Voices*, 7 February 2022; Courtenay J. Werleman, "Rising Violence Against Muslims in India Under Modi and BJP Rule", in *Insight Turkey*, Spring 2021, vol. 23, no. 2, pp. 39–49; Sunita Viswanath, "Modi's Religious Nationalism Hurts India's Hindus, Too", *Foreign Policy*, 26 May 2021; Annie Gowen and Manas Sharma, "Rising Hate in India", *The Washington Post*, 31 October 2018.

challenging the constitutional validity of the law.[57] These petitions are still pending and the government has defended the CAA as a law to protect persecuted religious minorities in the above-mentioned three neighbouring countries comprising a Muslim majority population. The UN Office of the High Commissioner for Human Rights gave a statement calling the CAA "fundamentally discriminatory" and a law which would "undermine [...] India's obligations under the International Covenant on Civil and Political Rights and the Convention for the Elimination of Racial Discrimination".[58]

Simultaneously, the government took steps to implement a programme called the 'National Register of Citizens' ('NRC') in an attempt to create a comprehensive list of all Indian citizens. This exercise involves the verification of documents. The purpose behind the NRC, as stated by the Union Home Minister Amit Shah at a December 2019 rally, is to "expel all intruders before 2024" through a nation-wide exercise.[59]

A combination of the CAA and the NRC (though the two are not linked by legislation) has the effect of ensuring that most Hindu residents in India are included in the NRC regardless of their ability to prove citizenship or lawful entry into the country because of the CAA exemption for Hindus who may be able to trace their entry from Afghanistan, Pakistan, or Bangladesh. Simultaneously, the claim of Muslim residents to citizenship may be rejected through the bureaucratic verification process of the NRC. Muslims could then be declared illegal migrants without the protection of the CAA, and be placed in detention centres or expelled.

The NRC verification process has been conducted in Assam, and has led to reports that it is a flawed and harrowing process.[60] The Indian government has stated that 143,466 persons have been declared as foreigners as of 31 December 2021. In addition, 329 people have been deported. However, the flaws in the NRC system are clear from the fact that the names of a staggering 121,598 persons were not included in the NRC as citizens, although they have actually been declared citizens by the Foreigners Tribunals. In spite of this, the cases of as many as 123,829 persons are pending before these Tribunals as on 31 December

57 Murali Krishnan, "In 10 Points, Supreme Court Hearing on Citizenship Act Petitions Explained", *Hindustan Times*, 30 August 2020.

58 UN Office of the High Commissioner for Human Rights, "Press Briefing on India", 13 December 2019.

59 "Will Expel All Intruders Before 2024 Polls: Amit Shah Sets Nation-Wide NRC Deadline", *India Today*, 2 December 2019.

60 Sushanta Talukdar, "National Register of Citizens in Assam: Trauma of Exclusion", *Frontline*, 11 October 2019.

2021.[61] As of June 2021, it is reported that about 500 persons are incarcerated in detention centres.[62]

The passage of the CAA, and the political announcements surrounding the NRC and a related exercise called the National Population Register ('NPR'), led to widespread but peaceful protests primarily by Muslim women. One of the first such protests (and the most easily recognizable) was at Shaheen Bagh, an area in south-east Delhi, where Muslim women led the public in a peaceful sit-in protest and inspired many others across the country.

6.5.3. Hate Speech by Political Leaders and Communal Riots in Delhi

Elections to the Delhi Legislative Assembly were scheduled to be held on 8 February 2020. In the run-up to the elections, leaders of the BJP made provocative, divisive speeches and demonized anti-CAA protestors.

On 20 December 2019 in a 'peace' march in central Delhi to counter the protests, the BJP candidate Kapil Mishra shouted "*Desh ke gaddaron ko, goli maaron saalon ko*" (Shoot the bloody traitors of the nation).[63] He also posted a video of the march on social media.[64]

Mishra described Shaheen Bagh as a "mini-Pakistan", saying "Pakistani hooligans have captured the streets of Delhi".[65] A few other speeches delivered by Mishra are not available, having been taken down by Twitter apparently because of their vile content.

"Shoot the bloody traitors" became a popular slogan among the right-wing establishment, and was used at a rally by Anurag Thakur, a Minister in the Government of India. He chanted the first line of the slogan and provoked or encouraged his supporters to chant the second line. In his rather facile defence, he stated that he merely asked his supporters what should be done with traitors and they responded in the manner they did (for which he is not responsible).[66] Similarly, another legislator, Parvesh Sahib Singh Verma, gave a speech demonizing the protestors at Shaheen Bagh, claiming that they "will enter your houses,

---

61 "Assam's Foreigners Tribunals Have Declared 143,466 People as Foreigners, Says Minister", *The Economic Times*, 10 February 2022.

62 Angana P. Chatterji, Mihir Desai, Harsh Mander and Abdul K. Azad, "Detention, Criminalisation, Statelessness: The Aftermath of Assam's NRC", *The Wire*, 9 September 2021.

63 Times Now, "Tweet", *Twitter*, 21 December 2019.

64 "'Goli Maaro Saalo Ko': BJP's Kapil Mishra Posts Video of His 'Peaceful' March Supporting the CAA", *Scroll*, 21 December 2019.

65 "'Pakistan Has Entered Shaheen Bagh': BJP's Kapil Mishra Raises Political Temperature in Delhi", *Hindustan Times*, 23 January 2020.

66 Liz Matthew and Abhinav Rajput, "Minister Anurag Thakur Chants Desh Ke Gaddaron Ko, Poll Rally Crowd Completes Goli Maaro …", *The Indian Express*, 28 January 2020.

rape your sisters and daughters, kill them".[67] The Election Commission exercised its powers and ordered the removal of Thakur and Verma as star campaigners of the BJP with effect from 29 January 2020.[68]

Two days after Anurag Thakur raised the "shoot the traitors" slogan on 27 January 2020, a 17-year-old shot bullets at anti-CAA protesters and injured one university student.[69] On 1 February 2020, in a second incident, a man fired bullets in the air at the Shaheen Bagh protest site. The police were standing behind him and made little attempt to immediately restrain him. When his gun jammed, he ran away but was later caught by the police.[70]

Yati Narsinghanand Saraswati, a prominent religious leader gave a speech in Delhi on 25 December 2019 in which he stated (with reference to anti-CAA protestors),

> I am once again appealing to Hindus, today the time has come, if even today we don't stand up then we won't survive. I want to tell Hindus that this is the final battle, if you lose this battle then nothing will remain.[71]

Later in the day, he gave interviews to several channels and in one of them he said:

> These people [the anti-CAA protestors] are enemies of the country, they should be put in jail. And if they do not reform after being jailed, they should be sentenced to death.[72]

A report prepared by HRW titled 'Shoot the Traitors' examined the February 2020 riots and noted that incendiary speeches by political leaders were immediately followed by Hindu mobs gathering in parts of north-east Delhi, "armed with swords, sticks, metal pipes, and bottles filled with petrol, began chanting nationalist slogans".[73] The mobs inflicted widespread violence, "killing Muslims and burning their homes, shops, mosques, and property".[74] The HRW report notes that "Hindu mobs stopped men in the streets demanding to

---

67 Asian News International ('ANI'), "Tweet", 28 January 2020.

68 Aishwarya Paliwal, "EC Orders BJP to Remove Anurag Thakur, Parvesh Sahib from Star Campaigners List for Delhi Poll", *India Today*, 29 January 2020.

69 "Man Fires Gun at Protestors at Jamia, Shouts 'Yeh Lo Aazadi'", *The Wire*, 30 January 2020.

70 Saurabh Shukla and Deepshikha Ghosh, "Firing at Shaheen Bagh, Delhi's Second in 3 Days at an Anti-CAA Protest", *NDTV*, 1 February 2020.

71 Alishan Jafri, Shehlat M. Wani and Siddharth Varadarajan, "Just Before Delhi Riots, Militant Hindutva Leader Called Repeatedly for Muslims to be Killed", *The Wire*, 3 March 2021.

72 *Ibid.*

73 "'Shoot the Traitors': Discrimination Against Muslims Under India's New Citizenship Policy", *HRW*, 9 April 2020.

74 Hannah Ellis-Petersen, "Inside Delhi: Beaten, Lynched and Burnt Alive", *The Guardian*, 1 March 2020.

see their identity cards. If anyone refused, they were forced to show whether or not they were circumcised, as is common among Muslim men".[75] According to the official records, over 50 people were killed and over 200 injured.[76]

A political activist approached the police for registering complaints against Parvesh Verma and Anurag Thakur but was unsuccessful. The trial judge also did not find any merit in her request that a complaint should be lodged against these two persons. In appeal, the High Court of Delhi declined to intervene[77] and now the case is pending in the Supreme Court of India.[78]

6.5.4. Allegations of State Complicity in the Riots in Delhi

The police force in Delhi is controlled by the Union Government and not the State government. Therefore, although the government in place in Delhi is formed by the Aam Aadmi Party ('AAP'), a political party which does not espouse Hindu fundamentalism, the Government of India exercises control over law and order in the national capital region. Police inaction and alleged complicity in the February riots in Delhi and their unwillingness to act against Hindu mobs is quite apparent. The HRW report references contemporaneous news reports which show that "Available evidence indicates that the police often did not intervene to stop the Hindu mobs and, in some cases, encouraged them or took part in beating Muslims".[79] In one incident captured on video, police officers are seen beating five Muslim men who had been injured during a mob attack, taunting them, and ordering them to sing the national anthem. One of these men later died.[80]

Several other reputable sources have concluded that the Delhi police were complicit in perpetuating violence to target Muslims. Amnesty International produced an Investigative Briefing which observed that the speeches by political leaders were immediately followed by the riots, that the police's actions in preventing the riots were "inadequate", and in fact they actively participated in the violence. The briefing notes allege that the police's complicity extended to "the

75 "Shoot the Traitors", 9 April 2020, see *supra* note 73.

76 "It's Official: Police Says 53 Dead, 200+ Injured, 2200 Arrests in Delhi Riots", *The Wire*, 8 March 2020.

77 Sofi Ahsan, "Hate Speech Case: If Said with Smile, No Criminality, Says Delhi HC", *The Indian Express*, 26 March 2022.

78 ET Bureau, "Supreme Court Seeks Police, Govt Response on Plea for FIR Against Anurag Thakur, Parvesh Verma in Hate Speech Case", *The Economic Times*, 17 April 2023.

79 Jeffrey Gettleman, Sameer Yasir, Suhasini Raj and Hari Kumar, "How Delhi's Police Turned Against Muslims", *New York Times*, 12 March 2020.

80 "Delhi Riots: 'My Brother Died After Police Beating'", *BBC*, 3 March 2020; Imran A. Siddiqui, "Delhi Police Identifies Three Policemen Who Forced Five Muslim Youths to Sing National Anthem", *The Telegraph*, 20 August 2021.

denial of medical services to victims, failure to rescue them, excessive and arbitrary use of force on protesters and differential treatment of assemblies. The briefing then demonstrates a pattern of torture and ill-treatment meted out on riot survivors and detainees by the Delhi police after the violence, followed by the harassment and intimidation of survivors and peaceful protesters".[81]

The Delhi Minorities Commission is a statutory body intended to oversee the welfare of minority communities. Post the communal riots in Delhi, it tasked a fact-finding committee to report on the events. The committee produced a report in June 2020,[82] finding that the Delhi Police were complicit in the riots and abetted the violence. The report also noted that the riots began immediately after Kapil Mishra gave another one of his provocative "shoot the traitors" speeches.[83]

It is therefore very clear that hate speeches by political leaders in late January 2020 and early February 2020 encouraged hatred and violence against Muslims. However, the police have not initiated any criminal action against Mishra, Thakur, or other speakers whatsoever. In the midst of the riots, civil society activists moved the Delhi High Court seeking, *inter alia*, the registration of criminal cases against these persons for their hate speeches.[84] A bench of the High Court heard the case and on 26 February 2020 played four video clips in open court, which showed the speeches of Thakur, Verma, Mishra and a fourth political leader repeating the 'shoot the bloody traitors' slogan. The Delhi High Court played the clips in response to the Solicitor General of India's assertion that he had not seen any of the videos and did not have any information about the allegedly inflammatory speeches given by these leaders. The High Court directed the police officials present to review the material and take a decision on registering a criminal case against the makers of the speeches by the next day, that is 27 February 2020.[85]

In what appears to be the Union Government's complicity in protecting its own party leaders, the presiding judge who questioned the government's inaction and played the hate speech videos in open court was transferred to a different High Court through an unprecedented order issued close to midnight on

81 "Six Months Since Delhi Riots, Delhi Police Continue to Enjoy Impunity Despite Rights Violations", *Amnesty International*, 27 August 2020.

82 Delhi Minorities Commission, "Report of the Fact-Finding Committee on the North-East Delhi Riots of February 2020", 1 July 2020, p. 30 (https://www.legal-tools.org/doc/vbvghc/).

83 Aneesha Bedi and Simrin Sirur, "Delhi Police Abetted, Was Complicit in February Riots, Says Minorities Panel Probe Team", *The Print*, 16 July 2020.

84 High Court of Delhi, *Harsh Mander & Anr. v. GNCT of Delhi and Others*, Writ Petition (Criminal) No. 565/2020.

85 High Court of Delhi, *Harsh Mander & Anr. v. GNCT of Delhi and Others*, Order, 26 February 2020, Writ Petition (Criminal) No. 565/2020 (https://www.legal-tools.org/doc/y6uvv9/).

26 February 2020.[86] The case was then taken up for consideration by a Bench presided over by the Chief Justice of the Delhi High Court, who proceeded to grant the government time until 13 April 2020 to take a decision – a markedly less urgent approach, demonstrating the disinclination of the Bench towards ensuring prosecution. This prompted the petitioners to move the Supreme Court, and on 4 March 2020 the Supreme Court directed the High Court to hear the matter earlier than scheduled, on 6 March 2020, and to dispose of the petitions "as expeditiously as possible".[87] The Delhi Police defended their inaction before the Delhi High Court, stating that there was no material showing any instigation or participation by Thakur, Mishra or Verma.[88] Eventually, some parties withdrew their plea for registration of a criminal case from the High Court on 27 July 2020. However, other petitioners persisted with their pleas, which had not been heard or decided even until December 2021, forcing them to return to the Supreme Court,[89] which again requested the High Court to decide the matter "expeditiously", and "preferably within […] three months"[90] (at the time of writing the present chapter, three months have elapsed since the aforementioned order was passed and the Delhi High Court has neglected to pass any directions in the matter). Events like this have diminished respect for the constitutional courts and the judiciary in the country.

Aside from the hate speech cases, several courts have observed that the attitude of the Delhi Police towards investigating the 758 criminal cases registered with regard to the riots has been "lackadaisical" and "callous".[91] The police have been blatantly complicit in not investigating a case where police officers were filmed kicking and beating four Muslim men, in particular. The mother of a deceased man in that incident has been forced to move the High Court for an investigation into her son's death, which the Court has noted leaves much to be

86 "Centre Notifies Transfer of Justice Muralidhar From Delhi HC to P&H HC", *LiveLaw*, 26 February 2020.

87 Sanya Talwar, "'Long Adjournment Unjustified', SC Requests Delhi High Court to List Riots Cases on March 6", *LiveLaw*, 4 March 2020.

88 Karan Tripathi, "No Evidence to Indicate Role of Anurag Thakur, Kapil Mishra & Parvesh Verma in Delhi Riots: Delhi Police Tells Delhi HC", *LiveLaw*, 14 March 2020.

89 Supreme Court of India, *Mohd. Nazim and Others v. Union of India and Others*, Writ Petition (Criminal) No. 448/2021.

90 Supreme Court of India, *Mohd. Nazim and Others v. Union of India and Others*, Order, 17 December 2021, Writ Petition (Criminal) No. 448/2021 (https://www.legal-tools.org/doc/xts3h5/).

91 Nupur Thapliyal, "'Sorry State of Affairs, Lackadaisical': 10 Times When Courts Slammed Delhi Police Over Riots Probe in 2021", *LiveLaw*, 31 December 2021.

desired.[92] State resources were instead spent on filing multiple criminal cases against student leaders and anti-CAA activists, some of whom spent more than a year in jail and some of whom continue to be incarcerated.[93] Many of them have been charged under the anti-terror law – The Unlawful Activities (Prevention) Act, 1967[94] – and with the offence of sedition.

Unfortunately, hatred coupled with violence did not seem to have sufficiently moved the judiciary in Delhi at the appropriate time.[95]

6.5.5. Journalists and Hate Speech

A young Dalit lady (belonging to a 'lower caste') was brutally gang raped by young men of an upper caste in a village in the Indian State of Uttar Pradesh. She later died and her body was cremated by the police during the night and without the knowledge or consent of her family. In his capacity as a journalist, Siddique Kappan was on his way to the village to report on the story. He was arrested by the Uttar Pradesh police on 5 October 2020 before he could reach the site. He was accused of an offence under Section 295A of the IPC (deliberate and malicious acts, intended to outrage religious feelings of any class by insulting its religion or religious beliefs) and sedition. He was incarcerated for over two years, and released on bail finally in February 2023.[96] The Editors Guild of India issued a statement to the effect that it was deeply disturbed by reports of the "inhuman treatment being meted out to journalist Siddique Kappan". The Editors Guild stated that it was "shocking that the Supreme Court of India has yet not intervened in this case to ensure a fair trial of the journalist, even though the Habeas Corpus petition challenging his arrest has been pending before the court for the past six months".[97]

---

92 Nupur Thapliyal, "'Status Report Neither Here Nor There': High Court Questions Delhi Police Probing Death of Man Forced to Sing National Anthem During Delhi Riots", *LiveLaw*, 22 February 2022.

93 See, for instance, The Hindu Bureau, "SC Issues Notice to Delhi Police on Bail Plea of Umar Khalid in UAPA Case Related to 2020 Delhi Riots", *The Hindu*, 18 May 2023.

94 India, The Unlawful Activities (Prevention) Act, 1967, 30 December 1967 (https://www.legal-tools.org/doc/41175f/).

95 The author, Justice Lokur, chaired a citizens' committee to examine the causes and trajectory of the violence of the 2020 riots and analyse the role of the state, media and criminal justice system. The report of the committee is titled "Uncertain Justice: A Citizens Committee Report on the North East Delhi Violence 2020", *Constitutional Conduct Group* (available on its web site).

96 Hannah Ellis-Petersen, "Indian journalist freed on bail after being jailed for two years without trial", *The Guardian*, 2 February 2023.

97 "Treatment Meted Out to Siddique Kappan in UP 'Should Stir Nation's Conscience': Editors Guild", *Scroll*, 26 April 2021.

On 19 December 2021, Suresh Chavhanke, the editor-in-chief of a news television channel appeared at an event organized by the Hindu Yuva Vahini, a right-wing youth group, at India's capital New Delhi.[98] At the event, Chavhanke administered an 'oath' to the members of the group, which included the statement: "In order to make this country a Hindu nation and to keep it a Hindu nation, and to move forward, we will fight, die and kill, if required". The attendees at the event responded to the oath and stood with hands outstretched in a salute.

Chavhanke himself tweeted a video of the event, tagging the Chief Minister of Uttar Pradesh, Yogi Adityanath. The Hindu Yuva Vahini claims to have been founded by Adityanath. The strong connections to political leaders and the political establishment explains the impunity with which a group like this one operates, and more pointedly, the laxity on the part of the police to investigate offences allegedly committed by them. A First Information Report ('FIR') was not registered by the police despite their power to do so. It has fallen to private citizens to seek the registration of criminal cases – one complaint was filed by private citizens on 27 December 2021 and addressed to the Commissioner of Police[99]; another was filed directly before a Delhi district court judge[100] under a provision in India's criminal procedure code which allows the court to direct an investigation by the police.[101] While this is better than no case being filed at all, the lack of any urgency shown in such a serious issue is a matter of concern. The delay in the district court – the case was scheduled to be taken up for consideration on 29 March 2022 – exacerbates the harm caused by State inaction.[102]

Chavhanke is a public figure well known for his strong right-wing connections and ideology, which he disseminates through his Hindi news channel

---

98 "Suresh Chavhanke Gives Call to 'Fight, Die, Kill' to Make India a 'Hindu Rashtra'", *The Wire*, 23 December 2021; "In Delhi, Hindutva Groups Vow to 'Fight, Die & Kill' to Make India Hindu Rashtra", *The Quint*, 23 December 2021.

99 Nupur Thapliyal, "Complaint Filed Against Suresh Chavhanke Over Alleged Hate Speech Against Muslims at Hindu Yuva Vahini Event", *LiveLaw*, 28 December 2021.

100 Nupur Thapliyal, "Suresh Chavhanke's Alleged Hate Speech at 'Hindu Yuva Vahini' Event: Delhi Court to Hear Plea on January 27", *LiveLaw*, 22 January 2022.

101 India, Code of Criminal Procedure, 25 January 1974, Section 156 (https://www.legal-tools.org/doc/29b68e/):

> Police officer's power to investigate cognizable case.
> (1) Any officer in charge of a police station may, without the order of a Magistrate, investigate any cognizable case which a Court having jurisdiction over the local area within the limits of such station would have power to inquire into or try under the provisions of Chapter XIII. (2) […]. (3) Any Magistrate empowered under section 190 may order such an investigation as above-mentioned.

102 Nupur Thapliyal, "Suresh Chavhanke's Alleged Hate Speech at 'Hindu Yuva Vahini' Event: Delhi Court Seeks Action Taken Report", *LiveLaw*, 27 January 2022.

'Sudarshan News'. He has been a life-long member of the ideological mentor body of the BJP and does not pretend to be a neutral journalist, but regularly invokes press freedom as a justification for his actions. In 2013, the Ministry of Information and Broadcasting issued a notice to his channel for violating broadcasting policies and instigating violence in Muzaffarnagar, a district in Uttar Pradesh where deadly communal riots were taking place.[103] In April 2017, Chavhanke was arrested by police for promoting religious enmity in the Sambhal district of Uttar Pradesh on his channel and then following it by announcing that he would visit the district and lead a rally there.[104]

The Supreme Court has had occasion to evaluate claims that Chavhanke's channel – and indeed the programme hosted by him – promotes speech targeting the Muslim community. In August 2020, Chavhanke and the channel began to promote a series called 'UPSC Jihad'. The series alleged that the highly competitive qualifying examination to the Indian administrative services through the Union Public Service Commission ('UPSC') was biased in favour of the Muslim community, with false claims about Muslims being the beneficiaries of a higher age limit and more attempts at the examinations.[105] The entry of Muslims into the services was therefore referred to as "jihad" and "infiltration".[106]

Injunctions were sought against the broadcast on the grounds that it was an attempt to vilify Muslim students and the community at large and disturbed communal harmony. Initially, the Supreme Court was reluctant to impose 'prior restraint', that is a pre-broadcast injunction, on the basis of a clip from the promotional videos for the show. Consequently, some episodes were broadcast between 11 and 14 September 2020. This was in keeping with the judiciary's general tendency to favour the right to the media's freedom of expression, including when claims of defamation are made. After the programmes were broadcast, the petitioners were able to make detailed arguments pointing to the undoubtedly hateful nature of the programme. It was also pointed out that on social media, the shows had become a "focal point" for hate-filled comments about the Muslim community.

---

[103] Manu Balachandran, "TV Channel under Lens Over Muzaffarnagar Riots", *Business Standard*, 12 September 2013.

[104] Ashutosh Bharadwaj, "Held for 'Promoting Enmity', TV Channel Head is Proud of It", *The Indian Express*, 14 April 2017; "Sudarshan TV Channel Editor Suresh Chavhanke Arrested for Inciting Communal Hatred", *India Today*, 13 April 2017.

[105] Ayush Tiwari and Anna Priyadarshini, "Sudarshan News Claimed Its 'UPSC Jihad' Show was 'Misquoted'. It Didn't Fly With I&B Ministry", *Newslaundry*, 20 November 2020.

[106] Pooja Chaudhuri, "A List of All the False Claims Made in Sudarshan TV's 'UPSC Jihad' Show", *The Wire*, 24 September 2020.

On 15 September 2020, the Supreme Court issued an important injunction order, noting that it was apparent that:

> [t]he intent, object and purpose of the episodes which have been telecast is to vilify the Muslim community. An insidious attempt has been made to insinuate that the community is involved in a conspiracy to infiltrate the civil services. Several statements in the episodes, which have been drawn to the attention of the Court are not just palpably erroneous but have been made in wanton disregard of the truth. [...]. The drift, tenor and content of the episodes is to bring the community into public hatred and disrepute. [...]. Any attempt to vilify a religious community must be viewed with grave disfavour by this Court as the custodian of constitutional values. Its duty to enforce constitutional values demands nothing less.[107]

These statements from the Supreme Court are heartening, because of the manner in which the Court ignored the government's attempt to detract from the issue by refusing to engage with the actual facts, taking no stand against the channel, and insisting that the case was part of a broader issue regarding media regulation. Given that the 'UPSC Jihad' programme was in breach of existing broadcasting policies (in this case, the Cable and Television Networks (Regulation) Rules, 1994), the government's attempts to deflect the Court's attention clearly indicated their complete disregard for actually enforcing the law. It is also important to note that the Supreme Court made no mention of the potential of the programme to cause violence.

Both the 'UPSC Jihad' case and the *Amish Devgan* case centre on the conflict between freedom of expression and specifically, freedom of the press and hate speech. In both cases, the Supreme Court refused to shield the perpetrators of the speech from consequences under civil or criminal law. What remains to be seen is how the news media evolves in response. At present, the Supreme Court's decisions in these cases do not appear to have completely deterred news organizations from spreading falsehoods about religious communities. For example, one news channel broadcast a programme alleging that Muslims are spitting into food for sale.[108] Clearly, certain sections of the news media are unafraid of the criminal or civil consequences of their actions, or are confident that they will ultimately prevail. Chavhanke's hate speech in Delhi in December 2021 displays a determination to spread his message of Hindu supremacy and use any available platform to do so. In light of the multiple incidents of

---

[107] Supreme Court of India, *Firoz Iqbal Khan v. Union of India and Others*, Order, 15 September 2020, (2021) 2 SCC 591 (https://www.legal-tools.org/doc/0rs2yz/).

[108] Meghnad S. and Deepanjali Pal, "Bloodlust TV: Aman Chopra Spitting Hate on Minorities with His 'Thook Jihad' Show", *Newslaundry*, 18 November 2021.

this nature, Indian courts must start taking more serious note of the ecosystem in which hate speech operates, rather than focus on facts of a case isolated from context.

6.5.6. Haridwar Hate Speeches, December 2021

Between 17 and 19 December 2021, a three-day event called a '*Dharam Sansad*' (religious parliament) was held at Haridwar, a holy city for Hindus in the northern State of Uttarakhand. The '*Dharam Sansad*' served as a platform for several speeches preaching violence against the Muslim community. One of the main participants was Yati Narsinghanand, the head priest of a temple who is already accused in various criminal cases. At the event, Narsinghanand called for a "war against Muslims" and urged "Hindus to take up weapons" to ensure a "Muslim didn't become the Prime Minister in 2029".[109] He also reportedly warned the attendees about "Islamic jihad" capturing India and that Hindus need to retaliate with economic boycott and weapons. Another participant, Prabodhanand Giri, President of the Hindu Raksha Sena (Hindu Protection Army), a right-wing organization, explicitly urged Hindus to conduct a "cleansing drive" akin to that in Myanmar (referring to the Rohingyas).[110] Giri is a prominent figure and has often been photographed with senior members of the governing political dispensation including Chief Ministers of the States of Uttarakhand (where the event took place) and Uttar Pradesh (a neighbouring State). Giri told the media that he was "not ashamed" of what he had said, "not afraid" of the police and that he stood by his statement.[111] Another participant, Pooja Shakun Pandey, alias 'Sadhvi Annapurna', was urging violence against Muslims. "If you want to finish them off, then kill them [...]. We need 100 soldiers who can kill 20 lakh (two million) of them to win this." Pandey later echoed Giri's conviction that nothing wrong had been done, informing a news outlet that: "The Constitution of India is wrong. Indians should pray to Nathuram Godse [Mahatma Gandhi's assassin, a militant Hindu nationalist]. I am not afraid of the police".[112]

Videos of the speeches were widely circulated on social media soon after the event. However, despite the availability of material and admissions by the perpetrators, the police reacted slowly. Initially the police stated that no complaint had been lodged by a private person, and therefore the incident had not

[109] Avaneesh Mishra, "Haridwar Hate Speeches Target Minorities, Call for Violence; DGP Says Illegal", *The Indian Express*, 24 December 2021.

[110] "India Monks Call For 'Muslim Genocide' in Hate Speech Summit", *TRT World*, 23 December 2021.

[111] Saurabh Shukla and Deepshikha Ghosh, "Hate Speech-Givers in Haridwar Tell NDTV 'Neither Regrets Nor Fear'", *NDTV*, 23 December 2021.

[112] Saurabh Shukla and Anindita Sanyal, "After Massive Outrage Over Haridwar Hate Speeches, Case Filed, 1 Named", *NDTV*, 23 December 2021.

been registered as an offence, and the police were only "monitoring the situation" although they were aware of the videos. Later, an FIR for the registration of a criminal offence was registered on the night of 23 December 2021 under Sections 153A (promoting enmity between religious groups) and 295A (hurting religious sentiments) of the IPC. A second FIR was registered on 3 January 2022 invoking Section 295A of the IPC (deliberate and malicious acts intended to outrage religious feelings of any class by insulting its religion or religious beliefs) and in the meantime, a Special Investigation Team was also formed to investigate the incident.[113] The first arrest (of a fourth person) took place after three weeks on 14 January 2022.[114] Shockingly, Narsinghanand was not arrested until 15 January 2022 – nearly a month after the incident, and he was granted bail in less than a month, on 7 February 2022[115] although he advocated ethnic cleansing if not genocide.

The manner in which the State and the judiciary have dealt with this case illustrates the slow decline of the rule of law in India in dealing with hate speech and religious extremism.

Firstly, Narsinghanand is a known perpetrator of hate crimes and unlawful actions – he has more than 20 different criminal cases against him. In March 2021, one of his disciples brutally assaulted a 14-year-old Muslim boy who entered a temple premises to drink water.[116] He has been open about his plans to train Hindu men to fight and propagate children in order to "outnumber Muslims" and enforce Hindu hegemony.[117] The police's laxity in acting against the December speeches by such a well-known perpetrator of hate displays their negligence towards the safety and security of the Muslim community.

Secondly, the police inaction has been selective, clearly demonstrating a bias in favour of groups belonging to the majority community, and particularly those with political connections or backed by the establishment. It is not the case that the police in India are generally lax or inactive, but it is worth comparing and contrasting the response of the State in the case of Thogadia and Narsinghanand. The case of Thogadia shows that the police and the establishment have the authority and power to act preventively and prohibit a rally or gathering

[113] Avaneesh Mishra, "Second FIR filed, SIT Set up to Probe Haridwar Hate Speech Case", *The Indian Express*, 3 January 2022.

[114] "Hate Speech at 'Dharma Sansad': Uttarakhand Cops Make First Arrest", *The News Minute*, 14 January 2022.

[115] "Haridwar Dharma Sansad Case: Dasna Temple Chief Priest Yati Narsinghanand Gets Bail", *The Times of India*, 8 February 2022.

[116] Bismee Taskin, "'Mandir was Open for All Before, Now Drinking Water Also Crime': Dad of Thrashed UP Muslim Boy", *The Print*, 15 March 2021.

[117] Tenzin Zompa, "Controversial UP Priest Yati Narsinghanand is Now a Top Leader of India's Largest Akhara", *The Print*, 22 October 2021.

which is likely to breach public order. However, in the case of Narsinghanand, no action was taken against him for several days after his hate speech and the exercise of authority and power became selective.

Thirdly, judicial treatment of the case and bail granted to Narsinghanand is a case study in the problems with the grant of bail in India. For 'serious' offences under Indian criminal law, courts have a discretionary power to grant bail. Bail may be granted upon the satisfaction of several conditions, which is highly subjective. One of the problems with this discretionary system is the preponderance of judicial views from the Supreme Court and the High Courts on the factors to be considered before granting bail. District courts are usually the first to hear and decide applications for bail after arrest, and they must implement the principles laid down by the Supreme Court and High Courts. Unfortunately, the requirement to consider multiple factors – including the severity of the offence, the maximum punishment for the offence, the likelihood that the offence has been committed and may be repeated, and the likelihood that the person may be a flight risk or intimidate witnesses – leads to a situation where courts can pick and choose factors in order to arrive at differing conclusions in similar cases.

In Narsinghanand's case, the district judge chose to grant bail because the alleged offences carried a maximum sentence of just three years' imprisonment and he had not been convicted in any other case. The fact that video recordings of the incident clearly displayed his intention to incite ethnic cleansing if not genocide was entirely ignored.[118] The district court essentially followed the principle of 'bail is the rule, jail the exception', as elucidated by Supreme Court Justice Krishna Iyer in 1977.[119] This is an admirable principle and undoubtedly one that should be followed. It is also important to adhere to this principle in the Indian context where case pendency means that trials can take several years to conclude. Appropriately exercised judicial discretion for bail is therefore valuable because unjustified and malicious prosecution can lead to individuals being imprisoned for years – as is being realized under the anti-terror statute which restricts judicial discretion. But the comparatively quick grant of bail to Narsinghanand highlights the fact that the judiciary does not apply the laid down principles uniformly or fairly, especially in cases like that of journalist Siddique Kappan[120] or others where the offence is far less 'serious' in that in some cases,

---

[118] Sparsh Upadhyay, "Local Court Grants Bail to Yati Narsinghanand in Haridwar Dharam Sansad Case", *LiveLaw*, 7 February 2022.

[119] Supreme Court of India, *State of Rajasthan, Jaipur v. Balchand alias Baliay*, Judgment, 20 September 1977, (1977) 4 SCC 308 (https://www.legal-tools.org/doc/ag1jyu/).

[120] Samar Halarnkar, "The Siddique Kappan Case and the Assault on India's Constitution", *Scroll*, 2 October 2021.

the alleged offences have not even occurred – and there was no intention to commit or incite the commitment of an offence or violence whatsoever.

The eagerness of the police to clamp down on free speech and press freedom in the case of Kappan (and others), is clearly in contrast to their laxity in a few other cases. This discriminatory action or inaction emboldens right wing activists who are now unafraid of police investigations, as was freely admitted by the perpetrators of the Haridwar hate speeches. Selective and biased policing is playing a crucial role in the spread of hate speech and terror.

6.5.7. Beyond Verbal Abuse: Targeting Muslim Women

Indian law accepts that hate speech may not necessarily be a verbal manifestation – it could also be through written words or by signs or by visible representation. This is best illustrated by the hosting of an application on 4 July 2021 on the GitHub platform. The app called 'Sulli Deals' was noticed posting pictures of at least 84 Muslim women as 'deals of the day' to be 'auctioned'. The incredible trauma that a woman feels when she is put up for 'auction' is best described by one of the victims of this horror:

> The stages of not knowing, disbelief in what you are beginning to understand, waves of horror, despair, and then rage are agonisingly slow. Every emotion has a taste and feel. I remember vividly feeling foggy and I had a hard time following conversations. Things looked blurry.[121]

Some of the pictures were taken from the social media profiles of the women, who described the experience as incredibly traumatic.[122] The word 'sulli' is a derogatory slur for Muslim women, and the app appears to have been created to harass, humiliate, and degrade them, with the app generating vile comments and threats of sexual abuse on social media, with at least ten Twitter handles resharing the content.[123] Many of the women filed criminal complaints[124] and the app was taken down after its contents were publicized, but no arrests were made until the next year.

However, before any arrests were made, yet another similar but hateful application was discovered on GitHub in January 2022 called 'Bulli Bai', which also posted pictures of Muslim women, including some allegedly doctored

[121] Hana M. Khan, "The Dread of Discovering I'm on an App That Auctioned Me", *India Today*, 4 January 2022.

[122] Ivan Mehta, "GitHub Shutters Site 'Auctioning' Muslim Women for Online Abuse", *The Next Web*, 7 July 2021.

[123] Bismee Taskin, "Delhi Police File Charge Sheets in Sulli Deals & Bulli Bai Cases, Call Them 'Illegal, Inhuman'", *The Print*, 8 March 2022.

[124] "We Don't Want an FIR, We Want Arrests, Say Muslim Women Listed For 'Auction' on Bulli Bai App", *India Today*, 3 January 2022.

photographs, with threatening and abusive comments. One of the women complained that her doctored picture had been displayed "in an improper, unacceptable and clearly lewd context".[125] Five people were finally arrested in January 2022.[126]

The offensive, hate-filled content on these two applications was followed by activity on a social audio app called 'Clubhouse'. This is a live page and in a widely circulated recording, dozens of participants carried out a discussion in which derogatory and sexually explicit remarks were made about Muslim women.[127] Sexual violence against Muslim women was discussed as also body parts.[128] It appears that Hindu women who came out in support of Muslim women were also targeted in the chat.[129]

The UN Special Rapporteur on Minority Issues condemned the incidents, saying they were "a form of hate speech".[130] The Indian State appears to have agreed, as criminal cases have been registered with reference to Sections 153A (Promoting enmity between different groups on ground of religion), 153B (Imputations, assertions prejudicial to national integration) and 295A (Deliberate and malicious acts, intended to outrage religious feelings, *et cetera*) of the IPC. Other offences alleged include sexual harassment, stalking, insulting the modesty of a woman, defamation, and publishing obscene material online.[131]

The fact that the extended meaning of hate speech has been invoked is a positive sign that these incidents are recognized by the State as not just instances of sexual harassment but also of religion-based hatred. The experience shows that the underlying intent to vilify a community can be identified even when the expression may not have an overt reference or incitement to violence. It is hoped that the eventual outcome of the case will affirm that non-violent 'hate speech' is punishable under Indian law.

---

[125] "Bulli Bai App Controversy: All You Need to Know", *The Times of India*, 2 January 2022.

[126] "Delhi Police Arrests Mastermind Behind Sulli Deals App from Indore", *The Economic Times*, 8 January 2022.

[127] Jignasa Sinha, "Clubhouse Group Targeting Muslim Women: Police Zero in on 4–5 Speakers, Set to Bring Them in for Questioning", *The Indian Express*, 20 January 2022.

[128] Naomi Barton, "Clubhouse and the Fantasy of Sexual Violence Against Muslim Women", *Livewire*, 21 January 2022.

[129] *Ibid.*

[130] "UN Official Says App Targeting Muslim Women Form of Hate Speech, Must Be Condemned", *The Indian Express*, 13 January 2022.

[131] Sharmeen Hakim, "Bulli Bai App Case: Defence Argues Accused's Talent Misused by Manipulating Him; Mumbai Police Opposes Bail", *Livelaw*, 17 January 2022.

6.5.8. A New Generation of Extremists

The events pertaining to the two apps, Sulli Deals and Bulli Bai, also show that we are now dealing with a new generation of hateful extremism. The people arrested in these cases are all young, with some being just 20 or 21 years of age. At least two accused are undergraduate college students, and two have completed their education and are in their late twenties. All have multiple social media and email accounts and are well-versed in anonymous online activity. The motivations behind such hate speech are not easy to understand. Is it possible that young, educated people having access to information and opportunities are becoming radicalized? A proactive and preventive approach is necessary to combat the possibility of hate being internalized in the youth.

6.5.9. Politics and Hate Speech

In February and March 2022, elections were held to the Legislative Assemblies of five Indian States. While there have been reports of provocative speech during electioneering, two highly objectionable speeches made by candidates in Uttar Pradesh in February 2022 stand out.

Two criminal cases were registered against a sitting Member of the Legislative Assembly ('MLA'), a leader of the ruling dispensation (also a functionary of the Uttar Pradesh chapter of the Hindu Yuva Vahini). The MLA reportedly gave a speech in which he called any Hindus who did not vote for him "traitors" and having "Muslim blood", since no Muslims would vote for him.[132] He has also been recorded saying that if he is re-elected, Muslims would have to stop wearing their skullcaps and be forced to put '*tilaks*' (a Hindu religious symbol drawn on the forehead). He made several comments pitting the Hindu and Muslim communities against each other, accusing Muslim men of being goons and criminals who made it unsafe for women and children to be in public, and using a highly derogatory term for Muslim men. In the face of some outrage against his remarks, he defended them as being intended to "counter rising Islamic terrorism".[133] No action was taken against him by the political party he belongs to or the Election Commission despite his remarks being circulated on social media.

However, on 22 February 2022, the Election Commission took action against a candidate, Mayankeshwar Singh, belonging to a political party now in governance, for making hateful comments while campaigning for the assembly elections in Uttar Pradesh. In a video, Singh was seen addressing a crowd of voters during one of his campaigns saying: "If the Hindus are awakened, we will

[132] "FIR against BJP Legislator Raghvendra Pratap Singh for Objectionable Remark: Police", *The Indian Express*, 24 February 2022.

[133] "UP BJP MLA Says 'No More Skull Caps, Muslims Will Put Tilaks' if He Is Re-Elected", *The Wire*, 15 February 2022.

pull out the beards and make a chotia [a ponytail sported by Brahmin Hindus]. If you want to stay in Hindustan you will have to say "Radhe Radhe" [a Hindu chant] else, just like at the time of partition people had gone to Pakistan, you should also go".[134] He was restricted from campaigning for 24 hours. A criminal case was also registered against him under Section 298 of the IPC[135] and Section 125 of the Representation of the People Act, 1951.[136] The Election Commission said the statements made by the candidate were "utterly irresponsible and provocative that have the undertone and propensity to disturb religious harmony of society".[137]

6.5.10. No Stopping Hatred

The question that sometimes arises is whether matters have now gone beyond redemption? Two recent events of February and March 2022 may be considered. In the first incident, the State government of Karnataka issued an order on 5 February 2022 to the effect that the dress code or uniform prescribed by schools and pre-university colleges must be adhered to by students. This effectively disabled Muslim girls from wearing the *hijáb*. When this was objected to by some students, Hindu students insisted on wearing a saffron scarf, perhaps as a 'retaliatory' measure against Muslim girls and to adversely impact their dignity. The issue reached the High Court of Karnataka, which held that wearing a *hijáb* was not an essential religious practice and therefore the State could insist on strict adherence to the prescribed uniform.[138] Was this controversy at all necessary and what has been the impact on the minority community? Perhaps, it is too early to tell.

The second incident occurred in March 2022 and this is equally if not more shocking. In a particular district in the State of Karnataka, Muslim traders

---

[134] "Hate Speech by Mayankeshwar Singh, BJP MLA From Amethi", *YouTube*, 17 February 2022 (available on YouTube).

[135] IPC, Section 298, see *supra* note 2.

Uttering words, etc., with deliberate intent to wound religious feelings. —Whoever, with the deliberate intention of wounding the religious feelings of any person, utters any word or makes any sound in the hearing of that person or makes any gesture in the sight of that persons or places any object in the sight of that person, shall be punished with imprisonment of either description for a term which may extend to one year, or with fine, or with both.

[136] India, The Representation of the People Act, 17 July 1951, Section 125 (https://www.legal-tools.org/doc/f9v9qf/).

[137] "Inflammatory Speech: EC Bans BJP Candidate in UP From Giving Public Statements for 24 hours", *The Indian Express*, 22 February 2022.

[138] High Court of Karnataka, *Smt. Resham v. State of Karnataka and Ors.*, Order, 15 March 2022, Writ Petition No. 2347 of 2022 (https://www.legal-tools.org/doc/n8fjod/); "Hijab Ban: Karnataka High Court Upholds Government Order on Headscarves", *BBC*, 15 March 2022.

were not allowed to participate in a bidding process to set up stalls and shops during the five-day annual religious fair. This discriminatory treatment is due to pressure on temple authorities from Hindu right-wing groups aligned to the political party governing the State. Multiple banners and hoardings had been put up stating that "shops will be given only to Hindus".[139] It appears that the restriction is spreading to other districts in the State, with the intention of discriminating against Muslim traders and prohibiting them from setting up shops and stalls in the vicinity of Hindu temples on festive occasions.[140]

The matter has further escalated with non-Hindu women being prohibited from performing a traditional dance on festive occasions inside a temple in the State of Kerala.[141] There is also objection to the sale of *halal* meat which is being described as "Economic Jihad".[142] The list is growing.

6.6. Sedition: A Misused and Unnecessary Provision

Punishment for hate speech and hate crimes (not of a heinous nature such as lynching) is usually punishable with a maximum of three years imprisonment. This makes obtaining bail relatively easy for the accused. However, opposition to policies of the government are also treated as expressions of hate in Indian jurisprudence and individuals (particularly journalists) are targeted and accused of sedition. This offence is rather serious and, as provided in Section 124A of the IPC, it involves bringing or attempting "to bring into hatred or contempt, or excite or attempt to excite disaffection towards the Government established by law". The key word here is 'hatred'. It is, therefore, quite easy for the police to accuse a dissenting or opposing voice to make an accusation that a dissenter is committing the offence of sedition because he or she is bringing or attempting to bring the government of the day into 'hatred' by opposing a particular policy or decision. Because of the nature of the accusation and the possibility of life imprisonment on conviction, bail is not usually granted by courts in India thereby effectively punishing a person for an offence not committed.

[139] "Muslim Traders Barred from Temple Fairs: Karnataka Govt Seeks Report", *Hindustan Times*, 23 March 2022.

[140] "Karnataka Govt Defends Move by Temples to Ban Muslim Traders From Fairs", *Hindustan Times*, 24 March 2022.

[141] Rickson Oommen, "Kerala Bharatanatyam Artist Barred From Performing in Temple Over Religion", *India Today*, 28 March 2022.

[142] "Halal Food is 'Economic Jehad': BJP Gen Secy C T Ravi", *The Indian Express*, 29 March 2022; "Karnataka: BJP Leader Demands Ban on Halal Meat, Says It Is Part of 'Economic Jihad'", *The Wire*, 30 March 2022.

In *Kedarnath Singh v. State of Bihar*[143] the Supreme Court held that only acts "involving intention or tendency to create disorder, or disturbance of law and order, or incitement to violence" could be punished for sedition. The element of possible violence is embedded in the understanding of sedition. This narrowing down of the offence of sedition was necessary to protect and uphold the right of citizens to free speech in a democracy.

This was illustrated by the Supreme Court in *Balwant Singh v. State of Punjab*[144] where two men were arrested and later convicted for raising an objectionable slogan in a public place. The context of the slogan was the assassination of the then Prime Minister of India Smt. Indira Gandhi. The Supreme Court overruled their conviction, holding that:

> Raising of some lonesome slogans, a couple of times by two individuals, without anything more, did not constitute any threat to the Government of India as by law established nor could the same give rise to feelings of enmity or hatred among different communities or religious or other groups.

6.6.1. Misuse of the Sedition Law

Despite the 'reading down' of the offence of sedition through the Supreme Court's judgments in cases such as *Kedarnath Singh* and *Balwant Singh*, sedition remains a flagrantly misused law. In October 2021, three college students were arrested and accused of sedition for allegedly celebrating the Pakistan cricket team's win against India in a cricket T20 World Cup match. They spent five months in jail before being granted bail by the High Court.[145] A charge of sedition is also frequently used against journalists. Six senior journalists and a Member of Parliament faced a criminal case of sedition in January 2021 for "posting tweets and deliberately circulating fake news" about the death of a farmer during the farmers' protests in Delhi.[146]

Since 2010 as many as 867 cases of sedition have been filed against more than 13,000 Indians. Since 2018 as many as 40 journalists have been accused of

---

[143] Supreme Court of India, *Kedar Nath Singh v. State of Bihar*, Judgment, 20 January 1962, Criminal Appeal No. 169/1957, AIR 1962 SC 955 (https://www.legal-tools.org/doc/yw74ig/).

[144] Supreme Court of India, *Balwant Singh and Others v. State of Punjab*, Judgment, 1 March 1995, Criminal Appeal No. 266/1985, (1995) 3 SCC 214 (https://www.legal-tools.org/doc/vk17yt/).

[145] "Kashmir Men Spend Over 100 Days in Jail for Cheering Pakistan Win", *Al Jazeera*, 16 February 2022; "After 5 months, Allahabad HC Bail to Kashmiri Students Charged with Sedition For 'Celebrating Pakistan's T20 win'", *The Times of India*, 31 March 2022.

[146] "Sedition in India: Colonial Legacy, Misuse and Effect on Free Speech", *Economic and Political Weekly ('EPW') Engage*, 17 February 2021.

sedition for reporting about, among other things, Covid-19, a gang rape and murder, the CAA and for being critical of the government.[147]

The misuse of the sedition law is so blatant that the Chief Justice of India questioned the Indian government on the necessity of sedition remaining on the statute books.[148] Several petitions have been filed at the Supreme Court challenging the constitutional validity of the section.[149] In its response to these cases in May 2022, the government indicated that it had "decided to re-examine and re-consider" the law. In light of the government's stand, the Supreme Court took the unusual step of ordering that it would be "appropriate" to discontinue the usage of the sedition law until the government's re-examination exercise was completed.[150] The order has the effect of disapproving of the registration of fresh criminal cases for the offence of sedition, and keeping all pending proceedings "in abeyance" with respect to sedition.

It is worth noting that the language of the Court's May 2022 order is somewhat less definite than an ordinary stay of operation of the law. The order states that the court "hope[s] and expect[s] that […] Governments will restrain from registering any FIR, continuing any investigation or taking any coercive measures" with respect to sedition. It seems to accept the possibility that cases will still be filed, providing that in case any "fresh case" is registered, parties will be permitted to "approach the concerned Courts for appropriate relief" (which does not provide any new relief to parties but merely affirms their existing right to seek legal remedy) and that in such a situation, the courts should "examine the reliefs sought" in light of the government's stand and the Court's order. This language falls short of a clear stay order which would prevent the registration of any new sedition case and, in the event a fresh case was filed, would result in the automatic abeyance of such a case. At the time of writing, the case is still pending, with the government claiming to be at an advanced stage of the re-examination process.[151] Until a formal repeal or invalidation of the law, it is important for us to contend with its impact on free speech.

---

147 "A Decade of Darkness: The Story of Sedition in India", *Article 14* (available on its web site).

148 "Colonial-era Sedition Law Misused Often, Why Don't You Scrap It, SC asks Centre", *Firstpost*, 15 July 2021.

149 "Constitutionality of Sedition: SG Vombatkere v. Union of India", *Supreme Court Observer* (available on its web site).

150 Supreme Court of India, *S.G. Vombatkere v. Union of India*, Order, 11 May 2022, Writ Petition (Civil) No. 682/2021 (https://www.legal-tools.org/doc/et0fpr/).

151 Supreme Court of India, *S.G. Vombatkere v. Union of India*, Order, 1 May 2023, Writ Petition (Civil) No. 682/2021 (https://www.legal-tools.org/doc/qnjryb/).

6.6.2. Distinction Between Sedition and Free Speech

In August 2018, the Law Commission released a Consultation Paper ('Consultation Paper') to study the "pros and cons" of sedition.[152] The Consultation Paper affirms the right to free speech and raises questions about the "relevance of [sedition] in an independent and democratic nation". It was also noted that the United Kingdom abolished the offence of sedition in 2009.[153]

In the Consultation Paper, the Law Commission noted that sedition is an offence against the State and not against an individual. Therefore, it is subject to higher standards of proof for conviction, which is necessary to "protect fair and reasonable criticisms and dissenting opinions from unwarranted State suppression. Legitimate speech must be protected and care must be taken that the grounds of limitation are reasonable and just".[154]

The above-mentioned observation in the Consultation Paper identifies the distinction between hate speech and sedition law, when approached from the point of view of potential for abuse. Hate speech is classified as an offence against public tranquillity in the IPC but is essentially an offence against an individual or a group of individuals, as distinct from the State. The targets of hate speech cannot unilaterally misuse or abuse the law to suppress free speech simply by alleging that it is hate speech. Therefore, the existence of anti-hate speech laws does not pose any large-scale threat to free speech.

On the other hand, the State is the potential target of seditious speech, and is also capable of employing the law whenever it finds it necessary. All governments have an inherent interest in minimizing criticism and opposition. This leads to the reasonable conclusion that there is a greater likelihood of the misuse of sedition laws, which pose a more significant threat to free speech. Therefore, a higher standard of proof and higher degree of harm is reasonable in accusations of sedition.

The distinction between sedition and hate speech is sometimes blurred by courts when they are dealing with broad issues of freedom of speech and expression. The Supreme Court has included sedition within its discussion in both *Pravasi Bhalai Sangathan* and *Amish Devgan*, even though the questions before the Court pertained only to hate speech. In *Amish Devgan* the Court reiterated that the expression of opinions on political issues should not be construed as

[152] Law Commission, "Consultation Paper on Sedition", 30 August 2018 (https://www.legal-tools.org/doc/dx3aom/).

[153] Clare Feikert-Ahalt, "Sedition in England: The Abolition of a Law From a Bygone Era", *LOC Blogs*, 2 October 2012 (available on the Library of Congress' web site).

[154] Consultation Paper, para. 7.3, *see supra* note 152.

sedition. However, the Supreme Court emphasized that violence or a possibility of violence is necessary for the prosecution of sedition.

Discussing sedition and hate speech in the same decision could confuse, and be potentially problematic for, courts dealing with cases of only hate speech. As discussed previously, violence is not a necessary ingredient of hate speech. It should also not be artificially imported into hate speech jurisprudence. Broadening the concept of hate speech to include dynamic forms of derogatory speech and behaviour is now necessary to protect the equality and dignity of all. This is urgently required, because the overview of just a few recent incidents of hate speech demonstrates the grave situation facing us today.

6.7. Conclusion

Constitutionally guaranteed free speech in India is at a crossroads. It must be appreciated that hate speech can never be protected, whether it is direct or inferential, whether it is verbal or non-verbal. Therefore, a clear definition of hate speech is necessary. While it is true that it may eventually be difficult to have a precise definition of hate speech, a beginning is necessary. Time, it is said, is a great healer and the gradual passage of time can also bring about a balance in the definition that may be needed for a clearer understanding of the distinction between free speech and hate speech.

The Supreme Court of India has accepted the content, intent and impact or harm as a working module for defining hate speech. This must be carried forward, although the authors believe that the 'impact or harm' factor as understood by the Supreme Court is narrow. Hate speech need not result in violence or a possibility of violence. Hate speech can disturb the mental equilibrium of any person who is targeted and this can manifest itself in psychosocial problems and trauma. These are not visible manifestations of the impact or harm caused by hate speech but are nevertheless quite real and must be recognized.

In this context, it would be worth exploring the possibility of introducing the theory of absolute liability to criminalize hate speech. The Supreme Court has observed that hate speech has no redeeming or legitimate purpose other than hatred towards a particular group (or an individual). If that be so, with the introduction of absolute liability, the likelihood of possibility of harm or an adverse impact on a group or a person loses its relevance. As long as the content test and the intent test are met, it might be possible to successfully prosecute the maker of hate speech.

Hate speech in India is resulting in polarization and divisiveness. In the absence of any clear understanding on what constitutes hate speech, the police are virtually having a free hand on whom to prosecute and to let off. This also puts the courts in a quandary, especially in matters relating to the grant of discretionary bail. Unless hate speech is checked immediately, its impact will be long-term and dangerous to society and perhaps the country itself. It is time for the executive arm of the government as well as the political governance structures to display sagacity and shout out that enough is enough and put a stop to recurring incidents of hate speech, both verbal as well as non-verbal.

The judiciary too should be alive to the consequence of hate speech not being punished suitably and in time. It is often said that 'delay defeats justice'. But what is more problematic with delay in punishing hate speech is not that justice is denied, but that freedoms in a free society get compromised or corroded to the detriment of targeted individuals, groups or communities. The Supreme Court appears to have taken notice of the urgency of policing hate speech. In a petition seeking redress against the proliferation of hate speech, the Court in October 2022 directed three state police forces to take immediate action to register cases against any incidents of hate speech in their jurisdictions, "even if no complaint is forthcoming".[155] The Court extended its order to all states in April 2023.[156] It remains to be seen, however, whether state authorities use this order to prosecute genuine cases of hate speech.

No democracy can afford to have sections of society lose these freedoms and allow hate to take over. Therefore, the time is ripe for India to introspect and take the lead – and the time starts now.

---

155 Supreme Court of India, *Shaheen Abdulla v. Union of India and Others*, Order, 21 October 2022, Writ Petition (Civil) No. 940/2022 (https://www.legal-tools.org/doc/ogaw3i/).

156 Supreme Court of India, *Shaheen Abdulla v. Union of India and Others*, Order, 28 April 2023, Writ Petition (Civil) No. 940/2022.

7

Patterns and Risks in Contemporary Religion-Based Hate Speech in India

Medha Damojipurapu*

7.1. Introduction

The present chapter aims to delineate, through concrete examples, the nature of hate speech, hateful expression and violence, directed against Muslims in the name of Hinduism in India. The purpose of this chapter is to provide a factual basis to assess the true threat posed by hateful utterances (such as incitement to violence, discrimination or genocide) against minority Muslims in India. While doing so, the chapter also attempts to identify overarching themes in the language that constitutes contemporary hate speech against Muslims and provides some reflections on the historical and cultural contexts within which certain stereotypical notions of Indian Muslims developed and which form the basis of much of the hate-filled rhetoric against them today. For the purposes of this chapter, the author has confined her analysis to hate speech that has been employed against Muslims in India since 2014, with particular focus on incidents that have transpired since 2020, during the second term of the Bharatiya Janata Party's ('BJP') rule in India.

Hateful utterances and violence against members of the Muslim community in India have been growing rapidly over the recent past, and more so with the development of social media and online modes of transmitting hate speech, which allow the perpetrators to remain anonymous while still having a wide reach in terms of audience and accessibility.

Certain stages in India's history marked the development of ideology that forms the basis of the content of contemporary hate rhetoric against Muslims. The delineation of definite religious identities in India during British colonial

---

* **Medha Damojipurapu** is a CILRAP Fellow and an Advocate enrolled with the Bar Council of India. She holds a B.A., LL.B. (Hons.) degree from NALSAR University of Law, Hyderabad, India. She has previously worked as a Law Clerk-cum-Research Assistant to late Justice Mohan M. Shantanagoudar at the Supreme Court of India. An earlier version of this chapter was published as Medha Damojipurapu, "Language and Connotation in Contemporary Hate Speech in India", Occasional Paper Series No. 11 (2022), Torkel Opsahl Academic EPublisher, Brussels, 2022. The chapter originates from the author's presentation at the Florence conference addressing "Language and Connotation in Contemporary Hate Speech in India", CILRAP Film, 8 April 2022, Florence (https://www.cilrap.org/cilrap-film/220408-damojipurapu/).

rule, the 'divide and rule' policy adopted by the British and the rise of Hindu nationalism were some of the developments that exacerbated the purported distinctiveness between the Hindu and Muslim communities in India, that were hitherto less pronounced or non-existent.

It is alarming to note that in recent times hate rhetoric has triggered large-scale, systematic violence against Muslims in the country. Coupled with impunity from law enforcement authorities and apathy from elected representatives, the result is that India is increasingly becoming a politico-religiously-charged environment in which Muslim minorities fear for their safety and are often targeted, demonized and ostracized.

This chapter seeks to contribute to the discourse on hate speech, hateful expression and violence against Indian Muslims. It is the modest hope of the author that the knowledge generated through this chapter will eventually inform attempts to find tools to encourage members of religious communities to refrain from engaging in vocalization and transmission of hate speech in the name of their faiths.

7.2. Historical and Cultural Connotations of Language Used

An analysis of the language used in contemporary hate rhetoric against Muslims in the name of Hinduism in India reveals certain underlying themes. In an attempt to break down and understand such hate rhetoric, this author has sought to analyse the significance and origin of its underlying themes.

7.2.1. Historical Context

Hinduism is an amorphous religion. The term 'Hinduism' was first used by foreigners to refer to what they *perceived* as the indigenous religion of India.[1] The use of the terms 'Hindu' and 'Hinduism' to denote the indigenous religion of India is, therefore, a recent development and one that has been conferred on Hindus externally. As renowned historian Romila Thapar has pointed out, the first use of the term 'Hindu' is as a *geographical* nomenclature.[2] The term 'Hindu' originally was the Indo-Aryan word for 'river', and, as a proper noun, it referred to the great river on the north-west of the subcontinent, that is, the Indus River, also known as the Sindh River (which now lies in the territory of Pakistan). The term 'Hindu' therefore was used to refer to the inhabitants of the lands beyond the Indus.

It is important to note that in pre-modern times in India, various religious sects co-existed, each having its own unique deity, rituals and practices,

1 Shashi Tharoor, *Why I Am a Hindu*, Aleph Book Company, 2018, p. 4.

2 Romila Thapar, *The Past as Present: Forging Contemporary Identities Through History*, Aleph Book Company, 2014, p. 119.

scriptures, *et cetera*. Hinduism as it is called in contemporary parlance comprised of these numerous religious sects, rather than being a formal, singular religion.[3] Caste formed the basic unit of organization of Indian society and, in turn, shaped and structured religion. Therefore, the term 'Hinduism' used by the British was an umbrella term which subsumed the multiplicity of beliefs, practices and doctrines that had evolved over time. Foreigners were often confounded by Hinduism, especially since unlike other world religions,

> the evolution of Hinduism is not a linear progression from a founder through an organizational system, with sects branching off. It is rather the mosaic of distinct cults, deities, sects and ideas and the adjusting, juxtaposing, or distancing of these to existing ones, the placement drawing not only on belief and ideas but also on the socio-economic reality.[4]

On the other hand, religions such as Islám, Christianity, Buddhism and Jainism base their evolution on interpretations of the original teachings of the religion and draw some strength from the structure of an ecclesiastical organization. However, Hindu sects had a distinct and independent origin. The belief systems of each sect were distinct as well. The religion did not conform to "a shared creed, catechism, theology, and ecclesiastical organization".[5] In fact, Hinduism is devoid of any rigid dogmas, a singular sacred text or a single holy religious site or religious temple.

The early interactions between the people of India and those associated with Islám was through various avenues, such as in the form of traders, *Ṣúfí* and Indian mystics, and attachments to conquerors. Such association predates the invasion by Muslim rulers later on:

> For a long while in India, they were referred to by the same terms as were used in earlier times for people from west and central Asia, suggesting that their coming was viewed in part as a historical continuity. And there are good historical grounds to explain such a continuity. The coming of the Europeans and the colonisation of India by Britain, was an altogether different experience. They came from distant lands, were physically different, spoke languages which were entirely alien and in which there had been no prior communication; their rituals, religion and customs were alien; their exploitation of land and labour exceeded that of the previous period; and above all they did not settle in India. The assumption that the west Asian and central Asian interventions after the eighth

3 *Ibid.*, pp. 138–140.

4 Romila Thapar, "Imagined Religious Communities? Ancient History and the Modern Search for a Hindu Identity", in *Modern Asian Studies*, 1989, vol. 23, no. 2, p. 216.

5 *Ibid.*, p. 218.

> century A.D. and that of the British were equally foreign to India, in origin and intent, would, from the historical perspective, be difficult to defend.[6]

Early followers of Islám who arrived in India were confounded that the Indian society at the time lacked the concept of conversion, as one was regarded as being born into one's caste.[7]

Today, Indian Hindus and Muslims are viewed as two distinct communities – a view that has often been projected back into the past.[8] There are differing accounts as to whether strong religious identities existed in pre-colonial times or if they were crystallized during British rule in India.[9] Further, there is also disagreement as to whether communal antipathy between these two groups was a result of British colonialism in India, which adopted the cynical policy of 'divide and rule', or whether such rivalry existed prior to British colonization of India.[10] Regardless, the division of the Indian population into discrete religious communities formed a part of the British colonial strategy.[11]

7.2.2. The Increasing Prominence of Concrete Religious Identities During the British Colonial Period

The 'First War of Independence' or the 'Revolt of 1857' ('Revolt') was an uprising against the rule of the British East India Company, which functioned as a sovereign power in India, on behalf of the British Crown. The Revolt was sparked by the use of new cartridges by the British army for the Enfield rifle, which Hindus and Muslims believed were greased with pig and cow fat (pigs are considered unclean by Muslims and Hindus consider cows to be holy animals). Loading the cartridge required tearing it open with one's mouth, which offended the religious sentiments of both Muslims and Hindus and sparked the rebellion. As a result of the rebellion, the East India Company's rule over India came to an end and thereafter, the British Crown assumed direct authority over India.

---

6 Romila Thapar, "The Tyranny of Labels", in *Social Scientist*, 1996, vol. 24, nos. 9–10, pp. 5–6.

7 Thapar, 1989, p. 223, see *supra* note 4.

8 Cynthia Talbot, "Inscribing the Other, Inscribing the Self: Hindu-Muslim Identities in Pre-Colonial India", in *Comparative Studies in Society and History*, 1995, vol. 37, no. 4, pp. 692–722.

9 Zaheer Babur, "Religious Nationalism, Violence and the Hindutva Movement in India", in *Dialectical Anthropology*, 2000, vol. 25, no. 1, pp. 61–76.

10 Frederic M. Bennett, "Muslim and Hindu: The Sensitive Areas", *The Atlantic*, February 1958; Ajay Verghese, "Did Hindu-Muslim Conflicts in India Really Start with British Rule?", *Scroll*, 5 June 2018.

11 Babur, 2000, p. 64, see *supra* note 9.

The end of the East India Company's rule heralded a transformation in the British policy in India.[12] The British gave up its annexationist approach and instead focused on appeasing Indian princes to secure their loyalty to the British Crown. The British feared that if any feelings of community and unity developed among the various castes and creeds of India, British rule could be under serious jeopardy.[13] Several administrative strategies were put in place by the British which, in effect, categorized people and produced a particular set of political identities in India. For example, a religious dimension to the census was brought in by the British in 1871 and the categories of 'Hindu' and 'Muslim' were created, notwithstanding the fact that in pre-colonial times, identities in India "were multiple and not fixed".[14]

The introduction of English as the official language of India and as the medium of higher education also had a significant impact on shaping identity and politics in colonial India. Hindus more readily took to Western education and learning, whereas Muslims, particularly the elite, rejected British ideas and teachings and instead sought to look inwards and revive Islám. Further, the British attitude towards Muslims also had a hand to play in keeping Muslims away from modern education. The British believed that Muslims were more responsible for the Revolt than Hindus and questioned the former's loyalty to the British Crown. They favoured the recruitment of Hindus to the administrative services and the fact that a far larger number of Hindus had knowledge of Western education than Muslims was an added bonus.[15]

Therefore, although the Revolt was unsuccessful, it marked a turning point in the British attitude towards India and set the stage for the delineation of concrete religious identities.

7.2.3. The Rise of Hindu Nationalism in India

Christian missionaries, established on an increased scale in India after 1813, undertook education and proselytizing activities. Several reforms to Hinduism were also undertaken by the British administration such as abolition of certain Hindu customs. In response to these perceived threats, several high-caste Hindus attempted to reform their religion in order to "adapt to Western modernity while preserving the core of Hindu tradition, which they defined mainly in

12 Neil Stewart, "Divide and Rule: British Policy in Indian History", in *Science & Society*, 1951, vol. 15, no. 1, pp. 49–57.

13 *Ibid.*

14 P.P. Abdul Razak, "Census Modality and The Making of Muslim Community of Malabar", in *Proceedings of the Indian History Congress*, 2008, vol. 69, pp. 771–780.

15 Ranbir Vohra, *The Making of India: A Political History*, Routledge, 2013, pp. 99–103.

Brahmanical terms".[16] The Arya Samaj was one such organization founded in 1875, by Dayanand Sarasvati, which sought to preserve the social order and culture of Hindus while adapting the traditions to take account of the Western society. The Arya Samaj was opposed to certain aspects of the Hindu religion such as the caste system and idolatry. However, the movement was averse to Christian proselytization and English-Western and Muslim influence over language, culture and education. The genesis of Hindu nationalism was derived from such socio-religious reform movements.[17]

Hindu nationalist groups such as the Hindu Mahasabha (earlier known as the Sarvadeshak Hindu Sabha) emerged in the early twentieth century, when India found herself under the oppressive rule of predominantly the British but also the French and the Dutch, to counter what they viewed as "a growing Muslim menace".[18] The Hindu Sabha was formed by local Arya Samajists in Punjab. In 1906, the All-India Muslim League was formed. At this juncture, the British were anxious to appease the minority Muslims and garner their support and thus granted them several concessions, such as the setting up of separate electorates in 1909 (the Indian Councils Act, 1909, commonly referred to as the 'Morley-Minto Reforms', provided for separate electorates with seats reserved for Muslims). This kind of discrimination aroused feelings of vulnerability and an inferiority complex in some Hindus.[19] It was in this backdrop that the Hindu Mahasabha was formed in 1915. It was "conceived as an articulation of Hindu assertiveness and strength in reaction to Muslim communitarian organization, presented to Muslim organizations a living proof and justification of their program of separate constituencies".[20]

The Hindu nationalist ideology marked the first attempts to organize and mobilize Hindus as a unified group. The ideology of Hindu nationalism was first codified in 1922, when Vinayak Damodar Savarkar, a leading figure of the Hindu Mahasabha, published his polemic titled 'Hindutva: Who is a Hindu?', which "perfectly illustrates the mechanisms of Hindu nationalist-identity building through the stigmatisation and emulation of 'threatening Others'".[21]

---

[16] Christophe Jaffrelot, *The Hindu Nationalist Movement in India*, Columbia University Press, New York, 1998, p. 14.

[17] *Ibid.*, p. 11.

[18] Manu Bhagavan, "Princely States and the Hindu Imaginary: Exploring the Cartography of Hindu Nationalism in Colonial India", in *The Journal of Asian Studies*, 2008, vol. 67, no. 3, p. 884.

[19] Jaffrelot, 1998, p. 18, see *supra* note 16.

[20] Thomas Blom Hansen, *The Saffron Wave: Democracy and Hindu Nationalism in Modern India*, Princeton University Press, Princeton, New Jersey, 1999, p. 77.

[21] Jaffrelot, 1998, p. 25, see *supra* note 16.

A few years later, Keshav Baliram Hedgewar established the Rashtriya Swayamsevak Sangh ('RSS', the ideological counterpart of the present-day ruling political party in India, that is, the BJP). The RSS and the Hindu Mahasabha were sister organizations and stood at the forefront of the Hindu nationalist movement. Another prominent leader of the RSS, Madhavrao Sadashivrao Golwalkar (the protégé of Hedgewar), also espoused some of the ideas that form the basis of contemporary hate speech against Muslims in India. Understanding Savarkar's work and Golwalkar's ideas in the early stages of development of Hindu nationalism is important to understanding the kind of rhetoric that is currently used in hateful utterances against Muslims in the name of Hinduism-Hindutva.

7.3. Themes in Contemporary Hate Speech

7.3.1. 'Othering' of Muslims and the Need to Unite Hindus in the Fight Against a Common Enemy

The Hindu nationalist ideology was formed in response to what were perceived as the 'threatening Others'.[22] The idea of the Muslim 'other', that is now reverberant in right-wing Hindu rhetoric aimed at attacking Indian Muslims, can be traced back to Savarkar's conceptualization of India as a Hindu land – he called Muslims and Christians "foreign invaders" of India:

> Hindutva took to the extreme – or, some would say, to its inevitable conclusion – the liberal idea of primordial "nations" (communities with essential, indivisible master identities) tied strictly to pieces of land, and therefore it was concerned with regenerating an "ancient," "pure" race by fulfilling its destiny – that is, by reclaiming the race's rightful homeland and purging it of all "impure" peoples. In this context, Savarkar called Muslims and Christians foreign invaders of a Hindu India. The relationship with Nazism and fascism apparent in this worldview is more than coincidental, as Savarkar and his colleagues were open admirers of Adolf Hitler.[23]

The central presumption of Savarkar was that the Aryans who he believed to have settled in India at the dawn of time formed a nation now embodied in the Hindus. Savarkar's way of defining Hindus was focused not so much on religious homogeneity (which was rather impossible given the complex religious differentiation within Hindu society), but was based on three common characteristics – geographical unity, racial features and a common culture. Savarkar espoused that Hindus were descendants of Aryans, who allegedly first

22 *Ibid.*, p. 81.

23 Bhagvan, 2008, p. 885, see *supra* note 18.

settled on the banks of the river Indus (a theory that is not supported by historical studies).[24] Savarkar defined a Hindu as:

> a person who regards this Land of Bharat Varsha, from the Indus to the Seas as his Fatherland as well as his Holy Land, that is, the cradle land of his religion.[25]

Thus, this definition not only sought to consolidate Hindu identity, but also to alienate Muslims and other non-Hindus. A Hindu was one who could identify India as both his Holy Land and his Fatherland, whereas those who followed religions of non-Indian origin had to seek another identity. He explained that:

> Hindudom is bound and marked out as a people and a nation by themselves not by the only tie of a common Holyland in which their religion took birth but by the ties of a common culture, a common language, a common history and essentially of a common fatherland as well. It is these two constituents taken together that constitute our Hindutva and distinguish us from any other people in the world. That is why the Japanese and the Chinese, for example, do not and cannot regard themselves as fully identified with the Hindus. Both of them regard our Hindusthan as their Holyland, the land which was the cradle of their religion, but they do not and cannot look upon Hindusthan as their fatherland too. They are our co-religionists; but are not and cannot be our countrymen too. We Hindus are not only co-religionists, but even countrymen of each other.[26]

According to Savarkar, the term 'Hindu' referred to all those people whose religions were born out of the soil of India – as a result, Buddhists, Jains, Sikhs and people belonging to the various Hindu sects would all fall under the umbrella of a 'Hindu'. This definition seemed to exclude those religious groups – Christians and Muslims – which could potentially pose a political or cultural threat to Hindus. Christians and Muslims were viewed as having "extraterritorial loyalties", and since their "holy lands" was outside India, they could not be considered Hindus.[27]

Golwalkar's views are best described in the following terms by renowned historian Ramachandra Guha:

> Golwalkar saw three principal threats to the formation of a Hindu nation – Muslims, Christians and communists. All three were

[24] Jaffrelot, 1998, pp. 26–28, see *supra* note 16.

[25] Amalendu Misra, "Savarkar and the Discourse on Islam in Pre-Independent India", in *Journal of Asian History*, 1999, vol. 33, no. 2, p. 149.

[26] Vinayak D. Savarkar, *Hindu Rashtra Darshan*, 1949, p. 5.

[27] Hansen, 1999, p. 79, see *supra* note 20.

> foreign in origin, and the last were godless to boot. Golwalkar saw Muslims, Christians and communists as akin to the demons, or rakshasas, of Indian mythology, with the Hindus as the avenging angels who would slay them and thus restore the goodness and purity of the Motherland. The RSS itself was projected by Golwalkar as the chosen vehicle for this national and civilizational renewal of the Hindus.[28]

In the 1930s, the RSS professed admiration for the policies of the National Socialists of Germany. Parallels can be drawn between the Nazi ideals and Golwalkar's ideas, such as the love for the mystical Motherland (that is, India). Golwalkar espoused a "(blood and soil) kind of nationalism", according to which only Hindus were true lovers of the nation and could restore it to its former glory.[29]

From Golwalkar's speeches, it is evident that he harboured and propounded the belief that today underlies the idea behind anti-conversion laws, *love jihád* and *ghar wapsi* (reconversion programmes) being carried out in India. In his conception, Christians and Muslims are not indigenous to India, but have been converted to Christianity and Islám and hence have no love or reverence for India:

> They are born in this land, no doubt. But are they true to its salt? Are they grateful towards this land which has brought them up? Do they feel that they are the children of this land and its tradition and that to serve it is their great good fortune? Do they feel it a duty to serve her? No! Together with the change in their faith, gone are the spirit of love and devotion for the nation.
>
> Nor does it end there. They have also developed a feeling of identification with the enemies of this land. They look to foreign lands as their holy places. They call themselves 'Sheikhs' and 'Syeds'. Sheikhs and Syeds are certain clans in Arabia. How then did these people come to feel that they are their descendants? That is because they have cut off all their ancestral national moorings of this land and mentally merged themselves with the aggressors. They still think that they have come here only to conquer and to establish their kingdoms. So we see that it is not merely a case of change of faith, but a change even in national identity. What else is it, if not treason, to join the camp of the enemy leaving their mother-nation in the lurch?

28 Ramachandra Guha, "The Hindu Supremacist: M.S. Golwalkar", in *The Makers of Modern India*, Penguin India, 2012, p. 371.

29 *Ibid.*, p. 372.

> Everybody knows that only a handful of Muslims came here as enemies and invaders. So also only a few foreign Christian missionaries came here. Now the Muslims and Christians have grown in number. They did not grow just by multiplication as in the case of fishes. They converted the local population. We can trace our ancestry to a common source, from where one portion was taken away from the Hindu fold and became Muslim and another became Christian. The rest could not be converted and they have remained as Hindus.[30]

The Hindu right-wing's purported paranoia over the alleged conspiracy of Muslims to outnumber Hindus and overtake India by creating a Muslim majority can also be traced back to Golwalkar's speeches. He accused Muslims of pursuing an aggressive strategy in two respects – one was to achieve, through direct aggression, the creation of the state of Pakistan, carved out of the motherland of Hindus. The second, he said, was to:

> increase their numbers in strategic areas of our country. After Kashmir, Assam is their next target. They have been systematically flooding Assam, Tripura and the rest of Bengal since long. It is not because, as some would like us to believe, East Pakistan is in the grip of a famine that people are coming away into Assam and West Bengal. The Pakistani Muslims have been infiltrating into Assam for the past fifteen years.[31]

From the above analysis, it is apparent that historical developments, particularly the rise of Hindu nationalism and the Hindutva ideology, form the bedrock of contemporary hate rhetoric through which religious intolerance and hatred is spread and minority communities are ostracized.

7.3.2. Excessive Use of the Term '*Jihád*'

Contemporary hate speech against Muslims in India has seen the evolution of several terms or labels, suffixed by the term '*jihád*'. *Jihád* is used loosely and often in hate speech against Muslims in India. It is therefore important to analyse the meaning of this term as well as its modern-day usage.

Jihád is regarded as one of the central duties of a Muslim, however, there is ambiguity as to what this duty precisely entails. The West, and more particularly Americans, have often misconstrued *jihád* to mean 'holy war'. However, a more accurate translation of the word in Arabic is to 'struggle' and the importance of the term is rooted in the Qur'án's command to 'struggle or exert' oneself in the path of God. The concept encompasses not only external struggle

---

[30] Madhav S. Golwalkar, *Bunch of Thoughts*, Vikrama Prakashan, Bangalore, 1966, Part II, Chapter XI, Section "Call to Shake Off Slavery".

[31] *Ibid.*

against enemies of Islám and idolaters (external *jihád* or lesser *jihád*), but also a struggle for self-improvement (internal *jihád* or greater *jihád*). In certain situations, it could also include physically standing up against oppressors in the absence of any alternatives.[32] However, *jihád* does not preclude the possibility for non-violent resolution of issues.[33]

Thus, *jihád* may refer to warfare engaged against non-Muslims but it may also refer to non-violent struggle in the cause of God. The use of military force constitutes only one dimension of *jihád*.[34] Scholars have noted that the Qur'án is ambivalent in its attitude towards warfare – while some passages clearly condemn warfare against the weak and declare that believers should only fight in self-defence, some passages appear to provide justification for warfare against non-believers. The meaning of *jihád* has evolved over time, depending on the historical predicaments faced by the Muslim community – it unfolded from a pacifist character, to defensive, and thereafter to a belligerent form in order to eliminate idolatry and other immoral practices, as also to spread the influence of Islám.[35] The conflicting verses of the Qur'án and the lack of a central religious authority (the Caliph) make it difficult to delineate the contours of military *jihád*.[36]

Modern day Islámist movements across the world appear to defend militant *jihád* as their religious duty.[37] Such movements usually fall within the ambit of Islámist fringe groups and terrorist organizations who have often adopted the term *jihád* in order to frame their cause and used religious philosophies to justify their actions.[38] As a consequence of the use of the term *jihád* in the context of military warfare, the understanding of *jihád* as a religiously sanctioned armed struggle became popular.[39] In the second half of the twentieth century, several political ideologies developed which based their notions on Islám and over time:

> the concept of jihad has been used and misused; used by resistance and liberation movements and hijacked and misused by extremist and terrorist organizations to legitimate, recruit, and motivate their

32 Brian Handwerk, "What Does 'Jihad' Really Mean to Muslims?", *National Geographic*, 24 October 2003.

33 *Ibid.*

34 Onder Bakircioglu, "A Socio-Legal Analysis of the Concept of Jihad", in *The International and Comparative Law Quarterly*, 2010, vol. 59, no. 2, p. 423.

35 *Ibid.*, p. 433.

36 Bakircioglu, 2010, p. 438, see *supra* note 34.

37 Madeeha Bajwa, "Reconciling Approaches to Terrorism, Militant 'Jihad' and Human Rights", in *Strategic Studies*, 2005, vol. 25, no. 2, pp. 142–168.

38 Handwerk, 24 October 2003, see *supra* note 32.

39 Sebastian Kusserow and Patryk Pawlak, "Understanding Jihad and Jihadism", *European Parliamentary Research Service* ('EPRS'), May 2015 (available on the EPRS' web site).

> followers. The trajectory of jihadist movements has moved from a national to a transnational or global agenda.[40]

In the aftermath of the 11 September 2001 terror attacks in the United States, Western media tended to conflate the distinction between terrorists, Muslims and Arabs. Moreover, Western media is alleged to have played a role in "creating the illusion that all Muslims are radical fundamentalists".[41] The obsession with using the term *jihád* in hate speech rhetoric against Muslims in India appears to be a combination of three factors: (i) the Hindu right-wing's need to identify a common enemy against which the Hindu masses could be mobilized and their unity strengthened – this was done through their propaganda of 'othering' Muslims and depicting them as foreign to the territory of India and a threat to the safety and existence of Hindus; (ii) the use of the term *jihád* by radical Islámic outfits to describe and justify their militant methods, which can be traced back to the second half of the twentieth century; and (iii) the portrayal of all Muslims as terrorists by the Western media in the aftermath of the 11 September 2001 terror attacks.

This obsession with *jihád* is evident in the use of the term to denote alleged terrorist activity or conspiracy on the part of Indian Muslims. Through this chapter, we notice that hate rhetoric in India delineates several modes of so-called *jihád* – *land jihád*, *love jihád*, *corona jihád*, *thook jihád*, *civil services jihád* and *redi jihád* are examples of terminology developed by Hindu extremists to describe alleged conspiracies being carried out by Muslims against Hindus in India. While *thook jihád* and *corona jihád* are explained in more detail in the next section of this chapter, the other terms are worth elucidating here.

Land jihád. In the context of Legislative Assembly elections in Assam (27 March 2021–6 April 2021), a state in the north-eastern region of India which allegedly has a long history of illegal immigration from neighbouring countries such as Bangladesh, the BJP's election manifesto introduced the concept of '*land jihád*'. *Land jihád* is the allegation that there is an underground conspiracy among Indian Muslims to acquire land across the country, especially in areas that are predominantly Hindu-populated, as a means to "take over the country".[42] There have been claims of *land jihád* involving Muslims in the states of

[40] John L. Esposito, "Islam and Political Violence", in *Religions*, 2015, vol. 6, pp. 1067–1081.

[41] Brendon Tagg, "Jihad, Race and Western Media, Post-September 11", in *Societies Without Borders*, 2009, vol. 4, no. 3, pp. 317–342.

[42] Alishan Jafri, "Is Uttarakhand Government's 'Demographic' Probe of Property Deals a Play on 'Land Jihad' Bogey?", *The Wire*, 5 December 2021.

Rajasthan and Uttarakhand as well.[43] Assam BJP President Swapnaneel Baruah is quoted as saying that:

> Land jihad is a way to force people sell off their lands — it happens anywhere where there are *miyas* (Bengali-origin Muslims in Assam). Cases have been reported from Sorbhog, Dhubri and border immigrant-majority areas.
>
> They corner the land owner, making the land uninhabitable, sometimes by stealing cattle and throwing chopped heads of cattle into courtyards. Ultimately, the owner is forced to sell the land. A third party comes into play and an offer is made to the owner for purchase of the land. A broker gets involved, and the land is captured.[44]

Civil services jihád. On 11 September 2020, an Indian news channel, Sudarshan News, broadcasted a show on "Muslim infiltration" in the Union Public Service Commission ('UPSC') examination, in which it alleged that Muslim aspirants are favoured in the exams by virtue of the provision of several benefits to the exclusion of Hindu aspirants.[45] Sudarshan News also claimed that there was a sudden increase in the number of Muslims who were clearing the UPSC exams.[46] While the Supreme Court of India initially refused to issue a pre-broadcast interlocutory injunction against the airing of the show on the basis of an unverified transcript of a promotional clip, after a few episodes of the show were broadcast, the Supreme Court interdicted any further telecast, noting that there had been a "change of circumstances" and that *prima facie* it appeared that the intent, object and purpose of the episodes which were telecast was to "vilify the Muslim community". The Supreme Court also noted that "[a]n insidious attempt has been made to insinuate that the community is involved in a conspiracy to infiltrate the civil services".[47] The matter is currently *sub-judice*.

Redi jihád. On 18 June 2021, a Muslim fruit vendor was allegedly brutally beaten up in Uttam Nagar, New Delhi by men chanting "*Jai Shree Ram*" (Glory to Lord Rama). Two days later, Hindutva activists allegedly blocked a main road in the area to protest against what they claimed to be violence and encroachment

---

[43] "Now, BJP MLA Claims There is 'Land Jihad' in Rajasthan Town", *The Indian Express*, 18 September 2021.

[44] Karishma Hasnat, "What Is 'Land Jihad', and Why BJP Has Promised a Law Against It in Assam Election Manifesto", *The Print*, 26 March 2021.

[45] Pooja Chaudhuri, "A List of All the False Claims Made in Sudarshan TV's 'UPSC Jihad' Show", *The Wire*, 24 September 2020.

[46] "'UPSC Jihad': Sudarshan News Head Claims 'Sudden' Increase in Muslims Clearing Civil Services Exams", *Scroll*, 27 August 2020.

[47] Supreme Court of India, *Firoz Iqbal Khan v. Union of India and Others*, Order, 15 September 2020, (2021) 2 SCC 591 (https://www.legal-tools.org/doc/0rs2yz/).

by *jihádi* fruit vendors. Anti-Muslim slogans were chanted and the activists also allegedly recited the *Hanuman Chalisa* (which is a hymn devoted to Hanuman, a Hindu god).[48]

Thus, the usage of the term *jihád* has now become commonplace in hate speech against Muslims, in order to connote alleged conspiracies by Muslims in various forms which pose, in the eyes of right-wing Hindus, a legitimate threat to Hindu interests in India.

It is interesting to note that Hindu right-wing groups have often projected Hinduism as an inherently non-violent religion. However, violence was often accepted as necessary in "certain worldly contexts, especially in the presence of forces which challenged the dharmic order".[49]

7.4. Language Used

7.4.1. Protests Against the Citizenship (Amendment) Act and the National Register of Citizens

The pogrom in Delhi that occurred between 23–27 February 2020 took place in the backdrop of widespread protests against the passage of the Indian Citizenship (Amendment) Act, 2019 ('CAA'). The CAA was enacted by the Indian Parliament on 11 December 2019. To understand the climate prior to the Delhi pogrom, it is important to trace the incendiary speeches and remarks that were being made from the very beginning of anti-CAA protests in December 2019.

The CAA proposes to provide a pathway to Indian citizenship for illegal immigrants fleeing religious persecution from Pakistan, Bangladesh and Afghanistan. Under the CAA, Hindus, Buddhists, Jains, Christians, Parsis and Sikhs who had migrated to India from the aforementioned three countries prior to 2014 will no longer be considered illegal immigrants and can more readily obtain Indian citizenship through naturalization.[50] The new law effectively amends India's Citizenship Act, 1955, which requires an applicant to have resided in India for 11 years in order to be eligible for citizenship. The CAA relaxes the requirement to five years. The CAA conspicuously excludes Muslims from the groups that can claim this concession and the reason cited is that Muslims do not comprise a religious minority in the above-mentioned three countries. However, the choice of these countries, in particular when Muslims are facing persecution in neighbouring countries such as Myanmar and Sri Lanka,

---

48 Alishan Jafri, "The 'Hindutva Ecosystem' Has a New Anti-Muslim Narrative: This Time the Street Vendors are the Target", *The Wire*, 28 June 2021.

49 Ankur Barua, "Encountering Violence in Hindu Universes: Situating the Other on Vedic Horizons", in *Journal of Religion and Violence*, 2017, vol. 5, no. 1, pp. 49–78.

50 India, The Citizenship (Amendment) Act, 2019, 12 December 2019 (https://www.legal-tools.org/doc/6tus7j/).

prima facie would seem to be otherwise motivated. A law that seeks to create different routes for seeking citizenship on the basis of religion or country of origin is inherently discriminatory:

> Parallels have already been drawn with Nazi laws and policies that resulted in the holocaust and genocide of millions in the 1930s and 1940s in German-occupied Europe. The exclusion of Muslim refugees has particularly been a point of denunciation of the new law, especially in a context where Muslims of diverse sects and ethnicities have been subjected to persecution and genocide not just in Sri Lanka, China, and Myanmar but even in Muslim majority nations of Afghanistan, Bangladesh, and Pakistan. The supporters of the law, especially from the government, have frequently (and wrongly) cited these latter set of countries as safe havens for the persecuted Muslims from the region.[51]

Demonstrations also ensued in the north-eastern states of India "against the possibility of floodgates getting opened for non-Muslim Hindu refugees who have already settled in these areas over several decades, but especially after the 1947 partition and the 1971 Bangladesh Liberation War".[52] The massive protests were fuelled by anxiety over an influx of settlers, with an imagined potential to cause economic, political and social marginalization and stress on resources brought on by the anticipated demographic change facilitated by the CAA.[53] The people of Assam view the CAA as a unilateral violation of the Assam Accord. The Assam Accord, signed by the Government of India, the Government of Assam, the All-Assam Students' Union and the All Assam Gana Sangram Parishad in 1985, was agreed upon to tackle the issue of illegal immigrants in Assam. The Assam Accord declared that a resident of Assam is an Indian citizen if he or she could prove his presence, or an ancestor's presence, in Assam prior to 25 March 1971.[54] As a result of the CAA, the cut-off date of 1971 set by the Assam Accord for the acceptance of illegal immigrants would be rendered ineffective and Assam would have to accept several hundred thousand 'illegal' immigrants who entered the country between 1971 and 2014.[55]

---

51 D. Parthasarathy, "Citizenship (Amendment) Act: The Pitfalls of Homogenising Identities in Resistance Narratives", in *Economic & Political Weekly*, 2020, vol. 55, no. 25.

52 *Ibid.*

53 Manavi Kapur, "India's New Citizenship Act and National Register of Citizens are Both Inspired by "paranoia"", *Quartz India*, 16 December 2019.

54 "Explained: What CAA+NRC Means to You", *The Indian Express*, 25 December 2019.

55 Chandan Kumar Sarma and Obja Borah Hazarika, "Anti-CAA Protests and State Response in Assam: Identity Issues Challenge Hindutva-Based Politics", in *Economic & Political Weekly*, 2020, vol. 55, no. 14.

Residents from this region are also concerned about the National Register of Citizens ('NRC'), which is proposed to be a comprehensive list of all Indian citizens. The verification process for the NRC has been conducted in Assam and reports suggest that approximately four million people were excluded from the NRC due to lack of proper documentation.[56] Although a large number of persons who were excluded were Hindus, the effect of the CAA would protect them from deportation, while Muslims would not be extended the same benefit.

The potential consequences of the CAA and the NRC together on Muslims is best explained in legal terms as follows:

> The implications are clear: if the government goes ahead with its plan of implementing a nation-wide National Register of Citizens, then those who find themselves excluded from it will be divided into two categories: (predominantly) Muslims, who will now be deemed illegal migrants, and all others, who would have been deemed illegal migrants, but are now immunised by the Citizenship Amendment Bill, if they can show that their country of origin is Afghanistan, Bangladesh or Pakistan.[57]

The combined effect of the CAA and NRC together created panic among Indian Muslims that should they be subject to exclusion from the NRC (due to lack of documentation to prove citizenship or ancestry), they would be rendered 'illegal immigrants' and the CAA's discriminatory provisions would preclude the possibility of obtaining Indian citizenship thereafter.

Protests against the CAA and NRC ensued from mid-December 2019 onwards in various places across the country. Police forces, particularly in Delhi, employed excessive force to quell protests, which were largely peaceful, and entered university campuses of Jamia Millia Islamia University ('Jamia') in Delhi and Aligarh Muslim University in Uttar Pradesh (both prominent Muslim educational institutions) and subjected students protesting against the CAA to beating and violence using batons and tear gas and caused the destruction of campus property.[58] Union Home Minister Amit Shah, on 26 December 2019, accused the Aam Aadmi Party ('AAP'), the ruling party in the National Capital Region of Delhi, of creating confusion over the CAA, stating that "it's time to

---

[56] Angana P. Chatterji, Mihir Desai, Harsh Mander and Abdul Kalam Azad, "Detention, Criminalisation, Statelessness: The Aftermath of Assam's NRC", *The Wire*, 9 September 2021.

[57] Gautam Bhatia, "A Bill that Undercuts Key Constitutional Values", *The Hindu*, 7 October 2019.

[58] Sidharth Ravi, "Video of Police Brutality in Jamia Milia Islamia Library Goes Viral", *The Hindu*, 16 February 2020; "60 AMU Students Injured in Police Violence, University Closed Till January 5", *The Wire*, 16 December 2019.

teach Delhi's tukde-tukde gang a lesson and the people should do it".[59] By '*tukde* gang', he meant a gang that wants to divide the country.

Following the police crackdown at Jamia, protests against the CAA gained momentum. Several students from Jawaharlal Nehru University ('JNU') and Delhi University protested outside the Police Headquarters in the Income Tax Office area in Delhi that same night. Students from universities across the country soon followed suit.

The Shaheen Bagh protest in Delhi was a peaceful sit-in protest started by a group of women on 15 December 2019 which continued for 101 days until 24 March 2020, when the Shaheen Bagh site was cleared by the police in light of the lockdown imposed due to the Covid-19 pandemic.[60] In conjunction with the incendiary and hateful speeches made by leaders of political parties and Hindu right-wing organizations, there were attempts to intimidate and harm anti-CAA protestors in Delhi – on 30 January 2020, one Rambhakt Gopal fired his gun at protesters at the gates of Jamia, injuring a student. On 1 February 2020, one Kapil Gujar fired two bullets at the Shaheen Bagh protest site; however, no one was injured.[61] Despite being surrounded by policemen, Gopal managed to spend approximately two minutes brandishing his pistol before firing it, without any resistance from the police, highlighting the breakdown of law and order in the country and complicity of police officials.[62]

In response to the country-wide protests against the CAA, several members of the BJP and other right-wing organizations made inflammatory speeches against the protestors and threatened them with dire consequences for speaking out against the CAA. At a pro-CAA rally, a local BJP Member of the Legislative Assembly ('MLA'), Somashekar Reddy, from Bellari district of Karnataka, warned that:

> It's just a caution for those who are protesting against the CAA (Citizenship Amendment Act). We are 80 per cent and you (Muslims) are 18 per cent. Imagine what will happen if we take charge [...]. Beware of the majority when you live in this country. This is our country. If you want to live here, you will have to, like the Australian Prime Minister said, follow the country's traditions [...]. So, I warn you that CAA and NRC are made by Modi and Amit

59 "People in Delhi Must Teach 'Tukde-Tukde' Gang a Lesson: Amit Shah", *The Quint*, 26 December 2019.

60 "Shaheen Bagh's 101-Day Protest: Timeline of Sit-In Against CAA", *The Indian Express*, 24 March 2020.

61 Somya Lakhani, "Delhi: Two Days After Jamia, Firing in Shaheen Bagh as Well", *The Indian Express*, 2 February 2020.

62 Deepshikha Ghosh, "As Teen Pulls Gun at Jamia, Police Watch, Don't Rush into Action", *NDTV*, 30 January 2020.

> Shah. If you will go against these acts, it won't be good […]. If you wish, you can go to Pakistan. We don't have any issues. Intentionally, we would not send you […]. If you will act as enemies, we should also react like enemies.[63]

As evidenced above, the atmosphere in Delhi and other parts of India was already communally charged in the backdrop of anti- and pro-CAA protests. The situation in Delhi was further exacerbated by the prospect of the upcoming Delhi elections.

7.4.2. Delhi Legislative Assembly Elections of 2020

Just as protests against the CAA gained momentum in many parts of the country, political parties began gearing up and campaigning for the Delhi Legislative Assembly elections, which were scheduled to be held on 8 February 2020. Several speeches with communal and Islámophobic overtones were made in the lead up to the Delhi elections. There was fraught rivalry between the two large political parties vying to take over the Delhi government – the AAP and the BJP.

The violence that took place in Delhi in February 2020 was preceded by mobilization of Hindutva groups spewing hatred against those protesting the passage of the CAA.[64] Attempts were made to cast the Shaheen Bagh protests in a negative light. Election rallies were used as a battleground to augment anti-Muslim sentiments, with the agenda of stoking communal tensions in the hopes of securing more votes.

The Election Commission of India asked Twitter to take down a tweet posted by Kapil Mishra, BJP member and former MLA, on 23 January 2020, in which he likened the upcoming Delhi elections to an India versus Pakistan cricket match[65] and claimed that India and Pakistan (a metaphor for Hindus and Muslims respectively) will fight on the streets of Delhi. In another tweet, he termed sites where protests against the CAA were taking place as "mini-Pakistans":

> Aam Aadmi Party and Congress have created mini-Pakistans like Shaheen Bagh. In response, Hindustan will face them on February 8. Whenever the anti-nationals create a Pakistan in India, the nationalists' Hindustan will face them.[66]

---

63 "BJP MLA 'Warns' Anti-CAA Protesters, Says 'We Are 80% and You Just 17%'", *India TV*, 4 January 2020.

64 Sagar, "Delhi Violence Unmasked: Part One", *The Caravan*, 1 March 2021.

65 "Delhi Elections: India vs Pakistan Match on February 8, Tweets BJP Leader Kapil Mishra", *Scroll*, 23 January 2020.

66 *Ibid.*

Such statements were clearly intended to imply that the 'enemy' was Pakistan – that is, anyone who did not support the BJP was a supporter of India's ultimate enemy, Pakistan.

On 27 January 2020, during a Delhi election rally, BJP Union Minister of State for Finance Anurag Thakur was caught on camera leading a crowd of BJP supporters who chanted "*goli maro saalon ko*" (shoot the traitors) in response to his shouts "*Desh ke gaddaron ko*" (traitors of the nation).[67] To put it simply, a Union Minister asked an entire crowd of people gathered at an election rally to shoot at 'traitors'. While he did not make any overt references to Muslims, he was evidently referring to anti-CAA protestors, who were predominantly Indian Muslims. The slogan "shoot the traitors" caught on and was thereafter used frequently against anti-CAA protestors across the country.[68]

Shortly thereafter, BJP Member of Parliament ('MP') Parvesh Varma stated that the voters in Delhi must carefully choose which government they wanted to elect to power:

> Arvind Kejriwal says I am with Shaheen Bagh, the deputy Chief minister Manish Sisodia says I am with Shaheen Bagh. The people of Delhi know the fire that once broke out in Kashmir, where the sisters and daughters of Kashmiri Pandits were raped […]. The same fire broke out in Uttar Pradesh, in Hyderabad, in Kerala, now the same fire has broken out in a corner of Delhi. Lakhs of people gather there [Shaheen Bagh]. The people of Delhi will have to carefully and thoughtfully make a decision. These people will enter your homes, they will pick up your sisters and daughters and rape and kill them. Today there is time. Tomorrow Modi ji won't come to save you, Amit Shah won't come to save you. The people of Delhi are safe only till Modi ji is the prime minister of India.[69]

Here, a reference was made to the violence against Kashmiri Pandits (Hindus) during the height of the insurgency in the territory of Indian-administered Kashmir or the erstwhile state of Jammu and Kashmir in the 1990s, suggesting that the same perpetrators were behind the protests at Shaheen Bagh. A

---

67 "Order Regarding Removal of Sh. Anurag Thakur and Sh. Parvesh Sahib Singh from the List of Star Campaigners of BJP", *Election Commission of India*, 29 January 2020; Aishwarya Paliwal, "EC Orders BJP to remove Anurag Thakur, Parvesh Sahib from Star Campaigners List for Delhi Poll", *India Today*, 29 January 2020; "Anurag Thakur Leads Crowd to Chant 'Shoot the Traitors'", *The Wire*, 27 January 2020.

68 "Watch: 'Goli maaro saalon ko' Slogans Repeated at Pro-Citizenship Act Rally in Nagpur", *Scroll*, 22 December 2019; Rohit Khanna, "After Delhi, 'Goli maaro...' Slogans Now in Kolkata", *Times of India*, 2 March 2020; "BJP MLA Abhay Verma Leads East Delhi March with 'Goli maaro saalo ko' as Mob Violence Continues", *Scroll*, 26 February 2020.

69 "Shaheen Bagh Protestors will 'Rape Your Sisters and Daughters', says BJP MP on Women-Led Protest", *Scroll*, 28 January 2020.

peaceful, democratic protest against a discriminatory law made by the Indian Parliament was likened to an insurgency that was carried out by terrorist outfits in Jammu and Kashmir.

On 28 January 2020, in another election campaign conducted by the BJP in Ranhoula village in west Delhi, Parvesh Varma publicly expressed his opposition to anti-CAA protestors and promised to clear Shaheen Bagh of protestors and to demolish all mosques in his constituency if the BJP came to power.[70] In light of the outrage sparked by these videos and the complaints filed against those making incendiary speeches, the Election Commission of India ordered the BJP to remove Thakur and Varma from their list of star campaigners.[71]

On 29 January 2020, Mr. Tarun Chug, National Secretary of the BJP, referring to the Shaheen Bagh protestors (predominantly Muslim women), who had blocked a main road connecting south-east Delhi to Noida, tweeted that:

> We will not let Delhi become Syria and allow them to run an ISIS-like module here, where women and kids are used. They are trying to create fear in the minds of people of Delhi by blocking the main route. We will not let this happen. (We will not let Delhi burn). #ShaheenBaghKaSach.[72]

On 2 February 2020, Mr. Ajay Bisht (popularly known as Yogi Adityanath), the Chief Minister of the Indian state of Uttar Pradesh ('U.P.'), addressed two election rallies in Delhi where he attacked BJP's opponent and AAP leader Arvind Kejriwal, accusing him of "feeding biryani" (a traditional Muslim delicacy) to the protestors at Shaheen Bagh and causing anarchy and unrest instead of working for the development of the people of Delhi:

> (Arvind) Kejriwal and his mandali (group) are trying to fan unrest and anarchy by tacitly supporting the Shaheen Bagh protests. These protests are nothing but a way for some section of people to show their objections against the scrapping of Article 370 and the construction of Lord Ram's grand temple in Ayodhya.[73]

Yogi Adityanath was indirectly attacking Indian Muslims, including Kashmiris, who have been protesting against the Indian Government's action of scrapping Article 370 of the Constitution of India of 1950 ('Indian Constitution')

---

70 "'Will Remove Shaheen Bagh Protestors, Mosques on State Land': West Delhi BJP MP Parvesh Verma's Poll Promise", *Firstpost*, 28 January 2020.

71 "ECI Orders Removal of Anurag Thakur, Parvesh Verma from BJP Star Campaigners List", *The Hindu*, 29 January 2020.

72 "Won't Allow Delhi to Become Syria, says BJP Leader Tarun Chugh on Shaheen Bagh Protest", *National Herald*, 30 January 2020.

73 Neelam Pandey and Regina Mihindukulasuriya, "Shaheen Bagh, Biryani, Bullets, Pakistan – What Yogi Adityanath said at Delhi Rallies", *The Print*, 2 February 2020.

(which provided Jammu and Kashmir with special autonomous status) and the Supreme Court's verdict in *M. Siddiq (D) Through Lrs. v. Mahant Suresh Das and others*[74] (commonly known as the *Ayodhya* verdict), through which the Court unanimously allowed the construction of a temple by Hindus on the disputed land in question, which Hindus claim to be the birthplace of the Hindu god Lord Rama, while Muslims, who claim to have been worshipping at the site for centuries, were directed to be allotted a separate piece of land. Yogi Adityanath exhorted the people to elect a BJP government in Delhi, which would promote all religions but warned that where "boli" (words) doesn't work, "goli" (bullets) would.[75]

On 5 February 2020, Tejasvi Surya, BJP MP, made Islámophobic statements against the Shaheen Bagh protests:

> What is extremely disappointing, what is extremely troubling is that the opposition of this country, knowing fully well that these legislations, especially the citizenship amendment act, have nothing whatsoever to do with taking citizenship away from anyone, has gone around the country indulging in a campaign of lies, campaign of slander, misguiding the people of this country [...] what is happening today in Shaheen Bagh in Delhi is a stark reminder that if the majority of this country is not vigilant, if the patriotic Indians do not stand up to this, the days of Mughal Raj coming back and revisiting Delhi is not very far away. Sir, what is happening in Shaheen Bagh is fanatic Islamism, masquerading in the garb of constitutional secularism. Sir, and therefore we must exercise vigilance to ensure that this country is on the path to true secularism.[76]

The rhetoric employed in likening the election campaign to a contest between Hindus and Muslims foreshadowed the targeted violence against Muslims that would follow later that month.

7.4.3. The Delhi Pogrom

Communal violence erupted in Maujpur in north-east Delhi on 23 February 2020 between a Hindu mob and protestors opposing the CAA, which marked the beginning of three days of communal violence. It soon spread to other parts

74 Supreme Court of India, *M. Siddiq (D) Through Lrs. v. Mahant Suresh Das and Others,* Judgement, 9 November 2019, (2020) 1 SCC 1 (https://www.legal-tools.org/doc/7lrgi2/).

75 Neelam Pandey and Regina Mihindukulasuriya, "Shaheen Bagh, Biryani, Bullets, Pakistan – What Yogi Adityanath said at Delhi Rallies", *The Print*, 2 February 2020.

76 "'Mughal Raj Not Far Away If…': BJP's Tejaswi Surya on Anti-CAA Protestors", *NDTV*, 5 February 2020.

of the city.[77] The pogrom resulted in 53 deaths (the majority of them Muslims), approximately 250 injured and around 2,000 displaced.[78] On the night prior, a group of local Muslim women protesting the CAA had caused a blockade ('*chakka jam*') on the Jafrabad-Maujpur road in Delhi. In the morning of 23 February 2020, Anupam Pandey, a ward-level president in BJP's Delhi unit, berated the nation's Hindu population in a Facebook post for not rising up against anti-CAA protestors:

> Sit in your homes till they block roads to our homes. Shame on 100 crore people![79]

Through a series of Facebook posts over the rest of the morning, he exhorted his "Hindu brothers" to gather at Maujpur square in as large a number as possible.

Throughout the day, he posted live streams of himself and his party colleagues gathering at Maujpur square. Videos show a gathering of a large number of members from the BJP's several wings, such as the Kisan Morcha (farmer's wing) and the Bharatiya Janta Yuva Morcha (BJP's youth wing) chanting slogans such as "*Hindu Ekta Zindabad*" (Hail Hindu Unity) and "*Jai Shree Ram*" (Glory to Lord Rama).[80] Later that evening, Akash Verma, a district executive in BJP's youth wing, also started a live stream on his Facebook account from Maujpur, where the crowd is seen using communal slurs and abuses to refer to Muslims, such as "mullah" or "katua". Calls were made encouraging Modi to beat the protestors ("Modiji, *tum latth bajao*") and for the traitors to be shot ("*Desh ke gaddaron ko, goli maaro saalo ko*").[81]

The important takeaway from these videos and live streams is that the Hindu mob that gathered at Maujpur did not do so spontaneously, rather it had been mobilized by Hindu extremists by using the rhetoric of Hindu unity and the need to protect themselves and defend the country against CAA protestors, thus inciting them to commit violence.

On 23 February 2020, Kapil Mishra took out a pro-CAA protest rally in Jaffrabad, New Delhi, less than a kilometre away from the sit-in protest being

77 "Delhi Violence Unmasked: Part One", 1 March 2021, see *supra* note 64.

78 Aiman Khan and Ishita Chakrabarty, "Why the 2020 Violence in Delhi Was a Pogrom", *Al Jazeera*, 24 February 2021.

79 "Delhi Violence Unmasked: Part One", 1 March 2021, see *supra* note 64. A crore is equal to 10 million.

80 *Ibid.*

81 Sagar, "Delhi Violence Unmasked: Part Two", *The Caravan*, 1 March 2021.

led by Muslim women against the CAA.[82] He urged people through Twitter to gather at the location and "prevent another Shaheen Bagh" protest from taking place. He also issued an ultimatum through a tweet to the Delhi police to clear the roads of anti-CAA protestors.[83] He addressed the rally (in the presence of the Deputy Commissioner of Police for north-east Delhi Ved Prakash Surya):

> This is what they wanted. This is why they blocked the roads. That's why a riot-like situation has been created. From our side not a single stone has been pelted. DCP is standing beside us. On behalf of all of you, I am saying that till the time [US President] Trump goes back [from India], we are going to go forward peacefully. But after that, we will not listen to the Police if roads are not cleared after three days. By the time Trump goes, we request the Police to clear out Jafrabad and Chaand Bagh. After that, we will have to come on the roads. Bharat mataki jai! Vande Mataram![84]

Within hours of Kapil Mishra's speech, violence broke out in several parts of north-east Delhi.[85] His incendiary speeches are widely regarded as being the trigger for the violence and bloodshed that ensued in Delhi from 23 to 27 February 2020.[86] Over the course of these days, Muslims were subject to targeted, organized and systematic violence. Mobs comprising anywhere between 100–1,000 persons attacked Muslim individuals, shops, houses, mosques, vehicles and other property, chanting slogans like "*Jai Shree Ram*" (Glory to Lord Rama), "*Modiji, kaat do in Mullon ko*" (Modi, cut these Muslims into pieces), "*Aaj tumhe Azadi denge*" (Today, we will give you freedom).[87] As per the Delhi Minorities Commission's Fact-Finding Report on Delhi Riots 2020, the violence was not spontaneous but appeared to have been carefully planned, evidenced by the fact that perpetrators positioned themselves strategically in residential areas, they came armed with lathis, iron rods, tear gas cylinders, *et cetera*, and specifically targeted people on the basis of their faith (that is, being Muslim), whereas Muslims were not armed with weapons and only engaged in violence in self-

[82] Delhi Minorities Commission, "Report of the Fact-Finding Committee on the North-East Delhi Riots of February 2020", p. 30 ('Delhi Minorities Commission, "Fact-Finding Committee Report 2020"') (https://www.legal-tools.org/doc/vbvghc/).

[83] "BJP's Kapil Mishra Has Issued an 'Ultimatum' to the Delhi Police. But Who Is He?", *The Wire*, 24 February 2020.

[84] "Won't Listen After 3 Days: Kapil Mishra's Ultimatum to Delhi Police to Vacate Jafrabad Roads", *India Today*, 23 February 2020; "Kapil Mishra Among These 4 Videos Delhi High Court Made Police Watch on Hate Speeches by Politicians", *YouTube*, 27 February 2020 (available on *YouTube*).

[85] Delhi Minorities Commission, "Fact-Finding Report 2020", p. 33, see *supra* note 82.

[86] *Ibid.*, p. 99.

[87] *Ibid.*, p. 100.

defence.[88] Mobs vandalized Islámic religious symbols such as copies of the Qur'án as well as plundered mosques and madrasas, while leaving places of worship of other religions (in the same area) untouched.[89]

Police complacence and complicity in repeated instances of communal violence in India is evidenced by the fact that in several instances communal violence was triggered by the utterance of hateful expressions in public with impunity in the presence of senior police officials. Police officials routinely ignored complaints against BJP leaders and others engaged in leading and luring mobs to commit violence in Delhi.[90]

On 11 March 2020, a 'Group of Intellectuals and Academicians' – which is purported to be a forum for socially-committed professional women but, in fact, appears to be a bogus, pro-government group, created to support and lend public legitimacy to the activities of the Modi government and the RSS – submitted a so-called a fact-finding report on the Delhi pogrom to the Union Home Minister, Amit Shah. The report alleged that:

> The Delhi riots are not genocide or a pogrom targeted at any community. They are a tragic outcome of a planned and systematic radicalization of the minorities by a far left-Urban Naxal network operating in universities in Delhi. Both communities have suffered greatly as a consequence. The presence of Jihadi organizations like Popular Front of India (PFI) at dharna sites has been observed.[91]

The report further alleged that the riots were caused not because of a pogrom targeted at any particular community but by the "systematic radicalization of the minorities by a far left-Urban-Naxal network operating in universities in Delhi".[92] The report claimed that there was evidence of a "Urban-Naxal-Jihadi network that planned and executed the riots".

On 29 May 2020, another such report titled 'Delhi Riots: Conspiracy Unraveled' – Report of Fact-Finding Committee on Riots in North-East Delhi during 23.02.2020 to 26.02.2020', prepared on behalf of a group called Call for Justice, was submitted to the Home Minister. The report alleged that the Delhi riots involved targeted attacks against the Hindu community:

> The Hindu community was totally unaware about the attacks while the attackers belonging to the Muslim community meticulously

[88] *Ibid.*

[89] *Ibid.*, pp. 40–60.

[90] Prabhjit Singh, "Dead and Buried: Delhi Police Ignored Complaints Against Kapil Mishra, Other BJP Leaders for Leading Mobs in Delhi Violence", *The Caravan*, 21 June 2020.

[91] Group of Intellectuals and Academicians, "Delhi Riots 2020: Report from Ground Zero – The Shaheen Bagh Model in North-East Delhi: From Dharna to Danga", p. 1

[92] *Ibid.*

> planned not only the manpower and other resources but also the timing as well as the pre-defined targets.[93]

The allegations made in the two reports above are in stark contrast to the findings of the report by the Delhi Minorities Commission and to the facts evidenced by videos and reports circulated at the time of the Delhi pogrom. It appears that the sole purpose of these two reports is to engage in distortion of facts and the chronology of events during the Delhi pogrom and place the blame for the communal violence in Delhi solely at the doors of the Muslim minority community in India. The spread of misinformation, albeit through means that appear *prima facie* legitimate (such as through purportedly reliable fact-finding reports) is another weapon in the BJP's arsenal to spread hatred and distrust against the Indian Muslim community among Hindus and feeds into the already-widespread rhetoric that Hindus are in imminent danger of being attacked and targeted by Muslims.

In October 2022, a Citizens' Committee comprising retired judges and former civil servants, chaired by Hon'ble Justice Madan B. Lokur (retired Judge, Supreme Court of India), released a report titled 'Uncertain Justice: A Citizens Committee Report on the North East Delhi Violence 2020'. The report analysed the manner in which certain sections of the media along with select politicians were instrumental in spreading rhetoric and messaging that was "geared to promote paranoia and suspicion over the intentions of anti-CAA protesters and Muslims in the same breath" and formed "powerful foundations of an architecture of hate".[94] The report also decried the:

> total lack of a robust institutional will to act against hate speech, particularly that which is wilfully employed by political leaders during elections, is very concerning. The Election Commission of India in particular has a crucial role to play to prevent elections from becoming easy platforms for the spread and normalization of hateful content.

With India's general elections slated to take place in May 2024, it is sincerely hoped that law enforcement authorities and the Election Commission are able to uphold their constitutional duty to maintain the sanctity of such elections in the world's largest democracy.

---

93 Call for Justice, "'Delhi Riots: Conspiracy Unraveled' – Report of Fact-Finding Committee on Riots in North-East Delhi During 23.02.2020 to 26.02.2020", 2020, pp. 8–10.

94 Constitutional Conduct Group, "Uncertain Justice: A Citizens' Committee Report on the North East Delhi Violence", 18 October 2022 (https://www.legal-tools.org/doc/whh08c/).

7.4.4. Hate Speech and Violence Against Kashmiris

The territory of the erstwhile princely state of Jammu and Kashmir has been a major bone of contention between India and Pakistan, since the time of India's partition in 1947. India and Pakistan have been locked in an international armed conflict over the disputed region for decades and each state occupies a portion of the disputed region. Two of the three wars fought between India and Pakistan were regarding the Kashmir issue.

Indian-administered Kashmir, or the erstwhile state of Jammu and Kashmir, was granted special status and certain autonomies under the Indian Constitution. Over the years, this autonomy has been substantially eroded through orders that attempted to bring about Jammu and Kashmir's integration with India and the application of national laws to the region.[95]

An insurgency began in the Kashmir Valley soon after elections took place in 1987 (these elections were widely perceived to have been rigged) and Kashmiri Muslims began a separatist movement from India. The beginning of the insurgency was marked by an incident where the main insurgent organization in Jammu and Kashmir, the Jammu and Kashmir Liberation Front, kidnapped the daughter of the Indian Minister of Home Affairs at the time and used her kidnapping as a bargaining chip to secure the release of members of their group.[96] The Indian state employed collective repression as a measure of response to the Kashmir insurgency.[97] The violence that resulted from the insurgency caused a mass exodus of Kashmiri Pandits (Hindus) in the early 1990s, due to a combination of reasons such as selective assassinations and the panic created by the situation.[98] Since the outbreak of insurgency in 1989, ethnic-stereotypes also emerged wherein the displaced Kashmiri Pandits view Kashmiri Muslims as plunderers and barbarians, whereas Kashmiri Muslims distrust the Kashmiri Pandits.[99]

Although there are different views as to whether Pakistan was responsible for the outbreak of the insurgency itself or whether it merely provided support to the insurgents, the Indian state blamed Pakistan for the insurgency. Pakistan, in turn, appears to have taken advantage of the situation in Jammu and Kashmir

---

95 Sameer P. Lalwani and Gillian Gayner, "India's Kashmir Conundrum: Before and After the Abrogation of Article 370", *U.S. Institute of Peace*, 2020. See Constitution of India, 26 January 1950, Article 370 (https://www.legal-tools.org/doc/9ov6kt/).

96 "The Kashmiris' Problem", in *Economic and Political Weekly*, 1989, vol. 24, no. 50, p. 2743.

97 Ahsan I. Butt, *Secession and Security: Explaining State Strategy Against Separatists*, Cornell University Press, Ithaca, 2017, p. 109.

98 Lalwani and Gayner, 2020, see *supra* note 95.

99 Sumit Ganguly, "Explaining the Kashmir Insurgency: Political Mobilization and Institutional Decay", in *International Security*, 1996, vol. 2, no. 2, pp. 87–88.

and tacitly supported the separatist movement by providing training, arms, fighters and sanctuary to the insurgents.[100] The insurgency also saw the involvement of some extremist organizations such as the Hijbul Mujahideen (which was supported by Pakistan) and the Lashkar-e-Taiba.[101]

The involvement of Pakistan led Indian security forces to respond with greater repression and brutality, harbouring the threat of not only a Kashmiri nationalist movement but also a potential Pakistani invasion. Kashmiris were viewed as a traitorous and disloyal population, "in bed with an enemy state".[102] The origin of such sentiment can also be traced to the Partition in 1947 and the fact that a majority of Kashmiris are Muslim.[103] The religious colouring of the Kashmir insurgency and the state response can be viewed in light of the fact that the Kashmir insurgency coincided in timing with the demolition of the Babri Masjid in Ayodhya and the subsequent communal riots that broke out in Bombay in December 1992. To this day:

> India portrays the Kashmiri struggle for self-determination as a fanatical religious movement, a jihad against India – an image that helps project Kashmir as an issue of "terrorism".[104]

Over the years, India has engaged in serious human rights violations against Kashmiris and has given wide powers to armed forces to quell dissent in the region, often by resorting to violence. The human rights violations in Jammu and Kashmir, especially by state authorities, which occurred prior to August 2019 have been widely documented, for example, by the Office of the United Nations ('UN') High Commissioner for Human Rights ('OHCHR') in its two reports on Kashmir.[105]

The situation worsened in August 2019, when the Indian Government abrogated Article 370 (which conferred Jammu and Kashmir with special status) and Article 35A (which empowered the Jammu and Kashmir state legislature to define permanent residents of the territory) of the Indian Constitution. The state of Jammu and Kashmir was dissolved and bifurcated into two union territories,

---

100 Butt, 2017, p. 115, see *supra* note 97.

101 *Ibid.*, p. 116.

102 *Ibid.*, p. 118.

103 *Ibid.*

104 Idrisa Pandit, "India Is Escalating Kashmir Conflict by Painting It as Terrorism", *Open Democracy*, 2 December 2019 (available on Open Democracy's web site).

105 OHCHR, "Report on the Situation of Human Rights in Kashmir: Developments in the Indian State of Jammu and Kashmir from June 2016 to April 2018, and General Human Rights Concerns in Azad Jammu and Kashmir and Gilgit-Baltistan", 14 June 2018 (https://www.legal-tools.org/doc/4z0mih/); OHCHR, "Update of the Situation of Human Rights in Indian-Administered Kashmir and Pakistan-Administered Kashmir from May 2018 to April 2019", 8 July 2019 (https://www.legal-tools.org/doc/xiskxp/).

which means that the Central Government in India retains direct control and authority over both.

In the days and weeks prior to the abrogation, the Indian Government deployed approximately 30,000–40,000 troops of security personnel in Jammu and Kashmir in addition to the 500,000 already present there,[106] abruptly put a stop to the Amarnath Yatra (an annual Hindu pilgrimage) and evacuated tourists under the pretext of anticipated attacks by Pakistan-based militants in the region.[107] Shortly before announcing its decision to abrogate Article 370, the Indian Government imposed an unprecedented communications blackout in Jammu and Kashmir by shutting down access to Internet, mobile and landline services.[108] Further, restrictions were imposed under Section 144 of the Indian Code of Criminal Procedure, 1973 in order to prevent persons from assembling in groups. Thus, the abrogation of Article 370 of the Indian Constitution was accompanied by a curfew, restriction on the freedom to assemble, heavy militarization and a communications blockade which were escalations of events over the preceding year.[109]

Several politicians, members of civil society, human rights activists and businessmen were placed under house arrest or detention under the preventive detention legislation known as the Jammu and Kashmir Public Safety Act, 1978 – "a lawless law"[110] – with approximately 240 persons taken to prisons outside the state.[111]

Apart from the apparent human-rights violations against Kashmiris, hate speech is often openly used to target Kashmiri Muslims. For example, Vikram Randhawa, a former BJP legislator from the Jammu region, called for violence – "skin them alive" – against Kashmiri Muslims, who allegedly supported the Pakistan cricket team in a match of the T20 World Cup that was held in the

106 "India Jailed Thousands in Kashmir Crackdown – Official Data", *TRT World*, 12 September 2019 (available on TRT World's web site).

107 Claire Parker, "India's Clampdown on Kashmir Continues: Here's What You Need to Know", *The Washington Post*, 13 August 2019.

108 Sarbani Sharma, "Chicaneries of Power and Subterfuge: Constitutional Laws on Kashmir", *Association for Political and Legal Anthropology*, 5 August 2020.

109 Anuradha Bhasin Jamwal, "The Inheritance of Loss Progression", *The Caravan*, 5 August 2020.

110 "India: A 'Lawless Law': Detentions Under the Jammu and Kashmir Public Safety Act", *Amnesty International*, 21 March 2011.

111 Ather Zia, Haley Duschinski and Mona Bhan, "A Year of Siege: Politics of Annexation and Settler Colonialism in Kashmir", *Association for Political and Legal Anthropology*, 30 July 2020.

United Arab Emirates in 2021.[112] Further, journalists reporting on-ground realities in Jammu and Kashmir are often targeted for being anti-national and proscribed as terrorists under the severe Unlawful Activities Prevention Act, 1967 ('UAPA').[113] Soon after the abrogation, Union Minority Affairs Minister Mukhtar Abbas Naqvi commented that separatists and terrorists had turned Kashmir into a "hell of terror" using Article 370 of the Indian Constitution as a shield and suggested that Article 370's abrogation would aid in tackling terrorism in the Kashmir Valley.[114]

It is worth mentioning here that the release of an Indian film depicting the exodus of Kashmiri Pandits from the Kashmir Valley in the 1990s, titled 'The Kashmir Files', in March 2022, resulted in a fresh wave of Islámophobia, distortion of historical facts and demonization of Kashmiri Muslims. The film was endorsed by Hindu nationalist groups and even Prime Minister Modi himself and was allowed tax waivers in several BJP-run states.[115] However, viewers were divided in their response to the authenticity of the film. While some lauded the film for allegedly portraying a true picture of the violence against and the exodus of Kashmiri Pandits during the height of militancy in Jammu and Kashmir, the Kashmiri Muslim community decried the movie as being "far from the truth", as it failed to show the struggles of the Muslim and the Sikh communities during the militancy in Jammu and Kashmir, and of being made with the objective of fanning communal tensions.[116] Following the release of the film, there were reports of genocidal slogans being raised against Muslims at screenings of the film, such as "*goli maaro saalo ko*" (shoot the traitors), "*Bharat Mata ki Jai*" (victory of Mother India) and "*Vande Mataram*" (praise to the Motherland).

In a video clip, one of the viewers is seen requesting the audience not to watch Bollywood movies, especially those starring Muslim actors.[117] A Dalit man was allegedly assaulted by a group of eleven people and forced to rub his

112 Rifat Fareed, "'Skin Them Alive': Kashmir BJP Politician Booked for Hate Speech", *Al Jazeera*, 2 November 2021.

113 Shakir Mir, "Use of UAPA Against Journalists is Last Nail in Coffin for Press Freedom in Kashmir", *The Wire*, 26 April 2020.

114 "Kashmir was Turned Into 'Hell of Terror' Under Article 370: Mukhtar Abbas Naqvi", *India Today*, 12 October 2019.

115 Umang Poddar, "How the BJP Is Promoting 'The Kashmir Files': Modi's Endorsement, Tax Breaks, Leave from Work", *Scroll*, 17 March 2022.

116 "The Kashmir Files Far from Truth: Omar Abdullah", *Maktoob Media*, 18 March 2022.

117 "Genocidal Slogans Raised at Kashmir Files Screening", *Maktoob Media*, 14 March 2022.

nose on a temple platform for criticizing the film.[118] Evidently, the film triggered further religious polarization, hate speech and violence in India.

7.4.5. Tablighi Jamaat and *Corona Jihád*

The Tablighi Jamaat ('Society of Preachers') is a revivalist Muslim organization in India, founded by a Deobandi Islámic scholar Maúlana Muḥammad Ilyas al-Kandahlawí in 1926. The purpose of the organization is to 'revive' Islám, by educating local Muslims about correct Islámic beliefs and practices.

The Tablighi Jamaat holds congregations around the world. One such congregation was held in mid-March of 2020, at the Nizamuddin Markaz in Delhi, the headquarters of the Tablighi Jamaat. Later that month, it was reported that there had been a cluster outbreak of the novel coronavirus at the conference.[119] In the weeks and months that followed, news outlets vilified the Tablighi Jamaat for being involved in an alleged conspiracy to spread coronavirus in the country.

From 8 to 15 March 2020, more than 2,000 devotees from around the world met at the Nizamuddin Markaz. The meeting continued two days after an order was issued by the Delhi government on 13 March 2020 whereby it directed that "all sports gathering (including IPL [Indian Premier League]/conferences/seminars beyond 200 people are prohibited in NCT [National Capital Territory] of Delhi for the purpose of prevention and control of the outbreak of epidemic disease namely COVID-19".[120] The order dated 13 March 2020 was vague and appeared to restrict only those gatherings which were related to sports events. Thereafter, the Delhi government issued an order on 16 March 2020 which explicitly imposed restrictions on religious gatherings as well.[121] By the time the order dated 16 March 2020 had been issued, several of the delegates had begun dispersing across the country while others stayed back at the Nizamuddin Markaz.[122]

---

118 "Criticised Kashmir Files, Dalit Man Assaulted on Temple Platform", *Maktoob Media*, 24 March 2022.

119 Vidya Krishnan, "Modi Government's Targeting of Minorities for COVID Repeats Old Mistakes of HIV Pandemic", *The Caravan*, 2 May 2020.

120 India, Government of National Capital Territory ('NCT') of Delhi, "Delhi State Health Bulletin for Containment of Covid-19", No.10/13 March 2020 (https://www.legal-tools.org/doc/wd07w6/); Aditya Menon, "Covid-19 in Nizamuddin: Who's to Blame – Govt. or Tablighi Jamaat?", *The Quint*, 1 April 2020.

121 India, Government of NCT of Delhi, "Delhi State Health Bulletin for Containment of Covid-19", 16 March 2020, no. 13 (https://www.legal-tools.org/doc/65k10m/).

122 Seema Chisthi, "The Nightmare: The Modi Government's Persecution of the Tablighi Jamaat", *The Caravan*, 30 January 2021.

The Modi government announced a nationwide lockdown on 24 March 2020, by which time several attendees of the Nizamuddin Markaz had moved to different parts of the country to attend smaller gatherings at local mosques. Around 960 foreign nationals were held in quarantine centres in Delhi for months. In some other states such as Uttar Pradesh, Jharkhand, Maharashtra, Karnataka and Tamil Nadu, the attendees were sent straight to jail.[123] Reports began pouring in that dozens of delegates who had attended the conference had tested positive for the novel coronavirus in various parts of the country.[124]

On 30 March 2020, the Chief Minister of Delhi, Arvind Kejriwal, ordered the authorities to take legal action against the Markaz administration.[125] Several states filed First Information Reports ('FIRs') against delegates who had attended the congregation, including many foreigners, and charged them under various sections of the Indian Penal Code 1860 ('IPC'), the Epidemic Diseases Act 1897, the National Disaster Management Act 2005 and the Foreigners Act 1946, for allegedly defying government restrictions and violating visa conditions for entry into India. High Courts of different Indian states later went on to quash few or all of the FIRs.[126]

Republic TV, a far-right news-channel, led by controversial news anchor, Arnab Goswami, took an active part in condemning the Tablighi Jamaat and by extension, the entire Muslim community. On 31 March 2020, for six minutes, Goswami vilified the Tablighi Jamaatis on air:

> the Tablighi Jamaat Markaz of Nizamuddin in Delhi has become the biggest coronavirus super-spreader but still the organizers are unrepentant. They have broken every law of this country, they have been spreading hate against the lockdown, and they have told their followers to do everything possible to defy and defeat the national lockdown, and as of now, as of this minute, at least 118 coronavirus positive cases come from this Islamic congregation alone. This Islamic congregation has also at least effectively 3000 corona suspects. All those who broke the lockdown and all those who attended the Tablighi Jamaat Markaz, a congregation of Muslim clerics from 16 countries, many of them coronavirus affected, and

[123] Sukanya Shantha and Mukul Singh Chauhan, "Tablighi Jamaat: A Year On, Some Attendees Still Await Trial, Others Struggle to Return Home", *The Wire*, 9 March 2021.

[124] Chisthi, 30 January 2021, see *supra* note 122.

[125] "Nizamuddin Congregation: Arvind Kejriwal Orders FIR Against Maulana", *India Today*, 30 March 2020.

[126] "'Chosen to Make Them Scapegoats': Bombay HC Quashes FIRs Against Tablighi Jamaat Members", *The Wire*, 23 August 2020; Arushi Thapar and Zaid Wahidi, "'Unjust and Unfair': What Three High Courts Said About the Arrests of Tablighi Jamaat Members", *Scroll*, 24 August 2020.

> 19 states, these people came together and not only did they break the lockdown but they actually asked their followers everywhere to break the lockdown […] they made fun of our national effort and they used religious teachings to claim that the lockdown announced by Narendra Modi needs to be defeated […] these are dangerous people, they have compromised us all. We were just winning, when they did everything to defeat us. We will now defeat the lockdown cheats.[127]

He continued:

> And where the hell is the PFI (People's Front of India), which chops the hands of people calling them non-believers, promotes terrorism, now has the gall to say that the Tablighi people are being victimized, that this is a systemic failure? Let us tell the PFI tonight that if they also lack the courage to name and shame these corona super-spreaders of the Tablighi Jamaat Markaz, then they have no right to be on Indian soil. The Modi government should initiate draconian steps, unforgiving steps to teach groups like Markaz a lesson, make them pay, destroy their financial base, put huge fines on them, lock up their leadership in jail, but for God's sake, don't let them abuse Indian democracy anymore. The people of India who can't move ambulances in Shaheen Bagh, the suffering citizens of India for months we have seen people dying in traffic jams caused by Shaheen Bagh are now dying because of the singular determination of the Tablighi Jamaat to spread the coronavirus in my country.[128]

The rhetoric used by Arnab Goswami makes it appear as if the members of the Tablighi Jamaat committed a crime of conspiracy against India, when it is in fact unclear whether the Markaz was ever in violation of any of the orders passed by the Delhi Government or the Government of India. Members of the Tablighi Jamaat have been termed "corona suspects", as if to suggest that being infected with the virus was a crime.

Suresh Chavhanke, the head of Sudarshan News, another right-wing news channel, opened his show *Bindaas Bol* on 31 March 2020 with the following statement:

> In today's Bindaas Bol, I bring you a very serious issue and appeal to the Narendra Modi government that the Tablighi Jamaat be banned. If India's mosques are posing a threat to Indians, and human bombs carrying coronavirus are roaming around freely,

[127] "Arnab Goswami's Lead Story – Markaz Lockdown Violation: How Can One Group Put All at Risk?", *Republic World*, 31 March 2020 (available on *YouTube*).

[128] *Ibid.*

> wouldn't you call it 'corona jihad'? We should keenly monitor these jihadis and the jihadis should be strictly punished under law.

In the aftermath of the Tablighi Jamaat congregation, several government officials publicly harped on the congregation as the reason for the spread of the coronavirus in India. While many agree that the holding of the event was irresponsible and endangered many lives, the event, and Muslims in general, received a disproportionate amount of blame and criticism over this incident. The Union Minority Affairs Minister Mukhtar Abbas Naqvi, who ironically is a Muslim himself, said that the Tablighi Jamaat had committed a "Talibani crime".[129] Amit Malviya, the National Convenor of the BJP's IT cell, tweeted as follows:

> Delhi's dark underbelly is exploding! Last 3 months have seen an Islamic insurrection of sorts, first in the name of anti-CAA protests from Shaheen Bagh to Jamia, Jaffrabad to Seelampur. And now the illegal gathering of the radical Tablighi Jamaat at the Markaz. It needs a fix![130]

Sangeeth Som, BJP MLA, stated that the manner in which members of the Tablighi Jamaat congregated at the Nizamuddin Markaz despite the warnings given by the government can be termed as "Corona Terrorism" – and that the matter ought to be investigated. Referring to the FIR filed by the Delhi police against Maualana Saad, who led the Tablighi Jamaat congregation in Delhi, and others, he stated that they should be given the same punishment as terrorists.[131] He further alleged that members of the Tablighi Jamaat were hiding in mosques in almost every district as part of a larger conspiracy to spread Covid-19 across India. It was also suggested that Tablighi members were attempting to spread the virus by spitting and other means, and that this constituted a new type of conspiracy and *jihád*.[132]

Karnataka BJP MLA MP Renukachary stated that:

> Those who attended Tablighi Jamaat congregation and have not come out for treatment and escaped, government should not protect them. It is not wrong to shoot them with a bullet.[133]

---

129 "This is a 'Talibani' Crime by Tablighi Jamaat: Naqvi on Nizamuddin Markaz Gathering", *The Print* (available on *YouTube*).

130 Amit Malviya, tweet @amitmalviya, 1 April 2020 (last accessed on 6 June 2022).

131 "'This is Corona Terrorism', Says BJP's Sangeet Som over Nizamuddin Markaz", *ABP Live*, 1 April 2020.

132 *Ibid.*

133 "Not Wrong to Shoot Hiding Tablighi Jamaat Attendees, Says Karnataka BJP MLA", *News18*, 7 April 2020.

Such rhetoric contributed to aggravating anti-Muslim sentiment in an already communally charged environment in India. Several Indian news channels spread fake news and misinformation which contributed to the growing Islámophobia and scapegoating of Muslims.[134] A video later went viral which allegedly depicted several members of the Jamaat admitted in a Ghaziabad hospital roaming around nude and misbehaving with hospital staff.[135] When this video was fact-checked, it came to light that the clip was from a video originally shot at a mosque in Karachi, Pakistan in August 2019.[136]

On 4 April 2020, a Hindi daily, *Amar Ujala*, published an article claiming that Jamatis admitted in quarantine centres in Sahranpur district of Uttar Pradesh had demanded non-vegetarian food, tossed aside the food that was served to them and defecated in the open in protest. Similar stories were also reported by another prominent daily called *Patrika*. The Sahranpur police investigated these claims and found them to be untrue. The posts by the two dailies have since been deleted.[137] Tweets with hashtags such as #BioJihad, #CoronaJihad and #CoronaTerrorism also began flooding Twitter and were shared several times.[138]

As such, an entire set of vocabulary was developed which linked the spread of coronavirus in India to the Muslim community, in one way or another. Such Islámophobic Covid-19-related hate speech vocabulary and imagery were amplified and circulated by the mainstream media, thereby abandoning norms of unbiased reporting.[139]

7.4.6. *Thook Jihád*

On 15 November 2021, a video of a Muslim eatery worker from Loni, Ghaziabad, in Uttar Pradesh, was circulated on social media and by right-wing media outlets. The video, which purportedly depicted a Muslim eatery worker spitting into food that he was preparing, was widely circulated using the hashtag #ThookJihad – *thook* literally translates to 'spit'. The video was shot by

[134] Shawn Sebastian, "After Covid-19 Outbreak at Tablighi Jamaat Conference, Fake News Targeting Muslims Abounds", *The Caravan*, 4 April 2020.

[135] "Shocking! Tablighi Jamaat Patients Make Vulgar Signs, Roam Naked, Demand Cigarettes in Ghaziabad Hospital", *ABP Live*, 2 April 2020.

[136] Jignesh Patel, "Old Video from Pakistan Falsely Viral as Tablighi Jamaat Member Roaming Naked in Isolation Ward", *AltNews*, 8 April 2020.

[137] *Ibid.*

[138] Rana Ayyub, "Opinion: Islamophobia Taints India's Response to the Coronavirus", *The Washington Post*, 6 April 2020; Billy Perigo, "It Was Already Dangerous to Be Muslim in India. Then Came the Coronavirus", *Time*, 3 April 2020.

[139] Equality Labs, "Coronajihad: An Analysis of Covid-19 Hate Speech and Disinformation", 2020 (https://www.legal-tools.org/doc/99bd0t/).

members of the Hindu Raksha Dal, a far-right group that works closely with the BJP and is based out of Ghaziabad.[140]

On 16 November 2021, in the Indian news channel News18's show titled '*Desh Nahi Jhukne Denge*', anchor Aman Chopra held a debate over the video wherein he made several Islámophobic statements and contended that this "*ri-waaz-e-thook*" (a purported 'tradition of spitting') was a conspiracy by Muslim eatery workers against Hindus through the contamination of food.[141] The video and the tweets were later taken down from YouTube and Twitter by the news channel.

In a similar vein, right-wing Hindus targeted Bollywood actor and super-star, Shah Rukh Khan, in relation to a video of him offering prayers at the funeral of a famous Bollywood playback singer, Lata Mangeshkar. For a split second in the video, the actor is seen taking off his mask and bending towards the body to blow air. The gesture of blowing air after reading a *duá* (prayer) is a traditional Islámic practice during funerals, which is intended to ward off evil.[142] The act of blowing air after offering prayers was misinterpreted as spitting.

7.4.7. Targeting Muslim Women

In April 2022, a video was circulated on social media, depicting a Hindu priest clad in saffron robes addressing a gathering in Sitapur, Uttar Pradesh, and threat-ening to kidnap and publicly rape Muslim women if any Muslim man harasses Hindu girls in the area.[143] The misogyny and humiliation of Muslim women by Hindu extremists has often characterized anti-Muslim hate-rhetoric in India. The sexualization and targeting of Muslim women is a means to silence and oppress them. The environment of impunity when it comes to hate speech, intimidation and violence against Muslims and other minorities in India appears to have en-couraged and emboldened hate-mongers engaging in such propaganda. Given below are a few examples of hateful expression against Muslim women in India in the recent past.

---

140 Alishan Jafri, "'Thook Jihad' is the Latest Weapon in Hindutva's Arsenal of Islamophobia", *The Wire*, 20 November 2021.

141 Meghnad S and Deepanjana Pal, "Bloodlust TV: Aman Chopra Spitting Hate on Minorities with His 'Thook Jihad' Show", *Newslaundry*, 18 November 2021; Alishan Jafri, "'Thook Jihad' is the Latest Weapon in Hindutva's Arsenal of Islamophobia", *The Wire*, 20 November 2021.

142 Nootan Sharma, "Shah Rukh Khan Didn't Spit at Lata Mangeshkar's Funeral. This Is What His Gesture Meant", *The Print*, 7 February 2022.

143 Alok Pandey, "Hatemonger's Rape Threat to Muslim Women, UP Cop Files Case After 6 Days", *NDTV*, 8 April 2022.

7.4.7.1. The Hijáb Row

Late in December 2021, a group of six Muslim female students wearing a *hijáb* (headscarves worn by many Muslim women) was removed from their class in a pre-university government college in Karnataka's Udupi district, for allegedly being in violation of the dress code.[144] The students protested against the restriction, filed a writ petition before the High Court of Karnataka and approached the National Human Rights Commission with their grievances.[145] Triggered by the mounting resistance to the restriction on *hijábs*, several Hindu students held counter demonstrations and donned saffron scarves and shawls (the saffron colour is associated with Hindu nationalism), garments not ordinarily worn by them[146] and called for a *hijáb* ban.[147] Many such Hindu students identified themselves as being members of the Akhil Bharatiya Vidyarthi Parishad ('ABVP', the student wing of the BJP) and the Hindu Jagarana Vedike (an organization affiliated to the RSS).[148]

Following suit, several other government-run educational institutions in Karnataka banned Muslim female students from wearing the *hijáb*.[149] Muslim students who arrived at educational institutions wearing a *hijáb* were later allowed entry but made to sit in separate rooms, which evoked concerns regarding segregation.[150] Reports also emerged of Muslim female students wearing the *hijáb* being heckled by Hindu men wearing saffron scarves.[151]

The admission forms of the six female Muslim students who initially protested against the *hijáb* ban, containing their home addresses, telephone numbers and the names of their parents, were allegedly leaked by the college. Following this breach of privacy, the girls allegedly began receiving threatening

---

[144] Rushda Fathima Khan, "What's Behind the Escalating Row Over Hijabs in India?", *Al Jazeera*, 15 February 2022.

[145] Mekhala Saran, "'Hijab Case Verdict Today: What Did Petitioners Argue? What Did State Say?", *The Quint*, 15 March 2022.

[146] Muhammed Sabith, "'Saffron Controversy, Not Hijab Controversy': Muslim Women Protest Across Karnataka", *The Wire*, 8 February 2022.

[147] "Hijab Ban in Indian State Violates Religious Freedom: US Official", *Al Jazeera*, 12 February 2022.

[148] "Karnataka Hijab Ban: CM Suspends Classes for Three Days", *Maktoob Media*, 8 February 2022.

[149] Muhammed Sabith, "'Saffron Controversy, Not Hijab Controversy': Muslim Women Protest Across Karnataka", *The Wire*, 8 February 2022.

[150] "Udupi: Hijab Wearing Students Allowed into College, Made to Sit in Separate Room", *The Wire*, 7 February 2022.

[151] "Hijab-wearing Student Heckled by Boys Wearing Saffron Scarves in Manday College", *The Hindu*, 8 February 2022.

phone calls and messages.[152] In a viral video, an ABVP activist in Karnataka's Vijayapura is seen calling for the killing of Muslims. In a speech that was delivered publicly and garnered much applause, she stated:

> If you want Hijab all over India, we will chop you all into pieces with Shivaji's sword.[153]

On 15 March 2022, the High Court of Karnataka ruled that wearing the *hijáb* is not "essential religious practice" of Islám, but is rather recommendatory. The High Court thus effectively upheld the ban on wearing the *hijáb* in educational institutions, stating that the restriction on wearing the *hijáb* was in adherence with the school dress code, and hence did not infringe upon the petitioners constitutionally protected right as it applied to all students, regardless of their religious backgrounds.[154] On 13 October 2022, a two-judge bench of the Supreme Court of India delivered a split verdict on an appeal against the Karnataka High Court's decision, thereby necessitating the referral of the case to a larger bench to resolve the deadlock.[155]

A Muslim exam invigilator was suspended for wearing a *hijáb* to invigilate state-level examinations.[156] The *hijáb* ban is the latest in a string of actions that target Muslim religious practices and symbolizes the growing intolerance in Indian society. Recently, complaints have also been made about the use of loudspeakers by mosques in order to transmit the *Azaan* (Muslim call to prayer), which happens five times a day.[157] The use of Urdu terms (Urdu is considered a Muslim language) in connection with a Hindu festival (Diwali) in an advertisement caught the ire of right-wing Hindus.[158]

7.4.7.2. *Bulli Bai* and *Sulli Deals* Apps

When it comes to the systematic dehumanization and vilification of Indian Muslims, Muslim women bear the additional burden of being sexualized, targeted

---

152 Nikhila Henry, "Karnataka Hijab Row: College Leaks Addresses, Numbers of Protesting Muslim Girls", *The Quint*, 9 February 2022.

153 Priyanka Rudrappa, "'Will Cut Them Into Pieces': ABVP Activist Calls for Genocide Against Muslims in Karnataka", *NewsNine*, 26 February 2022.

154 High Court of Karnataka, *Smt. Resham v. State of Karnataka and Others*, Order dated 15 March 2022, Writ Petition No. 2347 of 2022, 15 March 2022 (https://www.legal-tools.org/doc/n8fjod/).

155 Supreme Court of India, *Aishat Shifa v. the State of Karnataka and Ors.*, Judgment, 13 October 2022, (2023) 2 SCC 1 (https://www.legal-tools.org/doc/atvz99/).

156 "Muslim Invigilator Suspended for Wearing Hijab in Karnataka SSLC Exams", *Maktoob Media*, 28 March 2022.

157 "MP: Hindu Right Groups Threaten to Drown Out Azaan with Loudspeaker Music", *The Wire*, 14 February 2022.

158 Bilal Kuchay, "Hate Campaign in India Against Urdu for Being a 'Muslim' Language", *Al Jazeera*, 27 October 2021.

and humiliated. 'Bulli Bai' is an app that came to light on 1 January 2022 on Github, a Microsoft-owned platform for developing and hosting software and open-source projects. Approximately 100 Muslim women's profiles and pictures were made available on the web site, including those of prominent women journalists and civil society actors. These profiles, which were created without the consent of the women in question, were used to invite bids for auction of the women.[159]

Six months earlier, in July 2021, another app by the name 'Sulli Deals' was developed to auction Muslim women. Both apps were hosted on 'Github' and targeted vocal Muslim women in an attempt to humiliate and degrade them.[160] It is pertinent to mention that both '*Sulli*' and '*Bulli*' are derogatory terms for Muslim women in local slang.[161] They are alterations of the term '*Mulli*', which is often used by the right wing to offend Indian Muslim women.[162]

Based on a complaint by journalist Ismat Ara in New Delhi, an FIR was lodged by the Delhi Police's Cyber Crime Unit against unknown persons, invoking various sections of the IPC, including Section 153A (promoting enmity on grounds of religion) and Section 153B (imputations prejudicial to national integration) for harassing and insulting Muslim women on social media platforms using doctored pictures.[163] A complaint was also filed in Mumbai against the app developers. However, women seemed apprehensive that officials would take any action, since the complaints filed against Sulli Deals six months prior had not yet been acted upon.[164]

7.4.8. Calls to Genocide and Ethnic Cleansing of Muslims

India is witnessing an alarming rise in hateful expression and incitement to violence against minorities, particularly Muslims, in public settings. Few such incidents are highlighted below.

159 "Bulli Bai: Sulli Deals 2.0? All You Need to Know About the Online 'Auction' of Muslim Women", *Outlook*, 3 January 2022.

160 Unnati Sharma, "After 'Sulli Deals', Now 'Bulli Bai' App Lists Muslim Women 'for Sale'. Delhi Police Lodges FIR", *The Print*, 2 January 2022.

161 Srishti Jaiswal, "Bulli Bai: India's Muslim Women Again Listed on App for 'Auction'", *Al Jazeera*, 2 January 2022.

162 Mariya Salim, "'Bulli Bai', 'Sulli Deals': On Being Put Up for 'Auction' as an Indian Muslim Woman, *The Wire*, 16 January 2022.

163 Jaiswal, 2 January 2022, see *supra* note 161.

164 *Ibid.*; Asmita Bakshi, "Sulli Deals: Indian Muslim Women Offered for Sale in 'Auction'", *Al Jazeera*, 12 July 2021.

7.4.8.1. The 19 December 2021 Event Organized in Delhi by Hindu Right-Wing Groups

One such event calling for violence against Muslims was organized by Hindu right-wing groups, including the Hindu Yuva Vahini, and Sudarshan News Editor-in-Chief Suresh Chavhanke in Delhi on 19 December 2021. In a video recording of the event, Chavhanke and others present at the gathering are seen taking an oath to "fight, die and if required, kill" in order to transform India into a Hindu *Rashtra* (nation) at any cost.[165] When the Chairperson of the Congress (a political party in India) Minority Cell Imran Pratapgarhi condemned the hate speech, Chavhanke responded that Pratapgarhi was one of "those who took the oath of [Mughal Emperor] Aurangzeb".[166]

Aurangzeb Alamgir was the sixth Mughal Emperor of India, who ruled almost the entire Indian subcontinent for a period of approximately 49 years, shortly before British colonization of India. In popular conception, Aurangzeb has been construed as a Hindu-hating bigot, murderer, and a religious zealot. It is popularly believed that Aurangzeb was a brutal oppressor of Hindus who tried to convert them to Islám, and when he failed in his mission, massacred them in millions. Unsurprisingly, Aurangzeb is depicted in popular imagination as a pious Muslim king (which might not always have been the case in reality), which serves a specific purpose:

> From a divisive Hindu nationalist perspective, Babur and Aurangzeb are to some degree interchangeable as oppressive Muslim conquerors. In this sense Aurangzeb stands in for an entire category of "orthodox Muslims" who are supposedly implicated in unsavory aspects of India's past and, consequently, unwelcome in India's present. It is not incidental that Aurangzeb is widely believed to have been the most pious of the Mughal kings. Aurangzeb thus typifies zealous Muslims overall—both past and present—who allegedly threaten Indian society by virtue of their religiosity. In this formulation Indian and Hindu cultures are collapsed into a single, flattened entity that offers little breathing room for other religious groups.[167]

Aurangzeb's characterization as a ruthless and barbaric ruler owes its origin in some part to the British, who engaged in mud-slinging of Mughal

[165] "In Delhi, Hindutva Groups Vow to 'Fight, Die & Kill' to Make India Hindu Rashtra", *The Quint*, 23 December 2021.

[166] Ayesha Jain, "Delhi Hate Speech: 5 Days Since Vow to 'Kill' for Hindu Nation, No Police Action", *The Quint*, 24 December 2021.

[167] Audrey Truschke, *Aurangzeb: The Life and Legacy of India's Most Controversial King*, Stanford University Press, 2017, p. 16.

emperors, in an attempt to make their colonial project in India appear civilized and acceptable.[168]

The colonial-era image and rhetoric regarding Mughal emperors created by the British, more particularly that of Babur and Aurangzeb, lives on in Indian society and is often used to character-assassinate and vilify Indian Muslims. For Hindu nationalists, Muslims allegedly pose a threat to India's identity as a fundamentally Hindu nation.[169] Therefore, they engage in likening Indian Muslims to Aurangzeb, who they depict as a reviled and bigoted Islámist tormentor and hater of Hindus. It is also popularly believed that Aurangzeb systematically plundered and destroyed thousands of Hindu temples[170] and hence, posed a threat to Hinduism. Terms like "*Babur ki aulad*" (Babur's progeny) and "*Aurangzeb ki aulad*" (Aurangzeb's progeny) have often been used as terms of abuse against Indian Muslims, especially during the late 1980s and early 1990s, at the time of the demolition of the Babri Masjid in Ayodhya by a right-wing Hindutva mob.[171]

7.4.8.2. The Haridwar Event (Dharam Sansad Row)

From 17 to 19 December 2021, a *Dharam Sansad* (religious parliament) was held in Haridwar in the Indian state of Uttarakhand, which saw several Hindu right-wing leaders, monks and activists come together. The *Dharam Sansad* was organized by a militant Hindu priest, Yati Narsinghanand. Yati Narsinghanand, who heads the Dasna Devi temple in Uttar Pradesh, has a history of making Islámophobic hate speeches in public. Much before the Haridwar *Dharam Sansad*, he reacted to the stabbing of militant Hindutva leader Kamlesh Tiwari in Lucknow in October 2019 by threatening to eradicate Islám from India:

> Muslims around the world are celebrating because a Hindu lion has been killed and all our homes are in mourning. I am telling every one of those bastards, telling the Muslims, if I don't make you mourn the way Kamlesh Tiwari's house is mourning today, then I am not my father's son. As long as I am alive, I will use weapons. I am telling each and every Muslim, we will eradicate Islam from the country one day.[172]

---

168 Audrey Truschke, "A Much-Maligned Mughal", *Aeon*, 5 April 2017 (available on Aeon's web site).

169 *Ibid.*

170 *Ibid.*; Truschke, 2017, p. 17, see *supra* note 167.

171 Teesta Setalvad, "We Can't Let Hindu Nationalists Rewrite India's History", *Alternet*, 13 January 2018 (available on Alternet's web site).

172 Alishan Jafri, Shehlat Maknoon Wani and Siddharth Vardharajan, "Just Before Delhi Riots, Militant Hindutva Leader Called Repeatedly for Muslims to Be Killed", *The Wire*, 3 March 2021.

Videos of the three-day event revealed that several instances of hate speech, targeted verbal attacks and jibes against the Indian Muslim community were made at this event. The event was attended by around 150 people, including 50 *Mahamandaleshwars* (monks).[173] Ex-Delhi BJP spokesperson, Ashwini Upadhyay, was also present at the event. The event soon garnered international attention for its calls for violence amounting to genocide[174] and massacre of Muslims in India.[175]

One of the *Mahamandaleshwars* present at the event, Annapurna Maa, who is also the General Secretary of the Hindu Mahasabha, stated that:

> Nothing is possible without weapons. If you want to eliminate their population then kill them. Be ready to kill and be ready to go to jail. Even if 100 of us are ready to kill 20 lakhs of them (Muslims), then we will be victorious, and go to jail […]. Like [Nathuram] Godse, I am ready to be maligned, but I will pick up arms to defend my Hindutva from every demon who is a threat to my religion.[176]

Swami Prabodhanand, President of the Hindu Raksha Sena, a Hindutva organization based in Uttarakhand, urged the crowd:

> We have to make preparations. And I'll tell you what those preparations are. I will make myself clear, this is the solution, and if you follow this solution, then the path is made for you […] in Myanmar, Hindus were being chased away. The politicians, government, and police were just standing and watching. They started by killing them by cutting their necks, and not only this, but they began to cut them in the streets and eat them. The people-watching thought we are going to die, we are not going to live.[177]

In a video of the event, since deleted, a senior member of the right-wing Hindu Mahasabha political party, Pooja Shakun Pandey, reportedly stated that:

> If 100 of us become soldiers and are prepared to kill 2 million (Muslims), then we will win […] protect India, and make it a Hindu nation.[178]

---

173 Waquar Hasan, "'Can Kill 20 Lakh of Them': Call for Muslim Genocide at Haridwar Event Attended by 50 Hindu Monks", *Maktoob Media*, 23 December 2021.

174 "Militant Hindutva Leader Yati Narasinghanand Arrested in 2 Cases, Sent to 14-Day Judicial Custody", *The Wire*, 17 January 2022.

175 Dhirendra K. Jha, "Unholy Orders: The Haridwar Dharma Sansad is a Reflection of the RSS's New Strategy with Sadhus", *The Caravan*, 1 March 2022.

176 Hasan, 23 December 2021, see *supra* note 173.

177 *Ibid.*

178 Rhea Mogul and Swati Gupta, "India's Hindu Extremists are Calling for Genocide Against Muslims. Why is Little Being Done to Stop Them?", *CNN*, 15 January 2022.

At the same event, in an interview to the right-wing news channel Sudarshan News, Yati Narasinghanand stated that:

> This is our second Dharm Sansad. Our message is this that India, which is speedily becoming an Islamic state, should quickly be reversed, and it should become a Sanatan Vedic Rashtra.[179]

Yati Narasinghanand led the congregation in taking an oath, where he and the others made a vow to protect their religion:

> All of you raise your hands and repeat after me. I, *your name*, here on the banks of the Ganga, I take this vow, for Sanatan Dharm for my family, to keep my sisters and daughters protected. Anything in the world, whatever problems, whatever person, even thinks about causing loss to my religion, my family and my children, my women, I will not let him live. We will live for our religion. We will die for our religion. Islam's jihad will be finished. Long live Sanatan Dharm. May the enemies of Sanatan be destroyed.[180]

At the congregation, Narasinghanand also exhorted Hindus to come together to protect Hinduism from the alleged threat of becoming an Islámic state and encouraged his followers to take up violence if necessary to fulfil their duties of protecting their religion. He publicly offered a money reward to any Hindu youth who was willing to come forward and become "Hindu Prabhakaran". Narasinghanand was referring to Velupillai Prabhakaran, the founder and leader of the Liberation Tigers of Tamil Eelam ('LTTE'), an armed organization which sought an independent state for Sri Lankan Tamils and is banned in India. LTTE and its leader Prabhakaran were responsible for the assassination of former Prime Minister of India, Rajiv Gandhi.[181] The implications of such a call are serious to say the least – a Hindu priest publicly exhorted fellow Hindus to emulate the activities of an armed, militant organization in their purported quest to protect their religion.

Narasinghanand was later arrested in the *Dharma Sansad* case. Shortly after Narasinghanand was released on bail, he attended events in New Delhi and Una, Himachal Pradesh where anti-Muslim speeches were made, in clear violation of his bail conditions.[182]

---

179 "Yati Narasinghanand Offers Rs 1 Crore Award to Become 'Hindu Prabhakaran'", *The Wire*, 22 December 2021.

180 *Ibid.*

181 *Ibid.*

182 Alishan Jafri and Naomi Barton, "With Call for Violence Against Muslims at Burari, Yati Narasinghanand Violates Bail Conditions", *The Wire*, 4 April 2022; "Yati Narasinghanand Violates Bail Conditions Again, Makes Provocative Remarks in Una", *The Wire*, 18 April 2022.

More than a month after the Haridwar *Dharam Sansad*, the core committee of the Haridwar *Dharam Sansad* held a *Sant Sammelan* (gathering of saints) in Prayagraj, Uttar Pradesh, where the speakers again made hate speeches against Muslims and demanded that India be declared a "Hindu *Rashtra*".[183] They demanded the release of Narasinghanand and Jitendra Tyagi, both of whom had been arrested in connection with the Haridwar *Dharam Sansad.* Swami Anand Swaroop, a Hindu leader, also issued an ultimatum for their release:

> Our third demand is that if our religious warriors (Yati Narsinganand and Jitendra Tyagi) were not released within a week, this campaign will get aggressive. Not just aggressive, the result of it will be horrible. Maybe, the incarceration of these two warriors will cause us to do what Bhagat Singh did to the Assembly (bombing).[184]

Swaroop was referring to the bombing of the Central Legislative Assembly in 1929 by Indian freedom fighter Bhagat Singh in protest against British Rule in India. He also stated that the declaration of India as a secular state was a "constitutional mistake", one which the Prime Minster (Modi) ought to correct.[185]

The Haridwar *Dharam Sansad* is not the first instance in which Yati Narasinghanand has been video-taped engaging in hate speech and incitement against Muslims. In recent times, Narasinghanand has emerged as somewhat of a Hindutva icon.

While addressing a press conference organized by the Akhil Bharatiya Sant Parishad (Ghaziabad) at the Press Club of India in April 2021, Narasinghanand made insulting remarks against the Prophet Mohammad. In a video clip, he is seen addressing the congregation and telling them that:

> If the Muslims of the world become aware of the truth about Prophet Mohammad, then they will be embarrassed about being Muslims [...] once Muslims realize that the Prophet they are following was a plunderer, thief and dacoit, that he is a rapist and has engaged in the trafficking of women, [...] they will be ashamed [...]. It is the politicians of India who have glorified the dirty Islam [...]. As long as India's Hindus, who are now in the guise of Muslims, remain in that guise, they will be like animals and their goal

183 Waquar Hasan, "Declaring India Secular State a 'Constitutional Mistake': Hindu Priests at the Prayagraj Sammelan", *Maktoob Media*, 30 January 2022.

184 *Ibid.*

185 *Ibid.*

> would be to take advantage of others' daughters. But when Muslims realize the truth about Islam, they will change [...].[186]

In a video circulating on the Internet, he is seen stating that:

> [t]he situation today is that Islam's jihadis are killing us in various ways. They are raping our sisters and daughters. In the whole world, there is no one to listen to our voices, because Islamic Jihadis have money and power bestowed on them by politicians. There is no one to listen to our grievances. They are expanding their population as part of a larger conspiracy. It is possible that by 2039, India will have a Muslim Prime Minister.[187]

Following the blasphemous remarks made by Narasinghanand at the Press Club of India, AAP MLA and Chairman of the Delhi Wakf Board Amanatullah Khan filed a police complaint against Narasinghanand. An FIR was lodged by the Delhi police against Narasinghanand under Section 153A (promoting enmity between different groups) and Section 295A (deliberate and malicious acts intended to outrage religious feelings) of the IPC.[188]

7.4.8.3. Hate Speeches Made at Jantar Mantar in Delhi (August 2021)

On 8 August 2021, hate speech and violent slogans were chanted against Muslims at Delhi's Jantar Mantar, a couple of kilometres from the seat of the Indian Parliament. These speeches and slogans were shouted at a public meeting of organizations and supporters which came together as a result of a call made by former BJP spokesperson Ashwini Upadhyay.[189] Videos surfaced online capturing the sloganeering at the event. Uttam Upadhyay, a 26-year-old resident of Ghaziabad, Uttar Pradesh, is seen in the video chanting "*Jai Shri Ram. Mulle kaate jayenge, Ram Ram chilaayenge*" (Glory to Lord Rama. Muslims will be cut down while chanting Lord Rama's name).[190] In an interview given to the news media outlet Newslaundry, Uttam Upadhyay encouraged people to engage in the "economic boycott of Muslims [...] to save the country. Stop buying goods from them. Only then we'll be able to break them".[191] The meeting was also attended by Sushil Tiwari, a member of a group called the Hindu Army, who stated that "*Jo Bharat murdabad kahe, uske seene mein goli ho*" (whoever

186 "Yati Narsinghanand Saraswati Sparks Another Controversy, Abuses Prophet Muhammad in Press Conference", *The Logical Indian*, 3 April 2021 (available on *YouTube*).

187 *Ibid.*

188 Ismat Ara, "FIR Filed After AAP MLA's Complaint Against Hardline Dasna Priest for 'Blasphemous' Speech", *The Wire*, 3 April 2021.

189 Shivangi Saxena, "'Population Jihad Must Be Stopped': Meet the Men Who Shouted Anti-Muslim Slogans in Delhi", *Newslaundry*, 10 August 2021.

190 *Ibid.*

191 *Ibid.*

says "down with India" should have a bullet in their chest).[192] Six persons were later arrested in connection with the speeches made at Jantar Mantar.[193]

7.4.8.4. Other Speeches Indicating an Intent to Eliminate the Muslim Community in India

Back in 2014, Rajeshwar Singh, head of the Hindu outfit called 'Dharm Jagran Manch', said that "[w]e have so far ensured 'ghar wapsi' (reconversion) of three lakh Muslims and Christians back to Hinduism. By 2021, we will finish Islám and Christianity".[194]

BJP Bihar MLA Haribhushan Thakur told reporters on 25 February 2022 that as "Muslims were given a separate country at the time of Partition in 1947, they should leave for Pakistan. And if they live in India, they should live like second-class citizens. We urge the government to take away Muslims' voting rights".[195]

On 5 July 2021, at a *mahapanchayat* (congregation of people) organized by the Vishwa Hindu Parishad ('VHP'), a Hindu right-wing organization, in Pataudi, Haryana against alleged *love jihád* and religious conversions in the area, a young man allegedly exhorted youth present at the event to "kidnap Muslim women" as revenge for *love jihád* (explained below).[196] At the same event, Suraj Pal Amu, the spokesperson for the BJP's Haryana unit, stated in his speech, referring to Muslims, that "[t]hey cut their moustaches, we can cut throats [...]. We will pick them (Muslims) off one by one (*chun chun ke thokenge*)".[197] He continued:

> Bharat humari mata hai, aur Pakistan ke hum baap hai, aur yeh Pakistani kutto ko hum ghar kiraye par nahi denge. Inn huramjado ko iss desh se nikalo, yeh prastaav paas hoga (India is our mother, and we are the father of Pakistan, and we will not rent out our houses to these Pakistani dogs. Remove these scoundrels from this country, pass this proposal).[198]

---

192 *Ibid.*

193 "Communal Sloganeering at Jantar Mantar: BJP's Ashwini Upadhyay Among 6 Arrested by Delhi Police", *India Today*, 10 August 2021.

194 "Hindu Outfit Plans to 'Finish' Islam, Christianity by 2021", *The Indian Express*, 19 December 2014. A lakh is equal to 100,000.

195 "Hate Speech: Bihar BJP MLA Says Take Away Muslims' Voting Rights", *Maktoob Media*, 25 February 2022.

196 "Teenager Makes Provocative Speech at Pataudi 'Mahapanchayat'", *The Hindu*, 5 July 2021.

197 "After 'Can Cut Throats' Speech by Haryana BJP Official, No Police Action", *NDTV*, 9 July 2021.

198 Prabhjit Singh, "Muslims Advocate Restraint, Peace, Question Police Amid Haryana 'Mahapanchayat' Hate Speeches", *The Caravan*, 31 July 2021.

7.4.9. *Love Jihád*, *Ghar Wapsi* and Religious Conversion Laws in India

The Sangh Parivar (an umbrella term referring to all the Hindu nationalist organizations affiliated to the RSS) has always believed that India belongs to Hindus and that non-Hindus (particularly Christians and Muslims) are outsiders who ought to leave India to the Hindus. Other religious groups such as Jains, Buddhists and Sikhs are believed to come under the larger fold of Hinduism and hence, exempted from falling under the classification of non-Hindus, while the Parsi community is considered to be too small to be of significance.[199] The term *ghar wapsi* literally translates to homecoming, and refers to the idea of bringing members of other religions (back) into the fold of Hinduism. The idea of *ghar wapsi* thereby reinforces the notion that the minority religions do not belong to the *ghar* or the nation, which belongs exclusively to Hindus.[200] The *ghar wapsi* programme constructs the idea that those belonging to minority religions are prodigal offspring who need only to return to the home to find acceptance.[201] Promoting this programme serves a dual purpose for Hindu nationalists: it serves as a means of dealing with unwanted minorities (and is seen as a more viable alternative to wide-scale mass-killing and ethnic cleansing of minorities), while simultaneously increasing the population of Hindus through conversions.[202]

The notion of *ghar wapsi* can best be described as follows:

> In fact, it is not even acknowledged to be conversion, because it is represented as a form of shuddhi or "purification", rather than as conversion: as such, members of the minorities are understood to have been defiled by the "other" religion, rather than as belonging to it. They are therefore simply returning to their "true" religion, through ghar wapsi; but they do need to be "cleansed off" the other religion, not just converted from it. This speaks volumes about the attitude of the majoritarian community towards the minorities. They are not simply members of another religion, in a neutral, equanimous way; not even just "other" and alien, in some fundamentally irreconcilable, but still broadly neutral way. They are viewed as fundamentally polluting, impure, anathema to the sanctity of the "Hindu", and actively requiring elimination – hence the need for purification, not just conversion.

The desire to maintain and even substantiate numerical superiority and hence the political power of Hindus in the country is one of the main driving

[199] Prem K. Vijayan and Karen Gabriel, "Hindutva's Psychological Warfare: The Insidious Agendas of 'Ghar Wapsi'", in *Economic and Political Weekly*, 2015, vol. 50, no. 11, pp. 22–24.

[200] *Ibid.*

[201] *Ibid.*

[202] *Ibid.*

factors that underlies the *ghar wapsi* programme.[203] In reality, *ghar wapsi* programmes across the country have been characterized by intimidation, violence and bloodshed for decades. The goal of these programmes has not been so much as to instil converts (or re-converts, as Hindu nationalists view them) to Hinduism with knowledge about the tenets, scriptures and beliefs of the Hindu religion, but rather to ensure a de-Islámization or de-Christianization of the targeted communities.[204]

Love jihád is an example of how love is being weaponized in India and the agency of adult women, especially with respect to choosing their life partners and their religion or faith, is being systematically undermined. According to fringe Hindu groups such as the Shri Ram Sena, the VHP and the Bajrang Dal, *love jihád* is a looming threat to Hindus. Their theory is that Hindu women are abducted, sexually violated and used by Muslim men to increase their own population and power over Indian society. It is alleged to be a large-scale conspiracy by Muslim men to lure and deceptively marry innocent Hindu women and then force them to have a large number of children, thereby exponentially increasing the population of Muslims in India.

In a documentary made by *Al Jazeera*, titled 'Love and Faith in India – 101 East', the news channel documents a session of a training camp conducted by the Bajrang Dal (a Hindu youth organization with links to the BJP) in Saharanpur, a city in Uttar Pradesh.[205] In the words of Kapil Moda, who runs the Bajrang Dal camp: "Love Jihad is a massive conspiracy to turn India into a Muslim country by 2050".[206] The camp run by the Bajrang Dal claims to teach Hindu girls and boys how to protect themselves from *love jihád*. Moda alleges that women are treated as baby-making machines by Muslim men who disguise themselves as Hindus and prey on Hindu girls.

In the interview, Kapil Moda is seen explaining to a group of Hindu boys gathered as a part of the training camp, that Muslims and Christians are scattered in several countries around the world, whereas India is the only country belonging to Hindus. He proclaims that *love jihád* is a conspiracy against the last remaining 900 million Hindus in India. It is this rhetoric that is especially detrimental and amounts to hate speech – it creates panic that the Hindu population is at risk and under threat of becoming marginalized. One of the attendees,

203 Manjari Katju, "The Politics of Ghar Wapsi", in *Economic and Political Weekly*, 2015, vol. 50, no. 1, pp. 21–24.

204 *Ibid.*

205 "Love and Faith in India|101 East", *Al Jazeera*, 27 January 2022 (available on *YouTube*).

206 *Ibid.*

referring to Muslims, stated that "these Taliban-loving traitors should be thrown out of this country".[207]

Several public figures have made statements warning Muslims of dire consequences if they engage in *love jihád*. Yogi Adityanath, the Chief Minister of Uttar Pradesh, was caught on video, stating at a rally that if Muslim men would abduct one Hindu woman, Hindu men would abduct hundred Muslim women in retaliation.[208]

The case of a 25-year-old Hindu woman named Akhila, who converted to Islám and took a new name, Hadiya, garnered national attention in recent times.[209] While Hadiya insisted that she had voluntarily converted to Islám and subsequently married a Muslim man, Shafin Jahan, the High Court of Kerala, on the basis of a petition filed by Hadiya's father, ordered her confinement in her father's home and annulled her marriage.[210] The matter reached the Supreme Court of India, which eventually recognized her agency and reversed the orders of the High Court.[211]

In October 2020, an advertisement by a popular Indian jewellery brand, *Tanishq*, faced immense backlash from the Hindu right-wing for depicting an interfaith marriage and allegedly promoting *love jihád*. The advertisement featured a baby shower being organized for a Hindu bride by her Muslim in-laws.[212] The advertisement was taken down by the jewellery brand, which cited "hurt sentiments" and safety of its employees as the reasons for doing so.[213] Several advertisements have, over the last few years, faced criticism for depicting Hindu-Muslim unity.[214]

Despite the fact that Article 25 of the Indian Constitution protects the right to 'propagate' religion,[215] several states in the country have passed anti-

---

207 *Ibid.*

208 "Love Jihad: BJP's Yogi Adityanath Hate Speech Caught on Camera", *NewsExpress*, 27 August 2014 (available on *YouTube*).

209 Rahul Bhatia, "The Year of Love Jihad in India", *The New Yorker*, 31 December 2017.

210 "A Welcome Quietus: On Hadiya Case Verdict", *The Hindu*, 12 March 2018 (available on The Hindu's web site); High Court of Kerala, *Asokan K.M. v. The Superintendent of Police*, Judgement, 24 May 2017, Writ Petition (Criminal) No. 297 of 2016 (S) (https://www.legal-tools.org/doc/ztjrey/).

211 Supreme Court of India, *Shafin Jahan v. Asokan K.M.*, Judgement, 9 April 2018, Criminal Appeal No. 366 of 2018 (https://www.legal-tools.org/doc/arikp3/).

212 "Tanishq: Jewellery Ad on Interfaith Couple Withdrawn After Outrage", *BBC*, 13 October 2020.

213 *Ibid.*

214 Surbhi Gupta, "Tanishq Pulls Down Ad After Social Media Uproar", *The Indian Express*, 14 October 2020.

215 Constitution of India, Article 25, see *supra* note 95.

conversion legislations that criminalize religious conversions. Although these legislations are specific to each state, their content and purpose are largely similar. These laws are ironically termed 'freedom of religion' laws and intend to prohibit religious conversions that have been brought about through "fraudulent" or "forcible" means or by "allurement" or "inducement". Odisha was the first Indian state to adopt an anti-conversion law, that is, the Odisha Freedom of Religion Act, 1967. At present, a total of nine out of 29 states in India have passed anti-conversion laws – Odisha, Arunachal Pradesh, Madhya Pradesh, Chhattisgarh, Gujarat, Himachal Pradesh, Jharkhand, Uttarakhand and, most recently, Karnataka.

The judicial sanction for these laws can be traced back to the Supreme Court's judgment in *Rev. Stainislaus v. State of Madhya Pradesh* ('*Rev. Stainislaus*'), in 1977, wherein the Court opined that Article 25 of the Indian Constitution, which deals with freedom of religion, does not include the right to convert someone to another religion.[216] Article 25 contains two prongs to the freedom of religion – the freedom of conscience and the right to freely profess, practice and propagate religion.[217] The Court explained its interpretation of the term 'propagate' as it appears in Article 25 and made what may be seen as an arbitrary distinction between spreading the tenets of one's religion and converting another person to one's religion:

> [W]hat the Article grants is not the right to convert another person to one's own religion, but to transmit or spread one's religion by an exposition of its tenets. It has to be remembered that Article 25 (1) guarantees "freedom of conscience" to every citizen, and not merely to the followers of one particular religion, and that, in turn, postulates that there is no fundamental right to convert another person to one's own religion because if a person purposely undertakes the conversion of another person to his religion, as distinguished from his effort to transmit or spread the tenets of his religion, that would impinge on the "freedom of conscience" guaranteed to all the citizens of the country alike.[218]

Despite severe criticism of the Supreme Court's judgment in *Rev. Stainislaus* for being overly broad and vague and posing the risk of including within the ambit of prohibited conversions even those that have been carried out voluntarily, the judgment holds fort even today. *Rev. Stainislaus* grants legitimacy to anti-conversion laws passed by various states, which are often misused

---

[216] Supreme Court of India, *Rev. Stainislaus v. State of Madhya Pradesh*, Judgement, 17 January 1977, (1977) 1 SCC 677 ('*Rev. Stainislaus*') (https://www.legal-tools.org/doc/uc7djo/).

[217] Constitution of India, Article 25, see *supra* note 95.

[218] *Rev. Stainislaus*, see *supra* note 216.

to prohibit inter-faith marriages by claiming that such marriages involve forced conversions, or in other words, *love jihád*.[219] In this manner, anti-conversion laws across the country follow a pattern of legalized discrimination. An analysis of these issues raises an interesting question regarding the threat perception from minority religions that has prompted the passage of anti-conversion laws in India, given the staggering majority that Hindus enjoy in terms of population and demographics.

7.4.10. Cow Vigilantism in India

India is facing increasing instances of violence against Muslims in the name of protecting cows, which have long been considered to be holy animals by Hindus. A few prominent examples of lynching conducted by mobs in the name of cow protection are worth mentioning here.

On 28 September 2015, Mohammed Akhlaq was dragged from his home (the only Muslim home in a locality of Rajputs in Dadri, Uttar Pradesh) and killed by a frenzied mob on the suspicion of consuming and storing cow meat in his home.[220] His son was also severely beaten up and wounded during the lynching.[221] The lynching came after a local Hindu temple in the area announced that a cow had been slaughtered.[222] On the topic of Akhlaq's killing, BJP MP Sakshi Maharaj, referring to cows as Hindus' 'mother', stated that: "We won't remain silent if somebody tries to kill our mother. We are ready to kill and get killed".[223]

On 1 April 2017, Pehlu Khan, a 55-year-old man, left his village Nuh in Haryana, to purchase cattle. Later that day, he and his sons were lynched by a mob of men in Alwar, Rajasthan for transporting cattle.[224] On 21 April 2017, a mob brutally attacked five members of a nomad cattle-herding family in Jammu, on the suspicion that they were taking their cattle for slaughter. The victims included a nine-year-old girl child. A video of the incident emerged on social media, where two women are seen begging for mercy while the mob mercilessly beat an elderly man with rods and sticks while chanting slogans and eventually

---

219 "India's Love Jihad Anti-Conversion Laws Aim to Further Oppress Minorities, and It's Working", *The Conversation*, 3 September 2021 (available on The Conversation's web site).

220 Sukrita Baruah and Abhishek Angad, "Dadri Lynching: No Question of Returning Home, Just Hope Case Moves Quickly, Says Akhlaq's Kin", *The Indian Express*, 28 September 2018.

221 Aishwarya S. Iyer, "Dadri Lynching Trial Begins: How Akhlaq's Kin Waited for 5 Years", *The Quint*, 26 March 2021.

222 Abhimanyu Kumar, "The Lynching that Changed India", *Al Jazeera*, 5 October 2017.

223 "BJP MP Sakshi Maharaj Says Ready to Kill and Get Killed for Our Mother, Calls SP's Azam Khan a 'Pakistani'", *News18*, 6 October 2015.

224 "No One Killed Pehlu Khan", *Maktoob Media*, 14 August 2019.

breaking and burning down the family shelter.[225] One day before Eid in 2017, a 15-year-old boy named Junaid was stabbed to death in a local train in Delhi. Just before the incident, he was mocked for being Muslim and a “beef-eater”.[226]

The cow has come to be regarded as a sacred animal by most Hindus, especially Brahmins. Right-wing groups use this belief as a means to differentiate against groups that cause harm to the sacred animal, that is, Dalits, Christians and Muslims.[227] However, as American Indologist Wendy Doniger points out in her book ‘On Hinduism’, early religious texts of Hindus made references to cows as food and the sacrifice of cows was done on the arrival of guests.[228] The practice of refraining from eating cows developed in later texts. As Romila Thapar points out:

> Eventually it became a matter of status to refrain from eating beef and the prohibition was strengthened by various religious sanctions. Significantly, the prohibition was prevalent among the upper castes.[229]

The increasing religious diktats concerning beef and the renunciation of cow meat became a symbol of upward social and economic mobility among Hindus, especially the Brahmins. In later years, Hindus’ belief in the sacredness of the cow became a ploy to enable the ‘othering’ of Muslims and Christians who slaughtered and consumed the animal. Those who ‘invaded’ the Hindus’ homeland, that is, Muslim rulers and British imperialists, consumed beef and hence the cow became a symbol of the fight to protect the homeland from foreign invaders in political and religious movements.[230]

In modern times, the beef issue has become a serious bone of contention between Hindus and Muslims, resulting in large-scale violence and vigilantism by Hindu right-wing mobs. In India, the term ‘beef’ usually represents an umbrella term that includes cow meat and the meat of buffalos or oxen. In the south Indian state of Kerala and in many north-eastern states, beef forms an integral

225 “Chilling Video Seems to Show How Jammu Cow Vigilantes Brutally Attacked a Family of Nomadic Herders”, *Scroll*, 23 April 2017.

226 Apoorvanand, “What is Behind India’s Epidemic of ‘Mob Lynching’?”, *Al Jazeera*, 6 July 2017.

227 Mohammed Sinan Siyech and Akanksha Narain, “Beef-Related violence in India: An Expression of Islamophobia”, in *Islamophobia Studies Journal*, 2018, vol. 4, no. 2, pp. 181–194.

228 Wendy Doniger, *On Hinduism*, Aleph Book Company, New Delhi, 2013, pp. 502–503.

229 Romila Thapar, *The Penguin History of Early India: From the Origins to 1300*, Penguin Books, London, 2002, p. 115.

230 Siyech and Narain, 2018, pp. 181–194, see *supra* note 227.

part of the daily diet. These are also the states that currently do not have a beef ban in place.[231]

Since the BJP came to national power in 2014, there has been a spur in communal rhetoric in the country which has given rise to vigilante groups purportedly acting for the protection of cows, who have perpetrated violence against Muslims and others suspected of consuming, buying or selling beef.[232] According to a Human Rights Watch ('HRW') report titled 'Violent Cow Protection in India: Vigilante Groups Attack Minorities', between May 2015 and December 2018, at least 44 people, a large majority of them being Muslims, have been killed across 12 Indian states, while approximately 280 people have been injured across the country in cow-related violence.[233] According to the United States Commission on International Religious Freedom ('USCIRF'):

> Since the BJP came to power in 2014, there have been over 100 attacks, amounting to over 98 percent of such attacks since 2010. Lynching victims, rather than the perpetrators, are often arrested under these laws.[234]

There are several instances of hate speech against those who do not regard the cow as sacred and kill cows for consumption, which are veiled attacks on Dalits, *adivasis*, Muslims and Christians in India:

> Muslims can continue to live in this country, but they will have to give up eating beef. The cow is an article of faith here.[235]
>
> We will hang those who kill cows.[236]
>
> I had promised that I will break the hands and legs of those who do not consider cows their mother and kill them.[237]

Communal rhetoric around cow protection had also been used by Prime Minister Modi and his aides in the run-up to the 2014 general elections at the national level:

---

[231] Komal Deol, "Cow Protection Was a Sensitive Subject in India Even When the Constitution Was Being Framed", *Scroll*, 7 July 2021.

[232] "India: Vigilante 'Cow Protection' Groups Attack Minorities", *Human Rights Watch*, 18 February 2019 (https://www.legal-tools.org/doc/3xy1e1/).

[233] *Ibid.*

[234] United States Commission on International Religious Freedom, "Annual Report, 2020", April 2020 (https://www.legal-tools.org/doc/3o8jz4/).

[235] Varinder Bhatia and Nirupama Subramanian, "Muslims Can Live in this Country, But Will Have to Give Up Eating Beef, Says Haryana CM Manohar Lal Khattar", *Indian Express*, 16 October 2015.

[236] "Will hang those who kill cow: Chhattisgarh Chief Minister Raman Singh", *India Today*, 2 April 2017.

[237] Anindita Sanyal, "'Will Break Limbs of Cow Killers': Legislator Accused in Muzaffarnagar Case", *NDTV*, 27 March 2017.

Modi ko matdan, gai ko jeevadan [Vote for Modi, give life to the cow], *BJP ka sandesh, bachegi gai, bachega desh* [BJP's message, the cow will be saved, the country will be saved].[238]

Cow protection was one of the key conditions on the basis of which the VHP and the RSS agreed to back Modi as the prime ministerial candidate.[239]

7.4.11. Communal Violence at the Time of Ram Navami Celebrations in India (April 2022)

In India, a concerning trend is developing – religious festivals and processions are being used as playgrounds to fuel communal tensions and intolerance to religious practices and customs. This trend places additional onus on the local administration and law enforcement authorities to isolate epicentres of such violence and contain its spread, a responsibility that local administrations in most states in India have failed to discharge or simply refused to shoulder.

Ram Navami is a Hindu festival that celebrates the birth of Lord Rama, believed to be an incarnation of the Hindu god, Lord Vishnu. Ram Navami celebrations in India in April 2022 were besmirched with incidents of communal violence. In at least six Indian states – Delhi, West Bengal, Gujarat, Jharkhand, Madhya Pradesh and Karnataka – communal clashes broke out during processions being carried out to celebrate Ram Navami. It was reported that in Gujarat, Hindus celebrating the festival led processions into Muslim-dominated areas and allegedly hurled slurs at local Muslims, accusing them of mocking the Ram Navami festivities, which triggered violent clashes between Hindus and Muslims, including stone pelting and arson. Muslim shops, mosques and other property were set on fire and there appeared to be a deliberate and conscious attempt to provoke Muslims. The VHP and the Bajrang Dal purportedly put out calls on their social media inviting Hindus to such processions – the posters containing such invites were reported to have stated "*Jai Hindurashtra*" (victory of Hindu Nation) and "*Aao mil kar kare Ram Rajya ka Nirmaan*" (come, let's realize the goal of the Rule of Lord Rama).[240]

In Khargone, Madhya Pradesh, a Ram Navami procession was carried out in the Muslim-dominated area of Talab Chowk. Communal violence broke out between the members of the procession and Muslim residents of the area.[241] The violence was characterized by stone pelting and arson, prompting the police to

238 Elizabeth Soumya, "Sacred Cows and Politics of Beef in India", *Al Jazeera*, 20 April 2014.

239 *Ibid.*

240 Tarushi Aswani, "'Organised Violence': How Mosques, Dargahs, Muslim Houses Were Vandalised in Gujarat on Ram Navami", *The Wire*, 12 April 2022.

241 "Madhya Pradesh: Curfew in Khargone City After Stone-Pelting at Ram Navami Process Triggers Arson", *The New Indian Express*, 11 April 2022.

impose a curfew in the region.[242] Similar incidents of violence, stone-pelting and arson were also reported during Ram Navami processions in Goa's Vasco district[243] and in Karnataka's Kolar district.[244]

On 10 April 2022, violence erupted on the JNU campus in Delhi, leaving several students injured, over an alleged disagreement over non-vegetarian food being served in the hostels. There are different versions as to what triggered the violence. While a section of students belonging to ABVP claim that some 'leftists' wanted to disrupt and prevent a Ram Navami '*havan*' (a Hindu ritual in which offerings such as ghee and grains are burned on a special occasion) from taking place, another section of students claimed that ABVP students had objected to a vendor delivering chicken to be cooked in the hostel during the ABVP's Ram Navami *havan*, which had triggered the clashes.[245]

7.4.12. Jahangirpuri Clashes and the Bulldozer Demolition Drive

Communal violence flared up in Delhi's Jahangirpuri area, after hundreds of people, including several members of Hindu right-wing organizations took out a Shobha Yatra procession in celebration of Hanuman Jayanti (birth of Hindu god Hanuman) on 16 April 2022. The Jahangirpuri neighbourhood of Delhi predominantly consists of a Bengali-speaking Muslim population, and local BJP leaders alleged that a large proportion of them were illegal Bangladeshi immigrants.[246] While Hindus and Muslims blame each other for the clashes, it is reported that during the Hanuman Jayanti procession in Jahangirpuri, Hindu men were seen wearing saffron clothing, brandishing swords and chanting slogans. It is alleged that members of the Hanuman Jayanti procession waved a saffron flag in front of a mosque in Jahangirpuri, which ignited violence.[247]

In the wake of the communal clashes, BJP leader Kapil Mishra claimed that Jahangirpuri was known to harbour "Bangladeshi infiltrators" and that people had been mobilized from the area during the Delhi riots in 2020. He reportedly suggested that the incident should be treated as a terror attack. He stated that:

---

242 The Print, "MP: Five Held for Killing Man During Communal Violence; Three Others Absconding", 22 April 2022.

243 Herald Goa, "Tension Erupts in Baina as Groups Belonging to Two Communities Clash", 11 April 2022.

244 "Violence in 7 States on Ram Navami: One Dead in Gujarat, One in Jharkhand", *The Quint*, 11 April 2022.

245 "Violence in JNU After ABVP Allegedly Tried to Stop Non-Veg Being Cooked on Ram Navami", *The Wire*, 11 April 2022.

246 "Jahangirpuri: Shock and Anger in Delhi After Religious Violence", *BBC News*, 18 April 2022.

247 Arfa Khanum Sherwani, "Watch: How Communal Clashes Broke Out in Delhi's Jahangirpuri", *The Wire*, 21 April 2022.

They should be identified and their homes should be bulldozed.[248]

Following the communal tensions in the Jahangirpuri neighbourhood of Delhi, Delhi's local civic body, the Municipal Corporation of Delhi (run by the BJP government), carried out what it called a routine anti-encroachment drive in Jahangirpuri purportedly to clear all illegal constructions in the area.[249] The North Delhi Municipal Corporation demolished several shops, houses, carts and even the outer gate of a mosque in the area, which had been at the centre of communal clashes in the neighbourhood the previous week. No warning or notice had been issued to the alleged encroachers prior to the demolition drive.[250] The demolitions are alleged to have been the consequence of a letter written by Delhi BJP Chief Adesh Gupta to the Mayor of Delhi, requesting him to identify illegal constructions by "rioters" and demolish them.[251] The demolition drive was carried out along with the deployment of heavy police and paramilitary forces, despite being termed a "routine exercise" by the Delhi Mayor. The Supreme Court agreed to hear a petition challenging the anti-encroachment drive and stayed the activities of the Delhi civic body.[252]

A demolition drive was also carried out by the BJP government in the state of Madhya Pradesh, including in Khargone, allegedly selectively targeting the homes and properties of those believed to be involved in the communal clashes on the occasion of Ram Navami celebrations in the area on 10 April 2022. Reportedly, areas where maximum rioting had taken place were identified and the district administration had sought to demolish "illegal structures" constructed on encroached government land in those areas to "send a message" to rioters. Although officials claimed that there is no correlation between the demolitions and the communal violence,[253] bulldozers targeted and destroyed the homes of Muslims accused (but not convicted) of throwing stones at Hindus during the incident in Khargone.[254] Soon after the communal violence broke out, the State Home Minister for Madhya Pradesh Narottam Mishra stated that "*Jis*

---

248 "Jahangirpuri Violence: Arvind Kejriwal Appeals for Calm, Kapil Mishra Calls It Terror Attack", *The Indian Express*, 17 April 2022.

249 Nitin Srivastava, "Jahangirpuri: How Religious Violence Razed Homes and Dreams", *BBC News*, 21 April 2022.

250 Akhil Kumar, "14 Teams, 9 Bulldozers, 1500 Cops: How Delhi Demolition Was Carried Out", *NDTV*, 20 April 2022.

251 *Ibid.*

252 "Jahangirpuri Eviction Drive Updates: Demolition Drive Stopped After Supreme Court's 'Status Quo' Order", *The Hindu*, 20 April 2022.

253 Neelam Pandey, "'Stone Pelters Will Be Greeted with Bulldozer': BJP Defends MP Govt Action on Khargone Riot", *The Print*, 14 April 2022.

254 Gerry Shih and Anant Gupta, "How Bulldozers in India Became a Symbol of Hindu Nationalism", *The Washington Post*, 27 April 2022.

ghar se patthar aaye hai, us ghar ko hi pattharon ka dher banayenge" (The houses from which stones were pelted will be turned into rubble).[255] Mishra further directly blamed Muslims for the communal violence during Ram Navami celebrations, stating that "If Muslims carry out such attacks then they should not expect justice".[256]

The anti-encroachment drive in Delhi soon spread to other neighbourhoods.[257] A demolition drive was set to take place in the Shaheen Bagh neighbourhood; however, it was halted due to resistance and protests by residents, activists and media personnel.[258] Two weeks after the demolition drive in Jahangirpuri, the BJP-ruled South Delhi Municipal Corporation carried out similar demolitions in Delhi's Tughlakabad area.[259]

The bulldozer has thus become a symbol of the brute force of the Indian state, its complicity in targeting minorities, especially Muslims (since the demolition drives primarily targeted Muslim-dominated neighbourhoods) and apathy towards growing instances of communal violence in the country. News reports were flooded with images of bulldozers razing shops and houses to the ground, as locals looked on, too stunned and helpless to react.[260]

7.4.13. BBC Documentary Ban

On 17 January 2023, the British Broadcasting Company ('BBC') released the first episode of its two-part investigative documentary titled 'India: The Modi Question'. The documentary examines the intense communal riots that broke out in the western state of Gujarat in 2002, at which time Narendra Modi was Gujarat's Chief Minister. The riots were set off by an incident on 27 February 2002, in which coaches of the Sabarmati Express train, carrying several Hindu pilgrims, were set on fire at the Godhra railway station, resulting in the death of 59 people. The Muslim minority was blamed for the incident and in retaliation, for three consecutive days, an organized mob killed approximately 1,180 people,

[255] Bismee Taskin, "'Message to Rioters' or 'Anti-Encroachment Drive' – What Exactly Happened in Khargone After Riot", *The Print*, 16 April 2022.

[256] Anurag Dwary, "Madhya Pradesh Home Minister Blames Muslims for Ram Navami Clashes", *NDTV*, 12 April 2022.

[257] "Anti-Encroachment Demolition Drive Underway in Several Parts of Delhi Today", *Livemint*, 20 May 2022.

[258] Shreya Basak, "The Demolition Drive at Shaheen Bagh that Never Happened, but Did It Give a Message?", *Outlook*, 10 May 2022.

[259] "Demolition Drive Underway in Delhi's Tughlakabad Area", *Scroll*, 4 May 2022.

[260] Zoya Mateen, "Madhya Pradesh: Why an Indian State Is Demolishing Muslim Homes", *BBC News*, 15 April 2022.

the majority being Muslims.[261] The documentary references a hitherto unpublished investigative report by the British Foreign Office, which concluded that Modi was "directly responsible" for the "climate of impunity" enabling the communal violence, which the report described as reaching the level of ethnic cleansing. The report also suggests that the violence was premeditated by the VHP and that "the attack on the train at Godhra on 27 February provided the pretext. If it had not occurred, another one would have been found".[262]

The inquiry by the British government also reportedly stated that:

> Extent of violence much greater than reported. At least 2,000 killed. Widespread systematic rape of Muslim women. 138,000 internal refugees. The targeted destruction of all Muslim businesses in Hindu and mixed Hindu-Muslim areas.[263]

Modi has long been accused of failing to protect the Muslim minority community from the right-wing Hindu mobs and even implicitly supporting their actions during the Gujarat riots. There are several accounts of police officials standing by while rioters wreaked havoc against Muslim victims, targeting their businesses and homes and even raping Muslim women. In 2008, the Supreme Court of India constituted a Special Investigation Team ('SIT') headed by R.K. Raghavan (former Director, Central Bureau of Investigation) to investigate the Godhra incident as well as the subsequent pogrom. In 2012, the SIT filed a closure report, giving a clean chit to Modi and others, stating that there was no prosecutable evidence against them. In June 2022, the Supreme Court dismissed a plea filed against the findings of the SIT[264] – in essence, absolving Modi of any responsibility or liability in the Godhra riots of 2002.

The BJP government's response to the BBC documentary is illustrative of the painful demise of free speech in India, the world's largest 'democracy'. Arindam Bagchi, the official spokesperson for India's Ministry of External Affairs, termed the documentary "a propaganda piece designed to push a particular discredited narrative" and contended that "the bias, the lack of objectivity, and frankly a continuing colonial mindset is blatantly visible".[265] Rishi Sunak,

---

261 Vidya Krishnan, "What the BBC's "Modi Question" Reveals About India", *The Caravan*, 28 January 2023.

262 Hartosh Singh Bal, "BBC Row: UK Report States VHP Planned Gujarat Violence in Advance, Godhra a 'Pretext'", *The Caravan*, 23 January 2023.

263 Ashis Ray, "New BBC Documentary Puts Narendra Modi Back in the Dock", *Frontline*, 19 January 2023.

264 Supreme Court of India, *Zakia Ahsan Jafri v. State of Gujarat and Anr.*, Judgment, 24 June 2022, (2022) SCC OnLine SC 773 (https://www.legal-tools.org/doc/uvc22o/).

265 "India Government Criticises BBC's Modi Documentary", *BBC News*, 20 January 2023.

United Kingdom's Prime Minister, stated that he disagrees "with the characterisation" of Modi in the BBC documentary.[266]

While the documentary was not made available by BBC in India, unauthorized clips were circulated across YouTube and Twitter. The Information and Broadcasting Ministry invoked emergency powers under the Information Technology Rules, 2021 to direct YouTube and Twitter to block links sharing the documentary.[267] Attempts to screen the documentary at JNU and Jamia were allegedly halted by officials by cutting off electricity supply and access to the Internet.[268]

By reflecting on the Godhra riots of 2002 and incidents across the country over the last decade, such as the lynching of Muslims by cow vigilantes, the Delhi pogrom in February 2020, the calls for ethnic cleansing of Muslims and the bulldozer demolition drive, to name a few, a recurring pattern of targeted violence and othering of Muslim minorities emerges. The message sent out to Muslims in India today is that they live at the mercy of the Hindu majority, who enjoy unbridled impunity to commit atrocities against them, dehumanize them and question their loyalties to the nation. The message was loud and clear, when in August 2022, the Indian government approved the premature release of 11 men convicted and sentenced to life imprisonment for gang-raping a pregnant Muslim woman named Bilkis Bano and killing several members of her family during the 2002 Gujarat riots (including her three years-old daughter), on grounds of good behaviour.[269]

7.5. The Statutory Framework in India

Having highlighted several recent incidents of communal violence and hateful expression against Muslims in the name of Hinduism, it is important to draw attention to the legal framework on hate speech in India. There is no legal definition for hate speech in India. Neither is there a universally accepted definition of hate speech within the international legal framework. Article 19(1) of the Indian Constitution gives all citizens of India the right to freedom of speech and expression. However, this right is subject to reasonable restrictions "in the interests of the sovereignty and integrity of India, the security of the State, friendly

---

[266] "Rishi Sunak Defends PM Modi in UK Parliament Over BBC's Gujarat Riots Doc", *The Indian Express*, 22 January 2023.

[267] Rhea Mogul, Manveena Suri and Aliza Kassim Khalidi, "India Bans BBC Documentary on PM Modi's Role in Gujarat Riots", *CNN*, 23 January 2023.

[268] "Jamia, JNU: India Students Angry After Screenings of BBC Modi Documentary Blocked", *BBC News*, 25 January 2023.

[269] "Bilkis Bano Case: SC Promises to Form New Bench to Hear Plea Against Early Release of Convicts", *The Hindu*, 8 February 2023.

relations with foreign States, public order, decency or morality or in relation to contempt of court, defamation or incitement to an offence".[270]

7.5.1. The Indian Penal Code of 1860

The IPC contains several sections that deal with hate speech. Section 153A of the IPC penalizes "promoting enmity between different groups on grounds of religion, race, place of birth, residence, language, etc. and doing acts prejudicial to the maintenance of harmony". The means of promoting or attempting to promote such enmity includes a broad range of activities, such as "by words, either spoken or written, or by signs or by visible representations or otherwise" or by the commission of acts which are "prejudicial to the maintenance of harmony between different religious, racial, language or regional groups or castes or communities, and which disturbs or is likely to disturb the public tranquillity", with the effect of such acts being to promote "disharmony or feelings of enmity, hatred or ill-will between different religious, racial, language or regional groups or castes or communities".[271] Punishment for the commission of the above-mentioned offence shall be imprisonment which may extend to three years, a fine, or both. If such an offence is committed in a place of worship, he or she shall be punished with imprisonment which may extend to five years and shall also be liable to a fine.

Section 153B of the IPC prohibits imputations and assertions against members of any religious, racial, regional or linguistic group which are prejudicial to national integration.[272] The punishment for an offence under this section is the same as for the commission of an offence under Section 153A.

Section 295A of the IPC penalizes deliberate and malicious acts intended to outrage religious feelings of any class by insulting its religion or religious beliefs.[273] Punishment for this offence is imprisonment for a term which may extend up to four years, or with fine, or both.

Section 298 of the IPC penalizes the deliberate wounding of religious feelings of any person, by the utterance of any word, or by making any sound in the hearing of that person or by making any gestures in the sight of that person, or by placing any object in the sight of that person.[274] Punishment for the commission of an offence under Section 298 is imprisonment up to a term of one year, or with fine, or both.

---

270 Constitution of India, Article 19(2), see *supra* note 95.

271 Indian Penal Code, 6 October 1860, Section 153A (https://www.legal-tools.org/doc/6a8f6b/).

272 *Ibid.*, Section 153B.

273 *Ibid.*, Section 295A.

274 *Ibid.*, Section 298.

Section 124A of the IPC deals with the offence of sedition (hatred, contempt, disaffection towards the Government of India),[275] while Section 505(2) penalizes the offence of public mischief: whoever makes, circulates or publishes any statement or report containing any rumour or alarming news with the "intent to create or promote, or which is likely to create or promote, on grounds of religion, race, place of birth, residence, language, caste or community or any other ground whatsoever, feelings of enmity, hatred or ill-will between different religious, racial, language or regional groups or castes or communities" is liable to be punished with imprisonment up to three years, or with fine, or with both.[276]

Sections 8, 123(3A) and 125 of the Representation of the People Act, 1951 ('RPA') deal with electoral malpractice.[277] Section 8 of the RPA provides for disqualification of persons convicted of offences under, *inter alia*, Section 153A of the IPC or sub-sections (2) and (3) of Section 505 of the IPC. Section 123 of the RPA defines what constitute 'corrupt practices' within the context of elections in India. Section 123(3A) defines a 'corrupt practice' as: "the promotion of, or attempt to promote, feelings of enmity or hatred between different classes of the citizens of India on grounds of religion, race, caste, community, or language, by a candidate or his agent or any other person with the consent of a candidate or his election agent for the furtherance of the prospects of the election of that candidate or for prejudicially affecting the election of any candidate". Section 125 of the RPA provides that an offence committed under Section 123(3A) of the RPA shall be punished with up to three years of imprisonment, or with fine, or both.

Section 95 of the Indian Code of Criminal Procedure, 1973 ('CrPC') empowers the state governments to declare forfeited any newspaper, book or document, which contains matter the publication of which is punishable under, *inter alia*, Sections 124-A, 153-A or 153-B of the IPC.[278] Section 107 of the CrPC serves as a measure of preventive justice and empowers an Executive Magistrate to prevent a breach of peace or disturbance of public order that may occur within his local jurisdiction (including as a consequence of hate speech).[279] Similarly, Section 144 of the CrPC authorizes a District Magistrate, a Sub-Divisional Magistrate or any other Executive Magistrate specially empowered by a state government in this behalf, to pass orders in urgent cases of nuisance or apprehended

---

275 *Ibid.*, Section 124A.

276 *Ibid.*, Section 505.

277 India, The Representation of the People Act, Sections 8, 123(3A), and 125, 17 July 1951 (https://www.legal-tools.org/doc/f9v9qf/).

278 India, Code of Criminal Procedure, 25 January 1974, Section 95 (https://www.legal-tools.org/doc/29b68e/).

279 *Ibid.*, Section 107.

danger to human life, health or safety, or a disturbance of the public tranquillity, or a riot, or an affray.[280] As can be seen from these provisions of the CrPC, Indian state governments enjoy wide discretion in determining what publications contain material the content of which is punishable under the hate speech provisions of the IPC as well as what situations warrant danger to public order and human life.

7.5.2. The Supreme Court's Jurisprudence on the Meaning of Hate Speech

In the Supreme Court case *Ramji Lal Modi v. State of Uttar Pradesh*,[281] the petitioner argued that Article 19(2) of the Indian Constitution only allowed for restrictions on the freedom of speech in the interests of public order, however, the ambit of Section 295A was much wider, since it criminalized all speech that was intended to outrage religious feelings. The Supreme Court clarified the rationale behind the restriction of speech under Section 295A of the IPC as follows:

> In the first place clause (2) of Article 19 protects a law imposing reasonable restrictions on the exercise of the right to freedom of speech and expression "in the interests of" public order, which is much wider than "for maintenance of" public order. If, therefore, certain activities have a tendency to cause public disorder, a law penalising such activities as an offence cannot but be held to be a law imposing reasonable restriction "in the interests of public order" although in some cases those activities may not actually lead to a breach of public order. In the next place Section 295-A does not penalise any and every act of insult to or attempt to insult the religion or the religious beliefs of a class of citizens but it penalises only those acts of insults to or those varieties of attempts to insult the religion or the religious beliefs of a class of citizens, which are perpetrated with the deliberate and malicious intention of outraging the religious feelings of that class. Insults to religion offered unwittingly or carelessly or without any deliberate or malicious intention to outrage the religious feelings of that class do not come within the section. It only punishes the aggravated form of insult to religion when it is perpetrated with the deliberate and malicious intention of outraging the religious feelings of that class. The calculated tendency of this aggravated form of insult is clearly to disrupt the public order and the section, which penalises such activities, is well within the protection of clause (2) of Article 19 as being a law imposing reasonable restrictions on the exercise of the

---

280 *Ibid.*, Section 144.

281 Supreme Court of India, *Ramji Lal Modi v. State of Uttar Pradesh*, Judgement, 5 April 1957, AIR 1957 SC 620 (https://www.legal-tools.org/doc/bi4001/).

> right to freedom of speech and expression guaranteed by Article 19(1)(a). Having regard to the ingredients of the offence created by the impugned section, there cannot, in our opinion, be any possibility of this law being applied for purposes not sanctioned by the Constitution. In other words, the language employed in the section is not wide enough to cover restrictions both within and without the limits of constitutionally permissible legislative action affecting the fundamental right guaranteed by Article 19(1)(a) and consequently, the question of severability does not arise and the decisions relied upon by learned counsel for the petitioner have no application to this case. For the reasons stated above, the impugned section falls well within the protection of cl. (2) of Art. 19 and this application must, therefore, be dismissed.[282]

Therefore, any speech that has a tendency to create public disorder could be penalized. Through the above interpretation, it is seen that the Supreme Court created a "legal fiction".[283] The Court assumed that insults to a religion uttered with the deliberate and malicious intention of outraging the religious feelings of a class would necessarily tend to cause public disorder and hence, ought to be penalized.

In *Bilal Ahmed Kaloo v. State of Andhra Pradesh*,[284] the Supreme Court distinguished between the provisions of Sections 153A and 505(2) of the IPC. The Court held that the common ingredient between both sections is the promotion of feelings of enmity, hatred or ill-will between different religious or regional groups or castes or communities. While under Section 153A, promotion of such feelings is done by a person through "words, either spoken or written, or by signs or by visible representations", under Section 505(2), such feelings are promoted by making and publishing or circulating any statement or report containing alarming news or rumours.[285] *Mens rea* is a necessary ingredient of both offences.[286] Further, both sections refer to promotion of feelings of enmity, hatred and ill-will "between different" religious, racial, linguistic or regional groups and hence the Court concluded that "it is necessary that at least two such groups or communities should be involved. Merely inciting the feeling of one community or group without any reference to any other community or group

[282] *Ibid.*, para. 9.

[283] Gautam Bhatia, "'Blasphemy law' and the Constitution", *Mint*, 19 March 2016.

[284] Supreme Court of India, *Bilal Ahmed Kaloo v. State of Andhra Pradesh*, Judgement, 6 August 1997, (1997) 7 SCC 431 (https://www.legal-tools.org/doc/n4aknu/).

[285] *Ibid.*, para. 10.

[286] *Ibid.*, para. 11.

cannot attract either of the two sections".[287] The Court explained the distinction between the two sections in the following terms:

> The main distinction between the two offences is that while publication of the words or representation is not necessary under the former, such publication is sine qua non under Section 505. The words "whoever makes, publishes or circulates" used in the setting of Section 505(2) cannot be interpreted disjunctively but only as supplementary to each other. If it is construed disjunctively, anyone who makes a statement falling within the meaning of Section 505 would, without publication or circulation, be liable to conviction. But the same is the effect with Section 153-A also and then that section would have been bad for redundancy. The intention of the legislature in providing two different sections on the same subject would have been to cover two different fields of similar colour. The fact that both sections were included as a package in the same amending enactment lends further support to the said construction.[288]

The definition of hate speech remains elusive and unsettled both within the Indian statutory framework as well as in the international legal framework. In *Pravasi Bhalai Sangathan v. Union of India* ('*Pravasi Bhalai*'),[289] the Supreme Court of India drew on the understanding of hate speech espoused by the Supreme Court of Canada in *Saskatchewan (Human Rights Commission) v. Whatcott*, which explained the meaning of hate speech as follows:

> Hate speech is an attempt to marginalize individuals on the basis of their membership of a particular group. Using expression that exposes the group to hatred, hate speech seeks to delegitimize group members in the eyes of the majority, reducing their social standing and acceptance within society. Hate speech therefore rises beyond causing distress to individual group members. It can have societal impact. Hate speech lays the groundwork for later, broad attacks on vulnerable that can range from discrimination to ostracism, segregation, deportation, violence, and, in the most extreme cases, genocide. Hate speech also impacts a protected group's ability to respond to the substantive ideas under debate, thereby placing a serious barrier to their full participation in our democracy.[290]

---

[287] *Ibid.*, para. 15.

[288] *Ibid.*, para. 12.

[289] Supreme Court of India, *Pravasi Bhalai Sangathan* v. *Union of India*, Judgement, 12 March 2014, (2014) 11 SCC 477, para. 8 ('*Pravasi Bhalai Sangathan*') (https://www.legal-tools.org/doc/6drbwq/).

[290] Supreme Court of Canada, *Saskatchewan (Human Rights Commission) v. Whatcott*, Judgment, 27 February 2013, [2013] 1 S.C.R (https://www.legal-tools.org/doc/ojtnu8/).

This understanding of hate speech places emphasis on speech that can cause actual material harm through the social, economic and political marginalization of a community. It is something that feeds into a larger context of discrimination. The idea of discrimination lies at the heart of hate speech as explained above. This definition of hate speech is also important in that it focuses on speech that targets the social standing of a group and does not dwell on causing of distress to individuals.[291]

The Indian Supreme Court in *Pravasi Bhalai* also requested the Law Commission of India to consider, *inter alia*, a definition for hate speech.[292] The Law Commission of India, in its Report on Hate Speech of 2017, explained the idea of hate speech as follows:

> Hate speech generally is an incitement to hatred primarily against a group of persons defined in terms of race, ethnicity, gender, sexual orientation, religious belief and the like (sections 153A, 295A read with section 298 IPC). Thus, hate speech is any word written or spoken, signs, visible representations within the hearing or sight of a person with the intention to cause fear or alarm, or incitement to violence.[293]

The Law Commission recommended the insertion of new provisions in the IPC to elaborately address the issue of hate speech. Accordingly, the Law Commission proposed a draft amendment bill, The Criminal Law (Amendment) Bill, 2017, which proposed the insertion of two new sections in the IPC: Section 153C (prohibiting incitement to hatred) and Section 505A (intentionally causing fear, alarm or provocation of violence in certain cases).[294] In this sense, the Law Commission seems to have been aware of the dangers of hate speech in terms of its potential to incite both violence and hatred. However, the recommendations of the Law Commission have not been accepted to date.

In a recent case, *Amish Devgan v. Union of India and Others* ('*Amish Devgan*'),[295] the Indian Supreme Court analysed its jurisprudence on hate speech and once again underscored the importance of 'public order' as the rationale behind the curtailment of free speech. The Supreme Court also emphasized that one of the objectives behind criminalizing hate speech was 'dignity':

---

[291] Gautam Bhatia, *Offend, Shock, or Disturb: Free Speech under the Indian Constitution*, Oxford University Press, 2018, pp. 137–173.

[292] *Pravasi Bhalai Sangathan*, para. 29, see *supra* note 289.

[293] Law Commission of India, 267th Report on Hate Speech in India, 23 March 2017, para. 6.31 (https://www.legal-tools.org/doc/l6puhr/).

[294] *Ibid.*, para. 6.33.

[295] Supreme Court of India, *Amish Devgan v. Union of India and Others*, Judgement, 7 December 2020, (2021) 3 SCC 306 (https://www.legal-tools.org/doc/lrh6yj/).

> At this stage, it is necessary to clarify what is meant by the expression 'dignity' in the context of 'hate speech' – for an expansive meaning, if given, would repress and impede freedom to express views, opine and challenge beliefs, ideas and acts. Dignity, in the context of criminalisation of speech with which we are concerned, refers to a person's basic entitlement as a member of a society in good standing, his status as a social equal and as bearer of human rights and constitutional entitlements. It gives assurance of participatory equality in inter-personal relationships between the citizens, and between the State and the citizens, and thereby fosters self-worth. Dignity in this sense does not refer to any particular level of honour or esteem as an individual, as in the case of defamation which is individualistic. The Supreme Court of the United States of America in Beauharnais v. Illinois, while upholding conviction for hate speech, had emphasised that such speech should amount to group defamation which though analogous to individual defamation has been traditionally excluded from free speech protection in America. Loss of dignity and self-worth of the targeted group members contributes to disharmony amongst groups, erodes tolerance and open-mindedness which are a must for multi-cultural society committed to the idea of equality. It affects an individual as a member of a group. It is however necessary that at least two groups or communities must be involved; merely referring to feelings of one community or group without any reference to any other community or group does not attract the 'hate speech' definition.

Thus, in the Supreme Court's understanding of the statutory provisions on hate speech in India, particularly Sections 153A and 505(2) of the IPC, in order for hateful utterances to constitute 'hate speech', it must refer to two distinct groups and attempt to create enmity between the two.

Further, in *Amish Devgan*, the Supreme Court has construed hate speech as speech that is in the nature of incitement to hatred or violence and that promotes or is likely to promote public disorder:

> Therefore, anti-democratic speech in general and political extremist speech in particular, which has no useful purpose, if and only when in the nature of incitement to violence that 'creates', or is 'likely to create' or 'promotes' or is 'likely to promote' public disorder, would not be protected.
>
> 55. Sometimes, difficulty may arise and the courts and authorities would have to exercise discernment and caution in deciding whether the 'content' is a political or policy comment, or creates or spreads hatred against the targeted group or community. This is of importance and significance as overlap is possible and principles have to be evolved to distinguish. We would refer to one

> example to illustrate the difference. Proponents of affirmative action and those opposing it, are perfectly and equally entitled to raise their concerns and even criticise the policies adopted even when sanctioned by a statute or meeting constitutional scrutiny, without any fear or concern that they would be prosecuted or penalised. However, penal action would be justified when the speech proceeds beyond and is of the nature which defames, stigmatises and insults the targeted group provoking violence or psychosocial hatred. The 'content' should reflect hate which tends to vilify, humiliate and incite hatred or violence against the target group based upon identity of the group beyond and besides the subject matter.

Thus, it can be seen from the above analysis that the Supreme Court has on several occasions considered the exact import of statutory provisions on hate speech within the Indian context. The Supreme Court's analysis in both *Amish Devgan* and *Pravasi Bhalai* provide the basis to understand the need to maintain a balance between free speech guaranteed under the Indian Constitution and the need to curtail hate speech within the Indian context, given the rising instances of Islámophobia, genocidal slogans against minorities and religious polarization. While the Court in *Amish Devgan* does not mention ostracization or discrimination as one of the consequences arising from hate speech, this is explicitly referred to in the definition favoured by the Court in *Pravasi Bhalai* and the definition adopted by the UN Strategy and Plan of Action on Hate Speech.[296] Hate speech as a tool to discriminate, stigmatize and destabilize the Muslim community and incite violence against them is playing out in real time in India.

7.6. Conclusions

Hate speech and violence can have serious consequences for the social fabric of a country, especially one as diverse and multicultural as India. The rise in hate speech and calls for violence and genocide by Hindu extremists against Muslims has reached an alarming level in recent years. The simultaneous development of social media platforms, which are used as tools to spread hate rhetoric and discrimination against minority groups, has become a form of psychological warfare, which normalizes intolerance and acts as an omnipresent weapon against members of a group defined by religion, race, caste or other markers. In January 2022, Dr. Gregory Stanton, Director of Genocide Watch, warned that India is exhibiting early warning signs of genocide and that several stages of genocide have been fulfilled in India.[297] The United States Holocaust Memorial Museum's

---

[296] UN Secretary-General, "United Nations Strategy and Plan of Action on Hate Speech", May 2019, p. 2 (https://www.legal-tools.org/doc/5rrb5b/).

[297] Karan Thapar, "Watch | 'US Congress Must Pass Resolution Warning India on Genocide': Gregory Stanton", *The Wire*, 19 January 2022.

Early Warning Project has ranked India second in its list of countries at risk for mass-killing in 2021–22[298] and eight in its 2022-23 list.[299]

While the danger of hate speech and hateful expression are well acknowledged in so far as incitement to violence is concerned, less emphasis is placed on the intangible effects of hateful utterances – the effect on the psyche and morale of the targeted community and their social standing and perception within society. Social media is a powerful tool which ensures that hateful utterances continue to circulate long after they are uttered and have the potential to cause continuing harm. In this manner, hateful utterances can form an endless loop of stigmatization, ostracization and discrimination against the targeted communities and when allowed to continue unchecked, can reach unprecedented levels. It is important to accord importance to the devastating effects of verbal violence, not just as a precursor to physical violence but as a source of emotional and psychological distress for the targeted community and their ability to live a life with dignity.

The Hindu right-wing's efforts in 'othering' Muslims have resulted in the development of a false sense of victimhood among Hindus and triggered feelings of alienation and anxiety among the Muslim community in India.[300] Another regrettable consequence of hate rhetoric is the reduction of Hindus, Muslims and other minorities solely to their religious identities,[301] thereby attempting to obliterate any sense of nationhood and belonging among the various religious groups in India. Further, there appears to be a dearth of national reconciliation mechanisms to address, among other things, inter-religious conflict and historical impunity and injustice.[302]

Given this background, it is of the utmost importance to understand the real threat posed by religion-based and -related hate speech and the factors that motivate it. This has been the endeavour of the present chapter in the context of India, and indeed of the Centre for International Law Research and Policy ('CILRAP')'s project on 'Religion, Hateful Expression and Violence' as a whole

298 United States Holocaust Memorial Museum, Simon-Skjodt Center for the Prevention of Genocide: Early Warning Project, "Countries at Risk for Mass Killing 2021-22: Statistical Risk Assessment Results", November 2021.

299 United States Holocaust Memorial Museum, Simon-Skjodt Center for the Prevention of Genocide: Early Warning Project, "Countries at Risk for Mass Killing 2022-23: Statistical Risk Assessment Results", November 2022.

300 Nissim Mannathukkaren, "The Slow Poison of Hate Speech Harms in Obvious and Insidious Ways", *The Wire*, 8 April 2022.

301 *Ibid.*

302 Global Action Against Mass Atrocity Crimes ('GAAMAC'), "Preventing Hate Speech, Incitement, and Discrimination: Lessons in Promoting Tolerance and Respect for Diversity in the Asia Pacific", 2021, pp. 160–195 (https://www.legal-tools.org/doc/9ak28w/).

in the global context. The present chapter aims at providing a mapping of the language used and symbolic acts committed by religious actors (or in the name of their faiths) that amount to religion-based or -related hate speech or hateful expression. This chapter also attempts to provide some reflections on the cultural and historical context of such hateful utterances or acts. Such utterances not only serve to intimidate, marginalize and discriminate against Muslims in India, but also result in real acts of violence against them. Understanding the root causes of hateful utterances and expressions against Muslims is an important step towards tackling the problem of hate speech, as is also reflected in one of the key commitments in the UN Strategy and Plan of Action on Hate Speech.

The ideology of Hindutva and its articulation have remained much the same since the early 1920's. In the words of Christophe Jaffrelot:

> I do not think that Hindu nationalism has fundamentally changed over time, since its creation one hundred years ago. If you read Savarkar – and Golwalkar even more – you will find the same ideas as those which Hindutva leaders articulate today: the reading of history is the same, the enemies are the same, the objective – a Hindu Rashtra where some Indians will be more equal than others – is the same.[303]

Given the close interlinking between Hindu nationalist groups and the ruling political party in India today, that is, the Sangh Parivar and the BJP respectively, it is often difficult to segregate political hate speech and religious hate speech. In fact, since religion in India forms the medium through which electoral votes are rallied, it is often religious leaders (who also hold key political positions within the ruling party, across state and national levels) who engage in hate rhetoric and calls for violence against members of minority communities, particularly Muslims.

Formal measures to combat hate speech through legislation and prosecution are indeed extremely important and relevant. Condemnation and criticism by the international community of a state's complicity in hateful utterances and violence against a minority religious group may also serve to bring about a positive effect in combating hate speech. This was evident in the international outrage over remarks made by BJP National Spokeswoman Nupur Sharma and Delhi Media Operation Head Naveen Kumar Jindal insulting the Prophet Muhammad in June 2022. Over fifteen nations, including several Arab States and Indonesia (which has the largest population of Muslims in the world) as well as the Organisation of Islamic Cooperation, strongly condemned the remarks made

---

303 Ajoy Ashirwad Mahaprashasta, "'Not Hindu Nationalism but Society Has Changed': Christophe Jaffrelot", *The Wire*, 25 January 2020.

by the BJP members and called upon the Modi government to take strict action.[304] Several states such as Qatar, Kuwait, Iran and Pakistan summoned Indian envoys and ambassadors stationed in their countries to express their displeasure at the BJP officials' statements.[305] There were reports of a Kuwaiti supermarket pulling Indian products from its shelves in response to the derogatory remarks.[306] Succumbing to the diplomatic backlash and the impending threat of an economic boycott, the BJP suspended Sharma and expelled Jindal from the party. Deepak Mittal, the Indian Ambassador in Doha, sought to distance the Modi government from the statements made by Sharma and Mittal, claiming that the views expressed were those of "fringe elements".[307] Given that the actions taken by the Modi government were clearly in response to international pressure, it is safe to assume that in the absence of such pressure, government authorities may feel no obligation to intervene and contain a communally charged situation in India. In fact, Modi is infamous for his deafening silence in the face of mounting religious tensions and violence.[308]

There is therefore a need to adopt a multi-pronged approach and make use of measures internal to religious communities to prevent or reduce hateful expression in the name of religion. In the absence of a central authoritative religious figure for Hindus, measures can be taken to identify *de facto* religious leaders who have sufficient religious authority in local communities within cities, towns and villages and impress upon them the need to impose informal sanctions against those members of the community who engage in hateful expression and violence in the name of religion.

Outreach programmes can also be conducted in local contexts to rationalize baseless hatred, hostility and stereotypes against Muslims. A recent study by the Pew Research Center revealed that an overwhelming majority of Hindus in India still respect Islám as an Indian religion and believe that it is very important to respect all religions to be "truly Indian", although they see little in common among all the religions in India and prefer to live separately.[309] This

304 "The Full List of 20 Countries and Bodies That Have Condemned the BJP Leaders' Remarks", *The Wire*, 7 June 2022.

305 "Condemnation, Summons for Indian Envoys in Gulf After BJP Leaders' Remarks on Prophet", *The Wire*, 6 June 2022.

306 "In Kuwait, Indian Products Pulled From Shelves Over Prophet Remarks", *NDTV*, 7 June 2022.

307 Gerry Shih, "India Scrambles to Contain Fallout Over Insulting Comments About Islam", *The Washington Post*, 7 June 2022.

308 "Ex-Bureaucrats Urge Narendra Modi to End 'Deafening' Silence", *The Telegraph*, 27 April 2022.

309 Neha Sahgal *et al.*, "Religion in India: Tolerance and Segregation", *Pew Research Center*, 29 June 2021 (https://www.legal-tools.org/doc/5e0dts/).

may be viewed as a positive sign that there is still hope to bring about peaceful coexistence of religious communities in India and that further harm may be prevented, or at the very least, minimized, by undertaking measures to curb hate speech and incitement to violence against minorities.

As Professor David J. Luban concluded in his presentation during CILRAP's conference on 'Religion, Hateful Expression and Violence' held in Florence, Italy on 8-9 April 2022: "religious hate speech is most likely to motivate violence when the society is fracturing for other reasons".[310] The task then is to recognize the fissures that belie Indian society and which provoke people to engage in hateful expressions and violence in the name of religion, and to work towards healing these fragments.

[310] David J. Luban, "Is There Anything Intrinsic to the World's Religions That Makes Them Especially Prone to Hateful and Violence-Inspiring Speech?", CILRAP Film, Florence, 8 April 2022 (https://www.cilrap.org/cilrap-film/220408-luban/).

8

Religion-Based Hate Speech or Free Speech: Indian Courts in a Quandary

Usha Tandon and Harleen Kaur*

8.1. Introduction

One of the biggest challenges to the fundamental exercise of freedom of expression in any democratic nation is the codification of hate speech and to balance it with the right to freedom of expression guaranteed to its citizens while ensuring, at the same time, that such freedom is not put to indiscriminate use, especially by those who are powerful, resulting in discrimination against religious minorities. Additionally, incendiary words not only cause harm but also disrupt public order leading to violent consequences such as hate crimes, amongst other violent results. In India, which is a land of diversity in terms of caste, creed, religion *etcetera*, responsible speech is particularly important, as is ensuring that the principles of liberty and democracy enshrined in the Constitution of India, 1950 ('Constitution') are adequately backed: it is in this context that hate speech becomes an exception to the right to freedom of speech and expression guaranteed to Indian citizens.

However, over the years, the growing menace of religion-based hate speech in India has been witnessed to have resulted in violence such as mob lynching, communal riots in addition to attracting penal provisions and thereby putting religious freedom under grave and constant attack. Further, *sans* any specific law defining the expression 'hate speech' in India, complaints against hate speech pertaining to creative and artistic expressions, religious reforms, academic research and other forms of speech are dealt with under the Constitution and the general law as contained in the Indian Penal Code, 1860 ('IPC') and

* Dr. **Usha Tandon** is Dean, Faculty of Law, University of Delhi, and Senior Professor at Campus Law Centre, University of Delhi. She has over 30 years of teaching experience and is a recognized scholar in human development, focusing on women empowerment and environmental protection. A CILRAP Conversation on World Order with Professor Tandon is available at https://www.cilrap.org/cilrap-film/190221-tandon/. Dr. **Harleen Kaur** is an Assistant Professor of Law (Senior Scale) in the Campus Law Centre, Faculty of Law, University of Delhi. From the same institute, she holds an LL.B. (Gold Medallist), an LL.M. and a Ph.D. For an audio-visual recording of their statement to CILRAP's conference in Florence in April 2023 on the topic of this anthology, please see https://www.cilrap.org/cilrap-film/220408-kaur/.

other laws. Indian courts, over the years, have also adopted varying norms in deciding similar hate speech cases to attract criminal prosecution and thereby reflecting procedural and substantive asymmetries. While some cases have created room for legitimate criticism of religion if it is in a restrained language and appears to be rational, at the same time, other cases have narrowed down the scope, thereby resulting in the evolution of a blurred and obscure jurisprudence on hate speech in India calling for the standardization of law in this regard.

Therefore, this chapter aims to highlight the growing menace of religion-based hate speech in India and the fact that the application of varying standards and the adoption of different procedural approaches in similar cases have not only led to chaos in the already confusing jurisprudence on hate speech, but have also created an urgent need to define the contours of hate speech and to put in place a well-defined law curtailing unbridled speech, in addition to the adoption of a consistent procedural and proactive approach by courts with a genuine commitment of preventing the circulation of inflammatory speech. This chapter also proposes various suggestions as an endeavour to curb the evil of religion-based hate speech in India.

8.2. Exploring Contours of Hate Speech

8.2.1. Defining Hate Speech

As Newton Lee wrote, "there is a fine line between free speech and hate speech. Free speech encourages debate whereas hate speech incites violence, intolerance and poses complex challenges to freedom of speech".[1] Hate speech not only undermines the roots of a society, it eventually leads to deep divides in social cohesion.

In the context of Indian laws, hate speech does not get defined anywhere and therefore, as such, it continues to exist within the realm of debate and interpretation. One may refer to Black's Law Dictionary which identifies 'hate speech' as the "speech that carries no meaning other than expression of hatred for some group, such as a particular race, especially in circumstances in which the communication is likely to provoke violence".[2] The Supreme Court of India ('Indian Supreme Court') also, in the case of *Pravasi Bhalai Sangathan v. Union of India* ('*Pravasi Bhalai Sangathan*'),[3] described hate speech as "an effort to

---

1. Newton Lee, *Counterterrorism and Cybersecurity: Total Information Awareness*, Springer, 2013.
2. *Black's Law Dictionary*, 9th edition.
3. Supreme Court of India, *Pravasi Bhalai Sangathan v. Union of India*, Judgment, 12 March 2014, 2014 (11) SCC 477. A public interest litigation was filed before the Supreme Court of India seeking guidelines on hate speech during elections. The Court did not go beyond the purview of existing laws to penalize hate speech as that would amount to 'judicial overreach' (https://www.legal-tools.org/doc/6drbwq/).

marginalise individuals based on their membership in a group" and one that "seeks to delegitimise group members in the eyes of the majority, reducing their social standing and acceptance within society".[4] While recognizing the adverse and discriminatory impact of hate speech on individuals, the Indian Supreme Court in *Pravasi Bhalai Sangathan* also expressed the difficulty of "confining the prohibition to some manageable standard"[5] and therefore requested the Law Commission of India ('Law Commission') to examine the issue thoroughly and, if it "deems proper", to define hate speech and make recommendations to the Parliament of India to strengthen the Election Commission of India in order to curb the menace of "hate speeches" irrespective of when it is made. It was then that the Law Commission, after consulting the laws and various judgments on hate speech, submitted its Report No. 267 titled "Hate Speech" before the Government of India in March 2017 for consideration, and in this report, defined hate speech as "an incitement to hatred primarily against a group of persons defined in terms of race, ethnicity, gender, sexual orientation, religious belief and the like". It is pertinent to mention here that the 267th Law Commission Report in 2017 also suggested that separate offences with a focus on hate speech should be included in the IPC, to avoid clubbing tangentially similar offences to charge someone for committing hate speech and therefore accordingly recommended incorporation of the following two provisions:

- *Section 153C*: To cover offence committed when any person uses threatening words either spoken or written, signs, visible representations, which are intended to cause fear or hatred including violence on the grounds of race, caste, religion, sex, gender identity and other characteristics.
- *Section 505A*: To include provisions penalizing causing of fear, alarm or provocation of violence.

However, none of the recommendations have been acted upon, and to an extent, it has led to an increase in the ambiguity in construing hate speech by various constitutional courts.

Thus, broadly speaking, the term hate speech takes within its ambit derogatory speech made towards someone else.[6] However, in the present era, the ambit of 'hate speech' appears to have broadened and it is now generally understood to encompass speech that is offensive, insulting, derogatory, discriminatory, provocative or even such which incites and encourages use of violence or results in violent backlashes. Thus, hate speech has transformed into a heinous

4 *Ibid.*, para. 7.

5 *Ibid.*, para. 25.

6 Gautam Bhatia, *Offend, Shock or Disturb: Free Speech Under the Indian Constitution*, Oxford University Press, 2016, p. 139.

type of hate crime causing direct physical attacks to the victims in the form of lynchings, leading to chilling effects on the victims' right to free speech and expression, resulting in exclusion from participation in the democratic process and public discourse.[7]

Internationally, there is no agreed definition of hate speech either. According to the United Nations ('UN'), hate speech is defined as:

> any kind of communication in speech, writing or behaviour, that attacks or uses pejorative or discriminatory language with reference to a person or a group on the basis of who they are, in other words, based on their religion, ethnicity, nationality, race, colour, descent, gender or other identity factors.[8]

However, despite there being no universal definition of hate speech, there seems to be a universal understanding on what its core components are, that is, a malicious expression of hatred against a person or an idea which causes harm. In the Indian context, one can refer to numerous laws that address the issue of hate speech. For instance, the IPC penalizes sedition,[9] promotion of enmity,[10] deliberate and malicious acts intended to outrage religious feelings or religious beliefs,[11] uttering of words with intent to harm religious beliefs[12] and publication of any statement which causes enmity or ill-will among classes.[13] On a similar note, the Representation of People Act, 1951[14] prohibits promotion of enmity on grounds of religion, caste and community as a corrupt electoral practice. The Cable Television Network Regulation Act, 1995 also prohibits transmission of any programme through a cable network which does not adhere to the prescribed code.[15] In addition to it, the Cinematograph Act, 1952 also contains provisions concerning hate speech and its prevention.[16] Certain instances of hate speech styled as offence to protect historically marginalized communities from hate

---

7 Anandita Yadav, "Countering Hate Speech in India: Looking for Answers Beyond the Law", in *ILI Law Review*, 2018, vol. 2, p. 2.

8 United Nations, "United Nations Strategy and Plan of Action on Hate Speech", 18 June 2019, p. 2 (https://www.legal-tools.org/doc/5rrb5b/).

9 India, The Indian Penal Code, 6 October 1860, Section 124A (http://www.legal-tools.org/doc/6a8f6b/).

10 *Ibid.*, Section 153A.

11 *Ibid.*, Section 295A.

12 *Ibid.*, Section 298.

13 *Ibid.*, Section 505.

14 India, The Representation of People Act, 1951, 17 July 1951, Sections 8, 123(A), and 125 (https://www.legal-tools.org/doc/f9v9qf/).

15 India, The Cable Television Network Regulation Act, 1995, 25 March 1995, Sections 5, 6, and 7.

16 India, The Cinematograph Act, 1952, 21 March 1952, Sections 4, 5B, and 7.

speech can also be found under the Protection of Civil Rights Act, 1955[17] and Scheduled Caste and Scheduled Tribes (Prevention of Atrocities) Act, 1989.[18] However, this web of legal provisions dealing with one or the other form of hate speech makes it nearly impossible to comprehend exactly what is that particular 'hate speech' which is banned within the Indian jurisdiction. As a consequence, incidents of hate speech have been on the rise and all the aforesaid laws, put together, have not proved to be very effective in this aspect. Therefore, it becomes a matter of urgent concern to not only regulate hate speech but also to adopt such practices that can undo the damage that hate speech is causing.

8.2.2. Adjudication of Hate Speech Cases in India and the Tests Applied

One of the biggest challenges to the fundamental exercise of freedom of expression in any democratic nation is the codification of hate speech and to balance it with the right to freedom of expression guaranteed to its citizens while at the same time ensuring that such freedom is not put to indiscriminate use, especially by those who are powerful, thereby resulting in discrimination against religious minorities. In fact, most democracies in the world today *ban* hate speech due to the fact that incendiary words not only cause harm but also disrupt public order, leading to violent consequences such as hate crimes amongst other violent results. Since hate speech is against the mandate of the fundamental right of freedom of expression conferred by a society upon its members, it has become a highly debatable topic especially in countries upholding democratic values and the individual rights of citizens. In fact, hate speech has always been a live debate in India. The shared fear is that laying down of a definite standard may be counterproductive to the freedom of speech discourse and may in fact lead to curtailment of free speech, and this fear has prevented the judiciary from defining hate speech in India. However, while dealing with cases of hate speech, various high courts and the Indian Supreme Court have constantly sought assistance from well-established principles of law, long practices and tests, which stand acknowledged and approved by international and national courts alike. Courts have also referred to international instruments and practices, scholarly articles and law commission reports to analyse the permissible limitations on free speech and to distinguish free speech from hate speech. The various tests applied by courts, in different contexts, concerning hate speech are described in the following sections.

---

17 India, The Protection of Civil Rights Act, 1955, 8 May 1955, Section 7 (https://www.legal-tools.org/doc/kcg70x/).

18 India, The Scheduled Caste and Scheduled Tribes (Prevention of Atrocities) Act, 1989, 11 September 1989, Sections 3(1)(r), 3(1)(s), 3(1)(u), and 3(1)(v).

8.2.2.1. Incitement to Violence as a Key Identifying Factor

While the Indian judiciary has refrained from outlining a definition of hate speech, a common factor that has been identified and has gained universal acceptance is the incitement or provocation of violence.[19] The incitement of violence and immediacy of the threat has been considered as a relevant factor in determining whether a form of speech should be prohibited or not. However, it is apposite to say that incitement to violence cannot be the sole test for determining whether a speech amounts to hate speech or not. Even speech that does not incite violence has the potential of marginalizing a certain section of the society or individuals. In the age of technology, the anonymity of the Internet allows a wrongdoer to easily spread false and offensive ideas. These ideas need not always incite violence but they might perpetuate the discriminatory attitudes prevalent in the society. Thus, incitement to discrimination is also a significant factor that contributes to the identification of hate speech.

8.2.2.2. Public Order and Reasonable Restriction Test

The limitations on freedom of speech are often justified on the grounds of maintenance of public order. In the cases of *Ramji Lal Modi v. State of Uttar Pradesh* ('*Ramji Lal Modi*'),[20] *Romesh Thappar v. State of Madras*[21] and *Brij Bhushan v. State of Delhi*,[22] it has been held that restrictions may be validly imposed in the interest of public order. It was also held by the Indian Supreme Court that the expression in the 'interest of public order' mentioned in Article 19(2) is much wider than 'maintenance of public order'. Therefore, even if an act does not actually cause breach of public order, its restriction 'in the interest of public order' will be deemed reasonable. However, later the Indian Supreme

[19] Supreme Court of India, *Amish Devgan v. Union of India*, Judgment, 7 December 2020, 2020 SCC Online SC 994, para. 15 ('*Amish Devgan*') (https://www.legal-tools.org/doc/lrh6yj/).

[20] Supreme Court of India, *Ramji Lal Modi v. State of Uttar Pradesh*, Judgment, 5 April 1957, AIR 1957 SC 620 ('*Ramji Lal Modi*') (https://www.legal-tools.org/doc/bi4001/). The Indian Supreme Court upheld the validity of Section 295A of the IPC for having published an article in a magazine against Muslims.

[21] Supreme Court of India, *Romesh Thappar v. State of Madras*, Judgment, 26 May 1950, 1950 AIR 124 (https://www.legal-tools.org/doc/psh81n/). Petition was filed challenging state's decision to ban entry and circulation of petitioner's leftist journal. It was argued that the restriction put in the guard of public order was too broad. The Indian Supreme Court quashed the order of the state government whereby the newspaper was banned. The judgement is still authoritative insofar as it adjudicates whether restriction imposed on speech and expression falls within the ambit of reasonable restriction.

[22] Supreme Court of India, *Brij Bhushan v. State of Delhi*, Judgment, 26 May 1950, 1950 AIR 129. The Indian Supreme Court upheld the liberty of the press and that pre-censorship was in violation of the right to freedom of speech and expression (https://www.legal-tools.org/doc/15t621/).

Court, in *Superintendent, Central Prison Fatehgarh v. Ram Manohar Lohia* ('*Ram Manohar Lohia*'),[23] rationalized the test laid down in *Ramji Lal Modi* and held that there must be a proximate link between speech and public disorder, and not merely a vague or a fanciful connection.[24] The reasoning of *Ram Manohar Lohiya* was further strengthened in the case of *S. Rangarajan v. P Jagjivan Ram*[25] in which the State Government of Tamil Nadu wished to censor a tamil movie, *Ore Oru Gramathile*, which revolved around the controversial reservations in the state. The State Government took a stand that public order shall be at risk in case the movie was allowed to be screened. The Indian Supreme Court, while evaluating the concern raised by the State Government, ruled that the standard which was required to be demonstrated by the State Government was whether the action be the 'spark in the powder keg' which, if not interfered with, will cause disorder.[26] Therefore, the standard laid down was that the expression must be 'intrinsically dangerous to public order'.

8.2.2.3. Proximate and Real Connection Test

This proximate and real connection test as laid down in *Ram Manohar Lohiya*,[27] wherein the Indian Supreme Court held that the restriction must have proximate and real connection with public order while observing that the nexus must not be far-fetched, hypothetical or too remote to the concerns of public order and it must not also be excessive in relation to the object sought to be achieved. Recently, this test was again applied in the case of *Nuzhat Perween v. State of Uttar Pradesh* ('*Nuzhat Perween*'),[28] where the detention order of Prof. Kafeel Khan was set aside by the Allahabad High Court for not having a proximate and real connection with the interests of public order. In this case, as a result of a speech delivered by Prof. Khan at Aligarh Muslim University, he was detained by the State Government of Uttar Pradesh on the allegation that the speech delivered by him allegedly had the effect of inciting feelings of Muslim students at the university. In his speech, Prof. Khan had stated that:

> We will be made second class citizens by the way of CAA [Citizenship (Amendment) Act, 2019] and after that by implementation

---

23 Supreme Court of India, *The Superintendent, Central Prison Fatehgarh v. Ram Manohar Lohia*, Judgment, 21 January 1960, 1960 SCR (2) 821 ('*Ram Manohar Lohia*') (https://www.legal-tools.org/doc/n9p3c6/).

24 *Ibid.*, p. 11.

25 Supreme Court of India, *S. Rangarajan v. P. Jagjivan Ram*, Judgment, 30 March 1989, 1989 (2) SCC 574 (https://www.legal-tools.org/doc/io5jdm/).

26 *Ibid.*, para. 45.

27 *Ram Manohar Lohia*, see *supra* note 23.

28 High Court of Allahabad, *Nuzhat Perween v. State of Uttar Pradesh*, Order, 1 September 2020, 2020 SCC Online All 984 ('*Nuzhat Perween*') (https://www.legal-tools.org/doc/fs12zv/).

> of NRC [National Register of Citizens] they will trouble you by saying your father's documents are not correct you will be made to run around. This is a fight for existence and we will have to fight.[29]

The recitals aforesaid were treated as an effort to create disharmony and enmity towards Hindus, Sikhs, Christians and Parsi in the minds of the Muslim students of Aligarh Muslim University and deemed to have adversely affected public order resulting into continuous violence. It also developed fear, insecurity and anger amongst the people of sensitive district Aligarh. The Allahabad High Court bench comprising of Chief Justice Govind Mathur and Justice Saumitra Dayal Singh allowed the habeas corpus writ petition filed by the doctor's mother, Nuzhat Perween, seeking release of Prof. Khan, and stated that Prof. Khan's speech did not promote any kind of hatred or violence observing:

> A complete reading of the speech prima facie does not disclose any effort to promote hatred or violence. It also nowhere threatens peace and tranquility of the city of Aligarh. The address gives a call for national integrity and unity among the citizens. The speech also deprecates any kind of violence. It appears that the District Magistrate had selective reading and selective mention for few phrases from the speech ignoring its true intent.[30]

Thus, criticizing the district magistrate for his narrow interpretation and acknowledgement of only a few sayings from the speech while completely neglecting the speech's real intentions, this proximate nexus test aided the Allahabad High Court to come to the conclusion that there was no negative effect on public order done by the delivered speech. The same test was also applied in the case of *Shreya Singhal v. Union of India*[31] to hold Section 66A of the Information Technology Act, 2000 ('IT Act') as imposing unreasonable restrictions on freedom of speech and expression. In this case, the Mumbai Police arrested two girls in 2012, namely Shaheen Dhada and Rinu Srinivasan, on the allegations that they had expressed their displeasure, by posting their comments on Facebook, at a *bandh* (period of mourning) called during the time of death of Bal Thackery, the Shiv Sena Chief. In view of the widespread public protests, these girls were released later, and a decision was taken to close and end the criminal cases against them. However, there was a feeling that there was gross misuse of power by the police invoking Section 66A of the IT Act, as it amounted to violation of the freedom of speech and expression since it failed to create a proximate link

[29] *Ibid.*, p. 11.

[30] *Ibid.*, pp. 31–32.

[31] Supreme Court of India, *Shreya Singhal v. Union of India*, Judgment, 24 March 2015, AIR 2015 SC 1523 (https://www.legal-tools.org/doc/gvk8zj/).

between the restriction and the Act. Therefore, applying two tests – that is, clear and present danger and the probability of inciting hatred – Section 66A of the IT Act was held to have not passed these two tests, since it was quite clear that the Facebook posts for which the girls were jailed did not incite public hatred or disrupted law and order. In doing so, the Indian Supreme Court laid out three categories of speech – discussion, advocacy and incitement. Of the three categories, the Indian Supreme Court held that only speech that amounted to incitement could be as adjudicated as illegal.

8.2.2.4. Test of Necessity and Proportionality

It is equally well established that limitations on freedom of speech are necessarily to further constitutionally-recognized objectives, as pointed out in the case of *Anuradha Bhasin v. Union of India*,[32] wherein it was held that Articles 19 and 21 of the Constitution require that any action of the state must demonstrate five essential features: (i) backing of a 'law', (ii) legitimacy of purpose, (iii) rational connection of the act and object, (iv) necessity of the action, and (v) when the above four are established, then the test of proportionality.

8.2.2.5. Content, Context and Intent Test

Courts have often distinguished between offensive speech and a speech made with a malicious intent to incite violence. The latter attracts penal consequences.

As discussed above, in *Ramji Lal Modi*,[33] the Indian Supreme Court held that only aggravated form of insult to religion, when perpetuated with deliberate and malicious intent to outrage the religious feelings of the targeted group, can be penalized. The mode of exercise of free speech, the context and the extent of abuse of freedom are important in determining the contours of permissible restrictions.

In the context of hate speech, there is a widely accepted practice of reviewing the contents of alleged hate speech, written or oral, to conclusively adjudicate criminal proceedings, as has been witnessed in numerous cases; for

---

[32] Supreme Court of India, *Anuradha Bhasin v. Union of India*, Judgment, 10 January 2020, (2020) SC 1725 (https://www.legal-tools.org/doc/4kr19f/). The Indian Supreme Court was called upon to determine the constitutionality of the communication shutdown imposed in Jammu and Kashmir on 5 August 2019. The petition was filed by Ms. Anuradha Bhasin, an executive editor of the Kashmir Times Srinagar Edition who argued Internet to be essential for the modern press and the government failed to consider whether the Internet shutdown was reasonable and proportionate to the aims it pursued. The Court held that the orders of Internet shutdown must meet the tests of necessity and proportionality in the sense that some web sites may be allowed to be assessed including medical, e-banking and essential services and other relaxations subject to continuous reviews.

[33] *Ramji Lal Modi*, see *supra* note 20.

example, *Amish Devgan v. Union of India* ('*Amish Devgan*'),[34] where the Indian Supreme Court reviewed the script of the television show hosted by the petitioner to deny the relief he claimed in the form of quashing of first-information-reports ('FIR') registered against him. Similarly, in *Nuzhat Perween*,[35] the Allahabad High Court conducted an in-depth scrutiny of the speech delivered by the petitioner to hold that the contents and context of the speech were not of such a nature to warrant the detention of Prof. Khan. Also, in *Harsh Mander v. Government of National Capital Territory of Delhi*,[36] the Delhi High Court played the video clips in open court to question the executive on the non-registration of FIR's against certain politicians. Thus, the 'content' test which was elaborated in *Amish Devgan*, besides the subject matter, is basically that the objected content must have the tendency to vilify, humiliate and incite hatred or violence against the targeted group based on its religious identity. As such, the question on intent and purpose takes centre stage during the adjudication of any case concerning hate speech.

8.2.2.6. Reasonable Man Test

This test has been applied by courts especially in hate speech cases pertaining to written as well as spoken words, to justify relief or deny the same by allowing continuance of criminal proceedings against the alleged perpetrator. As per this test, the deliberate and malicious intent has to be necessarily gathered from the stand point of a reasonable man. However, what amounts to a reasonable man remains void of a definite standard in relation to hate speech jurisprudence, for when adjudication relates to religious sentiments of an individual or a community, the matter becomes excessively subjective. In the recent *Amish Devgan* case, the Indian Supreme Court elaborated on this test and the Court's final analysis has been a subject matter of much criticism for setting an excessively wide standard for a reasonable man. The analysis of the Indian Supreme Court fails to provide any clarity on the positioning of this reasonable man in terms of religion, caste, creed or gender or whether the standard of this reasonable man must be derived from someone in the targeted group.

8.2.2.7. Presence of Two Communities Test

A specific test involving the essential presence of two communities (the targeted and the one invoking violence) has also been employed by courts. In *Manzar*

---

34 *Amish Devgan*, see *supra* note 19.

35 *Nuzhat Perween*, see *supra* note 28.

36 High Court of Delhi, *Harsh Mander v. Government of National Capital Territory of Delhi*, Order, 26 February 2020, 2020 SCC Online Del 2124 (https://www.legal-tools.org/doc/y6uvv9/).

Sayeed Khan v. State of Maharashtra[37] and *Bilal Ahmed Kaloo v. State of Andhra Pradesh*,[38] the Indian Supreme Court noted that, in order to trigger the provisions of Sections 153A and 505(2) of the IPC, involvement of at least two groups or communities is necessary.

8.2.2.8. Judicial Review of Executive Actions

In addition to the above-mentioned tests, courts have also subjected the subjective satisfaction of the executive to scrutiny in cases concerning hate speech. It is no longer *res integra* that the subjective satisfaction of the executive is not completely immune from judicial review. In cases of hate speech, where there have been instances of detaining authorities functioning under political influence, the judicial reviewability becomes essential in the protection of rights of individuals and to prevent abuse and misuse of power. In *Nuzhat Perween*[39] the subjective satisfaction of the detaining authority was subjected to scrutiny by the Allahabad High Court and the Court held that satisfaction was not reached on consideration of objective material available on record and that satisfaction was not reached in a legal and regular manner but on whims and caprice, which is against the principles of natural justice.

However, despite the Indian Supreme Court having handed down various constitutional principles, there has been a continuous failure by the law enforcement agencies to check the indiscriminate invocation of these provisions. The true and harsh reality is that a large number of persons in various fields, including actors, writers and artists, have borne the brunt of this draconian provision irrespective of the political ideologies professed by the concerned state governments. Even the judiciary, despite vast powers having been conferred on it under the scheme of the Constitution, it has not exercised the same in a uniform manner in cases concerning hate speech. While in a few cases the judiciary has demonstrated a pragmatic approach, addressing the serious concerns and threats posed to pluralism and democracy in the Indian context, in various other occasions, especially the Indian Supreme Court, the judiciary has conveniently

[37] *Manzar Sayeed Khan v. State of Maharashtra* reflects the position that the speech, whether in form of spoken or written word, must be looked at in its entirety. Strongly worded, isolated, offensive passages cannot be solely relied upon to attract penal provisions. In this case, the Indian Supreme Court directed the respondents to not proceed against Prof. Laine, author of the book titled *Shivaji: Hindu King in Islamic India*, for offences under Sections 153, 153A and 34 of the IPC, Supreme Court of India, *Manzar Sayeed Khan v. State of Maharashtra*, Judgment, 5 April 2007, (2007) 5 SCC 1 (https://www.legal-tools.org/doc/hnli2i/).

[38] Supreme Court of India, *Bilal Ahmed Kaloo v. State Of Andhra Pradesh*, Judgment, 6 August 1997, (1997) 7 SCC 431 (https://www.legal-tools.org/doc/n4aknu/).

[39] *Nuzhat Perween*, see *supra* note 28.

excused itself in cases that warranted prompt and efficient action leading to staunch criticism.

In fact, the Law Commission also, in its 267th report on 'hate speech', after analysing the decisions of different state jurisdictions, identified certain parameters such the extremity of the speech, incitement, status of the author of the speech, status of victims of the speech, and context of the speech, *etcetera*, to determine hate speech.

8.3. Fighting Religion-Based Hate Speech and Balancing Freedom

In the context of religion-based hate speech, it sometimes becomes very difficult to trace the dividing line between the types of offensive language or statements that may disturb one's religious sentiments while at the same time protecting freedom of expression. In India, which is a secular country and has no state religion of its own, and where one can witness vast disparities in language, culture and religion, any unwarranted and malicious criticism or interference in the faith of others indeed constitutes a very serious danger to the way of life to which people are pledged under the Constitution. Over the years, incitement to religious and communal hatred has become an issue of considerable concern in India for capturing headlines following violent clashes, mostly – but by no means exclusively – between Hindus and Muslims, in different parts of the country. These clashes, which have claimed thousands of lives, have become a real and growing threat to the survival of the nation itself as a cohesive secular entity.

In India, law permits healthy discussions on religious matters, but in the guise of such discussions, deliberate intention to wound the religious feelings of others is not permissible. Freedom of speech and expression, which is the hallmark of Indian democracy, is protected under Article 19(1)(a) of the Constitution. This right, however, is not expressed in absolute terms, rather it is subject to Article 19(2), which allows the state to make laws imposing 'reasonable restrictions' upon freedom of speech and expression in the interests of 'the sovereignty and integrity of India', 'the security of the state', 'friendly relations with foreign states', 'public order', 'decency or morality' or in relation to 'contempt of court, defamation or incitement to an offence'. It is under the ground of 'public order' that India has prohibited and penalized 'hate speech'.

Also, to curb factors which are responsible for inciting religious animosities and to prevent religious riots and crusades, the IPC contains several provisions restricting freedom of expression (whether through written or spoken words) where it incites violence or promotes enmity between religious groups, *etcetera*. For instance, Section 153A of the IPC prohibits promoting or attempting to promote (by words, signs or visible representations) disharmony or feelings of enmity, hatred or ill-will between different religious, racial, language, or regional groups or castes or communities. Section 153B of the IPC penalizes imputations and assertions prejudicial to national integration and therefore safeguards the interests of class of persons and, above all, national integration. Section 295 of the IPC penalizes injuring or defiling any place of worship, or any object which any class of persons holds sacred, done either with an intention or knowledge that such act is likely to be considered as an insult to their religion by any class of persons. Section 295A of the IPC penalizes deliberate and malicious acts intended to outrage the religious feelings of any class by insulting its religion or religious beliefs. Section 298 of the IPC, similarly, classifies the offence of uttering words with the deliberate intent to wound the religious feelings of any person. Similarly, Section 505(2) of the IPC renders any statement that is made with a view to create or promote enmity, hatred or ill will between classes of society punishable and state governments may confiscate copies of newspapers, documents or books found to violate these provisions. Section 95 of the Criminal Procedure Code, 1973 ('CrPC') allows the widest discretion to the state governments to forfeit and seize publications that 'appear' to be in violation of Sections 295A, 124A, 153A, 153B, 292 and 293 of the IPC before the matter is even entertained by a court and no prior notice or hearing is contemplated before action is to be taken under Section 95 of the CrPC is to be taken. Similarly, Section 144 of the CrPC permits the issuance of temporary orders in urgent cases of nuisance or apprehended damage, and Section 107 of the CrPC gives power to a magistrate to execute the maintenance of peace with the help of people that will be required for implementing such bonds. Also, since the offences pertaining to hate speech are cognizable in nature and having serious repercussions on liberties of citizens therefore, a police officer, under Section 155 of the CrPC, is empowered to make arrest without orders from a magistrate.

In consonance with the theme of this chapter, the authors, in the present paper, dwell elaborately on the invocation of Section 295A along with Section 153A of the IPC which, over the years, have become a potent weapon in the hands of purported 'aggrieved' persons to file ill-motivated and vexatious complaints because of what they perceive to be deliberate and malicious acts against their religion. As Section 295A of the IPC has been classified as a cognizable, non-bailable and non-compoundable offence, meaning thereby that the police can arrest the 'accused' without a warrant, when this is coupled with the long time passed before criminal cases are heard and decided, it surely casts a chilling effect upon the freedom of speech and expression.

8.3.1. Evolution of Section 295A: Legislative Response

It is pertinent to note that the laws pertaining to religion and blasphemy do not find a place in the Constitution. In fact, the legal and constitutional landscape seems to be unfamiliar with the term 'blasphemy' because the Indian judiciary has since long emphasized the inclusive and plural nature of Hinduism, which makes a concept such as blasphemy incoherent. However, Section 295A of the IPC has been used as a blasphemy law, having been added by the Criminal Law Amendment Act, 1927, and owing its existence in the IPC to the upheaval caused by the decision of Lahore High Court in the case of *Raj Paul v. Emperor* ('*Raj Paul*'),[40] more famous by the name of the 'Rangila Rasul' case. Therein, the accused was convicted under Section 153A of the IPC for writing scandalous details about the sexual life of the Prophet Muhammad in his allegedly derogatory pamphlet 'Rangila Rasul'. In fact, the height of communal agitation coincided with Raj Paul's acquittal on appeal before the Lahore High Court, which could only happen after several years of legal battle, during the course of which the petitioner was convicted twice by lower courts. The Lahore High Court set aside the conviction of Raj Paul on the ground that the word 'classes' does not include religious denominations but means 'races', and that criticism or satire on a religious teacher is not within the purview of the section. At the same time, the court drew attention to the fact that this lacuna in law deserved to be taken care of at the earliest. Subsequently, a division bench of the same High Court in *Devi Sharan Sharma v. Emperor*,[41] popularly known as the '*Risala-i-Vartaman*' case, held that scurrilous and vituperative attack on a religion or its founder, did attract Section 153A of the IPC. The judgment in *Raj Paul* was, however, not cited at the time when this case was being adjudicated. In this case, the state had, under Section 99A of the then CrPC, 1898, prohibited a published work and the editor Gian Chand Pathak (who was also the printer and publisher of the journal *Risala-i-Vartaman* along with Devi Sharan Sharma, the author of the article "Sair-i-Dozakh" published in it, were charged under Section 153A of the IPC. The Lahore High Court held that "it was difficult to distinguish an attack on the founder of a religion from an attack on the religion founded by him" for the purposes of taking it from the substantive part of Section 153A of the IPC. Then, in the case of *Kali Charan Sharma v. Emperor*,[42] the Allahabad High Court, while dissenting from the judgment passed in *Raj Paul*, held that the book titled *Vachitra Jiwani* with an alternative title displayed on the front page that read *jiwan ki bichitra aur rahasya-mayi ghatnaen*, dealing with the life of the Prophet Muhammad, generated animosity and enmity between Hindus and Mohammadans, which triggered Section 153A of the IPC, holding as well that the word '*rahas*' has a variety of meanings, most of which, however, are associated with

40 High Court of Lahore, *Raj Paul v. Emperor*, Judgment, 4 May 1927, AIR 1927 Lah 590.

41 High Court of Lahore, *Devi Sharan Sharma v. Emperor*, Judgment, 6 August 1927, AIR 1927 Lah 594.

42 High Court of Allahabad, *Kali Charan Sharma v. Emperor*, Judgment, 24 February 1927, AIR 1927 All 649.

the notion of pleasure or merriment. Further, while analysing the subject matter of various chapters of the book, Justice Lindsay held that:

> the earlier portions [purport] to describe the perverted morals of Arab society at the time of the appearance of the Prophet. Here reference is made to the general prevalence at that time of drunkenness, superstition, adultery, incest and bestiality and it is asserted that although the Prophet posed as a reformer of morals he became in fact "a victim of all the vices just enumerated". [...] The later portions of the book are devoted to a narrative of incidents in the history of the life of the Prophet interspersed with caustic and provocative comment on the part of the author. Many of the passages here are difficult to describe temperately. They abound in vituperation and sarcasm expressed with the grossest obscenity which cannot fail to suggest that they were written deliberately for the purpose of holding up Mohammad to odium and derision so as to present him to the reader as a man wholly unworthy of the reverence of the millions who believe in him and in his doctrine.[43]

Justice Lindsay – as well as Justices Walsh and Banerji, who issued statements in assent at the end of the judgment – decided that it was not possible to make this distinction, and therefore Kali Charan Sharma's application to have the forfeiture of the *Vichitra Jivan* overturned was dismissed.

The conflicting interpretations on the applicability and interpretation of Section 153A of the IPC led to a considerable confusion regarding the appropriate application of the law as a consequence of which, the Indian Legislative Assembly passed Section 295A of the IPC marking a distinct transition from 'intermittent intervention' to major executive and judicial action.

In fact, the first case to reach the Indian Supreme Court, post-independence, challenging the statutory restrictions of speech, was the case of *Ramji Lal Modi v. State of Uttar Pradesh*[44] which also set the foundation for modern Indian expressive freedom jurisprudence by affirming the constitutionality of Section 295A of the IPC by a quorum of five judges. In this case, Section 295A was held to be valid and constitutional and well within the ambit of Article 19(2) of the Constitution. The case concerned the prosecution of an editor of a cow-protection magazine for writing an article that allegedly hurt the sentiments of Muslims. The sessions court acquitted the editor from the charge under Section 153A of the IPC, but convicted him under Section 295A of the IPC and sentenced him to 18 months of rigorous imprisonment and also imposed a fine of 2,000 rupees in default of payment of which the accused was to further ordered to undergo

---

43 *Ibid.*, para. 15.

44 *Ramji Lal Modi*, see *supra* note 20.

rigorous imprisonment for four months. In appeal proceedings before the Allahabad High Court, while the bench maintained the conviction, it however reduced the sentence of imprisonment to 12 months as well as the fine from 2,000 to 250 rupees. The matter was carried further to the Indian Supreme Court in a Special Leave Petition ('SLP') which was dismissed. The petitioner thereafter presented a petition under Article 32 of the Constitution praying for a stay of the sentence imposed on him. The Indian Supreme Court in the present case opined that the words appearing in Article 19(2) of the Constitution, namely 'in the interest of public order', have a very wide meaning and in order to prevent public disorder from being caused by these hate speeches, Section 295A of the IPC is a valid restriction on the freedom of speech and expression. The Indian Supreme Court also said that Section 295A of the IPC does not penalize any and every act of insult or attempt to insult the religion or religious feelings of any community, but only covers such insults which are made 'deliberately' and with 'malicious intention' to hurt the religion or religious feelings of any community. The Indian Supreme Court further went on to say that the clause would only apply to serious forms of religious insult having tendency to disrupt public order. At the time of writing, this case, though decided in 1957, still acts as a precedent over the cases brought under Section 295A of IPC.

8.3.2. Invocation of Section 295A: State Response

Though Section 295A of the IPC requires the act to be malicious or deliberate, and only an aggravated form of insult to religion which tends to disrupt public order can be punished, there have been numerous instances where the offence of hate speech was used not only on the grounds of what was seen to be distasteful by the government, but on some flimsy grounds as well. The police has also continued to harass activists, journalists and critics of the government by filing unjustified cases against them for dissenting views, protesting or covering protests, and the courts also, in view of divergent different approaches in similar cases, have failed to come up with effective redressal. Therefore, Section 295A of the IPC has witnessed having been abused, read and re-read according to the courts' interpretations and administrative whims and fancies. There are countless similar instances where the Section was invoked for frivolous reasons with no legal backing to substantiate the arguments, and a majority of these FIRs were quashed by the courts later on.

In February 2009, the police arrested Ravindra Kumar and Anand Sinha, respectively the editor and the publisher of a Kolkata-based English daily named *The Statesman*, for allegedly hurting Muslim sentiments. The police charged these two persons under Section 295A of the IPC for reprinting an article from *The Independent* published by its columnist, Johann Hari, titled "Why Should I

Respect Oppressive Religions?". The article stated Hari's belief that the right to criticize any religion was being eroded around the world.[45]

Thereafter, in November 2012, the Maharashtra Police arrested Shaheen Dhada, 21 years of age, for questioning the total shutdown in the city for Bal Thackeray's funeral in a Facebook post, and also her friend Renu Srinivasan, 20 years of age, for liking her post. Although no religious issue was involved, the two were charged under Section 295A of the IPC for hurting religious sentiments, in addition to Section 66A of the IT Act. However, the charges under Section 295A of the IPC were later dropped and the girls were charged for creating or promoting enmity, hatred or ill-will between classes under Section 505(2) of the IPC.

In a separate instance, Ravi Shastri, a former test cricketer, was arrested for hurting Hindu religious sentiments by allegedly eating beef in Johannesburg during the India–Pakistan test series.[46] The case was filed by the Bajrang Dal stating that their feelings were hurt as Shastri made a comment saying that even though he was a Brahmin, he could not prevent himself from eating beef. Similarly, in 2017, a complaint was filed because the complainant was 'disappointed' by seeing the cover page of a magazine which had a picture of Lord Vishnu with the face of Mahendra Singh Dhoni with a caption that read "The God of Big Deals".[47] This was quashed by the Indian Supreme Court on the ground that the "allegations remotely did not satisfy the essential ingredients of the offence". In September 2014, a police complaint came to be filed against a Bollywood actor Salman Khan, who was alleged to have insulted Muslim sentiments when, in a fashion show which was organized by his non-governmental organization "Being Human", a model walked the ramp with an Arabic word inscribed on her t-shirt.[48] A case was also registered against another Bollywood actor, Aamir Khan, for hurting religious sentiments through a scene shown in his film *PK* where the actor was shown as Lord Shiva while pulling a rickshaw on which two *burqa*-clad women were sitting.[49]

In November, 2020, the police filed a criminal case under Section 295A of the IPC, for insulting religious feelings, against two executives of Netflix, the online streaming platform, by reason of the strong exception having been taken

---

45 Jerome Taylor, "Editor arrested for 'outraging Muslims'", *The Independent*, 12 February 2009.

46 "Case filed against Ravi Shastri for eating beef", *Zee News*, 23 December 2006.

47 Supreme Court of India, *Mahendra Singh Dhoni v. Yerraguntla Shyamsundar*, Judgment, 20 April 2017, AIR 2017 SC 2392, para. 10 ('*Mahendra Singh Dhoni*') (https://www.legal-tools.org/doc/zmwdrr/).

48 "Salman too was accused of hurting Muslim sentiments", *Times of India*, 22 April 2017.

49 "FIR against amir Khan for hurting religious sentiments hile shooting for PK", *IndiaToday*, 11 October 2013.

by fanatic Hindu nationalists with regard to an interfaith couple kissing in a temple in a television production of *A Suitable Boy* which was based on a novel by Vikram Seth. The case was opened following an order of investigation into such content by the state home minister.

Similarly, Muslim stand-up comic Munawar Faruqui and his five associates – including three Hindus, a Muslim and a Christian – were arrested under Section 295A of the IPC for jokes he apparently did not perform but which allegedly hurt Hindu sentiments, on the basis of the complaint made by the leader of a Hindu nationalist group. On approaching the Madhya Pradesh High Court for bail, the Court denied it stating it was not a case fit for grant of bail. In fact, during Faruqui's bail hearing, the judge is also reported to have made remaks to the effect that 'such people must not be spared'. Faruqui appealed before the Indian Supreme Court, which granted him bail noting that the allegations in the case were vague and that the police had failed to follow proper procedure before his arrest. It is to be noted that Faruqui had spent 37 days in prison before he obtained bail from the Indian Supreme Court. Thus, the way the Indore police acted to wrongfully detain Munawar Faruqui until the Indian Supreme Court finally had to intervene is a glaring example of abuse of power by police authorities, especially when the offence is a cognizable one.[50]

Similarly, in another incident, comedian Kiku Sharda was sent to 14-days of judicial custody for hurting the sentiments of followers of Baba Gurmeet Ram Rahim Singh Insan on account of his mimicking the Godman, which in turn rekindled one more time the debate over India's regressive speech laws. The Haryana government later came to the decision of applying for quashing the FIR which had been filed against the comedian.[51]

Recently, senior politician P.C. George on two occasions was accused under Sections 153A or 295A of the IPC of making incendiary remarks against the Muslim community while delivering a public speech on Ananthapuri Hindu Maha Sammelan on 29 April 2022, uttering that "[t]ea laced with "drops causing impotence" were sold in Muslim-run restaurants to cause impotence to achieve their agenda of establishing Muslim country by sterilising men and women of other faith". However, the very same day, a judicial magistrate of the first class in Thiruvananthapuram granted him bail. While the member of legislative assembly was expected to have understood the effects of hate speech, he could not and thus on 10 May 2022, the police in Palarivattom at Kochi, registered *suo moto* a second case against him for again uttering a speech on communal lines

[50] High Court of Madhya Pradesh, *Munawar Faruqui v. State of Madhya Pradesh*, Order, 28 January 2021, 2021 SCC Online MP 152 (https://www.legal-tools.org/doc/ldc4cn/).

[51] "Haryana govt seeks to quash FIRs against Kiku Sharda for mimicking Gurmeet Ram Rahim", *First Post*, 9 September 2017.

at a temple in Vennala. A magisterial court cancelled his bail for not adhering to the bail conditions imposed upon him earlier. However, upon approaching the Kerala High Court, he was granted bail on the ground of there being no possibility of him fleeing from justice.[52]

In fact, if one peruses the data brought out by the National Crime Records Bureau, it is revealed this Section 153A of the IPC has a very high rate of arrest but, at the same time, a remarkably low conviction rate. Apparently, the Section is being used as a weapon to supress dissent. While there was a twofold increase in the number of cases registered under Section 153A of the IPC in 2017 (934 cases were registered, when compared with the 447 cases registered in the year 2016), there were 1076 cases registered in 2018, and in 2019, 1055 cases were registered.[53] Year 2020 witnessed the highest number of cases, that is, 1804 which is almost 70 per cent higher when compared to the previous year, 2019.[54] During the five-year period of 2015–2020, there was a four-fold increase in the number of cases registered under this Section 153A of the IPC. Though only 15.3 per cent of the cases ended up in conviction in 2016, this increased to 26.4 per cent in 2019. However, it again fell to 20.4 per cent in 2020.

8.4. Explicating the Judicial Trends

8.4.1. Religion-Based Hate Speech: Reflection of Procedural and Substantive Asymmetries

It cannot be denied that, over the years, hate speech against religious beliefs became deeply engrossed within the Indian society. There have been countless statements made by people around the nation to hurt the religious beliefs of other communities. As mentioned above, it seems to be unfortunate that, while in certain cases the judiciary has demonstrated a pragmatic approach addressing the serious concerns and threats posed to pluralism and democracy in the Indian context, in others, especially the Indian Supreme Court, the judiciary conveniently excused itself, when cases would have warranted a prompt and efficient action leading to staunch criticism. In a country where religion leads the way of life of millions, the consequences of inaction, especially where hate speech targets the religious sentiments of any community, are grave and may, as they have done in the past and worldwide, lead to imminent lawlessness and violence. The failure to impute accountability not only endangers the democratic and constitutional values of the nation, but could also potentially manifest its consequences in the form of loss of lives of real people. In fact, a reading into the

[52] "PC George granted bails by Kerala high court in 'hate speech'", *Times of India*, 27 May 2022.

[53] National Crime Records Bureau, *Crime in India 2019*, vol. 1, New Delhi, 2019, p. 39.

[54] *Ibid.*

approach adopted by the judiciary in hate speech cases, especially in the context of religion, points towards significant procedural and substantive asymmetries. Whereas, in a few cases, the judiciary has been prompt and sensitive while addressing the issue at hand, that is to say, the courts have identified and acknowledged the urgency and gravity of the situation to grant immediate relief to the aggrieved, there have been instances where the situation demanded immediate action, but unfortunately the courts, the Indian Supreme Court and high courts alike, have failed to walk the desired route, leading to undue delay in the initiation and advancement of legal proceedings.

For instance, in cases that warranted *suo moto* cognizance by the Indian Supreme Court, most recently the *Dharam Sansad* case, where hate speeches were delivered in Haridwar calling for genocide of Muslims and other minorities in the name of protecting Hinduism, the Court does not seem to have fulfilled its mandate as envisaged under the Constitution. The necessity for judicial intervention in the instant case was pointed out by the letters from 76 eminent lawyers of the Indian Supreme Court drawing attention to the inaction of police authorities. Despite the registration of FIRs, no arrests were made in this regard for a period of over a month. The letters further highlighted the threat posed to the integrity and unity of the country and the lives of Muslim citizens. In the preliminary hearing of the public interest litigation filed by journalist Qurban Ali,[55] the Indian Supreme Court issued notice to the concerned state authorities. However, the hesitance in the Court's intervention was apparent from the oral remarks of the Chief Justice of India N.V. Ramana who observed: "There are penal laws, there is a judgment of the Supreme Court as per the counsel, there are enough laws. What law can we lay down now?".[56] In other cases, like the plea filed by activist Harsh Mander for registration of FIRs against certain politicians for delivering hate speeches and inciting violence in the context of the 2020 Delhi riots, the courts failed to adjudicate the matter expeditiously. The petitioner moved the Delhi High Court in February 2020, and when aggrieved by the long adjournments, raised the matter with the Indian Supreme Court. The Court refused to hear the transcripts of the speeches provided by Mander and did not even allow his lawyer to argue. Ultimately, frustrated with the futility of the process, Mander withdrew his petition. The case is still pending before a district court. Where the matter concerns life and death, it is necessary that courts exercise their extraordinary powers in a much more prompt manner, but currently the judiciary is lacking in that regard.

---

55 Supreme Court of India, *Qurban Ali v. Union of India*, Order, 26 April 2022, Writ Petition (Civil) No. 24/2022 (https://www.legal-tools.org/doc/dza8lp/).

56 Thyagarajan Narendran, "Supreme Court Refuses To Stay Dharam Sansad Event At Himachal Pradesh, Directs Petitioners To Approach Local Authorities In State", *LawBeat*, 13 April 2022.

The issue of hate speech again came to the forefront in the case against the Sudarshan TV news channel when the telecast of a show titled *Bindaas Bol*, which aimed to expose Muslim community penetration into the Indian civil services, was announced. Initially, in its interim order dated 28 August 2020, the Indian Supreme Court did not find favour in imposing a pre-broadcast ban on the telecast of the allegedly controversial programme called *Bindaas Bol*. However, subsequently, in the order dated 15 September 2020, the Indian Supreme Court changed its view and imposed a pre-broadcast injunction over the remaining episodes of the programme after having been shown a transcript of the promotional clip of around 49 seconds. The three-judge bench of the Indian Supreme Court were of the *prima facie* view that the intent, object and purpose of the episodes which had been telecast was to 'vilify the Muslim community' and that an "insidious attempt has been made to insinuate that the community is involved in a conspiracy to infiltrate the Indian civil services". The Indian Supreme Court further observed in its interim order that:

> The edifice of a democratic society committed to the rule of law under a regime of constitutional rights, values and duties is founded on the co-existence of communities. India is a melting pot of civilizations, cultures, religions and languages. Any attempt to vilify a religious community must be viewed with grave disfavour by this Court as the custodian of constitutional values. Its duty to enforce constitutional values demands nothing less.[57]

Apparently, this interim order was passed with a view to ensuring that an equilibrium is maintained while protecting the right to free speech.

However, it is apposite to state that the approach adopted by the Indian Supreme Court, in this case, was in contrast to its approach adopted earlier in the case of *State of Karnataka v. Dr. Praveen Bhai Thogadia*,[58] wherein the Indian Supreme Court adopted the 'basic-structure-doctrine' theory to justify preventive action by the executive in order to prevent a person or group of persons from spreading hatred and thereby creating an atmosphere of disharmony and disturbing the equilibrium with their inflammatory speech.

---

57 Supreme Court of India, *Firoz Iqbal Khan v. Union of India*, Order, 28 August 2020, (2021) 2 SCC 596; and Supreme Court of India, *Firoz Iqbal Khan v. Union of India*, Order, 15 September 2020, (2021) 2 SCC 591 (https://www.legal-tools.org/doc/0rs2yz/).

58 Supreme Court of India, *State of Karnataka v. Dr. Praveen Bhai Thogadia*, Judgment, 31 March 2004, (2004) 4 SCC 684 (https://www.legal-tools.org/doc/qpmao9/). In this case, the petitioner challenged the impugned order passed by the District Magistrate, Belgaum, debarring him to visit communally sensitive areas in Belgaum District. The Karnataka High Court set aside the order of District Magistrate. However, Indian Supreme Court reversed the order of Karnataka High Court and upheld the ban.

In fact, the most apparent inconsistency in terms of procedure adopted by courts in cases of hate speech is the application of the principle of the exhaustion of alternative remedies. Often, in hate speech cases, a writ petition before the Indian Supreme Court is preferred under Article 32 of the Constitution, either praying for the criminal law to be set in motion or to stay the criminal proceedings initiated against the petitioner. In accordance with the law of the land, the Indian Supreme Court is not the court of first instance in either of the abovementioned scenarios. The criminal justice system provides for alternative remedies that the aggrieved party may avail before invoking the writ jurisdiction of the Indian Supreme Court. Whenever infringement of fundamental rights is in question, redressal can be sought by invoking the jurisdiction of high courts under Article 226 of the Constitution. The Indian Supreme Court has also stated in numerous cases that a petitioner complaining of the infraction of his or her fundamental right should approach the high courts first, rather than the Indian Supreme Court in the first instance.[59] Though, it is an equally well settled principle that the existence of alternative remedy is not an absolute bar to a writ petition, but is merely a self-imposed restriction.[60] However, one can see a considerable inconsistency in the approach of the Indian Supreme Court when addressing cases of similar nature concerning hate speech. For instance, recently in *Nupur Sharma v. State of West Bengal*,[61] where four FIRs were registered in relation to *OP India*'s (a news portal) reports on communal violence at Bhadreswar Teriipaia against Nupur Sharma and other *OP India* journalists, the Indian Supreme Court stayed the investigation proceedings and subsequently quashed the FIRs, thereby granting the relief claimed by the petitioners. Further, the Court observed that the state force must not be used to browbeat political opinions, and that "[i]n a country which prides itself on its diversity, there are bound to be different perceptions and opinions which would include political opinions. That is the very essence of a democracy". However, for the purpose of this chapter, what is to be noted is that the Court entertained the plea and granted an *ex-parte* stay on multiple FIRs, without directing the petitioners to the appropriate high court to avail the relief sought.

---

59 Supreme Court of India, *Kanubhai Brahmbhatt v. State of Gujarat*, Judgment, 18 February 1987, AIR 1987 SC 1159 (https://www.legal-tools.org/doc/ptjo29/).

60 Supreme Court of India, *Sakiri Vasu v. State of Uttar Pradesh*, Judgment, 7 December 2007, (2008) 2 SCC 409 (https://www.legal-tools.org/doc/k4vnq9/). It was observed, in reference to non-registration of an FIR, that the high courts may be moved only when the remedies under Sections 154 (3), 156 (3), 200 of the CrPC have been exhausted. Though there is no absolute bar in filing a writ petition under Section 482 of the CrPC, if there is an alternative remedy available, the high court must not interfere.

61 Supreme Court of India, *Nupur J. Sharma v. State of West Bengal*, Order, 9 December 2021, Writ Petition (Criminal) No. 155/2020 (https://www.legal-tools.org/doc/rtty41/).

In contrast, in the case concerning the detention of Prof. Kafeel Khan[62] with regard to the speech delivered by him at Aligarh Muslim University criticizing the then recently passed legislations (the Citizenship (Amendment) Act, 2019 and the National Register of Citizens), the Indian Supreme Court refused to interfere in the matter and directed the petitioners to move the Allahabad High Court. It must also be noted that high courts, while dealing with the cases referred by the Indian Supreme Court, especially concerning hate speech, have shown a progressive approach and have addressed the issues in a comprehensive manner, often observing the menace that hate speech poses to the constitutional fabric of the country. Setting aside the order of detention and upholding the right to freedom of speech and expression, in Prof. Kafeel Khan's case, the Allahabad High Court observed:

> The system of governance is to promote fraternity with assurance to maintain the dignity of every individual as well as unity and integrity of the Nation. The strong and valuable fabric of our Nation is well designed with support of fundamental rights given in Part-III of the Constitution.

However, the cases concerning hate speech often demand prompt intervention, as the failure to act swiftly often leads to undue delay in proceedings and relief. For instance, delays may lead to extended detention of the aggrieved person, impacting directly his or her right to life and dignity. Though the petitioner must ordinarily move the high courts of its jurisdiction, when a petition has been presented before the Indian Supreme Court, the Court must exercise its original jurisdiction rather than stres the invocation of its powers as an appellate authority.

In fact, an altogether different approach was adopted by the Indian Supreme Court in *Amish Devgan*,[63] where it went into the merits of the case and engaged itself in an in-depth analysis of the available facts, and provided an overview of the comparative jurisprudence on the issue of hate speech and the surrounding concerns more generally. The Court concluded that the charges against the petitioner needed to be probed further and ordered the consolidation of the FIRs against the petitioner – a journalist – in relation to the comments made by him in his talk show. In this case, journalist Amish Devgan, news anchor for *News18 India*, in his news debate show called *Aar Paar*, referred to the revered *Ṣúfī* Saint Khwaja Moinuddin Chisthi, also known as Khwaja Gareeb Nawaz, as an '*aakranta* (attacker) *Chishti*' and '*lootere* (looter) *Chishti*'. This incited waves of fury across the nation, and later on there were multiple police complaints and FIRs which were filed against Amish Devgan under Sections

62 *Nuzhat Perween*, see *supra* note 28.
63 *Amish Devgan*, see *supra* note 19.

295A, 153A, 505 and 34 of the IPC, all alleging that the journalist had incited religious sentiments and had provoked violence against the Muslim community. Following this, Devgan apologized on his show and claimed that his mistake was unintentional. He also tweeted in a similar fashion. Subsequently, Amish Devgan also approached the Indian Supreme Court in a writ petition praying for quashing of the FIRs. While the Indian Supreme Court declined to grant the relief claimed by Devgan, it, however, granted him interim protection subject to his joining and co-operating in the process of investigation until its completion.

Throughout the judgement, the Court stressed the importance of protection of individual and community dignity while upholding the fundamental freedom of expression. The judgment cites, among other cases, the case of *Ramesh S/O Chotalal Dalal v. Union of India*,[64] wherein it was observed that, "the effect of the words used must be judged from the standards of reasonable, strong-minded, firm and courageous men, and not those of weak and vacillating minds, nor of those who scent danger in every hostile point of view". The judgment extensively relies upon the wisdom of various foreign jurisdictions as well as the Indian Supreme Court's own precedents to re-examine the definition of hate speech. The judgment notes:

> It remains difficult in law to draw the outmost bounds of freedom of speech and expression, the limit beyond which the right would fall foul and can be subordinated to other democratic values and public law considerations, so as to constitute a criminal offence.

The Court further observed:

> Persons of influence, keeping in view their reach, impact and authority they yield on general public or the specific class to which they belong, owe a duty and have to be more responsible.[65]

The judgment goes on to state that,

> a speech by 'a person of influence' such as a top government or executive functionary, opposition leader, political or social leader of following, or a credible anchor on a T.V. show carries a far more credibility and impact than a statement made by a common person

[64] Supreme Court of India, *Ramesh S/O Chotalal Dalal v. Union of India*, Judgment, 16 February 1988, AIR 1988 SC 775 ('*Ramesh Dalal*') (https://www.legal-tools.org/doc/bweb1s/). The petitioner filed a writ petition under Article 32 of the Constitution of India declaring '*Tamas*', a series of four episodes created out of Shr. Bhishma Sahni's book which tells the story of the Hindu-Muslim and Sikh-Muslim tensions and violence before India was partitioned, as violating Section 5(b) of the Cinematograph Act 1952, and as violating the fundamental rights under Articles 21 and 25 of the Constitution, and constituting an offense under Section 153A of the IPC.

[65] *Amish Devgan*, para. 51, see *supra* note 19.

on the street. Latter may be driven by anger, emotions, wrong perceptions or mis-information.

However, at the same time the Indian Supreme Court was quick to clarify that "[t]his is not to say that persons of influence like journalists do not enjoy the same freedom of speech and expression as other citizens, as this would be grossly incorrect understanding of what has been stated above". This observation, however, adds to the ambiguity surrounding adjudication and jurisprudence of hate speech. It is a concern of many that imputing a higher degree of accountability and responsibility upon people of influence, may prove to be counterproductive as it may introduce undue subjectivity in adjudication. This observation may disproportionately affect the right to freedom of speech and peaceful dissent of well-known scholars, activists and journalists especially those who frequently voice their concerns against state actions. Stricter standards may foreseeably provide room for interpretation convenient to the state and may even lead to malicious prosecution against those who put forward a discourse not aligning to that of the state.

Another crucial aspect which arises here is the question of how a court will identify the persons who occupy positions of power and influence. By the term 'social leader of following' did the Indian Supreme Court mean 'social media influencers'? Further, what quantitative test will the Indian Supreme Court adopt in identifying 'social leaders of following' is something which remains ambiguous.

The *Amish Devgan* judgment brings to light the manner in which the Indian Supreme Court has exercised discretion to go into the merits in some cases while refraining from commenting, or even providing an opportunity of hearing, in others. Thus, the difference in approach of the Indian Supreme Court is highlighted when it is read through the judgment passed in this case. Such discrepancies have adversely affected the development of hate speech jurisprudence.[66]

In the case of *Patrica Mukhim v. State of Meghalaya*,[67] the Indian Supreme Court quashed an FIR against Shillong Times editor Patricia Mukhim who had spoken out against the physical attack on non-tribal people, a small minority, by local tribal youth in a Facebook post in July 2020. The editor's agony was directed against the apathy shown by the then chief minister of Meghalaya, the director general of police and the Dorbal Shnong (the local tribal council) in not taking action against the culprits. While the Meghalaya High Court turned down the petition filed by the petitioner, whereby the quashing of

66 Mani Chander, "Supreme Court's Curious Judgment in the Amish Devgan Case: Numerous Questions", *The Leaflet*, 23 December 2020.

67 Supreme Court of India, *Patrica Mukhim v. State of Meghalaya*, Judgment, 25 March 2021, 2021 SCC Online SC 258 (https://www.legal-tools.org/doc/sbc4ep/).

the FIR was sought, the Indian Supreme Court allowed it. The Court expanded the expression by raising the threshold of what could constitute 'hate speech'. The judges noted that disapprobation of governmental inaction cannot be branded as an attempt to promote hatred between different communities. The Court observed that calls for justice, equality and protection of a particular community in cases where government authorities have turned a blind eye can never be considered as 'hate speech'. In this case, the bench held that the citizens' right to free speech cannot be stifled by implicating them in criminal cases, unless such speech has the tendency to affect public order.

Despite there being guidance from the Indian Supreme Court in the form of judgment passed in *Amish Devgan*, the uncertainty around the interpretation of hate speech still looms and resulted in the adoption of varying standards. The Madras High Court, in *M. Maridoss v. State Represented by The Inspector of Police*,[68] quashed an FIR alleging hate speech involving targeting of minorities by holding that the 'YouTuber' is entitled to protection under Article 19(1)(a) of the Constitution, and distinguished this case from the application of the 'Who? What? Where?' test laid down in *Amish Devgan*. *Per contra*, the same high court, in the case of *Fr. P. George Ponnaiah v. Inspector of Police*,[69] gave no relief to the petitioner by holding him to be a person of influence. In this case the catholic priest had remarked that the Bhartiya Janta Party member of legislative assembly from Tamil Nadu, M.R. Gandhi, walked barefoot, but not Christians. "We wear shoes. Why? Because the filth of Bharat Mata should not contaminate us. The Tamil Nadu Government has given us free footwear. This *Bhuma devi* is dangerous, you could catch scabies from it." Stating that the priest painted '*Bhuma Devi*' and '*Bharat Mata*' as sources of infection and filth, the bench observed: "By referring to Bharat Mata and Bhuma Devi in the most offensive terms, the petitioner has *prima facie* committed the offence under Section 295A of IPC".[70]

68 High Court of Madras, *M. Maridoss v. State Represented by The Inspector of Police*, Order, 14 December 2021, (2021) 6 CTC 838 (https://www.legal-tools.org/doc/r7rv65/). The Madras High Court quashed the FIR registered against YouTuber Maridoss under Sections 292A, 295A, 153A and 505(2) of the IPC for posting his YouTube video criticizing the Tablighi Jamaat conference, held in Delhi in March 2020, when congregations and meetings were fully banned in the wake of Covid-19 pandemic and therefore accusing its attendees to be spreaders of Covid-19. It was held that the petitioner relied solely on the news resources then available in the public domain and criticism of an organization cannot be taken as a criticism of a community.

69 High Court of Madras, *Fr. P. George Ponnaiah v. Inspector of Police*, Order, 7 January 2022, 2022 SCC Online Mad 81 (https://www.legal-tools.org/doc/x64xat/).

70 *Ibid.*, para. 13.

The instances mentioned above clearly bring to light the apparent discrepancy in the manner in which courts have engaged with matters concerning hate speech and the incongruity which has caused further degeneration of the discourse on hate speech. Such divergent decisions also expose the lack of established legal standards in defining hate speech, especially that propagated via the digital medium.

8.4.2. Literary and Artistic Works

8.4.2.1. Lack of Proactive Judicial Intervention

While dealing with creative and artistic expression and academic research, the higher judiciary in India has endeavoured to strike a balance between these two interests by considering both 'internal' factors, such as the tenor and tone and the language used, and 'external factors', such as whether there already are a vitiated atmosphere or tensions between communities, while recognizing the freedom to express diverse view points and the freedom of creativity and art, as long as the mode of delivery and the language used do not indicate a deliberate and malicious intention to hurt sentiments or outrage feelings. Academic material is also protected unless the language used is crude or coarse, and the reader or viewer which is generally taken as the standard is a reasonable, strong and courageous person, rather than a weak person with a vacillating mind that scents danger in every point of view.[71] However, despite these standards, academicians and performers have found themselves to be at the receiving end of backlash even while expressing a legitimate or fair opinion on religion, as can be witnessed in several cases involving artists, such as Kiku Sharda, Munawar Faruqui and M.F. Hussain, as well as writers, such as Taslima Nasreen, Salman Rushdie and Wendy Doniger. All of them seem to be victims of the indiscriminate invocation of Section 295A of the IPC by the law enforcement machinery and of the courts' failure to exercise proactive judicial intervention.

8.4.2.2. From Recognition of Right to Criticism Towards Narrowing Down the Scope of Religious Debate

Today, when courts are presented with petitions where a literary work is challenged for portraying a community or a part of it in a bad light, judges are posed with the arduous task of attempting to balance three factors: social interests, liberty of thought and expression, and public safety. But in a nation like India, very often, even a mere dissenting opinion can cause a stir amongst the masses. Thus, authors find themselves spending more time self-censoring or battling in court. In India, it is not just books, magazines and films that have been banned or have faced the ire of a particular community, but also, time and again,

71 *Ramesh Dalal*, see *supra* note 64.

attempts have been made to ban events that involve controversial literature, films or eminent personalities.

It will be apposite, at this juncture, to look into the approach adopted by the judiciary in a chronical sequence of some of the leading cases in which renowned journalists, activists, authors and dissenters were implicated in criminal proceedings under Section 295A of the IPC due to the despotic and arbitrary nature of the authorities and various groups or political parties, in their endeavour to curb such expression in the films, books and other literary works which fell out of their taste, sometimes on flimsy grounds. It is apparent that while on numerous occasions the Indian judiciary has recognized the right of authors and publishers to deal with critique of religion by evolving broad consensus in law, at the same time it has applied varying standards and has adopted an altogether different procedural approach in similar cases.

For instance, in *Ramji Lal Modi*,[72] the Indian Supreme Court upheld the validity of Section 295A of the IPC and the conviction of Ramji Lal Modi for having published an article in a magazine against Muslims, by holding the petitioner's action to be deliberate and malicious, thereby falling within the scope of Section 295A of the IPC. Therefore, the restriction imposed upon the petitioner by the state under the guise of maintaining public order was upheld by the Indian Supreme Court, widening the scope of the said provision and, at the same time, narrowing the scope for fair criticism of religion. What the Court completely lost sight of was the fact that not every insult of religion may necessarily lead to a 'law and order' situation.

However, later, in *Ram Manohar Lohia*,[73] the Indian Supreme Court rationalized the test laid down in *Ramji Lal Modi* and held that "there must be a proximate link between speech and public disorder, and not a far-fetched, remote or fanciful connection".

In the case of *Veerabadran Chettiar v. E.V. Ramaswami Naicker*,[74] the Indian Supreme Court was confronted with the question of whether the breaking of a clay idol of the god Ganesha, not belonging to any temple and not being part of a religious procession, by a social reformer who led the Dravidian movement along with two other persons, amounted to insulting religious beliefs in a way that invokes the provisions of Sections 295 and 295A of the IPC. The Court of the District and Session Judge of Tiruchirapalli and the Madras High Court declined to convict the accused persons by holding that Sections 295 and 295A of the IPC required a person to insult religious beliefs and breaking a clay idol

[72] *Ramji Lal Modi*, see *supra* note 20.

[73] *Ram Manohar Lohia*, see *supra* note 23.

[74] Supreme Court of India, *Veerabadran Chettiar v. E.V. Ramaswami Naicker*, Judgment, 25 August 1958, AIR 1958 SC 1032 (https://www.legal-tools.org/doc/p5me52/).

of Ganesha did not amount to insulting any religious beliefs since the idol neither belonged to a temple, nor was it a part of any religious procession. However, in appeal before the Indian Supreme Court, the order of the trial court and high court was reversed and the Supreme Court opined that even though the idol broken by the accused was privately owned and was not a sacred idol, it was still a sacred object within the meaning of Section 295 of the IPC. Further, the Indian Supreme Court held that any object, however trivial or devoid of real value, if considered to be sacred by a class of persons, would be covered within the ambit of Section 295 of the IPC. The Court even expanded the ambit of the section to include objects that may not be worshipped at all. The Court also held that the judiciary must be very respectful of the religious sentiments of people and must not sit in judgment of those beliefs, even if it does not share those beliefs or find them rational. The Court, in this case, clearly mentioned that recurrence of such a behaviour by any person against any community would invite action under Section 295 of the IPC. However, considering that the case had already dragged for over five years, the Court found the matter 'stale' and refused to direct any further inquiry. Thus, while the Court set a very loose standard of which object could be considered as 'sacred', it narrowed the scope for religious debate and criticism; and, by suppressing further procedures on the ground of declaring the matter as stale, the Court ignored the fact that a legal battle never becomes stale until it is given a quietus by the court of law.

In the case of *N. Veerabrahmam v. State of Andhra Pradesh* ('*N. Veerabrahmam*'),[75] dealt with a notification issued under Section 99A of CrPC, 1898, which failed to mention any grounds: the State of Andhra Pradesh ordered the confiscation of a book titles *Bible Bandaram* authored by the petitioner, which pointed at the incongruities and inconsistencies in the Bible. The book also raised doubts about its authorship and made controversial claims such as that Jesus was a product of an adulterous union and that the immaculate conception theory was a cover-up. This judgment was rendered by a three judge bench, with a majority of two. The majority judgement upheld the notification passed by the state government and observed that setting forth the disputed passages in the notification was enough, and no grounds were required in support of the notification since the passages themselves were enough to show that they were promoting disharmony amongst the Christian community. The majority judgement also held that both volumes of the book were to be regarded as one book and that forfeiture of both volumes was correct.

However, in his minority judgement in this case, Justice Bhimasankaram held that as there were no grounds put forth in the notification, that by itself was

[75] High Court of Andhra Pradesh, *N. Veerabrahmam v. State of Andhra Pradesh*, Judgment, 12 March 1959, AIR 1959 AP 572 ('*N. Veerabrahmam*').

enough to revoke the notification. He further went on to hold that in case the passages would be read separately, then they could harm the religious sentiments and beliefs of the Christian community, but when the book was read as a whole, the theme of the book would not insult the religious beliefs of the community. He also pointed out that the volumes of the book were different and contained different things. Forfeiture of both the volumes by regarding them as one book should not have stood, and the volumes should have been regarded as two different books. Although this opinion by Justice Bhimasankaram was only a minority judgement in the present case, it was taken as the majority view in many cases.

On the other hand, in similar circumstances, an altogether different approach came to be adopted by the Indian Supreme Court in the case of *Lalai Singh Yadav v. State of Uttar Pradesh* ('Lalai Singh Yadav').[76] In this case, the state government of Uttar Pradesh,with a notification, ordered forfeiture of a book titled *Samman ke liye dharma parivartan karen*, which was a compilation in Hindi of the speeches made by Late Dr. B.R. Ambedkar. Twenty-four passages of the book were cited in the notification, objected to because they allegedly promoted or attempted to promote disharmony or feelings of enmity, hatred or ill-will between different religions, castes or communities, and insulted the religion or religious beliefs of a class, rendering the publication of the book punishable under Sections 153A and 295A of the IPC. When the matter arrived before the Allahabad High Court, the Court observed that, though a reading of the passages independently might outrage the religious feelings of any community, when the book is read as a whole, keeping in mind the theme of the book with which it was intended to be written, none of the passages complained of can be held to be punishable. The Allahabad High Court eventually allowed the application and ordered the impugned notification to be set aside. Through this case, the Allahabad High Court clarified that when some literary work is published, it should be read as a whole, according to its theme, rather than not separately in parts. It was also held that that mandatory procedure under Section 99A of the CrPC, 1898 was not fulfilled by the State of Uttar Pradesh, as no grounds were mentioned in the notification which forfeited the books. Being dissatisfied with the judgment, the State of Uttar Pradesh appealed against it before the Indian Supreme Court and contended that writing down the passages of the book in the notification itself formed the ground for passing the notification to forfeit the book.

The Indian Supreme Court held that noting down the passages in the notification was not sufficient and that not mentioning separate grounds in the

[76] High Court of Allahabad, *Lalai Singh Yadav v. State of Uttar Pradesh*, Judgment, 14 May 1971, 1971 CriLJ 1773.

notification was a legal impropriety on part of the state. On this reasoning, the Indian Supreme Court upheld the judgment of the Allahabad High Court.[77] The Indian Supreme Court did provide its opinion on the merits of the case, but only dealt with the issue of the legal procedure that the State of Uttar Pradesh was required to be followed. The Indian Supreme Court, however, made it clear that in order to penalize any literature under Section 295A of the IPC, with the judicial procedure outlined in Section 99A of the CrPC, 1898 should be strictly followed and that the absence of any ingredient could render the act of the state illegal. Further, the Court clearly opined that in order to test whether an act is to be penalized under Section 295A of the IPC, the full purpose of the act should be viewed rather than just a single act.

The issue of hate speech in a book was also examined in the case of *Gopal Vinayak Godse v. Union of India*,[78] in which the book in question, *Gandhi-hatya Ani Mee* (*Gandhi-assassination and I*), dealt with all the true facts and sequences that led to the death of Mahatma Gandhi, and with the life of the author and of other acquitted accused persons after they were let out of prison. The ground for forfeiting the book, as given by the government while passing the notification, was that the author, through this book, had tried to promote enmity between the Muslim and Hindu communities. The Indian Supreme Court held that, when the book was read as a whole, it just mentioned the true facts that took place, and that from the book the author did not seem of the intention to instigate any insult in the minds of the members of any community. According to the bench, there could be several central themes of the book, but none of them could be regarded as being an act punishable under Section 153A of the IPC. The author, through the book, showed that the assassination of Gandhi was due to his appeasement policy towards Muslims. The Indian Supreme Court held that the passages appearing in the notification did not, either by themselves or as read in the context of the book as a whole, promote feelings of hatred between the two communities. Hence, the order of forfeiture was set aside. However, despite having the chance to expand the horizon of the quintessential freedom of speech that forms the core of the democratic values prescribed by the Constitution, the Court chose to act against it. The Court proceeded to provide for two more conditions that may result in having a chilling effect on the freedom of speech. It held that, in a case involving Section 153A of the IPC, it is not necessary to prove that enmity or hatred was in fact caused or that there was any intention to cause hatred. If the language of the text is of such a nature that it

---

[77] Supreme Court of India, *State of Uttar Pradesh v. Lalai Singh Yadav*, Judgment, 16 September 1976, AIR 1977 SC 202 ('*Lalai Singh Yadav*') (https://www.legal-tools.org/doc/lxtoah/).

[78] High Court of Bombay, *Gopal Vinayak Godse v. Union of India*, Judgment, 6 August 1969, AIR 1971 Bom 56.

could promote feelings of enmity and hatred, then Section 153A of the IPC could be applied. This case firstly did away with the necessary criteria of *mens rea* required in cases of criminal trials, and secondly it discharged the burden on the prosecution to prove the impact that the speech had on the public. Further, it even went on to remove a truthful account of history as a defense to the charge under Section 153A of the IPC. The Court observed that in fact, greater the truth, greater the impact of the writing on the minds of its readers, if the writing is otherwise calculated to produce mischief.

Similarly, the case of *Maqbool Fida Husain v. Rajkumar Pandey*[79] came up for consideration before Delhi High Court in the 2007, in which a painting made by the petitioner was alleged to insult Hindu religious feelings along with the nationalistic feelings of the citizens of the country. The painting depicted the abstract and graphical representation of India in the form of a nude woman whose flowing hair formed the Himalayas, thereby showing the agony of the woman. The painting was said to be obscene and vulgar, depraving the minds of the nationals. On the issue of obscenity, the Indian Supreme Court applied the 'Hicklins Test'[80] that was accepted in the Indian legal system since the decision in the case of *Ranjit D. Udeshi v. State of Maharashtra*.[81] According to this test, mere nudity in art is not *per se* obscene and the work should be seen as a whole, and it should be tried to find out whether obscenity tends to deprave or corrupt the minds of common people. On the application of this test, the Court decided that this painting, when viewed as a whole, did not deprave the minds of the common person and hence it was decided that it was not obscene.

Further in this case, the Court also pointed out that when a matter concerns a painting, it should be looked at from the point of view of the artist and that the theme of the painting should be kept in consideration while deciding any related question. Regarding the offence under Section 298 of the IPC, the Court held that the idea of the artist in depicting India in the form of a nude distressed woman was "to show the disconsolate India which is entangled in various problems like corruption, criminalisation, crisis of leadership,

79 High Court of Delhi, *Maqbool Fida Husain v. Rajkumar Pandey*, Judgment, 8 May 2008, 2008 Cri LJ 4107 ('*Maqbool Fida Husain*') (https://www.legal-tools.org/doc/de6lvo/).

80 Hicklins Test was evolved in the case of *Regina v. Hicklin*, 29 April 1868, L.R. 3 Q.B. 360 (1868), in which anything was said to be obscene when the matter, interpreted as a whole, was such as "to deprave and corrupt those whose minds are open to such immoral influences".

81 Supreme Court of India, *Ranjit D. Udeshi v. State of Maharashtra*, Judgment, 19 August 1964, AIR 1965 SC 881 (https://www.legal-tools.org/doc/m9rs07/). Ranjit D. Udeshi was one of the four partners of a book stall. He along with his partners was convicted for selling a book, *Lady Chatterly's Lover*, which allegedly was obscene. Applying the Hicklin's Test, the Indian Supreme Court held the book to be depraving the minds of the people and hence was held to be obscene.

unemployment, poverty, over population, low standard of living, fading values and ethics etc.".[82] Thus, the Court held that the painting *Bharat Mata* was not intended to insult the religious sentiments of any person, but instead was drawn in this manner to depict the current state of the nation. The Court also held that looking at the photo would bring any person to tears and would bring him or her into the realization that the country is suffering from various evils, instead of depraving their minds.

Then, in the case of *Sujato Bhadra v. State of West Bengal*,[83] in which the State of West Bengal had passed a notification forfeiting all the copies of the book *Dwikhandita* written by Taslima Nasreen of Bangladesh. This book was the third part of the autobiography of the author and depicted the current situation of her home country. According to the book, after the acceptance of Islám as the national religion of Bangladesh, women in the country were not independent and were mistreated. The validity of this notification was challenged before the Calcutta High Court, raising the issue as to whether the book *Dwikhandita* could be proscribed in India. The contention of the state was that the author was not a citizen of India and hence she did not enjoy the fundamental rights to freedom of speech and expression. The Calcutta High Court, however, held that though the author was not a citizen and was not guaranteed the freedom of speech and expression, the petition was filed by a reader of the book who was the citizen of India, and the petition was filed because his freedom of speech and expression – including freedom to seek, receive and impart information from the said book – was being infringed by the forfeiture of the book. Therefore, he claimed himself to be a person who falls within the ambit of the expression "any person having any interest in any […] Book" as provided in Section 96 of the CrPC. Thus, the Calcutta High Court held that the petition would stand and then went on to decide the case on merits.

The Calcutta High Court held that the author had no deliberate and malicious intention to hurt the religious feelings of any community. Rather, by her novel, she wanted to show the world the reality of her own country and that women in her country were distressed by the nation's situation. If an author writes something in good faith with the object to facilitate some social reform by administering a shock to the people of the religion, then such a work cannot be regarded to be insulting to the religious feelings of any community. In the words of the Calcutta High Court:

> Many ills and maladies ingrained in the society have been eradicated or removed mostly through the people following the same

---

82 *Maqbool Fida Husain*, para. 98, see *supra* note 79.

83 High Court of Calcutta, *Sujato Bhadra v. State of West Bengal*, Judgment, 22 Septemeber 2005, 2006 Cri LJ 368.

> religion by their own emancipating thoughts and ideologies and sometimes striking very hard at the faiths and beliefs of the followers of that particular custom/system sanctioned by religion.[84]

In this case, the Calcutta High Court again reiterated that, in order to find something worth penalizing under Section 295A of the IPC, individual paragraphs or pages should not be looked into, the whole book should rather be read as a whole and that, while reading the 'insulting paragraphs' or 'pages', the theme of the book should always be kept in mind. The Calcutta High Court held that, since *Dwikhandita* was written with the intention to show the real condition of women in Bangladesh and not to insult the religious feelings of any religion, it cannot be regarded as a book worth of being forfeited. Hence, the Calcutta High Court set aside the notification of the State of West Bengal forfeiting all the copies of the book in the state.

In another case, *Delhi Administration v. Rajpal Singh Shastri*,[85] the accused, an editor and publisher of Hindi monthly journal titled *Madhur Lok*, was notified by the crime branch under Sections 153, 295 and 505 of the IPC on the ground that the articles published in the journal were written with a view to promote enmity and hatred between Sikhs and the Muslims. On appearance, the editor denied that he had written the articles to promote any hatred or disharmony in any community, rather what he had written was *bona fide* and was written with the intention to promote communal harmony and peace in the country. He pleaded not guilty and claimed trial. The trial court, upon appreciation of the evidence on record, acquitted him. On appeal, the Delhi High of Court held that the decision of the trial court was not perverse, and although another view was possible, it was not sufficient to reverse the judgement of acquittal. The trial court in this case acquitted the accused on the ground "that the article read as whole does appear to be an attack on the muslim religion but it attempts to expose certain mohammaden leaders who in the name of the religion exploit the muslim masses for their selfish ends".[86]

However, in the case of *Poojaya Sri Jagadguru Maate Mahadevi v. Government of Karnataka*,[87] a book titled *Basava Vachna Deepthi* was banned in 1998 by the State of Karnataka on the ground that the author substituted the

---

84 *Ibid.*, para. 9.3.

85 High Court of Delhi, *Delhi Administration v. Rajpal Singh Shastri*, Judgment, 23 February 2005, 2005 (81) DRJ 209.

86 *Ibid.*, para. 5.

87 "Kannada Author Loses Plea Against Ban on Her Book, SC Dismisses It Without Reasoned Order", *The Wire*, 20 September 2017. See also Supreme Court of India, *Poojaya Sri Jagadguru Maate Mahadevi v. Government of Karnataka*, Order, 20 September 2017, Criminal Appeal No. 491/2009.

original words in Lord Basava Vachanas, as she changed the pen name of Basaveshwara from "Kundalasangamadeva" to "Lingadeva", thereby hurting the feelings of the Veerashaiva Community in the state. The Indian Supreme Court upheld the ban on the book without giving any reasoned order, thus ignoring the implications that such order could have on free speech. This order of the Indian Supreme Court forms part of the list of the cases which call into question the common belief of every citizen who regards the highest branch of India judiciary as a custodian of fundamental rights. In cases such as this one, the Indian Supreme Court does not appear to have seen the right as a trump, but rather as an abstract notion that lies at the state's whimsical behest. In this case, without even a minimal analysis as to how the impugned action on part of the accused could satisfy the aggravated test result, the Court read deliberate intentions on a fragile ground, that the author changed the name of a book because she wanted to impose her philosophy through the name of Lord Basaveshwara.

Another book, *Maharishi Balmik: Ekk Samastik Adhyan*, was also sought to be brought within the ambit of Section 295A of the IPC, when an FIR was filed against its author. This came up for consideration in the case of *Manjula Sahdev v. State of Punjab*.[88] In this book, the author of the book Dr. Manjula Sahdev, a professor in the department of religious studies of Punjab University, had published her research work on the life of Balmiki. An FIR was filed against her in 2009 by a person belonging to the Balmiki community on the ground that the petitioner had depicted Balmiki as a '*Dakoo*' (thug) in her book, which had hurt the religious sentiments of the whole Balmiki community. The book was for the first time written and published in 1980. In defence, a primary contention regarding the FIR being time barred was raised by the petitioner on the ground that the FIR in question was filed 29 years after the book was first written and published, which was accepted by the Punjab and Haryana High Court.

The Punjab and Haryana High Court further observed that there were only two pages in the whole book which mentioned that Maharishi Balmiki was a '*Dakoo*' before becoming the saint he is known to be today, and that these two pages also mentioned that this fact was written after relying on two other books. The book written by the author was a work of thesis and hence was a compilation of work done by various other authors. The Punjab and Haryana High Court also held that a bare perusal of the statements written on those two pages did not show that the author had any intention to hurt the religious feelings of any community. The Court further held that "it is not the task of the criminal law to punish the individuals merely for expressing unpopular views, unless it is

88 High Court of Punjab and Haryana, *Manjula Sahdev v. State of Punjab*, Order, 23 April 2019, Criminal Main No. 18590/2010 (https://www.legal-tools.org/doc/6ktnlq/).

proved that the accused has done it in a mala fide manner".[89] Thus, the Court allowed the petition and quashed all the proceedings emanating from the impugned FIR.

Furthermore, in the case of *Mahendra Singh Dhoni v. Yerraguntla Shyamsundar*,[90] a complaint was filed under Section 200 of the CrPC against the petitioner when a magazine published as the cover page an image of him portrayed as Lord Vishnuwhile holding various commercial brands, including a shoe in his hands, with the caption "God of Big Deals". The complainant alleged that the photo had hurt the religious beliefs of Hindus by showcasing the petitioner as a god. The Indian Supreme Court held that a mere publication of a photo of the petitioner on the cover page of a magazine as an advertisement would not amount to be an insult to the religious sentiments of any community and could be considered to be an aggravated form of insult. Thus, the complaint against the petitioner was set aside. Concerned by the misuse of Section 295A of the IPC, which provides up to three years' jail term for hurting religious sentiments, the Indian Supreme Court limited the applicability of the penal provision to deliberate and malicious acts rather than casual observations that are not driven by malicious intent.

Along with books and paintings, Section 295A of the IPC has also been brought into play in certain movies and Internet series. In the case of *Sony Pictures Releasing of India Ltd. V. State of Tamil Nadu*,[91] the movie *Da Vinci Code*, based on a novel by Dan Brown, was prohibited from being exhibited in the State of Tamil Nadu for two months on the ground that the movie had the tendency to disrupt harmony in the state by hurting the religious sentiments of Christians. The petitioners, before releasing the movie in the theatres, had obtained a certificate of exhibition from the Central Board of Film Certification and in fact, prior to issuing the said certificate, the movie was shown to a few leaders of the Christian community, who suggested its release in the theatres after adding a few disclaimers at the beginning and at the end of the movie. In the words of the Madras High Court, "when the statutory body had granted permission to screen the film as per the guidelines, the local authority, without 'thinking' had stopped the screening".[92]

The Madras High Court held that, since the petitioners had already received the certificate to exhibit the film, there was no need to invoke Section 13 of the Cinematograph Act, 1952. The Madras High Court further held that it is

---

89 *Ibid.*, para. 22.

90 *Mahendra Singh Dhoni*, see *supra* note 47.

91 High Court of Madras, *Sony Pictures Releasing of India Ltd. v. State of Tamil Nadu*, Order, 7 July 2006, 2006 (4) CTC 193 (https://www.legal-tools.org/doc/5uysaz/).

92 *Ibid.*, para. 36.

the duty of the state to maintain peace and security within the state and that, if there appeared a chance of public disorder owing to the screening of the film, it would be the duty of the state to maintain public order and to also secure the locations in which the film was being released.

The Madras High Court further held that mere instances in the movie, especially since the movie was a work of fiction, cannot be deemed blasphemous or hurtful for the religious feelings of a community. The Madras High Court pointed out that the movie was not only released in India but worldwide, including in countries where the Christian community was in the majority, and that since the movie did not tend to disrupt the harmony in such places or hurt the religious feelings of people in such countries, it would likewise not do so in India. The impugned order was held to be clearly violating the petitioner's right to freedom of speech and expression and was set aside.

Similarly, in another case of *Aparna Purohit v. State of Uttar Pradesh*,[93] the makers of the web series *Tandav* approached the Indian Supreme Court for interim protection from arrest after the police, on the ground that the series had hurt Hindu religious sentiments, initiated investigations in six states based on complaints under Section 295A and others of the IPC. However, the Indian Supreme Court refused the prayer. In the series, caste and community-related utterances had been alleged to have been made deliberately to affect public peace. Some of the dialogues that lead to outburst were:

> Bholenath, you are very innocent, do something new, Infact tweet something new, something sensational, some flaming blaze, like (Thinking) Yes, "All students of Campus became traitors, they are raising slogans of freedom-freedom" and "When a man of a lower caste dates a woman of a higher caste, he is taking revenge for the centuries of atrocities from that one woman".

In this background, the makers were accused of provoking communal tension *via* its dialogues.

The Indian Supreme Court refused to grant interim protection from arrest and asked the petitioners to approach the high courts across the country for anticipatory bail. The Indian Supreme Court simply allowed the clubbing of FIRs, but refused prayers to quash despite the fact that objectionable scenes were deleted from the series and an unconditional apology was also rendered. The Allahabad High Court observed that it was becoming a trend in the country to insult Hindu gods and goddesses to gain popularity from it and if this trend was not curbed in time, it would tend to bring disastrous consequences in the Indian

93 Supreme Court of India, *Aparna Purohit v. State of Uttar Pradesh*, Order, 5 March 2021, Petition for Special Leave to Appeal (Criminal) No. 1983/2021 (https://www.legal-tools.org/doc/mnd1ou/).

social, religious and communal order, and therefore rejected the petitioner's plea stating that:

> the fact remains that the applicant had not been vigilant and has acted irresponsibly making her open to criminal prosecution in permitting streaming of a movie which is against the fundamental rights of the majority of citizens of this country and therefore, her fundamental right of life and liberty cannot be protected by grant of anticipatory bail to her in the exercise of discretionary powers of this court.

The Allahabad High Court further stated that "the conduct of the applicant shows that she has scant respect for the law of the land and her conduct further disentitles her to any relief from this court".[94] However, later on, the Indian Supreme Court granted protection from arrest to the Indian head of Amazon Prime Video, Aparna Purohit, subject to her co-operating in the investigation.

In fact, over the years a new trend has emerged to use Section 295A of the IPC against publication of material or screening of movies based on historic figures like Shivaji, Rani Padmavati, *etcetera*, who cannot, by any stretch of imagination, be called as religious figures. It is in this context, the screening of a Bollywood movie titled *Padmaavat* was challenged and various FIRs were filed under Section 295A of the IPC on the ground that several scenes tend to hurt the religious sentiments of the Rajput community. One such FIR came up for consideration when filmmaker Sanjay Leela Bhansali, director of the *Padmaavat*, filed a petition in the Rajasthan High Court seeking its quashing.[95] The FIR was registered even before the movie started being filmed and relied on the information from news channels and newspapers reporting that a movie on the life of Maharani Padmavati was being filmed, in which there was twisting and distorting of various historical facts and events. The Rajasthan High Court commented that Maharani Padmavati was a historical and not a religious figure, therefore the offence mentioned under Section 295A of the IPC could be invoked. The Rajasthan High Court also held that the FIR in the present case was filed when the movie had not even been released, thus no question of public harmony being disturbed could be raised. Further, when the movie was completed, it received the certificate of exhibition by the Central Board of Film Certification, and the Indian Supreme Court also passed the order that not allowing the movie to be released in theatres of certain states would be in gross violation

94 High Court of Allahabad, *Aparna Purohit v. State of Uttar Pradesh*, Order, 25 February 2021, (2021) SCC Online All 179 (https://www.legal-tools.org/doc/o1lc1e/).

95 High Court of Rajasthan, *Sanjay Leela Bhansali v. State of Rajasthan*, Judgment, 6 February 2018, Crim. Misc. (Pet.) No. 737/2017 (https://www.legal-tools.org/doc/xzdyyi/).

of the issued certificate. Thus, the Rajasthan High Court allowed the petition and quashed the FIR against the movie.

Thus, from the discussion above, it appears that Indian courts have not laid down any clear standards to ascertain the relevance of context, though, however, context-specific observations have been made in some instances. Within the Indian legal doctrine, there are two distinctive strands of thought when it comes to penal provisions regulating insult to religion, hurting community sentiments and promoting enmity between communities. The first is described by Justice Krishna Iyer in *Lalai Singh Yadav*[96] as "the constitutional value of ordered security" wherein Justice Iyer identified ordered security as a constitutional value that is to be safeguarded, implying that courts should give regard to the state if their intent is to protect safety and peace.[97] Here, the principle of ordered security is enunciated as a positive principle, without which creativity and freedom are meaningless. The second strand of doctrine is from Justice Bhimasankaran's dissenting judgement in *N. Veerabrahmam*, a decision of the Andhra Pradesh High Court,[98] wherein the majority held that free thinking does not involve the freedom to make scurrilous attacks on the religion and religious beliefs of other sects with impunity. In his dissent, Justice Bhimasankaran held that the Constitution does allow citizens to offer insults to religions if such insults are not made with deliberate and malicious intention of outraging the religious feelings of that class. Further, he called for society to get used to a greater tolerance of intolerance, holding that "curbs on freedom of expression are a greater evil than any consequences that may follow by exercise of such freedom and that one must not be afraid of error so long as truth is free to combat it". Justice Bhimasankaran's dissent is one of the most powerful articulations of a robust, free speech-oriented approach to claims of hurt of religious sentiment and is cited repeatedly in cases dealing with hate speech.[99]

To put it crudely, the former strand puts public order over free speech, while the latter does not. Religious sentiment and feelings have always been a crucial aspect when it comes to hate speech.[100]

96 *Lalai Singh Yadav*, see *supra* note 77.

97 Suvidutt M.S. and Aditya Tomer, "Hate Speech Laws In India And Australia: A Comparative Analysis", in *Amity International Journal of Juridical Sciences*, 2020, vol. 6, no. 1, p. 4.

98 *N. Veerabrahmam*, see *supra* note 75. The Andhra Pradesh government ordered for seizure of copies of Veerbrhamam's book *Bible Bandaram* under Section 99A of the CrPC and the constitutionality of the same was challenged.

99 Siddharth Narrain, "Hate Speech, Hurt Sentiment, and the (Im)Possibility of Free Speech", in *Economic and Political Weekly*, 2016, vol. 51, no. 17, p. 122–23.

100 *Ibid.*

Thus, what emerges from the discussion above is that by and large the judicial doctrine in India has recognized and accepted reasoned, rational and academic speech, and that any speech which is intended to hurt sentiments or outrage feelings has been considered to be a sign of hateful speech evincible from its form. If the form is vituperative, coarse, abusive or offensive, it is surely to be considered as 'hateful'. Further, historical or other truth is not seen as always acceptable, as truth that is used towards promoting enmity or outraging feelings will continue to fall on the side of unacceptable speech. The court will only protect claims of truth if they are shown in proper light. It is not the search for truth but the idea of a larger public interest that would prevail, and through this lens, truth and public interest would not always be compatible.

8.5. Conclusion and Suggestions

From the discussion in this chapter, it is evident that the uncertainty around the exact meaning of 'hate speech' has resulted not only in the adoption of inconsistent procedural and substantive approaches by the courts, but has also reflected upon the lack of proactivity on their part. The manner in which the Indian Supreme Court has exercised discretion to go into merits of the matter in some cases, while refraining from commenting or even providing an opportunity of hearing in others, has indeed resulted in the evolution of a blurred and obscure jurisprudence on hate speech in India, calling for the standardization of legislation dealing with this matter. However, despite the inconsistencies in the procedural and substantive approaches adopted by the higher judiciary, it must be noted that the courts have also meticulously tried to balance the principles of separation of powers with the fundamental freedoms guaranteed under the Constitution to the citizens. While refraining from stepping into the executive and legislative domain of state machinery, the courts have furthered, promoted and protected the freedoms that form the very fabric of our nation and have also laid emphasis on the right–duty dynamics concerning hate speech. The developments that have taken place, especially in the past few years with regard to academicians, scholars and artists being trapped in the net of Section 295A of the IPC, have made it imperative to review the provision as it stands, and to consider whether it sufficiently addresses the complexities of the religious discourse on hate speech and freedom of speech and expression. Since the protection of critical, dissenting views in a democratic setup is non-negotiable as it is closely and intricately linked to the values of tolerance, integrity, fraternity, liberty, pluralism and non-discrimination that form the essence of the Indian nation, it is with these considerations as guiding factors that the content of Section 295A of the IPC requires review and revision, for the simple reason that it is vaguely worded and, as such, leaves the scope for unwarranted space, risk of non-uniform application, judicial inaction as well as overreach. Additionally, the extant provision does not define or even provide guidance as to which religious sentiments are protected or what amounts to a 'religion' for the purpose of the section. Surprisingly, the Constitution does not contain any definition of 'religion' or 'religious feelings'. It can surely be asked as to whether 'religion' includes only mainstream religions like Hinduism – calling Hinduism a religion is also a much-debated topic, as the Indian Supreme Court in *Dr. Ramesh Yeshwant Prabhoo v. Shri Prabhakar Kashinath Kunte* ruled that it is not a religion, but a way of life.[101] Though any religion by its nature is a way of life, and by attributing this fundamental characteristic of religion solely to Hinduism, the Indian Supreme Court created an artificial inequality among equals. Furthermore, whether Hinduism includes within itself other religions such as Buddhism, Christianity, Islám or Sikhism, or it assimilates countless sects, is another issue. Even the Indian Supreme Court has recognized that the term religion is "incapable of specific and precise definition". The Court has held that it is not something that has a 'rigid definition', and by its very nature is "difficult, if not impossible to define". Moreover, the Section 295A of the IPC does not provide for a threshold of insult; therefore, drawing a line between criticism and insult often results in limiting the scope of fair criticism, as is evident from the frequent prosecutions of various artists, movie producers, academicians, authors and scholars for expression, written or oral, that hardly warrants such an action.[102] In fact, the risks posed by provisions that are vague have been aptly captured by the Indian Supreme Court in the following words:

> Vague laws may trap the innocent by not providing fair warning. Such a law impermissibly delegates basic policy matters to police men and also judges for resolution on an ad hoc and subjective basis, with the attendant dangers of arbitrary and discriminatory application. More so uncertain and undefined words deployed inevitably lead citizens to steer far wider of the unlawful zone […]

---

[101] Supreme Court of India, *Dr. Ramesh Yeshwant Prabhoo v. Shri Prabhakar Kashinath Kunte*, Judgment, 11 Decemeber 1995, 1996 SCC (1) 130 (1996) (https://www.legal-tools.org/doc/qf0jk2/), wherein the election of a candidate was impugned on grounds of having appealed to voters on religious grounds of Hindutva. It was held that an appeal based on Hindutva did not qualify as an appeal based on religion.

[102] For instance, the producers of *A Suitable Boy* were prosecuted for a kissing scene in the movie between a Hindu and a Muslim couple. Stand-up comedian Munawar Faruqui along with four other persons – Nalin Yadav, Prakhar Vyas, Edwin Anthony and Priyam Vyas – were prosecuted for allegedly passing 'indecent remarks' about Hindu deities. FIR was lodged against Amazon Prime India's head for screening of web series *Tandav*. The threshold for prosecution lacks clarity and must be defined.

> than if the boundaries of the forbidden areas were clearly marked.[103]

Thus, the provision in its current form creates space for unregulated subjectivity in the adjudication of cases, which, in turn, manifests arbitrariness in the process. Therefore, to prevent the provisions from being obsolete and to facilitate objective findings and incorporate sufficient guidance to the judiciary, it is important to redefine and revise the existing provisions so that they meet the unique demands of present-day society. The limitation on speech and expression must be confined to a minimum. The amendment is necessitated not only to impute accountability on those entering the legally prohibited side of speech and expression, but also to protect those legitimately exercising their right protected by the Constitution, especially those engaging in non-state conforming socio-political discourses. The provision must further, and not restrict, legitimate discussions and expressions even on topics that may not be the most convenient to be discussed and voice opinions on. Since there is an all-round development in the jurisprudence surrounding religious hate speech worldwide along with judicial precedents, there is ample guidance to carry out the necessary amendments and the provisions to fit in, meet the demands of the present day, and strike a balance between freedom of speech and expression and the promotion of fraternity and religious harmony.

As stated above, there have been numerous instances where the offence of hate speech was configured not only on the ground of what was seen to be distasteful by the government, but even on the whims and fancies of the executive, and the police has continued to harass activists, journalists and critics of the government by filing unjustified cases against them for dissenting views, protesting or covering protests. The courts, in view of divergent approaches in similar cases, have also failed to come up with an effective redressal. The cases, which have been on rise, have not only led to a chaos in the already confusing jurisprudence on hate speech, but have shown the urgent need to define the contours of hate speech and to have in place a well-defined law curtailing unbridled speech, in addition to the adoption of a consistent procedural approach by courts with a genuine commitment to preventing the circulation of inflammatory speech. Additionally, it is essential that the discretion of the executive is kept to the minimum, which may be done by providing for judicial scrutiny at the initial stages of the prosecution and time frames for various stages of the proceedings to ensure accountability, transparency and efficiency, especially since most of the existing penal provisions dealing with hate speech belong to the pre-Internet era. Moreover, to combat the growing menace of hate speech, an internal high-

[103] Supreme Court of India, *Kartar Singh v. State of Punjab*, Judgment, 11 March 1994, 1994 SCC (3) 569, para. 130 (https://www.legal-tools.org/doc/7tlwhn/).

power committee can be constituted by high-ranking executive members and former judges from the high court and the Indian Supreme Court, so that their assistance can be sought by courts while evaluating evidence on record pertaining to allegations of hate speech. Further, since the provisions governing hate speech are non-bailable, the legality of preventive action could also be analysed by such a committee in order to avoid harassment of innocent victims. Even though there does not appear to be any fundamental variance when one compares online hate speech and offline hate speech cases, it is only in the nature of interactions in which such cases occur that one can find the difference, along with the use and spread of specific words, accusations and conspiracy theories. As hateful messages can go viral in hours or even minutes, to regulate the content of online publishers of news and current affairs and curated audio-visual content, the Information Technology (Intermediary Guidelines and Digital Media Ethics Code) Rules, 2021 ('IT Rules') were released by the Ministry of Electronics and Information Technology on 25 February 2021 and came into effect on 25 May 2021. The IT Rules are a model framed by the Government of India after a thorough analysis of similar guidelines which have been adopted by countries like Singapore, Australia, the European Union and the United Kingdom, in order to curb the abuse of social media for spreading fake news and to strengthen the legal framework and make social media platforms accountable under the applicable law with a three-level grievance redressal instrument for digital media working in India, in consonance with the judgments of the Indian Supreme Court, including the Sudarshan News hate speech case from the end of 2020, that believes in regulation of 'venomous' Internet news medium. However, currently the rules are under challenge before several courts on the ground of being vague and suffering from excessive delegation of powers. To avoid multiple or contrary orders, the Indian Supreme Court is currently examining the merger of all of the individual petitions against the IT Rules over the country into one case to be heard by the Court itself.[104] Thus, the need of the hour is to put in place a specialized legislation governing hate speech propagated *via* the Internet and especially social media. In this regard, reference can be drawn to the Australian federal law known as "Criminal Code Amendment Act, 2019", which holds liable Internet service providers if it comes to light that they were aware that any abhorrent violent material, which has been defined to include material that a reasonable man would regard as offensive, is accessible through the service provided by them. Therefore, taking clue from best international standards, it is important that specific and durable legislative provisions which effectively combat hate speech, especially that which is propagated online and

[104] Supreme Court of India, *Skand Bajpai v. Union of India*, Order, 9 May 2022, Writ Petition (Civil) No. 799/2020 (https://www.legal-tools.org/doc/fmb6e1/).

through social media, be brought into force by amending the IPC as well as the IT Act.

SECTION C: ALLEGED HATE SPEECH IN THE NAME OF CHRISTIANITY: THE SITUATION IN THE BALKANS

9

Religious Leaders and Nationalist Propaganda: The Serbian Orthodox Church

Svein Mønnesland[*]

9.1. Introduction

The Yugoslav conflict in the 1990s was not a religious war in the sense that it was fought to convert to or impose a faith.[1] The war was triggered by the fall of Communism and the disintegration of the Yugoslav Federation. Political disagreement and conflicting ambitions led to war. Most politicians were former Communists and Yugoslavia was a secularized society. The origin of the conflict was the wish to form greater states on the ruins of Yugoslavia.

Religion was nevertheless of great importance. Even before the war, the churches were promoting nationalist propaganda, and when the conflict became a fact, religion was used by the politicians. Although some religious leaders were moderate, many supported the aims of the war, and some even supported war criminals or participated in battles. The churches were thus involved in a propaganda war. The most striking examples of complicity of church leaders in

---

[*] **Svein Mønnesland** is Professor Emeritus at the University of Oslo. He is a member of the Norwegian Academy of Sciences and the Academy of Sciences and Arts of Bosnia and Herzegovina. He is among the leading experts on Slavic Philology and Yugoslav culture, history and politics in the Nordic countries. Among his numerous publications is the 2013 monograph National Symbols in *Multinational States: The Yugoslav Case*. For an audio-visual recording of his statement to CILRAP's conference in Florence in April 2022 on the topic of this anthology, please see https://www.cilrap.org/cilrap-film/220408-monnesland/. The translations of quotations in this chapter which are not available in English are provided by the author.

[1] See Paul Mojzes, *Balkan Genocides*, Rowman & Littlefield, Lanham, 2011, p. 143; Sergej Flere, "Was the Bosnian War a Full-fledged Religious War?", in Gorana Ognjenović and Jasna Jozelić (eds.), *Politization of Religion and the Power of State, Nation, and Faith*, Palgrave Macmillan, New York, 2014. This statement by Sells is exaggerated:

> The violence in Bosnia was a religious genocide in several senses: the people destroyed were chosen on the basis of their religious identity; those carrying out the killings acted with the blessing and support of Christian Church leaders, the violence was grounded in a religious mythology that characterized the targeted people as race traitors and the extermination of them as a sacred act.

Michael Sells, *The Bridge Betrayed: Religion and Genocide in Bosnia*, University of California Press, Berkeley, 1996, p. 144. It cannot be taken seriously that Radovan Karadžić on several occasion said that it was a religious war, see Radovan Karadžić, *Intervjui i govori*, Međunarodni odbor za istinu o Radovanu Karadžiću, Belgrade, 2005, p. 319.

nationalist enterprises are to be found among the Serbian clergy. The following discussion will concentrate on the role of the Serbian Orthodox Church.

There are several reasons why religion became important with regards to the conflict.

9.2. Religion and National Identity

To understand the role of religion in nationalistic discourse, it is necessary to discuss the connection between religion and national identity in the South Slavic area. The Croats, Serbs and Bosniaks are not distinguished so much by language; therefore, religion became the main distinctive feature of national identity. To be a Serb means to be Orthodox, to be a Croat means to be Catholic and to be a Bosniak means to be Muslim. This is not a matter of personal belief, as one is born into a religion – meaning cultural tradition, holidays, naming tradition, *et cetera*. This ethno-religious identity developed from the end of the nineteenth century.

The Croatian national ideology was mainly historical and political, based on legal arguments, not linguistic or cultural ones.[2] In defence against Habsburg and Hungarian centralism, the Croats insisted on their historical state right as a 'political people'. The Croats were regionally so divided that it was difficult to create a united national movement in the nineteenth century. The movement was called 'Illyrianism', since the name Croat was associated with one region (Zagreb) and 'Illyrian' had a South Slavic reference. Due to its universalist nature, the Catholic Church could not easily become a national church. As it was said: "The ideologists of Croat nationhood, almost to the last practicing Catholic, resisted the equation of Catholicism and Croatdom".[3] This did not prevent individual clergymen from being exponents of Croatian nationalism, but the role played by Croatian bishops was, in general, moderate.

The Serbs had a different situation, with an old identity between Serbdom and Orthodoxy. The Serbian Church has always been a national church, due to the historically close relationship between the Orthodox autocephalous church and the national state, a tradition inherited from the Byzantine Empire. The concept of *symphonia*, the equal partnership of church and state, expressed by Emperor Justinian, implied close ties between the church and the state.[4] That this idea is still alive can be seen from a statement by Patriarch Pavle in 2002: "In

---

2 Ivo Banac, *The National Question in Yugoslavia*, Cornell University Press, Ithaca, 1984, pp. 85–93.

3 *Ibid.*, p. 108.

4 Irina Papkova, *The Orthodox Church and Russian Politics*, Oxford University Press, 2011, p. 71.

our view, the best relation between state and church and the one that used to be – a symphony of the state, the society, and the Church".[5]

From medieval times, the Serbian Orthodox Church was the guardian of Serbian culture in the Ottoman Empire, that is, "the sole privileged Serbian institution within the Ottoman Muslim state".[6] The Church kept the memory of the medieval Serbian state under the Nemanjić dynasty (from the twelfth to the fourteenth century). It was noted that "[i]t is impossible to underestimate the historical role of the church in keeping alive the idea of Serbia and its notion that one day the old state would, Christ-like, be resurrected".[7]

However, when modern nationalism developed among Serbs in the nineteenth century, the situation changed, probably due to the dream of a Great Serbian state also embracing a non-Orthodox population. For the creator of the Serbian literary language, Vuk Karadžić, who played an important role in the national movement in the first part of the nineteenth century, religion was not defining the Serb nation, but the language. He spoke of "Serbs of three faiths" – Orthodox, Catholic and Muslim, united by a common language, that is, all those who spoke the Shtokavian dialect.[8] He thus included Muslims and many Croats in the Serbian nation. Also, Ilija Garašanin, the creator of the first political programme of Great Serbia, promoted a national unity of Serbs and Muslims.[9] A different stand was taken, as we shall see, by the Montenegrin Bishop-Prince Njegoš, who saw the Slavs who had converted to Islám as a threat to Montenegrin independence.[10]

From the end of the nineteenth century, religion began to be closely connected to national identity. The Austro-Hungarian occupation of Bosnia-Herzegovina in 1878 created a multireligious state. The Austro-Hungarian minister and administrator of Bosnia-Herzegovina, Benjamin von Kállay (1882–1903), tried to create a common Bosnian nationality (*bosnjastvo*), but it was too late.[11] Nationalism was strong in the adjacent countries of Croatia and Serbia, and, in

5 *Danas*, 5–7 January 2002, cited in Milan Vukomanović, "The Serbian Orthodox Church: Between Traditionalism and Fundamentalism", in Ulrika Mårtensson, Jennifer Bailey, Priscilla Ringrose and Asbjørn Dyrendal (eds.), *Fundamentalism in the Modern World, Vol 1: Fundamentalism, Politics and History: The State, Globalisation and Political Ideologies*, I.B. Tauris & Co., London, 2011, p. 159; see "Struggle Over Patriarch's Legacy", in *Helsinki Bulletin*, no. 47, December 2009.

6 Banac, 1984, p. 64, see *supra* note 2.

7 Tim Judah, *The Serbs*, Yale University Press, New Haven, 1997, p. 46.

8 Vuk Stefanović Karadžić, "*Srbi svi i svuda*", in *Kovčežić za istoriju, jezik i običaje Srba sva tri zakona*, Vienna, 1849; Banac, 1984, p. 80, see *supra* note 2.

9 *Načertanie* ('Outline'), 1844.

10 See below Section 9.4.3.

11 Banac, 1984, p. 360, see *supra* note 2.

Bosnia-Herzegovina, Orthodoxy became a sign of Serbdom, whereas Catholicism signalled Croatian nationality. Serbian, Croatian and Bosniak nationalisms became connected to their religious differences. The Bosniak national ideology, being developed from the end of the nineteenth century, was based on Islám and on the opposition to the two other national identities in Bosnia. In the interwar period (1918–1939), there was a political party called the Yugoslav Muslim Organization. However, religious leaders did not play any important role.

The definition of nation by religion is thus of newer date. Religion was not central to the nationalist projects aiming at the formation of the first Yugoslav state in 1918, or in the first part of the interwar period. The political leaders were not religious and church leaders played no important role, although the state, dominated by Serbs, promoted the Orthodox Church, which almost became the state religion, as it had been in the Kingdom of Serbia. The major state holiday was the Serbian commemoration of the Kosovo battle, *Vidovdan* (Saint Vitus' Day).

9.3. Politicization of Religion

Towards the end of the interwar period, religion began to play a role in nationalist discourse. In 1935, the Yugoslav government planned to sign a treaty, a concordat, with the Vatican. The Serbs opposed the concordat; the Orthodox Church claimed that it "would eventually make our country and state subordinated to the Roman Curia".[12] The treaty was not signed and there was a mobilization of the churches during 1937–1941. The Serbs commemorated the Kosovo battle in 1939, and the Croats planned to celebrate the one-thousand-three-hundredth anniversary of Christianity for the Croat people.[13]

An influential and controversial theologian in the pre-war period was Nikolaj Velimirović, Bishop of Žica. Together with the theologian Justin Popović, Velimirović developed a special Serbian Orthodox theology called *svetosavlje*, based on the teaching of Saint Sava, the founder of the Serbian Church in the twelfth century. *Svetosavlje* was a combination of theology and national mythology, based on the Kosovo myth of Serb suffering. Velimirović "adapted this mindset of Serbian suffering to the modern conditions of the nation-state, transforming the suffering of the church into the suffering of the Serbs as a *nation*".[14]

---

12 Vjekoslav Perica, *Balkan Idols: Religion and Nationalism in Yugoslav States*, Oxford University Press, 2002, p. 18. See also Sabrina P. Ramet, *Balkan Babel: The Disintegration of Yugoslavia From the Death of Tito to the Fall of Milosevic*, Westview Press, Boulder, 2002, pp. 103–104.

13 Perica, 2002, pp. 20–21, see *supra* note 12.

14 Ger Dujzings, *Religion and the Politics of Identity in Kosovo*, Hurst & Company, London, 2000, p. 179. That, *svetosavlje* is a very unclear concept is shown by Mirko Djordjević, *Negativna svetosavska paralipomena*, VPA, Novi Sad, 2015.

Although Velimirović was a supporter of Dimitrije Ljotić, the Serbian fascist leader and Nazi collaborationist, he was arrested by the Nazis.[15] After the war, he emigrated to the United States ('US'). His propaganda in exile was anti-Communist and anti-Catholic, and he was accused of anti-Semitism.[16] In fact, he "was the first to charge that genocide was committed by Croats against Serbs".[17] In the early 1990s, *svetosavlje* again became popular in the Serbian Orthodox Church. In 1991, the relics of Velimirović were solemnly transferred from the US, and, in 2003, he was canonized. For the Croats, it was provocative that Velimirović, an ardent anti-Croat, was made a saint. Additionally, Archimandrite Justin Popović, who was "the most important twentieth-century Serbian Orthodox theologian [and] the teacher of the aggressively nationalist bishops who are presently playing the dominant role in the Serbian Orthodox Church",[18] was also canonized in 2010.

World War II was partly a civil war in Yugoslavia. In the so-called Independent State of Croatia ('NDH'), occupied by Germany and Italy, the Croatian fascist Ustasha regime committed genocide against the Serb population. Hundreds of monasteries and churches were destroyed and hundreds of Serb priests were liquidated. For the Serbian Orthodox Church, the war was a catastrophe, and the notion of Serb suffering was reinforced. Several Catholic clergies were active Ustasha members and some were also involved in NDH crimes. In general, the Catholic Church supported the Ustasha regime.[19] Catholicism was, however, not an essential part of the Ustasha national ideology, and their state was not recognized by the Vatican. That religion was seen as a sign of national affiliation is obvious from the fact that the Ustasha regime forced Serbs to convert to Catholicism, that is, to become Croats.

The Serb nationalist and royalist Chetnik movement fought the Communist partisan forces, but was also responsible for massacres against the civilian Muslim population of Bosnia. The Serb historian Vladimir Dedier characterized the Chetnik atrocities as genocide against the Bosniaks.[20] Many

---

15 "Ljotić enjoyed close relations with the Serbian Orthodox Church, in which he held an official position": Philip J. Cohen, *Serbia's Secret War: Propaganda and the Deceit of History*, Texas A&M University Press, College Station, 1996, p. 15.

16 Jovan Byford, "From 'Traitor' to 'Saint': Bishop Nikolaj Velimirović in Serbian Public Memory", in *Analysis of Current Trends in Antisemitism*, 2004, no. 22, pp. 4–5.

17 Perica, 2002, p. 26, see *supra* note 12.

18 Branimir Anzulovic, *Heavenly Serbia: From Myth to Genocide*, New York University Press, 1999, p. 126.

19 *Ibid.*, p. 24.

20 Vladimir Dedier, Antun Miletić, *Genocid nad Muslimanima 1941–1945: Zbornik okumenata i svjedočenja*, Svjetlost, Sarajevo, 1990.

Orthodox priests supported the Chetniks.[21] The Orthodox Church was anti-Communist and nationalist. The religious factor was obvious; they were continuing the old Serbian struggle against Islám. When the Yugoslav crisis developed in the 1980s and 1990s, the Serbian Church took up its historical support of the Chetnik movement. The Church supported, in 2015, the rehabilitation of Dragoljub (Draža) Mihailović, the Chetnik leader who was executed by the Communists as war criminal. The Church honours Mihailović and holds memorial services.

After the war, Yugoslavia became a secularized Communist society. The Communists carried out a massive retaliation against their enemies. It was noted that: "Persecution of clergy was an earmark of this period".[22] Josip Broz Tito, fromer President of the Yugoslavia, was hostile to religion, especially to the Catholic Church, the main ideological challenger to Communism. Also, Muslim activists were persecuted, as was the case with the 'Young Muslims' (*Mladi Muslimani*), whose members were arrested from 1946–1949, among which was the later President Alija Izetbegović.[23] Tito nevertheless recognized the Bosniaks as a separate nationality in the 1971 census, with the name 'Muslims' (in an ethnic sense).[24]

Since nationalism was forbidden, the churches became the only fora where nationalist narratives could exist. The Communists thus strengthened religious nationalism. From 1975 to 1984, the Croatian Catholic Church staged a grandiose nine-year jubilee in honour of the conversion of the Croats to Christianity, including massive liturgical events with thousands of faithful in attendance. It was, however, mainly after Tito's death in 1980 that the churches became politically influential. It has been pointed out that a renationalization of the Croatian Catholic Church took place in the second half of the 1980s.[25] After the fall of Communism in 1990, the churches became central political factors: "The Serbian Orthodox Church became a dynamo for the reawakening of Serb nationalism and belligerence".[26]

---

21 *Ibid.*, p. 23. See also Cohen, 1996, p. 45, see *supra* note 15: "Roughly Three Quarters of Yugoslavia's Serbian Orthodox Priests Supported the Chetniks Throughout the War".

22 Perica, 2002, p. 26, see *supra* note 12; see also Stella Alexander, *Church and State in Yugoslavia Since 1945*, Cambridge University Press, 1979, p. 224.

23 Sead Trhulj, *Mladi Muslimani*, Globus, Zagreb, 1991.

24 See Tone Bringa, *Being Muslim the Bosnian Way: Identity and Community in a Central Bosnian Village*, Princeton University Press, 1995, pp. 27–28.

25 Perica, 2002, pp. 72–73, see *supra* note 12.

26 Paul Mojzes, "Religion and the Yugoslav Wars (1991–1999)", in Branislav Radeljić and Martina Topić (eds.), *Religion in the Post-Yugoslav Context*, Lexington Books, Lanham, 2015, p. 11.

Under Communism, the official narrative did not allow nationalist discourse to be exposed in public life and many aspects of the war were suppressed. Memories of World War II were revived when the Yugoslav crisis developed in the 1980s. Symbols became important in the propaganda war between the Serbian Orthodox Church and the Croatian Catholic Church, such as the role of Cardinal Aloysuis Stepinac during the war. For the Croats, Stepinac was a patriotic symbol, while for the Serbs he was a symbol of their martyrdom. In answer to Serbian allegations that Stepinac was "the spiritual investigator" of genocide, the Catholic Church announced that he saved the lives of "several hundred" Jews. In 1998, the beatification of Stepinac was met with Serbian protests.[27]

The Ustasha death camp Jasenovac became the most important symbol for the Serbian Orthodox Church, only next to Kosovo. The two myths became connected as the main sites of Serb suffering. The Serbian Church drew parallels between Jasenovac, Golgotha and Auschwitz.[28]

In the independent Republic of Serbia after the break-up of Yugoslavia and end of state-enforced atheism, the Serb religious leaders could hope that Orthodoxy would again become the religion of state. It was natural for the Serbian Orthodox Church to support the state, just as the Russian Church did after the fall of Communism. However, the first head of state, Slobodan Milošević, was not inclined towards religion. Only after the fall of Milošević on 5 October 2000 did the Church begin to have official contacts with the state.

9.4. Historical Myths

There are several Serbian historical myths, important for the growth of nationalism, all connected to the Church. It is typical for Orthodox churches to have national-religious myths: "The Orthodox churches, like the ancient religions, are the churches of their respective nations, their myths being the myths of their respective nations".[29] For the Serbian Orthodox Church, the most significant is the Kosovo myth.

9.4.1. The Kosovo Myth

The Kosovo battle in 1389 was probably less decisive for Ottoman occupation of Serbian lands than the battle of Maritsa in 1371, but achieved enormous symbolic importance, since both the Serbian Prince Lazar and the Ottoman Sultan Murad were killed. Soon after the battle, the Serbian Orthodox Church created

---

[27] *Ibid.*, pp. 176–177.

[28] David Bruce MacDonald, *Balkan Holocausts?: Serbian and Croatian Victim-Centred Propaganda and the War in Yugoslavia*, Manchester University Press, 2002, pp. 160–170.

[29] Sabrina P. Ramet, "The Politics of the Serbian Orthodox Church", in Sabrina P. Ramet and Vjeran I. Pavlaković (eds.), *Serbia Since 1989: Politics and Society Under Milosevic and After*, University of Washington Press, Seattle, 2005, p. 255.

a legend, a religious narrative, about Prince Lazar. The Serbian Patriarch Danilo wrote that the sacred Prince chose a heavenly kingdom instead of one on earth. This following description was disseminated by oral traditional poetry: 'On the eve of the battle, Lazar is visited by Prophet Elijah disguised as a grey falcon. Elijah asks Lazar to choose between the heavenly and earthly kingdom. Lazar opts for the Kingdom of Heaven, sacrificing the material world for spiritual glory'. The Kosovo legend was kept alive through the centuries in Orthodox monasteries and by local bards. Prince Lazar thus became a saint.

In the nineteenth century, nation-builders made the oral tradition describing the Kosovo battle into a national ideology, influenced by the prevailing European ideology at the time – nationalism.[30] The narrative was important in the struggle against the Turks in the nineteenth century and continued to be a cornerstone of Serbian nationalism in the twentieth century.

The Kosovo myth contains several (very different) notions. Prince Lazar symbolizes Serbian sacrifice and martyrdom, but also Serbia as a 'heavenly nation'. The legendary Miloš Obilić, who, according to tradition, was the one who killed Sultan Murad, symbolizes Serbian heroism. Vuk Branković, who fought the battle but afterwards, according to the legend, co-operated with the Turks, symbolizes betrayal and internal rivalry. The oral tradition gave birth to additional symbolic figures, as the mother (Majka Jugovića) who loses nine sons at the battle, or the Kosovo Maiden (Kosovka devojka), who brought water to wounded soldiers. When Kosovo was handed over to Serbia by the Turks in 1912 in the First Balkan War, this was celebrated as a 'revenge' for the Kosovo battle. Soldiers kissed the sacred soil of Kosovo.

The first official commemoration of the battle was arranged in 1939, on the five-hundred-and-fiftieth anniversary. In the 1980s and 1990s, the notions from the Kosovo myth – Serbian suffering, heroism and betrayal – were taken up by nationalist intellectuals and politicians.

In the folk tradition, the expression 'Kosovo covenant' has played an important role. It meant sacrificing for a higher cause. 'It is better to die in battle than to live in shame', as it is expressed in a folk song.

> This pseudo-religious avowal evoked the ultimate goal of sacrifice for the fatherland and a determination to end in the heavenly kingdom. […] On the ground of Lazar's resolution and determination to gain the heavenly kingdom, the idea of a 'heavenly' Serbian

30 Noel Malcolm, *Kosovo: A Short History*, Macmillan, London, 1998, p. 79.

> people was launched, suggesting an eternal sinless national tradition.[31]

In 2007, the Serbian Orthodox Church published a luxury volume, *The Holy Prince Lazar and the Kosovo Pledge (Sveti Knez Lazar i kosovski zavet)*, in 100,000 copies, an enormous number for a history book in Serbia. The aim was to evoke patriotism.[32]

In 2016, a monument of Prince Lazar was erected in Kosovska Mitrovica. The Serbian Minister for Kosovo, Marko Djurić, stated: "Lazar will stay here, because the Serbs will stay here, and let this be our pledge in front of God and the holy Prince Lazar". The 10-metre-high sculpture was blessed by Bishop Teodosije of Raša-Prizren, stating: "Today, here in front of Lazar, we report to the Holy Prince that we remain decided, [...] that we are devoted to the heavenly kingdom".[33]

Instead of Prince Lazar's spiritual choice, Obilić's heroic choice was seen as more attractive for nationalist activists. What could be called 'Obilić's pledge' implies heroic fight and revenge.[34]

The way the Serbian Orthodox Church created myths that were taken up by politicians can be compared to the situation in Russia. The Kievan myth, the reign of Vladimir or Volodymyr, Prince of Kiev, is used to justify Russian claims on Ukraine. However, its historical basis is doubtful:

> Volodymyr the Rus was no more a Russian than Charlemagne the Frank had been a Frenchman. 'Russia' did not exist in his day, any more than 'France' existed in Charlemagne's. Unfortunately, when the Russian Orthodox Church came on to the scene five centuries later, it laid monopoly claims to the Kievan heritage; and modern Russian propaganda has done everything in its power to suppress rival claims and traditions, notably among the Ukrainians.[35]

31 Marko Šuica, "The Image of the Battle of Kosovo (1389) Today: A Historic Event, a Moral Pattern, or a Tool of Political Manipulation", in Robert Evans and Guy P. Marchal (eds.), *The Use of the Middle Ages in Modern European States*, Palgrave Macmillan, London, 2015, p. 171. See also Malcolm, 1998, p. 80, see *supra* note 30. About the Kosovo myth and myths in general in the Yugoslav context, see Vjekoslav Perica and Darko Gavrilović (eds.), *Political Myths in the Former Yugoslavia and Successor States: A Shared Narrative*, Institute for Historical Justice and Reconciliation, Republic of Letters, Dordrecht, 2011.

32 *Ibid*., p. 172.

33 "Marko Đurić Unveiled Monument to Prince Lazar of Serbia", *Office for Kosovo and Metohija*, 28 June 2016; "Đurić na Vidovdan u Kosovskoj Mitrovici: Lazar je tu da ostane, jer su Srbi tu da ostanu", *Radio Mitrovica*, 28 June 2016.

34 Ivan Čolović, "Koji zavet?", in *Vreme*, 4 April 2018 (available on its web site).

35 Norman Davies, *Europe: A History*, Oxford University Press, 1996, p. 326.

In the same way, it is unhistorical to claim that Kosovo was the cradle of medieval Serbia. The capital or centre of the medieval state was never in Kosovo. The Patriarchate of the Serbian Orthodox Church was located at Peć in Kosovo towards the end of the medieval period, that is, 1346–1463.

9.4.2. The Great Migration

In addition to the Kosovo battle, the most important church narrative is connected to the 'Great Migration' of Serbs (*Velika seoba*). The Austrian army reached Kosovo in 1689 but was routed by the Ottomans. Tens of thousands of Serbs, who had risen in support of the imperial army, were led by Patriarch Arsenije III in 1690 to settle in Austrian lands in Southern Hungary. A second migration took place in 1737 under Patriarch Arsenije IV and, in 1766, the Patriarchate of Peć was abolished by the Sultan. All Serbs are familiar with the painting by Paja Jovanović, showing the Patriarch leading his people away from Kosovo.

The Great Migration became a symbol of Serbian suffering. The migration changed the demographic structure of the population in Kosovo, leading to a gradual Albanian majority. The Church and many Serbian historians saw this as the most tragic event in Serbia's history. In 1990, a voluminous book on the Great Migration was published. A historian, Nikola Samardžić, wrote:

> The Great Migration three hundred years ago gave the Serbs a blow from which they never recovered. This was the beginning of the Albanian invasion in Kosovo and adjacent areas, and the expulsion of Serbs from the heart of their former kingdom. Until this day, this is the most important and most dangerous invasion of intolerant and destructive Islam in Europe. [...] It was the beginning of genocide in Kosovo and the sad exodus of the Serbian people, forced by Albanian terror to leave the homes of their forefathers.[36]

In the volume, Patriarch German, who was a Serbian patriarch from 1958–1990, summarized Serbian history, claiming that the Serbs have always been attacked by enemies:

> All came with the same aim, to enslave us and take our land, to destroy our Church, to destroy our spiritual centres and burn our holy places. All came with the same aim, to Islamize Serbs to make them Turks, or to make them Latin [Catholic] or Uniate, to destroy our national soul.[37]

For nationalist politicians, wanting to restore Serbian dominance in Kosovo, the celebration of the three-hundreth anniversary of the Great Migration in 1990 became a useful propaganda tool. In the following decades, the Great

---

[36] Ljubisav Andrić (ed.), *Velika seoba*, Bigz, Belgrade, 1990, p. 512.

[37] *Ibid.*, p. 502.

Migration was frequently used as a symbol of Serb suffering. In 2013, the Serbian Patriarch Irinej stated:

> In 1690, Patriarch Arsenije hoped that they would soon return to Kosovo, that the Austrians would help them to come back to their homes and holy places. Unfortunately, that did not happen, and it is repeated today. Today, like then, we hope that we will return to Kosovo. We believe that our Lord will not abandon us. As long as the holy objects of Kosovo are in our hearts and souls, as long as we pray to God with endurance, faith and hope, Kosovo will be ours.[38]

9.4.3. A Bishop Praising Ethnic Cleansing

The Kosovo myth was developed into a claim for revenge by Prince-Bishop Petar Petrović Njegoš, the religious leader and political ruler of Montenegro, who ruled during 1830–1851. He is the author of several books and is considered the Serbs' national poet and highly esteemed by Montenegrins as well. In his main work, *The Mountain Wreath* (1847), the Kosovo covenant is central, and he urges the Serbs to fight and sacrifice – claiming that resurrection requires martyrdom:

> Your destiny it is to bear the Cross
> of the fierce fight against brothers and foes!
> The wreath's heavy, but the fruit is so sweet!
> Without death there is no resurrection.[39]

The Mountain Wreath is controversial. The topic is the extermination of Montenegrins who had converted to Islám, the so-called *poturice*. It is a historical drama, describing what happened in 1709 when Bishop Danilo decides to attack his Muslim countrymen. This happens in a world where the small Montenegro is under constant threat from Ottoman Turks. The massacre should therefore be seen in its historical context. However, it remains extraordinary that Bishop Njegoš, writing in the nineteenth century, could see this as a heroic deed. Montenegro was still a less civilized Balkan country. At Njegoš's monastery, heads of killed Turks were exposed.

---

38 "Patriarh Irinej: Ponavljaju se seobe", *Novosti*, 3 November 2013.

39 Petar II Petrović-Njegoš, *The Mountain Wreath*, Vasa D. Mihailovich (trans.), Charles Schlacks Jr. Publisher, Irvine, 1986, p. 85. Njegoš's work is presented in Andrew Baruch Wachtel, *Making a Nation, Breaking a Nation: Literature and Cultural Politics in Yugoslavia*, Stanford University Press, 1998, pp. 45–51, 99–110. The topic of ethnic cleansing is discussed in George L. Scheper, "Reverberations of the Battle of Kosovo: The Mountain Wreath and Ethnic Cleansing", in Elrud Ibsch, Douwe Fokkema and Joachim von der Thüsen (eds.), *The Conscience of Humankind: Literature and Traumatic Experiences*, Rodopi, Amsterdam, 2000, pp. 393–414.

Njegoš has traditionally been admired for his poetry and philosophy, and his work is indeed admirable. In our time, however, many have pointed to the topic as a blueprint for ethnic cleansing and genocide. Indeed, Serb nationalists have referred to Njegoš and his fight against the Turks as a background to the fight in Bosnia against Muslims. *The Mountain Wreath* was learned by heart and played an important role in the forming of the attitude that Muslim Slavs were, as Njegoš says, "traitors of Serbian blood and Christ's faith". Political, military and religious leaders in Bosnia all referred to Njegoš. One example is of Metropolitan Amfilohije of Montenegro, who in 2014, stated:

> Many today reproach Bishop Danilo that he dared to do that. It is indeed terrible to kill people, however, still worse is the spiritual death that those false people spread around them, with their false belief. Thanks to this sacrifice Bishop Danilo saved Montenegro. Had that not happened, there would not have been any Orthodox in Montenegro today.[40]

Later the same year, Bishop Amfilohije stated:

> There is a sickness in Montenegro, conversion to Islam [*poturčenjaštvo*]. A part of our nation, as Njegoš says "rash and greedy converted to Islam", have changed their faith, abjured the holy cross and the fidelity to Nemanjić [Lazar] and become Muslims. Today everyone has the right to choose one's life, but one should always choose what is good and not what is bad.[41]

This shows that among at least a part of the Serbian Orthodox Church, the influence of Njegoš is still very much alive. The head of the Islámic community in Montenegro, Reis Rifat Fejzić, called it "a classical example of hate speech".[42]

9.5. Milošević, Political Nationalism and the Church

Slobodan Milošević, who came to power in Serbia in 1987, was a socialist and atheist and did not use the Serbian Orthodox Church in his nationalist propaganda. However, he adopted many of the ideas that had been developed by the Church.

9.5.1. It Started With Kosovo

The Kosovo myth was, as we have seen, created by the Church, but it was also used by Milošević. Well known is the speech held by Milošević on 28 June 1989, *Vidovdan* (Saint Vitus' Day), the commemoration of the battle of Kosovo. In his

40 Dragana Šćepanović, "Amfilohije: Istraga poturica spasila Crnu Goru", *Vijesti*, 3 August 2014.

41 V. Radojević, "Reis islamske zajednice: Amfilohije je preterao", *Novosti*, 11 November 2014.

42 *Ibid.* See also "Mitropolit Amfilohije opravdava ubistva muslimana u Crnoj Gori", *Islamska zajednica u Bosni i Hercegovini*, 5 August 2014.

speech, he did not rule out an armed conflict in Yugoslavia. Less known is the fact that the celebration was initiated and prepared by the Serbian Orthodox Church. A year earlier, the bones of the martyr of the Kosovo battle, Saint Prince Lazar, were carried from the Ravanica monastery on a year-long tour to monasteries throughout the Serb-populated areas of Yugoslavia, only to reach Kosovo on 19 June 1989. Bishop Pavle of Ras-Prizren (the later Patriarch) greeted the Saint Prince:

> The Holy Great Martyr Prince Lazar has come to Kosovo to perform a spiritual and national review and for the suffering Serbian people to bow to him and thereby confirm their fidelity and loyalty to the holy Kosovo covenant and determination for the Kingdom of Heaven and God's Justice.[43]

A huge procession carried the relics to the battlefield (Gazimestan) where the Patriarch held a service, and then to the Gračanica monastery near the battlefield. Church ceremonies were carried out for a week with thousands of participants from all over Kosovo. On 27 June 1989, Patriarch German led a procession of 300 Serb priests in scarlet robes at the Gračanica monastery and served a midnight liturgy. The next day, on Saint Vitus' Day, the Patriarch held a speech at the battlefield.[44] When Milošević delivered his speech the same day, the entire leadership of the Serbian Church was present, led by the Patriarch. Pictures of Prince Lazar were held up in the crowd alongside those of Milošević.

The Serbian Church even initiated the composition and publication of popular songs about Kosovo, as the one entitled 'Za Vidovdan 1989'.[45]

The Albanians, the majority population of Kosovo, conceived this manifestation as an expression of extreme Serb nationalism. Serbian nationalists focused on what they saw as suppression of Serbs. This is a text describing the situation at the time of the manifestation in 1989:

> I leave aside all the sabotage by the Šiptar (Albanian) rulers in Kosovo, who on the very day of the Vidovdan celebration denied even drinking water to a thirsty gathering of two million Serbian people, and in Priština they also damaged and contaminated the water supply the next day, when Saint Prince Lazar was leaving Pristina. We will also leave out all those various Šiptar boycotts and sabotages, crimes and fires, various obstructions and destructions, which occur almost daily in Kosmet (Kosovo and Metohija) and for which

43 Projekat Rastko Gračanica–Peć, "Godina 1989" (available on the Rastko.rs web site).

44 *Ibid.* See also Perica, 2002, p. 128, *supra* note 12.

45 Radina Vučetić, "Kosovo 1989: The (Ab)use of the Kosovo Myth in Media and Popular Culture", in *Comparative Southeast European Studies*, 2021, vol. 69, nos. 2–3, p. 230.

> no one is blamed or answered to. Because "everything is allowed" for Arnauts (Albanians), since Turkish times.[46]

The Kosovo myth triggered Serb nationalism long before the celebration in 1989. The notion of 'Holy Land' was kept alive under Communism. At the memorial service for Bishop Nikolaj in 1966, Archimandrite Justin Popović stated:

> The Holy Serbia did not die in Kosovo! No, it has continued its way through terrible slavery, the path of the eternal Serbian Church, struggling through history in the way of the Holy Serbia, and to this day – until our day, the Holy Serbia![47]

Already while Tito was alive, after Albanian demonstrations in 1968, the Serbian Orthodox Church began to appeal to the Communist authorities about the bad conditions for Serbs in Kosovo. The Serbian Orthodox Church was the first Serb institution that dared to state publicly that Kosovo Albanians allegedly persecuted the Church and expelled the local Kosovo Serbs. The Serbian migration from Kosovo was presented as due to Albanian assaults, rape, *et cetera*, although it happened mostly for economic reasons. Tito had given the Albanian majority population rights that made the Serbs feel discriminated. This political situation was exploited by the Church. The Communist Party was, however, negative to the growing nationalism. Since nationalism was suppressed otherwise in the society, the Serbian Church was the only carrier of Serbian ethnic nationalism.

In 1981, only a year after Tito's death, serious demonstrations broke out among the Albanians in Kosovo. They demanded that Kosovo should get the status of constituent republic, not only an autonomous province within Serbia. The Serbian Patriarchate at Peć was set on fire. This Albanian nationalism triggered a Serbian reaction. In May 1982, 21 clergymen (priests and monks) published an 'Appeal for the Protection of the Serbian Populace and Its Holy Sites in Kosovo' ('Appeal'), addressed to the communist leadership. The politicians were accused of forgetting Kosovo. The language was new and radical:

> For Serbs the Kosovo issue is not only a biological one or about 'region,' 'province' or 'republics' […] it is about the spiritual, cultural or historic identity of the Serbian people. […] Kosovo is our memory, our hearth, the focus of our being. And to take away from a nation its memories means to kill it and destroy it spiritually. […] Kosovo is for Serbs what Jerusalem is for the Jewish people. […]

---

46 "Godina 1989", see *supra* note 43.

47 Vladimir Cvetković, "From 'Merciful Angel' to 'Fortress Europe': The Perception of Europe and the West in Contemporary Serbian Orthodoxy", in *Erfurter Vorträge zur Kulturgeschichte des Orthodoxen Christentums*, 2015, no. 13, p. 14.

> We ask what kind of infernal and irrational forces are able to achieve, during a few decades in peace paid with blood, what Turks did not manage during the five hundred years of Turkish yoke. […] It is no exaggeration to say that a well-planned genocide is being executed against the Serbian population of Kosovo. […] There are no sufferings from history that have not been repeated during the last twenty years. […] It seems that the centuries long battle of Kosovo will end in our days with the final expulsion of Serbs, the final defeat. […] What is going on with that proud, patriarchal people [the Albanians] whose children, youth and men burn churches, destroy graveyards, rape, and torture their neighbours through centuries?[48]

During the 1980s, the wording of this Appeal, as extremely radical as it seemed, became mainstream discourse in Serbian cultural life. It was noted that: "By exploiting the Kosovo issue, the Serbian Orthodox Church saw a chance to regain much of its political influence after forty years of forced submission to communist rule".[49] The Church issued several petitions about Albanian terror in Kosovo. It had achieved a growing impact on Serbian cultural life. New churches were built, and work was taken up to finish the Saint Sava cathedral in Belgrade, the largest Orthodox church in the world.

In 1986, the Serbian Academy of Sciences published a document called *Memorandum,* repeating the claims of the Church that Serbs were subjected to persecution and genocide in Kosovo and that the Yugoslav authorities were responsible. The *Memorandum* demanded the abolition of the autonomous status of the province of Kosovo and its incorporation into Serbia.

The Serbian Communist leader Slobodan Milošević was no nationalist. More or less against his own will, he became an exponent of Serbian nationalism, when he understood that nationalism could be an instrument to gain power. He was surprised when he saw the Serb anger over conditions in Kosovo and stood up to protect the Kosovo Serbs during a visit to Kosovo in April 1987. But it was only when Yugoslavia was falling apart that he understood the value of myths and religious symbols. Now the nationalistic ideas of the Serbian Orthodox Church became useful, and he took some steps to normalize the relationship between church and state.

---

48 "Apel za zaštitu srpskog življa i njegovih svetinja na Kosovu", *Pravoslavlje*, 15 May 1982; "Od Kosova do Jadovna (Putni Zapisi)" (From Kosovo to Jadovn (Travel Records)), *Svetosavlje*, 26 January 2011.

49 Dujzings, 2000, p. 179, see *supra* note 14.

9.5.2. Anti-Croatian Propaganda

Besides the Kosovo myth, the Ustasha terror was used in nationalist propaganda. Already in 1984, the theologian, and later bishop, Atanasije Jeftić published the book *From Kosovo to Jadovno*, which dealt with the suffering of Serbs (Jadovno was the name of an infamous Ustasha camp).[50] He travels to areas of Serb 'martyrdom'. From Kosovo, he reports about rapes and atrocities against Serbs, mostly unknown to the public. From Croatia, he writes about the killing of Serbs during World War II. He also refers to shocking testimonies by witnesses, such as of massacres against civilians inside Orthodox churches and killing of priests.

In 1990, the Serbian Orthodox Church issued two statements on the 'almost occupation-like conditions' in Croatia and requested to explore pits into which Serbs had been thrown during the war. It was noted to be an "enormous help for Slobodan Milošević to draw attention away from domestic problems to problems in other places".[51] The exhumations were made with much publicity; the remains were buried with great commemorations in Croatia and Bosnia-Herzegovina. The object was to tell Serbs in Croatia that they could again be exposed to genocide and that parts of Croatia should be included in Serbia.

The Serbian Orthodox Church saw the different worlds of Orthodoxy and Catholicism as a 'clash of civilizations'. In 1987, an article in the Church's news organ *Pravoslavlje* stated:

> The world which developed under 'Byzantine influence' [...] differs from the world which evolved under 'Western-Roman influence', not only in its religion, but also in its culture, historical development, ethics, psychology, and mentality. The Byzantine world cannot envision a common survival in the same state with the members of the Western-Roman tradition, particularly not after the Second World War.[52]

The Yugoslav wars started in Croatia with the uprising of the Serb minority, supported from Belgrade. Already, in December 1990, the Serbs proclaimed an independent republic, *Krajina*, with Knin as main centre. The situation of the Croatian Serbs had been neglected or suppressed in Yugoslav politics. The Serbian Orthodox Church was, however, very active in promoting the history and culture of the Serbian population in Croatia. Dalmatia was especially in the focus, the core of what was to become the *Republika Srpska Krajina*. The

---

50 Amfilohije Radović (ed.), *Od Kosova do Jadovna*, George B. Markovina (trans.), Atanasije Jevtić, Belgrade, 1984.

51 Milorad Tomanić, *Srpska crkva u ratu i ratovi u njoj*, Medijska knjizara Krug, Belgrade, 2001, p. 33.

52 Svetozar Dušanić, in *Pravoslavlje*, 1 October 1987, quoted in Ramet, 2005, p. 256, see *supra* note 29.

Orthodox Eparchy of Dalmatia covered the area of Zadar, Šibenik, Split, Knin and Bosanski Petrovac. Here were old Serbian settlements and three old monasteries.

Already in 1939, on the occasion of the 550th anniversary of the battle of Kosovo, national celebrations were organized in Dalmatia and a book entitled *Kosovo – A Popular Reader* was published. In 1989, a volume with the same title was published by the Serbian Orthodox Church.[53] The subtitle was 'Dalmatian Kosovo'. This is the name of a village located between Knin and Drniš. The name may originate from immigrants from Kosovo some centuries ago. In any case, the existence of a Kosovo in Croatia was exploited by the Church. The volume contains articles and literary excerpts showing that this area has a very strong Orthodox tradition. This is a historical fact, but in the context, at the break-up of Yugoslavia and with militant Serb nationalism, the content contributed to the notion of Dalmatia being a 'Serbian land'. For politicians wanting to exclude this area from Croatia and include it in a greater Serbia, the Church's narrative was welcome. In September 1990, a group of Orthodox priests accused the Croatian authorities of neglecting the difficult situation in Croatia:

> Daily cases of terror and intimidation, insults, loss of jobs, demolition of homes, assaults and even proven cases of murder and rape […] the major targets of the violence being Orthodox priests, their families, and especially children.[54]

Patriarch German died in 1990 and was followed by Pavle (born Gojko Stojković). Patriarch Pavle, although known to be among the more moderate church leaders, had close contact with extreme nationalists and supported the disintegration of Yugoslavia and formation of a great Serbian state by Serbia's annexation of regions in Croatia and Bosnia-Herzegovina.

In May 1991, Patriarch Pavle held a meeting of the *Sabor* (Holy Assembly of Bishops) at Jasenovac, the site of the Ustasha concentration camp. In the propaganda, the atrocities committed at Jasenovac were exaggerated. Instead of the 80,000–90,000 victims (Serbs, Jews and Roma) as documented by the Jasenovac Memorial Site, Serbs claimed that 700,000 or even 1,000,000 Serbs were killed there. The Serbian Orthodox Church began to consider Jasenovac a religious site of Serb suffering and mourning. Patriarch Pavle stated:

> Nothing can be worse than Jasenovac, where during four years of war, 700,000 people were killed […]. Jasenovac is the scene of the most important horrors committed against the Serbs, the place of

---

53 Nikolaj Mrđa (ed.), *Kosovska narodna čitanka 1989: Dalmatinsko Kosovo*, Dalmatinska eparhija SPC, Odbor za proslavu Šestogodišnjice kosovske bitke i mučeničkog prestavljenja sv. kneza Lazara i kosovskih mučenika, Šibenik, 1989.

54 *Pravoslavlje*, 1 October 1990, cited in Perica, 2002, pp. 144–145, see *supra* note 12.

> […] their annihilation, their extermination, their execution, their torture, where they suffered under a blood lust, the like of which could not be paralleled by the antichrist himself. […] This is the new crucifixion of Christ. This is the sin of sins.[55]

In 1991, four bishops, Metropolitan Jovan of Zagreb-Ljubljana, Bishop Vasilije of Srem, Bishop Stefan of Žica and Bishop Lukijan of Osijek-Dalj-Baranja visited a training centre for Serbian voluntaries at Erdut, preparing for the war in Croatia. Here, they met the notorious mafia boss and paramilitary leader Željko Ražnatović, known as Arkan. In the report, the bishops stated that the activity was not nationalistic – its aim was to restore Orthodoxy, which had been suppressed for centuries.[56] Arkan stated in October 1991: "Patriarch Pavle is our supreme commander".[57] Patriarch Pavle called Arkan 'defender of Serbia'.

9.6. Church Leaders and the Greater Serbia Project

The Serbian Orthodox Church had historical traditions that coincided with the political ambitions of the new political leaders after the fall of Communism. Nationalist Serbian intellectuals and politicians adopted the ideas and discourse used by the Church already for decades.

The greater Serbia project coincided with the Church's concept that the extension of Serbian Orthodoxy was to be the Serbian state. This included Kosovo, Bosnia-Herzegovina, Montenegro, parts of Croatia and Macedonia. Kosovo was, according to the Church, 'holy Serb land'. The Montenegrins were considered to be Serbs, the Bosnian Muslims were converted Serbs, and large parts of Croatia were inhabited by Serbs, or were, in fact, Serbs without knowing it, as in Dubrovnik. The Macedonians were called 'south Serbs', and therefore could have no independent Orthodox church. This corresponded to the greater Serbian plan that some intellectual nationalists had been preparing.

When Yugoslavia fell apart and Milošević sought to create a great Serbian state, the Serbian Orthodox Church fully supported this political aim. There are many testimonies of how Orthodox leaders argued for a Great Serbia and the dissolution of Yugoslavia. Metropolitan Amfilohije of Montenegro said in an interview:

> there cannot be reconciliation over the graves of innocents, there will be no reconciliation until the Croatian people renounce the evil […] Today we Serbs are all determined to build a country of our own, and at the same time we must respect the centuries-old

---

[55] Quoted in MacDonald, 2002, p. 163, see *supra* note 28. Here is a discussion on the number of victims at Jasenovac. See also the statistics on the Jasenovac Memorial Site's web site.

[56] Srđan Barišić, "Srpska pravoslavna crkva i Jugoslavija", in *YU historija*, 2015, p. 12.

[57] In a Studio B interview, see Sonja Biserko, *Yugoslavia's Implosion: The Fatal Attraction of Serbian Nationalism*, The Norwegian Helsinki Committee, Oslo, 2012, p. 177.

> desires of our brethren Roman Catholic Croats and Slovenes to establish their national states.[58]

Patriarch Pavle supported the disintegration of Yugoslavia and formation of a great Serbian state by Serbia's annexation of ethnically cleansed regions in Croatia and Bosnia. In 1991, in a letter to Lord Carrington, the negotiator for the European Community, Patriarch Pavle stated:

> Our compatriots of the same faith and blood have only one fatal choice: either to fight for their lives with a weapon in their hand in order to stay in the same state as the rest of the Serbian nation, or to be forced to leave this new Independent State of Croatia sooner or later. There is no third alternative. The Serbian state thus must defend them by all legitimate means, including armed self-defence of Serbian lives and of all Serbian borderlands. The territories where the Serbian people has been living for centuries and where it has had an ethnic majority in April 1941, before the genocide by the Croatian quisling regime, cannot remain within any independent Croatia whatsoever but must be placed within one state with today's Serbia along with all other Serbian provinces. One must understand that the victims of genocide and their one-time perpetrators, and may be future, cannot live together. […] In the moment when the Croats declared independence, the Serbs in Croatia used the same right of self-determination and decided to live in Rest-Yugoslavia, in the state which is the Serbs' homeland. If not, they [Serbs in Croatia] would sooner or later lose their national identity, their faith, and names and perhaps experience expulsion and physical extermination. […] Those who through centuries have made Serbs Uniates and Catholics, and in World War Two even physically exterminated them, cannot be trusted. This must be realized by all former Yugoslavs and civilized Europe. The Serbian Orthodox Church is thus working not only for the historical and democratic rights of the Serbian nation but wishes to take the side of justice and truth, universal and Christian principles, which should regulate the relations between nations.[59]

Patriarch Pavle's relationship with Milošević was, however, problematic; he considered Milošević to be too much of a Communist. In June 1992, the Patriarch joined anti-Milošević protesters on the streets of Belgrade. The target of the protest, though, was not Milosević's nationalism but his neo-Communist ways. The Patriarch and other church leaders did, however, support the Serbian

58 Perica, 2002, p. 158, see *supra* note 12.

59 "Pavlovo pismo Karingtonu", *Pravoslavlje*, 1 November 1991.

nationalist leaders in Bosnia and Croatia. Bishop Atanasije said: "We blame Milošević not for trying to defend the nation, but for failing".[60]

In January 1992, Pavle announced that the Church and Serb people have

> never recognized AVNOJ [Anti-Fascist Council for the National Liberation of Yugoslavia] borders [post-World War II] and that no agreement whatsoever is binding for the nation as a whole without its consent and the blessing from its mother Serb Orthodox Church.[61]

The chief editor of *Pravoslavlje*, the magazine of the Serbian Orthodox Church, Dragan Terzić, wrote in March 1992:

> The Bosnian Serbs don't want to live in a Jamahiriyah like Libya, and to be under the rule of mujahideens and have the same status as Christians in Islamic states, i.e., being slaves, which they [the Serbs] had already experienced during the five hundred years of Islamic occupation.[62]

Metropolitan Amfilohije of Montenegro gave his vision of Greater Serbia in the spring of 1992:

> By international dictate, dwarfish states are emerging just to tear apart again crucial parts of the body of the Serb nation [...] Despite all hardships, the backbone of those unified lands is formed anew – by Serbia and Montenegro. Further these territories include Eastern Herzegovina, a considerable portion of Bosanska Krajina, as well as Srpska Krajina [...] The outlines of those Serb lands have already become evident in all recent developments. Unfortunately, Srpska Krajina's cry for help has not met a proper answer in due time.[63]

Patriarch Pavle stated, in 1994, that the West was guilty of the war; that the three sides "had agreed to divide Bosnia into three states, but then the West recognized a unitary state".[64]

The Serbian Orthodox Church even had a wider perspective of Greater Serbia than Milošević himself, since it advocated the thesis that the Macedonians were Serbs. The Macedonian Orthodox Church declared autocephaly in 1967 but was not recognized by the Serbian Orthodox Church. According to the

---

60 See Blane Harden and Carlotta Gall, "Crisis in the Blkans: The Serbian Orthodox; Church of Milosevic's Rise Now Sends Mixed Message", *New York Times*, 4 July 1999.

61 "Struggle over Patriarch's Legacy", *Helsinki Bulletin*, December 2009.

62 Tomanić, 2001, p. 129, see *supra* note 51.

63 *Duga*, 20 April 1992, cited in Sonja Biserko (ed.), *Kovanje Antijugoslovenske Zavere: Knjiga 1*, Helsinški odbor za ljudska prava u Srbiji, Belgrade, 2006, p. 291.

64 Norman Cigar, *Genocide in Bosnia: The Policy of 'Ethnic Cleansing'*, Texas A&M University Press, College Station, 1995, p. 39.

Serbian Church, the Macedonian Church could not be recognized since there was no Macedonian nation.[65] This view was also promoted by extreme Serbian politicians. Vuk Drašković proposed a Great Serbia including Macedonia. Metropolitan Amfilohije stated that the era under Tito resulted in the division of a unitary Serbian nation into four separate nations, among them the Macedonians:

> Macedonia owes its freedom to the bones of Serb warriors […]. Macedonia is covered with Serbian bones, not to mention churches and historical memory. The majority of the population feels, in spite of the brain washing, that they belong to the Serbian tree.[66]

There were serious conflicts between the two churches, as in 2003, when the Serbian Church denied the Macedonian Church access to the Prohor Pčinjski monastery, located near the Macedonian border and important for Macedonian history. After six decades of denying the Macedonian Church, in May 2022 the Serbian Church recognized its autocephaly. This was announced by Patriarch Porfirije, following an earlier decision by the Ecumenical Patriarch Bartolomew I of Constantinople.[67]

When the international community proposed that Bosnia-Herzegovina should be an independent state with an internal division based on ethnic criteria, the Serbian Church protested and argued for a great Serbian solution. The Church could not accept the river Drina as Serbia's western border and became an active political participant during the international negotiations. When the Contact Group presented its plan in 1994, the Church protested. The Serbian bishops issued 'An Appeal to the Serbian Nation and the World Public':

> With full responsibility before God and our nation and human history we call the whole Serbian nation to stand up in defence of their old rights and liberties, their vital interests necessary for the physical and spiritual existence in the land of their fathers and ancestors. […] Today we cannot agree to or accept the decisions made in Geneva about percentages and maps. We cannot remain without our heritage: the monastery Žitomislići on the river Neretva or the Sabor Church in Mostar or the church of Sopotnica on the river Drina, the monasteries Krka or Krupa in Dalmatia, Ozren and Vozuća in Bosnia, Prebilovci in Hercegovina or Jasenovac in Slavonia.[68]

---

65 About 'The Macedonian Schism', see Ramet, 2005, pp. 268–271, see *supra* note 29.

66 Tomanić, 2001, pp. 110–111, see *supra* note 51; *Duga*, 12 April 1992, cited in Biserko, 2006, see *supra* note 63.

67 Sinisa Jakov Marusić, "Serbian Patriarch Brings 'Good News' to Newly-Recognised Macedonian Church", *Balkan Insight*, 24 May 2022.

68 Tomanić, 2001, p. 110, see *supra* note 51.

Several statements by bishops testify their adherence to the Great Serbia project at an early stage in the conflict. Nikanor (Bogunović), Bishop of Karlovac, stated in April 1991:

> Where Serbian blood is spilled and Serbian bones fall, it must be Serbian land. [...] The Serbs are victims – the Ustashas are bloodthirsty criminals. We are defending the Serbian land, liberating it from the Ustasha terror, which never ended in these areas.[69]

When Atanasije (Jevtić) was installed as Bishop of Banat on 7 July 1991, he stated:

> Again, the Serbian nation is crucified, both in Kosovo, Dalmatia, Krajina, Slavonia, Banija, Lika, Kordun, Srem, and Bosnia-Herzegovina. This is a nation accustomed to carry a cross because that is our fate. [...] May God give that this crucifixion leads to resurrection, not only for us, but also for those who allegedly stood up in the name of Christ against the cross with three fingers [that is, the Serbs]. Unfortunately, they have been doing that for centuries in company with the crescent against the Serbian nation with three fingers.[70]

The vision of a Great Serbia was kept for decades after the disintegration of Yugoslavia, at least among the more extreme church leaders. Irinej (Bulović), Bishop of Bačka, stated in 2021:

> Old Serbia stretches from Kaimakčalan [on the border between North Macedonia and Greece] to the present-day lands of Slovenia, where Serbs live.[71]

9.7. Church Leaders and the War in Bosnia-Herzegovina

When the war broke out in Bosnia in April 1992, many Bosniaks were surprised that they were persecuted and killed just because they were Muslims. However, they were not killed because of religious affiliation, but because they belonged to a nationality which, according to political leaders, was hindering their political projects. In a policy of making ethnically 'clean' territories, all non-Serbs were enemies, regardless of their religion. Even when Serb politicians and intellectuals used an anti-Muslim rhetoric, the aim was more to take control over a territory than to fight Islám. The Serbs' century-old struggle against the Turks was, however, a useful tool in the hands of cynical politicians.

---

69 M. Đorđević, "Ratni krst srpske Crkve", *Republika*, 16 November 2001.

70 Tomanić, 2001, p. 46, see *supra* note 51.

71 "Serbian Bishop: Old Serbia Stretches from Kaymakcalan in North Macedonia to Present-Day Slovenia", Novinite.com, 17 November 2021.

The Serbian Church supported the Serb attack on Bosnia-Herzegovina in the spring of 1992. The Church denied alleged Serbian war crimes. When rumours of Serb concentration camps began to be published, a statement was given by the Synod ('The Holy Episcopal Synod of the Serbian Orthodox Church in Response to the False Accusations against the Serbian People in Bosnia-Herzegovina') in June 1992:

> In the name of God's truth and on the testimony from our brother bishops from Bosnia and Herzegovina and from other trustworthy witnesses, we declare, taking full moral responsibility, that such camps have neither existed nor exist in the Serbian Republic of Bosnia-Herzegovina or in the Serbian Krajinas.[72]

According to Cigar, Patriarch Pavle continued to deny the camps: "Some church leaders, such as Patriarch Pavle, in fact, never came to terms fully with this issue, for he continued to cast doubt on the existence of the camps long after such a tack had been abandoned by other Serb spokesmen". In an interview with an Italian journalist in early 1994, when asked about the camps, he still replied: "I do not believe that this is organized, but rather that what may be happening are actions by individuals".[73]

When Bishop Atanasije (Jevtić), in the autumn of 1992, visited the US, he told an American congressmen that he did not negate "certain bad things committed by Serbs in Bosnia, but this was mainly incidents of angry revenge by crazy individuals. Such examples are found also among Serbs, for example, a Serb in Gacko killed his family with a machine gun".[74]

When reports came about rapes, this was also denied. In an official statement, the Serbian Orthodox Church called such reports 'monstrous', made up by foreign countries to 'annihilate' the Serbs. There is no reason to believe that the Church leadership was not informed about the atrocities.

When Milošević wanted to accept the peace plan in 1994, Church leaders opposed it, as mentioned, and supported Karadžić. From that moment on, the relationship with Milošević was very negative. On 10 August 1994, the Bishops' Conference issued a statement demanding a 'just peace', mentioning the responsibility before God's Final Judgement. The Serbian authorities were criticized:

> The Pontius Pilate act of washing their hands in the blood of weary brethren will not resolve anything. [...] We cannot believe that the strongest powers in the world today would wish to test their strength and power on those who have been several times

72 Sells, 1996, p. 84, see *supra* note 1; Cigar, 1995, p. 89, see *supra* note 64.

73 Cigar, 1995, pp. 89–90, see *supra* note 64.

74 Tomanić, 2001, p. 83, see *supra* note 51.

> downtrodden, and not once butchered, on those who have defended the human dignity of civilized Europe with their bones.[75]

On 14 August 1994, the Patriarch visited Pale and blessed Karadžić and Mladić and insisted that they should not accept any peace plan. When the Serbian assembly at Pale rejected the peace plan in September 1994, Bishop Amfilohije stated:

> Today the people and the Assembly of Republika Srpska are face-savers for the entire Serb Orthodox nation; and they are saving our dignity not with empty words and unprincipled compromise but with their blood and lives they have been sacrificing for the defense everything this nation holds holy and honourable, and for the defense of Eastern Orthodoxy for the whole world to see. [...] Today in Bosnia-Herzegovina they are battling for the golden freedom and honour of Eastern Orthodoxy, for the soul and justice in the entire world, for the holiness of human dignity. [...] May God give our brothers in Bosnia-Herzegovina all help and good strength to withstand the pressure from the world, which Our Lord has already overcome. May he give our brothers in Republika Srpska such help and strength and give us the strength and wisdom that we do not lose our soul forever.[76]

In 1994, Pavle said to an Italian journalist: "I believe Serbs must fight, now as never before, to save not only the church but themselves".[77] In November 1993, Karadžić stated: "God has helped us. He has turned toward us, just as we have turned toward Him, after many years of errors".[78] Karadžić stated in early 1994 that the relations between the Church and the state were excellent. He said: "Our clergy is present in all our analyses and decisions, and the Church's voice is listened to as the highest authority".

There are pictures showing Radovan Karadžić and Ratko Mladić together with Patriarch Pavle and the Bosnian Metropolitan Bishop Nikolaj (Mrđa), the Senior Serb Orthodox Cleric in Bosnia during 1992–2015.[79] Present are also Bishop Jovan, Bishop Atanasije, Bishop Vasilije and Momčilo Krajišnik, speaker of the People's Assembly of *Republika Srpska*. The pictures are taken

---

75 Milan Milošević and Velizar Brajović, "Pictures from Pale: A Magnificent Landscape, Poisonous Atmosphere, Pigheaded People", in *Vreme News Agency*, 15 August 1994, no. 151.

76 *Pravoslavlje*, 1–14 September 1994, quoted in Srđan Barišić, "Legitimation of the Extreme Right-Wing", in Sonja Biserko (ed.), *Extremism: Recognizing a Social Evil*, Helsinki Committee for Human Rights, Belgrade, 2014, p. 44; see also Tomanić, 2001, p. 143, see *supra* note 51.

77 Cigar, 1995, p. 68, see *supra* note 64.

78 *Ibid.*, p. 69.

79 Some of the pictures from the ceremony can be seen at: "Dr Radovan Karadžić i đeneral Ratko Mladić", *Pogledi*, 10 March 2013.

on 2 July 1995 at Sokolac, the temporary seat of the Bosnian Metropolitan, a small place half-way between Sarajevo and Srebrenica. The occasion is the celebration of Saint Vitus' Day, the day of the battle of Kosovo in 1389. The day of Saint Vitus is 28 June, but, in Bosnia at that time, a spiritual assembly (*duhovna akademija*) was organized on the following Sunday. The Serbian Orthodox Church had recently consecrated a local church to Lazar, the Serbian Prince who fell in the battle. Sokolac is situated on the mountain of Romanija, famous in Serbian heroic epic tradition as the home of the *haiduks*, who fought the Turks. The *Lazarica* Church made the mountain of Romanija another Kosovo. In addition to the historical Kosovo and Dalmatian Kosovo in Serbian Krajina in Croatia, now there was a Kosovo also in the Serb part of Bosnia. There are also pictures, taken a few days before the Serbs attacked Srebrenica on 6 June 1995, depicting Mladić and Karadžić as they are being blessed by the Patriarch. They are the present-day Kosovo heroes, again fighting the Turks, although now they are their fellow citizens who are Muslims. When this blessing took place, they had already planned to take the United Nations secure zone of Srebrenica and execute the male population of the town. From 11 to 14 July 1995, approximately 8,000 unarmed captives from Srebrenica were exterminated.

This meeting was not accidental. The Bosnian Metropolitan Nikolaj embraced militant nationalism. Until 1992, he was Bishop of Dalmatia and played a role in the Serb uprising in Croatia. He stated in an interview, in 1993, that General Mladić accepted all of his suggestions. He said: "We have always won the wars. God will not abandon us this time either. [...] The fight is in the interest of the Serbian people".[80] The Metropolitan also blessed Serb troops, including those on the hills surrounding Sarajevo, from where the town was being mercilessly shelled.

At Sokolac a year earlier, on 3 June 1994, Metropolitan Nikolaj presented icons to Ratko Mladić and Radovan Karadžćić at the Celebration of the Army of *Republika Srpska*, on Saint Lazar's Day. He proclaimed that those who accepted the leadership of Karadžić and Mladić were "following the difficult road of Christ".[81] In 1994, Nikolaj was assigned the Nemanjić Order by the Serb Parliament at Pale for his help to create the Serb Republic in Bosnia.

At the Saint Vitus' Day ceremony of the Bosnian Serbian Army in the Serbian Orthodox Church of Bijeljina, on 28 June 1995, a few days before the

80 Cigar, 1995, p. 68, see *supra* note 64.

81 Noreen Herzfeld, "Lessons from Srebrenica: The Danger of Religious Nationalism", in Ronald A. Simkins, "The Context of Religion and Violence", in *Journal of Religion and Society*, 2007, Supplement Series No. 2, p. 111.

attack on Srebrenica, Mladić spoke to his soldiers about the importance of the Battle of Kosovo:

> Prince Lazar gave his army Communion, and bowed for the Heavenly Empire, defending fatherland, faith, freedom, and the honour of the Serbian people. We have understood the essence of his sacrifice and have drawn the historical message from it. Today we make a winning army, we do not want to convert Lazar's offering into a blinding myth of sacrifice.[82]

When the town was taken and the genocide started, Ratko Mladić said:

> Here we are, on the eleventh of July, in Serbian Srebrenica. On the eve of yet another Serbian religious holiday, we present this town as a gift to the Serbian nation. Finally, the day has come, that, after the revolt against the *dahijas* [when Serbs were killed in 1804], we will have vengeance against the Turks in this area.[83]

A video shown in The Hague at the trial of Mladić shows how Bishop Vasilije Kačavenda of Zvornik-Tuzla arrives in Srebrenica on 12 July 1995 at the celebration of *Petrovdan* (Feast of Saint Peter and Paul).[84] This was the day after the fall of the town and mass killings were going on. After the mass in the local church at Vlasenica, a place near Srebrenica, Bishop Vasilije Kačavenda participates at a lunch with Serbian soldiers and officers. Colonel Milenko Živanović holds a flaming speech about how happy he is because the day before the Serbian flag was planted in liberated Srebrenica and he hopes that all Serbian territories will soon be liberated. During the speech, he often makes the sign of the cross, while the Bishop is listening and approving. Bishop Vasilije Kačavenda then makes a speech saying:

> The blood is crying for revenge. By avenging, the Serbian nation has crushed the mightiest empires, and now we are expecting happy days. We are gradually approaching the moment when the Serbian people, after the battle of Kosovo, anew will unite and restore the Serbian state. […] God, may our brothers the Greeks liberate Cyprus from the Turks, liberate Constantinople, that it again may be the centre of Orthodox spirituality.[85]

During the mass, he stated:

---

[82] Ljiljana Bulatović, *General Mladić*, Evro, Belgrade, 1996, p. 154.

[83] "The Mladić Files: Mladić Entering Srebrenica – July 11, 1995", *Youtube*, 21 October 2011.

[84] The film was presented in the programme '*60 minuta*' and is found on YouTube: "Vasilije Kacavenda, Zvonko Bajagic, Milenko Zivanovic – Vlasenica 12/07/1995 Vlasenica", *Youtube*, 15 January 2018; "60 minuta – Kako je Vladika Kacavenda slavio pad Srebrenice", *Youtube*, 30 September 2012.

[85] Žarka Radoja, "Kačavendino blagosiljanje genocida", *Peščanik*, 21 April 2011.

> God has come close to our people, and heaven has never been nearer than now. We feel that God is with us. We feel that the hand of God is guiding us, because isn't it a miracle of God, brothers and sisters, that after so many sacrifices alone at Srebrenica, the old Serbian capital of Uroš, isn't it a miracle and the grace of God that here in three days brave Serbian warriors have liberated Serbian land occupied since Ottoman times, a land where the holy cross used to shine but was removed by the ugly crescent.[86]

Bishop Vasilije was clearly anti-Islámic. He stated in March 1993 that "we Serbs know very well that for a segment of the Muslims [...] the more 'unbelievers' they kill, the closer they come to heaven".[87]

The 'Scorpions' was a Serbian paramilitary unit involved in war crimes in Croatia, Bosnia-Herzegovina and Kosovo. They operated under the umbrella of the Serbian Ministry of Internal Affairs and, more specifically, its State Security Service.[88] They participated in the Srebrenica massacre in 1995. In 2005, a video showing the 'Scorpions' killing six Bosniak prisoners, some of them youngsters, was shown in The Hague at the trial of Slobodan Milošević.[89] The video was filmed by a 'Scorpions' member. In another video, taken with the same camera, a blessing ceremony was shown. Before the 'Scorpions' went to Srebrenica, Hieromonk Gavrilo, head of the Privina Glava Monastery in Serbia, blessed all the members of the paramilitary unit. Father Gavrilo states:

> Brothers, Turks have raised their ugly heads once again. They are bent on destroying Serbian sacred and holy institutions and monuments. In the name of the Father, the Son and the Holy Spirit, let God help his faithful army by providing it with the courage to prevail over a hostile people.[90]

When the documentary was shown in Serbia, it caused a veritable shock and admission of guilt, but no connection between the 'Scorpions' and official Belgrade, although the film explores the former's tie to the Ministry of Internal Affairs.

The Serbian Orthodox Church did what they could to diminish Serbian guilt for atrocities committed in Bosnia. In 1996, a book entitled *The Lamb of*

---

86 *Ibid.*

87 Cigar, 1995, p. 67, see *supra* note 64.

88 Iva Vukušić, "Nineteen Minutes of Horror: Insights from the Scorpions Execution Video", in *Genocide Studies and Prevention: An International Journal*, 2018, vol. 12, no. 2, p. 39.

89 The films can be found in material used at the International Criminal Tribunal for the former Yugoslavia ('ICTY'): "Blessing of 'Scorpions' – Đeletovci, Serbia" and "Prisoner Execution Footage", in *Srebrenica: Genocide in Eight Acts*, SENSE Agency, 2016 (available on its web site).

90 Biserko, 2012, p. 302, see *supra* note 57.

God, and the Beast from the Abyss: Philosophy of War was published by the Metropolitanate of Montenegro and the Littoral.[91] The volume contains contributions by 15 participants at a symposium held during the Days of Saints Cyril and Methodius, organized by Metropolitan Amfilohije at Cetinje. The aim was to justify the war in Bosnia. Bishop Atanasije (Jevtić) writes: "Our Serbian wars have always been defensive".[92] Bishop Amfilohije tries to explain how Petar, Bishop of Cetinje who ruled during 1784–1830 and who became a saint, could also be a warrior. The authors connect the war to the notion of *svetosavlje*, the mythical combination of theology and nationalism that was developed by the Serbian Orthodox Church in the 1930s ("They created a *svetosavlje* that was a war ideology").[93] Bishop Atanasije writes that "it is better to have war than a peace that separates us from God".[94] Among the contributors, was Radovan Karadžić who states:

> That is why I bow deeply to the only people, the Christ-like martyr, the Serbian people in Bosnia, who "regularly receive all the blows of fate", and whose bravery needs another science and another Clauzewitz. For now, they seem to be understood only by God himself.[95]

In 1997, three declarations were published in Belgrade in several languages, signed by sixty Serbian intellectuals, including four bishops, signed and blessed by Patriarch Pavle. One is the 'Declaration against the Genocide of the Serbian People':

> Processes of annihilation of the Serbs in the most diverse and brutal ways have been going on continuously. Through their whole history they have faced the fiercest forms of genocide and expulsion, threatening their very existence. They have, however, always been self-defenders of their own existence, spirituality, culture, and democratic convictions.[96]

---

91 Radoš M. Mladenović and Hierodeacon Jovan Ćulibrk (eds.), *Jagnje božije i zvijer iz bezdana*, Svetigora, Cetinje, 1996, pp. 70–72.

92 *Ibid.*

93 Djordjević, 2015, p. 74, see *supra* note 14. The editor Mirko Djorđević wrote very critically about the notion of *svetosavlje* and the right-wing factions of the Serbian Orthodox Church, its nationalism, use of the Kosovo myth and close connection to the state.

94 Mladenović and Ćulibrk (eds.), 1996, p. 71, see *supra* note 91.

95 *Ibid.*

96 "Sta Sadrzi deklaracija protiv genocida nad srpskim narodom: Poziv savesti (celog sveta)", *Naša borba*, 25 April 1997; see also Đokica Jovanović, "Legalitet ili diskretna odbrana nacionalizma", in Ivana Spasić and Milan Subotić (eds.), *Revolucija i poredak: O dinamici promena u Srbiji*, Institut za filozofiju i društvenu teoriju, Belgrade, 2001, pp. 110–111.

The other two declarations, from September 1997, were issued by 'The Commission for defence of Serbs against the Hague Tribunal'.[97] The first one explains who were responsible for the war:

> Tito's anti-Serbian and anti-Yugoslav regime, which prepared the break-up of Yugoslavia, and his pupils – the Croatian, Muslim, and Slovene destroyers of Yugoslavia (Tudjman, Izetbegović, Kučan) and at last the foreign helpers who behind the scenes helped the destroyers of Yugoslavia, first of all the German Foreign Minister Hans-Dietrich Genscher and his Austrian colleague Alois Mock.

The declaration also explains the war:

> All Serbian positions in the civil war 1991–95 were self-defensive. […] Karadžić and Mladić were leading a threatened nation in its struggle for existence […].
>
> We expect from the Tribunal that it will disclose the propaganda that has encircled the innocent Serbian nation and let this nation be illuminated by the light of truth and dignity. […] The manoeuvres of the Hague Tribunal cannot hide the disgusting crimes that were committed by Muslims and Croats against Serbs.

The second declaration was one that demanded that the ICTY criminal charges brought against Radovan Karadžić, the President of the Republic of Srpska, be repealed. This was after Karadžić was indicted, but before he was arrested. These declarations show the engagement of the Serbian Orthodox Church, since they were signed and blessed by the Patriarch:

> Today it is clear that the pressure made by the international community against Dr. Radovan Karadžić has no legal basis and no connection to international law and the functioning of judiciary in the world. The pressure against Karadžić is a pressure against the whole Serbian nation. World forces are trying to paralyze any political and social activity of the Serbian nation by trying to completely isolate Dr. Karadžić and threatening to arrest him. Where does this hate against the personality of Karadžić come from? This pressure comes from the fact that even the enemies of Serbs have understood the extraordinary abilities and authority of Karadžić, as uncompromising defender of his nation. […] Therefore, Karadžić is a thorn in the eye for all enemies of the Serbian nation and all those who accuse him, with accusations that are anti-legal. It is sufficient to mention that the war in Yugoslavia was started by Alija Izetbegović and Franjo Tudjman, in the name of holy centres

[97] *Druga deklaracija o obustavljenju postupka Haškog tribunala protiv dr. Radovana Karadžića*, Agencija "Doktor Radulović", Belgrade, 1996. Both Declarations can be found on the Nova Srpska politička misao (NSPM) Archive.

> of power. [...] The chase against Dr. Radovan Karadzic and the daily pressure has no basis in facts. Falsifications are used as documents in order to manipulate the public opinion.[98]

In Bosnia-Herzegovina, priests were involved in violent activities. In Trebinje, an Orthodox priest led a group of Serbs in expelling Muslims from their homes.[99] According to Velikonja, some Orthodox priests took active part in the war:

> There are even reports of forced conversions of Muslims to Orthodoxy: group baptisms took place, for example, in Bijelina. A number of Orthodox priests took up arms, including Nikodin Čavić, who was to be found 'wherever Serbs and Serb nationhood were threatened'.[100]

The role of religious symbols is obvious from the number of sacred buildings and monuments that were destroyed during the war in Bosnia-Herzegovina. It is estimated that about 1,000 mosques, 340 Orthodox and 450 Catholic churches and monasteries were destroyed.[101] Nearly all the mosques in Serb-held territory were destroyed. In Banja Luka, all the 16 mosques were levelled to the ground in half a year.

9.8. Serb Exoduses from Croatia and Kosovo

The result of the war in Croatia in 1995 was a disaster according to leaders of the Serbian Orthodox Church, due to the massive Serb exodus. Additionally, the Kosovo conflict in 1999 ended with a Serb exodus. These were modern parallels to the Great Migration.

9.8.1. The 'Storm'

The Croatian military operation 'Storm' (*Oluja*) in August 1995, that triggered a massive Serb refugee movement from Croatia to Serbia and Bosnia is presented as the worst catastrophe in Serb history. Interestingly, Milošević was made responsible, at least by some church leaders. Bishop Atanasije (Jeftić) called Milošević "a criminal, tyrant and traitor". He also stated that Milošević

---

98 *Ibid.*

99 MacDonald, 2002, p. 241, see *supra* note 28.

100 Mitja Velikonja, *Religious Separational and Political Intolerance in Bosnia-Herzegovina*, Texas A&M University Press, College Station, 2003, p. 266.

101 Gerald Powers, "Religion, Conflict, and Prospects for Peace in Bosnia, Croatia and Yugoslavia", in Paul Mojzes (ed.), *Religion and the War in Bosnia*, Oxford University Press, 1998, p. 240.

has "betrayed and sold" the Serbian population in Krajina.[102] In August 2016, at a commemoration of the exodus, Patriarch Irinej stated:

> Today we remember the suffering of our people at hands of the Croat military and police in the operation "Storm" in August 1995. The aim of that crime was to expel Serbs from the provinces, towns, and villages where they lived for many centuries and to cleanse Croatia from Serbs and Orthodox Christianity. Thus continued the terror against Serbs in Croatia from the Second World War. Then, we remember, in the Croat fascist Ustasha state Serbs were murdered in concentration camps […] the Ustasha regime even set up a concentration camp for Serb children with more than 120,000 innocent child victims, most of which died from hunger and thirst […]. Only Jews and Armenians, besides Serbs, have seen such a Golgotha […].[103]

The Patriarch participates in the state-organized Remembrance Day of the Victims and Exiles of the Serbs in the Operation 'Storm' every year.

9.8.2. The Kosovo War

The Serbian Orthodox Church was deeply involved in Serbian politics concerning Kosovo in the years leading up to the war in 1999, but not only as hardliners. Bishop Artemije (Radosavljević) of the Raška-Prizren Diocese, who was installed in 1991, had been viewed as a hardliner, but assumed a more moderate posture. He was afraid that Milošević's policy would produce a disaster for the Serbs in Kosovo. In August 1997, a church assembly under the leadership of Bishop Artemije convened in Prizren. It criticized the activities of the Serbian special forces as well as the Albanian Kosovo Liberation Army. Specifically, it opposed the Albanian aim of independence for Kosovo and suggested that Albanians try to find a satisfactory status in a "democratic Serbian state".[104]

During the Rambouillet negotiations in 1999, a plan was presented for a division of Kosovo, a 'cantonization', with five cantons to be reserved for the Serbs. The great majority of the cantons would be allotted to Albanians where they were a distinct majority. The interference of Patriarch Pavle and Bishop Artemije in the negotiations enraged Milošević. He regarded this as treasonous and dismissed them.

---

102 Atanasije Jeftić, "Najgori od svih mogućih ratova", in Radoš M. Mladenović and Hierodeacon Jovan (eds.), *Jagnje Božije i Zvijer iz bezdana*, Svetigora, Cetinje, 1996.

103 Vjekoslav Perica, "Serbian Jerusalem: Religious Nationalism, Globalization and the Invention of a Holy Land in Europe's Periphery, 1985–2017", in *Occasional Papers in Eastern Europe*, 2017, vol. 37, no. 6, p. 71.

104 Veselin Kesich, "Kosovo in the history of the Serbian Church", *Orthodox Research Institute*, 2017; see Cvetkovic, 2015, pp. 31–34, see *supra* note 47.

Bishop Artemije made several visits to Washington, D.C. and European capitals with the proposal to divide Kosovo, which was not what the international community wanted. The Serbian Orthodox Church was strongly against any compromise with the Albanians, and therefore opposed the Rambouillet agreement. Patriarch Pavle opposed the agreement with the words: "Our forefathers went there to defend their freedom and hearth, their land and faith that are ours now".[105] When William Walker, head of the Kosovo Verification Mission, asked why Serbs objected to be a national minority, Bishop Artemije answered:

> Was he [Walker] sent here to make of us what we are not and what we cannot ever be, and to forbid us to be what we are and have been for over eight hundred years in these parts – namely, our own masters in our own land?[106]

At a memorial service at the Cetinje Monastery, Metropolitan Amfilohije stated:

> The godless and tyrannical bombings and NATO violence is a continuation of Nazism and fascism of the twentieth century. […] European peoples, once Christian, marked the second millennium of their Christian history by these bombings of Holy lands, Christian shrines, especially of Kosovo and Metohija. This is a sign that will be remembered by generations and that will serve as a measure of everything that happened late in the twentieth to early twentyfirst centuries.[107]

In March 1999, when the war started, Patriarch Pavle stated:

> It is clear that there was no other choice. This war was imposed on us. This war is a just one because it is defensive […] and therefore blessed by God.[108]

The Serbian Orthodox Church accused the North Atlantic Treaty Organization ('NATO') of deliberately targeting and destroying Serbian monasteries in Kosovo, although no evidence of such destructions was provided.[109]

When the Kumanovo Agreement was signed in June 1999, stating that all Serbian military forces and police had to leave Kosovo and international forces were to take over, the Serbian Orthodox Church reacted very negatively.

---

105 Biserko, 2012, p. 237, see *supra* note 57.

106 *Ibid.*, p. 239

107 "Metropolitan Amphilohije: 'NATO bombings are a continuation of Fascism'", *Orthodox Christianity*, 30 March 2014.

108 *Duga*, 10–23 April 1999, cited in Biserko, 2006, see *supra* note 63.

109 Ramet, 2005, p. 261, see *supra* note 29.

Patriarch Pavle requested that Milošević should resign. He criticized Milošević for 'allowing' the bombardment instead of solving the crises beforehand.[110]

After the end of the NATO air campaign, several Serbian religious objects were blown up by vengeful Albanians, and there was an exodus of Serbs from Kosovo in fear of Albanian reprisals. It is no wonder that the Serbian Orthodox Church reacted against the violence and enforced their demand that Serbs should be protected and Kosovo returned to Belgrade's control. Bishop Artemije criticized NATO for not protecting the Serb minority and even filed a lawsuit in the European Court of Human Rights in Strasbourg against Germany, Italy, France and the United Kingdom. However, the Synod of the Serbian Orthodox Church forced Bishop Artemije to withdraw the case.[111]

The NATO war against Yugoslavia in 1999 was made into a narrative of Serb suffering. Metropolitan Amfilohije, referring, in 2014, to NATO Secretary General Anders Fogh Rasmussen, stated:

> Rasmussen made a statement that the bombing was done by Europe and America to defend Kosovo from genocide. The 1999 war was not a defence from genocide, but a continuation of genocide in Kosovo and Metohija which has lasted for 630 years.[112]

9.9. Montenegro: A Nationalist Metropolitan Bishop

In 1993, an Autocephalous Montenegrin Orthodox Church was proclaimed but not recognized by the Serbian Orthodox Church, which continued to keep the Cetinje monastery and most of the church property in Montenegro. The 'schismatic' Montenegrin Church was supported by independence-minded Montenegrins, including President (later, Prime Minister) Milo Djukanović, but condemned by pro-Serbian Montenegrins.[113] When Metropolitan Mihajlo was enthroned in 1998, violent demonstrations broke out. The rival Metropolitan, presenting the Belgrade Patriarchate, was Amfilohije.

Amfilohije (Radović), Metropolitan Bishop of Montenegro and the Littoral from 1990 to 2020, is an example of a religious leader responsible for nationalist propaganda (several of his statements are already cited in this chapter). He was one of the most influential church leaders, as a member of the Holy Synod of the Serbian Orthodox Church, and was among the three candidates for the Serbian Patriarchate in 2010. He was a professor at the Faculty of Theology in Belgrade and author of several books.

---

[110] Tomanić, 2001, p. 189, see *supra* note 51.

[111] Cvetković, 2015, p. 37, see *supra* note 47.

[112] "Neo-fascism dividing Ukrainians and Russians", *B92*, 13 May 2014.

[113] About the 'Ecclesiastical Dissension in Montenegro', see Ramet, 2005, pp. 264–268, see *supra* note 29.

Amfilohije was a declared Serb nationalist and his views coincided with the nationalist policy in Serbia. He advocated unification of all Serb lands and saw the conflict as Serbia being attacked by enemies from both West and East: "the lightning and thunder of the Catholic and Protestant West and the Ismaelite Islámic Middle East clash over the Serbian People".[114] One of his statements was:

> Our destiny is to carry the cross on this blazing divide between different worlds. Therefore, it [the Serbian people] is also divine [...] Our people [...] preserves in its bosom, in its collective memory, Jerusalem's holiness.[115]

Amfilohije saw the objective of the war as the destruction of Orthodoxy in Serbia. He considered Serbia as "the last island on which holiness is preserved. [...] Therefore, all the demonic forces are directed against the last redoubt of unsullied holiness, of untroubled and unpolluted truth".[116]

He was anti-Catholic. During the siege of Dubrovnik in 1991, Amfilohije played the *gusle* (a stringed instrument) and sang old nationalistic songs to Yugoslav Montenegrin troops. According to him, Dubrovnik is Serbian. He was also anti-Western and very critical of Euro-Atlantic integration, stating that "NATO is the Fourth Reich, that is, continuation of Fascism, seeking to dominate the whole world", and claiming that "NATO is a continuation of the Austro-Hungarian occupation".[117] He also compared NATO with the Bulgarian Tsar Samuil, "a tyrant, a rowdy", who was not satisfied with his Bulgaria and tried to take the Byzantine Empire. He said that the Orthodox churches, especially the one in Montenegro, are crucified and persecuted, "a calvary".[118] He hailed the Chetnik leader Draža Mihailović as a leader of Serbian fight for freedom.

Amfilohije was, in the beginning, an admirer of Slobodan Milošević. He stated that Milošević did not fight just for the freedom and honour of his own nation, but "for the freedom and honour of everything that is honourable and elevated in Europe". He added:

> The name of Slobodan Milošević will be written with golden letters in the history of Montenegro and Serbia as a man who to the very end sacrificed himself. His sacrifice was what Njegoš talked about when he spoke of Miloš Obilić. His sacrifice is noble. It is a

[114] Vladimir Tismaneanu, *Fantasies of Salvation: Democracy: Nationalism, and Myth in Post-Communist Europe*, Princeton University Press, 1998, p. 78.

[115] Cigar, 1995, p. 74, see *supra* note 64.

[116] *Ibid.*, p. 78.

[117] "Church Dignitary Likens NATO to 'Fourth Reich'", *B92*, 1 July 2013; "Amfilohije: NATO je nastavak austrougarske okupacije", *Politika*, 30 August 2016.

[118] "Mitropolit Amfilohije pisao Markoviću: Golgota Crkve u Crnoj Gori", *IN4S*, 12 May 2017.

> sacrifice that cannot be wiped out, just as his heroic achievements against the vampire-like neo-Fascist spirit in Europe and in the Balkans.[119]

When Milošević broke with the Bosnian-Serb leadership over the Vance-Owen plan in 1993, Amfilohije supported the Bosnian leaders and broke with Milošević. When the Bosnian-Serbian parliament in 1994 rejected the peace plan of the Contact Group, Amfilohije sent a message of joy, stating that this was a sign of God's justice, showing the dignity of the Serbian people. Instead of a peace plan, he wanted the Serbs to continue the war. When the Montenegrin parliament supported the plan, Amfilohije said:

> Damned be the hand that builds walls between himself and his brother in trouble, trice damned and accursed. [...] If the Montenegrin Assembly upholds this treacherous judgement, if it supports it selfishly and sycophantically, then it must know that it has signed its own sentence and that of every man who backed it.[120]

During the war in Bosnia, Amfilohije was a strong supporter of Serb warfare. He made many visits to Serb soldiers in Bosnia to give his support. He had close contact with Radovan Karadžić, whom he called "a good man" and a close friend and praised Karadžić for cleaning the Serbian land of Muslims.[121] His support for Ratko Mladić was also publicly stated.

On two occasions, Amfilohije invited the Serb warlord Željko Ražnatović, Arkan, and his paramilitary group, the Tigers, to guard the Cetinje Monastery. Arkan was a professional criminal, bank-robber and state security 'hitman' who was wanted by Interpol. He was popular among church leaders; he made generous donations to the Serbian Orthodox Church, especially for the rebuilding of churches in Kosovo.[122] Arkan was a convinced Serb nationalist, just like Amfilohije.

However, Amfilohije was extremely unpopular among Montenegrin nationalists. He declared that "[i]n history, there never existed a Montenegrin nation" and that "the Montenegrin nationality was invented in the laboratory of Tito and Djilas".[123] At the time when Metropolitan was enthroned as the head of the Montenegrin Church in 1990, Yugoslavia's disintegration led to nationalist tensions in all Yugoslav republics. In Montenegro, many nationalists wanted an independent Montenegrin Orthodox Church, but for the regime in Belgrade it

119 "Dva ratna druga: Aleksandar Vučić i Amfilohije Radović", *Al Jazeera*, 24 February 2020.

120 Milošević and Brajović, 1994, see *supra* note 75.

121 Perica, 2002, pp. 173–174, see *supra* note 12.

122 *Ibid.*, p. 174.

123 Slobodan Jovanović, "Mitropolit Amfilohije, zakleti neprijatelj Crne Gore", *Radio Skala*, 31 August 2017.

was important to preserve church unity. As long as Serbs and Montenegrins were united in a common Serbian Orthodox Church, Montenegrins could be considered to belong to the Serbian nation. Amfilohije strongly opposed Montenegrin religious separatism, and the adherents of an autocephalous Montenegrin Church organized protest meetings.

One such event was on 12 July 1991, *Petrovdan*, the feast of Saint Peter and Saint Paul. When people outside tried to get into the monastery, Arkan's gunmen opened fire at the crowd and several were wounded.[124] This incident contributed to the sharpening of ethnic tensions in Montenegro. Nationalists saw the Serbian Orthodox Church as an anti-Montenegrin organization led by Belgrade with the aim of eliminating Montenegrin identity.

Arkan was also invited to the Cetinje monastery on Orthodox Christmas in 1992. He had recently returned from the battlefields in Croatia. From the Cetinje monastery, Arkan announced: "Skadar shall be ours".[125] Skadar is the Serbian name of the Albanian town Shkodër.

When Arkan, in February 1995, was married to the Serbian folk-pop-singer Ceca, Bishop Vasilij of Tuzla-Zvornik was present at the wedding, which was conducted in mythological style with Arkan dressed as a Serbian Kosovo hero and Ceca as the Maiden of Kosovo. Here, Arkan stated: "We are fighting for our religion, the Serbian Orthodox Church".[126]

Amfilohije had close contact with Bosnian-Serb nationalist leaders, among them Biljana Plavšić, Vice-President of *Republika Srpska*. In 1993, he declared:

> At this moment my words cannot save the soul of our people, nor can the words of anyone writing or uttering them. At this moment and on this day the soul of our people is in the safe hands of Biljana, Republika Srpska and Srpska Krajina. In the same way as Vuk Karadžić guarded and protected our mother tongue, at this moment his namesake [Radovan Karadžić], together with Ms. Plavšić, a new Maiden of Kosovo, and together with Krajišnik, safeguard us all and our souls, as they set themselves this very night on the course of the holy Prince Lazar. Like Prince Lazar in the battle of Kosovo, they have opted for the hearth and home of our soul in the Heavenly Kingdom.[127]

[124] František Šistek, "Clericalization of Nationalism", in András Máté-Tóth and Cosima Rughinis (eds.), *Spaces and Borders: Current Research on Religion in Central and Eastern Europe*, De Gruyter, 2011, p. 125.

[125] Šerbo Rastoder, "Religion and Politics 1991–1999, The Montenegrin Perspective", 2003 (available on the *Academia.edu* web site).

[126] Sells, 1996, p. 82, see *supra* note 1. See also Velikonja, 2003, p. 265, see *supra* note 100.

[127] *Borba*, 30 April 1993, quoted in Barišić, 2014, see *supra* note 76.

As we see, Metropolitan Amfilohije compared Biljana Plavšić with the 'Maiden of Kosovo', the most positive woman in Serbian national mythology, who took water to wounded Serbian soldiers after the Kosovo battle, described in Serbian folk poetry. Plavšić, a biologist and former dean of the Faculty of Natural Science and Mathematics in Sarajevo, was an extreme nationalist. In 1994, she stated:

> It was genetically deformed material that embraced Islam. And now, of course, with each successive generation it simply becomes concentrated. It gets worse and worse. It simply expresses itself and dictates their style of thinking, which is rooted in their genes. And through the centuries, the genes degraded further.[128]

She also had reflections on rape:

> Rape unfortunately belongs to the war strategy of Muslims and some Croats towards Serbs. For Islam rape is normal, for that religion tolerates polygamy. Throughout 500 years of Turkish occupation both begs and agas were entitled to spend the first night with a recently married woman from the 'mob'.[129]

Michael Sells comments on the statements by Plavšić, stating:

> At moments of crisis, the Kosovo ideology helps efface the boundaries between notions of religion and race and turns religious nationalism into the most virulent form of racist ideology.[130]

Biljana Plavšić was eventually sentenced to 11 years of imprisonment by The Hague Tribunal.[131]

That other religious leaders also had anti-Muslim attitudes is seen from a statement made by Atanasije (Jevtić), Bishop of Zahumlje and Herzegovina, former dean of the Theological Faculty in Belgrade:

> Those are people with unpleasant sweating, Muslims, because they eat fat. Do you know what happened in the village of Brdarići? A kind man, who let people, travellers, sleep in his house, had one day two men staying there. Afterwards his wife was cleaning the

128 Quoted in Michael Sells, "Islam in Serbian Religious Mythology", in Maya Shatzmiller (ed.), *Islam and Bosnia: Conlflict and Resolution and Foreign Policy in Multi-Ethnic States*, McGill-Queen's University Press, Montreal, 2002, p. 58.

129 *Borba*, 8 February 1993, quoted in Renaud de la Brosse and Mato Brautović (eds.), *Reporting Attacks on Dubrovnik in 1991, and the Recognition of Croatia*, Cambridge Scholars Publishing, Newcastle upon Tyne, 2017, p. 110.

130 Sells, 1996, p. XV, see *supra* note 1.

131 ICTY, *Prosecutor v. Plavšić*, Trial Chamber III, Sentencing Judgment, 27 February 2003, IT-00-39&40/1-S (https://www.legal-tools.org/doc/f60082/).

> room but complained that it was still smelling. The husband said: It is not the room, *they* stink, they are Muslims.[132]

Metropolitan Amfilohije strongly supported the establishment of a Serb Republic in Bosnia, although it was created through war and ethnic cleansing (see Section 9.7). He even considered that the Serbs of *Republika Srpska* were better Christians than Serbs in Serbia or Montenegro:

> Only a soul that honourably carries its cross and a nation that carries that cross with dignity and suffers for its faith, truly understand the secrets of the original Christian way of being. [...] The Serbs in Republika Srpska did undergo crucifixion, which is why they are somewhat better than half-Christian Montenegro and un-Christian Serbia.[133]

As other Serbian nationalists, Amfilohije did not recognize that a genocide had taken place in Srebrenica. He claimed that the genocide in Srebrenica was revenge for crimes committed by the Bosniak commander Naser Orić.[134]

9.10. Religious Leaders' Activity after 2000

On 28 June 2001, Saint Vitus' Day, Milošević was arrested and transferred to The Hague. Metropolitan Amfilohije reacted with the following words:

> By doing that just on St. Vitus' Day, they could not have given Milošević a greater honour, and themselves and their nation a bigger shame in history. One is afraid that by taking this silly act, they have written themselves out of history. I ask what shall we do now? Those who have not lost their St. Vitus enlightenment, and those are still many in this nation and our state, know what to do and how. They will do anything possible to keep their personal and national honour and a common state.[135]

Patriarch Pavle died in November 2009 and was succeeded by Irinej, born Miroslav Gavrilović, who was Serbian patriarch in 2010–2020. He gave several nationalist statements. In 2013, he advocated for the restoration of the Serbian monarchy. About the Serb entity in Bosnia, he stated that it is created "by God's justice and truth", "God willing, we will soon be one", and that, for now, "it is enough that we are one as a nation, as the Orthodox Church, and that we are on

[132] "Justin je fino mirisao", *Vreme*, 5 April 2004.

[133] "Amfilohije: Republika Srpska je jedina krštena srpska zemlja, Crna Gora je polukrštena, a Srbija je nedokrštena", *Telegraf*, 1 April 2016.

[134] "Amfilohije: Srebrenica je bila osveta", *YouTube*, 1 June 2013.

[135] B92 television's program *Insajder*, episode of 20 November 2010.

the same path of Saint Sava and Christ".[136] In 2017, Irinej received Vojislav Šešelj at the Patriarchate.

9.10.1. The Serbian Church and Vojislav Šešelj

Vojislav Šešelj conveys an example of a relationship between a political leader and religious leaders. Šešelj was the leader of the Serbian Radical Party and paramilitary commander of a militia responsible for ethnic cleansing in Croatia and Bosnia. He was indicted by the ICTY and was arrested when he voluntarily came to The Hague.

In 2004, Šešelj requested a visit by Bishop Filaret (Mičević), but this was denied by the Court, since there was a ban on the Bishop from entering any member state of the European Union ('EU'). Filaret became 'famous' because of a picture. During the war in Croatia, in September 1991, he was photographed near the front (at the Komogovina Monastery, south of Zagreb) with a machine gun (an M–53) in front of an armoured vehicle with Serbian flag and paramilitary soldiers. Filaret was known to be an extreme nationalist, an ardent adherent of Šešelj. Later, in 1998, Filaret was promoted to Bishop of Mileševa in Serbia.

In November 2014, Šešelj was temporarily released from his trial for cancer treatment and returned to Belgrade, where he led nationalist protests and made a series of hard-line statements. On 27 January 2015, Šešelj was awarded the Order of the White Angel medal at the Mileševa Monastery by Bishop Filaret. The award was supported by Patriarch Irinej.[137] Bishop Filaret declared that Šešelj was "a Chetnik duke and a victor over the Hague Tribunal".[138] Šešelj was being given the honour, the Bishop explained, "for his love for the Serbian Church, and especially for his love for the Mileševa monastery, which is celebrating its 800th anniversary". On this occasion Bishop Filaret said:

> Dear friend, brother Vojo, God has given you the task to clean the blemish from the Serbian nation, although difficult, and we congratulate you for your brave struggle, a Serb struggle, a heroic struggle.[139]

On 25 June 2015, Šešelj was ordained by Metropolitan Amfilohije with the Order of the Montenegrin ruler Peter II. The Metropolitan gave him this decoration for "following the holy law of God's justice by defending the truth at the Hague Tribunal, which stinks of inhumanity". The Metropolitan saw the decoration "as an encouragement to continue his brave efforts to defend the soul and the honour of the Serbian people". Amfilohije further stated:

---

136 "'God willing, Serbs in Serbia, Bosnia will be one'", *B92*, 15 November 2010.

137 "Slučaj 'Orden za Šešelja': Irinej na Filaretovom putu", *Radio Slobodna Evropa*, 1 June 2015.

138 Sells, 2002, p. 58, see *supra* note 128.

139 "Zbog čega je Filaret odlikovao Šešelja", *Mondo*, 29 January 2015.

> Justice has never been humiliated and crushed as much as today, not even under Fascism, and primarily in our land. One of those who defend God's justice is Mr. Šešelj. […] The Hague Tribunal is exclusively an instrument for chasing Serbs. […] The case against Karadžić is a punishment of the whole Serbian nation. Throughout their history, the Serbs have been victims of the most brutal forms of genocide and expulsion, threatening their existence, and always they were defending their existence, their culture and democratic conviction. […] During the destruction of Yugoslavia, the Serbs went through the greatest sufferings and were driven from their historical homes in Croatia and Bosnia-Herzegovina. In this period the Serbs were exposed to physical extermination and spiritual genocide.[140]

Šešelj was first acquitted by the ICTY, then sentenced to 10 years in prison in 2018 by the Appeals Chamber of the Mechanism for International Criminal Tribunals.[141]

9.10.2. Against Independence of Kosovo

The main concern of the Serbian Orthodox Church after the wars in the 1990s has been the situation in Kosovo. One scholar noted that the "military loss of Kosovo and the massive exodus of Kosovo Serbs invoked the mythical narratives and inspired the religious discourse in Serbian nationalism".[142] The existence of a considerable Serbian cultural and religious heritage was used to show the Serbian historical right to Kosovo. Already in 1987, the Serbian Orthodox Church published an extensive edition on Serbian 'Sacred endowments' in Kosovo.[143] In 2001, the Serbian Church published an encyclopaedia showing the several hundred churches, monasteries and cemeteries in Kosovo.[144] Referring to Kosovo, Patriarch Pavle stated:

> It is the wellspring of the Serbian spiritual tradition, and of our statehood; the heart and soul of our nation – indivisible and essential. That is why our forefathers consecrated its soil with thousands of beautiful garlands: adorning the land with magnificent churches and monasteries dedicated to the glory of God.[145]

140 "Amfilohije odlikovao Šešelja, 25. jun 2015.", *YouTube*, 26 June 2015.

141 Mechanism for International Criminal Tribunals, *Prosecutor v. Šešelj*, Appeals Chamber, Judgment, 11 April 2018, MICT-16-99-A (https://www.legal-tools.org/doc/96ea58/).

142 Perica, 2017, p. 31, see *supra* note 103.

143 Atanasije Jevtić (ed.), *Zadužbine Kosova: spomenici i znamenja srpskog naroda*, Eparhija Raško-Prizrenska i Bogoslovski fakultet, Belgrade, 1987.

144 Slobodan Mileusnić (ed.), *Monasteries of Serbia: Large Illustrated Encyclopedia*, vols. 1–2, Pravoslavna reč, Novi Sad, 2002 (English edition).

145 Perica, 2017, p. 31, see *supra* note 103.

On another occasion, Patriarch Pavle stated:

> For us, Kosovo is just another name for the noblest principles, truth and justice, for law and order, whereas the Kosovo pledge is our New Testament. Therefore, the issue of Kosovo and Metohija is inseparable from the issue of Serbia and destiny of Serb nation.[146]

When the question of the independence of Kosovo came on the international agenda, Bishop Artemije, in 2004, appealed to the US Congress not to support independence:

> The independence of Kosovo, in a situation where most elementary standards of rule-of-law simply do not exist, would lead directly to the final eradication of the Serbian Christian presence in the historic heart of its nation. It would further destabilize the region which is so desperately in need of peace and stability.[147]

Kosovo's declaration of independence on 17 February 2008 triggered sharp reactions from the Serbian Orthodox Church. The Church supported the Serbian policy of resisting recognition of Kosovo and claiming that it should remain a part of Serbia. The state used the Church to promote the Serbian view on Kosovo to an international public, and the Church became a tool in Serbia's diplomatic efforts. In 2013, a 'Serbian Medieval Cultural Exhibition' was shown in London and New York. In 2014, an English-language monograph on the heritage of Kosovo was published in the US.[148]

The Serbian Orthodox Church opposes any compromise on the status of Kosovo and urges Serbs to abstain from participation in political institutions in Kosovo. The 'Kosovo covenant' was also recalled. In 2008, the bishops stated in their Easter message:

> We lived and died with the Kosovo covenant: "The earthly kingdom [is] small, the heavenly is forever". [...] We urge all Serbs to fulfill this covenant, the covenant of Lazar. If we fulfill this covenant no one can take Kosovo and Metohija from us, not in this or in any other century, just as nobody could take away from the Jewish people their holy Jerusalem.[149]

---

146 "Poruka patriarha Pavla", *Pravoslavlje*, 15 March 2007.

147 Quoted in Radmila Radić and Milan Vukomanović, "Religion and Democracy in Serbia Since 1989: The Case of the Serbian Orthodox Church", in Sabrina P. Ramet (ed.), *Religion and Politics in Post-Socialist Central and Southeastern Europe*, Palgrave MacMillan, 2014, p. 184.

148 Bishop Maxim Vasiljević (ed.), *The Christian Heritage of Kosovo and Metohija: The Spiritual, Historical and Aesthetic Heart of the Serbian People*, The Episcopal Council of the Serbian Orthodox Church in North America, Sebastian Press, Los Angeles, 2014.

149 "Vaskršna poslanica 2008. godine", *Srpska Pravoslavna Crkva*, 18 April 2008.

Patriarch Irinej presents Kosovo as a sacred land, stating: "For Serbs, Kosovo is not a geographic space but a holy land with their greatest holy sites. The Serbian Church will never accept that Kosovo is given away".[150] He called the international recognition of Kosovo a "sin".[151] In 2013, he stated:

> Kosovo is an occupied Serbian land. It cannot be traded or partitioned. We must fight for a united Kosovo and Metohija. The Serbian people has not lost Kosovo. As long as our churches are there, Kosovo will remain ours. If a just solution is not found, Kosovo will be a powder keg. Kosovo is the heart and soul of Serbian history, culture and people, a land bathed in the blood of thousands of martyrs, wetted by the tears of people who have suffered for 500 years. Kosovo is our most holy land and the cornerstone of everything we call ours. It is what Jerusalem is for Jews, Rome for Catholics, Kremlin for Russians.[152]

Metropolitan Amfilohije also used very harsh words about the situation in Kosovo. He considered that the situation was worse now than during the Nazi occupation:

> Hitler was wise enough to let the northern part of Kosovo belong to Serbia, although under Nedić and occupied. [...] Hitler's solutions, started in 1941, are being continued today, not only in Kosovo but also wider.[153]

Blessing the Church of Holy Trinity at Kolašin in 2013, Metropolitan Amfilohije said the following about Kosovo and Serbia's relationship with Europe:

> Now it's not only the tyranny of Murat [the Ottoman Sultan] but of NATO, the EU and the US as well, actually of all those following in the footsteps of the crusading, inquisitional, Napoleonic and Bolshevik tyranny [...] Our rulers should think twice. We need to join Europe but what Europe after all? This Europe of today – rascally, tyrannical and the one that tramples the poor – is that the Europe we need?[154]

In his 2017 Christmas message, Patriarch Irinej stated:

> Especially, we pray for the crucified Kosovo and Metohija, our spiritual and national cradle, the land that the great bishop-poet Njegoš named "the grand tribunal of history". As long as Serbs

150 "Patriarch: Kosovo nije geografski prostor, nego sveta zemlja", *Blic*, 11 July 2012.

151 "Serbian Patriarch Irinej calls Kosovo recognition a 'sin'", *Southeast European Times*, 4 October 2010.

152 "Patriarh SPC: Kosovo je okupirana zemlja", *Intermagazin*, 20 March 2013.

153 "Amfilohije: Republika Srpska je jedina krštena srpska zemlja, Crna Gora je polukrštena, a Srbija je nedokrštena", 2016, see *supra* note 133.

154 *Naše novine*, 1 July 2013, quoted in Barišić, 2014, p. 37, see *supra* note 76.

> live, Kosovo lives also! Kosovo is soul of the Serb! For that reason, Kosovo will always be Serb land, because our Golgotha and our Jerusalem are there![155]

In 2020, Irinej (Bulović), Bishop of Bačka, stated that Kosovo was occupied and added:

> Those who want to take a part of our territory, don't want only Kosovo, they want all our land! They want us not to exist! Kosovo is only a beginning. Therefore, we say: Kosovo is the heart of Serbia – they are hitting the very essence. If we accept that they take Kosovo, we will disappear from the earth.[156]

Patriarch Irinej died in November 2020 and was followed by Patriarch Porfirije, who continued the nationalistic discourse concerning Kosovo. In 2021, Patriarch Porfirije stated:

> A referendum about Kosovo took place in 1389 on the battle day. Kosovo is for us not only our nation's cradle, but it is also a reliquary filled with relics of our saints.

At Saint Vitus' Day in 2022, Patriarch Porfirije served the liturgy in Gračanica Monastery in Kosovo. In front of a thousand believers, he stated:

> Without Gračanica, without Vidovdan, without all the saints in Kosovo and Metohija, we are simply not what we are, we are not what God called us to. […] Vidovdan is our eye, Saint Lazar is our ear, the saints of Kosovo and Metohija are our mind. Here we see, here we hear, here we understand, not only our past, not only our origin, but we also understand what our goal is, why we are invited to this world.[157]

Archimandrite Damjan (Cvetković) said, in reference to Kosovo, that "it is the bleeding wound of the Serbian Church", and added:

> It seems to me that nothing can be compared to Kosovo because this is the most important part, the soul of the Serbian people and Church. […] Kosovo is our heart and never under any circumstances will we betray our Kosovo. It is simply impossible and absolutely out of question for us.[158]

The Serbian Orthodox Church's discourse about Kosovo was borrowed by Serbian politicians. The Jerusalem metaphor, coined by the Church and used

155 "Božićna poslanica Patrijarha Irineja: 'Dok je Srbija, biće i Kosova i Metohije, ono će ostati naša zemlja'", *Blic*, 3 January 2017.

156 "Ako pristanemo da nam uzmu Kosovo, nestaćemo sa lica zemlje!", *Vijesti Srpske*, 7 January 2021.

157 "Patriarh Porfirije: Vidovdan je naše oko", *YouTube*, 28 June 2022.

158 "Kosovo is our heart", *Orthodox Christianity*, 28 June 2022.

by the politician Vuk Drašković, already in the 1980s, was taken up by Serbian politicians and used by Foreign Minister Vuk Jeremić in 2011.[159]

9.10.3. The Dream of Great Serbia Is Alive

The dream of Great Serbia was not forgotten. Patriarch Pavle said in an interview in 2001:

> Throughout its history – including the twentieth century – the Church had to neglect its primary duties in favor of active engagement in the struggle for unification of the Serb nation, the struggle in which a priest has simultaneously been a teacher, a judge and an armed man defending himself and his family.[160]

In October 2017, during his visit to the Serb Republic in Bosnia-Herzegovina, Patriarch Irinej made the following statement:

> Wherever Serbs live, there is Serbia: not just in Serbia proper but in Bosnia-Herzegovina, Vojvodina, Montenegro, and other places. All Serbs, wherever they live in the world, should unite in the thinking about our people's glorious history. […] The twentieth century was so glorious yet tragic for the Serbs, that human history never recorded such a grave suffering of a people. It seems that the suffering of the Serbs exceeded the gravity of the calamities of Jewish and Armenian peoples.[161]

The Serb Orthodox Church has been very active in marking and 'serbianising' the territory of *Republika Srpska* by erecting church buildings in Muslim villages and neighbourhoods; sometimes even on private Muslim properties.[162]

Vojvodina is another contested province. The Serbian Orthodox Church protested against giving more autonomy to Vojvodina, even for the establishment of Vojvodina's Academy of Arts and Sciences. In a letter to the Serbian Parliament and Premier in February 2009, the Holy Synod of the Serbian Orthodox Church stated:

> As a guardian of Serbs' spiritual being and national identity for centuries, even at a time a Serb state was non-existent, the Serb Orthodox Church expresses its anxiety over sovereignty and territorial integrity of the state of Serbia jeopardized firstly by the seizure and occupation of Kosovo and Metohija, and then by the

159 Perica, 2017, p. 31, see *supra* note 103.

160 "Interview with Patriarch Pavle", *Danas*, 5–7 January 2001.

161 See Perica, 2017, p. 71, see *supra* note 103.

162 Hariz Halilovich, "25 Years After Srebrenica: 'Local' Genocide in a Global Context", in Sead Turčalo and Hikmet Karčić (eds.), *Bosnian Genocide Denial and Triumphalism: Origins, Impact and Prevention*, Faculty of Political Science, University of Sarajevo, 2021, p. 122 (https://www.legal-tools.org/doc/x1xcmh/).

> attempt to turn the Autonomous Province of Vojvodina into a new state within the state of Serbia.[163]

In Montenegro, the position of the Serbian Orthodox Church has created serious political conflicts. Most Montenegrins belong to the Serbian Orthodox Church,[164] although 45 per cent declared themselves as Montenegrins and only 28.7 per cent as Serbs in the census of 2011. The Serbian Orthodox Church claims all of them to be Serbs. In 2020, Patriarch Irinej stated, with regards to the Montenegrins:

> We are all one nation, notwithstanding how much they deny it. The split between Serbia and Montenegro is meaningless and unreasonable. I cannot understand that a Montenegrin does not recognize Serbdom as his native nation. Also in Serbia we are divided between people from Šumadija, Bosnia, Vojvodina, but our native root is in one nation – the Serbian.[165]

In a referendum on 21 May 2006, 55.5 per cent of Montenegrins voted to end the federation of Serbia and Montenegro and, on 3 June 2006, Montenegro declared independence. The Serbian Orthodox Church reacted against Montenegrin independence. Metropolitan Bishop Amfilohije stated:

> It is not up to us to create this or that identity. […] Montenegro was born in Jajce by Broz [Tito], it is a child of AVNOJ [the communist constitution of Yugoslavia], which was Godless; against Heaven's soul and kingdom did they build their strength and glory, but everything that is built against God and God's Church is temporary in history.[166]

When NATO membership came on the agenda for Montenegro in 2016, Metropolitan Amfilohije used harsh words about his fellow citizens, stating that they were "struggling to become cogs in the tyrannical and godless machine of NATO":

> The Church of God opposes this NATO. The Serbian Orthodox Church first of all condemns this satanic violence against human beings. The Church is against everything that enslaves and undermines human dignity, both physical and spiritual. […] What is NATO? It is nothing but the continuation of Nazism and Fascism of the twentieth century. Hitler was building a new world order and

---

163 "Struggle over Patriarch's Legacy", 2009, see *supra* note 5.

164 According to the 2011 census, 72 per cent of Montenegrins identify as Orthodox and about 70 per cent of this number follow the Serbian Orthodox Church, while 30 per cent identify with the Montenegrin Orthodox Church.

165 See Mirko Djordjević, *Kišobran Patriarha Pavla*, Peščanik, Belgrade, 2010, p. 142.

166 "Amfilohije: Crna Gora građena protiv Boga", *RTCG*, 6 June 2016.

> thus shed blood of millions of people in Europe and Asia, which has flooded Europe and the whole world with blood.[167]

When the Montenegrin government decided, in 2019, to transfer church property from the Serbian Orthodox Church to the non-recognized Montenegrin Orthodox Church, huge demonstrations broke out. Montenegrin nationalists accused Serbia of using the Church to promote Serbian identity and to influence Montenegrin politics. Serbia accused Montenegro of stealing Serb church property. In 2021, the tensions in Montenegro broke out in serious riots. After the death of Metropolitan Amfilohije, the new Metropolitan Joanikije was to be inaugurated. A large group of angry people barricaded the road from the capital to Cetinje to prevent the Serbian Patriarch Porfirije from attending the ceremony. The Patriarch and Metropolitan had to be flown in on a military helicopter to the monastery under heavy police protection. Many were arrested and at least 60 people injured. The conflict is not so much religious as it is political, and concerns Montenegro's relation to Serbia. It is indeed a strange situation for a country to have a Metropolitan who does not recognize the country's right to exist and nationhood. It seems that Metropolitan Joanikije is also supposed to continue the politics of Amfilohije and is very much against Montenegro's NATO membership and has stated that "the invitation to join NATO is like the five hundred years of slavery under the Turks".[168]

The Serbian Orthodox Church is against not only NATO, but also Serbian EU membership. Metropolitan Amfilohije had said that it is demanded that Serbia shall join the EU "without its head, that is Kosovo", and that to join the EU with only the body, without the head, would mean to join as a dead nation, one that has ceased to exist.[169] Bishop Atanasije (Jevtić) stated, in 2004:

> Gentlemen, who paid a visit riding tanks in 1914? Europe! Who came here in 1941? Was it Europe? We shall be liberating ourselves from such Europe for another two centuries. We shall still have uprisings here.[170]

The Serbian Orthodox Church reacted in opposition to the verdicts against Mladić and Karadžić. Bishop Lavrentije of Šabac-Valjevo stated, in 2003, that "people consider Karadžić and Mladić to be national heroes and

167 "Metropolitan Amfilohije: NATO Is Flooding Europe and the Whole World with Blood", *Orthodox Christianity*, 1 November 2016.

168 "Joanikije izabran za mitroploita crnogorsko-primorskog", *Radio Slobodna Evropa*, 29 May 2021.

169 "Ne u EU bez glave, tj. Kosova", *B92*, 19 October 2011.

170 *Vreme*, 19 February 2004, quoted in Barišić, 2014, p. 37, see *supra* note 76.

patriots and hide them wisely".[171] In November 2017, Patriarch Irinej called the life sentence given to Ratko Mladić by the ICTY, 'the work of [the] devil':

> One more Serb has been convicted in The Hague. We knew Ratko Mladić would be convicted and that everything would play out this way. Unfortunately, we cannot do anything about it. [...] This is all happening because the many global wielders of power are doing the devil's work and we are suffering the consequences. It is not new that it turns out only the Serbs are guilty for everything, while others are innocent.[172]

Atanasije (Jevtić), Bishop of Herzegovina, stated, with reference to Karadžić, in 2004:

> They will not find him. They will not find him, and they are angry. However, I know from reliable sources that they have no proof that Karadžić is a war criminal. All his orders are in accordance with international rules [...] Karadžić has clean hands.[173]

The Serbian Orthodox Church continued to negate the Srebrenica genocide. Regarding the Srebrenica Memorial Cemetery at Potočari, Patriarch Irinej stated:

> More than 50% of those buried at Potočari are soldiers who fought in or around Srebrenica, which shows that Potočari, which they try to present as a graveyard of victims from Srebrenica, in fact is a military graveyard.[174]

In July 2022, on the anniversary of the Srebrenica massacres, the extreme pro-Russian organization Eastern Alternative (Istočna Alternativa) screened a documentary film about 'The Liberation of Srebrenica'. The screening took place at the Holy Despot Stefan Lazarević Serbian Cultural Centre at the local Orthodox parish house in Srebrenica. According to Eastern Alternative, Mladić "played a historical role in these events". It stated that, through the screening, it "wanted to mark the day of liberation, the creation of peace and life in Podrinje [Drina Valley]". The Metropolitanate of Dabar-Bosnia did not respond to

---

[171] *NIN*, 10 April 2003, cited in Sonja Biserko, *Human Rights and Accountability: Serbia 2003*, Helsinki Committee for Human Rights in Serbia, Belgrade, 2004, pp. 260–261.

[172] "Patriarh Irinej: Presuda Mladiću je djelo đavola", *Oslobođenje*, 24 November 2017; "Patriarch: Mladic Verdict Is Work of Devil", *B92*, 24 November 2017.

[173] *Vreme*, 15 April 2004, cited in Egdunas Racius, "Orthodox Churches and the 'Othering' of Islam and Muslims in Today's Balkans", in *Journal of Muslims in Europe*, 2020, vol. 9, no. 3, p. 401.

[174] "Preminuo patrijarh Irinej: Čovjek koji je negirao genocid u Srebrenici i promovirao ideju Velike Srbije", *RTV Glass Drine/Dnevni avaz*, 20 November 2020.

inquiries of how this could take place when denial of genocide and other war crimes is banned by the High Representative.[175]

9.10.4. The Role of the Church in Society

During the period dominated by the Serbian Progressive Party, which has been the ruling party since 2012 (Aleksandar Vučić, having been Prime Minister (2014–2017), and being President at the time of publication (2017–)), the Serbian Orthodox Church has gained a prominent position in society. Subotić summarizes her article on the role of the Serbian Church in the following way:

> The Serbian Orthodox Church continues to serve as a political force in Serbian society – a fundamental source of Serbian national identity and an organization deeply immersed in contemporary Serbian politics. It is a Church that is deeply conservative, opposed to change, and primarily interested in preserving its status and privilege in Serbian society.[176]

The Serbian Church's anti-Westernism coincided with nationalist Serbian politics. Also, the insistence on the exclusive use of the Cyrillic alphabet, which the Church saw as the only Serbian script, coincided with nationalist concepts among intellectuals.

The Serbian Church argues that it is wrong to characterize Serbs or itself as nationalists. Bishop Atanasije (Jevtić) stated the following about nationalism:

> Why are Serbs called nationalists, why is it not valuable that we are connected to our nation and that we honour that God's gift? Nobody talks about Jews being nationalists, or Germans or Americans; they call it something else, American strategic interest. But they are worse than the Fascists and Nazis, those same Americans.[177]

Bishop Atanasije opposed the critics of Serbian nationalism, especially those coming from Brussels:

> This high-calibre anti-Serbian tirade, which surpasses both Ottoman and Communist achievements in the domain of fabrication, moaning, and slandering […] creating a confusion, based on malicious but carefully worded disinformation […] by the new, self-

[175] Nejra Dzaferagic, "Nationalists to Show Film Praising Serb Forces on Srebrenica Anniversary", *Balkan Insight*, 1 July 2022.

[176] Jelena Subotić, "The Church, the Nation, and the State: The Serbian Orthodox Church After Communism", in Sabrina P. Ramet (ed.), *Orthodox Churches and Politics in Southeastern Europe*, Palgrave Macmillan, 2019, p. 85.

[177] *Radio Slobodna Evropa*, 29 May 2021, see *supra* note 168.

> appointed unilateral, and one-party agit-prop, or Central Committee from Brussels.[178]

The role of the Serbian Orthodox Church in the present-day political landscape in Serbia is analysed by Sonja Biserko:

> Serbia is the only country in the region to renounce its anti-fascist past, having adopted a policy since 2000 of marginalizing the role played by the Communist partisans in World War II while declaring the Chetniks to have been a right-wing anti-fascist movement. [...] Serbian nationalists are increasingly turning for ideological inspiration to such twentieth-century champions of conservative thought as Nikolaj Velimirović, Justin Popović, Dimitrije Ljotić, and Milan Nedić who was prime minister of a Nazi-backed collaborationist regime in Serbia in World War II. The SPC [Serbian Orthodox Church] plays a singularly important role as authoritative promotor of such values.[179]

Biserko claims that the synthesis of Orthodox clericalism and an 'organic' concept of society, distinguishing Dimitrije Ljotić and his 1930s' movement Zbor, "has been revived by many political parties".[180] The Serbian Helsinki Committee, in 2003, concluded:

> The downfall of Milošević marked the end of the Communist ideology. The ensuing political vacuum was filled with anti-Communism, monarchism and Orthodox religion. The Serbian Orthodox Church gained a prominent position in society, which enabled it to launch a campaign for the retraditionalisation of both spiritual and public life.[181]

The connection between state and religion in modern Serbia can be seen from an interview given in 2005 by the Minister of Religious Affairs Milan Radulović on the occasion of preparing a law on religion:

> Every normal democratic state today understands that the Church organization is more powerful, more profound, and older than any other organization, because the Church has outlived numerous states and remained one and the same, while society changed all the time. There is now awareness that democratic society has to

[178] Atanasije Jevtić, "Tri kruga napada na vladiku Nikolaja" (Three rounds of attacks on Bishop Nikolaj), in *id.* (ed.), *Sveti Vladika Nikolaj Ohridski i Žički* (Holy Bishop Nikolaj of Ohrid and Žiča), Sveti Manastir Žiča, Kraljevo, 2003, p. 567.

[179] Biserko, 2012, p. 300, see *supra* note 57.

[180] *Ibid.*

[181] Helsinki Committee for Human Rights in Serbia, *Ljudska prava u senci nacionalizma: Srbija 2002*, Helsinški odbor za ljudska prava u Srbiji, Belgrade, 2003, p. 142.

> recognize the Church as a constant. It is an organism which is permanent and a guidepost for the state.[182]

To see the Serbian Orthodox Church as an 'organism' and 'guidepost for the state' reflects a traditional view among conservative Orthodox theologians, going back to the teachings of Velimirović. Velimirović's popularity is linked to the emergence of right wing organizations:

> Since 2000, Serbia has witnessed the emergence of a number of extremist Christian right-wing political organizations, which propagate a mixture of political conservatism, clerical nationalism, and to varying degrees – antisemitism.[183]

The Serbian Orthodox Church supports the most extreme political movements in Serbia, such as the right-wing political party Dveri. They have taken up the concept of *svetosavlje* as their political basis. The party leader, Boško Obradović, stated in 2022:

> The Serbian movement Dveri is deeply convinced that *svetosavlje* is the foundation of the Serbian national identity and that the Serbian Orthodox Church is the cradle where our justice, literature, script and art were born.[184]

Subotić states that these extreme movements are involved in violence against Roma, dissident intellectuals and the lesbian, gay, bisexual, transgender or queer ('LGBTQ') population, and that this is largely sanctioned or condoned by the Serbian Orthodox Church:

> There are a number of extremely violent right-wing groups associated with the Serbian Orthodox Church (*Obraz*, *Dveri*, *Pokret 1389*), which attack minorities and political opponents with criminal impunity. For example, one of the leaders of *Obraz* issued a statement confirming that "not one of his organization's activities was carried out without the support and blessing of the Church".[185]

According to Barišić, what distinguishes the Serbian extreme organizations from similar groups in other European countries "are the overemphasized sacral (clerical) elements of their identity".[186] At the elections in 2022, extreme right-wing parties, including Dveri and Obraz, took 17.6 per cent of the votes.[187]

---

182 Milan Radulović, "Prednacrt zakona o verskim slobodama", *Pravoslavlje*, 15 December 2005.

183 Byford, 2008, p. 117, see *supra* note 178.

184 "Značaj i uloga SPC i tradicionalnih verskih zajednica", *Direktno*, 20 March 2022.

185 Subotić, 2019, p. 95, see *supra* note 176.

186 Barišić, 2014, p. 32, see *supra* note 76.

187 "Did Serbia's Elections Signal a Further Tilt to the Right?", *Balkan Insight*, 8 April 2022.

The Serbian Orthodox Church is an ally of extreme views on internationalization and globalization, on homosexuality, liberalism and secularization.[188] The Pride Parade in 2010 was characterized by Metropolitan Amfilohije as "the so-called Pride Parade, actually a shame parade, a parade of Sodom and Gomorrah".[189] In 2012, Patriarch Irinej said the following with reference to the Pride Parade:

> I think that's a disease and those people need help to overcome their abnormality. […] The Church does not condemn a sinner but a sin. […] Such parades insult morality of the absolute majority not only Christians but also other believers and should not be allowed.[190]

The Serbian Orthodox Church is engaged in the fight against low natality (*bela kuga*, 'the white plague'), supporting a proposal to introduce a tax on unmarried people and married couples without children.[191]

President Aleksandar Vučić has also introduced the habit to consult the Church on political matters. In May 2022, when Serbia was the only country in Europe that had not introduced sanctions against Russia because of the war in Ukraine, Vučić had a meeting with the Patriarch and bishops to hear their opinion. All the clergymen were unanimously against any sanctions.[192]

9.10.5. Relationship with the Russian Orthodox Church

The Serbian Orthodox Church has very good relations with the Russian Orthodox Church. There are similarities in the concept of the two churches' theology and role in society. The close contact between the two churches has long historical roots. Russia supported Montenegro already in the eighteenth century and Bishop Njegoš visited Russia twice. In the nineteenth century, Russia used the ideology of Orthodox unity in its support for the national movements among Orthodox Balkan nations in their struggle against the Ottoman Turks. This Orthodox pan-Slavism was also an instrument for Russian expansion in the Balkans.

Both churches advocate pan-Slavism and pan-Orthodoxy. Based on the pan-Slavic myth, relations are close, not only among the churches. During the war in Bosnia-Herzegovina, hundreds of Russian volunteers joined the Army of

188 See Ramet, 2005, pp. 271–275, see *supra* note 29; see also Subotić, 2019, see *supra* note 176.

189 Subotić, 2019, p. 96, see *supra* note 176; Barišić, 2014, p. 35, see *supra* note 76.

190 Barišić, 2014, p. 36, see *supra* note 76.

191 "Šta je bećarski porez", *B92*, 20 February 2005.

192 Nenad Kulačin, "Ručak sa SPC-om koji je osokolio Vučića", *Al Jazeera Balkans*, 30 May 2022.

Republika Srpska.[193] Like the Serbian concept that Montenegrins, Macedonians and Bosnians are, in fact, Serbs, the Russian Orthodox Church has maintained that Belarussians and Ukrainians are Russians. This was reflected in President Putin's article published in 2021[194] and in his speech on 22 February 2022, just before the invasion of Ukraine, where he stated: "Ukraine is not just a neighbouring country for us. It is an inalienable part of our own history, culture, and spiritual space".[195] Putin has introduced the term '*russkiy mir*', or the 'Russian world', just as President Vučić in Serbia talks about '*srpski svet*', or the 'Serbian world'. This concept coincides with the Orthodox churches view of Orthodox unity. The Russian Orthodox Church posits that the Russians, Ukrainians and Belarusians are one united civilization due to the postulated common origin in Kievan Rus. It is argued that, in 988, Prince Volodymyr I of Kiev accepted Christianity and established a kingdom that both Russians and Ukrainians see as their predecessor. In his 2021 article, Putin stated:

> I said that Russians and Ukrainians are one people – a single whole […] Russians, Ukrainians, and Belarusians are all descendants of Ancient Rus, which was the largest state in Europe. […] The spiritual choice made by St. Vladimir, who was both Prince of Novgorod and Grand Prince of Kiev, still largely determines our affinity today.[196]

Both in Russia and Serbia, the Orthodox churches are closely connected to the state. In Russia, the relationship was not always easy in the period after the collapse of the Soviet Union.[197] With Putin, the ties are very close. As Betsy Prabo, professor of religious studies at the Western Illinois University, noted: "As representatives of the Russian Orthodox Church and the Russian state, Patriarch Kirill and President Putin are both players in a century-long symphony of church–state relations".[198] In Serbia, the relationship between the Patriarch and Milošević was strained, but President Vučić frequently consults the Patriarch and bishops on important state matters.

A common feature is the anti-Westernism and insistence on traditional values. As in Serbia, these concepts were transferred from the church to

---

193 Vjekoslav Perica, "A Post-Communist Serbo-Russian Romance: Eastern Relic of the Pan-Slavic Myth", in Perica and Gavrilović, 2011, p. 38, see *supra* note 31.

194 Russia, Presidency, "Article by Vladimir Putin: 'On the Historical Unity of Russians and Ukrainians'", 12 July 2021 (https://www.legal-tools.org/doc/tt382m/).

195 Russia, Presidency, "Address by the President of the Russian Federation", 24 February 2022 (https://www.legal-tools.org/doc/gvwvru/).

196 Putin, 2021, see *supra* note 194.

197 Papkova, 2011, see *supra* note 4.

198 Betsy Perabo, "Russia's Unfinished Symphony of Church and State", *Political Theology*, 2 July 2018.

politicians. Patriarch Kirill "managed to sell the concept of traditional values, the concept of Russkiy Mir, to Putin, who was looking for conservative ideology".[199] Kirill has called Putin's long tenure "a miracle of God".[200] In Russia, a National Security Strategy approved by the President in 2021 states that "the Russian spiritual and moral ideals and cultural and historical values […] are the foundation for the further development of the country". That the state has adopted the Russian Orthodox Church's anti-Western attitude, is seen from the same document where it is stated that "traditional Russian spiritual, moral, cultural and historical values are under active attack from the United States and its allies".[201] Lucian N. Leustean argues that religion is also important for Russia's foreign policy, stating that "Russia's security strategy gives prominent weight to concerns about traditional religious values".[202] During Orthodox Easter in 2022, while the war in Ukraine was going on, Putin wrote in a letter to Kirill:

> It is gratifying to know that under your guidance the Church is engaging in fruitful interaction with the state, making a tremendous contribution to promoting traditional spiritual, moral, and family values in society, educating the younger generation, and strengthening concord and mutual understanding between people in these trying times.[203]

Russian leaders adopted a discourse on Crimea akin to the Serbian one on Kosovo. Putin justified the annexation of Crimea by stating that Crimea has "a sacred meaning for Russia, like the Temple Mount for Jews and Muslims", and that Crimea is "the spiritual source of the formation of the multifaceted but monolithic Russian nation".[204]

Just as Kosovo is called "the heart of Serbia", the Donbas is called "the Heart of Russia". The Russian business magazine *Ekspert* published, in 2014,

---

[199] Statement by Sergei Chapnin, a senior fellow in Orthodox Christian studies at Fordham University who worked with Kirill in the Moscow Patriarchate, see Jason Horowitz, "The Russian Orthodox Leader at the Core of Putin's Ambitions", *The New York Times*, 21 May 2022.

[200] *Ibid.*

[201] President of the Russian Federation, Presidential Decree No. 400 validating the National Security Strategy of the Russian Federation, The Kremlin, Moscow, 22 July 2021 (https://www.legal-tools.org/doc/siyy7s/).

[202] Lucian N. Leustean, "When Will Russia's War on Ukraine End? Religion And Security Strategies", *Religion Unplugged*, 23 May 2022.

[203] Joseph Gedeon and Nahal Toosi, "The Pro-Russian Preacher the U.S. Won't Touch", *Politico*, 22 June 2022.

[204] Cited in Perica, 2017, p. 65, see *supra* note 103.

this slogan on its front page, together with a reprint of a Soviet poster from 1921 with the same title, showing the Donbas as a bleeding heart.[205]

The close ties between the Serbian Orthodox Church and Russia, both with church leaders and politicians, can be seen from the many orders that were awarded. In 2007, the Holy Synod of the Serbian Orthodox Church decided that Vladimir Putin should be awarded the Saint Sava Order of the First Degree,

> for his active love towards the Serbian Orthodox Church and Serbian people, particularly shown in a brave and persistent protection of the faithful people, churches, monasteries in Kosovo and Metohija, as well as the preservation of the integrity of the Republic of Serbia.[206]

When Putin visited Belgrade in 2011, Patriarch Irinej awarded him with this highest order of the Serbian Orthodox Church on the occasion of Putin's visit to Saint Sava's Cathedral. The finishing work in Saint Sava's Cathedral was supported by the Russian state and the Russian Orthodox Church. Irinej stated: "Vladimir Vladimirovič Putin is a greater European than all the bureaucrats in Brussels, he returns God into the constitution of the new, right, Christian and Orthodox Russia".[207] Additionally, two Russian ambassadors were bestowed with the Saint Sava Medal on a Cross – Ambassador Alekseyev (2008) and Ambassador Konuzin (2012).

In 2013, Patriarch Kirill visited the town of Niš in Serbia to attend the ceremony marking the 1700th anniversary of the Edict of Milan. In November 2014, Kirill visited Belgrade and stated that "the common faith, common culture [and] close historical ties, the common blood spilled in the name of common victories – all this unites our peoples".[208] The Montenegrin Metropolitan Amfilohije stated, in 2014, that:

> Who is not faithful to Russia, which is of the same language and same faith as us, let his flesh fall off him, let him be cursed three times and 3,000 times by me. This is what Saint Petar of Cetinje learnt his fellow Montenegrins.[209]

---

[205] "Донбасс, сердце России" (Donbas, The Heart of Russia), *Ekspert*, 9–16 June 2014; see Irena Chalupa, "Direct Translation: 'Donbas, the Heart of Russia'", *Atlantic Council*, 13 June 2014.

[206] "Russian Prime Minister Vladimir Putin Awarded the Serbian Orthodox Church's Highest Distinction", *Serbian Orthodox Church*, 24 March 2011.

[207] "Patriarh Irinej on Putin's Visit: A Great Friend and Brother is Coming!", Srbin.info, 16 January 2019.

[208] "Patriarch Kirill urges Europe to Return to Christian Values, Warns against 'Rewriting History'", *Orthodox Christianity*, 14 November 2014.

[209] "Amfilohije: Ko izda Rusiju, dabogda živo meso sa njega otpalo I neka je proklet", *Novosti*, 29 April, 2014.

In 2002, Patriarch Pavle was awarded by the Russian Orthodox Church for his "[e]xtraordinary efforts to unite the Orthodox peoples".[210] In 2021, it was announced that a statue of Patriarch Pavle would be placed at the (Serbian) Church of Saints Peter and Paul in Moscow near the Kremlin.[211]

Milan Dodik, President of the *Republika Srpska*, was awarded the Order of the Holy Emperor Nicholas in 2014 for his merits in the strengthening of friendly relations between Russia and Serbia. Specifically, Patriarch Kirill mentioned that the Dodik was felicitated for "the outstanding work for consolidation of the unity of Orthodox nations and promotion of Christian values in the life of society". Milorad Dodik is known to destroy Bosnia-Herzegovina by demanding sovereignty for *Republika Srpska*. Metropolitan Amfilohije of Montenegro was awarded the same order for his efforts to the glory of the Orthodox Church.[212] Patriarch Irinej stated, in 2012:

> We must resume the guiding values of our spirituality and history. Our faith has guided us towards the East. We must rope our little boat to the big ship of our great Slav brotherly nation to which we are connected by blood and faith.[213]

In 2020, Patriarch Irinej stated:

> The Lord gave the holy Russian people two great personalities that are important not only for Russia, but for the whole Orthodox world and even more broadly: Russian Patriarch Kirill and Russian President Vladimir Putin.[214]

For Serbia, friendship with Russia is important for securing support for the status of Kosovo as a Serbian province. The Russian Patriarch Kirill was active in appealing to the West to help Serbia preserve Kosovo. In 2013, he stated: "We unconditionally support the just stance of the Serbian Orthodox Church concerning Kosovo and Metohija".[215] In 2020, Patriarch Irinej received Foreign Minister Lavrov at the Serbian Patriarchate in Belgrade. It was noted that:

210 "Njegova svetost Patriarh Pavle vratio se iz Moskve", *Informativna služba SPS*, 23 January 2002.

211 "Patriarh Pavle dobije spomenik u centru Moskve", *Politika*, 3 March 2021.

212 Srđan Barišić, "The Role of the Serbian and Russian Orthodox Churches in Shaping Governmental Policies", in Sonja Biserko (ed.), *The Warp of the Serbian Identity*, Helsinki Committee for Human Rights in Serbia, Belgrade, 2016, p. 115.

213 *Večernje novine*, 26 November 2012, quoted in Barišić, 2014, see *supra* note 76.

214 "Patrijarh Lavrovu: Očekujemo veliku pomoć Rusije i Ruske crkve da sačuvamo Kosovo", *Danas*, 18 June 2020.

215 Barišić, 2016, p. 117, see *supra* note 212.

> Minister Lavrov reiterated the support of the Russian government for the territorial integrity and sovereignty of the Republic of Serbia in Kosovo and Metohija. Minister Lavrov expressed his support for the Serbian Orthodox Church in Montenegro as well and pointed out that only by strengthening the unity of Orthodox peoples.[216]

After the meeting, Irinej said: "We want Serbia to retain Kosovo, and hope that God will help us, with the assistance of Russia and wise and honourable people in the world".[217] When Putin, in 2022, used the Western recognition of Kosovo as an argument for declaring two independent states in Donbas, this came as a shock in Serbia, although Serbia continued to rely on Russian support in international fora.

The Russian Orthodox Church also supports the Serbian Orthodox Church's view on Montenegro. Patriarch Kirill has reportedly stated: "All Orthodox Churches consider Montenegro to be part of the canonical territory of the Serbian Patriarchate".[218]

The notion of 'holy war' was a common heritage. In 2016, Kirill stated that "a Christ-loving military never performs evil and unjust acts", but "always fights for justice against evil".[219] Just as the Serbian Church supported Serbian warfare in Yugoslavia, Patriarch Kirill supported Russia's war against Ukraine from the start. He "provided spiritual cover for the invasion of Ukraine".[220] The Patriarch described those opposing the invasion as the 'forces of evil'. A few days after Russia invaded, Kirill said:

> God forbid that the current political situation in fraternal Ukraine, which is close to us, should be aimed at ensuring that the evil forces that have always fought against the unity of Rus and the Russian Church gain the upper hand.[221]

Kirill urged his followers to rally against what he called Moscow's external and internal enemies. Just like Serbian bishops, he awarded icons to officers. "Let this image inspire young soldiers who take the oath, who embark on the path of defending the fatherland", Kirill had intoned as he gave a gilded icon to General Viktor Zolotov during a service at Moscow's Christ the Savior

216 "Russian FM Lavrov Expressed His Support for Serbian Orthodox Church in Montenegro", *Orthodox Times*, 19 June 2020.

217 "Lavrov sa patriarhom Irinejem o Kosovu, Crnoj Gori I SPC", *N1*, 18 June 2020.

218 Barišić, 2016, p. 119, see *supra* note 212.

219 Betsy Perabo, "Russia's Unfinished Symphony of Church and State", *Political Theology Network*, 2 July 2018.

220 Horowitz, 2022, see *supra* note 199.

221 Jeanne Whalen, "Russian Orthodox Leader Backs War in Ukraine, Divides Faith", *The Washington Post*, 18 April 2022.

Cathedral. The precious gift, the General had responded, would protect the troops in their battles against Ukrainian 'Nazis'.[222]

On 27 April 2022, when the war in Ukraine had lasted for more than two months, a talk took place between Patriarch Kirill and Patriarch Porfirije of Serbia through remote video communication. Participating in the talk from the Russian Orthodox Church were also Metropolitan Hilarion and Archpriest Nikolay Balashov. From the Serbian Church, Bishop Irinej of Bačka also participated. As to this meeting, an official Russian report stated:

> During a prolonged brotherly talk, they discussed the events going on in Ukraine. Special attention was given to the humanitarian situation in Donbass. Patriarch Kirill thanked the Patriarch of Serbia for the support and solidarity of the canonical Ukrainian Orthodox Church. "There is the firm belief that in this grave time the Serbian Church is with us", His Holiness said. […] His Holiness Patriarch Porfirije said that the events in Ukraine directly touched his heart and the hearts of fellow-bishops and all the Orthodox Serbian people who also endured hard trials in the end of the twentieth century. "We share your feelings and pray for you and ready to do all that is possible to support the Russian Orthodox Church and the faithful people in Russia and in Ukraine", said the Primate of the Serbian Orthodox Church.[223]

However, unlike the Russian and Serbian churches, the Ukrainian Orthodox Church (Moscow Patriarchate) condemned the Russian invasion of Ukraine. Metropolitan Onufriy criticized Kirill for supporting the war. On 27 May 2022, the Ukrainian Orthodox Church formally cut ties with Moscow and declared independence.[224]

The EU accused Kirill of supporting the invasion of Ukraine and acting as a propagandist for Putin's regime and planned to include him on a list of individuals subject to sanctions, but Hungary objected.[225] The British government, however, imposed sanctions: "Patriarch Kirill has made multiple public statements in support of the Russian invasion of Ukraine".[226] No similar action was made by the EU towards Serbian religious leaders during the wars in the 1990s.

---

222 *Ibid.*

223 "His Holiness Patriarch Kirill's talk with Primate of Serbian Orthodox Church", *Russian Orthodox Church*, 27 April 2022.

224 "The Ukrainian Church of Onoufriy Announced Autonomy from the Patriarchate of Moscow", *Orthodox Times*, 28 May 2022.

225 Jorge Liboreiro, Efi Koutsokosta and Shona Murray, "Patriarch Kirill excluded from EU sanctions after Hungary's Objection", *Euronews*, 2 June 2022.

226 Gedeon and Toosi, 2022, see *supra* note 203.

9.11. Conclusion

In the South Slavic area, national identity is closely connected to religious affiliation. The Serbian Orthodox Church sees itself as a national institution and as the guardian of Serbian culture and traditions. When the Yugoslav conflict developed in the 1980s and the Communist Party's grip gradually loosened, nationalist politicians and intellectuals took up nationalist narratives from the Serbian Orthodox Church. Many members of the former Communist elite adopted a religious nationalistic discourse.

Under Communism, narratives about Serb suffering and victimization were not allowed in public life but were preserved by the Serbian Orthodox Church. Old religious narratives triggered nationalist politics when nationalism substituted Communism. In the period after 1987, the Serbian Orthodox Church actively supported Slobodan Milošević and helped his populism be accepted by carrying pictures of Saint Lazar in political manifestations.

The reason why the Serbian Orthodox Church supported a policy of war and ethnic cleansing can be found in the traditional close relationship between the Serbian Orthodox Church and the state. During the wars that followed the disintegration of Yugoslavia, religious leaders, patriarchs and bishops of the Serbian Orthodox Church, played an important role for the Serbian regime's propaganda and military activities. Religious discourse was an important element in nationalist discourse. However, at a crucial point during the Yugoslav conflict, the Serbian Orthodox Church did not support the head of state, Slobodan Milošević, whom they found too weak and not consistently defending the plan of Greater Serbia. Instead, they supported more extreme nationalists and found such leaders in Bosnia-Herzegovina, where the Orthodox Church was made into a state ideology. Biljana Plavšić was praised by bishops, despite her extreme views. President Karadžič and General Mladić were blessed by the Patriarch and bishops a few days before the Srebrenica massacre. Although some bishops were moderate, even Patriarch Pavle to some extent, the spokesmen of the Serbian Orthodox Church were hardliners.

Church leaders supported the Greater Serbia project and played a direct political role by issuing statements about the actual political situation, writing letters to international peacemakers, protesting peace plans, *et cetera*. The Serbian Orthodox Church denounced all peace plans because the Serbian side was note assigned enough land (the Vance-Owen plan in 1993, the Contact Group plan in 1994, and the Dayton Accords in 1995).

Priests blessed soldiers before they went to the front. Although it was well known that war crimes were committed, the Serbian Orthodox Church denied them. Bishops awarded orders to extreme nationalists and praised their efforts. Two bishops gave orders to Vojislav Šešelj, an extreme chauvinist. Bishops celebrated holidays with paramilitary leaders known to be criminals, such as the infamous Arkan. The Serbian Orthodox Church protested the indictment of Ratko Mladić and Radovan Karadžić.

In post-Milošević Serbia, the Serbian Orthodox Church gained a prominent role in society. The Church supports extreme nationalist movements and political parties. The role of the Serbian Church can be compared to the role that the Russian Orthodox Church plays in Russian politics and cultural life.

It should not be forgotten that there is a process of reconciliation, a Catholic–Orthodox ecumenical rapprochement. Vjekoslav Perica finds that this process began in 2019 and that there are some positive results; he stated that "it seems that moderates have prevailed over zealots. The far right, however, did not cease its hateful propaganda and mythmaking".[227]

The close contact between some religious leaders and extreme nationalists and warmongers made church leaders supportive of the views of these politicians and the crimes of the warlords. By not protesting hate speech or crimes, they became accomplices.

No religious leaders were indicted or investigated by the International Criminal Tribunal for the former Yugoslavia.

[227] Vjekoslav Perica, "All Victims Matter: Reconciliation of the Balkan Faiths and Peoples. An Assessment of Recent Progress", in *Occasional Papers on Religion in Eastern Europe*, December 2020, vol. 40, no. 10, p. 1.

10

Religion and Ethno-Nationalist Extremism in Bosnia and Herzegovina

Majda Halilović*

10.1. Introduction

This chapter draws on two research projects carried out by the Atlantic Initiative in Bosnia and Herzegovina ('BiH') from December 2019 to January 2021.[1] Both projects examined far-right and ethno-nationalist discourse, messaging, narratives, and activities and their impact in communities, politics, and online spaces. This research moved away from the prevailing focus on radicalization and violent extremism linked to the foreign fighter phenomenon and radical Salafism, which the Atlantic Initiative has studied extensively since 2012.[2]

The projects that underpin this chapter produced vast amounts of data, collected through online and in-person surveys, focus groups and individual interviews, in order to document the discourses of ethno-nationalist extremism deployed by all three 'constituent' groups in BiH. However, for the purpose of this anthology, the data and analysis presented in this chapter relates to Serb ethno-nationalism and far-right movements and the Serbian Orthodox Church. Indeed, our research documented a strong and direct relationship between the Serbian Orthodox Church and Serb ethno-nationalism, including many examples of the messaging, language and symbolism of the Church reflected in the

* **Majda Halilović** is Research Manager at the Center for Security and Justice Research (Atlantic Initiative), Sarajevo. She holds a Ph.D. in Sociology and Social Policy from the Open University, and a Master's degree in Sociology of Education from Cambridge University. Since 2000, she has worked on research exploring mental health, social exclusion and discrimination. She is the co-author (with Nejra Veljan) of the 2021 report 'Exploring Ethno-Nationalist Extremism in Bosnia and Herzegovina', published by the Atlantic Initiative. For an audio-visual recording of her statement to CILRAP's conference in Florence in April 2022 on the topic of this anthology, please see https://www.cilrap.org/cilrap-film/220408-halilovic/.

1 One project was funded by the MATRA programme of the Embassy of the Netherlands in BiH; the other by the United States Agency of International Development Office of Transition Initiatives.

2 For example, see Edina Bećirević, *Salafism vs. Moderate Islam: A Rhetorical Fight for the Hearts and Minds of Bosnian Muslims*, Atlantic Initiative, Sarajevo, 2016; Vlado Azinović and Muhamed Jusić, *The New Lure of the Syrian War: The Foreign Fighters' Bosnian Contingent*, Atlantic Initiative, Sarajevo, 2016.

ideas, aspirations and way of life of ethno-nationalist Serbs in BiH and the region.

Thus, it is worth examining how religious leaders within the Serbian Orthodox Church have engaged in hate speech, or at least hate*ful* speech, against Muslims in the former Yugoslavia – particularly Bosniaks[3] – especially when this speech has legitimized the use of violence. This chapter will attempt to uncover the motivations for such speech from the Church and will discuss some of the current regional circumstances that have operated as amplifiers of ethno-nationalist extremism, including the Covid-19 pandemic, the migrant crisis and Montenegro's adoption of its law on religious freedoms. The role of the Serbian Orthodox Church in interpreting events from the politico-military to the medical will also be explored. This is crucial to understand, given that a majority of the populations in Serbia, Montenegro and the Bosnian entity of *Republika Srpska* are members of the Church, which is estimated to have some eight million adherents across its canonical jurisdiction.[4]

10.1.1. Methodology of the Research

From December 2019 to March 2020, the Atlantic Initiative collaborated with a number of civil society organizations and researchers across BiH to explore ethno-nationalism and violent ethno-nationalist extremism in the country for the project, 'The Prevention of Ethno-nationalism and Violent Extremism in Bosnia and Herzegovina', supported by the MATRA funding scheme. This research captured the views of 758 respondents, identified with the help of local researchers from among ethno-nationalist political party members, football hooligans, religious representatives and members or sympathizers of nationalist or far-right organizations. The aim of the research, to improve our understanding of ethno-nationalist extremism in BiH, marked a turn from the focus on Salafism that has dominated extremism research in BiH for a number of years. The project examined individuals, groups and narratives inspired by Serb, Croat and Bosniak ethno-nationalism, and the analysis it produced drew attention to the push and pull factors that lead people to join or support extremist groups, as well as to

---

3 In 1971, Muslims in (the Yugoslav Republic of) BiH were recognized as constituting a unique national identity, but the religious term 'Muslim' (*Muslimani*) was used as a catchall, encompassing even Bosnians who viewed themselves as ethnically, but not religiously, Muslim. Upon independence in 1992, the term 'Bosniak' was widely adopted to refer to ethnic and cultural identity, apart from religious identity. In other words, one can identify as 'Bosniak' but not as religious; and, of course, non-Bosniaks in BiH can be Muslim, such as Roma and Albanian Muslims. Still, in the discourse of the Serb far-right, the terms 'Bosniak' and 'Muslim' are used interchangeably.

4 For more, see Catholic Near East Welfare Association, "The Orthodox Church of Serbia", 19 February 2021.

how these factors relate to mainstream narratives and the politics of grievance. Data was collected from survey responses, which were triangulated, and from far-right web sites, Facebook groups, and other online platforms in both BiH and the region.

From the end of 2020 through the beginning of 2021, the Atlantic Initiative undertook a second project, to investigate the differences between research participants who were attracted to radical content and those who were not. Data was collected in focus groups and surveys that allowed researchers to assess the characteristics of individuals who follow or engage with extreme and far-right online content, to capture why they find the narratives of key influencers appealing, and to explore which parts of these narratives most resonate with them. Altogether, 485 individuals from different parts of BiH completed an online survey, complemented by 12 focus groups comprising 101 participants of different ages and genders. Though focus groups were mostly conducted *via* the Zoom platform, they nonetheless tended to gather participants from the same areas of BiH (meaning, participants from towns in Herzegovina were in one group, those from Sarajevo in another, and so on).

Both of these projects provided in-depth data related to the ideas, motivations, grievances and beliefs of people who sympathize with or espouse far-right narratives; and this data facilitated the contextualization of real-life expressions of extremism and radicalism through the lens of sociological and psychological theory. Notably, these research efforts found that far-right groups within the Bosniak, Croat and Serb ethnic communities in BiH and the region share many characteristics, and these commonalities are discussed in a paper published in 2021.[5] Members of these groups, across ethnicities, have a tendency to socially distance from other groups, feel that their religion and ethnicity is under threat, self-report high levels of religiosity, exhibit animosity towards migrants and sexual minorities and aspire to re-traditionalize society, including by returning women to their 'traditional roles'.

10.2. The Far-Right in Bosnia and Herzegovina and Serbia

In order to understand and map far-right extremist organizations in BiH, as well as their narratives, ideologies and propensities for violence, researchers were faced with the challenge of contextualizing the far-right in BiH. Still, some elements of far-right extremism are relatively universal, and far-right ideologies

[5] Majda Halilović and Nejra Veljan, *Exploring Ethno-Nationalist Extremism in Bosnia and Herzegovina*, Atlantic Initiative, Sarajevo, 2021.

typically feature most, if not all, of five key characteristics: nationalism, racism,[6] xenophobia, calls for a strong state and an anti-democratic attitude.[7] In fact, many far-right groups reject democratic constitutionality and the principle of equality. In the Western Balkans, some of these groups also advocate for the revision of established borders.

Far-right groups rely strongly on populism, especially in BiH. While populism and nationalism are often conflated, as both can serve to accentuate social divisions and promote the idea that a collective is central to an ideal society, they are not interchangeable concepts. Populism positions the people against elites; nationalism positions an in-group against an out-group.[8] In the rhetoric of far-right extremism, however, populism may be instrumentalized to define various out-groups, especially by framing 'the elite' as a homogenous, corrupt entity that cannot be trusted by 'the people'.[9]

In BiH, the complex structure of the Bosnian state itself also plays a role in the rhetoric and goals of far-right extremists. As Norris and Inglehart argue, "[p]opulist leaders knock-down safeguards on executive power by claiming that they, and they alone, reflect the authentic voice of ordinary people and have the capacity to restore collective security against threats".[10] For example, Serb and Croat far-right extremists prefer a weak Bosnian state, aiming at the least to strengthen and empower their own ethnic and identity groups, or in some cases, to undermine the Bosnian state entirely; while Bosniak far-right extremists desire a strong state, in which they dominate political spaces.

Though the relationships between far-right movements and mainstream political parties in BiH are opaque, it is safe to say, as Tamir Bar-On has noted, that political parties which promote nationalism provide the 'master concept' and 'master frame' for far-right extremism with a populist tone and an ambiguous relationship with fascism.[11] This is an extremism driven by perceived threats to national or cultural identity, and because far-right extremists in BiH view

---

6 It is important to understand that Bosniaks have been effectively 'racialized' (within the former Yugoslavia and outside it). This is evident in the ways many Serb and Croat far-right groups characterize Bosniaks and fuels Islámophobia in these groups.

7 Nikki Sterkenburg, "Far-Right Extremism: A Practical Introduction", in *Radicalisation Awareness Network*, 5 December 2019, p. 6.

8 Daphne Halikiopoulou, "'Far Right' Groups May Be Diverse – But Here's What They All Have in Common", *The Conversation*, 27 September 2018.

9 Sterkenburg, 5 December 2019, p. 6, see *supra* note 7.

10 Pippa Norris and Ronald Inglehart, *Cultural Backlash: Trump, Brexit, and Authoritarian Populism*, Cambridge University Press, 2019, p. 6.

11 Tamir Bar-On, "The Radical Right and Nationalism", in Jens Rydgren (ed.), *The Oxford Handbook of the Radical Right*, Oxford University Press, 2018, p. 44.

multiculturalism as a threat, their ideology manifests in a strong opposition to immigration, a longing for ethno-states, fears that the European Union ('EU') is undermining national sovereignty and the condemnation of foreigners as criminal. Indeed,

> [t]he politics of fear drives the search for collective security for the tribe – even if this means sacrificing personal freedoms. In this regard, the 'tribe' refers to an imaginary community demarcated by signifiers of us versus them – our people versus the others.[12]

Across the region, the far-right generally has a strong relationship with religion as well. Orthodox Christian and Catholic extremist groups claim Christianity is under threat in the same way that Salafist groups claim Islám is under threat. Far-right groups in BiH also celebrate the 'traditional family' and other patriarchal norms. Through this lens, a family is comprised of an exclusively heterosexual couple of the same religion and ethnicity, and as many children as possible – which is said to be necessary in order to sustain their endangered ethnic group.

This research shed a bit of light on the kinds of people who are attracted to far-right ideologies in BiH, but as is often true in research of this nature, their diversity belies a 'profile' or easy generalization. Still, it is worth mentioning several studies that have focused on the cognitive and psychological bases of far-right and right-wing attitudes and prejudices. A 2015 meta-analysis found, for instance, that people with lower cognitive ability are more likely to adhere to right-wing attitudes and tend to be more prejudiced toward ethnic minority groups, whereas those with higher cognitive ability are more likely to endorse left-wing beliefs and be less prejudiced.[13] A more recent study that examined emotional abilities (to identify, understand, express and regulate emotions) found similarly that people adhering to right-wing ideologies exhibited lower emotional ability and were more likely to endorse authority and strong leadership and find inequality acceptable.[14]

This question of emotional ability was notable in the context of this research, in which respondents who espoused far-right beliefs also presented themselves as concerned for and responsive to suffering in their communities. Researchers found, however, that there were constraints on this apparent empathy. For example, the organization *Levijatan* (Leviathan) attracted attention for

---

12 Norris and Inglehart, 2019, p. 7, see *supra* note 10.

13 Emma Onraet *et al.*, "The Association of Cognitive Ability with Right-Wing Ideological Attitudes and Prejudice: A Meta-Analytic Review", in *European Journal of Personality*, 2015, vol. 29, no. 6, pp. 599–621.

14 Alain Van Hiel *et al.*, "The Relationship Between Emotional Abilities and Right-Wing and Prejudiced Attitudes", in *Emotion*, 2019, vol. 19, no. 5, pp. 917–922.

the very real concern they showed for the well-being of animals in Serbia and the region, and their efforts to highlight alleged cruelty to animals, yet this same empathy was not extended to people perceived by the organization as being part of an out-group. They intimidated and attacked vulnerable Roma children whom they accused of mistreating animals, as well as migrants they claimed presented a danger.

Far-right groups often coalesce around conspiracy theories, and members often assert that they are more capable than mainstream media or experts of analyzing, synthesizing and making sense of information. This way of thinking is often referred to in far-right circles as 'taking the red pill' or 'getting redpilled', terms used to describe an awakening akin to the journey taken by the character Neo in the film *The Matrix*. The implications of this 'awakening' depend on the context and can manifest as everything, from Holocaust denial to anti-immigrant rhetoric or to anti-vaccine advocacy.[15]

Conspiracy theories can become legitimized on a particularly large scale when should-be experts play a role in shaping and spreading them. Among prominent far-right voices in Serbia, for instance, is Dr. Jovana Stojković – a medical doctor and psychiatrist, and a fierce opponent of mandatory vaccinations.[16] The issue of vaccination is one that is commonly used by far-right groups to attract members because it is a topic that can be wrought with anxiety and confusion for parents, and 'anti-vax' Facebook groups often attract more members than 'pro-vax' groups. As Terje Emberland has noted, conspiracy theories combined with extremist ideals can act as "radicalization multipliers" that have the potential to "lead to a feeling of alienation from and hostility toward society and increase the likelihood of individuals to engage in violence".[17]

Far-right groups in BiH and Serbia have been quick to exploit any political or international crisis over the last several years. The Covid-19 pandemic offered an on-ramp for many individuals who were fearful of the pandemic or skeptical of vaccines to far-right ideas, and the Russian invasion of Ukraine has again presented far-right groups with an opportunity to show their allegiance with perceived allies and step up their activities. In Serbia, for example, Predrag Petrović has described the speed with which anti-migrant groups, fascist groups and neo-Chetniks have come together to support the Russian invasion of

[15] Samantha Kutner, "Swiping Right: The Allure of Hyper Masculinity and Cryptofascism for Men Who Join the Proud Boys", in *International Centre for Counter-Terrorism*, May 2020.

[16] Stojković took on the issue of conspiracy theories in a video she recorded, referring to them as the ability to anticipate events and form different and critical thinking to that offered by the authorities.

[17] Terje Emberland, "Why Conspiracy Theories Can Act as Radicalization Multipliers of Far-Right Ideals", *RightNow!*, 24 February 2020 (available on its web site).

Ukraine.[18] On the streets of Belgrade, as well as in BiH and Montenegro, and in the online space, Serb ethno-nationalists have declared that Russians and Serbs are brothers, that Crimea is Russia, that Kosovo is Serbia and that Serbia sits firmly on the side of Russia. These same groups often demonstrate their support for Serb war criminal Ratko Mladić.

Petrović notes that extreme far-right organizations such as *Narodna patrola* (Peoples' Patrole), an anti-migrant organization made up of members who behave as if they are in a paramilitary, present themselves as saviors of the Serb nation from its enemies, especially Muslim migrants. The group regularly stops and intimidates migrants and would like to conduct citizens arrests. Though originally registered under the name 'No surrender to Kosovo', *Narodna patrola* quickly adjusted their focus as the migrant crisis gained significant media attention. Now, the group is a fierce supporter of the Russian invasion of Ukraine and an example of how the far-right in Serbia and in BiH views Putin's Russia.[19]

According to Petrović, the common denominator among Serb extreme far-right organizations is an ideology known as 'Saint Sava nationalism'. The ideology originated in the 1930's as the brainchild of Nikolaj Velimirović, bishop of the Serbian Orthodox Church, and combines Serb nationalism with Orthodox clericalism. It elevates the Serb nation to the rank of a saint, describes Serbs as a 'heavenly people', and advocates for a return to 'traditional' (that is, medieval) values such as piety, chivalry and the establishment of an Orthodox monarchy within historical borders. Adherents of the ideology resolutely reject Western culture, globalization, democracy, liberalism, human rights, republicanism and anti-fascism, but also ecumenism.[20] There is an undeniable symmetry between these ideals and the values promoted by Aleksandar Dugin, the Russian philosopher close to Putin who blames global elites for war and advocates the return of pre-modern values in the frame of a 'civilizational struggle'. Like Serb ethno-nationalists in the Western Balkans who dream of a 'Greater Serbia', Dugin envisions a 'Greater Russia' and has referred to Russians as "the people of the Empire".[21] For Dugin, Serbia thus holds a special status, not only because he sees it as a small state willing to stand up to the 'global elite', but because he

18 Predrag Petrović, "'Srbi i Rusi braća zauvek': Podrška ekstremnih desničara invaziji Putinove Rusije na Ukrajinu", *Atlantic Initiative*, 28 March 2022 (available on the Atlantic Initiative's web site).

19 *Ibid.*

20 *Ibid.*

21 Alexander R. Ross and Shane Burley, "Into the Irrational Core of Pure Violence: On the Convergence of Neo-Eurasianism and the Kremlin's War in Ukraine", in *The New Fascism Syllabus*, 4 March 2022 (available on its web site).

views it as the rightful heir to all of the Western Balkans, and believes Serbia should control this territory, with the support of Russia.[22]

Achieving Serb dominance in the region requires that homogenous Serb identities are built across the Western Balkans, and our research found that the Serbian Orthodox Church plays a decisive role in this effort by providing a frame for the opinions of many Serbs (even those who are not associated with far-right groups), introducing new ideas to adherents and influencing the behavior of Serbs as it relates to everything from their lifestyle to the political choices they make. In this sense, the degree to which the Church creates a supportive context for the expansionist politics of Serbs in both BiH and Serbia must be acknowledged. The Church did not assume this role overnight, but has been engaged in a systematic project of expansionism for centuries, which continues today and evolved amid the wars waged by Serbia in the 1990s.

10.3. The Role of the Serbian Orthodox Church in Promoting and Maintaining Serb Ethno-Nationalism and Far-Right Extremism in the Western Balkans

In his 2001 book, *Srpska pravoslavna crkva u ratu i ratovi u njoj* (The Serbian Church in war and wars within it), Milorad Tomanić provides a thorough account of the history of the Church and its role in the wars that followed the breakup of Yugoslavia.[23] He discusses the position of the Church during Serbia's turbulent social, economic and political transition, and contextualizes this against the long period of communist rule, when religion and religious expression were suppressed and relegated to private spaces. Indeed, under Tito's socialist government, following World War II, it was unpopular to openly declare any attachment to religion or to practice religious rituals, and thus, many people detached themselves from faith and the Church. It was popular to view this as the atheization of socialist society, but sociologists of religion at the time saw it as an indicator of the process of secularization.[24]

As Yugoslavia weakened, the Church sought to avoid conflict with those holding political power. After the death of Tito in 1980, some Church circles began establishing and strengthening their presence in public and media spaces. Then, in the early 1980s, new forces in the Church started to rehash Serb grievances related to the autonomy of Kosovo, and linked these grievances to threats to Serbs from 'others'. They called to spiritually and literally protect Serbs in

[22] Petrović, 28 March 2022, see *supra* note 18.

[23] Milorad Tomanić, *Srpska pravoslavna crkva u ratu i ratovi u njoj*, Medijska knjižara Krug, Belgrade, 2001.

[24] Mirko Blagojevic, "Desecularization of Contemporary Serbian Society", in *Occasional Papers on Religion in Eastern Europe*, 2008, vol. 28, no. 1, pp. 37–50.

Kosovo and Metohija.[25] Previously communist politicians and Serb intellectual elites welcomed the opportunity to engage another actor (the Church) in their political agenda and to use Orthodox Christianity as a means of consolidating national and religious sentiment. As Tomanić notes, Vuk Drašković and other communists and Marxists who had once criticized religion as the opium of the masses came rushing into Orthodox churches, displacing religious grannies and forming an even stronger bond with Church leaders.[26]

As this period of religious revival unfolded, nationalist intellectual elites in Serbia did not stand idly by, drawing the Church further into daily life and politics through their role as interpreters of social and political conditions. Tomanić shows that Serb nationalists used the grievances of Serbs *vis-à-vis* the status of Kosovo and claims that Serbs were surrounded by enemies, to mainstream a concept of Serb victimhood by the 1980s. They rather deftly employed narratives that were steeped in national mythology, which is not inherently inciteful and can be sources of cultural pride, but which served during conflict as a way to encourage militancy, brutality and mass hysteria.[27] Indeed, the great appeal of the Church to Serb ethno-nationalists is its capacity to provide an ideology, legitimacy and mystical appeal to the idea of a Greater Serbia, especially in times of turmoil and crisis; something that politicians alone have been incapable of doing, demonstrates Tomanić.

This combination – of politics, influential intellectuals, religion and propaganda – is a recipe for the manipulation of citizens and was used successfully during the war in BiH (1992–1995) to draw Serbs into a bloody conflict under the guise of righteous defense of Serbs. Following the Bosnian referendum on independence, and subsequent international recognition of BiH as an independent state, Serbia commenced a military onslaught that lasted three and a half years. From the start, the Serbian Orthodox Church openly supported Serb military and paramilitary formations, seemingly indifferent to the systemic mass atrocities carried out by these forces against non-Serbs, much less the genocide committed against Bosniaks. Church leaders offered prayers and blessings to those who fought for Serbs and Serb unity across the region and promoted the idea that wherever Serbs live and bury their dead should be a part of Serbia. Senior priests even traveled to the war zone to bless the Serb forces that were shelling civilians in besieged Sarajevo; and anointed soldiers known to have

25 Tomanić, 2001, see *supra* note 23.

26 *Ibid.*

27 *Ibid.*

engaged in the most brutal atrocities, including those from Chetnik formations who were responsible for the mass rape of Bosniak and Croat women.[28]

In her book *Genocide on Drina River*, genocide scholar Edina Bećirević explains in detail how Serb leaders managed to mobilize and radicalize so many Serbs, including those who had previously lived in peace with non-Serbs, to such a degree that they were prepared to commit horrific and habitual crimes. According to Bećirević, this was only possible due to a centuries-long process in which notions of Serb victimhood were carefully crafted through ideology, propaganda and myth, but also through the real history of battles won and lost. Over time, Muslims became the primary target of Serb animosity and were framed as the most significant threat to their survival, which served as a platform for mobilization in the 1990s.[29] When the North Atlantic Treaty Organization's ('NATO') military intervention on Serb military positions brought the war in BiH to an end in 1995, and especially after NATO engaged yet again in Serbia in 1999 to end the war in Kosovo, Serb nationalist politicians filtered these interventions through the lens of Serb victimhood, framing any tragedy emanating from the conflicts as a tragedy for Serbs. In this way, they effectively strengthened Serb unity.

During the wars in BiH and Kosovo, the fact that Orthodox priests played a role in lifting spiritual morale and providing guidance and encouragement to soldiers and paramilitary formations imbued the conflicts with a religious relevance. In the years after the wars, the Serbian Orthodox Church has only grown more potent in public and more present in media, which has intensified its impact even in secular institutions. In BiH, for instance, it has become a common practice for Orthodox priests to bless or 'baptize' schools or public institutions. The Church has become omnipresent in any part of BiH where Serbs make up the majority, assuming a role it has never played before in modern times. Its activities have contributed significantly to creating the perception that the Bosnian entity of *Republika Srpska* is an exclusively Serb territory – an idea strongly supported by influential political and media circles in Serbia. This symbolic conquest of space has included joint celebrations for Bosnian Serbs and Serbs as well as pan-Serbian holidays, and has facilitated the clericalization of politics and society across borders.

---

28 The Chetniks are a Serb nationalist and monarchist paramilitary and political organization, formed initially during the Ottoman Empire's domination of the Balkans. During World War II, they collaborated with the Italians and Germans in the fight against communist partisans. With the rise of communist Yugoslavia, they were pushed out of public view, but in the 1990s, were mobilized by Serb ultra-nationalists for the wars waged by Serbia as a paramilitary force.

29 Edina Bećirević, *Genocide on the Drina River*, Yale University Press, New Haven, 2014, pp. 39–44.

As part of this process of clericalization, the Church has used symbolism, stories of martyrdom and the assertion that others, especially Muslims, are enemies of Orthodoxy and therefore less worthy, leading them down the dangerous path of dehumanizing Bosniaks. Though this process began long before the war, it was historically less obvious, shrouded in and communicated through art, poetry, fairy tales and music. Now, this culture and mythology of supremacy remain, but they exist alongside overt hate speech and derision regularly directed at Bosniaks, and the negation by the Church of Bosniak identity, language, culture and religion. This rhetoric can compel some citizens with similar views to be manipulated and mobilized towards potential conflict.

As Mitja Velikonja has observed:

> Religions, their traditional symbols and rhetoric remain important and extremely persuasive elements of contemporary national and political mythologies and their iconography. Although latently present all the time, they are particularly exposed during the critical periods in a nation's history. As such, they must not be treated as something that is neither *a priori* tolerant nor militant; neither in advance conciliative nor destructive; neither necessarily oriented toward friendship nor toward enmity; neither *a priori* zealot nor well-intentioned. In short, they are neither hateful nor peaceful in advance: their current interpretations and practical activities make them become such. The cross and the crescent are easily transformed into the sword, and the brilliance of faith, as comprehended by believers, into the glare of the blade. The step from mythomaniac theory to bloodthirsty terror is a small one; any creed can be transformed into a ruthless beast.[30]

This is true across contexts and cultures, but the potential for religion to spark real crisis in the Western Balkans is frequently on display. For instance, as some of the research from which this chapter is drawn was underway in late December 2019, a major crisis in Montenegro was triggered by the adoption of a law on religious freedoms, which provoked nationwide protests by Serbs in Montenegro and led to heated debates around the region.[31] Several satellite demonstrations were also held in *Republika Srpska*. By putting many properties of the Serbian Orthodox Church in Montenegro under the official control of the

---

30 Mitja Velikonja, "Religious Symbolism in the Balkan Wars 1991–1995", in *International Journal of Politics, Culture, and Society*, 2003, vol. 17, no. 1, pp. 25–40.

31 Montenegro, Law on the Freedom of Religion and Beliefs and Legal Status of Religious Communities, 27 December 2019 (https://www.legal-tools.org/doc/34ssyi/). According to the law, *inter alia*, if religious communities in Montenegro cannot prove property ownership extending to before 1918 (when Montenegro joined the Kingdom of Serbs, Croats and Slovenes), their property belongs to the state.

government, the aim of the law was to mitigate the power and growth of the Church, which acts as an agent of Serbian politics in Montenegro. Yet, the Church used passage of the law as an opportunity to strengthen its position and led protests against the government of Milo Đukanović from December 2019 until the elections in August 2020.

These protests took the form of public liturgies (*litija*) and occurred in an environment of palpable tension, raising security concerns in cities across Montenegro. Substantial support for these protests came from the political establishments in both Serbia and *Republika Srpska*, including from opposition parties. Politicians, public figures, musicians and people of all generations demonstrated together in an undeniable expression of the power of the Serbian Orthodox Church to unite Serbs by positioning Serbdom over state. As these liturgies took place during the height of the Covid-19 pandemic, despite bans on public gatherings, they offered another opportunity for the Church to illustrate that it is above the law and is not subject to secular rules.

The demonstrations led by the Church contributed to the unseating of Montenegro's pro-Western government in favour of the rule of pro-Serb and pro-Russian parties. And, a year after the controversial law was passed, the new government of Montenegro amended it to remove any elements perceived as taking power from the Serbian Orthodox Church. Emboldened, the Church celebrated the inauguration of its new Metropolitan with defiance. The decision to anoint Bishop Joanikije II as head of the Church at a historic monastery associated with Montenegrin independence in Cetinje, the former capital of Montenegro, offended many citizens and provoked ethnic tensions and violent clashes with the police; but the new Metropolitan arrived to his inauguration by helicopter under the protection of police, who dispersed hundreds of protesters with tear gas before the ceremony got underway.

10.4. The Covid-19 Crisis as an Amplifier of Extremism

In 2020, the Soufan Center predicted that the "fallout from the coronavirus pandemic" could present "devastating opportunities for recruiting extremists of all shades" – from religious extremism which instrumentalizes the idea that a pandemic is either 'God's will' or 'God's judgment' to far-right extremism which claims that ethnic minorities (and policies that welcome them) are the source of disease.[32] On top of this, the pandemic increased isolation, while the opportunity to spread ideas online remained; and in the meantime, systems developed to help and support vulnerable people have in many cases weakened. Research undertaken by the Atlantic Initiative confirms this prediction of the Soufan Center.

[32] "IntelBrief: The Coronavirus Will Increase Extremism Across the Ideological Spectrum", *The Soufan Center*, 13 April 2020.

We have also observed how exploitation of the Covid-19 crisis by far-right groups has fed a rise in radicalization, inside and outside of BiH, and we expect this to have both short- and long-term effects.

In the short term, the impacts of this radicalization are likely to disrupt social cohesion, and, in BiH, this may increase social segregation among ethnic communities. But longer-term shifts in regional views of the West are also emerging from the far-right rhetoric that has developed during the pandemic. For example, pro-Russian narratives that were already key to the discourse of many Serb ethno-nationalist groups have been harnessed more broadly to damage perceptions of the West. The pandemic has served as a springboard for extremist groups to emphasize the corruption of Western countries and their lack of international solidarity, along with various other negative effects of globalization. Anti-European and anti-American sentiment is pervasive, not only in far-right ethno-nationalist and anti-vaccination groups, but in the mainstream media. This could negatively affect the image of Euro-Atlantic allies in BiH and the region for some time and potentially change the views of citizens on Euro-Atlantic integration.

To that end, citizens in the region are acutely aware that the EU has not only failed to garner solidarity among its own members in recent years, but has failed Western Balkan countries specifically. The only country in the region that managed to roll out a successful vaccination programme is Serbia, which acquired early donations of vaccine from Russia and China, bypassing the EU entirely. In fact, from the beginning of the pandemic, both Russia and China engaged in a battle for the ‘hearts and minds’ of people across the region, first by providing medical aid and then by providing vaccines. This has presented various challenges from the standpoint of democracy-promotion in a still-consolidating state, in part because it is hard to explain why authoritarian countries demonstrate more international solidarity than liberal democratic ones.

It is also more difficult in these circumstances to engage in discussion about the ways in which Russia and China represent malign influences in the Western Balkans; and it is fair to assume that this kind of very public pandemic diplomacy is at least partly intended to have this effect. Hence, many citizens in the region may accept the narrative that the Chinese and Russian governments value their lives more than Western governments and NATO allies do. The pandemic has marked a historic moment, and it is disappointing that Western allies have not shown more willingness to seize it by providing swift and consistent aid to the region. When the Covid-19 crisis began, the only relevant battle for ‘hearts and minds’ in BiH was the one fought over vaccines, which Moscow and Beijing recognized while Washington, D.C., and Brussels did not. The focus of Western governments on promoting inclusive narratives and fighting conspiracy theories in BiH is important, but they must also show concern for the individual well-being of everyday Bosnian citizens.

Unfortunately, the Serbian Orthodox Church showed almost no such concern during the pandemic and has suffered little for it. The role of the Church was especially prominent in the midst of the crisis, as people turned towards religion for comfort, but it ignored Covid-19 protection measures and gave license to adherents to do so, too. Even at the height of the pandemic, the Church held services in small, poorly ventilated buildings and continued to offer holy communion. Serb participants in our research largely justified the Church's noncompliance with measures to mitigate the spread of Covid-19 and most were reluctant to criticize the Church or the refusal of individual priests to introduce protection measures in their own congregations. Participants were asked, for instance, about the fact that these measures were not followed during the burials of both Montenegrin Metropolitan Amfolohije or Serbian Patriarch Irinej, and most explained this away as a function of deep beliefs that are hard to articulate, saying that Church has its own ways of doing things and should not be questioned. Still, it was a somewhat astonishing scene at the funeral of Amfilohije, who died of Covid-19, when thousands of people crowded around his dead body, many kissing him on the forehead. Needless to say, more Covid-19 related deaths followed in the Church, yet the Church has not publicly reflected on how its practices shaped or contributed to this tragic outcome.

The Church also promoted some of the various conspiracies that emerged in online spaces during the pandemic, especially related to vaccination. Before his death, Amfilohije dismissed the vaccine, claiming that "religious pilgrimages act as 'God's vaccine'".[33] This made the Church bedfellows with a number of far-right groups and figures that fiercely opposed mandatory vaccination. The Church very much played into this agenda and was nearly crippled by its own radicalizing narratives. Not only did Amfilohije and Irinej both die from Covid-19 in succession, the latter after presiding over the funeral of the former, but weeks later, the bishop who conducted part of Irinej's service also tested positive for the virus (for a second time). On top of this, Montenegro's new Metropolitan had also contracted the virus, so that his high-profile and security-laden inauguration was followed by weeks of isolation. Ironically, as outcry grew that the Church was being irresponsible, and criticism was levelled even by Serbian President Aleksandar Vučić, Church officials and priests awaited direction from the Holy Synod, which could not deliberate because three of its five members

33 Guy Delauney, "Serbia Coronavirus: The Church Losing Its Leaders to the Pandemic", *BBC*, 20 November 2020.

were either dead or severely ill with the virus.[34] Under pressure, the Church did shift to some extent on this issue, and Serbian Patriarch Porfirije has encouraged both vaccination and respect for protection measures. However, few Orthodox priests have made it a requirement for congregants to wear masks during weekly services or other religious ceremonies.[35]

10.5. Islámophobia as a Driver of Extremism

The people of BiH suffered untold horrors during the 1992–1995 war, which was instigated by leaders in Belgrade with the aim of establishing a Greater Serbia by ethnically cleansing the country's Muslim population. This project was ideologically supported by propaganda that spanned politics, religion and media in order to demonize Bosnian Muslims, resulting in at least 100,000 deaths, 30,000 enforced disappearances, the rape of some 30,000 women and girls and genocide in Srebrenica. Thus, the majority of victims were Bosniaks, many of whom were buried in hidden mass graves across the country that are still being discovered nearly 30 years later. The Islámophobic nature of the Serb aggression in BiH manifested in the deliberate destruction by Serb (and Croat) forces of an estimated 600 mosques and other Islámic religious objects.

When the 1995 Dayton Peace Agreement brought the war to an end, it did so by cementing the bulk of on-the-ground gains of the Serb campaign of aggression and genocide, which stopped the fighting in the short term but almost certainly deepened divides in the long term. The post-war years did not bring about a systematic reckoning with mass atrocities by those who committed them either, which left space for the development of multiple historical narratives of the war. Eventually, historical revisionism presenting the victims as perpetrators emerged among Serbs to justify the mass atrocities and brutal destruction of the conflict. Coupled with the fact that aspirations for a Greater Serbia are still very much alive in BiH and in Serbia, these revisionist narratives have the potential to powerfully influence regional relations. Thus, it remains crucial that interreligious understanding and tolerance are strengthened in BiH, while acknowledging complex and painful shared histories.[36]

Muslims in BiH have been the target of hateful speech and actions since the 1990s, sometimes expressed more openly, sometimes more symbolically; and sometimes expressed through violence. The environment that makes this possible is due in part to the role of the Serbian Orthodox Church and Serb

34 *Ibid.*

35 "Serbian Patriarch Tests Positive for Covid-19", *Euractiv*, 11 January 2022.

36 Hikmet Karčić, "Islamophobia in Bosnia and Herzegovina: National Report, 2019", in Enes Bayraki and Farid Hafez (eds.), *European Islamophobia Report*, Foundation for Political, Economic and Social Research (SETA), 2020.

political establishment in supporting and glorifying internationally indicted war criminals and denying the responsibility of Serbs for war crimes. One especially disturbing illustration of this was the case of Fata Orlović, which received significant media attention across the world when it reached the European Court of Human Rights. Orlović, a Bosniak who lost 22 family members in the Srebrenica genocide, returned to her home in nearby Konjević Polje after the war to find that an Orthodox church had been built in her backyard, right next to her destroyed home. She rebuilt her house and then began what would be a two-decade battle to remove the church. The symbolism of this choice by the Church, to erect a new house of worship on Orlović's property, is rather evident and her protest was to be expected. Yet, neither the Church nor the local Serb population showed any sympathy for her struggle, instead subjecting her to threats, intimidation, and hate speech for years. Nonetheless, she finally won her legal fight in 2021 and the Church was removed on the order of the Court in June of that year.[37]

Over the past decade, the rise of the Islamic State in Syria and Iraq has fueled a growth of Islámophobia in BiH. Though the country has seen few terrorist attacks, the new focus on global terrorism and the departure of foreign fighters from the Balkans and Europe to join the Islamic State reinforced the already strong Islámophobia of Serb ethno-nationalists. It mattered little that the Islámic community in BiH made concerted efforts to distance itself from radical Islámism and that security agencies surveilled anyone perceived as a threat to security or known to be practicing radical Islám.[38] In fact, numerous significant co-ordinated efforts between Bosnian security agencies, non-governmental organizations and other institutions to combat terrorism, including radical Islám, were exploited by Serb and Croat extremists to frame Islám as a danger to modernity and Christianity and to stigmatize all Muslims as a terror threat.

Another phenomenon that has fed Islámophobia in the region has been the international migrant crisis that first hit Europe in 2015. Beginning in 2017, migrants found their way to BiH when Serbia and Hungary closed their borders and Serbian authorities encouraged migrants to travel to BiH to ease their own domestic burden. The Croatian police were also in the habit of capturing migrants and sending them back over the border to BiH. This influx of migrants, many from Asia and Africa, helped feed the conspiracy theories pushed by many Serb ethno-nationalist politicians and media in BiH and drove new waves of Islámophobia, which was clearly reflected in our research.

---

[37] "Illegal Serbian Orthodox Church on Bosniak Woman's Land Is Demolished", *Los Angeles Times*, 5 June 2021.

[38] For more on the foreign fighter phenomenon, see Azinović and Jusic, 2016, see *supra* note 2.

Increasingly, Islámophobia is converging with the political rhetoric of mainstream Serb and Croat politicians in BiH as well, and this appears to be having an effect at the community level. In 2019 alone, Islámophobic incidents were recorded across the country, ranging from symbolic to violent. Among them, the Srebrenica Genocide Memorial in Potočari was desecrated with a bag of pork intestines. On a shared Instagram account, two Serb members of the Bosnian Armed Forces posted a video of themselves singing songs containing hate speech against Muslims. The entrance to the women's section of the Čaršijska Mosque in Prijedor and the garage belonging to the mosque were vandalized with offensive Serb nationalist graffiti. In Kozarac, near Prijedor, Bosniak returnee Azrin Hodžić was physically and verbally attacked for having a Bosnian flag sticker on his truck.[39]

Karčić has identified three categories of people who are central to spreading Islámophobia in BiH: (i) academic and semi-academic circles in Serbia and *Republika Srpska*, most notably Serbian 'experts' on security, terrorism and Islám; (ii) certain high-ranking officials in the Serbian Orthodox Church; and (iii) politicians, including Bosnian Serbs and Bosnian Croats, as well as Serbians and Croatians. These groups all make statements that are either anti-Muslim or are derisive about Bosniaks.[40] Just one example of this is a statement made in 2018 by Milorad Dodik and published in the media, in which he used the very derogatory term *arlaukanje* (inarticulate, beastly shouting) to refer to the Muslim call to prayer.

The hate directed towards Muslims by these groups of influencers is recycled at the community level and in online spaces. Many instances of speech that dehumanizes Muslims, includes offensive political rhetoric, or frames Sarajevo as a dangerous place for non-Muslims have been identified by researchers, including during in-person interactions with study participants. For instance, when asked how they perceive Sarajevo, some participants said they view it as 'the city of Balije' (a derogatory term for Bosnian Muslims) or 'the city of Muslims', or that it makes them think of '*mújahidín*'. Some even compared the Federation of BiH to the Islamic State. Similar sentiments were captured in our analysis of far-right online spaces, where Muslims are referred to as 'Turks' or diminished as 'Serbs who adopted Islám'. It is also common to find examples online of genocide denial, verbal abuse directed against Muslims as a

39 Karčić, 2020, see *supra* note 36.

40 *Ibid.*

community and the ridicule of Islámic practices including the choice by some women to wear *hijáb*.[41]

10.6. New Generations of Extremist Expression

Throughout both of the research projects that underlie this chapter, we encountered young people whose realities are framed by concerning social trends. They view a high degree of social distance and animosity against the 'other' as norms, and lack any perspective regarding how different ethnicities can live together in inclusive community.[42] Many of these young people are university-educated or current students, which gives them a sense of confidence that they are viewing the events and dynamics of the Balkans and the world with clarity. They worry about the future, tend to talk about the threat faced by their religious or ethnic group and are preoccupied by what they view as Western conspiracies to frame Serbs in a negative light. These youth have not been exposed to forms of social interaction that would mitigate the norm of social distance to which they are accustomed; apparently, the life lived by their parents in the former Yugoslavia, where social distance based on religion or ethnicity was viewed as shameful and politicly incorrect, is the distant past. In fact, a significant number of these young respondents said they would not marry someone from a different ethnic group and would prefer not to have political representatives, teachers or professors of a different ethnicity.

A very strong view, expressed by a radicalized Serb research participant from *Republika Srpska* is indicative of the way social distance is often reflected in rhetoric of the far-right as a defensive posture in response to past betrayals:

> While Croats gave birth to Croats, Muslim women gave birth to Muslims, Serb women gave birth to Yugoslavs. The Serbian people feel that today and that is why these online pages that fight against chauvinism were created. There was a knife in the back three times, now maybe a fourth […]. I mean, it won't happen again. There is no more brotherhood and unity.

---

41 See, for example, Sead Turčalo and Hikmet Karčić (eds.), *Bosnian Genocide Denial and Triumphalism: Origins, Impact and Prevention*, Faculty of Political Science, University of Sarajevo, 2021; Edina Bećirević, "25 Years After Srebrenica, Genocide Denial Is Pervasive. It Can No Longer Go Unchallenged", *Euronews*, 11 July 2020.

42 Affective social distance is among the greatest causes of concern among sociologists. Defined by Emory Bogardus, who created the Bogardus Social Distance Scale, affective social distance refers to the degree to which a person from one group feels sympathy or empathy for persons from other groups. The Bogardus scale measures this distance by establishing the willingness of a person to interact with people from other groups. See Darin M. Mather, Stephen W. Jones and Scott Moats, "Improving upon Bogardus: Creating a More Sensitive and Dynamic Social Distance Scale", in *Survey Practice*, 2017, vol. 10, no. 4.

Social distance alone is not a predictor of radicalization, but it is directly linked with the formation of prejudices and biases. Thus, it has the potential to deepen discrimination among groups and can be the cause of a lack of dialogue and further exclusion, which are pull factors for radicalization. Several Serb research participants shared individual experiences to which they attributed the development of their own increased animosity towards other ethnic groups. However, these experiences may have served instead as a confirmation bias for already existing beliefs and animosities. For example, one woman felt a man in the Federation of BiH had been rude to her because she wore a cross, and this had led her to hold generally negative views of Bosniaks. Another participant said his dislike of Bosniaks was cemented when he got into a fistfight in a Sarajevo bar after sharing his very offensive and derogatory views of Bosniaks, which he took as proof that Bosniaks are incapable of dialogue.

United Nations Development Programme ('UNDP') research indicates that social ties and connections in BiH have experienced a decline over the past decade, with a notable decrease in friendships and interactions between individuals of diverse ethnic backgrounds.[43] Still, measures of social distance are simply indicators of underlying issues that lurk beneath the surface, and in this case, these respondents had already exhibited an attraction to or affiliation with ideologies that promote social distance. It is worth noting with caution, however, that a high degree of social distance may be a predictor of potential violence, as it is associated with low levels of empathy for others.

Across all demographics, young people are voracious consumers of online content, so it was an important finding of our research that online Orthodox religious content is quite popular among young Serbs who express extremist views. This content gained more attention and popularity in 2020 as a result of the tensions surrounding the Serbian Orthodox Church in Montenegro. Young respondents who participated in our research said they follow content that offers wisdom and concern for the future of Serbs. Gojko Perović, a priest of the Serbian Orthodox Church in Montenegro, is among the figures they view as wise, intelligent and interesting. Montenegrin politician Zdravko Krivokapić is also popular because he is seen as a champion of Serbs. And a few participants said they follow Serbian politician Vojislav Šešelj because they support his party. Some also mentioned the Canadian psychologist and conservative influencer Jordan Peterson, who they believe is applying reason in a time of "shaky

43 UNDP, "Social Inclusion in Bosnia and Herzegovina. 2020 National Human Development Report", 2020, p. 110.

Western civilization values".[44] Several participants said they follow Arno Guyon as well. Guyon, who promotes far-right narratives of Serb grievance and ethno-nationalism, was appointed in 2020 by the Serbian government to serve as acting director of the Directorate for Cooperation with the Diaspora and Serbs in the region.[45]

Across respondents in the focus groups for this research, the most popular online content made claims about protecting the interests of the in-group, or 'their' people, and preserving the "truth about the suffering of their people". Religious and ethnic affiliation was very important to almost all of these respondents, who were identified by their ties to or sympathies for far-right groups, and this was particularly visible among Serbs, many of whom follow online groups that promote 'tradition' and the safeguarding of the homeland. One Serb respondent commented that "people who do not have the respect for their traditions are not a whole people and cannot be considered a strong people". Another stressed the importance of national symbols, flags, historic dates and figures and Serb history in general to his identity, which he said makes him "spiritually rich". Interestingly, some participants appear to have joined nationalist groups as a reaction to critiques of Serbian politics from liberal Serbs. One described these critiques as destructive and threatening to Serbs and asserted that they are aimed at wiping out history and all things sacred to the Serb people. He offered this as a key reason he had joined a group that publicizes the historical grievances suffered by Serbs.

In online spaces, algorithms meant to keep users engaged are designed to foster confirmation bias. In other words, by searching for information on perceived threats to a group, one is likely to be led to more content that confirms this threat. In fact,

---

44 Peterson, who has become an internet celebrity, asserts that feminists have "an unconscious wish for brutal male domination", has called developing nations "pits of catastrophe", and told a reporter that he supports "enforced monogamy". See Zack Beauchamp, "Jordan Peterson, the Obscure Canadian Psychologist Turned Right-Wing Celebrity, Explained", *Vox*, 21 May 2018.

45 Although the public in Serbia knows Guyon as a humanitarian who helps Serbs in Kosovo, his political activity in France is marked by participation in the extreme right-wing Bloc of Identitarians – a movement founded in 2003 by members of the far-right group Unité Radicale, which was banned after a sympathizer attempted to assassinate French President Jacques Chirac in 2002. From France, the extremist Identitarian movement has spread to other parts of Europe. Guyon was appointed acting director of the Directorate for Cooperation with the Diaspora and Serbs in the region on 26 November 2020. See Nevena Bogdanović, "Arno Guyon – od ekstremne desnice do funkcije u Vladi Srbije", *Radio Slobodna Europa*, 27 November 2020.

> [m]ost social media platforms use algorithms to *make sure* people find more of the same information and feel confirmed in their beliefs […]. They want to comfort people and not unsettle them. If information is perceived as too unsettling, people might start avoiding the platform (emphasis added).[46]

This kind of confirmation bias in a sort of constant feedback loop has almost certainly informed the narratives, behaviours and expression of beliefs we encountered among young research participants, some of whom exhibited very concerning extremist sympathies. These respondents grew up in a climate of 'othering' that has been fed by the anonymity of online engagement, where the propensity to stigmatize others is common. In these spaces, many young Serbs are reviving centuries-old grievances and nurturing a collective identity based on religious teachings of sacrifice, and on notions of victimhood and nationalism. The increased religiosity observed in these youth and their tendency to follow religious teachings without question, may make them susceptible to radicalization; but it also normalizes a certain degree of cognitive dissonance, required to engage deeply with the excruciating details of their own people's suffering while denying the well-documented atrocities committed by their people against others. [47]

It can be very difficult for youth to escape the yoke of nationalism, especially because those who do leave far-right groups and begin to think more critically or promote tolerance and respect are often branded as traitors. Indeed, the Serbian Orthodox Church long had a tradition of belittling so-called traitors and condemning them to hell. The analysis of Kecmanović, that this cohort of young extremist Serbs has been systematically pushed towards obedience as a function of their low threshold of tolerance towards others, is helpful. Their opinions have been formed through the strong 'voices of ethno-national interpreters' who claim that the fate of Serbs is in their hands while simultaneously relieving themselves of any responsibility when their followers act hatefully.[48]

---

[46] "RAN C&N Meeting: A Psychological and Neuroscientific Perspective on How Extremist Propaganda Works and How to Effectively Counter It", in *Ex Post Paper*, 7 and 8 February 2018.

[47] Dušan Kecmanović, *Psihopolitika mržnje*, Prosveta, Belgrade, 1999, p. 130, cited in Maja Kaninska, "Psychology of Nationalism and Religion in the Example of the Serbian Orthodox Church During the 80s and After the XX Century", in *Second International Conference on Research in Social Sciences and Humanities*, 10–12 December 2020.

[48] *Ibid.*

10.7. Common Characteristics of Far-Right Extremism in Bosnia and Herzegovina

Demonstrations of extreme ethno-nationalism among research participants ranged from a readiness to support far-right ideals at a rhetorical level to a readiness to justify and directly support acts of violence or commit acts of violence themselves. However, the research also revealed potential ways in which resilience to extremism can be fostered. For example, there were strong indications that respondents who interacted more regularly with people from other ethnic and identity groups were much less likely to support violence, even if they harboured strong ethno-nationalist views and were recognized as extremists within their communities.

The analysis offered here represents a departure from previous research on extremism in BiH in two ways. First, because previous research has largely focused on foreign fighters and Salafi communities; and second, because it emphasizes commonalities among ethno-national extremists that cut across Bosniak, Croat and Serb identities. While acknowledging that the ideologies espoused by far-right members in each of these identity groups are based in opposition to each other, research findings show that the attitudes and world views of ethno-nationalist extremists from all three Bosnian communities are more similar than different.

Ethno-nationalism is on the rise against a backdrop of complex political and social conditions, and this analysis helped expand our understanding of how far-right and extremist ideas are emerging in BiH and the ways in which regional and international contexts contribute to this process. The same issues and themes that animate the far-right in the rest of Europe have been observed in BiH: anti-immigration and Islámophobic narratives; opposition to gender equality; the promotion of conspiracy theories; and the exploitation of the Covid-19 crisis. There has been a growth of conservative religious discourse as well, which has not been adequately challenged. And in BiH, far-right narratives integrate and mirror the ethno-nationalism of political parties, which is then shaped further at the community level and online, taking these narratives further and developing them through a language of othering and a culture of affective social distance. This undermines efforts to advance the rights of women, achieve reconciliation and build peace in the country.

This research found that religion and its radical interpretations plays a particularly significant role in the lives of extremist respondents, with 74 per cent claiming to accept all the teachings and demands of their religion. But research participants were more likely to accept violence if they also had lower levels of education or were dissatisfied with their income, family life and prospects. Notably, a direct relationship was observed between respondents' views on gender equality and their support for violence, with those who reject gender equality and espouse 'traditional values' expressing more support for violence. On the other hand, respondents were less likely to accept or support violence if they were open to the idea of reconciliation with other ethnic and identity groups, understood that the celebration of war criminals from their group is offensive to other groups, and did not strongly oppose the idea of mixed marriages, befriending people outside their ethnic group or having them as their civic representatives, doctors and teachers.

Trust in democracy was another factor that strongly correlated to lower rates of support for violence among these extremist research participants. Still, a majority of respondents (61 per cent) felt a strong leader is *more* important than a democracy. This is somewhat inconsistent with the fact that most respondents cited corruption and organized crime as serious security threats, which tend to be worse in authoritarian regimes, but consistent with the fact that many also identified current domestic politicians as a serious security threat. And, despite the extreme ethno-nationalist views of these respondents, a majority (51 per cent) said they would choose to leave BiH in the case of renewed conflict, meaning they would refuse to take up arms. This was true across ethnic groups, and this analysis clearly demonstrated a significant degree of commonality among all extremists in BiH. Perhaps more than anything else, it points to the considerable correlation between a strong sense of religiosity and the feeling that violence is justified to defend or avenge a given ethnic and religious group, and demonstrates how radical interpretations of religion serve to intensify the sentiments of extreme ethno-nationalism.

10.8. Conclusion

The sense among many analysts and civil society activists in BiH is that the country is more radicalized now than it was before the war started in 1992; a sense that has only grown with the Russian invasion of Ukraine. The data presented in this chapter supports the validity of such an assessment, as it confirms the entrenchment of a culture of 'othering' in which stigmatization, high degrees of social distance and hate speech have been normalized in some communities. And while much of the research discussed here was focused on individuals who exhibit sympathy for or affiliation with far-right extremism, the extremism observed even in mainstream political discourse is alarming to many citizens and leaves them in a constant state of fear regarding a potential future conflict.

This chapter gave significant attention to the role of the Serbian Orthodox Church in shaping far-right discourse, because it has become ever more apparent in the last few years that the Church is actively taking part in processes of radicalization. Unfortunately, Montenegro had to face a significant crisis for this to become visible in the media. Clearly, the mythology and narratives of victimhood, threat and Serb supremacy espoused by the Church are dangerous in many ways. This rhetoric creates a culture of distrust and demonizes others, further weakening the already fragile and insecure political and economic reality of BiH.

An analysis by Srđan Puhalo, a psychologist from Banja Luka, poignantly summarized the relationship between the Serbian Orthodox Church, Serb ethnonationalism and the Bosnian education system, which is relevant for this chapter. Reflecting on a primary school celebration of Saint Sava in Banja Luka, he referred to it as "*retro, ethno and deadly*".[49] At this school in BiH, the children celebrated only Serbia on this day, singing songs about Kosovo, imagining the wartime suffering of Serbs, and playing out scenarios of sons being drafted to war and mothers crying mournfully for them. The strong message of this curriculum was that there is glory in death; but as Puhalo put it: "Why not celebrate life, celebrate school, celebrate knowledge, because that is why we send our children to schools, not to prepare them for death and dying".[50] This sentiment is not necessarily an outlier in BiH, where many people maintain a grassroots spirit of multicultural inclusion; yet across the country, similar celebrations in public schools frame *Republika Srpska* as a Serb space and imply to young children that they face threats from people who live in their own communities.

The messaging and narratives analyzed in this chapter, whether from the Serbian Orthodox Church or ethno-nationalist politicians, contribute to a context in which 'others' are seen as unworthy of humanity and identity. But, as we know all too well, denying the identity, culture and religion of people, and framing them as the enemy, is a path to destruction. We have seen it in BiH and are witnessing it now in the Russian invasion of Ukraine. These narratives may not be new to the region, but before 1992, they were restricted to private conversations among family; now, they are present in everyday life and framed as valid and factual. This was reflected in the confident declaration by one Serb research participant: "There is one language here and it is Serbian. Serbian lands are made up of parts of today's Croatia, Bosnia, Montenegro, and Macedonia. That is not an opinion I have, it is an indisputable fact".

In a 2019 article, Cichocka and Cislak characterized nationalism as a form of collective narcissism.[51] The traits of ethno-nationalists described in this chapter echo features of the collective narcissism they described – which does not benefit out-group or in-group members, but undermines social cohesion within

---

49 Srđan Puhalo, "Sveti Sava u raljama etna, retra i nacionalizma", *ФРОНТАЛ*, 28 January 2020 (available on the Frontal.ba web site).

50 *Ibid.*

51 Aleksandra Cichocka and Aleksandra Cislak, "Nationalism as Collective Narcissism", in *Current Opinion in Behavioral Sciences*, 2020, vol. 34, pp. 69–74.

and between these groups. This collective narcissism predicts undesirable inter- and intra-group outcomes, as it serves the self over other members. The authors argue that a hypersensitivity to threat links collective narcissism to prejudice, especially towards groups perceived as the enemy. National collective narcissism has also been linked to support for extreme intergroup violence and aggression, as well as political violence, especially in radicalized social contexts, which gives us many reasons to be concerned in BiH.

PART III: OVERARCHING NORMATIVE FRAMEWORKS

SECTION D: THE INTERNATIONAL LAW FRAMEWORK

11

Freedom of Expression and International Criminal Law

Matthias Neuner*

11.1. Introduction

This chapter discusses the origin and codification of freedom of expression, the limitations of this human right, including which offences of international criminal law and relevant modes of criminal liability exist to adjudicate severe abuses of this freedom. Section 11.7 analyses relevant case law of international tribunals.

11.2. Origins of Freedom of Expression

The philosophical origins of freedom of expression can be found in the literature of ancient Greece and authors of the European Enlightenment. The first legal codifications occurred between 1588 and 1791 in domestic jurisdictions: in England, Sweden, Denmark-Norway, Virginia, France and the United States of America ('USA').

11.2.1. Ancient Greece

In the fifth century BC, ancient Greek authors first expressed the idea of freedom of expression, particularly Euripides (484–407 BC). In his writings, the Greek word Παρρησία ('*parrhēsia*') appeared.[1]

Henry George Liddell and Robert Scott translate *parrhēsia* as:

> *outspokenness, frankness, freedom of speech,* claimed by the Athenians as their privilege [...] 2. In bad sense, *license of tongue* [...]

---

* **Matthias Neuner** is a Barrister in Berlin and Düsseldorf and former Trial Counsel, Offices of the Prosecutor ('OTP') of the Special Tribunal for Lebanon ('STL') and the International Criminal Tribunal for the former Yugoslavia ('ICTY'). The views expressed in this chapter are those of the author and do not necessarily reflect the views of ICTY, ICTY, or the European Union Advisory Mission for Ukraine. Some of his academic writings appear in Torkel Opsahl Academic EPublisher publications such as the 2020 anthologies *Integrity in International Justice* and *Colonial Wrongs and Access to International Law*. For an audio-visual recording of his statement to CILRAP's conference in Florence in April 2022 on the topic of this anthology, please see https://www.cilrap.org/cilrap-film/220408-neuner/.

1 Michel Foucault, "Discourse and Truth: The Problematization of Parrhesia (Six Lectures Given by Michel Foucault at Berkeley, Oct–Nov. 1983", p. 2 (available on the *Foucault.info* web site).

> 3. *freedom of action*; […] *license, permission*, […] *without fear* […] 4. *liberality, lavishness* […] *speak freely, openly*, […] *free expressions*.[2]

Robert W. Wallace understands *parrhēsia* to mean "open and candid speech in private and public life".[3]

Michel Foucault writes:

> 'Parrhesia' is ordinarily translated into English by 'free speech' (in French by 'franc-parler', and in German by 'Freimüthigkeit'). 'Parrhesiazomai' or 'parrhesiazesthai' is to use parrhesia, and the parrhesiastes is the one who uses parrhesia, i.e., is the one who speaks the truth.[4]

Wallace observes:

> Modern values of free speech protect the rights of individuals against society or government. The Athenians did not share this perspective. They had no experience of heavy bureaucratic oppression. They did know about tyranny. In Athens' democracy, every citizen had the freedom to speak. However, community interests came first. The power to shout down stupid or windy speakers was democratic freedom. The denial of that freedom was oligarchy or tyranny.[5]

Kyriakoula Papademetriou observes that the most common dictionaries of ancient Greek language translate *parrhēsia* into English in three ways: freedom of speech and action, openness, and boldness of speech.[6] He therefore concludes that "[f]reedom of speech and free speech, courage and self-confidence, clearness and sincerity, openness and honesty, senses with distinct differences, are consolidated under the name of παρρησία [*parrhēsia*]".[7]

---

2 Henry G. Liddell and Robert Scott, *A Greek–English Lexicon*, Oxford University Press, 1996, p. 1844.

3 Robert W. Wallace, "The Power to Speak – and Not to Listen – in Ancient Athens", in Ineke Sluiter and Ralph Rosen (eds.), *Free Speech in Classical Antiquity*, Brill, 2004, p. 221.

4 Foucault, 1983, p. 2, see *supra* note 1.

5 Wallace, 2004, p. 227, see *supra* note 3.

6 Kyriakoula Papademetriou, "The Performative Meaning of the Word παρρησία in Ancient Greek and in the Greek Bible", in Peter-Ben Smit and Eva van Urk (eds.), *Parrhesia Ancient and Modern Perspectives on Freedom of Speech*, Brill, 2018, p. 17, with further references in note 4.

7 *Ibid*., p. 34.

11.2.2. Desiderius Erasmus Roterodamus

In 1516, during the Renaissance period, Erasmus of Rotterdam introduced the idea of freedom of speech in one of his books through one character who stated "[i]n a free country, tongues likewise should be free".[8]

11.2.3. John Milton, William Walwyn and John Lilburne (1644–1645)

In the early seventeenth century, the printing press in England was regulated by complex mechanisms including by pre-printing approval and oversight through the printers' and booksellers' guild. Qualified licensers' pre-approved books had subsequently to be entered in the Stationers' company registers.[9] Initially, a royal licensing regime had been in place, though the English parliament overturned it in 1641 by issuing a series of stopgap orders and by summoning authors, printers and sellers who had committed violations of the legal regime on an *ad hoc* basis.[10]

On 14 June 1643, the English parliament issued an ordinance for the regulation of printing ('England's Printing Ordinance').[11] It reinstated, among others, pre-publication approval providing that, instead of old episcopal licensers, godly and orthodox divines should do the licensing.[12]

In the weeks following the adoption of this ordinance, the publishers, Mathew Simmons[13] and 'T.P.', published the book 'The Doctrine and Discipline of Divorce' without mentioning any author.[14] The second and third editions of this book published in 1644 and 1645 mentioned, as author, "J.M."[15] – the

---

8 Desiderius Erasmus, *The Education of a Christian Prince*, Columbia University Records of Civilization, Octagon Books, New York, 1963, p. 232.

9 David Como, "The Origins of the Concept of Freedom of the Press", in Robert Ingram, Jason Peacey and Alex W. Barber, *Freedom of Speech, 1500–1850*, Manchester University Press, 2020, pp. 98–99.

10 Randy Robertson, "Debating Censorship: Liberty and Press Control in the 1640s", in Christopher D'Addario and Matthew Augustine (eds.), *Texts and Readers in the Age of Marvell*, Manchester University Press, 2018, p. 132 ('Robertson, Censorship in England').

11 England, An Ordinance for the Regulating of Printing, 14 June 1643, in Charles H. Firth and Robert S. Rait, *Acts and Ordinances of the Interregnum, 1642–1660*, Her Majesty Stationary Office, London, 1911, vol. 1, p. 184.

12 *Ibid.*, p. 108.

13 Simmons had an office in Goldsmiths Alley in London in 1643 (compare Henry R. Plomer, *A Dictionary of the Booksellers and Printers Who Were at Work in England, Scotland and Ireland From 1641 to 1667*, vol. 1, Bibliographical Society, 1907). The first edition of the book 'The Doctrine and Discipline of Divorce' (see *infra* note 14) shows as one publisher "M.S." in London's Goldsmiths Alley.

14 Anonymous, *Doctrine and Discipline of Divorce*, M.S., London, 1 August 1643.

15 Compare the 1644 edition ("The_Doctrine_and_Discipline_of_Divorce – Milton (1644)", available on the *Wikisource* web site) and the 1645 edition ("The John Milton Reading Room:

initials of John Milton. His authorship for each edition of this book is nowadays no longer in doubt; though, in the seventeenth century, it had been published anonymously and without license.[16]

The book received critical reviews. One appeared in the form of a pamphlet by an anonymous source.[17] Thereby, an intellectual debate about divorce occurred between two persons who did not associate their own names to their arguments. On the other hand, Herbert Palmer, a puritan clergyman, openly appeared in front of both chambers of the English parliament criticizing the "wicked book" which was "uncensured", adding that it deserved to be "burnt".[18] Exemplary for this stage of censorship in England, this book resulted in intellectual debates between participants, some wearing helmets with open visors and some with closed visors, combined with calls for licensing or even burning Milton's anonymously published book on divorce. This situation, arising out of the English parliament's ordinance for the regulation of printing and its prepublication approval, prompted Milton to write a critique of the licensing system existing in England at the time.[19]

On 23 November 1644, Milton, using his full name, published 'Areopagitica'. He advanced several arguments against censorship, including but not limited to "[w]here there is much desire to learn, there of necessity will be much arguing, much writing, many opinions; for opinion in good men is but knowledge in the making".[20] He further argued that "[w]ho kills a man kills a reasonable creature, god's image, but he who destroys a good book, kills reason itself [...]".[21] And "[i]f we think to regulat[e] Printing, thereby to rectif[y]

The Doctrine & Discipline of Divorce", available on the Darthmouth University's *Milton Host* web site).

16 Stephen B. Dubranski, *The Cambridge Introduction to Milton*, Cambridge University Press, 2012, pp. 101, 110, 113, 117, 126 ('Dubranski, Milton').

17 Anonymous, *The Doctrine and Discipline of Divorce, or, A Plea for Ladies and Gentlewomen, and All Other Maried Women Against Divorce Wherein Both Sexes Are Vindicated From All Bondage of Canon Law, and Other Mistakes Whatsoever*, William Lee, London, 1644.

18 Herbert Palmer, *The Glasse of Gods Providence Towards His Faithfull Ones*, Th. Vnderhill, London, 1644, p. 57; Leo Miller, *John Milton Among the Polygamophiles*, Loewenthal Press, New York, 1974, p. 122; Dubranski, Milton, 2012, pp. 18, 114, see *supra* note 16.

19 Dubranski, Milton, 2012, p. 117, see *supra* note 16; Robertson, Censorship in England, p. 136, see *supra* note 10; Daniel F. Sullivan, "Milton's Areopagitica & Freedom of Speech on Campus", in *Liberal Education*, 2006, vol. 92, no. 2, pp. 56–59.

20 Ernest Sirluck (ed.), *Complete Prose Works of John Milton*, vol. II, Yale University Press, New Haven, 1953–1982, p. 554.

21 John Milton, *Areopagitica and other Political Writings of John Milton*, Liberty Fund, Indianapolis, 1999, p. 7.

manners, we must regulat[e] all recreations and pastimes, all that is delightfull to Man".[22]

On 28 December 1644, a warden of the Stationer testified in front of the English parliament referring to Milton as an author of scandalous books.[23]

Milton was not the only author criticizing England's Printing Ordinance. A month before he would publish 'Areopagitica', an anonymous author published 'The Compassionate Samaritan'.[24] This work is attributed to William Walwyn,[25] who criticized the censors in this book:

> [T]hey brand men with the name of Hereticks […] their next interest is to be masters of the Presse of which they are lately become by an Ordinance for licensing of Bookes […]. In the stopping of honest mens writing that nothing may come to the Worlds view but what they please, unless men will run the hazard of imprisonment (as I now doe) fo[r] that in publike the may speak what they will, write what they will, they may abuse whom they will and nothing can be said against them: well may they presume of making themselves masters of the people having these foundations laid, and the people generally willing to beleeve they are good.[26]

John Lilburne also criticized the English licensing system and the English parliament, having examined the situation, sent him to jail for this.[27] In 1649, the English authorities arrested and questioned Lilburne, Walwyn and other authors in relation to their publications and ended up trying Lilburne in court, where a jury acquitted him.[28]

In 1695, England effectively abolished pre-publication approval when the House of Commons omitted to renew the Licensing of the Press Act of 1662,[29] which therefore expired.[30] The omission to renew the law was caused by mutual

---

22 *Ibid.*, p. 22.

23 Robertson, Censorship in England, p. 136, see *supra* note 10, referring to *The British Index*, 28 December 1644.

24 Anonymous, *The Compassionate Samaritan*, 1st ed., 1644 ('Compassionate Samaritan').

25 Compare Robertson, Censorship in England, p. 136, see *supra* note 10.

26 Compassionate Samaritan, pp. 38–40, see *supra* note 24.

27 John Lilburne, *A Copie of A Letter, Written by John Lilburne Leut. Collonell to Mr. William Prinne Esq.*, London, 1645; Robertson, Censorship in England, p. 138, see *supra* note 10.

28 Robertson, Censorship in England, pp. 140–142, see *supra* note 10.

29 Its Section II provided for pre-publication approval: John Raithby (ed.), "Charles II, 1662: An Act for Preventing the Frequent Abuses in Printing Seditious Treasonable and Unlicensed Bookes and Pamphlets and for Regulating of Printing and Printing Presses", in *Statutes of the Realm: Volume 5, 1628–80*, 1819, vol. 5, pp. 428–435.

30 Charles A. Ruud, "Limits on the 'Freed' Press of 18th- and 19th-Century Europe", in *Journalism & Mass Communication Quarterly*, 1979, vol. 56, p. 521; Eckhart Hellmuth, "Towards

suspicion leading to an inability of the political parties to agree on how to limit the press, and not by their desire to grant more freedom to the press.[31]

11.2.4. Baruch or Benedict de Spinoza: Theological-Political Treatise (1670)

In 1665, Spinoza wrote to Henry Oldenburg that he was in the process of composing a treatise. He added that one of several considerations for doing so was the "freedom of *philosophizing and saying what we think*, which I want to defend in every way; here [in the Netherlands] the preachers suppress it as much as they can with their excessive authority and aggressiveness".[32]

In 1670, the 'Theological-Political Treatise' was published anonymously in Amsterdam.[33] The second edition of this book appeared in 1672 stating as author, the initials "B.D.S.".[34] These initials could stand for Baruch or Benedict de Spinoza.

Though the book could never be freely sold and was banned, for example, in the Netherlands in 1674 and, subsequently, by other governments and ecclesiastical authorities including France and the Vatican, it must have been available at least within certain circles because it was criticized by scholars within the Netherlands and abroad, for instance, in Germany and England.[35]

In the Theological-Political Treatise, Spinoza argued that people,

> communicate their thoughts to others […]. Hence, a government which denies each person freedom to speak and to communicate what they think, will be a very violent government whereas a state where everyone is conceded this freedom will be moderate. However, we cannot altogether deny that treason may be committed as much by words as by deeds. Consequently, if it is impossible

Hume – the Discourse on the Liberty of the Press in the Age of Walpole", in *History of European Ideas*, 2018, vol. 44, p. 160.

31 Raymond Astbury, "The Renewal of the Licensing Act in 1693 and Its Lapse in 1695", in *Library 33*, 1978, no. 4, pp. 296–322.

32 "Letter 30 from *Spinoza* to *Henry Oldenburg*", 1 October 1665, in *Collected Works of Spinoza*, vol. II, Princeton University Press, 2016, pp. 14–15, no. 3 (emphasis added).

33 Anonymous, *Tractatus Theologico-Politicus*, Amsterdam, 1670; Paola de Cuzzani, "Baruch de Spinoza: Democracy and Freedom of Speech", in Guttorm Fløistad (ed.), *Philosophy of Justice*, Springer, Berlin, 2015, p. 79 ('Cuzzani, Spinoza's Democracy and Freedom of Speech'); Benedict de Spinoza, *Theological-Political Treatise*, Jonathan Israel (ed.), Michael Silverthorne and Jonathan Israel (trans.), Cambridge University Press, 2007, pp. ix, xxxi ('Spinoza, *Theological-Political Treatise*').

34 Benedictus Spinoza, *Tractatus Theologico-Politicus*, Henrik Künraht, 1672. The book was published in Amsterdam (compare Spinoza, *Theological-Political Treatise*, p. xxxi, see *supra* note 33).

35 *Ibid*., pp. xxxi–xxxii.

> altogether to deny subjects this freedom, it is, on the other hand, likewise very dangerous to concede it without any restriction.[36]

Spinoza argues in favour of freedom of expression while acknowledging that such freedom should have limits. As to the reason for said limits, he considers that treason can also be committed by words.

Spinoza holds that the purpose of the state is to allow people's

> minds and bodies to develop in their own ways in security and enjoy the free use of reason, and not to participate in conflicts based on hatred, anger or deceit or in malicious disputes with each other. Therefore, the true purpose of the state is in fact freedom.[37]

He argues that people

> can think and judge and consequently also speak without any restriction, provided they merely speak or teach by way of reason alone, not by trickery or in anger or from hatred or with the intention of introducing some alteration in the state on their own initiative.[38]

Spinoza concludes that,

> freedom of judgment must necessarily be permitted and people must be governed in such a way that they can live in harmony, even though they openly hold different and contradictory opinions. [...] this is the best way of ruling, and has the least disadvantages, since it is the one most in harmony with human nature. In a democratic state (which is the one closest to the state of nature), all men agree [...] to act – but not to judge and think – according to the common decision. That is because people cannot all have the same opinions, they have agreed that the view which gains the most votes should acquire the force of a decision, reserving always the right to recall their decision whenever they should find a better course. The less people are accorded liberty of judgment, consequently, the further they are from the most natural condition and, hence, the more oppressive the regime.[39]

With these arguments, Spinoza has afforded reason, individual liberty, and freedom of expression, a central role for democracy and in his political theory. Within it, the capability to use reason and one's own judgment is key, as

36 *Ibid.*, pp. 251–252.

37 *Ibid.*, p. 252.

38 *Ibid.*

39 *Ibid.*, p. 257.

freedom of thought and expression results in public debates, thereby playing a "constitutive role" for democracy.[40]

11.2.5. Voltaire

François Marie Arouet, who carries the pen name 'Voltaire', lived in England from 1726 to 1728. As a result of his stay and knowledge of the English society, he used his pen name when publishing a series of 24 essays in 1733.[41] In essay XX,[42] Voltaire observed:

> There are about eighthundred Persons in England who have a Right to speak in publick, and to support the Interest of the Kingdom; and near five or six Thousand may in their Turns, aspire to the same Honour. The whole Nation set themselves up as Judges over these, and every man has the Liberty of publishing his Thoughts with regard to publick affairs; which shews, that all the People in general are indispensable oblig'd to cultivate their Understandings.[43]

Voltaire's description of the state of affairs in England was more optimistic than its reality. As demonstrated in this chapter, even decades after Voltaire had published his thoughts on freedom of speech and writing, Milton, Walwyn and Lilburne, who were just examples of many English authors, either chose anonymity or otherwise faced hardship when publishing their thoughts. Compared to this reality in England, decades later, Voltaire's intention in essay XX becomes apparent. He chose to portray freedom of speech and writing in England in a more positive light than it really was in order to indirectly criticize the then existing French political system, which was an absolutist kingdom and therefore not as free as the English system at the time.

One year later, in 1734, the French version was published, with only the initials of its author provided on the cover – "M.D. V***" – probably referring to Marie de Voltaire, thereby omitting his given name François.[44] Lanson described the effect of Voltaire's book as the "first bomb launched against the old [French] regime".[45] The authorities reacted by issuing an arrest warrant against

---

[40] Cuzzani, Spinoza's Democracy and Freedom of Speech, pp. 90–91, see *supra* note 33.

[41] Voltaire, *Letters Concerning the English Nation*, C. Davies in Pater-Noster-Row and A. Lyon in Russel Street, London, 1733.

[42] The essay's title is "On Such of the Nobility as Cultivate the Belles Lettres" in François Voltaire, *Letters on the English*, The Harvard Classics, 1909–1914.

[43] *Ibid.*, p. 193.

[44] Marie D. Voltaire, *Lettres Ecrites de Londres sur les Anglois et Autres Sujets*, A. Basle, 1734. Nowadays, the book is referred to as 'Lettres philosophiques'.

[45] In the original, "premièr bomb launcée contre l'ancien régime" (Gustave Lanson, *Voltaire*, Librairie Hachette et Cie, Paris, 1906, p. 52).

Voltaire for publishing without royal license, detaining the printer in the Bastille and confiscating the remaining copies of the book. On 10 June 1734, the parliament of Paris prohibited the book, copies of which were burned in the justice palace.[46] Voltaire fled France.

In 1765, Voltaire added to the third edition of his 'Philosophic Dictionary' the essay 'Freedom of Thought', in which he created a fictitious dialogue between a man from Portugal and another from England, and which advocated freedom of speech.[47] Voltaire sought to dismiss the concern of his Portuguese character that freedom of speech combined with independent thought could lead to confusion. Rather, he suggests this combination could propel society and its individuals forward into a new state of mind in which citizens are increasingly happy.[48]

In 1765, Voltaire published 'Questions sur les miracles', consisting of a series of letters or anonymously published pamphlets. In letter XIII, he further elaborated on freedom of expression:

> Soutenons la liberté de la presse, c'est la base de toutes les autres libertés, c'est par là qu'on s'éclaire mutuellement. Chaque citoyen peut parler par écrit à la nation, et chaque lecteur examine à loisir, et sans passion, ce que ce compatriote lui dit par la voie de la presse. Nos cercles peuvent quelquefois être tumultueux: ce n'est que dans le recueillement du cabinet qu'on peut bien juger. C'est par là que la nations anglaise est devenue une nation véritablement libre. Elle ne le serait pas si elle n'erait pas éclairée; et elle ne serait point éclairée, si chaque citoyen n'avait pas chez elle le droit d'imprimer ce qu'il veut.[49]

An unofficial translation reads:

> Let us support the freedom of the press, it is the basis of all the other freedoms, it is through this that we mutually enlighten each other. Each citizen can speak to the nation in writing, and each reader can examine leisurely and without passion what his compatriot submits to him through the press. Our circles can sometimes be tumultuous: it is only in the contemplation of the reading room that one can judge well. This is how the English nation

---

46 Jonathan I. Israel, *Enlightenment Contested: Philosophy, Modernity and the Emancipation of Man, 1670 – 1752*, Oxford University Press, 2006, p. 754.

47 Voltaire, "Freedom of Thought", in Voltaire, *Philosophical Dictionary*, 3rd ed., Amsterdam, 1765.

48 Compare Mary E. Gregory, *Freedom in French Enlightenment Thought*, Peter Lang, New York, 2008, p. 143.

49 Voltaire, "Letter XIII, Addressed by Mr. Covelle to His Dear Fellow Citizens, Questions sur les miracles", in Voltaire, *Œuvres complètes de Voltaire*, vol. 25, Garnier, 1879, p. 419.

> became a truly free nation. It would not be if it were not enlightened; and it would not be enlightened if each citizen did not have at home the right to print what he wants.

11.2.6. David Hume: Of the Liberty of the Press (1741–1778)

David Hume, a Scottish Enlightenment philosopher, wrote several versions of his essay 'Of the Liberty of the Press'. Around the age of 30, he had the first version of this essay published anonymously in 1741 in Scotland.[50] There, prepublication censorship still existed (unlike in England).[51] Throughout his life, Hume amended this essay. From 1753 onwards, this and other essays were added to Hume's treatises and re-published and, at least from this moment onwards, the essay on freedom of press bore his full name.[52]

Against the background of England, which was neither purely monarchical nor republican at the time, Hume argued in all versions of his essay that mixed political systems "beget a mutual watchfulness and jealousy".[53] Despotic powers could begin to steal people's liberty unless the people were "extreme[ly] watchful to prevent [the despot's] progress", unless there was an easy method and means to ring the alarm bell throughout the whole country.[54] Hume argued that the liberty of the press would mean that "all the Learning, Wit, and Genius of the nation may be employed on the side of liberty".[55] In the first version of his essay, Hume proclaimed that the liberty of the press is accompanied with so few inconveniences that it could be seen as a "common Right of Mankind".[56]

Skjönsberg interprets that Hume proclaimed a 'civic right', meaning a right granted by government to its citizen, as opposed to a natural right of a person which could be upheld against a government restricting the freedom of

---

[50] Anonymous, "Essays, Moral and Political", R. Fleming and A. Alison for A. Kincaid, Edinburgh, 1741 ('Anonymous, Essay on Press Freedom 1741'). In 1748, Millar and Kincaid contributed to the publication of the second edition of this book.

[51] Max Skjönsberg, "David Hume and 'Of the Liberty of the Press' (1741) in Its Original Contexts", in Ingram, Peacey and Barber, 2020, p. 172, see *supra* note 9 ('Skjönsberg, Hume's Essay in Context').

[52] David Hume, *Essays and Treatises on Several Subjects, in Two Volumes*, 4th ed., A. Millar, Strand, and A. Kincaid and A. Donaldson, Edinburgh, 1753.

[53] *Ibid.*, p. 9; Anonymous, Essay on Press Freedom 1741, p. 12, see *supra* note 50; David Hume, *Essays and Treatises on Several Subjects*, vol. I, J. Williams, (No. 21) Skinner-Row, Dublin, 1779, p. 11 ('Hume, Essay on Press Freedom 1779').

[54] *Ibid.*, p. 14.

[55] *Ibid.*

[56] *Ibid.*, p. 15

the press.[57] Other contemporaneous authors had issued similar claims regarding the nature of freedoms of the press or of expression, as 'rights'.[58]

Within this debate, Hume's impulse – made when he was about 30 years old – is remarkable insofar as, 30 years later, he may have *retracted* his claim that freedom of the press assumes the character of a right. He upheld this new position until his death in 1776. At least in all versions of his essay on freedom of the press from 1770 onwards (particularly in 1772 and 1779), Hume omitted the last section of his earlier essay on freedom of the press. The omitted final section of the essay was substantial in a qualitative and quantitative sense. It accounted for about one-third of the initial length of his essay. Substantively, the omission contained the discussion about the advantages and disadvantages of press freedom with an optimistic tone, crystallizing in the claim that this liberty should have the status of a "common Right of Mankind". Following a complete omission of this section in the 1770 edition, Hume added, for the 1772 edition, a new final paragraph: "the unbound liberty of the press […] is one of the evils attending those mixt forms of government".[59]

With this move, the aging Hume changed his earlier, optimistic tone on press freedom, to a cautionary one. At least since 1772, he considered the "unbound" version of this freedom to be an "evil". In the same token, he cautioned in the last version of his essay that it is "difficult, perhaps impossible, to propose a suitable remedy" to unbound liberty of the press.[60]

In conclusion, Hume's contribution to press freedom was to analyse the interplay between a free press and the existing political structure of a state. He saw press freedom, if approached with caution, as contributing to the delicate balance of power within mixed political systems.

---

57 Skjönsberg, Hume's Essay in Context, 2020, p. 180, see *supra* note 51.

58 As early as 1712, an anonymous writer claimed that "there never was a good government that stood in fear of freedom of speech, which is the *natural liberty of mankind*" (Anonymous, *Thoughts of a Tory Author Concerning the Press*, A. Baldwin, London, 1712, p. 13 (emphasis added)). Two scholars believe the anonymous author was Joseph Addison (Leonard W. Lewy, "On the Origins of the Free Press Clause", in *U.C.L.A. Law Review*, 1984, vol. 32, p. 184; Louis E. Ingelhart, *Press and Speech Freedoms in the World, from Antiquity Until 1998: A Chronology*, Greenwood Press, 1998, p. 86). In 1738, James Thomson produced a foreword to a republished Areopagitica in which he portrayed press freedom as the "best of human rights" (James Thomson, *A Speech of Mr. John Milton for the Liberty of Unlicens'd Printing, to the Parliament of England*, Millar Publisher, London, 1738, p. iii).

59 David Hume, *Essays and Treatises on Several Subjects*, vol. I, T. Cadell, Strand, and A. Kincaid and A. Donaldson, Edinburgh, 1772, p. 12.

60 Hume, Essay on Press Freedom 1779, p. 12, see *supra* note 53.

11.2.7. Carl Friedrich Bahrdt: Of Freedom of the Press and Its Limits (1787)

Karl Friedrich Bahrdt, a German theologian and professor, published anonymously, in 1787, the book 'Freedom of the Press and Its Limits – For Regents, Censors and Writers to Heed'. He argued:

> Die Freyheit, seine Einsichten und Urtheile mitzuteilen – es sey mündlich oder schriftlich, ist ebenso wie die Freyheit zu denken, ein heiliges und unverletzliches Recht der Menschheit, das, als allgemeines Menschenrecht, über das Recht der Fürsten erhaben ist.[61]

An unofficial translation reads:

> The freedom to communicate one's views and judgments, whether orally or in writing, is as the freedom to think a sacred and inviolable right of mankind which as general human right is superior to the right of the sovereign.

Bahrdt proclaimed freedom of expression to constitute a general human right. He went further than David Hume did. Until 1769, in all editions of his book 'Of the Liberty of The Press', Hume had proclaimed that (only) the freedom of the press constitutes a common right of mankind, before he omitted this proclamation from 1770 onwards and instead qualified "unbound" freedom of the press as an "evil". Bahrdt went beyond freedom of the press, in proclaiming that freedom of expression deserves the status of a general human right.

11.3. Domestic Codifications Before World War II

Various relevant codifications of the freedom of expression before World War II occurred on the domestic level, in England, Denmark-Norway, Sweden, France and the USA.

11.3.1. England, Bill of Rights (1688)

The first codification of freedom of speech occurred with the English Bill of Rights in 1688.[62] Its Article 9 stated:

> The Freedome of Speech and Debates or Proceedings in Parlyament ought not to be impeached or questioned in any Court or Place out of Parliament.

---

[61] Anonymous, *Preßfreiheit und ihre Gränzen – Zur Beherzigung für Regenten, Censoren und Schriftsteller*, Berlin, bei Friedrich Vieweg, 1787, p. 44 (compare also p. 46). The 1794 edition of this book, published in Züllichau, carried as author 'D. Carl Friedrich Bahrdt'.

[62] United Kingdom ('UK'), Bill of Rights, 1688. The Act received Royal Assent on 16 December 1689 (https://www.legal-tools.org/doc/acxss1/).

This privilege amounts to parliamentary immunity and constitutes a manifestation that "courts and parliament are both astute to recognize their respective constitutional roles"[63] by ensuring that parliamentarians could utter their thoughts in England without facing the risk of impeachment or criminal sanctions. The group of persons carrying this right were members of the parliament of England. Thus, this freedom of speech applied to a limited group within the British society.

11.3.2. Sweden, Freedom of Print Act (1766)

Inner political struggles, particularly in Sweden,[64] combined with progressive thoughts on freedom of the press and access to information in the writings of proponents of the Enlightenment, including but not limited to Anders Chydenius[65] in Finland and Peter Forsskål[66] in Sweden, culminated in a parliamentary committee of 15 members preparing, over months, a draft law which the Swedish parliament adopted in 1766: His Majesty's Gracious Ordinance Regarding the Freedom of Writing and of the Press.[67] Section 5 of this law stated in its relevant part:

> [E]veryone shall have the unrestricted right to express his thoughts on all matters that touch upon the rights and duties of the citizen

[63] Richard Clayton and Hugh Tomlinson, *The Law of Human Rights*, Oxford University Press, 2000, paras. 11.31, 11.32.

[64] Matti Klinge and Kaarle Nordenstreng, "Painovapauden aate ei ole suurmieshistoriaa", in *Helsingin Sanomat*, 25 January 2016; Rolf Nygren, "The Citizen's Access to Official Records – A Significant Principle in Swedish Constitutional Life Since 1766", in Günter Buchstab (ed.), *Die Zugänglichkeit von Parlamentsakten und die audiovisuellen Materialien in Parlaments und Parteiarchiven*, Academia Publisher, Sankt Augustin, 1999, pp. 22, 28.

[65] Anders Chydenius, "Mietintö kirjoitus – ja painovapaudesta (Report on the Freedom of the Press), 1765", in *Chydeniuksen valitut kirjoitukset* (Selected writings by Chydenius), WSOY (Werner Söderström Corporation) Publishers, Porvoo, 1929, pp. 165–170; Juhani Kortteinen, Kristian Myntti and Lauri Hannikainen, "Article 19", in Gudmundur Alfredsson and Asbjørn Eide (eds.), *The Universal Declaration of Human Rights: A Common Standard of Achievement*, Martijn Nijhoff Publishers, The Hague, 1999, p. 394.

[66] Peter Forsskål wrote "So, the life and strength of civil liberty consist in limited Government and unlimited freedom of the written word", in *Tankar om borgerliga friheten* (Thoughts on Civil Liberty), Stockholm, 1759, Section 7, pp. 15–16.

[67] Ere Nokkala, "World's First Freedom of Writing and of the Press Ordinance as History of Political Thought", in Ulla Carlsson and David Goldberg (eds.), *The Legacy of Peter Forsskål – 250 years of Freedom of Expression*, Nordicom, Göteborg, 2017, pp. 39–42; Jonas Nordin, "The Swedish Freedom of Print Act of 1776 – Background and Significance", in *Journal International Media & Entertainment Law*, 2017/2018, vol. 7, no. 2, p. 139 ('Nordin, Swedish Act of 1776'); Jonas Nordin and John Christian Laursen, "Northern Declarations of Freedom of the Press: The Relative Importance of Philosophical Ideas and of Local Politics", in *Journal of the History of Ideas*, 2020, vol. 81, p. 227 ('Nordin and Laursen, Freedom of Press').

> and which may lead to some improvement or the prevention of harmful consequences [...].[68]

Unlike Article 9 of the English Bill of Rights which was limited to parliamentarians, the Swedish law applied to "everyone". Also, the Swedish law provided for citizens' public access to official documents.[69]

The granted freedom of expression was limited, however, in four aspects, namely, if a person expressed thoughts or opinion (i) against the protestant faith, (ii) the royal house or foreign powers, (iii) in the form of defamatory remarks, or (iv) by publishing indecent or obscene thoughts.[70]

The new law resulted in a wave of new publications including eight new periodicals, the establishment of Sweden's first daily newspaper in 1769 and, from 1769 to 1772, publications for an average of 434 political pamphlets per year.[71]

However, in 1772, the Swedish King Gustavus III assumed absolute power over the parliament and, in 1774, issued a new 'Ordinance Concerning Printing' which re-introduced prior censorship, to be carried out by printers which were held strictly responsible.[72]

11.3.3. Denmark-Norway (1770)

Until 1770, rigid censorship rules existed in Denmark-Norway. For example, a code issued by the Danish-Norwegian king Christian V provided for pre-censorship of books by universities, and of publications relating to the king, his government or the administration, by a person appointed by the king.[73] Further measures included that, in 1737, the General Church Inspection College obtained the authority to censor religious books and, in 1738 and 1756, censorship of (news)papers was introduced.[74]

---

68 The translation was done by Ian Giles and Peter Graves at the Department of European Languages and Cultures ('DELC'): Scandinavian Studies, University of Edinburgh in October 2016, "Kongl. Maj:ts Nådige Förordning, Angående Skrifoch Tryckfriheten", in *Haus Der Pressefreiheit*, 2 December 1766.

69 *Ibid.*, Articles 5–11; compare Nordin, Swedish Act of 1776, p. 138, see *supra* note 67.

70 Sweden, Majesty's Gracious Ordinance Regarding the Freedom of Writing and of the Press (Konglige Majestäts Nådige Förordning, Angående Skrif-och Tryck-friheten), 2 December 1766, Articles 1–3.

71 John C. Laursen, "Censorship in the Nordic Countries, ca.1750–1890: Transformations in Law, Theory, and Practice", in *Journal of Modern European History*, 2005, vol. 3, no. 1, p. 104 ('Laursen, Censorship').

72 *Ibid.*, p. 105.

73 Henry Commager, "Freedom of the Press in Denmark", in *Scandinavian Studies and Notes*, 1927, vol. 9, no. 8, p. 260 ('Commager').

74 *Ibid.*

In 1763 and 1764, German physician Struensee wrote, in the Danish-administered Altona, articles for periodicals which were banned.[75] Struensee suspended his ambition as a writer.[76]

Years later, in the autumn of 1770, when he worked for, advised and thereby exerted influence over the Danish-Norwegian king Christian VII, Struensee himself prepared, within days, a cabinet order lifting censorship in Denmark-Norway.[77] Unlike in Sweden, the preparation of this document was not preceded by scholarly, public or parliamentarian discussion in Denmark-Norway.[78] The order, issued in German, stated:

> von nun an Niemand schuldig und verbunden seyn soll, seine Bücher und Schriften, die er dem Druck übergeben will, der bishero verordnet gewesenen Censur und Approbation zu unterwerfen.[79]

An unofficial translation reads that:

> from now on, nobody should be bound or obligated to submit to censorship and approbation his books or writings which he intends to submit for printing.

Subsequently, Struensee circulated an elaborate reasoning for this cabinet order to bishops, universities and the Sorø Academy:

> [I]t is as harmful to the impartial search for truth as it is to the discovery of obsolete errors and prejudices, if upright patriots […] are hindered from being free to write according to their insight, conscience, and conviction, attacking abuses and uncovering prejudices. […] [W]e have decided to permit […] in general an unlimited freedom of the press of such a form, that from now on no one shall be required and obliged to submit books and writings that he wants to bring to the press to the previously required censorship and approval, and thus to submit them to the control of those who have undertaken the business until now of inspecting them […].[80]

---

75 Johann F. Struensee and David Panning, *Monatsschrift zum Nutzen und Vergnügen* (six editions published in Hamburg, 1763); Johann F. Struensee, *Zur Beförderung der Wissenschaft, der Künste, des Geschmacks und der Sitten*, Altona, 1764; Laursen, Censorship, p. 106, see *supra* note 71; Nordin and Laursen, Freedom of Press, p. 228, see *supra* note 67; Commager, p. 261, see *supra* note 73.

76 Commager, p. 261, see *supra* note 73.

77 Nordin and Laursen, Freedom of Press, p. 227, see *supra* note 67.

78 *Ibid.*, p. 235.

79 Holger Hansen, *Kabinetsstyrelsen i Danmark*, vol. I, Copenhagen, 1916, pp. 46–47 ('Hansen').

80 Denmark, National Archives: Kabinetssekretariatet 1766–1771: Kgl. ordrer til kabinetssekretariatet, John Christian Laursen (trans.), Cabinet Order of 4 September 1770; John C. Laursen, "David Hume and the Danish Debate about Freedom of the Press in the 1770s",

This order marked the abolition of censorship in Denmark-Norway. Politically, this society was an absolute monarchy and therefore the abolition occurred by way of an "opinion guided absolutism",[81] meaning, without preceding discussions but simply from above, by Struensee, with King Christian VII's approval.[82]

Voltaire congratulated the Danish-Norwegian king for this bold move.[83] The promulgation of freedom of the press resulted in volumes of publications, but quantity does not always mean quality. At least David Hume's essay 'On Freedom of the Press' was published in the Danish language in 1771.[84] The pamphlets seldom mentioned Spinoza and, even then, rarely in relation to freedom of the press; but they sometimes criticized him.[85] Many pamphlets mimicked or criticized those in power, less King Christian VII, but mainly Struensee, who found himself being the object of personal slander.[86]

Struensee, in the meantime, acting as the *de facto* Prime Minister of Denmark-Norway, reacted by way of Cabinet Order of 7 October 1771, which introduced restrictions on press freedom. The order stated:[87]

> 1) In order that the freedom to write and print granted on 14 September 1770 may not be misused to thereby transgress other civilian laws, all libel, lampoon, and rebellious publications shall in the future, as before, be subject to the established punishment.[88]

---

in *Journal of the History of Ideas*, 1998, vol. 59, no. 1, pp. 167–172, translated from the original German in Rasmus Nyerup (ed.), *Luxdorphiana, eller Bidrag til den danske Literairhistorie*, Copenhagen, 1791, pp. 1–2; compare Hansen, pp. 46–47, see *supra* note 79.

81 Nordin and Laursen, Freedom of Press, pp. 236, 229, see *supra* note 67.

82 Following the enactment of the decree, the Danish-Norwegian King wrote to the German authorities inquiring about the status of freedom of the press there (Commager, p. 262, see *supra* note 73).

83 Voltaire, "Épître 109 au Roi de Danemark, Christian VII, sur la liberté de la presse accordée dans tous ses états, January 1771", in Louis Moland (ed.), *Œuvres completes de Voltaire*, vol.10, Garnier, Paris, 1877, pp. 421–427.

84 Laursen, Censorship, p. 110, see *supra* note 71; Nordin and Laursen, Freedom of Press, pp. 229, see *supra* note 67.

85 Nordin and Laursen, Freedom of Press, pp. 230–231, see *supra* note 67; Laursen, Censorship, p. 110, see *supra* note 71.

86 Nordin and Laursen, Freedom of Press, p. 235, see *supra* note 67; Laursen, Censorship, p. 111, see *supra* note 71; Commager, pp. 263, 265, see *supra* note 73.

87 Translation into English, as published by Laursen, Censorship, p. 111, see *supra* note 71.

88 The original ordinance states in the German language that: "Die Pressfreyheit muss nicht gemisbraucht werden um dadurch andere bürgerliche Gesetze zu übertreten, weswegen alle Injurien, Pasquille und aufrürische Schriften nach wie vor den Bestrafungen unterworfen bleiben" (compare Commager, p. 265, see *supra* note 73).

> 2) Although all censorship is abolished, nevertheless every author who writes something shall be responsible that it is not contrary to existing laws and ordinances.
>
> 3) Printers cannot be allowed to print any book or publication if he [sic.] does not know who the author is, as he is to be responsible if he cannot name the author, to which end no book may be printed that does not contain the author's or printer's name.

For reasons unrelated to this order, Struensee was arrested, tried and executed in 1772. Following his death, the Danish-Norwegian regime tightened its grip, restricting freedom of the press step by step. Yet, discussions over the necessity, benefits and risks of stricter laws, diverging positions of Bolle Willum Luxdorph and Henrik Stampe, divided the new state council and chancellery.[89] Temporarily, a strategy of discrete suppression combined with a few signal cases was chosen.[90]

On 20 October 1773, police controls limited to daily and weekly periodicals were introduced in the form of past censorship.[91] On 27 November 1773, the restrictions were extended to other forms of publications.[92] In December 1790, judicial review over publications was introduced, replacing the police constable's assessment.[93]

Struensee's expansion of press freedom had, after his death, led his political successors to counter-react, including by way of curtailments in Denmark-Norway, but hardly to a complete return to the limits of the prior full censorship.[94]

11.3.4. Virginia, Declaration of Rights (12 June 1776)

Since 6 May 1776, the Virginia Convention met in Williamsburg, in Virginia. In mid-May 1776, the Convention formed a committee to draft, among others, a bill of rights for Virginia. While heading this project, George Mason produced handwritten notes between 20–26 May 1776 which, together, are considered a draft of ten articles proposed for the future bill of rights of Virginia.

The last proposed article read:

---

89 Thomas Munck, "Absolute Monarchy in Later Eighteenth-Century Denmark: Centralized Reform, Public Expectations, and the Copenhagen Press", in *The Historical Journal*, 1998, vol. 41, p. 210; Ulrik Langen and Frederik Stjernfelt, *The World's First Full Press Freedom*, Walter de Gruyter, 2022, pp. 441–445 ('Langen/Stjernfelt').

90 *Ibid.*, pp. 445–449.

91 *Ibid.*, pp. 449–450; Laursen, Censorship, pp. 105, 112, see *supra* note 71; Commager, p. 266, see *supra* note 73.

92 Langen and Stjernfelt, p. 453, see *supra* note 89; Commager, p. 266, see *supra* note 73.

93 Laursen, Censorship, p. 122, see *supra* note 71.

94 *Ibid.*

> That the freedom of the press, being the great bulwark of Liberty, can never be restrained but in a despotic government.[95]

Sources available online claim that, while the document is generally in George Mason's handwriting, its last section which includes press freedom is in Thomas Ludwell Lee's handwriting.[96] Indeed, the handwriting on the last page of the holograph manuscript changes to a different one in the article on freedom of the press.[97] Whether Lee himself may have proposed to insert this provision is contentious. William Wirt Henry believes Lee did so,[98] but other scholars are cautious. Rutland, while acknowledging Lee's handwriting, argues that "it is hazardous to say categorically that [the proposal on freedom of the press] originated either with Lee or George Mason".[99] Mellen, acknowledging the uncertainty regarding the authorship, argues that the three Lee brothers "acted as a major force" behind the draft on freedom of the press.[100] By contrast, other scholars claim that the committee authorized by the Virginia Convention proposed and drafted the article on freedom of the press.[101]

In conclusion, the exact authorship of the first draft on freedom of the press for Virginia's Declaration of Rights is unknown. In comparison to this first draft, the committee formed by the Virginia Convention made more stylistic changes.[102] However, no minutes of the debates or votes exist.

On 12 June 1776, the fifth convention at Williamsburg unanimously adopted the Virginia Declaration of Rights. Its Article 12 states that "the Freedom of the Press is one of the great Bulwarks of Liberty, and can never be restrained but by despotic Government".

---

95 George Mason, "The Virginia Declaration of Rights", Accession 51818, Personal Papers Collection, Library of Virginia, Richmond, Virginia, 1776.

96 "Historical Documents of the Founders of the United States of America", USA National Archives, National Historical Publications and Records Commission and University of Virginia Press; "The Virginia Declaration of Rights – First Draft", George Mason's Guston Hall.

97 George Mason and Thomas L. Lee, "First Draft of the Virginia Declaration of Rights", 26 May 1776, USA, Library of Congress, Manuscript Division, p. 3.

98 William W. Henry, *Patrick Henry: Life, Correspondence and Speeches*, vol. 1, Charles Scribner's Sons, 1891, p. 428.

99 Robert A. Rutland, *Papers of George Mason*, vol. 1, University of North Carolina Press, 1970, p. 281.

100 The three *Lee* brothers were named, Thomas Ludwell, Richard Henry and Arthur. See Roger Mellen, "The Lee Family and Freedom of the Press in Virginia", in *Journalism History*, 2017, vol. 43, p. 128 ('Mellen').

101 Brent Tarter and Robert L. Scribner (eds.), *Revolutionary Virginia: The Road to Independence*, University Press of Virginia, 7th ed., 1983, p. 277, note 21; Wendel Bird, *Press and Speech Under Assault: The Early Supreme Court Justices, the Sedition Act of 1798, and the Campaign Against Dissent*, Oxford University Press, 2016, pp. 187–188.

102 Compare Mellen, pp. 123, 126, *supra* note 100.

11.3.5. France, Declaration on Human and Civic Rights (1789)

In Europe, the period of enlightenment culminated in the French Declaration on Human and Civic Rights, 1789.

On 11 July 1789, Marquis de Lafayette presented to the French National Assembly a draft which contained the following proposal on freedom of expression:

> Tout homme nait avec des droits inaliénable et imprescriptibles; tells sont la liberté de toutes ses opinions, […] la communication de ses pensées par tous les moyens possible.[103]

An unofficial translation reads:

> Every human is born with inalienable and imprescriptible rights; these are the liberty of all his opinions, […] the communication of his thoughts by all possible means.

Marquis de Lafayette's draft afforded the freedom of expression to any human being by birth and did not provide for the possibility to limit this right.

On 13 August 1789, the sixth committee of the French Assembly proposed narrower language through draft Article 19 of the French Declaration on Human and Civic Rights:

> La libre communication de pensées étant un droit de citoyen, elle ne doit ètre restraint qu'autant qu'elle nuit aux droits d'autruit.[104]

An unofficial translation reads:

> The free communication of thoughts is a citizen's right, which should only be restricted to the extent as it harms the rights of others.

The sixth committee limited the freedom of expression to "citizens" of the French Republic in contrast to Lafayette who wanted to afford it to every human. Further, the committee's draft provided for limitations of this freedom insofar as its exercise could harm the rights of third parties.

On 24 August 1789, the French Assembly discussed the proposed Article 19. During the debate, the Duke of Rouchefoucauld tabled a different wording which, after some debate, was adopted:

> La libre communication des pensées et des opinions et un des droits les plus précieux à l'homme; tout citoyens peut donc parler,

[103] France, Assemblée nationale constituante (1789–1791), archives parlementaires de 1787 à 1860, 11 July 1789, p. 222.

[104] France, Assemblée nationale constituante (1789–1791), archives parlementaires de 1787 à 1860, 12 August 1789, p. 432.

> écrire, imprimer, librement, sauf à répondre des abus de cette liberté, dans le cas prévues par la loi.[105]

An unofficial translation reads:

> The free communication of ideas and of opinions is one of the most precious rights of man. Any citizen may therefore speak, write and publish freely, except what is tantamount to the abuse of this liberty in the cases provided for by law.

Rouchefoucauld explained that the inclusion of the press would be advantageous as this would destroy despotism and fanatism.[106] Barrère de Vieuzac and Maximilien Robespierre supported this, adding that freedom of the press would form an "inseparable part" of the free communication of ideas.[107] Other proposals were rejected and the article as proposed by the Duke of Rouchefoucauld was accepted by vote. The adopted article remained *verbatim* and was two days later, on 26 August 1789, listed as Article 11 when the French Assembly adopted the *Déclaration des Droits de l'Homme et du Citoyen* (Declaration of Human and Civic Rights).

11.3.6. United States of America, First Amendment to the Constitution (1791)

More than two years later, by 15 December 1791, Virginia, as the eleventh state of the then 14 states of the USA, ratified the First Amendment to the Constitution of the USA ('USA Constitution') bringing the total number of ratifications[108] to a three-fourths[109] majority. Together, this first and nine other amendments to the USA Constitution are often referred to as the 'Bill of Rights'. The relevant part of the First Amendment states that "Congress shall make no law [...] abridging the freedom of speech, or of the press [...]".

A comparison between American and French approaches reveals commonalities and differences. Both legislations proclaim the right of the individual for freedom of expression. The French approach focuses on the *person* emphasizing his freedom to speak, write and publish. By contrast, the First Amendment to the USA Constitution focuses on the *legislator* by limiting his power to curtail the freedom of expression and of the press. As the American approach expressly mentions the Congress, the argument may be made that the right of the

---

[105] France, Assemblée nationale constituante (1789–1791), archives parlementaires de 1787 à 1860, 24 August 1789, p. 482 ('French Archives 24 August 1789').

[106] *Ibid.*

[107] *Ibid.*, p. 483.

[108] New Jersey, Maryland, North Carolina, South Carolina, New Hampshire, Delaware, New York, Pennsylvania, Rhode Island, Vermont and Virginia.

[109] USA Constitution, 4 March 1789, Article V (https://www.legal-tools.org/doc/bc3d56/).

individual binds public authorities only, but not private companies, if the latter choose to adopt measures limiting freedom of speech.

The First Amendment to the USA Constitution differs from its initial proposal. On 8 June 1789, James Madison Jr. had proposed a different focus, stating that the "*people* shall not be deprived or abridged of their right to speak, to write, or to publish their sentiments".[110]

This approach focused on the people emphasizing their freedom and was therefore similar to the French one. However, the Special Committee and the Senate later modified Madison's approach and adopted the version now known as the First Amendment to the USA Constitution.

Insofar as the American approach is concerned, it aims to limit and check legislative power, thereby indirectly enabling the individual's right for freedom of expression; yet also, the French legislator was conscient of the role of the state. Before the adoption of the article on freedom of expression, Barrère de Vieuxzac claimed that the freedom of expression would be the great maxim and then the French "constitution and laws would adapt this freedom to the principle and nature of the government. You must make the declaration of human rights to the code of the legislator himself. This is the type on which legislative power will form all of its institutions".[111]

11.4. International Human Rights Treaties after the Second World War

This section discusses international codifications of freedom of expression through the Universal Declaration of Human Rights ('UDHR') and the main regional human rights treaties on each continent.

11.4.1. Universal Declaration of Human Rights (1948)

On 6 January 1941, in the midst of the Second World War, Franklin D. Roosevelt, then President of the USA, delivered to the Congress his State of the Union address that is commonly referred to as the 'Four Freedoms'. He promised to ensure that the world would be founded upon four essential human freedoms, the first being the freedom of speech and expression.[112]

His wife, Eleanor Roosevelt, chaired the drafting committee of the Commission on Human Rights in its preparation of the UDHR, under the auspices of the emerging United Nations ('UN') years later.

[110] United States Congress, *The Debates and Proceedings in the Congress of the United States*, vol. I, Gales and Seaton, Washington, 1834, column 451, 8 June 1789 (emphasis added).

[111] Unofficial translation; French Archives 24 August 1789, see *supra* note 105.

[112] Franklin D. Roosevelt, "Annual Message to Congress", Records of the United States Senate, SEN 77A-H1, Record Group 46, 6 January 1941 (https://www.legal-tools.org/doc/0ao7w5/).

On 14 December 1946, the UN General Assembly ('GA') called freedom of information "a fundamental human right and the touchstone of all freedoms to which the UN is consecrated".[113]

In June 1947, the UN Secretariat prepared a first draft of the UDHR which contained, in Article 15, the right to freedom of expression: "Everyone has the right to form, to hold, to receive and to impart opinions".[114]

Also, a proposal of the UK contained an article on freedom of expression, but unlike the proposal of the UN Secretariat, it provided for several options to *limit* the right to freedom of expression by way of "necessary restrictions, penalties or liabilities".[115] One such possibility of limitation would have been if a publication incites persons to alter, by violence, the system of government.[116] The UK proposal was maintained for the purposes of the first report of the UN's drafting committee, but was omitted in its second report.[117] The latter report contained a proposal by the Union of Socialist Republics ('USSR') which asked not to tolerate incitement to war between nations.[118]

However, neither the proposals of the UK and the USSR nor Article 17(2) of the Draft Covenant on Human Rights[119] agreed to in April 1948, all of which would have offered explicit possibilities for states to limit the freedom of expression, were included in the final version of the UDHR, which stated in Article 19:

> Everyone has the right to freedom of opinion and expression; this right includes freedom to hold opinions without interference and

---

[113] Calling of an International Conference on Freedom of Information, UN Doc. A/RES/59, 14 December 1946 (https://www.legal-tools.org/doc/5tb5c7/).

[114] Draft Outline of International Bill of Rights, UN Doc. E/CN.4/AC.1/3, 4 June 1947 (https://www.legal-tools.org/doc/yip7t9/).

[115] Text of Letter from Lori Dukeston, the UK representative on the Human Rights Commission, to the Secretary-General of the UN, UN Doc. E/CN.4/AC.1/4, 5 June 1947, Annex 1, Article 14(c) (https://www.legal-tools.org/doc/zxmupb/); compare Report of the Drafting Committee to the Commission on Human Rights, UN Doc. E/CN.4/21, 1 July 1947, Article 14(3) (https://www.legal-tools.org/doc/1q8tos/).

[116] UN Doc. E/CN.4/AC.1/4, 5 June 1947, see *supra* note 115.

[117] *Ibid.*, Article 14(3) and Report of the Drafting Committee to the Commission on Human Rights, UN Doc. E/CN.4/95, 21 May 1948, Articles 17, 18 ('UN Committee UDHR, Second Report') (https://www.legal-tools.org/doc/3onjgq/).

[118] UN Committee UDHR, Second Report, 1948, see *supra* note 117. Compare also USA Department of State Bulletin, 2 January 1949, vol. XX, no. 496, publication no. 3385, p. 20.

[119] Compare Article 17 of Draft Covenant of Human Rights, as contained in Final Act, UN Conference of Information with Draft Convention on Information, Geneva, UN Doc. E/CONF-6/79-EN, 23 March 1948–21 April 1948, Annex B, Section II (1) and (2) (https://www.legal-tools.org/doc/sndoqv/).

> to seek, receive and impart information and ideas through any media and regardless of frontiers.[120]

In conclusion, the UDHR adopted the freedom of expression *without* any express mentioning of limits to this freedom. This omission by the UDHR's drafters was conscious, as they knew of the proposed limitations contained in the UK and Soviet proposals and in Article 17(2) of the Draft Covenant on Human Rights. The latter had provided for several possibilities to limit the freedom of expression, including the imposition of *penalties*:

> The right to freedom of expression carries with it duties and responsibilities and may, therefore, be subject *to penalties, liabilities or restrictio*ns clearly defined by law, but only with regard to:
>
> (a) Matters which must remain secret in the interests of national safety;
>
> (b) Expressions which incite persons to alter by violence the system of government;
>
> (c) Expressions which directly incite persons to commit criminal acts;
>
> (d) Expressions which are obscene;
>
> (e) Expressions injurious to the fair conduct of legal proceedings;
>
> (f) Infringements of literary or artistic rights;
>
> (g) Expressions about other persons natural or legal which defame their reputations or are otherwise injurious to them without benefiting the public;
>
> (h) The systematic diffusion of deliberately false or distorted reports which undermine friendly relations between peoples and States; […].

The comparison between the above Article 17(2) of the Draft Covenant on Human Rights and Article 19 of the UDHR reveals that the latter chose a different approach, omitting any references to possible restrictions of the freedom of expression.

On 10 December 1948, the GA adopted the UDHR as Resolution 217. Of the 58 states comprising the UN at the time, 48 voted in favour, eight states, including Poland, Czechoslovakia, the USSR, the Byelorussian Soviet Socialist Republic, the Ukrainian Soviet Socialist Republic and Yugoslavia abstained, with two states not casting a vote.[121]

---

[120] UDHR, UN Doc. A/RES/217(III), 10 December 1948, Article 19 (https://www.legal-tools.org/doc/085437/)

[121] Record of 183rd Plenary Meeting, Continuation of the Discussion on the Draft UDHR: Report of the Third Committee (A/777), UN Doc. A/PV/183, 10 December 1948, p. 933 (https://www.legal-tools.org/doc/0j0vp8/).

Separate votes were taken on each article, including on Article 19 of the UDHR which contained the freedom of expression. Forty-five states adopted Article 19 and four states abstained.[122] The UDHR is a resolution of the GA which, as such, has no binding force.[123] The resolution lacked the character of an international treaty and was therefore not open to ratification or accession by states.

11.4.2. Subsequent International Human Rights Treaties

The definition of the UDHR of freedom of expression forms the basis for subsequent legal developments on the level of regional or international treaties. Starting by the mere wording of Article 19 of the UDHR, this section adopts a comparative approach. The objects of comparison are relevant international treaties in chronological order:

Date	Instrument
1950	Article 10 of the European Convention on Human Rights ('ECHR')[124]
1966	Article 19 of the International Covenant on Civil and Political Rights ('ICCPR')[125]
1969	Article 13 of the American Convention on Human Rights ('AmCHR')[126]
1981	Article 9 of the African Charter on Human and Peoples' Rights ('ACHPR')[127]
2012	Article 23 of the Association of Southeast Asian Nations Human Rights Declaration ('AHRD')[128]

Table 1: List of international treaties selected for comparative analysis.

Article 19 of the UDHR can be broken down into six components:

1. The right to freedom of opinion and expression includes freedom,
2. to hold opinions,

---

[122] *Ibid.*

[123] Articles 10 and 11(1) of the UN Charter, 26 June 1948 (https://www.legal-tools.org/doc/6b3cd5/) speak of "recommendations" in relation to actions by the GA. A provision similar to Article 25 of the UN Charter for decisions of the Security Council does not exist with regard to actions of the UNGA.

[124] Council of Europe ('CoE'), ECHR, Council of Europe Treaty Series 005, 4 November 1950 (https://www.legal-tools.org/doc/c809a3/).

[125] ICCPR, 19 December 1996, p. 171 (https://www.legal-tools.org/doc/2838f3/).

[126] AmCHR, 22 November 1969 (https://www.legal-tools.org/doc/1152cf/).

[127] ACHPR, 27 June 1981 (https://www.legal-tools.org/doc/f0db44/).

[128] AHRD, 18 November 2012 (https://www.legal-tools.org/doc/545db2/).

3. without interference;
4. to seek, receive and impart information and ideas,
5. through any media,
6. regardless of frontiers.

Comparing these components with the subsequent human rights treaties shows the commonalities of the definitions:

UDHR Article 19	ECHR Article 10	ICCPR Article 19	AmCHR Article 13	ACHPR Article 9	AHRD Article 23
freedom of opinion and expression	freedom of expression		freedom of thought and expression		freedom of opinion and expression
hold opinions	hold opinions	hold opinions		express and disseminate opinions	
without interference	without interference by public authority	without interference			without interference
seek, receive and impart information	receive and impart informatio and ideas	seek, receive and impart information and ideas	seek, receive and impart information and ideas	receive information	seek, receive and impart information
through any media		orally, in writing or in print, in the form of art, or through any other media of his choice	orally, in writing, in print, in the form of art, or through any other medium of one's choice		orally, in writing, or through any other medium of that person's choice
regardless of frontiers	regardless of frontiers	regardless of frontiers	regardless of frontiers		

Table 2: Provisions of select international human rights treaties recognizing the right to freedom of expression.

The commonalities of language in the definitions in the various human rights instruments are striking. Only Article 9 of the ACHPR does *not* contain certain language. These omissions are marked against a black background. However, the African Commission on Human and Peoples' Rights ('AfCommHPR') addressed these omissions by establishing principles in 2019. For example, the (third) element 'without interference', though missing in the text of Article 9 of the ACHPR, has been subsequently added through Principles 2 and 38 of the Declaration of Principles of the Freedom of Expression and Access to Information in Africa ('2019 Declaration on ACHPR').[129] The element 'regardless of frontiers' has also been added through Principle 10 of the 2019 Declaration on ACHPR.

In conclusion, the international definition of freedom of expression gained momentum in 1948 through Article 19 of the UDHR. Since then, international and regional human rights treaties have adopted the major elements of this definition. The only continent where the human right of freedom of expression has not been subject to a continent-wide definition is Asia. Only the ten states belonging to Association of Southeast Asian Nations ('ASEAN') ratified the definition of freedom of expression through Article 23 of the AHRD.[130] Hence, the remaining Asian states are only bound, through ratification of the ICCPR, to the definition of freedom of expression contained in its Article 19. Yet, this approach *via* Article 19 of the ICCPR does not work for seven Asian states which neither signed nor ratified this treaty.[131] Further, on 5 October 1998, the People's Republic of China signed the ICCPR, but it has not yet ratified it at the time of writing this chapter.

11.5. Limitations of Freedom of Expression

Having clarified the definition and codification of freedom of expression, this section discusses which limitations, if any, are recognized by international law for the freedom of expression.

Any authority which guarantees the freedom of expression has to engage in a balancing exercise. It has to reconcile two sets of partially overlapping, partially diverging values. The first set consists of allowing (i) open debate, (ii)

[129] AfCommHPR, 65th session, 21 October 2019–10 November 2019, compare also Principles 5, 13(1) and (4), 17(1) and (2), 18(2).

[130] Brunei, Cambodia, Indonesia, Laos, Malaysia, Myanmar, the Philippines, Singapore, Thailand and Vietnam.

[131] Bhutan, Brunei Darussalam, Malaysia, Myanmar, Oman, Saudi Arabia, Singapore and the United Arab Emirates.

individual autonomy, and (iii) development of the individual and society as a whole. On the other hand, the authority is obligated to (i) prevent attacks on vulnerable communities, ensure (ii) equal, non-discriminatory participation of all individuals in public life, and (iii) public order. This second set of values may demand restrictions to the freedom of expression. Yet restrictions must be *exceptional*, subject to narrow conditions and strict oversight. Such oversight is provided in Europe through the European Court of Human Rights ('EuCtHr'), in Africa through the African Court on Human and People's Rights, and in the Americas and on the UN level through international commissions which have the competence to receive individual complaints as part of review mechanisms.[132]

The various human rights treaties providing possibilities for limitations of freedom of expression need to be distinguished as some provide for narrow and defined options to limit and others for broad based authorizations to limit this liberty.

11.5.1. Broad Authorizations

The broadest possibilities for authorities to restrict the freedom of expression are provided for by Article 11 of the French Declaration of Human Rights and Article 9 of the ACHPR. The relevant part of the French provision refers to "speak, write […] with freedom, except what is tantamount to the abuse of this liberty in the cases determined *by law*" (emphasis added). Similarly, Article 9 of the ACHPR states "everyone shall have the right to express and disseminate his opinions *within the law*" (emphasis added).

These authorizations to limit the freedom of expression are *broad*, as all a government is required to do is to enact a law curtailing the freedom. The literal interpretation of these provisions suggests that not even observance of the principle of proportionality is required. However, the AfCommHPR subsequently rectified this omission through Principle 9 of the 2019 Declaration on ACHPR:

> (1) States may only limit the exercise of the rights to freedom of expression and access to information, if the limitation:
>
> a. is prescribed by law;
>
> b. serves a legitimate aim; and

[132] Compare, for example, ECHR, Articles 34, 32, 33, see *supra* note 124 (https://www.legal-tools.org/doc/8267cb/); Protocol to the African Charter for Human and People's Rights on the Establishment of an African Court on Human and Peoples' Rights, 10 June 1998, Article 5(3) (https://www.legal-tools.org/doc/b9eae8/); AmCHR, Article 44, see *supra* note 126; Optional Protocol to the ICCPR, 16 December 1966, Articles 1, 2 (https://www.legal-tools.org/doc/4841b8/).

> c. is a necessary and proportionate means to achieve the stated aim in a democratic society.

Further, sub-paragraph 4 clarifies that to be necessary and proportionate, the limitation shall:

> a. originate from a pressing and substantial need that is relevant and sufficient;
>
> b. have a direct and immediate connection to the expression and disclosure of information, and be the least restrictive means of achieving the stated aim; and
>
> c. be such that the benefit of protecting the stated interest outweighs the harm to the expression and disclosure of information, including with respect to the sanctions authorised.

11.5.2. Pre-Defined Reasons for Measures

The four international human rights instruments discussed in this section not only recognize that limitations must be prescribed by law and be proportionate, but also pre-define legal interests or the aim which may justify the limitation of the freedom of expression. These are Article 10(2) of the ECHR, Article 19(3) of the ICCPR, Article 13 of the AmCHR, and Article 8 of the AHRD.

These instruments commonly provide that four legal interests or aims can justify the limitation of the freedom of expression: (i) national security, (ii) public safety, sometimes referred to as public order, (iii) (public) health or morals, or (iv) protection of reputation or rights of others.

Further, Article 10(2) of the ECHR lists four additional legal interests or aims, which are not mentioned in the other international human rights treaties, as justifying the limitation of the freedom of expression: (i) territorial integrity, (ii) prevention of disorder or crime, (iii) preventing the disclosure of information received in confidence, or (iv) maintaining the authority and impartiality of the judiciary. Only Article 8 of the AHRD allows for an additional legal interest which may justify limitations: the general welfare of peoples in a democratic society.

11.5.3. States' Treaty Authorization to Penalize

Among all human rights treaties which define the freedom of expression, only the ECHR expressly allows that states may limit abuse of freedom of speech by way of penalization. Article 10(2) ECHR mentions the "exercise of these freedoms […] may be subject to formalities, conditions, restrictions or *penalties*" (emphasis added). However, the ECHR's reference to penalties constitutes an authorization of states to punish the most severe violations of freedom of speech. The use of the verb "may" indicates that no obligation of states to penalize was created. To decide whether indeed an obligation to criminalize certain conduct involving the freedom of expression is created, due attention is to be given to the verbs used in human rights treaties.

11.5.4. Treaty Obligation to Prohibit by Law

Article 20(1) and 20(2) of the ICCPR mention that states shall *prohibit by law* propaganda for war or hatred and incitement to discrimination, hostility or violence.

The drafting process of the ICCPR supports that the formulation 'shall prohibit by law' authorizes, but does *not* require, a state to impose criminal sanctions for the specified abuse of freedom of expression. Namely, this formulation was preferred over the alternative phrase "constitutes a crime and shall be punished by the law of the state".[133] Further, the UN Special Rapporteur on the Promotion and Protection of the Right to Freedom of Opinion and Expression also argued that Article 20(2) of the ICCPR does not require states to criminalize such expressions amounting to incitement to violence.[134]

In *Rabbae et al. v. the Netherlands*, four members of the UN Human Rights Committee expressed their views that states can meet the obligation to 'prohibit by law' if they offer civil or administrative sanctions.[135]

How far-reaching the obligation of 'prohibit by law' is for states is revealed by a comparison of Article 20 of the ICCPR with Article 13(5) of the AmCHR. The latter provision states that propaganda for war and incitement to lawless violence "shall be considered as offenses punishable by law". This language is stronger than the 'prohibit by law' phrase of the ICCPR as the AmCHR specifically speaks of an offense which is *punishable* and not generally of a prohibition only. However, states are just asked to *consider*, which involves careful thinking before decision-making. The obligation to consider does not predict the outcome of the process.

Principle 23(1) of the 2019 Declaration on ACHPR does not even require states to prohibit 'by law', but simply to prohibit incitement to hostility, violence or certain types of discrimination. It follows that a prohibition by civil or

---

[133] Draft International Covenants on Human Rights, UN Doc. A/2929, 1 July 1955, Chapter VI, para. 194 (https://www.legal-tools.org/doc/qg02x2/).

[134] Report of the Special Rapporteur on the Promotion and Protection of the Right to Freedom of Opinion and Expression, UN Doc. A/67/357, 7 September 2012, para. 47 ('Special Rapporteur Report on Freedom of Opinion') (https://www.legal-tools.org/doc/o6o0t6/).

[135] UN Human Rights Committee, *The Case of Rabbae et al. v. the Netherlands*, Views Adopted by the Committee under Article 5(4) of the Optional Protocol, Concerning Communication No. 2124/2011, Concurring Opinion of Cleveland and Politi, 14 July 2016, para. 4 and Concurring and Partly Dissenting Opinion of Shany and Rodley, para. 3 (https://www.legal-tools.org/doc/zixinh/); William A. Schabas, *UN ICCPR – Novak's CCPR Commentary*, 3rd ed., Engel Publisher, Kehl, 2019, Article 20, para. 24 ('Schabas ICCPR Commentary').

administrative action may suffice. Only in the "most severe cases" and "as a last resort" should states criminalize prohibited speech.[136]

11.5.5. Treaty Obligation to Penalize

Other international treaties are more specific about the obligation of states to create a criminal offence. In particular, the Convention on the Prevention and Punishment of the Crime of Genocide ('Genocide Convention') obligates states to "provide effective penalties", for example, for incitement to genocide.[137] The International Convention on the Elimination of All Forms of Racial Discrimination ('CERD') requires states to "declare an offence punishable by law" with regards to the dissemination of ideas based on racial superiority or hatred and incitement to racial discrimination.[138] The phrase to 'declare an offence' in Article 4(a) of the CERD is more prescriptive than to 'prohibit by law' as used in Article 20 of the ICCPR.

The Committee on the Elimination of Racial Discrimination ('CERD Committee') emphasized that Article 4 was the "principal vehicle for combating hate speech" and further reasoned that criminalization of forms of racist expression should be left for "serious" cases, while stressing that less serious cases should be addressed by measures *other* than criminal law.[139]

Furthermore, the mere creation of criminal offences by States Parties to the CERD is insufficient, as its *effective* implementation, meaning sanctions by the competent national tribunals and other state institutions, matters as well.[140] What is relevant is investigating and, where appropriate, prosecuting in an expedient manner.[141] However, it depends on the details of each case. In *TBB-Turkish Union v. Germany*, Judge Velazquez argued that:

> [CERD] does not require the criminal prosecution of every expression of ideas of racial superiority or every statement inciting to racial discrimination. Rather, the Convention leaves States parties with discretion to determine when criminal prosecution would best

[136] 2019 Declaration on ACHPR, 10 November 2019, Principle 23(2) (https://www.legal-tools.org/doc/rs94e6/).

[137] Genocide Convention, 9 December 1948, Articles 5, 3(c) (https://www.legal-tools.org/doc/498c38/).

[138] CERD, 21 December 1965, Article 4(a) (https://www.legal-tools.org/doc/43a925/).

[139] UN Committee on the Elimination of Racial Discrimination, General Recommendation 35, UN Doc. CERD/C/GC/35, 26 September 2013, paras. 8, 12 ('CERD Committee Recommendation 35') (https://www.legal-tools.org/doc/d3c55a/).

[140] *Ibid.*, paras. 13, 17; CERD Committee, *TBB-Turkish Union in Berlin/Brandenburg v. Germany*, 4 April 2013, Communication No. 48/2010, CERD/C/82/D/48/2010, para. 12.3 ('*TBB-Turkish Union v. Germany*') (https://www.legal-tools.org/doc/suck1q/).

[141] *Ibid.*, para. 17.

> serve the goals of the Convention while safeguarding the principles of UDHR [...].[142]

Article 23(2) of the 2019 Declaration on ACHPRobligates states to criminalize the most severe cases of prohibited speech as a last resort.

Within the European Union, all Member States shall "ensure" that intentional public incitement to violence or hatred directed against a group or a member of such a group is punishable.[143] The European Commission against Racism and Intolerance ('ECRI') of the CoE requests its Member States to "take action [...] through the use of criminal law" against hate speech which incites acts of violence, intimidation, hostility or discrimination against those targeted by it.[144]

11.5.6. Conclusion

While some international human rights treaties define abuses of freedom of expression, they do *not* contain the obligation for states to create offences enabling criminal prosecution and convictions. This applies to Article 20 of the ICCPR and Article 9 of the ACHPR. However, in Africa, for the most severe cases of prohibited speech, an obligation for states to create offences is constituted through Article 23(2) of the 2019 Declaration on ACHPR. In the Asian continent, no regional human rights treaty currently obligates a state specifically to create offences punishing speech or speech crimes.

In conclusion, some international treaty law does partially contain an obligation to criminalize certain abuses of freedom of speech,[145] while other speech-related conduct is still seen as to be 'prohibited' by states, *stopping short* of the obligation to create penal offences, investigate and punish. However, even if no explicit obligation for states to punish may exist regarding some abuses of freedom of expression, the mere classification as 'prohibited' is still indicative of the severity of the speech-related conduct.

---

142 *TBB-Turkish Union v. Germany*, Individual Opinion of Committee Member Mr. Carlos Manuel Vazquez (Dissenting), 4 April 2013, CERD/C/82/3, para. 10 (https://www.legal-tools.org/doc/5n6y25/).

143 Council of the European Union, Council Framework Decision, 28 November 2008, 2008/913/JHA, Article 1(a) ('EU Council Decision 2008') (https://www.legal-tools.org/doc/45b60e/).

144 ECRI, General Policy Recommendation No. 15 on Combating Hate Speech, 8 December 2015, Recommendation X ('CoE Recommendation No. 15') (https://www.legal-tools.org/doc/hb51n3/).

145 Genocide Convention, Article III(c), see *supra* note 137; CERD, Article 4(a), see *supra* note 138.

11.6. Treaty Obligations to at Least 'Prohibit'

This section looks at the (regional or worldwide) scope of the prohibitions of certain abuses of freedom of expression; particularly regarding dissemination of information about racial superiority of a group and the dissemination of hatred as well as of propaganda for war. Finally, the scope of the prohibition of incitement is discussed particularly regarding which objects of incitement are prohibited and, ultimately, penalized.

11.6.1. Dissemination of Information About Racial Superiority

Article 4(a) of the CERD obliges states to declare as an offence any dissemination of ideas based on racial superiority.

By mid-June 2022, 182 of 197 states had ratified the CERD[146] which makes this treaty almost universal. However, particularly with regard to Article 4 of the CERD and its obligation on states to create domestic penal legislation, 19 states issued observations or made reservations.[147]

11.6.2. Advocacy of (National, Racial or Religious) Hatred

Regarding advocacy of hatred, one needs to distinguish between the forms of hatred and whether the treaty in question creates an obligation to prohibit (only) or rather to create an offence.

11.6.2.1. Racial Hatred

Three instruments, on the worldwide (Article 4(a) of the CERD) and regional levels (for the Americas: Article 13(5) of the AmCHR, and for the European Union: Article 1(a) of the 2008 EU Council Decision), oblige states to declare an offence of racial hatred. This is an indication that the creation of an offence of racial discrimination and thus the sanctioning of speech crimes, in this regard, is certainly mandatory, at least in the Americas and Europe and otherwise almost universally, though 19 states have made observations or declared reservations against Article 4 of the CERD.

11.6.2.2. National or Religious Hatred

Regarding the dissemination of national or religious hatred, the focus of this anthology, the situation is not as strong. First, the relevant universal instrument, Article 20(2) of the ICCPR, only obliges states to "prohibit" national, racial or

---

[146] Among the 15 states which had not yet ratified CERD were seven constituting pacific islands: Cook Islands, Nauru, Niue, Palau, Samoa, Tuvalu and Vanuatu. Naura and Palau have signed CERD. See the database of the UN Office of Legal Affairs.

[147] Antigua and Barbuda, Australia, Austria, Bahamas, Barbados, Belgium, France, Grenada, Ireland, Italy, Japan, Malta, Monaco, Nepal, Papua New Guinea, Switzerland, Tonga, the UK and the USA.

religious hatred, stopping short of a state obligation to create offences and to investigate and impose penal sanctions.

Regionally, in the European Union and in the Americas, states are obligated to create offenses relating to national or religious hatred.[148] In Africa, speech advocating for national or religious hatred is in general only "prohibited", except for the "most severe cases" for which states are obligated to penalize as a last resort.[149] By contrast, states in Asia neither carry the obligation to create offenses relating to national or religious hatred, nor to investigate and punish such cases.

11.6.3. Propaganda for War

Only states in the Americas are obligated to create an offence and sanction propaganda for war.[150] By contrast, Article 20(2) of the ICCPR, only obliges states to "prohibit" by law, an obligation which states can meet if they provide for civil or administrative sanctions.[151] A general prohibition clause in domestic penal or other law suffices.[152]

Further, the definition and scope of the terms 'propaganda' and 'war' are vague and thus susceptible to abuse.[153]

11.6.4. Conclusion

This section discussed various treaty prohibitions of speech-related conduct which falls squarely within the ambit of hate speech: dissemination of racial superiority, advocacy of (national, racial or religious) hatred and propaganda for war. All these speech-related activities are prohibited on the international level. Whether or not international treaties obligate states to penalize relevant conduct has been discussed in detail. Arguably, states are under a treaty obligation to penalize the dissemination of information relating to racial superiority and speech relating to racial hate. However, differences in treaty obligations exist on each continent. The situation is further complicated by the reservations and observations of 16 states to Article 20 of the ICCPR, and of 18 states to Article 4

---

[148] AmCHR, Article 13(5), see *supra* note 132; EU Council Decision 2008, Article 1(a), see *supra* note 143. Regarding Europe, compare also CoE, Problems Arising From the Coexistence of the UN Covenants of Human Rights and the European Convention on Human Rights, CoE-1970-EN–H-(70)7, 1 August 1970, para. 187.

[149] 2019 Declaration on ACHPR, Principle 23(1) and (2), see *supra* note 136.

[150] AmCHR, Article 13(5), see *supra* note 132.

[151] Schabas ICCPR Commentary, 2019, Article 20, paras. 24, 13, see *supra* note 135.

[152] Karl J. Partsch, "Freedom of Conscience and Expression and Political Freedom", in Louis Henkin (ed.), *International Bill of Rights*, Columbia University Press, New York, 1981, p. 228.

[153] Schabas ICCPR Commentary, 2019, Article 20, paras. 9, 12, see *supra* note 135; Amal Clooney and Philippa Webb, "The Right to Insult in International Law", in *Colombia Human Rights Law Review*, 2017, vol. 47, pp. 44, 54.

of the CERD. Insofar as the few critical voices are concerned, they treat these activities as states acting as 'persistent objectors' thereby preventing the crystallization of customary international law. Judge Meron observed that:

> no state party has objected to such reservations [of states to the ICCPR and CERD]. The number and extent of the reservations reveal that profound disagreement persists in the international community as to whether mere hate speech is or should be prohibited, indicating that Article 4 CERD and Article 20 of the ICCPR do not reflect a settled principle. Since a consensus among states has not crystallized, there is clearly no norm of customary international law criminalizing mere hate speech.[154]

11.6.5. A Focus on Incitement

With regards to incitement, what matters is the object of the incitement. Generally, there are distinctions in (treaty) law, as shown in Table 3 below.

Object of incitement:	Treaty obligation:
Genocide	Article 3(c) of the Genocide Convention Articles 6 and 25(3)(e) of the Statute of the International Criminal Court ('ICC') Article 4(3)(c) of the Statute of the ICTY Article 2(3)(c) of the Statute of the ICTR
(Lawless) Violence	Article 4(a) of the CERD Article 20(2) of the ICCPR Article 13(5) of the AmCHR Article 1(a) of EU Council Decision 2008 Recommendation X of CoE Recommendation No. 15
Racial Discrimination	Article 4(a) of the CERD Recommendation X of CoE Recommendation No.15
Intimidation and Hostility	Article 20(2) of the ICCPR Recommendation X of CoE Recommendation No. 15

Table 3: Provisions of international treaties with respect to the object of incitement.

[154] International Criminal Tribunal for Rwanda ('ICTR'), *Prosecutor v. F. Nahimana et al.*, Appeals Chamber, Judge Theodor Meron, Partially Dissenting Opinion, 28 November 2007, ICTR-99-52-A, para. 5 ('Meron, Dissenting Opinion to ICTR AC, Judgment Media Case') (https://www.legal-tools.org/doc/4ad5eb/); compare also the *amicus curie* brief submitted by the Open Society Justice Initiative in the appeals proceedings in this case, pp. 4, 18.

11.6.5.1. Definition

Incitement is generally defined by the UN, and incitement to genocide is defined by the statutes of the ICTY, ICTR and ICC as well as ICTR jurisprudence.[155]

The UN adopted a definition first advocated by 'ARTICLE 19', a non-governmental organization, which states that incitement is a statement about national, racial or religious groups that creates an imminent risk of discrimination, hostility or violence against persons belonging to those groups. [156]

11.6.5.2. Incitement to Genocide

The *travaux préparatoires* of the Genocide Convention demonstrate that incitement to genocide was seen by the drafters as essential and thus included in the UN Secretary-General's draft Genocide Convention. [157] Its Article II(II)(2) stated:

> The following shall likewise be punishable:
>
> [...] 2. Direct public incitement to genocide, whether the incitement be successful or not.[158]

The commentary of the Secretary-General explained:

> It refers to direct appeals to the public by means of speeches, radio or press, inciting it to genocide. [...] It may well happen that the lightly or imprudently spoken words of a journalist or speaker himself incapable of doing what he advises will be taken seriously by some of his audience who will regard it as their duty to act on his recommendation. Judges will have to weigh the circumstances and show greater or lesser severity according to the position of the criminal and his authority, according to whether his incitement is premeditated or merely represents thoughtless words.[159]

States reacted by offering alternative proposals. The proposal of the USA read:

> Direct and public incitement of any person or persons to any act of genocide, whether the incitement be successful or not, when such

[155] For incitement to genocide see *infra*, Sections 11.6.5.2, 11.7.2 and 11.8.1.

[156] Special Rapporteur Report on Freedom of Opinion, para. 44(c), see *supra* note 134, referring to ARTICLE 19, "Camden Principles on Freedom of Expression and Equality", 2009, Principle 12.1(iii).

[157] Draft Convention on the Crime of Genocide, UN Doc. E/447, 26 June 1947, Article II (II)(2) ('First Draft Genocide Convention') (https://www.legal-tools.org/doc/a2d995/).

[158] *Ibid.*

[159] *Ibid.*, p. 31.

> incitement takes place under circumstances which may reasonably result in the commission of acts of genocide.[160]

The French proposal read:

> Any attempt, provocation or instigation to commit genocide is also a crime.[161]

The USSR draft stated:

> Direct public incitement to commit genocide, regardless of whether such incitement had criminal consequences.[162]

China proposed:

> It shall be illegal to […] incite persons, to commit acts of [genocide].[163]

Following discussions, the Ad Hoc Committee of the UN Economic and Social Council ('ECOSOC') tabled a second draft which stated:

> The following acts shall be punishable […] I direct incitement in public or in private to commit genocide whether such incitement be successful or not.[164]

On 22 April 1948, during the fifteenth meeting, the ECOSOC's Ad Hoc Committee on Genocide retained incitement to genocide following affirmative votes on several elements of the definition.[165]

The draft of the Ad Hoc Committee underwent further changes before ECOSOC discussed it on 26 and 27 August 1948 and passed it on to the GA, without changes.[166] On 9 December 1948, 56 states in the GA adopted the Genocide Convention unanimously and without abstentions.[167] Acknowledging the unanimity leading to the adoption in the GA, the International Court of Justice

---

160 USA, Draft Convention on Genocide, UN Doc. E/623, 30 January 1948, p. 14.

161 France, Draft Convention on Genocide, UN Doc. E/623/Add.1, 5 February 1948.

162 USSR, Basic Principles of a Convention on Genocide, UN Doc. E/AC.25/7, 7 April 1948, Article V(2) (https://www.legal-tools.org/doc/61ezrc/).

163 China, Draft Articles for the Inclusion in the Convention on Genocide, UN Doc. E/AC.25/9, 16 April 1948, Article I (https://www.legal-tools.org/doc/q6bt4n/).

164 Ad Hoc Committee on Genocide, Draft Convention on the Prevention and Punishment of Genocide, UN Doc. E/AC.25/12, 19 May 1948, Article IV(c) ('Second Draft Genocide Convention') (https://www.legal-tools.org/doc/8zoi6x/).

165 Ad Hoc Committee on Genocide, Commentary on Articles Adopted by the Committee, UN Doc. E/AC.25/W.1/Add.1, 27 April 1948, p. 2 ('ECOSOC Ad Hoc Committee, Commentary') (https://www.legal-tools.org/doc/pqzzn6/).

166 Records of the 218th Meeting, UN Doc. E/SR.218, 26 August 1948 (https://www.legal-tools.org/doc/3tsqmg/); and ECOSOC, Records of the 219th Meeting, UN Doc. E/SR.219, 27 August 1948 (https://www.legal-tools.org/doc/yizvor/).

167 Records of the 179th Meeting, UN Doc. A/PV.179, 9 December 1948 ('GA Debate and Adoption Genocide Convention') (https://www.legal-tools.org/doc/nkok90/).

('ICJ') emphasized the convention was "nevertheless the result of a series of majority votes".[168]

Article III provided for "direct and public" incitement to commit genocide as a 'punishable act'.

Further, Article V contained the states' obligation to "provide effective penalties" for persons guilty of any act enumerated in Article III. Algeria and Myanmar submitted mere observations to Article III which did not amount to reservations. Thus, the states' obligation to provide for penalties for incitement to commit genocide was adopted *without* reservations.

The GA's intention was to adopt a convention which was universal in scope.[169] The prohibition of genocide under the Genocide Convention constitutes *jus cogens*. Particularly, the ICJ ruled repeatedly on this issue. In its Advisory Opinion, the ICJ spoke, in 1951, of a crime which "shocks the conscience of mankind" which is "contrary to moral law" and elaborated that "the principles underlying the Convention are principles which are recognized by civilized nations as binding on States, even without any conventional obligation".[170] In its 1996 preliminary objections judgment in the case *Bosnia and Herzegovina v. Yugoslavia*, the same Court ruled "the rights and obligations enshrined by the [Genocide] Convention are rights and obligations *erga omnes*".[171] In 2007, the ICJ ruled that the norm prohibiting genocide was assuredly a peremptory norm of international law (*jus cogens*).[172]

The Genocide Convention's definition of incitement to genocide was *verbatim* included in the statutes of three international criminal tribunals.[173] However, incitement to genocide is not expressly contained in Article 4 of the Law

---

[168] ICJ, *Reservations to the Convention on Genocide*, Advisory Opinion, 28 May 1951, ICJ Rep. 1951, p. 22 (https://www.legal-tools.org/doc/52868f/).

[169] *Ibid.*, p. 12

[170] *Ibid.*, p. 23.

[171] ICJ, *Case Concerning the Application of the Convention on the Prevention and Punishment of the Crime of Genocide (Bosnia and Herzegovina v. Yugoslavia)*, Judgment on Preliminary Objections, 11 July 1996, ICJ Rep. 1996, p. 615, para. 31 ('*RBiH v. Yugoslavia*') (https://www.legal-tools.org/doc/356fe2/); confirmed by ICJ, *Case Concerning Armed Activities on the Territory of the Congo (Democratic Republic of the Congo v. Rwanda)*, Judgment on Jurisdiction of the Court and Admissibility of the Application, 3 February 2006, ICJ Rep. 2006, p. 31, para. 64 (https://www.legal-tools.org/doc/1d7775/).

[172] *RBiH v. Yugoslavia*, 26 February 2007, para. 161, see *supra* note 171.

[173] Rome Statute of the International Criminal Court, 17 July 1998, Articles 25(3)(e), 6 ('ICC Statute') (http://www.legaltools.org/doc/7b9af9/); Statute of the International Criminal Tribunal for the Former Yugoslavia, S/RES/ 827, 25 May 1993, Article 4(3)(c) ('ICTY Statute') (http://www.legal-tools.org/doc/dc079b/); Statute of the ICTR, S/RES/955, 8 November 1994, Article 2(3)(c) ('ICTR Statute') (http://www.legaltools.org/doc/8732d6/).

on the Establishment of the Extraordinary Chambers in the Courts of Cambodia ('ECCC').[174]

11.6.5.3. Incitement to (Lawless) Violence

The prohibition of incitement to (lawless) violence stops short of being universal.

First, it is banned through Articles 4(a) of the CERD and 20(2) of the ICCPR. The latter provision does not require penal sanctioning and the former provision has been subject to the observations and reservations of 19 states, so that the universal nature of this ban is not clear.

Regionally, in the Americas and in Europe, states are required to penalize this form of incitement.[175] In Africa, Principle 23(1) of the 2019 Declaration on the ACHPR demands that states prohibit incitement to violence, but sub-paragraph 2 demands the criminalization of speech only in the "most severe" cases. In Asia, incitement to violence is not banned on the level of regional international human rights treaties.

11.6.5.4. Incitement to Racial Discrimination or Hatred

States are asked to criminalize incitement to racial discrimination and hatred through Article 4(a) of the CERD. As stated above, this ban's universal nature is unclear. Within the UN system, the Durban Conference and the GA have reminded states of their obligation to create penal offences for incitement to racial discrimination: the Durban Conference in 2001, the Durban Review Conference in 2009 and the GA in 2015, all affirmed the states' obligation to create an offence of incitement to racial discrimination.[176] In 2019, the 40th UN Educational, Scientific and Cultural Organization Conference urged its Member States to

[174] Cambodia, Law on the Establishment of the Extraordinary Chambers in the Courts in Cambodia for the Prosecution of Crimes Committed During the Period of Democratic Kampuchea, 27 October 2004, NS/RKM/1004/006 (https://www.legal-tools.org/doc/9b12f0/).

[175] Compare AmCHR, Article 13(5), *supra* note 132, and CoE Recommendation No. 15, Recommendation X, see *supra* note 144; for *intentional* incitement, see EU Council Decision 2008, Article 1(a), see *supra* note 143.

[176] Combating Glorification of Nazism, neo-Nazism and Other Practices That Contribute to Fuelling Contemporary Forms of Racism, Racial Discrimination, Xenophobia and Related Intolerance, UN Doc. A/RES/70/139, 17 December 2015, paras. 28(a), 29 (https://www.legal-tools.org/doc/up7vg5/); UNHCR, Durban Review Conference, Outcome Document, HR/PUB/09/4, 24 April 2009, para. 13 (https://www.legal-tools.org/doc/q7rock/); Report of the World Conference Against Racism, Racial Discrimination, Xenophobia and Related Intolerance, A/CONF.189/12, 8 September 2001, paras. 147(b), 145 (https://www.legal-tools.org/doc/cli7ol/).

reject incitement to racial hatred or racial hate crimes and to "combat them by all legal means".[177]

Nevertheless, on the regional level, no significant efforts or human rights treaties contain the obligation of states to criminalize incitement to racial discrimination. At least for the Americas, Article 13(5) of the AmCHR, which mentions incitement to "any other similar action" against any person or group, can be interpreted so that this general clause, depending on gravity, may encompass also incitement to racial discrimination.

11.6.5.5. Incitement to Discrimination

Article 20(2) of the ICCPR asks states to "prohibit" incitement to discrimination, but stops short of requesting them to create penal offences.[178] Regionally, only in Europe, states are required to create penal legislation against incitement to discrimination.[179] Thus, the obligation to penalize incitement to discrimination only exists for member states of the CoE, while otherwise at the international level no such obligation to punish exists at the time of writing of this chapter.

11.6.5.6. Incitement to Intimidation or Hostility

The same situation is valid for incitement to intimidation or hostility. Article 20(2) of the ICCPR asks states to "prohibit" such form of incitement, stopping short of requesting states to penalize this conduct.[180] Thus, at this point in time, incitement to intimidation and hostility cannot be regarded as constituting a punishable act on the international level except for member states of the CoE which carry the obligation to penalize such conduct.[181]

11.6.5.7. Conclusion on Incitement

All acts of incitement discussed above are prohibited. However, one needs to distinguish with regard to states' obligation to penalize. The obligation to punish incitement to genocide constitutes *jus cogens*. Even states who did not ratify the Genocide Convention are bound to create an offence and investigate and punish it.

Almost worldwide, meaning all states which ratified CERD and did not issue reservations, states should punish incitement to racial discrimination and hatred.

---

[177] UNESCO, Records of the General Conference, 40th session, 27 November 2019, Section 39 entitled "Elimination of Racial Discrimination, Racial Hatred and Racial Hate Crimes in the World", para. 1.

[178] Special Rapporteur Report on Freedom of Opinion, 2012, para. 47, see *supra* note 134.

[179] CoE Recommendation No. 15, 2015, Recommendation X, see *supra* note 144.

[180] Special Rapporteur Report on Freedom of Opinion, 2012, para. 47, see *supra* note 134.

[181] CoE Recommendation No. 15, 2015, Recommendation X, see *supra* note 144.

Regarding all other acts of incitement, the states' obligation to punish differs per region: only states in the Americas, Europe and, for severe cases, Africa, are obligated to penalize incitement to (lawless) violence. In Asia, no such obligation exists at the regional treaty law level.

The obligation to penalize incitement to discrimination, intimidation or hostility exists only for member states of the CoE. States on all other continents are not obligated to create offences and punish these forms of incitement, at least not under international treaty law.

11.7. (Inter)national Adjudication of Speech-Related Crimes

The international criminal tribunals produced relevant case law on speech-related crimes. Particularly, several judgments discussed whether severe forms of hate speech may amount to persecution, a crime against humanity.

11.7.1. Persecution

The International Military Tribunal ('IMT') in Nuremberg, its successor organization, the Military Tribunal, the ICTY, the ICTR and the Appeals Chamber of the International Residual Mechanism for International Criminal Tribunals ('IRMCT') ruled on the issue of whether certain forms of hate speech may amount to persecution. However, at the time of publishing this chapter, the ICC has not yet issued a substantive ruling on this subject.

11.7.1.1. International Military Tribunal in Nuremberg

The IMT in Nuremberg convicted Julius Streicher, editor of the infamous anti-Semitic Nazi publication *Der Stürmer*, for incitement to murder and exterminate the Jewish people, qualifying this conduct as persecution on political and racial grounds.[182] Particularly, the IMT ruled that "[i]n his speeches and articles, week after week, month after month, [Streicher] infected the German mind with the virus of anti-Semitism and incited the German people to active persecution".[183] The judges based the conviction for persecution on Streicher's own speeches and writings as well as on the writings of others which had been published in *Der Stürmer*,[184] the newspaper founded, owned and published by him.

By contrast, the judges' majority at the IMT acquitted Hans Fritzsche, the head of the Radio Division in the German Reich's Ministry of Popular Enlightenment and Propaganda since 1942, for incitement to war crimes and crimes

---

182 IMT, Judgment, 1 October 1946, in *Trial of Major War Criminals Before the International Military Tribunal, Nuremberg, Volume XXII*, p. 502 ('IMT Nuremberg, Judgement') (https://www.legal-tools.org/doc/d1427b/).

183 *Ibid.*, p. 501.

184 *Ibid.*, pp. 501–502.

against humanity.[185] Particularly, the majority observed anti-Semitism in speeches of Fritzsche, but emphasized that his words did "not urge persecution or extermination of Jews".[186]

Judge Nikitchenko dissented, arguing that Fritzsche should have been convicted for incitement and encouragement of the commission of war crimes and crimes against humanity, as he would have served as high commander of the entire German radio system, particularly considering that this means he would have spread propaganda and served as "one of the most important and essential factors in the success of conducting an aggressive war".[187] In his views, Fritzsche,

> participated energetically in the development of the propaganda campaigns preparatory to the acts of aggression against Czechoslovakia, Poland and Yugoslavia and he would have headed the German press campaign falsifying reports of Germany's aggressive war against England, France, Norway, USA, USSR and the other States.[188]

11.7.1.2. German Courts

Not only Russian judge Nikitchenko disputed the judges' majority findings at the IMT on Hans Fritzsche, but subsequently also by the German judiciary. During the so-called denazification procedures, a regional German appeals chamber confirmed a domestic conviction of Fritzsche, thereby *de facto* reversing the reasoning of the majority of the IMT. The German judges held:

> The judgment of the IMT ruled that Fritzsche positioned himself decidedly anti-Semitic. Though his speeches would have not called for the extermination of the Jews. The Appeals Chamber adds to these findings that [Fritzsche] has extraordinarily multiplied through propaganda the hatred stirred up by National Socialists against Jews. Though he did not directly call for the extermination of Jews, he nevertheless aided in an outstanding manner to create within the German people a mood which was beneficial for the persecution and extermination of Jews.[189]

---

185 *Ibid.*, p. 526.

186 *Ibid.*

187 *Ibid.*, p. 538.

188 *Ibid.*, p. 539.

189 Court of Appeal of Nuremberg-Fürth, *Prosecutor v. Hans Fritzsche*, Appeals Chamber I, Judgment, 30 September 1947, Ber.-Reg-Nr. BKI/695, p. 10, unofficial translation of the author (https://www.legal-tools.org/doc/cq8zo7/). The German original reads:

> Im Urteil des IMT ist festgestellt, dass Fritzsche ausgesprochen antisemitisch eingestellt war. Seine Ansprachen hätten aber nicht zur Verfolgung der Ausrottung der Juden

In conclusion, Appeals Chamber I in Nuremberg-Fürth applied a looser standard on persecution in that it affirmed a conviction issued by a German first instance court for propagandistic[190] and anti-Semitic speeches *without* requiring a call for violence.[191] The German judges convicted Fritzsche (merely) for his uttered words *without* requiring a temporal or causal link to specific crimes of persecution committed by the audience.

11.7.1.3. USA Military Tribunal IV in Germany

In the so-called *Ministries* case, Military Tribunal IV of the USA in Nuremberg convicted Otto Dietrich, Hitler's Reich's Press Chief and State Secretary in the Reich's Ministry of Public Enlightenment and Propaganda for war crimes and crimes against humanity (persecution). Particularly, the judges ruled:

> These Press and Periodical Directives were not mere political polemics, they were not aimless expressions of anti-Semitism […]. Their clear and expressed purpose was to enrage Germans against the Jews, to justify the measures taken and to be taken against them, and to subdue any doubts which might arise as to the justice of measures of racial persecution to which Jews were to be subjected. By them Dietrich consciously implemented, and by furnishing the excuses and justifications, participated in, the crimes against humanity regarding Jews.[192]

The USA Military Tribunal IV convicted Dietrich for his propaganda and press related activities *without* requiring a temporal or a causal link between *Dietrich*'s actions and specific acts of persecution committed by the audience.[193]

The above jurisprudence, from the IMT in *Streicher*, the USA Military Tribunal IV in *Dietrich* and the Appeals Chamber I of Nuremberg-Fürth in *Fritzsche*, indicates that, until the late 1940s, a certain body of case law had emerged which points to an emerging practice to consider and, depending on the

---

aufgefordert. Die Berufungskammer ergänzt diese Feststellungen dahin, dass der Betroffene den von den Nationalsozialisten geschürten Hass gegen das Judentum seinerseits durch Propaganda ausserordentlich vermehrt hat. Wenn er auch nicht direkt zur Verfolgung und Ausrottung der Juden aufgefordert hat, so half er doch in hervorragendem Masse mit, im deutschen Volk eine Stimmung zu schaffen, welche der Verfolgung und Ausrottung des Judentums günstig war.

190 The judgement mentions Fritzsche's propaganda activities which would have subjected wide circles of the German people acting in good faith to Nazi ideology (see Spruchkammer I, Stadtkreis Nuremberg, Judgment, 31 January 1947, Az. 1/2398, p. 4).

191 Wibke K. Timmermann, "Incitement in International Criminal Law", in *International Review of the Red Cross*, 2006, vol. 88, p. 830 ('Timmermann').

192 United States Military Tribunal IV, *The USA v. E. von Weizsaecker, O. Dietrich et al.*, 11 April 1949, Case No. XI, para. 576 (https://www.legal-tools.org/doc/eb20f6/).

193 Timmermann, 2006, p. 832, see *supra* note 191.

circumstances of each case, possibly enter convictions for persecution based on severe forms of speech-related crimes.

11.7.1.4. Case Law from the *Ad Hoc* International Criminal Tribunals

The case law from the *ad hoc* international criminal tribunals demonstrates that it depends on the circumstances of each case whether a conviction for persecution based on severe forms of speech-related conduct can be entered. The ICTR issued jurisprudence against the background of genocide in Rwanda in 1994. It continued the practice of post-World War II courts in Nuremberg by qualifying severe forms of speech-related conduct as persecution.

However, Trial Chamber III of the ICTY applied caution in this regard entering acquittals in the *Kordić* and *Šešelj* cases. In the latter case, the IRMCT Appeals Chamber reversed the acquittal entering a conviction for persecution.

At the time of publishing this chapter, the ICC has not yet made a substantive ruling on persecution committed by speech crimes.[194]

11.7.1.4.1. International Criminal Tribunal for Rwanda

In *Prosecutor v. Nahimana et al.*, the Trial Chamber ruled:

> Unlike the crime of incitement, which is defined in terms of intent, the crime of persecution is defined also in terms of impact. It is not a provocation to cause harm. It is itself the harm. Accordingly, there need not be a call to action in communications that constitute persecution. For the same reason, there need be no link between persecution and acts of violence.[195]

Thus, ICTR Trial Chamber I ruled, similarly to the IMT in the *Streicher* case[196] and the EuCtHR in *Féret v. Belgium*, that criminal convictions for hate speech do not necessarily require the perpetrator to call for criminal action. In the latter case, the majority of the EuCtHR ruled: "[L]'incitation à la haine ne requiert pas nécessairement l'appel à tel ou tel acte de violence ou à un autre acte délictueux".[197]

---

[194] The only ruling regarding persecution is a 'no case to answer' decision, see ICC, *Prosecutor v. Sang*, Trial Chamber V(a), Decision on Defence Applications for Judgments of Acquittal, 5 April 2016, ICC-01/09-01/11 (https://www.legal-tools.org/doc/41dc5f/).

[195] ICTR, *Prosecutor v. Nahimana et al.*, Trial Chamber I, Judgment, 3 December 2003, ICTR-99-52-T, para. 1073 ('ICTR TC, Judgment Media Case') (https://www.legal-tools.org/doc/45b8b6/).

[196] See Section 11.7.1.1.

[197] EuCtHR, *Féret v. Belgium*, Majority Judgement, 16 July 2009, Case No. 15615/07, para. 73 ('EuCtHR, Majority judgement, *Féret v. Belgium*') (https://www.legal-tools.org/doc/5a3794/). Judge Sajó supported by judges Zagrebelsky and Tsotsoria disagreed ruling:

In the *Media* case, the majority of the ICTR Appeals Chamber found that after the beginning of the genocide on 6 April 1994, hate speeches issued by Radio Télévision Libre des Mille Collines ('RTLM') were accompanied by calls for genocide against the Tutsi group and each speech took place in the context of a massive campaign of persecution with the campaign characterized by acts of violence (killings, torture, ill-treatment and rape). The Appeals Chamber required *contemporaneousness* between Kangura's and RTLM's hate speeches and widespread and systematic attack, for example, the massive campaign of persecution.[198] The judges found the speeches broadcasted by RTLM equivalent in gravity to other crimes against humanity.[199] The judges found that the "hate speeches and calls for violence against the Tutsi made after 6 April 1994 […] *themselves* constituted underlying acts of persecution".[200]

Judge Meron dissented from the majority's finding arguing that there would be no settled norm of customary international law which would criminalize hate speech.[201] Particularly, he pointed out that proposed Article III of the 1947 Genocide Convention's draft and proposals from the USSR, which would have allowed to penalize mere hate speech, was dismissed in the subsequent drafting process and thus not adopted in the final version of the Genocide Convention.[202]

> Les propositions qu'il fait n'invitent pas à la commission d'actes de discrimination privés mais simplement au soutien à un parti politique se présentant à une élection ainsi qu'à l'activité politique et parlementaire de son leader. Il est possible qu'un certain nombre des opinions recensées soient partagées par des personnes indéniablement racistes mais on ne saurait déclarer quelqu'un coupable en l'associant à autrui en particulier pour des propos.

Id., Judge A. Sajó, Dissenting Opinion, p. 29.

198 See, in particular, footnote 2259 which ruled out that hate speech *prior* to 6 April 1994 could amount to persecution as for these the persecutorial campaign in form of a contemporaneous widespread and systematic attack was missing. Due to lack of contemporaneousness, defendant Ngeze was acquitted for articles in Kangura as these were all published *before* 6 April 1994 (see ICTR, *Prosecutor v. Nahimana et al.*, Appeals Chamber, Judgment, 28 November 2007, ICTR-99-52-A, para. 1013 ('ICTR AC, Judgment Media Case') (https://www.legal-tools.org/doc/04e4f9/)).

199 *Ibid.*, para. 988 and particularly the partly dissenting opinion of Judge F. Pocar, para. 3.

200 ICTR AC, Judgment Media Case, para. 988, see *supra* note 198 (emphasis added).

201 Meron, Dissenting Opinion to ICTR AC, Judgment Media Case, para. 8, see *supra* note 154.

202 *Ibid.*, para. 6, referring to First Draft Genocide Convention, Article III, see *supra* note 157, and the Report of the Committee and Draft Convention Drawn up by the Committee, UN Doc. E/794, 24 May 1948 ('Ad Hoc Committee, Genocide Report 1948'), referring at pp. 9–10 to a proposal from the Soviet Union rejected on 27 April 1948 (https://www.legal-tools.org/doc/d88e33/).

11.7.1.4.2. International Criminal Tribunal for the former Yugoslavia

The ICTY Prosecutor had accused Dario Kordić of engaging in a campaign of widespread or systematic persecution by "encouraging, instigating and promoting hatred, distrust and strife on political, racial, ethnic or religious grounds, by *propaganda*, *speeches* […]".[203] Trial Chamber III acquitted the accused regarding this specific allegation, ruling that "criminal prosecution of speech acts falling short of incitement finds scant support in international case law".[204]

The majority of the same Trial Chamber III, but in a completely different composition, ruled in 2016 in *Prosecutor v. V. Šešelj* that speech crimes could not form the basis for persecution. This time, the Chamber's majority argued less with the absence of an international (customary) law prohibition of speech crimes, but with the real significance and impact of speeches, meaning with their scale. Though the majority did not use the word 'gravity', the following considerations would fit into this scheme:

> The mere use of an abusive or defamatory term is not sufficient to demonstrate persecution. Furthermore, the Prosecution did not offer any contextual evidence that would allow one to measure the real significance or impact of the speeches in Hrtkovci or Vukovar; bearing in mind that the Chamber, by a majority […] distinguishes between speeches and actions that stem from a conflict between the communities and actions that stem from deliberate and discriminatory criminal violence. […] the Chamber, by a majority, […] does not consider that the Prosecutor has proven the existence of persecutory acts. Even if he had, these criminal acts would not suffice to convict, since this is a Tribunal whose jurisdiction is confined to acts the magnitude of which is sufficient to be qualified as crimes against humanity.[205]

In essence, the judges' majority was not convinced that Šešelj's speeches in two towns met the gravity test for crimes against humanity and that there was a widespread and systematic attack against civilians in Hrtkovci.[206]

Judge Lattanzi, dissenting, argued that "no reasonable trier of fact could have denied that the Hrtkovci speech – taken separately from the other underlying acts of persecution, but within the context of the grave conflict in which it

[203] ICTY, *Prosecutor v. D. Kordić et al.*, OTP, Amended Indictment, 30 September 1998, T-95-14/2, para. 37(c) (emphasis added) (https://www.legal-tools.org/doc/15d8ed/).

[204] ICTY, *Prosecutor v. D. Kordić et al.*, Trial Chamber III, Judgment, 26 February 2001, T-95-14/2-T, para. 209, fn. 272 ('ICTY TC, Judgment Kordić') (https://www.legal-tools.org/doc/6cf007/).

[205] ICTY, *Prosecutor v. V. Šešelj*, Trial Chamber III, Judgment, 31 March 2016, IT-03-67-T, paras. 283, 284 (https://www.legal-tools.org/doc/9a8e36/).

[206] *Ibid.*, paras. 196–198, 283.

was made – demonstrated a level of gravity equal to the other crimes against humanity" listed in Article 5 of the Statute of the ICTY.[207]

Referring to the Rwandan context of genocide following 6 April 1994, Judge Lattanzi argued with the findings of the ICTR in the *Ruggiu*, *Media* and *Bikindi* cases and the IMT's conviction of Streicher,[208] emphasizing elements of gravity, such as the content and impact of the words uttered and their scale. Judge Lattanzi emphasized the findings in the *Bikindi* case according to which, depending on the message conveyed and the context, it may be possible to find persecution.[209] Emphasizing CERD Recommendation No. 35's approach to take contextual factors into account, she argued with the notion in human rights law, particularly the ECHR, that an individual's freedom of expression could be restricted and racist discourse combated if the person claiming to use this freedom abuses it by denigrating a person or group or when the "gravity of the denigrating or 'hate' speech […] amounts to the destruction of fundamental values of the convention".[210]

11.7.1.4.3. International Residual Mechanism for Criminal Tribunals

The IRMCT Appeals Chamber reviewed the dispute between the majority of Trial Chamber III and Judge Lattanzi regarding the gravity of Šešelj's speech in Hrtkovci and whether it could have amounted to persecution as a crime against humanity:

> by instigating the forcible expulsion of Croatians from Hrtkovci, Šešelj incited violence against them, in violation of their right to security. […] Šešelj's speech denigrated the Croatians of Hrtkovci on the basis of their ethnicity, in violation of their right to respect for dignity as human beings. […] Šešelj's speech rises to a level of gravity amounting to the *actus reus* of persecution as a crime against humanity.[211]

The Appeals Chamber further held that, following his speech, members of Hrtkovci's civilian Croat population were increasingly harassed and subjected to repeated mistreatment, threats and violence, resulting in a large percentage of them leaving. Thus, *Šešelj*'s speech discriminated and was delivered

[207] ICTY, *Prosecutor v. V. Šešelj*, Trial Chamber III, Partially Dissenting Opinion of Judge Lattanzi, 31 March 2016, IT-03-67-T, paras. 71, 69 (https://www.legal-tools.org/doc/9eda6a/).

[208] *Ibid.*, paras. 51, 53.

[209] *Ibid.*, para. 53 referring to ICTR, *Prosecutor v. Bikindi,* Trial Chamber, Judgment, 2 December 2008, ICTR-01-72-T, para. 395 (https://www.legal-tools.org/doc/a7213b/).

[210] *Ibid.*, paras. 55–57 referring to CERD Committee Recommendation 35, para. 15, see *supra* note 139, and EuCtHR, Majority Judgement, *Féret v. Belgium*, para. 73, see *supra* note 197.

[211] MICT, *Prosecutor v. V. Šešelj*, Appeal Chamber, Judgment, 11 April 2018, MICT-16-99-A, para. 163 ('MICT AC, Judgment *Šešelj*') (https://www.legal-tools.org/doc/96ea58/).

with discriminatory intent, and this conduct formed part of a widespread and systematic attack against the civilian population.[212] The IRMCT Appeals Chamber found that *Šešelj*'s speech met the gravity test and constituted a violation of the right to security amounting to persecution as a crime against humanity.[213]

11.7.1.5. Canada

On 22 November 1992, in Kabaya, Rwanda, about 16 months before the genocidal acts in this country broke out, Léon Mugesera spoke in front of about 1,000 persons, mainly members of the National Revolutionary Movement for Development, a Hutu party. In his speech, Mugesera used the word 'Inyenzis' 29 times, a derogatory reference to persons from the Tutsi ethnic group which translates into English as 'cockroaches.' For example, he told the audience we should:

> 'not allowing ourselves to be invaded' in the country, you know people they call 'Inyenzis' (cockroaches), no longer call them 'Inkotanyi' (tough fighters), as they are actually 'Inyenzis'. These people called Inyenzis are now on their way to attack us.[214]

After some time following his speech, the Rwandan authorities issued an equivalent of an arrest warrant, so Mugesera left the country and, in 1993, applied to immigrate in Canada.

When the content of his speech became known there, the Canadian authorities issued a deportation order. Mugesera invoked all remedies, so the Canadian Federal Court of Appeal had to rule:

> A speech such as Mr. Mugesera's, which actively encouraged ethnic hatred, murder and extermination and which created in its audience a sense of imminent threat and the need to act violently against an ethnic minority and against political opponents, bears the hallmarks of a gross or blatant act of discrimination equivalent in severity […] Hate speech, particularly when it advocates egregious acts of violence, may constitute persecution. In this case, it does.[215]

The Canadian judiciary found that hate speech may, particularly if it "advocates egregious acts of violence" and "creates a sense of imminent threat", amount to persecution.

[212] *Ibid.*, para. 164.

[213] *Ibid.*, paras. 163, 165, 175.

[214] Supreme Court of Canada, *Mugesera v. Canada (Minister of Citizenship and Immigration)*, Judgment, 28 June 2005, [2005] 2 R.C.S. p. 179, para. 13 and Appendix III (Speech Made By Léon Mugesera at a Meeting of the M.R.N.D. Held in Kabaya on November 22, 1992), compare also, p. 130, para. 69 (https://www.legal-tools.org/doc/f2cf94/).

[215] *Ibid.*, p. 157, para. 148.

11.7.1.6. International Criminal Court

At the moment, there is no substantial ruling of the ICC which analyses various sources of evidence and their reliability to prove or disprove hate crimes amounting to persecution.

However, in *Prosecutor v. Sang et al.*, the majority of Pre-Trial Chamber II found substantial grounds to believe that Mr. Sang by virtue of his position within the Kiss FM radio as key broadcaster, fanned violence through the spread of hate messages explicitly revealing the desire to kill the Kikuyus in Kenia.[216] Further, the majority of judges found substantial grounds that Mr. Sang would have broadcasted false news regarding murders or general offences against the Kalenjin, thereby instilling fear within this group.[217]

Following the close of the Prosecution's case, Judge Fremr observed that the only incriminatory evidence on hate speech came from witnesses and that "not a single press report or recording of any of the alleged 'hate speeches' was entered into evidence" and "to amount to hate speech or calls for violence or crimes, it would need to be of a significantly different level and nature than the words the relevant witnesses attributed to […] Mr. Sang".[218] Hence, the majority of Trial Chamber II vacated the charge of persecution and discharged Mr. Sang.

11.7.1.7. Conclusion on Persecution

At least six courts generated relevant case law on hate speech possibly amounting to persecution: the IMT, Military Tribunal IV of the USA in Nuremberg, the Appeals Court Nuremberg-Fürth, the ICTY, the ICTR and the Canadian Federal Court of Appeal. The ICC issued a 'no case to answer' decision based on the evidentiary situation, but has yet to issue a substantive ruling on this topic discussing the legal and substantive basis for hate speech including whether, and if so, under which conditions, it may amount to persecution.

Ahead of such an ICC ruling, a few points emerge. Hate speech is subject to a gravity test considering (i) the specific content of words, (ii) their scale and context, (iii) their impact, and (iv) the contemporaneousness between the speech and crimes. However, courts differ whether hate speech *as such* can, depending on the circumstances and its gravity, including whether it is connected with a

---

216 ICC, *Prosecutor v. Sang et al.*, Pre-Trial Chamber II, Majority Opinion on Decision on the Confirmation of Charges Pursuant to Article 61(7)(a) and (b) of the Rome Statute, 23 January 2012, ICC-01/09-01/11, paras. 355, 358, 363 (https://www.legal-tools.org/doc/96c3c2/).

217 *Ibid.*, para. 357.

218 ICC, *Prosecutor v. Sang et al.*, Trial Chamber V (A), Separate Reason of Judge Fremr, Decision on Defence Applications for Judgments of Acquittal, 5 April 2016, ICC-01/09-01/11, para. 130 (https://www.legal-tools.org/doc/6baecd/).

call for criminal acts, suffice to be considered an attack on the civilian population.[219]

11.7.2. Incitement to Genocide

The ICTR issued several judgments for incitement to genocide. In essence, 18[220] accused were convicted and eight[221] were acquitted. No other international criminal tribunal has issued judgments on incitement to genocide at the time of writing of this chapter.

Incitement to genocide is drafted as a form of participation in the crime of genocide in the Genocide Convention.[222] The statutes of the *ad hoc* international criminal tribunals and of the ICC Statute contain the relevant words of the Genocide Convention *verbatim*. However, the drafters of various statutes of international criminal tribunals transferred this quote into different sections of the founding instruments. In the ICC Statute, the passage on incitement to genocide from the Genocide Convention was transferred into the section 'General Principles of Criminal Law' in an article entitled 'Individual Criminal Responsibility'.[223] In contrast, even though the ICTY and ICTR Statutes contain a distinct article on 'Individual Criminal Responsibility', the drafters transferred the phrase on incitement to genocide to the 'crimes,' within the article on genocide, but in a separate sub-paragraph.[224] Thereby, the drafters observed the distinction of the Genocide Convention between genocide and 'other acts'.

Furthermore, a year before the Rome conference on the ICC, a proposal had been tabled to extend the incitement provision to crimes *other* than genocide:

219 Affirmative, MICT AC, Judgment *Šešelj*, paras. 163, 164, see *supra* note 211; ICTR TC, Judgment Media Case, para. 1073, see *supra* note 195; Cautious and Critical, ICTR AC, Judgment Media Case, para. 987, see *supra* note 198; ICTY TC, Judgment Kordić, 2001, para. 209, see *supra* note 204.

220 In alphabetical order: Akayesu, Bikindi, Kajelijeli, Kalimanzira, Kambanda, Kanyabashi, Karemera and Ngirumpatse, Muvunyi, Nahimana, Ngeze, Ndayambaje, Ngirabatware, Niyitegeka, Nteziryayo, Nzabonimana, Ruggiu and Serugendo.

221 In alphabetical order: Barayagwiza, Bicamumpaka, Bizimungu, Mugenzi, Mugiraneza, Nsabimana, Nyiramasuhuko and Semanza.

222 Genocide Convention, Article III(c), see *supra* note 137; see William A. Schabas, *Genocide in International Law*, 2nd ed., Cambridge University Press, 2009, p. 307 ('Schabas, Genocide').

223 ICC Statute, Article 25(3)(e), see *supra* note 173.

224 Compare ICTY Statute, Article 4(3)(c) and ICTR Statute, Article 2(3)(c) with Article 7 of the ICTY Statute and Article 6 of the ICTR Statute, see *supra* note 173.

> A person is criminally responsible and liable for punishment for a crime […] if that person: […] (f) [directly and publicly] incites the commission of [such a crime] [genocide] […].[225]

The second expression in square brackets indicates that some delegates envisaged during the drafting process that crimes *other* than genocide could have also been the object of incitement. However, this extension to incitement was not adopted and the narrower version, referring only to incitement to genocide as initially adopted in the Genocide Convention, was *verbatim* included into the ICC Statute.

The *travaux préparatoires* and the elements of incitement to genocide will be discussed in the next sub-section.

11.8. Modes of Liability

Speech crimes can be committed in various modes of liability. This section takes a focused approach discussing only three variants, namely incitement to genocide, instigation and joint criminal enterprise ('JCE') or common purpose. Other variants, such as aiding and abetting or co-perpetration, superior responsibility or ordering may be also applicable with regard to speech-related crimes, but the three modes discussed here have been chosen for this analysis because a certain volume of relevant case law exists at this point in time.

11.8.1. Incitement to Genocide

At this stage, most international treaties contain the obligation of states to 'prohibit' certain acts of incitement. This stops short of the obligation to criminalize other acts of incitement. Keeping the reservations of certain states in mind regarding the obligation to criminalize incitement to racial discrimination (Article 4 of the CERD), the remaining act of incitement, universally accepted as being subject to criminal sanctions at the international level, is incitement to *genocide*. Article 3(c) of the Genocide Convention and, following the *verbatim* transfers, its sister provisions Article 4(3)(c) of the ICTY Statute, Article 2(3)(c) of the ICTR Statute and Article 25(3)(e) of the ICC Statute, all contain the provision criminalizing the incitement to genocide.

225 Preparatory Committee on the Establishment of an ICC, Decisions Taken by the Preparatory Committee at its Session from 11–21 February 1997, UN Doc. A/AC.249/1997/L.5, 12 March 1997, p. 22, Article B b., c. and d., section (f) (https://www.legal-tools.org/doc/c0d16c/); Report of the Preparatory Committee on the Establishment of an ICC, UN Doc. A/CONF.183/2/Add.1, 14 April 1998, Article 23(7)(f) (https://www.legal-tools.org/doc/816405/).

The drafting process reflects attempts to include in the ICC Statute a broader reference to incitement, namely, to acts *other* than genocide.[226] However, none of these efforts found their way into the final version of the ICC Statute. Thus, while providing for the mode of liability of incitement, the ICC Statute limits it to acts of genocide. This approach is consistent with the Genocide Convention and the ICTY and ICTR statutes.

11.8.1.1. Genocide Convention: Propaganda Excluded

In May 1948, during the drafting process for the Genocide Convention, in the ECOSOC Ad Hoc Committee on Genocide, the USSR tabled a draft proposing to include propaganda into the Genocide Convention:

> All forms of public propaganda [press, radio, cinema, *etcetera*] aimed at inciting racial, national, or religious enmities, or hatreds, or at provoking the commission of acts of genocide.[227]

However, opposition arose that such an approach would be open to misinterpretation which could restrict the freedom of information.[228] Further, repression of hateful propaganda would be outside the scope of a genocide convention.[229] The majority of drafters voted against this proposal.[230] Subsequent efforts of the USSR during discussions in the Sixth Committee of the GA aimed at reintroducing incitement by way of propaganda into the Genocide Convention failed again.[231] Thus, the word 'propaganda' was omitted when the draft Genocide Convention was submitted for final adoption.

On the day of adoption, Katz Suchy, representing Poland, regretted that the text would not reflect the direct connection between the propaganda of racists sponsoring the regime and the crime of genocide.[232]

---

[226] The relevant part of the formulation stated: "[directly and publicly] incites the commission of [*such a crime*] [genocide]" (emphasis added), *ibid.*

[227] Compare Ad Hoc Committee, Genocide Report 1948, p. 23 (see no. 2), see *supra* note 202.

[228] Report of the Ad Hoc Committee on Genocide, UN Doc. E/AC.25/W.4, 3 May 1948, p. 13, Section 2 ('ECOSOC Ad Hoc Committee, Report Genocide') (https://www.legal-tools.org/doc/tvwj9u/).

[229] *Ibid.*

[230] Compare Second Draft Genocide Convention, 1948, p. 23 (see No. 2), see *supra* note 164; ICTR AC, Judgment Media Case, para. 692, fn. 1658, see *supra* note 198; Meron, Dissenting Opinion to ICTR AC, Judgment Media Case, para. 5, see *supra* note 154.

[231] USSR, Amendments to the Draft Convention on Genocide (E/794), UN Doc. A/C.6/215/Rev.1, 9 October 1948, para. 4 proposes to add a letter (f) to Article IV (https://www.legal-tools.org/doc/es13xv/); Sixth Committee, Record of the Third Session, 87th Meeting, UN Doc. A/C.6/SR.87, 29 October 1948, p. 253 (https://www.legal-tools.org/doc/tc5vmx/); ICTR AC, Judgment Media Case, para. 692, fn. 1658, see *supra* note 198.

[232] GA Debate and Adoption, Genocide Convention, 1948, pp. 839, 841, see *supra* note 167.

With the omission of propaganda, the adoption occurred and the text on incitement to genocide stated:

> The following acts shall be punishable: [...] (c) Direct and public incitement to commit genocide.[233]

In conclusion, the repeated and failed efforts of the USSR to include propaganda demonstrate that the majority of the drafters sought to criminalize only *specific* acts of direct and public incitement to commit genocide and exclude broader schemes such as programming of speeches from other persons, hate propaganda or propaganda tending to provoke genocide.[234]

11.8.1.2. Genocide Convention: Public v. Private Incitement

The first draft of a genocide convention, the Secretary-General's draft from 1947, in its Article II(2), omitted private incitement providing instead only for "direct public incitement to any act of genocide, whether the incitement be successful or not".[235]

While 'public' incitement was explicitly provided for, *private* incitement was omitted also in the Secretary-General's explanation:

> It refers to direct appeals to the public by means of speeches, radio, or press, inciting it to genocide. [...] It may well happen that the lightly or imprudently words of a journalist or speaker himself incapable of doing what he advises will be taken seriously by some of his audience who will regard it as their duty to act on his recommendation. Judges will have to weigh the circumstances and show greater or lesser severity according to the position of the criminal and his authority, according to whether his incitement is premeditated or merely represents thoughtless words.[236]

In the early stages of the negotiations, the drafters added the word "private" and adopted the formulation, "incitement in public *or in private*", by majority vote.[237] The comments stated:

> Incitement is public in form when made in public speeches or in the press, through the radio, the cinema or other ways of reaching the public. It is private when it is conducted through conversations, private meetings or messages.[238]

---

233 Genocide Convention, Article III(c), see *supra* note 137.

234 Compare ICTR AC, Judgment Media Case, paras. 726, 718, see *supra* note 198.

235 First Draft Genocide Convention, 1947, Article II(2), see *supra* note 157.

236 *Ibid.*, p. 32.

237 Second Draft Genocide Convention, Article 4(c), see *supra* note 164 (emphasis added); ECOSOC Ad Hoc Committee, Commentary, 1948, p. 2, see *supra* note 165; ECOSOC Ad Hoc Committee, Report Genocide, p. 11, Article 4(c), see *supra* note 228.

238 ECOSOC Ad Hoc Committee, Commentary, 1948, p. 2, see *supra* note 165.

Subsequently, Belgium launched a proposal seeking, among others, to delete the expression "in private".[239] Chile concurred arguing that punishing incitement in private "might encroach on the actual liberty of the individual".[240] The Belgian proposal was, against objections from Venezuela and Iran,[241] finally adopted by majority (26 votes in favour, 6 against and 10 abstentions).[242]

11.8.1.3. Jurisprudence on 'Public' Incitement

The ICTR Appeals Chamber commented that the GA's "Sixth Committee chose to specifically revise the definition of genocide in order to remove private incitement, understood as more subtle forms of communication such as conversations, private meetings, or messages, from its ambit".[243]

Incitement to genocide occurring *in private* may be subject to other modes of liabilities, including conspiracy, planning or complicity.[244]

The ICTR Appeals Chamber dismissed twice the element of "public" incitement in situations where a perpetrator instructed or talked to staff manning a checkpoint because the recipients were not the general public and the means used did not involve a form of mass communication, such as public speech.[245]

The importance of mass communication *via* the media is acknowledged in the case law of two international tribunals. The IMT in Nuremberg, judging the incitement to persecution (the offence of genocide did not exist at the time), emphasized the importance of the media in their conviction of Julius Streicher.[246]

---

239 Draft Convention (B/794) and Report of the Economic and Social Council, UN Doc. A/C.6/217, 5 October 1948 (https://www.legal-tools.org/doc/0vt1rc/).

240 Record of the 84th Meeting, UN Doc. A/C.6/SR.84, 26 October 1948, p. 217 ('GA, Sixth Committee: 84th Meeting') (https://www.legal-tools.org/doc/hu2xg9/).

241 Venezuela argued in "private" could include "individual consultation, by letter, or even by telephone" (*ibid.*, pp. 208, 214, 215).

242 Sixth Committee, Record of the 85th Meeting, UN Doc. A/C.6/SR.85, 27 October 1948, p. 230 ('GA, Sixth Committee: 85th Meeting') (https://www.legal-tools.org/doc/h72xbw/).

243 ICTR, *Prosecutor v. Kalimanzira*, Appeals Chamber, Judgement, 20 October 2010, ICTR-05-88-A, para. 158 ('ICTR AC, Judgement Kalimanzira') (https://www.legal-tools.org/doc/fad693/).

244 Compare, International Law Commission ('ILC'), Draft Code of Crimes Against the Peace and Security of Mankind, contained in Report of the ILC on the Work of its Forty-eighth Session, UN Doc. A/51/10, 6 May–26 July 1996, p. 22, Article 2, para. 16 ('ILC Draft Code CPSM') (https://www.legal-tools.org/doc/bb5adc/); Schabas, Genocide, p. 319, see *supra* note 222.

245 ICTR AC, Judgment Media Case, para. 862, see *supra* note 198; ICTR AC, Judgement Kalimanzira, paras. 165, 159–164, see *supra* note 243.

246 IMT Nuremberg, Judgement, *supra* note 182, p. 120: Streicher "infected the German mind with the virus of anti-Semitism and incited the German people to active persecution. Each issue of *Der Stürmer*, which reached a circulation of 600,000 in 1935, was filled with such articles [...]".

Various judgments of the ICTR discussed the importance of the mass communication and media in the context of public incitement to genocide.[247]

In conclusion the element of 'public' in incitement to genocide involves consideration of three factors: (i) the place; (ii) the number of people addressed; and (iii) the medium of the speech.[248]

11.8.1.4. 'Direct' Incitement

Direct incitement means the public has to be concretely urged or provoked to take immediate criminal action,[249] specifically in the form of an act of genocide.[250] By contrast, hate speech inciting to one or more acts of hatred, discrimination or violence that does not reach the level of an act of genocide is neither criminalized by incitement to genocide nor is the jurisprudence relating to hate speech inciting to hatred, discrimination or violence directly applicable.[251]

The incitement to genocide should not be in the form of a vague or indirect suggestion.[252] What matters is how the *intended* audience in its (cultural) context could understand the speech in order to determine its true message.[253] The ICTR Appeals Chamber held that the:

> principal consideration is thus the meaning of the words used in the specific context: it does not matter that the message may appear ambiguous to another audience or in another context. On the other hand, if the discourse is still ambiguous even when considered in its context, it cannot be found beyond reasonable doubt to constitute direct and public incitement to commit genocide.[254]

---

[247] ICTR, *Prosecutor v. Karemera and Ngirumpatse*, Appeals Chamber, Judgement, 29 September 2014, ICTR-98-44-A, para. 499 (speech broadcasted over the radio) (https://www.legal-tools.org/doc/372a64/); ICTR, *Prosecutor v. Nzabonimana*, Appeals Chamber, Judgement, 29 September 2014, ICTR-98-44D-A, para. 125 (mass media, for example, radio or television) ('ICTR AC, Judgment Nzabonimana') (https://www.legal-tools.org/doc/a1abb4/).

[248] ICTR AC, Judgment Nzabonimana, para. 231, see *supra* note 247; ICTR, *Prosecutor v. Akayesu*, Trial Chamber I, Judgement, 2 September 1998, ICTR-96-4-T, paras. 556, 673(i), (ii) ('ICTR TC, Judgment Akayesu') (https://www.legal-tools.org/doc/b8d7bd/); ILC Draft Code CPSM, p. 22, Article 2(f), para. 16, see *supra* note 244.

[249] ICTR TC, Judgment Akayesu, paras. 557, 558, see *supra* note 248; compare ICTR AC, Judgment Media Case, para. 696, see *supra* note 198.

[250] Specifically, an act referred to in Article II of the Genocide Convention, Article 2(2) of the ICTR Statute, Article 4(2) of the ICTY Statute, Article 6 of the ICC Statute, see *supra* note 173 (ICTR AC, Judgment Media Case, paras. 692, 693, see *supra* note 198).

[251] ICTR AC, Judgment Media Case, para. 693, see *supra* note 198.

[252] ILC Draft Code CPSM, Article 2(3)(f), para. 16, see *supra* note 244; ICTR TC, Judgment Akayesu, paras. 557, 558, see *supra* note 248.

[253] ICTR AC, Judgment Media Case, paras. 715, 700, 713, 739, see *supra* note 198.

[254] *Ibid.*, para. 701.

The assessment of the directness is made on a case-by-case basis and consideration includes the cultural and linguistic content of the message.[255]

11.8.1.5. Causality Between Incitement and Subsequent Acts

Even though the ICTR Appeals Chamber ruled that, with regards to incitement to genocide, causality between incitement and subsequent genocidal acts would *not* be required, this issue is not finally settled as it is debatable whether the ILC Draft Code CPSM and the ICC Statute reflect a different dogmatic viewpoint on this issue. The ICC has yet to rule whether causality is required (or not).

11.8.1.5.1. International Law Commission

In 1996, the ILC Draft Code CPSM contained, in its first section, a general part on criminal law.[256] Within this general part, the ILC created a separate article on 'individual responsibility' in which it listed incitement as a *mode of liability*. Particularly, Article 2(3)(f) required causation between incitement and subsequent acts:

> An individual shall be responsible for a crime […] if that individual: […] (f) [d]irectly and publicly incites another individual to commit such a crime *which in fact occurs* […].[257]

This causality requirement was not limited to incitement to genocide, because the ILC spoke about incitement to "crime". This is to be understood as including the crimes listed within the ILC Draft Code CPSM meaning, apart from genocide, crimes against humanity, war crimes, crimes against the UN and associated personnel, as well as the crime of aggression.[258] Thus, the scope of incitement in this draft was much wider than in the Genocide Convention, which may explain why the ILC thought that including the requirement of causality was necessary. The ILC limited this approach to its own code, pointing out that it would not limit the application of general principles and Article III(c) of the Genocide Convention.[259]

What legal weight is to be attached to the ILC's causality requirement is unclear at this point. One reason for the uncertainty is that the ICC Statute has not settled this question and clarifying jurisprudence is yet to come from the ICC.

---

[255] ICTR AC, Judgment Media Case, para. 700, see *supra* note 198; ICTR TC, Judgment Akayesu, para. 557, see *supra* note 248.

[256] ILC Draft Code CPSM, Articles 1–15, see *supra* note 244.

[257] *Ibid.*, Article 2(3)(f) (emphasis added).

[258] *Ibid.*, Part 2, Articles 16–20.

[259] *Ibid.*, p. 20, para. 8, particularly note 45.

11.8.1.5.2. The International Criminal Court Statute's Approach

Mirroring the systematic approach of the ILC Draft Code CPSM, the drafters of the ICC Statute also created a general part on criminal law and, within it, a separate article on 'individual criminal responsibility' where they inserted incitement: Article 25(3)(e) of the ICC Statute contains incitement to genocide as a *mode of liability*. The restriction of incitement to genocide to a mode of liability and not qualifying it as an offence, or punishable "act" as Article 3(c) of the Genocide Convention does, may be interpreted to mean in ICC law that incitement would only be criminal if it resulted in an act of genocide being carried out. Thus, Davies criticized that limiting incitement to genocide to a mode of liability could require causality between the act of incitement and a genocidal act.[260]

However, whether Article 25(3)(e) of the ICC Statute has to be interpreted to require causality is questionable. First, this provision reflects Article 3(c) of the Genocide Convention *verbatim*. The drafting process of the Genocide Convention suggests that a requirement of causality or the nexus between incitement and subsequent act of genocide was seen, but consciously dismissed. During debates within the Sixth Committee of the GA about six weeks before the adoption of the Genocide Convention, seven states pointed out that direct and public incitement to genocide should be punishable even if *not* followed by genocidal acts.[261] The drafter's intention was to create an autonomous infraction in form of incitement to genocide.[262]

Further, during the drafting of the Elements of Crimes of the ICC Statute, a USA proposal requiring causality between the act of incitement to genocide and an underlying crime was *not* adopted. The rejected proposal stated:

> the following elements would simply be added as a prerequisite for considering the offence: […] 2. That the accused committed a public act that had the direct effect of causing one or more persons to commit the crime of genocide in question.[263]

---

260 Thomas Davies, "How the Rome Statute Weakens the International Prohibition on Incitement to Genocide", in *Harvard Human Rights Journal*, 2009, vol. 22, pp. 269–270; Joshua Wallenstein, "Punishing Words: An Analysis of the Necessity of the Element of Causation in Prosecutions for the Incitement of Genocide", in *Stanford Law Review*, 2001, vol. 54, pp. 397–398.

261 GA, Sixth Committee: 84th Meeting, pp. 208 (Venezuela), 215 (Poland), 216 (Yugoslavia), 219 (Cuba, USSR), see *supra* note 240; GA, Sixth Committee: 85th meeting, pp. 222 (Uruguay), 223 (Egypt), 226 (Poland), 227 and 230 (USSR), see *supra* note 242.

262 Schabas, Genocide, pp. 319, 329, see *supra* note 222.

263 Preparatory Commission for the ICC, Proposal Submitted by the USA, UN Doc. PNICC/1991/DP.4/Add.3, 4 February 1999, Article 25.3(e) (https://www.legal-tools.org/doc/aae2ca/).

11.8.1.5.3. International Criminal Tribunal for Rwanda

The ICTR Appeals Chamber reasoned the causality requirement advanced in the ILC Draft Code CPSM would *not* reflect customary international law.[264] Indeed the ILC's work remained a draft which was never ratified. Schabas criticized the ILC approach requiring causation, portraying it a "serious misunderstanding".[265] The ICTR Appeals Chamber held, in *Prosecutor v. Nzabonimana*, that "direct and public incitement is an inchoate crime [...] that [...] is punishable even if no act of genocide has resulted therefrom".[266]

The ICTR Appeals Chamber argued, in *Prosecutor v. Bikindi*, that "the offence of direct and public incitement to commit genocide is, *in and of itself*, a serious offence warranting serious punishment, notwithstanding that no physical act of genocide may have been committed".[267] Similarly, ICTR Trial Chamber I held, in *Prosecutor v. Akayesu*, that "direct and public incitement to commit such a crime must be punished as such, even where such incitement failed to produce the result expected by the perpetrator".[268]

11.8.1.5.4. Discussion

The jurisprudence of the ICTR is helpful to interpret the *travaux préparatoires* of the Genocide Convention. The provisions which the judges interpreted, Article 2(3)(c) of the ICTR Statute and Article 3(c) of the Genocide Convention, have the same basis and are thus suitable for a literal and systematic interpretation. The norm in the ICTR Statute quotes the text of the Genocide Convention *verbatim* and their systematic positions within the ICTR Statute and the Genocide Convention are similar. Both international instruments treat incitement to genocide in one provision and as an offence *and* mode of liability.

By contrast, the ICC drafters' decision was to detach incitement from its neighbourhood with the offence of genocide and other definitions of crimes. The drafters moved it to Part III, on the 'general principles of criminal law', in a provision on 'individual criminal responsibility', which is suggestive of incitement to genocide being treated as a *mode of liability*. Whether from the decision of the drafters the conclusion follows that incitement to genocide as a liability requires treatment according to the accessory principle (*Akzessoritätsprinzip*),

---

264 ICTR AC, Judgment Media Case, para. 678, note 1614, see *supra* note 198, referring to ILC Draft Code CPSM, p. 20, Article 2(3)(f), para. 7, note 45, see *supra* note 244.

265 Schabas, Genocide, p. 324, see *supra* note 222.

266 ICTR AC, Judgment Nzabonimana, para. 234, see *supra* note 247; compare also ICTR AC, Judgment Media Case, paras. 678, 720, see *supra* note 198; ICTR, *Prosecutor v. Bikindi*, Appeals Chamber, Judgement, 18 March 2010, ICTR-01-72, para. 146 (https://www.legal-tools.org/doc/e112dd/).

267 *Ibid.*, para. 146 (emphasis added).

268 ICTR TC, Judgment Akayesu, para. 562, see *supra* note 248.

meaning that an act of incitement should have caused the actual perpetration of an underlying crime of genocide, is for the ICC judges to decide.

At this juncture, the drafters' intention becomes relevant. The text of the Genocide Convention alone contains three references to prevent[269] acts of genocide which would suggest that no causality is necessary. Subsequently, the drafters of the statutes of the ICTY, ICTR and ICC quoted the relevant text of incitement to genocide *verbatim*, which suggests they felt bound by the spirit and intention of the drafters of the Genocide Convention. To move the incitement provision to the general part of criminal law in the ICC Statute reflects a civil law approach, but not necessarily that the drafters had in mind to make the requirements for incitement stricter, particularly as the drafters did not adopt a USA draft on the elements of crimes of Article 25(3)(e) of the ICC Statute which would have required causation.

The ICC judges can clarify issues, including what is, in their view, the current state of causality regarding incitement to genocide under customary international law.

11.8.1.6. Mens Rea

The perpetrator's state of mind when inciting to genocide has to be twofold: first, to intend to directly prompt or provoke a person to commit genocide, meaning the perpetrator has the desire to create a state of mind necessary to commit genocide, in the mind of the person(s) he or she is so engaging.[270] Secondly, the perpetrator of incitement must also have the *dolus specialis*, the special intent to destroy in whole or in part a national, ethnical, racial or religious group, as such.[271]

11.8.2. Instigation, Soliciting and Inducing

This section discusses (i) the terminology, (ii) *mens rea*, (iii) causality, and (iv) compares instigation with incitement.

11.8.2.1. Terminology and *Actus Reus*

The terminology differs in the statutes of the *ad hoc* tribunals and the ICC. While the former refer to 'instigation', the latter mentions 'soliciting or inducing'.[272]

---

[269] See the title of the convention, its Articles 1 and 8 (Genocide Convention, *supra* note 137).

[270] ICTR TC, Judgment Akayesu, para. 560, see *supra* note 248; ICTR TC, Judgment Media Case, para. 1012, see *supra* note 195.

[271] *Ibid.*

[272] Compare ICTY Statute, Article 7, 2nd variant ("instigated"), see *supra* note 224; ICTR Statute, Article 6, 2nd variant ("instigated"), see *supra* note 224; ICC Statute, Article 25(3)(b), 2nd and 3rd variants ("solicits or induces"), see *supra* note 223.

ICC's Pre-Trial Chamber I ruled the term 'instigation' would encompass ordering, inducing and soliciting, a conduct by which a person is influenced by another to commit a crime.[273] ICC's Trial Chamber VII distinguished that the notions of inducing and soliciting are distinct and should not be conflated. Soliciting involves the perpetrator asking or urging the addressee to commit a certain criminal act, without the presupposition of the accessory being in a certain relationship with the physical perpetrator of the offence(s).[274]

In contrast, during the process of inducing, a person "exerts influence over the physical perpetrator, either by strong reasoning, persuasion, or conduct implying the prompting of the commission of the offence".[275] In conclusion, inducing is a stronger method of instigation than mere soliciting.[276]

Instigation, soliciting or inducing have to be more than mere facilitation, which suffices for aiding and abetting.[277]

What matters is that the instigator prompts[278] another person to commit an offence in the sense that the instigator brings about the "final determination" in the future principal perpetrator to commit the crime.[279] By contrast, a person who influences, through further encouragement or moral support, a principal perpetrator who had already definitely decided to carry out a certain criminal act (*omnimodo facturus*), cannot be an instigator, but still an aider and abettor.[280]

273 ICC, *Prosecutor v. Gbagbo*, Pre-Trial Chamber I, Decision on the Confirmation of Charges Against Laurent Gbagbo, 12 June 2014, ICC-02/11-01/11, para. 243 (https://www.legal-tools.org/doc/5b41bc/). Different: Trial Chamber II of the ICTY pointing out the difference between 'instigation' and 'ordering', the former implying "at least a factual superior-subordinate relationship", while instigation would "not presuppose any kind of superiority" yet involve "inciting, soliciting or otherwise inducing" the future principal perpetrator (ICTY, *Prosecutor v. Orić*, Trial Chamber II, Judgement, 30 June 2006, IT-03-68-T, paras. 271, 272 ('ICTY TC, Judgment Orić') (https://www.legal-tools.org/doc/37564c/)); compare ECCC, *Prosecutor v. Kaing Guek Eav alias Duch*, Judgement, 26 July 2010, 001/18-07-2007/ECCC/TC, para. 522 ('ECCC TC, Judgment Duch') (https://www.legal-tools.org/doc/dbdb62/).

274 ICC, *Prosecutor v. Bemba et al.*, Trial Chamber VII, Judgment Pursuant to Article 74 of the Statute, 19 October 2016, ICC-01/05-01/13, para. 75 (https://www.legal-tools.org/doc/fe0ce4/).

275 *Ibid.*, para. 76.

276 *Ibid.*

277 ICTY TC, Judgment Orić, paras. 271, 282, see *supra* note 273.

278 ICTY, *Prosecutor v. Kordić*, Appeals Chamber, Judgement, 17 December 2004, IT-95-14/2-A, para. 27 ('ICTY AC, Judgment Kordić') (https://www.legal-tools.org/doc/738211/).

279 ICTY TC, Judgment Orić, para. 271, see *supra* note 273.

280 *Ibid.*

11.8.2.2. Mens Rea

The *mens rea* of the solicitor or inducer is the intention to provoke or induce the commission of the crime and the awareness of the substantial likelihood[281] that, in the ordinary course of events,[282] a crime would be committed in the execution of that instigation. Instigating with this awareness is considered as accepting the crime.[283]

11.8.2.3. Causality

In civil law jurisdiction, instigation follows the principle of accessory (*Akzessorietätsgrundsatz*), in that its criminal liability depends on the commission of the principal act. Thus, without a principal act, there is no liability for an instigator.[284] Instigation requires a nexus between the instigating conduct and the principal crime committed.[285] This link is of a mere causal relationship which does not have to reach the level of *conditio sine qua non*.[286]

281 ICTY AC, Judgment Kordić, para. 32, see *supra* note 278; ICTR, *Prosecutor v. Karera*, Appeals Chamber, Judgment, 2 February 2009, ICTR-01-74-A, para. 317 (https://www.legal-tools.org/doc/5bf368/); ICTR AC, Judgment Media Case, para. 480, see *supra* note 198; ICTR, *Prosecutor v. Ndindabahizi*, Appeals Chamber, Judgment, 16 January 2007, ICTR-01-71-A, para. 117 (https://www.legal-tools.org/doc/0f3219/); ICTY, *Prosecutor v. Limaj et al.*, Trial Chamber II, Judgment, 30 November 2005, IT-03-66-T, para. 514 ('ICTY TC, Judgment Limaj') (https://www.legal-tools.org/doc/4e469a/); ICTY, *Prosecutor v. Brđanin*, Trial Chamber II, Judgment, 1 September 2004, IT-99-36-T, para. 269 ('ICTY TC, Judgment Brđanin') (https://www.legal-tools.org/doc/4c3228/); ECCC TC, Judgment Duch, 2010, para. 524, see *supra* note 273.

282 ICC, *Prosecutor v. Ntaganda*, Pre-Trial Chamber II, Decision Pursuant to Article 61(7)(a) and (b) of the Rome Statute on the Charges of the Prosecutor Against Bosco Ntaganda, 9 June 2014, ICC-01/04/02/06, para. 153(c) (https://www.legal-tools.org/doc/5686c6/).

283 ICTY AC, Judgment Kordić, para. 32, see *supra* note 278.

284 ICTR TC, Judgment Akayesu, para. 482, see *supra* note 248.

285 ICTY TC, Judgment Limaj, para. 514, see *supra* note 281.

286 ICTY AC, Judgment Kordić, para. 27, see *supra* note 278; ICTY, *Prosecutor v. Blaškić*, Trial Chamber I, Judgment, 3 March 2000, IT-95-14-T, para. 270 ('ICTY TC, Judgment Blaškić') (https://www.legal-tools.org/doc/1fdc7f/); ICTY TC, Judgment Brđanin, para. 269, see *supra* note 281; ICTY TC, Judgment *Orić*, para. 274, see *supra* note 273; ICTY TC, Judgment Limaj, para. 514, see *supra* note 281.

It suffices if the instigation constitutes a "substantial"[287] or "clear contributing factor" to the subsequent commission of the principal crime.[288] The ICTR Appeals Chamber specified that the fact alone that a person enjoys a "certain influence" in a community is, in the absence of further evidence such as a formal superior–subordinate relationship, insufficient to establish responsibility as an instigator.[289]

11.8.2.4. Contemporaneousness

Apart from holding that causality is required, the ICTR Appeals Chamber requires *contemporaneousness* between the instigation and subsequent acts. Ideally, a speech act would have 'substantially contributed' to the commission of acts of genocide. In the *Media* case, the ICTR ruled about RTLM broadcasts which had been disseminated days, weeks and even months *before* the genocide in Rwanda had started on 6 April 1994. The ICTR Appeals Chamber ruled on the question of whether these media activities could have amounted to instigation:

> evidence of a link between the broadcasts aired on RTLM before 6 April 1994 and the acts of genocide committed against the individuals so named seems, at the very least, tenuous [...] Thus the longer the lapse of time between a broadcast and the killing of a person, the greater the possibility that other events might be the real cause of such killing and that the broadcast might not have substantially contributed to it.[290]

The ICTR ruling is an example of the Latin maxim *nova causa interveniens*.

---

[287] ICTY AC, Judgment Kordić, para. 27, see *supra* note 278; ICTY TC, Judgment *Orić*, para. 274, see *supra* note 273; ICTY TC, Judgment Limaj, para. 514, see *supra* note 281; ICTR, *Prosecutor v. Gacumbitsi*, Appeals Chamber, Judgement, 7 July 2006, ICTR-2001-64-A, para. 129 (https://www.legal-tools.org/doc/aa51a3/); ICTR AC, Judgment Media Case, para. 480, see *supra* note 198; ICTR, *Prosecutor v. Bagilishema*, Trial Chamber I, Judgement, 7 June 2001, ICTR-95-1A, para. 30 (https://www.legal-tools.org/doc/aa51a3/); ECCC TC, Judgment Duch, para. 522, see *supra* note 273; compare ICTR, *Prosecutor v. Kamuhanda*, Trial Chamber II, Judgement, 22 January 2004, ICTR-99-54A, para. 590 (https://www.legal-tools.org/doc/4ac346/).

[288] ICTY TC, Judgment Blaškić, para. 270, see *supra* note 286; ICTY TC, Judgment Brđanin, para. 269, see *supra* note 281.

[289] ICTR, *Prosecutor v. Kamuhanda*, Appeals Chamber, Judgement, 19 September 2005, ICTR-99-54A-A, paras. 65, 61 (https://www.legal-tools.org/doc/bd4762/).

[290] ICTR AC, Judgment Media Case, para. 513, see *supra* note 198.

11.8.2.5. Differences Between Incitement and Instigation

The purposes of incitement to genocide and instigation are common, insofar as both activities seek to prompt or create a state of mind necessary to have the addressee(s) commit the crime(s).

Firstly, however, incitement to genocide and instigation differ as regards the addressees. Incitement relates to the general public while instigation targets a specific person or group.

Secondly, the way in which incitement has to be carried out to be criminal is stricter than instigation. Incitement to genocide must be direct and public while instigation does not demand such requisite elements.

Thirdly, according to the jurisprudence of the ICTR, incitement to genocide is an inchoate offence,[291] which requires neither a subsequent act of genocide nor causality[292] between the incitement and the intended crime.

By contrast, instigation is only punishable if the principal crime indeed occurred and if the instigation was a substantially (or clearly) contributing factor to the principal crime.

11.8.3. Joint Criminal Enterprise or Common Purpose

Speech-related crimes have also been adjudicated in connection with liability for JCE or common purpose.

On the level of international criminal tribunals, the ICTY convicted the Bosnian Serb political leaders Radovan Karadžić and Momčilo Krajišnik based on JCE liability for speech-related crimes.

The requirements for JCE are as follows.

11.8.3.1. Actus Reus

The actus reus consists of three elements:

1. Plurality of persons.[293] This requirement needs no further explanation.

---

[291] Kai Ambos, *Rome Statute of the International Criminal Court: Article-by-Article Commentary*, 4th ed., Beck/Hart/Nomos Publishers, 2022, Article 25, para. 46 ('Ambos').

[292] ICTR TC, Judgment Media Case, paras. 1015, 1029, see *supra* note 195. The ICC's position on this point is not yet known.

[293] ICC, *Prosecutor v. Lubanga*, Appeals Chamber, Judgment on the Appeal of Mr. Thomas Lubanga Dyilo Against His Conviction, 1 December 2014, ICC-01/04-01/06 A 5, para. 445 ('ICC AC, Judgment Lubanga') (https://www.legal-tools.org/doc/585c75/); ICTY, *Prosecutor v. Duško Tadić*, Appeals Chamber, Judgement, 15 July 1999, IT-94-1-A, para. 227(i) ('ICTY AC, Judgment Tadić') (https://www.legal-tools.org/doc/8efc3a/).

2. Existence of an expressly or implied agreement, common plan or purpose.[294] The Appeals Chamber of the ICC held:

> As to the question of whether the common plan must be 'designed to further a criminal purpose' […] it is not required that the common plan between individuals was specifically directed at the commission of a crime.[295]

The Appeals Chamber agreed with the approach of the majority of ICC Trial Chamber I in requiring as a "minimum", a "critical element of criminality" of the common plan.[296] Namely, the majority of Trial Chamber I had argued that the common plan's "implementation embodied a sufficient risk that, if events follow the ordinary course, a crime will be committed".[297]

3. Participation in this common design.[298] To participate in the common design, it suffices that the perpetrator engages in a "significant" contribution to the common design, plan or purpose.[299]

11.8.3.1.1. The Significant Contribution Standard and the Standard for Instigation

The 'significant' contribution standard required for JCE is lower than the 'substantial' contribution standard required for instigation. The ICTY ruled that a substantial contribution is generally *not* required for participation in a JCE. In *Prosecutor v. Brđanin*, the ICTY Appeals Chamber ruled "although the contribution need not be necessary or substantial, it should at least be a significant

---

[294] ICC AC, Judgment Lubanga, para. 445, see *supra* note 293; ICTY, *Prosecutor v. Vasiljević*, Appeals Chamber, Judgment, 25 February 2004, IT-98-32-A, paras. 100, 109 ('ICTY AC, Judgment Vasiljević') (https://www.legal-tools.org/doc/dbe7c4/).

[295] *Ibid.* The ICTY Appeals Chamber is stricter requiring a "common plan, design or purpose which amounts to or involves the commission of a *crime* provided for in the Statute" (ICTY AC, Judgment Tadić, para. 227(ii), see *supra* note 293 (emphasis added)).

[296] *Ibid.*, paras. 446 and 451 referring in note 822 to ICC, *Prosecutor v. Lubanga*, Trial Chamber I, Judgment Pursuant to Article 74 of the Statute, 14 March 2012, ICC-01/04-01/06, para. 984 (https://www.legal-tools.org/doc/677866/); critical Ambos, Article 25, para. 11, see *supra* note 291.

[297] *Ibid.*

[298] ICTY AC, Judgment Tadić, para. 227(iii), see *supra* note 293.

[299] ICTY, *Prosecutor v. Brđanin*, Appeals Chamber, Judgment, 3 April 2007, IT-99-36-A, para. 430 ('ICTY AC, Judgment Brđanin') (https://www.legal-tools.org/doc/782cef/); ICTY, *Prosecutor v. Krajišnik*, Appeals Chamber, Judgment, 17 March 2009, IT-00-39-A, para. 695 ('ICTY AC, Judgment Krajišnik') (https://www.legal-tools.org/doc/770028/); ICTY, *Prosecutor v. Šainović et al.*, Appeals Chamber, Judgment, 23 January 2014, IT-05-87-A, para. 985 ('ICTY AC, Judgment Šainović') (https://www.legal-tools.org/doc/81ac8c/); Special Court for Sierra Leone ('SCSL'), *Prosecutor v. Sesay et al.*, Appeals Chamber, Judgment, 26 October 2009, SCSL-04-15-A, para. 611 ('SCSL AC, Judgment Sesay') (https://www.legal-tools.org/doc/133b48/).

contribution to the crimes for which the accused is to be found responsible".[300] The same Chamber ruled slightly more strictly in *Prosecutor v. Kvočka*:

> in general, there is no specific legal requirement that the accused make a substantial contribution to the JCE. However, there may be specific cases which require, as an exception to the general rule, a substantial contribution of the accused to determine whether he participated in the JCE. In practice, the significance of the accused's contribution will be relevant to demonstrating that the accused shared the intent to pursue the common purpose.[301]

11.8.3.1.2. Nature of Significant Contribution

There is *no* requirement that a significant contribution has to be criminal *per se*, or would involve the commission of a specific crime,[302] or that the perpetrator engaging in a significant contribution to the JCE would have to perform a part of the *actus reus* of the perpetrated crime.[303] Particularly, the ICTY Appeals Chamber ruled, in *Prosecutor v. Tadić*, that such participation may take the "form of assistance in, or contribution to, the execution of the common plan or purpose".[304] In *Prosecutor v. Vasiljević*, the same Appeals Chamber ruled that it suffices if participatory acts would "in some way" be "directed to the furtherance of the common design".[305]

11.8.3.2. Mens Rea

The *mens rea* requirements differ according to the form of JCE or common purpose: 'JCE I' requires shared intent regarding the crime in pursuance of the criminal enterprise or common purpose.[306] 'JCE II' relates to systemic wrong found in concentration or detention camps and therefore requires awareness of the nature or system of ill-treatment and intention to participate in or further its

---

[300] ICTY AC, Judgment Brđanin, para. 430, see *supra* note 299.

[301] ICTY, *Prosecutor v. Kvočka*, Appeals Chamber, Judgment, 28 February 2005, IT-98-30/1-A, para. 97 ('ICTY AC, Judgment *Kvočka*') (https://www.legal-tools.org/doc/006011/).

[302] ICTY AC, Judgment Šainović, para. 985, see *supra* note 299; ICTR, *Prosecutor v. Ntakirutimana*, Appeals Chamber, Judgment, 13 December 2004, ICTR-96-10-A and ICTR-96-17-A, para. 466 (https://www.legal-tools.org/doc/af07be/).

[303] ICTY AC, Judgment Brđanin, para. 427, see *supra* note 299; ICTY AC, Judgment Krajišnik, para. 695, see *supra* note 299; SCSL AC, Judgment Sesay, para. 611, see *supra* note 299.

[304] ICTY AC, Judgment Tadić, para. 227(iii), see *supra* note 293; ICTY AC, Judgment Vasiljević, para. 100, see *supra* note 294. Summarizing jurisprudence from the Second World War, the ICTY Appeals Chamber stated the perpetrator "in some way actively participated in enforcing the system, i.e., encouraged, aided and abetted or in any case participated in the realisation of the common criminal design" (ICTY AC, Judgment Tadić, para. 202(iii), see *supra* note 293).

[305] ICTY AC, Judgment Vasiljević, para. 102(i), see *supra* note 294, compare also para. 119(i) and ICTY AC, Judgment Šainović, para. 1177, see *supra* note 299.

[306] ICTY AC, Judgment Tadić, paras. 220, 228, see *supra* note 293.

common design of ill-treatment, meaning its criminal purpose.[307] 'JCE III' relates to acts and crimes outside the common design or purpose and requires that the perpetrator shared the intent necessary for the crime and regarded the act or crime as a natural and reasonably foreseeable consequence of the realization of that common purpose, and willingly took this risk.[308] The ICC Appeals Chamber, referring to the second alternative in both Articles 30(2)(b) and 30(3) of the ICC Statute, ruled that consequence 'in the ordinary course of events' means that "the standard for the foreseeability of events is *virtual* certainty. Absolute certainty is not required".[309] The ICTY Appeals Chamber had required awareness that the actions "most likely" led to the result.[310]

11.8.3.3. Relevant Case Law

The ICTY conducted two cases involving speech crimes and JCE liability.

11.8.3.3.1. Prosecutor v. Krajišnik

From late 1991 until November 1995, including during the entire war in Bosnia and Herzegovina, Krajišnik had been, among other positions, President of the Bosnian Serb Assembly of the entity *Republika Srpska* ('RS Assembly'). Trial Chamber I ruled that Krajišnik did not act as a neutral parliamentary speaker although "he was not generating or echoing extreme political views himself, his method was to lend support to aggressive elements in the Assembly by giving them a platform for their views".[311] Further, the Trial Chamber found no evidence that Krajišnik ever tried to moderate extreme views against Muslim people or confront proponents of anti-Muslim or anti-Croat views uttered by others in the RS Assembly he was chairing.[312]

The Appeals Chamber found that both activities could arguably constitute a "significant" contribution to the JCE, particularly as the Trial Chamber had found that Krajišnik's contribution to the JCE had not been limited to his "failure to prevent other members of the Bosnian-Serb Assembly from making inflammatory statements".[313]

The Trial Chamber had further found that Krajišnik had supported, encouraged, facilitated or participated

[307] *Ibid.*, paras. 202, 203, 220, 228.

[308] *Ibid.*, paras. 204, 220, 228; ICTY AC, Judgment Kvočka, para. 86, see *supra* note 301.

[309] ICC AC, Judgment Lubanga, para. 447, see *supra* note 293; critical Ambos, Article 25, para. 11, see *supra* note 291.

[310] ICTY AC, Judgment Tadić, para. 220, see *supra* note 293.

[311] ICTY, *Prosecutor v. Krajišnik*, Trial Chamber I, Judgment, 27 September 2006, IT-00-39-T, para. 954 (https://www.legal-tools.org/doc/62a710/).

[312] *Ibid.*, para. 955.

[313] ICTY AC, Judgment Krajišnik, 2009, para. 217, see *supra* note 299.

> in the dissemination of information to Bosnian Serbs that they were in jeopardy of oppression at the hands of Bosnian Muslims and Bosnian Croats, that territories on which Bosnian Muslims and Bosnian Croats resided were Bosnian Serb land, or that was otherwise intended to engender in Bosnian Serbs fear and hatred of Bosnian Muslims and Bosnian Croats.[314]

In conclusion, the Appeals Chamber, dismissing Krajišnik's appeal, found that his contribution within the RS Assembly had amounted to a 'significant' contribution to the JCE.[315]

11.8.3.3.2. Prosecutor v. Karadžić

In July 1992, the President of the *Republika Srpska* had delivered, in the Bosnian-Serb Assembly, a speech claiming the conflict in Bosnia and Herzegovina had been "roused in order to eliminate the Muslims […]. They think they are being nationally established, but in fact they are vanishing".[316]

The Prosecution had advanced this speech excerpt to prove Karadžić's genocidal intent. ICTY Trial Chamber III reviewed the *context* of Karadžić's words which demonstrated that he had in the same speech also referred to the emerging Bosnian-Serb state for which he sought "to ensure that [the non-Serb ethnicities] have all the rights that we [Bosnian Serbs] have, under the condition that they are not hostile and that they leave the weapons". The judges concluded that they were *not* convinced that Karadžić intended to destroy part of the Bosnian-Muslim and Bosnian-Croat communities. [317] The judges found the "speeches and statements made by [Karadžić] and the Bosnian Serb leadership denigrated Bosnian Muslims and Bosnian Croats, portrayed them as their historic enemies, and exacerbated ethnic tensions" in Bosnia and Herzegovina which amounts to persecutorial intent:

> to create an ethnically homogeneous Serb state in Bosnia and Herzegovina, to separate from Bosnian Muslims and Bosnian Croats, and remove them from Bosnian Serb controlled territory. It also shows that [Karadžić] and the Bosnian Serb leadership advocated a position that co-existence with non-Serbs within Bosnian Serb-controlled territory […] was impossible.[318]

The Trial Chamber observed that the identity of the Bosnian Muslims as a nation or a people was called into question, that references to historic

---

314 *Ibid.*, para. 1121(c).

315 ICTY AC, Judgment Krajišnik, 2009, para. 217, see *supra* note 299.

316 ICTY, *Prosecutor v. Karadžić*, Trial Chamber III, Judgment, 24 March 2016, IT-95-5/18-T, para. 2601 (https://www.legal-tools.org/doc/173e23/).

317 *Ibid.*

318 *Ibid.*, para. 2596.

grievances against the Serb people, including allegations of genocide in World War II against them, were used and these "speeches also had the effect of creating fear and inciting inter-ethnic hatred amongst the [Bosnian Serb] population".[319] Acknowledging the "highly inflammatory speeches and statements" by Karadžić and other JCE members who spoke about 'disappearance', 'annihilation', 'vanishing', 'elimination' and 'extinction' of the Bosnian Muslims, and placing the totality of this evidence in context, the judges found persecutorial intent and stopped short of genocidal intent, as they were not convinced that the only reasonable inference was to infer from the speeches and statements Karadžić's intention to physically destroy a part of the Bosnian Muslim or Bosnian Croat group.[320]

The Prosecution appealed this finding, but the majority of the ICTY Appeals Chamber upheld the reasoning of the Trial Chamber and dismissed the appeal.[321]

11.9. Conclusion

The idea of freedom of expression was first conveyed in ancient Greek literature in the fifth century BC. Other philosophical foundations for freedom of expression and of the press were laid in the period of the Enlightenment by various authors from several countries including, but not limited to, writers from England, Finland, France, Germany, the Netherlands, Scotland and Sweden. The first codifications of freedom of expression or of the press and the dissemination of information occurred at the domestic level in Europe, namely in Denmark-Norway, England, France, Sweden, at the federal level of the USA and in Virginia. Following the Second World War, the UDHR and the ICCPR human rights treaties codified freedom of expression at the international level. Regional human rights treaties also contain freedom of expression, though in Asia such a right is internationally codified only for ASEAN states.[322]

Certain human rights treaties provide for limitations of the freedom of expression and at least oblige states to *prohibit* certain severe abuses of this freedom. Regarding incitement to genocide, states are obliged by international treaty law to *punish* such conduct. The same generally applies for conduct disseminating or advocating ideas of racial superiority and hatred, though 19 states have issued declarations or reservations to Article 4 of the CERD. Incitement to

[319] *Ibid.*, paras. 2597, 2598.

[320] *Ibid.*, para. 2599.

[321] MICT, *Prosecutor v. Karadžić*, Appeals Chamber, Judgment, 20 March 2019, MICT-13-55-A, paras. 741–746 (https://www.legal-tools.org/doc/jt3mc2/).

[322] Regional codifications in chronological order: ECHR (1950), AmCHR (1969) and ACHPR (1981). In Asia, for the ASEAN states, see Article 23 of the AHRD, see *supra* note 128.

(lawless) violence, discrimination, intimidation or hostility is prohibited. Yet, states' treaty obligation to create penal offences, investigate and punish such abusive behaviour differs from continent to continent.

(Inter)national adjudication resulted in convictions for severe abuses of freedom of speech for (i) persecution in front of the IMT, USA Military Tribunal IV, in Germany, Canada, at the ICTR and the MICT, and (ii) incitement to genocide in front of the ICTR. The ICC has not yet issued judgments on persecution and incitement to genocide for speech crimes.

Regarding the most relevant modes of liability for speech crimes, this chapter discussed (i) incitement to genocide, (ii) instigation, and (ii) JCE or common purpose. Incitement to genocide is an inchoate offence and, as such, requires no causality between the inciting conduct and subsequent crime. However, the systematic placement of incitement to genocide in the article on individual criminal responsibility in the ICC Statute and the ILC Draft Code CPSM have triggered discussions as to whether causality between speech and subsequent act may be required. The ICC still has to rule on this issue.

The causal link between prohibited speech and subsequent crime differs with regard to instigation and JCE or common purpose. For instigation, a 'substantial' contribution or effect is required, while for JCE or common purpose it suffices if the speaker makes a 'significant' contribution or effect to the common enterprise or purpose.

12

Freedom of Religion and the Prohibition of Incitement to Religious Hatred Under International Human Rights Law: Conundrums and the Way Ahead

Mona Elbahtimy*

12.1. Introduction

The nature of states' obligations pursuant to international human rights law ('IHRL') regarding the prohibition of incitement to religious hatred have taken on increased importance within the public space and have become a controversial issue within multilateral human rights diplomacy. This chapter provides an explanatory framework for the multiple conundrums associated with the regulation of incitement to religious hatred. This is preceded by examining the unique and underdeveloped nature of freedom of religion within IHRL and identifying five internal features of the international norm prohibiting incitement to hatred that generate multiple interpretation and implementation dilemmas. The chapter also explains how the complexities associated with the regulation of incitement to religious hatred have contributed to the failure of recent standard-setting attempts within the UN in this area. Finally, it explores the way ahead in light of the impasse reached in relation to finding a comprehensive universal normative framework for the prohibition of religion-based incitement to hatred.

---

* **Mona Elbahtimy** holds a Ph.D. from the University of Cambridge focusing on hate speech in international human rights law, and has long practical experience in multilateral human rights diplomacy, governmental human rights machineries, and regional human rights bodies. Her monograph *The Right to Protection from Incitement to Hatred: An Unsettled Right* was published by Cambridge University Press. The book traces the journey of the norm against hate speech within international law in three analytical domains: its emergence, relevant supranational jurisprudence, and standard-setting attempts within the United Nations ('UN'). For an audio-visual recording of Dr. Elbahtimy's statement to CILRAP's conference in Florence in April 2022 on the topic of this anthology, please see https://www.cilrap.org/cilrap-film/220408-elbahtimy/.

12.2. Freedom of Religion: A Unique and Underdeveloped Freedom Under International Human Rights Law

Article 18 of the International Covenant on Civil and Political Rights ('ICCPR') contains the core obligations under international law on the protection of freedom of religion. It stipulates that:

> 1. Everyone shall have the right to freedom of thought, conscience and religion. This right shall include freedom to have or to adopt a religion or belief of his choice, and freedom, either individually or in community with others and in public or private, to manifest his religion or belief in worship, observance, practice and teaching.
> 2. No one shall be subject to coercion which would impair his freedom to have or to adopt a religion or belief of his choice.
> 3. Freedom to manifest one's religion or beliefs may be subject only to such limitations as are prescribed by law and are necessary to protect public safety, order, health, or morals or the fundamental rights and freedoms of others.
> 4. The States Parties to the present Covenant undertake to have respect for the liberty of parents and, when applicable, legal guardians to ensure the religious and moral education of their children in conformity with their own convictions.

Freedom of religion is a 'unique' freedom within IHRL.[1] The construction of that freedom must deal with elements of *constraint* (religion is a self-imposed constraint on freedom) as well as *liberty* (the absence of constraint), and so the interpretation of religious freedom is more complicated than that of other rights.[2] Religions have their own value systems[3] embedded therein and international standards on freedom of religion create another normative framework that might not necessarily be in conformity with the normative underpinnings of religions. However, other human rights are not connected with an alternative normative system.[4] The international norm on religious freedom does not rest on the

---

1 Anat Scolnicov, *The Right to Religious Freedom in International Law: Between Group Rights and Individual Rights*, Routledge, London, 2010, p. 1.

2 *Ibid.*

3 "Interview with Kenan Malik", in Michael Herz and Peter Molnar (eds.), *The Content and Context of Hate Speech: Rethinking Regulation and Responses*, Cambridge University Press, 2012, p. 82; Scolnicov, 2010, p. 1, see *supra* note 1.

4 Scolnicov, 2010, p. 1, see *supra* note 1.

internal truths, revelations or beliefs of any *particular* religion. Nevertheless, it adopts a position of neutrality or impartiality between religions and beliefs.[5]

Freedom of religion embodies '*expressive*' (religion as liberty) as well as '*collective*' (religion as identity) dimensions. The former relates to the right to manifest religion and express religious ideas and mostly appears in worship, teaching, practice and observance,[6] whereas the 'collective aspect' indicates the affiliation with a group that adopts the same set of theological beliefs.[7] Freedom of religion protects the group identity of religious believers, which is often the basis for discrimination based on religion.[8] Enjoyment of freedom of religion can thus be either *individual* (as a matter of liberty) or *communal* (as a matter of equality).[9] The perception of religion as both a personal-individual choice and a collective identity creates challenges pertaining to subjecting religious freedoms to legal regulation, in particular with regard to balancing the values of liberty and equality (mirroring the individual and collective aspects of freedom of religion).

Finding universal consensus or even wide agreement among states on the contours of freedom of religion is fraught with a number of difficulties. There are considerable and wide differences among states in relation to the status of religions within the structure of societies and states.[10] In a number of societies, both the entire social structure and the national identity are significantly embedded within the highest authority of a specific religion. The relationship between state and religion is addressed differently in national legal systems. A 'state's self-definition' is largely shaped by whether there is complete or partial

---

5 Kevin Boyle, "Freedom of Religion in International Law", in Javaid Rehman and Susan C. Breau (eds.), *Religion, Human Rights and International Law: A Critical Examination of Islamic State Practices*, Martinus Nijhoff Publishers, Leiden, 2007, p. 28.

6 Tseming Yang, "Race, Religion, and Cultural Identity: Reconciling the Jurisprudence of Race and Religion", in *Indiana Law Journal*, 1997, vol. 73, p. 138; Scolnicov, 2010, p. 208, see *supra* note 1.

7 Thomas J. Gunn, "The Complexity of Religion and the Definition of Religion in International Law", in *Harvard Human Rights Journal*, 2003, vol. 16, p. 200.

8 Mohamed Saeed M. Eltayeb, "The Limitations on Critical Thinking on Religious Issues Under Article 20 of ICCPR and Its Relation to Freedom of Expression", in *Religion and Human Rights*, 2010, vol. 5, no. 2–3, p. 122; Gunn, 2003, pp. 203–204, see *supra* note 7; UN Human Rights Coucil, Implementation of General Assembly Resolution 60/251 of 15 March 2006 Entitled "Human Rights Council", UN Doc. A/HRC/2/6, 20 September 2006, para. 38 ('Implementation of GA Res. 60/251') (https://www.legal-tools.org/doc/ap60uw/); Rex Ahdar and Ian Leigh, *Religious Freedom in the Liberal State*, Oxford University Press, 2013, p. 376.

9 Richard Moon, *Putting Faith in Hate: When Religion Is the Source or Target of Hate Speech*, Cambridge University Press, 2018, pp. 20, 61.

10 Scolnicov, 2010, p. 23, see *supra* note 1.

separation or union between state and religion.[11] Such differences among states create many disagreements among them when negotiating international standards on freedom of religion, including the right to change religion and scope of restrictions on the manifestation of religion and belief.[12] This is understandable since such standards are related in a direct manner to the constitutional structures of states as well as their identities.[13] Such considerable areas of disagreements justify the non-expansion of legally binding international standards on freedom of religion within IHRL.

In the early 1960s, the United Nations General Assembly adopted a resolution to draft a declaration on racial and religious discrimination, as a first step to prepare a Convention on this area. Nevertheless, member states later agreed that racial and religious discrimination should be addressed in separate legal instruments against the backdrop of controversies related to negotiating detailed standards on religious discrimination.[14] The declaration on racism was adopted in 1963, followed by the International Convention on the Elimination of All Forms of Racial Discrimination ('ICERD') in 1965. However, the draft Declaration on the Elimination of Religious Intolerance ('1981 Declaration') became the subject of tough and lengthy debates among states for two decades. It was finally adopted in 1981 and comprised only eight articles.[15]

The exact scope of religious freedom in IHRL remains uncertain. Its normative content remains largely underdeveloped.[16] The 1981 Declaration does not include a provision prohibiting incitement to religious discrimination comparable to Article 4 of the ICERD prohibiting racist speech. Furthermore, the

11 *Ibid.*, p. 2.

12 Joshua Foster, "Prophets, Cartoons, and Legal Norms: Rethinking the United Nations Defamation of Religion Provisions", in *Journal of Catholic Legal Studies*, 2009, vol. 48, no. 1, p. 20.

13 Scolnicov, 2010, p. 114, see *supra* note 1.

14 Paul M. Taylor, *Freedom of Religion: UN and European Human Rights Law and Practice*, Cambridge University Press, 2005, p. 9.

15 Kevin Boyle and Anneliese Baldaccini, "A Critical Evaluation of Human Rights Approaches to Racism", in Sandra Fredman (ed.), *Discrimination and Human Rights*, Oxford University Press, 2004, pp. 148–149; David A.J. Richards, *Free Speech and the Politics of Identity*, Oxford University Press, 1999, p. 178; Natan Lerner, *The UN Convention on the Elimination of All Forms of Racial Discrimination*, Sijthoff & Noordhoff, Alphen aan den Rijn, 1980, p. 1.

16 Racism, Racial Discrimination, Xenophobia and All Forms of Discrimination: Situation of Muslims and Arab Peoples in Various Parts of the World – Report by Mr. Doudou Diène, Special Rapporteur on Contemporary Forms of Racism, Racial Discrimination, Xenophobia and Related Intolerance, UN Doc. E/CN.4./2006/17, 13 February 2006, para. 33 (https://www.legal-tools.org/doc/avvwtg/); Richards, 1999, p. 179, see *supra* note 15; Foster, 2009, p. 20, see *supra* note 12.

1981 Declaration did not address the interconnectedness between the freedoms of religion and expression. The sub-commission on what became the Declaration proposed a number of clauses in its drafts addressing religion-based incitement. These clauses obliged states to prohibit by law the "promotion or incitement to religious intolerance or discrimination",[17] "incitement to hatred or acts of violence whether by individuals or organizations against any religious group or persons belonging to a religious community", and "organizations which promote and incite to religious discrimination".[18] A number of Western states opposed the inclusion of clauses prohibiting incitement on the ground that they would constitute a violation of freedom of expression. These clauses were later deleted from the final text of the 1981 Declaration.[19] It was evidently difficult to reach consensus at the international level on how to strike the balance between the freedoms of religion and expression, or how to determine the threshold for prohibiting the exercise of freedom of expression on the basis of incitement to religious discrimination.[20] The precise determination of the contours of the exercise of freedom of religion, including religious expression, has been among the most contentious areas during international negotiations related to that freedom and has been an intractable issue within IHRL.[21]

In light of the difficulties encountered in achieving agreement on the 1981 Declaration, no initiative has been taken since then to draft a convention on the elimination of religious discrimination or to propose new legal obligations on states in this area.[22] Therefore, although international legal instruments prohibiting racial and gender discrimination have been adopted, the international community has failed to reach consensus on similar elaborate obligatory legal standards addressing religious discrimination. This reflects the complexities and

---

17 Note by the Secretary-General Containing in An Annex The Draft Convention Prepared by the Sub-Commission on Prevention of Discrimination and Protection of Minorities, UN Doc. E/CN.4/920 (on file with the author).

18 UN Commission on Human Rights, Report on the Twentieth Session, Economic and Social Council Official Records: Thirty-Seventh Session Supplement No. 8, UN Doc. E/3873, 17 February – 18 March 1964 (https://www.legal-tools.org/doc/7e6kfd/).

19 Kevin Boyle "Religious Intolerance and the Incitement of Hatred", in Sandra Coliver (ed.), *Striking a Balance: Hate Speech, Freedom of Expression and Non-discrimination*, Article 19, London, 1992, p. 65 (available on Article 19's web site).

20 Report of the UN High Commissioner for Human Rights on the Implementation of Human Rights Council Resolution 7/19 Entitled "Combating Defamation of Religions", UN Doc. A/HRC/9/7, 12 September 2008, para. 67 ('Report on the Implementation of HRC Res. 7/19') (https://www.legal-tools.org/doc/g0w2qi/); Boyle, 1992, p. 65, see *supra* note 19.

21 Taylor, 2005, pp. 2, 25, see *supra* note 14.

22 Javaid Rehman and Susan Breau, "Introductory Reflections", in *id.* (eds.), 2007, p. 47, see *supra* note 5.

sensitivities of the issues involved and the lack of universal agreement on the exact contours of the exercise of religious freedoms that states should respect and protect.

12.3. The Prohibition of Incitement to Hatred Under International Human Rights Law: Five Internal Features

There are provisions relevant to incitement to hatred in three different instruments of IHRL: the Universal Declaration of Human Rights ('UDHR'), ICERD and ICCPR. Nevertheless, Article 20(2) of the ICCPR embodies the most comprehensive concept of the international norm prohibiting incitement within IHRL.

Article 7 of the UDHR obliges states to provide protection against incitement to discrimination. Such prohibition is thus integral to the definition of the right to equality and the right to non-discrimination. The article provides protection only against one category of harms resulting from incitement which is discrimination. It does not address the other harms of incitement that Article 20(2) of the ICCPR proscribes; which are hostility and violence.

Article 4 of the ICERD obliges states parties to declare the following offences punishable by law: the dissemination and promotion of ideas based on racial superiority or hatred, incitement to racial discrimination and incitement to, and acts of, racially motivated violence. Furthermore, the article obliges states to legally prohibit the provision of assistance to racist activities and the establishment of organizations that promote and incite racial discrimination. The article is restricted only to the *racial* ground of incitement and does not address the other two grounds of incitement that Article 20(2) of the ICCPR addresses, which are the *religious* and *national* grounds. The ICERD imposes wider restrictions on racist speech than the ICCPR as it not only obliges states to prohibit incitement to racial discrimination and violence; it also prohibits the mere dissemination and promotion of ideas based on racial superiority or hatred.

Turning now to Article 20(2) of the ICCPR,[23] it states that "[a]ny advocacy of national, racial or religious hatred that constitutes incitement to discrimination, hostility or violence shall be prohibited by law". The scope of the international legal norm against incitement in this article is wider than that of Article 7 of the UDHR. It proscribes one act which is advocacy of hatred which causes incitement to three different categories of harms: (i) discrimination, (ii) hostility, and (iii) violence. It covers more grounds of incitement, compared to ICERD; race, nationality and religion.

[23] ICCPR, 23 March 1976 (https://www.legal-tools.org/doc/2838f3/).

Article 20(2) is a peculiar provision within the ICCPR – it is different from other articles codifying human rights and fundamental freedoms. The other articles use terms such as 'all persons' and 'everyone' and oblige states to refrain from interfering with the exercise of particular rights and freedoms. The articles codifying human rights are subject to a general provision stipulating that states adopt laws only 'as may be necessary' to give effect to these rights. Limitations on the exercise of freedoms within the ICCPR are of a permissive rather than prescriptive nature, permitting states to impose such limitations (which must be enacted in law) at their discretion. However, Article 20(2) explicitly incorporates a *positive* obligation on states to issue laws prohibiting specific expressions, rather than merely authorizing them to issue such laws. Article 20(2) is the only article in the ICCPR whose wording incorporates the phrase "shall be prohibited by law".

There are five internal features of the norm prohibiting incitement to hatred that provoke enduring controversies pertaining to its exact normative definition, interpretation and implementation. These internal features create challenges in reaching wide international agreement on the norm's exact meaning and scope and explain the current underdeveloped state of the international legal framework on hate speech.

The first internal feature of the norm prohibiting incitement to hatred is its 'emotional' component. Article 20(2) uses the term 'hatred' to describe the content of expressions that should be prohibited if they incite particular harms. It also recognizes incitement to hostility as a category of harm that justifies the prohibition of advocacy of hatred. More precisely, the norm obliges states to make their national laws intolerant of an extreme emotion – hatred – if its advocacy incites, *inter alia*, the emotional harm of hostility towards targeted groups. The descriptive objects of the two terms, 'hatred' and 'hostility', belong to the realm of emotive states. Both terms are unrelated to concrete practice, being concerned instead with intangible states of mind, attitudes and psychological states of abhorrence, detestation and enmity. The formulation of the norm in emotive language renders its clear interpretation challenging within an international legal context. Furthermore, the emotional component makes the norm's interpretation and implementation relative or contextual, as emotions are by-products of conceptions on morals, and morals are inherently relative and changeable.

The second internal feature: the 'incitement' component which relates to the nature of the causal or likelihood-based relationship between advocacy of hatred and its alleged harms. The prohibition of advocacy of hatred is justified only if that advocacy constitutes incitement to discrimination, hostility, or violence. In reality, proving sufficient causality to establish the existence of incitement is a complex exercise, and difficult to establish without contestation, given its indirect, cumulative, and mentally and emotionally mediated nature. The 'emotional' nature of both the content of the expressions involved and one particular category of their possible harms (that is, hostility) exacerbate the difficulties of proving incitement. This makes the first two features of the norm inter-related. It is difficult to provide a definitive answer to the question of how tightly the causal connection between advocacy of hatred and its possible harms must be drawn before restricting the former, as context determines whether incitement exists. This adds another relativist challenge to the norm's interpretation and implementation.

The first two features of the norm against incitement to hatred thus demonstrate the inherent difficulties in reaching wide international agreement on the definition and conditions of expressions prohibited pursuant to the right. These two features highlight the problematic nature of the shift from the moral denunciation of hate speech to its international legal prohibition.

The third important feature of the international norm prohibiting incitement to hatred is that it embodies tensions between the speakers' and targeted listeners' rights to liberty and equality and not, as frequently claimed in hate speech literature, between the values of liberty and equality in the abstract. The interaction of the two values of liberty and equality in the right is multifaceted and complex. The right takes effect by restricting speakers' freedom of expression. Yet liberty as a value is not enhanced only through the protection of a wider range of expressions; liberty can be at risk for members of targeted groups if they are not provided with protection against the harms of hate speech, as this can have a 'silencing effect' on them. Enhancing the equality of members of targeted listeners is the major underlying rationale of the right. However, equality, as a value, can also be at stake for speakers if their freedom of expression is unwarrantedly infringed upon. Thus, the interpretation and implementation of the norm should not be reduced to solving perceived tensions or even conflicts between equality and liberty and then giving primacy to one value over the other. Nevertheless, they require a delicate and difficult balance to be struck between the speakers' and targeted listeners' rights to equality and liberty.

The right's fourth internal feature is its 'group identity' aspect. Both hateful content itself and the harms of prohibited expressions affect specific collective identities. The right is integral to the protection of groups' rights and identities through the prevention of communal harms. It therefore involves tension between individual and group rights. Drawing a sharp dividing line between the two categories of protection (the individualized and the collective) is inherently difficult, given that hate speech targets individuals based on their group-defining characteristics or identity. The group identity component of the right also raises the dilemma of distinguishing between the protection of groups from the collective harms of hate speech and the protection of their group-defining characteristics. The lines separating these two interlinked forms of protection are blurred.

The religion component of the norm prohibiting incitement to hatred creates an additional source of tensions between the expressive and collective identity aspects of freedom of religion, both in relation to those who express offensive religious views and the religious followers who are targeted by such instances of expression. This fifth internal feature is examined in more detail in the next section.

Any regulatory regime that provides protection from incitement to discrimination, hostility, or violence has to grapple with the definitional challenges (the first and second features) and tensions underlying these internal features (the third, fourth and fifth features). The five features are inextricably interconnected and mutually reinforced. On the one hand, the emotional component of the right and the uncertainty in proving incitement make striking the balance between the targeted audience and speakers' rights to liberty and equality, as well as between individual and group rights, more complex. On the other hand, addressing the definitional uncertainties of the norm, in particular the emotive and incitement components, becomes more intractable under the effect of its underlying tensions manifested in the third, fourth and fifth internal features.

12.4. The Prohibition of Incitement to Religious Hatred Under International Human Rights Law: Additional Conundrums

The regulation of incitement to religious hatred carries a number of additional conundrums when compared to other grounds of incitement to hatred since it is intrinsically related to freedom of religion. While the prohibition of discrimination is the main rationale for providing protection against the harms of hate speech, the prohibition of religious hate speech is specifically justified by an additional rationale: protecting the religious freedoms of targeted religious groups. This extra rationale, however, adds complexity pertaining to the identification of the exact nature and scope of expressions that fall under the category of religion-based incitement.

The legal regulation of religious hate speech requires striking a delicate, and often very difficult, balance between respecting freedom of religious expression of speakers, on the one hand, and of targeted religious adherents, on the other. The intrinsic connection between protection from religious incitement and freedom of religion is evident in relation to the 'expressive' as well as 'collective' dimensions of that freedom. The protection provided in IHRL from incitement based on religious grounds impacts the expressive aspect of freedom of religion in two different ways. First, such protection limits the exercise of religious expressions when such exercise constitutes incitement to discrimination, hostility or violence (in relation to speakers). Second, the ICCPR recognizes the causal nexus between incitement to religious hatred and the infrigment upon the freedom to express and manifest religion in relation to religious groups that are targeted by such religious hate speech. Accordingly, once the threshold for religious incitement has been met in connection to any case, this constitutes a violation of freedom of religion infringing on the rights of members of religious groups targeted by such hateful incitement to practice and express their religion. Thus, Article 20(2) of the ICCPR protects both the collective-identity and expressive aspects of freedom of religion of religious groups targeted by religion-based incitement. Besides its implications on the exercise of freedom of religion, there are additional factors that complicate the drafting, interpretation and implementation of legal norms on religion-based incitement to hatred when compared to other grounds.

Firstly, the conditions in which specific expressions on religious matters might reach the threshold of incitement to religious hatred differ among different religions and beliefs.[24] Religious sensibilities might even be contradictory, given that religions are "fundamentally opposed belief systems"[25] and "are in a competitive position with regard to one another".[26] Expressions on religious matters that promote the supremacy of one religion might cause offense for – or even incite hatred against – believers of another religion.[27] Certain expressions that amount to incitement to religious hatred could be justifiable on the ground of the speakers' perception of the theological underpinnings or sacred texts of their religion or other religions or beliefs, which leads to problems in the interpretation and implementation of incitement to religious hatred offences.[28]

Secondly, religious sensitivities change across time and place; they evolve as the perceptions of adherents of religions evolve, which leads to

---

24 Taylor, 2005, p. 106, see *supra* note 14; Anthony W. Jeremy, "Religious Offences", in *Ecclesiastical Law Journal*, 2003, vol. 7, no. 3, p. 138.

25 Susannah C. Vance, "Permissibility of Incitement to Religious Hatred Offenses Under European Convention Principles", in *Transnational Law & Contemporary Problems*, 2004, vol. 14, p. 244.

26 Ivan Hare, "Blasphemy and Incitement to Religious Hatred: Free Speech Dogma and Doctrine", in Ivan Hare and James Weinstein (eds.), *Extreme Speech and Democracy*, Oxford University Press, 2009, p. 308.

27 "Interview with Robert Post", in Herz and Molnar, 2012, p. 36, see *supra* note 3; Jeremy Waldron, *Liberal Rights: Collected Papers 1981–1991*, Cambridge University Press, 1993, p. 138.

28 Peter Cumper, "Outlawing Incitement to Religious Hatred – A British Perspective", in *Religion and Human Rights*, 2006, vol. 1, no. 3, p. 263.

different, and maybe even competing, interpretations of offences on incitement to religious hatred.[29]

Thirdly, the increasingly multi-religious composition of societies against the backdrop of rising migration waves creates 'a standing danger' that religious believers might be stigmatized and stereotyped, and subsequently attacked on the basis of their religion.[30]

Fourthly, political debates often embody religious dimensions, for example, in relation to criticisms of public policies on religious grounds.[31] In many cases, religious leaders enter the public sphere and participate in public debates on matters of public controversy such as abortion, homosexuality and the status of women in society.[32] Also, debates on governmental policies on combating terrorism allegedly committed in the name of religion, and public debates of religious fundamentalism, in many cases complicate the separation between socio-political critiques of religion, political speech and religious speech.[33]

Fifthly, freedom of religion embodies the freedom to change one's religion, which requires open and critical debate about religions and beliefs. Categorizing expressions that are offensive to the religious feelings of others as incitement to religious hatred might undermine the exercise of freedom of religion itself.

Sixthly, it is difficult to distinguish between incitement to hatred against religious *believers* and *beliefs* or to distinguish between defamation of *religious groups* and defamation of *religions themselves*. As Waldron notes, "defaming the group that comprises all Christians, as opposed to defaming Christians as members of that group, means defaming the creeds, Christ and the saints. Defaming the group that comprises all Muslims, may mean defaming the Koran and the prophet Muhammad".[34] The distinction between the two categories of

29 European Commission for Democracy Through Law, "Report on the Relationship between Freedom of Expression and Freedom of Religion: The Issue of Regulation and Prosecution of Blasphemy, Religious Insult and Incitement to Religious Hatred" ('Venice Commission Report'), 23 October 2008, paras. 51, 79 (https://www.legal-tools.org/doc/2qqcxw/).

30 Jeremy Waldron, *The Harm in Hate Speech*, Harvard University Press, 2012, p. 130.

31 Vance, 2004, p. 246, see *supra* note 25; Hare, 2009, p. 300, see *supra* note 26; Robert Post, "Religion and Freedom of Speech: Portraits of Muhammad", in *Constellations*, 2007, vol. 14, no. 1, p. 77.

32 Hare, 2009, p. 308, see *supra* note 26; Ian Cram, "The Danish Cartoons, Offensive Expressions, and Democratic Legitimacy", in Hare and Weinstein (eds.), 2009, p. 324, see *supra* note 26.

33 Moon, 2018, p. 62, see *supra* note 9; Vance, 2004, p. 245, see *supra* note 25.

34 Waldron, 2012, p. 123, see *supra* note 30.

defamation is not easy.[35] Many religious groups consider defamation of their most sacred religious principles or symbols as tantamount to incitement to religious hatred against them, and to group defamation, since they identify themselves primarily by their religious convictions.[36] Moreover, in practice, expressions that defame religions are often perceived as inciting hatred against religious groups and are frequently used as a pretext to such incitement in an indirect manner.[37] It is more difficult to draw the boundary lines between anti-religion speech and hate speech, especially in the case of minority religions.[38] Rosenfeld clarifies:

> anti-Islam attitudes [in Europe] can easily and imperceptibly slip into anti-Muslim sentiments in a way that anti-Catholicism is not at all likely to denigrate into anti-French in France or anti-Italian in Italy.[39]

In a predominantly religious society, defamation of religion may offend the religious feelings of adherents to the predominant religion, but it will preclude religious practice for them.[40] Thus, expressions that defame religions could be considered as precluding the practice of religion, especially if that religion is not the predominant one, although this is not inevitably the case.[41] Incitement to violence, discrimination or hostility targeting a specific religion can cause restrictions in relation to manifesting or practicing religion (for example, the establishment of places of worship) and may therefore amount to a violation of freedom of religion. Proving the causal link or proving the likelihood-based

---

35 Eric Barendt, "Religious Hatred Laws: Protecting Groups or Belief?", in *Res Publica*, 2011, vol. 17, no. 1, p. 46.

36 Cumper, 2006, p. 265, see *supra* note 28.

37 Marloes van Noorloos, *Hate Speech Revisited: A Comparative and Historical Perspective on Hate Speech Law in the Netherlands and England & Wales*, Intersentia, Cambridge, 2011, p. 28; Eltayeb, 2010, p. 130, see *supra* note 8; Pnina Werbner, "Islamophobia: Incitement to Religious Hatred – Legislating for a New Fear?", in *Anthropology Today*, 2005, vol. 21, no. 1, p. 9.

38 Michel Rosenfeld, "Hate Speech in Constitutional Jurisprudence: A Comparative Analysis", in *Cardozo Law Review*, 2003, vol. 24, pp. 1523–1568..

39 *Ibid.*

40 Luis L. Guerra, "Blasphemy and Religious Insult: Offenses to Religious Feelings or Attacks on Freedom?", in Josep Casadevall, Egbert Myjer, Michael O'Boyle and Anna Austin (eds.), *Freedom of Expression: Essays in Honour of Nicolas Bratza President of the European Court of Human Rights*, Wolf Legal Publishers, 2012, p. 310.

41 Guerra, 2012, pp. 309–310, see *supra* note 40.

connection between advocacy of religious hatred and the harm caused to the adherents of the targeted religion is particularly challenging.[42]

In its recently issued General Comment No. 34 on freedom of expression, the Human Rights Committee recognized Article 20(2) as the benchmark for determining whether blasphemy and defamation of religious laws are in conformity with IHRL. The Committee affirmed that "prohibitions of displays of lack of respect for a religion or other belief system, including blasphemy laws" are incompatible with the ICCPR, *except under* "the specific circumstances" stipulated in Article 20(2).[43] The Committee added that such prohibitions must comply with the strict requirements of Article 19(3), as well as Articles 2, 5, 17, 18 and 26 of the ICCPR.[44] It emphasized that such laws should not discriminate in favour of, or against, any particular religion or belief system, or in favour of religious believers over non-believers.[45] Furthermore, the Committee added that laws prohibiting defamation of religion should not be employed to "prevent or punish criticism of religious leaders or commentary on religious doctrine and tenets of faith."[46] The Committee's stance is therefore symptomatic of its recognition of possible overlaps between the prohibition of defamation of religion and states' obligations under Article 20(2). Similarly, Frank La Rue, the former UN Special Rapporteur on Freedom of Expression, emphasized that Article 20(2) is the benchmark for determining whether anti-religious expressions represent legitimate exercise of freedom of expression. He opined that:

> the right to freedom of expression includes the right to scrutinize, debate openly, make statements that offend, shock and disturb, and criticize belief systems, opinions and institutions, including religious ones, *provided that they do not advocate hatred that incites hostility, discrimination or violence*.[47]

Although laws prohibiting defamation of religion and laws providing protection against incitement to religious hatred have different ideological rationales and targets of protection (beliefs and believers), they both involve the protection of religious *feelings* (the emotional component of the norm against

---

42 Lorenz Langer, "Recent Development: The Rise (and Fall?) of Defamation of Religions", in *Yale Journal of International Law*, 2010, vol. 35, no. 1, pp. 257–263.

43 General Comment No. 34: Article 19: Freedoms of Opinion and Expression, UN Doc. CCPR/C/GC/34, 12 September 2011 (https://www.legal-tools.org/doc/113be6/).

44 *Ibid.*, para. 48.

45 *Ibid.*

46 *Ibid.*

47 "Letter Dated 3 October 2012 from the Permanent Representative of Paraguay to the United Nations Addressed to the President of the General Assembly", UN Doc. A/67/537, 19 October 2012, para. 53 (emphasis added) (https://www.legal-tools.org/doc/53a29i/).

incitement to hatred). Given that the latter are defined by reference to religious beliefs, the protections provided by these two categories of laws are extended to religious beliefs *qua* religious feelings. It is difficult to determine precisely when the threshold of incitement to religious hatred is met, while completely avoiding an assessment of the significance of the expressions in question in relation to the doctrinal tenets of the targeted religious groups. Additionally, the psychological harms resulting both from defamation of religion and expressions that clearly incite hatred against religious groups have similar effects in relation to the members of targeted religious groups.[48] The distinction between incitement to hatred against religious believers and defamation of religions themselves can be made at the abstract level, as these two concepts represent separate analytical categories of expressive act. Nevertheless, it is indeed complicated to establish *empirically* whether the level of incitement against religious believers has been reached in the case of religious defamation or anti-religious speech, thus justifying the legal prohibition of such expressions.[49]

12.5. Recent Standard-Setting Attempts at the United Nations in the Area of Incitement to Religious Hatred

The most recent phase of multilateral negotiations on the norm prohibiting incitement to hatred took place in the aftermath of the 11 September 2011 terror attacks. Islámic states reacted to the rise of hate speech targeting Muslim communities in the West following the terrorist attacks of 9/11, by calling for the development of complementary international legal standards prohibiting incitement to religious hatred. The standard-setting efforts led mainly by Islámic states started with a series of UN resolutions on combating defamation of religion, adopted between 1999 and 2010. These resolutions sought to recognize defamation of religion as a human rights violation prohibited pursuant to Article 20(2) of the ICCPR.

Given the non-binding nature of these resolutions, however, Islámic states did not consider them sufficient to fully address their concerns. They redoubled their efforts through the establishment, in 2006, of the UN Ad Hoc Committee on the Elaboration of Complementary Standards, which had the explicit mandate of creating new international binding standards on incitement to racial and

---

48 Waldron, 2012, p. 122, see *supra* note 30.

49 Ahdar and Leigh, 2013, p. 434, see *supra* note 8; Scolnicov, 2010, p. 33, see *supra* note 1; Peter Cumper, "Inciting Religious Hatred: Balancing Free Speech and Religious Sensibilities in a Multi-Faith Society", in Nazila Ghanea, Alan Stephens and Raphael Walden (eds.), *Does God Believe in Human Rights? Essays on Religion and Human Rights*, Martinus Nijhoff Publishers, Leiden, 2007, pp. 238–239, 241; David Norris, "Are Laws Proscribing Incitement to Religious Hatred Compatible with Freedom of Speech?", in *UCL Human Rights Review*, 2008, vol. 1, no. 1, p. 110.

religious hatred. Islámic states, with the support of most African states, argued that Article 20(2) had normative gaps that necessitated the development of new complementary international legal standards. The standards proposed by Islámic states aimed at obliging states to legally prohibit the negative stereotyping and defamation of religion, as well as the derogatory profiling and stigmatization of both individuals and groups on the basis of religion.

The standard-setting efforts led by Islámic states involved direct engagement with the scopes of both freedom of expression and freedom of religion. Islámic states considered defamation of religion, negative profiling of religious adherents, insult to religious feelings and offensive attacks on matters regarded as sacred by religious followers not only as violations of the right to be protected from incitement to religious hatred, discrimination and violence, but also as violations of freedom of religion.[50] Islámic states therefore sought to strike a new balance between the freedoms of religion and expression, as well as the right to be free from religious discrimination, a balance grounded in the right to be protected from the harm of religious hate speech.[51]

The direct interaction of Islámic states' proposed standards with the definition and scope of freedom of religion under IHRL added further complexities to their standard-setting attempts. National legal systems across the world adopt different approaches as to what constitutes prohibited forms of expression on religious matters at both normative and jurisprudential levels.[52] These different approaches reflect various views on whether, and to what extent, respect for religious beliefs and feelings should limit freedom of expression. The varying status of religions in states' structures contributes to such differences; a clear distinction exists between states that recognize state religion whose protection preserves national identity and those who do not, with the latter group including secular states in particular.[53] The difficulties associated with reaching broad agreement on the contours of freedom of religion have precluded the attempts

---

50 Racism, Racial Discrimination, Xenophobia and Related Forms of Intolerance: Follow-Up to and Implementation of the Durban Declaration and Programme of Action: Report Submitted by Mr. Doudou Diène, Special Rapporteur on Contemporary Forms of Racism, Racial Discrimination, Xenophobia and Related Intolerance, UN Doc. A/HRC/7/19, 20 February 2008, para. 10 (https://www.legal-tools.org/doc/3uj7ba/).

51 Report of the Ad Hoc Committee on the Elaboration of Complementary Standards on its Second Session: Annex I – Attendance, UN Doc. A/HRC/13/58, 21 January 2010 (https://www.legal-tools.org/doc/9lkw39/).

52 Report on the Implementation of HRC Res. 7/19, 12 September 2008, para. 67, see *supra* note 20.

53 Foster, 2009, p. 56, see *supra* note 12; Allison G. Belnap, "Defamation of Religions: A Vague and Overbroad Theory That Threatens Basic Human Rights", in *Brigham Young University Law Review*, 2010, no. 2, p. 680.

to develop the normative content of the right to protection from religious incitement. There is a particularly wide gap between Islámic and Western states in this regard. Polarized conceptions of the rationales underpinning freedoms of religion and expression therefore lead not only to different positions on their boundaries and mutual relations, but also complicate standard-setting in the area of religious hate speech.

Western states strongly criticized both the general approach and conceptual framework of resolutions on defamation of religions as being incompatible with IHRL, which, in their view, should not provide protection to religions, entities or ideologies. They did not view defamation of religion as meeting the criteria for prohibited incitement under Article 20(2) of the ICCPR. They voted against these resolutions in the UN. Furthermore, they resisted completely the development of new international standards providing protection from incitement to hatred, in particular incitement based on religious grounds.

One major controversy that arose between supporters and opponents of standard-setting efforts was whether contempt of religion and offence to religious feelings constituted violations of freedom of religion. Islámic states believed that they did and assumed an automatic causal relationship between such categories of expressions and infringement of targeted adherents' religious freedoms that in turn justify the prohibition of these categories of expressions. The proposed standards delineated the normative scope of freedom of religion so as to include the right to protection from defamation of religion, negative profiling of religious groups and offence or insult to religious feelings. Conversely, Western states excluded any possible causal relationship between contempt of religions or offence to religious feelings and infringement upon freedom of religion. Along with a number of Latin American states, they firmly resisted the creation of new international binding standards on religious hate speech.[54]

The question of whether hate speech against a religion should be equated with hate speech against religious adherents proved to be the most controversial aspect of states' varying conceptions of the norm prohibiting incitement to religious hatred.

---

54 Statement by Finland on Behalf of European Union Member States Delivered at the UN Human Rights Council on A/HRC/1/L.16, 30 June 2006 (https://www.legal-tools.org/doc/jrcfyt/); Statement of the United States Delivered at the UN Human Rights Council on A/HRC/16/L.38, 24 March 2011 (https://www.legal-tools.org/doc/k8ui0o/); Statement of Canada Delivered at the UN Human Rights Council, 2009 (available on the UN *Webcast* web site); Statement of Brazil Delivered at the UN Human Rights Council on A/HRC/L.4/12, 30 March 2007 (https://www.legal-tools.org/doc/datqya/); Statement of Argentina Delivered at the UN Human Rights Council, 2007 (available on the UN *Webcast* web site).

Certain characteristics of the period during which Islámic states proposed their standards on religious hate speech at the UN are particularly relevant to understanding the resistance of Western states to those standards. First, these normative debates at the UN took place while the boundaries of freedom of expression relating to religious matters re-emerged forcefully as a contentious and sensitive issue in the West, creating friction and violence in many communities. Growing religious diversity – resulting from migration – led to demands from religious minorities, met mostly with fierce resistance, that Western democracies realign the boundaries of freedom of expression in order to advance multiculturalism.

Second, blasphemy offences in the West became mostly *de jure* abolished or *de facto* deactivated.[55] The legal protection of Christian religious beliefs, doctrine and symbols has a long tradition in the West and originally evolved at a time when religion and the state were closely interwoven.[56] With the gradual decoupling of state and religion in Western states, blasphemy offences have become increasingly irrelevant.[57] The change of religion's place in the secular state, where freedom of religion has become more dependent on the state's neutrality in religious issues, has changed the boundaries of protection accorded to religious speech in the West.[58] Blasphemy offences, the "world's oldest hate speech provisions",[59] have become "the most arcane and archaic pieces of European legislation"[60] and have "waned to the point of near universally recognized obsolescence".[61] The number of prosecutions pursuant to blasphemy laws has decreased to the point where the laws are rarely activated[62] and punishments

55 Blasphemy offences exist in a small number of countries of Council of Europe – Austria, Denmark, Finland, Greece, Ireland, Italy, Liechtenstein, the Netherlands and San Marino. See Venice Commission Report, para. 19, *supra* note 29.

56 Dieter Grimm, "Freedom of Speech in a Globalized World", in Hare and Weinstein (eds.), 2009, p. 17, see *supra* note 26.

57 Robert C. Blitt, "The Bottom Up Journey of 'Defamation of Religion' From Muslim States to the United Nations: A Case Study of the Migration of Anti-Constitutional Ideas", in *Studies in Law, Politics, and Society*, 2011, vol. 56, no. 1, p. 7.

58 Grimm, 2009, p. 18, see *supra* note 56.

59 Miklos Haraszti, "Forward: Hate Speech and the Coming Death of the International Standard Before It Was Born (Complaints of a Watchdog)", in Herz and Molnar (eds.), 2012, p. xvii, see *supra* note 3.

60 Cecile Laborde, "The Danish Cartoon Controversy and the Challenges of Multicultural Politics: A Discussion of the Cartoons That Shook the World", in *Perspectives on Politics*, 2011, vol. 9, no. 3, p. 603.

61 Geoffrey B. Levey and Tariq Modood, "The Muhammad Cartoons and Multicultural Democracies", in *Ethnicities*, 2009, vol. 9, no. 3, p. 436.

62 Jytte Klausen, *The Cartoons That Shook the World*, Yale University Press, 2009, p. 144.

thereunder have "passed into history".[63] In the past few years, European Union institutions have issued recommendations calling upon European states to review their offences on blasphemy, religious insult and insults to religious feelings.[64] These recommendations were justified by invoking "the greater diversity of religious beliefs in Europe and the democratic principle of the separation of state and religion".[65] Opponents to the introduction of the concept of defamation of religion perceived it to be "blasphemy in new clothes".[66] In their opinion, the concept mixes two normative systems, law and religion, which should be kept separate, with the former's content not being influenced by the latter.[67] Accordingly, efforts to create new international standards obliging states to prohibit defamation of religions ran counter to contemporaneous trends in the West regarding blasphemy offences. The standard-setting efforts were therefore perceived as an attempt to turn the clock back in Western states.[68]

Third, the standard-setting efforts of Islámic states coincided temporally with the increasing delegitimization, by the UN human rights machinery, of domestic legislation restricting freedom of expression based on religious defamation, blasphemy or insult to religious feelings. In the context of reviewing state parties' periodic reports, the Human Rights Committee has expressed negative views on blasphemy laws and similar legal provisions on the basis that they discriminate against adherents of specific religions and thereby restrict religious expression. A number of UN Special Rapporteurs have criticized blasphemy laws and other similar provisions for restricting the legitimate exercise of freedom of expression, especially inter-religious and intra-religious criticism. They have also condemned their frequent discriminatory application, which has

63 Robert F. Drinan, *Can God & Caesar Coexist?: Balancing Religious Freedom and International Law*, Yale University Press, 2004, p. 220.

64 Venice Commission Report, para. 89.c, see *supra* note 29; Council of Europe, Parliamentary Assembly, "Blasphemy, Religious Insults and Hate Speech Against Persons on Grounds of Their Religion", Recommendation 1805 (2007), paras. 10–11 (https://www.legal-tools.org/doc/9l6lcc/).

65 Council of Europe, Committee on Culture, Science and Education, "Blasphemy, Religious Insults and Hate Speech against Persons on Grounds of Their Religion", Doc. 11296, 8 June 2007 (https://www.legal-tools.org/doc/n9u7bp/).

66 Lorenz Langer, *Religious Offence and Human Rights: The Implications of Defamation of Religions*, Cambridge University Press, 2014, p. 260.

67 Langer, 2014, p. 260, see *supra* note 66.

68 Grimm, 2009, p. 17, see *supra* note 56.

infringed upon the rights of religious minorities and exacerbated religious intolerance.[69]

There are recognized links, commonalities and blurred lines between expressions that are defamatory of religions and expressions that are likely to raise or strengthen hostile feelings or hatred *vis-à-vis* religious adherents. While the right to protection from religious hate speech clearly prohibits the latter, Islámic states also sought prohibition of the former under IHRL. Their proposed standards presumed an automatic causation between expressions that defame, convey contempt or insult religions, on the one hand, and incitement to harms that infringe upon the rights of religious adherents, on the other, which was refuted completely by opponents to these standards.

In fact, the correlation between defamation of religion and incitement to religious discrimination, hostility, or violence is neither automatic nor inevitable, as Islámic states presumed; but neither is it impossible, as implied by Western states' positions. Instead, it should be empirically examined without holding predetermined assumptions.[70] Defamation of religion could (under certain circumstances and within specific contexts) overlap, in practical terms if not in strictly normative or conceptual terms, with incitement against religious adherents.[71] As addressed in detail in Section 12.4. of this chapter, the issue of distinguishing between incitement to hatred against religious *ideas* and incitement to hatred against religious *adherents* is a complex one. The emotional and group identities components of the norm against incitement to religious hatred contribute significantly to such complexity, in addition to the intersection of the norm with the freedoms of religions and expression.

A number of UN Special Rapporteurs had recognized that the "exercise of freedom of expression could *in some extreme cases* affect the right to manifest the religion or belief of certain identified individuals" (emphasis added).[72]

---

69 Heiner Bielefeldt, Frank La Rue and Githu Muigai, "Joint Submission to OHCHR Expert Workshops on the Prohibition of Incitement to National, Racial or Religious Hatred: Expert Workshop on Africa", 6–7 April 2011 (https://www.legal-tools.org/doc/2o8hrq/); "'Freedom of Expression and Incitement to Racial or Religious Hatred', Joint Statement by Githu Muigai, Asma Jahangir and Frank La Rue", OHCHR Side Event during the Durban Review Conference, Geneva, 22 April 2009 ('Joint Statement 2009') (https://www.legal-tools.org/doc/dwylqx/); Civil and Political Rights, Including the Question of Freedom of Expression: Report of the Special Rapporteur Protection of the Right to Freedom of Opinion and Expression, Mr. Abid Hussain, Submitted in Accordance with Commission Resolution 2000/38, UN Doc. E/CN.4/2001/64 (Annex V), 13 February 2001 (https://www.legal-tools.org/doc/yej4pm/); Implementation of GA Res. 60/251, para. 42, see *supra* note 8.

70 Levey and Modood, 2009, p. 435, see *supra* note 61.

71 Rosenfeld, 2003, p. 277, see *supra* note 38.

72 Joint Statement 2009, see *supra* note 69.

However, they considered it "conceptually inaccurate" to "present 'defamation of religions' *in abstracto* as a conflict between the right to freedom of religion or belief and the right to freedom of opinion or expression".[73] Asma Jahangir, the former UN Special Rapporteur on Freedom of Religion or Belief held that "defamation of religions may offend people and hurt their religious feelings but *does not necessarily or at least directly* result in a violation of their rights, including their right to freedom of religion".[74] She has convincingly affirmed that:

> [the question] as to whether criticism, derogatory statements, insults or ridicule of one religion may actually negatively affect an individual's right to freedom of religion or belief can only be determined objectively and, in particular, by examining whether the different aspects of the manifestation of one's right to freedom of religion are accordingly negatively affected.[75]

By the year 2010, standard-setting attempts had been brought to a halt, indicating that the opponents to these attempts were much more effective than their supporters in advancing their normative agendas.

The terminological shift in UN Human Rights Council Resolution 16/18 on 'combating intolerance, negative stereotyping and stigmatization of, and discrimination, incitement to violence and violence against, persons based on religion or belief' as a replacement resolution to defamation of religions does not in itself address the areas of contention between states on the regulation of hate speech. The new resolution adopted by consensus uses the same terminology as Article 20(2) of the ICCPR. However, the debates accompanying standard-setting efforts indicate that Article 20(2) does not constitute a clear universal benchmark for assessing the content and effects of hate speech that should be prohibited. Moreover, both sides invoked other human rights norms such as freedom of religion and prohibition of discrimination to justify their polarized stances. This means that these rights also refer to different normative content, in some aspects related to the scope of limitations on freedom of expression *vis-à-vis* religion.[76]

The consensual adoption of Resolution 16/18 may have ended the visible diplomatic rift between Islámic and Western states on the concept of defamation of religion, but it has by no means ended the normative dilemmas pertaining to defining the meaning and scope of the international norm prohibiting incitement to religious hatred. The Resolution does not, therefore, appear to represent any

---

73 *Ibid.*

74 Implementation of GA Res. 60/251, para. 37, see *supra* note 8 (emphasis added).

75 *Ibid.*, para. 39.

76 Langer, 2014, p. 259, see *supra* note 66.

substantial progress towards a new consensus on the empirical or practical implications of this norm.

12.6. The Way Ahead

As this chapter has demonstrated, finding a universal normative content for protection from incitement to religious hatred is very challenging. Securing broad agreement on an approach that moves beyond the current level of abstraction by adding specificity to the content and effects of prohibited advocacy of religious hatred seems far-fetched from reality. The conundrums associated with the regulation of incitement to religious hatred (that are embedded in the five internal features of the norm) prevent the progressive normative development of IHRL in this area. This is the case even though the contemporary challenges associated with the globalized dynamics of hate speech require a different response from IHRL.

In order for the international community to overcome such paralysis, one possible approach is to focus on the *procedural* development of the international norm prohibiting incitement to religious hatred rather than the legal or textual development. This approach would not provide a universal substantive solution to the dilemmas associated with determining the precise legal threshold of Article 20(2) in relation to advocacy of religious hatred; rather, it would address how to determine such threshold within different national contexts.

National authorities need guidance in implementing their international legal obligation to prohibit incitement to religious hatred. Such guidance is crucial to avoid the excessively prohibitive laws that suppress legitimate speech, inconsistent implementation of laws, and restrictive interpretations of laws in ways that jeopardize the obligation's preventive function – its central value from a policy perspective. Rather than legal or textual development, the efforts of the international community can be directed towards the provision of such guidance to states in the form of a *procedural* manual for the enforcement of the prohibition of incitement to religious hatred. This approach allows states to take into consideration their own national contexts when seeking to resolve the threshold dilemmas and inherent tensions underlying the norm prohibiting religious hate speech. This falls under *regulatory relativism*, in which the means of achieving protection from the harms of incitement to religious hatred is determined in accordance with the specific relevant context.

The relativist challenge facing the norm prohibiting incitement to religious hatred is evident; its interpretation and implementation are highly context-dependent, undermining the possibility of reaching a universally agreed-upon definition. Religions' statuses within states' structures differ significantly; constitutions and national laws address the relationship between state and religion in various ways. These variations generate different approaches to the legal regulation of incitement to religious hatred. Indeed, appeals to context frequently arose during the drafting history of Article 20(2) of the ICCPR and the more recent UN debates pertaining to standards-setting in the area of religious hate speech. The jurisprudence developed by supranational human rights–monitoring bodies indicates that they have to a great extent accepted relativist appeals through taking a cautious approach towards scrutiny of religious hate speech regulation. They have conceived of national authorities as best positioned to determine the formulation and application of hate speech laws, particularly with regard to the content of prohibited expressions and the assessment of their likelihood to incite harms.

Even among liberal democracies, there are many variations when it comes to the religious hate speech legal landscape. Different criteria are applied to determine the threshold of free speech and hate speech. The laws and judicial practices related to addressing hate speech are predicated upon different conceptions of the content of prohibited expressions, the scope of recognized harms of hate speech and the standards of causality between advocacy of hatred and its alleged harms. The prohibition of religious hate advocacy that constitutes clear and unambiguous incitement to immediate violence or illegal acts is the aspect of the norm against hate speech that enjoys most transnational resonance, since it easily crosses cultural and ideological boundaries. Nevertheless, legal regulation of hate advocacy on religious grounds that fall short of incitement to violence but create a social climate conducive to hostility and discrimination, does not enjoy the same universal resonance.

The differing national regulatory responses to incitement to hatred are also symptomatic of the vague international normative framework. Despite the fact that the international human rights paradigm seeks to influence norms at a national level, there is a lack of clarity on precisely what Article 20(2) requires from states in practice. A *procedural* approach would, therefore, contribute to making Article 20(2) more practicable for states through the provision of guidance to prosecutorial and judicial authorities about the sound application of national laws prohibiting incitement to hatred.

The Rabat Plan of Action on the prohibition of advocacy of national, racial or religious hatred that constitutes incitement to discrimination, hostility or violence[77] is an important step in this procedural development path. It was the outcome of a series of regional expert workshops organized by the Office of the UN High Commissioner for Human Rights in 2011 on the freedom of expression

[77] Annual Report of the UN High Commissioner for Human Rights on the Expert Workshops on the Prohibition of Incitement to National, Racial or Religious Hatred: Addendum, UN Doc. A/HRC/22/17/Add.4, 11 January 2013 (https://www.legal-tools.org/doc/oymwge/).

and the prohibition of incitement to national, racial, or religious hatred as reflected in Articles 19 and 20 of the ICCPR. These expert workshops attracted wide participation from government representatives, civil society, academia, UN treaty bodies and Special Rapporteurs of the Human Rights Commission. Their objectives were three-fold: firstly, "to gain a better understanding of legislative patterns, judicial practices and policies regarding the concept of incitement to national, racial, or religious hatred, while ensuring full respect for freedom of expression as outlined in Articles 19 and 20 of the ICCPR"; secondly, "to arrive at a comprehensive assessment of the state of implementation of the prohibition of incitement in conformity with international human rights law"; and, thirdly, "to identify possible actions at all levels". A 'wrap-up' expert workshop was convened in Rabat in October 2012 with the aim of bringing together the conclusions and recommendations from the previous different workshops: it led to the elaboration of the Rabat Plan of Action. One of the main purposes of this Plan is to raise awareness and understanding of Article 20(2) and, in particular, to promote an interpretation of the article that is consistent with other human rights; in particular Articles 18 (freedom of religion or belief) and 19 (freedom of expression) of the ICCPR. This process brought more visibility to Article 20(2) and sought to address the interpretation dilemmas associated with it.

The Rabat Plan of Action proposed a six-part threshold test as a framework for determining the threshold of "advocacy of national, racial or religious hatred that constitute incitement to discrimination, hostility or violence" under Article 20(2) of the ICCPR. It suggested that judicial systems adopt a case-by-case analysis when applying the test to determine whether the threshold of incitement has been reached. The first of the threshold test's six elements is the social and political context prevalent at the time the expression was made and disseminated. It is interesting to note that this first element therefore refers to context. It reflects a clear recognition, after comprehensive study of relevant legislation and jurisprudence, that context is of great importance when assessing whether particular statements are likely to incite to discrimination, hostility or violence. The Rabat Plan of Action recognized that context "may have a direct bearing on both intent and/or causation". The second element is the speaker, in terms of his position or status in society and "standing in the context of the audience to whom the speech is directed". The third is intent, in terms of the "activation of a triangular relationship between the object and subject of the speech act as well as the audience". The fourth is the content and form of expression, in terms of "the degree to which the speech was provocative and direct, as well as the form, style and nature of arguments deployed in the speech". The fifth is the extent of speech, in terms of its reach, public nature, magnitude, size of audience, frequency and the medium of dissemination. The sixth and final element is the likelihood of the occurrence of the harm, in terms of identifying "some degree of risk of harm" and "reasonable probability that the speech would succeed in inciting actual action against the target group, recognizing that such causation should be rather direct".

A number of UN Special Rapporteurs, human rights experts and non-governmental organizations have endorsed this threshold test.[78] The Rabat Plan of Action has also been noted in Human Rights Council resolutions on "[c]ombating intolerance, negative stereotyping and stigmatization of, and discrimination, incitement to violence, and violence around the world against persons based on religion or belief".[79]

The Rabat Plan of Action represents a significant step in the road to a serious procedural engagement with some of the challenging aspects of the right to protection from incitement to religious hatred. The *procedural* development of the international norm prohibiting religious hate speech is not overloaded with navigational challenges when compared to the creation of *substantive* international legal standards outlining the content of expressions and harms prohibited pursuant to this norm. As such, this procedural approach could offer a partial substitute for the development of a strong universal or consensual normative content to Article 20(2) of the ICCPR.

78 *Ibid.*

79 *Ibid.*

13

The Relevance of International Law Standards to Religious Leaders

Ioana Cismas[*]

13.1. Introduction

Madame Cissé Zeinab Keita, *Chargé d'affaires* at Mali's Ministry of Religious Affairs, recalls that she was one of only three women religious leaders invited, "at the very last minute", to a legal training on conflict-related violence against women organized by the United Nations ('UN') Multidimensional Integrated Stabilization Mission in Mali ('MINUSMA'). One hundred and five imáms were also invited to participate. When she challenged the under-representation of female religious leaders at the event, which was focused on the experiences of and legal protection for Malian women, the organizers explained that the training was intended for 'imáms'. Madame Cissé observed:

> Il n'y a pas des [femmes] imams dans l'Islam, mais il y a des prédicatrices, ou bien des prêcheuses […]. Toujours on a ces problèmes – ils essayent de mettre les femmes de côté.[1]

This opening anecdote should, at the broadest level, invite reflection on the importance of context-sensitive conceptualization. Specifically, it portrays how the way we define religious leadership may result in excluding – in this case, along gender lines – actors to which international legal standards may be

---

* Dr. **Ioana Cismas** is Co-Director of the Centre for Applied Human Rights and Reader at the York Law School, University of York. The present chapter draws on research conducted for the project *Generating Respect for Humanitarian Norms: The Role of Religious Leaders in Influencing Parties to Armed Conflict* ('the Generating Respect Project'). Funded by the United Kingdom's Economic and Social Research Council, the project was developed in partnership with the humanitarian organization Geneva Call between 2020–2022. The views expressed in this article do not necessarily reflect those of project partners or affiliated institutions. The author wishes to thank Dr. Ezequiel Heffes, Dr. Piergiuseppe Parisi and Dr. Katharine Fortin for fruitful discussions or reading earlier drafts. Any errors remain the author's own. For an audio-visual recording of Dr. Cismas' statement to CILRAP's conference in Florence in April 2022 on the topic of this anthology, please see https://www.cilrap.org/cilrap-film/220409-cismas/.

1 "There are no [female] imams in Islam, but there are [female] preachers, or even priestesses […]. We always have this problem – they try to set women aside" (author's translation). The recollection is part of the digital story: Generating Respect Project, "GRP digital story: 'Madame Cissé, prédicatrice de l'équité'", 31 October 2021 (available on YouTube).

relevant and the action of whom may, in turn, be relevant for international law. Inspired by Madame Cissé's recollection, this chapter engages in a reflexive effort to unearth and problematize preliminary assumptions about the concepts employed in international legal scholarship and practice, in encounters with religions, with the aim of providing a more holistic understanding of the relevance of international law to religious leaders.

Reflexivity is commonly described as the "process of a continual internal dialogue and critical self-evaluation of [the] researcher's positionality as well as active acknowledgement and explicit recognition that this position may affect the research process and outcome".[2]

Whilst reflexivity is nowadays expected in research in social and health sciences, its utility (although seldom its use)[3] extends to legal sciences, including international legal scholarship and practice. Relevant elements that influence the positioning of international law scholars and practitioners in encounters with religion include personal characteristics, such as gender, race, nationality, age, beliefs, personal experiences, linguistic traditions and professional affiliations.[4] Importantly, this chapter will demonstrate that the methodological and theoretical background and preferences of legal scholars and practitioners, as elements of positionality, condition the analysis of which international standards are applicable to religious actors; whether, how and why such standards are (or can be) used and abused by them; and what accountability mechanisms are available to address violations. The chapter, thus, makes a case for informed, reflexive engagement between legal scholars and practitioners and religious leaders as a step change in enhancing the relevance of international law.

Structurally, the chapter is divided in seven sections. Section 13.2. examines how doctrinal, socio-legal methods and constructivist theory can shape the analytical inquiry into international law standards of relevance to religious actors. Section 13.3. delves into empirical, doctrinal and sociological approaches to defining religious leadership, so as to understand the 'actorhoods' they embody, the variety of affiliations they can have with religion, belief or spirituality, and the special legitimacy they claim. Section 13.4. explores the international legal standards applicable to religious leaders and the consequences of the various actorhoods they embody on their enjoyment of rights and obligations. A

---

2 Roni Berger, "Now I See It, Now I Don't: Researcher's Position and Reflexivity in Qualitative Research", in *Qualitative Research*, 2015, vol. 15, no. 2, p. 220.

3 For a welcome exception, or rather an invitation to reflexive practice in international law, see Julia Emtseva, "Practicing Reflexivity in International Law: Running a Never-Ending Race to Catch Up With the Western International Lawyers", in *German Law Journal*, 2022, vol. 23, no. 5, pp. 756–768.

4 This enumeration draws on Berger, 2015, pp. 219–234, see *supra* note 2.

specific focus will be the legal regime applicable to religious personnel under international humanitarian law ('IHL') and the conditions and implications of the loss of this protective status. The accountability avenues available to challenge abuse by religious leaders and increase their positive influence on third parties are examined in Section 13.5. Section 13.6. discusses the interaction between religious leaders, international human rights law ('IHRL') and IHL, beyond compliance with or abuse of these standards. The conclusion ties the argumentative threads of the chapter together and makes a plea for greater engagement between international law scholars and practitioners and religious actors as a norm compliance-generation strategy.

13.2. On Methods, Theories and Their Relevance

In approaching a legal problem, the first decision that lawyers make – including those writing on and practising international law – concerns the methods that they will utilize to study the problem. Curiously, law schools (still) often do not equip their students with the understanding that this decision is a conscious one, which, in turn, requires clear articulation and justification. Avid readers of legal literature would be more surprised to stumble upon articles that include a methodology section than upon those omitting such a discussion altogether.[5] Hutchinson and Duncan observe that many doctrinal legal scholars consider it "unnecessary to verbalise" their chosen methods.[6] This may well be because of the overwhelming dominance of doctrinal legal methodology in the study and practice of law – it is as if legal scholarship and the doctrinal method have gone hand in hand for such a long time that they cofound and confound each other.[7]

Along similar lines then, due to the dominance of legal positivism in international law scholarship,[8] specialist literature appears to conflate theory ("a

5 For a similar observation in the context of doctoral studies in international law, see Robert Cryer, Tamara Hervey, Bal Sokhi-Bulley and Alexandra Bohm, *Research Methodologies in EU and International Law*, Bloomsbury Publishing, London, 2011, p. 2.

6 Terry Hutchinson and Nigel Duncan, "Defining and Describing What We Do: Doctrinal Legal Research", in *Deakin Law Review*, 2012, vol. 17, no. 1, p. 99.

7 Westerman, for instance, notes that "[t]he legal system is not only the subject of inquiry, but its categories and concepts form at the same time the conceptual framework of legal doctrinal research", Pauline Westerman, "Open or Autonomous: The Debate on Legal Methodology as a Reflection of the Debate on Law", in Mark van Hoecke (ed.), *Methodologies of Legal Research: Which Kind of Method for What Kind of Discipline?*, Hart Publishing, London, 2011, pp. 87–110. For a critique of doctrinal legal methodology which assumes the "identity of subject and theoretical perspective", see Jan Vranken, "Methodology of Legal Doctrinal Research: A Comment on Westerman", in *ibid.*, pp. 111–122.

8 In their article which aims to outline "a modern and, we hope, enlightened view of positivism as the core of international legal discourse", Simma and Paulus also observe that "in reflecting on our day-to-day legal work, we realized that, for better or for worse, we indeed employ the

systematic knowledge-resource [that] informs the selection of a particular methodology"), methodology ("the theory of methods which explains and justifies the method(s) used in a particular instance"), and method ("a technique of acquiring knowledge").[9] Perhaps this is so because recognizing that positivism is just one legal theory among many, with its 'doctrine of sources' and its 'doctrine of treaty interpretation' as predilect, yet not sole methods, could be seen as a defeat in the hard-fought battle to achieve recognition for international law as a scientific and an objective discipline.[10] A simpler explanation is provided by Kammerhofer: "for the most part, 'default positivism' is semi-conscious and half-reflected, more part of one's legal socialisation and culture than of a conscious choice and reflection".[11] In contrast, D'Aspremont notes that "[o]ne's refusal to unpack one's modes of meaning" – which is how he defines methods – "does not mean that there are no modes of meaning at work, let alone that there is no awareness of such refusal".[12] The submission made in this chapter is that methodological and theoretical preferences are a central feature of a researcher's positionality, which therefore require open discussion: refusal to enter into such discussion is, at the very least, methodologically problematic. In the context of the present study, the chosen mix of methods and the underpinning theory significantly shape the thinking and the meaning of 'relevance' of international law standards to religious leaders – and, as demonstrated in Section 13.3. of this chapter, they also shape the definition of religious leadership.

Allow me then to switch to the (unusual in legal writing) first-person address and discuss the theoretical and methodological foundations of this chapter. As an international lawyer schooled in legal positivism, faced with the task at

---

tools developed by the 'positivist' tradition", Bruno Simma and Andreas L. Paulus, "The Responsibility of Individuals for Human Rights Abuses in Internal Conflicts: A Positivist View", in *American Journal of International Law*, 1999, vol. 93, no. 2, pp. 302–303.

9 The introduction to a recent and much-needed edited volume on *Research Methods in International Law* distinguishes between theory, methodology and methods, as the above citations illustrate, yet it appears to conflate these categories when it comes to what the authors call "doctrinal methods". See Rossana Deplano and Nicholas Tsagourias, "Introduction", in *id.* (eds.), *Research Methods in International Law*, Edward Elgar Publishing, Cheltenham, 2021, pp. 1–2. This is so, perhaps, because they use Ratner and Slaughter's work as an example – in that work, confusingly, method is defined as theory and methodology is understood as method. See Steven Ratner and Anne-Marie Slaughter, "Appraising the Methods of International Law: A Prospectus for Readers", in *American Journal of International Law*, 1999, vol. 93, no. 2, pp. 291–292.

10 See Richard Collins, "How to Defend International Legal Method?", in Deplano and Tsagourias (eds.), 2021, p. 11, see *supra* note 9.

11 Jörg Kammerhofer, "International Legal Positivist Research Methods", in *ibid.*, p. 97.

12 Jean d'Aspremont, "International Legal Methods: Working for a Tragic and Cynical Routine", in *ibid.*, p. 48.

hand, I am bound to engage in an analysis of the international legal sources that seek to regulate the rights and obligations of these actors. As such, taking Article 38 of the Statute of the International Court of Justice as a starting point, I will be aiming to offer an assessment of which hard law – and, since I am not a strict positivist, soft law – standards are applicable to religious leaders, and where claims of breaches by and against them can be brought. Sections 13.4. and 13.5. of this chapter propose this sort of analysis. Yet, this study goes further *because* it is underpinned by social constructivist theory and draws on qualitative and socio-legal methods.[13]

Social constructivism, whilst not a unitary theory, starts from the premise that states *and* non-state actors,[14] as norm entrepreneurs, epistemic communities and communities of practice, participate in social interactions that result in intersubjective meaning or shared understandings, which, in turn, lead to the "emergence, maintenance, development, fading, and diffusion" of norms.[15] Thus, "[c]onstructivism helps explain how international law can exist and influence behavior".[16] Landefeld, drawing on Finnemore and Toope, explains the particular utility of a constructivist lens to international legal analysis as follows:

---

13 For an overview of the turn towards socio-legal methods in international law, see Gregory Schaffer and Tom Ginsburg, "The Empirical Turn in International Legal Scholarship", in *American Journal of International Law*, 2012, vol. 106, no. 1, pp. 1–46; see also Ingo Venzke, "International Law and its Methodology: Introducing a New Leiden Journal of International Law Series", in *Leiden Journal of International Law*, 2015, vol. 28, no. 2, pp. 185–187.

14 Famously, in his 1992 seminal article, Wendt remarked that "[a]narchy is what states make of it": Alexander Wendt, "Anarchy Is What States Make of It: The Social Construction of Power Politics", in *International Organization*, 1992, vol. 46, no. 2, pp. 391–425. Social constructivist thinking has evolved to focus in a much more pronounced and systematic manner on the role of non-state actors in the emergence, development and implementation of norms, including international law norms. For classic texts, see Martha Finnemore, *National Interests in International Society*, Cornell University Press, London, 1996; Martha Finnemore and Kathryn Sikkink, "International Norm Dynamics and Political Change", in *International Organization*, 1998, vol. 52, no. 4, pp. 887–917; Jutta Brunnée and Stephen J. Toope, *Legitimacy and Legality in International Law: An Interactional Account*, Cambridge University Press, 2010, especially p. 36. For a more recent application, see Jacqueline Eggenschwiler and Joanna Kulesza, "Non-State Actors as Shapers of Customary Standards of Responsible Behavior in Cyberspace", in Bibi van den Berg and Dennis Broeders (eds.), *Governing Cyberspace: Behavior, Power and Diplomacy*, Rowman & Littlefield, Lanham, 2020, pp. 245–262.

15 Sarina Landefeld, "The Evolution of Norms and Concepts in International Law: A Social Constructivist Approach", in Rossana Deplano (ed.), *Pluralising International Legal Scholarship: The Promise and Perils of Non-Doctrinal Research Methods*, Edward Elgar Publishing, Northampton, 2019, pp. 49, 55.

16 Jutta Brunnée and Stephen J. Toope, "Constructivism and International Law", in Jeffrey L. Dunoff and Mark A. Pollack (eds.), *Interdisciplinary Perspectives on International Law and International Relations: The State of the Art*, Cambridge University Press, 2012, p. 120.

> Constructivists regard international law [...] as 'a broad social phenomenon deeply embedded in the practices, beliefs, and traditions of societies, and shaped by interaction among societies'. It is thus influenced by a variety of non-legal factors and dynamics which a doctrinal international law approach may fail to understand due to its conceptual and methodological limits.[17]

The social constructivist grounding of this chapter allows us to complexify our understanding of 'relevance' beyond that of *which* posited norms of international law are applicable to religious actors. Three specific features deserve emphasis at this stage. First, constructivism encourages an examination of what state and non-state religious leaders say and practise in respect to these international law standards and with what effect. The analytical effort here specifically draws on the critical constructivist insight that "local actors actively reconstruct foreign ideas, creating greater congruence with local beliefs and practices".[18] They may also ignore 'foreign ideas', or contest them, creating a buy-out. Acharya, for example, shows how changes in norm acceptance could be explained by "the differential ability of local agents to reconstruct [international] norms to ensure a better fit with prior local norms, and the potential of the localized norm to enhance the appeal of some of their prior beliefs and institutions".[19]

Second, norms (including legal norms) understood as social constructs "constrain, enable, and constitute actors in their choices".[20] At the same time, actors are not at the mere mercy of social structures, they retain agency to shape norms – in particular, "actors with the ability to influence intersubjective meaning are considered as being in a position of power".[21] As religious leaders are often societally influential, one could assume that they are powerful norm-shapers. This assumption is often, yet not always, true, as discussed in Section 13.3. of this chapter.

Third, the discourse and practice of religious leaders – shaped and reshaped, as they are, through interaction with third parties, including legal

---

17 Landefeld, 2019, p. 50, see *supra* note 15. See also, Martha Finnemore and Stephen J. Toope, "Alternatives to 'Legalization': Richer Views of Law and Politics", in *International Organization*, 2001, vol. 55, no. 3, p. 743.

18 Amitav Acharya, "How Ideas Spread: Whose Norms Matter? Norm Localization and Institutional Change in Asian Regionalism", in *International Organization*, 2004, vol. 58, no. 2, p. 239.

19 *Ibid.*

20 John Ruggie, "What Makes the World Hang Together? Neo-Utilitarianism and the Social Constructivist Challenge", in *International Organization*, 1998, vol. 52, no. 4, p. 875.

21 Landefeld, 2019, pp. 48–49, see *supra* note 15.

scholars and practitioners – encapsulate the possibility or the promise for change.[22] The argument that will be pursued in the conclusion of the chapter is that the engagement between legal scholars, practitioners and religious leaders can result in forging shared understandings to, on the one hand, increase the relevance of international law to religious leaders, and, on the other hand, legitimize legal standards in local contexts.

Consistent with its social constructivist theoretical inclination, the chapter embraces a socio-legal approach[23] and draws on empirical qualitative research methods. In particular, it relies on data collected as part of the Generating Respect Project, an applied research project that sought to examine the role of religious leaders in influencing parties to armed conflict towards greater (non-)compliance with IHL and IHRL norms.[24] Data was collected by the research team through over 250 semi-structured interviews with legal and religious scholars, humanitarian practitioners, experts on conflict dynamics, journalists, religious leaders, current and former members of armed actors and members of conflict-affected communities in Colombia, Libya, Mali, Myanmar, Syria and Yemen (the project's case study countries), as well as through digital stories and reflexive diarizing. This chapter will draw on some of this primary data to discern if, how and why international law standards are considered by religious leaders and whether, in turn, religious leaders can contribute to norm-compliance.

In brief, the employed doctrinal and socio-legal methods and the social constructivist theoretical insights create a three-pillared examination of the 'relevance of international law standards' to religious leaders:

1. Applicability
    i. Which hard and soft law standards seek to regulate the conduct of religious leaders?
2. Accountability
    ii. What avenues exist to pursue accountability for violation of rights and obligations of religious leaders?

22 Note that, whilst social constructivism was often regarded as an optimist theory because of the potential for change which it holds, scholars have demonstrated that change need not necessarily be positive. See Brunnée and Toope, 2012, p. 137, *supra* note 16.

23 A socio-legal approach views law not "as an autonomous force to which society is subjected, but rather shapes and is shaped by broader social, political and economic logics, contexts and relations". See Darren O'Donovan, "Socio-Legal Methodology: Conceptual Underpinnings, Justifications and Practical Pitfalls", in Laura Cahillane and Jennifer Schweppe (eds.), *Legal Research Methods: Principles and Practicalities*, Clarus Press, Dublin, 2016, p. 108.

24 See the home page of The Generating Respect Project's web site (https://www.generatingrespectproject.org/) and the biographical note above.

3. Discourse and practice
   iii. Do religious leaders use international law standards in their discourse or activities?
   iv. If they do, why, how and with what effect? If they do not, why?

Armed with this set of research questions, we turn next to the term 'religious leadership' to explore how its conceptualization interacts with the identified elements of 'relevance of international legal standards'.

13.3. Defining Religious Leadership

Religious leadership – unlike religious personnel, as we shall see in Section 13.4. – is not a legal concept. Posited international law does not, as such, define the term. Thus, an empirical approach to defining religious leadership may be a useful starting point instead. Let us take the United Nations Development Programme ('UNDP') Guidelines on Engaging with Faith-based Organizations and Religious Leaders as a reference, which note that "priests, imams, rabbis, clerics, monks, nuns, lamas, traditional indigenous spiritual guides such as shamans and sukias, and lay religious leaders" are religious leaders.[25]

Three questions immediately arise. First, would an atheist or a humanist actor be included in this definition? Interpretative practice[26] and jurisprudence on freedom of religion or belief[27] answer in the affirmative, irrespective of the fact that calling an atheist or a freethinker a *religious* leader may be somewhat grating for the individual in question. Certainly, the practice of the European Court of Human Rights ('ECtHR') has sought to ensure that Article 9 of the European Convention on Human Rights protects philosophical convictions which attain "a certain level of cogency, seriousness, cohesion and importance".[28] In brief, it would be difficult to argue that we should exclude any leaders whose beliefs meet this threshold, despite the uneasiness we, or they, may have with the attribute 'religious'.

---

[25] UNDP, "UNDP Guidelines on Engaging with Faith-based Organizations and Religious Leaders", 1 October 2014, p. 5 ('UNDP Guidelines, 2014').

[26] See, for example, United Nations Human Rights Committee, CCPR General Comment No. 22: Article 18: The right to freedom of thought, conscience and religion, UN Doc. CCPR/C/21/Rev.1/Add.4, 30 July 1993, para. 2 (https://www.legal-tools.org/doc/9df763/).

[27] See, for example, ECtHR, *Kokkinakis v. Greece*, Judgment, 25 May 1993, Application no. 14307/88, para. 31 (https://www.legal-tools.org/doc/c550f8/); European Commission on Human Rights, *Union des Athées v. France*, Commission's report, 6 July 1994, Application no. 14635/89, para. 79 (https://www.legal-tools.org/doc/ba4agm/).

[28] See, for example, ECtHR, *Union des Athées v. France*, *Leela Förderkreis e.V. and Others v. Germany*, Judgement, 6 November 2008, Application no. 58911/00, para. 80 (https://www.legal-tools.org/doc/altgaj/).

Turning to the second and third questions: Since the above enumeration includes only individuals, could religious leadership be exercised by formal and informal groups or organizations and institutions? What forms of actorhood do these entities take: are they non-state or also state actors? Both questions can be answered doctrinally – Sections 13.4. and 13.5. of this chapter do just that, by providing an overview of the implications of various actorhoods that religious leaders can embody for their rights and obligations under international law and the available accountability avenues. A purely doctrinal approach, however, does not fully capture the distinctiveness of religious leaders, which goes a long way to explain their potential to enhance or diminish the relevance of international law standards in local contexts.

As such, in an effort to achieve greater analytical rigour, researchers involved in the Generating Respect Project have sought to identify the definitional contours of religious leadership by drawing on an extensive, interdisciplinary literature review, analysing critically the terminology employed in guidelines or strategies for engagement between various UN bodies and faith-based actors as instantiations of relevant practice,[29] and relying on doctrinal legal analysis and empirical data. We have proposed that religious leaders are actors who:

1. Have a formal or informal affiliation to religion, spirituality or belief;
2. Make a claim of special legitimacy – anchored predominantly in charisma or tradition – to interpret religion and to persuade or command obedience from followers, communities and other actors;
3. Exercise leadership individually or collectively, through formal or informal groups, networks, organizations or institutions;
4. Can operate as state or non-state actors;
5. Are most often institutionally external to armed actors, yet can also be part of their political or military structures.[30]

This definition distinguishes itself through three main features: first, it introduces the new element "claim of special legitimacy"[31] as a core definitional

29 See, for example, Joint United Nations Programme on HIV/AIDS, "Partnership with Faith-based Organizations: UNAIDS Strategic Framework", December 2009; UNDP Guidelines, 1 October 2014, see *supra* note 25; United Nations High Commissioner for Refugees, "Partnership Note on Faith-based Organizations, Local Faith Communities and Faith Leaders", 6 June 2014; United Nations Environment Programme, "Engaging with Faith Based Organizations. UN Environment Strategy", 20 July 2018.

30 Ioana Cismas *et al.*, *Considerations and Guidance for the Humanitarian Engagement with Religious Leaders*, University of York, 2023, p. 14.

31 This element is taken from Ioana Cismas, *Religious Actors and International Law*, Oxford University Press, 2014, pp. 51–57.

concept; second, it recognizes informal types of affiliation to religion; and third, it includes collective forms of leadership within the definition of religious leadership itself, as opposed to separating them (artificially) into a new category of faith-based organizations.[32] At this stage, it is useful to examine these elements and their implications for achieving greater relevance for international law standards in various contexts.

13.3.1. A Claim of Special Legitimacy

This definitional feature assumes that religious leaders' legitimacy is 'special' because of the specific sources of legitimation upon which these actors draw when they put forward religious interpretations, including those that have a positive or negative bearing on international law standards. As argued elsewhere, the relationship between religious leaders and their followers, members or adherents can be regarded as one of complex command–obedience between an authority or power-holder and power-subjects.[33] This command-obedience can be equally evidenced in the case of a secular (or non-religious) democratic legislature and citizens. However, in the latter case, it is the legal-rational aspect of the law and governance structure that confers legitimacy to the authority and generates compliance with its commands. In contrast, the legitimate authority of religious leaders is primarily (whilst not necessarily exclusively) grounded in two other sources of legitimation, tradition or charisma.[34] As such, power-subjects follow a specific religious command or rule, because religious leaders are perceived to have legitimate authority by virtue of tradition or charisma to issue it.[35] These sources of legitimation upon which religious leaders draw are particularly important to the topic of this chapter due to their ability to localize international legal norms, as shall be argued in Section 13.6 of this chapter. Let us pause at this point to explore the concept of 'claim', which we have used to qualify the special legitimacy of religious leaders.

Much in keeping with constructivist thought, the 'claim' element seeks to portray power-subjects as agents, and not merely as objects, of commands. In

---

32 Contrast with the definition in the UNDP Guidelines, 1 October 2014, p. 5, see *supra* note 25 ("Religious leaders (RLs) are men and women with a *formal* affiliation to a religion or spiritual path who play influential roles within their communities and the broader civil society" (emphasis added)).

33 See, *ibid.*, and Ioana Cismas and Ezequiel Heffes, "Not the Usual Suspects: Religious Leaders as Influencers of International Humanitarian Law Compliance", in Terry D. Gill, Robin Geiß, Heike Krieger and Christophe Paulussen (eds.), *Yearbook of International Humanitarian Law*, T.M.C. Asser Press, The Hague, 2021, vol. 22, pp. 138–139.

34 Clearly, the analysis draws on Max Weber's work, see *ibid.*, and Max Weber, *Economy and Society*, Roth and Wittich (eds.), University of California Press, Berkeley, 1978, p. 215.

35 *Ibid.*

other words, not all religious leaders, not all the time, and not in respect to all matters will actually *enjoy* the special legitimacy which they claim, because power-subjects may choose not to comply with their commands for a variety of reasons. This observation is important because it recognizes that religious leaders may be influential – including in generating compliance with international law – but they need not necessarily be so. Findings of the Generating Respect Project suggest that we cannot assume that religious leaders' societal influence necessarily translates into an influence on norm acceptance and compliance among parties to an armed conflict. The Colombian context provides an apt illustration. In Colombia, the Catholic Church and many individual religious leaders command significant respect in society and enjoy a measure of legitimacy among some non-state armed groups and members of the Colombian Armed Forces. Whilst they have made strong appeals urging respect for humanitarian norms and urgent calls for peace,[36] these have not always been heeded by parties to conflicts.[37] Another illustration comes from Libya. Here we have examples of *Madkhali*[38] armed actors "acting on religious interpretation or using such interpretation to justify whether they should participate in hostilities, on which side, how to behave during the conflict and how to govern populations under their control".[39]

Yet, these groups have also been documented to engage critically with religious advice or *fatwás*, when these appear to discount the contextual reality of Libya or their political and economic interests.[40] The conclusion cannot be escaped: whilst the claim to special legitimacy is a necessary definitional element of religious leadership, the ability (or power) of religious leaders to act as

36 See, for example, Philipp Kastner, *Legal Normativity in the Resolution of Internal Armed Conflict*, Cambridge University Press, 2015, p. 112.

37 There are, of course, examples where they have been heeded. See Cismas and Heffes, 2021, p. 137, *supra* note 33; Jonathan Zaragoza *et al.*, "Mapping of Armed Conflicts and Religious Leaders in Colombia", The Generating Respect Project, 7 September 2020 (on file with the author); Mohammed Assaleh *et al.*, "Religious Leaders as Brokers of Humanitarian Norm-Compliance: Insights from the Cases of Colombia, Libya, Mali and Myanmar", in *Armed Groups and International Law*, 21 October 2020 (available on its web site).

38 Madkhalism is described as a quietist stream of the Salafist movement, drawing on the teachings of the Saudi cleric Rabiyy' al-Madkhali. See George Joffé, "The Trojan Horse: The Madkhali Movement in North Africa", in *The Journal of North African Studies*, 2018, vol. 23, no. 5, pp. 739–744.

39 Hasnaa El Jamali and Ioana Cismas, "The Multifactorial Influence of Madkhali Salafism on Libyan Armed Actors", in *Journal of Human Rights Practice*, 2023 (forthcoming).

40 *Ibid.*

norm-shapers or compliance-inducers is not always secured and a finer-grained analysis is required.[41]

In reference to the context of armed conflict, our research has shown that the influence of religious actors on humanitarian norm compliance should be seen as a relational process shaped by endogenous factors to both religious leaders and armed actors (such as values, objectives and ideology; religious, social and ethnic background; organizational structure, including financing; access and communication channels; position on IHL and IHRL norms), and contextual factors (such as conflict dynamics, security situation, applicability and clarity of IHL and IHRL norms, societal position or perception of religious leaders and armed actors, and involvement of third parties).[42]

13.3.2. Informal Affiliation to Religion and Collective Forms of Religious Leadership

Informal affiliation to religion, belief or spirituality and collective expression of religious leadership are analysed together in this section, because their inclusion in the definition of 'religious leadership' pursues the same aim. That is, we seek to capture the complex empirical reality of religious leadership on the ground more closely, and to correct for intra- and extra-religious exclusionary patterns, which manifest themselves, generally, in respect to women and minorities (ethnic, religious and youth).

This broadening exercise is the direct result of a process of reflexivity within the Generating Respect Project research team. In an early article, in which we articulated the conceptual framework of the project, we acknowledged the 'elephant' in the analysis: all the religious leaders discussed therein were men.[43] We asked ourselves where the women religious leaders were in our case study countries, namely, Colombia, Libya, Mali, Myanmar, Syria and Yemen? One of the project's local researchers, with deep knowledge of the country context, suggested that women tend to be excluded from religious leadership positions due to the reproduction of patriarchal societal patterns within the formal hierarchical religious structure. Whilst agreeing that this may be a plausible

---

41 One final observation relating to the 'claim' aspect is in order. Note also that the commands of religious leaders may also be heeded because power-subjects fear "the prospect of punishment for non-compliance" or are motivated by "rewards for compliance". See Craig Matheson, "Weber and the Classification of Forms of Legitimacy", in *The British Journal of Sociology*, 1987, vol. 38, no. 2, p. 200. This serves to underscore that in addition to, or alternatively to, legitimate authority, religious leaders' influence could rest on coercive or reward-based authority.

42 See Cismas *et al.*, 2023, pp. 22–30, see *supra* note 30; Cismas and Heffes, 2021, pp. 133–138, 143–144, see *supra* note 33.

43 Cismas and Heffes, 2021, p. 136, see *supra* note 33.

explanation, we also recognized that we may have not 'seen' women (and other 'minorities') because of the methods of data collection employed up to that stage – largely doctrinal and involving document analysis[44] – or because of the manner in which we had defined the concept of religious leadership. Embarking on in-depth, in-country interviews, relying on snowball sampling and ensuring that our interview guides were tailored to capture gender aspects, revealed a much more complex empirical reality on the ground. That reality, in turn, shaped our conceptualization of religious leadership and resulted in the definition proposed in Section 13.3.

Literature also supports the broad scope of the definition of religious leadership. As Gingerich *et al.* noted: "While women are leaders in some faiths, they are often not part of the traditional hierarchy"[45] – this observation could be normatively described as reflecting an intra-religious exclusionary pattern. As such, 'traditional definitions' of religious leadership, which "have tended to identify people with theological or ceremonial authority",[46] have often obscured or made invisible the leadership roles performed by women. Recall Madame Cissé's observation that women in Mali, whilst not being able to become imáms, certainly can and are preachers and priestesses. Another example encountered during fieldwork in relation to Myanmar is powerful. The woman we had interviewed did not possess formal religious authority, but solely indirect authority through her kinship with a pastor; yet, her discourse, actions, charisma and how she was perceived by societal and armed actors placed her firmly in the category of religious leaders with influence to shape behaviour.[47]

In many settings, including conflict contexts, women's religious leadership is expressed collectively, such as in the form of faith groups – whether sanctioned or not by the official religious authorities – and these forms of leadership tend to be "less publically visible".[48] For example, church groups formed of women were instrumental in the tensions that engulfed the Solomon Islands between 1998–2003. The Catholic Daughters of Mary Immaculate Sisters

---

44 See Ioana Cismas, "Religious Leaders' Influence on Parties to Armed Conflict: Reflexive Early Considerations on the Design and Implementation of the Generating Respect Project", presented at the Conference on Rules and Laws in Protracted Conflict: Concurrence, Negotiation and Friction, 28 October 2020 (on file with the author).

45 Tara R. Gingerich, Diane L. Moore, Robert Brodrick and Carleigh Beriont, "Local Humanitarian Leadership and Religious Literacy: Engaging with Religion, Faith, and Faith Actors", Harvard Divinity School Religious Literacy Project and Oxfam, 31 March 2017, p. 7.

46 Elena Fiddian-Qasmiyeh (ed.), "Gender, Religion and Humanitarian Responses to Refugees", UCL Migration Research Unit Policy Brief, 19 October 2016, p. 12.

47 See Chris Rush and Ioana Cismas, "Interview with Religious Leader", 2022 (on file with the author).

48 Fiddian-Qasmiyeh (ed.), 2016, p. 12, see *supra* note 46.

brought food to fighters of opposing parties in the armed conflict as a mediation tool and to alleviate the suffering of affected communities.[49] Distributing food to fighters is one of the "'low key' methods and 'self-effacing ethos'", which has allowed "women to pursue progressive, and often courageous, social agendas, in spite of their marginalization in national politics".[50] This kind of leadership – which, it should be noted, spilled over into key leadership roles in disarmament initiatives and transitional justice advocacy[51] – is less visible than poignant public statements made by bishops and other (usually male) high-ranking religious authorities. Yet, as the example discussed demonstrates, it may be no less important in terms of its potential to influence behaviour in armed conflict and post-conflict contexts.

The inclusion of 'informal' forms of affiliation to religion in the definitional scope of religious leadership captures various other local realities. Some social groups or organizations choose not to formally affiliate themselves with religion in order to preserve a certain independence from religious hierarchical authorities. Types of informal affiliation should also resonate with those local contexts where "religion remains interwoven with public life and local culture".[52] As Fiddian-Qasmiyeh notes, in such settings,

> many local organisations do not deem it necessary to explicitly identify themselves as 'faith-based'. This is even the case when their values and actions are understood through religious frameworks, which are effectively the norm in their local context. While this may be unproblematic in itself, when this is translated through a secular humanitarian framework, the 'faith' and 'religious' elements of the local organisation and the impact that 'religion' has on its work with refugees, remains invisible and unanalysed.[53]

The observation made by the author in the context of refugee protection is equally valid in relation to other areas of international legal practice. The

---

49 John Braithwaite, Matthew G. Allen and Sinclair Dinnen, *Pillars and Shadows: Statebuilding as Peacebuilding in Solomon Islands*, Australian National University EPress, Canberra, 2010, p. 31.

50 Elizabeth Snyder, "Waging Peace: Women, Restorative Justice, and the Pursuit of Human Rights in the Solomon Islands", in *Refugee Watch*, 2009, vol. 32, p. 773, pp. 67–79. See also, Bronwen Douglas, "Why Religion, Race, and Gender Matter in Pacific Politics", in *Development Bulletin*, no. 59, 1 October 2002, p. 12.

51 See Snyder, 2009, p. 72, *supra* note 50. See also discussions in Ioana Cismas, "Reflections on the Presence and Absence of Religious Actors in Transitional Justice Processes: On Legitimacy and Accountability", in Roger Duthie and Paul Selis (eds.), *Justice Mosaics: How Context Shapes Transitional Justice in Fractured Societies*, International Center for Transitional Justice, New York, 2017, pp. 316–318.

52 Fiddian-Qasmiyeh (ed.), 2016, p. 12, see *supra* note 46.

53 *Ibid.*

impact of religion on the potentiality of such groups to influence other actors in society, including armed actors, remains invisible, unless one acknowledges the 'informal' religious element underpinning their mission, activities and methods.

This 'informal affiliation' should be understood to extend to those groups or organizations whose affiliation to a certain religion is disputed or rejected by religious or state authorities due to legitimate or illegitimate reasons. For example, in Myanmar, the radical ultra-nationalist Buddhist organization known as Ma Ba Tha claims a strong affiliation to Theravada Buddhism despite having been disbanded by the State Sangha Maha Nayaka Committee.[54] Ma Ba Tha and monks associated with it continue to exercise religious leadership and significant influence on communities and some parties to armed conflicts in the country (possible even among the Myanmar military, or Tatmadaw).[55] According to scholars, the incitement to hatred and violence propagated by this organization paved the way for the serious rights violations of the Rohingya in Rakhine State.[56] Put differently, Ma Ba Tha's influence had a markedly negative bearing on IHRL and IHL protection, irrespective of the fact that the organization had been pushed into 'informality'.

Libya provides another example and an opportunity to reflect on the various connotations of 'informality'. The Nawasi Brigade, a Salafist-inspired armed group, which was nominally affiliated with the Ministry of the Interior of Libya's Government of National Accord, is alleged to have been involved in the destruction of *Ṣúfī* places of worship in 2011–2013 and again in 2017,[57] reflecting perhaps those Salafist interpretations which consider *Ṣúfīsm* heterodox.[58] Effectively, thus, *Ṣúfī* groups were pushed in the realm of 'informality' in the country.

54 See Chris Rush *et al.*, "Mapping of Armed Conflicts and Religious Leaders in Myanmar", *Generating Respect Project*, 3 October 2020 (on file with the author).

55 *Ibid.*

56 Zo Bilay, "The Characteristics of Violent Religious Nationalism: A Case Study of Mabatha against Rohingya Muslim in Myanmar", in *Journal of Human Rights and Peace Studies*, 2022, vol. 8, no. 1, pp. 86–106; Md. Ali Siddiquee, "The Portrayal of the Rohingya Genocide and Refugee Crisis in the Age of Post-Truth Politics", in *Asian Journal of Comparative Politics*, 2020, vol. 5, no. 2, pp. 89–103; International Crisis Group, "Buddhism and State Power in Myanmar", Crisis Group Asia Report No. 290, 5 September 2017; Htet Min Lwin, "Politicized Religion as Social Movement in a Nascent Democracy: The MaBaTha Movement in Myanmar", Master's dissertation, Central European University, 2016.

57 El Jamali and Cismas, 2023, see *supra* note 39; Wolfram Lacher and Peter Cole, "Politics by Other Means: Conflicting Interests in Libya's Security Sector", in *Small Arms Survey*, October 2014, pp. 77–78, note 53; Human Rights Watch ('HRW'), "Libya: New Wave of Attacks Against Sufi Sites", 7 December 2017 (available on its web site).

58 Katherine Pollock and Frederic Wehrey, "The Sufi-Salafi Rift", *Carnegie Middle East Centre*, 23 January 2018.

The term 'informality' in the above illustrations is used as an element of the analytical category 'religious leadership'. As such, it does not aim to pass value-judgements relating to the internal legitimacy of religious convictions or beliefs.[59] Equally, the element does not aim to assess whether the affiliation with religion, being informal, is less real or less strong compared to formal affiliation. As shown above, context may often explain why groups choose, or are forced into, an informal relationship, as opposed to a formal one.

13.4. The Consequences of Actorhood(s) and Special Legitimacy

The previous section argued that religious leaders can embody different state and non-state actorhoods, and that irrespective of variations in terms of religion, belief or spirituality and of formal or informal affiliations with religion, what binds these actors together is the claim that they make to enjoy special legitimacy to interpret religion and command obedience from followers. Let us now turn to the legal standards applicable to them to verify whether their claim to special legitimacy has any consequences on their enjoyment of rights and obligations under international law.

13.4.1. Legal Standards Applicable to State and Non-State Religious Leaders

Recognizing that religious leaders can occupy any point on the state–non-state continuum allows us to understand that their specific type of actorhood will likely determine which international law standards apply to them. What emerges is a matrix. When religious leadership takes the shape of a state (or a state-like construct), it will enjoy the full panoply of rights, privileges and obligations of states; when an inter-governmental organization conforms to the definition of religious leadership, legally it will be treated in a similar fashion to secular (or non-religious) international organizations; when religious leadership is expressed through a non-state legal entity, this will have rights and obligations analogous to non-religious organizations; and finally, individual religious leaders will enjoy rights and be subject to international legal obligations just like any other individuals. What needs to be verified is whether this matrix remains accurate, when we account for the special legitimacy that religious leaders claim. In other words, does their special legitimacy translate in a special legality regime

[59] This would appear to be consistent with international jurisprudence which requires a certain neutrality to be observed by state authorities in assessing the legitimacy of religious beliefs. ECtHR, *Eweida and Others v. the United Kingdom*, Judgement, 15 January 2013, Applications nos. 48420/10, 59842/10, 51671/10 and 36516/10, para. 81 (https://www.legal-tools.org/doc/aee735/); ECtHR, *Ancient Baltic religious association "Romuva" v. Lithuania*, Judgement, *8 June 2021, Application no. 48329/19,* paras. 118–119 (https://www.legal-tools.org/doc/8714um/).

under international law? Do they have special rights and lesser obligations compared to their non-religious peers? Previous work set out to systematically answer these questions by comparing like-for-like in terms of actorhood, with the only variable being the religious/non-religious aspect.[60] The analysis concluded that religious actors do not enjoy a special legality regime under international law due to their religiosity, but that some grey areas or qualifications exist. Some examples are in order at this stage.

The most complex case among religious states (or state-like constructs) – and perhaps among religious actors more broadly – is the Holy See.[61] Whilst personifying the apex of Catholic leadership, the Holy See invokes a dual personality under international law.[62] Over the years, the Holy See has sought to shift between its international legal personality as a state, so as to enjoy state privileges, including treaty-making powers and immunity from foreign jurisdiction in the context of clerical child sexual abuse litigation, and its personality *qua* church to enjoy the human right to freedom of religion.[63] This selective practice has been decidedly challenged in more recent years by UN treaty bodies and domestic courts.[64] The Holy See was called upon to acknowledge its 'state'

60 Cismas, 2014, see *supra* note 31; Ioana Cismas, "The Child's Best Interests and Religion: A Case Study of the Holy See's Best Interests Obligations and Clerical Child Sexual Abuse", in Elaine Sutherland and Lesley-Anne Barnes Macfarlane (eds.), *Implementing Article 3 of the United Nations Convention on the Rights of the Child: Best Interests, Welfare and Well-Being*, Cambridge University Press, 2016, pp. 310–325; Ioana Cismas and Stacy Cammarano, "Whose Right and Who's Right? The US Supreme Court v. The European Court of Human Rights on Corporate Exercise of Religion", in *Boston University International Law Journal*, 2016, vol. 34, no. 1, pp. 2–44.

61 I have advanced the argument that the Holy See is a state-like construct, which enjoys a single personality grounded in two sources: international custom (that recognizes the religious legitimacy of the Holy See) and the Lateran Treaty (which confers upon it a resemblance of statehood through the grant of the Vatican territory). Cismas, 2014, Chapter 4, see *supra* note 31.

62 See Committee on the Elimination of Racial Discrimination, Consideration of Reports Submitted by States Parties Under Article 9 of the Convention, Addendum: Holy See, Fifteenth Periodic Reports of States Parties due in 1998, UN Doc. CERD/C/338/Add.11, 26 May 2000, para. 4 (https://www.legal-tools.org/doc/wbb7px/); United States District Court, Western District of Kentucky, *O'Bryan et al. v. Holy See*, 2007, 490 F.Supp.2d 826 ('*O'Bryan*').

63 See Cismas, 2014, pp. 185–237, *supra* note 31.

64 Contrast the early practice of the Committee on the Rights of the Child with more recent one. Committee on the Rights of the Child, Consideration of Reports Submitted by States Parties under Article 44 of the Convention, Concluding Observations of the Committee on the Rights of the Child: Holy See, Tenth Session, UN Doc. CRC/C/15/Add.46, 27 November 1995, para. 14 (https://www.legal-tools.org/doc/phstl7/); *id.*, Concluding Observations on the Second Periodic Report of the Holy See, U.N. Doc. CRC/C/VAT/CO/2, 25 February 2014, paras. 29–30 (https://www.legal-tools.org/doc/kjpol6/). See also *O'Bryan, supra* note 62.

obligations under international human rights treaties, including, or in particular, when these have extra-territorial effects.[65]

The Cairo Declaration on Human Rights in Islam, developed by the Organisation of Islamic Cooperation ('OIC') in the early 1990s, could be regarded as an effort by this inter-governmental actor with "religious contours" to opt-out from the customary rules of treaty interpretation, and build instead, a 'religionalism', that is, a self-contained human rights regime entirely subject to (differing) *Sharí'ah* interpretations.[66] The Cairo Declaration has attracted significant critical attention from scholars and among states – the Parliamentary Assembly of the Council of Europe made a formal request to member states who are also members of the OIC to disavow the instrument.[67] A doctrinal lens allows us to put the document into context: the Cairo Declaration is a non-binding declaration that does not supersede the OIC member states' binding obligations under international human rights treaties.[68] A socio-legal approach that examines the actual practice of member states in relation to the Cairo Declaration would suggest that "the attachment of the OIC member states to the Cairo Declaration appears to have been minimal, at least when these were acting in UN fora".[69] In social constructivist terms, we may argue that OIC member states have not reached a shared understanding of 'human rights in Islám'. The new OIC Declaration on Human Rights adopted in 2020 would suggest that the religionalism project, outlined by the Cairo Declaration, has been, at least partly, abandoned.[70]

What then can be said about the international law standards applicable to non-state religious legal entities, such as churches and other religious organizations? Their rights, or rather their ability to claim breaches of their rights, depend on the admissibility criteria stipulated by various regional and international

65 Cismas, 2016, see *supra* note 60.

66 Cismas, 2014, Chapter 5, see *supra* note 31. For more recent work combining various disciplinary perspectives, see Turan Kayaoglu, *The Organization of Islamic Cooperation: Politics, Problems, and Potential*, Routledge, Abingdon, 2015; "The OIC's Human Rights Regime" and "The OIC and Children's Rights", in Marie Juul Petersen and Turan Kayaoglu (eds.), *The Organization of Islamic Cooperation and Human Rights*, University of Pennsylvania Press, Philadelphia, 2019.

67 Parliamentary Assembly of the Council of Europe, "Sharia, the Cairo Declaration and the European Convention on Human Rights", 22 January 2019 (available, along the reports of the various committees, on the Council of Europe's web site).

68 Cismas, 2014, pp. 253–284, see *supra* note 31.

69 *Ibid.*, p. 279.

70 Confusingly, the 2022 Declaration seems to be referred to both as the OIC Declaration on Human Rights and the Cairo Declaration of the Organisation of Islamic Cooperation on Human Rights, 2022, see OIC's web site. See also, Mohammad Hossein Mozaffari, "OIC Declaration on Human Rights – Changing the Name or A Paradigm Change?", Raoul Wallenberg Institute, December 2020.

treaties and the interpretation of their supervisory bodies. The regimes established by the European Convention on Human Rights ('ECHR'), the American Convention on Human Rights and the African Charter on Human and Peoples' Rights allow non-state religious actors, including religious legal entities, to seek redress for violations of their rights.[71] Successful claims were made in respect to the rights to freedom of religion, expression, association and assembly, property and fair trial.[72] In contrast, the *locus standi* provisions of the Optional Protocol to the International Covenant on Civil and Political Rights, and the restrictive interpretation of the Human Rights Committee, bar such access to legal entities.[73] Frustratingly, but similarly to other non-state legal entities, religious organizations have only limited *direct* obligations under international law. Yet, case-law provides some grounds for optimism. The procedural and substantive limitations placed on the right to church or religious autonomy can be understood to delineate a duty of religious legal entities to respect – if not protect and fulfil – the human rights of third parties.[74]

Two nebulous areas arise in relation to legal entities that claim to have religious objectives. The first refers to established or state churches. Were these actors to be considered state organs, they would trigger a state's responsibility for their actions or omissions in breach of international obligations. In its jurisprudence, the ECtHR has equated established churches with non-governmental organizations *stricto sensu*, as in organizations that do not participate in the exercise of governmental powers.[75] In *Holy Monasteries v. Greece*, this approach should be read as an effort to ensure that these organizations have the capacity

71 ECHR, text as amended by Protocols No. 11 and No. 14, 4 November 1950, Article 34 (https://www.legal-tools.org/doc/8267cb/); American Convention on Human Rights, 22 November 1969, Article 44 (https://www.legal-tools.org/doc/1152cf/); African Charter on Human and Peoples' Rights, 1 June 1981, Article 55 (https://www.legal-tools.org/doc/f0db44/); and the African Commission on Human and Peoples' Rights, "Information Sheet No. 3: Communication Procedure", 1987.

72 For an extensive discussion of religious entities rights under the ECHR regime, see Ioana Cismas, 2014, pp. 85–118, *supra* note 31. See also, Ioana Cismas, "Freedom of Religion or Belief and Freedom of Association: Intersecting Rights in the Jurisprudence of the European Convention Mechanisms", in Jeroen Temperman, Jeremy Gunn and Malcolm Evans (eds.), *The European Court of Human Rights and the Freedom of Religion or Belief: The 25 Years since Kokkinakis*, Brill, Leiden, 2019, pp. 260–281.

73 First Optional Protocol to the International Covenant on Civil and Political Rights, 16 December 1966, Articles 1 and 2 (https://www.legal-tools.org/doc/7b6b02/). See also, Manfred Nowak, *UN Covenant on Civil and Political Rights: CCPR Commentary*, N.P. Engel, Kehl, 2005, pp. 830–831.

74 For the development of this argument, see Cismas, 2014, pp. 119–152, *supra* note 31.

75 ECtHR, *Holy Monasteries v. Greece*, Judgment, 9 December 1994, Application nos. 13092/87 and 13984/88 (https://www.legal-tools.org/doc/b8427e/).

to hold and invoke rights under the ECHR against the state, since the alternative would leave them without redress for perceived violations. This approach, which equates established churches with non-state legal entities, however, needs to rest on a careful and contextualized analysis of the religion-state relations in a given state. Subsequent jurisprudence of the ECtHR failed to conduct such analysis.[76]

> As a consequence of *Hautaniemi v. Sweden*, it would seem that established churches are automatically considered to fulfil the non-governmental requirement without a contextual analysis; in this sense, the direct state responsibility framework under the ECHR was weakened. [The remaining option is indirect accountability]. The presumption being that a state would incur responsibility only if it fails to prevent or punish human rights abuses by established churches, under the positive obligations doctrine.[77]

A second development relates to domestic courts' more recent practice of affording freedom of religion protections to *for profit* corporate actors.[78] The practice is concerning – more so if it should be upheld by international human rights mechanisms[79] in as much as it may be indicative of the emergence of a special legal (sub-)regime for business entities that claim to also have religious goals. This jurisprudential trend has important socio-legal consequences: the increase and legitimizing of interferences by corporate actors with the rights of women and minorities, the muddling of the conceptual foundations of the right to freedom of religion[80] and the exacerbation of the existing power imbalance

---

[76] See European Commission of Human Rights, *Finska församlingen i Stockholm and Teuvo Hautaniemi v. Sweden*, Decision of 11 April 1996, 11 April 1996, Application No. 24019/94 (https://www.legal-tools.org/doc/t7r4dd/). See also Charlotte Smith, "A Very English Affair: Establishment and Human Rights in an Organic Constitution", in Peter Cane, Caroline Evans and Zoe Robinson (eds.), *Law and Religion in Theoretical and Historical Context*, Cambridge University Press, 2008, p. 183.

[77] Cismas, 2014, p. 90, see *supra* note 31.

[78] See discussions in Sandra Fredman, "Tolerating the Intolerant: Religious Freedom, Complicity, and the Right to Equality", in *Oxford Journal of Law and Religion*, 2020, vol. 9, no. 2, pp. 305–328; Cismas and Cammarano, 2016, see *supra* note 60.

[79] Note that the ECtHR has dismissed the case *Gareth Lee v. the United Kingdom*, Application no. 18860/19 on grounds of non-exhaustion of domestic remedies and has not pronounced itself on the merits of the case.

[80] Specifically, collective forms of manifestation of religion, including of religious legal entities, are derivative from the individual's right to manifest religion. Case law, such as *Hobby Lobby* severs these ties with profound conceptual and empirical implications. See Cismas and Cammarano, 2016, pp. 22–26, *supra* note 60.

between individuals and corporations,[81] coupled with restricted avenues of accountability for the latter.[82]

Finally, let us turn to individual religious leaders. The International Criminal Tribunal for Rwanda ('ICTR') convicted a number of religious leaders for their involvement in the Rwandan genocide.[83] The judgments signal that no one is above the law, not even men of God – we could infer, therefore, that religious leaders whose actorhood takes the shape of individuals enjoy rights and obligations under international law in a similar fashion to other human beings.[84] We must, nonetheless, recognize that a special regime, albeit not a self-contained one,[85] exists for situations where individualized actorhood intersects with their professional function. The first instantiation refers to clerical privilege, which is recognized in the rules of procedures of various international criminal courts. It is noteworthy that the "confidentiality relationship" between a cleric and a penitent receives protection in the same manner as that between a doctor and a patient or legal counsel and their client.[86] This functional professional privilege

81 *Ibid.*, pp. 34–42.

82 See Juan Calderon-Meza, "Seeking Accountability of Corporate Actors", in Nina Jørgensen (ed.), *The International Criminal Responsibility of War's Funders and Profiteers*, Cambridge University Press, 2020, pp. 362–395; Ioana Cismas and Sarah Macrory, "The Business and Human Rights Regime under International Law: Remedy without Law?", in James Summers and Alex Gough (eds.), *Non-State Actors and International Obligations*, Brill Nijhoff, Leiden, 2018, pp. 222–259.

83 ICTR, *Prosecutor v. Elizaphan Ntakirutimana and Gérard Ntakirutimana*, Trial Chamber I, Judgment and Sentence, 21 February 2003, ICTR-96-10 and ICTR-96-17-T (https://www.legal-tools.org/doc/30307b/); ICTR, *Prosecutor v. Elizaphan Ntakirutimana and Gérard Ntakirutimana*, Appeals Chamber, Judgment, 13 December 2004, ICTR-96-10-A and ICTR-96-17-A (https://www.legal-tools.org/doc/af07be/); ICTR, *Prosecutor v. Athanase Seromba*, Trial Chamber III, Judgment, 13 December 2006, ICTR-2001-66-I (https://www.legal-tools.org/doc/e0084d/); ICTR, *Prosecutor v. Athanase Seromba*, Appeals Chamber, Judgment, 12 March 2008, ICTR-2001-66-A (https://www.legal-tools.org/doc/b4df9d/).

84 See generally Andrew Clapham, "The Role of the Individual in International Law", in *European Journal of International Law*, 2010, vol. 21, no. 1, pp. 25–30; Anne Peters, *Beyond Human Rights: The Legal Status of the Individual in International Law*, Cambridge University Press, 2016, and for a critique of Peters' book, see, Tara J. Melish, "Beyond Human Rights: The Legal Status of the Individual in International Law. By Anne Peters. Cambridge, UK: Cambridge University Press, 2016. pp. xxxv, 602. Index", in *American Journal of International Law*, 2019, vol. 113, no. 3, pp. 654–664.

85 For the difference between the two concepts, see generally Fragmentation of International Law: Difficulties Arising from the Diversification and Expansion of International Law, Report of the Study Group of the International Law Commission, finalized by Martti Koskenniemi, UN Doc. A/CN.4/L.682, 13 April 2006, para. 216 (https://www.legal-tools.org/doc/dda184/).

86 International Criminal Court, Rules of Procedure and Evidence, 3–10 September 2002, ICC-ASP/1/3, Rule 73 (https://www.legal-tools.org/doc/8bcf6f/). See also Cismas, 2014, pp. 43–44, *supra* note 31.

may be limited when there is a reasonable expectation of disclosure.[87] The second case refers to religious personnel in armed conflict and requires a detailed examination.

13.4.2. Religious Personnel – A Test Case

Under treaty and customary IHL, applicable in both international and non-international armed conflict,[88] military and civilian religious personnel "exclusively assigned to religious duties must be respected and protected in all circumstances"; yet "[t]hey lose their protection if they commit, outside their humanitarian function, acts harmful to the enemy".[89] To be considered religious personnel, an individual would have to cumulatively fulfil two conditions: they must be assigned to their religious duties by a party to a conflict under whose control they are placed (attachment), and the assignment must be exclusive, limited to them in fulfilling their ministry work or spiritual function (exclusivity).[90]

The dual obligation to respect and protect religious personnel requires that parties to an armed conflict refrain from attacking them and take positive measure to help them in fulfilling their duties.[91] The religious personnel status entitles such individuals to wear the distinctive emblems of the Geneva Conventions.[92]

---

[87] See ICTR, *Prosecutor v. Ferdinand Nahimana, Jean-Bosco Barayagwiza and Hassan Ngeze*, Minutes of Proceedings, 30 November 2001, ICTR-99-52. See also Robert John Araujo, "International Tribunals and Rules of Evidence: The Case for Respecting and Preserving the Priest-Penitent Privilege under International Law", in *American University International Law Review*, 1999, vol. 15, no. 3, pp. 639–666.

[88] In what concerns the applicability of the obligation to respect and protect religious personnel in non-international armed conflict, the ICRC Study on Customary IHL notes, as treaty sources, Article 9 of the Additional Protocol II and Article 8(2)(e)(ii) of the Statute of the International Criminal Court, as well as specific references in military manuals (Canada, the Netherlands and the United Kingdom) in national legislation, some other state practice, and the absence of contrary practice. Jean-Marie Henckaerts and Louise Doswald-Beck (eds.), *Customary International Humanitarian Law, Volume I: Rules*, International Committee for the Red Cross, Cambridge University Press, 2005, Chapter 7, Rule 27 (Religious Personnel) and corresponding practice, and Rule 28 (Medical Units) and corresponding ('ICRC Study on Customary IHL').

[89] *Ibid.*, Rule 27 (Religious Personnel).

[90] *Ibid.* In respect to medical personnel (the special protection regime which is applied by analogy to religious leaders), Kolb and Nakashima note: "This definition is considered applicable in both IAC and NIAC, subject to the differences resulting from the presence of non-State armed groups". Robert Kolb and Nakashima Fumiko, "The Notion of "acts harmful to the enemy" under International Humanitarian Law", in *International Review of the Red Cross*, 2019, vol. 101, no. 912, p. 1174.

[91] See ICRC Study on Customary IHL, Rules 27 (Religious Personnel) and 30 (Persons and Objects Displaying the Distinctive Emblem), *supra* note 88.

[92] *Ibid.*

Can this protective status conferred upon religious personnel be considered an example of special 'rights'[93] of religious leaders? It is worth recalling that religious personnel are not unique, in that medical personnel, for example, also enjoy a special protective status under IHL. Indeed, the rights regime of medical personnel, and the conditions in which they may lose special protection, are applied *mutatis mutandis* to religious personnel. As such, it would be incorrect to conclude that the special legitimacy which religious actors enjoy translates into a unique IHL legality regime. Instead, they enjoy a special protective status because of the professional function that they fulfil in times of war, comparative in nature and scope to other actors with similar functions.[94] Let us thus examine the requirement of 'exclusivity' and the consequences of loss of protection, followed by the requirement of 'attachment'.

13.4.2.1. (Non-)Exclusivity and Loss of Protection

Exclusivity in reference to religious personnel refers to these actors' spiritual function and the involvement in the work of their ministry on the battlefield. In addition to providing spiritual guidance to combatants or fighters, leading in prayer, administering funerals and organizing religious fasts and feasts, religious personnel may carry out medical tasks, provide social services for combatants or fighters and their families and organize recreation – these activities would not be considered to taint the exclusivity criterion, yet pursuing another occupation on a full-time basis may be.[95] In some armed forces and organized armed groups, religious personnel are tasked with instructing combatants and fighters on military ethics, IHL or the norms on conduct in war of a particular religion.[96] Due to their direct institutionalized channels of communication to the higher ranks and ordinary combatants, religious personnel hold a great potential to influence the behaviour of armed actors through instruction and advice.[97] Notably, in a 2019

---

[93] Whether IHL gives rise to rights for individuals is a matter of doctrinal debate, see Lawrence Hill-Cawthorne, "Rights under International Humanitarian Law", in *European Journal of International* Law, 2017, vol. 28, no. 4, pp. 1187–1215; and Anne Peters, "Direct Rights of Individuals in the International Law of Armed Conflict", Max Planck Institute for Comparative Public Law and International Law Research Paper No. 23, 19 December 2019.

[94] ICRC Study on Customary IHL, Rule 25 (Medical Personnel), see *supra* note 88.

[95] Stefan Lunze, "Serving God and Caesar: Religious Personnel and Their Protection in Armed Conflict", in *International Review of the Red Cross*, 2004, vol. 86, no. 853, p. 75. See also, for activities performed by chaplains, Andrew Bartles-Smith, "Religion and International Humanitarian Law", in *International Review of the Red Cross*, 2022, nos. 920–921, p. 30; and Ron E. Hassner, *Religion on the Battlefield*, Cornell University Press, Ithaca, 2016.

[96] See Bartles-Smith, 2022, p. 30, *supra* note 95.

[97] Channels and means of communication have been identified by the Generating Respect Project as one of the relevant variables, based on which we can identify the influence of religious leaders on parties to armed conflict.

address, Pope Francis encouraged Catholic religious personnel to contribute to the socialization of combatants in the norms and spirit of IHL:

> Dear Ordinaries and military chaplains: as you carry out your mission to form the consciences of the members of the armed forces, I encourage you to spare no effort to enable the norms of international humanitarian law to be accepted in the hearts of those entrusted to your pastoral care.[98]

Whilst noting the important role that religious personnel could play in enhancing IHL compliance, Bartles-Smith observes that some have "accused military religious personnel of acting more like indoctrination agents than true clergy".[99] Which brings us to the question of the scope of non-exclusivity. Would indoctrination, religiously-grounded war propaganda or recruitment interfere with the exclusivity criterion, and if so, with what consequences?

In addressing this question, let us first establish the consequences of a loss of special protection for religious personnel – the IHL regime for medical personnel is applied *mutatis mutandis* to chaplains.[100] As such, religious personnel would lose their special protection if they commit "outside their humanitarian function, acts harmful to the enemy" ('AHTTE') or "hostile acts, outside their humanitarian function", terminology present in the First Geneva Convention, Additional Protocol I and respectively II, and taken to carry the same meaning.[101]

According to Kolb and Nakashima's analysis, *civilian* religious personnel involved in AHTTE would lose their special protection after they have been provided with a warning to cease the harmful conduct, a reasonable period to comply, and if the warning was not heeded.[102] As a consequence, they would fall back onto the general protection provided by their status as civilians. As such, the loss of special protection does not automatically make them subject to a direct attack – they would become targetable only if, and for such time, they are

---

98 Holy See Press Office, Summary of Bulleting, "Audience with the Participants in the Fifth International Course of Formation of Catholic Military Chaplains on International Humanitarian Law, 31 October 2019" (available on its web site). See also, Bartles-Smith, 2022, p. 30, *supra* note 95.

99 Bartles-Smith, 2022, p. 30, and the cited source, Hassner, 2016, see *supra* note 95.

100 See ICRC Study on Customary IHL, Rule 27 (Religious Personnel), see *supra* note 88. Note that the loss of protection of medical personnel draws on an analogy with the loss of protection of medical units and transports.

101 *Ibid.*, Rule 25 (Medical Personnel).

102 It remains debatable whether the warning requirement applies also in non-international armed conflict as a matter of customary international law. Kolb and Nakashima, 2019, p. 1183, see *supra* note 90.

engaged in direct participation in hostilities ('DPH').[103] Sassòli notes that "the expression 'acts harmful to the enemy' was elaborated for medical units and establishments, while 'direct participation in hostilities' refers to persons".[104] Premised on this difference, he posits that loss of special protection should occur only if civilian religious personnel are involved in DPH. Whichever view one takes – that AHTTE must amount to DPH to result in loss of social protection or that AHTTE is a wider concept not requiring DPH – for the purposes of targeting *civilian* religious personnel, there is, ultimately, no difference, because the DPH test would have to be applied anyway to establish the lawfulness of a direct attack.

Sassòli's premise would make a significant difference for *military* religious personnel. Kolb and Nakashima contend that the loss of special protection for military medical personnel, and thus analogously for military religious chaplains, results from their involvement in AHTTE and, after the requirements for the warning-prong have been met, with the consequence being that they will become liable to direct attack.[105] In other words, according to these authors' analysis, the loss of special protection means that military religious personnel revert to the status of fighter (combatants) and can be targeted at all times.[106] On Sassòli's submission, however, loss of special protection for military religious personnel would "be limited to acts that amount to direct participation in hostilities, because this notion would be a more relevant criteria for persons than the notion of acts harmful to the enemy, which had been developed for objects".[107]

This view appears to be supported by the Commentary to the First Geneva Convention, which notes that "[t]he consequences of medical or religious personnel committing an 'act harmful to the enemy outside their humanitarian

---

[103] See *ibid.*, p. 1195. The DPH test comprises three elements that must be cumulatively met: the threshold of harm, direct causation and belligerent nexus; see Niels Melzer, *ICRC Interpretative Guidance on the Notion of Direct Participation in Hostilities under International Humanitarian Law*, ICRC, Geneva, 2009, pp. 46–64.

[104] Marco Sassòli, "When do Medical and Religious Personnel Lose What Protection?", in *Vulnerabilities in Armed Conflicts: Selected Issues: Proceedings of the Bruges Colloquium*, 17–18 October 2013, p. 54.

[105] Kolb and Nakashima, 2019, p. 1195, see *supra* note 90.

[106] *Ibid.*

[107] The cited text is from Laurent Gisel, "The Protection of Medical Personnel under the Additional Protocols: The Notion of 'Acts Harmful to the Enemy' and Debates on Incidental Harm to Military Medical Personnel", in Fausto Pocar (ed.), *The Additional Protocols 40 Years Later: New Conflicts, New Actors, New Perspectives*, International Institute of Humanitarian Law, 40th Round Table on Current Issues of International Humanitarian Law, San Remo, 7–9 September 2017, p. 167, who summarizes Sassòli, 2013, p. 54, see *supra* note 104.

duties' need to be measured in a nuanced way".[108] Because the bindingness of the warning requirement in non-state armed conflict is unclear[109] and, as we shall see below, the application of the attachment requirement in respect to non-state parties is often muddled – thus potentially increasing the number of individuals that could be classed as military religious personnel. It seems that the more cautious approach is that of applying the DPH test to military religious personnel for the purposes of lawful targeting. This would be in line with "humanitarian considerations".[110]

Whilst being involved in AHTTE, and certainly in DPH, would result in non-exclusivity of religious personnel, state practice would not seem to support a literal interpretation of the term 'exclusive'.[111] Benson surveyed the practice of the United States and Israel, finding that strategic advice to military commanders, a certain level of indoctrination and even human intelligence collection[112] are part of the activities undertaken by some military religious personnel.[113] Hassner makes similar observations relying on historic and more recent cases.[114] From a legal doctrinal point of view, one can either conclude that some of these instances represent departures from the treaty and customary law provision on the exclusivity of chaplains or that the term is interpreted more broadly in state practice. A social constructivist lens would point either to a lack of a shared understating of what exclusivity means or that an understanding exists, or is emerging, which has faded the exclusivity norm away from its literal meaning.

108 Bruno Demeyere, "Article 24: Protection of Permanent Personnel", in *Commentary of 2016 on Convention (I) for the Amelioration of the Condition of the Wounded and Sick in Armed Forces in the Field of 12 August 1949*, ICRC, Geneva, 2016, para. 2008.

109 See *supra* note 102 and reference therein.

110 The 2016 ICRC Commentary to the First Geneva Convention, whilst differentiating between AHTTE and DPH, with the former being considered wider and the latter narrower, appears to allow for differing interpretations, "in view of the humanitarian values at stake, in case of doubt as to whether a particular type of behaviour qualifies as an act harmful to the enemy, it ought not to be considered as such". Demeyere, 2016, paras. 1998, 2002, see *supra* note 108.

111 Contrast with Holterhus, who argues precisely for such a literal reading of exclusivity. Till Patrick Holterhus, "Targeting the Islamic State's Religious Personnel Under International Humanitarian Law", in *Yearbook of International Humanitarian Law*, T.M.C. Asser Press, The Hague, 2019, pp. 216–218.

112 This would seem to amount to AHTTE and possibly DPH in respect to medical personnel, hence, by analogy also to religious personnel. See Kolb and Nakashima, 2019, p. 1195, *supra* note 90.

113 K. Benson, "The Chaplaincy Exception in International Humanitarian Law: American-Born Cleric Anwar Awlaki and the Global War on Terror", in *Buffalo Human Rights Law Review*, 2014, vol. 1, no. 20, pp. 1–36.

114 Hassner, 2016, see *supra* note 95.

How then can we answer the leading question of this section, whether indoctrination, religiously-grounded war propaganda or recruitment interfere with the exclusivity criterion, and if so, with what consequences? Whilst these activities may taint the exclusivity requirement (although state practice appears rather tolerant on this aspect), they would not amount to DPH,[115] and thus should not result in the lawfulness of targeting religious personnel, whether civilian or military.

13.4.2.2. Attachment

Attachment is the other condition that must be met by religious leaders to benefit from special protection under IHL.[116] Among this mixed category of 'attached' personnel, a crucial distinction to be made is that between military and civilian religious personnel because a loss of protection, as we have seen above, could result in different consequences for the purposes of targeting. Assignment to armed forces or wings of a party to a conflict will also often have clear implications for the ability of religious personnel to influence commanders, as well as rank and file members. This is so, because of the direct access and institutionalized channels of communications it provides. In the case of the Colombian Armed Forces, this observation has been confirmed by a former military chaplain.[117] Moreover, differentiating religious *personnel* and religious leaders *tout court*, is particularly pertinent when parties to an armed conflict have armed or military forces or wings, as well as humanitarian and political wings.

Let us engage critically with an example from literature to understand the various implications. Holterhus argues, in respect to the Islamic State ('IS'), that a loss of protection results in "IS-chaplains" – which he equates with military religious personnel due to their "membership in the IS organized armed group" – becoming lawful targets of direct military attacks.[118] In other words, due to

---

[115] See Melzer, 2009, p. 24, *supra* note 103. However, on propaganda, see Alexandre Balguy-Gallois, "The Protection of Journalists and News Media Personnel in Armed Conflict", in *International Review of the Red Cross*, 2004, vol. 86, no. 853, p. 12.

[116] Protocol Additional to the Geneva Conventions of 12 August 1949, and relating to the Protection of Victims of International Armed Conflicts, 8 June 1977, Article 8(d) ('Additional Protocol I') (https://www.legal-tools.org/doc/d9328a/). Article 15 of Additional Protocol I extends the scope of Article 24 of the First Geneva Convention and Article 36 of the Second Geneva Convention to provide protective status for civilian religious personnel, in addition to military religious personnel. The ICRC Study on Customary International Humanitarian Law notes that the "extension is widely supported in State practice [...] [and also] [...] by States not, or not at the time, party to Additional Protocol I". See ICRC Study on Customary IHL, Rule 27 (Religious Personnel), see *supra* note 88.

[117] Piergiuseppe Parisi and Yolvi Lena Padilla Sepulveda, "Interview with former military chaplain", Colombia, February 2022.

[118] Holterhus, 2019, pp. 213–216, 218, see *supra* note 111.

their non-exclusivity through involvement in war propaganda and recruitment (thus, arguably failing one criteria), but by continued attachment (meeting the other), they 'fall back' on the status of fighters.

> As members of the organized armed group IS, IS's religious personnel can, therefore, as every other ordinary member, legally be subjected to direct military attack at any time (within the limits of the IHL's principles of necessity, proportionality, humane treatment, etc.).[119]

As argued above, I consider the better approach, for the purposes of establishing loss of protection, to be engagement in DPH, for both civilian and military personnel. Be that as it may, Holterhus' analysis raises two other problematic aspects. First, the term "organized armed group" – the entity to which "IS-chaplains" are purportedly attached – appears to be understood by Holterhus as IS, the non-state party to a conflict, and not solely as IS' armed wing.[120] This is in stark contrast with interpretative practice. The International Committee of the Red Cross ('ICRC') Interpretative Guidance on the notion of DPH differentiates between military or armed wings, political wings and humanitarian bodies, and concludes that in respect to targeting, the term "organized armed group" needs to be understood as referring to the armed wing of a non-state party to a conflict.[121] Similarly, Article 8, paragraph (d) of Additional Protocol I stipulates that for a chaplain to be considered 'attached', they need to be attached to "the *armed forces* of a Party to the conflict"[122] – importantly, this provision is arguably also applicable in non-international armed conflict, thus in reference to armed wings of non-state parties as well.[123]

---

119 *Ibid.*, p. 218.

120 For Holterhus' analysis on this aspect, see Holterhus, 2019, pp. 213–216, *supra* note 111.

121 Melzer, 2009, p. 32, see *supra* note 103:

> it is crucial for the protection of the civilian population to distinguish a non-state party to a conflict (e.g., an insurgency, a rebellion, or a secessionist movement) from its armed forces (i.e., an organized armed group). As with state parties to armed conflicts, non-state parties comprise both fighting forces and supportive segments of the civilian population, such as political and humanitarian wings. The term organized armed group, however, refers exclusively to the armed or military wing of a non-state party: its armed forces in a functional sense. This distinction has important consequences for the determination of membership in an organized armed group as opposed to other forms of affiliation with, or support for, a non-state party to the conflict.

See also, for a supportive yet novel perspective that allows to address a potential accountability gap, Katharine Fortin, "Civilian Wings of Armed Groups: included within the concept of 'Non State Party' under IHL?", in *Armed Groups and International Law*, 13 October 2020 (available on its web site).

122 See Additional Protocol I, Article 8(d), *supra* note 116 (emphasis added).

123 See ICRC Study on Customary IHL, *supra* note 116.

The equivalency, operated by Holterhus, between the non-state armed group in its totality and its armed wing, potentially renders a very large number of religious leaders affiliated to IS' political wings and media apparatus or religious actors otherwise affiliated to one of IS' organizations – yet not attached, in the sense required by IHL, to their armed wing – classifiable as military religious personnel.[124] Concretely, let us look at members of the IS Research and *Fatwá* Department and staff of the *Dabiq* magazine. The first is IS' politico-religious department and the second is its English-language magazine – both are involved in religiously grounded war propaganda and likely in recruitment efforts.[125] They have published the most horrendous justifications of enslavement, sexual slavery and rape of girls and women, "as religiously meritorious: not just acceptable but a positive good. Rather than grudgingly grant its permissibility, or merely matter-of-factly assume its legality as most premodern texts do, IS proclaims enslavement a triumphalist reflection of its own legitimacy".[126]

Undoubtably, these are prosecutable international crimes.[127] Indeed, the Independent International Commission of Inquiry on the Syrian Arab Republic has used articles published in *Dabiq* among the evidence based on which it inferred 'intent to destroy', as an element of the crime of genocide.[128] Be that as it may, these remain actors that are part of IS' political wings and as such cannot be considered attached to its military wing.

---

[124] When a member of an "organized armed group" becomes targetable remains a contested matter. The ICRC Interpretative Guidance proposes a functional membership approach, that is, "membership in an organized armed group begins in the moment when a civilian starts *de facto* to assume a continuous combat function for the group and lasts until he or she ceases to assume such function". Melzer, 2009, p. 71 and Section ii.3, see *supra* note 103; see also, Gloria Gaggioli, "Targeting Individuals Belonging to an Armed Group", in *Vanderbilt Journal of Transnational Law*, 2018, vol. 51, no. 901, pp. 901–917. Contrast with Kenneth Watkin, "Opportunity Lost: Organized Armed Groups and the ICRC Direct Participation in Hostilities Interpretive Guidance", in *New York University Journal of International Law & Politics*, 2009, vol. 42, pp. 641–695.

[125] See, for example, Brendon Colas, "What Does Dabiq Do? ISIS Hermeneutics and Organizational Fractures Within Dabiq Magazine", in *Studies in Conflict and Terrorism*, 2017, vol. 40, no. 3, pp. 173–190; Emily Chertoff, "Prosecuting Gender-Based Persecution: The Islamic State at the ICC", in *Yale Law Journal*, 2017, vol. 26, no. 4, pp. 1050–1117.

[126] Kecia Ali, "Redeeming Slavery: The 'Islamic State' and the Quest for Islamic Morality", in *Mizan, Journal of Interdisciplinary Approaches to Muslim Societies and Civilizations*, 2016, vol. 1, no. 1, p. 6, pp. 1–22.

[127] See Chertoff, 2017, *supra* note 125.

[128] "ISIS explicitly holds its abuse of the Yazidis to be mandated by its religious interpretation and its public statements have provided an invaluable resource directly demonstrative of its intent". Independent International Commission of Inquiry on the Syrian Arab Republic, "'They came to destroy': ISIS Crimes Against the Yazidis", UN Doc. A/HRC/32/CRP.2, 15 June 2016, paras. 150–165 and citation at para. 151 (https://www.legal-tools.org/doc/24962f/).

A second problematic aspect ensuing from Holterhus' article is the presumption of attachment based on a religious leader's membership in IS. Doctrine presents attachment as an intentional act that must be undertaken by an authority, not the religious leader themselves. A person can be a member of the armed wing or forces whilst also (having qualifications as) a cleric; unless an authority assigns them to the armed entity or expressly accepts them as (military) religious personnel, the person will not enjoy special protective status, but be subject to the legal regime applicable to fighters.[129] Lunze notes that:

> The decision on the attachment of religious personnel rests with the competent military authorities and creates an official relationship between chaplain and armed forces. [...] A unilateral declaration of the religious ministers themselves or their religious community is insufficient to constitute chaplain status. Instead, they must be received into the group they are attached to, designated for or at least accepted by.[130]

The Commentary of 1987 on the Additional Protocols explains why the intentionality of attachment is a key element in the architecture of the religious personnel institution:

> the competent authorities of the Parties to the conflict therefore retain responsibility for designating, or at least accepting, religious personnel who will enjoy protection. It should be reme mbered that this restriction is justified by the fact that the authorities of the Parties to the conflict are responsible for the application of the Protocol, and in particular for ensuring that no abuses will be committed by protected persons. To automatically and generally attribute the right to protection to all medical or religious personnel would make such a task extremely difficult, if not impossible.

Consequently, the better view must be that military religious personnel would need to be *intentionally* attached to a non-state party's *armed wing* or a state party's *armed forces* to be eligible for special protection, whereas the attachment of the civilian religious personnel would be to their humanitarian or medical agencies.[131] Other religious leaders that are not assigned specifically as military or civilian religious personnel cannot claim special protection, but would certainly enjoy general protection as civilians. This interpretation is supported by the Commentary of 1987, when it notes that:

---

[129] Lunze, 2004, p. 75, see *supra* note 95. See also, Demeyere, 2016, paras. 1972–1976, *supra* note 108.

[130] Lunze, 2004, p. 75, see *supra* note 95.

[131] Note also, the provisions of Protocol Additional to the Geneva Conventions of 12 August 1949, and relating to the Protection of Victims of Non-International Armed Conflicts, 8 June 1977, Article 9(2) ('Additional Protocol II') (https://www.legal-tools.org/doc/fd14c4/).

> The majority of civilian religious personnel *in the usual meaning of the term*, i.e., those carrying out their function amongst the civilian population, are therefore not covered by this provision. However, special protection cannot be justified for such personnel, who, it should be remembered, remain covered by the general protection accorded the population and all civilian persons.[132]

The observation echoes empirical findings from the Generating Respect Project and other research. For example, in the Philippines, Bangsamoro Darul-Ifta', the Islámic council with authority over religious matters in the central Mindanao island group, was instrumental in facilitating the engagement between the UN and the Moro Islamic Liberation Front ('MILF') concerning the Action Plan on the Recruitment and Use of Children in Armed Conflict.[133] The plan led to the disengagement of almost 2,000 children from the ranks of the MILF's Bangsamoro Islamic Armed Forces ('BIAF').[134] A UNICEF report notes:

> To ensure the Action Plan received full acceptance by its forces from a religious point of view, the MILF first consulted its Darul Ifta (Religious Council), which deliberated and confirmed that the Action Plan did not contravene Islamic teachings and principles, and endorsed the agreement for signing by the MILF leadership. This mitigating step by the MILF leadership minimised possible resistance to the legitimacy of the Action Plan among the commanders and elements, greatly facilitating its implementation in later years.[135]

The actions of the Darul-Ifta' provide an extraordinary example of the influence of religious leaders on parties to armed conflict and their potential – or in this case, the actuality – to generate greater respect for IHL and IHRL. Be that as it may, unlike the BIAF's Department of Islamic Call and Guidance, "which oversees senior religious leaders from its rank who are given lead roles as *murshideen* and *murshidaat* to provide Islámic guidance to the BIAF and BIWAB [Bangsamoro Islamic Women Auxiliary Brigade] in all base

[132] Claude Pilloud, Yves *Sandoz, Christophe Swinarski* and *Bruno Zimmermann, Commentary on the Additional Protocols of 8 June 1977 to the Geneva Conventions of 12 August 1949*, ICRC, M. Nijhoff Publishers, Geneva, 1987, p. 195 (emphasis added).

[133] See, generally, Jeyashree Nadarajah, "Children in Armed Conflict: Philippines", UN International Children's Emergency Fund ('UNICEF'), 2019.

[134] *Ibid.*, p. ii.

[135] *Ibid.*, p. 20. See also, for a discussion of the legal argumentation of the MILF, Heyran Jo, "Non-State Armed Actors and International Legal Argumentation: Patterns, Processes, and Putative Effects", in Ian Johnstone and Steven Ratner (eds.), *Talking International Law: Legal Argumentation Outside the Courtroom*, Oxford University Press, 2021.

commands",[136] the Darul-Ifta' cannot be classified as military (or civilian) religious personnel, either on ICRC's functional approach or by employing formal criteria of membership in the armed wing.[137] Whilst the difference may appear one of scholarly pedantry, it is not – it may have very real implications for the targeting regime that these leaders will be subjected to in case of loss of protection; in particular, if such loss is considered to occur for AHTTE that do not amount to DPH.[138] It may signify the difference between being prosecutable or being killable. With this reflection in mind, let us turn to avenues for ensuring accountability for abuse.

13.5. (Rethinking) Accountability

Having established that religious leadership spans the state–non-state spectrum and their obligations under international law largely map onto the obligations of their respective non-religious peers, what then can be said about avenues of accountability? International law is a notoriously weak system when it comes to accountability – unsurprisingly given its anarchic and consensualist nature. Accountability is the system's "Achilles' heel" as Krieger noted in relation to IHL,[139] an observation that equally applies to other branches of international law, despite the mushrooming of international courts and quasi-judicial mechanisms that can be observed in recent decades. Be that as it may, is accountability more difficult to achieve when one deals with religious states and religious non-states actors, including individuals?

Beyond the anecdotal evidence provided by the initial accommodating treatment which the Holy See had received during its periodic review by UN treaty bodies, it is difficult to assert that the international system has a reticence to specifically hold religious actors to account. Among the states that various judicial and quasi-judicial bodies have sought to hold accountable, we can find religious states; international criminal courts have convicted individual clerics,

---

136 *Ibid.*, p. 4. For a wider discussion of the role of these religious leaders in legitimizing processes of vernacularization of IHL, see Dominic Earnshaw and Datuan Magon, "Engaging *Ulama* in the Promotion of International Humanitarian Law: A Case Study from Mindanao", in *Journal of Human Rights Practice*, 2023 (forthcoming), and Chris Rush, Annyssa Bellal, Pascal Bongard and Ezequiel Heffes, "From Words to Deeds: A Study of Armed Non-State Actors' Practice and Interpretation of International Humanitarian and Human Rights Norms", Moro Islamic Liberation Front/Bangsamoro Islamic Armed Forces, August 2022.

137 See, for a discussion of the two approaches, Melzer, 2009, *supra* note 103, in contrast to Holterhus, 2019, see *supra* note 111.

138 This chapter has emphatically argued against this interpretation.

139 Heike Krieger, "Introduction", in Heike Krieger (ed), *Inducing Compliance with International Humanitarian Law: Lessons from the African Great Lakes Region*, Cambridge University Press, 2015, p. 1.

and indeed even religious personnel.[140] When it comes to non-state legal entities, religious or otherwise, direct accountability under international law is largely absent, due to lack of personal jurisdiction. Against this background of generalized difficulty to ensure state and non-state actors' accountability, non-religious and religious, two interrelated trends are noticeable, in particular in the fields of IHRL and IHL. First, there is a turn towards soft law, arguably as a "complement" or "alternative" to hard law.[141] Second, we note a reconceptualization of accountability into a more holistic notion, which is achieved by widening its scope to include non-judicial and extra-legal mechanisms and processes.

Illustrative of both trends is the process which began with the adoption of the Rabat Plan of Action on the Prohibition of Advocacy of National, Racial or Religious Hatred that constitutes Incitement to Discrimination, Hostility or Violence ('Rabat Plan').[142] This instrument has succeeded in resetting the terms of discussion away from the 'defamation of religions' resolutions, championed by the OIC at the turn of the century, towards a much needed debate on hate speech that incites violence, "an area of human rights law which has long remained dormant and the implementation of which is lacking in many respects".[143] The Rabat Plan was followed by the Beirut Declaration on Faith for Rights, the 18 commitments on Faith for Rights and the subsequent operationalization through the #Faith4Rights toolkit, described as a "practical peer-to-peer learning and capacity-building programme".[144] Essentially, the Faith for Rights framework promotes the engagement between and among human rights scholars and practitioners and religious leaders. Its aim is to achieve a form of preventative accountability by creating shared understandings on human rights and religions.

[140] Emmanuel Rukundo, convicted by the ICTR was a chaplain in the Rwandan Armed Forces. See ICTR, *Prosecutor v. Emmanuel Rukundo*, Trial Judgment, 27 February 2009, ICTR-2001-70-T (https://www.legal-tools.org/doc/1c7819/).

[141] For a discussion of these terms, see the excellent article of Gregory C. Shaffer and Mark A. Pollack, "Hard vs. Soft Law: Alternatives, Complements, and Antagonists in International Governance", in *Minnesota Law Review*, 2009, vol. 94, pp. 706–799.

[142] United Nations Human Rights Council, Rabat Plan of Action on the Prohibition of Advocacy of National, Racial or Religious Hatred that Constitutes Incitement to Discrimination, Hostility or Violence, Conclusions and Recommendations Emanating from the Four Regional Expert Workshops Organized by OHCHR in 2011, and Adopted by Experts at the Meeting in Rabat, Morocco, on 5 October 2012, Appendix to the Report of the United Nations High Commissioner for Human Rights on the Expert Workshops on the Prohibition of Incitement to National, Racial or Religious Hatred, UN Doc. A/HRC/22/17/Add.4, 11 January 2013 (https://www.legal-tools.org/doc/oymwge/).

[143] Cismas, 2014, pp. 62–69 and in particular p. 68, see *supra* note 31.

[144] See "OHCHR and the 'Faith for Rights' Framework" (available on the OHCHR's web site); Ibrahim Salama and Michael Wiener, "Faith for Rights in Armed Conflict: Lessons from Practice", in *Journal of Human Rights Practice*, 2023 (forthcoming).

The approach is not dissimilar to that pioneered by An-Na'im, who encouraged already in the early 1990s, the exploration of "possibilities of cultural reinterpretation and reconstruction through *internal cultural discourse and cross-cultural dialogue*".[145]

In the past decades, humanitarian organizations have also increasingly sought to engage with religious leaders. This humanitarian engagement appears to represent an IHL compliance-generation strategy, complementary to direct engagement with the parties to an armed conflict.[146] Engagement as form of accountability, in this case, is understood less as an avenue to address the religious leaders' own liability for their actions and discourse in war, and more as a means to tap into their potential to influence state and non-state parties to conflicts towards greater humanitarian norms compliance. Let us look at some of the interactions that occur between religious leaders and IHL and IHRL, beyond use and abuse.

13.6. Interactions Between Religious Leaders and International Law – Beyond Respect and Abuse

In Section 13.4., this study has identified the rights and obligations of religious leaders under international law, in particular IHRL and IHL, and highlighted some instances of abuse. Beyond these instances, and with particular attention to the context of armed conflict, there is a multitude of activities and discourses put forward by religious leaders that have a bearing on humanitarian norms[147] and which have influenced the behaviour of parties to the conflict or the lived experiences of war-affected communities. In this sense, not only is international law relevant to religious actors, but the latter are relevant to international law. Drawing on literature and our own empirical research, the Generating Respect Project has identified the following typology of interaction of religious leaders with IHL and IHRL:

1. Direct implementation or facilitation;

[145] Abdullahi Ahmed An-Na'im, "Introduction", in Abdullahi Ahmed An-Na'im (ed.), *Human Rights in Cross-Cultural Perspectives: A Quest for Consensus*, University of Pennsylvania Press, 1992, p. 3 (emphasis in the original).

[146] Such initiatives are documented in Cismas and Heffes, 2021, see *supra* note 33. For a guidance document on humanitarian engagement with religious leaders, see Cismas *et al.*, 2023, pp. 22–30, see *supra* note 30. See also, the excellent blog of the ICRC, "Religion and Humanitarian Principles" (available on its web site).

[147] The Generating Respect Project has focused on three broad norms – the protection of civilians from attacks, the protection of detainees and the facilitation of humanitarian assistance – understood to be anchored in both IHL and IHRL. However, the fieldwork findings have relevance to other norms.

2. Processes of 'translation' of humanitarian norms, such as vernacularization;
3. Strategic avoidance;
4. Hybridization and selective application;
5. Rejection;
6. Silence.[148]

The first type of interaction may perhaps be surprising for some. Religious leaders are often direct implementers of IHL and IHRL in armed conflict, because of their strong links with local communities and their legitimacy among parties to conflict. In Myanmar, since the *coup d'état* of February 2021, religious leaders seemed to be the main, and at times the only, actors that manage, at great personal risk, to provide humanitarian assistance to internally displaced people, refugees and other civilians shielding from the violence unleashed by the military junta. One religious leader recounts:

> So people when they are fleeing, when they are running for their life they, they call us or they talk to their friends and their friends know us, and they got our numbers and they say please can you bring rice. So that's how we are working. We are working directly with the people who are really in the war zone [...] we are not working with other organizations.[149]

Interestingly, in some instances, an element of inter-faith co-operation can be observed:

> So, we went to the temples to talk with the Buddhist monks because Buddhist temples are big, big enough to receive all these [displaced] people [...] when we bring the rations, we give it to the monk because we trust them, they will not use it, you know, they will not do anything, so we, we give it to them to give out.[150]

In Colombia, Catholic religious leaders have often acted as mediators in hostage situations and their intervention often led to the release of both civilians and members of armed forces.[151] Similar interventions of Islámic religious leaders have been documented in Mali.[152]

A different context offers a most fascinating example of advocacy by religious leaders that contributed to greater gender equality within a non-state

---

[148] See Cismas *et al.*, 2023, pp. 30–38, *supra* note 30.

[149] Rush and Cismas, 2022, see *supra* note 47.

[150] *Ibid.*

[151] See Piergiuseppe Parisi and Adelaida Ibarra, "The Catholic Church and Conflict Actors: In Search of Legitimacy to Build", in *Journal of Human Rights Practice*, 2023 (forthcoming).

[152] See Piergiuseppe Parisi, "Confronting Rifles with Words: The High Islamic Council of Mali and Armed Actors", in *Journal of Human Rights Practice*, 2023 (forthcoming).

armed group. A member of the group approached influential religious leaders, explaining that women carry a significant burden in terms of domestic and auxiliary work, yet they "would like to contribute in the decision making room, not just supporting the men's wing".[153] The religious actors conveyed these views to the armed group's leadership, and subsequently the space was created for women to occupy decision-making positions in the group's political wing.[154]

The second type of interaction refers to translation processes of humanitarian norms by religious actors through vernacularization, localization or pluralization.[155] As stated above, religious leaders claim a special legitimacy drawing on tradition or charisma. Due to these sources of legitimization, a religious command that supports human rights and humanitarian norms may vernacularize or localize these norms in a manner, in which 'domestication' of international law through parliamentary acts on its own would not be able to achieve. This is much in keeping with the suggestions made in the seminal *The Roots of Restraint in War* study, that "humanitarian norms have received greater traction" by "linking the law to local norms and values", since this connection encourages individual members of the parties to a conflict to internalize the standards, which in turn promotes restraint in war in a more durable manner.[156] The role of the *'ulama'* in the development of rules of conduct in war for the MILF provides such an example of vernacularization.[157]

Strategic avoidance, a third type of interaction, is particularly motivating, because it demonstrates that religious actors are, at times, interested in promoting IHRL and IHL, and will find creative ways to do so in complex contexts where political and societal elites reject a rights-based discourse. Doffegnies and Wells identify religious leaders' initiatives in Myanmar who sought to address the violence against the Rohingya, yet consciously avoided using human rights language due to "popular rejection".[158] Similarly, for strategic reasons, some religious leaders with confirmed influence on non-state armed groups may prefer to address aspects of IHRL and IHL with these actors directly behind closed

153 Chris Rush and Ioana Cismas, "Interview with member of armed group", 2022. Information about the location of the group is suppressed to ensure anonymity.

154 *Ibid.*

155 For vernacularization, see, generally, Sally Merry, *Human Rights & Gender Violence: Translating International Law into Local Justice*, University of Chicago Press, 2006. Localization and pluralization are discussed and illustrated in Cismas *et al.*, 2023, pp. 32–35, see *supra* note 30.

156 Fiona Terry and Brian Quinn, *The Roots of Restraint in War*, 12 June 2020, p. 9.

157 See Earnshaw and Magon, 2023, *supra* note 136; see also the discussion in the same footnote.

158 See Amy Doffegnies and Tamas Wells, "The Vernacularisation of Human Rights Discourse in Myanmar: Rejection, Hybridisation and Strategic Avoidance", in *Journal of Contemporary Asia*, 2022, vol. 52, no. 2, p. 247.

doors. Thus, a lack of a public discourse of religious leaders on the topic should not necessarily be read as a complete absence of IHRL and IHL preoccupations. Interestingly, this type of framing which avoids mentioning human rights and resolves to pursue a quiet diplomacy around shared values is not unusual even outside conflict contexts.[159]

The fourth type of interaction, hybridization, describes a declarative adherence to IHRL or IHL by religious leaders, whilst imparting the norms with an own meaning, which, in turn, departs from the posited norm. Doffegnies and Wells refer to religious leaders in Myanmar who presented a vision of human rights that sometimes supported, rather than opposed, the exclusion of Muslim minorities.[160] An illustration of selective application of humanitarian norms comes from Mali, where some Christian religious leaders had been willing to engage with our researchers to discuss their discourse and activities with a bearing on IHL. Yet, they have refused to engage on human rights topics, perceiving the latter as a "problématique piège" as the discussion would, in their view, inevitably centre on the rights of sexual minorities.

During fieldwork conducted for the Generating Respect Project, we have encountered examples of Yemeni religious actors affiliated to the Houthis that have rejected humanitarian standards because of their perceived foreign origin. This firth type of interaction, rejection of IHL and IHRL, is a common theme for Islámist groups such as IS or Al-Qaeda and religious leaders affiliated with them.[161] A project of "critical comparativism", as is the one suggested by Badawi, that treats Islámic law on armed conflict and IHL "as alternative manifestations of power structures which, when contrasted against each other, help shed more light on the inherent bias in each legal system",[162] may provide useful insights into the rejection of humanitarian norms by some Islámist groups and the modalities that could be pursued to effectively engage with such actors.

Sixth, silence, a different concept to that of strategic avoidance, may hide religious leaders' lack of awareness of IHL and IHRL standards or an uneasiness

159 See Paul Gready, "The Implications of and Responses to Covid-19 in the City of York (UK)", in *Journal of Human Rights Practice*, 2020, vol. 12, no. 2, pp. 250–259.

160 See Doffegnies and Wells, 2022, p. 247, *supra* note 158.

161 See "From Words to Deeds: A Study of Armed Non-State Actors' Practice and Interpretation of International Humanitarian and Human Rights Norm, The Islamic State Group" and "From Words to Deeds: A Study of Armed Non-State Actors' Practice and Interpretation of International Humanitarian and Human Rights Norms Al-Qaeda", American University in Cairo, September 2022.

162 Nesrine Badawi, "Regulation of Armed Conflict: Critical Comparativism", in *Third World Quarterly*, 2016, vol. 37, no. 11, pp. 1990–2009.

with their own conduct in war.[163] This observation, in and of itself, represents a call for humanitarians and human rights actors to engage with religious leaders. Finally, reflexive research practice requires that we ask whether what we perceive as silence may simply be the result of our own narrow conceptualization of religious leadership. In other words, discourses and activities with a bearing on international law standards may well be put forward by religious leaders; however, because we do not regard the emitters as religious leaders, we fail to *see* their actions and understand their implications.

13.7. Conclusion

We return, thus, to Madame Cissé's observation from the opening vignette – that women are often excluded from discussions about law and religion, and that their role in generating norm-compliance is invisibilized. The lesson, we argued, that (international) lawyers should learn from this is the necessity to centre reflexivity in our scholarship and practice, in general and specifically in encounters with religions. Embarking on a reflexive process, this chapter acknowledged its anchoring in social constructivist theory and the embrace of a socio-legal approach, which mixes empirical and doctrinal legal methods to provide a more holistic understanding of the relevance of international law to religious leaders and *vice-versa*. The concept of relevance then comprises the applicability of legal standards and accountability and interactions of religious leaders with international law beyond use and abuse.

Shaped by our theoretical and methodological choices, religious leadership was defined broadly to refer to those actors that claim a special legitimacy grounded in charisma or tradition, have a formal or informal affiliation to religion, express leadership individually or collectively, and span the non-state or state spectrum of actorhood, whilst being institutionally external or internal to armed actors. This understanding of religious leadership has promoted our inquiry into whether these actors enjoy special rights and lesser obligations when compared to their non-religious peers. The analysis concluded that whilst some religious leaders, such as religious personnel, enjoy special rights, this is so because of the function that they fulfil within the system of international (humanitarian) law. In this sense, their special status does not disrupt the system's legality by engendering exceptions from international obligations due to their special legitimacy. Because avenues for seeking redress for violations of international law, whether by non-religious or religious actors, remain imperfect, we observed a move towards a broader approach to accountability. This approach

[163] This silence could be paralleled with the absence of some influential religious actors from transitional justice mechanisms, the absence of which can be linked back to the actors' own complicity in past violations. See Cismas, 2017, pp. 302–343, *supra* note 51.

centres the development of soft law and the engagement between human rights and humanitarian scholars and practitioners, and religious leaders.

Meaningful engagement, we submit, requires that religious leaders are understood to be right-holders and duty-bearers, as well as influencers of IHRL and IHL norms-compliance by third parties. In the context of armed conflict, the Generating Respect Project has documented religious leaders that directly implemented or facilitated, vernacularized, strategically avoided, hybridized, received with silence or rejected humanitarian norms. With this variety of interactions in mind, engagement would have to be sought not only with those religious actors that share the same human rights and humanitarian values or principles as legal scholars and practitioners, but also (and from the point of view of humanitarian organizations, bound as they usually are to engage with all parties to a conflict) particularly with those who do not. On this account then, we may have to (uncomfortably) acknowledge that engagement may have to take the shape of "critical comparativism" and not be premised on the supremacy of international law over religious law. The hope expressed here, a social constructivist one, is that continued engagement will construct relevance, in a thick, socio-legal sense, for international legal standards – that is, both crafting ownership for the standards among religious leaders and addressing the power imbalances within international law and its system.

Section E: Theological and Philosophical Frameworks

14

In the Name of Belief: Religious (In)tolerance, Hate Speech and Justice in Classical Greek and Roman Sources

Emiliano J. Buis*

14.1. Introduction

Although most of us would probably identify 'hate speech' when we see it, there is no simple definition of what it really is.[1] Paying attention to its multidimensional nature,[2] several definitions have attempted to explain its main features. The borders of the notion can be established over the basis of common elements. According to Cohen-Almagor, for example, hate speech should be considered "a bias-motivated, hostile or malicious speech aimed at a person or a group of people because of some of their actual or perceived innate characteristics".[3] In spite of its inherent negative content, however, this concept fails to acknowledge the emotional background which seems to be inherent in its scope.[4]

---

* **Emiliano J. Buis** is Professor of Public International Law, International Humanitarian Law, the Origins of International Law in Antiquity and Ancient Greek Language and Literature at the University of Buenos Aires and the Central National University in Azul, Argentina. He is also a CILRAP Research Fellow and a Researcher at the National Research Council for Science and Technology (CONICET). He is a former fellow at the Department of Classics, Brown University, the Max-Planck Institut für europäische Rechstgeschichte, the Harvard University Center for Hellenic Studies, the Alexander S. Onassis Public Benefit Foundation, the Center for Epigraphical and Palaeographical Studies (Ohio State University) and the Center for Hellenic Studies at Princeton University. He received his Ph.D. from the University of Buenos Aires, Argentina. For an audio-visual recording of his statement to CILRAP's conference in Florence in April 2022 on the topic of this anthology, please see https://www.cilrap.org/cilrap-film/220409-buis/.

1 On the problem of definition, see Ian Leigh, "Damned If They Do, Damned If They Don't: The European Court of Human Rights and the Protection of Religion From Attack", in *Res Publica*, 2011, vol. 17, no. 1, p. 63.

2 "Hate speech is a linguistic, social, cultural, technological and legal issue", according to Alexander Brown and Adriana Sinclair, *The Politics of Hate Speech Laws*, Routledge, London, New York, 2020, p. 1.

3 Raphael Cohen-Almagor, "Freedom of Expression v. Social Responsibility: Holocaust Denial in Canada", in *Journal of Mass Media Ethics*, 2013, vol. 28, no. 1, p. 43.

4 Because of this subjective stress, Ivan Hare and James Weinstein (eds.), *Extreme Speech and Democracy*, Oxford University Press, 2009, p. 4, have suggested to replace the expression with "extreme speech".

Considering its strong affective nature, we can say that hate speech is based on a negative feeling towards a collective 'other' who is seen through the eyes of superiority. Since the others are deemed to be 'inferior', hate speech makes use of a number of discriminatory epithets to insult and stigmatize others on the basis of their race, ethnicity, gender, beliefs, sexual orientation or other form of group membership.[5] In the context of this conference, when assessing the ways in which hate can be "articulated" in speech,[6] attention is paid on a discourse grounded on religious considerations.[7]

According to the Council of Europe, "hate speech" includes:

> [a]ll forms of expression which spread, incite, promote or justify racial hatred, xenophobia, anti-Semitism or other forms of hatred based on intolerance, including intolerance expressed by aggressive nationalism and ethnocentrism, discrimination and hostility against minorities, migrants and people of immigrant origin.[8]

Quite naturally, and because of its origins related to the fight against racism, the notion includes a language which cannot be isolated from our contemporary reality, in which the rights of minorities are legally protected.[9] The seriousness of the verbal offense is very clear: in its specific dimension, hate speech

---

5 According to the recent discursive approach of Claudia Bianchi, *Hate Speech. Il lato oscuro del linguaggio*, Laterza, Bari, 2021, p. 11:

> [l]'etichetta serve a identificare varie forme espressive (parole e frasi, ma anche immagini, simboli, gesti, caricature, condotte) ostili e offensive, volte a causare danno a individui e gruppi storicamente oppressi e marginalizzati, identificati da caratteristiche tutelate dalla legge (razza, etnia, nazionalità, religione, genere, orientamento sessuale, abilità e disabilità).

6 Hare and Weinstein, 2009, p. 4, see *supra* note 4.

7 "Religious hate speech can simply be described as speech that incites to hatred on the ground of the religion or belief of the targets of the hate speech, of the victims" (Erica Howard, *Freedom of Expression and Religious Hate Speech in Europe*, Routledge, London, 2018, p. 63).

8 Council of Europe, "Recommendation No. R (97) 20 of the Council of Ministers to Member States on 'Hate Speech'", 30 October 1997 (https://www.legal-tools.org/doc/rx2ckd/). Cf. the broader definition provided by the European Commission against Racism and Intolerance in its "ECRI General Policy Recommendation No. 15 on Combating Hate Speech", 8 December 2015 (https://www.legal-tools.org/doc/hb51n3/):

> Advocacy, promotion or incitement, in any form, of the denigration, hatred or vilification of a person or group of persons, as well as any harassment, insult, negative stereotyping, stigmatization or threat in respect of such a person or groups of persons and the justification of all the preceding types of expression, on the ground of 'race', colour, descent, national or ethnic origin, age, disability, language, religion or belief, sex, gender, gender identity, sexual orientation and other personal characteristics or status.

9 See Kevin Boyle, "Hate Speech – The United States Versus the Rest of the World", in *Maine Law Review*, 2001, vol. 53, no. 2, p. 489, stressing the "advocacy of hatred and discrimination" against specific groups.

is different from offensive speech, since its expression must "directly attack a person's immutable identity characteristics".[10]

In this context of human rights (where inherent characteristics are acknowledged and safeguarded), 'hate speech' has been perceived as the dark side of free speech. A first set of theoretical problems arises when discussing whether the freedom of expression can (and should) be controlled and reduced in these extreme circumstances. Most authors dealing with the gravity of the phenomenon have discussed whether law should be used to constrain some uses of hate manifestations, either directly or indirectly.[11] Many think that regulation is necessary in democratic regimes as a consequence of our solid commitment to human dignity and because of the respect owed for vulnerable minorities.[12] Others question the value of legal restrictions to hate speech.[13] In any case, the gap between supporters and detractors is still far from being overcome: the defenders of the establishment of legal bans and those who oppose them have embarked in heated debates on censorship or protection until today.[14]

Another interesting aspect in the legal approach to 'hate speech' is related to the tracking of its conceptual origins. Its discriminatory nature and this idea of 'group identity', on the one hand, suggest that hate speech is closely related with a contemporary reality embedded in human rights and postcolonialism, and has only developed very recently. On the other hand, there is a structural element behind hate speech – since it intends to allow those who are in power to use verbal assaults and offensive imagery with the purpose of preserving their preferred position in the existing social order – which cannot be reduced to modern times: in this sense, it should be recalled that the deployment of emotional strategies to legitimate power has accompanied the exercise of authority since the beginning of history.[15]

---

10 Caitlin Ring Carlson, *Hate Speech*, Massachusetts Institute of Technology Press, 2021, p. 12.

11 On "hate speech law", see Alex Brown, *Hate Speech Law: A Philosophical Examination*, Routledge, London, New York, 2015, p. 5. On the debate regarding the need to "tailor" specific legal answers in different countries according to their own traditions, see the chapters in Michael Herz and Peter Molnar (eds.), *The Content and Context of Hate Speech: Rethinking Regulation and Responses*, Cambridge University Press, 2012.

12 Jeremy Waldron, *The Harm in Hate Speech*, Harvard University Press, 2012.

13 An alternative proposal has been elaborated by Katharine Gelber, *Speaking Back: The Free Speech versus Hate Speech Debate*, John Benjamins Publishing Company, Amsterdam and Philadelphia, 2002, who has suggested a policy of "speaking back", through which institutional, material and educational support are granted to the victims of hate speech in order to facilitate their response.

14 Prohibitionists and oppositionists, according to Eric Heinze, *Hate Speech and Democratic Citizenship*, Oxford University Press, 2016, pp. 24–25.

15 Carlson, 2021, p. 12, see *supra* note 10.

Additionally, the idea of 'hate' and its target has changed over time as well: whereas today the concept refers narrowly to an individual's negative belief about the members of some group of people because of their origin, status or common features, in the past 'hate' covered the existence of intense dislike or hostility towards any object.[16] Can these historical differences be useful in explaining the unfortunate 'success' of 'hate speech' as a means to promote violence in modern times?

I am not interested in this chapter in taking a position on the first set of interesting deliberations related to the right social response to tackle hate speech; I would also be unable to provide such an assessment. My intention is rather to make a humble contribution in the 'historical' field by offering an 'outside' perspective on the real motivations behind the emergence and the justification of 'hate speech' through the lens of a legal historian. Even though 'hate speech' as such is hard to find in classical antiquity, the outlook I offer is mainly fed by a discussion of ancient sources dealing with the construction of enemies, the legal prosecution of religious dissenters, and the justification of massacres as a result of a subjective perception of 'otherness'.

In this chapter, I will attempt to find some textual examples of these topics, with the purpose of analysing them in a way that could be illuminating to understand the current scope and limits of the modern notion of religious hate speech. Attention here will be limited to Greek and Roman civilizations in pre-Christian times, since other contributions in this volume will enlarge the temporal scope and include references to early Christian sources.[17]

Firstly, in Section 14.2., I intend to offer a short description of the nature of freedom and frankness of speech in ancient Greece and republican Rome, taking into account in particular the presence of legal restrictions. In Section 14.3., I will briefly deal with the existence of jurisdictional prosecutions based upon religious considerations (especially in classical Athens), to see to what extent religion has been used as an argument to justify intolerance towards political adversaries. In Section 14.4., I will focus on the creation of 'enmity' and the negative description of adversaries, especially taking into consideration the ancient Greek and Latin vocabulary for 'hate'. Since there is a symptomatic lack of reference of these terms when inciting war and strife, I will then proceed to explain in Section 14.5. that, when it is possible to identify it, the emotion which

[16] Jack Levin, *The Violence of Hate: Confronting Racism, Anti-Semitism, and Other Forms of Bigotry*, Allyn and Bacon, Boston, 2002, p. 1.

[17] Several interesting contributions have explored hate speech in early Christianity, where the rhetoric of religious hatred was promoted and endorsed at a material level, see the excellent book by Eberhard Sauer, *The Archaeology of Religious Hatred in the Roman and Early Medieval World*, Tempus, Stroud, 2003.

is more frequently referred to in texts promoting collective violence is *anger*, since it becomes easier to justify it as a reaction to a previous injustice. In Section 14.6., I will show that religion has played little role in endorsing this anger, which is better described as political antagonism. This inference will allow me to conclude, in Section 14.7., that it does not seem to be necessary to identify arguments of 'hate' to endorse a speech that can incite severe ferocity against innocent minorities; in rhetorical terms – as we see in ancient Greek and Roman literary sources – sometimes the mere reference to rage and irritation hides a discourse of profound animosity that obscures pre-existing antipathy and helps to support an apparent legitimacy of hegemonic imposition. As a complement to what arguments for trials based on the commission of sacred crimes can show, the rhetorical use of political reasons can efficiently camouflage, in many cases, the religious nature behind campaigns of extermination.

14.2. Free and Frank Speech in Ancient Greece and Republican Rome

Although freedom of speech is not a concept that can be extrapolated to ancient times,[18] classical societies promoted the importance of granting the possibility of expression to all citizens. In democratic Athens, for instance, equal speech (*isēgoria*) was fully granted to all adult male Athenians. If we consider that these men only represented ten per cent of the population, this also meant that speaking openly in public fora was forbidden for a great part of the inhabitants of Attica.[19] Bearing this in mind, *parrhēsia* ('frank speech') is constantly mentioned with pride as a landmark of democratic participation in the Assembly, the Council and popular tribunals.[20] The close relationship between *isēgoria* and *parrhēsia* is therefore well established, since the ability to speak openly in democratic Athens was complemented by the fact that all words were granted the same power.[21]

Although *parrhēsia* has been frequently translated as 'free speech', it is true that the original concept is less related "to the passive language of rights"

---

18 David M. Carter, "Citizen Attribute, Negative Right: A Conceptual Difference Between Ancient and Modern Ideas of Freedom of Speech", in Ineke Sluiter and Ralph M. Rosen (eds.) *Free Speech in Classical Antiquity*, Brill, Leiden, 2004, pp. 197–220.

19 Richard Sorabji, *Freedom of Speech and Expression: Its History, Its Value, Its Good Use, and Its Misuse*, Oxford University Press, 2021, p. 9.

20 According to Arnaldo Momigliano, "Freedom of Speech in Antiquity", in Philip P. Wiener (ed.), *Dictionary of the History of Ideas: Studies of Selected Pivotal Ideas*, vol. 2, Charles Scribner's Sons, New York, 1974, p. 259, "*parrhesia* represented democracy from the point of view of the equality of rights".

21 Luigi Spina, *Il cittadino alla tribuna. Diritto e libertà di parola nell'Atene democratica*, Liguori Editori, Turin, pp. 25–43.

and more linked to "the active expression of one's true belief".[22] Therefore, the notion of 'frank speech' was associated to the open possibility of expressing ideas honestly, without fear of reprisals, in the democratic decision-making processes.[23]

At least in theory, it seems clear that those who dared to speak truth to power were much admired in this context, and therefore censorship was seen as an obstacle to honest discussion among peers. The whole Athenian political system was based upon the expectation that engaged citizens would actively take the word to speak about everything in the common interest of the *dēmos*.[24]

Even if, contrary to the situation in ancient Greece, there was no explicit word in Latin to identify freedom of speech,[25] there seems to have been ample room for free expression in republican Rome as well.[26] On the basis of *libertas*, this opportunity to speak one's mind was largely bestowed on citizens[27] and became not just a *licencia* granted by the state, but a comprehensive right to speak without restrictions in the political system.[28] In the words of Tacitus (*Annals*,

---

22 Arlene W. Saxonhouse, *Free Speech and Democracy in Ancient Athens*, Cambridge University Press, 2006, p. 86.

23 On *parrhēsia* as frank speech, see Sara Monoson, *Plato's Democratic Entanglements: Athenian Politics and the Practice of Philosophy*, Princeton University Press, 2000, pp. 52–53; Michel Foucault, *Fearless Speech*, edited by Joseph Pearson, Semiotexte(s), Los Angeles, 2001, p. 12. David Konstan, "The Two Faces of *Parrhêsia*: Free Speech and Self-Expression in Ancient Greece", in *Antichthon*, 2012, vol. 46, p. 4, explains:

> […] *parrhêsia* is perhaps better conceived as a license to express one's views, whatever the context. An Athenian citizen felt that he could speak up and did not have to defer to superiors, whether in a spirit of flattery or as an especially bold display of honesty under pressure: this was not a right guaranteed by law, or by a constitution, but an expectation, a feature of social life.

24 The famous expression τίς ἀγορεύειν βούλεται (who wants to speak?) was a typical formula in public gatherings at the Assembly. However, in certain specific contexts some words could be considered threatening; see Vincent Azoulay and Aurélie Damet, "Paroles menaçantes et mots interdits en Grèce ancienne: approches anthropologiques et juridiques", in *Cahiers "Mondes anciens"*, 2014, vol. 5, pp. 1–18.

25 This led Kurt A. Raaflaub, "Aristocracy and Freedom of Speech in the Greco-Roman World", in Sluiter and Rosen, 2004, p. 44, see *supra* note 18, to consider that probably there was a lack of such consciousness.

26 Laura Robinson, *Freedom of Speech in the Roman Republic*, Johns Hopkins University Press, Baltimore, 1940, p. 15: "only by the free expression of opinions could the Republican government function".

27 Stefan G. Chrissanthos, "Freedom of Speech and the Roman Republican Army", in Sluiter and Rosen, 2004, p. 342, see *supra* note 18.

28 José Manuel Díaz de Valdés, "Freedom of Expression in Rome", in *Revista de Estudios Histórico-Jurídicos [Sección Derecho Romano]*, 2009, vol. 31, p. 127, explains that "it is plausible that constant exercise of freedom of speech breed a conviction in citizens that this

13.49), for example, in the Senate "*licere patribus, quoties ius dicendae sententiae accepissent, quae vellent expromere relationemque in ea postulare*" ("the Senators, as often as they received the privilege of stating an opinion, were at liberty to say out what they pleased, and to claim that it should be put to vote").[29]

According to van Renswoude,[30] *parrhēsia* and *libertas* were considered highly valued political and social virtues, the closest ones to our notion of 'free speech' because of their importance and valuation in democratic times.[31] Nevertheless, in a time where human rights did not yet exist, nothing in these notions indicated an inherent and natural condition: as it was widely accepted (and encouraged) among equals in internal affairs, the liberty to speak was unsurprisingly denied to 'others', such as women, slaves or foreigners.[32] But, as already stated, with the exception of these categories, frankness of speech was a landmark of Athenian democracy, where the idea of *parrhēsia* seemed to be therefore associated with an indifference to *aidōs* ('shame', considered the respect for public opinion).[33]

Strongly determined by its conventional character, the extent of this free speech allowed for the permission of personal ridicule or denigration (*aiskhrologia*) to a certain degree. Since positive and negative elements could stem from this bluntness,[34] there has been discussion about the limits of this freedom, especially concerning personal invectives and verbal attacks on the comic stage of

was not a mere *licencia* granted by the state, but something to which they were entitled to, even legally".

29 The Latin text corresponds to the edition by Charles D. Fisher (ed.), *Cornelius Tacitus. Annales ab excessu divi Augusti*, Oxford University Press, 1906. The translation belongs to Alfred J. Church, William J. Brodribb and Sara Bryant (eds. and trans.), *Complete Works of Tacitus*, Random House, New York, 1942.

30 Irene van Renswoude, *The Rhetoric of Free Speech in Late Antiquity and the Early Middle Ages*, Cambridge University Press, 2019, p. 1.

31 Raaflaub, 2004, p. 49, see *supra* note 25.

32 Even today, Renswoude, 2019, p. 3, see *supra* note 30, considers that "[f]ree speech is not a natural given; it is a cultural construction, governed by social norms, legal rules, rhetorical conventions and scripted roles".

33 This is the thesis presented by Saxonhouse, 2006, see *supra* note 22, in her book. A note of caution should be added, though. As Konstan, 2012, p. 8, see *supra* note 23, expresses, "if *parrhêsia* suggests a shameless disregard of traditional values, then democracy must be unfaithful to its own founding principle if it represses even the most outrageous speech".

34 "General Introduction", in Sluiter and Rosen, 2004, pp. 4–6, see *supra* note 18.

Aristophanes and other contemporary playwrights.[35] For Halliwell,[36] for example, there was a local climate in Athens of "attitudes which accepted, permitted, and even encouraged the liberty of comedy", especially accepted in an official context of festive celebrations.[37] According to him, outside the limits of comedy, open *parrhēsia* could "engender conditions in which the dangerous scope of obloquy, calumny, and invective (*kakēgoria*, *loidoria*, *blasphēmia*, *diabolē*) will become especially apparent". But except for the realm of comedy, there seemed to be a risk of excesses that could emerge out of this frankness, and Athenians were aware of these dangers.[38] One of the examples of these legal limitations (although late) is mentioned by Plutarch in his *Life of Solon* (21.1):

> ἐπαινεῖται δὲ τοῦ Σόλωνος καὶ ὁ κωλύων νόμος τὸν τεθνηκότα κακῶς ἀγορεύειν. καὶ γὰρ ὅσιον τοὺς μεθεστῶτας ἱεροὺς νομίζειν, καὶ δίκαιον ἀπέχεσθαι τῶν οὐχ ὑπαρχόντων, καὶ πολιτικὸν ἀφαιρεῖν τῆς ἔχθρας τὸ ἀΐδιον. ζῶντα δὲ κακῶς λέγειν ἐκώλυσε πρὸς ἱεροῖς καὶ δικαστηρίοις καὶ ἀρχείοις καὶ θεωρίας οὔσης ἀγώνων· ἢ τρεῖς δραχμὰς τῷ ἰδιώτῃ, δύο δ᾽ ἄλλας ἀποτίνειν εἰς τὸ δημόσιον ἔταξε. τὸ γὰρ μηδαμοῦ κρατεῖν ὀργῆς ἀπαίδευτον καὶ ἀκόλαστον· τὸ δὲ πανταχοῦ χαλεπόν, ἐνίοις δὲ ἀδύνατον.
>
> Praise is given also to that law of Solon which forbids speaking ill of the dead. For it is piety to regard the deceased as sacred, justice to spare the absent, and good policy to rob hatred of its perpetuity. He also forbade speaking ill of the living in temples, courts-of-law, public offices, and at festivals; the transgressor must pay three drachmas to the person injured, and two more into the public treasury. For never to master one's anger is a mark of intemperance and lack of training; but always to do so is difficult, and for some, impossible.[39]

---

[35] A general overview of the debates can be found in Robert W. Wallace, "Law, Attic Comedy, and the Regulation of Comic Speech", in Michael Gagarin and David Cohen (eds.), *The Cambridge Companion to Ancient Greek Law*, Cambridge University Press, 2005, pp. 357–373.

[36] Stephen Halliwell, "Comic Satire and Freedom of Speech in Classical Athens", in *Journal of Hellenic Studies*, 1991, vol. 111, pp. 48–70.

[37] On this comic permission to embark upon personal attacks, see Rossella Saetta-Cottone, *Aristofane e la poetica dell'ingiuria. Per una introduzione alla λοιδορία comica*, Carocci, Rome, 2005.

[38] See Stephen Halliwell, "Aischrology, Shame, and Comedy", in Sluiter and Rosen, 2004, pp. 115–144, see *supra* note 18. For an opposing view, see Alan H. Sommerstein, "Harassing the Satirist: The Alleged Attempts to Prosecute Aristophanes", in Sluiter and Rosen, 2004, pp. 145–174, *supra* note 18, who considers that not even comedy was above the law regulating free speech.

[39] The Greek text and the English translation correspond to Bernadotte Perrin (ed.), *Plutarch's Lives*, Harvard University Press, 1914.

Other references to specific decrees containing concrete limitations on comic license during the Peloponnesian War (such as the decree of Syrakosios, for example) point in the same direction, although the veracity of these sources remains extremely doubtful.[40]

In Rome, free speech was also subject to checks and constraints. Already the XII Tables seemed to have regulated freedom of speech through an action against libel or defamatory writing.[41] During the second century BCE, a possible law on *iniuria* in comedy and a *lex maiestatis* from the period of the Gracchi were enacted.[42] In 91 BCE, the *lex Reminia* established sanctions against malicious lawsuits (such as *calumnia*) to discourage political attacks against public adversaries.[43] In the context of these restrictions, orators were trained in a proper use of free speech; as recommended in Quintilian's *Institutio oratoria*, rhetoric should teach about the appropriateness of speaking frankly in particular situations, taking into account the circumstances of time and place.[44]

During the Roman Empire, the value of frankness continued to be acknowledged in the public sphere as an efficient way for rhetorical self-presentation and reputational prestige. In this new post-classical environment, where power relations became heavily stratified, frank speech was considered an ethical asset of intellectual elites.[45] At the same time, in spite of the absence of laws

40 Max Radin, "Freedom of Speech in Ancient Athens", in *The American Journal of Philology*, 1927, vol. 48, no. 3, pp. 215–230, has identified some laws that were passed during this time to penalize the use of certain expressions. In his opinion, the fact that comedy did not include any forbidden word in a context in which personal and violent abuse were still present, shows that real limitations existed. This conclusion requires a deep analysis of available sources; I have revisited these references in Emiliano J. Buis, *El juego de la ley. La poética cómica del derecho en las obras tempranas de Aristófanes (427-414 a.C.)*, Dykinson, Madrid, 2019, pp. 95–105.

41 This interpretation was formulated by Díaz de Valdés, 2009, p. 137, see *supra* note 28.

42 On the *lex maiestatis*, see Tacitus, *Annals*, 1.72. It is said that in Augustus' time, at the beginning of the Empire, this *lex* was reinforced and expanded to cover "slanderous writing" against great people: defamation would now become a crime. On the expansion of the *lex maiestatis*, see also Richard Bauman, *Human Rights in Ancient Rome*, Routledge, London, New York, 2000, pp. 102–103. Once again, the evidence for these legal limitations is scarce and unclear.

43 On the limitations of freedom of speech and censorship in later Latin texts, see Frederick H. Cramer, "Bookburning and Censorship in Ancient Rome: A Chapter from the History of Freedom of Speech", in *Journal of the History of Ideas*, 1945, vol. 6, no. 2, pp. 157–196.

44 Quintilian, *Institutio oratoria*, 9.2.26–9, 3.8.48, 9.137. Renswoude, 2019, p. 2, see *supra* note 30, explains these passages claiming that "some people truly spoke freely, but as soon as persuasion came into play [...] 'free speech' was no longer free, but belonged to the realm of rhetoric".

45 This is the main thesis of the recent book by Dana Fields, *Frankness, Greek Culture, and the Roman Empire*, Routledge, London, New York, 2021.

against freedom of expression in late antiquity,[46] a common understanding about the appropriateness or not of certain types of speech generated some self-censorship on political expressions.[47]

14.3. Prosecuting for Religious Motives in Antiquity

In what sense did frank expression (and its limitations) involve a religious dimension in antiquity? A quick revision of some interesting examples of accusations of heresy, impiety and atheism in ancient times can be interesting to understand how intolerance made its way into the judicial systems.[48]

We should definitely begin by reflecting the Athenian trials for religious motivations, which have been the subject of many monographs interested in studying the famous condemnation of Socrates under the light of other precedents considered to be accurate descriptions of real proceedings.[49] However, the historical character of those court cases founded on religious motives has been called into question by authors such as Dover[50] and Wallace,[51] who sceptically showed the prejudices and incongruities of the sources, which for the most part are late testimonies situated centuries away from the moment in which the trials allegedly took place. In any case, a review of the sources can be useful, from a legal and political perspective, to better understand the 'religious' scope of the allusions to the law – mainly in terms of 'impiety' (*asebeia*) – in order to see the polemical nature of these disputes.[52]

---

46 See Anthony Kaldellis, *The Byzantine Republic: People and Power in New Rome*, Harvard University Press, 2015.

47 Edward Watts, "Introduction: Freedom of Speech and Self-Censorship in the Roman Empire", in *Revue belge de philologie et d'histoire*, 2014, vol. 92, no. 1, pp. 157–166.

48 Arnoldo Momigliano, "Freedom of Speech and Religious Tolerance in the Ancient World", in Sarah C. Humphreys, *Anthropology and the Greeks*, Routledge, Kegal Paul, London, Boston, 1978, pp. 179–193.

49 Eudore Derenne, *Les procès d'impiété intentés aux philosophes à Athènes au Ve et au IVe siècles avant J.-C.*, Vaillant- Carmanne, É. Champion, Liège, 1930.

50 Kenneth J. Dover, "The Freedom of the Intellectual in Greek Society", in *Talanta*, 1976, vol. 7, pp. 24–54.

51 Robert W. Wallace, "Private Lives and Public Enemies: Freedom of Thought in Classical Athens", in Alan L. Boegehold and Adele C. Scafuro (eds.), *Athenian Identity and Civic Ideology*, Johns Hopkins University Press, 1994, pp. 127–155.

52 See Gabriele Marasco, "I processi d'empietà nella democrazia ateniese", in *Atene e Roma*, 1976, vol. 21, pp. 113-131; David Cohen, "The Prosecution of Impiety in Athenian Law", in Gerhard Thür (ed.), *Symposion 1985. Vorträge zur griechischen und hellenistischen Rechtsgeschichte*, Böhlau, Cologne, Vienna, 1989, pp. 99–107; Lara-Louisa O'Sullivan, "Athenian Impiety Trials in the Late Fourth Century B.C.", in *Classical Quarterly*, 1997, vol. 47, pp. 136–152; Delfim Ferreira Leão, "Matéria religiosa: processos de impiedade (*asebeia*)", in Delfim Ferreira Leão, Livio Rossetti and Maria do Céu Fialho (eds.), *Nomos. Direito e sociedade na Antiguidade Clássica*, Ediciones Clásicas, Universidade de Coimbra, Madrid,

Two trials, against Anaxagoras of Clazomenes and Protagoras of Abdera, constitute our first examples. As far as Anaxagoras is concerned, it is said that his adversaries reproached him for his cosmic theory: whereas the theological gaze saw gods in the stars (like Helios, 'the Sun', or Selene, 'the Moon'), Anaxagoras considered them as incandescent masses.[53] Accused therefore of not respecting the gods and of reducing the stars to simple stones, he was apparently brought to justice in a trial for impiety, around 437 BCE, as underlined in the first mention of these facts by Diodorus Siculus (*Library*, 12.39.2):

> διόπερ ἐκκλησίας συνελθούσης περὶ τούτων, οἱ μὲν ἐχθροὶ τοῦ Περικλέους ἔπεισαν τὸν δῆμον συλλαβεῖν τὸν Φειδίαν, καὶ αὐτοῦ τοῦ Περικλέους κατηγόρουν ἱεροσυλίαν. πρὸς δὲ τούτοις Ἀναξαγόραν τὸν σοφιστήν, διδάσκαλον ὄντα Περικλέους, ὡς ἀσεβοῦντα εἰς τοὺς θεοὺς ἐσυκοφάντουν· συνέπλεκον δ᾽ ἐν ταῖς κατηγορίαις καὶ διαβολαῖς τὸν Περικλέα, διὰ τὸν φθόνον σπεύδοντες διαβαλεῖν τὴν τἀνδρὸς ὑπεροχήν τε καὶ δόξαν.
>
> Consequently, when the Assembly convened to consider the affair, the enemies of Pericles persuaded the people to arrest Pheidias and lodged a charge against Pericles himself of stealing sacred property. Furthermore, they falsely accused the sophist Anaxagoras, who was Pericles' teacher, of impiety against the gods; and they involved Pericles in their accusations and malicious charges, since jealousy made them eager to discredit the eminence as well as the fame of the man.[54]

The legal aspects of the episode are clear: there is an accusation (as suggested by the verb *katēgorein* and the noun *katēgoria*) based on the crime of *asebeia* ('impiety'; literally, lack of religious consideration).[55] Interestingly, the testimony makes a distinction between two religious offenses, since next to *asebeia*, there is an allusion to *hierosylia* ('sacrilege'), which mainly refers to those violations of sacred goods and to the attacks on the property of sanctuaries.

In modern terms, however, it could be said that the nature of the procedure describe was not strictly judicial but political: there are no references to judges

2004, 201–226; Chiara Pecorella Longo, "Il reato di empietà nel diritto attico", in Giovanni A. Cecconi and Chantal Gabrielli (eds.), *Politiche religiose nel mondo antico e tardoantico. Poteri e indirizzi, forme del controllo, idee e prassi di tolleranza* (Atti del convegno internazionale di studi, Firenze, 24–26 settembre 2009), Edipuglia, Bari, 2011, pp. 43–55; Jakub Filonik, "Athenian Impiety Trials: A Reappraisal", in *Dike*, 2013, vol. 16, pp. 11–96.

53 Plato, *Apology*, 26d; Diogenes Laertius, *Lives of Eminent Philosophers*, 2.8.

54 The Greek text and the translation correspond here to Charles H. Oldfather (ed.), *Diodorus of Sicily in Twelve Volumes, Vol. 4-8*, Harvard University Press, 1989.

55 On the importance of piety as a stepping-stone in ancient religion, see Louise B. Zaidman, *Le commerce des dieux : eusebeia, essai sur la piété en Grèce ancienne*, Éditions La Découverte, Paris, 2001.

but to the Assembly (*Ekklēsia*), and the specific relationship between the philosopher and Pericles is significant to understand the political foundations of the denunciations: the slanders (*diabolai*) and the fact that unfounded accusations were made (the verb *sykophantein*) indicate that, behind the intention to drag Anaxagoras to justice, there was obviously an implicit will to attack Pericles.[56] In the context of a complicated political atmosphere, then, Plutarch reproduces the spirit of the times to show that Anaxagoras was not the only one to be prosecuted before the Assembly. I will quote the passage in full (*Life of Pericles*, 32.1–3):

> περὶ δὲ τοῦτον τὸν χρόνον Ἀσπασία δίκην ἔφευγεν ἀσεβείας, Ἑρμίππου τοῦ κωμῳδοποιοῦ διώκοντος καὶ προσκατηγοροῦντος ὡς Περικλεῖ γυναῖκας ἐλευθέρας εἰς τὸ αὐτὸ φοιτώσας ὑποδέχοιτο. καὶ ψήφισμα Διοπείθης ἔγραψεν εἰσαγγέλλεσθαι τοὺς τὰ θεῖα μὴ νομίζοντας ἢ λόγους περὶ τῶν μεταρσίων διδάσκοντας, ἀπερειδόμενος εἰς Περικλέα δι᾽ Ἀναξαγόρου τὴν ὑπόνοιαν. δεχομένου δὲ τοῦ δήμου καὶ προσιεμένου τὰς διαβολάς, οὕτως ἤδη ψήφισμα κυροῦται, Δρακοντίδου γράψαντος, ὅπως οἱ λόγοι τῶν χρημάτων ὑπὸ Περικλέους εἰς τοὺς Πρυτάνεις ἀποτεθεῖεν, οἱ δὲ δικασταὶ τὴν ψῆφον ἀπὸ τοῦ βωμοῦ φέροντες ἐν τῇ πόλει κρίνοιεν. Ἅγνων δὲ· τοῦτο μὲν ἀφεῖλε τοῦ ψηφίσματος, κρίνεσθαι δὲ τὴν δίκην ἔγραψεν ἐν δικασταῖς χιλίοις καὶ πεντακοσίοις, εἴτε κλοπῆς καὶ δώρων εἴτ᾽ ἀδικίου βούλοιτό τις ὀνομάζειν τὴν δίωξιν. Ἀσπασίαν μὲν οὖν ἐξῃτήσατο, πολλὰ πάνυ παρὰ τὴν δίκην, ὡς Αἰσχίνης φησίν, ἀφεὶς ὑπὲρ αὐτῆς δάκρυα καὶ δεηθεὶς τῶν δικαστῶν· Ἀναξαγόραν δὲ φοβηθεὶς ἐξέπεμψεν ἐκ τῆς πόλεως. ὡς δὲ διὰ Φειδίου προσέπταισε τῷ δήμῳ, φοβηθεὶς τὸ δικαστήριον μέλλοντα τὸν πόλεμον καὶ ὑποτυφόμενον ἐξέκαυσεν, ἐλπίζων διασκεδάσειν τὰ ἐγκλήματα καὶ ταπεινώσειν τὸν φθόνον ἐν πράγμασι μεγάλοις καὶ κινδύνοις τῆς πόλεως ἐκείνῳ μόνῳ διὰ τὸ ἀξίωμα καὶ τὴν δύναμιν ἀναθείσης ἑαυτήν. αἱ μὲν οὖν αἰτίαι δι᾽ ἃς οὐκ εἴασεν ἐνδοῦναι Λακεδαιμονίοις τὸν δῆμον, αὗται λέγονται, τὸ δ᾽ ἀληθὲς ἄδηλον.
>
> About this time also Aspasia was put on trial for impiety, Hermippus the comic poet being her prosecutor, who alleged further

[56] Luisa Prandi, "I processi contro Fidia, Aspasia, Anassagora e l'opposizione a Pericle", in *Aevum*, 1977, vol. 51, nos. 1/2, pp. 10–26; Antonio Banfi, "I processi contro Anassagora, Pericle, Fidia ed Aspasia e la questione del 'circolo di Pericle': note di cronologia e di storia", in *Annali dell'Istituto italiano per gli studi storici*, 1999, vol. 16, pp. 3–85. On the historical context of the trial, see Jaap Mansfeld, "The Chronology of Anaxagoras' Athenian Period and the Date of His Trial", in *Mnemosyne*, 1979, vol. 32, nos. 1/2, pp. 39–69 and Jaap Mansfeld, "The Chronology of Anaxagoras' Athenian Period and the Date of His Trial. Part II. The Plot against Pericles and his Associates", in *Mnemosyne*, 1980, vol. 33, no. 1/2, pp. 17–95.

> against her that she received free-born women into a place of assignation for Pericles. And Diopeithes brought in a bill providing for the public impeachment of such as did not believe in gods, or who taught doctrines regarding the heavens, directing suspicion against Pericles by means of Anaxagoras. The people accepted with delight these slanders, and so, while they were in this mood, a bill was passed, on motion of Dracontides, that Pericles should deposit his accounts of public moneys with the prytanes, and that the jurors should decide upon his case with ballots which had lain upon the altar of the goddess on the acropolis. But Hagnon amended this clause of the bill with the motion that the case be tried before fifteen hundred jurors in the ordinary way, whether one wanted to call it a prosecution for embezzlement and bribery, or malversation. Well, then, Aspasia he begged off, by shedding copious tears at the trial, as Aeschines says, and by entreating the jurors; and he feared for Anaxagoras so much that he sent him away from the city. And since in the case of Pheidias he had come into collision with the people, he feared a jury in his own case, and so kindled into flame the threatening and smouldering war, hoping thereby to dissipate the charges made against him and allay the people's jealousy, inasmuch as when great undertakings were on foot, and great perils threatened, the city entrusted herself to him and to him alone, by reason of his worth and power. Such, then, are the reasons which are alleged for his not suffering the people to yield to the Lacedaemonians; but the truth about it is not clear.[57]

Alongside Anaxagoras' flight to avoid judgment, the text first shows the connection of these cases with other imputations of *asebeia*, such as the one directed against Aspasia. But from the legal point of view, what is interesting here is the allusion to the decree of Diopeithes which illustrates the scope of impiety. Under this charge, it was possible to prosecute those who "did not believe in gods, or who taught doctrines regarding the heavens". On the one hand then, it seems that *asebeia* implied the lack of belief in the gods, therefore becoming associated with our notion of atheism.[58] Secondly, it also covered the

[57] Both the Greek text and its translation correspond to Bernadotte Perrin (ed.), *Plutarch's Lives*, Harvard University Press, 1916.

[58] On atheism in antiquity, see Wilhelm Fahr, *ΘΕΟΥΣ ΝΟΜΙΖΕΙΝ. Zum Problem des Anfänge des Atheismus bei den Griechen* (Spudasmata, XXVI), Georg Olms, New York, 1969; Marek Winiarczyk, "Methodisches zum antiken Atheismus", in *Rheinisches Museum*, 1990, vol. 133, pp. 1–15; Marek Winiarczyk, "Antike Bezeichnungen der Gottlosigkeit und des Atheismus", in *Rheinisches Museum*, 1992, vol. 135, pp. 216–225; Jan N. Bremmer, "Atheism in Antiquity", in Michael Martin (ed.), *The Cambridge Companion to Atheism*, Cambridge University Press, 2007, pp. 11–26; Robert Parker, "Atheism", in Simon Hornblower, Antony Spawforth

teaching of new astrological thoughts or the dissemination of singular views surrounding the celestial phenomena. In both cases, these actions were an attempt against the traditional religious values of the community.

Despite the interest of the text, the absence of other allusions to the decree of Diopeithes led to the questioning of its veracity. According to Donnay,[59] this decree is more related to the repertoire of old comedy than to reality, being nothing but a dramatic fabrication.[60] Plutarch even makes it clear that the accusation against Aspasia comes from the sources of comedy, particularly the playwright Hermippus, who promoted the imputation.

In spite of this apparent comic basis, the vocabulary of the accusations in Plutarch responds to the real formalities of Athenian denunciations. In the famous charges against Socrates, as transmitted by Favorinus through a passage from *Diogenes Laertius* (2.5.40), similar terms are present:

> Ἡ δ᾽ ἀντωμοσία τῆς δίκης τοῦτον εἶχε τὸν τρόπον: ἀνάκειται γὰρ ἔτι καὶ νῦν, φησὶ Φαβωρῖνος, ἐν τῷ Μητρῴῳ· “τάδε ἐγράψατο καὶ ἀντωμόσατο Μέλητος Μελήτου Πιτθεὺς Σωκράτει Σωφρονίσκου Ἀλωπεκῆθεν· ἀδικεῖ Σωκράτης οὓς μὲν ἡ πόλις νομίζει θεοὺς οὐ νομίζων, ἕτερα δὲ καινὰ δαιμόνια εἰσηγούμενος· ἀδικεῖ δὲ καὶ τοὺς νέους διαφθείρων τίμημα· θάνατος.”
>
> The affidavit in the case, which is still preserved, says Favorinus, in the *Metron*, ran as follows: “This indictment and affidavit is sworn by Meletus, the son of Meletus of Pitthos, against Socrates, the son of Sophroniscus of Alopece: Socrates is guilty of refusing to recognize the gods recognized by the state, and of introducing other new divinities. He is also guilty of corrupting the youth. The penalty demanded is death”.[61]

The accusation against Socrates, as presented here, provides us with new information: *asebeia* was also meant to include the lack of recognition or acceptance of the same gods venerated by the city (οὓς μὲν ἡ πόλις νομίζει θεοὺς

and Esther Eidinow (eds.), *The Oxford Classical Dictionary*, Oxford University Press, 2013, pp. 193–194.

59 Guy Donnay, “La date du procès de Phidias”, in *L'Antiquité classique*, 1968, vol. 37, pp. 29–30.

60 The comic sources for our reconstruction of the decree of Diopeithes are from Aristophanes: *Knights*, 1085; *Wasps*, 380 and the late *scholia* to *Birds*, 988 (‘Birds’).

61 The Greek text and the English translation correspond to R.D. Hicks (ed.), *Diogenes Laertius. Lives of Eminent Philosophers*, Harvard University Press, 1972.

οὐ νομίζων) and the introduction of new deities (ἕτερα δὲ καινὰ δαιμόνια εἰσηγούμενος).[62]

Other cases deserve attention. We know that the philosopher Protagoras – one of the initiators of the sophistic movement and the father of man-based relativism – was the author of a volume called *On the Gods*, where he had exposed the reasons for his atheism. The evidence related to the existence of a lawsuit against him provides some information on the prosecution. According to Cicero (*On the Nature of the Gods*, 1.63),

> *nam Abderites quidem Protagoras, cuius a te modo mentio facta est, sophistes temporibus illis vel maximus, cum in principio libri sic posuisset "de divis neque ut sint neque ut non sint habeo dicere", Atheniensium iussu urbe atque agro est exterminatus librique eius in contione combusti; ex quo equidem existimo tardioris ad hanc sententiam profitendam multos esse factos, quippe cum poenam ne dubitatio quidem effugere potuisset. Quid de sacrilegis, quid de impiis periurisque dicemus?*[63]
>
> Since as for Protagoras of the Abdera, the greatest sophist of that age, to whom you just now alluded for beginning a book with the words 'About the gods I am unable to affirm either how they exist or how they do not exist,' he was sentenced by a decree of the Athenian assembly to be banished from the city and from the country, and to have his books burnt in the market-place: an example that I can well believe has discouraged many people since from professing atheism, since the mere expression of doubt did not succeed in escaping punishment. What are we to say about the men guilty of sacrilege or impiety or perjury?[64]

Cicero's testimony indicates that Protagoras could not express whether the gods existed or did not exist. The texts transmitting the anecdote, however, differ greatly in the information provided. Whereas the Roman orator and Diogenes Laertius (9.52) evoke Protagoras' hunting, Philostratus (*Life of Sophists*, 1.10.3) indicates that he fled, banished by decree or at the end of a trial, and Sextus Empiricus and Flavius Josephus affirmed that the sophist had fled to escape the death sentence pronounced against him. All these different versions (which, according to Lenfant, can be explained from the divergent

---

62 Myles F. Burnyeat, "The Impiety of Socrates", in *Ancient Philosophy*, 1997, vol. 17, no. 1, pp. 1–12; Guy Donnay, "L'impiété de Socrate", in *Ktèma*, 2002, vol. 27, pp. 155–160.

63 The Latin text corresponds to the edition by Otto Plasberg (ed.), *M. Tullius Cicero. De Natura Deorum*, Teubner, Leipzig, 1917.

64 The translation corresponds to Harris Rackham (ed.), *Cicero in Twenty-Eight Volumes, Vol. XIX. De Natura deorum. Academica*, Harvard University Press, 1967.

interpretations of the verb *pheugein*, meaning ‘to be banished’ but also ‘to flee’)[65] call into question their reliability and cast doubt on the existence of the prosecution itself.[66]

A passage from Flavius Josephus evoking all these Athenian cases (as well as others) allows us, in my opinion, to reflect on the reasons which explain these apparently false references (*Against Apion*, 2.262–268):

> οἱ δὲ κοινὴν εἶναι τὴν ἑαυτῶν δόξαντες πόλιν Ἀθηναῖοι πῶς περὶ τούτων εἶχον, Ἀπολλώνιος ἠγνόησεν, ὅτι καὶ τοὺς ῥῆμα μόνον παρὰ τοὺς ἐκείνων νόμους φθεγξαμένους περὶ θεῶν ἀπαραιτήτως ἐκόλασαν. τίνος γὰρ ἑτέρου χάριν Σωκράτης ἀπέθανεν; οὐ γὰρ δὴ προεδίδου τὴν πόλιν τοῖς πολεμίοις οὐδὲ τῶν ἱερῶν ἐσύλησεν οὐδέν, ἀλλ᾽ ὅτι καινοὺς ὅρκους ὤμνυεν καί τι δαιμόνιον αὐτῷ σημαίνειν ἔφασκεν ἢ διαπαίζων, ὡς ἔνιοι λέγουσι, διὰ ταῦτα κατεγνώσθη κώνειον πιὼν ἀποθανεῖν. καὶ διαφθείρειν δὲ τοὺς νέους ὁ κατήγορος αὐτὸν ᾐτιᾶτο, τῆς πατρίου πολιτείας καὶ τῶν νόμων ὅτι προῆγεν αὐτοὺς καταφρονεῖν. Σωκράτης μὲν οὖν πολίτης Ἀθηναίων τοιαύτην ὑπέμεινε τιμωρίαν. Ἀναξαγόρας δὲ Κλαζομένιος ἦν, ἀλλ᾽ ὅτι νομιζόντων Ἀθηναίων τὸν ἥλιον εἶναι θεὸν ὅδ᾽ αὐτὸν ἔφη μύδρον εἶναι διάπυρον, θάνατον αὐτοῦ παρ᾽ ὀλίγας ψήφους κατέγνωσαν. καὶ Διαγόρᾳ τῷ Μηλίῳ τάλαντον ἐπεκήρυξαν, εἴ τις αὐτὸν ἀνέλοι, ἐπεὶ τὰ παρ᾽ αὐτοῖς μυστήρια χλευάζειν ἐλέγετο. καὶ Πρωταγόρας εἰ μὴ θᾶττον ἔφυγε, συλληφθεὶς ἂν ἐτεθνήκει γράψαι τι δόξας οὐχ ὁμολογούμενον τοῖς Ἀθηναίοις περὶ θεῶν. τί δὲ δεῖ θαυμάζειν, εἰ πρὸς ἄνδρας οὕτως ἀξιοπίστους διετέθησαν, οἵ γε μηδὲ γυναικῶν ἐφείσαντο; νῦν γὰρ τὴν ἱέρειαν ἀπέκτειναν, ἐπεί τις αὐτῆς κατηγόρησεν, ὅτι ξένους ἐμύει θεούς· νόμῳ δ᾽ ἦν τοῦτο παρ᾽ αὐτοῖς κεκωλυμένον καὶ τιμωρία κατὰ τῶν ξένον εἰσαγόντων θεὸν ὥριστο θάνατος. οἱ δὲ τοιούτῳ νόμῳ χρώμενοι δῆλον ὅτι τοὺς τῶν ἄλλων οὐκ ἐνόμιζον εἶναι θεούς· οὐ γὰρ ἂν αὐτοῖς πλειόνων ἀπολαύειν ἐφθόνουν.[67]
>
> But the Athenians, who considered their city open to all comers – what was their attitude in this matter? Apollonius was ignorant of

[65] Dominique Lenfant, “Protagoras et son procès d’impiété : peut-on soutenir une thèse et son contraire ?”, in *Ktèma*, 2002, vol. 27, pp. 135–154.

[66] On book-burning as a means to silence religious dissidence in the context of ancient Greek sources, see Robert W. Wallace, “Book-burning in Ancient Athens”, in Robert W. Wallace and Edward M. Harris (eds.), *Transitions to Empire: Essays in Greco-Roman History, 360-146 B.C., in Honor of E. Badian*, University of Oklahoma Press, 1996, pp. 226–240. See also Cramer, 1945, pp. 157-196, see *supra* note 43.

[67] The Greek text corresponds to Benedictus Niese (ed.), *Flavii Iosephi opera*, Weidmann, Berlin, 1892.

> this, and of the inexorable penalty which they inflicted on any who uttered a single word about the gods contrary to their laws. On what other grounds was Socrates put to death? He never sought to betray his city to the enemy, he robbed no temple. No; because he used to swear strange oaths and give out (in jest, surely, as some say) that he received communications from a spirit, he was therefore condemned to die by drinking hemlock. His accuser brought a further charge against him of corrupting young men, because he stimulated them to hold the constitution and laws of their country in contempt. Such was the punishment of Socrates, a citizen of Athens. Anaxagoras was a native of Clazomenae, but because he maintained that the sun, which the Athenians held to be a god, was an incandescent mass, he escaped by a few votes only from being condemned by them to death. They offered a talent for the head of Diagoras of Melos, because he was reported to have jeered at their mysteries. Protagoras, had he not prompted fled, would have been arrested and put to death, because of a statement about the gods in his writings which appeared to conflict with Athenian tenets. Can any wonder at their attitude towards men of such authority when they did not spare even women? They put Ninus the priestess to death, because someone accused her of initiating people into the mysteries of foreign gods; this was forbidden by their law, and the penalty decreed for any who introduced a foreign god was death. Those who had such a law evidently did not believe that the gods of other nations were gods; else they would not have denied themselves the advantage of increasing the number of their own.

The text is too long to discuss here in detail, but it provides some insights that I would like to address, in particular the facts behind the charges. When discussing all these episodes together, it seems clear that the wrongful conduct attributed to each philosopher differs. This shows us the extremely flexible nature of *asebeia*, a crime under which not only behaviour, but also thoughts and opinions were included: thus, Socrates, for example, is said to have sworn according to new formulas and to have spoken of *daimones*, Anaxagoras considered the gods as objects, Diagoras mocked the mysteries, Protagoras contradicted the feelings of the Athenians on their gods, and the priestess Ninus introduced cults in honour of foreign deities. From an argumentative point of view, placing Socrates next to these other public figures makes it possible to link his destiny to that of a succession of intellectuals whose theories had not been understood and were considered dangerous for life in common.

In this sense, *asebeia* can be deemed the most civic of all religious offences: unlike violations of rites, which required sacrifices or acts of purification, *asebeia* had to be dealt with through public punishment because of its communal impact. In his *Life of Nicias* (23.4), Plutarch pointed out that all 'cosmic' philosophers – that is, those interested in *physis*, such as Protagoras, Anaxagoras, and Socrates – were considered a living danger to the *polis*, since they outraged the gods and, at the same time, infringed upon reason and social conventions.

In spite of the existence of specific acts under the technical scope of the crime,[68] there seems to be a considerable elasticity in the notion of *asebeia.* Its civic and political character was reflected not only in behaviour against gods and deities, but also against dead or alive parents.[69] At the same time, the procedures and actions available for *asebeia* were also quite broad, and Demosthenes shows well (*Against Androtion*, 22.27) that it was possible to act by arrest (*apagōgē*), by written accusation (*graphē*) – as it was against Socrates – by action before the Eumolpids, or by summons (*phasis*) before the archon-king. If we add that the decree of Diopeithes also included the possibility of an *eisangēlia* (an action before the Assembly), a plurality of legal remedies opened up to the accusers for them to select.

The Athenian rhetoric of litigation linked to religious accusations can also be seen in the case of the mutilation of the Herms and the desecration of the Mysteries in 415 BCE.[70] This religious and political scandal is narrated by Thucydides, who relates it to the crime of *asebeia* (6.53.1) and interprets it as a negative omen for the expedition to Sicily (6.27.3): the presence onboard of an atheist like Alcibiades would put the entire naval campaign at risk. The connection between religious offenses and political accusations is, once again, very clear here.[71]

---

[68] These actions were identified and summarized by Jean Rudhardt in Jean Rudhardt, "La définition du délit d'impiété d'apres la legislation attique", in *Museum Helveticum*, 1960, vol. 17, pp. 87–105: not believing in gods, teaching celestial phenomena, introducing new gods and committing ritual offences.

[69] Plato, *Symposion*, 188c ("ἀσέβεια φιλεῖ γίγνεσθαι [...] καὶ περὶ γονέας καὶ ζῶντας καὶ τετελευτηκότας καὶ περὶ θεούς"), and Plato, *Euthyphro*, 5c, 12e; Plato, *Cratylus*, 394e; Plato, *Republic*, 615c ('Republic'); Plato, *Laws*, 716d-718a, 907d-e. The Greek notion of *asebeia*, thus, goes beyond religion and refers to any behaviour which is open to criticism on ethical and religious grounds because it implies disrespect towards gods, the family or the community; see Delfim F. Leão, "Asebeia", in Roger S. Bagnall, Kai Brodersen, Craige B. Champion, Andrew Erskine and Sabine R. Huebner (eds.), *The Encyclopedia of Ancient History*, Wiley-Blackwell, Oxford, 2012, p. 815.

[70] For an overview, see Fritz Graf, "Der Mysterienprozess", in Leonhard Burckhardt and Jürgen von Ungern-Sternberg (eds.), *Prozesse im antiken Athen*, C.H. Beck, Munich, 2000, pp. 114–127. See also David M. Lewis, "After the Profanation of the Mysteries", in Ernst Badian (ed.), *Ancient Society and Institutions: Studies Presented to Victor Ehrenberg on His 75th Birthday*, Blackwell, Oxford, 1966, pp. 177–191.

[71] C.A. Powell, "Religion and the Sicilian Expedition", in *Historia*, 1979, vol. 28, pp. 15–31.

In 415 BCE, the orator Andocides was also denounced for having participated in the mutilation of the statues.[72] After his arrest, he obtained impunity by confessing his misdeeds and denouncing his accomplices. Authorized to return from exile in 403 BCE, thanks to the amnesty which followed the restoration of the overthrown democracy the year before, he was again involved in political participation; however, a few years later he was accused in court once more on the pretext that he had violated the decree. In his plea, the nexus between the use of *asebeia* and the democratic or oligarchic opposition is evident.[73] Politics and religion stand together in these proceedings. A speech falsely attributed to Lysias suggests the spiritual scope of the crime (*Against Andocides*, 6.19):

> ἐπεδείξατο δὲ καὶ τοῖς Ἕλλησιν ὅτι θεοὺς οὐ νομίζει. οὐ γὰρ ὡς δεδιὼς τὰ πεποιημένα, ἀλλ᾽ ὡς θαρρῶν, ναυκληρίᾳ ἐπιθέμενος τὴν θάλατταν ἔπλει. ὁ δὲ θεὸς ὑπῆγεν αὐτόν, ἵνα ἀφικόμενος εἰς τὰ ἁμαρτήματα ἐπὶ τῇ ἐμῇ προφάσει δοίη δίκην.
> He has made it plain to the Greeks at large that he does not revere the gods. For without a sign of misgiving for his actions, but with an air of assurance, he took to ship-owning, and went voyaging on the sea. But the deity was enticing him on, that he might return to his iniquities and pay the penalty at my instance.[74]

At the same time, the text recalls (6.11) the fact that Andocides himself had made a similar accusation of impiety (*dikē asebeias*) against an individual named Archippus. This interaction of crossed judicial attacks proves that the imputations were politically embedded.

Other interesting evidence of religious-flavoured prosecutions concerns playwrights, who had frequently been targets of indictments. In his comedy *Thesmophoriazusae*, for example, Aristophanes dealt widely with the scope of *asebeia* when pointing to the nature of those offenses for which Euripides was accused by women on stage (*Thesmophoriazusae*, 667–677):

> ἢν γὰρ ληφθῇ δράσας ἀνόσια,
> δώσει τε δίκην καὶ πρὸς τούτῳ
> τοῖς ἄλλοις ἀνδράσιν ἔσται
> παράδειγμ᾽ ὕβρεως ἀδίκων τ᾽ ἔργων
> ἀθέων τε τρόπων·
> φήσει δ᾽ εἶναί τε θεοὺς φανερῶς
> δείξει τ᾽ ἤδη

72 John L. Marr, "Andocides' Part in the Mysteries and Hermae Affairs 415 B.C.", in *Classical Quarterly*, 1971, vol. 21, no. 2, pp. 326–338.

73 Andocides, *On the Mysteries*, 1.36.

74 The Greek text and its translation correspond to Walter R.M. Lamb (ed.), *Lysias*, Harvard University Press, 1930.

πᾶσιν ἀνθρώποις σεβίζειν δαίμονας
δικαίως τ' ἐφέπειν ὅσια καὶ νόμιμα
μηδομένους ποιεῖν ὅ τι καλῶς ἔχει.
κἂν μὴ ποῶσι ταῦτα, τοιάδ' ἔσται·
αὐτῶν ὅταν ληφθῇ τις ὅσια <μὴ> δρῶν,
μανίαις φλέγων λύσσῃ παράκο-
    πος πᾶσιν ἐμφανὴς ὁρᾶν
ἔσται γυναιξὶ καὶ βροτοῖς
ὅτι τά παράνομα τά τ' ἀνόσια
θεὸς παραχρῆμ' ἀποτίνεται.[75]

> If we seize some impious fellow, woe to him! He will know how we punish the outrage, the crime, the sacrilege. The criminal will then acknowledge at last that gods exist; his fate will teach all men that the deities must be revered, that justice must be observed and that they must submit to the sacred laws. If not, then woe to them! If we seize some impious fellow, woe to him! Heaven itself will punish sacrilege; being aflame with fury and mad with frenzy, all their deeds will prove to mortals, both men and women, that the deity punishes injustice and impiety, and that she is not slow to strike.[76]

Aristophanes' verses are useful because the expressions used suggest a close relationship between civic injustice or outrages against men, on the one side, and offenses against the gods, on the other. This relationship is also present in other contemporary testimonies.[77] Additional references to *asebeia*-related trials against Euripides include Aristotle's mention of an accusation made by Hygienon (*Rhetoric*, III.15.8, 1416a28–35),[78] and Satyros' claim, in his *Life of Euripides*,[79] that the tragic poet was accused of *asebeia* by the demagogue Cleon.

[75] The Greek text corresponds to Colin Austin and S. Douglas Olson (eds.), *Aristophanes. Thesmophoriazusae*, Oxford University Press, 2004.

[76] The translation corresponds to Eugene O'Neill, *Aristophanes. Women at the Thesmophoria.* (The Complete Greek Drama), vol. 2, Random House, New York, 1938.

[77] On the close relationship between *asebeia* and *anomia*, see Isocrates, *Busiris*, 11.42; Xenophon, *Memorabilia*, 1.2.2; Euripides, *Bacchae*, 263, 387, 476, 502, 997, 1015; Xenophon, *Cyropaedia*, 8.8.7 ("τὴν ἐκείνων περὶ μὲν θεοὺς ἀσέβειαν, περὶ δὲ ἀνθρώπους ἀδικίαν"); Pseudo-Aristotle, *Virtues and Vices*, 1251a30 ("ἀδικίας δ' ἐστὶν εἴδη τριά, ἀσέβεια πλεονεξία ὕβρις").

[78] It concerns an action of *antidosis*, which is a property-related procedure in which, in fact, the religious aspect is not central.

[79] See Bruno Snell, Richard Kannicht and S.L. Radt, *Tragicorum Graecorum fragmenta*, Vandenhoeck & Ruprecht, Göttingen, 2004, T99.

In any case, the image of an impious Euripides was a *locus communis* in antiquity.[80]

A similar situation arises when adding to this study the alleged indictments against Aeschylus, since some sources indicate that he was accused of impiety for having violated the secret of the Mysteries of Demeter in one of his plays.[81] Finally, regarding Diagoras of Melos, a lyrical poet, Aristophanes indicates that, when he was sentenced to death – shortly before the performance of *Birds* in 414 BCE – he fled and a price was put on his head.[82]

Roman sources also dealt extensively with the idea of religious behaviour and its transgressions. Nevertheless, as opposed to the idea of *asebeia*, in both republican and imperial times, *impietas* – that is, the improper attitudes towards gods, parents and the community – was not considered to be a crime in itself.[83] For that reason, we lack information on the judicial context of religious prosecution before the expansion of the Roman Empire in late antiquity.

As it can been seen from the sources mentioned so far, we know that there were several cases in the Athenian context related to the idea of the prosecution of religious transgressions. This crime not only involved the performance of specific actions, but also covered opinions and verbal expressions. Two preliminary conclusions can be offered. Firstly, that the presence of these proceedings is indicative of the degree of religious intolerance among the Athenian citizens: the fact that prosecuting for *asebeia* seemed to be a frequent strategy shows that the jury was willing to endorse convictions on the basis of religious

80 See Mary R. Lefkowitz, "Was Euripides an Atheist?", in *Studi Italiani di Filologia Classica*, 1987, vol. 5, pp. 149–166, and Filonik, 2013, p. 51, see *supra* note 52.

81 Aristotle, *Nicomachean Ethics*, 3.1 (1111a8–10) ('Nicomachean Ethics'); see *Republic*, 563c, see *supra* note 69; Clement of Alexandria, *Stromateis*, 2.14; Aelian, *Varia Historia*, 5.19: ἀσέβεια. On these prosecutions, see Miryam L. Moreno, "El proceso por impiedad de Esquilo", in *Habis*, 2004, vol. 35, pp. 39–56.

82 Birds, 1072–1075, see *supra* note 60. See also Diodorus Siculus, *Library*, 13.6.7. A *scholium* to Aristophanes (*Scholium ad Aristophanis Aves*, v. 1073) mentions the existence of a decree and explains that Diagoras had been charged with impiety (around 416–415 BCE) for exposing the secret teachings of the Eleusinian Mysteries to the uninitiated. See Leonard Woodbury, "The Date and Atheism of Diagoras of Melos", in *Phoenix*, 1965, vol. 19, pp. 178–211, and Frank E. Romer, "Atheism, Impiety and the *Limos Mēlios* in Aristophanes' *Birds*", in *American Journal of Philology*, 1994, vol. 115, no. 3, pp. 351–365. Nevertheless, as is usually the case with late *scholia*, the information provided on the decree was probably an invention of Hellenistic and Roman biographers. This lack of precision in the information we count on is by no means surprising, taking into account what has been said so far.

83 Momigliano, 1978, p. 189, see *supra* note 48. On the "religious" nature of accusations of magic in Roman law, see James B. Rives, "Magic in Roman Law: The Reconstruction of a Crime", in *Classical Antiquity*, 2003, vol. 22, no. 2, pp. 313–339.

considerations.[84] The second conclusion is that in most cases, however, the charge of *asebeia* was invoked as a political strategy. In the social context of the *polis*, the bonds of religion were used in order to justify common values: since beliefs are part of the collective experience of a community, religious considerations become an effective means to consolidate a united dēmos.[85] By claiming that someone was against those shared values, it was possible to justify, in front of the jury, the exclusion of an outlaw.[86] An *asebēs*, therefore, could not be protected by the institutions of justice.[87]

14.4. The Rhetorical Construction of Enmity (ἔχθρα, *inimicitia*) and Hate (μῖσος, *odium*)

A question now arises: what is the relationship between those prosecutions and the emotional basis of religious intolerance? In ancient Athens the acknowledgment of enmity between individuals was generally avoided in the public arena. Forensic orators, for example, would embark in large discussions not to make the jury believe that personal animosity was the real motive behind the judicial action.[88] The explanation for this rejection is, to my mind, understandable in social and political terms. As explained in the previous section, in the context of a genre which is strongly committed to the unification of citizens as a cohesive group (so the speaker builds an idea of a 'we' to cover the whole *dēmos*

84 On the importance of these trials for *asebeia* to better understand religious (in)tolerance, see Ernst Sandvoss, "Asebie und Atheismus im klassischen Zeitalter der griechischen Polis", in *Saeculum*, 1968, vol. 19, pp. 312–319, Dover, 1976, see *supra* note 50; Momigliano, 1978, see *supra* note 48; Peter Garnsey, "Religious Toleration in Antiquity", in *Studies in Church History*, 1984, vol. 21, pp. 1–27.

85 Robin Osborne, "The Religious Contexts of Ancient Political Thought", in Ryan K. Balot (ed.), *A Companion to Greek and Roman Political Thought*, Blackwell, Oxford, 2009, pp. 118–30.

86 The strategic use to enforce religious conformity in Athens cannot be underestimated. In this sense, individual and collective behaviour was manipulated through an appeal to divine authority, as explained by Robert S. Garland, "Strategies of Religious Intimidation and Coercion in Classical Athens", in Pontus Hellström and Brita Alroth (eds.), *Religion and Power in the Ancient Greek World: Proceedings of the Uppsala Symposium 1993*, Ubsaliensis S. Academiae, Uppsala, 1996, pp. 91–99.

87 On the civic implications of these religious arguments, see Donald B. King, "The Appeal to Religion in Greek Rhetoric", in *Classical Journal*, 1955, vol. 50, pp. 363–371. The creation of an 'other' based on exclusions related to religion is a frequent landmark of intolerance and hate speech today. The contemporary use of the rhetoric of inclusion or exclusion – to which I will come back in the next section – has been explored by Damojipurapu in her discussion of Indian politics and society: Medha Damojipurapu, "Language, Themes and Responses to Hate Speech in India", Policy Brief Series No. 132 (2022), Torkel Opsahl Academic EPublisher, Brussels, 2022 (https://www.toaep.org/pbs-pdf/132-damojipurapu/).

88 Asako Kurihara, "Personal Enmity as a Motivation in Forensic Speeches", in *Classical Quarterly*, 2003, vol. 53, pp. 464–477, who offers a thorough revision of the available sources.

represented by the jury-members), the adversary needs to be depicted as a 'public' outsider who committed grave deeds against 'all of us' and not just the accuser.[89] Personal enmity could be seen as a manifestation of an isolated emotion that could put at risk the feeling of communal belonging.

The situation became also interesting when it involved interstate relations. In external affairs, the national 'we' of a specific *polis* required the construction of a foreign 'other' which could not be assimilated. There was a strong rhetorical intention to exclude the external adversary as an 'enemy' of the people. In fact, in the context of societies deeply pervaded by warfare, the identification of friends and enemies constituted an essential part of foreign relations. In classical civilizations, civic identity was determined by dynamic interactions of inclusion, which in many cases involved the consolidation of ethnic groups.[90] The enmity among Greeks and Romans was therefore the result of the logic of cohesion, insofar as the basic principle for the preservation of common value was the need to harm one's enemy in order to maintain honour.[91] Fighting, feuding and struggling to justify the full participation in the collective endeavour of the *dēmos* or the *res publica* was logical in the establishment of political rights. In order to endorse such rights, there was a strong rhetorical background in the creation of enmity.[92] In Greek, the 'enemy' was either designated as an *ekhthros* (the personal rival) or a *polemios* (the military foe).[93] The existence of two words to categorize the adversary shows a difference between an enmity related to an individual acknowledgment of the other and an antipathy expressed toward those who became dehumanized or assimilated to barbarians.

Back to the archaic period, in the case of the Trojan war, the *Iliad* offers an example of the ways in which enemies were perceived. When Agamemnon addressed his brother Menelaus and explained that the Trojans ought to be

89 This rhetorical strategy has been recently studied by Andreas Serafim, "'I, He, We, You, They': Addresses to the Audience as a Means of Unity/Division in Attic Forensic Oratory", in Andreas N. Michalopoulos, Andreas Serafim, Flaminia Beneventano della Corte and Alessandro Vatri (eds.), *The Rhetoric of Unity and Division in Ancient Literature*, De Gruyter, Berlin, 2021, pp. 71–98.

90 On the cultural and political role of ethnicity in Greek antiquity, for example, see the interesting study by Jonathan M. Hall, *Ethnic Identity in Greek Antiquity*, Cambridge University Press, 1997.

91 This ethical code of conduct was clearly staged (and sometimes subverted) in Athenian tragedy, as explained by Mary W. Blundell, *Helping Friends and Harming Enemies: A Study in Sophocles and Greek Ethics*, Cambridge University Press, 1989.

92 Andrew T. Alwine, *Enmity and Feuding in Classical Athens*, University of Texas Press, 2015, pp. 55–116, considers this rhetoric of enmity as a legal strategy.

93 David Konstan, "Anger, Hatred, and Genocide in Ancient Greece", in *Common Knowledge*, 2007, vol. 13, no. 1, pp. 182–183.

eliminated, there seems to be an implicit will to destroy the adversaries that could not be overcome (6.55–60):

> ὦ πέπον ὦ Μενέλαε, τί ἦ δὲ σὺ κήδεαι οὕτως
> ἀνδρῶν; ἦ σοὶ ἄριστα πεποίηται κατὰ οἶκον
> πρὸς Τρώων; τῶν μή τις ὑπεκφύγοι αἰπὺν ὄλεθρον
> χεῖράς θ' ἡμετέρας, μηδ' ὅν τινα γαστέρι μήτηρ
> κοῦρον ἐόντα φέροι, μηδ' ὃς φύγοι, ἀλλ' ἅμα πάντες
> Ἰλίου ἐξαπολοίατ' ἀκήδεστοι καὶ ἄφαντοι.[94]
>
> Soft-hearted Menelaus, why carest thou thus for the men? Hath then so great kindness been done thee in thy house by Trojans? Of them let not one escape sheer destruction and the might of our hands, nay, not the man-child whom his mother bears in her womb; let not even him escape, but let all perish together out of Ilios, unmourned and unmarked.[95]

But what is the origin of this longstanding animosity? The epic poem refers to the fact that Achaeans and Trojans had been close friends before they were parted: "αὖτ' ἐν φιλότητι διέτμαγεν ἀρθμήσαντε" (*Iliad*, 7.302). In this sense, the reason to eradicate all Trojans cannot be considered the result of a natural antagonism, since in the past both opponents had been close to each other. What was the emotional justification for hostilities, then?

In no verse of the *Iliad* is there reference to hate as the motive explaining the siege of Troy and the intention to destroy the local population. According to Konstan, "the inferiority of the Trojans is not invoked to justify the slaughter"; however, the idea of *ekhthros* is closely linked to hatred (*misos*, in Greek),[96] to the extent that on many occasions the noun *ekhthra* is related to a verb (*ekhthairein*) that joins the meaning of "hating" (*misein*).[97]

An allusion to the nature of hate as an emotion in ancient Greece could be useful here. It is clear that, in spite of the ambivalent meaning of the

---

[94] The Greek text corresponds to David B. Munro and Thomas W. Allen (eds.), *Homeri Opera*, vol. 1, Oxford University Press, 1920.

[95] Translation by Augustus T. Murray (ed.), *Homer. The Iliad*, vol. I–XII, Harvard University Press, 1924.

[96] David Konstan, "Hate and the State in Ancient Greece", in Thomas Brudholm and Birgitte S. Johansen (eds.), *Hate, Politics, Law: Critical Perspectives on Combating Hate*, Oxford University Press, 2018, p. 38. On this link, cf. Euripides, *Heracleidae*, 941–943.

[97] David Konstan, 2007, p. 182, see *supra* note 93; see also David Konstan, "La haine et l'inimitié: les deux pôles opposés de l'amitié", in Jocelyn Peigney (ed.), *Amis et ennemis en Grèce ancienne*, Editions Ausonius, Bordeaux, 2010, p. 220. According to Polybius, *Histories*, 1.14.4 ('Histories'), the enemies of one's friends should be hated (συμμισεῖν τοῖς φίλοις τοὺς ἐχθρούς). On this opposition between friends and enemies in classical Athens, see Blundell, 1989, *supra* note 91.

vocabulary related to hate in classical literature,[98] the presence of *misos* was linked to a state of animosity or antagonism.[99] There was no need for a personal attack for hatred to be born.[100] The importance of this *pathos* is well acknowledged, for example, in Thucydides' report of the Peloponnesian War.[101] According to the historian, the Corinthians "hated" the Corcyraeans because they did not respect their metropolis (*History of the Peloponnesian War*, 1.25.3): ἅμα δὲ καὶ μίσει τῶν Κερκυραίων, ὅτι αὐτῶν παρημέλουν ὄντες ἄποικοι ("they hated the Corcyraeans for their contempt of the mother country").[102] Similarly, the Plataeans were accused by the Thebans because they had opposed them out of "hate" and not for reasons related to justice (3.67.5):

> καὶ τὴν νῦν ἐρημίαν δι' ἑαυτοὺς ἔχουσιν· τοὺς γὰρ ἀμείνους ξυμμάχους ἑκόντες ἀπεώσαντο. παρενόμησάν τε οὐ προπαθόντες ὑφ' ἡμῶν, μίσει δὲ πλέον ἢ δίκῃ κρίναντες καὶ οὐκ ἀνταποδόντες νῦν τὴν ἴσην τιμωρίαν· ἔννομα γὰρ πείσονται καὶ οὐχὶ ἐκ μάχης χεῖρας προϊσχόμενοι, ὥσπερ φασίν, ἀλλ' ἀπὸ ξυμβάσεως ἐς δίκην σφᾶς αὐτοὺς παραδόντες.
>
> For their present desolate condition, they have themselves to blame, since they wilfully rejected the better alliance. Their lawless act was not provoked by any action of ours; hate, not justice, inspired their decision; and even now the satisfaction which they afford us is not adequate; they will suffer by a legal sentence, not as they pretend as suppliants asking for quarter in battle, but as prisoners who have surrendered upon agreement to take their trial.

Hate in Greek texts frequently appears in contexts where groups were despised. Such is the case of traitors, who are hated by Prometheus in Aeschylus' *Prometheus Bound* (1068). Arrogant men are also hated by Pindar in *Pythian* (4.284–286). In Euripides' *Hippolytus* (313–314), Phaedra concedes that she

[98] As recently stated by Philip Aubreville, *Der Hass im antiken Rom. Studien zur Emotionalität in der späten Republik und frühen Kaiserzeit* (Historia Einzelschriften 266), Franz Steine, Stuttgart, 2021, pp. 87–106.

[99] Konstan, 2007, p. 182, see *supra* note 93.

[100] "Hatred (*misos*), which for our purposes will include milder forms such as general hostility or dislike, is an easier emotion to arouse than anger, because no personal injury need be proved" (Ed Sanders, "'He Is a Liar, a Bounder, and a Cad': The Arousal of Hostile Emotions in Attic Forensic Oratory", in Angelos Chaniotis (ed.), *Unveiling Emotions. Sources and Methods for the Study of Emotions in the Greek World*, Franz Steiner, Stuttgart, 2012, p. 369). We will discuss the relationship between hate and anger in the next section of this chapter.

[101] Konstan, 2018, pp. 40–41, see *supra* note 96.

[102] Both the Greek text and the translation, here and elsewhere in this chapter, correspond to Richard Crawley (ed.), *Thucydides. The Peloponnesian War*, J.M. Dent, E.P. Dutton, London, 1910.

hates women who are chaste in words but secretly engage in ugly escapades, and Hippolytus admits hating all women (*Hippolytus*, 664–665).[103]

In Rome, enmity was described as *inimicitia* when the opposing political factions in the Republic were presented as expressions of group antitheses – especially concerning powerful figures as Pompey and Caesar. This enmity is connected here to hatred,[104] and the rhetorical use of hate (*odium*) in military contexts is well-attested.[105] Just like the *ekhthros*, an *inimicus* was constructed as an individual perceived in clear contradiction with the social relationship of friendship (*amicitia*).[106] In Latin, *odium* is conceived as an emotion strongly rooted in an irrepressible aversion felt towards someone or something.[107] In close connection with *odium*, *invidia* is used to describe the feeling of a person who envies another one as a result of his social superiority (*gloria*) or power (*potentia*).[108]

We have briefly discussed the surprising absence of hate in the pre-classic testimony of the *Iliad*, but a larger question needs to be asked. Was hate present, in classical times, as the justification of hostile speech against enemies? When explaining the Roman attitude towards Carthage at the end of the Second Punic War in 202 BC, Polybius (*Histories*, 15.4.2) described Scipio's reaction in order

103 Women are also hated in Aeschylus, *Seven Against Thebes*, 186.

104 In mediaeval times, *inimicitia* can be translated as "hatred", as explained in Daniel L. Smail, "Hatred as a Social Institution in Late-Medieval Society", in *Speculum*, 2001, vol. 76, no. 1, p. 90.

105 Aubreville, 2021, p. 114, see *supra* note 98.

106 On *amicitia* in civic and political terms, see Joseph Hellegouarc'h, *Le vocabulaire latin des relations et des partis politiques sous la République,* Les Belles Lettres, Paris, 1972, pp. 41–90. Paul-Marius Martin, "Un exemple parfait de haine politique : Cicéron et Antoine", in Marc Deleplace (ed.), *Les discours de la haine: Récits et figures de la passion dans la Cité*, Presses universitaires du Septentrion, Villeneuve d'Ascq, 2009, p. 49, explains that "[e]st *inimicus* celui avec lequel, qu'on ait ou – plus rarement – qu'on n'ait pas entretenu antérieurement avec lui des relations d'*amicitia*, on a des différends, de quelque ordre qu'ils soient, mais souvent politiques".

107 Hellegouarc'h, 1972, p. 191, see *supra* note 106.

108 Alfred Ernout and Antoine Meillet, *Dictionnaire étymologique de la langue latine. Histoire des mots*, Klincksieck, Paris, 1967, s.v. *invidia*; Hellegouarc'h, 1972, p. 195, see *supra* note 106. In its relationship to *odium*, *invidia* can be translated as "ill will" (and not as jealousy); see Cicero, *De Oratore*, 1.228: "*invidia et odio populi*", and Quintilian, *Institutio oratoria*, 6.2.16. Arina Bragova, "Cicero on *Odium*", in *Studia Antiqua et Archaeologica*, 2020, vol. 26, no. 2, pp. 213–229, has examined Cicero's use of the concept of *odium* as a negative emotion related to crimes (*scelera*) and wars (*bella*) and to the presence of vices (such as *libido* and *crudelitas*). In another contribution she discusses *invidia* in the same corpus, showing to what extent it is combined with the idea of hatred or envy, in opposition to positive *gloria*; see Arina Bragova, "Concept of 'Invidia' in Cicero's Writings", in *Scientific Research and Development Socio-Humanitarian Research and Technology*, 2017, vol. 6, no. 2, pp. 82–84.

to motivate his revulsion against the Carthaginians: instead of showing 'hate', he expressed a feeling of "anger" as a result of the fact that they had behaved treacherously:[109]

> οὐκέτι παραλαμβάνων εἰς τὴν πίστιν τοὺς ἐθελοντὴν σφᾶς αὐτοὺς ἐγχειρίζοντας, ἀλλὰ μετὰ βίας ἀνδραποδιζόμενος καὶ φανερὰν ποιῶν τὴν ὀργήν, ἣν εἶχε πρὸς τοὺς πολεμίους διὰ τὴν Καρχηδονίων παρασπόνδησιν·[110]
>
> This time he did not admit to mercy those who voluntarily surrendered, but carried all the towns by force, and enslaved the inhabitants, to show his anger (*orgē*) at the treachery of the Carthaginians.[111]

It seems clear that, when justifying actions, anger is a forward-looking and action-oriented emotion that became ideal to explain the desire related to the annihilation of the enemy.[112] In terms of emotional impulse, anger ends up being "a better candidate for the passion that moved people to massacre in classical Greece".[113] A similar conclusion can be reached when assessing Roman sources. Why is this and what can it tell us about our concept of hate speech today?

14.5. *Delendum esse*: The Rhetoric of Anger (ὄργή, *ira*) as a Justification for Harming the Enemy

In classical Greece anger or *orgē* was an emotion directly linked to the democratic exercise of citizen power, as it implied a common affection that could be

[109] On this passage, see David Konstan, "Mass Exterminations and the History of Emotions: The View from Classical Antiquity", in Thomas Brudholm and Johannes Lang (eds.), *Emotions and Mass Atrocity: Philosophical and Theoretical Explorations*, Cambridge University Press, 2018, pp. 31–32.

[110] The Greek text corresponds to Theodor Büttner-Wobst (ed.), *Polybius. Historiae*, Teubner, Leipzig, 1893.

[111] Translated by Evelyn S. Shuckburgh (ed.), *Polybius. Histories*, Macmillan, London, 1889. Regina M. Loehr, "Emotions in Polybius' Histories", Ph.D. dissertation, University of California, Santa Barbara, 2017, p. 99, offers an insightful statistical study of emotions such as anger, indignation, and hate in Histories, see *supra* note 97. Unfortunately, she does not draw a distinction between them in the corpus under study. More specifically on the importance of Roman anger in the text, see Andrew Erskine, "Polybius and the Anger of the Romans", in Douglas Cairns and Laurel Fulkerson (eds.), *Emotions Between Greece and Rome*, Institute of Classical Studies, University of London, 2015, pp. 105–127.

[112] Loehr, 2017, p. 140, see *supra* note 111, who also mentions Polybius' passages in 25.25.23, 15.25.28, 15.27.1 and 15.30.1 (Histories, see *supra* note 97).

[113] Konstan, 2007, p. 184, see *supra* note 93.

triggered in defence of political institutions.[114] The mention of anger in classical sources describing the functioning of the Athenian courts is not surprising.[115] Indeed, if the administration of the judicial system dealt with the punishment of that behaviour affecting the community and with the restoration of social bonds, then it follows that prosecutors would carry their cases before the courts by appealing to the jurors' indignation and collective anger.[116]

According to Aristotle (*Rhetoric*, II.2.1, 1378a–30–32):

> ἔστω δὴ ὀργὴ ὄρεξις μετὰ λύπης τιμωρίας φαινομένης διὰ φαινομένην ὀλιγωρίαν εἰς αὐτὸν ἤ τι τῶν αὐτοῦ, τοῦ ὀλιγωρεῖν μὴ προσήκοντος.
>
> Anger (*orgē*) is a longing, accompanied by pain, for a real or apparent revenge due to a real or apparent insult affecting a man or one of his friends, when such an insult is undeserved.[117]

---

114 On Greek anger, see Danielle Allen, *The World of Prometheus: The Politics of Punishing in Democratic Athens*, Princeton University Press, 2000; William V. Harris, *Restraining Rage. The Ideology of Anger Control in Classical Antiquity*, Harvard University Press, 2001; Susanna M. Braund and Glenn W. Most (eds.), *Ancient Anger. Perspectives from Homer to Galen*, Cambridge University Press, 2003; Kostas Kalimtzis, *Taming Anger: The Hellenic Approach to the Limitations of Reason*, Bristol Classical Press, Bristol, 2012. Its close relationship with democratic values has been highlighted by David Konstan, *The Emotions of the Ancient Greeks. Studies in Aristotle and Classical Literature*, University of Toronto Press, 2006, pp. 75–76.

115 See also the specific contributions of Danielle Allen, "Angry Bees, Wasps and Jurors: The Symbolic Politics of *orgê* in Athens", in Braund and Most, 2003, pp. 76–98, see *supra* note 114; Lene Rubinstein, "Stirring Up Dicastic Anger", in Douglas Cairns and Ronald A. Knox (eds.), *Law, Rhetoric, and Comedy in Classical Athens. Essays in Honour of Douglas M. MacDowell*, The Classical Press of Wales, Swansea, 2004, pp. 187–204; Lene Rubinstein, "Evoking Anger Through Pity: Portraits of the Vulnerable and Defenceless in Attic Oratory", in Angelos Chaniotis and Pierre Ducrey (eds.), *Unveiling Emotions II. Emotions in Greece and Rome: Images, Material Culture*, Franz Steiner, Stuttgart, 2013, pp. 135–165; Évelyne Scheid-Tissinier, "Le rôle de la colère dans les tribunaux athéniens", in Pauline S. Pantel and François de Polignac (eds.), *Athènes et le politique. Dans le sillage de Claude Mossé*, Albin Michel, Paris, 2007, pp. 179–198. I have offered a view of the subversion of the judicial normativity of anger in Old Comedy in Emiliano J. Buis, "Comic *Pathos* and the Legal Emotional Community: Destabilizing Judicial Pity and Anger in Aristophanes", in Viktoria Räuchle, Sven Page and Vibeke Goldbeck (eds.), *Pathos und Polis. Einsatz und Wirkung affektiver Elemente in der griechischen Welt*, Mohr Siebeck, Tübingen, 2022, pp. 194–199.

116 Allen, 2000, p. 50, see *supra* note 114, shows the importance of anger as an ethical basis for the construction of citizen ideology.

117 The Greek edition, here and elsewhere, corresponds to William D. Ross (ed.), *Aristotle. Ars Rhetorica*, Oxford University Press, 1959. The translation of the text, here and in the rest of the passages quoted, belongs to John H. Freese (ed.), *Aristotle*, vol. 22, Harvard University Press, 1926.

The Aristotelian view in the *Rhetoric* was that it is only possible to be angry at particular individuals:[118] *orgē* entailed certain pleasure, he affirmed, since it was gratifying to imagine inflicting a penalty on a person who deserved it. Its relationship with revenge has led some scholars to consider that anger in Athens was an emotion closely related to the democratic body, a collective emotion that could be unleashed when citizens were called to defend the *polis* and its institutions.[119] This was achieved by retaliating against a specific individual who had acted unjustly against him or her.[120]

The status of public anger was in fact ambiguous.[121] Even if self-restraint was much valued, in some cases inflaming anger was thoroughly accepted. In fact, anger was a manly emotion, one that "buttresses martial valor"[122] and that could be justified when speaking about the need to punish grave crimes. Anger represented an efficient tool to create, according to Harris,[123] a common emotion set in place to exclude the outlaw from the *polis*. This feature explains the frequent references to the verb *orgizein* in forensic oratory. In his *Against Lochites*, for instance, Isocrates (20.6) states that, after an act of *adikia*, free men needed to become angry and exact revenge. Similarly, if an injustice was committed on

[118] It should be noted that in Aristotle, *De Anima*, 403a26-27, Aristotle provided a different notion of anger (as a particular sort of motion with a cause and for the sake of a certain end) that seemed to be completely independent of the opponent's identity.

[119] According to Giulia Sissa, "De l'animal politique à la nature humaine : Aristote et Hobbes sur la colère", in *Anthropologie et Sociétés*, 2008, vol. 32, no. 3, p. 22, *orgē* is a political, social, and narrative passion. In its political sense,

> il y a davantage de valeur politique dans la colère : c'est une émotion généreuse. C'est parce que vous vous respectez vous-même que vous enregistrez le mépris : c'est donc d'abord une défense fondamentalement égoïste. Mais vous vous emportez aussi au nom de quelqu'un d'autre, si quelqu'un offense votre enfant ou vos parents ou votre femme ou vos amis, par exemple. La rage est la passion qui vous pousse à prendre les armes pour vos alliés, pour votre cité. Vous vous battez à la fois pour vous-même et pour vos proches. Le potentiel de la colère est aussi celui de la solidarité, ou de la démarcation entre les amis et les ennemis de l'intérieur et de l'extérieur. L'art de se fâcher définit un cercle : la communauté des gens qui sont vos proches, par rapport à ceux qui ne le sont pas.

[120] "Anger (*orgē*) is […] a difficult emotion for a speaker to arouse, because it is felt primarily in response to a personal slight" (Sanders, 2012, p. 364, see *supra* note 100).

[121] Harris, 2001, pp. 183–187, see *supra* note 114; Victor Bers, "Appeals to Pity and Displays of Anger", in Genos Dikanikon, *Amateur and Professional Speech in the Courtroom of Classical Athens*, Center for Hellenic Studies, Washington, D.C., 2009, pp. 93–94.

[122] *Ibid.*, p. 97. According to Maurice Sartre, "Les Grecs", in Georges Vigarello (ed.), *Histoire des émotions, vol. 1, De l'Antiquité aux Lumières*, Éditions du Seuil, Paris, 2016, p. 24: "le mâle, le puissant, seul est susceptible de colère, selon un schéma que l'on qualifierait volontiers de machiste".

[123] Harris, 2001, p. 189, see *supra* note 114.

purpose, Demosthenes explained that anger and punishment (*timōria*) should go hand in hand (*On the Crown*, 18.274).[124]

The Latin language seems somehow poorer than ancient Greek vocabulary when referring to anger.[125] *Ira* or *iracundia* are perhaps the most frequent words covering that semantic field and can be easily translated as 'anger', 'rage' or 'indignation'; the nouns *furor* or *indignatio* can also be used in the context of describing the violent reaction of hostility.[126] In general, this collective public anger was aroused by a sense of wrongness, so the notion – as it happens with *orgē* – was related to a shared resentment in front of offenses that had been committed. Thus, contrary to Seneca's negative interpretation of *ira* as a chaotic emotion in *De ira*, Latin epic confirms that anger in times of armed conflicts could inspire soldiers in battle and lead to positive results.[127]

Out of the context of war, for instance, in *De domo sua* (88), Cicero placed *iracundia* next to *invidia* with an evident political tone: *"Ac si me populus Romanus, incitatus iracundia aut invidia, e civitate eiecisset"* ("And if the Roman people had cast me out of the city stirred up by anger or indignation").[128] In these contexts, *invidia* can be distinguished from "hate" and becomes closer to the idea of a righteous "anger", as explained by Kaster.[129] Under the term *invidia*, degrees or levels of resentment at another's advantage could be found: from personal envy to indignation, something which the Roman orators were well aware of in their speeches.[130]

---

124 Judicial anger was sometimes encouraged; see also Isocrates, *Against Callimachus*, 18.4; Demosthenes, *Third Philippic*, 9.31, 18.61; Demosthenes, *On the Crown*, 18.18, 18.138; Demosthenes, *On the False Embassy*, 19.7, 19.265, 19.302; Demosthenes, *Against Midias*, 21.57, 21.123; Demosthenes, *Against Conon*, 54.42; Demosthenes, *Against Stephanus 1*, 45.7; Dinarchus, *Against Demosthenes*, 1.2. Of course, manipulating the emotions of the jurors by getting them angry could be risky, as indicated by Rubinstein, 2004, see *supra* note 115.

125 Jayne E. Knight, "The Politics of Anger in Roman Society: A Study of Orators and Emperors, 70 BCE-68 CE", Ph.D. dissertation, University of British Columbia, Vancouver, 2015, p. 26.

126 *Ibid.*, p. 27.

127 On the constructive value of *ira* in Silius Italicus' *Punica*, see Claire Stocks, "Anger in the Extreme? *Ira,* Excess, and the *Punica", in Phoenix*, 2018, vol. 72, no. 3/4, pp. 293–311.

128 The Latin text corresponds to Albertus C. Clark (ed.), *M. Tulli Ciceronis Orationes*, Clarendon Press, Oxford, 1909.

129 In fact, Robert A. Kaster, *Emotion, Restraint, and Community in Ancient Rome*, Oxford University Press, 2005, p. 85, draws attention to the entry in the *Oxford Latin Dictionary*, according to which there seems to be an implied distinction between "active" *invidia* (ill will, spite, indignation, jealousy, envy) that we feel toward some person or state of affairs – and "passive" *invidia* (assimilated to *odium* or 'dislike') directed against us.

130 Robert A. Kaster, "Invidia, νέμεσις, φθόνος, and the Ancient Roman Economy", in David Konstan and N. Keith Rutter (eds.), *Envy, Spite and Rivalrous Emotions in Ancient Greece*, Edinburgh University Press, 2003, pp. 253–276. On the importance of personal enmity as an

But how did the ancient Athenians and Romans imagine the difference between our modern notions of 'hatred' and 'anger'? In the case of the Greek sources, the insistence on anger as an alternative to the manifestation of hatred can be better understood if another passage of Aristotle's *Rhetoric* is quoted. When explaining the importance of *pathē* in the technical construction of persuasive argument, Aristotle casts some light on the relevant terminology and endorses anger (*orgē*) as a cause for enmity (*Rhetoric*, 2.4.30–31, 1382a1–14):

> περὶ δ᾽ ἔχθρας καὶ τοῦ μισεῖν φανερὸν ὡς ἐκ τῶν ἐναντίων ἔστι θεωρεῖν. ποιητικὰ δὲ ἔχθρας ὀργή, ἐπηρεασμός, διαβολή. ὀργὴ μὲν οὖν ἐστιν ἐκ τῶν πρὸς αὐτόν, ἔχθρα δὲ καὶ ἄνευ τοῦ πρὸς αὐτόν· ἂν γὰρ ὑπολαμβάνωμεν εἶναι τοιόνδε, μισοῦμεν. καὶ ἡ μὲν ὀργὴ ἀεὶ περὶ τὰ καθ᾽ ἕκαστα, οἷον Καλλίᾳ ἢ Σωκράτει, τὸ δὲ μῖσος καὶ πρὸς τὰ γένη· τὸν γὰρ κλέπτην μισεῖ καὶ τὸν συκοφάντην ἅπας. καὶ τὸ μὲν ἰατὸν χρόνῳ, τὸ δ᾽ ἀνίατον. καὶ τὸ μὲν λύπης ἔφεσις, τὸ δὲ κακοῦ· αἴσθεσθαι γὰρ βούλεται ὁ ὀργιζόμενος, τῷ δ᾽ οὐδὲν διαφέρει. ἔστι δὲ τὰ μὲν λυπηρὰ αἰσθητὰ πάντα, τὰ δὲ μάλιστα κακὰ ἥκιστα αἰσθητά, ἀδικία καὶ ἀφροσύνη· οὐδὲν γὰρ λυπεῖ ἡ παρουσία τῆς κακίας. καὶ τὸ μὲν μετὰ λύπης, τὸ δ᾽ οὐ μετὰ λύπης· ὁ μὲν γὰρ ὀργιζόμενος λυπεῖται, ὁ δὲ μισῶν οὔ. καὶ ὁ μὲν πολλῶν ἂν γενομένων ἐλεήσειεν, ὁ δ᾽ οὐδενός· ὁ μὲν γὰρ ἀντιπαθεῖν βούλεται ᾧ ὀργίζεται, ὁ δὲ μὴ εἶναι.
>
> As for enmity and hatred, it is evident that they must be examined in the light of their contraries. The causes which produce enmity are anger, spitefulness, slander. Anger arises from acts committed against us, enmity even from those that are not; for if we imagine a man to be of such and such a character, we hate him. Anger has always an individual as its object, for instance Callias or Socrates, whereas hatred applies to classes; for instance, everyone hates a thief or informer. Anger is curable by time, hatred not; the aim of anger is pain, of hatred evil; for the angry man wishes to see what happens; to one who hates it does not matter. Now, the things which cause pain are all perceptible, while things which are especially bad, such as injustice or folly, are least perceptible; for the presence of vice causes no pain. Anger is accompanied by pain, but hatred not; for he who is angry suffers pain, but he who hates does not. One who is angry might feel compassion in many cases, but one who hates, never; for the former wishes that the object of his anger should suffer in his turn, the latter, that he should perish.

---

explanation to many public trials at court during the Roman Republic, see David F. Epstein, *Personal Enmity in Roman Politics, 218-43 BC*, Croom Helm, London, 1987.

In terms which are not very different to its modern conception, Aristotle's passage indicates that hatred (*to misein*) constitutes a permanent emotion which is addressed to general actions performed by individuals who possess some noticeable characteristics as part of a class identified by shared moral vices. Whereas hatred is the contrary of friendship (*philia*) and remains a stable moral emotion (generated by the perception of fault),[131] anger is provoked when we suffer an act of injustice;[132] *orgē* is thus focused exclusively on the person who caused *adikia*.

In Rome, different types of anger can be found in opposition to hatred. The concepts of *ira*, *excandescentia*, *odium*, *inimicitia* and *discordia* are clearly distinguished by Cicero in the following terms (*Tusculanae Disputationes*, 4.21):

> *ut ira sit libido poeniendi eius qui videatur laesisse iniuria, excandescentia autem sit ira nascens et modo existens quae θύμωσις Graece dicitur, odium ira inveterata, inimicitia ira ulciscendi tempus observans, discordia ira acerbior intimo animo et corde concepta.*
>
> Anger is a desire to punish a person who is thought to have harmed one unjustly. Heatedness is anger at its inception, when it has just come to be, what Greeks call *thymosis*; hatred is old anger. Enmity is anger biding its time for revenge. Soreness of heart is a more bitter anger which has its birth in the depths of mind and heart.[133]

Just as it happens with the Greek antithesis between *misos* and *orgē*, the opposition here responds to the persistence of the former emotion (*odium*) and the immediacy of the latter (*ira*).[134] In addition, *ira* is here again the result of a previous unjust action. In spite of these differences, Latin sources show that there was a firm interdependence between anger and hatred. For example, Livy draws a regular connection between both concepts in political terms: *timor atque ira* (*The History of Rome*, 2.57) and *metus odiumque* (*The History of Rome*, 33.16), and frequently makes reference to *odio iraque*.[135] The expression "*recens ira ... vetus odium*" ("recent anger ... aged hatred") is common throughout

131 Konstan, 2018, p. 39, see *supra* note 96.

132 See also a similar idea in *Nicomachean Ethics*, 5.8, 1135b25–29, *supra* note 81.

133 The Latin text corresponds to the edition by Max Pohlenz (ed.), *M. Tullius Cicero. Tusculanae Disputationes*, Teubner, Leipzig, 1918. See also Knight, 2015, p. 28, see *supra* note 125.

134 Titus Livius (Livy), *The History of Rome*, 2.35.6; Seneca, *De Ira*, 3.41.

135 *Ibid.*, 1.54.7, 2.6.1, 2.22.4, 3.2.11, 5.1.1 and 5.27.10. Henry S. Blume, "Fear, Anger, and Hatred in Livy's Account of the Struggle of the Orders", Ph.D. dissertation, Ohio State University, Columbus, 2017, pp. 4–5, concluded that "whatever connection we, in the modern world, ascribe to anger and hatred, it was far more pronounced in the Roman world".

Livy's text and demonstrates the temporal dimension involved in the difference between both emotional states.[136]

The texts concerning the justification of armed attacks in Greece and Rome tend to avoid referring to a state of hatred toward the adversary and focus primarily on the necessity of the aggression after a previous illegal assault or incitement.[137] As a result, and taking into consideration Thucydides' insistence in preserving honour and prestige as a valid motive for action,[138] we find *orgē* as an emotional driver to endorse the persecution of others.

In the initial debate over Epidamnus, for example, it becomes clear that Corinth was angry with Corcyra because of the identification of their attitude as a transgression deserving punishment.[139] In *The Peloponnesian War* (1.40.3), they criticized Athenian neutrality as an implicit support of the Corcyreans, claiming:

> οὐ γὰρ τοῖσδε μόνον ἐπίκουροι ἂν γένοισθε, ἀλλὰ καὶ ἡμῖν ἀντὶ ἐνσπόνδων πολέμιοι· ἀνάγκη γάρ, εἰ ἴτε μετ' αὐτῶν, καὶ ἀμύνεσθαι μὴ ἄνευ ὑμῶν τούτους.
>
> For you cannot become their auxiliary and remain our friend; if you join in their attack, you must share the punishment which the defenders inflict on them.

In the episode of Plataea, in turn, hatred was hidden behind an official discourse built over anger. When Archidamus addressed the Lacedemonians and their allies, he mentioned the hatred against the Athenians (*The Peloponnesian War*, 2.11.2):

> δίκαιον οὖν ἡμᾶς μήτε τῶν πατέρων χείρους φαίνεσθαι μήτε ἡμῶν αὐτῶν τῆς δόξης ἐνδεεστέρους. ἡ γὰρ Ἑλλὰς πᾶσα τῇδε τῇ ὁρμῇ ἐπῆρται καὶ προσέχει τὴν γνώμην, εὔνοιαν ἔχουσα διὰ τὸ Ἀθηναίων ἔχθος πρᾶξαι ἡμᾶς ἃ ἐπινοοῦμεν.
>
> We ought not then to show ourselves inferior to our ancestors, or unequal to our own reputation. For the hopes and attention of all Hellas are bent upon the present effort, and its sympathy is with the enemy of the hated Athens.

Nevertheless, the Spartan leader would add shortly afterwards that the Athenians, even though they were well prepared, would only be expected to

---

136 *Ibid.*, 2.35.7; 2.35.8; 42.29.

137 "The evil character of the population was not typically invoked to justify enslavement. Self-interest and the right of the victor sufficed"; Konstan, 2007, p. 186, see *supra* note 93.

138 Aleksander Chance, "Motives Beyond Fear: Thucydides on Honor, Vengeance, and Liberty", Ph.D. dissertation, Boston College, The Graduate School of Arts and Sciences, Department of Political Science, 2012, pp. 82–87.

139 *Ibid.*, p. 99.

react and fight back in *anger* only after experiencing the consequences of destruction on their own soil (*The Peloponnesian War*, 2.11.6–7):

> ἡμεῖς δὲ οὐδ᾽ ἐπὶ ἀδύνατον ἀμύνεσθαι οὕτω πόλιν ἐρχόμεθα, ἀλλὰ τοῖς πᾶσιν ἄριστα παρεσκευασμένην, ὥστε χρὴ καὶ πάνυ ἐλπίζειν διὰ μάχης ἰέναι αὐτούς, εἰ μὴ καὶ νῦν ὥρμηνται ἐν ᾧ οὔπω πάρεσμεν, ἀλλ᾽ ὅταν ἐν τῇ γῇ ὁρῶσιν ἡμᾶς δῃοῦντάς τε καὶ τἀκείνων φθείροντας. πᾶσι γὰρ ἐν τοῖς ὄμμασι καὶ ἐν τῷ παραυτίκα ὁρᾶν πάσχοντάς τι ἄηθες ὀργὴ προσπίπτει· καὶ οἱ λογισμῷ ἐλάχιστα χρώμενοι θυμῷ πλεῖστα ἐς ἔργον καθίστανται.
>
> In the present instance, the city against which we are going, far from being so impotent for defence, is on the contrary most excellently equipped at all points; so that we have every reason to expect that they will take the field against us, and that if they have not set out already before we are there, they will certainly do so when they see us in their territory wasting and destroying their property. For men are always exasperated (*orgê*) at suffering injuries to which they are not accustomed, and on seeing them inflicted before their very eyes; and where least inclined for reflection, rush with the greatest heat (*thymōi*) to action.

Similarly, in *The Peloponnesian War*, 2.8.5, Thucydides had also spoken of *orgē* (and not of *misos*) to identify the Spartan feeling towards the enemy: "οὕτως <ἐν> ὀργῇ εἶχον οἱ πλείους τοὺς Ἀθηναίους, οἱ μὲν τῆς ἀρχῆς ἀπολυθῆναι βουλόμενοι, οἱ δὲ μὴ ἀρχθῶσι φοβούμενοι" ("So general was the indignation (*orgē*) felt against Athens, whether by those who wished to escape from her empire, or were apprehensive of being absorbed by it").

Thucydides ascribed genocidal violence to anger.[140] When the Athenians voted angrily to exterminate men and enslave women and children in Mytilene after its revolt, a reference was made again to wrath (*The Peloponnesian War*, 3.36.2) in these terms:

> περὶ δὲ τῶν ἀνδρῶν γνώμας ἐποιοῦντο, καὶ ὑπὸ ὀργῆς ἔδοξεν αὐτοῖς οὐ τοὺς παρόντας μόνον ἀποκτεῖναι, ἀλλὰ καὶ τοὺς ἅπαντας Μυτιληναίους ὅσοι ἡβῶσι, παῖδας δὲ καὶ γυναῖκας ἀνδραποδίσαι, ἐπικαλοῦντες τήν τε ἄλλην ἀπόστασιν ὅτι οὐκ ἀρχόμενοι ὥσπερ οἱ ἄλλοι ἐποιήσαντο, καὶ προσξυνελάβοντο οὐκ ἐλάχιστον τῆς ὁρμῆς αἱ Πελοποννησίων νῆες ἐς Ἰωνίαν ἐκείνοις βοηθοὶ τολμήσασαι παρακινδυνεῦσαι· οὐ γὰρ ἀπὸ βραχείας διανοίας ἐδόκουν τὴν ἀπόστασιν ποιήσασθαι.
>
> [...] and after deliberating as to what they should do with the former, in the fury [*orgē*] of the moment determined to put to death not only the prisoners at Athens, but the whole adult male

---

[140] Konstan, 2007, p. 184, see *supra* note 93.

> population of Mytilene, and to make slaves of the women and children. It was remarked that Mytilene had revolted without being, like the rest, subjected to the empire; and what above all swelled the wrath of the Athenians was the fact of the Peloponnesian fleet having ventured over to Ionia to her support, a fact which was held to argue a long-meditated rebellion.[141]

Only time managed to reduce that anger, to the extent that the following day the Athenians voted to reconsider their decision and only punish those who were deemed responsible (*The Peloponnesian War*, 3.36.4).[142] There was no argument to justify 'hating' all the Mytilenians, but only acting in response to the political uprising.

Other passages can be added to confirm this interpretation. In the episode of the Melian dialogue, for instance, the Athenian envoys looked insulted by the Melians' denseness when their persuasion failed (*The Peloponnesian War*, 5.105.3).[143] They pitied their wilful folly, but their perverse attitude did not merit any anger (*The Peloponnesian War*, 5.111.3).[144]

What is interesting in all these texts is that anger served to justify a violent attitude rooted on previous irresponsible acts. In this sense, the emotion came close with the concept of *hybris*. In his *Rhetoric* (2.2.5, 1378b), Aristotle explained the nature of this notion as an insult that, based upon a sense of superiority, generated injury to someone considered to be inferior, and thus deserved a rightful punishment:

> ἔστι γὰρ ὕβρις τὸ πράττειν καὶ λέγειν ἐφ' οἷς αἰσχύνη ἔστι τῷ πάσχοντι, μὴ ἵνα τι γίγνηται αὑτῷ ἄλλο ἢ ὅ τι ἐγένετο, ἀλλ' ὅπως ἡσθῇ· οἱ γὰρ ἀντιποιοῦντες οὐχ ὑβρίζουσιν ἀλλὰ τιμωροῦνται. Αἴτιον δὲ τῆς ἡδονῆς τοῖς ὑβρίζουσιν, ὅτι οἴονται κακῶς δρῶντες αὐτοὶ ὑπερέχειν μᾶλλον (διὸ οἱ νέοι καὶ οἱ πλούσιοι ὑβρισταί· ὑπερέχειν γὰρ οἴονται ὑβρίζοντες)· ὕβρεως δὲ ἀτιμία, ὁ δ' ἀτιμάζων ὀλιγωρεῖ· τὸ γὰρ μηδενὸς ἄξιον οὐδεμίαν ἔχει τιμήν, οὔτε ἀγαθοῦ οὔτε κακοῦ·

For insult (*hybris*) consists in causing injury or annoyance whereby the sufferer is disgraced, not to obtain any other advantage for oneself besides the

[141] Greek text and translation by Crawley, 1910, see *supra* note 102.

[142] Chance, 2012, p. 102, see *supra* note 138.

[143] "καὶ πρὸς μὲν τὸ θεῖον οὕτως ἐκ τοῦ εἰκότος οὐ φοβούμεθα ἐλασσώσεσθαι: τῆς δὲ ἐς Λακεδαιμονίους δόξης, ἣν διὰ τὸ αἰσχρὸν δὴ βοηθήσειν ὑμῖν πιστεύετε αὐτούς, μακαρίσαντες ὑμῶν τὸ ἀπειρόκακον οὐ ζηλοῦμεν τὸ ἄφρον." ("Thus, as far as the gods are concerned, we have no fear and no reason to fear that we shall be at a disadvantage. But when we come to your notion about the Lacedaemonians, which leads you to believe that shame will make them help you, here we bless your simplicity but do not envy your folly.").

[144] Clifford Orwin, *The Humanity of Thucydides*, Princeton University Press, 1994, p. 117.

performance of the act, but for one's own pleasure; for retaliation is not insult, but punishment. The cause of the pleasure felt by those who insult is the idea that, in ill-treating others, they are more fully showing superiority. That is why the young and the wealthy are given to insults; for they think that, in committing them, they are showing their superiority. Dishonour is characteristic of insult; and one who dishonours another slights him; for that which is worthless has no value, either as good or evil.[145]

As this passage shows, the idea of superiority and inferiority – which, as explained, is nowadays an inherent aspect of in-group and out-group identification present in hate speech – was not related to *misos* in the ancient Greek texts, but rather on reactions based on a specific ill-treatment against one's honour that required an appropriate answer to the shame that had been produced. This also happened with other ancient emotions, such as *phthonos* ("envy") or *nemesis* ("indignation"),[146] which could also be found as a cause of hostility[147] and which were both included in the Latin term *invidia*.[148]

In republican Rome, the destruction of Carthage is perhaps the best attested example of the will to eliminate an entire foreign population,[149] and has been therefore considered as one of the first recorded cases of genocide.[150]

---

145 Chance, 2012, pp. 84–85, see *supra* note 138, contends that Aristotle describes *hybris* as one manifestation of anger, which seeks "conspicuous revenge for a conspicuous slight".

146 On the importance and relationship between both concepts, see David Konstan, "*Nemesis* and *Phthonos*", in Geoffrey W. Bakewell and James P. Sickinger (eds.), *Gestures. Essays in Ancient History, Literature, and Philosophy Presented to Alan J. Boegehold*, Oxbow Books, Oxford, 2003, pp. 74–87. On *phthonos* in particular, see Ed Sanders, *Envy and Jealousy in Classical Athens. A Socio-Psychological Approach*, Oxford University Press, 2014, pp. 33–46, and Esther Eidinow, *Envy, Poison, and Death. Women on Trial in Classical Athens*, Oxford University Press, 2016, pp. 71–79.

147 Konstan, 2018, pp. 46–47, see *supra* note 96.

148 As indicated by Kaster, 2003, see *supra* note 130. *Ratione brevitatis*, I cannot expand here on these concepts, which would require an in-depth exploration well beyond the limits of this chapter.

149 The famous phrase "*delenda est Carthago*" ("Carthage must be destroyed"), attributed to Cato the Censor during the debates just before the Third Punic War in the second century BCE, clearly shows the genocidal intent. The sentence is indirectly mentioned in several ancient sources: Pliny the Elder, *Natural History*, 15, 20; Aurelius Victor, *De viris illustribus*, 47.8; Florus, *Epitome*, 1.31; Plutarch, *Life of Cato the Elder*, 27.

150 Ben Kiernan, "The First Genocide: Carthage, 146 BC", in *Diogenes*, 2004, vol. 203, pp. 27–28; Adam Jones, *Genocide: A Comprehensive Introduction*, Routledge, London, 2010, p. 464); David Colwill, "'Genocide' and Rome, 343-146 BCE: State Expansion and the Social Dynamics of Annihilation", Ph.D. dissertation in Ancient History, Cardiff University, 2017. A brief comparative study of antiquity was previously offered by Frank R. Chalk and Kurt Jonassohn, *The History and Sociology of Genocide: Analyses and Case Studies*, Yale University Press, 1990, p. 33, in their historical study of genocide.

However, when examining the *causa belli*, Livy (*The History of Rome*, 21.1.3) also endorsed anger (*ira*) as the right reason for conducting war against Carthage, and not just hatred (*odium*):

> *odiis etiam prope maioribus certarunt quam viribus, Romanis indignantibus quod victoribus victi ultro inferrent arma, Poenis quod superbe avareque crederent imperitatum victis esse.*
>
> The animosity, too, with which they fought was almost greater than their strength: the Romans were enraged that the conquered should be actually drawing sword upon their conquerors; the Phoenicians, because they believed that the conquered had been treated with domineering arrogance and greed.[151]

As indicated by Konstan, anger was here an appropriate emotion to rely upon, since it constituted an adequate reaction to the Carthaginians' perceived bad faith and deceitful character.[152]

Taking into consideration the examples provided in this section, could we therefore conclude that, according to the available sources, there were no ancient cases in which hatred could be offered as a valid reason to legitimate the desire to eliminate an enemy? It seems to me that, from a rhetorical perspective, anger, indignation and envy were sufficient emotional reasons that could be quoted to justify military campaigns without the need to frame a broader context of pre-established hatred or permanent animosity. But, additionally, a last question emerges in the context of our reflections: is it possible to identify cases in which racial or religious considerations were offered as valid grounds to endorse violence against a specific targeted population?

14.6. A Matter of Belief? Religion and Politics as Motives of Annihilation in Antiquity

Some historians consider that race is a misleading or anachronistic term when applied to ancient societies.[153] However, when discussing the existence of 'racism' among the ancient Greeks and Romans, Isaac[154] has tried to show that many

151 The Latin text and translation correspond to Benjamin O. Foster (ed.), *Livy. Books XXI-XXII*, Harvard University Press, 1929.

152 Konstan, 2018, p. 33, see *supra* note 96.

153 On the discussion concerning race in antiquity, see the excellent review articles by Denise E. McCoskey, "By Any Other Name? Ethnicity and the Study of Ancient Identity", in *The Classical Bulletin*, 2003, vol. 79, no. 1, pp. 93–109, and *id.*, "Naming the Fault in Question: Theorizing Racism Among the Greeks and Romans", in *International Journal of the Classical Tradition*, 2006, vol. 13, no. 2, pp. 243–267.

154 Benjamin Isaac, *The Invention of Racism in Classical Antiquity*, Princeton University Press, 2004. For a different view, see Félix J. Neto, "The Fear of Social Interaction: A Historiographical Essay on Ethnocentrism and Racism in Ancient Greece", in *Revista Brasileira de História*,

sources identify a strong element of discrimination and inequality that went beyond the perception of cultural differences or ethnic identities.[155] In any case, when trying to explain radical differences, sources generally reflect a sort of environmental determinism to ensure domination, but do not include the idea of fixed and immutable characteristics of a people or a nation.[156] It was only later on that these considerations became misunderstood and were appropriated: it is enough here to recall how, in modern times, many ancient arguments have been frequently misquoted in order to justify Western supremacy by means of a "well-rooted" historical narrative.[157]

In any case, whereas racism probably did not exist as such in classical societies, this does not mean that superiority was not frequently acknowledged as a result of autochthonous purity and even xenophobia.[158] In Roman times, a number of illustrious authors (including Tacitus, Sallust, Juvenal and Martial) devoted time to criticizing the presence of foreigners in the *urbs*; in many occasions this negative view was exacerbated by ethnic disparities.[159] In his *Annals*, for instance, Tacitus explained that during the reign of Emperor Nero, the Jews and other foreigners were blamed for almost all the disruptions in the city (15.44):

São Paulo, 2020, vol. 40, no. 84, pp. 1–20, who claims that racism can only be conceived as a result of colonialism and modern slave trafficking.

155 He will later identify these attitudes in the sources as "proto-racism" in Benjamin Isaac, "Proto-Racism in Graeco-Roman Antiquity", in *World Archaeology*, 2006, vol. 38, no. 1, pp. 32–47.

156 According to Eric D. Weitz, *A Century of Genocide: Utopias of Race and Nation*, Princeton University Press, 2003, pp. 17–18, this is the difference with the modern perceptions of human races today that facilitate the perpetration of genocide.

157 See Emily A. King, "The (Mis-)use of Greco-Roman History by Modern White Supremacy Groups: The Implications of the Classics in the Hands of White Supremacists", Thesis, State University of New York at New Paltz, 2019; and Curtis Dozier, "Hate Groups and Greco-Roman Antiquity Online: To Rehabilitate or Reconsider?", in Louie D. Valencia-García (ed.), *Far-Right Revisionism and the End of History: Alt/Histories*, Routledge, London, 2020, pp. 251–269.

158 Manuel G. Sánchez, "La invención de la alteridad: griegos y persas", in Francisco M. Simón, Francisco P.P.J.R. Rodríguez (eds.), *Xenofobia y racismo en el mundo antiguo*, Collecció Instrumenta no. 64, Universitat de Barcelona, 2017, p. 17. Susan Lape, *Race and Citizen Identity in the Classical Athenian Democracy*, Cambridge University Press, 2010, pp. 282–283, mentions that, in ancient Greece, the identification of racial autochthony was a way of justifying civic inclusion and participation: "Although we do not find the full-blown concept of race in classical Athens – that is, no one was seeking to divide humanity onto distinct and hierarchically ranked groups – we do find a conception of racial identity attached to citizenship".

159 On the ways in which Juvenal – frequently pointed out as xenophobic – builds some satiric characters (especially Umbricius) on a clear rejection of foreigners, see Gergő Gellérfi, "Xenophobic Utterances in Juvenal's Satires", in *Graeco-Latina Brunensia*, 2019, vol. 24, no. 1, pp. 81–91.

> *ergo abolendo rumori Nero subdidit reos et quaesitissimis poenis adfecit quos per flagitia invisos vulgus Christianos appellabat. auctor nominis eius Christus Tiberio imperitante per procuratorem Pontium Pilatum supplicio adfectus erat; repressaque in praesens exitiabilis superstitio rursum erumpebat, non modo per Iudaeam, originem eius mali, sed per urbem etiam quo cuncta undique atrocia aut pudenda confluunt celebranturque. igitur primum correpti qui fatebantur, deinde indicio eorum multitudo ingens haud proinde in crimine incendii quam odio humani generis convicti sunt.*
>
> Consequently, to get rid of the report, Nero fastened the guilt and inflicted the most exquisite tortures on a class hated for their abominations, called Christians by the populace. Christus, from whom the name had its origin, suffered the extreme penalty during the reign of Tiberius at the hands of one of our procurators, Pontius Pilatus, and a most mischievous superstition, thus checked for the moment, again broke out not only in Judæa, the first source of the evil, but even in Rome, where all things hideous and shameful from every part of the world find their centre and become popular. Accordingly, an arrest was first made of all who pleaded guilty; then, upon their information, an immense multitude was convicted, not so much of the crime of firing the city, as of hatred against mankind.[160]

The animosity towards the Jewish people, frequently mentioned in Roman texts during early imperial times,[161] can be seen in different ancient sources from Hellenistic times, where references were made to the hostilities between Greeks and Jews in Alexandria.[162] A delegation led by Philo, for example, was sent to Emperor Caligula in 38 CE to expound the Jewish position in this strife – identified by some as the Alexandrian 'pogrom', which clearly responded to ethnic motivations.[163]

160 The translation corresponds to Church, Brodribb and Bryant (eds. and trans.), New York, 1942, see *supra* note 29.

161 See Edith M. Smallwood, *The Jews Under Roman Rule: From Pompey to Diocletian*, Brill, Leiden, 1981.

162 On these first manifestations of hatred against Jews, see the recent contribution by Armin Lange, "Jew-Hatred in Antiquity: Cultural, Legal, and Physical Forms of Antisemitic Persecution", in Armin Lange, Kerstin Mayerhofer, Dina Porat and Lawrence H. Schiffman (eds.), *Comprehending Antisemitism through the Ages: A Historical Perspective*, De Gruyter, Berlin, pp. 41–78. In that volume, an updated bibliography of primary and secondary sources on the subject is provided at the end.

163 Konstan, 2018, pp. 42–43, see *supra* note 96.

Nevertheless, in the passages referring to this episode, racial or religious aspects are notoriously absent. As pointed out by Schäfer,[164] hostility to Jews in the ancient world was not grounded in religion, except in the sense that the Jews' religious objections to cults other than their own offended many people.[165] On the contrary, it seems that political and legal aspects played a far more important part in the conflict, taking into account that the Jewish community was depicted as opposing the basic rules imposed by Romans on their territory.[166]

It has been said that the identification of an essential distance between Greeks, Romans and Jews does not find ground in the available literary or epigraphical testimonies, which rather suggest a much less strict gap between the groups.[167] This, of course, does not mean that we cannot find sources where discrimination can be perceived quite blatantly.[168] For instance, when Flavius Josephus presented his defence of the Jews in his *Against Apion* (written by the end of the first century BCE), he invoked the existence of an ancient hatred, founded on ignorance (1.223–224).[169] The words used here to describe the feelings related to this deep-rooted dislike respond to the Greek vocabulary of hatred (*misein*) and enmity (*ekhthra*).[170] But in any case the identification of these

---

164 Peter Schäfer, *Judeophobia: Attitudes toward Jews in the Ancient World*, Harvard University Press, 1997.

165 See Robert Goldenberg, "On the Origins of Anti-Semitism and the Problem of Blaming the Victim", in *Jewish Studies Quarterly*, 1999, vol. 6, no. 3, p. 251.

166 In the words of Jan N. Bremmer, "Priestesses, Pogroms and Persecutions: Religious Violence in Antiquity in a Diachronic Perspective", in Jitse H. F. Dijkstra and Christian R. Raschle (eds.), *Religious Violence in the Ancient World: From Classical Athens to Late Antiquity*, Cambridge University Press, 2020, p. 56:

> When we look at the course of events, we can see that religion played an important but hardly the most important part in this pogrom. The abolition of the legal and political rights of the Judaeans was a more central concern of the pogromists, but by the forced introduction of imperial statues and the occupation of the synagogues […].

In any case, the problem here seems to have been the fact that Jews did not integrate in the Roman system, something contrary to what happened with the Greeks, who happened to be too ready to infiltrate Roman institutions quite extensively (W.J. Watts, "Race Prejudice in the Satires of Juvenal", in *Acta Classica*, 1976, vol. 19, p. 104).

167 "Greeks, Romans, and Jews […] had far more mixed, nuanced and complex opinions about other peoples" (Erich S. Gruen, *Rethinking the Other in Antiquity*, Princeton University Press, 2011, p. 2).

168 Marvin Perry and Frederick M. Schweitzer (eds.), *Antisemitism: Myth and Hate From Antiquity to the Present*, Palgrave Macmillan, New York, 2002, offer interesting insights on the ancient origins of anti-Semitism through the identification of a series of myths and misperceptions about Judaism.

169 On these ancient roots of anti-Semitism, see Jean Yoyotte, "L'Égypte ancienne et les origins de l'antijudaïsme", in *Revue de l'Histoire des Religions*, 1963, vol. 147, pp. 133–143.

170 Bernard Legras, "Κατὰ πολλὴν ἀπέχθειαν. Les discours de haine contre les Juifs dans l'Égypte ptolémaïque", in Deleplace (ed.), 2009, p. 33, see *supra* note 106.

emotions is part of a polemical work which had the purpose of dismantling the harsh criticism expressed by Apion in search for the recognition of equal rights.[171] It is notorious that the vocabulary of hatred is avoided in other passages, where the disapproval towards the Jews was presented as a reasonable response to rebellion and defiance.

In the context of what has been said throughout this chapter, nevertheless, this narrative strategy is not surprising. In my opinion, the rhetorical use of these differences in Greek and Roman sources allows us to conclude that religious loathing, based on the impossibility of accepting that those who do not share the same belief system are not equals, was usually concealed behind a 'political' argument: the argument that, from a political perspective, the specific group in question rejected the imposition of a legitimate imperial authority.

14.7. Preliminary Conclusions

Contrary to what may come to the eyes as a first impression, the current debates on the scope of hate speech can learn much from a comparative analysis of classical sources. One of the most dangerous features of hateful expressions now is the fact that violence in many cases does not overtly show the emotional background that endorses the will to eradicate an enemy group, and therefore these attempts become difficult to find and punish. As expressed by Weber,[172] hate speech can easily be concealed in statements "which at a first glance may seem to be rational or normal".

In this regard, ancient Greek and Roman sources can demonstrate that discourse performed to incite the destruction of an adversary does not require any evidence of consolidated 'hatred', but can very efficiently rely on less sophisticated emotional justifications (anger, envy, indignation) which are acceptable in light of a harm previously suffered or a pending danger impersonated by the enemy. With the language of enmity and the rhetoric of self-defence – which is widespread across history – there is always ample room for a consistent justification of violence.

The first lesson learnt from sources coming from Thucydides, Livy, Polybius or Cicero is that skilful orators could hide well-founded hatred behind less problematic arguments which can encourage collective support to genocidal intents and lead to the justification and material commission of 'legitimized' massacres.

Secondly, in many cases the argument of religious motivations was a basis allowing for the prosecution of political adversaries. As shown in the course

[171] See Aryeh Kasher, *The Jews in Hellenistic and Roman Egypt. The Struggle for Equal Rights*, J.C.B. Mohr, Tübingen, 1985.

[172] Anne Weber, *Manual on Hate Speech*, Council of Europe, Strasbourg, 2009, p. 5.

of the Athenian proceedings based on *asebeia*, in many cases, sacred charges would be able to hide a background reality in which the motivations for legal action were in fact not related to religion itself. The explanation for the use of religious arguments is clear: if common beliefs were a common ground for a community to stand upon, then the rupture of those collective viewpoints became an efficient argument to generate the exclusion of those individuals who had put those values at stake.

The third conclusion that can be reached is complementary to the second one. Ancient sources suggest that, when exploring the construction of speeches of agitation against those who *really* trusted in other beliefs, religion was not always a criterion which was openly manifest to fight against dissenters. As shown for example in the case of the Jews, the decision to discriminate a specific religious minority did not require any racial, ethnic or spiritual foundation: mere political opposition or civic turmoil could serve the same end.

Paradoxically, then, classical sources seem to show that religion has been used as an argument to look for punishment when in fact the motives were political, whereas at the same time political reasons could be mentioned to hide the religious animosity which, as the true intention, endorsed those acts.

This concluding section shows, finally, that the strong rhetorical character of ancient sources is useful for us to understand that ‘religious hate speech’ can always find alternative ways of manifesting itself, ways which become dangerous because they are subtler and craftier. At the same time, they illustrate the fact that the prosecution of ‘religious hate speech’ does not always allow us to identify the underlying reasons for a specific course of action against a specific group or specific individuals. These two aspects from ancient Greek and Roman practice, which I hope I have managed to explain, are a clear sign of alert that, without hesitation, remains distinctly helpful today, more than two millennia later.

15

Hate Speech: A Christian Perspective and a Reflection on Myanmar

Michael Marett-Crosby*

15.1. Introduction

The section of the present anthology pertaining to the 'Theological and Philosophical Frameworks of Religion, Hateful Expression and Violence' is rightly concerned with understanding what principles or core texts can inform a proper understanding of the nature of speech, hate speech and authentic responses to hate speech in religious discourse and public policy. My task in the present chapter is to offer brief reflections on this topic from a Christian perspective. I feel bound also to offer some thoughts on this in the context of Myanmar. Hate speech has been, and remains, a powerful force in a country that has been wracked by violence and is now afflicted by a military coup that is as unlawful as it is largely unwanted.

The Christian vision of speech, and its power to do good as well as evil, is introduced in the preface to this valuable volume by His Eminence Cardinal Charles Maung Bo. The Cardinal has long been a witness to truth in his country. I am informed in part by my own experience of faith.

At the outset, it may be pertinent to point out that I am not a theologian, and make no claim here to present a detailed theology of Word or words. I work in the practical realm of humanitarian aid and relief, and at the time of writing, I am responsible for some sixty activities that range across healthcare, education, human rights and humanitarian relief. The group of charities with which I am associated are not religious organizations. They are concerned with creating conditions wherein the people of Myanmar can live in freedom from fear, and are able to craft their own future without being overshadowed by the power of the gun, or the desires of those who wish more to steal than to lead.

---

* Dr. **Michael Marett-Crosby** is a Trustee of Prospect Burma, The Rangoon General Hospital Reinvigoration Charitable Trust, the Lucy Faithfull Foundation, and the Irrawaddy Policy Exchange. He holds an M.A. and D.Phil. from Oxford University, and trained as a Catholic priest. He has led numerous projects to implement the late Dr. Kofi Annan's Rakhine Advisory Commission's recommendations. For an audio-visual recording of his statement to CILRAP's conference in Florence in April 2022 on the topic of this anthology, please see https://www.cilrap.org/cilrap-film/220409-marett-crosby/.

Having been in Myanmar at the time of the coup in 2021, I am very fortunate not to be in prison. Professor Sean Turnell, an Australian economist and former economic policy advisor to State Counsellor Aung San Suu Kyi (who was in Myanmar at the invitation of the government to help craft an economic response to the pandemic) was arrested in the days following the 2021 coup and was only released late 2022. Many of my Myanmar friends are still detained, while some others have died. The military junta started in 2022 to execute those whom it imprisons, which has rightly brought upon it near universal condemnation.

Those who lost their lives were those who spoke up for freedom. A line from the 1984 British biographical film 'The Killing Fields', pertaining to the regime of the Khmer Rouge in Cambodia, comes to mind: "Only the silent survive". And yet many people in Myanmar still speak up. I am struck every day by the bravery of those who hold on to the possibility of freedom. The needs of the victims of the coup impel me to raise my voice.

In taking the time to contribute to this anthology, I hope readers will understand that these reflections are practical in orientation.

15.2. Theological Underpinnings of Speech: Insights from Christianity

The present chapter seeks to explore how Christianity might inform the reality of the events taking place in Myanmar since the 2021 coup. I start with the obvious beginning. Christianity is a religion of the book. It shares this with other great faiths, in that it holds in a place of special veneration a particular revelation granted by God. 'Scripture contains all things'; my fellow countryman and theologian Robert Grosseteste wrote in his commentary on Ecclesiasticus.

He does not mean that the Bible is an encyclopaedia of facts, but that it is for Christians a source of truth about God and the world. St. Augustine in his *Confessions* speaks of the Bible as "the means by which we should look for you and believe in you".

Erich Auerbach expresses the point almost more forcefully in his *Mimesis*:

> The Scripture stories do not, like Homer's, court our favour, they do not flatter us that they may please us and enchant us – they seek to subject us, and if we refuse to be subjected we are rebels.[1]

Perhaps, if I may be so bold, Goethe puts it best of all:

[1] Erich Auerbach, *Mimesis: The Representation of Reality in Western Literature*, Princeton University Press, 1968, p. 168.

> The book of all books was given to us that we might try to enter there as into a second world, where we lose ourselves, enlighten ourselves, perfect ourselves.[2]

To which I would only add that, in losing ourselves in Scripture we must remember to find ourselves too, and come out at the far side of these reflections with something that will make a difference in our engagement with the world.

The Hebrew Scriptures speak of the 'Word of God' and the 'Wisdom of God', present at the making of all things. That empowered Word opens the Book of Genesis and is "the first fruits of his fashioning, before the oldest of his works" (Proverbs 8:22). In a compelling image later in the same Book, Wisdom speaks of itself:

> Then I was by him, *as* one brought up *with him*: and I was daily *his* delight, rejoicing always before him;
>
> Rejoicing in the habitable part of his earth; and my delights *were* with the sons of men.[3]

Such personifications of wisdom occur elsewhere in the Hebrew Scriptures, most notably Wisdom 7:25–26, that "breath of the power of God" and "reflection of the eternal light". This image of the word and wisdom of God as the child of the divine, as one in God's pleasure with human-kind, may seem far from our exploration of the dark recesses of hate speech. But it matters because it places the Word, and words, in a fundamentally positive position. "In the beginning was the Word, and the Word was with God, and the Word was God."[4] '*Verbum erat apud Deum*' in the Latin Vulgate – the Word was at home with God.

In speaking of the Word in the Christian Scriptures, the writers knew their debt to the Hebrew tradition of wisdom literature. St. Paul, in the hymn to Christ that follows the opening thanksgiving in his letter to the Colossians, writes: "[He] Who is the image of the invisible God, the firstborn of every creature",[5] yet he is also the one who suffered, "having made peace through the blood of his cross".[6] The Word, Wisdom, becomes flesh. This is the central mystery of Christianity: "And the Word was made flesh, and dwelt among us, (and we beheld his glory, the glory as of the only begotten of the Father,) full of grace and truth".[7] In consequence, our words have power.

---

2 This passage is the opening quotation of Roberto Calasso, *The Book of All Books*, Tim Parks (trans.), Allen Lane, 2022

3 Proverbs 8:30–31, King James Version ('the Bible').

4 1 John 1:1, the Bible (in following footnotes, I do not indicate 'the Bible' to avoid repetition).

5 Colossians 1:15.

6 Colossians 1:20.

7 1 John 1:14.

That words, and the mere act of speaking them, have this power is often inconvenient for sure, and both the Hebrew and Christian Scriptures are full of characters who would rather this was otherwise. There is a supposed freedom that might be seen to come from disempowered speaking, to say what we like in the confidence that it does not matter.

The call of the Prophet Jeremiah is a paradigm example. The Lord says:

> Before I formed thee in the belly I knew thee; and before thou camest forth out of the womb I sanctified thee, and I ordained thee a prophet unto the nations.[8]

To which the prophet can only mumble, talking nonsense for a moment so as to say back to his Lord, "behold, I cannot speak: for I *am* a child".[9]

Moses too, early in the Book of Exodus, tries the same, telling the Lord "I *am* not eloquent, neither heretofore, nor since thou hast spoken unto thy servant: but I *am* slow of speech, and of a slow tongue".[10] To which the Lord responds by asserting the facts of Creation:

> Who hath made man's mouth? or who maketh the dumb, or deaf, or the seeing, or the blind? have not I the LORD?
>
> Now therefore go, and I will be with thy mouth, and teach thee what thou shalt say.[11]

Or, in the words the Lord gives to the Prophet Jeremiah when he touches his mouth in an act of consecration:

> Then the Lord put forth his hand, and touched my mouth. And the LORD said unto me, Behold, I have put my words in thy mouth.
>
> See, I have this day set thee over the nations and over the kingdoms, to root out, and to pull down, and to destroy, and to throw down, to build, and to plant.[12]

To put words into the mouth. Jeremiah's encounter with the lord who touches his lips is both a freedom from wrong speech and grants the power to speak the truth. Both parts of this are important. In the call of the Prophet Isaiah that begins the so-called Book of Emmanuel in First Isaiah, a seraph takes a live coal from the altar of the Lord and touches the mouth of the prophet:

> And he laid it upon my mouth, and said, Lo, this hath touched thy lips; and thine iniquity is taken away, and thy sin purged.[13]

---

8 Jeremiah 1:5.

9 Jeremiah 1:6.

10 Exodus 4:10.

11 Exodus 4:11–12.

12 Jeremiah 1:9–10.

13 Isaiah 6:7.

The prophet, as bearer of the truth of God, becomes the mouth of God and receives what in a later context would be called by Christian theologians the *gratia sanans*, the healing grace, that brings freedom from the sin of wrong speech. In an even more evocative image, the Prophet Ezekiel is commanded by the Lord to eat a scroll, which tasted sweet as honey.[14] This scroll is not associated so much with freedom from sin as much as the *gratia elevans*, the grace that lifts a person beyond himself with the help of God that enables the prophet to take the words of the Lord to the people:

> And he said unto me, Son of man, go, get thee unto the house of Israel, and speak with my words unto them.[15]

The case of Ezekiel is instructive because the words on the scroll are not words of comfort or peace. They are explicitly "lamentations, and mourning, and woe",[16] and the prophet must therefore be as defiant as those who are hearing him. The prophet is told that, "[a]s an adamant harder than flint have I made thy forehead: fear them not, neither be dismayed at their looks, though they be a rebellious house".[17]

I shall help you speak. I have put my words in your mouth. The Christian Scriptures build on these encounters between people who feel themselves speechless or sinful with a Word and words that empower. Thus, the synoptic gospels especially portray stories of the unheard, the silenced and the small gaining a voice to speak about what they know.

Pre-eminently, of course, that empowered word belongs to the person of Jesus Christ. Of many examples, perhaps the paradigm is the cure of the Centurion's Servant recorded in the gospels of Matthew, Luke and John. It comes in Luke at the end of a long section of teaching: "When he had come to the end of all that he wanted the people to hear", in the words of the evangelist.

It is at this point that Jesus hears news of a Roman centurion, a non-believer, whose sick servant is brought to his attention by the local leaders of the Jewish community. To be clear – this is news of a servant who is part of the household of a pagan, and both master and servant are far outside the community of believers. Still, they matter.

Jesus sets off towards the house, but his journey is interrupted by a message from the centurion:

> Then Jesus went with them. And when he was now not far from the house, the centurion sent friends to him, saying unto him, Lord,

[14] Ezekiel 3:3.

[15] Ezekiel 3:4.

[16] Ezekiel 2:10.

[17] Ezekiel 3:9.

> trouble not thyself: for I am not worthy that thou shouldest enter under my roof:
>
> Wherefore neither thought I myself worthy to come unto thee: but say in a word, and my servant shall be healed.[18]

Jesus need only say the word. This is a moment of perfect faith not only in the Saviour but in the power of speech, of the word, to effect change. No surprise then that the Latin Mass puts these words in the mouths of those who are to receive the sacrament: *Domine non sum dignus ut intres sub tectum meum, sed tanto dic verbo, et sanabitur anima mea* ('Lord, I am not worthy to have you under my roof, but only say the word and my soul shall be healed').

With this faith in the power of words so much at the centre of the New Testament, it is no surprise that the Pastoral Epistles emphasise the power of speech to do good. Paul made the remarkable assertion to Titus that God does not lie at the beginning of that epistle.[19] Instead, that He "hath in due times manifested his word through preaching, which is committed unto me according to the commandment of God our Saviour".20

It is no surprise, therefore, that Paul both warns against bad speech and upholds its central power in the work of preaching and teaching. "Let no corrupt communication proceed out of your mouth", St. Paul tells the Church of Ephesus, "but that which is good to the use of edifying, that it may minister grace unto the hearers".[21] "Seeing then that we have such hope", St. Paul says elsewhere, "we use great plainness of speech"[22] – if not great eloquence, then at least the confidence that words can be used to communicate truth.

This Pauline faith in bold speech comes from the *gratia elevans* of the message itself. So important is the message that the character or past of the messenger can be fortified by the message. "For I will give you a mouth and wisdom, which all your adversaries shall not be able to gainsay nor resist",[23] Jesus tells his disciples in his discourse on the destruction of the Temple.

One clear example of such utterance is presented in the person of Stephen, who in the Book of Acts is the first of those so obviously empowered to speak. This "man full of faith and of the Holy Ghost",[24] debates in the synagogue and his words cannot be refuted save by subterfuge:

---

18 Luke 7:6, 7:7.

19 Titus 1:2.

20 Titus 1:3.

21 Ephesians 4:29.

22 2 Corinthians 3:12.

23 Luke 21:15.

24 Acts 6:5.

> We have heard him speak blasphemous words against Moses and *against* God.
>
> And they stirred up the people, and the elders, and the scribes, and came upon *him*, and caught him, and brought *him* to the council,
>
> And set up false witnesses, which said, This man ceaseth not to speak blasphemous words against this holy place, and the law.[25]

These accusations are followed by an extended speech given by Stephen, one of the earliest homilies in the Christian tradition. In response to these words, his hearers can only grind their teeth, the characteristic action of the slanderer in Job 16:9.

Words built on truth – from Stephen and through the history of the New Testament and thereafter – are the building blocks of the Christian mission. In the language of the Christian hymn '*Tantum Ergo Sacramentum*': "How says trusty hearing? that shall be believed".

15.3. Contextualizing Learnings from Christian Scriptures: Reflections on Myanmar

Let us take these reflections from the Hebrew and Christian Scriptures on truth and its enemies to the present day. Elsewhere in this volume, there are expert contributions on the role played by social media in the magnification of hate speech. Here I cite first of all a reflection from Pope Francis during an October 2021 address:

> In the name of God, I ask the technology giants to stop exploiting human weakness, people's vulnerability, for the sake of profits without caring about the spread of hate speech, grooming, fake news, conspiracy theories, and political manipulation.[26]

Then, in the aftermath of the killing of George Floyd, Pope Francis said:

> It is necessary to confront together the populist discourses of intolerance, xenophobia, and aporophobia, which is hatred of the poor. Like everything that leads us to indifference, meritocracy, and individualism, these narratives only serve to divide our peoples, and to undermine and nullify our poetic capacity, the capacity to dream together.[27]

---

25 Acts 6:11–13.

26 Mark A. Kellner, "Block 'fake news,' Pope Francis Begs Social Media Firms, 'in the name of God'", *The Washington Times*, 19 October 2021.

27 The Holy See, "Video Message of the Holy Father Francis on the Occasion of the Fourth World Meeting of Popular Movements", 16 October 2021.

These are important words. They highlight the capacity of speech to divide. They also highlight what we lose by so dividing – what the Pope calls the poetic capacity, the capacity to share dreams.

At this juncture, it seems apt to of offer a reflection on the power of speech from contemporary Myanmar, which is the focus of my work. There is no doubt that the hate speech spread through Facebook across Myanmar was an important cause of the appalling violence against the Rohingya Muslim peoples. Hate speech has exacerbated difficult relationships between the many ethnicities of that tatterdemalion nation. But recently, amidst the dreadful consequences of an unlawful and unwanted military coup, speech has been used for good.

I allude to the dialogue between the different ethnicities of Myanmar that has produced a truly remarkable document, the Federal Democracy Charter ('Charter').[28] This Charter is the creation of the National Unity Government and National Unity Consultative Council of Myanmar, two of the means by which a new alliance of hope has been created in opposition to the coup. These groups have articulated a new vision for Myanmar in a document that is itself built upon hours and days of detailed speech. It has been my privilege, even as a foreigner to Myanmar, to witness some of these extraordinary conversations. They have been controversial, at times arduous, a bringing together of competing histories in the search for a common identity.

The Charter is a vision of a peaceful federal democratic union, with values of democracy, minority rights, equality, self-determination and pluralism built into it, as its *raison d'être*. It is to secure these values that the union is made. Most importantly, the Charter establishes the states of the union and the people as the "original sources of sovereignty".[29]

I commend this Charter to you as, in the words of Pope Francis, a shared dream. But unlike a dream, it is being built into a reality.

I conclude with this for two reasons. The first is to recall what I suggested at the beginning of this short paper, that the theological position of Christian thinking establishes the 'Word', and therefore speech, as empowered to do good. We see examples of that in Myanmar. The second reason is to suggest at this point, if I may, that some others with the power to speak out on the issue of Myanmar have chosen the meagre rather than the strong way. While it is important and valuable to sit together and deliberate as a means to seeking

---

28 Committee Representing Pyidaungsu Hluttaw, "Federal Democracy Charter (Consisting of a 'Declaration of Federal Democracy Union' and 'Interim Constitutional Arrangement')", Myanmar, 31 March 2021 (https://www.legal-tools.org/doc/rjyt92/).

29 International Institute for Democracy and Electoral Assistance, "Myanmar's Federal Democracy Charter: Analysis and Prospects", in *Constitution Brief Interregnum Series*, 2022.

solutions to the problems of hate speech, for such work to be meaningful, we should also examine our own speech, and our own silences.

Many reading the present chapter will already be empowered individuals, whose words matter. And for sure, some of those who have such power have exercised it for good with regard to Myanmar. But others have not. And I must in conscience use this opportunity to ask those who speak from the privileged place of the International Court of Justice to consider their decision to allow the junta to speak in that court.

I am not a lawyer. I am often glad of that. Instead, it has fallen to me to count the bodies of those who have been murdered by the junta. I have sent aid into towns attacked by soldiers, to have those soldiers then set light to the food we sent, so that people could watch hope burning. I have had doctors and nurses in my charities executed for their efforts to do good.

There is a vision for a Myanmar, built on truth and a belief that peoples long divided can come together to build a closer, better union. This belief in truth is tested by violence every day. On the other side, there are the blank deceits of the junta that opposes them. In between sit those with the power to tell the truth. "I have put my words in your mouth", the Lord told the Prophet Jeremiah.

The people of Myanmar are wondering how you use those words. We can condemn others for their use of hate speech, but it is no great thing to have the power to tell the truth and fail to do so.

They are waiting for your answer.

16

Incitement to Religious Hatred: An Examination of the Approaches of Extremists to Islámic *Sharí'ah*

Adel Maged*

> Hast thou not seen how God has struck a similitude? A good word is as a good tree – its roots are firm, and its branches are in the sky; it gives its produce every season by the leave of its Lord. So God strikes similitudes for people; haply they will remember. And the likeness of a corrupt word is as a corrupt tree – uprooted from the earth, having no establishment.[1]

16.1. Introduction

The international community has recently recognized that effective action against terrorism requires the mobilization of efforts to confront and eliminate its root causes, and that extremism and hate speech are the main drivers of violence and terrorist acts. Counter-terrorism efforts that used to be based on security confrontations and amounted in some instances to the use of military force, are now more focused on preventive policies and measures. Furthermore, the

---

* **Adel Maged** is Judge and Vice President of the Egyptian Court of Cassation (Criminal Chambers). He was appointed Public Prosecutor in 1987, and served as a Judge at the Courts of First Instance, Chief Prosecutor at the Criminal Division of the Court of Cassation, Judge at the Egyptian Court of Appeals, and was for several years on secondment to the Ministry of Justice of the United Arab Emirates as a Legal Advisor on International Law and Treaties. He is also a lecturer at National Centre for Judicial Studies and the Faculty of *Sharí'ah* and Law, Al-Ázhár Ash-Sharíf University in Cairo, and a founding member of the research group 'Islám, Law and Modernity' at Durham Law School. He has advised the International Criminal Court's Office of the Prosecutor and the Arab League of States on international criminal law issues. His publications include books and articles, in Arabic and English, on international criminal law, Islámic law, justice reform, transitional justice, combating extremism, terrorism and combating migrant smuggling and human trafficking. He holds a Bachelor of Law from Alexandria University; an LL.M. on Internationalization of Crime and Criminal Justice from Utrecht University; and a Diploma on International Law and Organization for Development from the Institute of Social Studies, The Hague. The author thanks Morten Bergsmo for his conceptual input, Ms. Medha Damojipurapu for her profound review and valuable comments, and Ms. Rawan Maged for her research assistance. For an audio-visual recording of Judge Maged's statement to CILRAP's conference in Florence in April 2022 on the topic of this anthology, please see https://www.cilrap.org/cilrap-film/220409-maged/.

[1] The *Qur'án*, 14:29–31.

legislative policy against terrorism is no longer based on a penal approach. Rather, it has become preoccupied with adopting a policy that embraces preventive measures in national legislations, for proactive and early elimination of the causes of these phenomena.

The Arab region was not spared the toxins of terrorism, which caused it to experience one of the hardest ordeals, attributable to perverted ideologies and abhorrent extremism. Such ideologies and extremism were fuelled, in some instances, by external forces seeking to fragment countries and plunder the wealth of people. This is done through the promotion of perverted ideologies that use religion as a tool to accomplish political goals, or through the fabrication of religious and sectarian wars that depict Islám as a destabilizing threat to society[2] and which in turn led to the rise of Islámophobia.[3]

Many violent incidents against both the military and civilians in the Arab region have mainly been a product of ideological extremism fuelled by hate speech. In some instances, perpetrators used the ideology of *takfír* ('accusing people of apostasy' or 'excommunication') to render legitimacy to their killings. As will be shown below, the ideology of *takfír* isan extensive form of the notion of religious hatred. This phenomenon has coincided with the rise of armed terrorist groups who commit the most heinous and grave crimes, against both civilians and the military, with no regard to the minimum principles of humanity, in order to undermine the state's sovereignty and territorial integrity. In doing so, terrorist groups use hateful utterances and the deviant *takfír* ideology, based on false interpretations of religious texts as a reference to recruit their followers and legitimize their own criminal acts.[4]

As stated by the Grand Imám of Al-Ázhár Ash-Sharíf ('Grand Imam' and 'Al-Azhar'), this issue poses a major threat to society as these heinous, barbaric crimes take the true religion of Islám as a cover, and label the dens where their crimes are plotted with names relating to Islám, in an attempt to project a false image of Islám as a religion that slaughters, beheads or expels whoever comes

2 Aḥmad Tamím, the Mufti of Ukraine, "Makhaṭir at-Taṭárruff wa-Dawr al-Márji'íyyat ad-Díníyyah fí Múajahatih", in *Al-Ghulú Wal-Taṭárruff*, by a Group of Scholars, Islamic Research Academy, Research Academy Series, 2015, 47th Year, Book II, p. 105.

3 For the purposes of my chapters in this anthology, this term means 'phobia of Islám' or 'fear of Islám'. For more information on the concept, its origins and development, see Muṣṭáfa Ibn Tamsuk, *Islámophobia: Muqárábah Jiú-Siyasíyyah*, Mo'minún Without Borders, Rabat, 2017.

4 For more information on the nature of crimes committed by these groups in the Arab region, see Adel Maged and Rawan Maged, "Huqúq al-Insan wa-Múajabahat al-Jama'at al-Irhabíyyah al-Musallaḥah" (Human Rights and Confronting Armed Terrorist Groups), in *Journal of Studies in Human Rights*, May 2018, no. 1, pp. 24–26.

in disagreement with it.[5] To justify their acts, when they attack military personnel or police officers, they describe the latter as infidels, and for them political and military leaders are *ṭáwághít* (tyrants). This is a form of the hateful utterances that they use. Hate speech promoted by these extremist groups is not exclusively directed against people, but also targets the state's key institutions, that is, the judiciary, the military and the police, with the aim of weakening people's trust in these institutions and destabilizing the country. Surprisingly, this sort of disgraceful speech was directed at Al-Azhar too, in an attempt to shake its underlying principles. However, these attempts to tarnish Al-Azhar were doomed to fail, thanks to the counteraction by its venerable scholars and the support of the people for its lofty message.

That said, like many counter-extremism experts, I have noticed that most research and articles published on the topic use a monocular perspective to address this phenomenon, whether social, religious, or otherwise related to specialized disciplines such as sociology, political science and political sociology. Recent studies addressing these phenomena suggest that their causes should be examined using a comprehensive perspective which combines the aforementioned disciplines. Therefore, it is no longer surprising to see the phenomena of extremism and terrorism being addressed by multidisciplinary approaches combining the above-mentioned disciplines. One advantage of this chapter, I presume, is that it presents both classical and contemporary *Islámic Sharí'ah* scholars' approaches to and views on the topic.

On the basis of the foregoing, this chapter aims to address one of the main drivers that leads to the spread of hate and violence in the Arab world, namely extremism induced by perverted ideologies and fuelled by hate speech. The present chapter highlights the main challenges facing society, including perverted ideologies and behaviour conducive to extremism and violence that potentially lead to terrorism.

The foundation of my argument is that extremism and hate speech are interconnected, hence we cannot confront hate speech unless we examine the mindset of those employing it and contemplate the essence of their ideologies and motives. Therefore, this chapter attempts to examine the meaning of these notions (perverted ideology, extremism and hate speech), establish the relationship between them, and explain their detrimental effects. To reach this goal, the chapter focuses on the notion of hate speech from a theological perspective. It explains how extremists employ hate speech to attain their malicious goals, and how hateful expression is used to recruit people and instigate violent extremism.

---

5 Speech of the Grand Imám of Al-Azhar, Ahmed Al-Ṭayyeb, *A'mal Mú'támar Al-Ázhár al-'alamí li-Múajahat at-Taṭárruff wal-Irhab*, Islámic Research Academy, First Book on Táṣḥíḥ al-Mafahím, Cairo, 2017, p. 13.

The chapter concludes by presenting the measures included in various international instruments to confront extremism and hate speech, especially when it is driven by religious hatred.

With respect to the methodology of my research – to guarantee authenticity – I rely on early-classical and original literature by eminent *Sharí'ah* jurists and contemporary prominent religious scholars (for example, the Grand Imám), as experience has proven that intermediary references to *Sharí'ah*, especially those written in non-Arabic languages or by authors who are not well-versed with the *Sharí'ah* rules of interpretation,[6] may not have authenticity and could disrupt the real meaning of the original sources, or at least not convey their authentic aroma. Unfortunately, the intermediary non-Arabic literature on *Sharí'ah* often cannot convey the letter and spirit of the text to the reader, which is perceived not only by Muslim jurists, but also by Western scholars. [7]

16.2. Challenges of Extremism and Hate Speech: Arab and Islámic *Sharí'ah* Perspectives

As noted above, this part will attempt to examine the basic challenges we are facing, including intellectual deviation and behaviours conducive to extremism and violence and potentially leading to terrorism. Meanwhile, necessary countermeasures will be identified together with a precise delineation of these challenges so that they are best understood. Equipped with this knowledge, researchers and students of religious institutions will be enabled to fulfil their duty to undermine perverted ideology, extremism and hate speech, using the proper counter-narrative.

Therefore, this section of the chapter discusses the basic relevant concepts and terminology in order to define requisite preventive measures. For the purpose of defining and interpreting these terms and concepts, reference will be made to relevant international instruments, national legislation and other credible sources.

16.2.1. Challenges of Extremism

The term 'extremism' has recently raised the public's attention and caused much controversy among scholars and intellectuals. It has also been notably disseminated in the media, as one of the main drivers of terrorism. Specialists almost unanimously agree that adequate confrontation of extremism which is

---

6 For more details on this argument, ser Adel Maged, "*Sharí'ah* Sources and Reflections on Integrity", in Morten Bergsmo and Viviane E. Dittrich (eds.), *Integrity in International Justice*, Torkel Opsahl Academic Publisher ('TOAEP'), Brussels, 2020 (https://www.toaep.org/nas-pdf/4-bergsmo-dittrich/).

7 Jeffrey Einboden, *Nineteenth-Century U.S. Literature in Middle Eastern Languages*, Edinburgh University Press, 2013, p. 55.

potentially conducive to violence and terrorism requires examination and analysis of the reasons and motives for extremism, regardless of its type, forms and channels.[8]

The term 'extremism' frequently raises a terminological legal problem due to its overlap with the concept of terrorism so that the former has been commonly used to indicate the latter and the term 'extremists' has been used to denote terrorists although both are clearly distinct.[9] With this in mind, it is necessary to explain the meaning and dimensions of the concept of extremism, with a focus on basic terminologies and concepts related to and emerging from it, using a bottom-up approach which would take us up to the term 'violent extremism'.

When it comes to the concept of 'extremism', it is important to differentiate between several concepts or terms which may cause confusion or overlap with it, such as fanaticism, radicalization,[10] ideological extremism, violent extremism and terrorism.

16.2.1.1. Definition of Extremism

Lexically, 'extremism' means to diverge from limits of moderation and deviate from standards, norms, customs, traditions or values that govern society.[11] Contextually, it is a state of delinquency in thought or behaviour, to the right or left extremes. In religion, an extremist is a person who transgresses its limits, rules and guidance.[12] All of these characteristics reflect the meanings of *ghulú* in Islámic jurisprudence, which implies divergence from the limits and the purposes of religion,[13] fanaticism for a certain ideology, race or sect, and the rejection of dialogue with others.

---

8 Former Grand Imám of Al-Azhar, Jad al-Ḥáq 'Alí Jad al-Ḥáq, "At-Taṭárruff ad-Díní wa-Ab'aduh: Amníyyann ... wa-Siyasíyyann ... wa-Jtima'íyyann", in *Jama'at Anṣár al-Sunnah al-Muḥammaddiyyah*, no. 8, p. 47.

9 'Amer Jáwhár, "Ishkalíyyat at-Taṭárruff wa-'Iláqátuh bil-'Unf wal-Irhab", in *Journal of Jíl al-Dirásat al-Siyasíyyah wal'Ilaqát ad-Dawlíyyah*, no. 11, October 2017, p. 93.

10 Linguistically, this term primarily means 'fundamentalism' and many dictionaries provide it as a meaning of the Arabic word *Al-jithríyyah* (or *Al-jizríyyah*) and it is used sometimes to refer to a 'radical change' which takes place in political contexts. However, it is used by some researchers to mean fanaticism or extremism. For the purpose of this chapter, it will be limited to the meaning of the Arabic word *Tashaddod* (radicalization).

11 Majma' Al-Lughah Al-'Árábíyyah, *Al-Mu'jam al-Wásít*, 3rd ed., vol. 2, Dar Al-Gumhúríyyah lil-Ṣaḥáfah, Cairo, 1985, p. 575.

12 Aḥmad K. Shárqáwí, "Dáwr Al-Ázhár fí Múajahat al-Ghulú Wat-Taṭárruf", in *Al-Ghulú Wat-Taṭárruff*, p. 57, see *supra* note 2.

13 *Ibid.*, p. 57.

Lexically, *ghulú* means going beyond the limit; anyone who exaggerates has gone beyond the limit.[14] Contextually, a person is said to have exaggerated in an issue or in religion if they "take an issue to the extreme, go beyond the limit or be excessive".[15] Some jurists consider *ghulú* as an abnormal state when compared to the familiar and well-known principles of religion. It is a form of deficient piety, inflicted on our predecessors which then affects us, causing doom.[16] Islámic jurists cite the Prophet's *ḥadíth*: "ruined are those who insist on hardship in matters of the faith";[17] it refers to people who fanatically probe into matters, insist on hardship and go beyond limits in their words and deeds.[18] Ignorant people with a perverted ideology who deviate in their thoughts will fall into prohibitions and will be overwhelmed by strong currents and waves of extremism and terrorism. Accordingly, they are susceptible to committing the most heinous crimes in the name of religion.

Many consider that extremism is rooted in the perversion of ideology that can manifest in verbal or actual behaviour in its various stages. Ideological deviation, in principle, is an issue related to the person in question which does not, in itself, constitute a violation of a social or criminal norm. However, once extremism evolves into an illegal or harmful act or behaviour in the form of an extremist manifestation, and becomes associated with violent behaviours which may inflict terror or panic on society for the sake of specific political or ideological goals, the indication is that the extremist person has been assimilated into the loop of violence and terrorism.[19]

---

14 Ibráhím Ṣ.A. Hudhud, "Al-Ghulú fí al-'Ahd al-Nabawí: Ṣúwáruh Wa-'ilajuh", in *Al-Ghulú Wat-Taṭárruff*, p. 14, see *supra* note 2.

15 *Ibid.*, p. 684.

16 Jalal A.D.M. Ṣáliḥ, *Al-Irhab al-Fikrí: 'Ashkaluh Wa-Mumarasatuh*, Centre for Studies and Research, Naif Arab University for Security Sciences (NAUSS), Riyadh, 2008, p. 158.

17 Related by Muslim, *ḥadíth* no. 2670.

18 Jalal ad-Dín 'Abd al-Ráḥman bin Abí-Bakr and al-Síúṭí, *Al-Díbaj 'ala Ṣáḥíḥ Muslim bin al-Ḥajjají, lil-Ḥáfiẓ Jalal ad-Dín 'Abd al-Ráḥman bin Abí Bakr al-Síútí (Shárḥ al-Síútí), Kitab al-'Ilm, al-Mujallad al-Awwal, Sharikat al-Árqám bin Abí al- Árqám*, vol. 1, Dar al-Kotob al-'Ilmiyyah, Beirut, 2006, p. 103.

19 Egypt, Anti-Terrorism Law No. 94 of 2015, 15 August 2015, Article 2 ('Anti-Terrorism Law') (https://www.legal-tools.org/doc/205c78/), defines a "terrorist act" as follows:

> A terrorist act shall refer to any use of force, violence, threat, or intimidation domestically or abroad for the purpose of disturbing public order, or endangering the safety, interests, or security of the community; harming individuals and terrorizing them; jeopardizing their lives, freedoms, public or private rights, or security, or other freedoms and rights guaranteed by the Constitution and the law; harms national unity, social peace, or national security or damages the environment, natural resources, antiquities, money, buildings, or public or private properties or occupies or seizes them; prevents or impedes public authorities, agencies or judicial bodies, government offices or local units, houses of worship, hospitals,

Some scholars of Islámic jurisprudence cite local and external factors as drivers of extremism. In this regard, the late Grand Imam of Al-Azhar, Jad al-Ḥáq 'Alí Jad al-Ḥáq (1982–1996), stated:

> In order to prevent extremism in general, and address its negative dimensions, at the security, political and social levels, we should familiarize ourselves with those dimensions and causes, differentiate between local and external causes and always remember that this country is a target of major forces in this era.[20]

The many characteristics of an extremist person include the inability to tolerate ideas that come in conflict with their basic beliefs[21] and fanaticism for one's own opinion and group, believing that their ideology, race or sect is the best and the most correct. This would lead them to hate others, with a desire to inflict harm or even annihilate other groups in some cases. In the meantime, such extremist people often believe in and uphold certain religious or racist slogans. Therefore, it is imperative to examine the extremist or terrorist personality,[22] understand how extremist ideologies are formed, and how an intellectually deviant person evolves from having an extreme ideology to committing violence which then potentially leads to acts of terrorism. Thus, it is necessary to explore the meaning of the term 'ideological extremism' – which, according to Al-Azhar, is denoted by the term 'intellectual deviation'.

---

institutions, institutes, diplomatic and consular missions, or regional and international organizations and bodies in Egypt from carrying out their work or exercising all or some of their activities, or resists them or disables the enforcement of any of the provisions of the Constitution, laws, or regulations. A terrorist act shall likewise refer to any conduct committed with the intent to achieve, prepare, or instigate one of the purposes set out in the first paragraph of this article, if it is as such to harm communications, information, financial or banking systems, national economy, energy reserves, security stock of goods, food and water, or their integrity, or medical services in disasters and crises..

20 "Al-Taṭárruff ad-Díní wa-Ab'aduh: Amníyyann ... wa-Siyasíyyann ... wa-Jtima'íyyann", p. 38, see *supra* note 8.

21 See, for example, UN Development Programme ('UNDP'), "Preventing Violent Extremism Through Inclusive Development, Tolerance and Respect for Diversity: A Development Response to Addressing Radicalization and Violent Extremism", 1 July 2016, p. 12 ('Preventing Violent Extremism') (https://www.legal-tools.org/doc/guylbf/).

22 For more information about the importance of studying the extremist and terrorist character and relevant theories, see Basmah J. ad-Dín 'Áṭwah, "Al-Iṭár al-Manhají li-Dirásat al-Shákhsíyyah al-Irhabíyyah: Naḥw Bina' Takamulí fí Dirásat al-Jarímah al-Irhabíyyah", in *Múajahat al-Jarímah al-Irhabíyyah wal-Muqtáḍáyat al-Wáṭáníyyah*, National Centre for Social and Criminological Research, 2019, pp. 68–71.

16.2.1.2. Basic Terminologies and Concepts Related to Extremism

Below I will shed some light on basic terminology and concepts related to extremism, namely: (i) intellectual or ideological deviation; (ii) radicalization; and (iii) violent extremism.

16.2.1.2.1. Ideological Deviation

Undoubtedly, extremism of all forms or degrees may always be attributed to a general intellectual pattern or a so-called ideology adopted by the person in question, reflecting the fundamental theoretical framework underlying these ideas,[23] potentially leading to fanaticism or extremism. Therefore, extremism may be driven by a perverted ideology which may be of a religious, material or philosophical nature, seeking to uphold a certain belief or ethnocentrism, to realize its content and implement it.[24] This ideology often evolves into fanaticism for its own adopted ideas, which is usually associated with discrimination against the 'other' on religious, ethnic,[25] racial, political, social or other grounds, indicated in international conventions and the Constitution of the Arab Republic of Egypt. Accordingly, a person may be driven to extremism, where he becomes more likely to commit violent acts that may amount to a terrorist crime.

In order for a person to reach this stage of extremism, they usually go through a series of stimuli or influences that start with the adoption of a simple thought which then evolves into *g͟hulú* and extremism. These stimuli and influences are rooted in perverted ideas affecting the target person's mentality and belief. This shift typically takes place as a result of the influence of those ideas or due to personal ambitions and political conflicts or involvement in certain organizations. The overall goal is to legitimize violent behaviour and acts of terror.

Therefore, it is argued that a terrorist ideology is merely a

> system of perverted beliefs and ideas which, regardless of their nature, are based on *gulhú* in their beliefs which come in conflict with the common sense. It exceeds the limits delineating how the mind

---

23 An ideology is usually organized around a set or system of values, beliefs, ideas or philosophies adopted by a certain group which is dedicated to them or acts to promote or direct them to a specific or non-specific group or groups. Therefore, an ideology is not limited to a single society. Rather, it may move across national borders from one community to another to prevail in a particular region or regions (see, for example, Mohammed Atwan, "Ideology and the False Consciousness", in 'Adab al-Baṣrah, 2015, no. 74, p. 198; 'Abd A.K.W.F.A. Isma'íl, *Fí al-Aydíúlújíyyah wal-Ḥaḍárah wal-'Awlamah*, 1st ed., Maktabat Bustan Al-Ma'rifah, 2001, p. 32).

24 Ṣaliḥ, 2008, p. 28, see *supra* note 16.

25 The word 'ethnic' used in the UN instruments means classifying human groups on the basis of their ethnic or racial origins.

> envisages the self and its perceptions, and determines the relationship with the "other" and their perceptions, including all their religious or intellectual heritage, and good or bad qualities.[26]

Moreover, some specialists believe that the approach pursued by the state in addressing the intellectual and ideological dimensions, as part of its counter-extremism and counter-terrorism efforts, is a decisive factor in bringing a person closer to or further from terrorist crimes.[27] As such, psychologists of terrorism have become preoccupied with observing behaviour associated with the perverted ideology in order to explain behaviour conducive to violence and terrorism. To this end, they study patterns conducive to terrorism, namely pathways leading to the growth and development of terrorist behaviour which causes a normal person to turn into a terrorist, bearing in mind that the modality by which a person adopts perverted and extremist ideologies conducive to violence and terrorism cannot be limited to a single pathway or explained by a specific theory.[28] Accordingly, counter-extremism measures should be based on a study of cognitive aspects and thought patterns[29] which also form the basis for studies on the topic of combating terrorist crimes.

Consequently, the intellectual factor has become an essential component in understanding the phenomena of *ghulú*, extremism and terrorism and envisaging measures to counter them, especially those targeting militias and terrorist armed groups who draw on the ideological factor to promote their false ideas.

It is surprising that these 'Islámized' groups promote themselves as the exclusive representatives of the correct understanding of Islám. A claim which is not true. The risk is that they employ their false narrative to corrupt people's faith. Their intellectual corruption and ideological deviations are manifested as follows:

- lack of knowledge of *Sharí'ah* purposes, rulings and ultimate ends;
- fanaticism to one's unilateral opinion and intolerance towards others;
- misperception of many religious and factual issues, resulting in *ghulú*;

---

26 Ṣaliḥ, 2008, p. 105, see *supra* note 16.

27 'Alí al-Ghanim, "Al-Dawlah wal-Mujtama': Ru'yah Náqdíyyah lit-Taríkh alIjtíma'í lil-Irhab (1952–2010)", in *Múajahat al-Jarímah al-Irhabíyyah wal-Muqtáḍáyat al-Wáṭáníyyah*, p. 92.

28 Muḥammad I. Muḥammad, "Saykúlújíyyat as-Súlúk al-Irhabí bayn Taḥlíl al-Masarát wa-Namúdhaj al-'aql al-Irhabí", *Diae Network for Conferences and Studies*, 17 May 2017.

29 "Al-Iṭár al-Manhají li-Dirasát al-Shakhṣíyyah al-Irhabíyyah: Naḥw Bina' Takamulí fí Dirasát al-Jarímah al-Irhabíyyah", 2019, pp. 121–122, *supra* note 22.

- and finally, narrow ambitions of the person or the group, rendering legitimate all means to realize their goals.[30]

As will be elaborated later, United Nations ('UN') agencies agree that ideological deviation and extremism are among the most dangerous factors conducive to violent extremism and terrorism. In this regard, the Ambassador and Permanent Representative of Egypt to the UN and the then Chair of the UN Security Council Counter-Terrorism Committee ('CTC') stated: "Acts of violence can never be justified on the basis of religious pretext".[31]

In short, the intellectual and ideological dimensions are the foremost factors conducive to extremism and violence, and consequently the perpetration of terrorist crimes.[32] From a legal perspective, international jurisprudence almost unanimously suggests that a terrorist crime usually arises from an individual or collective strategy driven by ideological motives,[33] driving a person to violent extremism and therefore to commit terrorist crimes.

Accordingly, ideological deviation can be defined as the divergence from reasonable limits which amounts to *ghulú* and the strict adherence to an ideology or a set of ideologies, be it religious, political, social or economic. Based on this ideology, the person believes that he holds the absolute and indisputable truth. In addition, as far as knowledge is concerned, he spurns any difference in opinion and rejects diversity and pluralism.[34] Accordingly, he lives in isolation from the general society and in separation from the social fabric of the community where he exists and belongs. As such, he suffers from alienation from his own self and from society at large[35] and poses a threat to society if his thought exceeds the limit.

---

30 "Speech of Professor Naẓīr Muḥammad Naẓīr, Secretary General of the Islámic Research Academy on behalf of the Grand Imam", Opening Session, 30th General Conference of the Supreme Council for Islámic Affairs, Cairo, 15 September 2019.

31 Ambassador Amr A. Aboulatta, "2030 Agenda – A Unique Opportunity to Address Conditions Conducive to the Spread of Terrorism", in *UN Chronicle*, 2015, vol. 52, no. 4 (available on the UN web site).

32 "Al-Dawlah wal-Mujtama': Ru'yah Naqdíyyah lit-Taríkh al-Ijtima'í lil-Irhab (1952–2010)", p. 94, see *supra* note 27.

33 See also on the definition of terrorism and elements that should be fulfilled in a terrorist crime: Aḥmad F. Súrúr, *Al-Múajahat al-Qánúníyyah lil-Irhab*, 2008, p. 58; Aḥmad Aḥmad F. Súrúr, *Ḥukm al-Qánún fí Múajahat al-Irhab*, Madbouly Bookshop, 2007, p. 6.

34 "Al-Tashríḥ al-Thaqáfí li-'Áqlíyyat al-Mutaṭárriff", 11th Cultural Salon, Ṭabah Research and Development Consulting Foundation (available on the Tabah Foundation's web site).

35 'Ala' Z. al-Rawashda, "At-Taṭárruff al-Aydíúlújí min Wijhat Naẓár al-Shabab al-'urduní", in *Al-Majallah al-'Árábíyyah lil-Dirasát al-Amnníyyah wat-Tadríb*, vol. 32, no. 63, Riyadh, 2015, p. 90.

An extremist person's mindset and ideological composition are created by many factors that bring about new patterns of extremism, attributed to intellectual, psychological, political or social reasons, or driven by economic and educational motives. With a balanced and comprehensive perspective, it can be asserted that the relevant drivers of extremism are intertwined and overlapping. Therefore, we should not address one single driver, as the phenomenon in question is complicated by many overlapping causes.[36] With intensive stimuli of intellectual deviation, the person progresses towards radicalization.

16.2.1.2.2. Radicalization

Radicalization is one of the main drivers for a person to fall into the trap of extremism and terrorism. Western jurists largely view radicalization as an upward process of radical change of thought which may be conducive to extremism and violence. The term is usually understood in relation to the context in which it is being used.[37]

In Egypt, and other Arab and Muslim countries, contemporary political science experts correlate the radicalization of certain groups of persons, who are already have fallen in the realm of deviating ideologies, to the influence of political Islám.[38]

The terms 'radicalization', 'fundamentalism' and 'hate speech' are used in terrorism-related studies to refer to the means employed by terrorist organizations to recruit people to their ranks. These terms denote the process used to influence a person to adopt a radical stance on topics of a social, political or religious nature, and then to encourage them to commit violence in support of these positions.

According to the UN, there is no reliable statistical data on reasons for individual radicalization. While easily recognizable trends and patterns exist, researchers agree only on a few areas. Qualitative research, which primarily used interviews, suggests that two main categories of drivers can be distinguished: 'push factors', namely the conditions conducive to violent extremism and the structural context from which it emerges; and 'pull factors', or the

---

36 Salih bin G. al-Sudlan, "Asbab al-Irhab wal-'Unff wat-Taṭárruff", in *Majallat al-Amn wal-Ḥayah*, Naif Arab University for Security Sciences, 2004, no. 286, p. 53.

37 Alex P. Schmid, "Radicalization, De-Radicalization, Counter-Radicalization: A Conceptual Discussion and Literature Review", International Centre for Counter-Terrorism (ICCT) Research Paper, March 2013, The Hague, p. 11.

38 See Nabil Abd al-Fatah, "Islamic Radical Changing Discourse", in Diaa Rashwan, *The Revisions: From the Islamic Jamaa to Jihad*, Al-Ahram Centre for Political and Strategic Studies, 2008, p. 95.

individual motivations and processes which play a key role in transforming ideas and grievances into violent extremist actions.[39]

Hate speech can be considered as a 'push factor' to radicalization. Extremists usually employ hateful expressions against the 'others' to instil malevolent and hostile ideas in the hearts of their followers against their adversaries – a modality used by militant groups operating in the Arab region to incite violence against their opponents.

According to contemporary Islámic jurisprudence, a person would embrace extremist religious ideology for reasons such as ignorance and lack of knowledge making a person susceptible to various interpretations, or adhering to the superficial meanings of texts, reliance on unreliable (*Sharí'ah)* sources, contaminating some school curricula with confused ideas, and finally enthusiasm and arrogance towards one's ideas and concepts that might lead a person to complete fanaticism for their hard-line thoughts. This amounts to the *takfír* of others and to a premise for their killing, causing a person to enter the loop of violent extremism.[40]

16.2.1.2.3. Violent Extremism

Violence is one of the most dangerous social phenomena threatening societies globally and posing a risk to peace and security.[41] Violent extremism is a new term for Muslims, emanating from the Western world. Some Western countries have agreed to the use of the term 'violent extremism', especially when it comes to dealing with radical or *takfír* terrorist groups. Subsequently, it has been adopted in many international and regional instruments.

I have noted above that the dangers of extremism are exacerbated when it turns from being a thought, belief and theoretical perception to a material expression using violent means, such as murder and threatening to murder. Accordingly, the phenomenon of extremism is placed under the umbrella of

39 UN Secretary-General, Plan of Action to Prevent Violent Extremism, UN Doc. A/70/674, 24 December 2015, para. 23 ('Plan of Action to Prevent Violent Extremism') (https://www.legal-tools.org/doc/ui69e3/).

40 Al-Sharíf Ibráhím Saliḥ al-Ḥusseiní, Chairman of the Nigerian Fatwa and Islámic Council), "Al-Ghulú wat-Taṭárruff wa-Dawr al-'Ulama' fí Muḥarábátihima", in Al-Ghulú wat-Taṭárruff, Islamic Research Academy, 2015, p. 92; Ibráhím Ráshid al-Muraíkhí, "Al-Ghulú wat-Taṭárruff wa-Dawr al-'Ulama' fí Múḥarábátihima", in Al-Ghulú wat-Taṭárruff, Islamic Research Academy, 2015, pp. 79–80.

41 "At-Taṭárruff ad-Díní wa-Ab'aduh: Amníyyann ... wa-Siyasíyyann ... wa-Jtima'íyyann", p. 7, see *supra* note 8.

'violent extremism'. It should be noted that 'violent extremism' is argued to be the natural incubator of terrorism.[42]

Violent extremism is a diverse phenomenon which lacks a clear definition.[43] Similar to the term 'terrorism', violent extremism has not yet received an agreed upon definition by states, especially in the Arab world. It is not exclusive to a certain region, nationality or system of belief. In essence, it is internationally agreed that violent extremism is a global phenomenon, driven by a combination of personal, intellectual and societal factors, and its manifestation varies between individuals and societies.[44]

In promoting the term 'violent extremism' and urging counteraction, the UN may have been driven by the emergence of armed groups using violence to achieve their goals. A further reason is that religious extremism has usually been a common feature between violence and terrorism committed by these groups. Therefore, a new trend has emerged at all international, regional and national levels seeking solutions to address this type of extremism, especially when it is associated with violence. The term 'violent extremism' was incorporated into international instruments, with special attention from the UN, the European Union ('EU') and other international organizations concerned with the study of this phenomenon and the design of policies and frameworks to prevent it.

It is noteworthy that, in 2017, the Permanent Mission of Egypt to the UN in New York undertook active efforts to persuade the UN Security Council ('UNSC') to issue a resolution (Resolution No. 2354 of 2017),[45] welcoming and putting into force the UN document titled 'Comprehensive International Framework to Counter Terrorist Narratives'.[46] The Egyptian Ministry of Foreign Affairs said then that: "The issuance of this resolution culminates Egypt's efforts in countering terrorist narratives and ideologies".[47]

---

[42] "Speech of Dr. Abdulaziz Ḥamad Al Awaishq", 30 October 2019, Common Vulnerabilities and Exposure Network's Second Workshop, General Secretariat of the Gulf Cooperation Council, Riyadh.

[43] Plan of Action to Prevent Violent Extremism, para. 2, see *supra* note 39; National Human Rights Council, Cairo Declaration on "The Role of Awareness Institutions in Confronting Violent Extremism and Incitement to Hate", 7 July 2017, preambular paragraph 2 ('Cairo Declaration on the Role of Awareness Institutions').

[44] Plan of Action to Prevent Violent Extremism, para. 59, see *supra* note 39.

[45] UNSC, Resolution 2354 (2017), UN Doc. S/RES/2354, 24 May 2017 (https://www.legal-tools.org/doc/9ae36f/).

[46] UNSC, Comprehensive International Framework to Counter Terrorist Narratives, UN Doc. S/2017/375 (Annex), 28 April 2017 (https://www.legal-tools.org/doc/43nh0x/).

[47] It should be noted here that the language of the Security Council resolution in its Arabic version uses the phrase "terrorist discourse" as a translation of the phrase "violent extremism" which is included in the English version of the resolution which has the same meaning as the

To explain what violent extremism is, some governments and research centres argue that it "reflects the beliefs and actions of persons who support or use violence to achieve ideological, religious or political goals".[48] The United States ('US') administration uses this term to refer to extremists who support or commit violence driven by ideological motives to achieve political goals. It considers terrorism as one of the means used by such extremists to reach their goals.[49]

According to Professor Ali Eddin Hilāl,

> [i]n order for a person to reach this stage of extremism, they usually go through a series of stimuli or influences which go beyond the mere adoption of a certain ideology to the violent extremism. This shift typically takes place as a result of the influence of astray or perverted ideas or due to personal ambitions and political conflicts, or the effects of involvement in certain organizations. The ultimate outcome is the "legitimization" of the behavior of violence and terrorism.[50]

As explained by one researcher, in order to explain how a person becomes a perpetrator of violent and terrorist acts, some specialists distinguish between 'extremism in opinion' and 'extremism in action'. In addressing the concept of 'extremism in opinion' as manifested in the phenomenon of 'Islámic extremism' – according to their classification – they divide persons who adopt extremist ideologies along a bottom-up hierarchical scale, starting with neutral persons at the bottom, going up to sympathizers and then to justifiers, all the way up to the top which is occupied by the *takfīr jihádist* ideologies. The 'extremism in action' phenomenon, on the other hand, starts at the bottom with motionless persons,

---

French version "l'extrémisme violent". Therefore, Egyptian media circulated this mistranslation in the news that was published related to the said resolution of the Security Council. It should be likewise noted that the Minister of Foreign Affairs used the term "violent extremism" in his official speeches, as I will address in detail when discussing the term 'violent extremism' in section four of the present chapter. Generally, according to the working procedures of the UN, should a text written in one of the official languages differ from the original text written in the two working languages (English and French), the two working languages shall prevail, as stipulated in Article 52 of the UN, Provisional Rules of Procedure for the General Assembly, UN Doc. A/71/Rev1, 28 April 1947 (English) (https://www.legal-tools.org/doc/77vh93/) and Rule 51 of the UN, Rules of Procedure for the General Assembly, UN Doc. A/520/Rev.19, 2021 (Arabic) (https://www.legal-tools.org/doc/z06j3e/).

48 Department of Parliamentary Services, Parliament of Australia, "Australian Government Measures to Counter Violent Extremism: A Quick Guide", 10 February 2015, Research Paper Series (2014–2015).

49 For more details, see the web site of the US Department of Homeland Security.

50 Ali E. Hilāl, "How Does Intellectual Extremism Turn Into Terrorism?", *Al-'Ain Analytics*, 13 August 2019.

and moves up through fanatics, radical and violent extremists and finally to terrorists.[51]

Figure 1 illustrates the above-mentioned process:

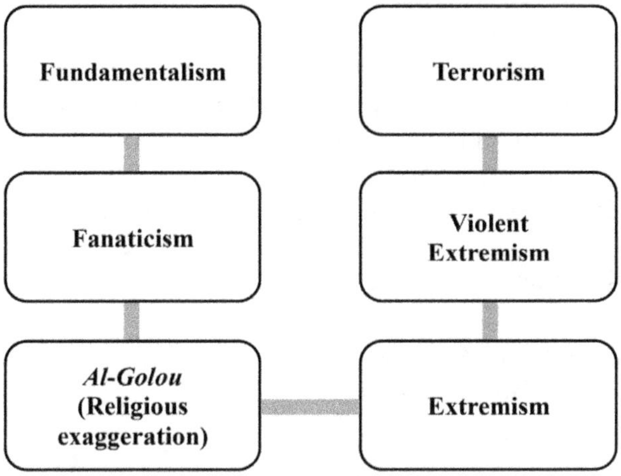

Figure 1: Visualization of the radicalization process.

The Cairo Declaration on Human Rights in Islam, adopted by the Egyptian National Council for Human Rights, highlighted the role of educational institutions in confronting violent extremism and incitement to hatred, stating that:

> Confronting violent extremism is a major challenge facing countries in the world today. It is considered the main source of terrorism, together with its catastrophic repercussions on human rights and the exacerbation of social conflicts and civil wars.[52]

Many instruments issued by the UN on combating violent extremism opine that violent extremism may be caused by many factors and that some groups are more vulnerable to violent extremism, due to which they have been recruited by international terrorist groups using extremist or radical rhetoric which results in violent extremism that may be conducive to terrorism.[53]

According to promoters of the term 'violent extremism', extremism reaching a certain threshold at which embracers of such extremism use violence to achieve their goals, goes beyond the boundaries and limits of usual extremism.

---

[51] Shiḥatah Zayyan, "'Irhab adh-Dhi'ab al-Munfaridah bayn Tawsí' Da'irat al-Ishtibah wa-Ḍámanat Huqúq al-Insan: Da'wah lil-Fahm", in *Múajahat al-Jarímah al-Irhabíyyah wal-Muqtáḍayat al-Wáṭáníyyah,* National Centre for Social and Criminal Studies, 2019, pp. 68–71.

[50] Cairo Declaration on the Role of Awareness Institutions, see *supra* note 43.

[53] See, for example, Preventing Violent Extremism, p. 5, see *supra* note 21.

Therefore, it was termed 'violent extremism'. In the West, the term 'violent extremism' was mostly introduced to address so-called 'Islámic extremism'. By the same standards, Western discourse should speak of 'violent racist extremism' if racism uses hateful expressions and violence to achieve its ill ideology against other races or ethnic groups.

However, it is incorrect to attempt to attribute violent extremism exclusively to 'Islámized' terrorist groups. The rationale for this is that many violent accidents of extremism and terrorism that have recently occurred in the West, involved Muslim victims. Therefore, the Al-Azhar Observatory believes that many acts of violent extremism and terrorism that have occurred in the West recently are a result of a racist ideology based on the rejection and hatred of Muslims and Islám that is reinforced by the Western discourse promoted on social media and mass media.[54]

In its Plan of Action to Prevent Violent Extremism, the UN attributed violent extremism to the following factors:

- lack of socio-economic opportunities;
- marginalization and discrimination;
- poor governance, violations of human rights and the rule of law;
- prolonged and unresolved conflicts; and
- radicalization in prisons.[55]

According to the UN, these factors were identified following a study and monitoring of specific recurring drivers which are common among a wide variety of countries and regions and which lead, sometimes in isolation and sometimes in combination with other factors, to radicalization and violent extremism.[56]

> Understanding factors causing the shift from politicization to violence is vital not only to understanding violence and terrorism incidents which take place around us, but also to developing counter-policies and programs and reduce their effects.[57]

In a previous study, I have expressed my apprehension that the term 'violent extremism' may be used exclusively to label deeds of 'Islámised' terrorist

---

54 "Ḥadit͟h Niyúzílandah al-Irhabi ... min Zawayah 'Uk͟hrá, Waḥdat Raṣd al-Lug͟hat al-Isbaníyyah, Marṣád Al-Ázhár", Al-Azhar, 9 April 2019 (available on Al-Azhar's web site).

55 Plan of Action to Prevent Violent Extremism, Section A, "Conditions Conducive to and the Structural Context of Violent Extremism", paras. 25–31, see *supra* note 39.

56 *Ibid.*, para. 24.

57 Hilāl, 13 August 2019, see *supra* note 50.

groups, rather than to describe terrorism.[58] This concern is justified especially given the fact that some of these groups receive illegitimate logistical and financial support and are not considered by some countries as terrorists. I uphold the position to exclude those who launch hostile armed terrorist attacks from any international protection and to counter any attempts to mitigate the actions of such groups, which must be labelled as 'terrorism', not merely as 'violent extremism'.[59]

Considering the foregoing, the Egyptian Minister of Foreign Affairs, Ambassador Sameh Shoukry stated, while addressing the Summit on Countering Violent Extremism held by the White House in Washington, D.C. from 17 to 19 February 2015, that "terrorist organizations exploit the violent extremist ideology to attract and recruit combative elements and legitimize their criminal acts", and that:

> a proper understanding of the phenomenon of extremism must begin with the recognition that all terrorist organizations under different names are linked to one ideological framework, be it ISIS, Boko Haram, Ansar al-*Sharí'ah*, al-Qaeda or others.[60]

Accordingly, the correct confrontation of these groups and their extremist ideology must be based on a comprehensive approach which encompasses not only essential security-based counter-terrorism measures, but also systematic preventive measures which directly address the drivers of violent extremism which cause people to join violent extremist groups.[61]

Notably, several legal systems in the Arab world have already criminalized some behaviours conducive to 'violent extremism'. The Egyptian legislator for example, prohibited, in Article (28) of Law No. 94 of 2015 on Combating Terrorism, the promotion of ideas and beliefs advocating the use of violence on the basis that they indirectly promote the commission of terrorist crimes.[62]

---

58 Adel Maged, "Múajahat al-Irhab fī Sayna': 'Istiratíjíyyat aḍ-Ḍárabat al-Istibáqíyyah (Confronting Terrorism in Sinai: Preemptive Attacks Strategy)", in *Kurrasat 'Istiratíjíyyah*, Al-Ahram Centre for Political and Strategic Studies, 2015, vol. 24, no. 257, p. 9.

59 For more information on armed terrorist groups operating in the Arab world using extremist religious thought to justify their violent behavior and achieve their political goals, see Adel Maged, "The Impact of Religion on Military Self-Interest in Accountability: An Islámic Sharīah Perspective", in Morten Bergsmo and SONG Tianying (eds.), *Military Self-Interest in Accountability for Core International Crimes*, TOAEP, Brussels, 2015, pp. 141–166 (https://www.toaep.org/ps-pdf/25-bergsmo-song-second/).

60 "Speech of Minister of Foreign Affairs Ambassador Sameh Shoukry", Summit on Countering Violent Extremism, Washington, D.C., 17–19 February 2015.

61 Letter dated 22 December 2015 from the Secretary-General to the President of the General Assembly, UN Doc. A/70/675, 24 December 2015 (https://www.legal-tools.org/doc/r2lv9n/).

62 Anti-Terrorism Law, Article 28, see *supra* note 19.

Definitely, a person who is under the influence of 'radicalization' or 'violent extremism' is easily incited and persuaded to commit terrorist crimes.

In light of the international standards established by international instruments on countering violent extremism, and in order to counter any attempt to circumvent the description of terrorism for crimes committed by extremist terrorist groups, I introduced, in a previous study, the following definition of violent extremism:

> A state in which an extremist person commits a form of verbal or actual violent behavior, individually or within a joint criminal project. This includes the promotion of views which would incite hate, instigate violence or encourage the commission of acts potentially conducive to terrorism, in support of the person's beliefs which are driven by religious, racial, ethnic, political or other motives influencing the relevant person's belief.[63]

As already noted, extremism takes various forms, most notably extremism on grounds of religious or racist beliefs.

16.2.1.3. Forms of Extremism

I have already explained above that extremism has varying degrees, starting at a point in which a person is influenced by astray ideologies, followed by the adoption of and fanaticism for that perverted ideology in a manner that is conducive to radicalization and then to extremism. This is usually associated with manifestations of visible behaviour which indicates and anticipates extremism. While extremism has various degrees, it also has different types; it is not exclusively religious as some would believe or argue. I uphold this claim as the phenomenon of extremism is often automatically and stereotypically linked to the concept of 'religious extremism'. As such, it has been limited to extremism stemming from a false religious thought. This is an incorrect approach as extremism may also be attributed to the adoption of ideas based on non-religious foundations. It may also arise on ethnic, ideological, political and racial grounds.

My focus in this chapter will be on religious and racial extremism.

16.2.1.3.1. Religious Extremism

As noted above, the prohibition of discrimination against persons or groups on the basis of religion has been a well-established international norm, recognized by all countries and peoples. It has been enshrined at the international level, for more than seventy years, in Article 2 of the Universal Declaration of Human

---

63 Adel Maged, "Bayn at-Taṭárruff wal-Irhab: Ru'yah Qánúníyyah" (Between Extremism and Terrorism: A Legal Prespective), in *Taḥaddíyyat a<u>th</u>-<u>Th</u>aqáfah al-Qánúníyyah fí al-'Alam al-'Árábí, al-Markaz al-'Árábí lil-Wa'y bil-Qánún*, December 2019, p. 45.

Rights. The norm has been codified in the 1965 International Convention on the Elimination of All Forms of Racial Discrimination ('ICERD'),[64] which established international responsibility for its violation. In the same vein, discrimination against persons on the grounds of religion or belief constitutes an affront to human dignity and a disavowal of the principles of the UN Charter.[65]

Therefore, the UN Commission on Human Rights expressed its deep concern at negative stereotyping of religions and manifestations of intolerance and discrimination in matters of religion or belief which are still evident in many parts of the world at present.[66] According to former UN Special Rapporteur on Freedom of Religion or Belief Heiner Bielefeldt, religious extremism typically implies the rejection of pluralism not only among religions but also – and often in even more aggressive ways – within the same religion.[67] Accordingly, the UN urges states to take all necessary actions to combat hate and fanaticism motivated by religious discrimination potentially conducive to extremism.[68]

In many of its instruments, the UN has also emphasized its condemnation of the employment of religion for narrow purposes. The 'Joint Declaration on Freedom of Expression and Countering Violent Extremism'[69] states that:

> Experience from different parts of the world shows that harnessing religion for narrow purposes of power politics nearly always results in setting groups of people against one another, thus often poisoning relations between communities that had previously coexisted peacefully.[70]

---

64 For more information on the ICERD, see, Adel Maged, "Mas'úlíyyat ad-Dúwal 'an al-Isa'ah 'ila al-'Adyan war-Rumúz ad-Díníyyah" (The Responsibility of States for Defamation of Religion and Religious Figures), in *Strategic Studies Series (The Emirates Centre for Strategic Studies and Research)*, 2007, no. 125, pp. 16–18.

65 UN General Assembly, Resolution on the Elimination of All Forms of Religious Intolerance, UN Doc. A/RES/50/183, 6 March 1996 ('UN Resolution on the Elimination of All Forms of Religious Intolerance') (https://www.legal-tools.org/doc/tku3p1/).

66 UN Commission of Human Rights, Resolution on Combating Defamation of Religions, UN Doc. E/CN.4/2005/3, 12 April 2005 (https://www.legal-tools.org/doc/46pw9a/).

67 Report of the Special Rapporteur on Freedom of Religion or Belief, Heiner Bielefeldt, Addendum: Mission to Jordan, UN Doc. A/HRC/25/58/Add.2, 27 January 2014 (https://www.legal-tools.org/doc/qniu9w/).

68 UN Resolution on the Elimination of All Forms of Religious Intolerance, para. 5, see *supra* note 65.

69 UN Special Rapporteur on Freedom of Opinion and Expression, the Organization for Security and Co-operation in Europe Representative on Freedom of the Media, the Organization of American States Special Rapporteur on Freedom of Expression and Special Rapporteur of the African Commission on Human Rights and Peoples on Freedom of Expression and Access to Information, "Joint Declaration on Freedom of Expression and Countering Violent Extremism", May 2015 (https://www.legal-tools.org/doc/ae7oa2/).

70 *Ibid.*

Religious extremism is also closely related to the concept of 'sectarianism' which means fanaticism towards a particular sect or doctrine. Sectarianism may encourage fanatics of one sect by depriving followers of another sect from practicing their rituals as a form of intellectual and ideological terrorism. As mentioned before, religious extremism in Egypt and many Arab countries was not limited to threatening the rights of Christian citizens, but went beyond to adopt a *takfīr* ideology targeting Muslims of the same sect. In his keynote speech at the International Institute for Strategic Studies Manama Dialogue, Egyptian President Abdel Fatah Al-Sisi stressed[71] that the escalation of sectarian differences has fuelled the continuation of conflicts in the Arab region, wasting the energy of the Arab states and threatening the assets of its peoples, in addition to causing severe damage to the role and prestige of the state. The national state concept is inevitably negatively affected by fuelling hateful sectarian tendencies.

It has become clear that the armed terrorist attacks that take place throughout the Arab world are based on this extremist *takfīr* ideology[72] which is disseminated through radical narratives and through the incitement of violence, encouraging followers of this narrative to carry weapons against their own countrymen. This type of radical narrative is dangerous as it is issued by *takfīr* groups seeking to *takfīr* and defame the other, in preparation of their elimination. Therefore, they would not hesitate to commit the most heinous crimes in the name of religion. To this end, they partly employ religion to serve their goals, by exploiting the naivety of certain groups or their sectarian tendencies and greed for power, or by tickling the feelings of those who belong to extremist political Islámic groups and by providing them with money and weapons to achieve their goals.[73] They do not hesitate to justify their wicked deeds with false interpretation of the *Qur'an* and the *Sunnah*, which are the main sources of Islámic law, as well as by citing historical radical precedents such as the Khawarij movement and Ibn Taymiyya's *fatwá*.

Based on the above arguments, a recent EU-funded research project considered abuse of religious thoughts and teachings as a substantial driver of radicalization and violent extremism among young people.[74]

---

71 "Speech of President Abdelfattah El-Sisi", Manama Dialogue Forum, Manama, Bahrain, 30 October 2015.

72 For more information, see "Múajahat al-Irhab fí Sayna': 'Istiratíjíyyat aḍ-Ḍárabat al-Istibáqíyyah", 2015, pp. 19–20, *supra* note 58; Adel Maged, "Miṣr wal- Ḥárb 'ala al-Irhab d-Dawlí, Al-Maṣry Al-Youm Newspaper", 21 January 2014, p. 12.

73 For more information on the risk of the extremist religious thought, see "The Impact of Religion on Military Self-Interest in Accountability", 2015, pp. 141–166, *supra* note 59.

74 Contexts of Violent Extremism in MENA and Balkan Societies (CONNEKT). The project explores the drivers of radicalization and violent extremism among young people aged from

Religious scholars and other specialists of psychology, social science and political sociology almost unanimously agree that religious radical ideology must be confronted on the basis of thought and dialogue. In this regard, the review process led by Al-Azhar scholars and the 'Al-Azhar Document to Renounce Violence and Commit to National Dialogue to Resolve Controversial Issues' is often cited. The document mainly seeks to renounce violence and deprive it of its political cover and protect the national fabric from sectarian strife and calls for racism. We have seen how religious institutions, namely Al-Azhar and the Egyptian Orthodox Church, managed to contain incidents of sectarian violence.

In any case, I share the opinion of the former UN Special Rapporteur on the Promotion and Protection of Human Rights and Fundamental Freedoms while Countering Terrorism, Ben Emmerson, in his warning against overemphasizing religious ideology as the driver of terrorism and violent extremism at the expense of other potential political, social or economic factors.[75]

Despite the role of religion as a substantial driver of extremism, if misused, the concept of extremism is not exclusive to religious extremism, but includes extremism arising from racist tendencies as well. In this context, I point out that the term 'racism' itself is associated with meanings of intolerance and extremism which amount to hatred of the other. Religious extremism and racism are both abhorrent terms, arising from feelings of self-overestimation and superiority compared to others. This is the very same arrogance that contradicts normal instinct and true religious feeling, which suggest moderation and balance.

16.2.1.3.2. Racial Extremism

Discrimination on the ground of race or ethnic background has certainly caused serious adversities that left many victims. We have seen how racial discrimination led to the killing of Egyptian citizens in some Western countries and was a cause for the killing of dozens of US citizens (by their fellow citizens and with weapons made in the United States itself).

---

12 to 30 in eight countries: Bosnia and Herzegovina, Bulgaria, Egypt, Jordan, Kosovo, Morocco, North Macedonia and Tunisia. It maps and establish interrelationships and specific significance of seven potential drivers (religion, digitalization, economic deprivation, territorial inequalities, transitional dynamics, socio-political demands, educational, cultural and leisure opportunities) within three different levels of analysis (global-state, community and individual).

[75] UN High Commissioner for Human Rights, Report on Best Practices and Lessons Learned on How Protecting and Promoting Human Rights Contribute to Preventing and Countering Violent Extremism, UN Doc. A/HRC/33/29, 21 July 2016, para. 15 (https://www.legal-tools.org/doc/p90c3n/).

Racism is a repugnant characteristic and a hateful term associated with the meanings of excessive self-esteem or egocentrism, exclusion, marginalization, humiliation or belittling of the other and dealing with them as inferiors. Therefore, it contributes to the formation of a heritage that reflects a state of arrogance which discriminates between people based on their racial and ethnic characteristics, social or economic status or religious affiliations.

Racism is usually associated with the worst forms of intimidation and discrimination reflected, for example, in the banning of some cultures and the ranking certain citizens of a particular race as second-class. Two cases in point are the racial segregation or apartheid seen in both the US and South Africa. Migrants are usually targets of discrimination, hate speech and intolerance, often under the pretext of maintaining ethnic and religious purity and preserving the cultural and linguistic heritage of a geographical region.[76]

A major feature of Egypt and its people is that the concept of racism and its manifestations, in their explicit linguistic meanings, do not exist in the vocabulary of Egyptians, which underscores their tolerance and resistance to any attempts to incite racism or sectarianism among them.

Combined with intolerance, racist discrimination will be conducive to extremism and violence in dealing with the 'other'. This was evident in several Western countries where bloody incidents seem to have been driven by racial discrimination, which is often fuelled by hate speech.

16.2.2. Challenges of Hate Speech

It was concluded above that the broad concept of extremism is not exclusive to religious extremism; rather, it goes beyond to include racial extremism as well. Indeed, religious extremism and racism are usually motivated by hate speech. As such, it is necessary to explain what hate speech is, its stance in Islám, its dangers and its counter mechanisms both at the international and national levels.

16.2.2.1. What Hate Speech Is

Hate speech is defined in some laws as "every statement or action that incites discord, strife, or discrimination between individuals or groups".[77] All these

[76] UN Human Rights Council, Report of the Special Rapporteur on Contemporary Forms of Racism, Racial Discrimination, Xenophobia and Related Intolerance, UN Doc. A/HRC/38/5225, 25 April 2018 (https://www.legal-tools.org/doc/pkidr7/).

[77] See United Arab Emirates, Federal Decree-Law No. (2) of 2015 Concerning Combating Discrimination and Hatred, 15 July 2015, Article (1) ('Federal Decree Law') (https://www.legal-tools.org/doc/s8g0gl/).

forms of behaviour are deemed 'hate crimes' by several laws.[78] Acts of incitement to hatred against a group of the population defined by a particular characteristic such as race or religion are criminalized by other laws as constituting a disturbance to public peace which is punishable, as stipulated in Article 130 of the German Criminal Code.[79]

Under international human rights law, there is no universal definition of hate speech as the concept is still widely disputed especially in relation to the freedom of opinion and expression, non-discrimination and equality.[80] However, in its efforts to reach a unified definition of the term globally, the UN Strategy and Plan of Action on Hate Speech defines hate speech as:

> Any kind of communication in speech, writing or behaviour, that attacks or uses pejorative or discriminatory language with reference to a person or a group on the basis of who they are, in other words, based on their religion, ethnicity, nationality, race, colour, descent, gender or other identity factor.[81]

Hate speech seeks to form stereotypes and create public opinion, which is directed towards intolerant tendencies, reflecting hate, and fuelling sentiments of hostility against the other on the grounds of religion or race, in order to marginalize or sometimes eliminate them. The danger of hate speech is intensified when it is targeted at oppressed or marginalized communities.

Therefore, hate speech is one of the most dangerous means of inciting extremism which is conducive to violent extremism and terrorism. Auspiciously, the international community is aware that hate speech has the potential to incite violence and undermine social unity and recognized that it has been a precursor to atrocity crimes, including genocide, over the past 75 years.[82]

The UN Secretary-General has unequivocally warned of the danger of hate speech. He said:

> Hate speech is in itself an attack on tolerance, inclusion, diversity and the very essence of our human rights norms and principles. More broadly, it undermines social cohesion, erodes shared values, and can lay the foundation for violence, setting back the cause of

78 For more information about the definition of hate crimes, see, Charles L. Nier, "Racial Hatred: A Comparative Analysis of the Hate Crimes Law of the United States and Germany", in *Dickinson Journal of International Law*, 1995, vol. 13, no. 2, p. 242.

79 Maged, 2007, p. 19, see *supra* note 64.

80 UN, "Understanding Hate Speech" (available on the UN web site).

81 UN Secretary-General, "United Nations Strategy and Plan of Action on Hate Speech", May 2019, p. 2 (https://www.legal-tools.org/doc/5rrb5b/).

82 UN Secretary-General António Guterres, "United Nations Strategy and Plan of Action on Hate Speech", 18 June 2019 (https://www.legal-tools.org/doc/ugpz03/).

> peace, stability, sustainable development and the fulfilment of human rights for all.[83]

Accordingly, the UN highlights that it is vital to prevent "advocacy of hatred that constitutes incitement to hostility, violence and/or discrimination".[84] As mentioned before, hate speech may target people, groups, or the state's institutions.

Thus, the prohibition of incitement to hatred and superiority-based propaganda are considered in many instruments issued by the UN which prohibit incitement to hatred in all its forms, especially cases relating to hate speech motivated by racism, including the dissemination of ideas of racial superiority or incitement to racial hatred.[85] The UN has also stressed that prohibiting the dissemination of ideas based on racial superiority or racial hatred does not contradict freedom of opinion and expression.[86] The same meaning was echoed by the European Court of Human Rights, which ruled that the right to freedom of expression shall be respected unless it implies incitement to disrespect or hatred.[87]

16.2.2.2. Prohibition of Hate Speech in Islámic *Sharí'ah*

Islám promotes good manners and prohibits hate speech. This has been illustrated in *Súrát Ibráhím* (the fourteenth chapter of the *Qur'án*). To uphold this line of thought, the Prophet Muhammad has asserted in his *ḥadíth* that: "The good word is a [benevolence] [charity]".[88] The call for 'good or pure words' has been repeated in the Prophet Muhammad's *ḥadíth*.

The term 'hate speech', as such, is not used in classical *Sharí'ah* literature. However, 'hate' and 'hateful utterances' are prohibited in various sources of Islámic *Sharí'ah*. Islámic *Sharí'ah* forbids hate speech as it contradicts the purposes of Islám (*maqáṣid ash-Sharí'ah*). Typically, all forms of speech, including hateful utterances, that aim to humiliate or degrade the honour of others or to fuel sentiments of hostility against the other are condemned in Islám. In his

---

83 *Ibid.*

84 "Joint Declaration on Freedom of Expression and Countering Violent Extremism", May 2015, see *supra* note 69.

85 International Covenant on Civil and Political Rights, 16 December 1966, Articles 19 and 20 (2) (https://www.legal-tools.org/doc/2838f3/); and ICERD, 21 December 1965, Article 4 (https://www.legal-tools.org/doc/43a925/).

86 Committee on the Elimination of Racial Discrimination, Report of the Committee on the Elimination of Racial Discrimination, UN Doc. A/48/18, 15 September 1993, General Recommendation XV (https://www.legal-tools.org/doc/ucve4z/).

87 European Court of Human Rights, *Giniewski v. France*, Judgment, Application No. 64016/00, 31 January 2006, para. 52 (https://www.legal-tools.org/doc/e1ed3d/).

88 Al-Bukhárí, *ḥadíth* no. 6023.

ḥadíth to his companions, the Prophet Muhammad (ﷺ) requested them to avoid hating each other. He said:

> Do not hate one another, nor be jealous of one another; and do not desert one another, but O Allah's worshipers! Be Brothers! And it is unlawful for a Muslim to desert his brother Muslim (and not to talk to him) for more than three nights.[89]

Noticeably, Islámic *Sharí'ah* prohibited all sort of behaviour that constitutes hate speech. All forms of disrespect of others are explicitly condemned in Islámic *Sharí'ah*. According to Islámic teachings, mockery and similar forms of behaviours that amount to hate speech should be avoided, especially at times of conflict and disputes. In *Súrat Al- Ḥujurát* people are warned against mocking or ridiculing others:

> O believers, let not any people scoff at another people who may be better than they; neither let women scoff at women who may be better than themselves. And find not fault with one another, neither revile one another by nicknames.[90]

In his commentary on the above verse of the *Qur'án*, Ibn Kathír asserts that Allah forbids scoffing at people as it implies humiliating and belittling them. This prohibition, according to Ibn Kathír, is stated for both men and women.[91] Further, in his commentary on the verse which stipulates "nor insult one another by nicknames", Ibn Kathír states: "you should not address people by nicknames that they dislike".[92] One reason behind this is that mockery reflects a feeling of superiority that may instil hatred among people.

The ideology of *takfír* comes at the top of the hate speech narratives employed by extremists' militant groups to legitimize their actions against their enemies. The *takfír* ideology advocates the killing of non-Muslims and Muslims by declaring them as unbelievers. Perpetrators of violence use the garb of such ideology to justify their actions. These groups may even go to the limit of *takfír* of everyone who does not accept or follow their misguided ideology, even permitting their killing using the *takfír* rhetoric.[93] One wonders how these groups pretend to represent true Islám while they violate the basic rules of Islámic faith.

---

89 Al-Bukhárí, *ḥadíth* no. 6076.

90 The *Qur'án*, 49:11.

91 *Tafsír Ibn Kathír (interpretation of Noble Qur'án in English)*, vol. 9, Darussalam, Riyadh, 2000, p. 198.

92 *Ibid.*, p. 201.

93 For more information on the phenomenon of *takfír*, see, Grand Imam, Ahmed al-Ṭayyeb, "Khuṭúrat at-Takfír, Táṣḥíḥ al-Mafaḥím", pp. 99–111.

They disregard the fact that the *Qur'án* has established centuries ago that there is no compulsion in religion.[94]

For the above-mentioned reasons, the Prophet Muḥammad was very keen to warn his followers about the detrimental consequences of declaring another Muslim as apostate. There are several *ḥadíth* in which the Prophet Muḥammad warned Muslims not to declare a person a disbeliever. In one of his *ḥadíth*, the Prophet said:

> If the man told his brother (Muslim): *ya kafir* (you are a disbeliever), then one of them is a disbeliever.[95]

Therefore, an eminent religious scholar is of the opinion that "a major calamity experienced by our communities are fatwas issued by wicked preachers who advocate the comprehensiveness of *takfír* and for the shedding of blood".[96] The Grand Imam of Al-Azhar confirms that "*takfír* is a plague which afflicted the society in the past and in the present; it is stated exclusively by someone who is infringing on the law of God or ignorant of its teachings".[97]

In order to confront hate speech adopted by *takfír* groups, some laws combat and criminalize the exploitation of religion in the *takfír* of individuals and groups. These laws set heavy penalties for criminal offenders, which may amount to the death penalty if *takfír* is combined with incitement to murder, and therefore the crime of murder occurs accordingly.[98]

16.2.2.3. Religious Hatred

Hate speech seeks, *inter alia*, to stir up strife among people which is meant to create or attempts to create disorder, division and dispersal. The danger of hate speech increases when it targets specific groups of people, citizens or otherwise, who share common characteristics or features, in a manner that stigmatizes them as inferiors, or attributes them with other downgrading characteristics thus ranking them as lower than other groups. The risk of this speech is not limited to being 'racist' – rather, it also constitutes an open invitation for hostility and attack, of whatever form, against them.

Religious belief is sometimes the source of putative cases of hate speech. In all cases, religion-based hate speech may cause discord between people of the same religion, or between people of different religions, or the so-called

[94] The *Qur'án*, 2:258.

[95] Al-Bukhárí, *ḥadíth* no. 6103.

[96] Tamím, 2015, p. 105, see *supra* note 2.

[97] "Speech of the Grand Imam, Professor Ahmed al-Ṭayyeb", Final Statement, Al-Azhar International Conference on Renovation of Islámic Thought, Cairo, 27–28 January 2020.

[98] See, for example, Federal Decree Law, Article 10, *supra* note 77.

'sectarian strife'.[99] In this context, hate speech is dangerous because it is usually associated with incitement to violence among people which constitutes a serious threat to public peace. Religion-based hate speech is frequently used by militant extremists in a form of 'propagandistic' hateful expressions directed against a certain group or sect.

Hateful expression could be used to attack religious beliefs causing humiliation and frustration to the attacked groups. If we are unable to rectify the frustration caused to the targeted group, this might lead to anger which could then be transformed in certain societies to violence, exactly like the violent incidents involving comic cartoons of the Prophet Muḥammad in the Danish newspaper *Jyllands-Posten* and the French publication *Charlie Hebdo*, which caused societal disturbance in the Arab and Muslim worlds.

A 2022 occasional paper published by TOAEP highlights the danger of religious hatred and how hateful expression, in this context, could be used to incite violence against minorities (particularly Muslims), in public settings. In some incidents hateful expressions included calls to genocide and ethnic cleansing of Muslims.[100]

On the other hand, it has been proven through many incidents that attacking Islám, Islámic *Sharí'ah* and its symbols, *per se*, incites hatred and fuels extremism. As concluded in the TOAEP publication:

> it is important to accord importance to the devastating effects of verbal violence, not just as a precursor to physical violence but as a source of emotional and psychological distress for the targeted community and their ability to live a life with dignity.[101]

Islámic militant groups employ the feelings of alienation, anxiety and frustration among the Muslim community subjected to incidents of hateful expressions to induce and recruit young Muslims to follow their violent policies.

The following Figure 2 illustrates how hate speech by targeted persons who are wreaked by perverted ideologies could enter the path of extremism:

---

99 See Rabab A. Es-Sayíed, "Al-Bina' al-Ma'rifí wal-'Amn al-Fikrí", Ḥurríyyat al-'Áqídah bayn al-Ḥáẓr wal-Ibaḥah fí Dú' Mashrú' Qánún Mukafaḥat al-Karáḥíah wal-'Unff b-Ism ad-Dín al-Muqáddam min Al-Ázhár Ash-Sharíf, 12–13 December 2017, Third International Scientific Conference of the Faculty of Islámic and Arabic Studies for Girls, Cairo, p. 95.

100 Medha Damojipurapu, "Language and Connotation in Contemporary Hate Speech in India", Occasional Paper Series No. 11 (2022), TOAEP, Brussels, 2022, p. 42 (https://www.toaep.org/ops-pdf/11-damojipurapu/).

101 *Ibid.*, p. 73.

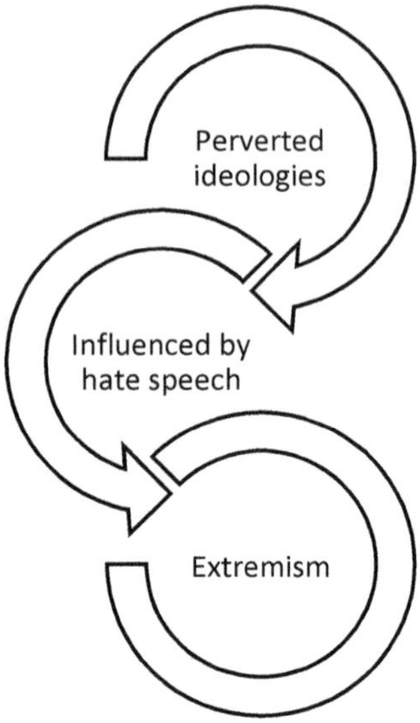

Figure 2: Visualization of the detrimental effects of hate speech.

To prompt their ideologies, members of extremist and racist groups call for the 'mobilization' against the other – this idea is being advocated for on social media platforms. Modern technologies are used by terrorist organizations as a platform to disseminate hate speech, incite violence and provide support for terrorist acts.[102]

16.2.2.4. Extremists and Information Technology

We have seen how extremist groups use information technology techniques, including social media, to promote hate speech by establishing and inciting racial discriminatory content and violent ideologies. Unfortunately, social media and other forms of communications are being exploited as platforms of bigotry.[103] These platforms are used as channels to spread hate speech against certain groups and to incite ethnic violence and assault against these groups. Therefore, the internet becomes a tool for inciting violence and terrorism when it is used for illegal purposes.[104]

---

[102] UNSC Resolution 1624 of 2005, UN Doc. S/RES/1624, 14 September 2005 (https://www.legal-tools.org/doc/65ab15/).

[103] "United Nations Strategy and Plan of Action on Hate Speech", May 2019, see *supra* note 81.

[104] Adel Maged, "Al-'Aúlamah wa-Atharuha 'ala at-Tawassu' fí Tajrím al- A'mal al-Táhḍíríyyah lil-Jara'im al-Irhabíyyah, al-Majallah al-'Árábíyyah lil-Fiqh wal-Qáḍá'", in *Arab Journal of Jurisprudence and Judiciary*, League of Arab States, October 2009, pp. 19–20.

The terrorist group Da'ish (also known as 'ISIS') benefited the most from non-traditional media, such as social media, Internet fora, blogs and other media platforms and means of communication on the Internet. This organization was closely acquainted with the jargon, secrets and paths of digital media which have become part of its propaganda strategy. Through this strategy, ISIS seeks to disseminate its extremist ideology, confront counter-ideas and groups, and attract fighters to support its combat operations or sympatric audience as a backup in countries where it has no terrorist arms.

Unfortunately, the inflammatory messages disseminated by violent extremist groups on social media, usually linked to hate speech, have achieved considerable success in attracting members, especially young women and men, into their ranks.[105] As such, these platforms have developed into a space for attracting sympathy with extremist and violent groups. It is on such platforms that these groups are praised and efforts are made to influence people to join them.[106]

Specialists in the field of combating extremist groups unanimously agree that these groups pursue policies which are based on giving priority to the group's interests over the state's interests. Therefore, they act to spread hate speech, combined with misconceptions, against the state's institutions.

The CTC observed in its study published in January 2016 that, according to the second "Global Survey of the Implementation of the Security Council Resolution 1624 (2005) by Member States",[107] the threat of incitement to commit acts of terrorism has increased significantly worldwide. This is attributed to the increase in the number of messages transmitted over information and communication technologies and in traditional institutions such as educational and religious ones, inciting violence and terrorist acts.

Recognizing the dangers of hate speech, Article 53(2) of the Egyptian Constitution stipulates that "Discrimination and incitement to hate are crimes punishable by law".[108] Criminal legislation in Egypt addresses some aspects of criminal behaviour that affects religious belief and practices in Articles 161 and 162 of the Egyptian Penal Code. Further, the Egyptian Penal Code criminalizes some forms of behaviour that call for the promotion of extremist ideas and for hatred. For instance, Article 98(f) of the Egyptian Penal Code prohibits the use of religion in promoting extremism, if the intent of this behaviour is to stir up

105 Plan of Action to Prevent Violent Extremism, para. 55, see *supra* note 39.

106 For more information on the phenomenon of foreign terrorist fighters, see Maged, 2019, p. 31, *supra* note 63.

107 CTC, Global Survey of the Implementation of Security Council Resolution 1624 (2005) by Member States, UN Doc. S/2016/50, 28 January 2016 (https://www.legal-tools.org/doc/bs463h/).

108 Constitution of Egypt, 18 January 2014, Article 53 (https://www.legal-tools.org/doc/632f2f/).

sedition, humiliate one of the heavenly religions or the sects belonging to it, or to harm national unity.[109]

To summarize, hate speech is a tool used by ill-minded persons to attract others to violent extremism. Its dangers are exacerbated when extremists employ religion to advocate their goals. Accordingly, it is crucial to adopt a counter-narrative to hate speech, in which religious institutions play a particularly important role. I will discuss some preventive measures to combat extremism and suitable narratives advocated by the religious leaders to confront hate speech in Chapter 29 below.

16.3. Conclusion

The present chapter has attempted to show that extremism finds its grounds in perverted ideologies and in reprehensible thoughts which are focused on the hate of others. Extremism is usually fuelled by hateful utterances which mainly aim to deepen rivalries, exacerbate grudges, and spread the culture of rejecting, hating and even eliminating the other, if necessary.

This chapter demonstrated how extremism has many ugly faces; it may be based on false religious motives, in which case it is called religious extremism, and it may be based on hateful racist motives, in which case it is called racist extremism. The repercussions of religious and racist extremism are so serious that they require action to prevent and fight calls for fanaticism which may lead to extremism, violence and terrorism. Earlier in this chapter, the author defined the phases through which extremism develops.

This chapter has recognized the specific harms inflicted by hate speech rhetoric and showed that hate speech is one of the most dangerous tools for instilling violent tendencies amongst the target audience, especially if it is issued by religious figures who distort religious texts and mix up religious concepts in order to corrupt religious belief and promote extremism. This is also the case if hate speech is employed by political leaders who use ethnic strife to lure followers, all for the sake of narrow-sighted interests or biased political goals. It also highlighted the serious consequences of incitement to religious hatred when employed by militant extremist groups, who use false and misleading narrative to fabricate the meaning of the religious texts. I have emphasized in different contexts that Islámic *Sharí'ah* prohibits hate speech, in all its forms and connotations, and explained that the ideology of *takfír* echoes an intensive form of religious hatred. The concept of religious hatred was examined and the proper

[109] For more information on national legal text applicable in the field, see, Adel Maged, "Bayn at-Taṭárruff wal-Irhab: Ru'yah Qánúníyyah", in *Kitab Muntada Taḥaddíyyat ath-Thaqáfah al-Qánúníyyah fí al-Wáṭán al-'Árábí, al-Markaz al-'Árábí lil-Wa'y bil-Qánún*, December 2019, pp. 40–47.

modalities to confront it, based on religious counter-narrative deducted from the *Qur'an* and the *Sunnah*, was presented. Chapter 29 contains an in-depth examination of the term 'counter-narrative', its meaning, dynamics and effectiveness.

In this chapter, the author has attempted to highlight the concept of 'violent extremism' while voicing his concerns regarding both the context in which this concept was adopted and its purposes. The author has also expressed concerns that the term 'violent extremism' may sometimes replace the term 'terrorism'. I encourage researchers to study different approaches used in this regard, and to determine the correct approach and framework which can be used by religious institutions to address it.

As a concluding comment, let me stress that proper understanding of the facts of Islám should be disseminated by establishing foundations of co-operation and coexistence among people to confront perverted ideologies and eliminate extremist dogmas. I also wish to indicate my awareness of the fact that the virtues of love and tolerance are inherent human qualities, while hate is a reprehensible one, a product of unwelcome political narratives and malicious interests. The harm caused by hate supersedes any justification for tolerating it on the basis of freedom of expression. It is only by spreading a culture of love and tolerance among people that narratives of extremism, hate and terrorism can be countered. I will reflect more on this approach in Chapter 29 of the present anthology.

17

Broader Normative Bases for Religious Leaders to Prevent Hate Speech

Gunnar M. Ekeløve-Slydal*

17.1. Introduction

A quote by China's most famous teacher, Confucius (551–479 BCE), states that you should not do unto others what you do not want to be done unto you. Similar teachings – often phrased positively as 'do to others as you would like them to do to you' or 'love your neighbour as yourself' – are included in the ethical doctrines of most world religions and belief systems. They are often not limited to people of the same creed, but refer to any human being. Sometimes even to enemies.

Illustrating the positive ethical contributions of world religions, in 1947, aimed as a contribution to the drafting process of the Universal Declaration of Human Rights, the United Nations ('UN') Educational, Scientific and Cultural Organization ('UNESCO') Philosophers' Committee received 56 answers to their questions on views on human rights from diverse religious and philosophical thinkers. In their answers, Chinese, Islámic, Hindu, Christian philosophical, scientific and political thinkers gave reasoned opinions on human rights principles. According to the Committee, overall, the results were encouraging,

* **Gunnar M. Ekeløve-Slydal** is Director of the Coalition for International Criminal Justice (CICJ) (which is a pro bono function); Deputy Secretary General of the Norwegian Helsinki Committee; and Adjunct Lecturer at the University of South-East Norway. He studied philosophy at the University of Oslo and worked for many years for the Norwegian Centre for Human Rights at the University of Oslo and as Editor-in-Chief of the *Nordic Journal on Human Rights*. He has written extensively on human rights, international institutions and philosophical themes, including textbooks, reports and articles. He has contributed chapters to several anthologies published by the Torkel Opsahl Academic EPublisher ('TOAEP'), including *Integrity in International Justice* (https://www.toaep.org/nas-pdf/4-bergsmo-dittrich) and *Colonial Wrongs and Access to International Law* (https://www.toaep.org/ps-pdf/40-bergsmo-kaleck-kyaw). For an audio-visual recording of his statement to CILRAP's conference in Florence in April 2023 on the topic of this anthology, please see https://www.cilrap.org/cilrap-film/220409-ekelove-slydal/.

indicating that the leading human rights principles were present in several cultural and religious traditions.[1]

Recent scholarship indicates that the UNESCO survey may have failed to comprehensively represent non-Western religious traditions' views and that its authors overplayed global consensus on human rights principles.[2] There is also a critical underpinning question of whether the universality of human rights can be constructed by such empirical research. In any case, it remains an indisputable fact that religion remains both a source and a target of hate speech and violence, in stark contravention of human rights principles and values. At the same time, it can contribute to reconciliation and building of bridges between conflicting parties by mobilizing norms and behaviours to that effect.

There are several complications related to religion as a source of hate speech, such as believers invoking scriptures or revelations of God's will which may be interpreted as justifying hatred for a group. It may be hard for courts and targeted people to know if they should take the quoted passages as a literal expression of the believer's view. Another complication is that religious beliefs are often deeply rooted and part of a shared culture. Believers may experience censorship by the state as an affront to their dignity and the standing of their group.[3]

Taking these complications into account, this chapter discusses normative bases for religious leaders to prevent hate speech and violence in the name of religion. Religious leaders may have considerable impact on preventing hate speech. They can probably be more influential than secular authorities or outside persons criticizing such abuse, especially if they can refer to esteemed teachers within their religious tradition or other respected teachers who aspire to create universal ethical bases for adherents belonging to different religions or life-stance traditions.

By 'religious leaders', I refer to persons recognized within a particular religion as having authority. The authority may be based on *formal* recognition by a prescribed body to persons that perform specific roles, such as priests, imams, preachers and so on. However, the authority may also be based on

---

1 Mary Ann Glendon, *A World Made New: Eleanor Roosevelt and the Universal Declaration of Human Rights*, Random House, New York, 2001, p. 76. For a critical account of the narrative that the 1947 UNESCO survey "demonstrated the universality of human rights through empirical evidence", see Mark Goodale, "The Myth of Universality: The UNESCO 'Philosophers' Committee' and the Making of Human Rights", in *Laws & Social Inquiry*, 2018, vol. 43, no. 3, pp. 596–617.

2 Extensive material and comments related to the UNESCO Survey on Human Rights are presented in Mark Goodale (ed.), *Letters to the Contrary: A Curated History of the UNESCO Human Rights Survey*, Stanford University Press, 2018.

3 Richard Moon, *Putting Faith in Hate: When Religion is the Source or Target of Hate Speech*, Cambridge University Press, 2018, pp. 115–16.

informal recognition by a group of persons, that is, granting a person *de facto* leadership.

Where can such leaders find norms to prevent hate speech and violence? First, norms against hate speech and violence are expressed in founding texts, religious discourse, religious philosophies and efforts at systematizing the religions' ethical teachings. Importantly, there exist religiously inspired inquiries that strive to establish *universal* moral teachings that adherents of different faiths can accept. I outline the approaches of Danish protestant Christian philosopher Søren A. Kierkegaard (1813–1855) and Knud E. Løgstrup (1905–1981). They were the two most influential Danish philosophers in the nineteenth and twentieth centuries.

While not addressing hate speech and violence in the name of religion specifically, they analyse foundational ethical demands inherent to human existence that consider 'care for the neighbour' the primary duty of human beings. Their account of human existence and the ethical demand is inspired by Christian conceptions, but aims to be valid for all human beings, regardless of their religious or philosophical outlook. They point to how religion may be used for ideological purposes, ossifying its proclamation into political and sometimes intolerant doctrines, instead of challenging individuals to believe in and serve God and their neighbour.

Second, while the discussion of Kierkegaard and Løgstrup is the main contribution of this chapter, I briefly point to other normative bases. In addressing hate speech, religious leaders may refer to norms about religious tolerance, freedom, spiritual- and life-view diversity, and epistemology of religion.

Third, they may refer to common messages by religious leaders of diverse creeds on human dignity, love for your neighbour, compassion and other values that can prevent hate speech. Part of this approach would be to refer to dialogue between representatives of religions to tackle hate and hate speech by or against members of religious groups. Values of dialogue, mutual respect, love and the ability to agree to disagree have been repeatedly expressed in the encounters of the fourteenth Dalai Lama (1935–) and the late South African Archbishop Desmond Tutu (1931–2021).

Another example is the Council for Religious and Life-Stance Communities in Norway, established in 1996 to promote equal treatment of religious and life-stance communities and respect and understanding among them through dialogue. The Council arranges meetings of senior religious leaders and has proved to be an effective tool in addressing sensitive issues and preventing conflicts among religious and life-stance communities.[4]

Fourth, religious leaders may refer to internationally recognized human rights as norms that protect freedom of religion or belief as embedded in a comprehensive set of rights to protect the integrity, dignity and well-being of all human beings. Reading the Universal Declaration of Human Rights as it was meant to be read by its framers, namely as a whole, makes it become "a common standard that can be brought to life in different cultures in a legitimate variety of ways". It was never intended as "a kind of menu of rights from which one can pick and choose according to taste".[5]

Referring to lesbian, gay, bisexual, transgender or intersex ('LGBTI') persons, persons belonging to religious minorities, or other groups at risk of discrimination and hatred as having the same rights as any other member of society may become a potent weapon against hate speech in the mouth of religious leaders. In the words of Eleanor Roosevelt (1884–1962), who led the UN drafting process of human rights, the Declaration may, in their practice, become "a bridge upon which we can meet and talk".[6] However, many religious leaders are sceptical about human rights, and one may need to find novel ways to start a conversation with them.

Fifth, religious leaders may refer to norms prescribing prudent relationships between religion and politics. Many examples of religious movements becoming a source of hate speech and violence against certain groups of individuals, organizations or even foreign states originate from abusing religion and religious institutions by politicians or religious leaders that operate like politicians. There may also be temptations for religious institutions that receive financial and other benefits from political leaders to compromise spiritual integrity. However, norms of prudence can guide religious leaders to avoid becoming 'useful tools' for politicians seeking to mobilize support for politics of conflict.

17.2. Understanding Religious Hate Speech

Religious hate speech is a sub-group of hate speech. A starting point for understanding such speech is a provision of the 1966 International Covenant on Civil and Political Rights ('ICCPR'), obliging States Parties to prohibit by law "[a]ny advocacy of national, racial, or religious hatred that constitutes incitement to discrimination, hostility, or violence". The 1965 International Convention on the

[4] More information about the Council for Religious and Life Stance Communities in Norway is available on its web site.

[5] Glendon, 2001, p. xviii, see *supra* note 1.

[6] Eleanor Roosevelt, "The UN and the Welfare of the World", in *National Parent-Teacher: The P.T.A. Magazine*, June 1953, vol. 47, p. 14.

Elimination of All Forms of Racial Discrimination ('ICERD') similarly obliges States Parties to "declare an offence punishable by law all dissemination of ideas based on racial superiority or hatred, incitement to racial discrimination, as well as all acts of violence or incitement to such acts against any race or group of persons of another colour or ethnic origin, and also the provision of any assistance to racist activities, including the financing thereof".[7]

The definition of hate speech inherent in these international provisions is *the advocacy of hatred that constitutes incitement to discrimination, hostility or violence*. Many states have enacted laws against hate speech, including incitement. Canadian law prohibits public statements that incite "hatred against any identifiable group where such incitement is likely to lead to a breach of the peace", while Danish Law prohibits comments "by which a group of people is threatened, derided, or degraded […]".[8]

The words 'deriding' and 'degrading' signifies another essential element, which is made clear in German law, prohibiting attacks on "the human dignity of others by insulting, maliciously maligning, or defaming segments of the population".[9]

Hate speech may then be characterized as *speech that attacks human dignity and incites discrimination, hostility or violence*. Racial and ethnic groups constituting minorities of the population are among the targets. In national laws, religious groups and some other minorities are also frequently protected. The Norwegian Penal Code defines hate speech as a "discriminatory or hateful statement" (which includes the use of symbols) that is "threatening or insulting a person or promoting hate of, persecution of or contempt for another person based on his or her a) skin colour or national or ethnic origin; b) religion or life stance; c) homosexual orientation; and d) reduced functional capacity".[10]

While hate speech in its most dangerous forms may contain all elements, it is not necessarily so with all forms of hate speech. Hate speech may attack the dignity of targeted groups without an explicit incitement element.[11] Understanding hate speech is, however, not only about knowing its elements. An equally important question is: what is the intended purpose of s*peech that attacks human*

---

7 ICCPR, 16 December 1966 (https://www.legal-tools.org/doc/2838f3/); ICERD, 21 December 1965 (https://www.legal-tools.org/doc/43a925/).

8 The quotation is from Jeremy Waldron, *The Harm in Hate Speech*, Harvard University Press, 2012, p. 8.

9 *Ibid.*

10 Norway, Penal Code, 20 May 2005, Section 185 (https://www.legal-tools.org/doc/aa2cee/).

11 UN Office on Genocide Prevention and the Responsibility to Protect, *Plan of Action for Religious Leaders and Actors to Prevent Incitement to Violence that Could Lead to Atrocity Crimes*, 14 July 2017, p. 2 (https://www.legal-tools.org/doc/8723g7/).

dignity and/or incites discrimination, hostility or violence against certain groups?

Slogans such as “do not trust Muslims”, “Muslims are about to take over our land, and they are even prepared to use violence to achieve that goal”, or “Muslims are full of hate, violence, and murder and are incapable of living peacefully among non-Muslims” clearly intend to mobilize defensive actions and in the end may be understood to signal that Muslims deserve ill-treatment.[12] However, the underlying message to members of the targeted group may be best summarized as ‘they should not feel safe here, they do not belong, they do not deserve the same rights as us and they had better leave’.

Jeremy Waldron (1953–) summarizes this inherent messaging of hate speech well:

> Don’t be fooled into thinking you are welcome here. The society around you may seem hospitable and non-discriminatory, but the truth is that you are not wanted, and you and your families will be shunned, excluded, beaten, and driven out, whenever we can get away with it. We may have to keep a low profile right now. But don’t get too comfortable. Remember what has happened to you and your kind in the past. Be afraid.[13]

For persons belonging to a targeted group, pressing questions will be: How many people feel this way about our presence here? Is the number increasing? And importantly, what do the government, the police and other powerful institutions think?

Discussions on how to react to hate speech may start from two opposing assumptions. It may be argued that, as disturbing as it may be for targeted persons, hate speech is mainly about people needing to express their frustrations and distorted views of certain social groups. Characterizing slogans as *hate speech* mainly refers to it as “a way in which one or another racist or Islámophobic element “lets off steam”, as it were, venting the hatred that is boiling up inside”.[14]

Or the argumentation may instead, more convincingly I think, take as a starting point that hateful expressions are mainly about rallying support for actions intended to drive certain people away, expel them or threaten them in such a way that they withdraw from society. Based on this assumption, hate speech should be understood as s*peech that attacks human dignity and incites*

---

12 Examples are from Moon, 2018, p. 9, see *supra* note 3.

13 Waldron, 2012, p. 2, see *supra* note 8.

14 *Ibid.*

discrimination, hostility or violence against certain groups to drive them away or underground.

Supposing that this understanding of hate speech is correct; how then to understand *religious* hate speech? The term 'religious' clearly indicates that religious belief plays a substantial role for those who express hate or that their role as representatives of religious institutions, religious leaders or adherents plays a part. The hate speech must be motivated, propagated or framed by persons in their capacity of belonging to a religious group or belief system. Typically, a monk, a minister or an imam express religious hate by attacking members of other religions or different interpretations of their religion or groups of society that adhere to lifestyles they deem to be sinful, such as members of LGBTI communities.

It may also take the form of attacking those who criticize, make caricatures or ridicule religion, as illustrated by the *Jyllands-Posten Muhammad cartoons controversy* in 2005–06. The Danish newspaper Jyllands-Posten published 12 editorial cartoons on 30 September 2005, depicting the Prophet Mohammad. The newspaper presented this as a contribution to the debate about criticism of Islám and self-censorship. Muslim groups in Denmark complained and there were worldwide protests, which included hate speech, deadly violence and riots in some Muslim countries.

One of the publications that printed the cartoons was the French satirical magazine *Charlie Hebdo*. On 7 January 2015, two gunmen attacked the Paris offices of the magazine, killing 12 people, including senior editorial staff members, in retribution for the magazine's provocative portrayals of the Prophet.[15]

Another prominent example is the *fatwá* (legal opinion) against the Indian-born British writer Salman Rushdie (1947–) because of his depiction of a character modelled after the Prophet Mohammad in his novel *Satanic Verses* (1988). On 14 February 1989, the spiritual leader of Iran, Ayatollah Ruhollah Khomeini (1902–1989), publicly condemned the book and issued a *fatwá* against Rushdie. A bounty of USD 3 million was offered to anyone who would execute him. Even though the Iranian government stated, in 1998, that it would not enforce the *fatwá*, a quasi-official foundation added USD 500,000 to the bounty in 2012.

In August 2022, Rushdie was attacked and seriously injured in Chautauqua, New York. The attacker, Hadi Mater, 24 years of age, motivated his actions by referring to Rushdie as "someone who had attacked Islam, he attacked their

[15] Encyclopedia Britannica, "Charlie Hebdo Shooting" (available on its web site).

beliefs, the belief systems".[16] The official reaction by the Iranian government was to deny any link to the attack, while underlining that freedom of speech did not justify Rushdie's insulting of Islám:

> In this attack, we do not consider anyone other than Salman Rushdie and his supporters worthy of blame and even condemnation.
>
> By insulting the sacred matters of Islam and crossing the red lines of more than 1.5 billion Muslims and all followers of the divine religions, Salman Rushdie has exposed himself to the anger and rage of the people.[17]

Since religious leaders may play important political roles, alongside being authorities on religious matters, religious hate speech can have substantial political repercussions. As has been the case in Myanmar, India, and current conflicts between Russia and Ukraine, religious leaders may play the role of political ringleaders, mobilizing support for violent or military actions to chase away or subjugate targeted groups. Muslims have been targeted by Buddhist nationalists in Myanmar and Hindu nationalists in India.[18] Despite Hindus constituting 81 per cent of the population in India, Hindu hate speech is becoming increasingly widespread (as discussed in detail in Chapters 6, 7 and 8 above), claiming that "Muslims pose an imminent threat to Hindus in India, and seek to undermine Hindu interests through several conspiracies. Thus, Hindus must unite against their common enemy, that is, Muslims".[19]

In the Russia-Ukraine conflict, Russian Orthodox leaders have supported military action against Ukraine while denouncing the establishment of an independent Ukrainian Orthodox Church. In a sermon on 6 March 2022, Russian Orthodox Patriarch Kirill depicted the ongoing war in spiritual terms: "We have entered into a struggle that has not a physical, but a metaphysical significance". He contended that some of the Donbas separatists were suffering for their "fundamental rejection of the so-called values that are offered today by those who

---

16 "Sir Salman Rushdie attack suspect 'only read two pages' of Satanic Verses", *BBC News*, 18 August 2022.

17 Statement by Iran's foreign ministry spokesperson Nasser Kanaani, quoted in "Salman Rushdie: Iran Blames Writer and Supporters for Stabbing", *BBC News*, 15 August 2022. According to some observers, the *fatwa* against Salman Rushdie contributed to radicalizing an entire generation of Muslims, both Shia and Sunni, cf. Kunwar Khuldune Shahid, "Iran's Rushdie Fatwa Radicalized an Entire Generation of Muslims", *Haaretz*, 15 August 2022.

18 Amresh Lavan Gunashingham, "Myanmar's Extreme Buddhist Nationalists", *The Interpreter*, 21 September 2021. Sameer Yasir, "As Hindu Extremists Call for Killing of Muslims, India's Leaders Keep Silent", *New York Times*, 24 December 2021.

19 Medha Damojipurapu, "Language, Themes and Responses to Hate Speech in India", Policy Brief Series No. 132 (2022), TOAEP, Brussels, 2022, p. 4 (https://www.toaep.org/pbs-pdf/132-damojipurapu/).

claim world power". According to him, this unnamed world power is posing a "test for the loyalty" of countries by demanding they hold gay pride parades to join a global club of nations with its ideas of freedom and "excess consumption".[20]

Throughout history, hate speech and violence against members of different interpretations or representatives of independent institutions within the same religion happened frequently. The conflict between the Moscow and Kyiv Patriarchates is a new chapter in that long and brutal history.

Is religious hate speech different from hate speech motivated by non-religious ideologies or racist ideas? There may be a few factors that make preventing and remedying religious hate speech especially hard. Since religious beliefs are often deeply rooted and part of a shared culture, it may be exceedingly difficult to convince adherents to change their course. Religious leaders are often highly respected, making it hard to persuade followers that they are wrong. Even secular courts and governments may find it difficult – and sometimes wrong – to go against religious leaders. Criticism from outsiders may be dismissed simply because religious leaders perceive it to be against religion and spiritual values.

17.3. Searching for Solutions

The role of religion in conflicts is nuanced and complex, depending on the context. Other factors may play more prominent roles in escalating disputes and violence. There exists, nevertheless, a widespread realization that religion matters in many of today's conflicts, both as conflict drivers and in efforts to solve them. Religion, it seems, can be a part of both the problem and the solution.

Linked to this realization is a second one concerning the understanding of religion as such. Religion is doctrine and values upheld by leaders, institutions, authoritative interpretations of scriptures, as well as efforts by theologians at adaption of core doctrines to new circumstances. A 'functional' one supplements this 'substantive' aspect of religion, that is, how doctrine, ritual, procedural rules and loyalty to a religious community affect individual or group behaviour, thoughts and choices.[21] It follows that religious leaders may need not only to understand religious doctrine and criticize misinterpretations, but must also excel in knowing community dynamics, loyalties and power structures

[20] Jonathan Luxmoore, "After Supporting Ukraine Invasion, Russia's Patriarch Kirill Criticized Worldwide", *National Catholic Reporter* ('*NCR*'), 15 March 2022; and Peter Smith, "Russia's Patriarch Kirill Defends Invasion of Ukraine, Stoking Orthodox Tensions", *NCR*, 8 March 2022. See also Jason Horowitz, "The Russian Orthodox Leader at the Core of Putin's Ambitions", *New York Times*, 21 May 2022.

[21] Sara Silvistri and James Mayall, *The Role of Religion in Conflict and Peace Building*, British Academy, 2015, p. 6.

within religious networks to confront hate speech effectively. The role of religion in conflicts may depend as much on its 'functional' as its 'substantive' aspects.

Another critical issue is the relationship between 'modernity' and 'religion'. In analysing religious fundamentalism, Ernest Gellner (1925–1995) defined it as the view that "faith is to be upheld firmly in its full and literal form, free of compromise, softening, re-interpretation or diminution. It presupposes that the core of religion is a doctrine, rather than ritual and that this doctrine can be fixed with precision and finality, which further presupposes writing".[22] The secularization thesis held that religion would gradually lose its influence in modern industrial societies, soften its edges progressively and lead to the religious doctrine being adapted to scientifically rooted life views; this, however, has not happened. Fundamentalism in the name of Islám has gained substantial popular support, in several cases in the form of intolerant and sometimes violent political ideology, based on particular and in no way uncontested interpretations of Islám.[23] Other world religions also have their versions of fundamentalism, often leading to intolerance, conflict and sometimes violence.1

Arguably, the collapse of communism during the late 1980s and the early 1990s has given religion a new upspring in former Soviet and East European countries. Under the slogan of defending 'traditional values', signifying anti-gay, family values and stigmatization of sexual and gender minorities, many governments in Europe, Asia, Africa and the Americas have used religion to mobilize support for policies that leads to increased intolerance. Such policies are often presented as a defence against globalization and harmful foreign influence, strengthening national sovereignty and revising the global order.

Russia has been a regional and global promotor of traditional values, including in the UN Human Rights Council, creating new coalitions of actors in opposition to sexual and gender rights and making respect for human rights dependent on 'responsible behaviour'.[24] In the words of Swedish political scientist Emil Edenberg,

> [t]he idea of Russia as an international beacon of "traditional values" echoes older missionary narratives of Russia's role in the

22 Ernest Gellner, *Postmodernism, Reason and Religion*, Routledge, London, 1992, p. 2.

23 Marit Tjomsland, "A Discussion of Three Theoretical Approaches to Modernity: Understanding Modernity as a Globalising Phenomenon", CMI Working Paper No. 2 (1996), Chr. Michelsen Institute, Bergen, 1996, p. 10. See also, Mustafa Akyol, *Islam Without Extremes: A Muslim Case for Liberty*, W.W. Norton & Company, New York, 2013.

24 For an account of Russia's attempts to redefine human rights in the UN Human Rights Council, see Maggi Murphy, "'Traditional values' vs human rights at the UN", *OpenDemocracy*, 18 February 2013 (available on its web site).

> world, such as the pre-revolutionary idea of Moscow as a "Third Rome" embodying true Christianity after the fall of the Roman and Byzantine empires, as well as the Soviet rhetoric of liberating workers across the world [...]. [T]he Russian state's turn to "traditional values" does not merely represent a defensive and inward-looking reaction to globalisation and perceived threats to established norms of gender and sexuality. On the contrary, this move constitutes an element of an activist and revisionist foreign policy, a soft power initiative that sends a message about Russia's importance in world affairs, as a purported leader in a transnational conservative axis.[25]

These developments point to significant challenges for human rights-based approaches to mobilizing religious leaders against hate speech, as pointed out in Morten Bergsmo's concept note for the research project of which this anthology forms part.[26] Fundamentalists, nationalists or specific schools of conservative religious leaders may not share the values and principles of human rights. Convincing them to become religious human rights defenders may prove exceedingly difficult. Such leaders may perceive international human rights as Western, secular and alien to their faith. Religious leaders embracing human rights are easier to attract, but their impact may be limited to those who already refrain from hate speech.

An alternative or supplementary approach, to be presented in the following, would be to mobilize *internal* normative bases against hate speech, assuming that world religions contain interpretative resources to fight hate directed against non-believers, those who believe differently or those who adhere to perceived sinful lifestyles. Detecting such resources may be an essential first step and fertilize the ground for introducing comprehensive human rights approaches at later stages.

For any approach, misuse of religion by political leaders remains a significant obstacle. Autocratic political leaders who use religion to build support for conflict-oriented and intolerant policies may meet religious leaders who actively prevent hate speech with hostility. Most democratic states restrict hate speech by law, particularly incitement to violence or discrimination. At the same time, courts in these countries try to strike a proper balance between such

---

[25] Emil Edenberg, "Homophobia as Geopolitics: 'Traditional Values' and the Negotiation of Russia's Place in the World", in Jon Mulholland, Nicola Montagna and Erin Sanders-McDonagh (eds.), *Gendering Nationalism*, Palgrave Macmillan, 2018, p. 78.

[26] See his Chapter 1 above. See also UN Office on Genocide Prevention and the Responsibility to Protect, *Plan of Action for Religious Leaders/Actors from the Asia-Pacific Region to Prevent Incitement to Violence that Could Lead to Atrocity Crimes*, 7 December 2016 (https://www.legal-tools.org/doc/lc4g5j/).

restrictions and legal norms to uphold freedom of expression. In authoritarian environments, religious leaders cannot rely on state authorities to comply with such norms, playing their part in restricting hate speech while upholding the right to freedom of expression.

The UN and other intergovernmental organizations have invested heavily in developing a human rights approach to fighting religious hate speech and violence, including the involvement of religious leaders in developing action plans and measures to prevent the misuse of religion. However, these plans do seldom challenge religious leaders to refer to broader normative bases outside human rights to act.

17.4. Broader Normative Bases

In the following sections, I discuss a few examples of such normative bases.

17.4.1. Internal Normative Bases Against Hate Speech

The Western Enlightenment period introduced a lasting shift in the role of religion. It is true that the death of religion (or God), as proclaimed by Friedrich Nietzsche (1844–1900), never occurred. Religion has survived despite philosophers' and scientists' critical assessments of its foundations and role in society. As stated by Morten Bergsmo, "rather than solemnly burying God, sixty-six years after Nietzsche's madman pronounced God dead, nations of the world raised a normative shield by declaring that 'everyone has the right to freedom of […] religion'" in the 1948 Universal Declaration of Human Rights.[27]

However, an enduring result of the Enlightenment and the rise of science is that Christianity gradually lost its status as the provider of *moral knowledge* in the Western world. Development took place, which resulted in the fact that there currently exists no moral *knowledge* or a 'science of ethics', as framed by American philosopher Dallas Willard (1935–2013).[28] He insists that even if many persons can provide clear outlines of their moral convictions, moral questions do not make up the subject matter of any systematic discipline that extends our moral knowledge by appealing to reason and evidence. Unlike scientific disciplines concerning non-normative issues, there is no institutional home for objective moral inquiry.

This situation is different from previous times. As late as 1903, the great English moral philosopher George E. Moore (1873–1958) compared disagreements in ethics to those in arithmetic. We are not surprised, he pointed out, when

---

27 CILRAP Concept and Programme, 220408-09 Conference (as of 220405), p. 2 (https://www.cilrap.org/events/220408-09-florence/).

28 Dallas Willard, Steven L. Porter, Aaron Preston and Gregg A. Ten Elshof (eds.), *The Disappearance of Moral Knowledge*, Routledge, New York, 2018.

there is a disagreement about the solution to a problem in arithmetic. We assume that there was a mistake somewhere and seek to locate it. It is similar in ethics, according to Moore. When we disagree, "though [...] we cannot prove that we are right, yet we have reason to believe that everybody, unless he is mistaken as to what he thinks, will think the same as we", once we have clarity on the question being asked.[29] The only difference is that in ethics, "owing to the intricacy of its subject matter, it is far more difficult to persuade anyone either that he has made a mistake or that that mistake affects his result".[30]

Moore's ethical-philosophical programme thus presupposed that the science of ethics existed. Knowledge of moral reality was achievable by sensible and thoughtful people, a conviction he shared with other philosophers at his time.

This conception is not around any longer and has not been for some time. During the twentieth century, ethics and its foundations became increasingly fragmented in the West and, due to Western influence, in other parts of the world. The role of Christianity and philosophy as sources of a compelling moral theory gave way to a plurality of approaches influenced by political ideologies and diverse philosophical or religiously inspired doctrines. The closest one that comes to a *universally* accepted set of norms today may be international human rights, interpreted not only as a body of legal norms, but as a statement by the international community of binding moral values.

When a compelling body of rational and evidence-based knowledge of morality does not exist, the risk is that too much is left to demagogues and interest-based approaches. Over time, this situation may have unfortunate consequences. A quotation from the preface to Willard's book on the disappearance of moral knowledge by Scott Soames (1945–) summarizes the situation well:

> Because morality is central to human life, we will always be concerned with it. The issue isn't whether we will pursue what we take to be moral, but how we will do so. Without the discipline and humanity forced on us by rational, evidence-based inquiry, we too easily become blind to our own moral limitations and intolerant of those who don't march in lockstep with us. As a result, purported answers to contentious moral questions come to be treated as moral certainties about which there can be no debate. Since no single moral perspective dominates all the others in society, intimidation, coercion, and condescension fill the gap left by the absence of moral reasoning.[31]

---

29 G.E. Moore, *Principia Ethica*, Dover Publications, Mineola, 2004, p. 123.

30 *Ibid.*

31 Willard, 2018, p. viii, see *supra* note 28.

How we ended up in this situation is a complex story. The shift from the firm belief held by philosophers from Socrates, Plato and Aristotle to George E. More and shared by theologians and politicians until the twentieth century, holding that moral knowledge existed and should guide the actions of individuals and societies, did not give way to the present disbelief due to specific discoveries or the presentation of definite arguments. Willard suggests several factors that led to a gradual change in perceptions that resulted in the current situation, such as the abdication of God as a guarantor of morality, the realization that moral principles and behaviour vary according to culture and shifts in perceptions of the human self, which is no longer seen as an integrated and rational agent capable of being the subject of moral knowledge.[32]

The French Enlightenment philosopher Marquis de Condorcet (1743–1794) predicted that a moment would come when the Sun only shines over "free people, who will not have any other master than their own reason".[33] His utterly optimistic view about the future of human society and well-being included progress in science and technology as well as in morals and in creating peaceful societies. Everything he detested would be overcome, such as slavery, repression and inequality. Medicine would keep humans healthy and society would be rid of friction and conflicts. Knowledge about how one can avoid conflicts and achieve results that benefit all would be incorporated into the laws and disseminated to the citizens.

Looking at today's world, one must conclude that only half of Condorcet's vision has come true. Science and technology ('hard' Enlightenment) have even outperformed his imagination of what would be achieved, while developments in morals and society ('soft' Enlightenment) lag far behind.[34] This is the broader picture that must be considered when pointing to the need for religious leaders to mobilize against hate speech and violence in the name of their religions. They must be specific in addressing hate speech, but they must also consider how they can contribute to a wider strengthening of a shared morality

[32] *Ibid.*, pp. 8–18.

[33] Marquis de Condorcet, *Esquisse d'un tableau historique des progrés de l'esprit humaine*, Masson et Fils Libraires, Paris, 1822, p. 271. The full quotation in French reads: "Il arrivera donc ce moment où le soleil n'éclairera plus sur la terre que des hommes libres, et ne reconnaissant d'autre maître que leur raison".

[34] Sven-Eric Liedman, Swedish historian of ideas, has called the two aspects of Condorcet's vision of human progress 'hard' and 'soft' Enlightenment. Condorcet conceptualized the Enlightenment project "as an indissoluble unity. In reality, however, hard enlightenment can work without the soft one". Sven-Eric Liedman, *Den moderne verdens idéhistorie: I skyggen av fremtiden* (The Modern World's History of Ideas: In the Shadow of the Future), Dreyers forlag, Oslo, 2016, p. 27.

against hate and violence. They must mobilize the ability to see the humanity and dignity present in all human beings.

Based on the above outline of the disappearance of moral knowledge and the failure of 'soft' Enlightenment, I argue that religious leaders should refer to religiously inspired universalist ethical teachings in addressing expressions of hate and violence. They should not only refer to scriptures and teachings specific to their religion, but to teachings that present fundamental ethical values valid for all.

Doing so, they help build that 'bridge upon which we can meet and talk'. They may also, in this way, provide elements for that 'science of ethics' which is much needed to confront abuse of religion in formulating slogans and hate speech.

17.4.2. Religiously Inspired Universalist Ethical Teachings

The essential values to be mobilized in preventing hate speech include respect for 'humanity' or 'dignity' inherent in every human being, treating neighbours and foreigners well, and tolerating people or communities who adhere to different beliefs or lifestyles. Such values promote equal treatment of human beings in some fundamental respects, although not all. Refraining from hate speech and violence does not mean that you must treat all humans equally in all respects, although this maximalist ideal is inherent in some religious teachings.

In the following, I present two protestant theologians and philosophers who contributed decisively to developing *ethics of individual responsibility and integrity*, inspired by Christianity but presented within the realm of philosophy and thus intended to be valid for anyone – religious or non-religious.[35] Inherent in their thinking are criteria to detect abuse of religion – by religious institutions, politicians and demagogues.

17.4.2.1. Søren Kierkegaard's Analysis of Existence

Danish religious philosophy has a personalistic and nearness-to-life approach as one of its most noticeable characteristics. Søren Kierkegaard is a great representative of this type of criticism and the prevailing thinking of his time (that is,

[35] The analysis of human existence to be found in Kierkegaard, and later in Martin Heidegger's (1889–1976) work *Sein und Zeit* (Being and Time), 1927, was influenced by the New Testament of the Bible, Augustine (354–430), and Martin Luther (1483–1546) and their accounts of the Christian proclamation. K.E. Løgstrup, *Kierkegaard's and Heidegger's Analysis of Existence and Its Relation to Proclamation: Translated with an Introduction and Notes by Robert Stern*, Oxford University Press, 2020, p. 75. The book was based on lectures held by Løgstrup at the Freie Universität in Berlin and first published in German as *Kierkegaards und Heideggers Existenzanalyse und ihr Verhältnis zur Verkündigung*, Erich Blaschker Verlag, Berlin, 1950.

the first part of the nineteenth century) which centred around state, church and society membership as the way for the individual to attain a meaningful life and salvation. 'Being Danish equals being Christian and in alignment with God' is a somewhat simplified summary of this mode of thinking. At the elite level in the Church, academia and among a wider circle of intellectuals, the sentiment was heavily influenced by Georg W.F. Hegel's (1770–1831) philosophy and conception of religion as a form of self-consciousness and a pre-stage to the absolute form of knowledge attained in philosophy.

Kierkegaard's philosophy is complex, explicated in an impressive sequence of books published between 1838 and 1855 by many pseudonyms and sometimes in Kierkegaard's name, either as an author, editor or publisher.[36] Extremely well-written as his books are, they nevertheless represent severe difficulties for the reader to fully apprehend their meaning and significance. He is not a philosopher who presents a view and then argues in favour of it. Instead, his texts include a variety of styles and the different pseudonymous authors refer to and argue with each other. 'Indirect communication', is Kierkegaard's term for this authorship practice, which is inspired by Socrates' (470 BCE–399 BCE) way of challenging his fellow Athenians by asking uncomfortable questions to detect misconceptions and inspire awareness of what can be known and what cannot. One of the results is that scholarship on, and influence by Kierkegaard, is vast and presents conflicting interpretations.

In the following, I restrict myself to focusing on Kierkegaard's analysis of human existence, including his concepts of the 'philistine' ('*Spidsborger*', from the German '*Spiessbürger*'), 'aesthetic', 'ethical' and 'religious' stages on life's way ('modes of existence', 'archetypes' or 'life views', as scholars tend to term them). Kierkegaard tells stories and stages various archetypical figures to show the reader how life can unfold, depending on which life view one has. The multiple characters' foremost task is to elicit self-knowledge in the reader, not to teach a lesson. There is no necessity to develop from one stage to another. However, there is no doubt that the religious stages in Kierkegaard's view represent the possibility for the individual to attain selfhood and escape from 'life

[36] The whole spectre of Kierkegaard's authorship, including both his published and unpublished books, his extensive journals, notes and papers is available online on the web site of Søren Kierkegaards Skrifter. His published and unpublished writings as well as his journals and notebooks are available in English translation, *inter alia*, in the Princeton University Press series *Kierkegaard's Writings* and *Kierkegaard's Journals and Notebooks*. For further information, see "Søren Kierkegaard", Princeton University Press.

in the crowd'. However, acquiring a new life view is always based on the individual's decisions and passionate striving to attain the truth.[37]

The precondition for Kierkegaard's expositions is his conception that humans are born with the possibility of becoming human beings entirely or becoming 'a self', as he explains in *The Sickness unto Death* (1849). He defines humans as a synthesis of 'soul' and 'body', the latter including the whole physical environment, which they are conscious of in 'reflection'. But humans are also a synthesis of 'infinity' and 'finitude', 'eternity' and 'temporality'. The self as a synthesis of body and soul refers to humans beings aware of their dual nature. In contrast, the relation between infinity and finitude refers to how the individual, through their *actions*, 'relates itself to itself'. In its actions, the individual responds to an *infinite demand*, which is how 'eternity' is present in human existence and by which a human being can become a self. It is through the self's response to the infinite demand, in a decision to obey or disobey it, that its relation to the infinite, God, is determined.[38]

Humans' relationship to God or eternity is not about cognition, as in speculative philosophy, but about action. Being a human means not only being conscious or knowledgeable, but rather that your existence is of fundamental concern to you. It is about being an ethical individual, placed in a decision-making situation by relating to the infinite demand. The demand does not come from outside the person; rather, it is a part of being human. It is, therefore, inescapable.

According to Kierkegaard, humans are metaphysically ambiguous beings. He is not alone in holding this conception of humans as having an inherent connection to eternity, as Platonism and various theological strands maintain. In the Bible, conceptions of humans being created by God include that eternity still has a place in their hearts, despite their sinful state. Genesis 1:26 teaches that every human being possesses the image of God. Ecclesiastes 3:11 declares that God has "set eternity in the hearts of men", while in Luke 17:21, Jesus proclaims, "The kingdom of God is within you". The apostle Paul teaches that every human being possesses an immaterial soul-spirit and that it is this part of us that connects with God (Hebrews 4:12).

However, Kierkegaard's view is that eternity's presence in human beings is not in the form of the knowledge of God, but as an infinite demand for our existence. This demand has not the form of a command, that is, God telling

[37] The 'aesthetic' and 'ethical' stages are presented by the pseudonymous author and publisher Victor Eremita in *Either/Or: A Fragment of Life* (1843) and by Hilarius Bogbinder, publisher of *Stages on Life's Way* (1844). The religious stage is presented in *Fear and Trembling* (1843) by Johannes De Silentio. Both the publishers and the authors of different parts of these books are pseudonyms. The real author is Søren Kierkegaard.

[38] Løgstrup, 2020, Chapter 2, see *supra* note 35.

humans to do certain things. The infinite demand does not have a specified content; it is rather *a demand that the individual expresses in existing, that they can do nothing themselves but is nothing before God.* Only by honouring this demand can the individual become a self and regain his life in society without being subject to life in the crowd.

The *philistines*, however, have not realized the possibility of becoming a self. Their way of life is characterized by never questioning whether life or society could be different. They are not aware of their choices, but let society's values and norms determine which path they choose to take. They flow with the flow and live up to the environment's expectations, doing like the others. The philistines think they have made their choices, but they have not. They are simply a product of the society they are part of. They cannot choose and are not aware that they have a choice. They let circumstances choose for them, are unaware of themselves, and live their life without passion and genuine commitment.

The *aesthetes* have realized that they have a choice and depart from the philistine way of life. However, according to Kierkegaard, their life is still marked by the despair of not wanting to be themselves, not choosing themselves "in their eternal validity", as he phrases it.[39] They are not bound by the norms of society, but consider life and others with an ironic distance. Despite all the cultural events they attend, they are eventually plagued by boredom and despair. They choose based on desire, sensuality, possibilities and the projected exciting outcome of their adventures. They cannot or will not make binding choices. Instead, they choose based on what they feel like in a given moment. Preoccupied with the exterior, beauty, fun and enjoyment, they stage themselves in different roles about what they want to achieve. They do not concern themselves with their actions' moral and ethical aspects, living a non-committal life without engaging with others or taking responsibility for the society of which they are a part. Love relations are based on lust and desire rather than commitment and responsibility.

The *ethicists*, on the other hand, perceive life as a task and have discovered life's inner and ethical dimensions. They choose out of duty and take responsibility for themselves and their choices without leaving out feelings, passion and love. Such unstable emotions, however, need support and direction by decisions based on duty. They stand by their choices and live a committed, moral, meaningful and duty-fulfilling life without hidden agendas for their surroundings and those closest to them.

---

[39] Victor Eremita (pseudonym of Søren A. Kierkegaard), *Either/Or: A Fragment of Life, 1843, Abridged, Translated and with an Introduction and Notes by Alastair Hannay*, Penguin Classics, London, 1992, p. 499.

The ethicists commit to themselves, their families, work and the community. They enforce the rules and norms around which society is built because they choose to participate actively in the culture of which they are part. In their view, God is behind its norms and provides for their validity.

Even for ethicists, however, life is not without anxiety and despair. They are, in a way, desperate to be themselves and fulfil their responsibilities. They are anxious about the consequences of their choices because they stand alone with the duties and responsibilities for themselves and their actions. There is a risk that the norms and responsibilities will crush them. They realize that it is difficult to live up to all the demands they set on themselves. They feel guilty about their mistakes and that there are things in the world they cannot change.

Ultimately, the ethicist may enter the *religious* stage, taking comfort in the idea that we are always wronged against God. The *religious* see themselves as created by God, the greatest all-embracing love that stands above society's norms. They see themselves as part of something bigger. God forgives and loves man unconditionally when he chooses to perceive himself as created by God and receive life as a gift and task.

The religious person leaps into the 70,000 fathoms of water and starts believing that God is the possibility in the impossible and that humans are created by something greater than themselves. God can forgive guilt and creates coherence and peace in their lives. God is the foundation the ethicists sought when they realized they could not change the world's cruelties. Neither the many rules they set up for themselves nor sublime humour was enough for them to step into character as themselves.

For Kierkegaard, the paradox of faith is that the individual is higher than the general. On this point, he opposes Hegel, who places the individual under society's norms and rules, as the ethicist exemplifies in his version of the Hegelian concept of '*Sittlichkeit*', or living according to the prevailing social norms.[40] These social norms are used to justify or prohibit actions within a community. For Kierkegaard, Christian faith is a matter of individual subjective passion, which cannot be mediated by the clergy, human artefacts or thinking. Faith is the most critical task for a human being because only based on faith does an individual have a chance to become an authentic self, to escape from living in the crowd. This self is the lifework that God judges for eternity.

---

40 See William McDonald's description of 'The Ethical stage' in "Søren Kierkegaard", in Edward N. Zalta (ed.), *The Stanford Encyclopedia of Philosophy*, Winter 2017 Edition, 2017; and Merold Westphal, "Kierkegaard and Hegel", in Alastair Hannay and Gordon M. Mariono (eds.), *The Cambridge Companion to Kierkegaard*, Cambridge University Press, 1998, Chapter 4.

The individual is thus subject to a heavy burden of responsibility. Humans are not only responsible for validating the prevailing norms through their primordial choice as the ethicists prescribe. The existential choice or leap of faith, without proof or even against reason, "by virtue of the absurd", as Johannes De Silentio (the pseudonymous author of *Fear and Trembling* (1843)) terms it, determines one's eternal salvation or damnation.

The concept of faith as holding certain dogmas to be true is thus replaced by Kierkegaard as a 'way of life', as 'a form of the will'. In *Fear and Trembling*, the emphasis on acting rather than thinking or reasoning is highlighted by the sheer irrationality of Abraham's faith, his belief, 'by virtue of the absurd', that he will get Isaac back when God asks him to sacrifice him.[41] Thus, faith cannot be reduced to a form of preliminary expressions of knowledge that philosophy or science can express better and more coherently. Kierkegaard believed that Christian civilization had effaced the true meaning of Christianity. Becoming a Christian had once entailed significant risk, but over time it had been reduced to merely being born to Christian parents in a Christian nation.[42]

Anxiety or dread ('*Angest*'), as outlined in *The Concept of Anxiety* (1844), is the presentiment of this freedom and responsibility when the individual stands at the threshold of momentous existential choice, as well as the Christian concept of 'sin', which together with 'absolute guilt' characterizes human standing in relation to God. The individual creates, through temporal choice, a self, which will be judged for eternity. Anxiety may be seen as the *symptom* of this freedom to choose oneself, not in a fantastic way, but within the social context and the human capabilities given to a specific person. 'Despair', another important Kierkegaardian concept outlined in *The Sickness unto Death* (1849), is when we instead attempt to be rid of ourselves.

Underpinning Kierkegaard's analysis is, as already noted, the view that in order to become a self, the individual must avoid "living a life that is governed by others and so is inauthentic, trapped within the humdrum and the mundane – a life in the crowd".[43] A person living in the crowd "finds being himself too risky, finds it much easier and safer to be like the others, to become a copy, a number, along with the crowd".[44] In this way, the person has allowed himself to be "cheated of its self by 'the others'".[45] Kierkegaard uses value-laden words about this situation, underlining that the person in this way may gain "all that is

---

41 Johannes De Silentio is referring to the story of Genesis 22:1–18.

42 See Ronald M. Green, "'Developing' Fear and Trembling", in Hannay and Mariono (eds.), 1998, Chapter 10, see *supra* note 40.

43 Robert Stern, "Introduction", in Løgstrup, 2020, p. xviii, see *supra* note 35.

44 Søren Kierkegaard, *The Sickness unto Death*, Penguin Books, 2004, p. 61.

45 *Ibid.*

required for a flawless performance in everyday life, yes, for making a great success out of life. Here there is no dragging of the feet, no difficulty with his self and its infinitizing, he is ground as smooth as a pebble, as exchangeable as a coin of the realm".[46]

This happens because temporal and worldly interests imprison human beings. Going under in the crowd presupposes that the human being is bound to the earthly in an immediate way, in which their whole life goes on. They put themselves in "an absolute relation only to relative ends", as stated in Kierkegaard's seminal philosophical work, *Unconcluding Scientific Postscript* (1946).

From this, it follows that one can never make a proper decision in this life. That decision, which is essentially only to be found in the individual, is sought after outside the self, in the opinion of the social environment, in public opinion and village gossip. In this life, there is only *action without any decision*, an action whose only point is that something in a superficial sense is accomplished as an undertaking.

17.4.2.2. Kierkegaardian Takeaways

Kierkegaard's analysis of human existence and the possibilities for humans to become a self puts some constraints on any religious proclamation, life or worldview. As Enlightenment philosophers put constraints on religions based on science and reason, Kierkegaard presents correspondence with the formal structure of human existence as preconditions for humans to become adherent freely and based on their comprehension of the proclamation. While in earlier times, philosophy made constraints on religious proclamation in the name of reason, Kierkegaard made it in the name of existence.[47]

Existence puts humans in a decision situation. They may choose to run away from this or to live as there is no demand on them. But living in this way is life in the loss of oneself. Humans may refer to their place in society, serving important institutions, or being members of religious or political movements as sufficient determinations of their meaning of life. But according to Kierkegaard, this is despair or not wanting to accept human life as it is, a life of responsibility, becoming, movement and repetition of choices.

While humans may become part of religious practices by being introduced to them and trained as children, they must still answer individually about why they adhere to a particular religion. In Kierkegaard, being religious by default does not exist. Everyone must choose for themselves.

---

46 *Ibid.*

47 Løgstrup, 2020, p. 75, see *supra* note 35. In the following, I render the main points of Løgstrup's interpretation of how philosophy and religion relate in Kierkegaard.

While the content of religion cannot be demonstrated, it must nevertheless be comprehensible. The fundamental relationship between philosophy and religion in Kierkegaard is that:

> the content of [religious] proclamation [must] correspond to the purely formal structure of human existence, that it lets itself be understood in the formal/empty determinations that result from the analysis of the structure of human existence. If that is not the case, if the proclamation is not comprehensible in the sense that the inner structure of existence is graspable, then the receiving or accepting of a proclamation would either involve allowing others to impose it upon one or imposing it on oneself. Faith without understanding is not faith, but coercion; the individual then imposes the proclamation on themselves not because they take it up and accept it for the sake of its content, but for other and therefore illegitimate motives. If a proclamation is not comprehensible in the sense that it corresponds to the structure of human existence, what would the difference then be between proclamation and obscure superstition? Philosophy as the analysis of existence can therefore serve to distinguish between faith and coercion.[48]

If there is an argument for the truth of Christianity in Kierkegaard, it is precisely based on his description of how its proclamation corresponds to the formal structure of human existence. Its truth cannot be objective and certain, but rather is paradoxical and even absurd. A religion presenting itself as objectively certain would make the existence wholly indifferent. The point here is, however, not to render Kierkegaard's argument for Christianity comprehensible, but to show how his philosophical analysis of existence puts forward constraints on any religion or life-view.

These constraints can be expressed in a series of questions:

1. Does the religious proclamation "leave the individual at the mercy of the crowd, or does it insist that the person who receives it lives their life as an individual"?[49]
2. "Does the proclamation seduce the human being into committing themselves to what has been realised, or does its content insist that the addressee remain true to the character of their existence as becoming and possibility"?
3. Does the proclamation let "the relation of the individual to the absolute [God] be hidden from the outsider, from the third"?

---

[48] *Ibid.*, p. 74.

[49] This and the following quotations are from *ibid.*, pp. 75–79.

4. Does the proclamation "give human beings an absolute certainty in their life and actions", or does it make "clear to the individual that they must live their life in uncertainty, in their responsibility, and their own guilt"?

If the proclamation does not leave the individual in uncertainty, having to rely on their understanding of how to realize their relationship with the absolute or God,

> the absolute and radical would become transformed and garbled into an idea, a principle, and a value; in other words, it would then be something thought, the product of reason or thought. And as thought, it would be a system, and ideology or a utopia.

Subordinating existence to thought effectively eliminates the human as an existing being. Instead, they would become mere tools for realizing a programme or a belief system. Their insight, humanity, personal commitment and the decision of the existing person would be put out of play. In short, there is a risk of the total dehumanizing of human beings, who become mere agents. If we let thought 'override existence' in this way, everything "can proceed wholly mechanically; only a purely technical calculation is necessary". The absolute and radical must remain beyond thinking; it must be given with human existence and "cannot be a freely thought-out idea, ideology, utopia, or freely thought-out principle".[50]

In other words, to be true to their existence as decisions, becoming and movement, humans must use their own understanding, insight and humanity to make clear to themselves what to do. There is plenty for thinking and insight to be involved with the "understanding of existence as a becoming, as a permanent possibility, and the connected understanding that the situation is always new and requires new decisions keeps thinking alive".

An important consequence of subordinating existence to thinking is contempt for the other human being. If one's existence is disregarded for the sake of realizing an idea which has been thought out once and for all, then the existence of the other person will be ignored as well. The subordination of one's own existence will lead to subordination in general. Only if thinking remains subordinate to existence and its infinite demand will thinking stay in the service of finding out what best serves the other. A final question to religious proclamation should therefore be posed:

5. "In proclamation, is the existence of oneself and the other there for the sake of thinking, or is thinking there for the existence of oneself and the other"?

The main takeaway from the Kierkegaardian analysis of existence is a consequential challenge to any proclamation in the name of religion: does it

[50] *Ibid.*, p. 78.

pretend that 'the absolute', 'God' or any other word one uses for the highest authority, can be realized in "an absolutely definite action, where one can see that it has been performed in obedience to the absolute because the absolute is a thought-out-ideology or utopia, that subordinates oneself and the existence of other human beings to thinking"?

The alternative, which Kierkegaard and Løgstrup present, is that individuals remain "true to the character of their existence as becoming and possibility". In doing so, they know that what they say and do, in virtue of their relation to the absolute, is said and done on their own responsibility and in complete uncertainty. They make efforts by thinking about how to best act for the sake of their own existence and other human beings. But they can never be sure that they did what was the best.

This is the way of thinking behind Kierkegaard's attack on the Danish Church's proclamation of his time. He criticizes it for leaving the individual to live in the crowd, complaining that it preaches it to be sufficient for someone to be Christian that they are born in a Christian nation, that nothing is disturbing in being Christian because we are all Christians by default. He also charges that ministers of the Church use 'aesthetic' categories in their Christian lectures without distinguishing them from ethical-religious categories.[51]

An important question remains as to whether religious leaders and thinkers should accept that philosophy in this way presents constraints on religious proclamation. Løgstrup presents Kierkegaard's analysis of existence as being influenced by Christian proclamation in the first place and opts for not simply accepting it as authoritative. Instead, a debate should be underway between philosophy and theology: "Ultimately, it is the same human existence, whether it is centred on philosophy or theology. The concern they share ought to allow fruitful interaction to seem wholly natural".[52]

Suppose that religious leaders reject the possibility of a philosophical critique of religious proclamation because the latter is based on revelation or holy scripture. In that case, they then assume that revelation does not need to correspond to the structure of human existence. They thereby claim that the proclamation must neither be rationally nor existentially comprehensible. Then, however, the difference between faith and coercion is annulled.

While Kierkegaard and Løgstrup are wrestling with this question within a Christian context, their conclusion is valid for everyone. If there is no

[51] Kierkegaard's series of pamphlets against the Danish Church called 'Øieblikket' ('The Moment') is available in English translation by Howard V. Hong and Edna H. Hong (eds. and trans.), *The Moment and Late Writings: Kierkegaard's Writings, XXIII*, Princeton University Press, 1998.

[52] Løgstrup, 2020, p. 80, see *supra* note 35.

understanding in faith, if it does not correspond to the formal structure of human existence, it is impossible to distinguish it from coercion, brainwashing or superstition.

For Løgstrup, the implication of the philosophical analysis of existence for the relationship between religion and politics is obvious: "Every political use of Christianity, for example, is open to critique by philosophical existence analysis, where Christianity is used as the reason or argument for a particular policy".[53] Of course, religious persons may engage with political issues, but the point is that they cannot deduce their *political* views from their religion. Any human being must use their reason and experiences to arrive at their opinions. Every mixing of religion and politics, each assertion that a specifically Christian, Muslim, Hindu, Buddhist, *et cetera* policy ought to be put forward, is open to criticism based on the philosophical analysis of existence.

The same goes for any purported religious ethics, which must pertain to the same considerations and disagreements as any other ethical knowledge. Religious leaders who assert to have special authorization from God to promote certain principles make God into something given and their relationship with God into a fact, which others may inspect and certify. However, the ethical demand asks us to serve the other person based on our insight and reason. In arguing for what we say and do to be ethically sound, we must refer to our reasons and not to an intention of fulfilling the ethical demand. Our relationship to God and the fulfilment of the ethical demand is a private affair, hidden from others.

Of course, religious leaders may claim that they represent the religious message or the ideals and values derived from that message. But they then make religion into an ideology "that is at one's disposal and can be directly applied and immediately realised".[54] Suppose that one thinks that religion can be reduced to a given set of messages or system of ideas without considering one's relation to them. In that case, religion is "ossified into an ideology that can be applied". The risk is that leaders or adherents start to believe that they are in a position to speak and act with absolute or divine certainty. To be religious would amount to being able to go beyond one's human limitations and to cut themselves off in political and ethical matters from the non-religious or adherents of other religions.

Ossifying religion into ideology includes a great risk that organized religion establishes itself as a political front and supports political leaders that purport to represent the ideology. By way of the analysis of existence and its constraints on religion that I have presented, we have now come to a point where

[53] *Ibid.*, p. 81.

[54] *Ibid.*, p. 82.

we can address some of the main problems we observe today. Religion is made into an ideology applied to separate and build fronts between people of different creeds and to build political power. Individual responsibility in relationship with God is replaced by responsibility for realizing an ideology which cannot be criticized or debated. Not only is one's own existence disregarded, but also the existence of the other human being, which is subordinated to that which is thought out once and for all.

A further unsound consequence of applying religion in this way, as an ideology that often involves coercion, is that one's conscience may remain completely clean: "it is after all the absolute, for which one bears responsibility that is realised".[55] The limits in our responsibility for others drawn by Kierkegaard and Løgstrup in their existential analysis, based on the fact that each individual has the task to live their lives as individual persons, are disregarded. According to these limits, responsibility for others can never consist in taking away their responsibility. We are all placed in the same human condition, to remain responsible for our own words and actions. From that follows that we have to respect that others are responsible for their lives, even though we care for them and want to help them according to our understanding of what is best for them.

In short, humans can never act as God's representatives.

17.4.3. Knud E. Løgstrup's Disclosure of the Ethical Demand

The analysis of human existence by Kierkegaard, Løgstrup and other philosophers inspired by them may help define constraints on religion and the way religion can be abused in politics and ethics. Løgstrup aims, however, to go a step further. He presented Kierkegaard's (and Heidegger's) existential analysis in a book from 1950, on which I have based the previous section.[56] In this book, it was clear, however, that as much he shared Kierkegaard's view that human existence includes an inherent ethical demand, he was not content with how Kierkegaard framed and explicated the demand.

According to Kierkegaard, every human being is a synthesis of temporality and eternity. Eternity is present in existence as an infinite demand, which we relate to either in obedience or disobedience. Unlike Heidegger (and Emmanuel Levinas (1905–1995), with whom Løgstrup has some affinities), Løgstrup agrees with Kierkegaard on this critical point. But while Kierkegaard maintains that the ethical dimension is primarily linked to the individual's relationship with God, for Løgstrup, the ethical demand confronts humans in their social, interdependent and vulnerable life with other human beings. The demand arises from situations where we are responsible for larger or smaller parts of fellow

---

55 *Ibid.*, p. 84.

56 See *supra* note 35.

human beings' lives, as he demonstrates in his ground-breaking analysis of primordial 'trust' in encounters between individuals.[57] The demand states that we should care for the other for their own sake, not basing our acts or words on our interests.

Løgstrup's philosophical account of this foundational demand inherent in human existence is expounded in his main work, *The Ethical Demand*, originally published in Danish in 1956.[58] His starting point is – in continuity with Kierkegaard and Heidegger – that for a religious proclamation to be relevant and comprehensible, it must correspond to features in our existence. We may be unaware of those features, so we need the proclamation to disclose them. But as soon as we have been made aware of and comprehended them, we can recognize them ourselves without needing a proclamation. We may even accept the features of our existence disclosed by the proclamation while rejecting the proclamation itself. In this way, the religious proclamation has both philosophical contents, revealing features of human existence that can be recognized by anyone regardless of their belief and a purely religious message which is up to everyone who hears it to believe or not.[59]

According to Løgstrup, the proclamation of Jesus of Nazareth touches on one feature of human existence in particular, namely our relation to other human beings. It is this feature that Løgstrup sets out to analyse, "what attitude to the other human being is implicit in Jesus's proclamation?".[60] While there is a content of Jesus' proclamation that "in a wholly ordinary and vague sense of the word is religious", there is also at play "an attitude to the other human being, which, although it is contained within the religious content of the proclamation, could still be formulated in purely human terms".[61]

The attitude that you should love your neighbour and even your enemy, as illustrated by the story about the Good Samaritan, is put in a purely religious

57 K.E. Løgstrup, *The Ethical Demand: Translated with an Introduction and Notes by Bjørn Rabjerg and Robert Stern*, Oxford University Press, 2020, pp. 67–75 ('*The Ethical Demand*').

58 The book made Løgstrup 'world famous' in Denmark and the Nordic countries. It is, however, only recently that authoritative translations into English of this and some of his other seminal works on ethics have been published. Oxford University Press publishes a series entitled Selected Works of K.E. Løgstrup, which currently consists of three volumes: *Kierkegaard's and Heidegger's Analysis of Existence and its Relation to Proclamation*, see *supra* note 35; *The Ethical Demand*, see *supra* note 57; and *Ethical Concepts and Problems: Translated with an Introduction and Notes by Kees van Kooten Niekerk, Kristian-Alberto Lykke Cobos*, Oxford University Press, 2020. *Controverting Kierkegaard* ('Opgør med Kierkegaard', 1968) is forthcoming in the series. Throughout this chapter, I refer to these translated versions of Løgstrup's books.

59 *The Ethical Demand*, p. 60, see *supra* note 57.

60 *Ibid*., p. 62 (*sic.*).

61 *Ibid.*

context in Jesus' proclamation. It states that the individual's relationship with God is decided through their relationship with another human being. Life is a gift from God, and God wants other human beings to be cared for. However, a precondition for this close relationship can be described in purely human terms, namely that we live our lives in interdependence and entanglement with each other. In Martin Luther's words, we are the 'daily bread' in one another's lives.

In disclosing the ethical demand and its origin in the interdependence of human existence, Løgstrup makes use of the phenomenological method he learned from the German philosopher Hans Lipps (1889–1941), who belonged to the famous Philosophical Society of Göttingen that gathered around Edmund Husserl (1859–1938) and Adolf Reinach (1883–1917). Lipps understood philosophy as a hermeneutics of reality, which is tied up with ordinary language. It is through language that reality, both in terms of objects and human beings, is revealed. The philosophical investigation must therefore follow the hints toward meaning and distinctions embodied in ordinary words and speech, clarifying those hints and explicating the understanding they contain. In contrast to Husserl's theory of the 'ideal unities of significance', Lipps emphasized the undetermined meaning of words and concepts whose exact meaning changes according to the context of the speech situation.[62]

According to Løgstrup, humans tend to treat the world and other human beings as mere means to their ends. We take undue credit for our achievements, but in fact, the features and deeper value structures of human existence can be known to us. Phenomenology, rather than scientific methods, can disclose our misconceptions of who we are and what the world really is. Just as the Christian proclamation can disclose our dependency on others and how we fail to take proper care of them, this can also be made sense of philosophically by applying a phenomenological method.

Løgstrup's short formulation of his undertaking is thus to make "the distinctions that are necessary in order to understand the silent, radical, one-sided, and unfulfillable character of the demand which is contained in the proclamation of Jesus".[63] In other words, his aim is to disclose the ethical demand as a feature of human existence in a way that can be understood independently of any religious proclamation.

He does that by outlining how our mutual interdependence and vulnerability put us under each other's power. That power can be used to do good or ill

62 Løgstrup's philosophy of language presented in *Vidde og Prægnans: sprogfilosofiske betragtninger* (Width and Meaning: Philosophical Considerations of Language), Gyldendal, Copenhagen, 1976, is inspired by Lipps. Løgstrup followed Lipps' lectures in the early 1930s and reiterated his dependency on his method throughout his works.

63 *The Ethical Demand*, p. 64, see *supra* note 57.

for the other person. We then fall under a demand to do good. Understanding the demand in this way, including providing it with specific content, honours Kierkegaard's concern that the individual becomes a self, living his or her life in a society without being subject to life in the crowd. The demand must not be confused with the requirements put on us by convention or ethical and legal requirements prevalent in the society where we live. It is neither to be identified with what the vulnerable person asks of us. To genuinely care for the other, therefore, we may have to go against their expressed wishes, instead using our own understanding of what is best for them. It therefore isolates and makes us responsible.

The demand being *unspoken* or *silent* in this way, leaving it to ourselves to decide how to act on it, results in a risk that we intrude on the other. There are, therefore, limits to be respected. We should neither make others the master of our deeds to take care of them, reducing us to mere tools in their hands, nor should we subjugate them to our understanding of life as a form of intrusion and encroachment.

In this way, "we are caught in a conflict between a consideration for others that is in fact indulgence, compliance, and flattery on the one hand, and on the other hand lack of consideration for others which in the interests of our understanding of life becomes an intrusion and an encroachment".[64] Addressing this conflict in a balanced way includes avoiding taking away a person's responsibility for themselves while at the same time not just doing what the other person asks of us. Including in the notion of 'respect' that individuals ultimately remain responsible for themselves, even if they depend on our help, is to appreciate that they may have another understanding of life.

Unlike social norms, the ethical demand presupposes that we act selflessly for the other person's good. We do not fulfil it for the sake of avoiding sanctions or to look good. Thereby lays the *radical* nature of the demand. Prevailing morality and law also often give rise to specific prescriptions or prohibitions of actions, while the demand leaves it to our understanding, insight and experience to decide how we should act. Moreover, the radical nature of the demand also includes other essential aspects. It does not only cover situations where it is pleasant for us to fulfil the demand. It also includes situations where we have our enemy's life, fate or well-being in our hands. Our enemy may also be dependent on us:

> Is not my enemy dependent on me to some degree, and on the manner in which I come to meet them? How much thinking is taken up with focusing on the enmity between us? Isn't a human being as

[64] *Ibid.*, p. 83.

> dependent on whom they hate, and often much more than on whom they love? The demand therefore consists in taking care of that part of the life of the other person which has been delivered up to me, regardless of whether they are someone who is closest to me or a stranger, and regardless of the manner in which they have been delivered up to me, whether it is through a trust that I welcome or through an enmity which arouses me to self-assertion.[65]

While other demands or requirements may involve *rights* claims, as they are established through contracts or are adopted by legitimate assemblies, the ethical demand is not grounded in such processes. The other person cannot present a claim that I fulfil the demand or fulfil it in a certain way. The demand must not be confused with the more or less well-founded claims we present on each other, based on past achievements or services we have provided. It must also be separated from views that our responsibility is limitless, regarding things which are not in our power to accomplish. Such views may, on the contrary, be a product of selfishness, an attempt to give significance to our own lives, or result in overzealous control over the lives of others.[66]

Given our tendency to disregard the ethical demand and act selfishly, we need social norms of 'law, morality, and convention' to protect us against each other and stabilize our lives and societies. They function well precisely because they, different from the ethical demand, do not require that we act selflessly. As long as we adhere to these norms, our motivations do not matter so much. They can therefore be enforced through threats of punishment or promoted by the promise of reward. As written or customary norms, they also require less engagement in terms of personal assessment and judgment on our side.

We may then ask if we need an ethical demand independent of the prevailing social norms of the society where we have our lives. Løgstrup offers some compelling answers to this key question:[67]

- Even if social norms are prescriptive, many are not completely determinate, and will still require some judgment from our side, including on what is best for the individual whose life is influenced by the fulfilment of the norms.
- In personal relations, acting only based on what is required by social norms, may severely reduce my ability to act properly. Without the attitude of love or care for the other (required by the demand), obeying social norms may not make my spouse or my children or wider family happy. Acting in

[65] *Ibid.*, p. 104.
[66] *Ibid.*, p. 105.
[67] *Ibid.*, pp. 115–120.

loveless manners results in a feeling that I am not present in or behind my deeds myself.

- If we dropped the ethical demand, we would lose the compass we need to assess the social norms and see if they result in good or not. Social norms need constant assessment as they can be damaging as well as beneficial to a good life. They vary according to time and place, and the ethical demand provides us with the capacity to assess them.

There is another key feature of the demand to care for the other's life in a way that best serves the other, namely that it is non-reciprocal or *one-sided*. There are many ways we can protest the demand, based on conceptions that it would be unreasonable to demand that we always put our own best interests aside to help the other. After all, life is conducive to basic rules of 'give and take'. Why should I act for you without ensuring that I get something in return? Løgstrup's answer is that the demand requires an understanding of life as a gift:

> For this reason, a human being has no basis in their existence on which to make a counterdemand to another human being. In view of the fact that what a human being owns is something that they have received, no counterclaim can be issued. The individual is a debtor, not by first committing some wrong, but simply because they exist and have received their life.[68]

The Christians as well as adherents of other religions that teach the world and humans to be created by a merciful God have an explanatory framework to make sense of this aspect of the demand. However, Løgstrup argues that atheists and those who do not share a belief in creation will also find enough fundamental phenomena in their lives that they cannot claim to have created themselves or be created by other humans to accept that 'life is a gift'. The primary examples are understanding, openness, love and compassion, which he in later works characterizes as 'sovereign expressions of life'.[69] The point is that these phenomena are pre-ethical and in some fundamental meaning given so that we can fulfil them or distort them, but not take credit for them.

These phenomena provide important elements in the account of life as a gift, namely, that their

---

68 *Ibid.*, p. 174.

69 In his final critical account of Kierkegaard's understanding of Christianity, *Opgør med Kierkegaard* (Controverting Kierkegaard), Gyldendal, Copenhagen, 1968, one of Løgstrup's main arguments is that Kierkegaard overlooks such spontaneous and life-upholding phenomena as love, trust and compassion, and therefore creates a false dichotomy of either love in relation to God as an infinite idea or conformity ('life in the crowd'). There is a third option, according to Løgstrup, and that is a life where one responds to the claim of the sovereign expressions of life.

> ethical structures are not something we bring about for ourselves but are a normative order in which we always already have our place. This then allows Løgstrup to make a clear distinction between the goodness of life itself, and the harm that we then bring to life by imposing our own self-created distortions upon it, as we turn trust into reservation, and love into selfishness.[70]

The ethical demand is *unfulfillable* in a fundamental sense. While the demand may arise out of natural love, the problem with the latter is that it often fails. It can easily dissipate, friends and loved ones losing the attraction they once had. A more fundamental problem, though, is that natural love is selective, only extending to some people but not all. In these circumstances, the ethical demand creates an obligation to replace love by doing what love would have done without being obliged to do it. In love as a pre-ethical relationship, there is no need for an ethical demand. Love is a 'given' for us; so, if we are capable of genuine love, this comes from the goodness of life itself, as a gift. However, our selfishness tends to distort love. In Løgstrup, there is an ontological optimism "concerning the goodness of human life and anthropological pessimism concerning the wickedness of human beings".[71]

The demand is thus unfulfillable in the sense that if I need to be told to do what is best for the neighbour, I have already failed to act out of love. Ethically demanded acts replace in this way the natural goodness and love that are inherent in human existence. The demand is thus not unfulfillable because it asks too much of us, but because it should not have been necessary. The Good Samaritan did not act after recognizing a demand to help, but did so spontaneously. In replacing this spontaneity, the demand also lets in other motives to help, such as self-righteousness and proving to others that we care.

In the final chapters of *The Ethical Demand* (Chapters 10–12), Løgstrup discusses whether his conception of the demand is compatible with science, anti-metaphysical philosophy (positivism of some sort), how it relates to poetry and finally how Jesus' proclamation related to the demand.

Science may give explanations for why we fail to love others, referring to biological factors, our upbringing or our environment, thereby taking away our responsibility. Løgstrup's response is that if we think of ourselves as selves at all, we must take responsibility for making the demand unfulfillable. But to think that we are to blame in this way is to go beyond any scientific or anti-metaphysical conception of life, so there remains an inevitable conflict with

70 Robert Stern, *The Radical Demand in Løgstrup's Ethics*, Oxford University Press, 2019, pp. 91–92.

71 Bjørn Rabjerg and Robert Stern, "Introduction", in *The Ethical Demand*, p. 43, see *supra* note 57.

science. When it comes to the problem of determinism, Løgstrup argues similarly to Luther and Calvin that, as long as the concept of the self is kept, a person can still be held responsible.

In Chapter 11, Løgstrup refers to poetry as an ally in helping to pay attention to often forgotten features of our existence. While "[p]hilosophy can at best make an understanding clear. Poetry can make it present".

In the book's last chapter, Løgstrup returns to the proclamation of Jesus. The question is whether Jesus is solely a teacher who taught us about the ethical demand, which we otherwise can understand in purely human terms, or whether he represented something more. The answer is that Jesus offers forgiveness to us for our failure to respond to the other with love. Here Jesus speaks with a particular kind of divine authority. In Løgstrup, as in Christianity, Jesus here speaks for God, and puts us in the decision situation of faith: do we believe him to be the son of God or not?

All the rest is made sense of in philosophical enquiry and open for every human being to understand, debate, criticize and *apply*.

17.4.4. How Can Religious Leaders Make Use of Kierkegaard and Løgstrup?

There are several ways religious leaders can make use of Kierkegaard's and Løgstrup's analysis of human existence in mobilizing against hate speech and violence in the name of religion.

Firstly, as already outlined above, the analysis provides a set of criteria for religious leaders to scrutinize religious teaching. Concepts such as 'holy land', 'holy religion' or 'holy war', for that matter, fail the test. They represent distortions by absolutizing ideas that humans have thought out and put into action. By making their own religion into an ideology, religious leaders may also be prone to attacking adherents of other religions on the basis that they are agents of rival religious ideologies with an aim to take over the land. The result may be religious hate speech, which denies others the right to stay and practice their religion.

Hate speech in the name of religion may in some circumstances be an unavoidable consequence of making religion into ideology, that is, a set of finalized ideas on how society should be organized as a fulfilment of religious doctrines. In this way, a front against the others is established. The others are portrayed as threats to the implementation of the ideology and should either leave or possibly convert. In attacking, conspiracies that the others have plans to take over the land and replace us are frequently used. An argument may be presented that, 'if we do not act decisively, others may do and it will be the end of us'.

Secondly, religious leaders should teach that individual responsibility always remains in religion. It is true that religious beliefs are often deeply rooted and part of a shared culture, but an important insight of the analysis of existence provided by Kierkegaard and Løgstrup is that the decisions to relate to God in one's life cannot be taken once and for all. Existence is movement and decisions must be repeated or changed on one's own account.

An argument may be presented that non-Western cultures are prone to putting the collective at a higher place than Western cultures do. However, while respect for the elderly, a sense of belonging to the family or a clan, as well as adherence to social norms may vary, becoming a self always includes taking responsibility for the cultural specificities one is placed under. There is no exit from this kind of responsibility in the life of humans if they decide to leave life in the crowd.

Thirdly, religious leaders should engage in and refer to conversations about the kind of universalist approach inherent to Kierkegaard and Løgstrup. Philosophers today have limited influence on policies and the way people think. In many contexts, religious leaders may play more decisive roles in placing the need for 'soft' Enlightenment on the agenda, that is, the need for moral knowledge that can challenge the way religious as well as non-religious communities and movements relate to ethical issues. Fragmentation of ethics is a dangerous route for everyone, and religious leaders should rather promote respect for our shared humanity as exemplified in Kierkegaard and Løgstrup than insist on exclusively religious ethics. The decisive point is not whether one accepts any of their accounts of human existence and its inherent ethical demand, but whether one engages with them and with similar projects in a serious and honest conversation.

In the above reference to American philosopher Dallas Willard's diagnosis of Western culture, I referred to his claim that moral knowledge has disappeared. His prescription of how moral knowledge can return, by presenting *a model of the good person*, underlines the contributions to ethical thinking of Løgstrup and Levinas. They present, according to Willard, descriptions of 'primitive personal interactions', attempting to describe (often overlooked) experiences of moral obligation. Løgstrup focuses on natural trust in human relationships while Levinas focuses on the experience of the human face and of human need beyond all classifications of the one in need. They do not make efforts of establishing rules or general principles but leave it to the individual to mobilize their own insight and understanding when meeting the other's face or being called to action by the ethical demand.[72]

[72] Willard, 2018, pp. 362–63, see *supra* note 28.

Religious proclamation often refers to 'good' or even 'holy' persons and tells stories of human interactions to exemplify good and evil. If Willard's prescription is right, religious leaders may play an important role in debating the main characteristics of good persons, based on experiences and tested values.

Last, but not least, both Kierkegaard and Løgstrup refer to 'love' as the fundamental expression of life in humans. Their conceptions are far from any Hollywood-style romantic cliché story. They rather represent a realistic analysis of life without overlooking the way human selfishness and hate may distort relations and even lead to deadly conflict and war.

Their understanding of life was nurtured by religion. They experienced plenty of challenges in their own life – Kierkegaard experienced the death of all his siblings but one brother in spite of him being the youngest, and Løgstrup experienced the breakdown of European culture during both world wars – but kept faith in life as a gift and love as the primary expressions of life.

This may also be an important inspiration for religious leaders, to talk about love, not only for adherents of their religion, but for humans.

17.5. Religious Tolerance, Freedom, Diversity and Epistemology

There are several ethical norms that can be found in religions as well as in reflections on diversity and the epistemology of religion, which can help religious leaders to confront hate speech and violence in the name of religion. I will mention just a few.

According to a recent survey by Pew Research Center, Indians feel their country has lived up to its post-independence ideals of creating a society where followers of many religions can live and practice freely. India's population, at the time of the survey of about 1.4 billion, consisted of 81 per cent Hindus, 12.9 per cent Muslims and 2.4 per cent Christians, as well as significant groups of Sikhs, Buddhists, Jains and other religions.[73]

The survey finds that Indians of all religious backgrounds overwhelmingly feel free to practice their faith. They see

> religious tolerance as a central part of who they are as a nation. Across the major religious groups, most people say it is very important to respect all religions to be "truly Indian". And tolerance is a religious as well as a civic value: Indians are united in the view

[73] The survey was based on nearly 30,000 face-to-face interviews of adults conducted in 17 languages between late 2019 and early 2020. Neha Sahgal *et al.*, "Religion in India: Tolerance and Segregation", *Pew Research Center*, 29 June 2021. In the following, I render the main points of the survey.

> that respecting other religions is a very important part of what it means to be a member of their own religious community.[74]

A remarkable feature discovered by the survey is that not only do most Hindus (77 per cent) believe in *karma*, but so do an identical percentage of Muslims. Further, 32 per cent of Christians and 81 per cent of Hindus say they believe in the purifying power of the Ganges River. However, despite sharing certain values and beliefs, members of different religious communities often do not feel they have much in common with one another. The survey found that 66 per cent of Hindus see themselves as very different from Muslims, and 64 per cent of Muslims return the sentiment. While a few of the smaller communities feel they have a lot in common with Hindus, people in the major religious communities tend to see themselves as very different from others and prefer to live with, have friends with and marry people from their own communities. In fact, 36 per cent of Hindus stated that they did not want to have Muslim neighbours.

While overwhelmingly expressing support for religious tolerance, most Indians seem to prefer segregation along religious divides. For example, 82 per cent of Hindus say they value tolerance, but do not want interreligious marriages of Hindu women. There is also a strong identification among Hindus of being 'truly' Indian and Hindu (64 per cent) and speaking Hindi (59 per cent). These groups also mainly support the ruling Bharatiya Janata Party ('BJP'), led by Prime Minister Narendra Modi (1950–), known for its Hindu nationalism. According to observers, the BJP's electoral success is largely attributed to Modi's charisma and the politics of religious polarization and strident nationalism.[75]

Based on this background, an important question is what 'tolerance' really means in the Indian context. Adding to a somewhat confusing picture, according to the survey, 65 per cent of Indians say violence between religious groups is a 'very big problem'. How can widespread tolerance go hand in hand with the wish for segregation and frequently occurring interreligious violence?

Religious tolerance has been defined as "the forbearance and the permission given by the adherents of a dominant religion for other religions to exist, even though the latter are looked on with disapproval as inferior, mistaken, or harmful". In contrast, religious 'liberty' or 'freedom' is understood as the recognition of equal freedom for all religions without discrimination. Toleration is something a ruler can easily withdraw, while freedom is harder to cancel.[76]

---

74 *Ibid.*

75 Soutik Biswas, "The Secret Behind Success of India's Ruling Party BJP", *BBC News*, 2 December 2020.

76 Perez Zagorin, *How the Idea of Religious Toleration Came to the West*, Princeton University Press, 2003, pp. 5–6.

The concept of tolerance had its breakthrough in the European eighteenth century Enlightenment in order to overcome religious conflicts and wars. The Enlightenment was usually seen to include, among its defining achievements, reason, civility, tolerance, commerce and freedom. Traditionally, research has pointed to the role of so-called *philosophes*, living in Paris, who tried to change the world with their writings, and in particular to take on the Catholic Church or religious fanaticism to introduce a modern, scientific and philosophical approach to developing society.

Recent scholarship has, however, to a degree redefined Enlightenment as an *Atlantic* and not a French or Western European phenomenon with a variety of national contexts and characteristics. The philosophy-centred research has given way to research on the many forms of Enlightenment culture. The black-and-white understanding of the Enlightenment as a secular and anti-religious movement has given way to perceptions that stress that several religious trends played important roles within the Enlightenment. There was a religious or Christian Enlightenment and even a Catholic one. The Enlightenment, therefore, is now seen as "a spectrum of many different, and even opposed, 'lights'. The Enlightenment is giving way to 'the Enlightenments'".[77]

While there is still considerable support for the view that science, political freedom, human rights and religious tolerance all have their origin in the Enlightenment, some modern scholars tend to complicate this perception. They have, *inter alia*, shown that the ideal of religious toleration "long preceded the Enlightenment, that religious persecution continued in many parts of Europe throughout the eighteenth century, and that Enlightenment thinkers not only held a vast range of religious and political ideas but also often advanced arguments for *both* tolerance and intolerance".[78]

However, while Enlightenment philosophers adhered to different views on many topics, they may all have shared a view that the principal enemy was of a religious nature: the 'abuse of spiritual authority', in the words of Jean le Rond d'Alambert (1717–1783), or 'ecclesiastical despotism' as Immanuel Kant (1724–1804) called it. They were not fighting religion as such; they "rather aspired to reform churches and beliefs so that they ceased to be an obstacle to political stability, social harmony, economic growth, and intellectual development".[79] In this endeavour, they were united with reform-oriented men inside the churches as well.

---

77 Juan Pablo Domínguez, "Introduction: Religious Toleration in the Age of Enlightenment", in *Journal of History of European Ideas*, 2017, vol. 43, no. 4, pp. 273–74.

78 *Ibid.*, p. 275.

79 *Ibid.*

In our context, it is important to note that tolerance was from its inception a narrower concept than religious freedom. The idea of toleration was used to differentiate between 'enlightened, acceptable citizens and intolerable fanatics'. Counter-Enlightenment could therefore point to their opponents being inconsistent, denying toleration to Catholics and advocating repression of atheists. Religious freedom, on the contrary, was closer to how religious people in opposition to the church thought, namely that every person should be permitted to decide on their religious views and adherence.

As illustrated by the Pew Research Center survey on India, supporting religious tolerance does not preclude Indians from supporting segregation, being against interreligious marriages and violence between religious groups remaining widespread. I, therefore, argue that religious leaders should aim at promoting 'religious freedom' rather than 'religious tolerance'. Tolerance is, of course, better than intolerance, being motivated by considerations on how to make society more peaceful even if it is divided along religious lines. Its solution is that we should simply accept 'others', while we do not have to make efforts to understand them better or interact with them.

Religious freedom goes deeper. It is aligned with existential analysis as presented above, underlining that the individual must take their own decision on how to relate to the religious proclamation. While Enlightenment philosophers were primarily concerned about religious institutions being subjugated to civil authorities, religious figures such as William Penn (1644–1718) propagated "the need to stop the persecution he and his fellow Quakers suffered at the hands of *civil* authorities".[80]

There may be discerned a different attitude to religious diversity in attitudes dominated by tolerance compared to attitudes dominated by freedom. While the tolerant reluctantly accepts diversity even if they do not like the 'others', those who profess religious freedom may even appreciate that in religious matters there can be no consensus, at least not without coercion.

There are three main views on religious diversity, the *pluralistic*, *exclusivist* and *inclusivist* theories. While pluralist approaches state that, within bounds, one religion is as good as another, exclusivists underline that one religion is uniquely valuable. Inclusivist theories agree with exclusivism that one religion has the most value but adds that others also have significant religious value.[81] While the concept of religious pluralism in some contexts is simply referring to a tolerant and sympathetic view of the various religions, it can also function as a normative principle, stating that people of different religions

80 *Ibid.*, p. 278.

81 Dale Tuggy, "Theories of Religious Diversity", *Internet Encyclopedia of Philosophy*.

should be treated the same. Religious leaders should, at least, by reflecting on religious diversity be cautious in judging those who believe differently, also taking into account that it may be impossible to prove that one belief is truer than others.

The question of evidence or proof adds an additional basis for religious leaders to promote religious freedom and confront intolerance. It comes from the fact that the *epistemology* of religious belief differs from other areas of human understanding. Contemporary epistemology of religion asks whether some sort of *evidentialism* applies to religious beliefs, or whether we should instead adopt a more permissive epistemology. Evidentialism says that a belief is justified only if "it is proportioned to the evidence".[82] However, religious belief is seldom if ever based on *the graduation of the likeliness that the religious propositions are true based on an assessment of evidence*.

Adherents of religious belief are hardly ever heard to be saying, when confronted with why they believe that the evidence they base their belief on justifies, for instance, a 60 per cent certitude, that their religion is true. Rather we believe based on a comprehensive interpretation of life experiences, and sometimes after listening to convincing preachers. Or the situation may be like Kierkegaard explained, there is no compelling evidence, but I mobilize my inner passion and fulfil the leap of faith. There may also be many adherents who did not seriously question why they believe because religion for them is more about belonging to a community and culture than questioning the truth of their faith.

Admitting this subjective dimension to religious belief, religious leaders should promote respect for individuals that chose differently.

17.6. Religious Dialogue and Human Rights

In confronting hate speech and violence against members of other religious communities, religious leaders may refer to norms and practices of dialogue. 'Dialogue' refers to ways of meeting and interacting with those who have other opinions, or with whom one has a conflict. It is a way of solving conflicts or at least understanding each other better through conversations that may be more or less structured.

Dialogue norms may vary, and even be subject to adoption in an initial phase of a specific dialogue. The following proposal for cross-cultural dialogue rules contains in my experience some of the most frequently referred to norms:[83]

[82] For a short introduction, see Peter Forrest, "Epistemology of Religion", in Edward N. Zalta (ed.), *The Stanford Encyclopedia of Philosophy*, Winter 2017 Edition, 2017.

[83] "Suggested Norms for Cross-Cultural Dialogue", *Harvard University* (available on its web site).

- Try on ideas. If someone expresses an idea, opinion or point of view new to you or different from your own, try it on; try to see it from within that other person's perspective.
- Practice 'both/and' thinking. We often practice 'either/or' thinking, believing that ideas, situations, plans and so on can only be 'this way' or 'that way'. What happens if both ideas – more than one plan or situation or perspective – can be meaningful, valuable or true?
- It is permitted to disagree, but not to shame, blame or attack another person.
- Use 'I' statements, speaking from your own personal experience rather than speaking of another's experience or generalizing about a group, whether that group is your own or another's.
- Take responsibility for your own learning: if there is something that you do not understand, ask for clarification. Seek out sources of new learning. Come to the conversation with an 'intent to learn', rather than an 'intent to control'.
- Respect confidentiality: it is good to share our learnings and experiences from dialogue with others, but it is not permitted to share another's story and to name that person unless that person gives specific permission to do so.
- It is allowed to be messy. Real dialogue, especially when it takes place across various kinds of differences, will be messy – inconclusive, sometimes uncomfortable or unclear. Welcome the messiness as a sign of authenticity and honesty. Practice bringing to the conversation a spirit of compassion and flexibility.
- Step up or step back: if you are a person who often remains silent in group conversations, step up to share your experience and perspectives. If you are someone who often speaks in such conversations, step back to leave space for others. Be intentional about both contributing to the conversation and sharing the 'air space'.

Such norms distinguish dialogue from *discussions, debates* or *deliberations*. In the latter, the emphasis is on agreeing on decisions, while debates involve argumentation in which two or more opposing sides on an issue make a case for their position. Discussions are informal and unstructured conversations without a goal to achieve specific outcomes. In dialogues, the aim may be to agree on decisions, but it can also be a collective act of sharing and listening to increase understanding of each other's perspectives and positions.

17.6.1. The Messaging of the Dalai Lama and Desmond Tutu

The encounters between the fourteenth Dalai Lama, Tenzin Gyatso, and the late Archbishop of Southern Africa Desmond Tutu were full of dialogue. Eventually, they became friends and published a book together on how joy in life can be achieved despite suffering and other troubles on life's way.[84]

They differ vastly in their background and religious outlook. The Dalai Lama is the spiritual leader of the Tibetan people and of Tibetan Buddhism, travelling extensively and promoting a message of kindness and compassion, interfaith understanding, respect for the environment and world peace. Aligned with the approach presented in this chapter, he has been a passionate advocate for a secular universal approach to cultivating fundamental human values. He has lived his life in exile in Dharamsala, India.

Desmond Tutu was a prominent leader in the struggle for justice and reconciliation in South Africa. In 1994, he was appointed Chair of the Truth and Reconciliation Commission, where he pioneered new ways for countries to address abuses, civil conflict and oppression. He was the Founding Chair of The Elders, a group of global leaders that promotes peace and human rights. He lived in Cape Town, South Africa.

From their different backgrounds, they had common experiences of struggles against powerful adversaries. As religious leaders, they have important political functions. And they have much to say on how humans and societies can deal with issues that for most people would seem insurmountable obstacles to progress on peace and human development. This is, however, not the point here. The point is that they both represented a deep understanding of what connects people of all creeds. They look to the deep respect for humanity in each person which religious belief, at its best, can instil. Religion has opened their eyes to what unites people on a very basic level, not to those articles of faith which may divide them.

After all, it is, as Løgstrup noted, the same human existence that religions, as well as philosophical thinking, refer to. In recommending how people should receive their message, they advised that:

> You don't need to believe us. Indeed, nothing we say should be taken as an article of faith. We are sharing what two friends, from very different worlds, have witnessed and learned in our long lives. We hope you will discover whether what is included here is true by applying it in your own life.[85]

[84] The Dalai Lama, Desmond Tutu and Douglas Abrams, *The Book of Joy*, Hutchinson, London, 2016.

[85] *Op. cit., p. x.*

They are outstanding persons whom religious leaders can learn and draw inspiration from.

17.6.2. Institutionalized Dialogue, an Example From Norway

Inspiration to adhere to norms of tolerance or freedom in religious matters may come from outstanding leaders. But it can also come from successful institutionalized dialogue and co-operation on developing common views and fighting hate and extremes across religious and life-view divides. I will present but one of the many examples of such dialogue around the world, the Council for Religious and Life Stance Communities in Norway, established in 1996.[86]

The Council's member communities include Bahá'í, Buddhists, Christians, Humanists, Hindus, Jews, Muslims and Sikhs. The main goals of the work of the Council are to promote equal treatment of religious and life-stance communities in Norway and to promote respect and understanding among religious and life-stance communities. In this way, the Council unites engagement for equal rights, and dialogue to increase understanding between the different communities. In addition to a national council, there are local councils in seven Norwegian towns.

The Council has been active on a range of political issues in education, workplaces, health institutions, detention centres, the military and graveyards. It is also developing common views on a number of ethical issues, such as protection of the environment, biotechnology, gender equality, sexual harassment within religious communities and the rights of refugees.

In its decision-making, the Council applies the principle of consensus, so that the opinion of each of the members has the same weight regardless of the size of the community. The Council can, however, make statements even if not all members agree, making explicit which religious or life-stance communities do not support a specific opinion. The Council provides advice and consultation to the Norwegian government.

There are some specific features, which may have contributed to the importance of the Council and made its prevention of hate speech and conflicts between religious communities effective. First, it provides co-operation among both religious and secular communities. Second, it provides a forum where both majority (the Protestant Church of Norway) and minority communities can take part on equal feet in defining and pursuing common political goals such as equal treatment of religious and life-stance communities. Third, the Council includes both Shí'ah, Sunní and Ahmadiyya communities, as well as different Christian communities, having different groups of Muslims and Christians sit at the same

86 More information about the Council for Religious and Life Stance Communities in Norway is available on its web site. All quotes in this section are from this web site.

table. Fourth, the Council has run projects to document and counter hate speech and discrimination based on religion or life-views. In this way, it has increased awareness of the problems and effectively promoted larger responsibility within the communities to counter such practices.

Another important factor is that the Council facilitates regular meetings of senior religious leaders. According to its own assessment,

> the level of mutual knowledge, trust and cooperation established within and supported by the Council, has proved to be an effective tool to address sensitive issues in the field of religious pluralism and has worked as a tool for conflict prevention in Norway among religious and life stance communities.

17.6.3. Freedom of Religion or Belief as a Human Right

The most relevant UN instrument for the topic of this chapter is the 1981 Declaration on the Elimination of All Forms of Intolerance and Discrimination Based on Religion or Belief.[87] It underlines in its Preamble that religion and belief is one of the fundamental elements in the 'conception of life' of anyone who professes either and "that freedom of religion should be fully respected and guaranteed":

> it is essential to promote understanding, tolerance, and respect in matters relating to freedom of religion and belief and to ensure that the use of religion or belief for ends inconsistent with the Charter of the United Nations, other relevant instruments of the United Nations and the purposes and principles of the present Declaration is inadmissible […].

The duty-bearers and potential perpetrators are, according to Article 2(1), both state and non-state actors ("any State, institution, group of persons, or person"). However, the operational provisions of the Declaration are addressed to states, which shall "take effective measures to prevent and eliminate discrimination on the grounds of religion or belief" (Article 4(1)), "enact or rescind legislation where necessary to prohibit any such discrimination" and take "appropriate measures to combat intolerance on the grounds of religion or other beliefs" (Article 4(2)).

A resolution of 12 April 2011 by the UN Human Rights Council adds substantial flesh to the Declaration's call for "effective measures".[88] The

[87] Declaration on the Elimination of All Forms of Intolerance and Discrimination Based on Religion or Belief, UN Doc. A/RES/36/55, 25 November 1981 (https://www.legal-tools.org/doc/hexdsg/).

[88] Combating Intolerance, Negative Stereotyping and Stigmatization of, and Discrimination, Incitement to Violence and Violence Against, Persons based on Religion or Belief, UN Doc. A/HRC/RES/16/18, 12 April 2011 (https://www.legal-tools.org/doc/0a86d2/).

Declaration has been followed up by a series of resolutions in the Council and concretized in the so-called Rabat Plan of Action of 2012.[89] In addition to calling upon states to respect and protect freedom of religion or belief for all, the resolution presents a list of eight recommended measures, including the creation of collaborative networks for dialogue and action in the fields of education, health, conflict prevention, employment, integration, media education, creating a mechanism within governments to address potential areas of tension between different religious communities and assisting with conflict prevention and mediation.

Several recommendations concern outreach to religious communities and encouraging religious leaders to discuss within their communities the causes of discrimination and how to counter these causes. State representatives should speak out against intolerance and religious hatred, and criminalize incitement to imminent violence. Other measures include education, awareness-building and "open, constructive and respectful debate of ideas, as well as interfaith and intercultural dialogue at the local, national and international levels".

These and other international initiatives endeavour to make religious leaders partners in fighting religious hate speech, but the question is whether their human rights- and state-oriented approach succeed. As referred to above, conservative religious leaders may acknowledge the benefits of the prohibition of discrimination and some other human rights for their own group, but are far more sceptical of the principled view that all human rights should be protected for everyone – regardless of their religion or belief, ethnicity, sexual orientation or gender identity. They may perceive international human rights as Western, secular and alien to their faith, aiming at emancipating people from religion, not within religion.

So how can a conversation with them on human rights start?

I think the first step should be to point to internal normative bases that reinforce the value placed on all humans – in religions, philosophy, as well as in human rights.

As recent scholarship has nuanced the view of the Enlightenment, pointing to the role of religious reformists in promoting religious tolerance and freedom, Samuel Moyn's research on 'Christian human rights' has nuanced the view on the role of religion in the drafting of the Universal Declaration. Conservative Catholic and Protestant Christians had before and during World War II adopted

[89] Rabat Plan of Action on the Prohibition of Advocacy of National, Racial, or Religious Hatred that constitutes Incitement to Discrimination, Hostility, or Violence: Conclusions and Recommendations emanating from the Four Regional Expert Workshops organized by the Office of the UN High Commissioner for Human Rights in 2011 and adopted by experts at the meeting in Rabat, Morocco, on 5 October 2012, UN Doc. A/HRC/22/17/Add.4, 11 January 2013 (https://www.legal-tools.org/doc/oymwge/).

a concept of 'dignity' that applied to all humans and not only privileged people. Their main motivation, according to Moyn was not to defend human emancipation in the tradition of the Enlightenment, but rather to defend a 'reinvented conservatism' inspired by personalism and religion – against both liberalism and totalitarian communism. Such ideas played, according to Moyn, a bigger part in the drafting of the Universal Declaration of Human Rights than previously admitted. The breakthrough of human rights in its secular form, and as an expanding part of international law, took place only in the 1970s.[90]

Moyn's thesis is not uncontroversial,[91] but it nevertheless illustrates how one may enter human rights from a variety of standpoints and motives, including from conservative religion. The point is that if one starts the conversation on human rights by introducing conceptions found in religion, which support human dignity, tolerance and freedom, one can create ownership and provide for an open discussion. Starting from external and perceived secular norms may close doors.

In line with this, the second step should be to ask religious leaders to do more than UN action plans usually ask them to. They should be asked to respect human rights by refraining from hate speech themselves and criticizing those who do. However, they should in addition be challenged to develop their own views on how hate speech and violence can be addressed based on broader normative bases. Part of that discussion should focus on how they can prevent religion from becoming a political front, an ideology.

From there, the conversation can take many different directions. By following this approach, however, the view that less religion is the solution to the problem of religious hate speech and violence is left out. Instead, the discussion will facilitate views on *how religious leaders can be more ambitious in fighting hate speech* and teaching religious tolerance, freedom and respect for diversity.

17.7. Religion and Politics: Norms of Prudence

Few have stated the demarcation between religion and politics as clearly as Pope Francis (1936–). The Pope, in a conversation on 16 March 2022 with Russian Orthodox Patriarch Kirill (1946–), told the Patriarch, who is a crucial supporter of President Vladimir Putin's aggressive war against Ukraine:

> Brother, we are not state clerics, we cannot use the language of politics but that of Jesus. We are pastors of the same holy people of God. Because of this, we must seek avenues of peace, to put an

---

90 Samuel Moyn, *Christian Human Rights*, University of Pennsylvania Press, Philadelphia, 2015.

91 See Ronald E. Osborn, "Conservatism by Other Means", in *The Hedgehog Review*, 2016, vol. 18, no. 1.

> end to the firing of weapons. [...] The patriarch cannot transform himself into Putin's altar boy.[92]

Kirill was elected in 2009 as the Patriarch of the Russian Orthodox Church, which has more than 100 million followers. Orthodox Christianity is the dominant faith both in Russia and Ukraine. Still, after Russia invaded Eastern Ukraine in 2014 and then attempted the invasion of the whole country starting on 24 February 2022, the Russian Orthodox Church has contributed to a rift between Moscow and Kyiv and between the Russian and the Ukrainian Orthodox churches.

In April 2022, Patriarch Kirill called on Russian soldiers to "love our fatherland [...] protect it, as only Russians can defend their country". He described those affected by the conflict in Ukraine as "people of Holy Russia. They are our brothers and sisters". He has lauded military service as "an active manifestation of evangelical love for neighbours".[93]

The relationship between Patriarch Kirill and President Putin helped justify the war. President Putin used the language of faith to support his political and military ambitions, while Patriarch Kirill used sermons to back the campaign on spiritual grounds, underlining Russia's broader struggle with Western countries that supports Ukraine and represent a decadent and God-less culture.

Patriarch Kirill's support for President Putin's latest war led to strong criticism within his church and internationally. Nearly 300 Russian priests and deacons signed an open appeal calling for a cease-fire.[94] In Ukraine, more than 320 priests signed a letter accusing the Patriarch of "heresy" and "moral crimes by blessing the war against Ukraine".[95]

The Pope's demarcation did not imply that religious leaders should not interfere in politics. Instead, he underlined that when doing so, they should use religious language, which is a language of peace and respect for human life. He also implied that the church must refrain from being instrumentalized by political power.

I did not find a more to-the-point criticism of Patriarch Kirill than the one expressed by the Pope, probably the world's most influential religious leader.

---

92 Timothy Bella and Sammy Westfall, "'Don't Be Putin's Altar Boy', Pope Warns Russian Orthodox Leader", *Washington Post*, 4 May 2022.

93 *Ibid.*

94 Jeanne Whalen, "Russian Orthodox Leader Backs War in Ukraine, Divides Faith", *Washington Post*, 18 April 2022.

95 "'Don't be Putin's Altar Boy', Pope Warns Russian Orthodox Leader", 4 May 2022, see *supra* note 92.

The norms underlying his criticism are based on centuries of mistakes and struggles to define the demarcation of religion versus politics.

17.8. Conclusions

There are several bases where religious leaders can find norms against religious intolerance, hate speech and violence.

I have pointed to universalist ethical approaches inspired by religious proclamation, as outlined by Kierkegaard and Løgstrup. Based on their philosophical analysis of human existence, they argue that the religious proclamation must correspond to human existence's structure and central features. If there exists no correspondence, religion becomes superstition, ideology and coercion. As such, it can lead to escalation of conflicts, abuse in the name of God and spreading of hate against those who represent other religions or beliefs or are excluded because of ethnicity, sexual orientation or other grounds.

The risk of religion developing into intolerant ideology can be effectively addressed by religious leaders, referring to the examples of open-minded and dialogue-oriented religious personalities such as the Dalai Lama and Desmond Tutu, religious traditions of tolerance, freedom and love for your neighbour, to diversity and epistemology of religion and to examples of institutionalized dialogue between religions and secular life-views. They can engage in debates about universalist ethical approaches and how to re-establish moral knowledge.

Religious leaders are frequently urged by the UN and other international organizations to abide by human rights norms and to refrain from using hateful expressions and criticize those who do. But they must also be challenged to mobilize internal normative bases to fight abuse of religion.

PART IV: MOTIVATIONS BEHIND HATE SPEECH

18

Motivations for Terrorism: Personality Factors, Situational Factors and Hateful Incitement

Ariel Merari*

The number of people who hold radical views and support violence against perceived political opponents is immensely larger than the number of people who actually commit terrorist acts. The main question that I seek to address in this chapter is: what is the difference between those who support violence but do not translate their beliefs into action, and those who actually resort to violence, often risking their own lives, or even commit suicide while killing others? Why does incitement to violence affect some people more than others?

The empirical findings on which this chapter is based are mostly derived from a series of studies conducted in Israel, in which Palestinian assailants were interviewed about their family and social background, interests, political and religious beliefs and activity, motivations for carrying out a terrorist attack, the process of planning, preparing and executing the attack, and their feelings and conduct before, during and after the attack. Assessment of the participants' personality characteristics and possible psychopathological conditions was obtained through interviews with experienced clinical psychologists and a battery of standard psychological tests.

---

* **Ariel Merari** is a Senior Research Fellow, International Institute for Counter-Terrorism, Interdisciplinary Center, Herzliya, and Professor Emeritus, Department of Psychology, Tel Aviv University. He served as Chair of Tel Aviv University's Department of Psychology (1982–1985). During the period of 1978–1989, he was a Senior Fellow at the Jaffee Center for Strategic Studies, where he established and directed the Terrorism and Low Intensity Conflict Program. From 1989 until his retirement, he was the Director of the Political Violence Research Unit at Tel Aviv University. He established Israel's Hostage Negotiations and Crisis Management Unit and commanded it for more than 20 years. In recent years he has headed a large study of suicide terrorism, publishing in 2010 the monograph *Driven to Death: Psychological and Social Aspects of Suicide Terrorism*. He has been a Visiting Professor at Berkeley and Harvard, and a Senior Fellow at the Kennedy School's International Security Program of the Belfer Center. He has studied political terrorism and other forms of political violence for more than thirty years. He received a B.A. degree in psychology and in economics from the Hebrew University in Jerusalem, and a Ph.D. in psychology from Berkeley. For an audio-visual recording of his statement to CILRAP's conference in Florence in April 2022 on the topic of this anthology, please see https://www.cilrap.org/cilrap-film/220409-merari/.

In this chapter, I shall describe some of the findings of these studies. But before I do that, I think that a general description of three of the participants, as revealed in their interviews, would help in forming an overview of the type of persons whom we studied and their motivations for carrying out terrorist attacks.[1]

18.1. Case 1: Rafik, Volunteered to Carry Out a Suicide Attack

Rafik was arrested with an explosive belt in his possession, as he tried to cross the border from the Palestinian Authority area into Israel, in order to carry out a suicide attack. He was a young man, 21 years old at the time of the attempted attack. Both his parents were college graduates. He had two brothers and two sisters. He evaluated the family's economic status as "middle class". He was first interviewed by an experienced former intelligence officer. In that interview, in response to a direct question about the reasons for his volunteering to carry out a suicide attack, he emphasized nationalist and religious motives. A dominant motive he mentioned was the Israeli occupation and the humiliation of Palestinians by Israel. At the same time, he viewed his attempted attack as fulfilling a religious obligation, doing Allah's will, and attributed his decision to carry out a 'martyrdom' attack to his love of *istishhad* (martyrdom) and his desire to go to heaven. He described himself as much more religious than his family.

However, a second interview, this time with an experienced clinical psychologist, revealed other layers in Rafik's personality and exposed different motivational forces. In the clinical interview, Rafik described himself as a loner since his childhood. Here are some excerpts from his interview:

> As a child I was a recluse […]. I had no friends in school. I had very few relationships. And it has been like this until now. I don't like to talk much with people. I'm not afraid, but embarrassed. And it's especially hard for me to talk with women. With my father I talked normally, but with my mother I only talked a little. When I wanted something, I asked my father. […] With my brothers and sisters, I didn't communicate much. Most of the time I locked myself in my room and watched television. Sometimes, when I am very nervous and no one can talk to me, then if somebody says 'hi' to me I can beat him up. On the other hand, when I see a small child crying, I may cry with him. I have these kinds of extremes.
>
> Then I made another friend – my father. We used to go out together. If there were problems, I would go to him and he'd come to me. We talked, did things together, not like father and son but

[1] The second part of the chapter is largely based on Chapter 7 of my book *Driven to Death: Psychological and Social Aspects of Suicide Terrorism*, Oxford University Press, New York, 2010.

> like friends. But he died. I tried to make other friends after he died, but it was hard for me. The mosque was the best place for me, going there, praying.

Rafik described himself as an explosive, impulsive person from childhood. He used to respond violently even to slight provocations.

His father's sudden death of a heart attack at the age of 78 years, when Rafik was 20 years old, was a very hard blow to him. Rafik took his father to the hospital, shook him, refused to accept his death, threatened to kill the doctor.

> After his death I did not want to go out. I thought, 'who would I be with, with whom would I talk without him?' I thought of committing suicide by cutting my veins, and had my mother not come into my room at that time, I might have done it.

He consulted with a Muslim cleric, who told him that suicide was forbidden, but martyrdom was considered meritorious in Islám. He then decided to join the ranks of a militant organization and, soon afterward, volunteered to carry out a suicide operation. He also mentioned that in prison, four days before the interview, he considered committing suicide with painkillers he had stocked.

On the basis of the interview and tests, Rafik was assessed as impulsive and unstable with a suicidal tendency.

18.2. Case 2: A Shahíd on Standby

Let us consider another assailant. Ahmad was 18 years old when he stabbed an orthodox Jew in Jerusalem. He was not a member of any group and carried out the attack on his own initiative. He was born in a village near Jerusalem. From birth, he suffered from a severe hearing and speech impairment. His parents divorced when he was 11 years old. His father used to beat him but after the divorce Ahmad did not see much of him. He was more religious than his family and used to pray five times a day in the village mosque.

Ahmad was very active in social media. He said that he had 1,500 friends on Facebook. Most of his communication on social media concerned the Israeli-Palestinian conflict and resistance activity. His logo on Facebook was 'a shahíd on standby'.

In a questionnaire about the motives for his attack, he marked as "very important" several different motives, including hatred of Jews, revenge for national humiliation, revenge for religious humiliation, a desire to die, a desire to be in heaven, a desire to prove himself and a desire to obtain social appreciation. In the interview, he insisted that he had been absolutely certain that he would be killed during his attack. When asked whether there were circumstances under which he would have changed his mind and cancel his planned attack, he said that there were no such circumstances because he was determined to die.

In this case too, the clinical psychological interview exposed and highlighted the more personal aspects of his motivation to carry out a terrorist attack.

Ahmed described himself as a loner. He felt that because of his hearing and speech impairment he was socially rejected and unwanted. He had no actual friends, only social media pals. He had no relations with girls. There was a girl he secretly loved but never dared approaching her in any way. Life was hard on him and he wanted to die.

Having finished high school several months before the attack, he spent his time at home, in the company of his computer. As he had always been politically aware and very religious, he was deeply influenced by the religious and nationalist incitement in the media. Against the backdrop of the wave of terrorist attacks by lone actors, which began in October 2015, many of whom were killed in the course of their attack, he thought that this was an appropriate way to achieve two goals: leaving this world and achieving a social status of an admired hero. In the interview, he said that he wanted that his tombstone would carry the inscription: "Here rests the Shahid General Ahmed". A couple of hours before he lunged at his victim, he posted a Facebook message: "Mother, I love you so much. Father, forgive me. I want to die in the ways of Allah. Allah is greater than me. People hate you, only Allah. I am going to stab a settler. Allah, may I be admitted to Heaven".

So far, I have focused on cases in which a desire to die was the dominant motivation for carrying out a violent attack. But not all assailants were suicidal. The motivation for carrying out terrorist attacks is seldom one dimensional, that is, propelled by a single sentiment. The balance between personal motives and ideological motives changes from person to person, but it is often possible to identify the dominant motivation. For some individuals, the desire to die is by far the strongest motive and the ideological component is just a small additional factor, whose main effect is to dictate the way of committing suicide and the choice of targets. In other cases, the personal factor and the ideological factors are equipotent or nearly so, and in still other cases, the main driving force is ideological conviction, a sense of burning hatred against a perceived enemy, which may or may not have a psychopathological basis, depending on the circumstances. The following is an example of an assailant whose main motivation for attack was ideological.

18.3. Case 3: Ideological Motivation and Sociopathic Personality Characteristics

Hashem was 20 years old when he participated in a shooting attack on Israeli civilians in a café in Tel Aviv, in which four people were killed and many others were wounded. He was born to a religious middle-class family and had partial university education. He was not a member of any political organization but emphasized that he was religious and his opinions were close to the Islamic State ('ISIS'). He said that in the course of the last year before the attack he was radicalized by contents he read on the internet and was especially influenced by ISIS messages. He used to follow ISIS pages for hours every day. He described himself as much more religious than his family and friends. Since he became very religious, he punctiliously made sure to pray all five required prayers every day.

The attack he carried out was not a spontaneous act. He planned and prepared it with a friend for months. He said that he never hesitated once he made the decision to carry out an attack. He mentioned three reasons that drove him to carry out the attack: Israel's humiliation and killing of Palestinian women,[2] revenge for the killing of the Dawabsheh family by Israeli terrorists[3] and defense of Al-Aqsa mosque. The nature of the victims did not bother him. He said that non-combatants, including children, were legitimate targets. He did not want to die although he was ready to die in the attack and had been certain that he would die. He said that, in retrospect, he was not satisfied with the attack because the number of victims was too small. In the clinical psychological interview, he described good relations with his parents and siblings. He talked much about his perception of true Islám, emphasizing that *jihád* is the highest obligation of every Muslim. He explained his attitude to the possibility of being killed in the attack, saying that he did not want to die but wanted to be in heaven. This differentiation may be philosophically meaningful, but practically entails unbridgeable contradiction. His true choice was shown by his attempt to escape the scene after committing the attack. Indeed, Hashem's clinical psychological evaluation found no suicidal tendency. He was assessed as having a sociopathic personality.

---

2 In September 2015, a radical Islámic women organization named 'Murabitat' conducted a series of provocative violent demonstrations at the Al Aqsa Mosque. Israeli police used riot control measures in clashes with the demonstrators. None of the demonstrators was killed or seriously wounded. In the course of the wave of lone actors' attacks that started in October 2015, several women assailants were killed by Israeli security forces. These events were mentioned by several male interviewees as one of the reasons that influenced their decision to carry out an attack against Israelis.

3 On 31 July 2015, at night, Jewish terrorists threw incendiary devices into the home of a Palestinian family in the village of Duma and set it on fire, causing the death of Saed and Riham Dawabsheh and their 18-months-old son Ali and the severe wounding of another son, four-years-old Ali. This shocking event was mentioned by several Palestinian assailants as a reason that prompted them to take revenge. The perpetrator of the attack on the Dawabsheh family, Amiram Ben-Uliel, was sentenced to three life sentences and additional 20 years in prison.

18.4. The Interaction Between Individual Mental State and External Influences

The first two participants described above, Rafik and Ahmad, were motivated to carry out an attack by both individual psychopathological conditions and ideological convictions. Clearly, however, the psychopathological condition, especially the desire to die, was the dominant element in their decision to engage in an act of terrorism. This mixture of motivations existed in most of the individuals whom we examined in our studies during the last two decades. In a recent study of independent attackers, in which 39 assailants (men and women) were interviewed and tested, two-thirds of the participants were diagnosed as suffering from one or more of the following: psychotic background, severe personality disorder and suicidality.[4] Somewhat lower but still high rates of psychopathology were found in several studies on terrorist lone actors in Western Europe and the United States, which based their assessments on secondary sources rather than on direct interviews and tests.[5] Thus, the accumulating evidence leaves little doubt that psychopathological states of mind and individual life circumstances play a major role in many (albeit not all) assailants' decisions to carry out a terrorist attack. Still, the question remains, why would a person, whose main motivation is to escape an unbearable personal situation, choose to do so by carrying out a terrorist attack? Why have those, whose main motivation was to cause their own death, done so in a manner that involves hurting other people?

The answer rests in the interaction between personality factors and external influences in generating violent behaviour which is ostensibly motivated by

[4] Ariel Merari and Boaz Ganor, "Interviews With, and Tests of, Palestinian Independent Assailants", in *Terrorism and Political Violence*, 2022, vol. 34, no. 8.

[5] Paul Gill, John Horgan and Paige Deckert, "Bombing Alone: Tracing the Motivations and Antecedent Behaviors of Lone-Actor Terrorists", in *Journal of Forensic Science*, 2014, vol. 59, no. 2; Emily Corner and Paul Gill, "A False Dichotomy? Mental Illness and Lone-Actor Terrorism", in *Law and Human Behavior*, 2015, vol. 39, no. 1, pp. 23–34; Jeanine De Roy van Zuijdewijn and Edwin Bakker, "Analysing Personal Characteristics of Lone-Actor Terrorists: Research Findings and Recommendations", in *Perspectives on Terrorism*, 2016, vol. 10, no. 2, pp. 41–48; Jeff Gruenewald, Steven M. Chermak and Joshua D. Freilich, "Distinguishing "Loner" Attacks from Other Domestic Extremist Violence", in *Criminology & Public Policy*, 2013, vol. 12, no. 1, pp. 65–91; Maarten Van Leyenhorst and Ada Andreas, "Dutch Suspects of Terrorist Activity: A Study of Their Biographical Backgrounds Based on Primary Sources", in *Journal for Deradicalization*, 2017, no. 12; Anton W. Weenink, "Behavioral Problems and Disorders Among Radicals in Police Files", in *Perspectives on Terrorism*, 2015, vol. 9, no. 2; Paul Gill, James Silver, John Horgan and Emily Corner, "Shooting Alone: The Pre-Attack Experiences and Behaviors of U.S. Solo Mass Murderers", in *Journal of Forensic Sciences*, 2017, vol. 62, no. 3, pp. 710–714; Lauren Richards, Peter Molinaro, John Wyman and Sarah Craun, "Lone Offender: A Study of Lone Offender Terrorism in the United States (1972–2015)", United States Department of Justice, Federal Bureau of Investigation, Behavioral Analysis Unit, November 2019.

political or religious sentiments and the susceptibility of the individual in question to these influences. These external influences include the attitudes and values of the assailants' reference groups, namely, their immediate social milieu and the national and religious community they belong to.

In the context of the Israeli-Palestinian conflict, a simple example of influential community values is the fact that while ordinary suicide is forbidden in Islám, '*istishhad*' – dying in a martyrdom operation – is highly recommended and adored. Whereas people who ordinarily commit suicide are believed to go to hell, *shahíds* are promised a glorious place in Paradise. But in a broader sense, in the context of nationalist or religious conflict, we can say that by choosing attacks on the perceived enemies of their religion or their ethnic group as a way to end their own lives, suicidal assailants use the socially accepted values of nationalism and defense of religion for justifying the socially unaccepted act of committing suicide. In the specific context of our studies, during the period under consideration, attacks by Palestinian individuals which resulted in the death of the perpetrators were at the centre of media coverage and public awareness. Social media posts in which young adults declared their intention to become *shahíds* gained overwhelming publicity in Palestinian society. Incitement to violence soars especially in periods of heightened confrontations. At these times, Palestinian inhabitants of the occupied territories were flooded with news, sermons, artwork and teachings that glorified the *shahíds* and praised their sacrifice. In a book based on first-hand impressions of Palestinian society at the time of the second intifada (2000–2004), Ann Marie Oliver and Paul Steinberg, who lived a long time among Palestinians in Gaza and the West Bank, described the Palestinian public's attitude to suicide attacks as follows:

> Support for suicide bombings went far beyond the military wings of the nationalist and Islamist movements. Parents dressed their babies and toddlers as suicide bombers and had them photographed in local photography studios. Children marched with suicide belts around their chests. University exhibitions included one that recreated an actual suicide bombing carried out in the Sbarro restaurant in Jerusalem, replete with pizza slices and bloody body parts. The Palestinian Authority named popular soccer tournaments after martyrs belonging both to Fatah and the rival Hamas, with even the suicide bomber who blew himself up during an Israeli family celebration of Passover, killing thirty of them, thus honored. On public TV, the Palestinian Broadcasting Corporation aired videos of men being lured away by the *hur*, the beautiful virgins of Paradise promised to martyrs, as if they were commercials or public service announcements. If the term *cult* did not suggest a

fringe phenomenon, we might begin to speak of a cult of martyrdom.[6]

Indeed, during the second intifada, in the Palestinian society, suicide attacks were established as a praiseworthy act, a generally admired expression of patriotism and sacrifice. All social agents of influence have shared this attitude, thus creating an overwhelming impact on people's opinions. Praise for suicide bombers has not been limited to media outlets representing the militant groups; mainstream newspaper editorials and Palestinian National Authority ('PNA') government television broadcasts voiced the same sentiments. Glorification of *shahíds* was embedded in the Palestinian education system and thus became a basic element in the formation of values of future generations. A study of 29 textbooks published in the school year 2004–2005 by the PNA Ministry of Education for fifth and tenth grades, found that these books were replete with phrases exalting *shahíds* and the glory of martyrdom.[7] Praise for martyrdom operations was introduced not only in Islámic education and history textbooks, but also in a matter-of-fact manner by using phrases glorifying *shahíds* as syntactic examples in grammar textbooks.

Indeed, praise for suicide bombers in all media outlets at the time of the second intifada created an overwhelming impact on people's opinions. This atmosphere was well reflected in public opinion polls. During the second intifada, rates of public support for suicide attacks against Israeli civilians reached nearly 80 per cent (even in relatively calm periods, they were usually in the range of 25–40 per cent of the population).[8] And during the wave of lone actors' attacks of 2015, a public opinion poll conducted by a highly reliable Palestinian pollster found that 67 per cent of a representative sample of the Palestinian population supported knife attacks against Israelis.[9]

Thus, for men and women who wanted to end their lives, this course of action not only became the most salient choice due to its public prominence, it was also an act that granted them a feeling of personal significance, because these attacks were admired by many people in their society as idealistic and heroic and endorsed as such by religious and political authorities.[10]

---

6 Anne Marie Oliver and Paul Steinberg, *The Road to Martyrs' Square: A Journey into the World of the Suicide Bomber*, Oxford University Press, New York, 2005, p. xxiii.

7 Noa Meridor, "A Study of Textbooks in the Palestinian Education System", Intelligence and Terrorism Information Center, Center for Special Studies, Israel, 16 April 2006.

8 See Merari, 2010, Chapter 7 and Appendix 1, see *supra* note 1.

9 Palestinian Center for Policy and Survey, "Palestinian Public Opinion Poll No. 58", 14 December 2015.

10 For an analysis of the importance of the search for significance as a motivation for suicide terrorist attacks, see Arie W. Kruglanski *et al.*, "Fully Committed: Suicide Bombers'

Another category of individuals, in addition to suicidal persons, who were affected by incitement and supportive public atmosphere, were persons characterized by excessive susceptibility to influence by other people, especially figures of authority. In a study of suicide bombers of the second intifada, 69 per cent of the would-be suicide bombers were assessed as having dependent-avoidant personality styles.[11] Dependent personality disorder characterizes individuals having pervasive psychological dependence on other people. Therefore, they tend to be particularly vulnerable to social pressure and are excessively influenced by public opinion and figures of authority. These are people who are more likely to turn to violence in response to incitement by authoritative religious or political leaders.

Thus, it is the interaction between personality characteristics and mental state on the one hand, and public atmosphere, accentuated with incitement by recognized authorities, on the other hand, that makes the combustible combination which leads specific types of individuals to commit acts of violence that are intended to kill others, perceived as enemies, while killing themselves at the same time.

Incitement has a critical role in creating public atmosphere that propels violent behaviour. Incitement is especially effective in moving people to aggressive action at times of acute conflict, when tempers flare. For completing the picture, the next part of the chapter brings examples of incitement by various sources of influence during the periods in which the assailants discussed above carried out their attacks.

18.5. Support for Violence by Sources of Authority

People's values are shaped by the culture they are born into. In all cultures, a variety of values are represented by historical or legendary figures, who symbolize different adored behaviours, such as defense of the religion, patriotism, generosity, *et cetera*. This is why the nature of a person's heroes can tell us much about the values he or she cherishes and, presumably, may be at least partly indicative of the motives that guide his or her behaviour. With this in mind, in a study of the characteristics of suicide bombers who committed deadly suicide attacks, we looked, *inter alia*, at the heroes whom the deceased bombers admired. [12] In that study, families of dead Palestinian suicide bombers were

Motivation and the Quest for Personal Significance", in *Political Psychology*, 2009, vol. 30, no. 3, pp. 331–357; David Webber *et al.*, "Divergent Paths to Martyrdom and Significance Among Suicide Attackers", in *Terrorism and Political Violence*, 2017, vol. 29, no. 5, pp. 852–874.

11 Ariel Merari *et al.*, "Personality Characteristics of 'Self Martyrs'/'Suicide Bombers' and Organizers of Suicide Attacks", in *Terrorism and Political Violence*, 2010, vol. 22, pp. 87–101.

12 Merari, 2010, Chapter 4, see *supra* note 1.

interviewed by Nasra Hassan, a Muslim woman from Pakistan who had worked for several years in the occupied territories with an international refugee organization. The families of 34 suicide bombers were interviewed in that study, and 20 of them described their dead sons' heroes. It turned out that all the heroes mentioned were various representatives of militant Islám.[13] Some of these heroes were also known in Islámic tradition for defying their families. This finding highlights the importance of religious tradition in shaping the values and motivation of youngsters who were willing to kill and die for these values. Yet the interpretation of this millennium-old tradition in the context of current events in a way that incited these youngsters to resort to extreme violence has been done by present day sources of authority, religious authorities in particular, but also other public opinion leaders, including journalists, politicians and academic authorities, as the following examples show.

18.6. Religious Authorities

At times of heightened conflict, such as during the second intifada, Palestinian religious authorities have unanimously praised suicide bombers (as well as other *shahíds*). Praise for *shahíds* and encouragement of martyrdom have been expressed not only by clerics associated with the militant Islámic groups but by those appointed by the PNA as well, such as the Mufti of the PNA, Sheik Ikrima Sabri,[14] the Chief Mufti of the PNA Police, Sheik Abd Al-Salam Shkhaydam[15] and many others.[16]

The legitimacy of Palestinian suicide attacks against Israeli civilians has spread beyond the Palestinian arena and gained support in part of the Islámic establishments of the Arab world. A leading figure among the Islámic authorities

---

13 Similarly, in a study in which 35 incarcerated Middle Eastern terrorists – most or all of them *not* suicide bombers – were interviewed, Post, Sprinzak and Denny found that the boyhood heroes of the Islámist terrorists were "religious figures, such as the Prophet, or the radical Wahabi Islamist Abdullah Azzam". However, the heroes of members of secular groups were revolutionaries such as Che Guevara and Fidel Castro. See Jerrold M. Post, Ehud Sprinzak and Laurita M. Denny, "The Terrorists in Their Own Words: Interviews with 35 Incarcerated Middle Eastern Terrorists", in *Terrorism and Political Violence*, 2003, vol. 15, no. 1, pp. 171–184.

14 "The Joy of the Mothers of Palestinian 'Martyrs'", Middle East Media Research Institute ('MEMRI') Inquiry and Analysis Series No. 61, 25 June 2001, quoting *Voice of Palestine Radio*, 25 May 2001.

15 *Ibid.*, quoting *Al–Hayat Al–Jadida (PA)*, 17 September 1999.

16 See "The Shuhada Cult of Martyrdom in Islamic Jihad", MEMRI Inquiry and Analysis Series No. 25, 24 February 2000; MEMRI Inquiry and Analysis Series No. 61, 25 June 2001, see *supra* note 14, and "Incitement in the Palestinian Authority After the Aqaba Summit", MEMRI Special Report No. 20, 22 August 2003. All the reports can be found on MEMRI's web site.

who has supported suicide attacks has been Sheikh Yúsuf al-Qáráḍáwí. Qáráḍáwí, an Egyptian Islámic cleric who lived and taught in Qatar for many years, has been one of the most influential religious authorities in the Islámic world in the twenty-first century, especially in the Middle East. He had a weekly program on the *Al-Jazeera* television, which exposed him to a vast Muslim audience. His *fatwás* (religious rulings) endorsing Palestinian suicide attacks have been widely publicized and often quoted. In a *fatwá* dated 22 March 2004, for example, he stated:

> The martyr operation is the greatest of all sorts of jihad in the cause of Allah. A martyr operation is carried out by a person who sacrifices himself, deeming his life [of] less value than striving in the cause of Allah, in the cause of restoring the land and preserving the dignity.[17]

In an earlier interview, Qaradhawi justified killing Israeli civilians as follows:

> Israeli society is militaristic in nature. Both men and women serve in the army and can be drafted at any moment. [On the other hand] if a child or an elderly is killed in such an operation, he is not killed on purpose, but by mistake, and as a result of military necessity. Necessity justifies the forbidden.[18]

Qaradhawi has been associated with the Muslim Brothers, a radical Islámic movement founded in Egypt in 1928, which has, among other things, spawned the Palestinian Hamas.[19] As such, his support for suicide attacks may not be surprising. However, support for suicide attacks has also been expressed by mainstream religious authorities in several Arab countries, especially Egypt. Cairo's Al-Ázhár University ('al-Azhar') – which Gilles Kepel, one the best scholars on Islámic movements in Egypt, described concisely as "the highest authority of Islam in Egypt; government controlled to some extent and therefore criticized by the Islamicist movement" – has been the home of several enthusiastic supporters of suicide attacks.[20]

The top Egyptian cleric of al-Azhar University, Sheikh Muhammad Sayyed Tantawi, initially opposed suicide attacks against civilians, ruling that "the suicide operations are of self-defense and a kind of martyrdom, as long as

---

17 "The Qaradawi Fatwas", in *Middle East Quartyerly*, 2004, vol. 11, no. 3, pp. 78–80.

18 "Debating the Religious, Political and Moral Legitimacy of Suicide Bombings Part 1: The Debate Over Religious Legitimacy", MEMRI Inquiry and Analysis No. 53, 2 May 2001, quoting *Al–Ahram Al–Arabi* (Egypt), 3 February 2001.

19 See "The Qaradawi Fatwas", 2004, see *supra* note 17.

20 Gilles Kepel, *Muslim Extremism in Egypt: The Prophet and Pharaoh*, University of California Press, Berkeley, 1993, p. 276.

the intention behind them is to kill the enemy's soldiers, and not women or children".[21] Later, however, apparently under pressure from other high-ranking Egyptian clerics, he modified his position, stating that martyrdom (suicide) attacks were the highest form of *jihád*, urging Palestinians of all factions to intensify them and saying that attacks against women and children were legitimate as long as the Israeli occupation continued.[22]

Other high-ranking religious authorities in Egypt who have endorsed Palestinian suicide attacks have included, *inter alia*, Sheikh Ali Abu Al-Hassan, Chairman of the Religious Ruling Committee at al-Azhar University,[23] Sheikh Dr. Ahmad al-Tayyeb, Egypt's Mufti,[24] who was later appointed President of al-Azhar University,[25] and his successor in the position of Egypt's Mufti, Dr. Sheikh 'Ali Gum'a. In an interview with the Egyptian newspaper *al-Haqiqa* in July 2003, Gum'a said:

> The one who carries out *Fedaii* [martyrdom] operations against the Zionists and blows himself up is, without a doubt, a *Shahid* because he is defending his homeland against the occupying enemy who is supported by superpowers such as the U.S. and Britain.[26]

18.7. Praise for Shahíds in Non-Palestinian Media

Palestinians' support for suicide attacks has been reinforced by the approving attitudes of public opinion in other Arab countries, which constitute the broader social, cultural and political milieu for the Palestinians. Many religious and secular opinion leaders in Arab countries have expressed support for suicide attacks, giving the Palestinian people a feeling that they are not crazy fanatics. Support for suicide attacks among radical Islámic circles and their media organs in

---

21 MEMRI Inquiry and Analysis Series No. 53, quoting *Sut Al–Ama* (Egypt), 26 April 2001, see *supra* note 18. See also "Debating the Religious, Political, and Moral Legitimacy of Suicide Bombings: Part III", MEMRI Inquiry and Analysis Series No. 65, 27 July 2001, quoting Ruz Al–Yussuf (Egypt), 18 May 2001.

22 "Leading Egyptian Government Cleric Calls For: 'Martyrdom Attacks that Strike Horror into the Hearts of the Enemies of Allah'", MEMRI Special Dispatch Series No. 363, 7 April 2002, quoting *Lailatalqadr*, a web site of the al-Azhar University.

23 "Wafa Idris: The Celebration of the First Female Palestinian Suicide Bomber - Part I", MEMRI Inquiry and Analysis Series No. 83, 12 February 2002, quoting *Afaq Arabiya*, Egypt, 30 January 2002, as cited in *Al–Quds Al–Arabi*, London, 31 January 2002. *Afaq Arabia* is an Egyptian Muslim Brotherhood's mouthpiece.

24 The *Mufti* is a top religious-legal advisor, appointed by the government, whose role includes issuing religious rulings (*fatwas*), usually in response to questions.

25 MEMRI Special Dispatch Series No. 363, quoting the al-Azhar web site *Lailatalqadr*, 4 April 2002, see *supra* note 22.

26 "The New Egyptian Mufti – Dr. Sheikh 'Ali Gum'a: Opinions About Jihad, Supporting Suicide Bombings, and Forbidding Muslims in the U.S. Militaryfrom Fighting Other Muslims", MEMRI Special Dispatch Series No. 580, 1 October 2003.

various Arab countries is not surprising and can be taken for granted. The fact that this support has permeated much broader echelons of society, however, is less obvious and arguably more important. In Egypt, for example, an editorial of *Al-Akhbar*, a government-sponsored daily, wrote, following a Palestinian suicide attack on passengers in a bus station inside Israel:

> [The operation] was the only effective answer to the [feelings of] bitterness and pain in our reality. This operation proved that the Palestinian individual is still capable of breaking through all forms of siege and oppression, when he is armed with steadfastness and the justice of his cause, and capable of reaching the depths of the Zionist entity in order to strike at it.[27]

The same sentiments in a more venomous form were expressed in *Al-Akhbar* by the columnist Bahjat Ibrahim Al-Dsuqi, who wrote that "the rats who came from the US, Europe, and Russia will flee". He also opined that "whoever blows himself up as a revenge against the enemies is a Shahid of the highest rank of Martyrdom, because he has sold his soul and bought Paradise. We are not afraid of [sacrificing] thousands of Martyrs".[28] Another *Al-Akhbar* columnist, Walid Badran, also thought that suicide attacks would drive Israeli Jews out of the country unless they reached an agreement with the Palestinians.[29]

Support for Palestinian suicide attacks was also expressed by Dr. Lutfi Nasif, a columnist for the Egyptian government daily, *Al-Gumhuriya*. He suggested that these attacks were praiseworthy because they spread fear among Jews who had immigrated to Israel and would help drive them out of the country, as well as deter others from coming. Therefore, in his words, "We salute all the Shahids and are sorry for their departure, but the freedom tax must be paid, even if it is expensive [...]".[30]

Following the first suicide attack by a Palestinian woman, Wafa Idris (27 January 2002), the Egyptian media was swamped with praise. Ahmad Bahgat, a columnist for the leading Egyptian daily *Al-Ahram*, a generally respected newspaper, wrote:

> Wafa revealed the meaning of the Palestinian personality; she revealed the heroism of the Palestinian woman and turned from a living creature walking on the Earth to a symbol that went down

27 "Debating the Religious, Political and Moral Legitimacy of Suicide Bombings Part II: The Debate Over Political and Moral Legitimacy", MEMRI Inquiry and Analysis Series No. 54, 7 May 2001, quoting *Al–Akhbar*, Egypt, 24 April 2001.

28 "Debating the Religious, Political, and Moral Legitimacy of Suicide Bombings: Part IV", MEMRI Inquiry and Analysis Series No. 66, 27 July 2001, quoting *Al–Akhbar*, Egypt, 1 June 2001.

29 *Ibid.*, quoting *Al–Akhbar*, Egypt, 3 June 2001.

30 *Ibid.*, quoting *Al–Gumhuriyya*, Egypt, 2 June 2001.

> in history, the trace of which cannot be eradicated. As a nurse, her work was like that of the merciful angels. She cared for the sick and injured, and rescued the wounded. And behold, she expanded the sphere of her work from saving individuals to saving the Palestinian nation.[31]

Another *Al-Gumhuriya* columnist, Abd Al-Wahab 'Adas, wrote:

> She gave, for the first time, a different example of women's heroism [...]. Wafa's pure spirit will join in waving the flag of Palestine above the dome of Al-Aqsa. Wafa Idris engraved her name with pride, with strength, and with honor [...] on the conscience of every Muslim Arab.[32]

The attitudes of Egyptian writers to suicide attacks are of particular interest because of Egypt's dominant cultural and ideological influence in the Arab world and because of its relative freedom of the press. However, favourable positions concerning suicide attacks have also abounded in Arab media in other countries. For example, following a suicide attack at a Tel Aviv discotheque, in which 22 Israeli teenagers were killed (1 June 2001), Dr. Ali 'Aqleh 'Ursan, head of the Syrian Arab Writers Union, wrote:

> Whoever denounces the operations of the Shahids joins the Arab politicians who apologize for the legitimate struggle. However, these do not represent the conscience of the nation, nor do they influence the public [...]. It is the blood that writes history, and the black ink cannot soil the golden pages written in the blood of the Shahids, on their way to liberate Palestine, the Golan, and South Lebanon.[33]

Justification of suicide attacks through dehumanization of the victims characterizes the commentary by Hamad Al-Majid, a columnist for the London-based Arabic weekly *Al-Sharq Al-Awsat*, who described the victims as:

---

31 "Wafa Idris: The Celebration of the First Female Palestinian Suicide Bomber - Part III", MEMRI Inquiry and Analysis Series No. 85, 14 February 2002, quoting *Al–Ahram*, Egypt, 3 February 2002. Ibrahim Nafi', Editor-in-Chief of *Al–Ahram*, also expressed understanding (albeit not enthusiasm) for Wafa Idris' suicide attack. He wrote:

> She decided to end her fresh young life at a moment of a profound sense of oppression such as no people had suffered as the Palestinians do. But before that, she decided that her death would reverberate so as to draw attention to the tragedy created by the Israelis, with their airplanes and tanks against a defenseless people (*ibid.*, quoting *Al–Ahram*, Egypt, 5 February 2002).

32 *Ibid.*, quoting *Al–Gumhuriya*, Egypt, 31 January 2002, as cited in *Al–Quds Al–Arabi*, London, 2 February 2002.

33 MEMRI Inquiry and Analysis Series No. 66, quoting *Al–Usb'u Al–Adabi*, Syria, 9 June 2001, see *supra* note 28.

> a riffraff of Zionists whose killing has brought happiness to any bereaved Palestinian mother and remedy to every injured family in Jerusalem […]. We wish that just like the Zionist airports were filled with those vagabond homosexuals on their way in, they will be filled once again on their way out, without anyone feeling sorry for them.[34]

18.8. Academic Authorities

Academic authorities are another source of influence on public attitudes. Academics in several countries have joined the media and the religious establishment in expressing support for suicide attacks. In Egypt, for example, Dr. Adel Sadeq, Chairman of the Arab Psychiatrists Association and head of the Department of Psychiatry at Ein Shams University in Cairo, said in an interview with *Iqraa*, a Saudi satellite television channel:

> The psychological structure [of the perpetrator of a suicide attack] is that of an individual who loves life. This may seem strange to people who see the human soul as most sublime. They are incapable of understanding [the suicide attack] because their cultural structure has no concepts such as self-sacrifice and honor. These concepts do not exist in a number of cultures, and therefore they offer stupid interpretations, attesting to ignorance […]. But we know this well, because our culture is one of sacrifice, loyalty, and honor […].
>
> When the martyr dies a martyr's death, he attains the height of bliss […]. As a professional psychiatrist, I say that the height of bliss comes with the end of the countdown: ten, nine, eight, seven, six, five, four, three, two, one. And then, you press the button to blow yourself up. When the martyr reaches 'one,' and then 'boom,' he explodes, and senses himself flying, because he knows for certain that he is not dead […]. It is a transition to another, more beautiful world, because he knows very well that within seconds he will see the light of the Creator. He will be at the closest possible point to Allah […]. None in the [Western] world sacrifices his life for his homeland. If his homeland is drowning, he is the first to jump ship. In our culture it is different […].
>
> There are no Israeli civilians. They are all plunderers. History teaches this […]. I am completely convinced that the psychological effect [of the attacks] on the Israeli plunderer is [the realization] that his existence is temporary […]. They have become completely convinced that their existence in this region is temporary […]. Remove the Apache [helicopter] from the equation, leave them one-

34 *Ibid.*, quoting *Al–Sharq Al–Awsat*, London, 5 June 2001.

> on-one with the Palestinian people with the only weapon [for both sides] being dynamite. Then you will see all the Israelis leave, because among them there is not even one man willing to don a belt of dynamite […].[35]

It is important to note that, as a result of severe criticism on his statements or because he reconsidered the issue, not long after he voiced his praise for suicide bombers, Dr. Sadeq published an article in the Egyptian daily *Hadith Al-Madina*, in which he expressed utterly opposite views on suicide attacks:

> First of all, we must ask the Palestinian youth to stop the suicide operations. We, the psychiatrists, are opposed to suicide; actually, we treat [people who attempt] suicide and protect our [mentally] ill from suicidal thoughts.
>
> Second, we must oppose spilling the blood of innocent people, children, women, old people, and the sick, on both the Palestinian side and the Israeli side. We must not rejoice over the killing of an Israeli child or an Israeli teenage girl. The war must be waged only between fighters. The ugly game now going on – in which a young Palestinian blows himself up on an Israeli bus and innocent people die and then Israel responds by firing missiles on Palestinian homes and innocent people die – must cease, because it is an insane and hellish cycle.
>
> Third, the Arab psychiatrists must meet with the Israeli psychiatrists to examine how we should call for peace. We must support the peace movement in Israel and in Arab countries […].
>
> Fourth, we, the Arab psychiatrists, must talk to the people through the media and call on them to stop the suicide and to stop the killing of innocent people. We must call for peace and create public opinion that will pressure the rulers and the governments in order to persuade them to surrender to peace […].[36]

But there have been other academic supporters of suicide attacks, of course. For example, Dr. Ibrahim Abrash, a lecturer on politics at the Rabat University in Morocco, asserted that Palestinian suicide attacks are legitimate from the point of view of international law and should not be regarded as terrorism.[37]

---

35 "Chairman of the Arab Psychiatrists Association Offers Diagnoses: Bush Is Stupid; Perpetrating a Suicide/Martyrdom Attack Is Life's Most Beautiful Moment; We'll Throw Israel Into the Sea", MEMRI Special Dispatch Series No. 373, 30 April 2002, quoting *Iqraa TV*, Saudi Arabia/Egypt, 24 April 2002.

36 "The Metamorphosis of the Secretary of the Arab Psychiatrists Association", MEMRI Special Dispatch No. 414, 23 August 2002, quoting the Egyptian daily *Hadith Al-Madina*.

37 MEMRI Inquiry and Analysis Series No. 66, quoting *Al–Quds Al–Arabi*, London, 25 May 2001, see *supra* note 28.

Dr. Muhammad Kamal Al-Din Al-Imam, a lecturer on Islámic law at the Alexandria University Faculty of law, justified the killing of Israeli civilians by suicide bombers:

> The [Israeli] society as a whole attacks the land of Palestine. They are all armed, they are all part of a military force, they are all recruited. They came from various countries in order to occupy someone else's land. Can someone who committed such a crime be treated as a civilian?!!

Al-Imam even suggested that it is permissible to kill Muslims along with the "heretics" if there is no other way of killing the enemy.[38]

18.9. Other Voices

These descriptions rightly convey the impression that the most important agents of influence in the Palestinian society – namely, the media, the educational system and religious authorities, those that form public opinion – have not only supported suicide attacks but glorified this behaviour as the utmost form of patriotism. Yet, there have also been other voices in Palestinian society and in the Arab world that have criticized this phenomenon, even during the heat of the second intifada. MEMRI recorded the uneven debate on suicide attacks in a series of publications. Interestingly, however, in most (albeit not all) cases even those who opposed suicide attacks justified their opposition by utilitarian rather than moral arguments (on the ground that the attacks arouse anti-Palestinian sentiments in the world).

One of the critics in the Palestinian community was Yassir Arafat himself, Chairman of the PNA. In a speech in May 2002, he declared that suicide attacks against civilians are "unacceptable", because they alienate the international community from the Palestinians.[39] Other high-ranking Palestinian critics of suicide attacks have included Abd Al-Razzaq Al-Yahya, Interior Minister at the time,[40] former Minister for Parliamentary Affairs Nabil Amru,[41] and Mamduh Nofal, Arafat's Advisor on Military Affairs at the time.[42] Others, such as Bassam

---

38 MEMRI Inquiry and Analysis Series No. 65, quoting *Al–Liwa Al–Islami*, Egypt, 14 June 2001, see *supra* note 21.

39 "The Palestinian Debate Over Martyrdom Operations Part I: The Debate Within the PA", MEMRI Inquiry and Analysis Series No. 100, 4 July 2002, quoting the Palestinian *al Ayam*'s report of Arafat's speech, 16 May 2002.

40 *Ibid.*, quoting *Al Hayat Al Jadida*, PNA, 14 June 2002.

41 *Ibid.*, quoting the Palestinian daily *Al Quds*, 29 May 2002.

42 *Ibid.*, quoting *Al Hayat Al Jadida*, PNA, 9 June 2002. Interestingly, in the 1970s, Mamduh Nofal was the head of operations of the Democratic Front for the Liberation of Palestine. In that capacity, he oversaw the operation in which about 100 high school children were taken hostage in the northern Israeli town of Ma'alot and 20 of them were killed. In later years,

Abu Sharif, have advised that suicide operations be limited to attacks against soldiers and settlers in the occupied territories while refraining from attacks against civilians inside Israel.[43]

In June 2002, following the escalation in suicide attacks inside Israel in the wake of the Defensive Shield operation during the second intifada, when Israeli forces re-entered Palestinian cities in the West Bank, 55 prominent Palestinians published a call to stop suicide attacks. The statement did not criticize all suicide attacks, only those directed against Israeli citizens inside Israel; thus, suicide attacks against Israeli security forces in Israel and the territories as well as attacks against Israeli civilians in the occupied territories were apparently considered acceptable. The call did not criticize suicide attacks against civilians on moral grounds. Rather, it argued that suicide attacks were damaging to Palestinian interests because they exacerbated the conflict, strengthened the right wing in Israel and provided excuses for the Israeli government to continue the war against Palestinian cities and villages.[44] A somewhat modified call with 315 signatories was published two days later. The modified version added a strong condemnation of:

> [A]ll measures implemented by the Israeli repression against our people, including the policy of incursions, assassinations, and siege, and stress that the occupation is the basis of the tragedy to which our people is subject and that resistance is a right and an obligation.[45]

Outside the Palestinian Territories, Dr. Abd Al-Hamid Al-Ansari, former Dean of *Shari'ah* (Islámic law) and the Law Faculty at Qatar University, observed that: "Today, no one blows himself up among women and children, in a restaurant, in a hospital, or on a subway except for Muslims, who continue to do so, terrorizing people". The association between suicide attacks and Islám damages Islám's image. Al-Ansari argued that Islám forbade killing women and children and that those who commit suicide are condemned to hell. He criticized Qaradhawi's *fatwás,* which allowed suicide attacks against civilians in Israel and Iraq, calling them a "fatal breach" of Islámic law, concluding that "[t]hese

Nofal moderated his position and became a supporter of political action and negotiation rather than armed struggle.

43 *Ibid.*, quoting *Al Sharq Al Awsat*, London, 2 May 2002. Bassam Abu Sharif was the Popular Front for the Liberation of Palestine spokesman in the 1970s–mid 1980s, who in 1986 joined Fatah and served as Arafat's political advisor.

44 "A Palestinian Communiqué Against Martyrdom Attacks", MEMRI Special Dispatch Series No. 393, 25 June 2002, quoting *Al–Quds*, Palestinian Authority, 19 June 2002.

45 *Ibid.*, quoting *Al–Quds*, Palestinian Authority, 21 June 2002.

*fatwa*s are a moral and ideological mark of shame, which we must purge from our Islam".[46]

18.10. Final Word: The Families of Suicide Bombers

Having discussed the views of opinion leaders, it seems to me appropriate to end the chapter with a note on the attitude of parents of suicide bombers to their sons' death. In the above-mentioned study in which 34 families of dead suicide bombers were interviewed, almost all of the parents said that they would have prevented their son from carrying out the attack had they known about his intention. In a dramatic expression of her feelings, one the mothers said: "Of course I would have tried to stop him! I would have cut open my chest with a knife, put him inside my heart and sewed him up tight inside, to keep him safe inside my heart". Other parents used expressions such as "I would tie him to his bed".[47]

Confirmation to the parents' testimony was found in another study, in which 14 Hamas, Islamic Jihad and Fatah commanders who had organized suicide attacks were interviewed.[48] One of the questions the participants were asked was how they had handled suicide candidates families' opposition to their sons' intended suicide mission. Eight out of ten who answered the question said categorically that the operation had to be cancelled immediately if the suicide's family learned about it, as the family would try to prevent it at any cost – including contacting the PNA or even the Israeli authorities. All the commanders said they had made no attempt to persuade the families as they believed such attempts to be futile. It seems, therefore, that at least in the struggle to prevent suicide attacks, potential assailants' families are good allies of law enforcement organizations.

---

46 "Leading Progressive Qatari Cleric: By Permitting Suicide Operations, Al-Qaradhawi and His Ilk Have Caused a Moral Crisis in Islam", MEMRI Special Dispatch Series No. 968, 25 August 2005.

47 Merari, 2010, Chapter 4, see *supra* note 1.

48 Ariel Merari *et al.*, "Making Palestinian 'Martyrdom Operations'/'Suicide Attacks': Interviews with Would-Be Perpetrators and Organizers", in *Terrorism and Political Violence*, 2010, vol. 22, pp. 102–119.

19

Hate Speech on Social Media Platforms: Evidence From the Victims' and the Perpetrators' Perspectives

Laura Dellagiacoma[*]

19.1. Introduction

The study of hate speech in social sciences is a relatively new field that was initiated when the phenomenon became increasingly visible and worrying on social media platforms. Social psychology contributes to this field by linking online hate speech with research on derogatory language, discrimination and intergroup relations.[1] Through well-established research, social psychology provides theoretical lenses to conceptualize hate speech without reducing its complexity. Moreover, thanks to its quantitative methodological approach, social psychology offers evidence-based insights to expand the current understanding of hate speech on social media, particularly in regard to prevalence, exposure, victimization and impact.

It is important to note that within social sciences hate speech is not defined according to legal definitions, but is conceived along a continuum: it consists of hateful expressions or images whose content ranges through different levels of discriminatory offence. The work presented in this chapter draws on Cohen-Almagor's definition of hate speech, namely as:

> bias-motivated, hostile malicious speech aimed at a person or a group of people because of some of their actual or perceived innate characteristics. It expresses discriminatory, intimidating, disapproving, antagonistic, and/or prejudicial attitudes toward those

---

* **Laura Dellagiacoma** is a Marie Skłodowska-Curie Actions (MSCA) Ph.D. candidate within the NETHATE ITN Consortium (funded by the European Union's Horizon 2020), working at the Institute for Democracy and Civil Society ('IDCS') in Jena, Germany. The research discussed in this chapter was presented at the International Workshop on "Hate Speech – an interdisciplinary approach", organized by the Minerva Center for the Rule of Law under Extreme Conditions of the Faculty of Law and the Geography and Environmental Studies Department of the University of Haifa.

1 For a review on the links between online hate speech and research on discriminatory language, see Carmen Cervone, Martha Augoustinos and Anne Maass, "The Language of Derogation and Hate: Functions, Consequences, and Reappropriation", in *Journal of Language and Social Psychology*, 2021, vol. 40, no. 1, pp. 80–101.

> characteristics, which include gender, race, religion, ethnicity, colour, national origin, disability, or sexual orientation. Hate speech is intended to injure, dehumanize, harass, intimidate, debase, degrade and victimize the targeted groups and to foment insensitivity and brutality against them.[2]

Not all cases of so-defined hate speech can be legally prosecuted, but they are as intentionally damaging for the targeted person as for the social group to which the person belongs or to which they ascribe.

Following the psycho-social quantitative approach, this chapter brings evidence from the perspectives of victims as well as perpetrators, drawing on the data of the 'Online Hate' project.[3] Conducted in Germany in 2019, the project consists of a representative online survey, in which 7,337 individuals took part.

Firstly, a descriptive intersectional analysis is used to understand which social groups are affected the most by hate speech on social media. The data are analysed based on age, gender, ethnic background and their intersections. Secondly, the focus is shifted towards the perpetration of online hate speech. The theoretical framework of the Dual Process Motivational Model by Duckitt and Sibley[4] is applied on the same data to investigate what motivates individuals to produce and use hate speech against others. Statistical analyses are conducted to study the role of the two main ideological attitudes: right-wing authoritarianism ('RWA') and social dominance orientation ('SDO'). Results are interpreted through Duckitt and Sibley's model, taking into account individual as well as contextual factors.

Results are then discussed from the victims' and perpetrators' perspectives, shedding lights on the implications for religious communities and leaders. While the Online Hate data do not allow for religion-based intersections in the German sample, the results presented in this chapter nevertheless provide relevant insights on the nature of hate speech spreading online.

19.2. Evidence from the Victims' Perspective: Intersectional Analysis

The Online Hate project collected data in 2019 with the aim of capturing to which extent hate speech on social media occurs in the German society.[5] With data from N = 7,337 respondents, it constitutes the survey on hate speech with

2 Raphael Cohen-Almagor, "Fighting Hate and Bigotry on the Internet", in *Policy & Internet*, 2011, vol. 3, no. 3, pp. 1–2.

3 Daniel Geschke *et al.*, "Hass im Netz: Der schleichende Angriff auf unsere Demokratie", IDZ - Institut für Demokratie und Zivilgesellschaft, Jena, 2019.

4 John Duckitt and Chris G. Sibley, "A Dual Process Motivational Model of Ideology, Politics, and Prejudice", in *Psychological Inquiry*, 2009, vol. 20, nos. 2–3, pp. 98–109.

5 Geschke *et al.*, 2019, see *supra* note 3.

the largest representative sample. The inclusion criteria to take part in the survey were a minimum age of 18 years, residence in Germany, and usage of online platforms with comments sections, such as social networks, blogs, fora, news sites, Messenger and other chat services.[6] In order to understand who is affected the most by online hate speech, the data are analysed based on the intersections between age, gender and migration status.[7]

The intersectional approach represents a critical, theoretical and analytical framework.[8] It was developed in the United States' context, thanks to academic critiques and political activism by Black feminists, highlighting that "the intersection of racism and sexism factors into Black women's lives […] cannot be captured wholly by looking at the race or gender dimensions of those experiences separately".[9] While intersectionality initially challenged social psychology, stressing that social categories are "building blocks of social hierarchies, not components of personal identity",[10] current social psychologists call for a wider and broader use of intersectionality within the field.[11] Bowleg underlines how crucial intersectionality is for social psychology:

> [intersectionality] highlights how multiple social identities such as race, gender, sexual orientation, socioeconomic status (SES), and disability (to name a few) intersect at the micro level of individual experience to reveal interlocking systems of privilege and oppression (i.e., racism, sexism, heterosexism, classism) at the macro social-structural level.[12]

In other terms, following the intersectional approach, data should be read and analysed as disaggregated not only by gender and race as separate axes, but through the full matrix, namely white women, white men, racialized men and

6 Representativity is ensured through statistical weight for age, gender, political behaviour (2017 elections) and education.

7 The 'migration status' includes immigrants and descendants living in Germany. Participants were asked about their own country of birth and of their parents and grandparents. No information was collected about the specific country of origin. Therefore, the data do not allow differentiating between individuals who come from European and non-European countries. This is problematic because individuals from non-European countries (and their descendants) face discrimination in Europe significantly more often.

8 As defined by Lisa Bowleg, "Intersectionality: An Underutilized but Essential Theoretical Framework for Social Psychology", in Brendan Gough (eds.), *The Palgrave Handbook of Critical Social Psychology*, Palgrave Macmillan, London, 2017, pp. 507–529.

9 Kimberle Crenshaw, "Mapping the Margins: Intersectionality, Identity Politics and Violence against Women of Color", in *Stanford Law Review*, 1991, vol. 43, no. 6, pp. 1241–1299.

10 Jeanne Marecek, "Invited Reflection: Intersectionality Theory and Feminist Psychology", in *Psychology of Women Quarterly*, 2016, vol. 40, no. 2, p. 178.

11 Bowleg, 2017, see *supra* note 8.

12 *Ibid.*, p. 509.

racialized women. Exclusively through this “matrix perspective”,[13] it is possible to conduct research that captures the everyday reality of individuals.

The intersectional descriptive analysis on the self-reported Online Hate data is presented in the following order: prevalence of exposure to hate speech, victimization, direct impact on targeted individuals, and indirect impact on platform users. Since the young adults, aged between 18 and 34 years, represent one fourth (n = 1,834) of the whole sample (N = 7,337) and reported to have faced hate speech online and its impact more often, the focus of the current analysis is set on young adults. In fact, while younger generations engage with social media platforms more often than older generations, it is also important to stress that young adults do so not only for leisure activities, but also with the aim of enriching their own network and finding socio-economic opportunities.[14] Indeed, they are increasingly required to take advantage of the technological tools also to enter today’s job market.[15]

19.2.1. Exposure to Online Hate Speech

Based on the 2019 Online Hate data, 42 per cent of the overall sample encountered hate speech online: that is, four out of ten respondents (N = 7,031). The percentage increases when focusing on young adults (n = 1,775):[16] more than two-thirds of respondents aged between 18 and 34 years affirmed that they noticed hate speech online (67 per cent). When considering further in detail the group of young adults and analysing the data for gender and migration background intersectionally[17] (see Graph 1), it emerges that young women with a migration background encountered hate speech slightly more often (72 per cent) than young women without a migration background (66 per cent). No differences were found in exposure to hate speech experienced by young male adults (with a migration background: 68 per cent; without: 67 per cent).

13 *Ibid.*

14 Ellen Helsper, “A Corresponding Fields Model for the Links Between Social and Digital Exclusion”, in *Communication Theory*, 2012, vol. 22, no. 4, pp. 403–426.

15 Jan van Dijk, *The Digital Divide*, Polity Press, 2020.

16 The differences in sample sizes are due to some missing responses. For example, in the case of young adults, the whole sample size is n = 1,834, but only n = 1,775 individuals answered the question ‘Have you noticed hate speech online’; therefore, responses by 59 young adults are missing.

17 When adopting an intersectional approach to read the data, the sample size further diminishes (n = 1,535) because of some missing information on either gender or migration background. However, as argued in the previous paragraphs, only through an intersectional perspective is it possible to capture, with data, the real experience of individuals.

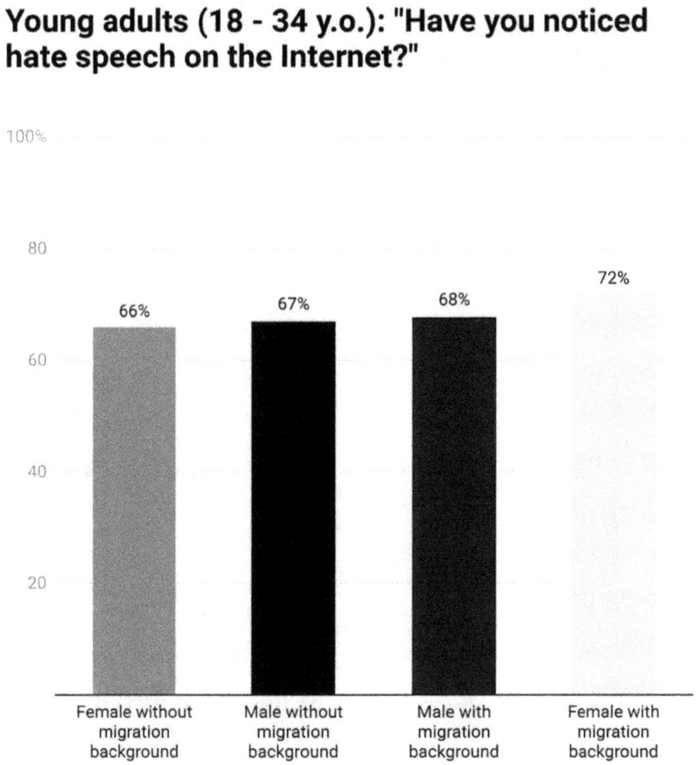

Graph 1: Young adults aged 18–34 years who noticed hate speech online (percentage) by gender and migration background (N = 1,535).

19.2.2. Direct Victimization of Online Hate Speech

Being exposed to hate speech online does not necessarily imply being directly targeted. In fact, 8 per cent of all respondents reported that they were directly victimized by hate speech. The rate strongly increases when disaggregating the data based on age: young adults were three times more likely to be directly targeted by hate speech (17 per cent) than respondents aged 35 years or older (5 per cent). Investigating the victimization of younger individuals by gender and migration background, the data show specific patterns (see Graph 2): young individuals with a migration background were more often directly targeted by hate speech than individuals without a migration background. More specifically, 27 per cent of young men and 19 per cent of young women with a migration background reported to have been the direct victim, while the percentages are lower for young individuals without a migration background (men: 14 per cent, women: 12 per cent).

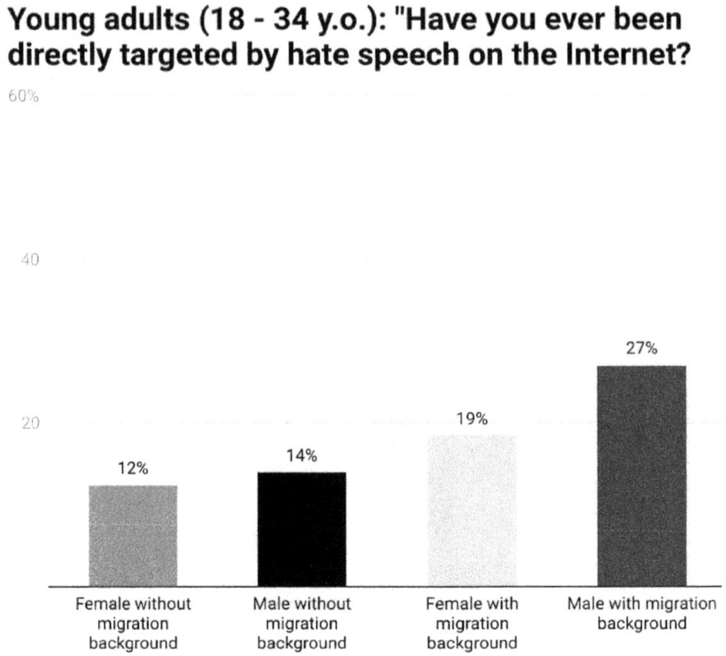

Graph 2: Young adults aged 18–34 years who have been directly targeted by hate speech online (percentage) by gender and migration background (N = 1,527).

19.2.3. Direct Impact of Hate Speech on Targeted Individuals

The Online Hate project thoroughly investigated the impact of online victimization, considering both social environment and individual well-being. At the social level, the most frequently reported direct effects were problems at work, with colleagues and within the educational and training system, while at individual level, these were problems with self-image and depression symptoms.

Several individuals among the overall direct victims (n = 586)[18] indicated that they faced problems at work and in the university or educational system because of hate speech (15 per cent). A higher number of respondents affirmed that they had to cope with depression and problems with their self-image because of hate speech (respectively, 19 per cent and 24 per cent).

[18] In this case, the sample size is n = 586 because it includes only those eight per cent of respondents who indicated that they were directly targeted by hate speech online. Individuals who affirmed that they have never been directly targeted were not asked about direct hate speech effects.

Young adults suffered from all the negative effects more frequently, as Graph 3 below shows. Young males with a migration background and young females in general faced the psychosocial consequences of being directly targeted by hate speech more often. In particular, young women without a migration background reported all the negative effects more often. Yet, young males with a migration background indicated having faced issues within the educational and training system because of online hate speech as frequently as females without a migration background. All groups mentioned depression symptoms.

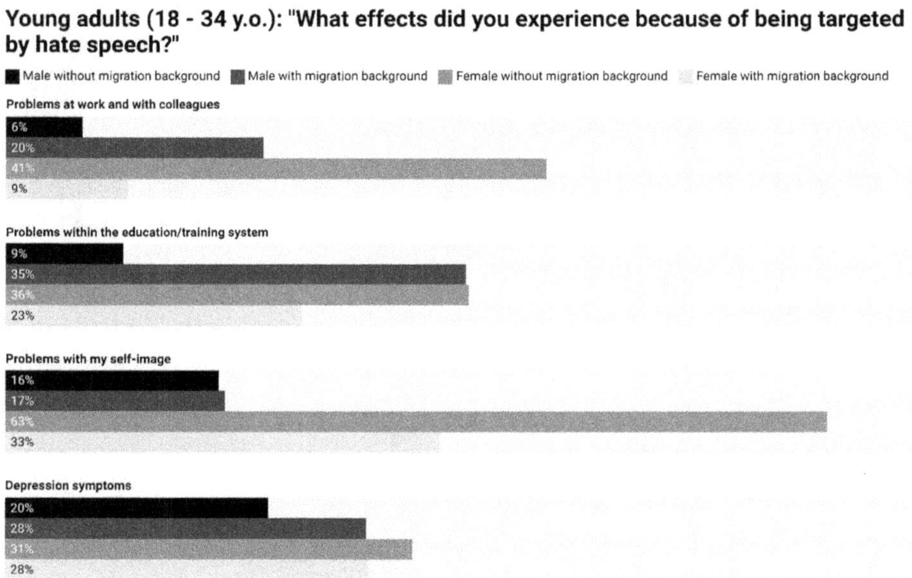

Graph 3: Young adults aged 18–34 years who were directly targeted by online hate speech and experienced the following negative effects (percentage) – by gender and migration background (N = 253).

19.2.4. Indirect Impact of Hate Speech on Platforms' Users

An assumption of hate speech research is that hate speech affects not only direct victims, but all platform users and the culture of discussion to a certain extent. Yet, whether this is the case, and to what extent, has rarely been quantitatively shown.

The intersectional approach applied to the Online Hate data allows to present some insights in this regard. Several consequences that have potentially spread across all platform users were investigated – thus, also those who were not direct victims of hate speech. The main indirect impact concerned issues of anxiety, such as being afraid of becoming a direct target of hate speech or that close people might be targeted, and avoidance behaviours, such as limiting one's own platform use and participation due to the presence of hate speech and the risks it implies.

Overall, one-fourth of all participants reported that they are afraid that someone among their friends and relatives might become a target of online hate speech (25 per cent). Slightly fewer affirmed to be afraid of becoming a victim of hate speech themselves (19 per cent). Over half of the respondents indicated that they avoid expressing their political views online because of hate speech (55 per cent) and almost half participate less in discussion online because of it (46 per cent).

Focusing on young adults through intersectional lenses (see Graph 4), a clear pattern emerges. Namely, individuals with a migration background reported those negative consequences more frequently (see below). In particular, young males with a migration background were most worried to become a target of hate speech online (36 per cent) or that a relative would (41 per cent). Moreover, the great majority of women with a migration background (71 per cent) affirmed that they avoid expressing their political views online because of hate speech on social media platforms.

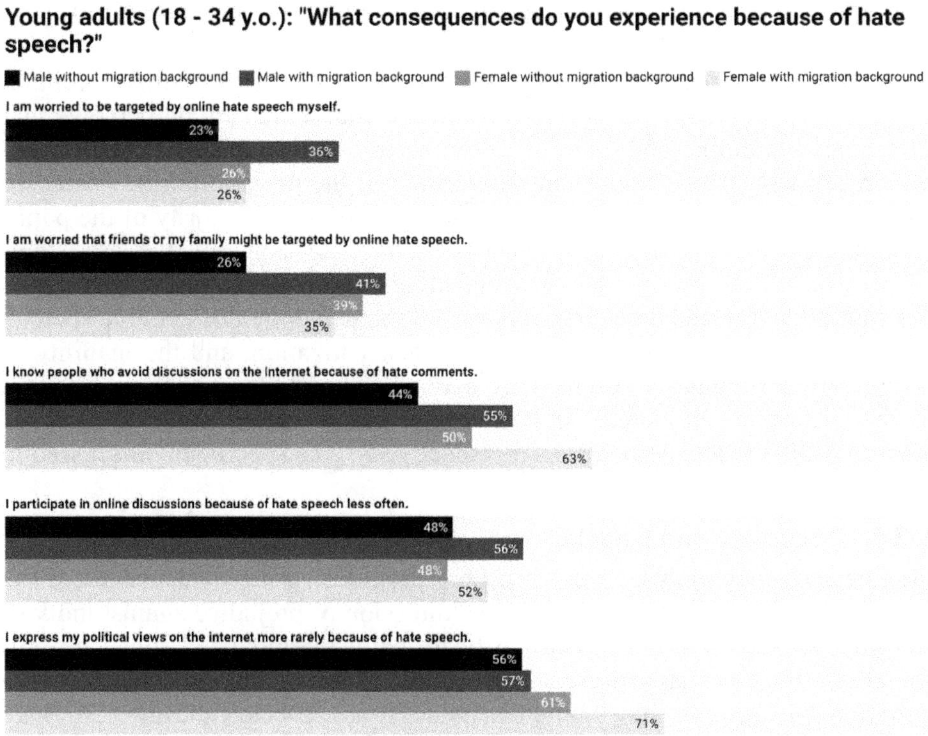

Graph 4: Young adults aged 18–34 years experiencing the following consequences because of online hate speech (percentage) by gender and migration background (N = 1,568).

The data shown in Graph 4 point out to silencing effects determined by hate speech on social media platforms:[19] by means of fear and anxiety of being victimized, hate speech intimidates individuals and disengages them from full use of social media platforms and the accompanying digital possibilities. The silencing effects of hate speech disempower individuals especially in regard to the fulfilment of their socio-political rights: individuals avoid participating in online discussion, in particular when political topics are discussed. Most importantly, the intersectional analysis shows that the silencing effects do not affect individuals equally. On the contrary, individuals who belong (or are ascribed) to specific social groups are affected the most: young men and women with a migration background. Consequently, diversity of content and opinions

[19] Marjan Nadim and Audun Fladmoe, "Silencing Women? Gender and Online Harassment", in *Social Science Computer Review*, 2021, vol. 39, no. 2, pp. 245–258.

on social media platforms is reduced: voices of diverse social groups are missing, because they are being silenced.

The lack of perspectives from minorities might lead to a misperception regarding how fractured the society actually is: individuals might perceive that hatred prevails online and, possibly, dominates offline as well.[20] This misperception can trigger self-reinforcing mechanisms: the more minorities perceive online hate speech as corresponding to the attitude of the majority of the population, the more they will opt for being silent and, consequently, the lesser their perspectives will be represented on social media. From the majoritarian perspective, instead, a reduced content diversity and the perception of extreme societal fractures can lead to looser social norms, desensitization, and the inability to recognize discriminatory offenses as hate speech.[21] Such a vicious circle is likely to determine an increase in hate speech and intergroup conflict, online as much as offline.[22] The perpetrators' perspective will be specifically discussed in Section 19.3.

19.2.5. Discussion and Conclusions

The intersectional analysis presented here provides strong evidence about the nature of hate speech: it constitutes the expression of prejudice against individuals that belong (or are ascribed) to historically marginalized social groups. Namely, in the German representative sample, young men and women with a migration background and women in general are affected the most by hate speech. This is confirmed by the higher prevalence rates in exposure, victimization and direct as well as indirect impact experienced by those social groups. The intersectional perspective demonstrates that although online hate speech targets one specific individual, its harm affects the whole community to which the individual belongs (or is ascribed). Indeed, the peculiarity of hate speech, recurring also in hate crime, consists in its symbolic message towards the entire minority: while the violent verbal or physical attacks might be directed at a single person, the symbolic message of hatred, intimidation and exclusion aims at the whole community. [23]

Results are particularly concerning when taking into account that young individuals are required to engage with social media and more broadly with

---

20 As also highlighted by Geschke *et al.*, 2019, see *supra* note 3.

21 Michał Bilewicz and Wiktor Soral, "Hate Speech Epidemic: The Dynamic Effects of Derogatory Language on Intergroup Relations and Political Radicalization", in *Advances in Political Psychology*, 2020, vol. 41, pp. 3–33.

22 Kyaw Yin Hlaing, "Socio-Political Factors that Can Motivate Hate Speech", *CILRAP Film*, Yangon, 9 April 2022 (https://www.cilrap.org/cilrap-film/220409-kyaw/).

23 Jennifer Schweppe and Barbara Perry, "A Continuum of Hate: Delimiting the Field of Hate Studies", in *Crime, Law and Social Change*, 2022, vol. 77, no. 5, pp. 503–528.

online tools to increase their social, educational and economic capital. For this reason, a limited Internet use can contribute to exacerbate offline socio-economic inequality, as stressed by relevant authors in the field of digital engagement.[24] More specifically, based on what the intersectional analysis shows, young women and men with a migration background are more likely to reduce their use of online platforms because of the presence of hate speech and their increased risk of being directly targeted. Therefore, online hate speech represents, particularly for individuals with a migration background, a threat to their online and potentially offline socio-economic opportunities.

While the data indicate that young male individuals with a migration background are more likely to be victimized, young female individuals with and without a migration background reported overall negative psychosocial effects more frequently. On the one hand, this could be explained by a higher propensity of female as compared to male participants to report those effects. On the other hand, previous research that found similar differences highlights that men and women are targeted through different types of online hate speech. Based on the study by Nadim and Fladmoe, men are more likely to receive hate speech based on their opinions, whereas women more often receive gendered hate speech, targeting "who they are" rather than "what they think".[25] It is, however, important to note that in this case, men with a migration background are likely to be targeted by hate speech because of their opinion and because of their social belonging as well. Women without a migration background are more likely to be targeted mainly because of their gender, whereas women with a migration background might be targeted because of all the three intersectional grounds: their opinion, social belonging and gender. In fact, the intersectional analysis demonstrates that young women with a migration background avoid expressing their political views online the most.

Overall, the high prevalence rates of exposure, victimization and direct and indirect impact on targeted individuals and on all platform users highlight the urgency of taking hate speech in serious consideration. Young adults are more frequently affected by online hate speech and they are not better equipped to deal with its consequences, which include psychosocial effects and can lead to intergroup conflicts. In fact, the intersectional analysis reveals the prejudice-based nature of hate speech spreading online, shown in the higher direct and indirect victimization and impact reported by young individuals with a migration background. While some social groups face the worst consequences in their individual, social and economic life, the effects of hate speech negatively

---

[24] Helsper, 2012, see *supra* note 14 and van Dijk, 2020, see *supra* note 15.

[25] Nadim and Fladmoe, 2021, see *supra* note 19.

influence the whole society: it threatens content diversity, societal diversity and intergroup relations in the online and offline spheres.

Lastly, it is necessary to highlight that these results would have not emerged without the intersectional approach. As Purdie-Vaughns and Eibach stress, 'intersectional invisibility' not only leads to an inaccurate picture, in this case, of the nature of hate speech and of its damaging effects, but also reproduces the same power imbalances at the origin of discrimination and hate speech.[26] Moreover, as an analytical tool, intersectionality allows testing of theoretical assumptions on differential effects on different social groups and it permits the linking of individual experience at the micro-level with systemic historical, cultural and economic intergroup disparities and conflicts at the macro-level.[27] Thus, intersectionality should be embraced more frequently and broadly in order to capture the complex and specific patterns of oppression experienced by individuals belonging to marginalized social groups.

In conclusion, the results presented in this section provide relevant information on the nature of hate speech spreading online from the victims' perspective, suggesting that certain power mechanisms are in place. In the next section, statistical analyses are applied to investigate the motivations and ideological attitudes of individuals perpetrating hate speech on social media.

19.3. Evidence from the Perpetrator's Perspective: Statistical Analyses

In order to theoretically understand and empirically test what motivates individuals to produce hate speech, the Dual Process Motivational Model by Duckitt and Sibley is adopted for statistical analyses.[28] The model draws on well-established theoretical and experimental research on the two ideological attitudes of RWA and SDO. This contribution investigates the effects of RWA and SDO on the perpetration of hate speech online, taking into consideration individual and contextual factors. Relevant differences emerge between individuals with higher levels of RWA and individuals with higher levels of SDO in the following statistical analyses.

19.3.1. Theoretical Framework: Right-Wing Authoritarianism, Social Dominance Orientation and the Dual Process Motivational Model

Psychological mechanisms behind socio-political behaviours and outgroup prejudice are studied within psychology through the ideological attitudes of RWA and SDO. In political psychology, RWA and SDO are considered as socio-

26 Valerie Purdie-Vaughns and Richard P. Eibach, "Intersectional Invisibility: The Distinctive Advantages and Disadvantages of Multiple Subordinate-Group Identities", in *Sex Roles*, 2008, vol. 59, pp. 377–391.

27 Bowleg, 2017, see *supra* note 8.

28 Duckitt and Sibley, 2009, see *supra* note 4.

political dimensions that develop along a continuum: every individual has higher or lower levels of RWA and SDO. In the case of RWA, higher levels indicate a strong conformity to the established authority and to traditional norms and values, while lower levels relate to valuing personal autonomy and openness.[29] Regarding SDO, instead, higher levels refer to a preference for hierarchical intergroup relations and the endorsement of a strong competitive motivation, as opposed to favouring egalitarian and collaborative relations in case of low SDO levels.[30] For a summary of the two different dimensions, see Table 1 below. Higher levels of RWA and SDO are usually more common among right-wing individuals; however, as psychological dimensions, they reach beyond the political left–right spectrum.[31] Research on these two dimensions allows for a more nuanced understanding of socio-political attitudes and behaviours. In fact, several studies showed that while related, RWA and SDO express different values. For instance, valuing order, structure and religion relate with RWA but not with SDO, while power and social Darwinism relate with SDO but not with RWA.[32] Moreover, conservative motivations and values of security, conformity and tradition were found to correlate with RWA, whereas anti-egalitarian motivations and self-enhancement, achievement, and hedonism strongly correlate with SDO.[33]

29 As confirmed by the work of Bob Altemeyer, *Right-Wing Authoritarianism*, University of Manitoba Press, 1981; Bob Altemeyer, "The Other 'Authoritarian Personality'", in *Advances in Experimental Social Psychology*, 1998, vol. 30, pp. 47–92; John Duckitt, "A Dual Process Cognitive-Motivational Theory of Ideology and Prejudice", in *Advances in Experimental Social Psychology*, 2001, vol. 33, pp. 41–111; John Duckitt and Chris G. Sibley, "Right–Wing Authoritarianism and Social Dominance Orientation Differentially Moderate Intergroup Effects on Prejudice", in *European Journal of Personality*, 2010, vol. 24, no. 7, pp. 583–601.

30 Felicia Pratto *et al.*, "Social Dominance Orientation: A Personality Variable Predicting Social and Political Attitudes", in *Journal of Personality and Social Psychology*, 1994, vol. 67, no. 4, pp. 741–763. Confirmed also by Duckitt, 2001, see *supra* note 29.

31 John Duckitt and Chris G. Sibley, "A Dual Process Motivational Model of Ideological Attitudes and System Justification", in John T. Jost, Aaron C. Kay and Hulda Thorisdottir (eds.), *Social and Psychological Bases of Ideology and System Justification*, Oxford University Press, 2009, pp. 292–313.

32 Altemeyer, 1998, *see supra* note 29; Duckitt, 2001, see *supra* note 29.

33 Charles Stangor and Scott P. Leary, "Intergroup Beliefs: Investigations from the Social Side", in *Advances in Experimental Social Psychology*, 2006, vol. 38, pp. 243–281.

	Socialization	Personality	Worldview	Motivational goal	Ideological beliefs
	Punitive	Conforming	Threatening/ dangerous	Social control/ security	Authoritarian/ conservative
RWA	versus	versus	versus	versus	versus
	Tolerant	Autonomous	Safe/secure	Personal free-dom	Autonomy/ openness
	Unaffectionate	Tough-minded	Competitive jungle	Superiority and dominance	Social dominance
SDO	versus	versus	versus	versus	versus
	Affectionate	Tender-minded	Co-operative harmony	Altruistic concern	Egalitarian-humanism

Table 5: The dimensions of high levels and low levels of authoritarianism and social dominance.[34]

By aggregating evidence from quantitative studies and experimental research on RWA and SDO, Duckitt and Sibley developed the Dual Process Motivational Model of Ideology (see Figure 1). According to the model, RWA and SDO result from a combination of personality traits and contextual factors that induce related worldviews and behaviours. More specifically, RWA originates from a social context that stresses social dangers and threats and from a personality that values social conformity over autonomy.[35] Subsequent studies on personality traits showed that RWA individuals score high in conscientiousness and low in openness. [36] Those societal and personality factors lead to a conception of the world as inherently dangerous and determine an uncertainty-driven motivation to establish and maintain collective security through a strong need for social cohesion, order and traditional norms. Instead, SDO is the product of a social context that highlights competition over status and power, and a personality with low levels of agreeableness, collaboration and sympathy.[37] The world is perceived as a 'competitive jungle' in which it is necessary to compete against other social groups and to demonstrate one's own superiority to survive. This

[34] Adopted by Duckitt, 2001, p. 53, see *supra* note 29.

[35] Duckitt and Sibley, 2009, see *supra* note 4.

[36] John Duckitt and Chris G. Sibley, "Big-Five Personality, Social Worldviews, and Ideological Attitudes: Further Tests of a Dual Process Cognitive-Motivational Model", in *Journal of Social Psychology*, 2009, vol. 149, no. 5, pp. 545–561. Patrick C.L. Heaven and Sandra Bucci, "Right-Wing Authoritarianism, Social Dominance Orientation and Personality: An Analysis Using the IPIP Measure", in *European Journal of Personality*, 2001, vol. 15, p. 49–56.

[37] *Ibid.*

leads to a competition-driven motivation to increase one's own social status and exert power over others.

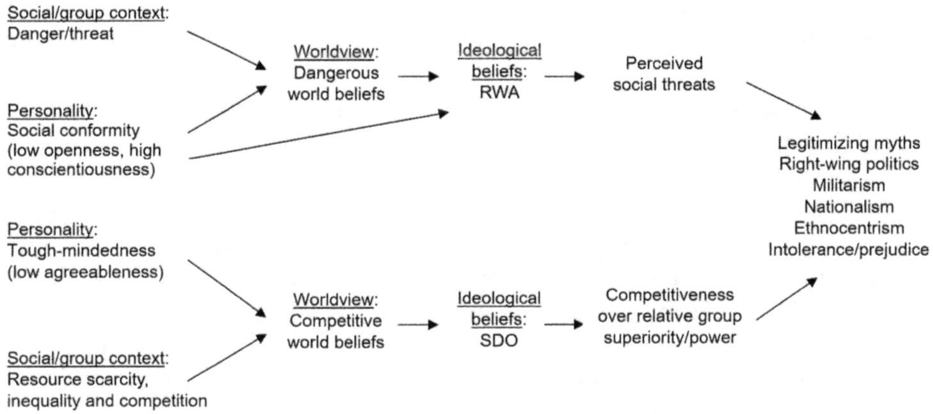

Figure 1: Causal model of the impact of social situation, personality and social worldviews on the two dimensions of RWA and SDO and their impact on socio-political attitudes and behaviour.[38]

Originating from different psychological and contextual bases and expressing different values and motivations, the ideological attitudes of RWA and SDO determine related, yet qualitatively different, socio-political intentions and behaviours. Quantitative research indicates that individuals with high levels of RWA are more likely to support parties that stress conservative and traditional values[39] and to advocate for war when it is perceived as 'protecting the own people against foreign threats'.[40] Individuals with high levels of SDO are, instead, more likely to vote for political parties that vouch for free-market capitalism and anti-welfare policies[41] and they would support war regardless of the human costs, aiming at blatantly conquering others' territories.[42] Furthermore, high-RWA individuals are more likely to develop outgroup prejudice, for instance, when migrants are described as 'dangerous' and 'threatening'[43] and

38 Duckitt and Sibley, 2009, p. 101, see *supra* note 4.

39 Duckitt and Sibley, 2009, see *supra* note 4.

40 Sam G. McFarland, "On the Eve of War: Authoritarianism, Social Dominance, and American Students' Attitudes Toward Attacking Iraq", in *Personality and Social Psychology Bulletin*, 2005, vol. 31, no. 3, pp. 360–367.

41 Duckitt and Sibley, 2009, see *supra* note 31.

42 McFarland, 2005, see *supra* note 40.

43 As emerged by several studies: Duckitt and Sibley, 2010, p. 101, see *supra* note 29; Jan C. Cohrs and Monika Stelz, "How Ideological Attitudes Predict Host Society Members' Attitudes Toward Immigrants: Exploring Cross-National Differences", in *Journal of Social Issues*, 2010,

when they are perceived as not willing to assimilate in the majoritarian culture.[44] On the contrary, high-SDO individuals endorse prejudice especially against 'derogated' and socio-economically disadvantaged outgroups,[45] and their aggressive intentions increase against migrants who do want to assimilate into the dominant culture.[46]

Longitudinal research,[47] cross-national research[48] and experimental research[49] have so far confirmed the Dual Process Motivational Model's theoretical reasoning and contributed to support its causal assumptions. As research summarized so far shows, ideological attitudes are influenced by personality traits as well as by the social environment, and they shape individual motivation and social values in return. Since they affect the perception of the socio-economic world, of hierarchies and of individuals belonging to different social groups, they might also affect the individual intentions to produce hate speech on social media platforms. The next sub-section focuses on research conducted on the links between RWA and SDO and hate speech.

19.3.2. The Dual Process Motivational Model Applied to Online Hate Speech

Bilewicz and Soral analysed the role of the ideological attitudes of RWA and SDO as predictors of outgroup prejudice and support for the prohibition of hate

---

vol. 66, no. 4, pp. 673–694; Frank Asbrock, Chris G. Sibley and John Duckitt, "Right-Wing Authoritarianism and Social Dominance Orientation and the Dimensions of Generalized Prejudice: A Longitudinal Test", in *European Journal of Personality*, 2010, vol. 24, no. 4, pp. 324–340.

44 Lotte Thomsen, Eva G.T. Green and Jim Sidanius, "We Will Hunt Them Down: How Social Dominance Orientation and Right-Wing Authoritarianism Fuel Ethnic Persecution of Immigrants in Fundamentally Different Ways", in *Journal of Experimental Social Psychology*, 2008, vol. 44, no. 6, pp. 1455–1464.

45 See *supra* note 43.

46 Thomsen, Green and Sidanius, 2008, see *supra* note 44.

47 Chris G. Sibley, Marc S. Wilson and John Duckitt, "Effects of Dangerous and Competitive Worldviews on Right-Wing Authoritarianism and Social Dominance Orientation over a Five-Month Period", in *Political Psychology*, 2007, vol. 28, no. 3, pp. 357–371; Asbrock, Sibley, and Duckitt, 2010, see *supra* note 43.

48 Duckitt and Sibley, 2009, see *supra* note 31; Cohrs and Stelz, 2010, see *supra* note 43.

49 Vincent Dru, "Authoritarianism, Social Dominance Orientation and Prejudice: Effects of Various Self-Categorization Conditions", in *Journal of Experimental Social Psychology*, 2007, vol. 43, no. 6, pp. 877–883. Jan C. Cohrs and Frank Asbrock, "Right-Wing Authoritarianism, Social Dominance Orientation and Prejudice against Threatening and Competitive Ethnic Groups", in *European Journal of Social Psychology*, 2009, vol. 39, no. 2, pp. 270–289.

speech on social media.[50] In two studies with adolescents (N = 653) and adults (N = 1,007), they proposed a list of hate speech examples and asked participants to rate, on a seven-point Likert scale, whether hateful messages should be permitted or prohibited. Their analyses revealed that both high-RWA and high-SDO were positively related with outgroup prejudice, indicating that individuals with high levels of RWA and SDO endorsed outgroup prejudice, as expected. Yet, they surprisingly found that only SDO was negatively correlated with the prohibition of hate speech, whereas RWA was instead positively related. Therefore, the higher individuals' levels of SDO, the less likely they are to support the prohibition of hate speech. In contrast, the higher individuals' levels of RWA, the more likely they are to support the prohibition of online hatred. Bilewicz and Soral argued that the support of high-RWA individuals for hate speech prohibition is in line with the normative aspects of RWA, as hate speech constitutes a severe violation of social norms. More specifically, "in societies with more strict norms of antidiscrimination, authoritarians would be more punitive toward those who violate theses norms – even if such violations would be in line with their worldviews".[51] Thus, the authors called for a more nuanced understanding of RWA, in particular for the development of countering measures.

Subsequently, the authors developed the 'Hate Speech Epidemic Model' on the spread of hate speech throughout society from the observer perspective.[52] When distinguishing between factors that inhibit or catalyse hate speech, they included RWA among the former, followed by social norms and empathy. As risk factors, they took into consideration desensitization,[53] normativity,[54] stereotype content, dehumanization and the emotion of contempt.[55] Based on their model, the more hate speech circulates, the less sensitive observers become, and the more socially accepted hate speech would be, leading to the inability of recognizing it as such. Yet, the role of the social dominance-oriented values of

50 Michał Bilewicz *et al.*, "When Authoritarians Confront Prejudice. Differential Effects of SDO and RWA on Support for Hate-Speech Prohibition", in *Political Psychology*, 2017, vol. 38, no. 1, pp. 87–99.

51 *Ibid.*, p. 96.

52 Bilewicz and Soral, 2020, see *supra* note 21.

53 Wiktor Soral, Michał Bilewicz and Mikołaj Winiewski, "Exposure to Hate Speech Increases Prejudice Through Desensitization", in *Aggressive Behaviour*, 2018, vol. 44, no. 2, pp. 136–146.

54 Wiktor Soral, James Liu and Michał Bilewicz, "Media of Contempt: Social Media Consumption Predicts Normative Acceptance of Anti-Muslim Hate Speech and Islamoprejudice", in *International Journal of Conflict and Violence*, 2020, vol. 14, no. 1, pp. 1–13.

55 Michał Bilewicz *et al.*, "From Disgust to Contempt-Speech: The Nature of Contempt on the Map of Prejudicial Emotions", in *Behavioural and Brain Sciences*, 2017, vol. 40, pp. 225.

competition over status and power and the sensitivity towards resource scarcity and inequality remained unexplored.

In sum, Bilewicz and Soral used the two ideological attitudes as theorized within Duckitt and Sibley's model to investigate the support for prohibitive measures against hate speech on social media, but they did not examine the perpetration of hate speech itself. Moreover, while the effects of RWA were taken into account in their analysis as potentially limiting the spread of hate speech, less attention was paid to the role of SDO. SDO, however, could represent a key factor to understand the motivations behind hate speech. For these reasons, the full Dual Process Motivational Model will be adopted to gather insights on the production of hate speech on social media.

19.3.3. The Present Analysis

The following statistical analyses are conducted on the basis of the data of the Online Hate project.[56] As previously mentioned, the dataset includes information from respondents (N = 7,349) aged between 18 and 95 years, living in Germany and using online platforms with commentary functions at least once per week. Representativity is ensured through statistical weight for age, gender, voting behaviour, education and population size.

The aim of the present analysis is to test whether the two ideological attitudes of RWA and SDO predict the production of online hate speech in opposite directions. Namely, drawing from the research described above, SDO is expected to positively relate to the perpetration of online hate speech, whereas RWA is expected to negatively relate to it. In other words, the higher the levels of SDO, the more likely individuals would be to perpetrate online hate speech (*hypothesis 1*); the higher the levels of RWA, the less likely individuals would be to perpetrate online hate speech (*hypothesis 2*). The hypotheses are theoretically in line with differential worldviews, values and motivations of the two ideological attitudes, as proposed in the Dual Process Motivational Model.[57] Moreover, they follow Bilewicz and Soral's findings on the differential effects of RWA and SDO on the support for online hate speech prohibition.[58] Thus, if confirmed, these hypotheses would corroborate and expand Bilewicz and Soral's results to the actual (self-reported) perpetration of online hate speech.

Additionally, the effects of SDO and RWA on the likelihood of perpetrating online hate speech are expected to remain statistically significant also when adjusting the analyses for the socio-economic factors of age, gender and education (*hypothesis 3*), and when controlling for the potential alternative

[56] Geschke *et al.*, 2019, see *supra* note 3.

[57] Duckitt and Sibley, 2009, see *supra* note 4.

[58] Bilewicz *et al.*, 2017, p. 96, see *supra* note 50.

explanations of political attitude and endorsing outgroup prejudice (*hypothesis 4*). In fact, representing broader ideological and psychosocial dimensions, intertwined with personality and with the social context, the two ideological attitudes of RWA and SDO are expected to predict the perpetration of online hate speech beyond the effects of the political and prejudice-related factors.

In order to test the hypotheses, the outcome variable '*perpetration of online hate speech*' is measured through a scale built on the two following items: '*I sometimes offend people that I do not know online*' and '*I post things that I would not say*' (online hate speech: $\alpha = 0.72$; $M = 1.32$; $SD = 0.62$; $N = 7{,}082$). The measures for the ideological attitudes of RWA and SDO are selected from the literature: a six-items scale (RWA: $\alpha = 0.75$; $M = 2.82$; $SD = 0.65$) based on Decker and colleagues[59] and Heitmeyer and Heyder[60] for RWA (for example, 'People should leave important decisions in society to leaders'; 'Established behaviours should not be questioned'), and a five-items scale (SDO: $\alpha = 0.72$; $M = 2.03$; $SD = 0.60$) from Cohrs and colleagues[61] for SDO (for example, 'To get ahead in life, it is sometimes necessary to have no regard for others'; 'All groups should have equal opportunities in life'; reverse item). Two further scales are used for controlling the results: a scale on the frequency of '*online platforms use*' ($\alpha = 0.81$; $M = 2.13$; $SD = 0.72$) and a scale on '*outgroup prejudice*' based on Zick and colleagues' work[62] on xenophobia in Germany ($\alpha = 0.89$; $M = 2.54$; $SD = 0.98$). All scales are rated through a Likert scale, with values ranging from one ('I strongly disagree') to four ('I strongly agree'). Further control variables are political attitude ($M = 5.69$; $SD = 2.00$), self-rated on a scale ranging from one (being politically left) to 11 (being politically right), and the socio-economic variables of age ($M = 48.18$, $SD = 16.07$), gender (female: 51.6 per cent) and education (high education: 29.6 per cent).

Multiple logistic regressions are used to analyse the data and to test the likelihood of perpetrating online hate speech in relation to the different levels of RWA and SDO. Results are summarized in Table 2 below.[63]

---

59 Oliver Decker, Johannes Keiss and Elmar Brähler, *Die enthemmte Mitte: Autoritäre und rechtsextreme Einstellung in Deutschland*, Psychosozial-Verlag, 2017.

60 Aribert Heyder and Wilhelm Heitmeyer, "Autoritäre Haltungen", in Wilhelm Heitmeyer (ed.), *Deutsche Zustände*, vol. 1, Suhrkamp, Frankfurt am Main, 2002, pp. 59–81.

61 Jan C. Cohrs *et al.*, "Befragung zum 11. September 2001 und den Folgen: Grundideen, Operationalisierungen und deskriptive Ergebnisse der ersten Erhebungsphase", in *PsychArchives*, 2002.

62 Andreas Zick, Beate Küpper and Daniela Krause, *Gespaltene Mitte - Feindselige Zustände*, Verlag J.H.W. Dietz Nachf. GmbH, 2016.

63 Odd Ratios ('OR') above value one (OR > 1) indicate a higher likelihood that an event will happen; in this case, online hate speech perpetration. Similarly, Odd Ratios below value one

	Model 1			Model 2			Model 3		
	OR	**95% CI**		**OR**	**95% CI**		**OR**	**95% CI**	
Online Platforms Use	4.08***	3.62	4.58	3.41***	3.00	3.86	3.47***	3.06	3.95
RWA	0.60***	0.52	0.69	0.67***	0.58	0.78	0.51***	0.42	0.62
SDO	2.80***	2.40	3.26	2.57***	2.20	3.00	2.18***	1.84	2.57
Age	-	-	-	0.97***	0.96	0.97	0.96***	0.96	0.97
Male = 1	-	-	-	1.91***	1.58	2.33	1.90***	1.57	2.31
Low Education = 1	-	-	-	1.24*	1.02	1.52	1.25*	1.03	1.53
Political Attitude	-	-	-	-	-	-	1.03	0.98	1.08
Outgroup Prejudice	-	-	-	-	-	-	1.37*	1.19	1.57
LR $\chi2$	910.31			1037.49			1062.41		
Pseudo R squared	0.27			0.31			0.32		
N	6546			6546			6546		

Table 2: Summary of results of logistic regressions on the dependent variable 'online hate speech perpetration'. Note: RWA = Right Wing Authoritarianism; SDO = Social Dominance Orientation; OR = Odd Ratios. 95 per cent CI = 95 per cent Confidence Intervals; Statistical significance: $*p < 0.05$. $***p < 0.001$.

Results indicate that individuals with high levels of SDO are more likely to perpetrate online hate speech, as compared to individuals with low levels of SDO (OR: 2.18***). On the contrary, individuals with high levels of RWA are less likely to perpetrate online hate speech, as compared to individuals with low levels of RWA (OR: 0.51***). Thus, *hypotheses 1* and *2*, proposing the differential effects of SDO and RWA on the perpetration of online hate speech, are confirmed. Including only the main predictors of RWA and SDO and the control variable of online-platform use, the statistical *model 1* is explaining most variance within the analysis (*Pseudo R squared* = 0.27). As expected, the effects of RWA and SDO on the perpetration of online hate speech slightly diminish after adjusting the analysis for the socio-economic factors (*model 2*), but they remain statistically significant, supporting *hypothesis 3*. The significant relations hold also when controlling for outgroup prejudice and self-rated political attitude

(OR < 1) indicate a lower likelihood. The Confidence Intervals (95 per cent CI) show the range in which the real value of the predictor can be found in 95 per cent of cases.

(*model 3*), thus supporting *hypothesis 4* and corroborating the theoretical assumption of RWA and SDO capturing broader psychosocial political dimensions.

19.3.4. Discussion and Conclusions

In order to understand the results of the logistic regressions, interpretations are drawn from Duckitt and Sibley's model and related research.[64] Indeed, the SDO core values of competition, self-enhancement and achievement[65] are well in line with the perpetration of online hate speech as a direct expression of prejudice and overt discriminatory behaviour. High-SDO individuals might perpetrate online hate speech in order to achieve a higher position within society by exerting power against other social groups. As previous studies investigating intergroup relations indicate, SDO-related aggressive intentions target individuals that are perceived by them as 'derogated': socio-economically disadvantaged groups, who might take advantage of the social system.[66] More specifically, high-SDO individuals are more likely to offend minorities and marginalized social groups when they want to gain assimilation into the dominant culture.[67] Thus, high-SDO individuals might use online hate speech to exclude individuals of other social groups from the socio-economic competition, increasing hierarchical relations within society and, at the same time, enhancing their own social status and power.

With regard to RWA, instead, results show that high-RWA individuals are less likely to perpetrate online hate speech. At first, this might seem counterintuitive, but the model's assumptions and previous research allow for a more nuanced understanding. Namely, the main principles of RWA are the need for stability, conformity to social norms[68] and the rejection of what deviates from one's (own) norm.[69] Previous research showed that high-RWA individuals develop aggressive intentions against minorities when those are perceived as "not willing to assimilate",[70] but they might accept those who want to assimilate, differently from high-SDO individuals. Moreover, high-RWA individuals are more likely to develop outgroup prejudice against social groups that are perceived as 'dangerous' and threatening, but not against socio-economically disadvantaged

---

64 Duckitt and Sibley, 2009, see *supra* note 4.

65 Stangor and Leary, 2006, see *supra* note 33.

66 See *supra* note 43.

67 Thomsen, Green and Sidanius, 2008, see *supra* note 44.

68 Stangor and Leary, 2006, see *supra* note 33.

69 John Duckitt, "Differential Effects of Right Wing Authoritarianism and Social Dominance Orientation on Outgroup Attitudes and Their Mediation by Threat from and Competitiveness to Outgroups", in *Personality and Social Psychology Bulletin*, 2006, vol. 32, no. 5, pp. 684–696.

70 Thomsen, Green and Sidanius, 2008, see *supra* note 44.

groups.[71] The current results show that, although they endorse outgroup prejudice,[72] high-RWA individuals are less likely to perpetrate online hate speech: they might avoid engaging with online hate speech because they consider it as a severe violation of social norms. This corroborates Bilewicz and Soral's findings on the positive relation between RWA and outgroup prejudice and the simultaneous support of RWA individuals to prohibit online hate speech.[73] Moreover, this seems in line with the RWA-related conservative motivations to protect the established social order and to adhere to social norms.[74] In other words, high-RWA individuals might refrain from perpetrating online hate speech to preserve stability and cohesion, thus choosing not to overtly express their prejudice against minorities.

It is important to take into account the social context in which the Online Hate data[75] were collected in 2019, as it can further explain the results. Since high-RWA and high-SDO individuals are sensitive to different social-context factors,[76] several elements require considerations. First, the German society has adopted a strong position against the production and sharing of hate speech on social media platforms (see, for example, the NetzDG framework),[77] addressing online hate speech as a possible threat to social stability and cohesion. Through legal efforts to increase social platforms' policies against hate speech, the German government and civil society have so far strongly reinforced social norms against hate speech. As high-RWA individuals are motivated to conform to social norms in order to preserve social stability and order, these normative and societal regulations that strengthen social norms are likely to have a positive impact of RWA individuals. On the contrary, if no regulations are implemented and, instead, social and political leaders engage with hate speech against minorities, either online or offline, the impact of such regulations on social norms

---

71 See *supra* note 43.

72 Before conducing the logistic regression, correlations were checked. A strong positive correlation between RWA and outgroup prejudice against migrants was found ($r = 0.58^{**}$). The correlation between SDO and outgroup prejudice was also positive but less strong ($r = 0.44^{**}$).

73 Bilewicz *et al.*, 2017, see *supra* note 50.

74 In line with research conducted by Duckitt and Sibley (Duckitt and Sibley, 2009, see *supra* note 4 and *id.*, 2009, see *supra* note 31), by Bilewicz and Soral (Bilewicz *et al.*, 2017, see *supra* note 50 and Soral, Bilewicz and Winiewski, 2018, see *supra* note 53) and Stangor and Leary (Stangor and Leary, 2006, see *supra* note 33).

75 Geschke *et al.*, 2019, see *supra* note 3.

76 As indicated by Duckitt and Sibley (Duckitt and Sibley, 2009, see *supra* note 4 and *id.*, 2009, see *supra* note 31) and in the meta-analyses by Cohrs and Stelz, 2010, see *supra* note 43.

77 The 'Network Enforcement Act' (Netzwerkdurchsetzungsgesetz or NetzDG) obligates social-media platforms to remove illegal content within 24 hours or within seven days, depending on the extent of the damaging content. The official document is made available by the German Ministry of Justice on its web site.

would be useless, and high-RWA individuals might become more inclined to produce hate speech on social media platforms.

Differently from high-RWA individuals, high-SDO individuals are neither positively affected by social norms and rules, nor by the values of social order or cohesion. On the contrary, high-SDO individuals are motivated by a strong sense of competition and the need to achieve higher status and power. They are particularly sensitive to social contexts and mechanisms that stress resource-scarcity, socio-economic inequality and social Darwinist views in which "the strong win and the weak lose".[78] These characteristics overlap with the neoliberal values of self-interest, free and 'fair' competition, financial success and (blind) meritocracy,[79] overwhelmingly present in (Western) market-based societies, including the German social-market society.[80] Whereas not all individuals are influenced to the same extent by such values, as Duckitt and Sibley's model indicates, high-SDO individuals are specifically triggered and influenced by these. In the specific case of hate speech on social media platforms, high-SDO individuals might be particularly motivated to use hate speech against minorities in highly competitive and hierarchical contexts. Online hate speech could, in fact, represent, for high-SDO individuals, a successful communicative strategy to disparage social groups and minorities, excluding them from the 'free' and 'fair' competition and the level playing field,[81] while increasing socio-economic inequality and improving their own position on the social ladder.

Some further aspects of the statistical analyses deserve specific attention. Political attitude (left versus right) is the only predictor in the statistical analyses that is not significantly associated with the production of hate speech on social media, contrary to expectations. Since the variable of political attitude has been measured through a self-report scale, this outcome could be influenced by the self-report measurement.[82] However, this also suggests that hate speech on

[78] Duckitt and Sibley, 2009, see *supra* note 31.

[79] See Bruno Amable, "Morals and Politics in the Ideology of Neo-Liberalism", in *Socio-Economic Review*, 2011, vol. 9, no. 1, pp. 3–30; Tim Kasser *et al.*, "Some Costs of American Corporate Capitalism: A Psychological Exploration of Value and Goal Conflicts", in *Psychological Inquiry*, 2007, vol. 18, no. 1, pp. 1–22; Jo Littler, "Meritocracy as Plutocracy: The Marketising of 'Equality' within Neoliberalism", in *New Formations*, 2013, vol. 80, no. 1, pp. 52–72; Laina Y. Bay-Cheng *et al.*, "Tracking Homo Oeconomicus: Development of the Neoliberal Beliefs Inventory", in *Journal of Social and Political Psychology*, 2015, vol. 3, no. 1, pp. 71–88.

[80] Stephanie L. Mudge, "The State of the Art: What is Neo-Liberalism?", in *Socio-Economic Review*, 2008, vol. 6, pp. 703–731.

[81] Amable, 2011, see *supra* note 79.

[82] Respondents were asked to rate their own political attitude on a scale from 1 (left) to 11 (right). The item derives from the European Social Survey.

social media is not attributable to right-wing 'extremists' only and raises questions, in particular, about individuals considering themselves as politically 'centre'. Research focusing on indirect forms of hate speech, such as based on sarcasm, black humour and blind forms of racism,[83] will hopefully contribute to gain better insights in the future, as no specific information has been found, so far, on the role of political attitude in indirect forms of hate speech. Currently, it can be affirmed that hate speech constitutes a complex socio-political phenomenon and the ideological attitudes of RWA and SDO represent a useful framework to investigate individual motivations and contextual factors underlying the perpetration of hate speech on social media platforms. Endorsing high levels of outgroup prejudice is significantly related with higher odds of perpetrating hate speech, as expected (*OR* = 1.37*); yet, the statistical analyses corroborate that RWA and SDO constitute the main predictors of online hate speech. Additionally, as mentioned above, individuals with high levels of outgroup prejudice are not equally likely to produce hate speech: high-RWA individuals are less likely to directly act upon their prejudice though hate speech, while high-SDO are more likely to do so. Lastly, with regard to the demographic factors, it is relevant to note that being male is positively related with higher odds of perpetrating hate speech (*OR* = 1.90***). This is in line with research conducted on gender-based online hate speech.[84] Furthermore, this result contributes to research on the links

---

[83] See Luiz V.P. Trindade, "Disparagement Humour and Gendered Racism on Social Media in Brazil", in *Ethnic and Racial Studies*, 2020, vol. 43, no. 15, pp. 2766–2784; Fabienne Baider and Maria Constantinou, "Covert Hate Speech: A Contrastive Study of Greek and Greek Cypriot Online Discussions with an Emphasis on Irony", in *Journal of Language Aggression and Conflict*, 2020, vol. 8, no. 2, pp. 262–287; Tirşe E. Filibeli and Can Ertuna, "Sarcasm Beyond Hate Speech: Facebook Comments on Syrian Refugees in Turkey", in *International Journal of Communication*, 2021, vol. 15, pp. 2236–2259; Ariadna Mataromos-Fernandez and Johan Farkas, "Racism, Hate Speech and Social Media: A Systematic Review and Critique", in *Television & New Media*, 2021, vol. 22, no. 2, pp. 205–224.

[84] See Sergio A. Castaño-Pulgarín, "Internet, Social Media and Online Hate Speech: Systematic Review", in *Aggression and Violent Behavior*, 2021, vol. 58, pp. 1–7; Simona Frenda *et al.*, "Online Hate Speech Against Women: Automatic Identification of Misogyny and Sexism on Twitter", in *Journal of Intelligent & Fuzzy Systems*, 2019, vol. 36, no. 5, pp. 4743–4752; Naganna Chetty and Sreejith Alathur, "Hate Speech Review in the Context of Online Social Networks", in *Aggression and Violent Behavior*, 2021, vol. 40, pp. 108–118; Valeriya Mechkova and Steven Wilson, "Norms and Rage: Gender and Social Media in the 2018 US Mid-Term Elections", in *Electoral Studies*, 2021, vol. 69, pp. 1–13; Francesca Dragotto, Elisa Giomi and Sonia Maria Melchiorre, "Putting Women Back in their Place: Reflections on Slut-Shaming, the Case Asia Argento and Twitter in Italy", in *International Review of Sociology*, 2020, vol. 30, no. 1, pp. 46–70; Trindade, 2020, see *supra* note 83; Nicola Döring and Mohsen R. Mohseni, "Fail Videos and Related Video Comments on YouTube: A Case of Sexualization of Women and Gendered Hate Speech?", in *Communication Research Reports*, 2019, vol. 36, no. 3, pp. 254–264; Anastasia Powell, Adrian J. Scott and Nicola Henry, "Digital Harassment

between sexism, SDO and RWA.[85] Previous research indicates that RWA is related to benevolent forms of sexism, such as portraying women as wonderful, fragile creatures. SDO, instead, relates with hostile forms of sexism, which aim at intergroup domination, especially against women who challenge male power.[86] It is also interesting to note that Bay-Cheng and colleagues found a strong positive correlation between SDO and neoliberal beliefs, indicating victim-blaming views on sexual violence against women.[87] Indeed, hate speech on social media platforms could represent an overt expression of hostile sexism to exert power against women and individuals of a diverse gender.

In sum, statistical analyses confirm the opposite effects of RWA and SDO on the perpetration of hate speech for individuals engaging with online platforms. Results indicate that right-wing authoritarians are less likely to produce hate speech and this might be linked with their conservative motivation of conforming to social norms and preserving the social order. As a direct expression of outgroup prejudice, hate speech might represent, for high-RWA individuals, a severe violation of social norms, threatening social stability. On the contrary, social dominance-oriented individuals are more likely to produce hate speech online: they might, for instance, achieve their competition-driven goals of exerting power over others and improve their position on the social ladder by spreading hate speech on social media.

This subtle, yet crucial difference between the ideological attitudes of RWA and SDO can be a starting point to design specific and successful strategies to counteract hatred, both online and offline. Social norms seem to play a key role for the prevention of hate speech, especially in the case of authoritarian individuals. Thus, officially and publicly condemning online hate speech is necessary to reinforce social norms against it. Hate speech on social media should be effectively counteracted both at individual- and group-level through counter-speech, as well as at platform-level, through the removal of hate speech against minorities and marginalized social groups and through deplatforming of haters. Yet, as social norms might have no influence on high-SDO individuals, legal measures should be in place in order to protect individuals from different social

and Abuse: Experiences of Sexuality and Gender Minority Adults", in *European Journal of Criminology*, 2020, vol. 17, no. 2, pp. 199–223.

85 See Jim Sidanius and Felicia Pratto, *Social Dominance: An Intergroup Theory of Social Hierarchy and Oppression*, Cambridge University Press, 1999; Chris G. Sibley, Marc S. Wilson and John Duckitt, "Antecedents of Men's Hostile and Benevolent Sexism: The Dual Roles of Social Dominance Orientation and Right-Wing Authoritarianism", in *Personality and Social Psychology Bulletin*, 2007, vol. 33, no. 2, pp. 160–172; Bay-Cheng *et al.*, 2015, see *supra* note 79.

86 Sibley, Wilson and Duckitt, 2007, see *supra* note 85.

87 Bay-Cheng *et al.*, 2015, see *supra* note 79.

groups and to prevent the escalation of intergroup conflicts. Since highly competitive contexts and hierarchical structures affect the motivations behind hate speech, countermeasures should be implemented to reduce socio-economic inequality offline as well. In fact, the online and offline lives of individuals are increasingly complementary[88] and it is not possible to solve a societal issue such as online hate speech without taking into account the offline world. Instead, it is crucial to build more equal and inclusive societies, in which socio-economic resources are more equally distributed and individuals from all social groups can truly benefit from diverse online and offline realities.

19.4. Implications for Religious Communities and Leaders

Relevant evidence-based information for religious community leaders can be drawn from the intersectional analysis on victimization and effects of hate speech (Section 19.2.) and from the results on the ideological attitudes behind the perpetration of hate speech on social media platforms (Section 19.3.).

The intersectional analysis provides insights on the nature of hate speech on social media, showing the higher prevalence of exposure, victimization and damaging effects experienced by individuals with a migration background. The different rates clearly indicate that hate speech constitutes the overt expression of prejudice against individuals that belong to minorities or specific social groups. Moreover, while the discriminatory verbal (or image-based) offences might target a specific individual, its symbolic message affects the whole community to which the individual belongs, as the intersectional data on indirect impact illustrate (Section 19.2.4.), confirming the theoretical conception of hate speech.[89] Being online or offline, the symbolic message of hate speech consists of bias-motivated hatred, intimidation and exclusion, which can lead to an escalation of intergroup violence.[90] It is necessary to highlight that hate speech develops and spreads especially along historically perpetuated socio-economic

---

[88] See Helsper (2012, *supra* note 14), van Dijk (2020, *supra* note 15), and Alexander Bor and Michael B. Petersen, "The Psychology of Online Political Hostility: A Comprehensive, Cross-National Test of the Mismatch Hypothesis", in *American Political Science Review*, 2021, vol. 116, no. 1, pp. 1–18.

[89] See Schweppe and Perry (2022, *supra* note 23), and Barbara Perry, "The Sociology of Hate: Theoretical Approaches", in Barbara Perry and Brian Levin (eds.), *Hate Crimes: Understanding and Defining Hate Crime*, Praeger Perspective, London, 2009, pp. 55–77.

[90] This has also been recognized by Global Action Against Mass Atrocity Crimes ('GAAMAC'), see GAAMAC, "Strengthening National Efforts to Address Hate Speech, Discrimination, and Prevent Incitement: Outcome Document of the Fourth Global Meeting (GAAMAC IV)", 15–18 November 2021 (https://www.legal-tools.org/doc/pi26u1/).

"fractures"[91] and chronic power imbalances within societies. For this reason, acknowledging hate speech as more than a matter of 'free speech' or differing political attitudes is crucial. Hate speech originates from systemic oppression mechanisms – such as colonialism, [92] racism, sexism, heterosexism,[93] *et cetera*, which are reproduced today through a slightly different, potentially subtler, neoliberal guise.[94] In fact, hate speech catalyses societal strain deriving from structural oppressive patterns and increased socio-economic inequality,[95] as stressed also in the United Nations Development Programme's 2016 report.[96] If power imbalances are not recognized and structural inequalities are denied, not only is the dominant societal group's power maintained at the expense of all racialized 'Others',[97] but the risk of misreading the causes of hate speech by blaming faith and religious beliefs becomes instead impelling and threatening for the whole society.

Investigating the predictors of hate speech production on social media, the statistical analyses, presented in Section 19.3., allow identification of some risk and protective factors that can determine or hinder hate speech. At the individual level, risk factors relating to social dominance orientation are the following: strong competitive attitudes, an inclination to disregard the opinion and needs of others,[98] and showing low empathy levels and low interest in collaborating with others,[99] especially in the case of minorities and/or individuals who are in a lower power position. Moreover, a preference for unaffectionate

91 See David Luban, "Is There Anything Intrinsic to the World's Religions that Makes Them Especially Prone to Hateful and Violence-Inspiring Speech?", *CILRAP Film*, Florence, 8 April 2022 (https://www.cilrap.org/cilrap-film/220408-luban/).

92 See Jacques P. Leider, "Colonial Prejudice and Discrimination Predicating Post-Colonial Hate Speech", *CILRAP Film*, Florence, 9 April 2022 (https://www.cilrap.org/cilrap-film/220409-leider/).

93 Perry, 2009, see *supra* note 89.

94 See James Carr, "Islamophobia, Neoliberalism, and the Muslim 'Other'", in *Insight Turkey*, 2021, vol. 23, no. 2, pp. 83–106; James Carr, *Experiences of Islamophobia: Living with Racism in the Neoliberal Era*, Routledge, 2016; Jo Littler, *Against Meritocracy: Culture, Power and Myths of Mobility*, Taylor & Francis, 2017; Littler, 2013, see *supra* note 79.

95 Kate Pickett and Richard G. Wilkinson, *The Spirit Level: Why More Equal Societies Almost Always Do Better*, Allen Lane, London, 2010.

96 United Nations Development Programme, "Preventing Violent Extremism through Promoting Inclusive Development, Tolerance and Respect for Diversity: A Development Response to Addressing Radicalization and Violent Extremism", 1 July 2016 (https://www.legal-tools.org/doc/guylbf/).

97 See Carr, 2021, see *supra* note 94.

98 Sidanius and Pratto, 1999, see *supra* note 85.

99 Heaven and Bucci, 2001, see *supra* note 36.

relations and to consider hierarchical intergroup relations as naturally deserved[100] also represent risk factors. Individuals holding such preferences, who are more likely to be young men with lower education and high levels of outgroup prejudice, would produce hate speech on social media possibly as a strategy to exert their own power and improve their position within the community. On the contrary, individual protective factors against the perpetration of hate speech include: greater conformity to social norms, valuing the established social order, concern for social stability within one's own community, and trust in authorities. Along with these, a preference for affectionate and equal relations and an inclination to collaborate and empathize with others, especially with minorities, should also be accounted as protective individual factors. At the social level, instead, highly unequal socio-economic contexts constitute risks factors: they encourage extreme competitive behaviours over resource scarcity, allowing 'the winner' to take all advantages with no regards for those left behind. It is worthy to note that extreme socio-economic inequality is increasingly recognized as a root cause of societal problems,[101] violent behaviour and extremism.[102] Therefore, less competitive, more cohesive and diverse social contexts can represent protective factors against the perpetration of hate speech, namely, facilitating collaborative behaviours, community life and increasing social trust.[103]

Furthermore, as emerged from the analyses and literature presented in Section 19.3., social norms play a crucial and dual role in preventing the use of hate speech. In fact, social norms prescribe what should and should not be overtly affirmed in the public sphere, both online and offline. Yet, social norms shift over time since they are influenced by social and historical environments and by social actors. As suggested by Bilewicz and Soral, social norms can prohibit the use of derogatory language and hate speech; however, if hate speech spreads exponentially, the individuals' ability to recognize discriminatory offenses as such would be affected and social norms against hate speech would become less effective.[104] On the one hand, strong social norms can prevent the production of hate speech, also in the case of authoritarian individuals with some levels of outgroup prejudice, thanks to their inclination to conform to social norms and rules – as shown in the statistical analyses. On the other hand, whether social norms are effective or not is linked with the behaviours of

[100] Pratto *et al.*, 1994, see *supra* note 30.

[101] Pickett and Wilkinson, 2010, see *supra* note 95.

[102] United Nations Development Programme, 2016, see *supra* note 96.

[103] See Richard Wilkinson and Kate Pickett, *The Inner Level: How More Equal Societies Reduce Stress, Restore Sanity and Improve Everyone's Well-Being*, Penguin Books, 2019.

[104] Bilewicz *et al.*, 2017, p. 96, see *supra* note 50.

relevant social actors as well. In fact, if social leaders do not take a clear stance against hate speech, social norms will be negatively affected, not only for authoritarian individuals but also for the whole society. Therefore, in order to make use of the inhibiting effects of social norms, it is important that hate speech against minorities and marginalized social groups is consistently and publicly delegitimized, online as much as offline.

In conclusion, religious leaders should acknowledge the complex nature of hate speech against minorities, which is intertwined with historical power imbalances and structural oppressive mechanisms. Therefore, as already stated in the Rabat Plan of Action[105] and in the Beirut Declaration,[106] it is crucial that religious leaders refrain from using hate speech. From a psychosocial perspective, they exert a pivotal influence on social norms and, thus, on whole communities. To instead prevent the production and spread of hate speech, it is recommended that religious leaders become aware of risk and protective factors at the individual and social levels, and identify them within their communities and in their specific socio-economic contexts. If aiming to actively strengthen social norms against hate speech, religious leaders should publicly take distance from community figures who use hate speech, regardless of whether the latter belong to secular or religious environments. The endorsement of a clear position against hate speech also constitutes a strategy to initiate reconciliation, recognized by the Beirut Declaration as a duty of religious leaders. Lastly, in order to effectively counteract and prevent hate speech, religious leaders should actively protect minorities, defending publicly their equal dignity and rights, thus promoting diversity and social cohesion. In practice, this can be enacted, on one hand, through technological tools, as suggested in the 18 Commitments on "Faith for Rights"[107] and confirmed by Stern.[108] This aim can also be pursued through inter- and intra-faith dialogue within and between communities, as recommended

[105] United Nations Office of the High Commissioner for Human Rights ('OHCHR'), Rabat Plan of Action on the Prohibition of Advocacy of National, Racial or Religious Hatred that Constitutes Incitement to Discrimination, Hostility or Violence, UN Doc. A/HRC/22/17/Add.4, Annex, 5 October 2012 (https://www.legal-tools.org/doc/jh1be1/).

[106] OHCHR, "Beirut Declaration Enhances Role of Religions in Promoting Human Rights", 29 March 2017 (https://www.legal-tools.org/doc/acp88f/).

[107] OHCHR, "18 Commitments on "Faith for Rights"", 29 March 2017 (https://www.legal-tools.org/doc/qp9nv2/).

[108] Peter J. Stern, "Reflections on the Potential of Social Media to Assist Religious Actors Who Seek to Prevent or Reduce Hate Speech", *CILRAP Film*, Florence, 9 April 2022 (https://www.cilrap.org/cilrap-film/220409-stern/).

in the framework of the United Nations Strategy and Plan of Action on Hate Speech.[109]

[109] United Nations Office on Genocide Prevention and the Responsibility to Protect, "United Nations Strategy and Plan of Action on Hate Speech", 31 May 2019, p. 2 (https://www.legal-tools.org/doc/5rrb5b/).

20

Colonial Prejudice and Discrimination Predicating Post-Colonial Hate Speech

Jacques P. Leider*

In Burma/Myanmar, subjection and inequality have been features of both the colonial law and order system and the post-colonial authoritarian regimes.[1] So are discrimination, prejudice and hate speech. But they are so in different ways and there is no simple cause-to-effect correlation between conditions under British rule and in independent Burma. In his study of indigenous concepts in the rise of xenophobic nationalism in colonial Burma, Phyo Win Latt characterizes the recent aggressive Islámophobia as inspired by anti-colonial phrases and 'outdated' concepts of the pre-World War II period.[2] Matthew J. Bowser argues, on the other hand, that Islámophobia takes its origin in the late colonial "Burmese fascism" which thrived on the socio-economic crisis of the 1930s.[3] While this latest research adds to a debate driven by the post-2012 violence, the cultural and socio-economic dynamics of the colonial period cannot explain how anti-Indian prejudice lived on and was re-enabled in novel contexts of Islámophobia.

---

* **Jacques P. Leider** is Lecturer, Ecole Française d'Extrême-Orient ('EFEO', French School of Asian Studies). He holds a doctorate from the Institut national des langues et civilisations orientales in Paris and has published widely on the early modern history of Arakan and Myanmar's Buddhist history. Since 2012, his research has contributed to the exploration of the historical background of the Rakhine State crisis. Alternating periods of academic research and teaching since 1995, he was in charge the EFEO research centres in Yangon, Chiang Mai and Bangkok. From 2017 to 2021, he was based in Bangkok as the Scientific Coordinator of Competing Regional Integrations in Southeast Asia (CRISEA), an interdisciplinary research project on integration within the Association of Southeast Asian Nations ('ASEAN') funded by the European Union. For an audio-visual recording of his statement to CILRAP's conference in Florence in April 2022 on the topic of this anthology, please see https://www.cilrap.org/cilrap-film/220409-leider/.

1 Burma's name was officially changed to Myanmar in 1989. As this chapter deals with successive historical periods, 'Burma/Myanmar' is used to include explicitly the periods before and after 1989.

2 Phyo W. Latt, "Protecting Amyo: The Rise of Xenophobic Nationalism in Colonial Burma, 1906–1941", Ph.D. dissertation, National University of Singapore, 2020, pp. xi and 236.

3 Matthew J. Bowser, "'Buddhism Has Been Insulted, Take Immediate Steps:' Burmese Fascism and the Origins of Burmese Islamophobia, 1936–1938", in *Journal of Modern Asian Studies*, 2022, vol. 55, no. 4, pp. 1112–1150.

A combination of organizational and ideological factors offers a more grounded explanation to establish a link between the colonial and the post-colonial regimes of inequality and subjection. The present chapter contends that Burma's post-independence leaders embedded prejudiced categories of foreignness and racial difference into their nationalist discourse and practices by maintaining the colonial state's mode of racialized classification from the 1930s. Under Burma's authoritarian military rule, ethnic difference was bureaucratized and determined civic status. At the same time, prejudice rooted in the colonial conditions of exploitation and communal frictions was never discontinued. It became normalized and functioned as a public resource to re-ignite opportunistic hate speech in contexts of state-driven political manipulation and economic distress. The nationalist discourse of Burma's ethnocentric governments did not decolonize, but rather reappropriated the racialized classification in its hierarchization of national belonging.[4]

Classification is one of the features of the colonial rhetoric which produced inequality. David Spurr explains that "the process by which one culture subordinates another begins with the process of naming and leaving unnamed or making on an unknown territory the lines of division and uniformity".[5] Organization is a crucial factor when the dynamics of hate speech spill out into mass violence.[6] There is nothing like *spontaneous* mass violence or dissemination of hate speech. Research on Indian riots led Paul Brass to coin the term "institutionalized riot system".[7] In his research on the clashes in Meikthilar (Upper Myanmar) in 2013–14, Ye Myint Win underscores that Islámophobic violence must be understood "as a systematically organized activity".[8] Both state

[4] Zaheer Baber has shown that "racialization" offers an alternative approach to the analysis of inter-communal conflict in modern India (Zaheer Baber, "'Race', Religion and Riots: The 'Racialization' of Communal Identity and Conflict in India", in *Sociology*, 2004, vol. 38, no. 4, pp. 701–718). Despite the differences of India and Burma, comparative work could contribute to a better understanding of the phenomenon of cultural racism in Myanmar which sorely lacks theoretically grounded research.

[5] David Spurr, *The Rhetoric of Empire – Colonial Discourse in Journalism, Travel Writing, and Imperial Administration*, Duke University Press, Durham, 1993, p. 4.

[6] Examples of external provocations leading to anti-Muslim violence in Myanmar between 2012 and 2014 are quoted in The Centre for Peace and Conflict Studies, *"This Is Not Who We Are": Listening to Communities Affected by Communal Violence in Myanmar*, CPCS, 2015, p. 6.

[7] Paul Brass, "The Development of an Institutionalized Riot System in Meerut City, 1961-1982", in Paul Brass, *Forms of Collective Violence*, Three Essays Collective, Gurgaon, 2006, pp. 65–102.

[8] Ye Myint Win, "A Case Study of Violence and Recovery in Meikhtilar", Master's thesis, Mahidol University, Myanmar/Bangkok, 2017, p. 1.

and non-state organizations have been exposed as playing an instrumental role in Islámophobic violence in contemporary Buddhist countries.[9]

Classification and organization are operational factors that underpin the course of violent cycles and cannot be separated from an ideological frame of thought-action providing meaning and direction. In Burma, an anti-Indian sentiment emerged before the eruption of anti-colonialism in the 1920s. Shared beliefs in ethnic hierarchies and racial differences lived on in the post-independence period and were overlaid by an increasingly anti-Muslim narrative that drove religiously and racially motivated violence in the early twenty-first century.[10] Over several decades, a rigidified classification of ethnicity tied to indigeneity moved Burma from racialized divisions in the colonial period to a range of subtle, ordinary and brutal forms of ethnoreligious exclusion that culminated in the excesses of violence against Muslims seen after 2012. In the transition from an anti-Indian to a predominantly anti-Muslim sentiment, the role of the state shifted. The colonial state drew its legitimacy from racial differentiation and superiority; the nationalist state exploited the categorization of otherness for its political goals.

What follows is organized in three parts. The first section highlights the colonial state's racial interpretation of the anti-Indian violence and the normalization of xenophobia in independent Burma. The second section addresses the racialization of the colonial classification in Burma censuses and its conceptual survival after independence. In post-colonial Burma, ethnic classification was perceived as natural because it became an unquestioned way of looking at ethnic diversity. As it became normative, it could be instrumentalized for the purpose of social and political exclusion. Taking the example of naming Muslims in Rakhine State ('Bengali' versus 'Rohingya'), the last section explains that the contending parties argue within the same ideological framework of racialization which essentializes ethnicity and indigeneity.

---

9 Iselin Frydenlund, "Religious Liberty for Whom? The Buddhist Politics of Religious Freedom during Myanmar's Transition to Democracy", in *Nordic Journal of Human Rights*, 2017, vol. 35, no. 1, p. 46; Iselin Frydenlund, "Buddhist Islamophobia: Actors, Tropes, Contexts", in Asbjørn Dyrendal, David G. Robertson and Egil Asprem (eds.), *Handbook of Conspiracy Theory and Contemporary Religion*, Brill, Leiden, 2019, pp. 279–302. Ye Myint Win points to the military regime's "culture of impunity to instigate anti-Muslim riots", Win, 2017, pp. 2, 31–32, see *supra* note 8.

10 Aspects of contemporary Islám in Myanmar, the politics of belonging and recent violence are discussed in Melissa Crouch, "Myanmar's Muslim Mosaic and the Politics of Belonging", in Melissa Crouch (ed.), *Islam and the State in Myanmar*, Oxford University Press, 2016, pp. 9–28 and Nyi N. Kyaw, "Islamophobia in Buddhist Myanmar: The 969 Movement and Anti-Muslim Violence", in *ibid.*, pp. 183–210.

20.1. Inequality, Racialization and the Normalization of Xenophobia

The anti-Indian sentiment which drove explosive violence in the late colonial period emerged before World War I. In a short essay written in 1913, Taw Sein Ko (1864–1930), a Sino-Shan colonial civil servant, reports on the "impression that Burmans have a prejudice against Indians".[11] Noting that there was little social intercourse between the two groups, Taw Sein Ko attributed the prejudice to the lack of a "liberal education and wide traveling" which prevented the Burmese from appreciating "their political status as citizens of the Indian Empire". As "fellow citizens of a common empire", he wrote, Burmese should be grateful for the "excellent services rendered to Burma by the Indians in the past".[12] The beneficial impact of Indian toil and enterprise for Burma and an implicit request for gratitude are central themes that appear both in administrative reports of the colonial period and in later historical overviews of the Indians in Burma.[13]

Indian immigration was primarily welcomed by the British for reasons of agricultural and commercial development. The praise meted out to Indians for their thrift was commonly trailed by hints at Burmese apathy.[14] In North Arakan, where wastelands were still widely available until the end of the nineteenth century, Chittagonian agriculturists (that is, coming from Bengal's Chittagong Division) settled numerously and formed 70 per cent of the rural population in the border township of Naaf (later renamed Maungdaw) in the 1880s.[15] In Arakan, as elsewhere in Burma, there were both temporary migrants as well as permanent settlers who took advantage of a favourable fiscal assessment of newly cultivated land. The Naaf River, today's international border between Bangladesh and Myanmar, was an internal administrative border from 1826 to 1937 and migrations of all sorts were a constant phenomenon. The decennial census records reveal the transformation of Arakan's north into a densely populated region. Regrettably, there are no year-by-year records to track the demographic growth during the late nineteenth century in greater detail. Reports on land assessments provide irregular but reliable data on the transformation of wastelands into rice fields. Cross-border circulation on the land routes was never put on record and, in the case of Arakan, port figures are rare and inconclusive to follow the flow of migrants.

---

[11] Taw Sein Ko, "Burmans and Indians", in *id.* (ed.), *Burmese Sketches*, British Burma Press, Rangoon, 1913, p. 316.

[12] *Ibid.*, p. 317.

[13] Usha Mahajani, *The Role of Indian Minorities in Burma and Malaya*, Vora and Co. Publishers, Bombay, 1960; Nalini R. Chakravarty, *The Indian Minority in Burma –The Rise and Decline of an Immigrant Community*, Oxford University Press, 1971.

[14] Frank B. Leach, *The Future of Burma*, British Burma Press, Rangoon, 1937, p. 45.

[15] *Report on the Settlement Operations in the Akyab District Season 1886–87*, Superintendent Government Printing, Rangoon, 1888, p. 3 (https://www.legal-tools.org/doc/1o4bkb/).

In Lower Burma, British efforts to attract Indian settlers and establish Indian farming colonies had largely failed in the 1880s. The number of Indian migrants increased nonetheless before World War I and drove an expanding sector of commercial and industrial occupations. From 1901 to 1911, Indian arrivals at the port of Rangoon grew on average 7.5 per cent per year, reaching nearly 270,000 in 1910–11.[16] The relative growth of the Indian population which chose to settle in Burma is difficult to extract from these data. Decennial census reports recorded every Indian who was in the country on the day of the census; they included temporary workers who likely returned to India after a few years. The Rangoon Port statistics reveal a yearly 'surplus' resulting from the subtraction of departures (called '"emigrants") from annual Rangoon port arrivals (called "immigrants"). The rise and decline of port arrivals reflect the dynamics of the labour market but tell us very little about the number of permanent settlers.[17] Until the 1920s, British officials remained optimistic about the proportion of Indians in Burma: "To a nation alive to the conditions, the present numbers of Indians and their rate of increase offer no menace. There will be room for them always".[18] Colonial officers were not worried by the risk of communal frictions, but rather "the continued existence of the Burmese race", as the supervisor of the 1911 Census report put it.[19] As the Indian population was growing, the legal framework of mixed marriages was the only issue where the colonial state intervened as a regulator with the introduction of the Special Marriage Act of 1872, the Revision of the Special Marriage Act in 1923 and the Buddhist Women's Special Marriage and Succession Act of 1939.[20]

While Taw Sein Ko's essay from 1913 shows that the anti-Indian sentiment preceded the manifestation of Burmese anticolonialism in the 1920s, it also exposes a colonial hierarchy where Indians ranked higher than Burma's native populations. The political lives of Indian and Burmese elites evolved separately. The Young Men's Buddhist Association (a Burmese cultural association

16 Morgan C. Webb, *Census of 1911, Volume IX: Burma, Part I. Report*, Office of the Superintendent Government Printing, Rangoon, 1912, vol. 1, p. 77 (https://www.legal-tools.org/doc/vcj9hs/).

17 From 1901 to 1908, the average surplus reached 27 per cent. The excess of immigrants over emigrants from 1901–08 totals 355,703 people, *ibid.*, p. 77.

18 Stanley G. Grantham, *Census of India 1921, Volume X: Burma, Part I. Report*, Office of the Superintendent Government Printing, Rangoon, 1923, p. 226 (https://www.legal-tools.org/doc/r84t1w/).

19 Webb, 1912, p. 75, see *supra* note 16.

20 After the 1938 riots, the *Interim Report of the Riot Inquiry Committee* noted that "one of the major sources of anxiety in the minds of a great number of Burmese was the question of the marriage of their womenfolk with foreigners in general and with Indians in particular". Government of Burma, *Interim Report of the Riot Inquiry Committee*, Government Printing and Stationery, Rangoon, 1939, p. 28.

founded in 1906) refused Indian members long before it became itself a hot-house of nationalist elements in the 1920s.[21] After World War I, the anti-Indian sentiment kept growing with the ongoing flow of Indians entering Burma's labour market. The causes of the communal violence hitting Indians in 1930, 1938 and 1942 are commonly attributed to a combination of socio-economic factors related to the global economic crisis after 1929, the anti-Muslim resentment springing from the legal complications of mixed marriages, and the forces driving Burma's rising nationalism. Contemporary analysts have pointed out that the scapegoating of the Indian community disguised systemic flaws of Burma's colonial capitalism characterized by unbridled competition on the labour market. But political tensions and social divisions were also fuelling discontent and may have had a more enduring impact. In a report of 1947, S.A.S. Tyabji, the Governor of Burma's adviser on Indian Affairs and a passionate defender of the social integration of Indians, noted that the ongoing deterioration of Burmese-Indian relations went back to the aftermath of World War I. He held the view that the separate communal representation of the Indians established by the Montagu-Chelmsford Reforms (1919) protected the interests of "Burmese Indians" but prevented their social and political integration. Moreover, Burma's Constitution of 1935 marking its separation from India did not provide an "option of declaring for citizenship of Burma".[22]

In 1938, violent attacks against mostly Indian Muslims started in Rangoon on 26 July, spread throughout the country, and lasted for a full month. A general strike brought economic life to a standstill. The events which caused the death of 204 people led to the creation of an investigative commission which produced a detailed report.[23] The anti-Indian riots of 1938 deeply shocked the British establishment as they undermined the rationale that the political and legal order that the British had created in Burma was sufficient to ensure popular contentment.[24]

The trigger of the violence was the slandering of Buddhism by a Muslim teacher ('Maung Shwe Hpi's book').[25] Rumours flared and were amplified by the press appealing to the "Burman Buddhists to protect their religion and their race". However, as the Riot Inquiry Committee concluded, this was merely the pretext for a "political campaign against Indians and other foreigners in Burma". The report determined that "the riots were not religious riots. They were

21 United Kingdom ('UK') National Archives, *Nationality Status of Indians in Burma*, 1947, M/4/2658, f. 86.

22 *Ibid.*, f. 87.

23 Government of Burma, *Final Report of the Riot Inquiry Committee*, Government Printing and Stationery, Rangoon, 1939 (https://www.legal-tools.org/doc/jyq4ev/).

24 Frank S.V. Donnison, *Burma*, Praeger, New York/Washington, 1970, p. 11.

25 Bowser, 2022, p. 2, see *supra* note 3.

political".[26] The Inquiry Committee also noted that the riots "were not spontaneous"[27] and explained: "When the time came, the ground had been well prepared in which to plant the seeds of anti-Indian rioting".[28] It blamed "political and racial passions" vented by the press, politicians, nationalist activists (the *thakin*) and politically engaged monks (the "hooligans in yellow robes").[29] In sum, organized violence could be attributed to the anti-colonial Burmese nationalists. However, the anti-Indian hate speech spread by Burmese nationalists was operational within an ideological framework supported by the state. The risk of collective violence was accepted by the state because racial differences and political passions could result in communal hostilities. The colonial state had at least a passive role in letting violence take place.

While it determined the 'political' character of the anti-Indian riots, the 1939 Inquiry Commission remained defensive on what was then called the 'Indian Question', the unrestricted migration of Indians to Burma. Thirty years later, Frank Donnison, who had been a member of the Commission, admitted that one million Indians in Burma "exercised an influence in the affairs of Burma altogether disproportionate to [their] numerical strength".[30] But in the eyes of the Inquiry Commission in 1939, the issue of Indian migration had been "politically misunderstood".[31] By deferring the colonial state's responsibility for immigration to a misunderstanding by the Burmese political class, the Inquiry Commission could then intimate an interpretation that displaced the anti-Indian violence into an entirely different sphere. The Commission stated: "there is the gravest danger of there arising, if it has not already arisen, a communal or racial question within Burma [...]. For it is no ordinary 'communal' question of caste or religion, but it is one of race and lies between Burma and India itself".[32] This racialization of the conflict's etiology was typical of the colonial ideology. It was a pervasive trait of the narrativization of social relations and of history itself. The British authorities, as they saw it, were blameless, because they were merely observers of events that unfolded as consequences of an inevitable conflict between races.

It seems rather unlikely that the Burmese and Indian elites in Rangoon in the late 1930s saw themselves and their communities expressly as actors in an inevitable racial conflict. The intellectual development of pre-war Burmese nationalism was affected by authoritarian-fascist and communist-leftist ideologies

---

26 Government of Burma, 1939, p. 287, see *supra* note 23.
27 *Ibid.*, p. 290.
28 *Ibid.*, p. 288.
29 *Ibid.*, p. 288.
30 Donnison, 1970, p. 91, see *supra* note 24.
31 Government of Burma, 1939, p. 288, see *supra* note 23.
32 *Ibid.*, p. 289. Donnison, 1970, see *supra* note 24, writing thirty years later, includes "dangerous racial [...] pressures" in his explanation of the riots.

which reached Burma notably via India and Indian political actors like Subhas Chandra Bose.[33] Nonetheless, Burma's nationalist organizations were ideologically fragmented and anti-colonialism connected Indians and Burmese to a certain extent.[34] But for the Burmese British colonialism had a distinctive Indian face, and the colonial trauma of the Burmese masses was entangled with the 'Indian question'. Indians formed 6.3 per cent of the total population and "disproportionately dominated Burma's colonial enterprise".[35] They were highly visible in the commercial quarters of towns and cities where over half of them lived but also at the institutional and administrative levels. Labour issues in the port of Rangoon, the rural debt crisis involving Chettiyar lenders, and the ensuing losses of agricultural land by Burmese farmers as well as dissatisfaction with Islámic inheritance laws for Buddhist women marrying Muslim men were issues that were publicly discussed over many years. In comparison, colonialism had only an occasional white face. Among 30,000 Europeans and "allied races", the British counted for less than one-third, that is less than 10,000, or 0.06 per cent of the total.[36]

For middle- and upper-class Indians, their community's economic importance generated a sense of entitlement of being in Burma. Indians opposed the separation of Burma from India due to their "natural fear that after separation the position of Indians resident in Burma might become difficult".[37] However, the status of Indians and people of Indian origins was hybrid during the entire colonial period and became insecure after independence. While the Indians were British subjects claiming their rights as citizens of the Empire, they were officially described as a foreign race in census reports. Indians were resented as too many and too dominant even though leading Indian Muslims had joined the anti-colonial struggle in Burma since the 1920s and were committed to social integration. Approximately half a million Indians left when the Japanese invaded

33 Hans-Bernd Zöllner, *Birma zwischen "Unabhängigkeit Zuerst – Unabhängigkeit Zuletzt". Die birmanischen Unabhängigkeitsbewegungen und ihre Sicht der zeitgenössischen Welt am Beispiel der birmanisch-deutschen Beziehungen zwischen 1920 und 1948*, Lit-Verlag, Hamburg, 1998, pp. 377–389.

34 The ideological fragmentation of Burma's independentist organizations in the 1930s and 1940s is highlighted in *ibid.*, pp. 411–479. On the fascination for fascist leaders in India during the same period, see also Baber, 2004, pp. 709–10, *supra* note 4.

35 Renaud Egreteau, "Burmese Indians in Contemporary Burma: Heritage, Influence, and Perceptions Since 1988", in *Asian Ethnicity*, 2011, vol. 12, no. 1, p. 33.

36 John J. Bennison, *Census of India 1931, Volume XI: Burma Tables*, Office of the Superintendent, Government Printing and Stationery, Rangoon, 1933, vol. 2, p. 245 (https://www.legal-tools.org/doc/7z9vl8/).

37 Leach, 1937, pp. 44–45, see *supra* note 14.

Burma in 1942.[38] Many Indians wanted to return after 1945, but the Burmese leaders were not accommodating and made sure that immigration regulations were introduced in 1947.[39] During the parliamentary period (1948–62), Indians still played a prominent social and political role. Divided by geographical origins, language, political ideologies and religion, their communities never formed a monolithic block. They discussed how much their communities should advocate for greater integration into the Burmese society, push for the recognition of communal interests or emphasize their religious concerns. The military dictatorship of General Ne Win (1962–88) put an end to these conflicted debates. The ethnopolitical order the General imposed was challenged by indigenous ethnic groups whose elites felt treated unfairly rather than Indians. But the military regime's nationalist politics soon targeted and marginalized the people with South Asian origins.

The nationalization of the economy (1964), the citizenship law of 1982, and, more generally, the politics of Burmanization under General Ne Win's regime were "disguised anti-Indian state policies", diminished the social and economic role of city-dwellers and drove many middle-class business people (referred to as 'Indians' or 'Pakistanis' until the 1960s) out of the country.[40] Looking back at Ne Win's rule in October 2001 when a wave of anti-Muslim violence swept through several Myanmar cities in the wake of the Islámist terror attacks in the United States, a Burmese journalist wrote:

> Ne Win's government exploited the people's hatred of Muslims. Whenever the country faced a political or economic crisis, Ne Win's government created religious clashes between the Burmese and Muslims in an effort to turn the public's attention away from the crisis.[41]

The Burmese saw the population growth of their western neighbour Bangladesh as a demographic threat.[42] The border with East Pakistan

---

38 Hugh Tinker, "A Forgotten Long March: The Indian Exodus from Burma, 1942", in *Journal of Southeast Asia Studies*, 1975, vol. 6, no. 1, pp. 1–15.

39 The Burma Immigration (Emergency Provisions) Act XXXI of June 1947 was primarily pointed at immigration from India. It made immigration permits and "visaed passports" mandatory. One of the reasons for its introduction was that "the absence of any legal provision […] enables any person to enter Burma freely by land or freely by sea and air, subject only to the difficulty of finding accommodation on steamer or aircraft". The Burma Immigration (Emergency Provisions), 1947, Act XXXI of 1947, FO 643/67 (https://www.legal-tools.org/doc/3efb59/).

40 Egreteau, 2011, p. 45, see *supra* note 35.

41 Maung M. Oo, "Terror in America, Backlash in Burma", in *The Irrawaddy Magazine*, 2001, vol. 9, no. 8.

42 Bohmu H. Myaing, *Report on the Arrival of Foreigners and the Situation in Rakhine State* (Nuiṅṅaṁ khrāḥ sāḥ myāḥ vaṅ rok hmu nhaṅ. rakhuiṅ prañ nay mha phrac rap a khre a ne

(Bangladesh since 1971) was porous and the site of smuggling and illicit crossings. In 1978, a mass flight of nearly 200,000 Muslims to Bangladesh happened after the security forces used excessive force during a campaign of immigration control in Arakan.[43] The Rohingya Patriotic Front, an armed organization active in the refugee camps, published accusations of serious human rights violations. But they were not investigated because the United Nations ('UN') oversaw the successful repatriation of the refugees together with the Burmese government in 1979.

Ne Win mistrusted people of South Asian origins in his own country. At the tenth Central Committee Meeting of the Burma Socialist Programme Party ('BSPP', 10–11 December 1979), he mused about the lesser loyalty one would expect from people who had mixed blood or who had been naturalized.[44] The preparation of a new citizenship law which followed the proclamation of the new Constitution in 1974 had followed a long process of internal debates and was complicated by an accumulation of citizenship issues that had not been resolved since independence. When the 1982 citizenship law was published, UK Ambassador Leeland commented that "[t]he new Law is blatantly discriminatory on racial grounds", explaining that the Burmese resented the economic success of Indians and Chinese.[45] Whatever the different motives, the ideology underpinning the new law with its three-tiered system (including associated and naturalized citizens with lesser rights) was immersed in the racialized conception of ethnic hierarchies inherited from the 1930s. When he presented the new law to the party's Central Committee on 8 October 1982, General Ne Win stated that "[r]acially, only pure-blooded nationals will be called citizens".[46] The Rohingyas immediately saw the 1982 citizenship law as the state's legal initiative to disenfranchise the Muslims of North Arakan. Many months before its proclamation, militant Rohingyas protested the "anti-Muslim socialist regime" (Rohingya Patriotic Front) and the foundation of the Rohingya Solidarity Organization, a new armed organization, in 1982 came in the wake of the announcement

akhyui), 1983 (on file with the author). This is a 'secret' report which can be found freely on the Internet.

43 Klaus Fleischmann, *Arakan – Konfliktregion zwischen Birma und Bangladesh: Vorgeschichte und Folgen des Flüchtlingsstroms von 1978*, Mitteilungen des Instituts für Asienkunde, Hamburg, 1981.

44 *Dispatch of the Embassy of the Federal Republic of Germany to the Ministry of Foreign Affairs, Bonn*, 17 December 1979, Politisches Archiv des Auswärtigen Amts, Berlin, Zwischenarchiv no. 110.467.

45 British Embassy Rangoon, "Letter from British Embassy Rangoon (Ambassador J.R. Leeland) to South East Asian Department", 25 November 1982.

46 General Ne Win, "Speech by General Ne Win at the Central Committee meeting held in the Central Meeting Hall, President House, Ahlone Road", 8 October 1982.

of the new citizenship law.[47] Contemporary scholars like Nyi Nyi Kyaw and Nick Cheesman have stressed bureaucratic lethargy and underscored that the discrimination that started to hit the Rohingyas a few years later was not due to the law as such, but to the lack of its fair implementation.[48] In sum, the racialized matrix which Burma inherited and which Ne Win's BSPP regime perpetuated did not *cause* discrimination *per se*, but it shaped the state's politics to restrict access to full citizenship. It also rationalized exclusion in the eyes of the public. Rather than overcoming the colonial trauma of foreign domination, Burma's unitarian nation-building projects failed to unshackle the country of the corrosive combination of anti-colonialism and opportunistic xenophobia.

Renaud Egreteau has demonstrated how the internalized Indophobia muted into an increasingly virulent Islámophobia under the State Law and Order Restoration Council-State Peace and Development Council regime (1988–2011).[49] At first sight, this development would suggest that the country followed an international trend where 'Islámism' was portrayed as an enemy of global security. More specifically, in the context of India's "New Burma Policy", where "'Hindu' India and 'Buddhist' Myanmar seemed to share the same enemy – Islamism", Egreteau points to the "repossessing" of Buddhism by Hindu nationalists in India "in order to establish a 'Hindu-Buddhist' alliance to fight Muslim expansionism".[50] Pace the internationalization of an Islámist threat and the ideological resources of Hindu mythology, the Burmese military regime mainly revised its xenophobic toolbox for domestic reasons by weaponizing Islámophobia in the 1990s and by ruthlessly exploiting Rohingyaphobia after 2012.

For over a century, Indian Muslims or Muslims of Indian origins were the biggest group of victims of violent attacks and xenophobia was the common denominator of their discrimination in the colonial and postcolonial contexts. While xenophobia is the prejudice against people from other countries, in modern Myanmar, the mistrust of foreigners was increasingly being associated with fear and a threat to the survival of the nation and Buddhist culture. The evolution from an outdated colonial Indophobia to an Islámophobia attuned to global trends did not shrink the space of discrimination. Nor did the rise of Islámophobia make xenophobia more specific in its targets, as the accusation of the

47 Rohingya Patriotic Front, "Muslim Rule in Arakan", in *Rohingya Daak*, January 1982, no. 2, p. 1 (type-written extract on file with the author).

48 Nyi N. Kyaw, "Unpacking the Presumed Statelessness of Rohingyas", in *Journal of Immigrant and Refugee Studies*, 2017, vol. 15, no. 3, pp. 269–286; Nick Cheesman, "How in Myanmar 'National Races' Came to Surpass Citizenship and Exclude Rohingya", in *Journal of Contemporary Asia*, 2017, vol. 47, pp. 1–20.

49 Egreteau, 2011, see *supra* note 35.

50 Renaud Egreteau, *Wooing the Generals: India's New Burma Policy*, Authors Press, Delhi, 2003, p. 115.

Rohingya genocide might suggest. 'Muslims' in general became typified as the expression of a quintessential and dreaded foreignness. It is therefore not a paradox that latent xenophobia has been shared by political foes. After reviewing statements of Daw Aung San Suu Kyi that relate to Burmese Buddhist anxieties about Muslims, Michał Lubina concluded that "she was not against Islam *per se*, but in Myanmar would rather keep [it] at arm's length".[51] At the same time, anti-Muslim prejudice was instrumentalized in vitriolic attacks against Aung San Suu Kyi herself when her picture was edited with Islámic headwear insinuating that she was pro-Muslim, adding to earlier slander about her so-called foreign connections (as she had married a British).[52]

In her work on the Association for the Protection of Nationality and Religion (founded in 2014 and widely known by its Burmese acronym 'MaBaTha'), Iselin Frydenlund has shown how the contemporary anti-Muslim narrative in Myanmar's mediascape draws on ancient history (such as the penetration of Islám, termed 'conquest', in India and maritime Southeast Asia which had once been Buddhist lands), the rise of contemporary Islámism (for example, Taliban rule in Afghanistan from 1996 to 2001), terrorist acts by fundamentalists, and finally, alleged plots of Muslims ('love jihad') trying to gain control over Buddhist Burma.[53] But even this plentiful repertoire seems open for further additions. Presenting a discussion among young, university-educated women about the military regime's switch from an anti- to a pro-ASEAN stance in 1996, Monique Skidmore recalls that one of her friends "repeated a common Rangoon rumour that Burma's entrance to ASEAN was part of a secret Muslim conspiracy that would result in the Buddhist architecture of Rangoon being replaced with Muslim mosque-style domes and minarets at the completion of (then Indonesian President) Suharto's visit to Rangoon".[54]

Such lurid speculations were not merely the outcome of an *ad hoc* anti-Muslim propaganda fitting the government's chauvinist agenda. They were the reflection of a widespread internalized mistrust of foreigners maintained by the country's memorialization of anticolonialism and its ethnocentric education. During the 1990s, the post-Ne Win military junta intensified the propagation of a Burma-centric nationalism which perpetuated the colonial notion that even long-time residents (such as people of Indian, mixed origins or non-Buddhists) could still be 'foreigners'. This instrumentalization of xenophobic prejudice was

---

51 Michał Lubina, *A Political Biography of Aung San Suu Kyi: A Hybrid Politician*, Routledge, London, 2021, p. 118.

52 "Altered Image: Burma's Aung San Suu Kyi 'in fake headscarf'", *BBC News*, 9 June 2014.

53 Frydenlund, 2019, see *supra* note 9.

54 Monique Skidmore, *Karaoke Fascism – Burma and the Politics of Fear*, University of Pennsylvania Press, Philadelphia, 2004, p. 130. For another telling example of Islámophobic hate speech in 1996, see *ibid*., p. 22.

facilitated, as the next section argues, by the confirmation of the racialized classification of Myanmar's ethnic diversity in the list of 135 races (or ethnic groups).

20.2. Classification: The Toxic Heritage of Racialized Categories

Categorizing is a helpful brain-function to simplify human encounters with a complex world. Classification counts both as a reasonable and a rational exercise in organizing sets of living beings, objects, data or ideas. For British administrators in the early nineteenth century, enumeration and classification were practical tasks to fulfil their obligation of assessing fiscal dues. Following the annexation of two Burmese provinces in 1826 (Tenasserim and Arakan) and the conquest of Lower Burma in 1852, categories of language, religion and ethnicity were applied in different ways to the people living in these three distinctive regions. The need for a comprehensive approach occurred with the creation of British Burma in 1862. For several years, the annual administrative reports show a keen interest in the presence of newly arrived Indian migrants. While the *Report on the Administration of the Province of British Burmah for the Year 1864–65* put Burmese, Arakanese and Mon in a single group of domestic Buddhists, it differentiated a group of Indian (mostly Muslim) immigrants, and a smaller one of indigenous Muslims (called 'Mahomedans of Burma').[55] This differentiation of indigenous and immigrant Muslims vanished with the organization of the decennial *Census of India* reports starting in 1872. From 1872 to 1911, Burma's population was mainly categorized according to language and religion. For the sake of a standardized enumeration, the categories applied in Burma were aligned with those of India. From 1872 to 1931, there were seven *Census of India* operations (1872, 1881, 1891, 1901, 1911, 1921 and 1931) including British Burma. From 1891 onwards, there were two (and occasionally three) volumes for each division or province, the first one containing a conclusive report and the second one, the "imperial tables", with the classified data. Starting in 1901, the censuses included "provincial tables" which provide a detailed view of the population composition at the township level. The colonial administration tracked the demographic evolution, the composition of the population by religion, ethnicity, language, age categories and gender distribution, as well as migration, literacy, infirmities and professional occupations. These categories were often combined in select sub-groups (focusing, for example, on urban development) and people were grouped in ever more detailed categories.

Categorizing people was not only a meticulous administrative activity for the sake of counting, taxing and ruling the population, it was also understood as

[55] *Report on the Administration of the Province of British Burma for 1865–66*, Foreign Department Press, Calcutta, 1866.

a methodically rational operation. Enumerators, however, became frustrated by Burma's ethnic and linguistic complexity which when observed on the ground, underwent seemingly endless change. Moreover, the standard categories imposed by the format of the census were, on the one hand, too elaborate, and on the other, insufficient. They were tailored to India's Hindu and Muslim populations and to the complexity of castes and sects. They appeared less useful for the record of Burma's still poorly explored ethnic diversity where the choice of language used by minority groups varied and ethnonyms fluctuated as exonyms competed with endonyms. Ethnic belonging could even become absorbed within a religious affiliation. Such was the case of the Chinese who, in regional settings where their numbers were very small, were simply added to the Buddhist category. But the linguistic classification was ultimately considered ineffectual, a criticism that emerged first in the 1911 Census. Twenty years later, Captain J.H. Green summed it up in his *Note on the Indigenous Races of Burma* and advised:

> [T]o obtain more accurate knowledge of the inter-relationship and culture of our tribes, a study of ethnology, anthropology, and folklore [...] is of the greatest importance. Unfortunately, practically nothing, so far has been done in this respect [...].[56]

Green summed up his criticism as follows:

> Up to the present time, language has been the only basis of classification of the races and tribes of Burma. Some of the races or tribes in Burma change their language almost as often as they change their clothes. The classification of the indigenous races has been further complicated as the names now applied to them are not their own names, but those given to them by their neighbours. In many cases, these originated as terms of abuse.[57]

With the rise of racist ideologies in Europe and America, 'race' came to be seen as a more reliable and potentially more scientific criterion to classify colonized people by "concentrating" on their "similarities in body measurements, customs, laws, arts, and religious beliefs" and grouping them into "stages of cultural evolution".[58] The focus on racial categories was therefore not new. However, the considerable effort put into racializing ethnic and linguistic diversity signalled a new approach after World War I. The conceptual shift is perceptible in the 1921 Census. Definitions of "race", "race-groups", "peoples", "home races", and the "distribution of races" were newly presented.[59] The use of 'caste' for the internal classification of Hindus and 'sects' for the Muslims altogether

[56] Bennison, 1933, p. 245, see *supra* note 36.

[57] *Ibid.*

[58] *Ibid.*

[59] Grantham, 1923, Chapter XI, "Race and caste", see *supra* note 18.

disappeared. But a comprehensive application of racialized categories took place only ten years later. The extensive use of "race" and "race-groups" in the 1931 Census' table of contents is revealing. Two examples may illustrate the racial turn of the 1931 Census.

- Imperial Table VII-A was called "Age, Sex and Civil Condition (Provincial Summary)" in 1911; it became "Age, Sex and Civil Condition by *Religion*" in 1921, and appeared as "Age, Sex and Civil Condition by *Race*" in 1931.
- The 1911 Burma Census contained an Imperial Table XIII which bore the imprecise title, "Caste, Tribe, Race or Nationality"; in 1921, Table XIII focused already exclusively on "Race" while in the 1931 Census, race-related content tripled, and was presented in three Tables (XVII, XVIII and XIX) with added subdivisions on "variation" and "distribution".

The emphasis on race did not just switch one marker for another or introduce a new tool to order people. It generated a different picture of the population. On the one hand, it de-individualized groups of people by pairing them with certain economic attributes or by including them in bigger "race-groups".[60] On the other hand, racial differences brought back to attention smaller communities like the Chinese, or split groups into two that had previously been united by their similar religious or linguistic affiliation.

In the *Schedule for Racial Map* of the 1931 Census, the population of Akyab District, the biggest of Arakan's three districts, the Arakanese "race" (today called 'Rakhine') was absorbed into the Burma "race-group" because the Arakanese were seen racially like the Burmese. The population groups previously profiled as "Hindus" or "Muslims" and collectively referred to as "Indians" were divided and classified either as "Indian races" or as belonging to a hybrid "Indo-Burman Race".

The reshaping of the categories reflected the progress of a racist mindset rather than new insights or determinations of ethnic or cultural markers. Fifteen "race-groups" were created which contained each a set of "Indigenous Races" who were "associated particularly closely with Burma, *even* if a greater part of their people live elsewhere".[61] Indigeneity, therefore, did not mean that people were exclusively living in Burma. Many ethnic populations belonging to the Tai, Kachin, Chin or Karen "race groups" lived indeed on two sides of the border. The author of the 1931 Census had to admit that the classification was "in fact chiefly linguistic though intended as a *tentative* ethnological classification". The

[60] One example is Provincial Table VI, "Race and Economic Function", of the 1931 Census (Bennison, 1933, see *supra* note 36).

[61] Grantham, 1923, p. 207, see *supra* note 18.

non-indigenous races, however, were not "classified ethnologically, but only collected into the five *convenient* groups of European, etc. Chinese, Indo-Burman, Indian and Others".[62] As a result, the classificatory grid of the 1931 Census was more detailed than earlier censuses and seemed to do away with ambiguities in the eyes of its creators. But the racialization of the 1931 Census did not cut through the perceived fuzziness of ethnolinguistic categories; it established arbitrary divisions which came to haunt the country after independence.

Our contemporary understanding of the interaction between different ethnic communities embraces social, economic and cultural relations where factors like influence, adaptation or dependence play out in multiple political and civic contexts. The authors of the colonial censuses did not see it that way. Their recurring expression was 'absorption' which denoted a zero-sum game where a dominating group was overcoming another by imposing its language or culture, or via hybridization where one group durably impacted another. 'Absorption' was implicitly understood as a function of racial superiority. Colonial administrators were generally enthusiastic about the racial impact of Indians on Burma's society which they saw historically as beneficial.[63] Their opinions were divided on whether the Burmese could hold their own in the racial contest. The colonial perspective of an ongoing ethnic and racial struggle is poles apart from the contemporary liberal understanding of equality, tolerance, social integration and, ideally, social harmony. John S. Furnivall described the colonial society as a "plural society", composed, as Lee Hock Guan summarizes:

> [O]f racial groups that are divided into separate sections, where each racial group is 'an aggregate of individuals rather than an organic whole'. Such a society is inherently unstable because there is no common social will to integrate the different ethnic sections.[64]

Strikingly, Furnivall's plural society still appears as a valuable description of Burma's post-independence society.[65] 'Burmanization' can be characterized

---

62 *Ibid.*, p. 251 (emphasis added).

63 This refers to the process of cultural transfer called 'Indianization'. It was long understood as a one-way transmission of Brahminic and Buddhist beliefs and practices from India to Southeast Asia. Contemporary scholars explain it as the adoption and creative adaptation of such practices and beliefs by Southeast Asian host cultures.

64 Lee H. Guan, "Furnivall's Plural Society and Leach's Political Systems of Highland Burma", in *Sojourn: Journal of Social Issues in Southeast Asia*, 2009, vol. 24, no. 1, p. 34.

65 Analyzing Burma's 1973 census, Ismael Khin Maung concluded that "considerable indigenization of the population" had taken place "as a consequence of the mass exodus of the nonindigenous groups" and that the "phenomenon of a plural society and the associated problem of achieving social integration […] have nearly disappeared", Ismael K. Maung, "The Population of Burma: An Analysis of the 1973 Census", in *East-West Center*, 1986, p. 17. The record

as an administrative juggernaut of the unitarian state which erodes cultural differences, and it has been described by ethnic minority people as a vicious state-centric attempt to destroy regional cultures. Mutual trust is lacking, prejudice lives on, and social discord and communal conflict can be instrumentalized. The collective fear of a Muslim threat hailing the annihilation of Burmese Buddhist culture, for example, can be seen as the pernicious outcome of a mindset steeped in essentialized colonial divisions. But it was not the colonial classification *per se* but rather the racist ideology linked to the binary of indigeneity and foreignness which poisoned interethnic relations. Where the winner takes it all, a 'common social will' cannot take root.

How did the inherited racialized classification become toxic? A first explanation is that the post-colonial avatars of the racialized classification rigidified ethnic categories. Colonial classifications were divisive, matter of fact and often arbitrary, but they were also experimental and potentially evolving. Western colonizers became obsessed with race, but 'race' was long perceived as fuzzy and its classificatory usability was not easily determined. Even in the 1911 Census, we still read that "race in Burma is not a fixed definite phenomenon capable of presentation in a set of tabular statements. It is vague and indeterminate and in a constant state of fluctuation".[66] Only ten years later, the 1921 Census stipulated that "for the purposes of the census […] [the] meaning [of race] is narrowed down to a consideration of the extent to which tribal or local subdivisions of groups of tribal people are to be separately tabulated […]. Race must be regarded as the generic name of the classes tabulated […]".[67] Hereafter, racial classification was not questioned and became normalized. The 1931 Census, however, does not expressly state either a subtotal of indigenous races or a total of all the 'races' in Burma. This would not have made much sense at the time because "European and allied populations" were wrapped up in a single diffuse category. If one leaves aside all Indian, Western and other 'races', the number of races listed in the 1931 census drops to 145. This is, as one may consider, the number that Burma enumerators started with after independence. Following the census operations of 1973, a list of 143 indigenous ethnicities (*taingyintha lumyo*) was published. It included a group called "Rakhine-Chittagong" unmistakably designating the Muslims of Rakhine State (with the exception of the Muslim Kaman, a small group that was listed separately), as well as three other

of Islámophobia and inter-ethnic violence of the last four decades does not confirm this interpretation.

66 Webb, 1912, p. 250, see *supra* note 16.

67 Grantham, 1923, p. 206, see *supra* note 18.

groups of Burmese Muslims.[68] The list was further revised and presented in 1989 as a list of 135 indigenous races divided among eight major ethnic groups.[69] In its present congealed form, it does not make sense as a definite record of indigenous people, either ethnically, historically or linguistically. Nonetheless, it became dogmatic and serves the practical purpose of a nationalist ideology. With the exception of Rakhine State's Kaman, Muslims became *de facto* excluded. This exclusion comprised the Rohingyas, but also those Burmese or Myanmar Muslims who had been listed as 'indigenous' by the British since the 1860s. Therefore, it is rather surprising how respectfully the list of 135 was treated by international observers and human rights groups after 2012. Advocating for the Rohingya to be recognized as the one hundred thirty-sixth group for the sake of their ethnic legitimacy comes close to a recognition of the antiquated racialized classification itself. Moreover, Myanmar is home to many other Muslims who could raise ethno-historical claims like those of the Rohingyas.[70]

A second reason to speak about a heritage that became toxic is the politicization of ethnicity. The racialized classification with its fundamentalist credo of ethnicity was not only owned by the ethnocentric state dominated by the Burmese army, but also by all the ethnic groups classified as 'indigenous'. It ensured status and political recognition within the Union. Despite the ruthlessness of military policies towards many of Myanmar's ethnic minorities, no ethnic group enjoying the state's recognition as an indigenous population rejected the existing ethnic grid, as it could work in their favour. The creation of Mon State and Arakan State by the Constitution of 1974 shows how the Mon and Arakanese moved upward within the state-sanctioned ethnic hierarchy. Mon and Rakhine leaders had fought for the creation of their own ethnically denominated states since the 1950s.

The Muslims in North Arakan, on the other hand, were a mixed population with pre-colonial and colonial roots which failed to gain formal ethnic

68 Final Compilation of the Census Lists: 143 Indigenous Union Races (Praññthoṅcu tuiṅḥ raṅḥ sāḥ lū myuiḥ 143 myuiḥ rhi sanḥ khoṅ cā raṅḥ kok ran pru cu thāḥ prīḥ prī), in Bothataung Gazette, 22 February 1973. Reproduced as Appendix X in Myint Thein (Abdus Salaam), "The Problem of Muslim National Identity in Myanmar", Ph.D. dissertation, International Islamic University (International Institute of Islamic Thought and Civilization), Kuala Lumpur, 2012, p. 397.

69 Maung, 1986, p. 16, see *supra* note 65:

> The 1973 Census secured information of race by directly inquiring about the race of respondents and their parents. Thus race was defined subjectively rather than by the criterion of respondents' language […]. Officially, three broad groups of races were identified: the indigenous races, nonindigenous or foreign races, and Burmese mixed with foreign races.

70 "UN Delegation Visits Myanmar, Interview with Kenneth Roth, Director of Human Rights Watch", *NPR*, 2 May 2018.

recognition even though they had enjoyed a semblance of regional autonomy from 1960 to 1964 (the 'Mayu Frontier Administration', or 'MFA'), ten years before the creation of Arakan State (named 'Rakhine State' after 1982). Branding identity papers established during this period is a way for Rohingyas to testify to the administrative recognition of their citizenship status and their chosen ethnonym. During the short period of the MFA, North Arakan Muslim leaders sought the public validation of a unique Rohingya Muslim identity and promoted a homogenous yet selective historical narrative of Muslims in Arakan. The bulk of North Arakan's Muslim population in 1948 were second, third or fourth generation descendants of Chittagonian migrants who had arrived in Arakan in the second half of the nineteenth and early twentieth century. Their elite was indifferent to Burma's political life until 1937, but its political awakening took place in 1942 when the Japanese invasion led to the collapse of British rule and the 'Chittagonians', as they were uniformly called by the British military administration, had to stand their own ground during a chaotic period. After the war, one of their most prominent leaders, Mohammed Abdul Gafar, pleaded in favour of the North Arakan Muslims (including the rebel *Mujahids*) arguing that they were not separatists, but loyal to the state and only wanted recognition as *taingyintha,* indigenous people.[71]

The Arakanese Buddhist majority traditionally acknowledged the long-established Muslim communities of Akyab, Kyauktaw and Mrauk U and recognized the tiny community of Kaman people in South Arakan as an ethnic Muslim minority, but it refused to accept the claims of indigeneity of the modern Rohingyas which they still saw as 'Chittagonians'. Unsurprisingly, the North Arakan Muslim leadership similarly saw the Buddhist majority as hostile to its territorial and political interests and rejected the creation of an Arakan State where both populations would have to live together. The Burmese nation-state did not mediate this political contestation but exploited the division for its own advantage. Hate speech and prejudice were predictably perpetuated until today. Each group cultivates its own version of history: the history of the Buddhist kingdom of Arakan and the Rohingya narrativization of precolonial Arakan as the history of an Islámized kingdom are irreconcilable.

The Rohingya leaders who needed to legitimize their claims did not reject the established ethno-racial classification. They did not contest the fact that people were categorized (and discriminated via their categorization) or call for

[71] Mohammed A. Gafar, "Memorandum Presented to the Home Affairs Minister of the Government of Burma", 10 November 1948 (Burmese text on file with the author). Nemoto states that the text was published in the English *Guardian Daily* on 20 August 1951, Kei Neimoto, "The Rohingya Issue: A Thorny Obstacle between Burma (Myanmar) and Bangladesh", unpublished, Tokyo, 2007, p. 3.

alternate forms of recognition in the Burmese nation-state. They rather wanted to gain recognition within the existing classificatory system to defend their rights and recognition as full citizens. This approach did not change until today. Politically, the Rohingya movement entered a downward cycle after 1964, because its early gains rapidly collapsed under General Ne Win's rule. The Muslim majority areas were re-integrated into the district of Sittway. As mentioned above, it was not 'Rohingya', but "Rakhine-Chittagong" that was listed as an ethnic identifier in 1973. But even this category was not applied in a coherent way. In the 1973 Census lists for Arakan State, it was the appellation "India-Pakistan" that was used to record people of allegedly South Asian origins.[72] Only in the late 1970s or early 1980s, the appellation 'Bengali' became the preferred administrative term for the majority of Muslims in Arakan. It was unacceptable to all those who affirmed a Rohingya identity, but it was not questioned internationally until 2012. From a global perspective, the name 'Rohingya' led a marginal existence until 2012. The unprecedented international reaction to the two waves of collective violence in Rakhine State in June and October 2012 also amplified the contestation of names and categories. The next section illustrates the latest chapter of this controversy.

In conclusion, the case of Arakan/Rakhine State's populations shows how in independent Burma, ethno-racial classification remained an instrument of inclusion (for the Buddhist majority) or marginalization and exclusion (for the Muslims). The racialized classification of the 1931 Census did not corroborate but eroded the historically grounded profile of indigenous Muslims. It also shows that while the categories or names within the classification were changing in response to evolving administrative (citizenship regimes) and political circumstances (East Pakistan becoming Bangladesh in 1971), the racial ideology which underpinned classification did not change. As a result, a persisting mistrust and an uncompromising stance on competing historical claims became the default mode of Buddhist-Muslim relations at the political level.

20.3. Names and Categories: Where the Colonial and Post-Colonial Overlap

The plight of the Rohingyas offers an extreme example of ethnoreligious discrimination in a context where anti-Indian resentment, barefaced racism and Islámophobia, as detailed above, were compounded by conflicting political and territorial interests, interethnic divisions, demographic pressure, illicit border crossings and a contested history of migrations. The link between ethnonyms (Rohingya, Bengali) and categories is another feature of this complexity. The

72 Socialist Republic of the Union of Myanmar, Home and Religious Affairs Ministry (Immigration), *Census of 1973 – Rakhine State*, Rangoon, 1974.

contestation of the self-identification of North Arakan Muslims as an indigenous ethnic Rohingya group exemplifies how the rigidity and the politicization of the racial classification generated incompatible claims. Rohingya writers reference the historical presence of Muslims in the former Arakanese kingdom and state that they are indigenous people. The Myanmar authorities have publicly denied their claim since the early 1990s, arguing that there is no historical evidence of a pre-colonial Rohingya ethnicity and call them 'Bengali'. The Arakanese (Rakhine) Buddhists look upon the Rohingyas as the descendants of colonial-period migrants.

When Myanmar moved out of several decades of isolation in 2011, the acrimonious debate about the competing names, Rohingya and Bengali, surprised newcomers to the country. Outsiders found it odd that 'Bengali' was an item of hate speech in contemporary Rakhine State and on social media, but not in Yangon's public space or the rest of Myanmar. Throughout the last decade, foreign media have annotated the use of 'Bengali' by the authorities with the explanation that the term unduly insinuates that in Rakhine State, Rohingyas were interlopers from Bangladesh. This is a correct, but incomplete clarification. Transborder movements were a contested issue between the neighbouring countries since the creation of an international frontier in 1947. Public discussions re-surfaced with every armed border clash, reports on human trafficking and refugee crises.[73] In 1978, the international press and UN observers did not deny that illegal migration was a reason behind the heavy-handed immigration controls and the panicked mass flight of 200,000 Muslims from Rakhine State to Bangladesh.[74] The international perception changed after the outbreak of violence in 2012 when analysts argued that poor people (from Bangladesh) would not move to an even poorer country where Muslims were discriminated. This argument makes sense but in a *longue durée* perspective, one should consider changes in the economic and political conditions on *both* sides of the border. Even during the colonial period, Chittagonian migration did not singularly depend on Arakan's appeal for landless migrants, but also on conditions in Bengal (overpopulation, the prospect of sufficient harvests, famine, drought, *et cetera*) that impacted emigration.

Before becoming a global household name for the victimization of a Muslim minority in Myanmar, the name 'Rohingya' had to be glossed when it was used outside the circle of UN organizations and non-governmental organizations reporting on the humanitarian situation and the statelessness of Rohingya

73 Jacques P. Leider, "Mass Departures in the Rakhine-Bangladesh Borderlands", Policy Brief Series No. 111 (2020), Torkel Opsahl Academic EPublisher, Brussels, 2020 (http://www.toaep.org/pbs-pdf/111-leider/).

74 The issue of illegal immigration is discussed in Fleischmann, 1981, see *supra* note 43.

refugees. It was neither well-known in Myanmar (outside of Rakhine State) nor in the wider region. Rohingya organizations had advocated for their cause and their chosen name for a long time, most recently following the second mass flight to Bangladesh in 1991–92 and in the wake of the irregular migrant boat crisis in the Bay of Bengal in 2009. However, they gained a wider hearing only when the two waves of violent clashes in Rakhine State made international headlines in 2012. The horrific impact of the brutal military operations in 2016–17 amplified the humanitarian resonance. For nearly a decade (2012–2021), the stream of images on social media documenting the condition of Rohingyas displaced in Rakhine State or driven into Bangladesh kept international attention at a high level.[75] The name 'Rohingya' became accepted in global media as an exclusive appellation for Muslims of Rakhine State. More Muslims in Rakhine State openly identified as Rohingyas. Adding to the hostile constellation of Myanmar security forces, Rakhine Buddhists and Rohingya Muslims opposed each to each other, international humanitarian, legal and mass media voices further complicated the narrative about Rohingya victimhood. As a consequence of the international recognition of the name 'Rohingya', 'Bengali', the government's preferred term, was perceived as a violation of the group's right to self-identify and rejected by media outside the country as part of Islámophobic speech. Nonetheless, there is a long history of naming and categorizing Muslims in Arakan/Rakhine State and both terms cannot be separated from the historical context of migrations, border politics and the cultural frontier.[76]

'Bengali' and 'Rohingya' denote different approaches to the historical genealogy of Muslims in ancient and modern Arakan. The case of the small precolonial Muslim community of the Kaman in South Rakhine State shows that acculturation could transform a Muslim group over time into an accepted ethnic community. In the case of the modern Rohingyas, it is not the process of their ongoing ethnification that is relevant for our analysis, but the political acceptance of a Rohingya ethnicity.

In 1948, North Arakan Muslim leaders referred to themselves as 'sons of the soil' and trusted that they could pass a 'racial' test and become accepted as an indigenous race of Burma. To ease political acceptance by Burma's leaders, they de-Indianized their community by denying foreign roots and pleaded

[75] Research led by the EFEO centre in Bangkok on Rohingya-related events shows that following the new international interest in the Rohingya plight between 2012 and 2016, the number of mixed academic-activist events, charity events and fundraisers quadrupled in 2017 and 2018.

[76] Jacques P. Leider, "From Aracan Mahomedans to Muslim Rohingyas – Towards an Archive of Naming Practices", in Surakarn Thoesomboon and Aurapin Khamson (eds.), *Past Identity and Authenticity of Ethnology Art and Archaeology*, Princess Maha Chakri Sirindhorn Anthropology Centre, Bangkok, 2018, pp. 213–270.

loyalty to the state. When the last Mujahid rebels surrendered their arms in 1961, Brigadier General Aung Gyi gave a speech where he generously acknowledged the desire of the rebels to be called 'Rohingyas'. This openness on behalf of the government was good politics, but Aung Gyi assimilated their situation with ethnic groups in the country who lived on two sides of the national borders. Aung Gyi's speech is commonly referenced as proof that the Burmese government recognized the Rohingyas as an indigenous ethnic group, but the Rohingyas have never seen themselves as a population living on two sides of the border. Refugee studies undertaken in the camps of Bangladesh have taught us much about the linguistic and cultural specificity of Rohingyas, but the issue of a, culturally speaking, Bengali Muslim heritage shared across the border is mostly left unspoken.[77]

One may take note that discussions about the recognition of the Rohingyas by the state before 1962 do generally refer to the acknowledgment of their citizenship rights in line with the 1947 citizenship law that defined a single kind of citizenship. Indigeneity was always taken for granted by the Rohingya leaders, but it became an object of political controversy only in public discussions that followed the 1982 citizenship law. Its three-tiered citizenship made indigeneity a condition of full citizenship.

The contestation about the name 'Rohingya' and about the indigenous character of North Arakan Muslims was a smouldering conflict before 1991. During the following decades, the confrontation gained momentum with printed and digital publications disseminating the related historical arguments. The intensity of the conflict was due to the fact that the contending parties argue within the *same* ideological framework with its essentialized understanding of ethnicity and indigeneity. 'Bengali' and 'Rohingya' function as names, but also as categories that prolong the colonial mode of racialized classification and hence prejudice. 'Bengali' denotes the linguistic, cultural and historical links of generations of Muslims with pre-colonial and colonial Bengal. It is the most frequent term found in the archive since Arakan's annexation in 1826. Referring to seasonal labourers and Muslims settling under British rule alike, in most contexts it is synonymous with 'Indian' and 'Chittagonian'. However, after World War I, British census officers differentiated Bengalis and Chittagonians (people coming from Bengal's Chittagong Division) because of the great number of Chittagonians. Chittagonians formed by themselves a quarter of all the Indians in Burma in the 1930s and most of them worked in Arakan. In the 1950s, the term 'Pakistani' was still temporarily in use. As Lower Bengal became East Pakistan

---

77 Kazi F. Farzana, "Music and Artistic Artifacts: Symbols of Rohingya Identity and Everyday Resistance in Borderlands", in *Austrian Journal of South-East Asian Studies*, 2011, vol. 4, no. 2, pp. 215–236.

in 1947, the government of Pakistan recognized that there were people in Arakan who had the right to claim Pakistani citizenship. As mentioned before, 'Bengali' became the standard administrative appellation in the 1970s and 1980s. The Myanmar government requests Rohingyas to accept the appellation 'Bengali' to enter the citizenship verification process. Such a condition goes against their self-identification and implicitly denies indigeneity. It may result in the obtaining of naturalized citizenship which encases Rohingyas in the same condition of social and political marginalization shared by other Muslims with Indian roots.

'Rohingya' denotes the territorial belonging of Muslims to Rohang, or Arakan, and their claim of being indigenous people of mixed South Asian origins, and *not* the descendants of recently arrived migrants from Chittagong. The implication of their classification as an indigenous group would be the recognition of first-class citizenship like Myanmar's eight official race-groups. Oral forms of the name 'Rohingya' are unquestionably old but lack written evidence. Rare occurrences are found in the writings of Francis Buchanan. Rohingyas saw their claims confirmed with the academic rediscovery around 2003 of Buchanan's article on the description of languages in the late eighteenth century. Muslims and Hindus residing in Arakan had been deported together with thousands of Buddhist Arakanese by the Burmese king to the capital Amarapura after the conquest of the kingdom in 1784.[78] Buchanan's Hindu Brahmin informers at the court of Amarapura referred to Arakan as "Rooinga" (a term used by Muslims) or "Rossawn" (as used by Hindus).[79] Both terms are vernacular forms of the classic Bengali word for Arakan, Roshanga.[80] Modern Rohingyas interpret the occurrence as proof that a self-identifying Muslim population using the name 'Rohingya' had existed in pre-colonial times. Hindus do not. The existence of pre-colonial Muslim communities in Arakan is uncontroversial. Arakanese slave-raiding along the coasts of Bengal went on until the 1770s and many of the deported Bengalis were forced to work on royal fields. Others were at the service of the court in Mrauk U. But there is no written vernacular evidence of

---

78 Francis Buchanan, "A Comparative Vocabulary of Some of the Languages Spoken in the Burma Empire", in *Asiatic Researches or Transactions of the Society instituted in Bengal for inquiring into the History and Antiquities the Arts, Sciences and Literature of Asia*, 1799, vol. 5, pp. 219–40. The text was reprinted by Full Professor Michael W. Charney in the *School of Oriental and African Studies (SOAS) Bulletin of Burma Research*, 2003, vol. 1, no. 1, pp. 40–57.

79 Former UK Ambassador Derek Tonkin pointed out via Twitter that Buchanan's manuscript diary kept at the British Library (Mss Eur C 13) proves that Buchanan did not receive his information on the people and languages spoken in Arakan from Muslim but from Hindu Brahmin deportees.

80 Thibaut d'Hubert, "Oral Communication", 3 August 2012, fully cited in Jacques P. Leider, "Rohingya: The Name, the Movement, the Quest for Identity", in *Nation Building in Myanmar*, Myanmar Egress/Myanmar Peace Center, Yangon, 2013, pp. 226–27.

the name, and it does not appear in British administrative or census reports after the annexation in 1826.

From the late 1940s to the early 1960s, however, various forms, such as 'Rwangya', 'Rawangya', 'Roewengya' or 'Ruhinja', circulated in English and Burmese publications and point to a revival of the old orally-used name. To emphasize a distinctive Muslim identity, local leaders and politically active Muslim students from North Arakan combined the name in the 1950s with their claim of a historically grounded and shared Muslim identity. The endeavour to obtain recognition for their name has always been considerable because the Rohingyas see it as an external confirmation of their ethnic identity. During the last decade, global acceptance pulled the name Rohingya from several decades of an obscure existence.

During the so-called parliamentary period under Prime Minister U Nu and the caretaker rule of General Ne Win (1948–62), the emerging Rohingya movement was a marginal, but nonetheless exceptional phenomenon in Burma's political landscape. Among the different Muslim communities which had historically formed in Myanmar's distant or more recent past (such as Burmese/Myanmar or Union Muslims, Indian Muslims, Pashu Muslims with Malay roots, Panthay Muslims descending from nineteenth-century Yunnan refugees, Myedu and Kaman of South Arakan, Shia Muslims with ancestors coming from Iraq in the late nineteenth century, *et cetera*), the Rohingyas were the only group that actively fought for the recognition of an indigenous ethnic status. Burmese/Myanmar Muslims could have made similar historically grounded claims of indigeneity because their ancestors lived in the coastal ports or served Burmese kings since the early modern period. To counter prejudice and bouts of Islámophobic violence by Buddhist chauvinists, Burmese Muslim leaders emphasized that they were Burmese and shared the same ethnic and cultural identity as Buddhists. North Arakan Muslim leaders, however, were afraid of being ruled by the Arakanese Buddhists. Different options seemed viable after the war. Following the ethnic cleansing in 1942 where thousands of Muslims were driven out of Central Arakan and Muslim settlers chased away the Buddhist population of Maungdaw, the population of the border area supported Allied war efforts and experienced a regime of quasi-autonomy under the British 'Military Administration of Arakan' until 1945. But when prompted to show their gratitude in 1947, the British refused to grant the region the status of a Muslim frontier state in recognition of the Muslims' auxiliary services during the war. A second option, joining Pakistan, was rejected by Pakistan's and Burma's respective leaders. A third option chosen by the Mujahid rebels fighting for an autonomous Muslim state within the Union of Burma made the region into a war zone for several years and ultimately failed.

In the middle of the political chaos of the late 1940s, North Arakan parliamentarian Mohammed Abdul Gafar fought hard to discard the reputation of being secessionists and, in November 1948, argued that the Muslims of North Arakan were a nation of their own.[81] While he did not use the name 'Rohingya', one may consider 1948 as the foundational moment of the modern Rohingya movement. But Gafar's seminal role passed by with little notice as the unity of Burma was threatened by civil war and the country on the brink of disaster in 1949. The political goal of Gafar and his colleague Sultan Ahmed was to shed the perceived foreignness of a population which the British administrators had invariably called 'Chittagonians' until 1947. In doing so, they wanted to level up with the Arakanese whom they saw as political rivals but who were not yet recognized as a group deserving its own ethnic state. But how could Gafar explain his novel claims as there was no agreement among the Muslim political class itself about a common identity? Sultan Mahmood, a rival political leader, wanted to stick with the established appellation of 'Arakan Muslims'. Some ten years later, between 1958 and 1965, a relative of Gafar, the young Mohammed Abdul Tahir Ba Tha (1932–2017), published a series of articles in English in *The Guardian* and a seminal book in Burmese, which sketched a cultural history of Arakanese Muslims as Rohingyas assimilating their case with the Kamans, the old ethnic Muslim community in Southern Arakan.[82] Ba Tha's work marked a break with earlier efforts to integrate the North Arakan Muslims of mixed origins into the history of Burmese Muslims. Muhammad Khalilur Rahman's *Tarikh-i-Islam: Arakan aur Burma* (1944) and Azadi G. Hasan's *Qaum-i-halat-imusulmanane Burma wa Rakhine* (1946), both written in Urdu, had tried to connect the history of Arakanese Muslims to the general history of Islám in Burma, but they did not claim that Arakanese Muslims were a distinct ethnic population.[83]

It is this history of the becoming of the modern Rohingyas which is poorly acknowledged by Rohingya communal leaders today and passed over in accounts that advocate for the rights of the group. After 2012, the co-production of knowledge on the Rohingyas was exclusively framed by the moral and legal representation of the group's refugee and victimhood status. Rohingya advocacy introduced them one-sidedly as passive victims who need international support

---

81 Gafar, 1948, see *supra* note 71.

82 Mohammad A.T. Ba Tha, *Rui haṅ gyā nhaṅ. Kaman lū myuiḥ cu myāḥ* (Rohingyas and Kamans), United Rohingya National League, Myitkyina, 1963. The book was translated into English by Abdul Faiz in 1998. Several of Ba Tha's articles can be found in "Arakania", available on the Network Myanmar's web site, under section S. 1959–1989.

83 Jacques P. Leider, "Rohingya: The History of a Muslim Identity in Myanmar", in David Ludden (ed.), *Oxford Research Encyclopedia of Asian History*, Oxford University Press, 2018.

and humanitarian intervention.[84] The process of disseminating an international message on the downtrodden Rohingyas also validated and invalidated names as acceptable or unacceptable.[85] 'Rohingya' entered international parlance as *the* sole politically correct term, while 'Bengali', the appellation used by the state authorities, was discredited as hate speech and implicitly prohibited.

20.4. Conclusion

Critical historical analyses tend to blur moral and legal categories of good and bad and right and wrong because they focus on the complications of agency and power relations. The dynamics of group actors such as Indian labour migrants, Burmese nationalists, Muslim elites, security forces, colonial administrators or ethnic minorities invariably create confusing storylines where motives and actions get enmeshed. The challenge for those who take a historical approach is therefore to disentangle and rebalance the threads and narratives that emerge from descriptive accounts.

The history of the condition of Indians and communities of Indian origins in Burma from the nineteenth to the early twenty-first century testifies to a loss of agency and power after 1937 and much more so after 1945 and 1962; in sum, it is the decline of the considerable social, economic and political roles they held under British rule and their collective marginalization in independent Burma. The introduction started with the observation that Muslims of Indian origins were disproportionately victims of hate speech and religiously motivated violence in Buddhist Burma. As their agency declined, their victimization increased. There is a stark contrast between the self-confident Rohingya movement of the 1950s, which competed successfully with the Arakanese nationalists, and the punishing treatment the Rohingyas incurred during the three decades that followed the first mass flight of 1978. However, even if patterns of violence are often similar, the conditions of discrimination and the production of hate speech in the colonial society were very different from those under which marginalization and violence against people with South Asian roots were created in authoritarian Burma. The colonial state was exploitative but indifferent to racial strife, while the military regime acted as a predator and manipulated ethno-racial

[84] Azeem Ibrahim, *The Rohingyas: Inside Myanmar's Hidden Genocide*, Hurst, London, 2016; Ronan Lee, *Myanmar's Rohingya Genocide: Identity, History and Hate Speech*, I.B. Tauris Bloomsbury Publishing, London, 2021.

[85] The quintessential example of Burmese hate speech has been *kalar*, denounced as a slur for Indian Muslims. In the twenty-first century, it ranks at the level of the unspeakable North-American 'n' word. The original meaning of *kalar* is a person from the West, commonly an Indian and more specifically a Muslim. The term still appears, though, in a variety of contexts where it has no racist connotations.

conflict for its interests. This insight led to the question if there is nonetheless a meaningful connection between both periods.

The contention of the article has been that prejudice and the relative ease to ignite racially and religiously motivated conflict were transmitted with the postcolonial state's entrenchment of colonial categories. The racialized classification which had evolved as an experimental 'ethnological' way of categorizing people in late colonial Burma was normalized in independent Burma. The second section described how the classification of the 1931 Census was adapted to the requirements of the nationalist ideology culminating in a dogmatic list of 135 ethnicities considered 'indigenous'. The marginalization and the exclusion of people with Indian origins, in particular Muslims, was rationalized via the differentiation of indigenous, mixed (less 'racially pure' in the language of the time) and foreign groups. Under military rule, the authoritarian state's administrative practice stressed ethno-racial otherness for the sake of marginalization. The 1982 citizenship law reflects the military regime's obsession with racial difference and its perceived need to create barriers to citizenship. The inflexible list of 135 ethnic groups proclaimed in 1989 was the result of a process of ideologizing indigeneity and racial belonging.

The third section focused on the case of the Rohingyas because the contestation of their name by the government since the 1990s is illustrative of the fact that names are not just names but tied to racial categories. Accepting the name 'Rohingya' signals the acceptance of indigeneity and the right for full citizenship, while the government's official appellation 'Bengali' denotes foreignness and raises suspicion of illegal residence. Only the recognition of indigeneity as defined by the state gives access to the right of full citizenship. Only a fluid and fairer understanding of ethnic identity and national belonging could lead to a different citizenship regime. But both sides partake of the same conceptual framework and remain attached to the existing racialized classification. As it has been argued above, in contemporary Myanmar, the '135' avatar of the late colonial classification remains the quasi-natural expression of the country's ethnic diversity and a shared ideological cornerstone of Myanmar's ethnic nationalisms. It authenticates inequality and does not bode well for the demise of prejudice, interethnic discord or a decrease of xenophobia.

21

Exploiting Social Influence: Embedded Human Agency and Perversion of Religion

Song Tianying*

21.1. Perversion of Religion Within Local Community

During the Khmer Rouge rule in Cambodia, the regime cited Buddhist teachings to support torture, killing and elimination of intellectual and urban life. The Buddhist concept of mindfulness was applied to improve a person's "revolutionary consciousness".[1] Buddhist teachings about detachment were used to rationalize severing one's personal relationships – family members should report on each other to Khmer Rouge leaders. Torturers and executioners were instructed to be good Buddhists who do not indulge in anger and exercise self-discipline when carrying out their tasks.[2]

Is there something in Buddhist teachings that is inherently conducive to atrocity? Certainly not. The wrong does not lie in general principles, norms, values, but in their local interpretation and application. Religious doctrines are not self-interpreting. They must be given "socially relevant interpretation".[3] The concrete interpretation is then applied by agents with pre-existing moral perception.[4] Interpretation can be done by persons both within and outside the religious institution. Throughout history, flexible and creative interpretation of religious script and canons has helped religions to survive, adapt to and

---

* Dr **Song Tianying** is a Researcher at the European University Institute, Law Department. She formerly served as a Legal Officer in the Regional Delegation for East Asia of the International Committee of the Red Cross (Beijing). She holds a Master's degree in international law and a Bachelor's degree in law from China University of Political Science and Law. She holds a doctoral degree from the European University Institute (Florence). She was awarded the 2016 M.C. Bassiouni Justice Award. For a film of her presentation at the CILRAP conference on Religion, Hateful Expression and Violence in Florence on 9 April 2022, see https://www.cilrap.org/cilrap-film/220409-song/.

1 Alexander Hinton, *Why Did They Kill? Cambodia in the Shadow of Genocide*, University of California Press, Berkeley, 2005, cited in Matthew Talbert and Jessica Wolfendale, *War Crimes, Causes, Excuses, and Blame*, Oxford Scholarship Online, 2018, p. 60.

2 *Ibid.*

3 Herlinde Pauer-Studer and James D. Velleman, "Distortion of Normativity", in *Ethical Theory and Moral Practice*, 2011, vol. 14, no. 3, p. 333.

4 *Ibid.*

contribute to major social transformations.[5] Yet religion as a human practice is not immune to human error. It can be used to legitimize and normalize hatred and violence. Those subscribing to such interpretations do not think their horrible atrocities violate religious teachings; on the contrary, they think their acts are permitted or even required by their faith. In other words, they are striving to conform to a thorough moral order, albeit a perverted one.[6] There is a confusion of immorality with duty. Religious teachings fail to impose moral scrutiny, and even sanctify immorality. This is a kind of "moral inversion".[7]

Contingent social factors mediate between abstract norms and their application in concrete situations.[8] Religious teachings filtered through hate speech can give a situation a "distorted normative significance".[9] There can be two kinds of mistakes here. The first one is failure of moral perception, that is, failing to see and evaluate the "morally questionable features" in a situation.[10] A terrorist sees his attack as solely serving a righteous cause, not as killing the innocent, such is a failure of moral perception. The second mistake is misinterpretation of the guidelines for action in the concrete situation.[11] The Nazi doctor thinks of gassing as a "humanitarian treatment" which spares victims of slow and painful death in the concentration camp, such is a misinterpretation of humanitarianism.[12] Hate speech parasitic on religion can help create erroneous perceptions and interpretations with serious consequences. It can enable moral disengagement through a kind of "cognitive restructuring".[13] This explains in some circumstances why noble principles and teachings do not deter atrocities but rather legitimize them.

Now I review four strategies commonly used in hate speech to create misperception and misinterpretation.

21.2. Strategies to Incite Intergroup Hatred and Violence

Hatred consists of "habitual bitter feeling and accusatory thought" and persisting "aggressive impulses toward a person or class of persons".[14] Hate speech, in

---

5 Samir Amin, *Eurocentrism*, 2nd ed., Monthly Review Press, 2010, p. 26.

6 Pauer-Studer and Velleman, 2011, see *supra* note 3.

7 *Ibid.*

8 *Ibid.*, p. 7.

9 *Ibid.*, p. 13.

10 *Ibid.*, pp. 6, 8.

11 *Ibid.*

12 *Ibid.*, p. 18.

13 Albert Bandura, "Selective Activation and Disengagement of Moral Control", in *Journal of Social Issues*, 1990, vol. 46, no. 1, p. 29.

14 Joanna Bourke, *An Intimate History of Killing: Face to Face Killing in 20th Century Warfare*, Granta Books, 1999, p. 139.

its potential to incite intergroup violence, is often directed against a certain group of people. Defining an enemy is the starting point. It serves to transform immoral and illegal acts into moral and even honourable acts. The ideal enemy is different, evil and dangerous. Group identity becomes the dominant form of identity. 'Us' and 'Them' become incompatible categories: our gain is their loss, our victory is their defeat. Intergroup relationship becomes a zero-sum game.

21.2.1. Group Identity Replacing Personal Identity

David Berreby proposes two modes of thought and feelings about others: one is to see individuals who possess traits; the other is to see traits that possess individuals.[15] They respectively emphasize individuality and commonality of human beings. They are natural ways for human beings to process information about others. When the traits-possessing individual thinking is manipulated, preconceived group traits completely overtake individual differences. Individuals are perceived as only components of the group, not whole in themselves. They are rendered 'interchangeable instances' of a certain human category. Obliteration of individuality is especially forced upon those who are seen as members of the enemy. The victim is no longer an individual with a unique history, character, but a "specimen"[16] of the enemy group. There is no conflict or clash between individuals involved, only collective struggles. Individual members of the enemy group are compelled to answer for everything their fellow members do.[17] The individual becomes a symbol, a mark, a means to the collective ends. Her worth and standing are determined by group membership. The fate of the group becomes the fate of its members. Total identification with the group makes 'your group is your destiny' a self-fulfilling prophecy.[18]

21.2.2. One Group Identity Overruling Other Identities

Following deindividuation, hate speech tends to insist on one particular group membership which sharply distinguishes one's own group and the enemy. People are fixed to a single group identity which is presented as permanent and inevitable. In doing so, it seeks to eliminate occasions where sympathy may arise out of similarities with the enemy. Natural human fellowship means people can easily see others belonging to many different groups and relate to some of these identities. It is not natural that a Buddhist cannot see anything in common with a non-Buddhist. It takes "powerful persuasion" to blind us to other people's

[15] David Berreby, *Us and Them: The Science of Identity*, University of Chicago Press, 2008, p. xiv.

[16] Arne J. Vetlesen, *Evil and Human Agency*, Cambridge University Press, 2005, p. 261.

[17] *Ibid.*, p. 176.

[18] *Ibid.*, p. 7.

multiple identities and their "potential as teammates".[19] The one-dimensional understanding of identity is completely artificial, "an ideologically concocted construct" that needs to be imposed from outside and actively sustained.[20] The individual is locked into one human category, all the time, in all contexts.[21] For example, stigmatization is used to paralyze "the normal shifting process" where people might see different identities of the same person in different contexts.[22] It impoverishes human imagination for alternatives. The result: a permanent "spoiled identity" – the stigmatized are always and only the bad kind of people.[23]

To reduce and entrap the individual to one identity reflects a dichotomous way of thinking, a kind of narrow-mindedness in its mild form, a real catastrophe when carried to extreme. In times of social crisis, of uncertainty and change, a simple approach to identity can be very persuasive. The dichotomous logic is typical of hate speech, war, ethnic cleansing and genocide. It freezes our perceptions with fear. When the "homogeneous and exclusivist" ideology successfully replaces the "heterogeneous and hybrid" reality,[24] the enemy is firmly established.

21.2.3. Dehumanization of 'Other'

Deindividuation1 and single group identity pave way for dehumanization. After eliminating possible overlapping social identities, hate speech tends to eliminate the one natural identity that is common to all human beings – the human identity. Dehumanization is the ultimate categorical distinction. When one sees another as a fellow human being, one tends to react to another's experience empathetically through perceived similar human qualities. Harming "humanized persons" can cause distress and self-censure because of "vicarious emotional activation".[25] Dehumanization divests people of human qualities.[26] It entails "psychological mechanisms of intellectualization, denial, and the isolation of affect".[27] The dehumanized are no longer seen as persons with feelings and thoughts, but as "subhuman" or "mindless" objects.[28] While human relationships are

[19] Berreby, 2008, p. 89, see *supra* note 15.

[20] Vetlesen, 2005, p. 156, see *supra* note 16.

[21] Berreby, 2008, p. 89, see *supra* note 15.

[22] *Ibid.*

[23] *Ibid.*, p. 232.

[24] Vetlesen, 2005, p. 156, see *supra* note 16.

[25] Bandura, 1990, p. 38, see *supra* note 13.

[26] *Ibid.*

[27] Philip Zimbardo, *The Lucifer Effect: Understanding How Good People Turn Evil*, Random House Trade Paperbacks, 2008, p. 223.

[28] Bandura, 1990, see *supra* note 13.

"subjective, personal, and emotional", dehumanized relationships are objectifying, analytical and empty of emotional or empathic content.[29] As such dehumanization excludes some human beings from "the moral order" of the human world.[30] Albert Bandura argues that the process of dehumanization is essential to the perpetration of inhumanities.[31]

When a group is dehumanized, its members cease to have moral worth or standing as fellow human beings. Individuals belonging to the enemy group are not fully human, not capable of thinking rationally and feeling pain. Degrading nicknames are invented to reinforce the prejudice and hatred towards the enemy. Dehumanizing names remind people of the inferior status, barbarous culture, or simply utter alienness of their enemy. Dehumanizing acts follow.

Through dehumanization, hate speech enables selective moral disengagement towards the enemy. Moral disengagement means suspension of morality which typically governs "reasoned actions" towards our fellow humans.[32] "Cognitive controls" that guide us to act "in socially desirable and personally acceptable ways are blocked, suspended, or distorted".[33] Together with traditional cognitive and moral constraints, all the natural human emotions, perception and judgment are suspended. This helps insulate or disassociate people's daily life from the hatred and ensuing violence incited by hate speech.[34] Bandura argues that dehumanization fosters self-exonerative thinking towards victims. People rationalize, rather than condemn, harmful conduct towards dehumanized persons.[35] By rationalizing, desensitizing hatred and violence towards the enemy, hate speech creates moral and psychological distance which facilitates harmful conduct. It amounts to "social production of moral indifference".[36] The intersubjective relationship between human beings is gone at all times, in all occasions. Evil thrives in "an ecology of dehumanization".[37]

---

29 Zimbardo, 2008, see *supra* note 27.

30 *Ibid.*, p. 307.

31 Bandura, 1990, see *supra* note 13.

32 Zimbardo, 2008, p. 307, see *supra* note 27.

33 *Ibid.*, p. 305.

34 Peter H. Wilson, "Defining Military Culture", in *The Journal of Military History*, 2008, vol. 72, no. 1, p. 35.

35 Bandura, 1990, p. 39, see *supra* note 13.

36 Zygmunt Bauman, *Modernity and the Holocaust*, Cornell University Press, Ithaca, 2001, cited in Jean-Jacques Frésard, *Roots of Behaviour in War: A Survey of the Literature*, International Committee of the Red Cross, 2004, p. 65.

37 Zimbardo, 2008, p. 223, see *supra* note 27.

21.2.4. Righteousness

While one side of hate speech is hatred, the other side is blinding self-righteousness. Group identity usually fosters a sense of pride, unity, shared fate, and importantly, righteousness. Within the group, the sense of self-righteousness is inflated and consolidated. Hate speech often capitalizes on such righteous feeling. Intergroup conflicts are ultimately about "whose 'right' is righter".[38] Intuitive superior feelings are perfectly rationalized no matter how remote they are from the reality. We are against them because they are 'bad'. We are noble, civilized, moral and intelligent; they, the enemy, are perfidious, barbaric, unethical and stupid. A "master narrative" keeps track of all the historical wrongs of and contemporary threats from the enemy.[39] The master narrative is part of the "collective memory" of the group, or some would rather say, the "collective instruction". It stipulates common ideas of significance and triggers predictable thoughts and feelings.[40] Hate speech delivers the satisfaction of winning the intergroup competition of righteousness. Religious concepts can be manipulated to support the group's perceived righteous cause.

It is no surprise that self-defence is frequently invoked in hate speech. We are always the victim, and they, the villain. If our group is not being harmed right now, it was harmed in the past or will be harmed in the future. Aggression is rationalized through retrospective vengeance (righting previous wrongs) and pre-emptive attack (preventing future attacks).[41] Aggression against the enemy, when equalled to one's own survival, becomes "imperative and necessary, not optional and avoidable".[42] As long as one is on the right side of the struggle, any means one employs to achieve the goal is justified.

By mythologizing history and perpetuating victimhood of self, the righteous narrative reverses the roles of perpetrator and victim: the victim is seen as the perpetrator and perpetrator as victim. A sense of "historical and moral entitlement" justifies worst atrocities.[43] Hate speech imparts this sense of self-righteousness through "cognitive restructuring":[44] harmful conducts are reconstrued as good and moral; evil lies in those who 'deserve' suffering. The "ideological preparation" convinces the perpetrator that her action is honourable, just and

---

[38] Robert Sapolsky, *Behave: The Biology of Humans at our Best and Worst*, Penguin Press, 2017, p. 509.

[39] Vetlesen, 2005, p. 151, see *supra* note 16.

[40] Susan Sontag, *Regarding the Pain of Others*, Penguin, 2004, p. 76.

[41] Vetlesen, 2005, p. 151, see *supra* note 16.

[42] *Ibid.*, p. 146.

[43] *Ibid.*, p. 151.

[44] Bandura, 1990, p. 29, see *supra* note 13.

immune from punishment; it blocks feelings of guilt, shame, or remorse towards the victims.[45]

In sum, hate speech monopolizes group identity, dehumanizes the enemy and exploits righteous feelings. It prevents the agent from seeing the morally salient features in the single-minded opposition with the perceived enemy. This helps create an atrocity-producing environment.

21.3. Embedded Human Agency and Power of Social Influence

How could it happen that people adopt rather than condemn hate speech? Why is it that so many cannot see hate speech as it is – a travesty of spirit, a distortion of reality and an exploitation of human vulnerability? Is not the wrong of hate speech axiomatic? Is not morality a central feature of our common humanity? It is assumed that every human being, in virtue of her humanity, should know certain acts are immoral and illegal. And that a 'normal' person should have the inner strength to resist bad social influences. Human beings aspire to be rational actors who can appraise their circumstances in a detached manner and always act in accordance with their judgment. We should not confuse aspiration with reality. When we judge others' behaviour *ex post facto* and declare it unthinkable, we take God's perspective. We erect a "seemingly impermeable boundary between Good and Evil", in great simplification of human experience.[46]

It takes concrete persons who are deeply embedded in their community to adopt and implement hate speech. Human beings are social beings whose attitudes and acts are guided and shaped by their social environment. If our genetics or disposition is like 'hardware', our 'cultural software' determines how this hardware functions. This cultural software is learned from society, not inherited.[47] Roberto Unger says that the human brain is individual, but the mind as consciousness is social. He argues that the "means by which we develop a subjective life, from language to discourse, from ideas to practice, are all a common possession and shared construction".[48] Bhikhu Parekh similarly reminds us that the individual is not "naturally given and biologically encapsulated" but "a social construction".[49] It is only through human interactions that we form and sustain an image of self.[50] It is a matter of "social practice" to draw boundaries

45 Vetlesen, 2005, pp. 176–177, see *supra* note 16.

46 Zimbardo, 2008, p. 211, see *supra* note 27.

47 Carmel O'Sullivan, *Killing on Command: The Defence of Superior Orders in Modern Combat*, Palgrave Macmillan, London, 2016, p. 188.

48 Roberto M. Unger, *The Religion of the Future*, Verso, 2016, p. 98.

49 "Introduction", in Bhikhu Parekh, *Ethnocentric Political Theory: The Pursuit of Flawed Universals*, Palgrave Macmillan, 2019, p. 12.

50 Unger, 2016, p. 85, see *supra* note 48.

between self and other and between human groups,[51] an insight often lost in discussions of human agency. The observations of Unger and Parekh concern fundamental human needs and social reality. To imagine the individual person with purely abstract features is to imagine an individual without context, without a history, a 'naked' individual. Such a "self-contained, singular and internally unified moral agent" does not exist in real life.[52]

Human identity is embedded and contextual. Culture and society constitute one's existence. Individuals develop their identity within a community where they are seen as competent and responsible speakers and actors.[53] Personal integrity depends on the integrity of "interpersonal relations of reciprocal recognition".[54] Selfhood is relative to the environment.[55] An individual's identity is heavily shaped by social groups and collective values. Religious identity remains one of the most powerful and salient forms of social identities.

Social engineering makes, at least in part, human experience and perception. Following the social code, people get the same lessons out of their experiences in life.[56] Culture and society predispose people to certain interpretations of situations and choices. Individuals are autonomous only in the sense that they can choose freely from the options offered by the society. Although many do not realize that their choice is 'pre-empted' by society's choice.[57] In particular, our visceral feelings of right and wrong do not arise in a social vacuum.[58] Moral intuition is "neither primordial nor reflexively primitive", but "end products of learning".[59] The Eichmann court pronounces that the wrongfulness of certain acts is so obvious and flagrant that it pierces the eye and revolts the heart, unless the eye is blind and the heart stony and corrupt.[60] The Eichmann court's belief in the wisdom of moral repugnance is widely shared in atrocity trials. But we should not overlook the second half of the court's pronouncement – that in a

---

51 Parekh, 2019, see *supra* note 49.

52 *Ibid.*

53 Arne J. Vetlesen, *Perception, Empathy and Judgment*, Pennsylvania State University Press, 1994, p. 319.

54 *Ibid.*

55 Richard Shapcott, *Justice, Community and Dialogue in International Relations*, Cambridge University Press, 2009, p. 34.

56 Berreby, 2008, p. 184, see *supra* note 15.

57 Vetlesen, 1994, p. 194, see *supra* note 53.

58 *Ibid.*

59 Sapolsky, 2017, p. 508, see *supra note* 38.

60 Supreme Court of Israel, *Adolf Eichmann v. The Attorney General*, Judgment, 29 May 1962, Criminal Appeal No. 336/61, para. 21 (http://www.legal-tools.org/doc/aceae7/), quoting an Israeli case, Israel Military Court, Central District 3/57, *Military Prosecutor v. Melinki*, Judgment, 13 October 1958, 17 Dist. Ct. Rep. 90.

certain social environment, a large part of the population has blind eyes and corrupted hearts. Our faith in the consistency of human conscience needs to be tempered by an understanding of social influence on personal morality. Moral intuition entails automatic, unconscious mental activities which are different from conscious reasoning. In fact, many have disclosed that moral reasoning is often "flagrantly illogical".[61] Arne Johan Vetlesen explains that our faculty of empathy, which is vital in our moral perception, is extremely vulnerable to societal manipulation.[62] Empathy can be selectively blocked *vis-à-vis* certain groups of people. When emotional abilities are suspended or impeded, the individual sees the other not as a relatable fellow human being, but as an abstract target. Our moral judgment is so indispensable yet so precarious.[63] It may be an unreliable guide when it is poisoned by a highly manipulative regime.

Empirical studies suggest that many people are capable of extreme violence under the right circumstances. Ervin Staub claims that it is the norm, not the exception that evil "arises out of ordinary thinking and is committed by ordinary people".[64] When linking research on mechanisms of moral disengagement to the historical chronicle of human atrocities, Bandura comments: "It requires conducive social conditions, rather than monstrous people, to produce heinous deeds. Given appropriate social conditions, decent, ordinary people can be led to do extraordinarily cruel things".[65] Manipulation of natural psychological processes such as motivations, thoughts and feelings can lead ordinary people to commit atrocities.[66] Philip Zimbardo's Stanford Prison Experiment shows that a permissive, enclosed prison environment can transform the moral standards of perfectly normal university students and cause them to mistreat their fellow students. Zimbardo observes that "total situations" can induce ordinary people to "act in irrational, stupid, self-destructive, antisocial, and mindless ways".[67]

Hate speech erodes moral perception and judgment. Participants in organized violence often do not lose all sense of morality, rather, they act according to inverted virtues, duty and practical wisdom.[68] Hate speech can initiate and

61 Sapolsky, 2017, p. 185, see *supra* note 38.

62 Vetlesen, 1994, p. 195, see *supra* note 53.

63 *Ibid.*

64 Cited in O'Sullivan, 2016, p. 143, see *supra* note 47.

65 Bandura, 1990, p. 39, see *supra* note 13.

66 O'Sullivan, 2016, p. 143, see *supra* note 47.

67 Zimbardo, 2008, p. 211, see *supra* note 27.

68 Talbert and Wolfendale, 2018, pp. 151–152, see *supra* note 1. Talbert and Wolfendale give the example of how the United States military quickly accepted and implemented so-called 'enhanced interrogation techniques' which amount to torture, in the aftermath of 9/11 terrorist attacks.

sustain a kind of "moral drift" – "a slide into evil" as people are "gradually acclimated to destructive norms".[69] What used to be unthinkable becomes normal. The "supportive organizational context" may well induce a "shared illusion" that members "are engaged in a legitimate enterprise".[70] That is, participants internalize the inverted moral order – their eyes blind and hearts corrupted. Hate speech parasitic on religion can significantly suppress available normative frameworks within a community through potent social influence. Mechanisms of social influence and engineering make the harm of hate speech serious and far-reaching.

Behavioural outcomes are results of complex interactions between the person and the situation.[71] There are numerous factors contributing to human atrocities; here, I focus on two social mechanisms hate speech typically exploits: social authority and group.

21.4. Mechanisms of Social Influence

Social influence links the individual to social structures. Use of authority, for example, is a form of social influence. Social influence induces change of behaviour, attitude or belief in the individual.[72] It happens because the individual feels compelled to comply with certain social norms, identifies with certain social roles, or internalizes certain social values. These are three processes of social influence proposed by Herbert Kelman: compliance, identification and internalization. By learning and adopting specific rules, role expectations and values of a society or group, the individual is socialized into the collective. Rule-, role- and value-orientations co-exist and are not mutually exclusive.[73] They are present in both authority and group situations.

21.4.1. Authority Defines the Situation and Interprets Religious Teachings

Through hate speech, religious and secular authorities can create normative frameworks which appropriate religion for their criminal causes. Authorities are particularly effective in shaping attitude and behaviour. Human beings have a natural tendency to obey authority, especially an apparently legitimate authority which is nearby. Stanley Milgram's experiments show that ordinary people are willing to administer electric shocks to a screaming victim at the polite, non-

---

69 John M. Doris, *Lack of Character: Personality and Moral Behavior*, Cambridge University Press, 2014, p. 57.

70 Herbert C. Kelman, "Violence without Moral Restraint: Reflections on the Dehumanization of Victims and Victimizers", in *Journal of Social Issues*, 1973, vol. 29, no. 4, p. 47.

71 Doris, 2014, p. 38, see *supra* note 69.

72 Herbert Kelman and V. Lee Hamilton, *Crimes of Obedience: Toward a Social Psychology of Authority and Responsibility*, Yale University Press, 1990, pp. 77, 78, 87.

73 *Ibid*., pp. 88–113.

coercive request of an experimenter. In these cases of voluntary obedience to a legitimate authority – such as the scientific staff – Milgram discerns 'an internalized basis' for obedience. That is, obedience is motivated by the actor's sense of obligation, not potential sanctions.[74] The obligation- or role-consciousness in ordinary people is an important basis for authority's social influence. People rarely realize how powerful and omnipresent social influence is. Once they are in an "action sequence", they tend to react "mindlessly" following routine scripts.[75] People often do not consciously choose to enact a script, they simply do what is expected of them in such a situation. Personal attitudes and preferences are not important to a person's entry into a script.[76] This role-based motivation is supplemented by fear of sanctions and internalization of values.

In the process of 'moral drift', authorization typically plays a key role in legitimizing previously illegitimate behaviours. Authority can influence through explicit order, implicit encouragement, tacit approval and permission. Hate speech is neither implicit nor tacit, it is open and direct incitement of hatred and hostilities. Religion, with its founding myths, history, customs, traditions, evokes profound spiritual and moral legitimacy among believers. Specific authorities, either religious or secular, also enjoy presumption of legitimacy among their constituencies. The sense of institutional legitimacy is transmitted through buildings, symbols, rituals, official documents, procedures, legal and administrative rules, appearance, *et cetera*. When local authorities issue specific statements and demands invoking religion, they combine their institutional legitimacy with that of religion and project strong normative influence on their constituency. When such statements and demands incite hatred and hostilities, they greatly enhance people's "readiness" to commit or at least condone abuses.[77] Kelman explains that behaviourally, official authorization carries "automatic justification" which makes it no longer necessary for actors to make judgment or choices themselves.[78] The actor is no longer an independent moral agent, but "an extension of the authority".[79] Sheer existence of authority suppresses individual agency, especially when the authority is trusted, legitimate, stable and nearby like a local religious or social authority.[80]

---

[74] Stanley Milgram, *Obedience to Authority: An Experimental View*, Harper and Row, New York, 1974, pp. 140–141.

[75] Kelman and Hamilton, 1990, p. 90, see *supra* note 72.

[76] *Ibid.*

[77] Kelman, 1973, p. 39, see *supra* note 70.

[78] *Ibid.*

[79] *Ibid.*

[80] Sapolsky, 2017, p. 470, see *supra* note 38.

In fact, people are willing to go very far to please the authority. Kelman argues that in situations of legitimate authority, individuals can focus on their role obligations at the expense of their personal interests and preferences.[81] He explains that authority can induce actions that call for considerable personal sacrifices on the part of the actor, as well as actions that go against the actor's personal judgment. This is possible because the actor has relinquished control and responsibility to authority.[82] For example, someone who personally disapproves killing and assault may easily perform these acts when commanded by authority.

It can be difficult for deeply-embedded members of the community to transcend the predominant normative framework in their immediate environment, and to think and act otherwise. Relatively few people have the resources needed to resist authority, or the authority's definition of the situation.[83] Unless the individual steps outside authority's definition of situation, she is not able to redefine the situation and challenge the legitimacy of the demand.[84]

21.4.2. Group Magnifies the Effect of Hate Speech

The normative framework created or endorsed by authority is disseminated and reinforced within the group. Hate speech does not stop at the immediate recipients, it spreads within the community and has a lasting effect. With its emphasis on intergroup conflict and single group identity, hate speech usually strengthens group thinking. Group thinking in turn intensifies emotions and radicalizes behaviours.

The group can be the main source of comfort, meaning and security for its members. The group imparts "a sense of limitless power" and "immortality" and provides emotional reliefs.[85] People rely on their immediate group to make sense of complex and ambiguous situations. Especially in times of social upheaval, there is a strong need to be protected and supported by "the formidableness of the group".[86] The commitment to the role of group member can be easily activated by group leaders' definition of the situation. Religion usually elicits strong emotions and intense feelings, which make conformity urgent and pressing.[87] An individual behaves differently when she is subject to group dynamics.

---

[81] Kelman and Hamilton, 1990, p. 97, see *supra* note 72.

[82] *Ibid.*, p. 96.

[83] Milgram, 1974, p. 6, see *supra* note 74.

[84] Kelman and Hamilton, 1990, p. 139, see *supra* note 72.

[85] Mark Osiel, "Obeying Orders: Atrocity, Military Discipline, and the Law of War", in *California Law Review*, 1998, vol. 86, no. 5, p. 1055; Sara Mackmin, "Why do Professional Soldiers Commit Acts of Personal Violence that Contravene the Law of Armed Conflict?", in *Defence Studies*, 2007, vol. 7, no. 1, p. 82.

[86] Cited in Mackmin, 2007, see *supra* note 85.

[87] Berreby, 2008, pp. 186–187, see *supra* note 15.

When an individual feels, experiences and acts emphatically as a group member, she may show hidden or dormant features which are not seen when acting alone.[88] French sociologist Gustave Le Bon comments already in the late nineteenth century that the group reduces the sense of individual distinctiveness hence responsibility, and spreads sentiments like a contagion. He observes that groups tend to adopt extreme attitudes: suspicions are turned into certainties, and antipathy into hatred.[89] While one's emotions are extraordinarily intensified in a group, her ability to 'think for herself' is significantly reduced.[90] Being in a group therefore can undermine individual ability for "moral deliberation".[91]

The needs to belong, to be transformed by the group are only human. Group thinking has no necessary moral direction.[92] It can be used for good or for evil. The "moral ambiguity" of this human tendency makes it "double-edged".[93] It is not unusual to see that with intensified obnoxious feelings such as anger or aggression, the group enables violent acts which the individual alone would not think of committing. The victim, the Other, becomes a convenient target for collective catharsis. Hate speech therefore has the potential to escalate and materialize itself in the group, with uncontrollable consequences.

Group dynamics can also compel reluctant members to follow the tide. The need to conform is so strong that it can override one's personal belief and judgment.[94] Disapproval of other members can be devastating when the group is the primary source of reference and security. Those who deviate from the group may be excluded, ostracized, or ridiculed. They are blamed for undermining group values and solidarity. A 'traitor' is as bad as, or even worse than an enemy. Going against the tide does not just cause emotional discomfort or social embarrassment. It can be deadly when violence reigns. It takes "great strength of character" to resist group norms.[95] Moral and behavioural autonomy in face of enormous group pressure is exceptional.

21.4.3. Reduced Senses of Agency and Responsibility Towards Harmful Conduct

Both authority situation and group dynamics reduce moral restraints by collectivizing and displacing agency and responsibility. They alienate an agent from

88 Vetlesen, 2005, p. 171, see *supra* note 16.

89 Cited in Frésard, 2004, p. 38, see *supra* note 36.

90 Vetlesen, 2005, p. 171, see *supra* note 16.

91 O'Sullivan, 2016, p. 179, see *supra* note 47.

92 Berreby, 2008, p. 43, see *supra* note 15.

93 *Ibid.*, p. 274.

94 Mackmin, 2007, p. 82, see *supra* note 85.

95 *Ibid.*

her own judgment and act. The individual's desire and "psychological ability" to experience herself as a distinct actor is "lacking or at least considerably hampered".[96] The agent feels she is shielded by the power of authority and anonymity within the group. Renouncing personal agency to authority and group minimizes emotional and moral conflicts caused by interpersonal violence. Individuals do not see their obedient or conforming acts as reflecting on them personally. They tend to see their actions as coming from external demands, not their internal agency.[97] The actor is alienated not only from her own act, but also from the consequences or responsibility of her act. When individuals feel they are not "the actual agent" of their actions, they tend to morally disengage from the consequences of their own actions.[98] Responsibility is diffused within the group and displaced to the authority.

Social structures of dominance and dependence amplify the effects of hate speech by "obscuring causal agency".[99] Kelman argues that when trying to understand atrocities, we need to look at factors weakening restraints against violence, more than factors motivating violence.[100] Hate speech, propagated in its typical social contexts and parasitic on religion, prepares ground for atrocity by reducing moral restraints at multiple levels.

21.5. "Dialectic between Circumstance and Transcendence"

Words and ideas matter. Hate speech inflicts intrinsic harm in the spiritual realm and derivative harm in the social realm. Social structure of dominance and dependence constitutes an inescapable human condition. Precisely because human behaviour and attitude are so attuned to social environment, the derivative harm of hate speech can be substantial. We can only be vigilant to bad social influences by acknowledging their power over us. If we proceed on the basis of the "old illusion of personal invulnerability",[101] we risk setting ourselves up to fail. We should not forget this when discussing moral and criminal responsibilities of those who propagate hate speech. More than a mere personal behaviour, hate speech is a particularly toxic social interaction. It contaminates the mind and the soul of those who look up to the promise of an ideal. Hate speech needs to be suppressed because we need to improve our normative and relational environment, not only our judgment and motivations which are so precious but so

---

96 Vetlesen, 2005, p. 146, see *supra* note 16.

97 Bandura, 1990, p. 34, see *supra* note 13.

98 *Ibid.*

99 *Ibid.*, p. 28.

100 Kelman, 1973, p. 38, see *supra* note 70.

101 Zimbardo, 2008, p. 447, see *supra* note 27.

vulnerable to social manipulation. In all of this, religion may represent one of humanity's few hopes of escape from disastrous social circumstances.

A revealing spiritual insight is that human beings can transcend their earthly dwelling. Social structure, together with our genetic endowment and past experiences, makes us who we are. Yet our physical composition and social context fail to exhaust us. There is more in us than our finite existence. The depth and reach of our spiritual experience are "unfathomable".[102] Such conception of the self as "embodied spirit"[103] carries the potential to challenge the social and conceptual regimes we inhabit. It reminds us of our ability to surprise, to act outside the script of both the social order and the individual character.[104] The spiritual dimension of our experience forms part of "the dialectic between circumstance and transcendence".[105] Yet when religion conspires with malicious social influences, it not only loses its critical force against other normative regimes, but lends credibility to them. It is a double blow to our already miserable human struggle. When religion itself is used to suppress spiritual freedom and impoverish human imagination, how can we transcend religion? Perverted religion dehumanizes, instead of humanizing or divinizing humanity. It diminishes the imminent spiritual seed, instead of nourishing it. It perpetuates social disaster instead of reversing it. By appropriating religion, hate speech therefore not only inverts our moral compass, but also blocks one of the few rescues to an inverted moral order. It completes our enslavement to an evil social structure.

[102] Unger, 2016, pp. 94, 124, see *supra* note 48.

[103] *Ibid.*, pp. 118–119.

[104] *Ibid.*, p. 130.

[105] *Ibid.*, p. 132.

22

The Use of Religious Themes to Islámize European Anti-Semitism and Motivate Hateful Expression in the Hamas Covenant

Eliyahu Stern*

22.1. Introduction

In this chapter, I discuss Hamas's founding document, "The Covenant of the Islamic Resistance Movement – Hamas" ('Hamas Covenant' or 'Covenant'), which appeared in 1988, attempting to show how the Covenant took from *The Protocols of the Elders of Zion* (also referred to as '*Protocols*') anti-Semitic motifs, which had been imported into the world of Islám from Europe during the twentieth century, and Islámized them.

The Covenant uses two methods to Islámize the *Protocols*: firstly, it presents the contents of the *Protocols* Islámized; and secondly, it elaborates this move by means of an intense poetics that shapes the reader's consciousness.

As for the contents, the *Protocols* portray the Jews as having been working for centuries to take over the world by undermining the economic, social and moral infrastructures of all countries. The Hamas Covenant incorporates these motifs into Islámic history, ties them to the Crusader and Mongol invasions in the Middle Ages, and positions the elimination of Islám as a central goal of the Jews and Zionism. The Covenant also positions *jihád* as the only remedy

---

* Dr. **Eliyahu Stern** is Associate Professor at the Department of Islamic and Middle Eastern Studies of Hebrew University, where he has taught Arabic and Islám since 1993. He holds B.A., M.A. and Ph.D. degrees from Hebrew University of Jerusalem. He is an expert on Islámic mysticism and its interrelations with theology and law, as well as the special poetics of *Ṣúfí* literature. His Ph.D. dissertation was on "Protection from Sin in al-Qushayri's Thought", 2010 (under the supervision of Professor Etan Kohlberg). He has also been involved in research and teaching on the relationship between Islám and Judaism. The author expresses his gratitude to Professor Vered Lev-Kanaan for her help in finalizing this chapter, and to Yigal Carmon, Founder and President of the Middle Eastern Media Research Institute ('MEMRI'), for sending an edited compilation of sermons and interviews, as well as for the rich materials regarding the distribution of the Protocols of the Elders of Zion in Arabic, Persian, Turkic and Urdu. For an audio-visual recording of Dr. Stern's statement to CILRAP's conference in Florence in April 2022 on the topic of this anthology, please see https://www.cilrap.org/cilrap-film/220409-eliyahu-stern/.

that can lead to the eradication of the Jews. It is, according to the Covenant, a *jihád* that lasts from the dawn of Islám to the end of days.

As for the poetics, the Covenant also Islámizes motifs from the *Protocols* by presenting them as intertwined with sacred Islámic sources, while employing very strong religious rhetoric. This rhetorical vehicle is a highly suggestive poetics with the power to deeply affect the feelings and worldview of a reader. One may suggest that the Covenant of Hamas is experienced as if it were an excellent sermon delivered by a particularly charismatic Islámic cleric, one who is famous among his audience as a high religious authority. The Covenant is attached to this chapter as an annex.

Throughout the chapters of the Covenant, the reader is presented with extremely harsh descriptions of the Jews and their actions.[1] Time and again the

---

[1] All the quotes of the Covenant of Hamas in this chapter use the translation in Menahem Milson, "The Covenant of the Islamic Resistance Movement – Hamas", *MEMRI Special Dispatch Series*, No. 3867, 26 May 2011. The Covenant, which is about 5,600 words long, has an introduction and 36 articles divided into five chapters and a conclusion. The titles of the chapters and sub-chapters of the Covenant are the following:

Preamble.

Chapter one, "Introduction to the Movement", contains eight articles arranged according to the following topics: "Ideological Premises; "The Relation between the Islamic Resistance Movement and the Muslim Brotherhood"; "Structure and Formation"; "The Islamic Resistance Movement – Dimensions of Time and Place"; "Distinctiveness and Independence"; "The Universality of the Islamic Resistance Movement"; "The Motto of the Islamic Resistance Movement".

Chapter two, "Goals", contains two articles gathered under one topic: "Causes and Goals".

Chapter three, "Strategy and Means", contains 12 articles arranged according to the following topics: "The Strategy of the Islamic Resistance Movement"; "Palestine Is an Islamic Waqf [that is, an Islámic religious endowment]"; "Homeland and Nationalism as Seen by the Islamic Resistance Movement"; "Peaceful Solutions, Initiatives and International Conferences"; "The Three Circles"; "Jihad for the Liberation of Palestine Is a Personal Duty"; "Educating the Next Generations"; "The Role of Muslim Women"; "The Role of Islamic Art in the War of Liberation"; "Social Solidarity"; "The Forces which Support the Enemy".

Chapter four, "Our Positions on:", contains 11 articles arranged according to the position of Hamas on the following topics: "A. The Islamic Movements"; "B. The Nationalist Movements in the Palestinian Arena"; "C. The Palestine Liberation Organization"; "D. Arab and Islamic States and Governments"; "E. Nationalist and Religious Groups and Organizations, Intellectuals, and the Arab and Islamic World"; "F. Followers of the Other Religions – "The Islamic Resistance Movement is a Humane Movement"; "G. The Attempt to Isolate the Palestinian People".

Chapter five, "Historical Evidence throughout the Generations regarding Confrontation with Aggressors", contains two articles.

Conclusion, "The Islamic Resistance Movement – Soldiers [for the Cause]", contains one article.

reader experiences the threat they pose to him, his society, Islám, and the whole world, repeatedly experiencing the religious obligation imposed on him to wage *jihád* against the Jews.

22.2. On the Penetration of Western Anti-Semitic Ideas from Europe into the World of Islám

It was common in Europe for hundreds of years to blame the Jews for the death of Jesus, for being in a pact with the devil, for poisoning wells, and spreading disease. These accusations joined the blood libel according to which Jews killed Christian children to use their blood to make Passover bread. And on top of all this, in modern times, there was *The Protocols of the Elders of Zion*, a fabricated text that was meant to prove that Jews were conspiring to destabilize societies and economies across the world, with the purpose of gaining political power and universal rule. These charges, both ancient and modern, have throughout history played an important role as a catalyst for anti-Jewish discrimination, legal persecution, violence, and mass destruction.

While classical Islám never produced anti-Semitism of that intensity, the traditional image of Jews in the textual sources of Islám is not good. The *Qur'án* and the *ḥadíth* – the traditions of the Prophet Muḥammad – preserves the memory of some six years of struggle between the Jews and the Prophet Muḥammad in the city of Al-Madínah.[2] Although the *Qur'án* mentions that few of the Jews welcomed Muḥammad's message, most Qur'ánic verses relating to the Jews say harsh things about them, such as: the Jews did not honour their religious obligations, God punished the Jews with arduous dietary restrictions,[3]

Hamas, its writings and ideology, as well as its social and political history, are the subject of a huge amount of research. For a few studies regarding the birth and political history of Hamas, see Litvak's references in his article: Meir Litvak, "'Martyrdom is Life': Jihad and Martyrdom in the Ideology of Hamas", in *Studies in Conflict and Terrorism*, 2010, vol. 33, no. 8, p. 730, note 2.

2 For two prominent studies on the Jews in the *Qur'án*, see Uri Rubin, "Jews and Judaism", in Jane Dammen McAuliffe (ed.), *Encyclopaedia of the Qur'ān*, Georgetown University, Washington, D.C., 2022; Meir M. Bar-Asher, *Jews and the Qur'an*, Princeton University Press, 2021. For the Jews in the *ḥadíth*, see Norman A. Stillman, "Yahūd", in Peri J. Bearman *et al.* (eds.), *Encyclopaedia of Islam*, 2nd ed., Brill, 2005, Section 3; Michael Lecker, *Muhammad and the Jews*, Yad Izhak Ben-Zvi, Jerusalem, 2014 (in Hebrew). See also, Haggai Ben-Shammai, "Jew-Hatred in the Islamic Tradition and the Koranic Exegesis", in Shmuel Almog (ed.), *Antisemitism Through the Ages*, Pergamon Press, Oxford, 1988, pp. 161–169.

3 In a few verses, it is mentioned that God cursed some of the Jews by turning them into monkeys and pigs as punishment for violating the Sabbath. Although the punishment of transformation into monkeys and pigs is mentioned only in a few verses, relating to very specific occasions, they nevertheless inspired a most common insult directed against Jews (and sometimes also Christians) throughout subsequent history. See Bar-Asher, 2021, pp. 54–55, see

the Jews falsified the Torah which Moses brought them, and they murdered some of their prophets. They are despised, humiliated and bear the brunt of God's anger. The Jews who in the *Qur'án* practice fraud and exploitation, take bribes, and bring about war are portrayed as the enemies of the Prophet and of Muslims.

However, the negative image of the Jews in Islám was much less threatening than the murderous and even diabolical picture painted of them by European anti-Semitism. Although the long history of Jews under Islám was not without persecution, it is important to emphasize that what classical Islám produced along these lines was much less widespread and horrifying than what we know from Europe.[4]

From a legal point of view too, the Jews of Islám had it easier than Europe's Jews, since Islám gave the non-Muslims they ruled over (including the Jews) the protected – albeit inferior – status of *dhimmí*. The *dhimmí* had, however, to pay a poll tax (*jizyah*) and were subject to various restrictions (not always strictly enforced), such as: a ban on the use of weapons, having to wear special clothing, avoiding worship in public as much as possible, and acknowledging the superiority of Muslims in social and economic life. But in exchange for the observance of these rules by the *dhimmí*, Muslim rulers had to protect their lives, property and ability, albeit circumscribed, to practice their religion.[5]

---

supra note 2. On the use of this insult in recent years to describe Jews in Friday sermons, political articles and even in educating small children, see Menahem Milson, a lecture delivered at the opening of the annual international conference of the Global Forum for Combating Antisemitism held in Jerusalem on 24 February 2008, *MEMRI Inquiry & Analysis Series*, No. 442, 29 May 2008. Meir Litvak mentions how Hamas activists present the *jihád* carried by the Palestinians against God's "enemies, the brothers of pigs and apes", see Litvak, 2010, p. 720, and see also his references in p. 731, note 25, see *supra* note 1.

4 There is extensive and longstanding research on Jews in the Islámic world. See, for example, Bernard Lewis, *The Jews of Islam*, Princeton University Press, 1987.

5 Bar-Asher quotes the translation of the Pact of 'Umar in Abdelwahab Meddeb, Benjamin Stora and Denis Charbit (eds.), *A History of Jewish–Muslim Relations from the Origins to the Present*, Princeton University Press, 2013, pp. 72–73, according to which the Christians of Syria wrote to the second Caliph, 'Umar, saying:

> [...] we asked you for a guarantee of security (*aman*) for ourselves, our offspring, our property and the people of our religious community (*milla*) and we undertook the following obligations toward you, namely:
>
> We shall not build in our cities or in their vicinity new monasteries, churches, hermitages, or monks' cells, nor shall we repair, by night or day, any of them that have fallen into ruin or which are located in the quarters of the Muslims.
>
> We shall keep our gates wide open for passersby and travellers.
>
> We shall provide three days' food and lodging to any Muslims who pass our way.
>
> We shall not give shelter in our churches or in our homes to any spy nor hide him from the Muslims.

A turn for the worse came with European control of Muslim countries in the nineteenth and twentieth centuries. Muslims adopted a variety of Western perspectives in science, government, society and philosophy, and regrettably European anti-Semitic thought penetrated Islám. Two prominent cases in point are the blood libel and *The Protocols of the Elders of Zion.*

The blood libel, according to which the Jews made use of the blood of non-Jewish children in the baking of *matzah* (the special bread for the Passover holiday), appeared in the Muslim world in the nineteenth century and spread

---

We shall not teach our children the Qur'an.
We shall not hold public religious ceremonies.
We shall not seek to proselytize anyone.
We shall not prevent any of our kin from embracing Islam if they so desire.
We shall show deference to the Muslims and shall rise from our seats when they wish it.
We shall not attempt to resemble the Muslims in any way with regard to their dress, as, for example, with the *qalansuwa* [a conical cap], the turban, footwear or parting of the hair.
We shall not speak as they do nor shall we adopt their kunyas [honorific bynames].
We shall not ride on saddles.
We shall not wear swords or bear weapons of any kind or even carry them on our persons.
We shall not engrave Arabic inscriptions on our seals.
We shall not sell alcoholic beverages.
We shall dress in our traditional fashion wherever we may be and we shall bind the *zunnar* [a distinctive belt] around our waists.
We shall not display our crosses or our books anywhere in the roads or markets of the Muslims.
We shall only beat the clappers in our churches very quietly.
We shall not raise our voices in our church services, nor in the presence of Muslims.
We shall not go outside on Palm Sunday or Easter nor shall we raise our voices in our funeral processions.
We shall not display lights in any of the roads of the Muslims or in the marketplaces.
We shall not come near them with our funeral processions [or: we shall not bury our dead near the Muslims].
We shall not take slaves who have been allotted to the Muslims.
We shall not build our homes higher than theirs.
(Another obligation – "We shall not strike any Muslim" – appears in an amendment).

According to the text, 'Umar approved the contents of the letter, but imposed two conditions on the Christians: "They will not be able to purchase individuals taken prisoner by Muslims. He who will have deliberately struck a Muslim will no longer benefit from any guarantee from this pact". See this and the rest of Bar-Asher's discussion of the Pact of 'Omar in Bar-Asher, 2021, pp. 112–116, see *supra* note 2. See also his references to Chapter 5, *ibid*, p. 146. For a most comprehensive reading of Islámic sources (the *Qur'án* and its classical exegesis, the *ḥadíth* and the early works of Islámic jurisprudence – *fiqh*) regarding Islám's attitude towards other religions, see Yohanan Friedmann, *Tolerance and Coercion in Islam – Interfaith Relations in the Muslim Tradition*, Cambridge University Press, 2003. On Hamas' perception that peace with the Jews contradicts the *dhimmí* rules, see Litvak, 2010, pp. 721, 727, see *supra* note 1.

like wildfire, and is still widely seen as a Jewish ritual one should be wary of. It is disseminated via a variety of media and information outlets, but because it is not mentioned in the Hamas Covenant it falls outside the scope of this chapter. The *Protocols*, which, as I mentioned, posits Jewish world domination, is very widespread in the Muslim world and is the focus of this chapter.

At this stage, I can summarize by saying that in contemporary Islámic anti-Judaic discourse, the Jews are represented negatively in line with the two traditional views of them: as transgressors against God and the enemies of Muslims, as portrayed in the *Qur'án*, and as bloodthirsty world-dominators as found in European anti-Semitism.[6]

We find motifs from these two lineages occurring very frequently in Islámic anti-Jewish discourse, in all the channels of information and discussion found in the Muslim world, including in the media, on the Internet, in films and TV series, books, articles, speeches and sermons.[7]

22.3. The Suggestive Poetics of the Hamas Covenant

In this chapter we discuss a test case in a rich, punctilious and lengthy piece of writing (weighing in at about 5,600 words), "The Covenant of the Islamic Resistance Movement – Hamas", issued in 1988 with the emergence of that organization. It is a decidedly religious text, displaying potent religious motifs which endow the believer with a hatred of Jews and strengthen a sense of obligation to go to war with them.

The Covenant of Hamas serves here as a case study, so one can learn from it how texts of similar Islámic bodies which use religious motifs encourage their readers to fight infidels generally and Jews in particular.

As many studies have shown, powerfully suggestive textual motifs call to deep parts of the reader or hearer's psychology, stirring up strong feelings and sometimes influencing cognitive processes.[8]

6 See also Milson's three major components of Arab anti-Jewish propaganda: "Anti-Jewish views derived from traditional Islamic sources; Antisemitic stereotypes, images and accusations of European and Christian origin; Holocaust Denial and equating Zionism with Nazism", in Milson, 26 May 2011, see *supra* note 3. The comparison of Zionism to Nazism is also found in the Hamas Covenant and will be mentioned later.

7 For an extensive review see *ibid.* Milson's conclusions were reached "on the basis of extensive monitoring by MEMRI of a wide variety of Arabic and Iranian publications and forums (newspapers, magazines, television programs, Friday sermons in mosques, books and websites)" over the first decade of the current century and a little earlier.

8 Eliyahu Stern, "Protection From Sin in al-Qushayrī's Thought", Ph.D. dissertation, Hebrew University, 2010, pp. 94–126, 368–377. References to the vast research endeavour in this area are beyond the scope of this chapter. Nevertheless, in light of the issue considered here – suggestive poetics – Reuven Tsur's extensive discussions in a discipline known as 'cognitive

A religious text has a particularly strong suggestive power, and it can impact the way the reader sees the world. Its power stems from the status of the text as a source of religious authority that expresses God's will. God is directly present in the text for the believer, who finds the text composed of sacred, literary layers. So, when in a text the Muslim believer identifies Qur'ánic verses, traditions of the *ḥadíth* spoken by the Prophet Muḥammad, and expressions of a clearly religious nature, such as prayers, sayings of venerated figures, and quotes from the *Sharí'ah*, he experiences himself in a sanctified religious space. To be in this space means to experience awe, excitement and a readiness to respond with devotion to divine command.

Now, with the reader in the arms of religious experience, he is open to suggestion, such that the various matters addressed by the text (for example: historical narratives, descriptions of the perfect society, and so on) take on the hues of absolute religious truth. This truth is authoritative, binding and even accompanied by an experience of sanctity.

Therefore, a statement in such a text reading that the Jew is an evil enemy who rules the world becomes part of the believer's religious worldview. It is an absolute view with great psychological force.

The Hamas Covenant is replete with literary-religious motifs conducive to sacred experience – it is sprinkled with dozens of quotes from the *Qur'án* and the *ḥadíth*, and many sayings familiar as expressions of religious devotion. A complete enumeration of these motifs is impossible in this chapter.[9]

In any case, it is worth devoting some words to the suggestive force of three main ingredients – two of which are the quotes from the *Qur'án* and from the *ḥadíth*, because they have a central role in motivating the reader of the

---

poetics' deserve mention. At the opening of his book *Toward a Theory of Cognitive Poetics*, Sussex, 2008, p. 1, he defines the field as follows:

> Cognitive Poetics is an interdisciplinary approach to the study of literature employing the tools offered by cognitive science. 'Cognitive science' is an umbrella term covering the various disciplines that investigate human information processing: cognitive psychology, psycholinguistics, artificial intelligence, and certain branches of linguistics, and of the philosophy of science. These explore the psychological processes involved in the acquisition, organization, and use of knowledge; in fact, in all information processing activities of the brain, ranging from the analysis of immediate stimuli to the organization of subjective experience. Cognitive Poetics explores the possible contributions of cognitive science to Poetics: it attempts to find out how poetic language and form, or the critic's decisions, are constrained and shaped by human information processing.

9 I counted the instances of poetic elements evoking religious excitement and devotion in the believer as he reads the Covenant of Hamas. These elements, including quotes from the *Qur'an* and the *ḥadíth*, lines of poetry, quotes from *shár'í* texts and distinctly Islámic terms (such as *Allah, Islám, Khalífah, Sunnah, Al-masjid Al-áqṣá, jihád, shahíd* and dozens of others) make up more than a third of the entire text.

Covenant of Hamas to take part in *jihád*; and the third ingredient is *jihád* itself as it appears in the Covenant of Hamas as a powerfully suggestive motif.

22.3.1. Quotes from the *Qur'án* in the Hamas Covenant

For Muslims, it is not only the contents of the *Qur'án* that come from God, but also its language – its style, its components and sounds. It is all a divine miracle, and beyond human power to imitate. To hear Qur'ánic verses is to hear the language of God, and is accompanied by great excitement, stirring up powerful devotion. Many verses are familiar to Muslims and repeated ritual recitation of the *Qur'án* is an ancient and popular custom.

The Hamas Covenant quotes more than 40 verses from the *Qur'án*, three of them at the very beginning and one to close the document. The three opening verses already contain severe charges against the Jews.

> You are the best nation that has been brought out for mankind. You command good and forbid evil and believe in Allah. If only the people of the Book [that is, Jews and Christians] had believed, it would have been well for them. Some of them believe, but most of them are iniquitous. They will never be able to do you serious harm, they will only be an annoyance. If they fight you, they will turn their backs and flee, and will not be succoured. Humiliation is their lot wherever they may be, except where they are saved from it by a bond with Allah or by a bond with men. They incurred upon themselves Allah's wrath, and wretchedness is their lot, because they denied Allah's signs and wrongfully killed the prophets, and because they disobeyed and transgressed. (*Qur'án*, 3:110–112)

The rest of the quotes are dispersed among its articles, imparting a seal of sacred religious truth. Every article which ends with a verse from the *Qur'án* lingers in the reader's consciousness as religious truth.

22.3.2. Quotes from the *Ḥadíth* in the Hamas Covenant

Quotes from the *ḥadíth* have a similar suggestive power. The *ḥadíth* is a vast literature containing a collection of sayings and actions of the Prophet, which Islám holds were transmitted orally through the generations in the first centuries of Islám until they were written down. The Prophet, according to a well-known Islámic theological principle, was protected by God from sin and error. His sayings and actions, therefore, express God's will. When a believer comes across a quote from the *ḥadíth*, he experiences religious devotion and veneration of the Prophet. Sayings of the Prophet's trustworthy friends (*ṣaḥábah*), especially those of the first four caliphs, also carry a tinge of religious truth, although to a lesser extent than those of the Prophet. Therefore, to quote their sayings is also to evoke an experience of religious amazement and awe.

The Hamas Covenant cites a number of traditions from the *ḥadíth* literature, which strengthen the authority and validity of the sections where they are cited.

22.3.3. The Use of *Jihád* as a Suggestive Poetic Element in the Hamas Covenant

The Covenant of Hamas also makes use of the powerful motif of *jihád*. The topic will be discussed at length later in the chapter,[10] but in the meantime, in order to emphasize the poetic power of the appearance of *jihád* in the Covenant, I will present a summary, as well as an emphasis on the poetic power of a quote from *Sharí'ah*.

Jihád and jihádists appear dozens of times throughout the document. The reader is commanded to join the Muslim fighters for *jihád*, who throughout history have fought infidels, including the Jews in Palestine, from the inception of Islám, through the Crusades and the Mongol invasions, up to our time, knowing that the war against the Jews will continue until the end of days. One can say that the reader feels himself to be within the 'sacred history of Islám'.

Moreover, in Article 12, the Hamas Covenant quotes a medieval *shár'í* source using language that is extremely authoritative in indicating a command of God, easily identifiable and imposing a personal religious obligation on the reader to engage in *jihád* in Palestine.

> When the enemy tramples Muslim territory, waging jihad and confronting the enemy become a personal duty of every Muslim man and Muslim woman. A woman may go out to fight the enemy [even] without her husband's permission and a slave without his master's permission.[11]

The term "personal duty" (*fárḍ 'ayn*) that appears in the paragraph quoted above is used in Islámic sources only in the context of *Sharí'ah* religious law. It reappears in the Covenant in the same context in Articles 14 and 15, including

---

[10] See Section 22.4.1.

[11] The reader recognizes the distinct *shár'í* legal style both in terms of the literary style characteristic of a *shár'í* text and particularly in mentioning the duty of the slave to engage in *jihád* in a world where the laws of Islámic slavery have not been implemented for generations.

A quick web search of the Al-Shámila Grand Library revealed the text quoted in the Covenant appearing in a number of *shár'í* sources. One of the earliest is the Ḥanafī scholar from Baghdad Imam al-Quduri (973–1037), *Mukhtasar al-Quduri*.

On Islámic slavery law, see Aharon Layish's legal introductions in *id.*, *Shari'a and the Islamic State in 19th-Century Sudan: The Mahdī's Legal Methodology and Doctrine*, Brill, Leiden, 2016, pp. 63–73. On women's physical participation in *jihád* fighting and on *jihád* as a personal duty (*fárḍ 'ayn*), see *ibid.*, pp. 246–247.

in the title of Article 15: "Jihad for the Liberation of Palestine Is a Personal Duty".

Along with the Hamas Covenant's focus on *jihád* are many mentions of the enemies who have occupied the land of Palestine, enemies one has to fight in *jihád* – sometimes called Jews, sometimes Zionists and sometimes just "the enemy".[12]

These terms take on a unique anti-Semitic tinge when, alongside the term "world Zionism" taken from literature based on *The Protocols of The Elders of Zion*, the adjective "Nazi" is also used to describe the enemies, the Jews and the Zionists.[13]

22.3.4. The Protocols of the Elders of Zion

The *Protocols* is a work of European anti-Semitism, widely read for more than a century.[14] Its 24 so-called 'protocols' are presented as if stolen from the Jews.

---

12 The three names given to the enemy are sometimes intertwined: The "Jews" are also the "enemies" (Preamble, Articles 15 and 20); the "Zionists" are also the "Jews" (Articles 7, 28 and 32); and the "Zionists" are also the "enemies" (Articles 17 and 22). Israel is mentioned in Articles 27 and 28, as well as in a quote at the beginning of the Covenant from Ḥasan al-Banná', the founder of the Muslim Brotherhood: "Israel will exist, and will continue to exist, until Islam abolishes it, as it abolished that which was before it".

Using the various terms in the Hamas Covenant to denote the same enemy is consistent with Milson's statement that "it should be emphasized that Arab antisemitic propaganda does not distinguish clearly between Jew, Zionist and Israeli; these three concepts are often used in Arab and Iranian anti-Jewish publications as though they were synonymous", Milson, 26 May 2011, see *supra* note 2.

13 Article 20 reads: "A society which is facing a wicked enemy with Nazi behaviour [...]. The Nazism of the Jews targeted both women and children"; Article 31 says: "The Nazi Zionist measures against our people will not succeed in prolonging the duration of their invasion"; Article 32 says: "All forces and capabilities must be pooled to confront this ferocious Mongol, Nazi onslaught [of Zionism]".

On the widespread identification between Zionism and Nazism in Arab and Islámic antisemitism, see Milson, 26 May 2011, see *supra* note 2.

On the book called 'World Zionism' (*Al-Ṣahyuniyya al-'Ālamiyya*) published in Egypt in 1956 by 'Abbas al-'Aqqád, one of the most prominent Egyptian intellectuals in the twentieth century, and its extensive influence on the dissemination of the worldview of the *Protocols* in the decades that have passed since then, see Menahem Milson, "A European Plot on the Arab Stage: The Protocols of the Elders of Zion in the Arab Media", *MEMRI Inquiry & Analysis Series*, No. 690, 20 May 2011.

14 *The Protocols of the Elders of Zion* are a subject discussed in thousands of studies. To offer an impression of just a little of the development of the research concerning them, including descriptions of trials that took place in the courts regarding them, I refer to two books: the relatively early book of the late judge Hadassa Ben-Itto, first published in 1998 and updated in 2005: Hadassa Ben-Itto, *The Lie that Will Not Die – The Protocols of the Elders of Zion*, Vallentine Mitchel, London, 2020, and Michael Hagemeister's most up-to-date book: Michael

They describe a malicious long-term plan to rule the world. To achieve this, the Jews have created social, governmental and economic chaos, and have stirred up revolutions and wars, all through deviousness, bribery and betrayal, along with out-and-out violence. They work through a secret organization, the Freemasons, and control the media; they have much wealth at their disposal, which they enlarge at the expense of the peoples of the world.[15]

The *Protocols*, written, some say, by the Russian secret police or perhaps by political agitators in Imperial Russia,[16] first saw the light of day as a book in 1905. By the beginning of the twentieth century, it had already sparked pogroms against Jews, had been translated into many languages and disseminated around the world, and had become particularly well known with its use by the Nazis in World War II. Although in the West, quite a few studies of the text have been made and a number of legal cases brought against it, during which it became clear that it was nothing but a forgery, the *Protocols* continue to be widely distributed, and Jewish influence is blamed for all kinds of new catastrophes which had not yet come to be when the document was written (for example, the Jews were blamed for the spread of the HIV virus in the 1980s[17] and, more recently, for the Covid-19 pandemic).

Arabic translations of the *Protocols* had already reached the Arab world during the first quarter of the twentieth century and achieved significant distribution. Until today, it is sold in many editions and one can find it in a wide variety of information channels – the media, Internet, films, political, and theoretical literature, syllabi, speeches and sermons. The State of Israel's struggle with the Arabs is also frequently portrayed as part of the programme of the *Protocols*.[18]

Hagemeister, *The Perennial Conspiracy Theory: Reflections on the History of the Protocols of the Elders of Zion*, Routledge, London, 2022. For the recommendation to choose Hagemeister's book, I owe thanks to Dr. Mark Volovici.

15 For extensive, albeit not comprehensive, details of the allegations against the Jews in *The Protocols of the Elders of Zion*, see Ben-Itto, 2020, pp. 9–15, see *supra* note 14.

16 Much of Ben-Itto's book is devoted to describing the role of people who belonged to the Russian secret police in forging the *Protocols*. Based on later research, Hagemeister presents a different approach and position as to their origin, see Hagemeister, 2022, p. 14, see *supra* note 14.

17 Ben-Itto, 2020, p. 371, see *supra* note 14. Ben-Itto mentions many other examples, a few of which are blaming the Jews for the destruction of the Twin Towers and the war in Iraq, see *ibid*, p. 380, and before that, in 1996, even for the war in Croatia, an accusation published in a local publication of *The Protocols of the Elders of Zion* (Croatia's case is mentioned in the Hebrew version of Ben-Itto's book, published by Dvir, Tel-Aviv, 1998, p. 339).

18 For an extensive review, see Milson, 20 May 2011, see *supra* note 13. See also, Ben-Itto, 2020, pp. 367–381, see *supra* note 14. See also an extensive discussion of the Protocols in the Arab

22.3.5. The *Protocols* in the Hamas Covenant

The picture of the world emerging from the *Protocols* is woven into the entire text of the Hamas Covenant and is explicitly found in nine of its articles (7, 16, 17, 22, 25, 28, 30, 32 and 36), and also has strong resonance in other articles (mainly 15, 27, 29 and 35).

The reader of the Covenant learns that Zionist Jews took over the media (Articles 17, 22 and 30) and finance (Articles 22 and 30), operated (and still operate) secret organizations devoted to espionage and destruction, which spread corruption and hazardous materials, threatening Islám and the Muslim society in general and Muslim women in particular, even the entire world (Articles 17, 22 and 28). They have invaded most countries of the world (Article 30) and used the colonialist forces under their control (Articles 22 and 32) against Islám, aiming to eliminate it (Articles 22 and 28). They even succeeded in bringing down the Muslim Caliphate (Article 22). Many forces are obedient to them (Articles 7, 16, 25 and 36) and, for decades, these forces have even placed obstacles in the path of the Muslim Brotherhood's *jihád* against the Jews, from 1936 up to the emergence of Hamas (Article 7).

Colonialism, which (according to Article 22) is led by the Jews, realized the plan conceived by the Crusaders to take over Muslim society through an intellectual and cultural invasion meant to sow ideological confusion and disrupt the culture of Muslims (Article 15): the Covenant emphasizes the need to rehabilitate and repair Muslim culture from the severe damage caused by this ideological invasion (Articles 15, 27 and 35; Article 29 will also be understood in this light).

---

world up to the early 1970s, Yehoshafat Harkaby, *Arab Attitudes to Israel*, Vallentine, Mitchell, London, 1972, pp. 227–255; see also pp. 181–186. The book contains a list of translations of the Protocols, see *ibid.*, p. 518. For further details of 37 books published in the Arab World up to the late 1960s that provide a summary of the Protocols, quote or rely on them, see Yehoshafat Harkaby, *The Arab Position in Their Conflict With Israel*, Dvir, Tel-Aviv, 1968, pp. 488–490 (in Hebrew).

For two recent publications about the Protocols in the Arab world in the past and present, as well as their widespread distribution in the Persian, Turkish and Urdu languages, see Yigal Karmon, "The Protocols of the Elders of Zion in the Arab and Muslim World – Past and Present", *MEMRI Daily Brief*, No. 493, 22 June 2023 (this publication contains about 200 links to analyses and appearances of the protocols in the media as published by MEMRI); "The Protocols of the Elders of Zion in the Arab and Muslim World – 120 Years Since Their Emergence", *MEMRI Inquiry & Analysis Series*, No. 1689, 21 April 2023 (this publication contains about 200 pages of analysis and review of the appearance of the Protocols in Persian, Turkish and Urdu).

Article 32 is the only section explicitly mentioning *The Protocols of the Elders of Zion* by name and is sometimes mentioned in this regard in studies on Hamas.[19]

> Today it is Palestine, and tomorrow some other country or countries, for the Zionist plan has no limits, and after Palestine they want to expand [their territory] from the Nile to the Euphrates, and when they finish devouring one area, they hunger for further expansion and so on, indefinitely. Their plan is expounded in *The Protocols of the Elders of Zion*, and their present [behaviour] is the best proof for what we are saying.

And yet the most detailed description of the world emerging from the *Protocols* is found in the first two-thirds of Article 22:

> The enemies have been planning expertly and thoroughly for a long time in order to achieve what they have achieved, employing those means which affect the course of events. They strove to accumulate huge financial resources which they used to realize their dream.
>
> With money they have taken control of the world media – news agencies, the press, publishing houses, broadcasting services, etc. With money they sparked revolutions in various countries around the world in order to serve their interests and to reap profits. They were behind the French Revolution and the Communist Revolution and [they are behind] most of the revolutions about which we hear from time to time here and there. With money they have formed secret organizations, all over the world, in order to destroy [those countries'] societies and to serve the Zionists' interests, such as the Freemasons, the Rotary Clubs, the Lions, the Sons of the Covenant [that is, B'nei B'rith], etc. All of these are organizations of espionage and sabotage. With money they were able to take control of the colonialist countries, and [they] urged them to colonize many countries so that they could exploit their resources and spread moral corruption there.
>
> There is no end to what can be said about [their involvement in] local wars and world wars. They were behind World War I, through which they achieved the destruction of the Islamic Caliphate, reaped material profits, took control of numerous resources, obtained the Balfour Declaration, and established the League of the United Nations [*sic.*] so as to rule the world through this organization. They were [also] behind World War II, through which they reaped enormous profits from commerce in war materials and paved the way for the establishment of their state. They [also]

[19] See, for example, Milson, 20 May 2011, see *supra* note 13.

> suggested the formation of the United Nations and the Security Council to replace the League of the United Nations [*sic.*] and to rule the world through this [new organization]. Wherever there is war in the world, it is they who are pulling the strings behind the scenes.

It is worth noting the suggestive connection that the Covenant creates between Article 22 and Article 32 by means of a unique poetic tool: in both articles, it quotes the same verse from the *Qur'án* (5:64), which suggests that the Jews ignite wars.[20]

Another suggestive poetic link between the two articles, in exactly the same context of igniting wars, is embodied in the designation of the Jews as "the warmongers" at the end of Article 32 just before the repeated verse mentioned above, which is used to firmly seal the article. "[T]he warmongers" is a one-of-a-kind sobriquet in the Covenant for the Jews and it ends the clause with a profanity that takes the reader sharply back to the description appearing in Article 22: "They were [also] behind World War II, through which they reaped enormous profits from commerce in war materials".[21]

22.4. Islámizing the *Protocols* in the Hamas Covenant

A reader of the Hamas Covenant comes to the *Protocols* as if it were an Islámic religious text. The reader is not aware at all of the possibility of being faced with a concept whose origin is neither religious nor Islámic. The world of the *Protocols* appears in the Covenant as part of sacred Islámic history intertwined with *jihád* over Palestine and against the Jews from the inception of Islám until the end of days. Moreover, the descriptions taken from the world of the *Protocols* are overlayed in the Covenant with poetic and other Islámic motifs to the extent that they are sometimes interwoven beyond recognition, almost as if they were part of the Islámic sources themselves.

In the next two sub-sections, I will discuss some characteristics of the Islámization of the Protocols in the Covenant: in the first sub-section, *jihád* and

---

20 Only one other verse (*Qur'án*, 58:21) appears twice in the Covenant, and it too makes a poetic link between two occurrences in the text of a particularly weighty issue. First, this verse is quoted (along with two others) at the end of the Preamble. Here, it is intended to intensify the call for the mobilization of all forces for the most significant battle against the Jews. Later in the text, in Article 29, the verse is quoted in a call on Muslims to defeat the Zionist invasion, just as they defeated the Crusaders and the Mongols. On the importance of the connection that the Hamas Covenant creates between the Jews' Zionist invasion and the Crusader and Mongol invasions, see Section 22.4.1.2.

21 Ben-Itto wrote a brief and somewhat incomplete summary of the allegations against the Jews based on the *Protocols* that appear in the Covenant of Hamas, Ben-Itto, 2020, p. 374, see *supra* note 14.

the sacred historical timeline it creates and, in the second sub-section, the Islámization of the Protocols in three prominent articles of the Covenant.

22.4.1. *Jihád* and Sacred Islámic History in the Hamas Covenant

22.4.1.1. *Jihád* in the Hamas Covenant

It can be argued that *jihád* is the most important motif in the Hamas Covenant.[22] To read the Covenant is to experience oneself as immersed in a world of religious war, a war in which one is required to fight in obedience to the command of God.

Jihád appears in the Hamas Covenant in its *s̲hár'í* sense of a Muslim war waged against the infidel enemy. According to the Covenant, *jihád* is waged throughout history, and today, in the immediate context of the readers' lives, it refers in particular to the war against Israel and the Jews.

Already in the Preamble to the Covenant, Hamas presents itself as a movement of *jihád* fighters: "[In doing this, Hamas] joins arms with all those who wage jihad for the liberation of Palestine".

Shortly thereafter, Article 3 states that: "The Islamic Resistance Movement is founded upon Muslims who [...] raised the banner of jihad in the face of the oppressors, in order to deliver the land and the believers from their filth, impurity and evil".

And especially important, in this regard, is the short Article 8, which declares that "The Motto of the Islamic Resistance Movement" is:

> Allah is its goal, the Prophet its model to be followed, the Koran its constitution, Jihad its way, and death for the sake of Allah its loftiest desire [...].[23]

The Covenant stresses that *jihád* makes Hamas unique: its readers will not find any other entity operating in the Palestinian and political arenas giving the same status to *jihád.*

Thus, Article 25, which deals with "The Nationalist Movements in the Palestinian Arena", provides that Hamas "emphasizes to all the members and supporters [of these movements] that it is a jihadist, ethical movement", and Article 12, which establishes the *S̲harí'ah* status of *jihád* as a personal duty applying to every Muslim, states: "There is nothing like this in any other political system – this is an indisputable fact".

---

[22] For an extensive review of Hamas' *jihád* ideology, written a little over two decades after the organization was founded, see Litvak, 2010, pp. 716–734, see *supra* note 1.

[23] The martyrdom involved in *jihád* is a central issue in the ideology of Hamas. See Litvak's discussion in *id.*, 2010, especially pp. 723–727, see *supra* note 1. On the concept of martyrdom in Islám, see Etan Kohlberg, "S̲hahīd", in Bearman *et al.*(eds.), see *supra* note 2.

The Hamas Covenant posits *jihád* as the only solution to the Jewish presence in Palestine and rejects any political or international solution. Article 13 sets this out while ruling out the involvement of the "infidels" in international attempts at a solution, and ties those "infidels" to the Jews and Christians by quoting a verse from the *Qur'án*:

> From time to time there are calls to hold an international conference in order to seek a solution for the [Palestinian] problem. Some accept this [proposal] and some reject it, for one reason or another, demanding the fulfilment of some condition or conditions before they agree to hold the conference and participate in it. However, the Islamic Resistance Movement – since it is familiar with the parties participating in the conference and with their past and current positions on the issues of the Muslims – does not believe that these conferences can meet the demands or restore the rights [of the Palestinians], or bring equity to the oppressed. These conferences are nothing but a way to give the infidels power of arbitration over Muslim land, and when have the infidels ever been equitable towards the believers?
>
> The Jews will never be content with you, nor will the Christians, until you follow their religion. Say: 'The guidance of Allah is the right guidance.' But if you follow their desires after the knowledge which has come to you, then you shall have no protector or guardian from Allah. (Koran, 2:120)

All the resources of society are mobilized for *jihád*. Not only is the nation one of *jihád* (Article 19), but every family is a *jihád*-fighting family, and every daughter must be educated so that she grows up to be a worthy mother to train her children for their role as *jihád* fighters (Articles 17–18), and all sectors, especially all those with various kinds of education – artists, writers and educators as well as media people and preachers, must play their part in the *jihád* (Articles 16, 19. 30). Even those who cannot take part in the physical fighting will take part in *jihád* as supporters of the fighters (Article 30).

Jihád enables the reader to experience his nationalism in a religious manner. The above quoted Article 12 states that:

> Nationalism, as seen by the Islamic Resistance Movement, is part of the [Islámic] religious creed. There is nothing that speaks more eloquently and more profoundly of nationalism than the following: when the enemy tramples Muslim territory, waging jihad and confronting the enemy become a personal duty of every Muslim man and Muslim woman.

At the same time, *jihád* also connects the reader to all the Muslims of the nation of Islám throughout the world, beyond local borders. The title of Article

7 is "The Universality of the Islamic Resistance Movement" and the first sentence of the article states that:

> Muslims who adopt the way of the Islamic Resistance Movement are found in all countries of the world, and act to support [the movement], to adopt its positions and to reinforce its jihad. Therefore, it is a world movement.

Muslims from all over the world are called upon to take part in Hamas' *jihád*, and the Arab and Muslim countries are required to allow *jihád* fighters to come to Palestine for the purpose of making war alongside their Muslim brethren (Articles 28 and 33).

Fighting the enemy also appears as a religious obligation in articles in which the word *jihád* itself is not found, but in which the reader is required to take part in the religious war against the "Nazi" enemy (Articles 20 and 31)[24] in the face of the terrible war crimes it commits (Articles 20 and 21). A proper Muslim education (Article 29) will help defeat the enemy, as it did in the past with the defeat of the Crusaders and the Mongols.

22.4.1.2. The Sacred Timeline of *Jihád* in the Hamas Covenant

The duty of *jihád* imposed on the reader of the Covenant is combined with another powerfully suggestive motif, appealing to the reader's feelings and worldview – a sacred timeline. The reader finds himself standing alongside *jihád*

---

[24] Article 31 actually declares that Hamas is a humane movement allowing Muslims, Christians, and Jews to live under the rule of Islám. But the article immediately takes a stand against members of the other religions, seeing them as competing with Islám for the region, quoting a Qur'ánic verse about the Jewish struggle against Muslims, and denouncing "Nazi Zionis[m]":

> Under the wing of Islam, the followers of the three religions – Islam, Christianity and Judaism – can co-exist in security and safety. It is only under the wing of Islam that safety and security prevail. Recent and ancient history provide the best evidence for this. The followers of the other religions should stop competing with Islam for sovereignty in this region, because, when they rule, there is nothing but carnage, torture and deportation, and they cannot get along with their own, let alone with followers of other religions. Both the present and the past are full of evidence for this.
>
> > They do not fight you together, except from within fortified villages, or from behind walls. They fight fiercely with one another. You consider them to be united, but their hearts are divided, for they are a people with no sense (Koran, 59:14).
>
> Islam accords to every person his rights, and prevents any infringement on other people's rights. The Nazi Zionist measures against our people will not succeed in prolonging the duration of their invasion, for the rule of injustice lasts but one hour, while the rule of the truth will last until the Hour of Resurrection.

On Islám's attitude towards other religions and on Hamas' perception that peace with the Jews contradicts the *dhimmí* rules, see *supra* note 5.

fighters throughout history from the rise of Islám, then during the Middle Ages, up to the present day, and looking forward to the day of resurrection.

The sacred timeline of *jihád* leaves a special imprint on the memory and religious motivation of the reader – it appears at the beginning of the Hamas Covenant and is amplified at the end. By appearing at beginning and end of the text, the sacred timeline creates within the reader's mind a vivid emotional signature that intensifies the appearances of the *jihád* timeline throughout the Covenant.

At the beginning of the sacred timeline – the inception of Islám: In the Preamble to the Covenant, when the reader first encounters the entity called Hamas, it is presented as a movement that arose to fight a *jihád* that has continued from the time of the rise of Islám to the present day.

> Then the Islamic Resistance Movement [Hamas] set out to play its role, marching onward for the sake of Allah. [In doing this, Hamas] joins arms with all those who wage jihad for the liberation of Palestine. The souls of its jihad fighters meet the souls of all those jihad fighters who sacrificed their lives for the land of Palestine, from the time when the Prophet's companions conquered it until the present.

At the end of the sacred timeline – the Day of Resurrection: The last chapter of the Covenant (Articles 34 and 35)[25] is called "Historical Evidence throughout the Generations regarding Confrontation with Aggressors", and is indeed devoted to history. Once again, the reader is placed within the timeline of an ancient and continuous *jihád*, this time continuing until the end of days according to a *ḥadí<u>th</u>* quoted in Article 34:

> Palestine is the center of the Earth and the meeting place of the continents; it has always been the target of greedy aggressors. This has been the case since the dawn of history. The Prophet, Allah's prayer and peace be upon him, points to this in his noble words with which he addressed his exalted companion, Mu'adh b. Jabal, saying: "Oh Mu'adh, Allah will give you the land of Al-Sha'm after my death, from Al-'Arish to the Euphrates. Its men, women and handmaids will be [constantly] stationed on the frontier until the Day of Resurrection, for any one of you who chooses [to live in] some part of the coastal plains of Al-Sha'm or Bayt Al-Maqdis [that is, Palestine], will be in a [constant] state of jihad until the Day of Resurrection.

The timeline is sanctified here by the Prophet's *ḥadí<u>th</u>*, and is thus linked to another *ḥadí<u>th</u>* of the Prophet cited in Article 7, according to which "[t]he

---

[25] It is followed only by a concluding clause, Article 36.

hour of judgment shall not come until the Muslims fight the Jews and kill them"[26]. The readers are placed, according to the first *ḥadíth* (Article 7), within the unending *jihád* fought against the Jews, wherever they are, and, according to the second *ḥadíth* (Article 34), within the unending *jihád* for Palestine.

It is also worth noting that the *ḥadíth* in Article 34 is the very last quotation from the *ḥadíth* in the Covenant, which gives it a particularly strong impact on the reader's memory as well as on his experience of religious devotion and willingness to fulfil his duty in the *jihád* war.

In the course of the sacred timeline – Crusaders from the West, Mongols from the East, and the Jews of the Elders of Zion: The sacred history of *jihád* also involves *jihád* war both in the Middle Ages and today. As a matter of fact, according to the Covenant, the *jihád* of the Middle Ages and the *jihád* of today are indeed distinct episodes in the history of one ongoing *jihád*.

Articles 34 and 35 are the two main articles that fill in the gaps in the sacred timeline of *jihád* between the rise of Islám and the day of Resurrection, with the wars against the Crusaders and the Mongols in the Middle Ages, and with the war against the Zionists in modern times. The articles state that only fighting *jihád* under the banner of Islám made it possible to repel the Crusader and Mongol invasions and call on the readers to learn these lessons of the past in order to defeat the Zionist invasion today as well. Article 34 says:

> The great armies of the Crusaders came there, bringing their religious creed and hoisting their cross. They managed to defeat the Muslims for a while, and the Muslims only managed to regain it when they fought under their religious banner, joined forces crying "Allah Akbar," and set forth in jihad under the command of Salah Al-Din Al-Ayyubi for nearly two decades, which led to a clear victory: the Crusaders were defeated and Palestine was liberated.
>
> This is the only way to liberation, and one cannot doubt the testimony of history. This is one of the rules of the universe and the laws of reality. Only iron can break iron, and their false, fabricated faith can only be overcome by the true faith of Islam, for religious faith cannot be attacked except through religious faith.

Article 35 provides:

> The current Zionist invasion was preceded by Crusader invasions from the west, and by Mongol invasion from the east. And just as the Muslims faced these invasions, made plans for fighting them and defeated them, they can [now] confront the Zionist invasion and defeat it. This not difficult for Allah, providing that intentions are sincere and resolve is strong, and that Muslims draw benefit

[26] For further discussion of Article 7, and especially of this *ḥadíth*, see Section 22.4.2.1.

> from the experiences of the past, shed off the influences of the intellectual invasion, and follow the ways of their predecessors.

The Hamas Covenant, however, does not consider the Crusader and Mongol invasions, on the one hand, and the Zionist invasion, on the other, as separate and unconnected historical events. In fact, the Covenant draws a direct line between the Crusaders and the Jews of today, and also asserts strong resemblance, to the point of identity, between the Mongols and the Jews of today. As for the Crusaders (mentioned in Articles 15, 27, 29, 34 and 35), the Covenant states that it was the Crusaders who conceived the Western ideological and colonial takeover of the Islámic world (Article 15), and it was the Jews who carried out this plan and brought colonialist occupation to the world of Islám (Article 22). As for the Mongols (Articles 29, 32 and 35), the Covenant describes both the Mongol and Zionist invasions as designed to take over the world and destroy human civilization.

Article 29 states that the whole of human civilization was saved by "defeating the Crusaders and routing out the Mongols, thus saving human civilization", and Article 35 mentions that:

> The Islamic Resistance Movement studies the defeat of the Crusaders at the hands of Salah Al-Din Al-Ayyubi, the liberation of Palestine from them, as well as the defeat of the Mongols at 'Ayn Jalut and the breaking of their military strength at the hands of Qutuz and Az-Zahir Baybars, and the delivery of the Arab world from the Mongol conquest which destroyed all aspects of human civilization.

Article 32 (according to which the plan of "World Zionism" to take over the world "is expounded in *The Protocols of the Elders of Zion*") refers to the Zionist invasion as "Mongol" and states that, "[a]ll forces and capabilities must be pooled to confront this ferocious Mongol, Nazi onslaught, lest homelands be lost, people be exiled, evil spread on the earth and all religious values be destroyed. Each and every person should know that he is responsible to Allah".

The Mongol East and the Crusader West: The comparison between the Crusaders and the State of Israel was already a longstanding and well-known motif in anti-Israel literature at the time the Hamas Covenant was written. But, in the Covenant, this trope is Islámized, serving as a powerful tool to impose on the reader a personal religious obligation to engage in *jihád* against the very Jews of the *Protocol*s who had implemented the Crusader plan and thus brought about the colonial (and cultural) invasion.

The comparison of the Mongols to the State of Israel, on the other hand, was extremely rare at the time of writing the Covenant, and perhaps had never been made.[27]

Indeed, just as with the motif of the Crusaders, the Mongols too are used in the Covenant both to establish the sacred timeline of *jihád*, within which the reader can situate himself, and as a lesson in religious history for the reader to learn so that he engages in *jihád* war against the Zionists.

However, the comparison with the Mongols in the Covenant serves another valuable religious purpose – the harsh Islámist negation of both East and West. Through the combination of the Crusaders and the Mongols, the Covenant links this Islámist negation of West and East, familiar in modern times, to the Middle Ages.

According to Islámist thought, the cultural influences from the East and the West (often referred to as the "communist East" and the "capitalist West") have severely damaged the world of Islám. Therefore, abandoning these influences and returning to Islám is the only solution to the ills of the Islámic world.[28]

This well-known negation of East and West in its modern Islámist context is also found in the Hamas Covenant. Article 25, which presents Hamas'

---

27 Throughout the years of my acquaintance with the Hamas Covenant, I have indeed been impressed that the comparison between the Mongols and Zionists is extremely rare. Nevertheless, in preparation for the writing of this chapter, I consulted with two of the most prominent experts in their fields. I learned from Professor Michal Biran that the literary image of the Mongols destroying the cultures they invaded was quite common, particularly in the description of their alleged destruction of the city of Baghdad. Biran has shown in her research that this conception of the Mongols is inaccurate. On the change in the attitude towards the Mongols in the Muslim world following the rise of nationalism, see Michal Biran, *Chinggis Khan*, OneWorld Publications, Oxford, 2007, pp. 128–136; for a re-evaluation of the Mongols' impact on the Muslim world, see, for example, Michal Biran, "Libraries, Books, and Transmission of Knowledge in Ilkhanid Baghdad", in *Journal of the Economic and Social History of the Orient*, 2019, vol. 62, nos. 2–3, pp. 464–502; or Michal Biran, "Baghdad Under Mongol Rule", in Jens Scheiner and Isabel Toral-Niehoff (eds.), *Baghdad: From Its Beginnings to the 14th Century*, Brill, Leiden, 2022, pp. 285–315. I am grateful to Prof. Biran for sharing some of her research and insights and, in particular, for her observation that the comparison between the Mongols and the Zionists was unprecedented.

I have also consulted with Professor Hillel Cohen and I am thankful to him for pointing out that the comparison between the Mongols and the Zionists was unfamiliar to him in Palestinian literature both before the time the Covenant was written and at the time it was written, and for drawing my attention to the writers who made such a comparison in later years.

28 On the Muslim Brotherhood's perception that the loss of Palestine in 1948 is "a symptom of a deeper moral and social malaise within the Muslim world that stemmed from the abandonment of Islam and the adoption of Western Ideologies and culture", see Litvak, 2010, p. 717, see *supra* note 1. An extensive discussion of the motif in Islámist thought, see Uriah Furman, *Islamiyyun – Religion and Society in Contemporary Islamist Thought*, Maarchot, Tel-Aviv, 2002, pp. 115–142 (in Hebrew).

perception of "The Nationalist Movements in the Palestinian Arena", states: "[The Islamic Resistance Movement] respects them and appreciates the conditions that surround and affect them. It supports them as long as they do not pay allegiance to the Communist East or to the Crusader West".[29] Article 26 begins in the very same spirit stating that, "The Islamic Resistance Movement – looking favourably as it does on the Palestinian nationalist movements that do not pay allegiance to the East or to the West".

The Covenant also makes anti-Semitic use of this motif in the spirit of *The Protocols of the Elders of Zion* and links to the actions of the Jews the harm caused by the East and West to the Islámic world. Thus, in Article 22 quoted above, the Covenant describes the Jews' takeover of the world's ruling powers and states that the "colonialist powers, both in the capitalist West and the communist East, support the enemy with all their might, both materially and with manpower, alternating one with the other in giving support". The article immediately further Islámizes the motif of 'the East and the West', noting: "When Islam appears, all the forces of unbelief unite to oppose it, for all unbelief is one denomination".[30]

Then, in Article 35, this motif of 'East and West' is used by the Covenant as a poetic means to link modern times to the Middle Ages and establish the ongoing history of *jihád*'s sacred timeline. The article does this by referring to the Crusaders as the people of the West and the Mongols as the people of the East ("The current Zionist invasion was preceded by Crusader invasions from the west, and by Mongol invasion from the east").

Thus, even though the West and East were earlier in the document put in modern context (Articles 22, 25 and 26), the reuse of the motif 'East and West' to indicate Mongols and Crusaders (Article 35) posits the contemporary context as a continuation of the medieval one – in the mind of the reader the East is Mongol now just as the West is Crusader.

The reader of the Hamas Covenant can therefore experience himself standing in battle, not only alongside the first Muslims in the seventh century, but also alongside Ṣáláḥuddín al-Ayyúbí, Quṭuz and Aẓ-Ẓáhir Bibárs, who led the *jihád* armies against the Crusaders and the Mongols in medieval times.

---

29 The Islámist discourse outside the Hamas Covenant also includes the use of the term 'Crusader West' alongside the 'Communist East'. See, for example, the appeal to Egyptian youth by the General Union of Students of the Arab Republic of Egypt in *Voice of Truth* (available in the *Ikhwanwiki* web site).

30 For further discussion of Article 22, and especially of the sentence quoted, see below Section 22.4.2.2.

It is quite possible that, for the reader, he and his medieval predecessors are fighting the same historical enemy.

22.4.2. The Islámization of the *Protocols* in Three Prominent Articles of the Covenant

22.4.2.1. Article 7: "The Universality of the Islamic Resistance Movement"

At the end of Article 7 of the Hamas Covenant is a very well-known *ḥadíth*. The article states that Hamas' war of *jihád* against the Jews is a continuation of the *jihád* of the Muslim Brotherhood of 1936, 1948 and 1968, and that *jihád* against the Jews is not restricted in time, because:"

> Although these links are far apart, and although the continuity of jihad was interrupted by obstacles placed in the path of the jihad fighters by those who circle in the orbit of Zionism, the Islamic Resistance Movement aspires to realize the promise of Allah, no matter how long it takes. The Prophet, Allah's prayer and peace be upon him, says: "The hour of judgment shall not come until the Muslims fight the Jews and kill them, so that the Jews hide behind trees and stones, and each tree and stone will say: 'Oh Muslim, oh servant of Allah, there is a Jew behind me, come and kill him,' except for the Gharqad tree, for it is the tree of the Jews. (Recorded in the Hadith collections of Bukhari and Muslim).[31]

This famous *ḥadíth* is taught in the textbooks of high schools in the West Bank and Gaza Strip[32] and is much quoted in sermons and propaganda outlets.

---

[31] The *ḥadíth* database 'sunnah.com' contains 16 major *ḥadíth* collections, both in their Arabic origin and in their translation into English, including the six collections considered the most reliable in the Sunní tradition. Two of the six, the collections of Al-Bukhárí and Muslim are considered the most reliable. Within the more than 630 traditions in which the word 'Jew' and its declensions appear, this *ḥadíth* appears 11 times, sometimes in the exact version presented in the Hamas Covenant and other times in close versions: Riyad as-Salihin, Book 18, *ḥadíth* 13; Muslim, Book 54, *ḥadíth* 103; Muslim, Book 54, *ḥadíth* 99; al-Bukhárí, Book 53, *ḥadíth* 139; Muslim, Book 54, *ḥadíth* 100; Muslim, Book 54, *ḥadíth* 101; Muslim, Book 54, *ḥadíth* 102; al-Bukhárí, Book 61, *ḥadíth* 100; al-Bukhárí, Book 56, *ḥadíth* 138; at-Tirmidhí, Book 33, *ḥadíth* 79; Ibn Majah, Book 36, *ḥadíth* 152. See also discussions of this *ḥadíth* in Bar-Asher, 2021, pp. 55–56, see *supra* note 2; Milson, 24 February 2008, see *supra* note 3; Litvak, 2010, pp. 727, 729, see *supra* note 1; David Cook, *The Mahdi's Arrival and the Messianic Future State According to Sunni and Shi'ite Apocalyptic Scenarios*, The Nehemia Levzion Center for Islamic Studies, The Hebrew University of Jerusalem, 2014, pp. 6–7.

[32] See "Remaining Antisemitism in Palestinian Authority Textbooks and Study Cards 2021–22 Grades 1–12", Institute for Monitoring Peace and Cultural Tolerance in School Education ('IMPACT-se'), London and Ramat Gan, March 2022, p. 12 (Section 16). I am thankful to Arik Agassi, Chief Operating Officer at IMPACT-se, for providing this valuable document along with other documents.

Today, it is even common to say that the Jews plant the Gharqad tree where they live because they know their end is not far off.[33]

Attention should be drawn to how, in Article 7, the Islámic and Western traditions are interwoven. The *ḥadíth* appears here as an Islámic religious solution to a problem derived from the *Protocols*, namely the worldwide powers now put into motion by Zionism. These powers put up obstacles in the path of *jihád* – that is, in the way of Islámic law and history, but in the *ḥadíth*, the Prophet promises that war against the Jews will go on forever. By placing the *Protocols* in the text between the holy *jihád* and the sacred prophetic tradition, the framers of the Covenant of Hamas ensure that from now on, etched into the brain of the believing reader as religious truth, is the reality of world-dominating powers activated by Zionism.

22.4.2.2. Article 22: "The Forces which Support the Enemy"

As mentioned before, the Hamas Covenant repeats many of the charges against the Jews originating in the *Protocols*, and many of its 36 articles feature them. The accusations taken from the *Protocols* are woven together with Islámic motifs in the Covenant of Hamas, so that the reader comes to perceive the world as run by a Jewish-Zionist conspiracy aiming not only at world domination and the spread of corruption as emphatically displayed in the European source, but also at the demise of Islám.

The most far-reaching accusation of those deriving from the *Protocols* is found in Article 22, at 300 words – the longest of the Hamas Covenant's articles. This article begins by describing how the conspiracy proceeds:[34] the enemy lays his plans well over many years, gathering much capital, gaining control of the media and instigating most of the revolutions in the world, while making use of secret organizations devoted to espionage and sabotage. The enemy controls the colonial powers and leads them to settle in many parts of the world. The enemy created and continues to create all wars – including the two world wars during which it brought down the Islámic Caliphate and established the infrastructure of its own state. In order to rule over the world, it created the League of Nations, later replacing it with the United Nations and the Security Council.

Then this relatively long text appears, which, after some 200 words, suddenly becomes Islámic and holy by the deployment of two verses from the *Qur'án* and one quote from *ḥadíth* literature. The first verse from the *Qur'án* appears hand-in-hand with a sentence blaming the Jews for bringing about all

33 MEMRI has edited a large collection of *ḥadíth* on the matter. On such a preacher in Hamas' *al-Aqsa* TV channel, see Litvak, 2010, p. 727, *supra* note 1.

34 For a full quotation see above Section 22.3.5.

wars, so that this originally 'Western' charge of being at the root of war becomes for the reader a Qur'ánic accusation:

> Wherever there is war in the world, it is they who are pulling the strings behind the scenes. "Whenever they ignite the fire of war, Allah extinguishes it. They strive to spread evil in the land, but Allah does not love those who do evil." (*Qur'án*, 5:64)

And now, immediately after this comes the following assertion:

> The colonialist powers, both in the capitalist West and the communist East, support the enemy with all their might, both materially and with manpower, alternating one with the other [in giving support] When Islam appears, all the forces of unbelief unite to oppose it, for all unbelief is one denomination.[35]

The expression at the end of this paragraph is a famous saying of the second Caliph, 'Umár, one of the two most authoritative figures in Sunní Islám after the Prophet Muḥammad,[36] and it gives the whole article religious force. The Jews of the *Protocols* lead the infidels of the *ḥadíth* in the struggle against Islám.

And now comes the second verse from the *Qur'án*, appealing directly to the reader:

> Oh you who believe, do not take as your intimate friends those outside your ranks, for they will spare no effort to harm you. They desire that which causes you suffering. Hatred has indeed come out of their mouths, but what they hide in their hearts is even worse. We have given you clear signs, if you understand. (*Qur'án*, 3:118)

And if that is not enough, the Covenant of Hamas concludes the Article with a suggestive rhetorical tool of potentially great emotional force, one of a kind in the document, returning to the last words of the verse: "It is not for nothing that the verse ends with His words 'if you understand'".

The reader of the Hamas Covenant, now being addressed directly by the *Qur'án*, is left fully imbued with religious experience.

Readers will note that it is not only rhetoric here presenting the *Protocols* as Islámic truth, but also that the actual content of the *Protocols* is now Islámic. The *Protocols* are now the programme of the enemies of Islám, as they work against Islám, and they were indeed successful in bringing down the Caliphate. The concept of the Islámic Caliphate, the political ruling entity replacing the Prophet's political authority, has great importance in Islámic religious

---

35 This passage is discussed above in reference to the use of the motif of 'West and East', see Section 22.4.1.2.

36 On the invaluable importance of 'Umár in Islámic tradition, see Hava Lazarus-Yafeh, "'Umar b. Al-Khaṭṭáb – Paul of Islam?", in *id.*, *Some Religious Aspects of Islam*, Brill, Leiden, 1981, pp. 1–16.

consciousness. Several Islámic movements, among them the Islámic State,[37] frequently call for the establishment of the Islámic Caliphate.

The fall of the Caliphate under the authority of the Ottoman Turks at the beginning of the twentieth century is a familiar symbol in modern Islámic discourse for the defeat of Islám by the infidels;[38] and in the Covenant of Hamas, thanks to the *Protocols*, the Jews, eternal enemies of Islám, turn out to be the ones who brought it down, leading the infidels in their struggle against Islám.

22.4.2.3. Article 28: "Arab and Islamic States and Governments"

Article 28 in the Covenant is of paramount importance to Hamas, as it calls on Arab and Islámic countries to assist in the *jihád* against the Jews. It is part of a concept that appears in a number of places in the Covenant, according to which Hamas is part of the Muslim Brotherhood, its activity being global and not bound only to Palestine. This article also evokes a religious experience with which Islámist discourse has been concerned for decades: it is the entire nation of Islám, with its more than one and a half billion followers, that stands up to the Jews in Israel.

The structure of Article 28 is therefore intended to inflame the feelings of the entire Muslim nation against the Jews. Its beginning, taken from the *Protocols*, indicates the danger to which the Islámic world is subjected by Zionism. The second part includes a demand on Arab and Islámic countries to support *jihád*; and the last part contains a pointed and virulent attack against the Jews, the enemies of the Prophet Muḥammad and Islám.

The Protocols of the Elders of Zion constitute more than the first half of the section. These passages appear shrouded with a poetic intensity that is not captured in the English translation but is most evident in the Arabic, with its suggestive influence on the reader. Thus, we see short and harsh statements, rich in the interplay of sound, rhythm and rhyme, decorated with derogatory and threatening adjectives, which appear in a cumulative sequence conducive to rising emotional tension, enthralling the reader. It is not for nothing that this is where the Covenant explicitly states that the goal of the Zionists is the elimination of Islám:

---

37 See the debate with ISIS regarding the Caliphate in Ella Landau-Tasseron, "Delegitimizing ISIS on Islamic Grounds: Criticism of Abu Bakr Al-Baghdadi by Muslim Scholars", *MEMRI Inquiry & Analysis Series*, No. 1205, 24 November 2015, especially Section 22.

38 See, for example, the presentation of Mustafa Kemal Atatürk as an emissary of the enemies of Islám to abolish the Caliphate and impose secularism, Furman, 2002, p. 83, see *supra* note 28. On the centrality of the comparison made by radical Muslims between the abolition of the Caliphate in 1924 by Atatürk and the elimination of the 'Abbásíd Caliphate by the Mongols in 1258, see Emmanuel Sivan, *Radical Islam: Medieval Theology and Modern Politics*, Yale University Press, 1985 (Hebrew edition: Am Oved Publishers, Tel Aviv, 1986, p. 68).

> The Zionist invasion is a cruel invasion, which has no scruples whatsoever; it uses every vicious and vile method to achieve its goals. In its infiltration and espionage operations, it greatly relies on secret organizations which grew out of it, such as the Freemasons, the Rotary Clubs, the Lions and other such espionage groups. All these organizations, covert or overt, work for the interests of Zionism and under its direction, and their aim is to break societies, undermine values, destroy people's honour, create moral degeneration and annihilate Islam. [Zionism] is behind all types of trafficking in drugs and alcohol, so as to make it easier for it to take control and expand.

Now that the article has described the unrestrained cruelty of the Zionist invasion,[39] it vehemently demands that the Arab and Islámic countries support the *jihád* of the Muslims in Palestine:

> We demand that the Arab countries around Israel open their borders to jihad fighters from among the Arab and Islamic peoples, so they may fulfil their role and join their efforts to the efforts of their brothers – the Muslim brethren in Palestine. As for the rest of the Arab and Muslim countries, we demand that they facilitate the passage of the jihad fighters into them and out of them – that is the very least [they can do].

In the last part of the article, at its emotional peak, the text turns aggressively against the Jews, accusing them of attempting to offend the dignity of the Prophet and of Muslims:

> We should not fail to remind every Muslim that when the Jews occupied the Sacred place [that is, Jerusalem] in 1967 and stood on the threshold of the blessed Al-Aqsa mosque, they shouted: "Muhammad is dead; his offspring are women" [...].

This story was probably invented in 1969 and became very common in literature and the media from the early 1970s.[40] It seems to indicate that the Jews mocked the Muslim armies, who failed – 'were women' – in the fighting against Israel in 1967. Even worse, the story also indicates an attempt to offend the Prophet's dignity by alluding to a familiar story from classical literature about his life. According to it, one of Muḥammad's opponents mocked the Prophet for

---

39 In various versions of the Covenant, the opening of the section "The Zionist Invasion" sometimes appears, and sometimes the "Crusader Invasion" does.

40 Saudi journalist and researcher 'Ali al-'Umaym found that the story first appeared in written publications in 1969 at the earliest: "Exposing a 52-Year-Old Fallacy", *Al Arabiya*, 25 June 2021.

leaving behind only daughters and not sons.[41] Insulting the Prophet has been known as a serious attack on Islám and Muslims throughout history, and its power to provoke rage and even violence is well known even today.

Article 28 now sharply summarizes the position of the Hamas Covenant regarding Judaism and Jews, and states: "Israel with its Jewish identity and Jewish people is challenging Islám and the Muslims".[42] These pointed words are now ingrained in the reader's memory by means of a short and intense quote from ancient Islámic sources, itself carrying a potential threat: "May the cowardly know no sleep".[43]

These are among the famous words attributed to Kh<u>á</u>lid Ibn al-Walíd (592–642) on his deathbed. Khálid Ibn al-Walíd, who was called by some 'the Sword of the Messenger of Allah', was one of the most important Muslim generals in the days of the Prophet and the first two caliphs. He was known for his many conquests in Iraq and Syria and especially for never being defeated in battle.[44]

22.5. A Closing Remark About Contemporary Media

I have used the Hamas Covenant in this chapter to show how Islámic religious motifs can be used to disseminate an anti-Judaic discourse: the Covenant is both an echo chamber for negative statements about Jews in the *Qur'án* and the *ḥadíth*, and for the *Protocols*, which has become an Islámic religious motif in its own right. The dissemination of these motifs in a diverse array of public outlets has made them known on a mass scale across the world.

Furthermore, a game-changer with threatening implications has just appeared in recent years in the form of social media. The power of social media – Telegram and TikTok currently stand out – to drive believers to violence is well known, both in Israel and the world.

A learned colleague (whose area of study includes social media) has informed me that the anti-Jewish motifs described in this chapter are repeated extensively in social media. While in the (quite recent) past it would have taken

41 Many sources indicate that it was al'áṣí Ibn Wa'il from the Tribe of Quraysh who mocked the Prophet for leaving behind only daughters. See, for example, one of the most well-known commentaries on the *Qur'án*, *Tafsír al-Jalalayn*, 1460–1505, p. 824.

42 In order to poetically capture the short and sharp sound of the Arabic source, I suggest the translation: 'Israel, with its Jewishness and its Jews, challenges Islám and Muslims'.

43 In Islámist discourse over the media, a more literal English translation is often used: 'may the eyes of the cowards never sleep'. The sentence is quoted in many classical Islámic sources, including, for example,
Ibn al-Qáyyim al-Jawziyyah (d. 1350), *Al-Furúsíyyah al-Muḥammadíyyah*, Dar Ibn Ḥazm, Beirut, 2019, p. 459.

44 See Patricia Crone, "Khālid b. al-Walīd", in Bearman *et al.* (eds.), 2005, see *supra* note 2.

months for an anti-Semitic Muslim preacher's defamatory statements about the Jews to reach the great masses of believers, today it can happen within an hour.[45]

[45] On the role of social media in 'lone wolf' attacks in recent years, see Harel Chorev, "Palestinian Social Media and Lone-Wolf Attacks: Subculture, Legitimization, and Epidemic", in *Terrorism and Political Violence*, 2019, vol. 31, no. 6, pp. 1284–1306. I am grateful to Dr. Dina Lisnyansky for the reference and for the valuable information she shared.

Appendix I: The Covenant of the Islamic Resistance Movement – Hamas

English translation by Menachem Milson, in *MEMRI Special Dispatch Series*, No. 3867, 26 May 2011

Palestine, Muharram 1, 1409 A.H./August 18, 1988

In the name of Allah the Merciful and the Compassionate

"You are the best nation that has been brought out for mankind. You command good and forbid evil and believe in Allah. If only the people of the Book [that is, Jews and Christians] had believed, it would have been well for them. Some of them believe, but most of them are iniquitous. They will never be able to do you serious harm, they will only be an annoyance. If they fight you, they will turn their backs and flee, and will not be succored. Humiliation is their lot wherever they may be, except where they are saved from it by a bond with Allah or by a bond with men. They incurred upon themselves Allah's wrath, and wretchedness is their lot, because they denied Allah's signs and wrongfully killed the prophets, and because they disobeyed and transgressed." (Koran, 3:110-112).

"Israel will exist, and will continue to exist, until Islam abolishes it, as it abolished that which was before it." [From the words of] The martyr, Imam Hasan al-Banna', Allah's mercy be upon him.

"The Islamic world is burning, and each and every one of us must pour water, even if it be a little, to extinguish whatever he can extinguish, without waiting for others." [From the words of] Sheikh Amjad Al-Zahawi, Allah's mercy be upon him.

In the name of Allah the Merciful and the Compassionate

Preamble

Praise be to Allah. We seek help from Him, we ask forgiveness from Him, we ask Him for guidance, and we rely on Him. Prayer and peace be upon Allah's messenger and upon his family and companions, and those who are loyal to him and spread his message and follow his *sunna* [the Prophet's custom]. Prayer and peace be forever upon them as long as heaven and earth exist.

Oh people, from the midst of great troubles and in the depths of suffering, and from the beating of believing hearts and arms purified for worship, out of cognizance of duty and in response to Allah's command - thence came the call [of our movement] and the meeting and joining [of forces], and thence came education in accordance with Allah's way and a resolute will to carry out [the movement's] role in life, overcoming all of the obstacles and surmounting the difficulties of the journey. Thence came also continuous preparation, [along with] readiness to sacrifice one's life and all that is valuable for the sake of Allah.

Then the seed took form and [the movement] began to move forward through this stormy sea of wishes and hopes, yearnings and aspirations, dangers and obstacles, pains and challenges, both locally [in Palestine] and abroad.

When the idea ripened, and the seed grew, and the plant shot its roots into the ground of reality, away from fleeting emotions and improper hastiness, then the Islamic Resistance Movement [Hamas] set out to play its role, marching onward for the sake of Allah. [In doing this, Hamas] joins arms with all those who wage jihad for the liberation of Palestine. The souls of its jihad fighters meet the souls of all those jihad fighters who sacrificed their lives for the land of Palestine, from the time when the Prophet's companions conquered it until the present.

The covenant of the Islamic Resistance Movement (Hamas) reveals its face, presents its identity, clarifies its stand, makes clear its aspiration, discusses its hopes, and calls out to help it and support it and to join its ranks, because our fight with the Jews is very extensive and very grave, and it requires all the sincere efforts. It is a step that must be followed by further steps; it is a brigade that must be reinforced by brigades upon brigades from this vast Islamic world, until the enemies are defeated and Allah's victory is revealed.

This is how we see them coming on the horizon: "And after a time you will come to know about it."(Koran, 38:88)

"Allah has written: It is I and My messengers who will surely prevail. Allah is Strong and Mighty." (Koran, 58:21)

"Say: This is my way. I call on Allah with certainty, I and those who follow me, and glory be to Allah, I am not among the polytheists." (Koran, 12:108)

Chapter One: Introduction to the Movement

Ideological Premises

Article One

The Islamic Resistance Movement: Islam is its way. It is from Islam that it derives its ideas, concepts, and perceptions concerning the universe, life, and man, and it refers to Islam's judgment in all its actions. It is from Islam that it seeks direction so as to guide its steps.

The Relation between the Islamic Resistance Movement and the Muslim Brotherhood

Article Two

The Islamic Resistance Movement is one of the wings of the Muslim Brotherhood in Palestine. The Muslim Brotherhood movement is a global organization and is the largest of the Islamic movements in modern times. It is distinguished by its profound understanding and its conceptual precision and by the fact that it encompasses the totality of Islamic concepts in all aspects of life, in thought and in creed, in politics and in economics, in education and in social affairs, in judicial matters and in matters of government, in preaching and in teaching, in art and in communications, in secret and in the open, and in all other areas of life.

Structure and Formation

Article Three

The Islamic Resistance Movement is founded upon Muslims who gave their allegiance to Allah and served Him as He ought to be served. "I did not create *jinns* and men except that they should serve me." (Koran, 51:56)

[These Muslims] recognized their duty towards themselves, their families and their homeland, fearing Allah in all of this. They raised the banner of jihad in the face of the oppressors, in order to deliver the land and the believers from their filth, impurity and evil. "We hurl the truth against falsehood and crush its head, and lo, it vanishes." (Koran, 21:18).

Article Four

The Islamic Resistance Movement welcomes every Muslim who embraces its creed, adopts its ideology, is committed to its way, keeps its secrets and desires to join its ranks in order to carry out the duty, and his reward is with Allah.

The Islamic Resistance Movement – Dimensions of Time and Place

Article Five

The temporal dimension of the Islamic Resistance Movement - in view of the fact that it has adopted Islam as its way of life - go back to the birth of the Islamic message and to the righteous early believers; Allah is its goal, the Prophet is its example to be followed, and Koran is its constitution.

Its spatial dimension: wherever there are Muslims who embrace Islam as their way of life, everywhere upon the earth. Thus, [Hamas] sends its roots deep into the ground, and it extends to embrace the heavens.

"Do you not see how Allah has given us a parable? A good word is like a good tree; its roots are firm and its branches extend to the heavens. It always bears its fruit at the right time in accordance with God's will. Allah recites parables to men so that they will take heed." (Koran, 14:24-25)

Distinctiveness and Independence

Article Six

The Islamic Resistance Movement is a distinct Palestinian movement that is loyal to Allah, adopts Islam as a way of life and works to raise the banner of Allah over every inch of Palestine. Under the wing of Islam, followers of other religions can all live safe and secure in their life, property and rights; whereas in the absence of Islam, discord arises, injustice spreads, corruption burgeons, and there are conflicts and wars. Allah bless the Muslim poet Muhammad Iqbal who said:

> When faith is gone, there is no safety,
>
> And there is no life to him who has no religion.

He who is content to live without religion
Has taken death as a consort of life.

The Universality of the Islamic Resistance Movement

Article Seven

Muslims who adopt the way of the Islamic Resistance Movement are found in all countries of the world, and act to support [the movement], to adopt its positions and to reinforce its jihad. Therefore, it is a world movement, and it is qualified for this [role] owing to the clarity of its ideology, the loftiness of its purpose and the exaltedness of its goals. It is on this basis that it should be regarded and evaluated; it is on this basis that its role should be recognized. Whoever denies its rights, refrains from helping it, becomes blind [to the truth] and makes an effort to blot out its role - he is like one who attempts to dispute with [divine] predestination. Whoever closes his eyes to the facts, intentionally or unintentionally, will eventually wake up [to find that] events have overtaken him and that the [weight of the] evidence has rendered him unable to justify his position. Precedence shall be given to those who come first [to the movement]. The iniquity of one's own relatives is more painful to the soul than the blow of a sharp sword.

"We have revealed to you the Book in truth, confirming the scripture that came before it and guarding it. Judge between them according to what Allah has revealed, and follow not their capricious will, turning away from the truth that was revealed to you. To each among you Allah has appointed a law and a way. If Allah had so desired, he would have made you a single nation. However, he desired to test you in all that he had given you. So vie with one another in good works. It is to Allah that you shall all return, and He will then reveal to you [the truth] about the matters in which you differed." (Koran 5:48)

The Islamic Resistance Movement is one link in the chain of jihad in confronting the Zionist invasion. It is connected and linked to the [courageous] uprising of the martyr 'Izz Al-Din Al-Qassam and his brethren the jihad fighters of the Muslim Brotherhood in the year 1936. It is further related and connected to another link, [namely] the jihad of the Palestinians, the efforts and jihad of the Muslim Brotherhood in the 1948 war, and the jihad operations of the Muslim Brotherhood in 1968 and afterwards. Although these links are far apart, and although the continuity of jihad was interrupted by obstacles placed in the path of the jihad fighters by those who circle in the orbit of Zionism, the Islamic Resistance Movement aspires to realize the promise of Allah, no matter how long it takes. The Prophet, Allah's prayer and peace be upon him, says: "The hour of judgment shall not come until the Muslims fight the Jews and kill them, so that the Jews hide behind trees and stones, and each tree and stone will say: 'Oh Muslim, oh servant of Allah, there is a Jew behind me, come and kill him,' except for the Gharqad tree, for it is the tree of the Jews." (Recorded in the Hadith collections of Bukhari and Muslim).

The Motto of the Islamic Resistance Movement

Article Eight

Allah is its goal, the Prophet its model to be followed, the Koran its constitution, Jihad its way, and death for the sake of Allah its loftiest desire.

Chapter Two: Goals

Causes and Goals

Article Nine

The Islamic Resistance Movement has found itself in a period when Islam is absent from everyday life. Consequently, the balance has been disturbed, concepts have been confused, values have been altered, evil people have come into power, injustice and darkness have prevailed, the cowardly have become tigers, the homeland has been ravished, the people have been driven away and have been wandering in all the countries of the world. The rule of righteousness is absent, and the rule of falsehood prevails. Nothing is in its proper place. Thus, when Islam is absent, everything is transformed. These are the causes.

As for the goals, they are to fight falsehood, vanquish it and defeat it so that righteousness shall rule, the homeland shall return [to its rightful owner], and from the top of its mosques, the [Muslim] call for prayer will ring out announcing the rise of the rule of Islam, so that people and things shall all return to their proper place. From Allah we seek succor.

"If Allah did not ward off one group of people by means of another, the earth would certainly be in a state of disorder. Allah is most kind to all beings." (Koran, 2:251)

Article Ten

The Islamic Resistance Movement - while marching forward - offers support to all who are persecuted and protects all who are oppressed with all its strength. It spares no effort in upholding the truth and eradicating falsehood, in word and in action, here and in every place within its reach and its influence.

Chapter Three: Strategy and Means

The Strategy of the Islamic Resistance Movement

Palestine Is an Islamic *Waqf* [that is, an Islamic religious endowment]

Article Eleven

The Islamic Resistance Movement maintains that the land of Palestine is *Waqf* land given as endowment for all generations of Muslims until the Day of Resurrection. One should not neglect it or [even] a part of it, nor should one relinquish it or [even] a part of it. No Arab state, or [even] all of the Arab states [together], have [the right] to do this; no king or president has this right nor all the kings and presidents together; no organization, or all the organizations together - be they Palestinian or Arab - [have the right to do this] because Palestine is Islamic *Waqf* land given to all generations of Muslims until the Day of Resurrection.

This is the legal status of the land of Palestine according to Islamic law. In this respect, it is like any other land that the Muslims have conquered by force, because the Muslims consecrated it at the time of the conquest as religious endowment for all generations of Muslims until the Day of Resurrection. This is how it was: when the conquest of Al-Sha'm and Iraq was complete, the commanders of the Muslim armies sent messages to the Caliph ‘Umar b. Al-Khattab, asking for instructions concerning the conquered land - should they divide it up among the troops or leave it in the hands of its owners or what? After discussions and consultations between the Caliph ‘Umar b. Al-Khattab and the Companions of the Prophet, they decided that the land should be left with its [original] owners to benefit from its crops, but the substance of the land, that is the land itself, should constitute *Waqf* for all the generations of Muslims until the Day of Resurrection. The tenure of the owners is only tenure of usufruct. This *Waqf* will exist as long as the heaven and earth exist. Any measure which does not conform to this Islamic law regarding Palestine is null and void. “This surely is the very truth. Therefore, praise the great name of your Lord.” (Koran, 56:95-96)

Homeland and Nationalism as Seen by the Islamic Resistance Movement

Article Twelve

Nationalism, as seen by the Islamic Resistance Movement, is part of the [Islamic] religious creed. There is nothing that speaks more eloquently and more profoundly of nationalism than the following: when the enemy tramples Muslim territory, waging jihad and confronting the enemy become a personal duty of every Muslim man and Muslim woman. A woman may go out to fight the enemy [even] without her husband’s permission and a slave without his master’s permission.

There is nothing like this in any other political system - this is an indisputable fact. Whereas the various other nationalist [ideologies] are connected to physical, human and regional factors, the nationalism of the Islamic Resistance Movement is [likewise] characterized by all of the above, and in addition - and most importantly - it is characterized by divine motives which endow it with spirit and life, since it is related to the source of the spirit, and to Him who gives life. [The Islamic Resistance Movement] is raising the divine banner in the skies of the homeland, so as to firmly connect heaven and earth.

> When Moses came and cast down his rod
>
> Both sorcery and sorcerer came to naught

“The right way stands out clearly from error; therefore, whoever renounces falsehood and believes in Allah, he has indeed grasped the firmest handhold, which never breaks, and Allah is Hearing and Knowing.” (Koran, 2:256)

Peaceful Solutions, Initiatives and International Conferences

Article Thirteen

The initiatives, the so-called peace solutions, and the international conferences for resolving the Palestinian problem stand in contradiction to the principles of the Islamic Resistance Movement, for to neglect any part of Palestine is to neglect part of the Islamic faith. The nationalism of the Islamic Resistance Movement is part of its [Islamic] faith. It is in the light of this principle that its members are educated, and they wage jihad in order to raise the banner of Allah over the homeland.

“And Allah has full control over His affairs; but most people do not know.” (Koran, 12:21)

From time to time there are calls to hold an international conference in order to seek a solution for the [Palestinian] problem. Some accept this [proposal] and some reject it, for one reason or another, demanding the fulfillment of some condition or conditions before they agree to hold the conference and participate in it. However, the Islamic Resistance Movement - since it is familiar with the parties participating in the conference and with their past and current positions on the issues of the Muslims - does not believe that these conferences can meet the demands or restore the rights [of the Palestinians], or bring equity to the oppressed. These conferences are nothing but a way to give the infidels power of arbitration over Muslim land, and when have the infidels ever been equitable towards the believers?

"The Jews will never be content with you, nor will the Christians, until you follow their religion. Say: 'The guidance of Allah is the right guidance.' But if you follow their desires after the knowledge which has come to you, then you shall have no protector or guardian from Allah." (Koran, 2:120)

There is no solution to the Palestinian problem except by jihad. Initiatives, proposals and international conferences are a waste of time and a farce. The Palestinian people is far too eminent to have its future, its rights and its destiny toyed with. As stated in the Hadith: "The people of Al-Sha'm are [Allah's] rod in His land. Through them, He wreaks vengeance on whomever He wishes among His servants. The hypocrites among them are not allowed to be superior to the believers among them, and they shall die in grief and distress." (Recorded by Al-Tabarani with a chain of transmitters to Muhammad, and by Ahmad [Ibn Hanbal] with an incomplete chain of transmitters to Muhammad which may be the accurate record, the transmitters in both cases being trustworthy - Allah alone is omniscient).

The Three Circles

Article Fourteen

The problem of liberating Palestine involves three circles: the Palestinian circle, the [pan-]Arab circle and the Islamic circle. Each of these three circles has its role in the struggle against Zionism and has its duties. It is a grave error and shameful ignorance to neglect any of these circles, for Palestine is an Islamic land. In it is the first of the two qiblas [directions of prayer] and the third most holy mosque, after the mosques of Mecca and Medina. It is the destination of the Prophet's nocturnal journey.

"Praise be to Him who carried His servant by night from the most sacred mosque to the farthest mosque whose surroundings We blessed, so as to show him Our signs. He is the One who is hearing and seeing." (Koran, 17:1)

This being the case, the liberation [of Palestine] is a personal duty of every Muslim, wherever he be. It is on this basis that one should consider the problem, and every Muslim should understand this. When the day comes and the problem is treated on this basis, and all the capabilities of the three circles are mobilized - the current circumstances will change and the day of liberation will draw near.

"You strike more fear in the hearts of the Jews than does Allah, because they are people who do not understand." (Koran, 59:13)

Jihad for the Liberation of Palestine is a Personal Duty

Article Fifteen

The day the enemies conquer some part of the Muslim land, jihad becomes a personal duty of every Muslim. In the face of the Jewish occupation of Palestine, it is necessary to raise the banner of jihad. This requires the propagation of Islamic consciousness among the masses, locally [in Palestine], in the Arab world and in the Islamic world. It is necessary to instill the spirit of jihad in the nation, engage the enemies and join the ranks of the jihad fighters.

The indoctrination campaign must involve ulama, educators, teachers and information and media experts, as well as all intellectuals, especially the young people and the sheikhs of Islamic movements. It is [also] necessary to introduce essential changes in the curricula, in order to eliminate the influences of the intellectual invasion which were inflicted upon them by the Orientalists and the missionaries. This invasion came upon the region after Salah Al-Din Al-Ayyubi defeated the Crusaders. The Crusaders then realized that it is impossible to vanquish the Muslims unless the way is first paved by an intellectual invasion that would confuse the [Muslims'] thinking, distort their legacy and impugn their ideals. Only after this [intellectual invasion] would there come invasion with troops. This [intellectual invasion] prepared the ground for the colonialist invasion, as [General] Allenby declared upon entering Jerusalem: "Now the Crusades have come to an end." General Gouraud stood at Salah Al-Din's tomb, and said: "Oh, Salah Al-Din, we are back!" Colonialism helped to intensify the intellectual invasion and helped it to take root. It still does. All this paved the way towards the loss of Palestine.

It is necessary to establish in the minds of all the Muslim generations that the Palestinian issue is a religious issue, and that it must be dealt with as such, for [Palestine] contains Islamic holy places, [namely] the Al-Aqsa mosque, which is inseparably connected, for as long as heaven and earth shall endure, to the holy mosque of Mecca through the Prophet's nocturnal journey [from the mosque of Mecca to the Al-Aqsa mosque] and through his ascension to heaven thence.

"Being stationed on the frontier for the sake of Allah for one day is better than this [entire] world and everything in it; and the place taken up in paradise by the [horseman's] whip of any one of you [jihad fighters] is better than this [entire] world and everything in it. Every evening [operation] and morning [operation] performed by Muslims for the sake of Allah is better than this [entire] world and everything in it." (Recorded in the Hadith collections of Bukhari, Muslim, Tirmidhi and Ibn Maja)

"By the name of Him who holds Muhammad's soul in His hand, I wish to launch an attack for the sake of Allah and be killed and attack again and be killed and attack again and be killed." (Recorded in the Hadith collections of Bukhari and Muslim)

Educating the Next Generations

Article Sixteen

It is necessary to educate the next Islamic generations in our region in an Islamic way, based on the performance of the religious duties, attentive study of Allah's book, study of the Prophet's *sunna* [custom], perusal of Islamic history and legacy based on reliable sources under the instruction of experts and scholars, and reliance on methods which will produce a wholesome outlook in thought and in faith. In addition, it is necessary to closely study the enemy and his material and human capabilities, to become familiar with his weaknesses and strengths, to recognize the powers that assist and support him. It is also necessary to be familiar with current events, follow new developments and study the analyses and commentaries regarding them. It is likewise necessary to plan for the future and to study each and every phenomenon, so that Muslims engaged in jihad will live with full awareness of their purpose, goal and way, and [with full awareness of] what is happening around them.

"Oh my son! If [a thing] is but the weight of a grain of mustard, though it be in a rock, or in the heavens, or on earth, Allah will bring it forth. Allah discerns even the smallest thing; He is omniscient. Oh my son! Keep up prayer and enjoin the good and forbid the evil, and persevere whatever may befall you; surely this [behavior] is worthy steadfastness. Turn not thy cheek in scorn away from people; do not walk haughtily in the land. Allah does not love the arrogant and self-conceited." (Koran, 31:16-18)

The Role of Muslim Women

Article Seventeen

The role of the Muslim woman in the war of liberation is no less important than that of the man, for she is the maker of men. Her role in guiding and educating the next generation is very important. The enemies have realized [the significance of] her role, and they believe that if they can educate her according to their wishes, guiding her away from Islam, they will have won the war. You find, therefore, that they continually make great efforts [to do this] by means of the media, the cinema and school curricula, through their agents who are incorporated in Zionist organizations that assume various names and forms such as the Freemasons, Rotary Clubs, espionage groups, etc. - all of which are dens of sabotage and saboteurs. These Zionist organizations have an enormous abundance of material resources, which enable them to play their game in [various] societies with the aim of realizing their purpose while Islam is absent from the scene and the Muslims are estranged [from their faith]. The followers of the Islamic movements should fulfill their role in countering the schemes of these saboteurs. When Islam is at the helm, it will totally eradicate these organizations, which are hostile to humanity and to Islam.

Article Eighteen

The woman in the jihadist home and family, as mother or sister, has the primary role in managing the household, raising the children according to the moral ideas and values inspired by Islam, and teaching them to perform the religious duties in preparation for the jihadist role that awaits them. Hence, it is necessary to pay close attention to the schools in which the Muslim girl is educated, and to their curricula, so that she will grow to be a good mother, conscious of her role in the war of liberation. She should have adequate awareness and understanding concerning the management of domestic affairs, since economy and avoiding wastefulness in family expenses are among the requirements in the ability to persist in the current difficult circumstances. She should ever be aware that available funds are like blood that must flow only in the veins for life to continue in both young and old.

"Muslim men and Muslim women, the believing men and women, the truthful men and women, the persevering men and women, the humble men and women, the charitable men and women, the fasting men and women, the men and women who guard their chastity, and the men and women who remember Allah frequently - for them Allah has prepared forgiveness and great reward." (Koran, 33:35).

The Role of Islamic Art in the War of Liberation

Article Nineteen

Art has rules and standards by which it is possible to determine whether it is Islamic or pagan. The Islamic liberation is in need of Islamic art that uplifts the spirit without subjecting one aspect of human nature to another, but rather uplifts all aspects in [perfect] balance and harmony. Man is a marvelous and unique creature made from a handful of clay and a breath of spirit. Islamic art addresses man on this basis, while pagan art addresses the physical body and gives dominance to the component of clay.

Books, articles, pamphlets, sermons, epistles, traditional songs, poems, [patriotic] songs, plays, etc. - when they have the characteristics of Islamic art, they are among the necessary means of ideological indoctrination. [They constitute] self-renewing sustenance for continuing the journey and refreshing the spirit, for the road is long, the suffering is great and the souls grow weary. Islamic art renews the energies, revives motion and awakens the soul to lofty ideals and wholesome conduct.

Nothing heals the soul when it is in retreat save moving from mode to mode.

All this is utterly serious and no jest, for the nation engaged in jihad knows no jest.

Social Solidarity

Article Twenty

Muslim society is characterized by solidarity. The Prophet, Allah's prayer and peace be upon him, says: "Blessed are the Banu Al-Ash'ar tribe. When they are afflicted with drought - whether in a town or on a journey - they would collect all that they have and divide it among themselves in equal shares." This is the Islamic spirit that should prevail in every Muslim society. A society which is facing a wicked enemy with Nazi behavior, that does not distinguish between men and women, old and young, has an even greater need to grace itself with this Islamic spirit [of solidarity]. Our enemy employs the method of collective punishment, depriving people of their homes and possessions. He pursued them [even] in their places of exile, breaking bones, shooting women, children and elderly people with or without reason. He established detention camps to imprison thousands and thousands [of people] in inhuman conditions, all this in addition to destroying houses, orphaning children and unjustly convicting thousands of young people to spend the best years of their youth in the darkness of prison. The Nazism of the Jews targeted both women and children. The terror they spread is directed at everyone. They fight people by destroying their livelihood, stealing their money and trampling their dignity. Their horrible treatment of people is like that of the worst war criminals. Deportation from one's homeland is a form of murder. In the face of such behavior, we must have social solidarity among the people, and we must face the enemy as one body, which, when one of its limbs is in pain, the rest of it reacts with sleeplessness and fever.

Article Twenty-One

Social solidarity means offering help to everyone who is in need, be it material or moral, or joining with him to complete some work. Members of the Islamic Resistance Movement should regard the interests of the masses as their own, and they should spare no effort to achieve them and protect them. They must prevent reckless playing with matters affecting the future of the next generations or causing losses to their society. The masses are of them and for them, and the strength of the masses is strength for them; their future is theirs. The members of the Islamic Resistance Movement should be with the people on joyous occasions and at times of grief. They should espouse the demands of the masses and strive to serve the masses' interests, which are indeed their own. When this spirit prevails, friendship will deepen and there will be cooperation and empathy, unity will increase and the ranks will be strengthened to confront the enemies.

The Forces which Support the Enemy

Article Twenty-Two

The enemies have been planning expertly and thoroughly for a long time in order to achieve what they have achieved, employing those means which affect the course of events. They strove to accumulate huge financial resources which they used to realize their dream.

With money they have taken control of the world media - news agencies, the press, publishing houses, broadcasting services, etc. With money they sparked revolutions in various countries around the world in order to serve their interests and to reap profits. They were behind the French Revolution and the Communist Revolution and [they are behind] most of the revolutions about which we hear from time to time here and there. With money they have formed secret organizations, all over the world, in order to destroy [those countries'] societies and to serve the Zionists' interests, such as the Freemasons, the Rotary Clubs, the Lions, the Sons of the Covenant [that is, B'nei B'rith], etc. All of these are organizations of espionage and sabotage. With money they were able to take control of the colonialist countries, and [they] urged them to colonize many countries so that they could exploit their resources and spread moral corruption there.

There is no end to what can be said about [their involvement in] local wars and world wars. They were behind World War I, through which they achieved the destruction of the Islamic Caliphate, reaped material profits, took control of numerous resources, obtained the Balfour Declaration, and established the League of the United Nations [*sic*] so as to rule the world through this organization. They were [also] behind World War II, through which they reaped enormous profits from commerce in war materials and paved the way for the establishment of their state. They [also] suggested the formation of the United Nations and the Security Council to replace the League of the United Nations [*sic*] and to rule the world through this [new organization]. Wherever there is war in the world, it is they who are pulling the strings behind the scenes. "Whenever they ignite the fire of war, Allah extinguishes it. They strive to spread evil in the land, but Allah does not love those who do evil." (Koran, 5:64)

The colonialist powers, both in the capitalist West and the communist East, support the enemy with all their might, both materially and with manpower, alternating one with the other [in giving support]. When Islam appears, all the forces of unbelief unite to oppose it, for all unbelief is one denomination.

"Oh you who believe, do not take as your intimate friends those outside your ranks, for they will spare no effort to harm you. They desire that which causes you suffering. Hatred has indeed come out of their mouths, but what they hide in their hearts is even worse. We have given you clear signs, if you understand" (Koran, 3:118). It is not for nothing that the verse ends with His words "if you understand."

Chapter Four - Our Positions on:

A. The Islamic Movements

Article Twenty-Three

The Islamic Resistance Movement looks on the other Islamic movements with respect and appreciation, for even if it is at variance with them in some given respect or thought, it agrees with them in many more respects or thoughts, and it views them - so long as their intentions are good and they are devoted to Allah - as falling under the rubric of legitimate opinion, that is, as long as their actions are within the bounds of the Islamic circle. Everyone who strives for truth receives his reward.

The Islamic Resistance Movement considers these movements as reinforcing it, and asks [Allah] to guide and direct us all. It never forgets to constantly raise the banner of unity and to strive assiduously to achieve unity in accordance with the Koran and the *sunna*. "Hold fast to Allah's rope, all of you. Do not be divided among yourselves, and remember Allah's favor to you. When you were enemies to one another, He brought your hearts together, and through his favor you became brothers. You were on the brink of a pit of fire, and He saved you from it. Thus Allah shows you His signs, so that you may follow the right way." (Koran, 3:103)

Article Twenty-Four

The Islamic Resistance Movement does not allow to impugn or to blacken the name of individuals or groups, for [true] Muslims do not impugn or curse others. One should make a clear distinction between this and positions or behavior, for the Islamic Resistance Movement does have the right to expose error and to deter people from it and to strive to make the truth known and to adopt it in an impartial way in every given case. Wisdom is what the Muslim looks for, and he takes it wherever he finds it.

"Allah does not like it when people speak ill in public, except for those who have been wronged. Allah hears all and knows all. When you do good openly, or in secret, or forgive a wrong [done to you], surely Allah is Forgiving and Almighty." (Koran, 4:148-149)

B. The Nationalist Movements in the Palestinian Arena

Article Twenty-Five

[The Islamic Resistance Movement] respects them and appreciates the conditions that surround and affect them. It supports them as long as they do not pay allegiance to the Communist East or to the Crusader West, and it emphasizes to all the members and supporters [of these movements] that it is a jihadist, ethical movement, conscientious in its worldview and in its treatment of others. It abhors opportunism, wants only good for the people, both as individuals and as groups, and does not strive to attain material gain or fame for itself. It does not seek reward from people, and it goes forth with its own resources and what it has at hand - “Muster against them all the force you can” (Koran, 8:60) - in order to carry out the duty and win Allah’s favor. It has no desire other than that.

It reassures all the nationalist [groups] of all orientations that are operating in the Palestinian arena for the liberation of Palestine that it shall never be anything other than a support and an aid for them, in word and in deed, at present and in the future. It joins together and does not separate, preserves and does not scatter, unites and does not divide, it values every kind word, every sincere effort and every praiseworthy endeavor. It closes the door in the face of petty disagreements. It pays no heed to rumors and biased remarks, but is fully aware of [its] right to defend itself.

Anything that opposes or contradicts this orientation is fabricated by the enemy or by their lackeys in order to cause confusion, divide the ranks and create distraction with side issues. “OH you who believe, if an evildoer brings you information [about any person], you should examine it carefully lest you hurt [innocent] people out of ignorance, and afterwards come to regret it.” (Koran, 49:6)

Article Twenty-Six

The Islamic Resistance Movement - looking favorably as it does on the Palestinian nationalist movements that do not pay allegiance to the East or to the West - does not refrain from discussing new developments concerning the Palestinian problem in the local and international arena in an objective manner, so as to find to what extent [these developments] agree or disagree with the national interests in the light of the Islamic vision.

C. The Palestine Liberation Organization

Article Twenty-Seven

The Palestine Liberation Organization [PLO] is closest to the heart of the Islamic Resistance Movement. [We regard it as] a father, brother or friend, and a true Muslim does not spurn his father, his brother or his friend. Our homeland is one, our misfortune is one, our destiny is one and we share the same enemy.

Owing to the circumstances that surrounded the establishment of the PLO, and [owing to] the intellectual confusion which prevails in the Arab world as a result of the intellectual invasion to which it has been subject since the defeat of the Crusaders, and which was intensified, and continues to be intensified by Orientalism and Christian missionary activities - the PLO has adopted the idea of the secular state, and we view [the PLO] accordingly. Secularist ideology stands in total contradiction to the religious ideology, and it is ideas which are the basis of positions, behavior and decisions.

Hence, with all our appreciation for the Palestine Liberation Organization and what it may yet become, and without belittling its role in the Arab-Israeli conflict, we cannot give up the Islamic identity of Palestine in the present and in the future to adopt the secularist ideology - for the Islamic identity of Palestine is part of our faith, and whoever is lax with his faith is lost. "Who spurns the religion of Abraham but one who has made himself into a fool?" (Koran, 2:130)

When the PLO adopts Islam as its way of life, then we shall be its troops and the fuel for its fire that will burn the enemies. But until this time comes - and we pray to Allah that it be soon - the position of the Islamic Resistance Movement vis a vis the PLO is that of a son towards his father, a brother towards his brother or a relative towards his relative. He shares the other's pain when he is pricked by a thorn, and supports him in facing the enemy, and he wishes for him to find divine guidance and [follow] the right path.

> Your brother, your brother before all others! He who has no brother
>
> Is like one who goes to war unarmed.
>
> Your cousin, you must know the strength of his wing,
>
> For how can the falcon rise up without wings?

D. Arab and Islamic States and Governments

Article Twenty-Eight

The Zionist invasion is a cruel invasion, which has no scruples whatsoever; it uses every vicious and vile method to achieve its goals. In its infiltration and espionage operations, it greatly relies on secret organizations which grew out of it, such as the Freemasons, the Rotary Clubs, the Lions and other such espionage groups. All these organizations, covert or overt, work for the interests of Zionism and under its direction, and their aim is to break societies, undermine values, destroy people's honor, create moral degeneration and annihilate Islam. [Zionism] is behind all types of trafficking in drugs and alcohol, so as to make it easier for it to take control and expand.

We demand that the Arab countries around Israel open their borders to jihad fighters from among the Arab and Islamic peoples, so they may fulfill their role and join their efforts to the efforts of their brothers - the Muslim brethren in Palestine. As for the rest of the Arab and Muslim countries, we demand that they facilitate the passage of the jihad fighters into them and out of them - that is the very least [they can do].

We should not fail to remind every Muslim that when the Jews occupied the Sacred place [that is, Jerusalem] in 1967 and stood on the threshold of the blessed Al-Aqsa mosque, they shouted: "Muhammad is dead; his offspring are women." Israel with its Jewish identity and Jewish people is challenging Islam and the Muslims. May the cowardly know no sleep.

E. Nationalist and Religious Groups and Organizations, Intellectuals, and the Arab and Islamic world

Article Twenty-Nine

The Islamic Resistance Movement hopes that these groups will stand by it in every respect, help it, espouse its positions, back its activities and strive to enlist support for it, so that the Muslim peoples will be a support and a reinforcement for it, and [will provide] strategic depth on all levels: [in terms of] human and material resources, information, in every time and every place. [This should be done] by holding conferences, publishing ideological pamphlets, and by indoctrination of the masses with regards to the Palestinian issue - what is facing [the Palestinians] and what is plotted against [them]. [Likewise they should work to] mobilize the Islamic peoples, ideologically, educationally and culturally, so that they will play their role in the decisive war of liberation just as they did in defeating the Crusaders and routing out the Mongols, thus saving human civilization. This is not difficult for Allah.

"Allah has decreed: 'I and My messengers shall prevail'; Allah is strong and all-powerful." (Koran, 58:21)

Article Thirty

Writers, intellectuals, media people, preachers in mosques, educators and all the various sectors in the Arab and Islamic world, are all required to fulfill their role and perform their duty. [This is necessary] due to the ferocity of the Zionist onslaught and the fact that it has infiltrated many countries and has taken control of the finances and media - with all the ramifications that follow from this - in most countries of the world.

Jihad is not limited to wielding arms and fighting the enemies face to face, for eloquent speech, persuasive writing, effective books, support and help - when [they are] performed with the sincere intention that Allah's banner will reign supreme - all constitute jihad for the sake of Allah.

[As the prophet said:] "Whoever equips a warrior fighting for the sake of Allah is [himself] a warrior, and whoever supports the family of a warrior [who has set out to fight for the sake of Allah] is [himself] a warrior." (Recorded by Bukhari, Muslim, Abu Da'ud and Tirmidhi in their Hadith collections).

F. Followers of the Other Religions

The Islamic Resistance Movement is a Humane Movement

Article Thirty-One

The Islamic Resistance Movement is a humane movement which respects human rights and is committed to the Islamic tolerance towards the followers of the other religions. It is hostile only to those among them who display hostility towards it or stand in its way, hampering its activities and foiling its efforts. Under the wing of Islam, the followers of the three religions - Islam, Christianity and Judaism - can co-exist in security and safety. It is only under the wing of Islam that safety and security prevail. Recent and ancient history provide the best evidence for this. The followers of the other religions should stop competing with Islam for sovereignty in this region, because, when they rule, there is nothing but carnage, torture and deportation, and they cannot get along with their own, let alone with followers of other religions. Both the present and the past are full of evidence for this.

"They do not fight you together, except from within fortified villages, or from behind walls. They fight fiercely with one another. You consider them to be united, but their hearts are divided, for they are a people with no sense." (Koran, 59:14)

Islam accords to every person his rights, and prevents any infringement on other people's rights. The Nazi Zionist measures against our people will not succeed in prolonging the duration of their invasion, for the rule of injustice lasts but one hour, while the rule of the truth will last until the Hour of Resurrection.

"Allah does not forbid you to show kindness and act justly towards those who do not fight you on account of your religion, and do not drive you from your homes. Allah loves those who act justly." (Koran, 60:8)

G. The Attempt to Isolate the Palestinian People

Article Thirty-Two

World Zionism and the colonialist powers attempt, by clever maneuvering and meticulous planning, to pull the Arab states, one by one, out of the circle of the conflict with Zionism, so as to ultimately isolate the Palestinian people. It has already taken Egypt out of the circle of conflict to a large extent through the treacherous Camp David Accords [of September 1978], and it is trying to pull additional [Arab] countries into similar agreements so that they leave the circle of conflict.

The Islamic Resistance Movement calls upon all the Arab and Muslim peoples to strive seriously and diligently to prevent this horrible scheme, and to alert the masses to the danger inherent in leaving the circle of the conflict with Zionism. Today it is Palestine, and tomorrow some other country or countries, for the Zionist plan has no limits, and after Palestine they want to expand [their territory] from the Nile to the Euphrates, and when they finish devouring one area, they hunger for further expansion and so on, indefinitely. Their plan is expounded in The Protocols of the Elders of Zion, and their present [behavior] is the best proof for what we are saying.

Leaving the circle of the conflict with Zionism is an act of high treason; all those who do this shall be cursed. "Whoever [when fighting the infidels] turns his back to them, unless maneuvering for battle or intending to join another [fighting] company, he incurs Allah's wrath, and his abode shall be hell. Most unfortunate is his fate." (Koran, 8:16)

All forces and capabilities must be pooled to confront this ferocious Mongol, Nazi onslaught, lest homelands be lost, people be exiled, evil spread on the earth and all religious values be destroyed. Each and every person should know that he is responsible to Allah.

"Anyone who does a grain's weight of good shall see it, and anyone who does a grain's weight of evil shall see it." (Koran, 99:7-8)

In the circle of the conflict against world Zionism, the Islamic Resistance Movement sees itself as a spearhead or as a step forward on the road [to victory]. It joins its efforts to the efforts of all those who are active in the Palestinian arena. It now remains for steps to be taken by the Arab and Islamic world. [The Islamic Resistance Movement] is well qualified for the upcoming stage [of the struggle] with the Jews, the warmongers.

"We have planted enmity and hatred among them [that is, among the Jews] until the Day of Resurrection. Every time they kindle the fire of war, Allah extinguishes it. They strive to spread evil upon the earth, and Allah does not love those who do evil." (Koran, 5:64)

Article Thirty-Three

The Islamic Resistance Movement - proceeding from these general concepts which are in harmony and agreement with the laws of nature, and following the current of divine destiny towards confrontation with the enemies and jihad against them in defense of Muslims, Islamic civilization and Islamic sanctities, primarily the Al-Aqsa mosque - calls on the Arab and Islamic peoples and their governments, and on their NGOs and official organizations, to fear Allah in their attitude toward the Islamic Resistance Movement and in their treatment of it. They should act towards it as Allah wants them to, namely back it, support it, assist it and continuously reinforce it, until Allah's word is fulfilled. Then the ranks will all be united, jihad fighters will join other jihad fighters, and the masses all over the Islamic world will rush out and answer the call of duty, shouting: "Hasten to jihad!" This call will penetrate the clouds in the sky and continue to ring out, until liberation is accomplished, the invaders are defeated and Allah's victory is revealed.

"Allah surely helps whoever helps Him; Allah is strong and mighty." (Koran, 22:40)

Chapter Five: Historical Evidence throughout the Generations regarding Confrontation with Aggressors

Article Thirty-Four

Palestine is the center of the Earth and the meeting place of the continents; it has always been the target of greedy aggressors. This has been the case since the dawn of history. The Prophet, Allah's prayer and peace be upon him, points to this in his noble words with which he addressed his exalted companion, Mu'adh b. Jabal, saying: "Oh Mu'adh, Allah will give you the land of Al-Sha'm after my death, from Al-'Arish to the Euphrates. Its men, women and handmaids will be [constantly] stationed on the frontier until the Day of Resurrection, for any one of you who chooses [to live in] some part of the coastal plains of Al-Sha'm or Bayt Al-Maqdis [that is, Palestine], will be in a [constant] state of jihad until the Day of Resurrection."

The aggressors coveted Palestine on many occasions. They attacked it with great armies in attempt to realize their greedy aspirations. The great armies of the Crusaders came there, bringing their religious creed and hoisting their cross. They managed to defeat the Muslims for a while, and the Muslims only managed to regain it when they fought under their religious banner, joined forces crying "Allah Akbar," and set forth in jihad under the command of Salah Al-Din Al-Ayyubi for nearly two decades, which led to a clear victory: the Crusaders were defeated and Palestine was liberated.

"Say to the unbelievers: You will surely be defeated and gathered in Hell. Most terrible shall be your resting-place." (Koran, 3:12)

This is the only way to liberation, and one cannot doubt the testimony of history. This is one of the rules of the universe and the laws of reality. Only iron can break iron, and their false, fabricated faith can only be overcome by the true faith of Islam, for religious faith cannot be attacked except through religious faith. And truth shall eventually triumph, for truth is the strongest.

"We have already given Our Word to Our servants, the messengers, that they would be helped to victory and that Our army will triumph." (Koran, 37:171-173)

Article Thirty-Five

The Islamic Resistance Movement studies the defeat of the Crusaders at the hands of Salah Al-Din Al-Ayyubi, the liberation of Palestine from them, as well as the defeat of the Mongols at 'Ayn Jalut and the breaking of their military strength at the hands of Qutuz and Al-Zahir Baybars, and the delivery of the Arab world from the Mongol conquest which destroyed all aspects of human civilization. [The Islamic Resistance Movement] studies these [events] seriously, and draws lessons and examples from them. The current Zionist invasion was preceded by Crusader invasions from the west, and by Mongol invasion from the east. And just as the Muslims faced these invasions, made plans for fighting them and defeated them, they can [now] confront the Zionist invasion and defeat it. This not difficult for Allah, providing that intentions are sincere and resolve is strong, and that Muslims draw benefit from the experiences of the past, shed off the influences of the intellectual invasion, and follow the ways of their predecessors.

Conclusion: The Islamic Resistance Movement- Soldiers [for the Cause]

Article Thirty-Six

The Islamic Resistance Movement, in its march forward, repeatedly emphasizes to all members of our people and of the Arab and Muslim peoples that it is not seeking fame for itself, or material gain, or social status, and that it is not aimed against any of our own people in an attempt to compete with them or to take their place - nothing of the kind. It does not oppose any Muslim, or any non-Muslim who is peaceful towards it, here [in Palestine] or elsewhere. It will always offer nothing but help to all groups and organizations that strive against the Zionist enemy and against its lackeys.

The Islamic Resistance Movement adopts Islam as its way of life. [Islam] is its creed and its law. [Any group that] adopts Islam as its way of life, here or elsewhere - be it an organization, association, state or any other group - the Islamic Resistance Movement will serve as its soldiers. We ask Allah to guide us, to guide [others] through us, and to judge between us and our people with truth.

"Oh, Lord, judge between us and our people with truth. You are the best of judges." (Koran, 7:89)

At the end, we beseech: Praise be to Allah, Lord of the Universe.

Part V: Measures Available to Prevent or Reduce Hateful Expression in Religious Communities

SECTION F:
EXTERNAL MEASURES

23

Relevant Activities and Recommendations of Intergovernmental Organizations on the Role of Religious Actors to Reduce Hate Speech, Including in Their Own Contexts or Communities

Kishan Manocha[*]

23.1. Introduction

Hate speech is a deep-rooted, complex and multidimensional phenomenon that has far-reaching and dangerous consequences in and for societies.[1] Its reported

---

[*] **Kishan Manocha** is Head, Tolerance and Non-Discrimination Department, at the Organization for Security and Co-operation in Europe ('OSCE') Office for Democratic Institutions and Human Rights ('ODIHR'). He holds degrees in psychology and medicine from the University of London and in law from the University of Cambridge, and has worked as a psychiatrist and also practised as a barrister in the areas of domestic and international criminal law. He has extensive experience in freedom of religion or belief and related human rights issues in Europe, North America, the Middle East and North Africa, and Central and South Asia, as an advocate, researcher and trainer. He serves on the International Religious Freedom or Belief Alliance's Global Council of Experts and on the Global Steering Committee of the United Nations ('UN') Plan of Action for Religious Leaders and Actors to Prevent Incitement to Violence that Could Lead to Atrocity Crimes, and was ODIHR Senior Adviser on Freedom of Religion or Belief between 2015 and 2020. For an audio-visual recording of his statement to CILRAP's conference in Florence in April 2022 on the topic of this anthology, please see https://www.cilrap.org/cilrap-film/220408-manocha/. Views expressed in this chapter do not necessarily reflect those of the author's current or former instutional affiliations.

[1] UN Secretary-General António Guterres, "United Nations Strategy and Plan of Action on Hate Speech", 18 June 2019 (available on the UN's web site):

> Hate speech is in itself an attack on tolerance, inclusion, diversity and the very essence of our human rights norms and principles. More broadly, it undermines social cohesion, erodes shared values, and can lay the foundation for violence, setting back the cause of peace, stability, sustainable development and the fulfillment of human rights for all.

Council of Europe ('COE'), "Recommendation CM/Rec(2022)16 of the Committee of Ministers to Member States on Combating Hate Speech", 20 May 2022, Preamble, para. 6 ('Recommendation CM/Rec(2022)16') (https://www.legal-tools.org/doc/lxa81b/):

> Realising that hate speech negatively affects individuals, groups and societies in a variety of ways and with different degrees of severity, including by instilling fear in and causing humiliation to those it targets and by having a chilling effect on participation in public debate, which is detrimental to democracy.

disturbing rise, particularly during the Covid-19 pandemic,[2] adds to the sense of urgency in tackling it. Cognizant of its damaging effects on the social fabric, a number of intergovernmental organizations in recent years have made efforts to tackle hate speech at both policy and programmatic levels and have set standards, issued recommendations, developed action plans and undertaken initiatives to deal with this problem; they also recognize that preventing and countering it requires multi-level and multi-stakeholder approaches. Religious actors – whether leaders or members of religious communities, religious institutions or faith-based organizations – are regarded to varying degrees as important actors in the co-ordinated, society-wide effort against hate speech. Religious communities are among the groups most targeted by hate speech, but, at the same time, some hate speech is perpetrated by religious actors or justified in the name of religion, so-called 'religious hate speech', which may lead to terrorism or atrocity crimes. Therefore, the contributions of religious actors are viewed with particular importance by the international community for both the peace and security of religious communities as well as that of wider society.

Debates on the precise definition and parameters of hate speech continue[3] and, to date, no authoritative, legally binding definition of hate speech exists at the international level despite the frequent usage of the term.[4] Consequently,

---

2 The proliferation of hate speech, particularly online, during the Covid-19 pandemic, has been observed and reported by numerous experts and international organizations. See, for example, OSCE, "OSCE Human Dimension Commitments and State Responses to the COVID-19 Pandemic", 17 July 2020, pp. 126–136; UN Human Rights Council ('UNHRC'), Report of the Special Rapporteur on Minority Issues, UN Doc. A/HRC/46/57, 3 March 2021 (https://www.legal-tools.org/doc/46g6nv/); UN Office of the High Commissioner for Human Rights ('OHCHR'), "Global Pledge for Action by Religious Actprs and Faith-Based Organizations to Address the COVID-19 pandemic in Collaboration with the United Nations", 7 July 2021 ('Global Pledge for Action by Religious Actors and Faith-Based Organizations'); International Dialogue Centre (KAICIID), "Expert Consultation on Countering Hate Speech: Findings", 20 April 2021, pp. 3–4 ('Expert Consultation on Countering Hate Speech').

3 "Being aware that hate speech is defined and understood in different ways at the national, European and international levels and that it is crucial to develop a common understanding of the concept, nature and implications of this phenomenon", Recommendation CM/Rec(2022)16, 2022, para. 13, see *supra* note 1.

4 Existing definitions and descriptions of the term are often political in nature and are formulated in a broad manner and cover speech that generates and amplifies hate and that is often also rooted in intolerance and hate. See, for example, COE, "Recommendation No. R(97)20 of the Council of Ministers to Member States on 'Hate Speech'", 30 October 1997 ('Recommendation No. R(97)20') (https://www.legal-tools.org/doc/rx2ckd/); International Convention on the Elimination of All Forms of Racial Discrimination, 21 December 1965, Article 4 (https://www.legal-tools.org/doc/43a925/); International Covenant on Civil and Political Rights, 16 December 1966, Article 20(2) ('ICCPR') (https://www.legal-tools.org/doc/2838f3/); Parliamentary Assembly of the Council of Europe ('PACE'), "Ending

terminological confusion abounds and the characterization of what is 'hateful' is controversial and disputed.[5] Nevertheless, a broad definition that distinguishes within it different layers of hate speech finds support in the approaches taken by, or under the auspices of, intergovernmental organizations.[6] For the purposes of this chapter, this broad approach will be followed and the term 'hate speech' will be used to cover a range of hateful expressions, offline and online, which vary in their severity, the harms they cause and their impact on members of particular groups in different contexts, including incitement to discrimination,

---

Cyberdiscrimination and Online Hate", Resolution 2144(2017), 25 January 2017, para. 2 ('PACE Resolution 2144(2017)') (https://www.legal-tools.org/doc/u0yz7o/); PACE, "The Role and Responsibilities of Political Leaders in Combating Hate Speech and Intolerance", Resolution 2275(2019), 10 April 2019, para. 1 ('PACE Resolution 2275(2019)'); ECRI, "ECRI General Policy Recommendation No. 15 on Combating Hate Speech", 8 December 2015, Preamble, para. 6 and Section B, paras. 8–21 ('ECRI General Policy Recommendation No. 15') (https://www.legal-tools.org/doc/hb51n3/); UN Office on Genocide Prevention and the Responsibility to Protect, "United Nations Strategy and Plan of Action on Hate Speech", 31 May 2019, p. 2 ('UN Strategy and Plan of Action') (https://www.legal-tools.org/doc/5rrb5b/); The Detailed Guidance on Implementation of the Strategy and Plan of Action for UN Field Presences notes, on p. 10, that the definition of hate speech contained in the Strategy "is for the purposes of supporting a common basis for the implementation of the Strategy by the UN, only. It does not give rise to any binding obligations upon States". UN Office on Genocide Prevention and the Responsibility to Protect, "United Nations Strategy and Plan of Action on Hate Speech: Detailed Guidance on Implementation for United Nations Field Presences", September 2020, p. 10 ('Detailed Guidance on Implementation for UN Field Presences'); Recommendation CM/Rec(2022)16, 2022, Appendix to the Recommendations, para. 2, see *supra* note 1.

5 UN Office on Genocide Prevention and the Responsibility to Protect, "Plan of Action for Religious Leaders and Actors to Prevent Incitement to Violence that Could Lead to Atrocity Crimes", 14 July 2017, p. 2 ('Plan of Action for Religious Leaders and Actors') (https://www.legal-tools.org/doc/8723g7/).

6 The Rabat Plan of Action on the prohibition of advocacy of national, racial or religious hatred that constitutes incitement to discrimination, hostility or violence does not mention hate speech, but refers to "three types of expression", namely "expression that constitutes a criminal offence; expression that is not criminally punishable, but may justify a civil suit or administrative sanctions; expression that does not give rise to criminal, civil or administrative sanctions, but still raises concern in terms of tolerance, civility and respect for the rights of others.", UNHRC, Annual Report of the UN High Commissioner for Human Rights, UN Doc. A/HRC/22/17/Add.4, 11 January 2013, para. 20 (https://www.legal-tools.org/doc/oymwge/). This largely corresponds to the approach taken in the UN Strategy and Plan of Action (see reference to "three levels of hate speech" on Detailed Guidance on Implementation for UN Field Presences, 2020, pp. 12–15, see *supra* note 4) and by the Recommendation CM/Rec(2022)16, 2022, Appendix to the Recommendations, para. 3, see *supra* note 1. The comment that, "[w]hile all incitement to discrimination, hostility or violence is hate speech, not all hate speech constitutes incitement", would seem to be in line with this approach to understanding what constitutes hate speech (Plan of Action for Religious Leaders and Actors 2017, p. 2, see *supra* note 5).

hostility or violence, the most serious form of hate speech,[7] as well as offensive, intolerant or harmful utterances that are not deemed to be of sufficient severity to warrant legitimate restriction.[8] The term 'religious actor' will be used in this chapter as shorthand for individuals and entities who are motivated by faith, whether a religious or non-religious belief system or conscientiously held worldview, to participate in the life of society. The category of religious actor includes, but is not limited to, religious leaders, individuals, communities, institutions, faith-based and faith-inspired organizations.

After a brief review of some of the reasons given by intergovernmental organizations for engaging religious actors in efforts to prevent and counter hate speech, including in their own contexts or communities and whether alone or as part of multi-stakeholder approaches, this chapter will present and discuss the most notable intergovernmental initiatives on hate speech, whether activities, action plans, consultative processes, strategies or recommendations, that have paid focused attention to the contribution of religious actors or assigned them a strategic role in such efforts. This is not intended to be an exhaustive mapping exercise of all relevant efforts, nor does it attempt an analysis of the normative basis for such engagement.[9] Consequently, it will not deal with the involvement of religious actors in areas that are somehow related to hate speech, such as preventing or countering violent extremism and terrorism, human rights protection, and the building of peaceful, equal and inclusive societies, unless their role in combating hate speech within these broader processes constitutes a distinct area of work.[10] The chapter will also explore a number of issues that have

---

7 "Incitement is a very dangerous form of speech, because it explicitly and deliberately aims at triggering discrimination, hostility and violence, which may also lead to or include terrorism or atrocity crimes": UN Strategy and Plan of Action on Hate Speech, 2019, Foreword, p. 2, see *supra* note 4. See also, Detailed Guidance on Implementation for UN Field Presences, 2020, pp. 12–14, see *supra* note 4.

8 This form of hate speech corresponds to the third layer of expression mentioned in para. 20 of the Rabat Plan of Action, the third level of hate speech described in the Detailed Guidance on Implementation for UN Field Presences, 2020, pp. 14–16, see *supra* note 4, and to "offensive or harmful types of expression which are not sufficiently severe to be legitimately restricted under the European Convention on Human Rights, but nevertheless call for alternative responses" in the Recommendation CM/Rec(2022)16, 2022, Appendix to the Recommendations, para. 3(b), see *supra* note 1.

9 For a discussion of the normative basis for action by religious leaders in the area of hate speech, see Chapter 17 in this volume by Gunnar Ekeløve-Slydal.

10 Consequently, documents such as the UN Secretary-General, Plan of Action to Prevent Violent Extremism, UN Doc. A/70/674, 24 December 2015 (https://www.legal-tools.org/doc/ui69e3/); UN Development Programme ('UNDP'), "Preventing Violent Extremism through Promoting Inclusive Development, Tolerance and Respect for Diversity: A Development Programme to Addressing Radicalization and Violent Extremism", 1 July 2016

emerged in relation to the intergovernmental-religious engagement on hate speech issues to date and, in light of these, will consider how religious actors can become more effective partners to intergovernmental efforts to address hate speech.

23.2. Reasons Why Intergovernmental Organizations Engage Religious Actors in Efforts to Prevent and Counter Hate Speech

Intergovernmental organizations have increasingly recognized that the multidimensional nature of hate speech, offline and online, requires a comprehensive and collaborative multi-actor approach if it is to be effectively combatted. Such a 'whole-of-society' response, mobilizing multiple stakeholders, is designed to tackle the root causes and drivers of hate speech as well as take due account of specific situations and broader contexts.[11] There is a varying recognition among intergovernmental organizations that religious actors, particularly religious leaders, are among the important stakeholder categories with which to increase collaboration and focus and to engage at all levels, particularly in relation to hate speech perpetrated by religious individuals or in the name of religion, but not only.[12] As the ensuing discussion will show, there is a move at least on the part of the UN for this engagement to be more proactive, deliberate and strategic.

('2016 UNDP Report') (https://www.legal-tools.org/doc/guylbf/); and the UNDP, "Jakarta Declaration on Violent Extremism and Religious Education", 28 December 2017, (https://www.legal-tools.org/doc/uy3tje/) adopted at a workshop sponsored by the UNDP in December 2017 are not discussed in this chapter. These documents are discussed by Morten Bergsmo in Chapter 1 of this volume.

11 A multi-stakeholder approach to countering hate speech is endorsed in documents such as ECRI General Policy Recommendation No. 15, the Plan of Action for Religious Leaders and Actors, the UN Strategy and Plan of Action on Hate Speech, and Recommendation CM/Rec(2022)16. See also, Article 19, "Tackling Hate: Action on UN Standards to Promote Inclusion, Diversity and Pluralism", 3rd. ed., 2020, p. 8 ('Tackling Hate').

12 The role of religious leaders in tackling hatred more broadly in society has been recognized, for example, in the UN Plan of Action to Safeguard Religious Sites which notes that:

> Religious leaders play a crucial role in building trust, fostering dialogue, stressing unity, solidarity, and mutual understanding, and in offering positive and moderate narratives in response to hatred and division. The active and sustained engagement of religious leaders to build and effectively communicate through all available channels a counternarrative to hatred and violent extremism as and when conducive to terrorism is crucial.

UN Alliance of Civilizations ('UNAOC'), "The UN Plan of Action to Safeguard Religious Sites", 12 September 2019, p. 9 ('UN Plan of Action to Safeguard Religious Sites'). Such recognition is not surprising given the growing awareness in the intergovernmental space of the extent to which religious actors, as integral members of civil society and contributors to public and political discourse, have proven to be responsible and valuable collaborators and partners to broader civil society, domestic policymakers, and regional and international organizations in many fields, including advancing human rights, refugee protection, addressing

The significant influence that religious leaders exert on the thinking, attitudes and behaviours of their co-religionists has been stressed by a number of leading intergovernmental officials in recent years. Of course, it is recognized that this influence can be used for positive or negative ends, including in relations to matters of tolerance: religious actors can contribute to countering hate speech or fomenting it.[13] In his foreword to the Plan of Action for Religious Leaders and Actors to prevent incitement to violence that could lead to atrocity crimes, the UN Secretary-General declared that,

> [r]eligious leaders can play a particularly important role in influencing the behavior of those who share their beliefs. Unfortunately, religion has sometimes been cynically distorted to justify incitement to violence and discrimination, and it is vital that religious leaders from all faiths show leadership.

He made similar comments when introducing the Global Pledge for Action by Religious Actors and Faith-Based Organizations to address the Covid-19 pandemic in collaboration with the UN in July 2020. In his message to the expert meeting convened by the OHCHR in Beirut in March 2017 on "Faith for Rights", the then High Commissioner, Zeid Ra'ad Al Hussein, stressed that "religious leaders, with their considerable influence on the hearts and minds of millions of people are potentially very important human rights actors".

Alongside the authority, influence and credibility that religious leaders hold within their communities, issues of access and reach are also regarded as important reasons why intergovernmental organizations choose to collaborate with them in efforts to counter hate speech, particularly the deep connections they have to people and communities in which many of the drivers of hate speech (individual, cultural, social, economic, political, religious) are rooted. Religious actors, especially religious minorities, are also often the first targets of hate speech and the experience of dealing with hate speech directly has given many religious actors an increased understanding and empathy, as well as the ability to assess the causes of hateful expressions and utterances stemming from within religious communities and to detect, prevent and counter it. Further, religious actors are also in a position to contribute to a solid foundation on which

---

the climate crisis and achieving sustainable development. For a discussion of such efforts to date and on new frameworks for engaging religious actors in multilateral diplomatic initiatives to address current and future global challenges, see Philip McDonagh, Kishan Manocha, John Neary and Lucia Vázquez, *On the Significance of Religion for Global Diplomacy*, Routledge, 2020.

13 See, for example, Plan of Action for Religious Leaders and Actors, 2017, p. 4, see *supra* note 5.

to address hate speech through interfaith and interreligious dialogue and partnerships.

23.3. Initiatives of Intergovernmental Organizations to Engage Religious Actors on Hate Speech Issues

23.3.1. Council of Europe

The COE is the first and only intergovernmental organization to have adopted an official definition of hate speech.[14] Its political bodies, particularly the Committee of Ministers and the Parliamentary Assembly, have set standards, including in the area of cyberhate,[15] issued recommendations[16] and provided guidelines to member States on how to counter hate speech and support victims; the organization has also engaged in a range of awareness-raising and capacity-building activities, notably the No Hate Speech Movement youth campaign.[17]

---

[14] Recommendation No. R(97)20, 1997, see *supra* note 4 states that:

> The term 'hate speech' shall be understood as covering all forms of expression which spread, incite, promote or justify racial hatred, xenophobia, anti-Semitism or other forms of hatred based on intolerance, including: intolerance expressed by aggressive nationalism and ethnocentrism, discrimination and hostility against minorities, migrants and people of immigrant origin.
>
> In Recommendation CM/Rec(2022)16, 2022, see *supra* note 1, hate speech is defined as: all types of expression that incite, promote, spread or justify violence, hatred or discrimination against a person or group of persons, or that denigrates them, by reason of their real or attributed personal characteristics or status such as 'race', colour, language, religion, nationality or ethnic origin, age, disability, sex, gender identity and sexual orientation.

Recommendation CM/Rec(2022)16, 2022, Appendix to the Recommendations, para. 2, see *supra* note 1.

[15] Most notably, COE, The Additional Protocol to the Convention of Cybercrime, Concerning the Criminalisation of Acts of a Racist and Xenophobic Nature Committed through Computer Systems, European Treaty Series No. 189, 28 January 2003 (https://www.legal-tools.org/doc/i4fbyh/).

[16] Most notably, Recommendation No. R(97)20, see *supra* note 4, and COE, "Recommendation No. R(97)21 of the Committee of Ministers to Member States on the Media and the Promotion of a Culture of Tolerance", 30 October 1997 (https://www.legal-tools.org/doc/117sod/); PACE, "Resolution 1510 (2006) on 'Freedom of Expression and Respect for Religious Beliefs'", 28 June 2006; PACE, "Recommendation 1805 (2007) on 'Blasphemy, Religious Insults and Hate Speech against Persons on Grounds of their Religion'", 29 June 2007; PACE, "Resolution 1928 (2013) on 'Safeguarding Human Rights in relation to Religion and Belief, and Protecting Religious Communities from Violence'", 24 April 2013 ('Resolution 1928'); PACE Resolution 2144(2017), 2017, see *supra* note 4; and PACE Resolution 2275(2019), 2019, see *supra* note 4.

[17] The No Hate Speech Movement youth campaign, launched in 2013, seeks to reduce the acceptance of hate speech both online and offline, through human rights education and awareness-raising, youth participation and medial literacy. It has developed and disseminated tools

However, only a small number of its instruments explicitly refer to the role of religious actors in addressing hate speech. The Committee of Ministers' groundbreaking Recommendation on "Hate Speech" adopted in 1997 is silent on the matter and the 2022 Recommendation and accompanying Appendix, which set out comprehensive legal and policy guidance to member States aimed at preventing and combating hate speech, contain one only recommendation to religious leaders: "to firmly and promptly condemn the use of hate speech, use counter-speech and alternative speech and promote intergroup understanding, including by expressing solidarity with those targeted by hate speech".[18]

With the exception of PACE Resolution 1510 on "Freedom of expression and respect for religious beliefs" in which the the Parliamentary Assembly of the COE "encourages religious communities in Europe to discuss freedom of expression and respect for religious beliefs within their own community and to pursue a dialogue with other religious communities in order to develop a common understanding and a code of conduct for religious tolerance which is necessary in a democratic society", no PACE documents explicitly refer to the role of religious actors in countering hate speech beyond endorsing interreligious dialogue as an important measure for cultivating tolerance, trust and mutual understanding in society.[19]

The European Commission Against Racism and Intolerance ('ECRI'), the human rights body of the COE, has drawn up a number of General Policy Recommendations ('GPRs') which make reference to hate speech. However, there are only a handful of suggested actions addressed to religious actors. ECRI's GPR No. 15 on Combating Hate Speech, adopted in 2015, states that "religious and community leaders [...] are in a position to make it clear that the use of hate speech is unacceptable in a democratic society" and also recognizes that they have a particularly important responsibility in speaking out against hate speech. In discussing the range of non-legal measures to be deployed in efforts to counter hate speech, ECRI notes that human rights information and awareness-raising should not just be a matter for formal education programmes but should also be the focus of ongoing discussion in faith communities and contexts. It also

---

and mechanisms for reporting hate speech, especially online, at the national level and has mobilized national and European partners to prevent and counter hate speech and intolerance offline and online. Under the umbrella campaign, national and local campaigns have been set up across Europe but these do not seem to have systematically engaged religious actors. See COE, "No Hate Speech Youth Campaign" (available on its web site).

18 Recommendation CM/Rec(2022)16, 2022, Appendix to the Recommendations, para. 53, see *supra* note 1. Member States are also called upon to promote interfaith dialogue (*ibid.*, para. 49).

19 See, for example, PACE, "Resolution 1510 (2006) on Freedom of Expression and Respect for Religious Beliefs", 28 June 2006 and Resolution 1928, 2013, see *supra* note 16.

recommends that interfaith and interreligious dialogue initiatives at various levels aimed at promoting greater awareness of the 'other' or 'others' in society should be undertaken or supported. Its GPR No. 5 on preventing and combating anti-Muslim racism and racial discrimination[20] identifies religious leaders, scholars and community representatives as relevant actors in the fight against anti-Muslim hate speech, and religious leaders at all levels and scholars are encouraged to "take responsibility for teachings at the grassroots level and avoid fueling anti-Muslim racism". Similarly, GPR No. 9 recommends that religious actors be involved in the fight against anti-Semitism, including anti-Semitic hate speech, and encourages religious leaders at all levels to "take responsibility for teachings at the grassroots level and avoid fueling antisemitism".[21]

23.3.2. European Union

As part of a comprehensive European Union ('EU') legal and policy framework aimed at tackling discrimination, racism and xenophobia,[22] Council Framework Decision 2008/913/JHA defines a common criminal law approach to racist and xenophobic hate speech and hate crimes and criminalizes illegal hate speech.[23] To further strengthen the legal framework on hate speech across the EU, the European Commission introduced, in December 2021, an initiative with the potential to lead to a decision by the European Council to extend the list of 'EU crimes' to hate speech and hate crime. However, to date, the main EU institutions have not seriously engaged religious actors in their efforts to address hate speech beyond referring to it in the context of a number of Article 17 dialogues

---

20 ECRI and COE, "ECRI General Policy Recommendation No. 5 (revised) on Preventing and Combating Anti-Muslim Racism and Racial Discrimination", 8 December 2021.

21 ECRI and COE, "ECRI General Policy Recommendation No. 9 (Revised) on Preventing and Combating Antisemitism", 1 July 2021.

22 The EU has recently adopted a comprehensive series of strategies aimed at fostering a Union of Equality package, including the European Commission, "Union of Equality: Gender Equality Strategy (2020–2025)", 5 March 2020, COM(2020) 152 final; EU, "Union of Equality: The Anti-Racism Action Plan (2020–2025)", 18 September 2020, COM(2020) 565 final ('The Anti-Racism Action Plan (2020–2025)'); EU, "Union of Equality: The LGBTIQ Equality (2020–2025)", 12 November 2020, COM(2020) 698 final; EU, "Union of Equality: Strategy for the Rights of the Persons with Disabilities (2021–2030)", 3 March, 2021, COM(2021) 101 final.

23 Hate speech as defined by Article 1 of the Framework Decision refers to "the public incitement to violence or hatred directed against a group or a member of such a group defined by reference to colour, religion, descent or national or ethnic origin". Council of the EU, "Council Framework Decision 2008/913/JHA on Combating Certain Forms and Expressions of Racism and Xenophobia by means of Criminal Law", 28 November 2008 (https://www.legal-tools.org/doc/45b60e/).

with religious leaders and actors since 2015.[24] Further, there has been no systematic engagement with religious actors on the part of the EU High Level Group on combating racism, xenophobia and other forms of intolerance which was established to support Union and national efforts in combating hate crime and hate speech or in the context of the work on anti-Semitic and anti-Muslim hate speech undertaken by the European Commissioner on combating anti-Semitism and fostering Jewish life and on combating anti-Muslim hatred, respectively.[25]

The EU Anti-Racism Action Plan, launched in September 2020, sets out a series of measures to step up action and to bring together actors at all levels in a common endeavour to address racism, including racist hate speech, more effectively; however, there is no mention of religious actors among the stakeholders the Commission expects to engage with in implementing its multi-layered plan.[26]

23.3.3. Organization for Security and Co-operation in Europe

A number of the political commitments of the participating States of the OSCE are relevant to preventing and countering hate speech and intolerant and discriminatory discourse. While the OSCE countries have recognized the primary character of the right to freedom of expression on numerous occasions,[27] they have also expressed their firm commitment against hate speech and have stressed that promoting tolerance and non-discrimination can contribute to

---

24 For example, on topics such as social cohesion, the promotion of human rights, migration and the European way of life. Established in the early 1990s, the European Commission dialogue with churches, religious associations and non-confessional organizations recognizes the specific contribution of churches, religious and non-confessional organizations to society. This dialogue now has a legal basis in Article 17 of the Treaty on the Functioning of the European Union which introduced a legal obligation on the EU to conduct an open, transparent and regular dialogue with churches, religious associations, and philosophical and non-confessional organizations. European Union, Treaty on the Functioning of the EU, Official Journal of the EU, 7 June 2016, vol. 59, C 202 (https://www.legal-tools.org/doc/15b8be/).

25 Combating anti-Semitic hate speech offline and online figures in the EU Strategy on Combating Antisemitism and Fostering Jewish Life (2021–2030), specifically under Pillar 1 on preventing and combating all forms of anti-Semitism: 1.2 – Combating anti-Semitic hate speech and hate crime and 1.3 – Tackling anti-Semitism online; however, there is no mention of the role of religious actors in this effort (EC, "EU Strategy on Combating Antisemitism and Fostering Jewish Life (2021–2030)", 5 October 2021, COM(2021) 615 final). The European Commission Coordinator on Combating Anti-Muslim Hatred has worked with civil society on anti-Muslim hate speech and has organized a range of meetings to this end, but there is no specific or dedicated strategy to engage religious actors in this regard.

26 The Anti-Racism Action Plan (2020–2025), 2020, see *supra* note 22.

27 See, for example, OSCE, "Document of the Copenhagen Meeting of the Conference on the Human Dimension of the CSCE", 29 June 1990.

eliminating the basis for it.[28] Furthermore, OSCE participating States have agreed on certain commitments related to "intolerant political discourse" and "racist, xenophobic and discriminatory public discourse" and have recognized its harmful impact, emphasized the need for consistently and unequivocally speaking out against manifestations of hate in political discourse, and stressed the positive role of political representatives in the overall promotion of mutual respect and understanding and in speaking out against hate-motivated acts and incidents in society.[29] Participating States have also been called on to address the increasing use of the Internet to advocate views constituting incitement to violence.[30] However, the lack of consensus on a definition of hate speech among OSCE participating States constrains the OSCE's ability to address hate speech more directly and comprehensively.

Although OSCE participating States do not refer explicitly to the role of religious actors in countering hate speech, their potential contribution may be inferred in light of commitments calling on them to speak out against violent extremism and radicalization that lead to terrorism and in offering alternatives to violent extremism messaging,[31] and those emphasizing the importance of interfaith and interreligious dialogue and partnerships in the context of fostering tolerance, mutual respect and understanding in the OSCE region.[32] Further, the importance placed by participating States on the right to freedom of religion or belief as an integral component of the OSCE's comprehensive concept of security[33] underscores the importance that they attach to the role of religious actors

---

28 OSCE, "Decision No. 6: Tolerance and Non-Discrimination", 7 December 2002, MC(10).DEC/6 ('Porto Document 2002').

29 OSCE, "Decision No. 10/05: Tolerance and Non-Discrimination: Promoting Mutual Respect and Understanding", 6 December 2005, MC.DEC/10/05 ('Ljubljana Document 2005'); OSCE, "Decision No. 13/06: Combating Intolerance and Discrimination and Promoting Mutual Respect and Understanding", 5 December 2006, MC.DEC/13/06 ('Brussels Document 2006').

30 OSCE, "Decision No. 10/09: OSCE High-Level Conference on Tolerance and Non-Discrimination", 2 December 2009, MC.DEC/10/09 ('Athens Document 2009').

31 OSCE, "Ministerial Council Declaration No. 4/15 on Preventing and Countering Violent Extremism and Radicalization that Lead to Terrorism", 4 December 2015, MC.DOC/4/15; OSCE, "Ministerial Council Declaration No. 1 on Strengthening OSCE Efforts to Prevent and Counter Terrorism", 9 December 2016, MC.DOC/1/16.

32 OSCE participating States have committed to promoting and facilitating open and transparent interfaith and interreligious dialogue and partnerships, see, for example, Porto Document 2002, 2002, see *supra* note 28; Ljubljana Document 2005, 2005, see *supra* note 29; OSCE, "Decision No. 3/13: Freedom of Thought, Conscience, Religion or Belief", 6 December 2013, MC.DEC/3/13 ('Kyiv Document 2013'); OSCE, "Declaration on Enhancing Efforts to Combat Anti-Semitism", 5 December 2014, MC.DOC/8/14 ('Basel Document 2014'); Ministerial Council Declaration No. 4/15, 2015, see *supra* note 31.

33 See, in particular, OSCE, "Conference on Security and Co-operation in Europe Final Act", 1975; Kyiv Document 2013, 2013, see *supra* note 32.

in contributing to the building of equal, inclusive and cohesive societies free of all manifestations of hate and intolerance.

The OSCE's autonomous institutions contribute in varying ways to efforts to prevent and counter hate speech in society, in line with their respective mandates, but none of them engages religious actors strategically in this work. The OSCE Representative on Freedom of the Media helps participating States abide by their commitments to freedom of expression and free media. Activities include efforts to combat hate speech in the media through awareness-raising projects, education and regular meetings with media outlets, editors and journalists. There has been no scope for involving religious actors in these efforts to date. In pursuance of its mandate to provide early warning and, as appropriate, early action in regard to tensions involving national minority issues that have the potential to develop into a crisis or conflict, the OSCE High Commissioner on National Minorities has paid attention to the importance of countering hate speech and xenophobic rhetoric against minorities,[34] but it has not addressed the role of religious actors in this area.

The OSCE Office for Democratic Institutions and Human Rights ('ODIHR') assists OSCE participating States to combat all forms of intolerance, discrimination and hate as well as the conditions conducive to their spread in communities.[35] In line with the OSCE's holistic approach to security and deploying strategies grounded in respect for human rights and fundamental freedoms, it works closely with civil society, including religious leaders, actors and communities, to tackle all manifestations of prejudice, negative stereotyping and bias, particularly through awareness-raising and capacity-building activities, including on freedom of religion or belief, and facilitates and supports inclusive interfaith and interreligious coalitions to address all forms of intolerance and hate in society. The knowledge, insights and skills acquired by religious actors through their engagement in these and related activities might prove helpful in their efforts to reduce hateful expressions both in wider society as well as in their own contexts. In terms of policy advice and recommendations, in its

---

34 For example, the conference marking the fifteenth anniversary of the OSCE, "OSCE High Commissioner on National Minorities' Policing Recommendations Remain Relevant 15 Years After Publication, Say Speakers at Anniversary Conference", 5 November 2021 (available on its web site); OSCE High Commissioner on National Minorities, *The Bolzano/Bozen Recommendations on National Minorities in Inter-State Relations*, OSCE, 2008; OSCE, *The Ljubljana Guidelines on Integration of Diverse Societies*, OSCE, 2012.

35 Relevant OSCE commitments in the area of tolerance and non-discrimination include Porto Document 2002, 2002, see *supra* note 28; Ljubljana Document 2005, 2005, see *supra* note 29; Brussels Document 2006, 2006, see *supra* note 29; Athens Document 2009, 2009, see *supra* note 30; Kyiv Document 2013, 2013, see *supra* note 32; Basel Document 2014, 2014, see *supra* note 32.

discussion of 'extremist' speech and literature and security in the 2019 publication, *Freedom of Religion or Belief and Security: Policy Guidance*, the ODIHR calls on the leaders of religious or belief communities to speak out strongly and promptly against hate speech that amounts to incitement to discrimination, hostility or violence and encourages religious or belief communities to engage in interfaith and interreligious dialogue and partnerships in order to strengthen the foundations of tolerance and understanding across society.[36]

23.3.4. United Nations

The UN has the most elaborate policy framework on hate speech among intergovernmental organizations; an increasingly prominent element of this framework is the specific attention given to the role and contribution of religious actors. The insight that religious actors should refrain from using hateful expressions and incite to hostility and violence and calls on them to promote tolerance, mutual understanding and religious pluralism can be found in a number of recent UN initiatives, including resolutions, declarations and action plans.

23.3.4.1. Human Rights Council Resolution 16/18 and the Istanbul Process

The UNHRC Resolution 16/18 on "Combating intolerance, negative stereotyping and stigmatization of, and discrimination, incitement to violence, against persons based on religion or belief", adopted in 2011, constitutes a common framework on how to tackle intolerance and discrimination on the basis of religion or belief and rests on the rationale that the promotion of inclusion, diversity and pluralism is the best antidote to intolerant expression. The Resolution deplores "any advocacy of discrimination or violence on the basis of religion or belief" and condemns "any advocacy of religious hatred that constitutes incitement to discrimination, hostility or violence". The eight-point action plan contained in paragraph five calls on States to take initiatives to tackle religious hatred and foster greater inclusion, diversity and pluralism; however, only one asks them to directly engage with religious actors as part of this overall effort.[37]

---

[36] OSCE and ODIHR, *Freedom of Religion or Belief and Security: Policy Guidance*, OSCE, 2019, p. 50 ('Freedom of Religion or Belief and Security: Policy Guidance').

[37] Namely, para. 5(d): "Encouraging the efforts of leaders to discuss within their communities the causes of discrimination, and evolving strategies to counter these causes": UNHRC, Resolution 16/18, Combating Intolerance, Negative Stereotyping and Stigmatization of, and Discrimination, Incitement to Violence and Violence against, Persons based on Religion or Belief, UN. Doc. A/HRC/RES/16/18, 12 April 2011 (https://www.legal-tools.org/doc/0a86d2/). Para. 5(h) recognizes that interfaith and intercultural dialogue at the local, national and international levels can play a positive role in combating religious hatred, incitement and violence.

The Istanbul Process is a series of meetings, initiated in 2011, to promote and guide implementation of Resolution 16/18. It was conceived of as a space for various stakeholders, including religious leaders and other actors, to exchange good practices and experiences of implementing the 16/18 action plan in their domestic contexts, outside of the sphere of multilateral politics. After a brief hiatus, the process was reinvigorated in November 2019 with a meeting hosted by the Netherlands. While this meeting was one of the most inclusive to date with a number of religious actors in attendance and signalled a renewal of political will in the process, attention still needs to be paid to securing the active involvement of a greater number and diversity of religious actors in future meetings.

23.3.4.2. Rabat Plan of Action

The Rabat Plan of Action on the prohibition of advocacy of national, racial or religious hatred that constitutes incitement to discrimination, hostility or violence, developed by international experts with the support of the OHCHR, provides non-binding practical and legal policy guidance to States on implementing Article 20(2) of the ICCPR, which requires them to prohibit certain severe forms of hate speech, including any advocacy of national, racial or religious hatred that constitutes incitement to discrimination, hostility or violence. Since its adoption in October 2012, it has received broad approval by the international community.

Many of the positive policy measures addressed in the Plan to tackle the root causes of discrimination find support in the UNHRC 16/18 action plan, but it differs in its emphasis on the role of non-State actors, including religious leaders, in speaking out against and countering incitement to discrimination, hostility or violence, including incitement to hatred in the name of religion. Indeed, one of the most important messages contained in the Rabat Plan of Action is that what is required above all in order to prevent and respond to incidents of incitement to hatred and other forms of hate speech are policies which promote a creative and productive use of freedom of expression, and the role of religious leaders in this regard. While falling short of issuing concrete recommendations to religious actors and using the explicit language of responsibilities, it does identify three principal contributions of religious actors, namely to speak out firmly and promptly against instances of hate speech; to refrain from using messages of intolerance or expressions which may incite to religious violence, hostility or discrimination; and to clearly understand that violence can never be tolerated as a response to incitement to hatred.[38] Further, civil society actors and

[38] OHCHR, Rabat Plan of Action on the Prohibition of Advocacy of National, Racial or Religious Hatred that Constitutes Incitement to Discrimination, Hostility or Violence, UN Doc.

national human rights institutions are called upon to create and support interreligious dialogue initiatives.[39]

The Rabat Plan of Action is the first intergovernmental initiative of its kind to indicate a role for religious actors in countering hate speech, whether in their own contexts or more widely in society. A major shortcoming, however, is its silence on the gender dimensions of discrimination and hate based on religion or belief and on the importance of the full and effective participation of female religious leaders in preventing and countering hate speech and promoting tolerance, inclusion and respect for diversity.[40]

23.3.4.3. The Beirut Declaration and its 18 Commitments on 'Faith for Rights'

Adopted in a workshop organized by the OHCHR on 28–29 March 2017 in Beirut and attended by some 30 faith-based and civil society actors and international experts working in human rights,[41] 'Faith for Rights' seeks to identify the potential for joint action and co-operation between those motivated by religion or belief and those motivated by human rights to foster the development of fair, just and peaceful societies based on respect for universal human rights principles. Specifically, the 'Faith for Rights' framework, comprising the Beirut Declaration and its 18 Commitments on 'Faith for Rights',[42] seeks to expand on what its signatories refer to as the three specific core responsibilities of religious actors against incitement to hatred as laid out in the Rabat Plan of Action.[43]

The signatories to the Declaration undertake "to combat any form of exploitation of such [theological] differences to advocate violence, discrimination and religious hatred"[44] and express the conviction that "religious actors should be enabled [...] to assume their responsibilities in defending our shared humanity against incitement to hatred".[45] Rather than focusing on theological and

A/HRC/22/17.Add.4, Annex, Appendix, 5 October 2012, para. 36 ('Rabat Plan of Action') (https://www.legal-tools.org/doc/jh1be1/).

[39] *Ibid.*, para. 56.

[40] See Tackling Hate, 2020, see *supra* note 11, for a discussion on this point.

[41] Including a number relevant UN Treaty Body members and UN Special Procedures.

[42] For the full text of the Declaration and commitments, relevant background and latest information on the implementation of the 'Faith for Rights' framework, see: OHCHR, "The Beirut Declaration and its 18 Commitments on 'Faith for Rights'", 29 March 2017 ('Beirut Declaration and its 18 Commitments on Faith for Rights') (https://www.legal-tools.org/doc/qp9nv2/ and https://www.legal-tools.org/doc/k178m1/).

[43] *Ibid.*, para. 22. The Beirut Declaration refers in p. 7 to the Rabat Plan of Action as its "founding precedent".

[44] The Beirut Declaration and its 18 Commitments on 'Faith for Rights', 2017, para. 4, see *supra* note 42.

[45] *Ibid.*, para. 8.

doctrinal divides, the Beirut Declaration favours the identification of common ground among all religions and beliefs to uphold the dignity and equal worth of all human beings, and is intended to be action-oriented and spawn multi-level collaborative action involving religious and other relevant actors.[46] Some of the most insightful passages in the Declaration concern the role of speech which is deemed as "fundamental to individual and communal flourishing" and "one of the most crucial mediums for good and evil sides of humanity", and, therefore, "one of the most strategic areas of the responsibilities" that the signatories commit to assume.[47] The Declaration acknowledges the potential, on the basis of the criteria articulated in the Rabat Plan of Action, of certain statements by religious leaders to meet the threshold of incitement to hatred in the name of religion.[48]

The 'Faith for Rights' initiative is rooted in the understanding of the Declaration's authors that both religious teachings and international legal frameworks attribute responsibilities to faith actors:[49] indeed, the Beirut Declaration and its 18 commitments serve as the first major self-articulation by 'faith actors' (defined in line with the Beirut Declaration's inclusive approach as religious leaders and other individuals of religious faith and those motivated by non-religious belief systems) of some of the human rights responsibilities they have assumed in relation to preventing and countering hate speech, particularly incitement to hatred in the name of religion.

'Faith for Rights' goes beyond the aforementioned contributions of religious leaders in preventing and countering hate speech as articulated in the Rabat Plan of Action[50] to embrace duties in relation to the understanding and interpretations of religious texts. These include commitments to promote constructive engagement on the understanding of religious texts and the encouragement given to critical thinking as a means to reach "enlightened religious

[46] *Ibid.*, paras. 9, 10(a), 12, 13.

[47] *Ibid.*, para. 20.

[48] *Ibid.*, para. 21.

[49] *Ibid.*, paras. 15 and 18. Article 2(1) of the 1981 UN Declaration on the Elimination of all Forms of Intolerance and of Discrimination Based on Religion of Belief states that "no one shall be subject to discrimination by any State, institution, group of persons or person on the grounds of religion or belief". UN General Assembly, UN Declaration on the Elimination of all Forms of Intolerance and of Discrimination Based on Religion of Belief, UN Doc.A/RES/36/55, 25 November 1981, Article 2(1) (https://www.legal-tools.org/doc/hexdsg/).

[50] Commitment VII is a pledge to "publicly denounce all instances of advocacy of hatred that incites to violence, discrimination or hostility [...] particularly when it is conducted in the name of religion or belief". The Beirut Declaration and its 18 Commitments on 'Faith for Rights', 2017, Commitment VII, see *supra* note 42.

interpretations";[51] the pledge to establish policies and methodologies within the respective areas of competence of the signatories; the pledge to monitor interpretations, determinations or other religious views that conflict with universal human rights norms;[52] and the pledge to reject exclusionary interpretations claiming religious grounds in a manner that would instrumentalize religions, beliefs or their followers to incite hatred for electoral purposes or political gains.[53] A notable new duty introduced by the Beirut Declaration for religious actors in their efforts to counter hate speech in the name of religions or beliefs is that of "remedial advocacy to reconciliation".[54] The gender dimension is introduced through a commitment "to revisit [...] those religious understandings and interpretations that appear to perpetuate gender inequality and harmful stereotypes or even condone gender-based violence",[55] and there is also a pledge to "refrain from, advocate against and jointly condemn any judgemental public determination by any actor who in the name of religion aims at disqualifying the religion or belief of another individual or community in a manner that would expose them to violence in the name of religion".[56] In recognition of the importance of long-term measures, the 18 commitments include an undertaking to refine the curriculums, teaching materials and textbooks wherever some religious interpretations, or the way they are presented, may give rise to the perception of condoning violence or discrimination.[57] Further, there is a pledge to defend academic freedom and the freedom of expression in accordance with international human rights law, in particular for academics who study religion,[58] which promotes the notion that religious belief can be subjected to new challenges and can be a source for facilitating free and creative thinking.

The declaration and accompanying commitments have subsequently been referred to by several UN entities, including Treaty Bodies and Special Procedures,[59] and have already spawned a number of practical initiatives, including capacity-building and collaborative events and workshops in various parts of the world which explore further the relationship between religions, beliefs and

[51] The Beirut Declaration and its 18 Commitments on 'Faith for Rights', 2017, Commitment III, see *supra* note 42.

[52] *Ibid.*, Commitment VIII.

[53] *Ibid.*, Commitment X.

[54] *Ibid.*, para. 22. See also reference to the duty of religious actors to "redress hate speech by remedial compassion and solidarity that heals hearts and societies alike", *ibid.*, para. 10(d).

[55] *Ibid.*, Commitment V.

[56] *Ibid.*, Commitment IX.

[57] *Ibid.*, Commitment XII.

[58] *Ibid.*

[59] For a listing, see OHCHR, "The Framework in Action: OHCHR and the 'Faith for Rights' Framework" (available on its web site).

human rights,[60] as well as webinars held in the context of the Global Pledge for Action by Religious Actors and Faith-Based Organizations to address the Covid-19 pandemic in collaboration with the UN.[61]

The 'Collaboration of Collonges' is the follow-up to the normative trajectory of the soft law standards emerging from the Rabat Plan of Action and the Beirut Declaration and Commitments. It seeks to fill the triple gap of education, research and training on faith and human rights, as identified in the Declaration, through the Faith for Rights toolkit.[62] This toolkit, launched in January 2020, translates the Faith for Rights framework into practical peer-to-peer learning and capacity-building exercises for religious actors, civil society representatives and educational institutions who engage in an interdisciplinary discussion on 'faith' and 'rights' in relation to 18 key topics mirroring each of the commitments on 'Faith for Rights'. The toolkit is designed to be interactive, results-oriented and conducive to critical thinking and is expected to be tailored and adapted to the specific context of the participants. Module 7 of the 'Faith for Rights' toolkit deals with incitement to hatred.

The 'Faith for Rights' framework is significant in that it raises consciousness of the human rights responsibilities of religious actors in addressing 'religious hate speech' to new levels. Although human rights as legal norms do not themselves constitute an overarching belief-system, the underlying principles – such as the respect for human dignity and the equality of all human beings – have substantive overlaps with many religious and non-religious belief systems and philosophical traditions. Human rights may therefore provide incentives for strengthening the awareness of the charitable messages contained in different religions or beliefs in order to build resilience against messages of hatred and violence. Achieving and maintaining a consensus on a set of human rights responsibilities for faith actors is not without its fair share of challenges and its risks, of course, and some of the 'Faith for Rights' commitments will no doubt prove challenging, controversial and impossible to uphold in certain quarters. Creating and sustaining an increasing number of spaces for cross-disciplinary reflection and action on the connections between religions and human rights will be critical to the success of the project and its impact on hate speech on the part of religious actors among other issues. In order to achieve this, 'Faith for Rights' will need a level of support and commitment from prominent and influential religious leaders and actors, representative of the diversity of the world's

60 These meetings were co-organized by the OHCHR and took place in Dakar, Rabat, Geneva, Tunis, Marrakesh and Djibouti between 2017 and 2019. For further information, see OHCHR, "OHCHR and the 'Faith for Rights' Framework" (available on its web site).

61 See sub-Section 23.3.4.5.of this chapter.

62 See OHCHR, "#Faith4Rights Toolkit" (available on its web site).

religious traditions, as well as local ownership, particularly from women and youth faith actors, in all parts of the world than is currently the case.[63] 'Faith for Rights' has proven itself to be more than just a nice set of ideals in that it has already given rise to a number of practical actions and projects but there is clearly a vital need for more.

'Faith for Rights' calls for introspection of the part of faith actors which, if acted on, should lead to a reduction in hate speech within religious communities. It recognizes that if religion is to contribute to social progress, then religious actors will need to reflect profoundly on those aspects of belief and practice that can create divisions and foster prejudice. In this connection, religious interpretations that appear to endorse or support inequality, discrimination and harmful stereotypes of whatever sort need to be revisited. The strong focus of 'Faith for Rights' on the understanding and interpretation of religious texts is therefore timely and important. However, by ignoring the role of religious actors in discerning, understanding and tackling the root causes and drivers behind hate speech and other manifestations of intolerance in their particular contexts, its ultimate efficacy as a tool for long-term hate speech prevention in religious communities is somewhat diminished.

23.3.4.4. Plan of Action for Religious Leaders and Actors to Prevent Incitement to Violence that Could Lead to Atrocity Crimes

Incitement to violence in public discourse and in the media is both a common warning sign and a precursor of atrocity crimes.[64] In response to the alarming spike in hate speech and particularly incitement to violence in recent years against individuals and communities on the basis of their identity and being cognizant of the role played by some religious leaders and actors in inciting discrimination, hostility and violence and in disseminating hate speech in the name of their religion, the UN Office of Genocide Prevention and the Responsibility to Protect ('UNOGP') organized a series of consultations between April 2015 and December 2016 to analyze and discuss the specific role that religious leaders

---

[63] The current list of supporters of the Declaration and its 18 Commitments can be found at OHCHR, "The Beirut Declaration and its 18 Commitments on 'Faith for Rights' – Report and Outlook", 17 March 2022, pp. 90–91 ('The Beirut Declaration and its 18 Commitments on 'Faith for Rights' – Report and Outlook'). While it contains a number of distinguished academic and other experts, including a number of UN Special Procedures and members of UN Treaty Bodies, it lacks support from high level and diverse religious actors, especially leaders.

[64] For the purposes of the Plan of Action, the term 'atrocity crimes' refers to the three legally defined international crimes, namely genocide, crimes against humanity and war crimes, and also ethnic cleansing (Plan of Action for Religious Leaders and Actors, 2017, Annex, p. 20, see *supra* note 5).

and actors[65] play in preventing incitement to violence that could lead to atrocity crimes.[66] The discussions at the first meeting in Fez, Morocco, resulted in a declaration of principles ('Fez Declaration') and a draft plan of action for religious leaders and actors to prevent incitement that could lead to atrocity crimes ('Fez Plan of Action'). The ensuing regional consultations sought to develop context-specific, human rights-grounded and gender-sensitive regional plans for religious leaders and actors and refine the Fez Plan of Action. Some 232 religious actors from 77 countries, drawn from a diversity of faith and non-faith backgrounds and including religious leaders and a range of faith-based organizations, participated in the extensive consultation process. The outcome was a final Plan of Action for Religious Leaders and Actors to prevent incitement to violence that could lead to atrocity crimes launched by UN Secretary-General António Guterres in July 2017, who called for its wide dissemination and implementation.

The Plan of Action for Religious Leaders and Actors is the most detailed and comprehensive set of options and recommendations for religious actors in the area of hate speech produced under the auspices of an intergovernmental organization to date. It is notable for the wide range of stakeholders that contributed to its development, the broad role it envisages for religious leaders and actors, and in the detail of its suggested actions. The Plan consists of nine groups of thematic recommendations organized into three main clusters: prevent (including specific actions to prevent and counter incitement to violence); strengthen (including enhancing education and capacity-building and fostering interfaith and intra-faith dialogue); and build (including building peace, inclusive and just societies through respecting, protecting and promoting human rights). While the focus of the Plan of Action for Religious Leaders and Actors is on incitement to violence, the actions it suggests are generally relevant to preventing and countering other forms of hate speech.

The scope of the Plan of Action for Religious Leaders and Actors is broader than what its title would tend to suggest and moves beyond prevention of incitement to violence to the significant question of how to bring about peaceful, inclusive and just societies. In this way, the Plan casts religious leaders and actors as key agents of change in society with influence in a broad range of sectors including the promotion and protection of human rights, the prevention of violent extremism and conflict, governance and peacebuilding. Further, while

[65] 'Religious leaders' were identified as those who were or are formally assigned leadership roles by their respective religious institution or communities and/or hold formal religious qualifications, while 'religious actors' covered those who work in or with non-governmental organizations in such areas interreligious affairs, or religious development and humanitarian entities as well as those who teach religion in academic contexts.

[66] KAICIID and the World Council of Churches also supported this consultation process.

the Plan of Action for Religious Leaders and Actors is intended primarily for religious leaders and actors, it is also an important part of a wider endeavour to counter atrocity crimes and so also includes detailed recommendations addressed to other relevant actors, including States and State institutions, civil society organizations, new and traditional media, and academic and educational institutions, with the hope and expectation that these different stakeholders will collaborate towards realizing this objective.

Among the notable recommendations to religious leaders and actors are those that call on them to understand, address and counter the causes and drivers of hate speech, including listening to and addressing the grievances of youth and engaging them in tackling injustice in a constructive way, and to establish national interreligious observatories to detect the causes and origins of hate speech. Religious actors are also encouraged to react to incitement as soon as it occurs; to learn how to differentiate between speech that merely causes offence and speech that could constitute incitement to violence; to monitor the media, including social media, to ensure that incitement to hatred is constantly identified and countered; to issue and disseminate religious statements and messages by religious leaders and authorities denouncing incitement; to offer alternative messages, particularly those which promote and reinforce positive values and human rights, including online; to identify influential and committed religious leaders and actors who can be appointed to disseminate counter and alternative messages; to discard ideas of superiority and exclusivity; to understand, dismantle and counter the arguments of those with extremist views using religious texts and messages; and to target and educate those who are particularly questioning as well as those who claim to know and interpret the religious texts and messages correctly. There are also recommendations calling on religious leaders and actors to actively reach out to, support and spiritually counsel community members, particularly youth, who are marginalized or otherwise vulnerable, and to educate young community members to understand and interpret religious teachings in order to identify and respond to positive and negative messages. A recommendation dedicated to preventing incitement to gender-based violence is specifically included, and academic and education institutions and civil society organizations are also called on to support the efforts of religious leaders and actors by providing training on the prevention of incitement to violence, including effective communication strategies to curb incitement. The Plan of Action for Religious Leaders and Actors also encourages collaboration between religious leaders and actors with traditional and new media to prevent and counter incitement, including the elaboration of new online strategies to reframe narratives and provide alternative ones. In turn, traditional and new media professionals and relevant civil society organizations are encouraged to provide suitable training opportunities for religious leaders and actors on how to use strategic communications, including the use of social media, to prevent incitement to violence.

A number of recommendations addressed to religious actors focus on the role of awareness-raising, education, capacity-building and dialogue to prevent incitement. These include identifying and sharing religious texts and influential theological writings that could be used to promote mutual respect and understanding; promoting critical thinking, respect for international human rights standards and the knowledge of the 'other' to ensure that religious identity does not become a source of division and tensions; and the inclusion in the training curricula for religious leaders' knowledge of different religions and beliefs and international norms on freedom of religion or belief and other human rights. Religious leaders and actors are specifically encouraged to engage in interfaith and intrafaith dialogue and co-operation to prevent incitement to violence through, *inter alia*, the building of cross-regional interfaith coalitions dedicated to this aim and to sharing good practices and lessons learned, including the development of an interfaith code of conduct for preventing incitement to violence while preaching. Other forms of partnership, including with non-religious believers, as a means of demonstrating the power of common action and solidarity across religious or belief boundaries, are also recommended, and religious institutions are called on to develop training programmes to support the participation of religious leaders in interfaith work. Intrafaith dialogue is often overlooked in initiatives to address hate speech so it is noteworthy that the Plan of Action for Religious Leaders and Actors suggests that religious leaders and actors engage in internal community dialogue processes to exchange experiences and good practices for building social cohesion and preventing incitement and as a means to ensure that all voices within a community are heard, including those who are hostile or who hold discriminatory or extremist views.

As already mentioned, the Plan of Action for Religious Leaders and Actors accords religious leaders and actors a specific role in building peaceful, inclusive and just societies. A number of recommendations in this regard call on them to advance and disseminate positive, pro-social messages of peaceful coexistence with others grounded in respect for universal human rights and fundamental freedoms. They are also specifically encouraged to serve as role models for these values both within and outside their communities.

The Plan of Action for Religious Leaders and Actors is implemented at regional, national and local levels under the overall stewardship of the UNOGP and with the guidance and support of a Global Steering Committee appointed in

2017.[67] The UNOGP is also responsible for evaluating activities and disseminating the good practices and lessons learned deriving from them. In February 2018, in Vienna, some 120 policy makers, including representatives of 53 member States, as well as religious leaders and actors explored ways to institutionalize support for and implement the Plan of Action for Religious Leaders and Actors. A number of challenges in disseminating and implementing the Plan were recognized, including lack of visibility and the need for systematization of efforts to ensure impact. In an attempt to formalize and widen support for the Plan of Action for Religious Leaders and Actors by religious leaders and actors, the UNOGP and the International Association for the Defence of Religious Liberty organized two Summits on Religion, Peace and Security in November 2016 and April 2019. The main objective of the second meeting was the establishment of an "International Platform on Religious, Peace and Security" aimed at connecting religious leaders and actors with other relevant stakeholders in efforts to address hate speech and counter incitement to violence and on matters pertaining to peace and security in general, and to systematize lessons learned from the global experience in these areas. Unfortunately, plans to establish this Platform have not yet materialized.

The Plan of Action for Religious Leaders and Actors discloses a wider horizon of possibilities for religious actors in the fight against hate speech beyond speaking out against hate speech and addressing matters of religious interpretation and understanding. It is unique among intergovernmental initiatives on hate speech involving religious actors in its emphasis on tackling the drivers of incitement to violence and other forms hate speech in the name of religion thereby showing due regard for the importance of contextual and other factors. Its suggestions that religious actors engage with social media, its recommendations on the prevention of incitement to gender-based violence and its focus on intrafaith dialogue and capacity-building are particularly innovative. The Plan of Action for Religious Leaders and Actors therefore contains guidance, which if successfully operationalized, could lead to a significant reduction in incitement to violence and other forms of hate speech both within religious contexts and communities and more widely in society. However, the Plan's efficacy as a programmatic tool is limited by a lack in places of specific, actionable guidance on combating unfolding incitement to violence and includes actions that are

67 Among the notable regional initiatives in support of the Plan of Action is the partnership between the UN Human Rights Regional Office for the Middle East and North Africa ('OHCHR-ROMENA') and the UNOGP which led to the launch in November 2021 of a booklet on 'Engaging Religious Actors to Counter Hate Speech, Prevent Incitement to Violence, and Build Inclusive and Peaceful Societies' (OHCHR-ROMENA and UNOGP, "Engaging Religious Actors to Counter Hate Speech, Prevent Incitement to Violence, and Build Inclusive and Peaceful Societies", 15 November 2021).

sometimes unrealistic and would seem to exceed the capacities of religious actors (for example, the establishment of national interreligious observatories to detect causes of hate speech) or for which significant guidance, support and resources would be needed to ensure sustainability and impact (such as fostering interfaith dialogue and coalitions to prevent and counter incitement). The Plan, at times, does read like a long wish list and is rather repetitious in parts; for example, many of the recommendations under the third cluster on 'Build' are a restatement of what appears in the clusters on 'Prevent' and 'Strengthen'. These challenges could well impede the Plan's ongoing implementation and support, which to date has indeed been somewhat uneven. Further, while the consultative process that gave rise to the Plan endeavoured to be as inclusive as possible, concern remains as to how well the input of religious leaders was elicited.[68]

23.3.4.5. Other United Nations Initiatives

Noting the growing trends of intolerance, stigmatization and hate speech around the world, the UN Secretary-General launched the UN Strategy and Plan of Action on Hate Speech on 18 June 2019.[69] The Detailed Guidance on Implementation for UN Field Presences was issued in September 2020.[70] The objectives of the UN Strategy and Plan of Action are twofold: to enhance UN efforts to address root causes and drivers of hate speech and to enable effective UN responses to the impact of hate speech on societies and victims. One of the four overarching principles of the UN Strategy and Plan of Action is that "tackling hate speech is the responsibility of all – governments,societies, the private sector". While a broad stakeholder approach to countering hate speech is clearly favoured in the UN Strategy and Plan of Action, the distinct lack of reference to the role of religious actors is surprising given the attention paid to them in hate speech initiatives elaborated under the auspices of the UN in the years immediately preceding.

Closely linked to the UN Strategy and Plan of Action is the UN Plan of Action to Safeguard Religious Sites, adopted a few months later in September 2019 in the wake of rising attacks against places of worship around the world.[71]

---

[68] For a helpful overview and critique of the Plan of Action for Religious Leaders and Actors, 2017, *supra* note 5, to prevent incitement to violence that could lead to atrocity crimes, see Sara E. Hall and Stephen D. Smith, *The Routledge Handbook of Religion, Mass Atrocity, and Genocide*, Routledge, London, 2022.

[69] The full text can be found at: UN Strategy and Plan of Action on Hate Speech, 2019, see *supra* note 4.

[70] The full text can be found at: Detailed Guidance on Implementation for UN Field Presences, 2020, see *supra* note 4.

[71] The full text can be found at: The UN Plan of Action to Safeguard Religious Sites, 2019, see *supra* note 12.

This Plan, developed by the High Representative of the UNAOC at the request of the UN Secretary-General and informed by a wide variety of actors, including religious leaders and communities, contains recommendations to support relevant stakeholders in their efforts to prevent possible attacks against religious sites. In this context, it encourages religious leaders to take a number of actions relevant to preventing and countering hate speech and intolerant discourse, including notably in their own contexts, such as engaging with women and youth, in particular: to build strong counter-narratives to hatred and alienation; to persuade those with whom they hold influence to avoid inflammatory speech; and to develop media content, including through the creation or strengthening of websites; to make religious texts and messages accessible to a wider audience; and to provide answers to challenges related to social exclusion and hatred.

Drawing on the experience gained from mobilizing faith actors to stand up for human rights through the 'Faith for Rights' process, the UN has been exploring innovative ways to engage religious leaders and faith-based organizations to address the multiple challenges related to the spread of Covid-19, including growing hate speech trends.[72] A Guidance Note on how to address and counter hate speech related to the Covid-19 pandemic, published by the Office of the Special Adviser on the Prevention of Genocide ('OSAPG') in May 2020, sets out recommendations to various actors and specifically calls on influential figures in society, including religious leaders and other faith actors, to actively speak out against Covid-19 related hate speech, misinformation, disinformation and conspiracy theories. Commitments by faith actors to partner in innovative ways in response to the current and future challenges posed by the pandemic, including in the area of hate speech, subsequently crystallized in the Global Pledge for Action by Religious Actors and Faith-Based Organizations to address the Covid-19 pandemic in collaboration with the UN. [73]

---

[72] UN, "United Nations Guidance Note on Addressing and Countering COVID-19 related Hate Speech", 11 May 2020, Introduction, p. 1:

> The COVID-19 pandemic has seen demonstrations of overwhelming solidarity between nations and communities working together to address the impact and challenges it poses. Unfortunately, the pandemic has also given rise to a new wave of hate speech and discrimination. 'COVID-19 related hate speech' encompasses a broad range of disparaging expressions against certain individuals and groups that has emerged or been exacerbated as a result of the new coronavirus disease outbreak – from scapegoating, stereotyping, stigmatization and the use of derogatory, misogynistic, racist, xenophobic, Islamophobic or antisemitic language. Closely linked to this is the dissemination of 'disinformation' or 'misinformation' related to COVID-19.

[73] The full text of this document can be found at: Global Pledge for Action by Religious Actors and Faith-Based Organizations, 2021, see *supra* note 2.

With the objective of translating the Global Pledge for Action by Religious Actors and Faith-Based Organizations into specific actions, the OSAPG, OHCHR and the UNAOC organized a series of webinars in 2020 and 2021 with religious actors on addressing and countering hate speech and discrimination related to Covid-19 and beyond. A number of peer-to-peer learning snapshots and recommendations for actions by religious actors, were identified during these webinars. It is expected that these recommendations together with the learning points shared in these online meetings will inform the development of a capacity-building tool to assist the work of religious actors in addressing Covid-19 related hate speech.

23.4. Some Reflections on Intergovernmental Organizations' Initiatives Engaging Religious Actors on Hate Speech Issues

From the above discussion, it is clear that the UN is the intergovernmental organization that has paid the most attention to the role of religious actors in combating hate speech in the name of religion, particularly incitement to violence, and has accumulated the most experience to date in this regard.

Initial strategies, as articulated in the Rabat Plan of Action, focused religious actors on reactive responses, principally refraining from intolerant and hateful messages and the prompt and robust denunciation of hate speech particularly arising from within their communities. These were retained in the subsequent 'Faith for Rights' framework and the Plan of Action to prevent incitement to violence, which in turn built on these and developed specific commitments and recommended suggested actions in a range of other areas thereby opening a wider role for religious actors. Prominent among these were calls to monitor, analyze and report hate speech; raise awareness within communities about hate speech, its reasons, forms and the harm it causes; understand and address the root causes, drivers and actors of hate speech, including incitement to violence; participate in interfaith and interreligious dialogue activities in order to foster tolerance, mutual respect and understanding as a means of addressing the root causes and drivers of hate speech; produce and disseminate counter- and alternative narratives to intolerant and hateful ones, both offline and online, particularly by promoting values of tolerance, non-discrimination, inclusion and respect for diversity; and join civil society networks, coalitions and partnerships to work collectively on hate speech issues in society.

In the absence of formal evaluations, it is difficult to assess whether and to which extent these three initiatives have been successful in combating hate speech generally or in affecting those religious actors most likely to engage in hate speech, particularly incitement to violence in the name of religion. While these efforts are commendable and offer potentially powerful recommendations to religious actors to prevent and counter hate speech, more information is needed in order to understand how religious actors have responded and how they have integrated newly acquired insights and skills in their daily lives and routines and what impact this has for their activity. Nevertheless, though intergovernmental-religious actor engagement on hate speech is still in its early stages, a number of insights and broader lessons have emerged. A useful way to think about these issues is in terms of content and process. This section will discuss a number of these issues and their implications for enhancing the effectiveness and impact of interventions by religious actors to tackle hate speech, particularly in their own contexts. It is by no means intended to be an exhaustive treatment of the many important issues involved.

23.4.1. Content Issues

23.4.1.1. Hate Speech – Causes, Context and Criteria

Mere platitudes and strongly worded statements distancing religious actors from hate speech are not entirely adequate to effectively prevent and combat hate speech, including hateful expressions in the name of religion. A focus on identifying, understanding and addressing its root causes and drivers, its deep societal context and its various articulations would seem crucial and central to any strategy aimed at long-term hate speech reduction on the part of religious actors.

The nature of hate speech and its possible consequences has led to the placing of much emphasis on the solutions to the problem and on how they should be grounded in international human rights norms. 'Faith for Rights' exemplifies this approach. Yet this very focus has also limited deeper attempts to understand the causes underlying the phenomenon and the dynamics through which certain types of content emerge, diffuse and lead – or not – to actual discrimination, hostility or violence in the religious context. There is therefore a need to ground interventions in empirical evidence, produce research that maps the emergence and diffusion of hate speech in the name of religion, and the need for studies examining the links between such hate speech and other social phenomena, ranging from access to education to rising inequalities and social marginalization. One can see in the Plan of Action for Religious Leaders and Actors to prevent incitement to violence a move from a focus on condemning hate speech to a more nuanced approach in which religious actors are encouraged to be more alert to the specific contexts – local, cultural, political – and reasons for such harmful behaviour while remaining sensitive to the contribution of religious or ideological factors such as narrow-minded and polarizing interpretations of religious traditions. This should enable them to contribute meaningfully towards tackling the problem of hate speech within their communities by, among other things, addressing some of the underlying factors contributing to intolerance and hate. Religious actors often have considerable local knowledge and this should be tapped into when devising context-specific responses to hate speech. A context-sensitive approach can also help reframe religious narratives to address the deep-rooted causes which generate grievances driving hate speech and intolerant discourse and tailor them to the unique circumstances of each case of hate speech.[74]

Religious actors, particularly community members, are usually unfamiliar with the different layers or forms of hate speech[75] and the criteria to assess these or with their effects. Increasing awareness of hate speech and how to deal with it within religious communities, particularly among children and youth and their parents or carers, would therefore seem essential. A related challenge facing religious actors is in distinguishing between the various forms of hate speech and particularly the boundaries between protected expression and incitement;[76] a lack of clarity concerning legal boundaries often contributes to hate speech being spread, sometimes unwittingly, within religious communities and across society more broadly. To help address this, religious actors might benefit from training on how to understand and apply the six-part test set out in the Rabat Plan of Action to determine whether the threshold of incitement to hatred is met or not.[77] Further, although non-legal measures, such as awareness-raising, education and interfaith and interreligious dialogue, can be successfully deployed to address all forms of hate speech, incitement to violence in the name of religion or belief requires a specific set of responses from religious actors and strategies developed by intergovernmental organizations should continue to take this into account. With respect to non-legal measures to address less egregious forms of hate speech, such as expressions that do not amount to incitement to hatred, religious actors could be additionally encouraged to collaborate across religious and belief boundaries on the development and systematic promotion of an etiquette of empathetic and civil expression rooted in the importance of language and how to use it responsibly as articulated in numerous religious traditions.

Effective reporting and recording of hate speech provides important information about its nature, form, scale, scope and prevalence and can therefore help target interventions accordingly and appropriately. Religious actors generally lack the skills and resources to report hateful expressions arising from

---

74 For an insightful discussion of the interplay between religious and contextual factors in driving hate and violence in the name of religion, see UNHRC, "Report of the Special Rapporteur on Freedom of Religion or Belief, Heiner Bielefeldt", UN Doc. A/HRC/28/66, 29 December 2014, pp. 3–7 ('Report of the Special Rapporteur on Freedom of Religion or Belief, Heiner Bielefeldt') (https://www.legal-tools.org/doc/46g6nv/).

75 See Expert Consultation on Countering Hate Speech, 2021, see *supra* note 2.

76 *Ibid.*

77 Namely, context, speaker, intent, content and form, extent of the speech act, and likelihood, including imminence (Rabat Plan of Action, 2012, para. 29, see *supra* note 38).

within their communities and so this should be factored into intergovernmental organization-led strategies and initiatives on hate speech.

When dealing with hate speech issues, religious actors should also be sensitive to intra- and inter-group dynamics within religious communities. Hate speech can target members of the same religious community, particularly minorities or those regarded as dissidents or heretics. Members of religious communities who speak out against hate speech in these circumstances often find themselves the targets of discrimination, harassment or exclusion. In light of this, religious actors should be encouraged to develop and implement appropriately tailored intra- and interfaith community hate speech intervention programmes.

Given the role of disinformation in creating the conditions for hate speech to emerge, religious actors, particularly religious leaders, have an important role in disseminating validated scientific-based information within communities and challenging disinformation and misinformation, including online. This should also be reflected in future intergovernmental organization hate speech initiatives involving religious actors.

23.4.1.2. Gender

In activities to counter hate speech, the gender dimension warrants special attention as women frequently suffer from complex and intersectional stigmatization that renders them particularly vulnerable to hateful expressions.[78] Religious actors engaged in this work, therefore, need to be committed to addressing all forms of gender-based hate in their responses. Intergovernmental organizations should ensure that their hate speech initiatives and plans involving religious actors are gender-mainstreamed, including the full and effective participation of female religious actors in the consultative process feeding into the design and development of these efforts.[79] To date, only a single gender-based specific recommendation is included in the 'Faith for Rights' framework and in the Plan of Action for Religious Leaders and Actors to prevent incitement to violence, respectively.

Applying a gender lens to hateful expressions within religious communities and contexts could focus the efforts of religious actors on such issues as evaluating the extent to which gender-based stereotypes is a factor driving advocacy of hatred, analyzing how gender is being deployed to advocate hatred,

[78] OSCE and ODIHR, "Gender-Based Hate Crime", 10 March 2021 (available on OSCE's web site); Tackling Hate, 2020, p. 21, see *supra* note 11.

[79] In this connection, it is worth noting that the expert meeting in Beirut that launched the eponymous Declaration and its 18 commitments was more or less gender balanced while women accounted for 30 per cent of all participants in the consultations that led to the formulation of the Plan of Action for Religious Leaders and Actors, 2017, *supra* note 5, to prevent incitement to violence that could lead to atrocity crimes.

in particular where it incites gender-based discrimination or violence including sexual violence, and considering how gender dimensions have contributed to the popularity and spread of hate speech in religious contexts. Women religious leaders could also be encouraged to educate young women in their communities about hate speech and its gendered impact.

23.4.1.3. Interfaith and Interreligious Dialogue Initiatives and Activities

Interfaith and interreligious dialogue and co-operation have a key function in all agendas to overcome hate speech in the name of religion.[80] Although people who meet regularly across religious or belief boundaries will not necessarily agree on all issues, they will realize that followers of other religions and denominations are not 'aliens' with totally different mentalities or feelings. This is an important experience and a precondition for overcoming discriminatory stereotypes, ignorance and fear which are prime motives for 'religious hate speech'. Discovering common concerns, worries and interests may also be the first step for developing joint action plans for tackling the root causes of hate speech in the name of religion more strategically. It is, therefore, encouraging to see a number of references to interfaith dialogue in the Plan of Action for Religious Leaders and Actors to prevent incitement to violence, and it should continue to feature prominently in future intergovernmental organization hate speech initiatives involving religious actors.

The potential of interfaith and interreligious communication for preventing and countering 'religious hate speech' is enormous.[81] However, it is important that any dialogue initiatives promoted by intergovernmental organizations are grounded in respect for universal human rights principles, particularly freedom of religion or belief and freedom of expression, and these should be taken into account when designing strategies or offering recommendations in this area. Chief among these is strict respect for the voluntary participation and autonomy of religious actors who remain free to establish interfaith and interreligious dialogue activities of their own accord and should not be coerced into

[80] For a general discussion about interfaith and interreligious dialogue and communication, including the role of the State in promoting it and the importance of grounding dialogue initiatives in a human rights approach, see UN General Assembly, Interim Report of the Special Rapporteur on Freedom of Religion or Belief, UN Doc. A/66/156, 18 July 2011, pp. 9–22 ('Interim Report of the Special Rapporteur on Freedom of Religion or Belief') (https://www.legal-tools.org/doc/gavxex/). For a discussion of the role and contribution of interreligious dialogue and communication to combating religious hatred, including hate speech in the name of religion, see Report of the Special Rapporteur on Freedom of Religion or Belief, Heiner Bielefeldt, 2013, pp. 11–12, see *supra* note 74.

[81] Interim Report of the Special Rapporteur on Freedom of Religion or Belief, 2011, pp. 9–22, see *supra* note 80; Report of the Special Rapporteur on Freedom of Religion or Belief, Heiner Bielefeldt, 2013, pp. 11–12, see *supra* note 74.

joining State-sponsored initiatives.[82] Further, interfaith and interreligious dialogue initiatives can accommodate a range of formats and settings and take place at all levels – local, national and international – and recommendations issued by intergovernmental organizations should be sensitive to this diversity. The role of informal activities at the grassroots level in advancing tolerance, mutual respect and understanding, and combating intolerance and hate remains particularly underexplored. These are important aspects of the interfaith dialogue process that should also be reflected in intergovernmental hate speech strategies engaging religious actors.

Intergovernmental organizations should also make it clear that interfaith and interreligious dialogue initiatives should follow an inclusive approach that, in keeping with freedom of religion or belief, accommodates the full diversity of religious or belief communities in a society, including newly-established and numerically smaller groups,[83] and ensure the full and equal participation of women and the substantive and substantial involvement of youth as they are usually under-represented in such activities.[84]

23.4.1.4. Online Hate Speech

In recent years, the digital space has become a forum for the expression of hate speech of varying degrees of severity, including incitement to discrimination, hostility or violence, including by religious actors or in the name of religion. Preventing and combating online hate speech poses specific challenges, as it can be disseminated as never before, worldwide, in a matter of seconds, and sometimes remain persistently available. [85] Pressure is mounting for effective

---

82 See on Freedom of Religion or Belief and Security: Policy Guidance, 2019, p. 45, see *supra* note 36.

83 *Ibid.*, pp. 45, 48 and 50.

84 *Ibid.*, p. 46. See also UN Plan of Action to Safeguard Religious Sites, p. 10, see *supra* note 12: "the role of women must be particularly recognized and supported; female religious actors have an important role to play to promote diversity, dialogue, respect and mutual understanding".

85 Recommendation CM/Rec(2022)16, 2022, Preamble, see *supra* note 1:

> Being aware that internet intermediaries can facilitate public debate, in particular through the digital tools and services they make available, while at the same time highlighting that those tools and services can be used to disseminate, quickly and widely, worrying volumes of hate speech.

ECRI, "ECRI General Policy Recommendation No. 6 on Combating the Dissemination of Racist, Xenophobic and Anti-Semitic Material via the Internet", 15 December 2000 ('ECRI General Policy Recommendation No. 6') (available on its web site):

> Recognising that the Internet offers unprecedented means of facilitating the cross-border communication of information on human rights issues related to anti-discrimination […] Deeply concerned by the fact that the Internet is also used for disseminating racist,

responses to hateful expressions online.[86] To date, no intergovernmental initiative on hate speech has explored the substantive role of religious actors in preventing and countering the phenomenon of online hate beyond a handful of recommendations in the Plan of Action for Religious Leaders and Actors to prevent incitement to violence.[87]

The coded and contextual nature of hate speech, the vast amounts and diversity of user-generated content greatly complicate the challenge of engaging religious actors in efforts to address online hate. Nevertheless, religious leaders in particular have an important educational responsibility to change attitudes, values and behaviours, particularly within their own communities as well as across society, as this is a necessary part of the solution. In addressing the role of religious actors in tackling hate speech online, intergovernmental organizations might want to consider how religious leaders can be supported in their

---

xenophobic and antisemitic material, by individuals and groups aiming to incite to intolerance or racial and ethnic hatred.

86 Among the notable recent intergovernmental responses to online hate are Recommendation CM/Rec(2022)16 which includes eight recommendations specifically addressed to Internet intermediaries (Recommendation CM/Rec(2022)16, 2022, Appendix to the Recommendations, paras. 30–37, see *supra* note 1) and the Digital Services Act, 2020 (EC, "Proposal for a Regulation of the European Parliament and of the Councilon a Single Market for Digital Services (Digital Services Act) and Amending Directive 1000/31/EC", 15 December 2020, COM(2020)825).

87 The Plan of Action for Religious Leaders and Actors, 2017, *supra* note 5 on preventing incitement to violence that could lead to atrocity crimes includes recommendations that religious leaders and actors "disseminate positive and alternative speech online and offline"; "amplify through new and traditional media the stories of religious leaders and communities responding to hate with expressions of love and solidarity"; "engage with traditional and new media organizations to counter prejudices and false rumours"; "engage popular social media organizations, including Facebook and Twitter, as active partners in advocacy to support counter speech and alternative narrative campaigns"; "discuss with social media the creation of positive adverts vis-à-vis content that aims to disseminate hatred and incite violence". There are also recommendations addressed to traditional and new media under the 'Strengthen' cluster. Although internet intermediaries are called upon to "establish effective co-operation with civil society organizations that work on hate speech" and to "support their efforts to improve policies, practices and campaigns to address hate speech" (Recommendation CM/Rec(2022)16, 2022, Appendix to the Recommendations, para. 35, see *supra* note 1), Recommendation CM/Rec(2022)16 does not make specific mention of religious actors in this regard.

Similarly, ECRI General Policy Recommendation No. 6, 2000, *supra* note 85, does not refer to the role of religious actors in countering online hate speech. The UN Secretary-General's 2020 Roadmap for Digital Cooperation, which addresses how the international community can better harness the opportunities presented by digital technologies while addressing their challenges, is also silent on the question of the possible role of religious actors (see UN General Assembly, Road Map for Digital Cooperation: Implementation of the Recommendations of the High-Panel on Digital Cooperation, UN Doc. A/74/821, 29 May 2020 (https://www.legal-tools.org/doc/pfr43y/).

efforts to help members of their communities to navigate falsehoods online; how they can be assisted in their own efforts to generate effective counter-speech against online hate, including its gendered dimensions, and help key users to do so; how they can reach out effectively to online hate mongers, hate entrepreneurs and agitators to help them change their views; and how they can put in place an educational process in their communities that help young people to develop a moral framework to deal with a polarized and deceptive online information environment and to express themselves using language that educates rather than denigrates.

23.4.2. Process Issues

23.4.2.1. The Challenge of Implementation and the Need for Tools, Capacity-Building and Support

Knowledge, human rights awareness, declarations, commitments and action plans alone are not sufficient to bring about lasting, sustainable impact and change. Challenges generally arise in the implementation phase, when regional or local sensitivities, combined with a lack of operational guidance and tools and a lack of readily available support from other key stakeholders such as domestic policymakers, wider civil society, statutory human rights and equality bodies, and intergovernmental actors can hinder the taking of action.[88] Policymakers, in particular, would seem to have the means to support the initiatives of religious actors in line with their pledges and commitments and multiply their positive effects. This would go a long way to ensuring sustainability of gains and impact. Securing the commitment of these and other relevant stakeholders to engage in such a process is a serious challenge that needs to be urgently addressed.

Religious actors often do not feel well equipped to deal with a problem as complex and emotive as hate speech, while remaining sensitive to the imperatives of ensuring full respect for human rights, particularly freedom of expression and freedom of religion or belief, or engage in effective prevention activities. To address this, it will be necessary to develop tailor-made tools that they can use in context where there are hate speech concerns. In this regard, the 'Faith for Rights' toolkit is a welcome contribution,[89] and there are also already existing educational manuals that address hate speech through human rights

[88] Expert Consultation on Countering Hate Speech, 2021, p. 4, see *supra* note 2.

[89] See sub-Section 23.3.4.3. of this chapter.

education, including through the use of counter-speech, that can be used or adapted for use by religious actors.[90]

Capacity-building, practical guidance and support will also assist religious actors in their efforts to translate commitments into tangible outcomes. This includes training and guidance in such areas as identifying, monitoring and reporting hate speech and on building and sustaining coalitions with other interested civil society actors, whether religiously affiliated or not, to counter hate speech.[91] A particularly pressing need is that of digital literacy. Religious actors often lack the knowledge, skills and confidence needed to engage proactively in online spaces as well as the skills to recognize misinformation and disinformation when presented online.[92] Training and support to those within religious communications who deal with social media would seem to be particularly important, including providing strategies for constructively curating conversations online when they take a hostile turn. Training for religious actors in communicative counter-strategies and counter-messaging, including shaping narratives on a wider level, online as well as offline, would also appear essential. Religious communities should feel encouraged to start initiatives of interfaith dialogue and co-operation, but in some cases public authorities and civil society organizations will need to proactively support these efforts, including where appropriate by resourcing.

Peer-to-peer learning programmes can enhance the skills of religious actors to address hate speech by empowering them with interdisciplinary knowledge and methodologies. The 'Faith for Rights' toolkit uses such a peer-to-peer learning approach; it will be important to translate this into a deliverable programme adapted to local contexts and needs and sustained over time. In addition to formal peer-to-peer learning initiatives, other spaces for exchange and the sharing of learning, offline and online, should be created. These will provide opportunities for voices of expertise and experience, including from the field, to share their insights and wisdom as well as good practice and to address gaps in

---

90 This includes the materials 'Bookmarks' and 'We CAN' developed for the Council for Europe's 'No Hate Speech Movement'. For information about these resources, see COE, "No Hate Speech Youth Campaign", see *supra* note 17.

91 By bringing together actors and groups with different skills, experiences, resources and connections, coalitions can be a powerful ways to bring about large-scale, enduring changes to address issues of intolerance, discrimination and hate. The ODIHR has developed a guide to help civil society actors in the OSCE region, including religious leaders and actors, a human rights-based approach and practical basis for building successful coalitions aimed at addressing hate and fostering more tolerant, inclusive and peaceful societies. See, OSCE and ODIHR, *Coalition Building for Tolerance and Non-Discrimination: A Practical Guide*, OSCE, Warsaw, 2018.

92 Expert Consultation on Countering Hate Speech, 2021, p. 4, see *supra* note 2.

the understanding among religious actors of their role and responsibilities. Intergovernmental organizations can use their convening power to moderate and facilitate such exchanges and spaces. These efforts could be supplemented by an online knowledge management tool which could serve as an open space for free capacity-building development opportunities and facilitate interaction among religious actors to perpetuate the benefits of exchanges on related initiatives.

Tackling the problem of hate speech is work of long duration calling for tangible and measurable steps with honest evaluation of progress. Monitoring mechanisms to assess the impact of current efforts such as 'Faith for Rights' and the Plan of Action for Religious Leaders and Actors to prevent incitement to violence will need to be established. At present, there are no guidelines on how to evaluate or report impact of these UN-led initiatives. Widespread awareness of and support for these initiatives among religious actors, particularly senior religious leaders, around the world is still not significant.[93] They need to be more vigorously promoted at national and local levels among all relevant stakeholders, translated into more languages and disseminated more widely. The endorsement of prominent religious actors, particularly women and youth, needs to be more assiduously and systematically cultivated.

23.4.2.2. Inclusivity

To ensure that as wide a diversity of insights, views and experiences as possible from the religious sector informs the scoping, design and development of strategies and action plans on hate speech, intergovernmental organizations should aim for inclusive engagement, including women and youth, from the outset. This will also help secure broad-based support for initiatives and assist in their sustainable implementation. While striving for inclusivity, representatives of non-Abrahamic religions were largely absent from the expert meeting that concluded the Beirut Declaration and its 18 Commitments on 'Faith for Rights'.[94] A wider diversity of the world's religious and non-religious belief systems were, however, involved in the consultative process that led to the development of the Plan of Action for Religious Leaders and Actors to prevent incitement to violence.[95]

[93] For a listing of participants in the regional consultations that led to the elaboration of the Plan of Action for Religious Leaders and Actors to prevent incitement to violence that could lead to atrocity crimes, see Plan of Action for Religious Leaders and Actors, 2017, Annex, pp. 23–26, see *supra* note 5.

[94] The original list of signatories to the Beirut Declaration and commitments can be found at: The Beirut Declaration and its 18 Commitments on 'Faith for Rights' – Report and Outlook, 2022, see *supra* note 63.

[95] See sub-Section 23.3.4.4. of this chapter.

Intergovernmental organizations should ensure that their outreach and engagement to religious actors is inclusive by involving members of numerically smaller communities, representatives of new religious movements, and non-believers. They should be careful to not focus mainly on those religions that can make a difference, that are politically influential, statistically significant or economically strong. This can lead to an implicit dichotomy between politically and socially 'relevant' and 'irrelevant' religions, with the danger that those belonging to the less relevant groups remain largely ignored. While some communities might benefit from increased attention and public awareness and recognition, others might lose out. This can lead to serious discrimination or new forms of ignorance or stigmatization. Therefore, in keeping with the universalistic spirit of freedom of religion or belief, religious engagement should be welcoming and inclusive of the prevalent religious and belief diversity in society, and intergovernmental organizations should be encouraged to explore new avenues for collaboration with minority and less prominent religious actors in efforts to counter hate speech and make these more visible in the process.

23.4.2.3. Engaging Religious Actors with Sensitivity

Efforts by intergovernmental organizations to engage religious actors and leaders in a meaningful response to hate speech require sensitive understandings of religious roles. The religious sector is broad, deep and complex. Intergovernmental organizations often assume that publicly visible figures holding formal titles or specific organized institutions are the most relevant religious interlocutors for a given community, but this is not always the case. In many settings, the direct influence of formal religious leaders – even in matters of religion – is questionable. Careful assessment of leadership patterns is needed: religious actors, particularly, leaders who actively put themselves forward or are chosen by intergovernmental organizations for this work do not necessarily have the greatest following or influence within communities. Religious leaders at the local and provincial level and other individuals of capacity in communities, including women and youth, are likely to be trusted and to have a more granular understanding of the specific issues facing their communities. When thinking about effective engagement within religion in any setting, it is important to understand how the concept of lived religion operates in that context. Recalibrating understanding of the religious sector to go beyond official religious authorities and formal institutions makes it possible to discern a far more complex religious landscape populated by a wide array of actors and voices. For example, although many religious traditions limit formal religious authority to older males, in practice women play a major role in shaping understandings and interpretations of religion – both within families and as public religious leaders. Focusing only on men can serve to reproduce male domination of the religious space and miss opportunities for more effective and impactful engagement. For similar reasons, younger or more junior leaders are often omitted from efforts to engage religious actors when they are often more credible and effective communicators, especially among their peers in local communities, and can play a particularly important role on social media in the fight against hate speech.

Training in religious literacy can help intergovernmental organization officials identify credible access points within a religious community and understand the different roles of various religious figures and how their relationship could affect community dynamics. The challenge of religious engagement demands wise interventions that start with strategic knowledge of religious communities and institutions and issues pertaining to religious leadership.

23.5. Concluding Remarks

There is great potential for religious actors to become more active – and more visible – as important collaborators with intergovernmental organizations in the fight against hate speech, particularly incitement to violence arising from within their own communities. While awareness of their role has clearly emerged within the UN, it needs further exploration even within this multilateral space to be fully understood. This is a fascinating area for practical experimentation, research and exchange of experiences. Indeed, recent UN-sponsored initiatives, particularly 'Faith for Rights' and the Plan of Action for Religious Leaders and Actors to prevent incitement to violence, have invited us to rethink the common assumptions about the role of religious actors in society. The tendency when discussing religious actors in the context of hate speech has been to assume that their primary role should be about providing counter-ideological messages or theological antidotes to extremist interpretations of religion. The approach has its merits but also its shortcomings. Positive and non-coercive measures, including messaging, that promote tolerance, mutual understanding, inclusion, pluralism and diversity are essential to fostering mutual understanding within and between groups and empowering people to speak out against hate. The key is to address the underlying prejudices that motivate those who engage in hate speech and religious actors have a critical part to play here. It is ultimately about changing hearts and minds.

The international community does not need more declarations, rather the focus should be on building the capacity of an ever-increasing pool of religious actors to prevent and counter hate speech through a range of results-oriented activities tailored to specific needs, contexts and the evolving nature of hate speech, and providing them with the operational guidance, practical support, tools and resources to do so. The Rabat Plan of Action, 'Faith for Rights' and the Plan of Action for Religious Leaders and Actors to prevent incitement to violence should be seen as important milestones in the wider effort of learning about the role and potential of religion to advance the cause of social peace. It is to be hoped that other intergovernmental bodies will be inspired and encouraged by the still fledgling but nonetheless determined efforts of the UN and that their own engagement with the religious sector on hate speech issues will become more strategic, purposeful and impactful.

24

The Law as a Tool Against Hate Speech in Religious Contexts: Some Theoretical Comments in View of the Israeli Experience

Gilad Noam[*]

This chapter explores the Israeli provision prohibiting incitement to racism (Sections 144a–144c of Israel's Penal Law) and the justifications for such a prohibition, with a focus on two notable clauses: no requirement of attendant harm in order to prosecute a perpetrator and a 'religious exception' that seemingly distinguishes between religious speech and other forms of speech. The author assesses the clauses alongside the varying justifications for prohibiting hate speech, the legislative history, and Israeli jurisprudence to determine how such clauses should be applied.

24.1. Introduction

The Israeli legislation regarding incitement to racism (known as 'hate speech' in other jurisdictions, which will be used interchangeably)[1] developed in response to country-specific history that made its codification necessary. The legislation had to contend with various fundamental, and perhaps contradictory, rights, the most obvious being freedom of expression, as well as freedom of

---

* Dr. **Gilad Noam** is Deputy Attorney General (International Law) at the Ministry of Justice of the State of Israel. He holds an LL.B. in law and humanities (Arabic literature), and an LL.M. and Doctorate in Laws (LL.D.) from the Hebrew University of Jerusalem. He has published on various international law issues, including international criminal law, treaty-making powers in Israel and the suppression of the financing of terrorism. The essay does not necessarily reflect the positions of the State of Israel. The author wishes to thank Adv. Efrat Hakak and Ms. Liana Bernstien for their valuable assistance. For an audio-visual recording of his statement to CILRAP's conference in Florence in April 2022 on the topic of this anthology, please see https://www.cilrap.org/cilrap-film/220409-noam/.

1 There are some who would claim that hate speech and incitement are distinct legal concepts, see Jeroen Temperman, *Religious Hatred and International Law*, Cambridge University Press, 2016, p. 181:

> Thus 'incitement' has as its focus a target group (for example, a group characterized by religion or ethnicity), but its *real audience* consists of third persons whom the inciter hopes to arouse to respond to the message of hate to the extent that they would engage in hostile acts such as violence or discrimination vis-à-vis the target group.

However, in the Israeli case, the term 'incitement' is used to indicate what others would call hate speech.

religion.[2] The conflict between freedom of expression and incitement to racism is clear, considering that the limitation of any kind of speech, including hate speech, would constitute a limitation on the freedom of expression, a fundamental right in any democratic State.

Another right that can come into conflict is that of freedom of religion. An unfortunate truth encountered by lawmakers and law enforcement everywhere is that despite the value of religious teachings and texts as ancient, multi-generational material, they can also reflect the racism and racial hierarchies that were endemic to the social order at the time of its writing. Examples of such texts can be found in virtually every religion practiced today, and when taught or preached, may come into conflict with prohibitions of hate speech.[3]

These conflicts raise the questions: how should liberal democratic societies react to racist speech within a religious context? To what extent should contemporary understandings of racism in a democratic-liberal society apply to expressions made in a traditional religious context? This chapter explores how criminal law can contend with hate speech, and religious hate speech specifically, using the Israeli experience as a springboard – the various theoretical justifications for such a law, the legislative history of Section 144 to Israel's Penal Law (the prohibition of incitement to racism)[4] and its interpretation.

---

2 Much of the legal literature about religion and hate speech focuses on hate speech about or against religion, such as prohibitions on blasphemy or profanity, or speech that denigrates religion; that type of hate speech has its own unique set of problems. See, for example, Lorenz Langer, *Religious Offence and Human Rights: The Implications of Defamations of Religions*, Cambridge University Press, 2014. See also European Commission for Democracy through Law (Venice Commission), *Report on the Relationship between Freedom of Expression and Freedom of Religion: The Issue of Regulation and Prosecution of Blasphemy, Religious Insult and Incitement to Religious Hatred*, 2008.

3 Richard Moon, *Putting Faith in Hate*, Cambridge University Press, 2018. The author provides examples of discriminatory religious teachings from different religions that preach anti-Semitism, Islámophobia, racism and anti-LGBTQ feeling (pp. 117–122); Medha Damojipurapu, "Language and Connotation in Contemporary Hate Speech in India", Occasional Paper Series No. 11 (2022), Torkel Opsahl Academic EPublisher, Brussels, 2022 (http://www.toaep.org/ops-pdf/11-damojipurapu/); Bart Duriez and Didier Hutsebaut, "The Relation Between Religion and Racism: The Role of Post-Critical Beliefs", in *Mental Health, Religion & Culture*, 2000, vol. 3, no. 1, pp. 85–102; United Nations Human Rights Council ('UNHRC'), "Gender-based violence and discrimination in the name or religion or belief: Report of the Special Rapporteur on freedom of religion or belief", UN Doc. A/HRC/43/48, 24 August 2020 (https://www.legal-tools.org/doc/ms3uhb/).

4 Throughout this article, the prohibition of incitement to racism, which is found in Sections 144a–144c will be referred to as 'Section 144'. This is merely out of convenience and refers solely to the Sections relevant to incitement to racism.

24.2. International Human Rights Law and Incitement to Racism

International human rights law sets a general framework that reflects the inherent tensions between freedom of expression and the obligation to protect against incitement to racism. The International Covenant on Civil and Political Rights ('ICCPR') guarantees freedom of expression in Article 19, but recognizes the limits of this right in Article 19(3), *inter alia*, for reasons of public order and national security.[5] The limits of freedom of expression are defined once again in Article 20, which calls upon States to prohibit propaganda for war, or "any advocacy of […] hatred that constitutes incitement to discrimination, hostility or violence".[6]

Article 20 of the ICCPR aims to protect values and rights that justify constraining, to some degree, the exercise of 'free speech'. Article 7 of the Universal Declaration of Human Rights ('UDHR') is even more explicit about the *right* to be protected against incitement. It states that: "All are entitled to equal protection against any discrimination in violation of this Declaration *and against any incitement to such discrimination*".[7] Article 4 of the International Convention on the Elimination of All Forms of Racial Discrimination ('CERD') requires States to take "immediate and positive measures" to end all incitement or discrimination regarding racial hatred, including (as stated in Article 4(a)) criminalizing incitement to racial discrimination.[8]

---

5 Article 19(3) of the ICCPR, 19 December 1966 (https://www.legal-tools.org/doc/2838f3/) stipulates that:

> The exercise of the rights provided for in paragraph 2 of this article carries with it special duties and responsibilities. It may therefore be subject to certain restrictions, but these shall only be such as are provided by law and are necessary: (i) For respect of the rights or reputations of others; (ii) For the protection of national security or of public order (ordre public), or of public health or morals.

6 See Stephanie Farrior, "Molding the Matrix: The Historical and Theoretical Foundations of International Law concerning Hate Speech", in *Berkeley Journal of International Law*, 1996, vol. 14, no. 1, pp. 1–98; Temperman, 2016, Chapter 3, see *supra* note 1; UNHRC, General Comment No. 34: Article 19: Freedoms of opinion and expression, UN Doc. CCPR/C/GC/34, 12 September 2011, paras. 50–51 (https://www.legal-tools.org/doc/113be6/); ARTICLE 19, "Policy Brief: Prohibiting incitement to discrimination, hostility or violence", December 2012.

7 Universal Declaration of Human Rights, 10 December 1948, Article 7 (https://www.legal-tools.org/doc/de5d83/).

8 The CERD Committee recommended that:

> the criminalization of forms of racist expression should be reserved for serious cases, to be proven beyond reasonable doubt, while less serious cases should be addressed by means other than criminal law, taking into account, *inter alia*, the nature and extent of the impact on targeted persons and groups. The application of criminal sanctions should be governed by principles of legality, proportionality and necessity.

National legal systems differ in the ways in which they chose to balance between free speech and suppressing incitement to racism.[9] Specifically, States' laws differ in defining hate speech[10] and the extent to which limitations on speech are imposed.[11]

24.3. Hate Speech Legislation in Israel

In Israel, the catalyst for criminalizing incitement to racism was the rise of the political party 'Kach', which was associated with the religious extremist rabbi, Meir Kahana, who promulgated a virulently racist, violent, extremist ideology.[12] Throughout the 1970s and 1980s, Kahane and his followers gradually gained political power, and with it worked to incite racism and violence, propose racist policies and deepen the divisions between various factions of Israeli society.[13] As the Israeli government attempted to contend with the unsavory behaviour of a politician and his followers, two laws were enacted to limit the power of

---

ICERD Committee, General Recommendation No. 35: Combating Racist Hate Speech, UN Doc. CERD/C/GC/35, 26 September 2013, para. 12 (https://www.legal-tools.org/doc/d3c55a/); see also, ICERD Committee, General Recommendation No. 15: Organized Violence based on Ethnic Origin (Art. 4), UN Doc. CERD/C/GC/15, 23 March 1993 (https://www.legal-tools.org/doc/a03003/).

9 For a succinct summary of some comparative law on these issues, see Itai Weschler-Be'er, Amir Fuchs and Mordechai Kremnitzer, "The Crimes of Incitement to Racism and Violence: A Rethinking", in *Israel Democracy Institute*, 2 December 2019, Chapter 2 (Hebrew); ARTICLE 19, 2012, see *supra* note 6; Alexander Tsesis, "Dignity and Speech: The Regulation of Hate Speech in a Democracy", in *Wake Forest Law Review*, 2009, vol. 42, pp. 521–531.

10 According to those comparative law surveys, certain States specify the protected groups, others are more general. Hungary, for example, includes the entire "Hungarian nation" in their prohibition of incitement; Germany has a more ambiguous list, which includes "national, racial, religious groups defined by their ethnic origin" and "segments of the population". Italy, Poland and England specify in their prohibitions an exhaustive list of what parameters could justify the use of the prohibition, such as incitement to discriminate on the basis of race, ethnic origin, nationality and religion.

11 There seems to be a spectrum of practice as to the scope of the prohibition. In Poland, the prohibition of incitement includes threatening or publically insulting a group of people or individuals. In Italy, the prohibition includes instigating or provoking violence. In Austria, the prohibition is defined as inciting hatred with the intention of harming human dignity. In Germany, the scope of the prohibition includes dissemination of certain propaganda. In Britain, there is a separate prohibition that specifically prohibits any racist chanting at football matches.

12 For a more detailed history of the background to its legislation, please see Chapter 3 by Justice Dorit Beinisch, "Drawing the Line Between the Preservation of Freedom of Religious Expression and the Fight Against Hate Speech and Incitement to Terrorism and Violence: The Perspective of a Judge and a Prosecutor" in this volume.

13 For an overview of Meir Kahane's and Kach's activity, see Shaul Magid, *Meir Kahane: The Public Life and Political Thought of an American Jewish Radical*, Princeton University Press, 2021, specifically Chapters 3 (Race and Racism) and 5 (Zionism).

'Kach', and Kahane specifically. Section 144 of the Israel Penal Law is one of such laws.[14]

The first provision, Section 144a, provides definitions for the rest of the article. In it, racism is defined as:

> persecution, humiliation, denigration, expression of hatred, threats or violence, or promoting feelings of resentment towards a community or sections of the population, solely due to color or belonging to a race or a national-ethnic origin.

Sections 144b and 144c detail what is and, perhaps more interestingly, what is *not* considered a violation of this offense (emphasis added):

Prohibition of publication of incitement to racism	144b. (a) A person who published material with the intent to incite to racism is liable to imprisonment for five years. (b) For the purpose of this section, *it is immaterial whether the publication led to racism or not*, or whether it contained truth or not.
Permitted publication	144c. (a) The publication of a correct record of an act described in section 144b shall not be deemed as an offence under that section, provided that it was not done with the intent to incite to racism. (b) *The publication of a quote from religious writings or prayer books, or the observance of a religious rite, shall not be deemed an offence under section 144b, provided that it was not done with the intent to incite to racism.*[15]

Table 1: Sections 144b and 144c of Israel's Penal Law.

Following these sections, Section 144e stipulates that any indictment under Section 144b is subject to written consent by the Attorney General.[16] The emphasized clauses of Sections 144b and 144c seem somewhat peculiar in the context of criminal law. Firstly, Section 144b is a conduct crime, meaning that only the prohibited conduct needs to be proven (namely, publishing material

[14] In addition to the prohibition of incitement to racism, Kach and Meir Kahane's actions led the Israeli Parliament ('Knesset') to add Article 7A to the Basic-Law: The Knesset (Israel, Basic-Law: The Knesset (5718-1958), 12 February 1958 (https://www.legal-tools.org/doc/tt9mvj/)). The new article authorized the Central Elections Committee to disqualify a political party list of candidates or individual candidate if their goals or actions include the negation of the State of Israel as a Jewish and democratic State, incitement to racism, or support for an armed struggle by a hostile State or by a terrorist organization against the country.

[15] Laws of the State of Israel, vol. 40, 5746-1985/86 (https://www.legal-tools.org/doc/043w3c/), authorized translation from Hebrew, prepared by the Ministry of Justice. Since the publication of the translation, the law has been changed slightly, and the translation provided here reflects those changes.

[16] Immediately following the prohibition of incitement to racism, Section 144d(2) of the Penal Law details the prohibition of incitement to violence. Incitement to violence and incitement to racism both require the consent of the Attorney General for indictment.

with the intent to incite racism), and there is no requirement of attendant harm. Interestingly, this could be gleaned from the text of Section 144b(a), which does not include any mention of attendant harm, but the lawmaker emphasized this further by stipulating that attendant harm was "immaterial" to the prohibition, as expressly clarified in Section 144b(b).

Secondly, Section 144c(b) provides that a quote from religious writings or prayer books, or the practice of religious rites, is not deemed an offence, as long as it is not done with intent to incite racism. This does not seem materially different from Section 144b, since the conditions are still the same as those mentioned previously, which raises the question as to why religious speech was afforded a special clause and whether this is meant to signal a different legal standard.

As mentioned, Israel's legislation was adopted against the background of a certain social and political reality. Both of the above-mentioned unique components in the landscape of criminal legislation may be the result of that reality. However, refining some theoretical aspects regarding the relations between the prohibition of incitement to racism and freedom of expression, and between the prohibition and freedom of religion, is also important to understanding the legal arrangements that were adopted in Sections 144b(b) and 144c(b) respectively.

24.4. Incitement to Racism versus Freedom of Expression: Theoretical Background

Much has been written about the importance of freedom of expression, but prominent scholars have also recognized the dangers of hate speech and how that may affect the legitimacy of expression.[17] It should be noted that delegitimizing hate speech by legal means does not necessarily entail using criminal law. Civil and administrative tools may be preferable.[18] However, since this chapter zooms in on Israel's Penal Law, that will be the focus of the theoretical analysis.

Three main justifications for criminalizing incitement to racism arise repeatedly throughout the academic literature: to protect the dignity of the victims of the racist speech, to allow the State to direct the behaviour of speakers (and thus prevent speech that the State considers distasteful), and to prevent *eventual* violence.[19] The first justification, that of protecting the *dignity* of the maligned groups, is meant, in Waldron's words, to protect the victims' "basic entitlement

17 David Kretzmer, "Freedom of Speech and Racism", in *Cardozo Law Review*, 1987, vol. 8, pp. 467–492; Jeremy Waldron, *The Harm in Hate Speech*, Harvard University Press, 2012; Langer, 2014, pp. 290–310, see *supra* note 2.

18 See *supra* note 8. ARTICLE 19, 2012, p. 24, see *supra* note 6.

19 Langer, 2014, p. 302, see *supra* note 2. See also Kretzmer, 1987, p. 465, see *supra* note 17.

to be regarded as a member of society in good standing, as someone whose membership of a minority group does not disqualify him or her from ordinary social interaction".[20] Waldron is careful to clarify that the protection of dignity differs from the protection from offense, since taking offense is a subjective experience, and dignity provides a certain objective standard.[21]

The second argument, that of directing behaviour by the State, differs from the first in that it focuses on the State's will to maintain a society with a certain standard of respectful discourse, rather than protection of the group to which the expression is directed. Through prohibiting incitement to racism, the State makes clear that racism and bigotry are not legitimate modes of discourse in a liberal society. This justification relies on the presumption that hate speech hurts society as a whole. The harm done to victims is not the focus here, but rather the domino effect that such harm has on public discourse and societal norms.[22] The State's attempt to regulate speech assumes that such regulation will change the behaviour of those who would otherwise partake in racist speech.[23] Whether such regulation can impact moral attitudes, and to what extent, can be disputed. There are cases where regulation was proven effective in changing the public discourse,[24] but the results are not unequivocal.[25]

The final justification, and the one I find most persuasive, is that of preventing eventual physical harm or violence. Much as the seeds of weeds that infiltrate a garden are unseen until they grow in spring, incitement to racism can cause violence long after the fact, and possibly without a discernable trace to the original speaker. The weeds that grow are undoubtedly the result of the seeds that made their way into the garden, despite the fact that it may be impossible to determine which specific seed caused each weed. The same can be said of hate

20 Waldron, 2012, p. 103, see *supra* note 17.

21 *Ibid.*, pp. 105–107.

22 Robert Post, "Hate Speech", in Ivan Hare and James Weinstein (eds.), *Extreme Speech and Democracy*, Oxford University Press, 2009, pp. 128–133.

23 See Anthony Oberschall, "Propaganda, Hate Speech and Mass Killings", in Pedrag Dojčinović (ed.), *Propaganda, War Crimes Trails and International Law*, Routledge, 2012, p. 171. Although it does not refer specifically to the prohibition of hate speech, see also Kenworthey Bilz and Janice Nadler, "Law, Moral Attitudes, and Behavioral Change", in Eyal Zamir and Doron Teichman (eds.), *The Oxford Handbook of Behavioral Economics and the Law*, Oxford University Press, 2014.

24 See, for example, Global Action Against Mass Atrocity Crimes ('GAAMAC'), "Preventing Hate Speech, Incitement, and Discrimination: Lessons on Promoting Tolerance and Respect for Diversity in The Asia Pacific", August 2021 (https://www.legal-tools.org/doc/9ak28w/); Kay Whitlock and Michael Bronski, *Considering Hate: Violence, Goodness, and Justice in American Culture and Politics*, Beacon Press, 2015.

25 Sandra Coliver (ed.), *Striking a Balance: Hate Speech, Freedom of Expression and Non-discrimination*, ARTICLE 19, 1992, pp. 1–6.

speech. Situations involving mass atrocities typically follow years of racist speech that dehumanized the victim and primed the perpetrators of the atrocities later committed (witness Nazi Germany, Myanmar and Pakistan as examples).[26] The rationale of such a justification is that waiting until the end of the line for imminent or even probable harm may be too late.

These justifications may seem convincing, and hate speech is undoubtedly lamentable, but there is also danger in making use of criminal law in such a context. A criminal offense could potentially be used in a way that would unduly infringe upon freedom of speech; and such a law could be misused by governments, thereby censoring imperative political speech and debate. It could also come dangerously close to the criminalization of thoughts and ideas, as opposed to actions, which negates the default principle of criminal law that requires harm, or at least a real possibility that harm could be caused, in order to punish the perpetrator.[27] Moreover, it is argued, primarily in the American legal tradition, that the proper response to harmful speech is not to limit it, but rather to allow "the marketplace of ideas" to flourish, letting "good" speech combat the harmful speech.[28]

A State that chooses to use its penal laws to address hate speech must be aware of the above-mentioned dangers. The Israeli case provides an example of a society where the dangers of racism are real, where polarization is deep, and where there is a history of violence. In such circumstances, it was deemed legitimate and moral to criminalize hate speech. Considering the aforementioned dangers, the crucial question is when and to what extent criminal law should be applied to instances of hate speech.

24.5. Israel's Hate Speech Legislation: Is There a Dominant Theoretical Rationale?

The 'no attendant harm' clause in Section 144b seems to be in line with the second and third theoretical justifications for incitement to racism prohibitions:

---

26 See Gordon W. Allport, *The Nature of Prejudice*, Addison-Wesley Publishing Company, 1954. Allport traces prejudice from its roots to its horrendous outcomes in multiple cultures (see, for example, pp. 285–339 which assesses Germany pre-World War II); GAAMAC, 2021, see *supra* note 24.

27 Jerome Hall, *General Principles of Criminal Law*, 2nd ed., Bobbs-Merill Co., 1960, pp. 18–19, 212–246.

28 It is not surprising, therefore, that in the American tradition, which limits free speech only in the presence of clear danger or imminent lawless action, a prohibition on racist speech, *per se*, would be nearly inconceivable. Even in Waldron, 2012 (see *supra* note 17), the author does not attempt to convince his American readers to criminalize such speech – he suffices with attempting to convince them that the European model of free speech which would allow for such criminalization is not illiberal, but rather based on a rational approach to speech in a liberal society.

to dictate societal norms and to prevent eventual harm. The most obvious indication is the fact that Section 144b(b) requires the speaker to have *intent* to incite, but it does not require any *likelihood* or probability of *harm.* During the law-making process, there were those who called for the addition of attendant harm, and the Supreme Court of Israel ('Supreme Court') has toyed with the idea of requiring such an element,[29] but ultimately the law has remained entirely conduct-dependent, with no required result.

In other provisions of the Penal Law, most notably the adjacent section prohibiting incitement to violence, one of the criminal elements requires that harm, or "a real possibility" of such harm, be proven. In the context of incitement to violence, the rationale of protecting the victim seems to be dominant, since any conviction is dependent on having caused harm or a real possibility of harm. However, considering that Section 144b stipulates *specifically* that the speaker's action does not need to have caused harm, it is clear that the first justification is not at the forefront of Section 144b, and the rationale seems to be related more to the second and third justifications – namely, dictating what constitutes appropriate societal behaviour and preventing eventual harm.[30]

24.6. Freedom of Religion in International Human Rights Law: The Legal Framework

Section 144c(b) stipulates that religious speech, texts and rites are not considered incitement to racism, as long as the speaker did not have the intent to incite racism. This Section, by mentioning religion specifically, raises the question whether the line between permitted and forbidden speech may be different in cases of religious speech. It adds another layer of complexity to the already-delicate balance between freedom of expression and incitement to racism.

[29] Supreme Court of Israel, *Rabbi Ido Elba v. State of Israel*, 50 (5) PD 221 [1996], Crim. A. 2831/95, 1996, para. 4 ('*Elba*') (https://www.legal-tools.org/doc/jmspn9/). The seminal case regarding Section 144b is the *Elba* case, wherein a rabbi published a 'clarification' about the Jewish Law (Halacha) concerning killing gentiles (non-Jews). The Court determined that, in accordance with the plain language of the law, attendant harm was not necessary in order to convict the defendant. However, the Court did not clarify what it considered to be the protected value behind the prohibition of hate speech. Kremnitzer explains that different protected values (or 'justifications' as I referred to them) could influence the Court's interpretation of the required *mens rea* or *actus reus* in Section 144b (see Mordechai Kremnitzer, "The Elba Case: A Clarification of the Laws of Incitement to Racism", in *Mishpatim*, 2018, vol. 30, pp. 109–110 (Hebrew)).

[30] Israel is not unique in such a provision. Other countries, such as Canada, the United Kingdom, France and Scandinavian countries, have hate speech prohibitions that are dependent on intent, rather than harm (see *supra* note 9). This seems to further strengthen the idea that prohibitions of hate speech are not solely to protect the group being spoken about, but rather to protect society as a whole.

Freedom of religion or belief is considered a universal right, as reflected in Article 18 of the UDHR and Article 18 of the ICCPR, among other international legal instruments.[31] The scope of the freedom of religion is viewed as having two 'sides': the negative side requires the government to avoid intervening in people's religion, belief or worship, while the positive side requires the government to protect the exercise of religions. The two sides of the right can be seen clearly in the structure of Article 18: the first part, one's right to *hold* beliefs and opinions is not to be infringed upon.[32] However, the second part of the right to freedom of religion – one's right to *manifest* one's religion – like most rights, is not absolute, and may be limited to protect, among other things, the "fundamental rights and freedoms of others".[33]

24.7. Freedom of Religion in Israel: A General Background

In Israel, freedom of religion has been recognized in the State's Declaration of Independence,[34] and has been regarded as a fundamental right in Israeli jurisprudence.[35]

---

31 Article 18 of the UDHR (see *supra* note 7) contains many of the elements that later appear in the ICCPR. See also the International Convention on the Elimination of All Forms of Racial Discrimination, 21 December 1965, Article 5(b)(vii) (https://www.legal-tools.org/doc/43a925/); the Convention on the Rights of the Child, 20 November 1989, Article 14 (https://www.legal-tools.org/doc/f48f9e/); United Nations General Assembly, Declaration on the Elimination of All Forms of Intolerance and of Discrimination Based on Religion and Belief, UN Doc. A/RES/36/55, 25 November 1981 (https://www.legal-tools.org/doc/hexdsg/); the Convention relating to the Status of Refugees, 28 July 1951, Article 4 (https://www.legal-tools.org/doc/9b8e7a/); the Convention Relating to the Status of Stateless Persons, 28 September 1954, Article 4 (https://www.legal-tools.org/doc/di2frl/); as well as a plethora of regional treaties, including the European Convention for the Protection of Human Rights and Fundamental Freedoms, 4 November 1950, Article 9 ('ECHR') (https://www.legal-tools.org/doc/8267cb/).

32 ICCPR, Article 18(2), see *supra* note 5.

33 *Ibid.*, Article 18(3). Note the differences between the ICCPR and ECHR in this respect. In the ICCPR, Article 18 is listed as one of the provisions that cannot be derogated from during a public emergency, according to Article 4(2), while Article 18(3) specifies the permitted limitations on the right to manifest one's religion. In the ECHR, Article 9 is not listed as one of the non-derogable provisions in time of emergency in Article 15(2). However, similar to the ICCPR, the permitted limitations apply only to the right to *manifest* one's religion in Article 9(2).

34 Israel's Declaration of Independence includes the following sentence: "[The State of Israel] will guarantee freedom of religion, conscience, language, education and culture […]" (translated from Hebrew), Declaration of Establishment of State of Israel, 14 May 1948 (https://www.legal-tools.org/doc/260670/).

35 See for example, Israel High Court of Justice, *Mitrael Ltd. v. The Prime Minister and Minister of Religious Affairs*, H.C.J. 3872/93, 22 October 1993 (https://www.legal-

The question of how to balance limitations on the manifestation of religion with other rights has long plagued liberal States. European courts, for example, have used tests such as determining the proportionality of the limitation,[36] requiring the State to provide "appropriate accommodation" for certain religious behaviours, [37] or exempting essential, or core, religious practices from any limitation, while narrowly delineating what is considered a core belief.[38]

In Israel, due to its religious diversity and polarization, as well as the deep respect afforded to religious beliefs, any limitation to freedom of religion must be undertaken with extreme caution. In one prominent case, *Emmanuel*, the Supreme Court had to determine the boundaries of the freedom of religion, within the context of religious instruction at schools.[39] Although religious instruction differs from incitement to racism, the tests used in the Court's ruling provide insight as to how the courts balance the right to freedom of religion with other basic principles of democratic society. There, the Court determined that any discrimination on the basis of religion may be justified only when it is (i) an *inherent* part of the belief system; (ii) *relevant* to the purpose of the distinction; and (iii) *necessary for the preservation* of the religion.[40] By applying these tests to

tools.org/doc/v23kb0/); Israel High Court of Justice, *Yisrael Soloduch v. City of Rehovot*, 1 August 2010, H.C.J. 10907/04, 2010 (https://www.legal-tools.org/doc/926pnn/).

36 John Bowers, "Accommodating Difference: How is Religious Freedom Protected When It Clashes with Other Rights: Is Reasonable Accommodation the Key to Levelling the Field", in *Oxford Journal of Law and Religion*, 2021, vol. 10, pp. 283–285; UNHRC, General Comment No. 22: Article 18 (Freedom of Thought, Conscience or Religion), UN Doc. CCPR/C/21/Rev.1/Add.4, 30 July 1993, para. 3.

37 Bowers, 2021, pp. 285–286, see *supra* note 36.

38 In England and Wales Administrative Court, *R (on the application of Playfoot (a minor) v. Governing Body of Millais School*, EWHC 1698 (Admin), 16 July 2007 (https://www.legal-tools.org/doc/otcnd8/), the Court determined that wearing a 'purity ring' at school was not a core tenant of the religion, and therefore not a protected right. This is similar to the case of Constitutional Court of South Africa, *MEC for Education KwaZulu-Natal and Others v. Pillay*, [2007] ZACC 21, 5 October 2007 (https://www.legal-tools.org/doc/anurqt/), which considered the wearing of a nose ring in South Africa. See also Farrah Raza, "Limitations to the Right to Religious Freedom: Rethinking Key Approaches", in *Oxford Journal of Law and Religion,* 2020, vol. 9, pp. 435–462.

39 Supreme Court of Israel, *Amutat "Noar K'Halacha" v. Ministry of Education*, H.C.J. 1067/08, 6 August 2009 ('*Emmanuel*') (https://www.legal-tools.org/doc/jrtn43/). In *Emmanuel*, primary school students were separated into different tracks depending on their religious tradition (a 'Hasidic track' and a 'general track'). Students in the Hasidic track were almost entirely of Ashkenazi ancestry, while students in the general track were typically of Sephardic ancestry. A physical wall separated the tracks within the building; the students had different uniforms and different hours for recess. Parents argued that the separation into tracks was racially motivated, rather than strictly pertinent to differences in religious education.

40 *Ibid.*, paras. 19 and 24 of Justice Edmond Levy's judgment.

the specific circumstances of *Emmanuel,* the Court found that the separation between students did not conform to the tests, and was therefore not protected under the students' right to religious manifestation.

The legal test adopted in the *Emmanuel* case can perhaps provide some guidelines for the purposes of Section 144c(b) *mutatis mutandis*, but the question of how religious customs and texts could be accommodated in the context of Section 144c(b) is not clear.[41] As will be discussed below, the Supreme Court has avoided any unequivocal determination of the appropriate balance between freedom of religion, freedom of expression and hate speech, and the role, if any, that Section 144c(b) has in such a determination.[42]

24.8. Freedom of Religion and Hate Speech in Israeli Law

As mentioned above, Section 144c(b) holds that:

> [t]he publication of a quote from religious writings or prayer books, or the observance of a religious rite, shall not be deemed an offence under section 144b, provided that it was not done with the intent to incite to racism.

It is not entirely clear what this Section adds to the prohibition of hate speech. In prior sections, it is already stipulated that if the perpetrator of racist speech did not have the intent of inciting racism, he is not criminally responsible, which would seemingly include speech spoken within a religious context, given the speaker has no nefarious intent. So why did religious speech merit a separate

---

41 In the past, when Israeli case law has addressed the conflict between religious freedom and other rights, it has separated the right of manifestation of religious identity from that of 'religious feeling' or an interest in maintaining a certain cultural norm, which do not merit the same constitutional-like status that the freedom of religion does. Supreme Court of Israel, *Lior Horev v. Minister of Transport*, H.C.J. 5016/96, 13 April 1997 ('*Horev*') (https://www.legal-tools.org/doc/xyspdw/); and Supreme Court of Israel, *Yaakov Gur Aryeh v. Second Television and Radio Authority*, H.C.J. 1514/01, 18 June 2001 ('*Gur Aryeh*') (https://www.legal-tools.org/doc/lc010y/). In the *Horev* case, in which residents of an ultra-orthodox neighborhood wanted to block the main road through the neighborhood on the Sabbath, the Court decided that the closing of the road was purely to satisfy religious feeling and a cultural interest, rather than a religious obligation on the residents of the neighborhood, and therefore was not superior to the secular residents' freedom of movement. In the *Gur Aryeh* case, religious people who observed the Sabbath were recorded for a television programme, and opposed the programme's broadcast on the Sabbath, since watching television would be a transgression of their religious law. The Court decided that since the petitioners would not be actively participating on the broadcast, but rather opposed that others would watch the programme, it was not a violation of their freedom of religion, and therefore did not supersede the broadcasting network's freedom of expression.

42 Supreme Court of Israel, *12 of Cheshvan The Movement for Strengthening Tolerance in Religious Education v. Attorney General*, H.C.J 2684/12, 9 December 2015, para. 61 (p. 32) of Justice Elyakim Rubinstein's opinion ('*Torat HaMelech*') (https://www.legal-tools.org/doc/8xn5hw/).

section – what can be learned from this Section about the relationship between freedom of religion, freedom of expression and the protection from incitement to racism? Does it give additional protection to religious writings and religious speech in general? Does the Section provide different elements of the crime than non-religious speech that incites to racism? Is it a superfluous clause, simply reiterating the *mens rea*, while not changing the substance of the offense?

The legislative history of the Section may assist in its interpretation. In the records of the Knesset, it becomes apparent that the Section was the result of a compromise[43] between religious Members of Knesset ('MKs'), who feared that any prohibition of hate speech would be used against "ordinary" religious speech,[44] and secular MKs, who feared that providing an exception for religious speech would allow for racist speech behind the facade of religion.[45] The final version of the section therefore provided a clause to specify that religious speech is not considered incitement to racism, but reiterated that this is only as long as there is no *intent* to incite racism.[46]

The confusion regarding whether Section 144c(b) affords religious speech a different standard than non-religious speech was evident from its inception. When the Knesset was discussing the law back in 1986, MK Kulas explicitly noted that the new clause was declarative and "educational".[47] Other

43 In 1986, after several long months of political back and forth and committee sessions to hammer out the details of the proposed bill on incitement to racism, the bill was returned to committee, in the middle of the final vote in the plenary. Among other changes, the requirement for 'intent' was added in by the government at the last minute (which was what triggered the proposal being pulled back to the Constitution Law and Justice Committee). This was in part an attempt to mitigate what would be a far-reaching criminalization of speech. The protocols provide a record of the discussions between MKs at the time, including the Constitutional Law and Justice Committee, Protocol No. 139 from 4 August 1986 which discusses the definitions used in the law, and Protocol No. 141 from 8 August 1986 (when it was pulled back to committee after near finalization in the plenary).

44 In Protocol No. 141, 1986, p. 5, see *supra* note 43, MK Avner-Hai Shaki questioned whether teaching Jewish religious laws like marrying 'out of the faith' would constitute a criminal offense. Note that at that point, there was still a question about whether or not the offense would include hate speech against other religions (not only other races or nationalities).

45 Protocol No. 139, 1986, p. 16, see *supra* note 43, MK Yitzhak Artzi's comment.

46 *Ibid.*, pp. 10–12.

47 235th Meeting of the 11th Knesset, 5 August 1986, p. 4014. See MK Kulas' comment (translated from Hebrew):

> A clause of 'permitted publication' means that anything that is done without the purpose of inciting racism [is not deemed an offense]. Therefore, if you read from the Holy Scriptures without such an intent, it is immaterial whether you read from the Holy Scriptures or other sources. This Section is more declarative, it comes to express an educational trend and not something else. Since the ultimate phrase of the Section says again: "[...] provided that it was not done with the intention of inciting to racism" [...] If you read from holy

MKs, however, perceived the section as providing extra protection to religious speech, and as such, fiercely opposed the proposed religious exception, even going so far as to call it "a weapon in the hands of the racists".[48] Still others believed that the new clause was meant to target only those manipulating the religious text for racist purposes.[49] In their view, it was inconceivable that the word of God could support racism, and it is inconceivable that a religious act or ritual would be racist.[50]

After the legislation passed in the Knesset, the Supreme Court, much like the legislators themselves, encountered difficulties when having to interpret the religious exception clause. In 1995, two justices (in an *obiter dictum*) set out the opposing interpretations of the religion text clause: Justice Mazza wrote that it "did not come to add anything that would otherwise not have been known and manifest",[51] while Justice Tal opined that "the law created a presumption of sorts, one which is rebuttable, that when a person quotes from religious texts, on the face of it, it is not his intention to incite to racism, but rather to promulgate the religion".[52] This judicial debate has never been settled, though the Court later clarified that religious texts are not categorically immune from prosecution.[53]

> writings, regardless of religion, with the intention of inciting to racism, it is a criminal offense. And that's what we are trying to prevent.

48 *Ibid.*, p. 4018. See MK Ran Cohen's comment, which believed the new wording legitimized religious racist speech instead of denouncing it (translated from Hebrew):

> Today you are ready to put weapons in the hands of racists who intend to use [religious] quotes to disguise their words and preach racism, and you are unwilling to say to yourselves that you're putting weapons in their hands? Not only are you not preventing them from undertaking racist acts, you are handing them a weapon for preaching racism.

49 *Ibid.*, p. 4014.

50 Protocol No. 141, 1986, p. 5, see *supra* note 43.

51 *Elba*, 1996, para. 23 of Justice Eliahu Mazza's opinion (p. 260), see *supra* note 29. The Israeli scholar Kretzmer agreed with this opinion:

> The requirement of purpose means that Section 144C.(b), relating to quotations from religious writings, etc. (introduced in order to meet the demand of the religious parties as a condition for their support of the bill), is totally superfluous. This section states that such quotations will not be an offence unless made with the purpose of inciting to racism. But as other categories of acts constitute offences only if done with such purpose there is nothing unique about quotations from religious writings.

See David Kretzmer, "Racial Incitement in Israel", in *Israel Yearbook on Human Rights*, 1992, vol. 22, p. 251.

52 *Elba*, 1996, p. 323, see *supra* note 29.

53 *Torat HaMelech*, 2015, para. 61 (p. 32) of Justice Elyakim Rubinstein's opinion, see *supra* note 42. The case dealt with 'Torat HaMelech', a book published in 2009 that argued that Jewish Law permitted the killing of non-Jews in certain circumstances. The Attorney General at the time had decided not to prosecute the authors with incitement to racism, in accordance with the provisions of Section 144e, due to his perception that the book was written in a

The legislative history and the scant references in the Supreme Court's jurisprudence show that Section 144c(b) may be understood either as redundant or as affording religious expressions an additional layer of protection. This second option adds an additional ball to the proverbial juggling act that already exists within the context of Section 144b, with freedom of religion joining the complicated maneuver between freedom of expression and prohibiting racial incitement.

In my opinion, the purpose of Section 144c(b) is twofold. On the one hand, it is meant to emphasize that religious leaders are not exempt from the hate speech prohibition in Section 144b, provided that they intended to incite racism. Such an addition seems important, especially considering the hesitation of the State to intervene when it comes to issues that are considered to be part of the religious autonomy. In fact, in many of the cases where the State has sought to prosecute hate speech, the speaker has often been a religious leader,[54] and Section 144c(b) has been explicitly referenced by the Court in order to prove that religion cannot act as a facade for racism.[55] On the other hand, by adding this section, the Israeli legislator showed awareness of the social, cultural and perhaps political sensitivities associated with restrictions on religious expressions, especially in a divided society like the Israeli society. Whether and how the addition of this section could affect the legal formula that balances between the need to suppress hate speech, freedom of expression and freedom of religion, remains a question for the courts to decide.

Considering the confusion surrounding Section 144c(b), and perhaps in part due to the understandable reluctance to restrict both freedom of expression and freedom of religion, it will come as no surprise, that in Israel, the prosecution practically limits the use of the criminal offense, particularly in religious contexts, to the most egregious examples of hate speech. A significant factor in deciding which cases to pursue seems to be the likelihood of harm.[56] By doing

general manner and did not call for violence. The High Court justices supported the Attorney General's decision not to prosecute in a split decision (2–1).

54 *Elba*, 1996, see *supra* note 29; *Torat HaMelech*, 2015, see *supra* note 42; Magistrate Court of Nazareth, *State of Israel v. Nazim Abu Salim*, 1 April 2012, Crim. C. 12629-11-10 (https://www.legal-tools.org/doc/3wgtm0/); Magistrate Court of Jerusalem, *State of Israel v. Halad Mughrabi*, Crim. C. 29733-11-15, 14 March 2016 (https://www.legal-tools.org/doc/edgyyy/); Magistrate Court of Jerusalem, *State of Israel v. Omar Abu Sara*, Crim. C. 44176-01-15, 23 March 2016 (https://www.legal-tools.org/doc/e37ges/).

55 *Elba*, 1996, para. 30 (p. 273) of Justice Mazza's opinion, see *supra* note 29; *Torat HaMelech*, 2015, paras. 12, 65 of Justice Rubinstein's opinion, see *supra* note 42.

56 *Torat HaMelech*, 2015, para. 56 to Justice Rubinstein's opinion and paras. 63–37 to Justice Joubran's opinion, see *supra* note 42; *Elba*, 1996, pp. 266–268 of Justice Mazza's opinion, see *supra* note 29.

so, the difference between incitement to racism and incitement to violence (a different section in Penal Law) becomes blurred.[57]

Comparative and international law may inform the prosecution, and ultimately, the courts, in formulating guidelines for deciding which cases of hate speech in religious contexts are suitable to prosecute. The Office of the High Commissioner for Human Rights' Rabat Plan of Action from 2012 ('the Rabat test') includes a six-part threshold test, with the following considerations: (i) context of the speech, (ii) status of the speaker, (iii) intent of the speaker, (iv) content and form of the speech, (v) extent of the speech act, and (vi) likelihood of harm, including imminence.

The Supreme Court has already acknowledged the Rabat test[58] and certain parts of the Rabat test are reflected in Israeli legislation and case law. For example, Part 3, which requires intent by the perpetrator to incite racism, mirrors Section 144b(a) and 144c(a–b) of the Penal Law. The other parts of the Rabat test are often considered by way of prosecutorial policy and in case law. These parts include Part 6, which requires the prosecution to consider the likelihood of harm, including imminence. In case law, this has been shown to be a consideration of both the prosecution and the courts.[59] Furthermore, consideration of the fact that the speech emanates from religious tradition or rites could be added in accordance with Parts 1, 4 and 5. This would also be the appropriate place to add consideration of the *Emmanuel* tests (*inherent*, *relevant* and *necessary*) in regard to the limitations on the freedom of religion. By using such tests, the Supreme Court would be able to determine whether religious teachings or acts with some type of discriminatory character would be considered 'incitement' or remain protected under the freedom of religion. Finally, Part 2 would allow the status of the speaker to be taken into account, such as cases where the speaker is a religious community leader.

24.9. Conclusion

The various sections of Israel's hate speech prohibition reflect the complicated balance that must be struck when different rights come into conflict. By looking at Section 144b through the lens of theoretical justifications, it becomes clear that the main goal of the State in such a prohibition is dictating what constitutes valid public discourse and preventing eventual harm by the perpetrator or those who adhere to their statements. Meanwhile, Section 144c(b) attempts to contend with situations that have an added layer of complexity: religious expressions, and by extension, the freedom of religion. Although the actual elements of the

57 See *supra* note 16.

58 *Torat HaMelech*, 2015, paras. 27–29 of Justice Rubinstein's opinion, see *supra* note 42.

59 See *supra* note 56.

crime are materially identical to Section 144b, when assessed alongside the political and judicial history that led to its legislation, this seemingly meaningless addition may actually change the application of Section 144c(b) to signal to the prosecution and the courts that religious texts do not absolve perpetrators from accountability, while also stipulating that the religious context should be taken into account.

Significant questions still remain regarding the proper balance between Section 144, freedom of expression, and freedom of religion. The sparse instruction provided by the judiciary creates added difficulty to such work,[60] while cases regarding incitement to racism are actively advanced by the State prosecution.[61] Israel's dealing with the challenges related to the fight against hate speech in religious contexts must be sensitive to the unique features of the Israeli society, and at the same time be able to draw from the experience accumulated in the international arena.

60 A study published recently by the Israel Religious Action Center ('IRAC') contends that there are suspect discrepancies between the amount of Arabs and Jews prosecuted under Sections 144b and 144c of Israel's Penal Law. The study is available online (in Hebrew): Ori Narov and Orly Erez-Likhovski, "On the Enforcement Policy of the Offenses of Incitement to Racism and Incitement to Violence", in *IRAC*, 2022, pp. 26–122. Note that the report does not always separate statistics according to the different prohibitions (incitement to racism or incitement to violence). An article summarizing some of the study's main findings (in English) is available online: Or Kashti and Chen Maanit, "77% of Incitement Charges in Israel Filed Against Arabs, Study Reveals", *Haaretz*, 1 August 2022.

61 Recently, for example, the State Attorney's Office alerted Michael Ben Ari, a former MK, that a prosecution against him is considered under Section 144b, following a series of incendiary tweets. Tobias Siega, "Prosecutors weigh indicting former far-right MK for incitement against Arabs", *Haaretz*, 10 August 2022.

25

Elements of the Local Osaka Ordinance that May Be Relevant to Community Self-Regulation

Ochi Megumi*

25.1. Introduction

People organize groups or communities based on their similar religious or ideological beliefs and to achieve some goals bigger than one's capacity. If the goal is to compete against or to limit the rights or privileges of certain other groups in a society, the group would let its members engage in demonstrations to send messages and make claims in public. If such claims have discriminatory contents, the words used for this purpose can be violent, degrading, or inhumane. The community leaders of religious or ideological communities are required to engage self-regulation policies to control the expressive behaviours of their members. For the law, the function of promoting such self-regulation can be another way to stop hate speech. If laws can enhance a community's self-regulation, it would have pragmatic deterrence effect rather than exercising administrative or judicial enforcement powers and putting a limit on individual freedoms.

In Japan, one of the largest cities, Osaka City, enacted an innovative ordinance on the measures available to the city mayor for dealing with hate speech, while legislative discussion shows limited progress in this regard in the National Diet. *Ōsakashi Heitosupīchi eno Taisho ni Kansuru Jōrei*, that is, the Osaka City Ordinance for Dealing with Hate Speech ('Osaka Ordinance') adopted in 2016, is a unique ordinance which does not contain a clause on punishment. The main

* **Ochi Megumi** is Associate Professor at the College of International Relations and the Graduate School of International Relations of Ritsumeikan University in Kyoto, Japan. She specializes in public international law and international criminal justice. She completed her Ph.D. in Law at Osaka University and LL.M. at Leiden University. She is a member of the Young Penalist Committee of the International Association of Penal Law and a Senior Fellow at CILRAP's Case Matrix Network. She has published the 2020 monograph *国際刑事手続法の体系—「プレミス理論」と一事不再理原則* (The System of International Procedural Criminal Law: The Premise Theory and the Principle of Ne Bis In Idem), and her second monograph *国際刑事手続法の原理—国際協働におけるプレミスの特定* (The Rationales of the International Procedural Criminal Law: Identifying the Premises in International Cooperation) is in course of publication. For an audio-visual recording of her statement to CILRAP's conference in Florence in April 2022 on the topic of this anthology, please see https://www.cilrap.org/cilrap-film/220409-ochi/.

tools put forward by the Osaka Ordinance to combat hate speech are two-fold: naming-and-shaming and awareness-raising. The elements of the Osaka Ordinance could provide ideas for self-regulation in religious or ideological communities and an example for city authorities in other urban concentrations where there are issues of religion or nationality-based or -related hate speech and violence, such as Yangon, Mandalay, Delhi, Belgrade, Banja Luka or Gaza. Local or regional governments could draw on the Osaka Ordinance as an example of lower-level state regulation in cities that may experience problems with hate speech in religious or nationality contexts.

This chapter examines how the emphasis on naming-and-shaming and awareness-raising in the Osaka Ordinance could be useful for self-regulation policies within religious or ideological communities. This chapter first provides an overview of hate speech laws in Japan and their background. Second, it introduces the Osaka Ordinance and its features, including the purpose, definitions of hate speech and the measures available to the mayor and the Osaka Hate Speech Review Board ('Review Board'). Third, it analyses the impacts of the Osaka Ordinance on self-regulation within communities and concludes that the Japan model has the potential to follow a multilateral approach to combating hate speech, by combining efforts by national and local authorities as well as civil society.

25.2. The Hate Speech Laws in Japan

25.2.1. Discrimination Against *Zainichi* Koreans

In Japan, recent news on hate speech mostly concerns activities against *Zainichi* Koreans (Koreans with permanent resident status in Japan).[1] The *Zainichi* Korean system was created to address one of the lasting effects of Japan's colonial policy over the Korean peninsula during World War II. Japan's annexation of Korea resulted in Koreans crossing over to Japan and becoming Japanese under

---

1 Higuchi Naoto, "Japan's Postcolonial Hate Speech", in Higaki Shinji and Nasu Yuji (eds.), *Hate Speech in Japan: The Possibility of a Non-Regulatory Approach*, Cambridge University Press, 2021, pp. 363–80. One of the most serious discrimination issues in Japan used to be the treatment meted out to so-called *Burakumin* (*Buraku* people). The *Burakumin* discrimination (or *Dōwa* (assimilation) issue) has a long history that stems from a caste system based on occupation and residential area that affected employment and marriage since before modern times. The national government enacted a series of laws on this issue. As for local governments, Osaka was actually at the centre of this issue, and Osaka Prefecture in 1998 enacted a relevant ordinance: Japan, 大阪府人権尊重の社会づくり条例 (The Osaka Prefecture Ordinances on Community Planning to Respect Human Rights), 30 October 1998 (https://www.legal-tools.org/doc/qf2o3v/). They also issued ordinances prohibiting investigation into whether a person lives in or comes from *Buraku*. See, Yamamoto Takanori, "Buraku Discrimination and Hate Speech: Complex Situations of Classical and Contemporary Discrimination in Japan", in Higaki and Nasu (eds.), 2021, pp. 107–24.

the law. The liberation of the Korean Peninsula followed the dissolution of the Japanese empire after Japan's surrender, but a significant number of Koreans who had already found their way to Japan continue to live there, despite the Japanese government's encouragement to return to their 'national homeland'.[2]

The *Mindan* (the Association of Koreans in Japan) achieved a favourable outcome in the negotiations aimed at normalizing the relationship between the newly formed South Korea and Japan. This led to the signing of the Treaty on Basic Relations in 1965 between the two nations. The negotiations for the treaty were initiated in 1964 and covered various topics, including property rights, economic co-operation and diplomatic relations. The treaty resolved compensation and claims between the two countries, including both individual and government claims. In the treaty, a permanent resident status was established for *Zainichi* Koreans who hold South Korean nationality.[3] Complicated negotiations under the purviews of developing international human rights instruments continued, and now all *Zainichi* Koreans including the second and third generations have access to the social security system in areas such as governmental pensions, childcare allowance and access to public hearings under national and international laws including the Agreement between Japan and the Republic of Korea Concerning the Legal Status and Treatment of the People of the Republic of Korea Residing in Japan and the Special Act on Immigration Control.[4]

Even though socioeconomic integrity had almost been achieved at the end of the last century, nationalistic xenophobic movements targeting *Zainichi* Koreans have spread rapidly on the Internet since the 2000s.[5] Those groups that target people from abroad in Japan on the Internet are collectively known as *Netto Uyoku* ('Net Far-Right').[6] One of the largest of these kinds of groups is "在日特権を許さない市民の会" ('Group of Citizens Who Do Not Tolerate Privileges for Ethnic Korean Residents in Japan' ('*Zaitokukai*')), a conservative civic group with specific emphasis on Japanese nationality and *Shintō* (Shintoism), which conducts hate demonstrations mainly against ethnic Korean residents and condemns their alleged privileges. *Zaitokukai* was founded by a former civil servant, Sakurai Makoto, in 2006. The original supporters were 500 in

2 *Ibid.* Japan sought its 'unmixing' policy based on the idea of ethnically homogeneous nation-state-building promoted by the United States anti-communism doctrine.

3 *Ibid.*

4 *Ibid.*

5 Ku Ryangok, "The Current Movement of Hate Speech", in Higaki and Nasu (eds.), 2021, pp. 125–50, see *supra* note 1.

6 *Ibid.*

number, but its membership had increased to more than 16,000 by 2016.[7] It had led many threatening hate demonstrations including three infamous incidents of oral violence committed in front of the Kyoto Korean Elementary School on 4 December 2008, 14 January 2009, and 28 March 2010 respectively. Some *Zaitokukai* members were arrested and criminally charged, and the Kyoto district court found *Zaitokukai* liable for damages in 2013.[8] The focus of academia and journalists covering the Japanese nationalist movement concentrates on this new and largest collection of extreme hate groups which use the Internet for recruitment and organization.[9]

25.2.2. Development of Local and National Laws

In Japan, between 2012 to 2015, there were 1,152 cases of demonstrations that contained references to attacking the lives and limbs of certain ethnic or other groups. 164 such cases were adjudicated in Osaka.[10] Some political leaders started discussing a possible scheme to regulate, or at least curb, hate speech in the wake of the Kyoto district court decision.[11] The pressure from the international community, such as from the Committee on the Elimination of Racial Discrimination ('CERD'), also enhanced such debate.[12]

Against this backdrop, a major legal development on the problem of hate speech in Japan has been seen since 2013. The Osaka City Mayor Hashimoto

---

7 Nagayoshi Kikuko, "日本の排外意識に関する研究動向と今後の展開可能性" (Research on Xenophobia in Japan: What are the Remained Tasks for Future Research?), in *The Annual Reports of Graduate School of Arts and Letters Tohoku University*, 2017, vol. 66, p. 89.

8 Kyoto District Court of Japan, 街頭宣伝差止め等請求事件 (Case of Request for Injunction Against Street Advertisings), Judgment, 7 October 2013 ('*Zaitokukai case*') (https://www.legal-tools.org/doc/pc2oc5/).

9 Jeffrey J. Hall, *Japan's Nationalist Right in the Internet Age: Online Media and Grassroots Conservative Activism*, Routledge, London, 2021. The mental disorder cases regarding *Zainichi* Koreans are becoming a serious problem. The special positions of *Zainichi* Koreans in Japan may be a cause of the high suicide rate of *Zainichi* Koreans compared to those of ethnic Japanese and other foreigners. See also, Kim Taeyoung, *Zainichi Koreans and Mental Health: Psychiatric Problem in Japanese Korean Minorities, Their Social Background and Life Story*, Routledge, London, 2021.

10 440 cases have taken place in Tokyo (between 2012 and 2015) and the number in Osaka is the second largest in Japan. See, Centre for Human Rights Education and Training, "ヘイトスピーチに関する実態調査報告書" (Report of a Fact-finding Survey Concerning Hate Speech), *Ministry of Justice of Japan*, March 2016 (available on its web site).

11 Higashikawa Koji, "Japan's Hate Speech Laws: Translations of the Osaka City Ordinance and the National Act to Curb Hate Speech in Japan", in *Asia-Pacific Law and Policy Journal*, 2017, vol. 19, p. 2.

12 Consideration of Reports Submitted by States Parties Under Article 9 of the Convention (ICERD), UN Doc. CERD/C/JPN/CO/3-6, 6 April 2010 (https://www.legal-tools.org/doc/ig8rkv/).

Toru, who was an experienced lawyer, promoted "大阪市人権施策推進審議会" ('Osaka City Human Rights Policy Promotion Council') and it began its discussion in September 2014. Meanwhile, Mayor Hashimoto held a public discussion meeting with the *Zaitokukai* leader Sakurai in person on 20 October 2014 where the latter demonstrated their discriminative beliefs and violent expressive stance.[13] Mayor Hashimoto commented later that the intent of the meeting was to shift the target to himself instead of the *Zainichi* community and to prove the urgent need for legislation.[14] Osaka City solicited public comments and issued the first draft of an ordinance on hate speech regulation following the meeting.

After intensive revisional discussions, Osaka City became the first city to enact an ordinance on hate speech. The Osaka Ordinance was promulgated on 18 January 2016.[15] The point that the Council report emphasized was not to focus on punishment but to construct a structure to defend the human rights of citizens and others.[16]

Furthermore, the Osaka City submitted an opinion paper to the Japanese Diet to initiate discussions over making effective legislation towards elimination of hate speech in 2015. The Act on the Promotion of Efforts to Eliminate Unfair Discriminatory Speech and Behavior Against Persons Originating from Outside Japan (the 'National Hate Speech Act') passed the Diet on 24 May 2016.[17]

25.3. The Osaka Ordinance and Its Characteristics

25.3.1. The Purpose of the Osaka Ordinance

The purpose of the Osaka Ordinance is explained in Article 1 of the Osaka Ordinance.[18] This provision indicates that the purpose of the Ordinance is to set

---

13 "橋下徹大阪市長と在日特権を許さない市民の会との意見交換" (Exchange of Opinions Between Mayor Hashimoto Toru and the Group of Citizens Who Do Not Tolerate Privileges for Ethnic Korean Residents in Japan), *Logmi Biz*, 20 October 2014 (available on its web site).

14 "橋下徹市長登庁会見" (Hashimoto Toru Mayor's Office Press Conference), *Logmi Biz*, 21 October 2014 (available on its web site).

15 Japan, *Ōsakashi Heitosupīchi eno Taisho ni Kansuru Jōrei* (The Osaka City Ordinance for Dealing with Hate Speech), 15 January 2016 ('the Osaka Ordinance') (https://www.legal-tools.org/doc/0v24j5/).

16 Nakamura Hideaki, "The Framework of the Hate Speech Local Ordinances", in Higaki and Nasu (eds.), 2021, pp. 207–22, see *supra* note 1.

17 Japan, 本邦外出身者に対する不当な差別的言動の解消に向けた取組の推進に関する法律 (The Act on the Promotion of Efforts to Eliminate Unfair Discriminatory Speech and Behavior against Persons Originating from Outside Japan (Provisional Translation)), 3 June 2016 (https://www.legal-tools.org/doc/zv95o4/).

18 > Recognizing that hate speech may harm the dignity of an individual and cause a sense of discrimination towards them, this Ordinance aims to protect the human rights of

rules for the City about the measures needed to combat hate speech and not impose any obligations on the population. The focus is not on punishment of those engaging in hate speech but the protection of targeted persons and deterrence of hate speech. Osaka City explains that the purpose of the Ordinance is not to regulate expressive activities directly, but to pay attention to the freedom of speech and stipulates the possible measures under existing laws.[19]

25.3.2. Definitions of Hate Speech in the Osaka Ordinance

The term 'hate speech' was unknown to Japanese law until the Osaka Ordinance introduced this concept. Whereas the National Hate Speech Act does not use the term 'hate speech' but merely defines the targeted acts in a vague way,[20] the Osaka Ordinance provides a detailed definition of hate speech. This is because

---

> the citizens and others through providing necessary rules concerning measures that the City applies to deal with hate speech and to seek to deter hate speech.

Article 1 of the Osaka Ordinance, see *supra* note 15. The English translation is not official.

19 "'大阪市ヘイトスピーチへの対処に関する条例' の解説及び審査の実例 (1 条)" (Explanation and Practice of Assessment related to the Osaka Ordinance on Suppression of Hate Speech Article 1), *Osaka City*, 12 April 2022 (available on its web site).

20 The definitions are provided in Article 2(1) of the Osaka Ordinance, see *supra* note 15:

> 'Hate speech' as used in this Ordinance is an act of expression that falls within all of the following descriptions:
>
> (1) The act has been committed with the purpose of any of the following (for the application of subsection (iii), the specified purpose must be clearly identifiable):
> - (i) To exclude any person or group of persons with specific attribute pertaining to race or ethnic origins (hereinafter 'the Specific Persons') from society;
> - (ii) To limit the rights or freedoms of the Specific Persons; or
> - (iii) To incite hatred or a sense of discrimination, or violence against Specific Persons.
>
> (2) The content or manner of the expression falls within any of the following:
> - (i) It insults or defames the Specific Persons; or
> - (ii) It poses a threat to the Specific Persons (or a substantial number of the Specific Persons if directed to a group).
>
> (3) The act has been committed in a place where, or in a way that, many and unspecified persons could know the content of the act.
>
> Cf. Article 2 of the National Hate Speech Act, see *supra* note 17:
>
> In this Act, "unfair discriminatory speech and behaviour against persons originating from outside Japan" shall mean unfair discriminatory speech and behaviour to incite the exclusion of persons originating exclusively from a country or region other than Japan or their descendants and who are lawfully residing in Japan (hereinafter referred to in this Article as "persons originating from outside Japan") from the local community by reason of such persons originating from a country or region other than Japan, such as openly announcing to the effect of harming the life, body, freedom, reputation or property of, or to significantly insult, persons originating from outside Japan with the objective of encouraging or inducing discriminatory feelings against such persons originating from outside Japan.

the Osaka Ordinance was envisaged to allow the city's mayor to adopt measures to prevent dissemination of such expressions and a clear definition was needed to ensure predictability.[21]

25.3.3. The Measures Available to the City Under the Osaka Ordinance

The Osaka Ordinance makes available several measures which the mayor may employ to combat hate speech in Osaka City, such as measures to prevent dissemination of hateful expressions, the public acknowledgment that certain expressions amount to hate speech, and awareness-raising.

25.3.3.1. Prevention of Dissemination and Publication of Recognition

Article 5 of the Ordinance provides measures to prevent dissemination and publication of recognitions that certain expressions amount to hate speech. First, it obliges the mayor to "take necessary measures to prevent dissemination of the content pertaining to said act in accordance with the facts of the case upon finding the following acts of expression as hate speech".[22] Article 5 also obliges the mayor, "upon finding the following acts of expression as hate speech" to "publish the fact that the act in question constitutes hate speech, the summary of the content of the expression, the measures taken by the mayor to prevent dissemination of the expression, and the name of the actor".[23]

The opinions of the Review Board must be heard on whether the acts in question constitute hate speech, so that the measures explained above may be taken. The Review Board is constituted by five selected experts or other people recognized as appropriate by the mayor with a two-year-term (Article 8). Articles 6 to 9 set the rules on the proceedings of investigation and deliberation by the Review Board. The Review Board may request the petitioners to submit a written opinion or materials and may have hearings with witnesses (Article 9). The hearings are equally available for the alleged perpetrator. Article 9(3) obligates the Review Board to provide opportunities to persons alleged to have

---

21 Nakamura, 2021, see *supra* note 16.

22 On the limits over the national legal framework to impose administrative responsibility on social networking service ('SNS') providers in Japan, see, Jitsuhara Takashi, "ヘイトスピーチ対策として SNS 事業者に対行政責任を課す場合の法的課題" (Legal questions about public law responsibilities of SNS providers to combat hate speech), in *Fukuoka University Review of Law*, 2021, vol. 66, no. 2, pp. 247–62.

23 Article 5 of the Osaka Ordinance, however, provides exceptions in three circumstances, including where if the mayor finds "that the publication will inhibit the purpose set by Article 1", "if the whereabouts of the actor are unknown", or "if the mayor finds otherwise that there is any special reason to do so". In these cases, "the mayor may withhold the name of the actor", see *supra* note 15.

engaged in hateful expressions to give their opinions unless the Review Board finds it unnecessary.

25.3.3.2. Awareness-Raising

Article 3 of the Osaka Ordinance that accompanies the above-mentioned measures stipulates that "[t]he City of Osaka, in recognition of the fact that hate speech may harm the dignity of an individual and cause a sense of discrimination against them, is to raise the awareness of the Citizens to increase interest in and understanding of the human rights violations caused by hate speech". The purpose of this provision is explained to confirm the need to raise awareness to deepen the interest and understanding of citizens about hate speech in order to foster a social climate that does not allow the expression of hate speech in the city.[24]

The actual measures for awareness-raising include posting posters created by the Ministry of Justice at ward offices and subway stations, creation and placement of enlightenment and educational leaflets, publishing articles in the City Human Rights Information Magazines ('OSAKA Lifelong Learning Information Magazine Icho Namiki' and 'Osaka City Human Rights News KOKORO Net') and posting of enlightenment materials on the City web site.[25]

Duties to engage in awareness-raising activities are also stipulated in the National Hate Speech Act. It not only declares the national government's duties but also the need for local governments' engagement in this issue.[26]

---

24 "'大阪市ヘイトスピーチへの対処に関する条例' の解説及び審査の実例 (3 条)" (Explanation and Practice of Assessment Related to the Osaka Ordinance on Suppression of Hate Speech (Article 3)), *Osaka City*, 12 April 2022 (available on its web site).

25 *Ibid.*

26 Article 7 of the National Hate Speech Act, see *supra* note 17:

(1) The national government shall spread awareness among the general public about the need to eliminate unfair discriminatory speech and behaviour against persons originating from outside Japan, and implement public relations activities for the purpose of furthering understanding thereof and other awareness-raising activities, and shall make the necessary efforts therefor.

(2) The local governments shall spread awareness among the local residents about the need to eliminate unfair discriminatory speech and behaviour against persons originating from outside Japan in accordance with the actual situation of the region, taking into account the sharing of appropriate roles with the national government, and implement public relations activities for the purpose of furthering understanding thereof and other awareness-raising activities, and shall make the necessary efforts therefor.

25.4. Impacts on Self-Regulation Policies Within Religious or Ideological Communities: The Japan Model

Due to the high-level protection of freedom of speech, Japan does not have any law punishing hate speech but relies on non-statutory measures to combat the aforementioned phenomenon. Nasu and Higaki suggest that the Japanese model is unique since on the one hand, it adopts non-regulatory means to combat hate speech, similar to the United States model, while on the other hand, it does not include statutory provisions defining hate crimes nor does it contain civil rights laws against hate speech or distinguish between individually directed hate speech and public hate speech.[27] The Japan model may be characterized by: (1) The liberal policy on freedom of speech; (2) the robust local autonomy system; (3) the combination of naming-and-shaming and awareness-raising measures; and (4) the collaboration with civil society.

25.4.1. Freedom of Speech and Naming-and-Shaming

25.4.1.1. Constitutional Guarantee of Freedom of Speech

Japan adopts a liberalistic policy with respect to freedom of speech with critical influence from United States law.[28] Article 21(1) of the Constitution of Japan ('Constitution') clearly and directly acknowledges that "[f]reedom of assembly and association as well as speech, press and all other forms of expression are guaranteed". It adds that "no censorship shall be maintained" (Article 21(2)). However, the restrictions provided by law are often admitted and sustained by the Japanese Supreme Court with references to the concept of 'public welfare' under Articles 12 or 13 of the Constitution.[29] Even though the Japanese jurisprudence tends to allow restrictions on expression when reasonable and necessary, such restriction must be taken with serious consideration especially in relation to preemptive restriction.[30] The negative views on penalization are the majority view among Japanese constitutional scholars.[31]

Because of the hesitant approach towards imposing restrictions on freedom of speech, Japan made a reservation to Article 4 of the International Convention on the Elimination of All Forms of Racial Discrimination ('ICERD')

---

27 Nasu Yuji and Higaki Shinji, "Introduction", in Higaki and Nasu (eds.), 2021, pp. 1–14, see *supra* note 1.

28 Higuchi, 2021, see *supra* note 1.

29 Matsui Shigenori, "Freedom of Expression in Japan", in Higaki and Nasu (eds.), 2021, pp. 35–57, see *supra* note 1.

30 Supreme Court of Japan, *北方ジャーナル事件* (*Hoppō Journal case*), Judgment, 11 June 1986, Civil Matters Jurisprudence Collection, vol. 40, no. 4, p. 872 ('Hoppō Journal case') (https://www.legal-tools.org/doc/evyor9/).

31 Higuchi, 2021, see *supra* note 1; Matsui, 2021, pp. 35–57, see *supra* note 29.

that obligates States Parties to criminalize and illegalize conduct spreading hatred. Japan's reservation on this provision declares that Japan fulfils these obligations to the extent compatible with the guarantee of the freedoms recognized under its Constitution.[32]

At the local governance level, the reluctant approach has long been widespread. For local authorities, hate speech issues would be relevant when the local population applies for the use of public spaces for hate demonstrations. Article 244(2) of the Local Autonomy Act stipulates that a local authority shall not refuse such use without a 'legitimate reason'. The 'legitimate reasons' are generally understood to include reasons such as non-payment of fees, excessive number of participants, risks posed to other uses, violation of the user rules and so on.[33] Even if the use may result in commission of hate speech and such result is anticipated, such anticipation is regarded as insufficient for the local authorities to ban the use of public space.[34]

25.4.1.2. The Court Rulings on Constitutionality of Naming-and-Shaming

A *Zaitokukai* member raised a lawsuit against Osaka City claiming that the publication of the applicant's username and real name as a measure to name-and-shame and thus combat hate speech is inconsistent with Articles 13, 21(1) and 31 of the Constitution.[35] On the freedom of expression stipulated in Article 21(1) of the Constitution, according to the applicant, the measures to prevent dissemination is a restriction over the freedom of expression, and such law should ensure that its withering effect is at a minimum.[36] The City argued in response that the Ordinance itself does not have any contents that restrict freedom of expression, and that it will not impact the personal dignity of those who engage in such

---

32 Japan's Reservation to ICERD:

> In applying the provisions of paragraphs (a) and (b) of article 4 of the [said Convention] Japan fulfills the obligations under those provisions to the extent that fulfillment of the obligations is compatible with the guarantee of the rights to freedom of assembly, association and expression and other rights under the Constitution of Japan, noting the phrase 'with due regard to the principles embodied in the Universal Declaration of Human Rights and the rights expressly set forth in article 5 of this Convention' referred to in article 4.

Ministry of Foreign Affairs of Japan, "International Convention on the Elimination of All Forms of Racial Discrimination (First and Second Report)", June 1999, Article 4 (available on its web site).

33 Matsumoto Hideaki, *逐条地方自治法*, 学陽書房, Tokyo, 2015, p. 61.

34 "第 190 回国会 参議院 法務委員会会議録" (Minutes of the 190th Legal Committee of the House of Councillor), 国会 (National Diet of Japan), 19 April 2016 (available on its web site).

35 Osaka Regional Court, *判例地方自治* (Cases Local Autonomy), 17 January 2020, No.468, p. 11.

36 *Ibid.*

hateful expression (the Constitution not protecting people's social reputation).[37] Furthermore, the City went further and said that hate speech as defined in the Ordinance denies an individual's dignity, violates the rights to live peacefully, of honour, of personality, not to be excluded from local society, or of equity and brings serious social disruption and will not be protected by the freedom of expression.[38] It also referred to the serious situation in Osaka wherein repeated demonstrations of a similar kind subjected the targets of such demonstrations to great suffering and resulted in the creation of a significant rift within the local society.[39]

The court noted that not all of the expressive conduct defined as hate speech in the Ordinance amounts to abuse of the freedom of expression and that the Ordinance's measures might restrict the exercise of such rights only in certain cases.[40] However, the court declared the compatibility of the Ordinance with the Constitution since the regulatory measures are within the ambit of reasonable and necessary measures for pursuing the public order.[41]

25.4.1.3. Combination of Naming-and-Shaming and Awareness-Raising

The key point of the Osaka Ordinance is that it has both measures for naming-and-shaming and awareness-raising. One such measure available to the Osaka City mayor is called 'doxing'. Doxing is "the deliberate release of personally identifiable information in a form that is easily accessible to others, usually with the aim of intimidating the identified person".[42] It removes the shield of anonymity or obscurity that may foster these forms of antisocial behaviour.[43] Doxing is often used by activists to shame persons who use hate speech on social media or participate in demonstrations that include discriminatory messaging.[44] Douglas articulated how doxing works as a tool for audience vigilantism through the following three stages: discovery, release and response.[45] Discovery

37 *Ibid.*

38 *Ibid.*

39 *Ibid.*

40 *Ibid.*

41 *Ibid.*

42 George Hawley, *The Alt-Right: What Everyone Needs to Know*, Oxford University Press, New York, 2018, p. 201; David M. Douglas, "Doxing: A Conceptual Analysis", in *Ethics and Information Technology*, 2016, vol. 18, no. 3, p. 199.

43 David M. Douglas, "Doxing as Audience Vigilantism against Hate Speech", in Daniel Trottier, Rashid Gabdulhakov and Huang Qian (eds.), *Introducing Vigilant Audiences*, Open Book Publishers, Cambridge, 2020, p. 259.

44 Mojca M. Plesničar and Pika Šarf, "'This Web Page Should Not Exist': A Case Study of Online Shaming in Slovenia", in Trottier, Gabdulhakov and Huang (eds.), 2020, see *supra* note 43.

45 Douglas, 2020, p. 268, see *supra* note 43.

is the stage where personally identifiable information is uncovered; release stage refers to releasing and announcing that information; and response stage is when the audience acts on that information.[46]

The release stage is often referred to as 'naming-and-shaming'. Naming-and-shaming is defined as a policy of punishment through publication of the fact of violation designed to inflict "reputational damage on moral grounds".[47] Naming-and-shaming is designed to "shine a spotlight on bad behaviour [in order to] help sway abusers to reform".[48] The goals for naming-and-shaming individuals include informal punishment, informing the public about their conduct, and expressing disapproval for that conduct.[49]

Naming-and-shaming and awareness-raising in the Osaka Ordinance might contribute to enhancing self-restraint within the discriminating community. Self-restraint "suppresses hate speech only incidentally, only as part of other purposes not specifically and never by name".[50] According to Jacobson and Schlink, "[i]t relies primarily, if not exclusively, on the energies and ambitions of institutions within civil society, not on compulsion by the state" and "reflects the interests, needs, and perspectives of those institutions which mark and modulate any stance toward hate speech the institution may take or any effect on hate speech it may have".[51]

Some commentators suggest the possibility that a naming-and-shaming system is "most appropriate culturally in Japan" since "[t]he obvious advantage of implementing Osaka's city ordinance on a wider scale would be that it is the least inhibitive towards free speech because it deters without criminalizing".[52]

While naming-and-shaming may encourage individuals and communities to refrain from propagating discriminatory expressions, naming-and-shaming or

---

46 *Ibid.*

47 Irene Kahn, "Understanding Corporate Complicity: Extending the Notion Beyond Existing Laws", Paper Presented at the Business Human Rights Seminar, London, 8 December 2005, p. 4.

48 Emilie M. Hafner-Burton, "Sticks and Stones: Naming and Shaming the Human Rights Enforcement Problem", in *International Organization*, 2008, vol. 62, no. 4, p. 690.

49 Jacob Rowbottom, "To Punish, Inform, and Criticise: The Goals of Naming and Shaming", in Julian Petley (ed.), *Media and Public Shaming: Drawing the Boundaries of Disclosure*, I.B. Tauris & Co., London, 2013, p. 1.

50 Arthur Jacobson and Bernhard Schlink, "Hate Speech and Self-Restraint", in Michael Herz and Peter Molnar, *The Content and Context of Hate Speech: Rethinking Regulation and Responses*, Cambridge University Press, Cambridge, 2012, p. 12.

51 *Ibid.*

52 Nichole Koontz, "Japan and the Potential for National Hate Speech Legislation: An International Consideration on Possibilities", in *Washington University Global Studies Law Review*, 2017, vol. 16, no. 2, p. 363.

release of personal information pertaining to those engaging in hate speech alone is insufficient to move to the next stage of doxing, that is, response. In order to foster public response after people receive information regarding those responsible for hate speech, grass-root awareness-raising is critical. Whereas it is difficult to assess the impact of awareness-raising, the example of the Japanese civil society's response, alluded to below, provides certain insights into the benefits of awareness-raising activities.

25.4.2. The Robust Local Autonomy System and Cooperation with Civil Society

25.4.2.1. Local Autonomy System

The Japan model also emphasizes a multilateral approach using national level and local level non-regulatory measures. Article 92 of the Constitution confirms that local autonomy is an essential element of an administrative body and the basic percept of the principle of local autonomy restricts the legislative power of the Diet. The Local Autonomy Act reinforced the democratic and self-rule aspects to the local governments, strengthening the local assembly's power, reducing oversight by the national government and so on.[53] However, since Japan is not a federal state, the local government's legislative power is subject to national laws and local ordinances must follow the Constitution and other national laws.[54]

Despite these limits, the local governments are expected to be responsible, within the limit, to take proactive efforts to eliminate discrimination under Article 4 of the National Hate Speech Act, because the local situation varies from region to region.[55] This provision corresponds to the norm stipulated in Articles

---

[53] Nakamura, 2021, see *supra* note 16.

[54] See Constitution of Japan, 3 November 1946 (http://www.legal-tools.org/doc/77ef9a/), Articles 94 and 98; Japan, 地方自治法 (Local Autonomy Act), 17 April 1947, Articles 14(1) ('Local Autonomy Act') (https://www.legal-tools.org/doc/ad4cgl/). Article 4 of the Osaka Ordinance provides on the supplementary nature of the measures available under it to combat hate speech, see *supra* note 15:

> Considering that the measures and publications under Articles 5 and 6 are enforced to protect the human rights of the citizens and others, they must be aimed to supplement the remedial measures of the State's remedial systems for human rights violations and must be implemented in coordination with the said systems.

To enforce the local ordinances, only the following methods are available: in general, administrative guidance, public disclosure of a lack of compliance and punishments restricted to "imprisonment with or without work for two years or less, a fine of not more than 1-million-yen, penal detention, a petty fine or confiscation" and "a civil fine of not more than 50,000 yen". Local Autonomy Act, Article 14(3).

[55] Article 4(2) of the National Hate Speech Act, see *supra* note 17:

2(1)(a), 2(1) (c) and 4(c) of the ICERD. Among the measures available in Japan, the Osaka Ordinance is outstanding. It was the first hate speech law in the whole of Japan, and predates the enactment of the National Hate Speech Act. The allocation of power to local authorities in relation to hate speech suppression also reflects the characteristics of the Japanese situation – hate speech issues are especially critical in some specific regions in Japan.

25.4.2.2. Collaboration with Civil Society

The combination of naming-and-shaming and awareness-raising resulted in widespread civil claims against discriminatory actions. Thus, the Japan model also encompasses the combination of national and local level legal measures with private campaigns. The professionals' discussions and court rulings stimulated and supported the civil movement by providing legal justifications and narratives against hate speech.

Lawyers initiated their anti-hate speech movement and created a legal basis for claiming injustice against discriminatory demonstrations that exceed the ambit of freedom of speech. Soon after the Kyoto School case, the Kyoto Bar Association issued its Statement on Harassment against Korean Schools, and the Federation of Bar Associations in Kansai area adopted a resolution "to criticize discrimination against Korean children in Japan" in 2010.[56]

The active use of the Internet to disseminate discriminatory movements conducted by *Netto Uyoku* provides a chance to the wider public to be aware of such activities and express shock and disgust at hateful and violent words used against victims.[57] The guilty verdict in the Kyoto Korean School case in October 2013 increased the number of news media reports regarding the issue and the term 'hate speech' was nominated and chosen as the top Japanese Buzzword of 2013.[58]

Ordinary citizens of Japan, most of whom do not have personal connections with *Zainichi* Korean people and have never been involved in any kind of civil society groups, started forming groups to counter surging hate groups

---

> The local governments shall endeavour to take measures in accordance with the actual situation of the region, taking into account the sharing of appropriate roles with the national government with respect to the efforts to eliminate unfair discriminatory speech and behaviour against persons originating from outside Japan.

56 Hatano Ayako, "Can Strategic Human Rights Litigation Complement Social Movements?: A Case Study of the Movement Against Racism and Hate Speech in Japan", in Kang Myungkoo, Marie-Orange Rivé-Lasan, Kim Wooja and Philippa Hall (eds.), *Hate Speech in Asia and Europe: Beyond Hate and Fear*, Routledge, London, 2020.

57 *Ibid.*

58 *Ibid.*

around 2009.[59] The Tokyo Anti-Discrimination March comprising around 2,000 people campaigned against recent hate rallies in September 2013 and this action was reported nation-wide. Counter-hate groups such as *Tai Reisisuto Koudou Shūdan* ('Counter Racist Action Collective', that is, 'C.R.A.C.')[60] or Anti-Racism Project[61] made use of the Internet to mobilize hundreds of participants against hate groups.

Local-based public-civil combined movements were also organized involving both political figures and citizens. In Kawasaki city, "ヘイトスピーチを許さない川崎市民ネットワーク" ('Kawasaki Citizen's Network against Hate Speech') was established with Not-for-Profit Organizations ('NPOs'), journalists, lawyers and members of the City Council as members.[62] The group disseminates information about racist movements and holds study meetings to share knowledge about the historical and the legal background of the issue and proposes negotiation and other effective measures of redressal.

25.4.3. The Impacts of the Osaka Ordinance

25.4.3.1. Practice in Statistics

The statistics of numbers of cases before Osaka City on hate speech is as follows:

	2016	2017	2018	2019	2020
Newly submitted cases	27	7	9	11	4
Finalized cases	1	9	3	4	5
(Cases that are recognized as hate speech cases)	0	4	2	2	1

Table 1: Statistics on the Number of Cases before Osaka City.[63]

The number of newly submitted cases was the highest in the first year and the number is decreasing. Cases are constantly being finalized. Approximately half of the remaining cases have been reviewed and concluded. The hate speech

59 *Ibid.*

60 According to the official site, C.R.A.C. "is a platform for those who are going to carry out various anti-racism action such as street protest, speech, photograph, art, music, petitions, lob[b]ying, events, workshop and so on. Any people who want to take action against racism, please contact C.R.A.C. to share your ideas and get together with others who are already in a fight with racists". *C.R.A.C.*, 1 October 2013 (available on its web site).

61 "Anti-Racism Project", *Facebook* (available on its web site).

62 "HS を許さない かわさき市民ネットワーク" (Kawashiki Citizens' Network Not Allowing Hate Speech), *Tumblr* (available on its web site).

63 This table is compiled by the author, citing "'ヘイトスピーチへの対処に関する条例' にかかる案件の取扱状況について" (On the Practice on the Issues Related to the Ordinance on Suppression of Hate Speech), *Osaka City*, 31 March 2021 (https://www.legal-tools.org/doc/jfd7a3/).

recognition roughly constitutes half of the finalized cases. Those acts considered as hate speech include video posting on the Internet, uploading articles as a listicle on the Internet, uploading audio files about public demonstrations on the Internet, and live-streaming and video publications of public demonstration.[64]

25.4.3.2. The *Dainamo* Case

While the impact of naming-and-shaming by international institutions on states behaviours has been both theoretically and empirically proven,[65] that of local governments on hate groups has not been discussed widely. The present section of this chapter introduces one of the cases that may indicate the impact of local ordinances in using measures of naming-and-shaming and awareness-raising in promoting self-restraint.

On 1 June 2017, Osaka City published a report regarding a case in which a person, with the handle name '*Dainamo*' uploaded a video to the Internet with open access that could amount to hate speech.[66] The video contained an audio-visual record of a demonstration march held on 24 February 2016 and its pre-demonstration meetings.[67] In the video, the participants of the demonstration referred to the *Zainichi* people as 'cockroach' and issued calls to 'kill' Korean people.[68] The Review Board started its work and decided to provide an opportunity to the questioned persons to be heard.[69] *Dainamo* did not respond to the message sent via the online video service provider and erased the video from the site.[70] The City mayor found that the video had been removed and that no further special prevention measures were necessary. The mayor made an official announcement and made the information regarding the real name and the handle name of the person who took this expressive activity of hate speech public.[71]

---

64 *Ibid.*

65 Jacqueline H.R. De Merit, "International Organizations and Government Killing: Does Naming and Shaming Save Lives?", in *International Interactions*, 2021, vol. 38, no. 5, pp. 597–621; James Meernik, Rosa Aloisi, Marsha Sowell and Angela Nichols, "The Impact of Human Rights Organizations on Naming and Shaming Campaigns", in *Journal of Conflict Resolution*, 2012, vol. 56, no. 2, pp. 233–56.

66 Japan, Osaka District Court, Case on the Request for Confirmation of Invalidity of Public Money Expenditure (resident lawsuit), Judgment, 17 January 2020, Local Governance Jurisprudence, no. 468, p. 11 ('*Dainamo case*').

67 *Ibid.*

68 *Ibid.*

69 *Ibid.*

70 *Ibid.*

71 *Ibid.*

25.4.3.3. Spill over to Other Local Authorities

Osaka Prefecture and other areas in Japan followed in the footsteps of Osaka City and enacted similar kinds of ordinances with the technical support of the Ministry of Justice.[72] Several local governments, including Tokyo Metropolitan Government, Kawasaki City, Kobe City, Setagaya Ward in Tokyo, Kunitachi City in Tokyo, and Komae City in Tokyo, have enacted ordinances against hate speech. The CERD and other international human rights organs welcomed such developments.[73] While some commented that a norm cascade took place in Japan that pushed the reaching consensus across parties, Higuchi's analysis presented another view that the National Hate Speech Act was enacted without norm cascade. According to Higuchi, "[i]t was as if different actors relayed a baton from civil society to the core of the ruling coalition".[74]

Meanwhile, Kawasaki City adopted another type of ordinance against hate speech that imposes criminal punishment. "川崎市差別のない人権尊重のまちづくり条例" ('Japan:Kawasaki City, Ordinance for Development of a Human-Rights-Based City without Discrimination' ('Kawasaki Ordinance')) imposes a fine of not more than ¥500,000 in cases of repeated discriminatory behaviour even after the recommendations issued by the city mayor (Articles 12, 14, 23). The prohibited actions include incitement or notification to displace or harm, or serious insult to those who are from abroad (Article 12).[75] It also expands the scope to human rights education and victim protection, stipulating that the city shall promote such education (Article 7) and provide counselling or information sharing support for victims of hate speech (Article 8).

---

72 "ヘイトスピーチに関する条例" (The Ordinance on Hate Speech), 地方自治研究機構 (RILG), 8 September 2021 (available on its web site). "'本邦外出身者に対する不当な差別的言動の解消に向けた取組の推進に関する法律' に係る参考情報" (The Reference Information on 'The Act on the Promotion of Efforts to Eliminate Unfair Discriminatory Speech and Behavior against Persons Originating from Outside Japan'), *Ministry of Justice of Japan* (available on its web site).

73 Concluding Observations on the Combined Seventh to Ninth Periodic Reports of Japan, UN Doc. CERD/C/JPN/CO/7-9, 26 September 2014 (https://www.legal-tools.org/doc/bpnnv0/); Concluding Observations on the Sixth Periodic Report of Japan, UN Doc. CCPR/C/JPN/CO/6, 20 August 2014 (https://www.legal-tools.org/doc/fnjxo9/).

74 Higuchi Naoto, "When Hate Becomes Illegal: Legislation Process of the Anti-Hate Speech Law in Japan", in Kang, Rivé-Lasan, Kim and Hall (eds.), 2020, see *supra* note 56.

75 The 'serious insult' requires "comparison, etc. of a person originally from outside of Japan with something other than a human". The law did not apply to the incident of hate demonstration conducted on 5 September 2020 by a group near Kawasaki Station that called non-Japanese people as liars and claimed for authorities to take harder measures to stop bank transfer scams conducted by foreigners; Mochida Joji, "Milestone or Minor Progress? Japan's Strongest Antihate Law Takes Effect in Kawasaki", *Nippon.com*, 29 December 2020.

25.5. Conclusion

Bottom-up legislation and non-statutory and network-based regulation are the characteristics of hate speech regulation in Japan. Although the Japan Model has shown some success in progressing towards anti-hate speech systematization, it may require the fulfilment of many other conditions to be entirely successful. The cultural, historical and regional features for assessing the effectiveness of such non-regulatory measures should also be taken into consideration.

Meanwhile, although the cases are still limited to demonstrating the practical impact on community self-regulation, the *Dainamo* case demonstrates that publication of real names, especially those of people who are hiding behind the Internet to spread fears has potential to deter such activities. The impact on the community's self-regulation is difficult to examine, but it is theoretically feasible if the expressors are hiding behind a community name and do not wish their names to be published. Such publication seems to have limited impact on the persons who have already expressed their discriminatory beliefs in public.[76] The naming-and-shaming approach might not always induce shame in the targeted person engaging in hate speech. Therefore, public narrative creation is required to result in the loss of status or reputation that directly affects the impact of discriminatory speech towards the public. Naming-and-shaming would in this way promote self-regulation within a community. Awareness-raising is a critical component of naming-and-shaming measures that might establish a social background that make those who had wished to conduct hateful demonstration hesitant.

It is still too early to conclude that the Japan model is the most effective way to solve the issue of hate speech for many reasons. Further development of the cases and comparative research is required to construct a general theory. Despite these significant limitations, this chapter hopes to be a start for such an academic avenue.

---

[76] The mayor found that posting of leaflets with discriminatory expression against Korean people to the individual residents in a residential area in Osaka City amounts to hate speech and publicized the name of the perpetrator. The leaflet dissemination was conducted by *Kawahigashi Dairyo*, a former deputy representative of *Zaitokukan* and now the leader of *Chōsenjin no Inai Nihon o Mezasu Kai* ('Association Seeking Japan Without Koreans') who had participated in the Kyoto elementary school case and been prosecuted. In 2019, this case became the first case in Japan wherein the real name of the perpetrator was publicly announced by the government, but this person has repeatedly committed similar acts of hate speech and his name was published again in 2021. "差別的なチラシ戸別配布: 'ヘイト' 認定し氏名公表: 大阪市" (Individual Posting of Discriminative Leaflet: Recognition of 'Hate' and Publication of the Name: Osaka City), *毎日新聞*, 14 December 2021 (available on its web site).

26

A Non-Governmental Perspective on the Relative Effectiveness of Multilateral and Bilateral Measures to Combat Hate Speech: An Analysis of Tools Deployed in Response to Religious Hate Speech in Iran

Bani Dugal*

26.1. Introduction

There are many well-documented cases throughout history of the denial of religious belief, which, regrettably, resulted in atrocity crimes. The Holocaust is one of the most extreme examples and did not happen suddenly or in a vacuum. The atrocities committed against the Jewish population took place in the context of centuries of anti-Semitism throughout Europe and many years of discriminatory laws and practices. This history illustrates how, as societies face political instability and insecurity of other types, violence and atrocity crimes can be triggered by ongoing narratives that spread hostility or incite populations to commit violence. At the heart of such acts lies the deeper malady of prejudice. Often rooted in narrow conceptions of identity, prejudice finds expression in narratives of 'us'

* **Bani Dugal** is the Principal Representative of the Bahá'í International Community to the United Nations ('UN'). She is currently the Vice-Chair of the Steering Committee of the Non-Governmental Organization ('NGO') Working Group on the Security Council; serves on the Faith-Based Advisory Council to the UN Inter Agency Task Force for Religion and Development; and is a Co-President and member of the World Council of Religions for Peace. She previously served, *inter alia*, as President of the NGO Committee on Freedom of Religion or Belief; Chair of the NGO Committee on the Status of Women; Co-Facilitator of the UN Gender Equality Architecture Reform Campaign (GEAR); Co-Facilitator of the Faith and Feminism Working Group; and Chair of the Global Forum of the NGO Committee on the UN International Children's Emergency Fund. She holds an LL.M. in Environmental Law from Pace University School of Law, New York, and an LL.B. from the University of Delhi, India. Prior to relocating to the United States in 1988, she practised law before the Supreme Court of India. She has participated in events such as the Global Conference of Human Fraternity in the United Arab Emirates (2019), fifth World Forum on Intercultural Dialogue in Baku (2019), World Economic Forum (2005, 2015–2019), and UN Women Intergenerational Dialogue Day at the fifty-ninth CSW/Beijing+20 (2015). For an audio-visual recording of her statement to CILRAP's conference in Florence in April 2022 on the topic of this anthology, please see https://www.cilrap.org/cilrap-film/220409-dugal/.

and 'them' and the pitting of groups against each other. It veils the truth that every individual forms part of a greater shared collective and undermines more unifying views that see all as protagonists on a common journey. As this deeper ailment is understood and addressed, efforts to combat hateful expressions will become increasingly effective and transformative.

One way in which prejudice is cultivated, often with dire consequences, is through hate speech, which can be one of the first steps towards incitement to violence. Defining what is hate speech may be subjective and therefore controversial. While there is no universal legal definition, hate speech was recently described by UN Secretary-General António Guterres as:

> any kind of communication in speech, writing or behaviour, that attacks or uses pejorative or discriminatory language with reference to a person or a group on the basis of who they are, in other words, based on their religion, ethnicity, nationality, race, colour, descent, gender or other identity factor.[1]

At the very least such speech divides, demeans and isolates its targets. While international law prohibits the incitement to discrimination, hostility and violence, which could lead to atrocity crimes, if hate speech does not reach the threshold of incitement to violence, international law does not compel States to prohibit it. This is concerning given the growth in media technologies over recent years which have served as vehicles for propagating online and offline hate speech in all parts of the world. Alarmed by such widespread incidents of hate speech on the basis of religious belief, the international community has increasingly turned its attention in recent years to the matter.

One case that can be considered in regard to such issues is that of the Islamic Republic of Iran. While Iran has claimed to support international efforts to combat hate speech, a systematic campaign of State-sponsored incitement to hatred is underway in that country. The target is the Bahá'í community, which has faced wide-ranging persecution at the hand of Iranian authorities for over a century, particularly since the Islámic Revolution. Since 1979, more than 200 Iranian Bahá'ís have been executed and thousands have been imprisoned. To date, they remain under severe social and economic restrictions. Increasing numbers are deprived of employment and property, young Bahá'ís are barred from higher education, and Bahá'í administrative institutions have been dismantled. All such acts seek to curtail virtually any opportunity for a viable community life. Regrettably, this repression has intensified over the last few years and

1 UN Office on Genocide Prevention and the Responsibility to Protect, "United Nations Strategy and Plan of Action on Hate Speech", 31 May 2019, p. 2 ('UN Strategy and Plan of Action on Hate Speech') (https://www.legal-tools.org/doc/5rrb5b/).

the systematic use of the media to convey hateful narratives has fuelled opposition to this population.

Section 26.2. of the chapter will provide a brief overview of some of the existing instruments within the international human rights framework that give effect to the "right to freedom of thought, conscience, and religion",[2] and the corollary duty to protect against discrimination and incitement to such discrimination. The chapter will describe the government of Iran's responsibilities within such a framework and set the scene for how its actions against the Bahá'ís have constituted a breach of those obligations.

Section 26.3. of the chapter will provide a more in-depth description of the State-sponsored strategy of the Iranian government and clergy to vilify the Bahá'ís on the basis of their religious belief. Accordingly, it will outline some of the main themes present in anti-Bahá'í propaganda in the country, provide a number of examples, including images that depict the extent of such hateful expression, and demonstrate the connection between that propaganda and the violence experienced by the Bahá'ís.

Section 26.4. of the chapter will provide an overview and analysis of the relative effectiveness of the main multilateral strategies pursued during my time as Principal Representative of the Bahá'í International Community's ('BIC') UN Office in response to the situation of the Bahá'ís in Iran. In doing so, the chapter will offer insights from a form of advocacy pursued by the BIC specifically assisting the Bahá'ís in Iran to receive rights that the government of that country has committed to providing to all individuals under its internationally-agreed obligations. Among the strategies discussed are the use of Charter of the United Nations' ('UN Charter') bodies and the Third Committee of the UN General Assembly, as well as engagement with the Special Rapporteurs mandated with investigating such atrocities. The chapter will outline the evolution of international instruments to increasingly engage faith actors to respond to hate speech and provide an analysis of the relative strengths and limitations of such measures. The chapter will also describe some of the bilateral reactions to the persecution experienced by the Bahá'ís in Iran, including the support of assorted national governments, parliaments and intergovernmental bodies, as well as individual leaders within Iran. Additionally, it will explore the response of both the Bahá'ís who face persecution themselves and the broader worldwide Bahá'í community, which has engaged with like-minded collaborators in contributing

[2] Universal Declaration of Human Rights, UN Doc. A/RES/217(III) A, 10 December 1948, Article 18 ('UDHR') (https://www.legal-tools.org/doc/085437/). Article 18 includes the "freedom to change [one's] religion or belief, and freedom, either alone or in community with others and in public or private, to manifest [one's] religion or belief in teaching, practice, worship and observance".

to socially, materially and spiritually prosperous, and cohesive societies founded on commitment to the principle of humanity's oneness, in all its diversity.

Having outlined the different responses and their effectiveness, the chapter will conclude with a call to action for the continued development of the international human rights framework, extending responsibilities to faith leaders and communities, and urging that human rights violations against the freedom of religious belief continue to receive due attention.

26.2. The International Community's Commitment to Combating Hate Speech and Violence

26.2.1. The International Human Rights Framework

The international community has widely recognized the need to confront incitement to hatred and violence directed against religious minorities. Since its founding in 1945, the UN has sought to establish equality of rights for all people, everywhere. Its Charter upholds "respect for human rights and for fundamental freedoms for all without distinction as to race, sex, language, or religion".[3]

The UDHR, approved in 1948 by the UN General Assembly, specifically identified the "right to freedom of thought, conscience and religion"[4] as a fundamental human right. Within that same article is contained the "freedom to change [one's] religion or belief, and freedom, either alone or in community with others and in public or private, to manifest [one's] religion or belief in teaching, practice, worship and observance".[5] A positive obligation is also included: that all people "are entitled to equal protection against any discrimination in violation of this Declaration and against any incitement to such discrimination".[6] In these clauses can be found the roots of a framework that forms the basis of recourse for individuals and communities who suffer human rights violations, indeed, any form of discrimination.

While the UDHR calls for the unconditional protection of the 'internal' right to freedom of religion, the 'external' right to manifest one's beliefs is subject to limitations. Governments are permitted to place restrictions on the right to freedom of religious belief for the purposes of "meeting the just requirements of morality, public order and the general welfare in a democratic society".[7] This latitude extended to States, however, has often been abused in efforts to quell minority populations and has raised questions about what constitutes legitimate governmental interference in manifestations of religion or belief.

---

3 UN Charter, 24 October 1945 (http://www.legal-tools.org/doc/6b3cd5/).

4 UDHR, Article 18, see *supra* note 2.

5 *Ibid.*

6 *Ibid.*, Article 7.

7 *Ibid.*, Article 29.

Notwithstanding, the right to freedom of religious belief has been reaffirmed and codified in numerous UN resolutions as well as international covenants and treaties – noteworthy among them, the International Covenant on Civil and Political Rights ('ICCPR' or 'Covenant').[8] The Covenant guarantees the right to freedom of expression,[9] and, in Article 18, spells out the right to freedom of religion or belief:

> 1. Everyone shall have the right to freedom of thought, conscience and religion. This right shall include freedom to have or to adopt a religion or belief of his choice, and freedom, either individually or in community with others and in public or private, to manifest his religion or belief in worship, observance, practice and teaching.
> 2. No one shall be subject to coercion which would impair his freedom to have or to adopt a religion or belief of his choice.
> 3. Freedom to manifest one's religion or beliefs may be subject only to such limitations as are prescribed by law and are necessary to protect public safety, order, health, or morals or the fundamental rights and freedoms of others.[10]

Condemnation of incitement to discrimination on the basis of religion is expressly articulated in Article 20 of the ICCPR which states that "[a]ny advocacy of national, racial or religious hatred that constitutes incitement to discrimination, hostility or violence shall be prohibited by law".[11] Though "incitement to discrimination" does not explicitly constitute hate speech, the implementation of these rights is inextricably linked with its prohibition.

In addition to differences of opinion around extending protection against instances of hate speech within this framework, the drafting of the ICCPR, together with other instruments such as the Declaration on the Rights of the Child as well as the Declaration and International Convention on the Elimination of All Forms of Racial Discrimination, have demonstrated how contested the

---

[8] See Nazila Ghanea, *Human Rights, the UN and the Bahá'ís in Iran*, George Ronald Publisher, 2002, p. 66, who describes that the UN Charter referenced non-discrimination in general, but not freedom of religion and belief. See also in that book a discussion on the ICCPR; International Covenant on Economic, Social and Cultural Rights, 3 January 1976 (https://www.legal-tools.org/doc/06b87e/); the Declaration on the Elimination of All Forms of Intolerance and Discrimination Based on Religion or Belief, UN Doc. A/RES/36/55, 25 November 1981, Article 2(1) ('Declaration on the Elimination of All Forms of Intolerance') (https://www.legal-tools.org/doc/hexdsg/); Convention on the Rights of the Child, 2 September 1990 (https://www.legal-tools.org/doc/f48f9e/); and UN General Assembly, Declaration on the Rights of Persons Belonging to National or Ethnic, Religious and Linguistic Minorities, UN Doc. A/RES/47/135, 18 December 1992 (https://www.legal-tools.org/doc/17hvwd/).

[9] ICCPR, 23 March 1976, Article 19 (https://www.legal-tools.org/doc/2838f3).

[10] *Ibid.*, Article 18.

[11] *Ibid.*, Article 20.

terrain has been around what constitutes a belief and the extent to which it should be protected.[12] Indeed, the drafting and adoption of such texts have involved robust debate and political compromise. Over the years, different aspects related to freedom of religion or belief have evolved, with clusters of rights emerging around non-discrimination, the rights of religious minorities in general and a broader right to hold or practise a specific religion or belief.[13]

In 2007, Asma Jahangir, the UN's Special Rapporteur on Freedom of Religion or Belief at the time, helped advance thinking around what constitutes the right to freedom of religion or belief, in particular asserting that it was not only limited to officially 'recognized' or 'traditional' religions. In her 2007 report to the Human Rights Council ('HRC'), Jahangir stated:

> [F]reedom of religion or belief is not limited in its application to traditional religions or to religions and beliefs with institutional characteristics or practices analogous to those of traditional religions. Furthermore, it has been established that article 18 of the International Covenant on Civil and Political Rights (ICCPR) 'protects theistic, non-theistic and atheistic beliefs, as well as the right not to profess any religion or belief'.[14]

Further multilateral instruments have evolved in response to a growing recognition of the need for more clarity surrounding the nature of the right to hold a religious belief, or not, and its associated protections. A number of these will be outlined in more detail in Section 26.4. Despite challenges of building consensus around such matters, these instruments have been consequential in the evolution of thought around the protection and lived experiences of religious minorities.[15]

Regrettably, however, communities worldwide continue to fall victim to severe hate crimes, including hate speech. More insidious have been those cases where the perpetrator is the State itself, particularly when that State has purported to uphold these internationally agreed upon ideals and obligations. One such case involves the situation of the Bahá'í community in Iran. But before outlining an account of the experiences of this religious minority, it is important to take note of the international obligations Iran has committed itself to, in order to contextualize the gravity of this breach of law.

---

12 Ghanea, 2002, p. 93, see *supra* note 8.

13 *Ibid.*

14 UN General Assembly, Report of the Special Rapporteur on the Freedom of Religion or Belief, Asma Jahangir, UN Doc. A/HRC/6/5, 20 July 2007, para. 6 (https://www.legal-tools.org/doc/r8dvwp/).

15 Ghanea, 2002, pp. 72–77, see *supra* note 8.

26.2.2. Iran's Obligations Under International Law

In 1976, Iran, a signatory to the UDHR, signed the ICCPR.[16] Diplomats representing the Islamic Republic of Iran have always claimed that they are striving to abide by the Covenant, and Iran has explicitly participated in its ongoing application, submitting regular reports to the international Human Rights Committee charged with monitoring its implementation.[17]

In 2005, Iran supported a resolution in the UN General Assembly that, among other things, deplored "the use of the print, audio-visual and electronic media, including the Internet, and any other means to incite acts of violence, xenophobia or related intolerance and discrimination towards Islam or any other religion".[18] And, in 2009, Iran put forward language at a UN conference on racism and related intolerance that expressed serious concern at "instances of defamation of religions which manifest itself in projecting negative insulting and derogatory images of religions and religious personalities, generalized and stereotyped associations of religions, in particular Islam".[19]

Iran has also actively participated in discussions on religious hatred in the UN, particularly as it relates to 'defamation' against Muslims, whose beliefs have been portrayed by some as fanatical and violent.[20] Negative stereotyping and intolerance – especially following the 11 September 2001 terrorist attacks – has indeed been a concern among nations with Muslim majorities. Iran was thus among a number of Islámic States that proposed a series of resolutions that ultimately resulted in a reaffirmation of the obligation to protect against religious discrimination and incitement to hatred, as well as a strongly worded, unanimously adopted resolution by the HRC in 2011.[21]

Despite the government of Iran's continued support of the right to freedom of religious belief and the need to protect against religious discrimination and incitement to hatred, it would seem incongruent that such a party would actively violate the very right it has sought to give voice to on an international level with increasing degrees of formalization. Yet, as described in the account that follows, Bahá'ís in Iran have consistently been the target of government-

[16] BIC, "Inciting Hatred: Iran's Media Campaign to Demonize Bahá'ís", 2011, p. 3 ('Inciting Hatred Special Report').

[17] *Ibid.*

[18] *Ibid.*, p. 28.

[19] *Ibid.*

[20] *Ibid.*, p. 3.

[21] *Ibid.*, p. 4. See also UNHRC, Combating Intolerance, Negative Stereotyping and Stigmatization of, and Discrimination, Incitement to Violence and Violence Against, Persons Based on Religion or Belief, UN Doc. A/HRC/RES/16/18, 12 April 2011 ('Istanbul Process') (https://www.legal-tools.org/doc/0a86d2/).

led discrimination and Iranian officials have repeatedly peddled obvious falsehoods, such as denying that Bahá'ís are persecuted and claiming that Bahá'ís are virtually non-existent as a group. At the heart of such denials is a claim made that the Bahá'í Faith is not a 'divine' religion in the understanding of Islám, as if such a fact would exclude the minority from the protection afforded by international guarantees of freedom of religion or belief.[22] Needless to say, such an assertion is flagrantly inconsistent with settled international parameters and definitions of human rights. It is in effect a declaration that the government will only respect the freedom of those deemed worthy of having freedoms, rendering the very understanding of inalienable human rights meaningless.

26.3. Background: The Situation of the Bahá'ís in Iran

The intention of the following section is not to provide an extensive account of the forms of persecution experienced by the Bahá'ís in Iran, which has already been documented in detail elsewhere.[23] Rather, it offers an illustration of the extent to which State-sponsored discrimination can find expression and how violence against a community can be fuelled through hate speech. It is hoped that this section can generate further attention around the situation of the Bahá'ís in Iran and provide further impetus for the development of the international human rights framework specifically in relation to the freedom of religious belief.

26.3.1. Historical Overview of Persecution

Ever since the Bahá'í Faith was founded in Iran in the mid-nineteenth century by Mírzá Ḥusayn-'Alí, known as Bahá'u'lláh, the religious establishment in Iran has sought to quench that community with fierce opposition, inciting violence against Bahá'u'lláh and his followers.[24] To the Iranian clergy, the Bahá'í Faith has represented both theological heresy and a threat to their influence and authority. The Bahá'í Faith's progressive principles, which advocate, among other beliefs, the advancement of scientific inquiry as being in harmony with religion and the independent investigation of truth, appealed to large segments of the populace and were, thus, perceived as a direct threat to the worldview and power of the clergy.[25] Beyond the challenge the Bahá'í Faith's social and spiritual teachings have posed to the orthodoxy, the very idea that there could be a divine

---

22 Inciting Hatred Special Report, p. 29, see *supra* note 16.

23 See, for instance, BIC, "Archives of Bahá'í Persecution in Iran" and *id.*, "Situation of Bahá'ís in Iran" (available on BIC's web site).

24 Such persecution involved the execution of the forerunner of the Bahá'í Faith,'Alí-Muḥammad, the Báb, and the exile of Bahá'u'lláh. See Inciting Hatred Special Report, p. 25, see *supra* note 16.

25 BIC, "The Bahá'í Question Revisited: Persecution and Resilience in Iran", October 2016, p. 68 ('The Bahá'í Question Revisited').

religion after Islám has been claimed impossible.[26] The faith has, therefore, long been cast as an illicit political movement or cult deserving eradication, sparking episodic outbursts of persecution.[27] From the killing of at least 4,000 of its earliest followers, to the torture and humiliation of thousands more, the oppression has been widespread from the outset.[28]

In the 1970s, immediately preceding the overthrow of the Pahlavi regime, the persecution both grew in scale and took a different form, with accusations specifically by the revolutionary cleric Ayatollah Khomeini that Bahá'ís were "centers of evil propaganda" or "agents of Western powers".[29] He even went so far as to state, when asked if the Bahá'ís would be given freedom under an Islamic Republic, that "they are a political faction. They are harmful. They will not be accepted".[30] And specifically in response to the question of whether they would be afforded religious freedom, he simply said, "No".[31]

By the end of the decade, with Khomeini's rise to political power, the oppression had also been extended into Iranian law.[32] Article 19 of the Constitution of the Islamic Republic of Iran ('Constitution'), for instance, states that "[a]ll people of Iran, whatever the ethnic group or tribe to which they belong, enjoy equal rights; colour, race, language, and the like, do not bestow any privilege".[33] Conspicuously absent in this clause, however, is any reference to religion, an absence that opens the door to discrimination based on religious belief. Article 13 of the Constitution also states, "Zoroastrian, Jewish, and Christian Iranians are the only recognized religious minorities".[34] Yet, the Bahá'í Faith – Iran's largest non-Muslim religious minority and a religion that was born in Iran – is entirely excluded from similar constitutional protection.[35]

---

26 *Ibid.*, p. 62.

27 *Ibid.*

28 Inciting Hatred Special Report, p. 25, see *supra* note 16.

29 Julia Berger, *Rethinking Religion and Politics in a Plural World*, Bloomsbury Academic, London, 2021, p. 60.

30 *Ibid.*

31 *Ibid.*

32 Inciting Hatred Special Report, p. 25, see *supra* note 16.

33 Iran, Constitution, 3 December 1979, Article 19 (https://www.legal-tools.org/doc/4205c7/).

34 *Ibid.*, Article 13.

35 The Bahá'í Question Revisited, p. 12, see *supra* note 25, which quotes a statement made by then UN Secretary General Ban Ki-moon in a report to the HRC on the situation of human rights in Iran (3 March 2016):

> The Iranian Constitution recognizes Christians, Jews and Zoroastrians as protected religious minorities, who are free to perform their religious rites, ceremonies and provide religious education, in accordance with the tenets of their faith. The Constitution does not extend such recognition to other religious groups, such as Bahá'ís, leaving them vulnerable to discrimination and judicial harassment and persecution.

The institutionalized nature of such discrimination, resulting from the wording of the Iranian Constitution, has had a devastating impact in courts as Iranian legislation is interpreted to the detriment of the Bahá'ís.[36] In court hearings, many Bahá'ís have been denied the right of redress or protection against assault, killings or other forms of persecution, and in many rulings Iranian citizens who killed or injured Bahá'ís were not held liable because their victims were considered "unprotected infidels".[37]

In 1980, all nine members of the national Bahá'í governing council, the National Spiritual Assembly of the Bahá'ís of Iran, were abducted and disappeared without a trace.[38] It seems certain that they were executed.[39] In the decade that followed, hundreds of Bahá'ís were killed and even more were tortured or imprisoned.[40] One form of psychological abuse during this period involved offering prisoners the promise of release, conditional upon recanting their faith, an act which they would refuse. This condition, however, constituted clear proof that the persecutions were based solely on religious belief.[41]

In the 1990s, after a series of UN resolutions condemned Iran's actions, the Iranian government ceased the outright killing of Bahá'ís and shifted its approach to a form of persecution which, though less blatant, was just as insidious.

---

36 *Ibid.*, p.11. In both criminal and civil cases, judges or prosecutors often merely need to cite the fact that a defendant or plaintiff is a Bahá'í as evidence against them. See also The Bahá'í Question Revisited, pp. 18–19, see *supra* note 25, as an example of the treatment of Bahá'ís in the courts. In that case, 24 Bahá'ís in Gorgan were summoned to court in December 2014, and their lawyer was given only 15 minutes to read 5,000 pages of court documents. Prior to the court hearing, the lawyer was threatened during a meeting with representatives of the Ministry of Intelligence and a cleric. In addition to judicial misconduct, Bahá'ís – like so many others in the Iranian judicial system – are often beaten or tortured while in custody. Several of the 24 in Gorgan were beaten during their interrogation. Other Bahá'ís have faced long stints of solitary confinement during their detention. Extreme verbal or psychological abuse is also common. For another case, see The Bahá'í Question Revisited, p. 21, see *supra* note 25, which outlines the trial of the seven Bahá'í leaders known as the Yárán or 'Friends in Iran'. In that case, the individuals were not told of the charges against them for their first year of detention, and had virtually no access to lawyers. During their trial, remarks from the bench indicated extreme prejudice on the part of the judge. According to one of their lawyers, Mahnaz Parakand,

> [t]he bill of indictment [...] was more like a political statement, rather than a legal document. It was a 50-page document [...] full of accusations and humiliations levelled against the Bahá'í community of Iran, especially our clients. It was written without producing any proof for the allegations.

37 *Ibid.*, p. 64.

38 *Ibid.*, p. 63.

39 *Ibid.*

40 *Ibid.*

41 *Ibid.*, p. 65.

The strategy involved the systematic social, economic and cultural exclusion of the Bahá'í community in every facet of life.[42] A significant feature of this approach was that it was supported and directed by the highest levels of the government, including through the direct participation of the Supreme Leader Ayatollah Ali Khamenei.[43] In 1991, for instance, a memorandum was drafted by the Supreme Revolutionary Cultural Council and signed by Khamenei.[44] Specifically addressed as "the Bahá'í Question", the memorandum established a national policy to promote the gradual eradication of the Bahá'í community as a viable entity in Iranian society.[45] The memorandum explicitly states that "their religious [...] activities should be answered by giving them religious and cultural responses, as well as propaganda", that "[p]ropaganda institutions (such as the Islamic Propaganda Organization) must establish an independent section to counter the propaganda and religious activities of the Bahá'ís", and that "[a] plan must be devised to confront and destroy their cultural roots outside the country",[46] evidence of which can be found in Yemen and other places.[47] This memorandum has never been rescinded, and continues to remain in effect by references to it in other more recent policy documents.[48]

In 2005, the crackdown on the Bahá'ís was deepened further by the former president Mahmoud Ahmadinejad, with more than 860 arrests, at least 240 Bahá'ís having been expelled from university, thousands more being blocked from enrolling in higher education, as well as over 950 specific incidents of economic discrimination.[49]

Further, in 2013, a series of '*fatwás*' by Ayatollah Khamenei were published declaring that any interaction with Bahá'ís was unlawful.[50] Taking various forms over the years, the government-initiated strategy has also involved directives that permit the expropriation of Bahá'í-owned property, the

42 Inciting Hatred Special Report, p. 26, see *supra* note 16.

43 The Bahá'í Question Revisited, p. 8, see *supra* note 25. See also Geoff Cameron and Nazila Ghanea, "Bahá'ís in the Middle East", in Paul S. Rowe (ed.), *Routledge Handbook of Minorities in the Middle East*, Routledge, London, 2018, p. 174.

44 The Bahá'í Question Revisited, p. 8, see *supra* note 25.

45 *Ibid.*

46 *Ibid.*, p. 95, which lays out the text of "the Bahá'í Question" memorandum.

47 Cameron and Ghanea, 2018, p. 180, see *supra* note 43.

48 *Ibid.*, p. 9.

49 The Bahá'í Question Revisited, p. 2, see *supra* note 25. These figures, as do all such statistics throughout this chapter, reflect the minimum number of incidents. Because of restrictions on the free flow of information, as well as the reluctance of Iranian Bahá'ís to complain or call attention to themselves, there are undoubtedly many more incidents of persecution than have been reported to the BIC.

50 *Ibid.*, p. 52.

destruction of Bahá'í Holy Places, the dismissal of Bahá'ís from many forms of work, the cancellation of pensions, the expulsion of Bahá'ís from universities and the denial of their higher education, the criminalization of membership on Bahá'í institutions and the surveillance by intelligence and police officials of the activities of the Bahá'ís.[51]

Since that time, the government has stepped up its harassment of the Bahá'ís. This has involved fine-tuning its policy of oppression with an escalation in revolving-door arrests and detentions, a rise in the number of Bahá'ís imprisoned, and a series of government memoranda that announce or reiterate explicitly anti-Bahá'í policies.[52] The approach, which still continues today, involves a process of 'othering' and seeks to portray the Iranian Bahá'ís as outsiders in their own land.[53] In summarizing the experience of the Bahá'ís, a top UN human rights official stated that the government-led persecution spans "all areas of state activity, from family law provisions to schooling, education, and security".[54] Put simply, the oppression of Iranian Bahá'ís extends from cradle to grave.

As mentioned above, this intolerance against the Bahá'ís has, regrettably, expanded throughout the Middle East through a campaign initiated by the Iranian government.[55] Notable is the influence that has extended to Yemen. On 23 March 2018, Abdel-Malek al-Houthi, the leader of the Houthis in Yemen, gave a speech vehemently vilifying and denouncing the Bahá'í Faith.[56] Within days of his speech, over twenty online news sites reiterated his negative comments about the Bahá'í Faith and a prominent Houthi writer and strategist commented on social media "we will butcher every Bahá'í".[57] For the purpose of this case study, however, the analysis will be limited to Iran.

The systematic persecution of the Bahá'ís in Iran can also be understood as the government's response to the Iranian people's struggle for a democratic transformation in the country, where the general population has made demands for greater freedoms and social progress. Indeed, the use of the Bahá'ís as a convenient scapegoat is part of a historical pattern of justifying authoritarianism

---

51 *Ibid.*; *ibid.*, p. 10. See also Berger, 2021, p. 61, see *supra* note 29.

52 Inciting Hatred Special Report, p. 26, see *supra* note 16.

53 *Ibid.*, p. 4.

54 The Bahá'í Question Revisited, pp. 2–3, see *supra* note 25. See also "Persecution of Baha'is in Iran Extends Across all Stages of Life", *Bahá'í World News Service*, 18 March 2013 (available on its web site).

55 Cameron and Ghanea, 2018, p. 180, see *supra* note 43.

56 BIC, "Inflammatory Speech by the Houthi Leader Targets Baha'is in Yemen with Genocidal Intent", 18 April 2018 (available on its web site).

57 *Ibid.*

through the construction of imaginary enemies, which is recognized as a means of urging a population to unite in uncritical obedience to their leaders.[58] Efforts to uphold the rights of the Bahá'ís, then, far transcend the security of just one minority group, but also extend to any fair-minded observer who values democratic safeguards.

26.3.2. Use of the Media

Beyond the physical acts of exclusion, one insidious element of this persecution has been the government's extensive use of the mass media to convey hateful messages, systematically denigrating and vilifying the Bahá'ís with potentially dire consequences. Since the 1979 Iranian Revolution, the government of Iran has waged a relentless anti-Bahá'í propaganda campaign in the media. This has continued and intensified in recent years, with more than 20,000 such items published or broadcast since the beginning of 2014.[59] Slanders and falsehoods are disseminated in State-controlled and State-sanctioned media through pamphlets, online and print articles, web sites entirely dedicated to condemning the Bahá'í Faith, online software databases, television programmes and radio series.[60] Anti-Bahá'í propaganda is spread from pulpits, in seminars, conferences, symposia, and at public exhibitions and events.[61] The government's campaign to demonize Bahá'ís through propaganda spans all aspects of the life cycle, even reaching children.[62] The diverse content of these attacks demonstrates tremendous effort and commitment of resources by the Islamic Republic.

Through such propaganda, the victims' humanity is denied. Bahá'ís are portrayed as the source of every conceivable evil including the economic and social problems of the country – and often the wider world – justifying their absolute mistreatment.[63] Notable in its volume and vehemence, its scope and sophistication, such propaganda is cynically calculated to stir up antagonism against the Bahá'í community. Even images of Bahá'í Holy Places recognized by the UN Educational, Scientific and Cultural Organization as a World Heritage

---

58 Inciting Hatred Special Report, p. 25, see *supra* note 16.

59 The Bahá'í Question Revisited, p. 50, see *supra* note 25.

60 Inciting Hatred Special Report, p. 1, see *supra* note 16.

61 *Ibid.*

62 *Ibid.*, p. 21. In an attempt to instil a lifelong prejudice among the young against Bahá'ís, on the last day of school in 2008, school authorities in Shiraz distributed to every primary school child a sealed envelope with a 'gift' from a local publishing company. Inside was a 12-page illustrated story book titled "The Deceitful Babak", which tells a disguised story of the Báb, the Prophet-Herald of the Bahá'í Faith, in an erroneous, mocking, and degrading manner. Other articles geared towards youth are portrayed in the name of enlightening them towards the path of 'truth'.

63 *Ibid.*, p. 3.

site possessing "outstanding universal value" have been graphically denigrated, not only conveying hurtful narratives about the Bahá'ís themselves, but also acting as a profound source of disrespect against the sacredness which the spots represent for the Bahá'ís.[64]

The increasing intensity of anti-Bahá'í propaganda is a sign of the degree to which Iran has shifted its strategy of persecution from overt to covert – all the while never relenting in its ultimate goal of neutralizing the Bahá'í community as a viable force in Iranian society.[65] After over 30 years of hate propaganda, it seems that the Bahá'ís have become an all-purpose scapegoat, so much so that the Iranian government now feels it can effectively denigrate its opponents by merely accusing them of being Bahá'ís, as if that were the most heinous crime.[66] The propaganda has become increasingly imaginative, weaving together a broad and often contradictory spectrum of inflammatory accusations in often absurd combinations.[67] A number of themes are often advanced, and are outlined in more depth below.

26.3.3. Main Themes of Anti-Bahá'í Propaganda

An analysis of the themes present in anti-Bahá'í propaganda shows a wide range of tactics employed by the government to reach a broad audience. On the one hand, anti-Bahá'í propaganda has purposely been designed to inflame the sensibilities of a traditionally religious audience, professing Bahá'ís as heretics.[68] On the other hand, attempts to appeal to a younger and more secular generation have added the additional layer of casting Bahá'ís as threats to the national identity and existence of Iran.[69]

64 *Ibid.*, p. 13.

65 The Bahá'í Question Revisited, p. 52, see *supra* note 25.

66 Inciting Hatred Special Report, p. 2, see *supra* note 16.

67 *Ibid.*, p. 5.

68 The Bahá'í Question Revisited, p. 51, see *supra* note 25.

69 *Ibid.*

Figure 1: This image (of the classic shrouded figure of death) has been used to illustrate a number of anti-Bahá'í articles on government-sponsored or pro-government web sites and blogs in Iran.

Many attacks are built on gross distortions of Bahá'í history and often use graphic imagery (see, for instance, Figure 1 above). Some attempt a strategy of guilt by association, by lumping Bahá'ís together with completely unrelated groups – such as 'Satanists' or the Shah's secret police.[70] Others deploy a tactic of connecting Bahá'ís with 'opponents' of the authorities, which allows the government to discredit both the Bahá'ís and its adversaries in a single transaction.[71] Internally contradictory or patently false, the messages are designed to have the greatest possible emotional impact on the wider population.[72] All of this is reinforced by the absence of more accurate narratives through the systematic censure of information, forbidding anyone to write or broadcast anything in support of the Bahá'ís.[73]

The BIC's examination of government-sponsored or government-enabled anti-Bahá'í propaganda reveals a number of recurring themes, some of them overlapping.[74] Though not exhaustive, the description that follows provides a broad picture of how the government has advanced a variety of harmful narratives about the Bahá'ís.

70 Inciting Hatred Special Report, p. 4, see *supra* note 16.

71 *Ibid.*

72 *Ibid.*

73 *Ibid.*

74 The Bahá'í Question Revisited, see *supra* note 25.

• *Bahá'ís were supporters of the Pahlavi regime and the late Shah of Iran, and have collaborated with SAVAK, the secret police.*[75] Under this narrative, the Bahá'í Faith is painted as a political organization opposed to the present Iranian government, thereby posing a security threat.[76] Such a portrayal is contrary to the fact that Bahá'ís are required by the basic principles of their faith to show loyalty and obedience to the government of the country in which they live. They therefore neither opposed the Pahlavi regime, nor the present government of the Islamic Republic of Iran. Indeed, members of the community have been obedient to the present government, including, for instance, adhering to the order to disband all Bahá'í administrative institutions.[77]

• *Bahá'ís are anti-Islámic, actively working to undermine Islám.*[78] This narrative conveys that the Bahá'ís have directly participated over the last two centuries in a number of incidents aimed at wiping out and destroying Islám.[79] The narrative also serves to categorize Bahá'ís as enemies of the Islamic Republic and more generally all Muslims.[80] Within this story, the Bahá'í Faith is cast as a 'misguided sect' or somehow associated with other 'deviant', 'cult-like' practices, such as Satanism. Bahá'ís are accused of engaging in acts such as brainwashing and controlling unwitting followers who are purported to have no autonomy to leave the faith if they wished.[81] Ironically, the Bahá'ís have also been accused of co-operating with a virulently anti-Bahá'í movement, the Hojjatieh, that is also perceived as anti-regime.[82] The Hojjatieh Society was founded in the 1950s to oppose the Bahá'í Faith as part of its mandate to protect and purify Islám. However, it was banned in the early years of the Islamic Revolution because its theological views clashed with those of Ayatollah Khomeini.

• *Bahá'ís are agents of Zionism or spies for Israel.*[83] Central to this narrative is the assertion that Bahá'ís are a threat to the existence of the Iranian nation. Framing Bahá'ís as spies for Israel, it also effectively plays on prejudices against Jewish Iranians and the increasing resort to anti-Semitic propaganda,

---

75 *Ibid.*, p. 54. See also Inciting Hatred Special Report, p. 19, see *supra* note 16. 'SAVAK' is the Anglicized acronym for Iran's secret police under the Shah, Sazeman-e Ettela'at va Amniyat-e Keshvar, the National Intelligence and Security Organization.

76 The Bahá'í Question Revisited, p. 54, see *supra* note 25.

77 *Ibid.*

78 Inciting Hatred Special Report, p. 16, see *supra* note 16.

79 *Ibid.*

80 *Ibid.*

81 *Ibid.*, p. 13.

82 *Ibid.*, p. 5.

83 *Ibid.*, p. 15.

such as President Mahmoud Ahmadinejad's denial of the Holocaust.[84] Iranian propaganda also makes much of the fact that the world headquarters and a number of important holy places of the Bahá'í Faith are located in Israel. What they fail to mention is that this historical circumstance was driven in large part by the Iranian rulers of the past who banished Bahá'u'lláh in 1868 to the Ottoman prison city of Acre – which now sits within the borders of modern-day Israel – and that the Bahá'í spiritual and administrative home of the faith had been fixed to that geographic spot by Bahá'u'lláh long before it became Israel.[85] From the latter years of Bahá'u'lláh's incarceration in Acre to the present day, the Bahá'í community has been respected by and has enjoyed a peaceful relationship with people of all religious backgrounds in the region.[86]

- *The Bahá'í Faith is 'anti-Iranian' and was created by – or has a historic connection with – imperialist powers, specifically Great Britain or Russia.*[87] This narrative seeks to portray a religion indigenous to Iran as a 'foreign conspiracy'.[88] One claim was that the Bahá'ís participated in – or even planned – the Ashura day protests of December 2009, including charges that they possessed arms and ammunition.[89] The government flooded the nation with anti-Bahá'í propaganda in the period immediately after the protests.[90] The suggestion

---

84 *Ibid.*

85 *Ibid.*, pp. 15–16. In the early years after the Revolution, Bahá'ís under interrogation were asked such questions as: 'How much money did you send to Israel?'. A number of Bahá'ís were executed on charges of 'spying' for Israel. More recently, the high-profile trial of seven national-level Bahá'í leaders in 2010 also included charges that they were 'spies' for Israel. On that false accusation and others they were convicted and imprisoned for 20 years.

86 *Ibid.*, pp. 15–16.

87 *Ibid.*, pp. 12–16. In early 2009, the state-run radio network Radio Maaref began broadcasting a weekly anti-Bahá'í programme called Saraab (Mirage). According to the web site Ayande-ye-Roshan, the programmes "analyze the deviant sects, Babism and Bahaism". Aimed at youth, the series reportedly sought to inform listeners about "the connection between Bahaism and western colonialism".

88 *Ibid.*

89 *Ibid.*, p. 17. In one example, on 11 January 2010, *Kayhan* newspaper published an article that accused Bahá'ís of not only participating in those protests, but of "managing" them. The article begins with a headline proclaiming: "The think tank behind the Green Movement turned out to be Bahá'ís". Its lead paragraph then promised to present "new clues about the active role played by the colonialist Bahaism party in the management of the green sedition". The article then makes a reference to the "detention of 10 Bahaist leaders" in connection to the protests. This appears to refer to the wrongful arrest, on 3 January 2010, of 10 Bahá'ís who were accused of playing "a role in organizing the Ashura protests" and namely for "having sent abroad pictures of the unrest". Some of the 10 were also accused of having arms and ammunition in their homes. The 10 were never convicted of these alleged crimes, which the BIC exposed as "a blatant lie".

90 *Ibid.*

that Bahá'ís are instigators of the opposition to the government in Iran – in addition to their alleged links to numerous other conspiracies – is a thinly veiled attempt to deflect criticism of the increasing social ills and economic problems confronting the Iranian nation. Yet, Bahá'ís are actively engaged in supporting social progress and justice in Iran, and are prevented by their religious principles from participating in partisan politics.[91] Such a narrative also claims that foreign broadcasters, in particular the British Broadcasting Corporation ('BBC') and Voice of America ('VOA'), are controlled by or under the influence of Bahá'ís because they cover stories about human rights violations against Bahá'ís, or that Bahá'ís have influence over anti-regime Iranian human rights activists.[92]

- *Bahá'ís are morally corrupt.*[93] This narrative seeks to incite anger among both a more traditionally conservative or religious population as well as a more secular one. Under such a narrative, Bahá'ís are claimed to engage in practices like marrying and having sexual relations with family members or to engage in orgies (see Figure 2 below, which has often accompanied such a narrative).[94] The fact that Bahá'í marriage is not recognized by the government has reinforced this narrative, denouncing Bahá'í wives as prostitutes and leading to charges that Bahá'ís engage in promiscuity and extra-marital affairs.[95] All of this is notwithstanding the fact that Bahá'ís have a strict moral code and attach great importance to good moral behaviour and to the institution of marriage. The principle of the equality of women and men, so central to the Bahá'í teachings, is also often reframed as the "mingling of men and women", a form of adultery, or the "promotion of feminism", implying that it is immoral or criminal instead of something to be welcomed.[96] The Bahá'í community's dedication to social progress, equality and justice is thus, in the inverted morality of the propagandists, a cause for its demoralization.[97]

[91] *Ibid.*, p. 16.

[92] *Ibid.*, p. 10. One example that is often cited is the Nobel Peace Prize Laureate Shirin Ebadi.

[93] *Ibid.*, p. 20.

[94] *Ibid.*

[95] *Ibid.*

[96] *Ibid.*, p. 21.

[97] *Ibid.*

Figure 2: This image has appeared on a number of pro-government, anti-Bahá'í web sites. It was used, for example, to illustrate an 8 January 2011 story on the *Kalameh News* site claiming that Bahá'ís in Tehran hold meetings on Shí'ah holy days in which men, women and girls pray together – and then shed their clothing, "listen to vulgar music, and celebrate".

Analysis of a wide range of media sources demonstrates that the government's tactic involves weaving together several of the above-mentioned themes in each piece of propaganda. One example that clearly demonstrates the nature of anti-Bahá'í propaganda through the use of multiple narratives at the highest levels can be found in a speech delivered in October 2010 by Supreme Leader Ayatollah Ali Khamenei in Iran's religious centre, Qom.[98] The Supreme Leader's anti-Bahá'í remarks were broadcast in their entirety on the national television service, Islamic Republic of Iran Broadcaster, and also reported on by the government's official news agency, the Islamic Republic News Agency ('IRNA').[99] The following are excerpts from the IRNA story, which ran that same day, reporting Khamenei as saying: "Enemies of the Islamic Revolution who intend to inflict damage on the revolution have two main targets, the religion of the people and their devotion to the revolution […]".[100] He further added that the country's enemies have raised doubts about religious values in an attempt to weaken the pillars of people's faith,

> especially the young generation through promoting immorality, false Sufism, promotion of Bahaism and promotion of home-based churches. These are tactics that enemies of Islam, today, carefully

98 *Ibid.*, pp. 6–7.

99 *Ibid.*

100 *Ibid.*

> study and plan with the objective of weakening religion in the society.[101]

Over the weeks following the Supreme Leader's comments, the media continued to provoke antagonism through articles that provided supporting analyses and commentaries of the speech, many of which amplified its anti-Bahá'í theme.[102]

Three significant points are worth noting about this article and its subject. First, the speech was given by Iran's Supreme Leader – whose word is taken to be tantamount to a divine directive. He stands at the top of the government hierarchy, above even the president. Second, the main thrust of the article is about enemies of Iran – and of Islám. It is an appeal both to nationalist and religious passions. By including Bahá'ís in the list of enemies, the Supreme Leader confers upon them a stigma of the worst category. Finally, as demonstrated by ensuing events, it is clear that the speech was part of a premeditated campaign to set a particular tone and direction in State policy.

Another case of a spike in anti-Bahá'í propaganda followed a meeting between Fariba Kamalabadi, a Bahá'í who had previously been sentenced to prison for being one of the seven Bahá'í leaders known as the Yárán or 'Friends in Iran', and another former prisoner who had shared a cell with her, Faezeh Hashemi, the daughter of former President Akbar Hashemi Rafsanjani in May 2016.[103] This meeting sparked a storm of anti-Bahá'í rhetoric and hate speech by officials and religious leaders.[104] One top Iranian government official – judiciary spokesman Gholamhossein Mohseni Eje – called the meeting "a very ugly and obscene act".[105] Scores of religious leaders joined in making assertions such as, "consorting with Bahá'ís and friendship with them is against the teachings of Islam" and that Bahá'ís are "deviants" who must be "isolated".[106]

Desecrating the name of anyone and propagating baseless slanders is enough to constitute an affront to anyone's dignity. Yet the challenge with these tactics is that they do not stop at a false accusation aimed to blame a scapegoat. Many of these false claims have been directly linked to an increase in physical violence against the Bahá'ís. There is tangible evidence that many instances of atrocity crimes against the Bahá'ís in Iran are linked to the messages found in

101 *Ibid.*

102 *Ibid.*

103 The Bahá'í Question Revisited, p. 56, see *supra* note 25.

104 *Ibid.*

105 *Ibid.*

106 *Ibid.*

the media that spread hostility and hatred or encourage or incite populations to commit violence against them.

26.3.4. Connection Between Propaganda and Violence

In the Iranian context, the incidence of hate propaganda has been marked by a rise in incidents of violence against Bahá'ís and Bahá'í properties, ranging from outright murder to simple vandalism, instigated by the government and carried out by unknown individuals and groups who have been influenced by the messages in the media. These attacks have come above and beyond an increase in arrests, detentions, imprisonments and confiscations undertaken by the government or its agents. Attacks, principally in the form of arson and vandalism on Bahá'í-owned businesses and properties (see, for instance, Figure 3 below), have grown over the last few decades, often accompanied by the sending of anonymous letters, the scrawling of anti-Bahá'í graffiti, and other scare tactics, some amounting to death threats.[107] Since 2005, Bahá'í cemeteries in more than a dozen cities and towns have been vandalized, bulldozed or subjected to fire bombings.[108] These acts are almost always carried out at night.[109]

Figure 3: A Bahá'í-owned shop in Rafsanjan, Iran, targeted by arsonists. Several businesses run by Bahá'ís there have suffered serious damage in a wave of attacks in the city since 25 October 2010. The attacks were accompanied by an anonymous letter warning "members of the misguided Bahaist sect" not to teach their faith.

[107] Inciting Hatred Special Report, p. 22, see *supra* note 16.

[108] *Ibid.*, p. 23.

[109] *Ibid.*

By way of illustration, during the period between 2008 and 2010, a series of incidents took place in the city of Semnan, which involved the firebombing of Bahá'í properties, the scrawling of hate graffiti on Bahá'í-owned buildings, the vandalizing of a Bahá'í cemetery and the denouncing of Bahá'í children in public schools.[110] Many of these incidents followed a two-part anti-Bahá'í lecture series held in the city, which, according to reports, sought to analyse the link between the Bahá'í Faith and Zionism.[111] Within weeks of those rallies, on 15 December 2008, the homes of some 20 Bahá'ís were raided by local authorities.[112] During the same period, unidentified arsonists attacked at least three Bahá'í-owned businesses, threw firebombs at several Bahá'í homes, and set fire to buildings at the Bahá'í cemetery.[113] These attacks were reinforced by a decision made in early 2009 by the Semnan Chamber of Commerce and some 39 associated trade unions to prohibit the issuing of business licences or managerial permits to Bahá'ís and to decline to renew existing ones.[114] On 14 September 2009, a mob gathered in front of the Semnan city hall and the provincial governor's office shouting slogans such as: "Death to Bahá'í" and demanding that greater pressure be put on the Bahá'ís.[115] The day before, a similar group had barged in during the burial service of a Semnan Bahá'í, uttering insults and threats to interrupt the service.[116] Reports have also emerged from Semnan that Muslim clerics during this period were invited to give presentations in classrooms that insult the Bahá'í Faith, and that Bahá'í schoolchildren had in some cases been segregated from their classmates.[117] On at least two occasions, Muslim students were encouraged to strike Bahá'í students.[118]

The case of Semnan is but one of many egregious accounts of action against the Bahá'ís as a result of the reinforcing interactions between government policy, action, and hateful speech in the media. Regrettably, such forms of aggression have been widespread throughout the country. Notwithstanding the openly criminal nature of the violations, attackers are rarely, if ever, prosecuted, reflecting a culture of impunity. In its public statements, the government of Iran has suggested that violence against Bahá'ís is a manifestation of popular

[110] *Ibid.*, p. 24.
[111] *Ibid.*
[112] *Ibid.*
[113] *Ibid.*
[114] *Ibid.*
[115] *Ibid.*
[116] *Ibid.*
[117] *Ibid.*
[118] *Ibid.*

prejudice beyond government control.[119] Yet the evidence suggests that most acts of violence against Bahá'ís and their properties are likely undertaken with government complicity.[120] The facts and details surrounding most of these incidents point beyond active ignorance to willing approval or encouragement by the government.[121] In a number of the attacks on cemeteries, for example, perpetrators have used heavy construction equipment (see, for instance, Figure 4 below); it is highly unlikely ordinary citizens could freely use bulldozers and other heavy equipment without involvement or support.[122] The government has made no effort to investigate these incidents – a minimum requirement under its international obligations – let alone prosecute or sentence the perpetrators.[123] To whom does a minority facing extreme persecution, in every facet of life, turn when the government itself is a party to such atrocities?

Figure 4: The Bahá'í cemetery in Yazd was destroyed in July 2007 by unknown attackers. The tracks and severity of the damage are from bulldozers or other heavy equipment – the use of which would not easily be possible without official sanction. Dozens of Bahá'í cemeteries have been desecrated in this way.

[119] The Bahá'í Question Revisited, p. 38, see *supra* note 25.
[120] *Ibid.*
[121] *Ibid.*, p. 45.
[122] *Ibid.*
[123] *Ibid.*

26.4. Responses to Hate Speech and the Associated Persecution of the Bahá'ís

A number of formal strategies have been pursued to generate international pressure on the government of Iran and to alleviate the suffering of the Bahá'ís in that country. The BIC has long worked within existing legal mechanisms, beginning with bilateral dialogue with the government of Iran, with Iran's Mission to the UN, and subsequently with the UN itself, by providing detailed information on the situation of the Bahá'ís to the UN Secretary-General as well as the High Commissioner for Human Rights.[124] At the heart of such engagement is a commitment to truth through a non-adversarial posture. This has included the provision of timely, accurate and verifiable information, as well as appealing to evidence, reason, and a desire to build trust with government officials through such a course of action. Though the rights of the Bahá'ís remain under threat, efforts at the international level have assisted in preventing the complete eradication of the Bahá'í community from the country. Equally important have been bilateral and grassroots initiatives. Indeed, the wide-ranging condemnation from the international community, activists, and, increasingly, ordinary citizens inside Iran have contributed to a decline in outright arrests and imprisonments of Bahá'ís. It has, however, meant that the government of Iran has shifted its tactics to less blatant, though still egregious, forms of persecution, such as economic, educational and cultural repression, fuelled in part by a strategy of anti-Bahá'í propaganda. As has already been described, these more subtle tactics constitute an attempt to conceal the government's ongoing efforts to destroy the Bahá'í community.

26.4.1. Multilateral Reactions

Much of the work on the international stage that has contributed to the protection of the Bahá'ís in Iran has been through the use of UN Charter bodies and the Third Committee of the UN General Assembly, as well through engagement with the Special Rapporteurs appointed to monitor and report on human rights concerns.[125] Rather than claiming 'minority status', the BIC has worked within these mechanisms to secure, on behalf of the Bahá'ís in Iran, the rights guaranteed to every individual.[126] In doing so, it has utilized existing international legal instruments and processes, which define specific rights holders as well as the limits to State action.[127]

124 Berger, 2021, pp. 61–64, see *supra* note 29.

125 Ghanea, 2002, pp. 104–105, see *supra* note 8.

126 Cameron and Ghanea, 2018, p. 170, see *supra* note 43.

127 *Ibid.*

The case of the Bahá'ís in Iran was first brought to the international community by the UN Sub-Commission on Prevention of Discrimination and Protection of Minorities following the 1979 Islamic Revolution in Iran.[128] It was from here that a resolution was adopted expressing "profound concern" for the safety of the Iranian Bahá'ís.[129] In 1982, the first resolution on the situation of the Bahá'ís was adopted by the Human Rights Commission.[130] Such expressions quickly moved up the UN architecture, and, in 1985, the General Assembly identified the government of Iran as a human rights violator.[131] Beyond the significance of this resolution for Bahá'ís, it represented the first occasion where a minority group suffering human rights violations had been specifically delineated in a General Assembly resolution.[132] In the years that followed, the UN Commission on Human Rights, subsequently the HRC, passed more than 20 resolutions that also explicitly mentioned the persecution of the Bahá'ís.[133] This was noteworthy, as references to specific religious communities were unusual at that time and expressions of diplomatic concern by the UN were often of a more general nature when it came to human rights violations and discrimination.[134] It is also significant that virtually all of these resolutions called on Iran to abide by the various international covenants on human rights that the government had freely signed.

The BIC has also worked with Special Rapporteurs who have consistently refuted Iran's denials and confirmed that the oppression of Bahá'ís is extensive, systematic and based on religious prejudice.[135] A 1960 report titled "Study of Discrimination in the Matter of Religious Rights and Practices" initiated by Arcot Krishnaswami, Special Rapporteur of the Sub-Commission on Prevention of Discrimination and Protection of Minorities,[136] opened the door for the engagement of NGOs accredited at the UN on issues related to freedom of religious belief, and provided a foundation for the adoption of resolutions and

128 Ghanea, 2002, p. 105, see *supra* note 8.

129 *Ibid.*

130 *Ibid.*, p. 108.

131 UN General Assembly, Situation of Human Rights in the Islamic Republic of Iran, 116th plenary meeting, UN Doc. A/RES/40/141, 13 December 1985 (https://www.legal-tools.org/doc/ccv46y/). See also Berger, 2021, p. 64, see *supra* note 29.

132 Berger, 2021, p. 64, see *supra* note 29. See also The Bahá'í Question Revisited, p. 72, see *supra* note 25.

133 The Bahá'í Question Revisited, p. 72, see *supra* note 25.

134 *Ibid.*

135 *Ibid.*

136 Arcot Krishnaswami, "Study of Discrimination in the Matter of Religious Rights and Practices", E/CN.4/Sub.2/200/Rev. 1, 1960 (https://www.legal-tools.org/doc/fitlrl/).

mandates condemning forms of discrimination.[137] The appointment of the Human Rights Commission's first Special Rapporteur on the Implementation of the Declaration on the Elimination of all Forms of Intolerance and of Discrimination Based on Religion or Belief in 1986 also contributed to raising awareness around specific country violations.[138] The discourse has also shifted over the years from one focused on eliminating intolerance to one enshrining the right to "a belief".[139] As mentioned earlier, however, there is still much tension surrounding the exact definition and scope of such a right.

The reports of the Special Rapporteur on Freedom of Religion or Belief have continued to be important instruments documenting the experiences of the Bahá'ís. The 2022 report of Ahmed Shaheed, titled "Rights of Persons Belonging to Religious or Belief Minorities in Situations of Conflict or Insecurity",[140] for instance, highlighted the increasing insecurity faced by the Bahá'ís and stressed that "State and non-State actors have exploited the identity of religious or belief minorities to further their political, economic, and military objectives".[141] The report highlighted that Bahá'ís in Iran and, regrettably, also Yemen have been targeted "through hateful rhetoric that seeks to mobilize the public against them and 'legitimize' policies and practices that harm them".[142] The report said that targeting Bahá'ís in this way entrenched widespread "fear, suspicion, and discrimination […] leaving many members of the Bahá'í community feeling more fearful and exposed to violence".[143] His report was also important in offering a number of concrete recommendations which involved an appeal for States to "recall their international human rights obligations towards

[137] See, for instance, Declaration on the Elimination of All Forms of Intolerance, see *supra* note 8; as well as UN General Assembly, Report of the UN High Commissioner for Human Rights on the Expert Workshops on the Prohibition of Incitement to National, Racial or Religious Hatred, UN Doc. A/HRC/22/17/Add.4, 11 January 2013 ('Rabat Plan of Action') (https://www.legal-tools.org/doc/oymwge/); and Istanbul Process, see *supra* note 21 (of which the BIC was directly involved in consultations leading to their adoption).

[138] Ghanea, 2002, p. 120, see *supra* note 8. See also UN Office of the High Commissioner for Human Rights ('OHCHR'), "Special Rapporteur on Freedom of Religion or Belief" (available on the OHCHR's web site). From the outset of the process, the BIC was committed to pushing for this mandate with other like-minded organizations.

[139] Ghanea, 2002, p. 64, see *supra* note 8.

[140] UN General Assembly, Rights of Persons Belonging to Religious or Belief Minorities in Situations of Conflict or Insecurity, UN Doc. A/HRC/49/44, 2 March 2022 ('Rights of Persons Belonging to Religious or Belief Minorities in Situations of Conflict or Insecurity') (https://www.legal-tools.org/doc/o1f68d/).

[141] *Ibid.*, Annex, "Experiences of Persons Belonging to the Baha'i Minority Community in Conditions of Increasing Insecurity".

[142] *Ibid.*

[143] *Ibid.*

religious minorities"[144] including the Bahá'ís; the encouragement of relevant agencies within the UN system to "adopt a more cohesive and coordinated approach"[145] in responding to the situation facing religious minorities; and a call for States and civil society to consider establishing new "platforms" to advocate for the rights of the Bahá'ís.[146]

Beyond efforts specifically directed at the situation of the Bahá'ís, a number of other international mechanisms have played a significant role in advancing dialogue in responding to instances of hate speech on the basis of religious identity. In October 2012, the OHCHR organized a series of workshops which resulted in the Rabat Plan of Action on the prohibition of advocacy of national, racial or religious hatred that constitutes incitement to discrimination, hostility or violence.[147] The Plan recognized how challenging it was to balance the tension between the prohibition of incitement to hatred and the freedom of expression, as well as how necessary it is for domestic legislation to increasingly reflect appropriate standards.[148] The Rabat Plan of Action also indicated that anti-incitement measures at the national level are still "too general, not systematically followed up, lacking focus and deprived of proper impact assessments".[149] Among the policy conclusions, the Rabat Plan of Action was significant in outlining that:

> religious leaders should refrain from using messages of intolerance or expressions which may incite violence, hostility or discrimination; but they also have a crucial role to play in speaking out firmly and promptly against intolerance, discriminatory stereotyping and instances of hate speech.[150]

Beyond this important reference, the Rabat Plan of Action does not articulate direct obligations of religious leaders.

Other instruments have since been developed, some calling for religious leaders to assume a more proactive role in contributing to the creation of cohesive communities. In 2017, building on the Rabat Plan of Action, the UN Human Rights Office hosted a two-day meeting that resulted in the Beirut Declaration

---

144 *Ibid.*

145 *Ibid.*

146 *Ibid.*

147 Rabat Plan of Action, 2013, see *supra* note 137.

148 *Ibid.*, para. 60 which states:

> [I]nternational human rights standards on the prohibition of incitement to national, racial or religious hatred still need to be integrated into domestic legislation and policies in many parts of the world. This explains both the objective difficulty and political sensitivity of defining this concept in a manner that respects the freedom of expression.

149 *Ibid.*, para. 11.

150 *Ibid.*

on Faith for Rights.[151] The declaration reinforced the objectives of the Rabat Plan of Action, outlined that prohibition of incitement is not enough, and added the obligation of "[r]emedial advocacy to reconciliation"[152] as a duty upon religious leaders. As outlined by Ibrahim Salama, Chief of the UN Human Rights Treaties Branch of OHCHR, "[r]ather than focusing on theological and doctrinal divides, the Beirut Declaration favours the identification of common ground among all religions and beliefs to uphold the dignity and worth of all human beings".[153] The declaration was followed by the formulation of 18 commitments on "Faith for Rights".[154] Important as these advances were, there still remained limitations in connecting religious leaders who were themselves perpetrators of human rights standards with the obligations contained in these instruments.

Commenting on the rise in hate speech over the years, in 2019, the UN Secretary-General said:

> Hate speech is a menace to democratic values, social stability and peace. And as a matter of principle, the UN must confront hate speech at every turn. Silence can signal indifference to bigotry and intolerance, even as a situation escalates and the vulnerable become victims.[155]

That year, the UN Strategy and Plan of Action on Hate Speech was launched.[156] This strategy recognized that hate speech has been a precursor to atrocity crimes, including genocide, over the last 75 years and that such speech is, itself, an attack on tolerance, inclusion, diversity, and human rights norms and principles.[157] The UN Strategy and Plan of Action is important in that it recognizes the need to foster peaceful, inclusive and just societies as a strategy to address the root causes and drivers of hate speech, including through the promotion of "intercultural, interfaith and interreligious dialogue and mutual understanding".[158]

In 2021, a further effort to respond to atrocities arising from hate speech included a meeting of the Global Action Against Mass Atrocity Crimes ('GAAMAC'). The meeting was important in articulating the link between

---

151 OHCHR, The Beirut Declaration on "Faith for Rights", 29 March 2017 (https://www.legal-tools.org/doc/k178m1/).

152 *Ibid.*

153 OHCHR, "Beirut Declaration Enhances Role of Religions in Promoting Human Rights", 29 March 2017 (https://www.legal-tools.org/doc/acp88f/).

154 OHCHR, "18 Commitments on "Faith for Rights"", 29 March 2017 (https://www.legal-tools.org/doc/qp9nv2/).

155 United Nations Strategy and Plan of Action on Hate Speech, see *supra* note 1.

156 *Ibid.*

157 *Ibid.*

158 *Ibid.*, p. 4.

deeply rooted prejudices in society and the use of hate speech, which in some instances could even lead to violence and loss of life as ingrained beliefs could cause perpetrators to view the illusory 'other' as less than human.[159]

In addition to instruments that specifically seek to root out hate speech, the UN Secretary-General has more broadly stressed the influence that faith actors can have on values, attitudes, behaviours and actions. Indeed, the case of religious clergy in Iran demonstrates the negative influence such leaders can exert on minority populations. Sadly, religion, whose very reason for being entails service to the cause of unity and peace, has long lent credibility to fanaticism, fuelling shameful outbursts of oppression and violence. Yet, the converse influence is also true. As leaders not only of congregations and worshippers, but also of communities and citizens, the voice of moral authority that religious leaders hold has the potential to move multitudes into positive, constructive action, such as preventing and mitigating atrocities and providing safe spaces for mediation. Recognizing this potential, the UN Office on Genocide Prevention and the Responsibility to Protect published a "Plan of Action for Religious Leaders and Actors to Prevent Incitement to Violence that Could Lead to Atrocity Crimes" ('Fez Plan of Action')[160] in July 2017. In its forward, the UN Secretary-General stated in relation to the need to combat hate speech that "[r]eligious leaders can play a particularly important role in influencing the behaviour of those who share their beliefs".[161] The aim of the Fez Plan of Action has been to prevent incitement to violence, foster interfaith dialogue, strengthen collaboration between faith leaders as well as with the media, establish networks between religious leaders, and build peaceful, inclusive and just societies that respect the full range of human rights.[162]

There have been other developments which, though not explicitly related to hate speech, represent a growing acknowledgement within the UN community of the important role of faith leaders and faith communities in society in addressing present day challenges. Such advances recognize the critical role that religious leaders can play in promoting cohesion across a diversity of groups in

---

159 GAAMAC, "Strengthening National Efforts to Address Hate Speech, Discrimination, and Prevent Incitement: Outcome Document of the Fourth Global Meeting (GAAMAC IV)", 15–18 November 2021, p. 1 (https://www.legal-tools.org/doc/pi26u1/). See, for instance, p. 3:

> [H]ate speech builds on the existence of all forms of prejudice and maximizes their reach. It may incite certain behaviours against constructed figures of the other–who may become an enemy–and incitement may generate a 'license to kill' this despised person who is no longer considered an equal human being.

160 UN Office on Genocide Prevention and the Responsibility to Protect, Fez Plan of Action, 14 July 2017 (https://www.legal-tools.org/doc/8723g7/).

161 *Ibid.*

162 *Ibid.*

society, a point which, as described earlier, is a valuable strategy in addressing the deeper causes of hate speech, namely prejudice. In April 2020, the UN Secretary-General, in his message to mark the start of Ramadan, called on religious leaders to play a key role in addressing the Covid-19 pandemic by working together and translating common values into action.[163] Building on this call, the UN Alliance of Civilizations, the Office on Genocide Prevention and Responsibility to Protect, and the OHCHR organized a virtual consultation one month later, bringing together diverse religious leaders and actors as well as faith-based organizations to discuss possible areas of action and collaboration with the UN in the common fight against the pandemic. This consultation resulted in the Global Pledge for Action, which was designed to advance and reinforce ongoing actions and stimulate new results-oriented activities by religious actors and faith-based organizations to counter the additional challenges posed by the Covid-19 pandemic.[164] Not only do these advances illustrate a heightened recognition within the international community of the role of religious leaders in responding to society's challenges, they also demonstrate the importance of connecting grassroots actors with international plans for their successful realization. Important then will be steps to empower and assist religious leaders to advance the overarching principles and obligations enshrined in the human rights regime, regardless of their familiarity with or even opinion of the numerous types of human rights instruments.

Together, these processes and plans of action recognize that though religion can be used as a means to elicit division and dissention, it has tremendous power to unite. The above-mentioned declarations and commitments have also contributed to a growing emphasis on and awareness of the limits to State control of individual conscience and the need to safeguard minority groups who would otherwise not have redress within their own jurisdiction. Together, they have been significant in ameliorating oppression against the Bahá'ís. As the violations described above have consistently been made known to the world through multilateral bodies and processes, the international community has responded, expressing its desire for the fulfilment of the human rights framework. One can look back to 1955, for instance, when the Shah of Iran heeded entreaties by the UN to stop the rampage against Bahá'ís following hateful radio broadcasts.[165] There is also little doubt that international pressure by the UN, governments and the media helped to curb the wholesale killing of Bahá'ís in the 1980s,

---

163 UN News, "UN Chief Calls for Unity to 'Build a Peaceful World', Ahead of Ramadan", 1 April 2020 (available on its web site).

164 OHCHR, "Global Pledge for Action by Religious Actors and Faith-Based Organizations to Address the COVID-19 Pandemic in Collaboration with the UN", 7 July 2021.

165 The Bahá'í Question Revisited, p. 87, see *supra* note 25.

though unfortunately, efforts by the authorities have continued through more subtle forms of oppression.[166] Significant as all these multilateral initiatives have been, there still is much work to be done by the international community if this religious minority and all who are oppressed within Iran are to be alleviated.

26.4.2. Bilateral Reactions

In addition to efforts by the UN and its subsidiary bodies and agencies, numerous national legislatures and regional bodies have spoken out against Iran's treatment of its Bahá'í community. Expressions of concern for Iran's Bahá'ís have come from the European Council, the European Parliament and from the legislatures of Australia, Brazil, Canada, Spain, the United Kingdom and the United States of America, among others.[167] Many Heads of State and Government have voiced their dismay over Iran's treatment of the Bahá'ís.[168] International and national NGOs have also risen to their defence. Amnesty International, the International Federation for Human Rights, Human Rights Watch and the International Commission of Jurists among other international human rights organizations, for instance, have compiled extensive reports on and called for action to stop the persecution of Iranian Bahá'ís.[169] At the national level, a number of prominent groups and individuals, including human rights lawyers and activists, journalists and filmmakers, as well as religious scholars inside Iran, have condemned, at great personal risk, the government's persecution of the Bahá'ís and are speaking out in support of 'Bahá'í rights' (see, for instance, Figure 5).[170]

166 *Ibid.*

167 See "'Exceptional solidarity': #StopHatePropaganda Reaches 88 Million in Support of Iran's Bahá'ís", *Bahá'í World News Service*, 21 August 2021 ('Exceptional Solidarity').

168 *Ibid.*

169 The Bahá'í Question Revisited, p. 73, see *supra* note 25.

170 *Ibid.*, pp. 73–75; "Nasrin Sotoudeh Speaks About the 7 Baha'i Leaders on the 7th Anniversary of Their Arrest", 20 May 2015 (available on YouTube). Among such individuals, Nobel laureate Shirin Ebadi; Akbar Ganji, a journalist; Ahmad Batebi, a student leader; Nasrin Sotoudeh, a human rights lawyer; Narges Mohammadi, a prominent women's rights activist; Mohammad Nourizad, a journalist and filmmaker; Muhammad Maleki, the first head of Tehran University following the Islamic Revolution; Masumeh Dehghan, an activist; the wife of Abdolfatah Soltani, a well-known lawyer who represented the Yárán; and Jila Baniyaghoob and Issa Saharkhiz, two prominent journalists who were previously in prison. And in May 2016, five prominent Iranian religious scholars – Abdolali Bazargan, Hasan Fereshtian, Mohsen Kadivar, Sedigheh Vasmaghi, and Hasan Yousefi-Eshkevari – published a statement saying that the "followers of the Bahá'í religion have been oppressed because of their religion and beliefs for decades".

Figure 5: In 2015, on the seventh anniversary of the arrest and imprisonment of the seven Iranian Bahá'í leaders, Iranian human rights lawyer Nasrin Sotoudeh bravely recorded a video message calling for their release. "Their sentences are unjust", she said. "It is definitely due to their particular beliefs that they are held in prison". Sotoudeh was herself imprisoned and for a time shared a cell with two of the Bahá'í leaders. She was released in 2013, shortly before Iranian President Hassan Rouhani's visit to the UN that year.

Numerous news media outlets have detailed, confirmed and condemned the persecutions of Iran's Bahá'í community, including Le Monde, the Times of India, the Times of London, the New York Times and the Washington Post, along with regional outlets such as the Daily Vox and the Daily Maverick in South Africa, Folha de São Paulo in Brazil, Today's Zaman in Ankara, Turkey, and the Tribune in Chandigarh, India,[171] as have international radio and television networks such as Al Jazeera, the BBC, CNN and VOA.[172] Moreover, a number of prominent Iranian journalists and commentators, both inside and outside Iran, have recently written articles in defence of their Bahá'í countrymen.[173] In 2013, for instance, Mohammad Nourizad, a former hard-line conservative columnist turned dissident, publicly displayed his regret for past actions by kissing the feet of a young child, whose parents were imprisoned because of their Bahá'í beliefs, and telling him: "My little boy, I apologize to you on behalf of all of those who,

---

[171] The Bahá'í Question Revisited, p. 76, see *supra* note 28. The major wire services, such as the Associated Press, Agence France-Presse, Deutsche Presse-Agentur, and Reuters, have also carried numerous dispatches on the persecution. See also "Why Iran Matters to Africa", *The Daily Vox*, 23 October 2018; and "Iranians Will Never Forget How Archbishop Desmond Tutu Stood up to the Teheran regime", *Daily Maverick*, 13 January 2022.

[172] The Bahá'í Question Revisited, p. 76, see *supra* note 25.

[173] *Ibid.*

in these Islamic years, have made you and your [Bahá'í] fellows face injustice" (see Figure 6).[174]

Figure 6: On 15 July 2013, Mohammad Nourizad kissed the feet of a 4-year-old Bahá'í boy named Artin and apologized for the treatment of the Bahá'ís in Iran.

Beyond such instances, where Iranian activists and journalists have risen up in support of their fellow countrymen, there are also an increasing number of accounts demonstrating that the majority of Iran's general populace do not view the Bahá'í community in the manner that the authorities portray them. Iranians of all religious backgrounds are standing up for the rights of Bahá'ís or taking smaller, day-to-day actions – such as shopping at Bahá'í-owned stores or providing employment to Bahá'ís – demonstrating their solidarity and their expectation that the government should show religious tolerance. Indeed, the BIC continues to receive accounts of Iranians praising the courage, patience and steadfastness of the Bahá'ís, or expressing that the Bahá'í ideals resonate with their vision for a future Iranian society.[175] This is all the more true as many from among the wider population are also suffering some form of oppression within the country – as students and academics, as journalists and social activists, as artists and poets, as progressive thinkers and proponents of women's rights and even as ordinary citizens.[176]

174 "Following Pope's Example, Iranian Dissident Kisses Feet of Baha'i Boy", *Radio Free Europe*, 16 July 2013.

175 Inciting Hatred Special Report, p. 32, see *supra* note 16.

176 *Ibid.*

Together, these expressions of support have been critical, not only in raising awareness about the situation of the Bahá'ís, but in providing a source of solace to Bahá'ís on the ground. Of particular impact has been the support from religious leaders themselves, which, as already described above, is increasingly being recognized as a potent influence in fostering cohesive societies. Among the most notable recent expressions of such support was that of prominent Muslim cleric Ayatollah Abdol-Hamid Masoumi-Tehrani, who illuminated a calligraphic manuscript featuring a quote from the Bahá'í writings as a gift to the Bahá'í world in 2014 (Figure 7).[177] The quote depicts a paragraph from Bahá'u'lláh's *Most Holy Book*, which reads:

> Consort with all religions with amity and concord, that they may inhale from you the sweet fragrance of God. Beware lest amidst men the flame of foolish ignorance overpower you. All things proceed from God and unto Him they return. He is the source of all things and in Him all things are ended.[178]

Ayatollah Masoumi-Tehrani explained on his web site that the calligraphic work was meant to serve as a "reminder of the importance of valuing human beings, of peaceful coexistence, of co-operation and mutual support, and avoidance of hatred, enmity and blind religious prejudice".[179] In 2015, he produced another work of calligraphy featuring a different passage from the Bahá'í writings, and expressed his hope that this act would "raise the conscience of my fellow countrymen by considering increasing their respect for human dignity and not focusing their attention on different ethnicities, languages and religions".[180] These experiences demonstrate the unique and powerful role religious leaders can play in building cohesive and resilient societies, and in countering calls to division and violence.

[177] The Bahá'í Question Revisited, p. 77, see *supra* note 25.

[178] Bahá'u'lláh, *Most Holy Book*, Baha'i World Centre, Haifa, 1992, para. 144, p. 72.

[179] The Bahá'í Question Revisited, p. 77, see *supra* note 25.

[180] *Ibid.*

Figure 7: Ayatollah Abdol-Hamid Masoumi-Tehrani perfecting an illuminated work of calligraphy. The words used in this piece are from the writings of Bahá'u'lláh.

26.4.2.1. The Worldwide Bahá'í Community's Response

Parallel to the efforts described above, national Bahá'í communities across the world have set up systems and processes to approach their governments, inform them of the situation of the Bahá'ís in Iran and ask for support in their defence. The co-ordinated and decentralized structure of the administration of the worldwide Bahá'í community – guided by the global governing body of the Bahá'í Faith, the Universal House of Justice – has enabled the development of a coherent strategy unfolding at the national and local levels, simultaneously reinforcing efforts on the international level. That same structure and system of co-ordination has also facilitated the efficient gathering and dissemination of verifiable information.[181] Other systems and processes within the Bahá'í community are dedicated to building capacity within Bahá'í institutions, communities and individuals to engage meaningfully and constructively in dialogue with those around them on matters of social import. Discussions on freedom of religious belief and the protection of the Bahá'ís in Iran have naturally formed part of these endeavours.[182] To this end, national affiliates have been working closely with government officials at the national level.[183] Bahá'í communities have been developing multimedia content to generate attention and have been supporting

[181] Berger, 2021, p. 62, see *supra* note 29.

[182] *Ibid.*

[183] *Ibid.*

worldwide awareness campaigns.[184] And local Bahá'ís have been involved in calling elected representatives, asking them to support relevant resolutions and declarations by national governing bodies regarding Iran's adherence to human rights conventions or treatment of its Bahá'í community. They also work with members of interfaith and human rights groups to bring awareness to the issue. It is this co-ordinated collective effort, including the interplay between grassroots action by individual Bahá'ís and communities together with the advocacy work carried out at the national and international levels, that forms the heart of the Bahá'í community's strategy and approach to advocacy.[185]

The framework for action that guides these endeavours also informs the broader efforts of the worldwide Bahá'í community to work towards the social, spiritual and material betterment of their societies. Whether through the holding of prayer gatherings open to all, the provision of moral education programmes, the creation of spaces to engage in meaningful dialogue on matters of social import, or the design and implementation of initiatives aimed at bringing about the social and material well-being of their communities, local Bahá'í communities across the globe are labouring at the grassroots to effect positive social transformation. All of these efforts are taking shape in concert with groups and individuals who are concerned about the betterment of their communities, irrespective of religion, race, gender or social background. These acts, carried out with the intention of contributing to the advancement of society, have had a positive synchronicity with efforts to dispel misinformation about the Bahá'ís and have contributed to building goodwill with public officials. By viewing first-hand the character and society-building approach of Bahá'í communities, many have come to acknowledge their contributions and to mobilize accordingly in support of their defence.

A few cases are worth briefly noting as an illustration of some of the efforts of Bahá'í communities to contribute to the promotion of cohesion within their societies. In Iraq, the Bahá'í community arranged a number of high-level public events together with other collaborators, with the aim of promoting peace, co-existence and the preservation of historical sites.[186] In Jordan, like many other countries, the Bahá'í community has focused on the empowerment of young adolescents.[187] Bahá'ís in Jordan are also increasingly being invited into

[184] See for instance Exceptional Solidarity, see *supra* note 167; "'Education Is Not a Crime' Gains Momentum", *Bahá'í World News Service*, 8 February 2015 (available on its web site); and "'Five Years Too Many' Campaign Gathers Momentum", *Bahá'í World News Service*, 12 May 2013 (available on its web site).

[185] Cameron and Ghanea, 2018, p. 180, see *supra* note 43.

[186] *Ibid.*, p. 180.

[187] *Ibid.*, p. 179.

civil society spaces to engage in dialogue, including with government officials, on matters related to conflict resolution, interfaith collaboration, citizenship and freedom of belief.[188] And, in Canada, the community has been involved in supporting refugees, especially those Bahá'ís fleeing persecution from Iran. This work has focused on integrating arrivals into their new societies, while offering to public discourse a framework on how newly resettled individuals can become beneficial resources contributing to the social fabric of the community.[189]

At the heart of the framework guiding the endeavours of the Bahá'í community is the principle of the oneness of humankind. Importantly, an appreciation of this principle contains within it the essential concept of diversity, which embraces the wealth of insight that can come from the harmonious interaction and collaboration between diverse perspectives and backgrounds. An implication of an appreciation of humanity's oneness necessitates constructive and unifying alternatives to adversarial forms of social change, such as violent protest and upheaval. Another implication of this acceptance involves a refusal to adopt any partisan or political agenda, which are often the source of divisiveness in society. These principles find expression in the manner in which Bahá'ís interact with and respond to the institutions of society, through a posture of obedience to one's government.[190] Such a posture of obedience, however, is not to be conflated with absolute agreement or promotion of political principles and policies, and Bahá'ís are forbidden from denying their faith. It is also not to be confused with passivity or an indifference to gross human rights violations. Indeed, such a posture does not preclude individual Bahá'ís from expressing their views in public, building coalitions with like-minded and sympathetic civil society actors, or seeking legal recourse when their rights have been infringed. It does not prevent them from highlighting standards to which governments are expected to adhere in safeguarding the interests of the citizens, which they hold in trust.[191] Recognizing the authority of government to advance the well-being of the nation, and responding in obedience to it, places an ever greater corollary duty on government to carry out its mandated responsibilities with increased vigour and fidelity.[192] In pursuit of transforming society, then, Bahá'ís recognize the paramount importance of redefining the nature of interactions between individuals,

---

188 *Ibid.*

189 Geoffrey Cameron, "The Bahá'í Community and Public Policy: The Bahá'í Refugee Resettlement Program (1981–1989)", in Geoffrey Cameron and Benjamin Schewel (eds.), *Religion and Public Discourse in an Age of Transition: Reflections on Bahá'í Practice and Thought*, Wilfrid Laurier University Press, Ontario, 2018, p. 266.

190 Cameron and Ghanea, 2018, p. 182, see *supra* note 43.

191 *Ibid.*, p. 182.

192 *Ibid.*, p. 174.

as well as between individuals and the governing institutions of society, as a critical component of the realization of justice.

26.4.2.2. The Bahá'í Community in Iran's Response to Persecution

As for those who are facing persecution directly, the Bahá'ís in Iran are not dispirited, demoralized or downtrodden. They, too, are working to apply, within their own context, the framework for action guiding the affairs and initiatives of the worldwide Bahá'í community, including its non-adversarial approach characterized by the principle of the oneness of humankind.[193] This orientation finds its origins in Bahá'u'lláh's example upon being exiled to Baghdad, and exhortations that his followers exemplify kindness and concern for their community.[194] It was this posture that contributed directly to the building of trust among sympathetic government officials at that time.[195] The Bahá'í community's concern for advancing the well-being of their societies continued to take shape in the late 1800s and early 1900s. These efforts included contributions to modern medicine in Iran, the development of modern schooling, as well as an increase in literacy levels, especially among young girls.[196]

The global governing body of the worldwide Bahá'í community, the Universal House of Justice, has described the response of this community in terms of "constructive resilience",[197] a response to oppression that seeks "neither to succumb in resignation nor to take on the characteristics of the oppressor".[198] Such a posture is not one of passivity or blind acceptance, but rather one of seeing in adversity an opportunity to contribute to the betterment of society.[199] A notable example of this kind of constructive response was the creation of the Bahá'í Institute for Higher Education ('BIHE'), an *ad hoc*, alternative university set up by the Iranian Bahá'í community to provide young Bahá'ís access to higher education, from which they had otherwise been barred by the

193 The Bahá'í Question Revisited, pp. 80–81, see *supra* note 25; Michael Karlberg, "Constructive Resilience: The Bahá'í Response to Oppression", in *Peace & Change*, 2010, vol. 35, No. 2, pp. 222–257.

194 Firaydoun Javaheri, "Constructive Resilience", in *Journal of Bahá'í Studies*, 2018, vol. 28, No. 4, p. 11. See also Cameron and Ghanea, 2018, p. 174, *supra* note 43.

195 *Ibid.*

196 *Ibid.* See also BIC, Office of Social Development, "For the Betterment of the World: The Worldwide Bahá'í Community's Approach to Social and Economic Development", 2018, p. 3 (available on its web site).

197 See Universal House of Justice, "To the Bahá'í Students Deprived of Access to Higher Education in Iran", 9 September 2007 (available on its web site). See also Universal House of Justice, "To the Bahá'ís of Iran", 14 May 2011 ('To the Bahá'ís of Iran') (available on its web site); and Karlberg, 2010, p. 35, see *spra* note 193.

198 See To the Bahá'ís of Iran, *supra* note 197.

199 Javaheri, 2018, p. 12, see *supra* note 194.

government.[200] Using correspondence courses and, later, online study offering university-level programmes in 17 academic subjects, the BIHE sought to provide the substance of a fully-fledged university education for the thousands of Bahá'í youth who were otherwise excluded from higher learning.[201] The government's response, however, was to try to shut down the initiative through raids, arrests, and, in 2011, the long term imprisonment of key faculty and staff as the efforts were cast as a "conspiracy against national security".[202] Yet, the BIHE's commitment to high academic standards, international collaboration, the pursuit of knowledge and truth, and an innovative teaching and learning environment was increasingly recognized internationally, and many of its graduates have been accepted into graduate-level programmes in other countries.[203] The initiative demonstrates a response characterized not by defiance, but rather by thoughtful collective self-empowerment and peaceful determination.[204]

Beyond efforts to improve their own welfare, the Bahá'ís of Iran, in the midst of oppression aimed at their very eradication, have been working for the betterment of Iranian society more broadly.[205] Students who have been denied access to education in Iran and forced to study abroad, for instance, have returned to assist in the development of their country.[206] Others have initiated, within the means available to them, social and economic development projects aimed at helping their fellow citizens, such as offering kindergarten education and tutorial programmes, as well as providing humanitarian assistance in the wake of disaster, for instance, following the earthquake in East Azerbaijan in 2012.[207] Still, others have contributed to public discourse on human rights, on subjects such as expanded civil rights or the removal of obstacles to the full participation of women, minorities, and other marginalized groups, all in a manner that avoids polarization.[208] Sadly, many of these initiatives to contribute to Iranian society have been met with resistance. Many individuals have been arrested, and their efforts portrayed as revolutionary acts of dissent.[209]

200 The Bahá'í Question Revisited, pp. 80–81, see *supra* note 25; and Karlberg, 2010, pp. 222–257, see *supra* note 193.

201 The Bahá'í Question Revisited, pp. 34, see *supra* note 25.

202 *Ibid.*

203 *Ibid.*

204 Javaheri, 2018, p. 13, see *supra* note 194. See also "Iran Closes 'University' Run Covertly by the Bahá'ís", *New York Times*, 29 October 1998, which called the efforts of the BIHE "an elaborate act of communal self-preservation".

205 *Ibid.*, p. 3.

206 *Ibid.*, p. 54.

207 *Ibid.*

208 Cameron and Ghanea, 2018, pp. 170 and 176, see *supra* note 43.

209 The Bahá'í Question Revisited, p. 80, see *supra* note 25.

By refusing to deny one's faith and seeking integration in Iranian society through active participation in civic life, the Bahá'ís have consistently worked to claim equal citizenship and the requisite rights to which every Iranian citizen is entitled. Instead of simply appealing for minority status, which reinforces norms and notions of separateness, the Bahá'ís in Iran call for the full recognition of their rights within a society to which they belong, and to which they are deeply committed.[210] The Bahá'ís of Iran, like their co-religionists around the world, respond in this manner because they are seeking to build a new and peaceful world, where means and ends are always in coherence.

26.5. Conclusion

The protection of the freedom of religion or belief must entail vigilance in safeguarding citizens from the forces of prejudice and corrupt forms of power, including from extreme orthodoxy. Hate speech and the incitement to violence, extremism, hostility, or even worse, atrocity crimes on the basis of religion, must be forcefully sanctioned and unreservedly condemned.

In many respects, the Bahá'í case demonstrates how the international human rights machinery, combined with support from civil society advocates, and accurate coverage from the news media, can be used to protect an oppressed minority. Thanks to international support for the Bahá'ís, along with growing support inside Iran and among Iranian expatriates, the Bahá'í community has been shielded from some of the most extreme attacks planned against it. History has shown that continued international pressure is the best method of restraining the Iranian government from acting on deeply held prejudices against Bahá'ís. The last three decades have proven that Iranian authorities are indeed cognizant of international opinion and that pressure to meet their obligations under international human rights law can have an effect.

Yet, these efforts, necessary as they are, are insufficient. The Bahá'í community in Iran still suffers oppression, and could continue to do so to even greater degrees were it not for the measures already taken. If the Islamic Republic of Iran is not held accountable, this ongoing campaign of State-sponsored hatred and religious persecution could easily lead to escalating violence and even the potential resumption of the executions that the Bahá'ís suffered in the 1980s.[211]

As of this writing, many Bahá'ís are currently in prison for their religious beliefs, and a greater number are out on bail or awaiting trial on fabricated charges. The government of Iran's systematic persecution of the Bahá'ís spans three generations, now affecting the grandchildren of children who were

[210] Cameron and Ghanea, 2018, pp. 170 and 172, see *supra* note 43.

[211] Inciting Hatred Special Report, p. 5, see *supra* note 16.

imprisoned or killed in the 1980s. The question remains: can the international community prevent its impact on another generation?

As for the government of Iran itself, if its leaders are sincere in desiring to open a new chapter in its international relations, there is no better indicator than bringing a swift end to the decades-long persecution of its Bahá'í minority. Concrete signs of such a move could include informing the world that the 1991 Bahá'í Question memorandum has been rescinded – and calling for an end to incitement of hatred against Bahá'ís. Another indicator would be Iranian diplomats candidly addressing the discrimination against their Bahá'í citizens, rather than denying that it occurs or refusing to discuss the topic, as is often the case currently. Bahá'ís desire no special privileges and have no political aspirations. They only wish to be free to worship as they choose and to contribute to the betterment of society in their native land.

The international human rights framework will also need to be further developed. As has already been described, there are numerous mechanisms that have helped provide relief to the Bahá'ís, but those who carry out such violations often do not accept the values enshrined in international instruments. And in a country where the government itself, despite being a party to these agreements, does not actively translate these principles into domestic law to be upheld by the courts, there is little recourse. Empowering religious leaders to advance the overarching principles and obligations enshrined in the human rights regime, irrespective of their familiarity with the numerous instruments, then, will be an important aspect of a strategy for combating hate speech.

As long as prejudice, on whatever basis, is normalized and allowed to take root in society, these incidents will continue. Complementing these measures to combat hate speech, then, must be efforts to overcome prejudice in society. As described, faith communities and religious leaders have tremendous power in this regard, and the formalization of international instruments recognizing this fact has been an important advancement and will no doubt need to continue to evolve. The endeavours of such communities, working to cultivate cohesive values in society between different groups, must continue to be showcased as examples of best practice and further supported and promoted. The efforts of the Bahá'í community with their collaborators are but one example of diverse populations working together to redefine patterns of relationships within society based on a fundamental appreciation of humanity's oneness. These responses recognize that the most enduring of remedies must embrace diversity as an essential element of this appreciation and that change must ultimately be effected in the human heart. Together, these strategies can serve to reinforce and develop the international human rights framework in a way that ensures humanity's noblest aspirations find actionable expression and are applied ever more consistently and universally.

SECTION G: INTERNAL MEASURES AVAILABLE TO RELIGIOUS LEADERS

27

How Should Responsible Religious Leaders React to Hate Speech in Their Community?

Mohamed Elewa Badar and Rana Moustafa Essawy*

27.1. Introduction

While religious leaders were commonly referred to as inciters of hatred, their significant role as human rights actors has been receiving increased attention in the last decade. In 2012, the Rabat Plan of Action on the prohibition of advocacy of national, racial or religious hatred that constitutes incitement to discrimination, hostility or violence – a result of four regional expert workshops organized by the United Nations ('UN') Office of the High Commissioner for Human Rights ('OHCHR') in 2011 – articulated three core responsibilities for religious leaders in combatting hate speech:

> (a) Religious leaders should refrain from using messages of intolerance or expressions which may incite violence, hostility or discrimination; (b) Religious leaders also have a crucial role to play in speaking out firmly and promptly against intolerance, discriminatory stereotyping and instances of hate speech; and (c) Religious

* Professor **Mohamed Elewa Badar** holds the Chair in Comparative and International Criminal Law at Northumbria University, Newcastle. His recent work on adjudicating hate propaganda before international criminal tribunals, hate speech as a crime against humanity of persecution, and the criminalization of *takfir* and incitement to religious hatred appear in the *International Criminal Law Review*, *International Journal of Human Rights*, and *Nordic Journal of Human Rights*. He is the Chief Editor of the Arabic version of the commentary in Lexsitus (https://cilrap-lexsitus.org/ar/clicc), and the Regional Liaison Officer for the Middle East and North Africa, War Crimes Committee of the International Bar Association. **Rana Moustafa Essawy** is Assistant Professor of Public International Law at the Faculty of Law, Alexandria University, Egypt. Her thesis 'The Doctrine of Implied Powers in International Law' (in Arabic) was awarded the Boutrous Boutrous-Ghali prize for the second-best Ph.D. in Egypt for 2018–19. She has published on various subjects of international law. Her most recent publication is "Human Rights, Pandemics, and the Infrastructure of Human Rights Institutions", in Christopher Sabatini (ed.), *Reclaiming Human Rights in a Changing World Order*, Chatham House-Brookings Institution, 2022, pp. 93–119. For an audio-visual recording of Professor Badar's presentation to CILRAP's conference in Florence in April 2022 on the topic of this anthology, please see https://www.cilrap.org/cilrap-film/220409-badar/. The authors would like to thank Mr. Hossam Ed-Deen Allam for his very valuable input. There are no words to express our gratitude to the Director of CILRAP, Morten Bergsmo, and his great team for the time and energy they invested in making this giant project a success.

> leaders should be clear that violence can never be tolerated as a response to incitement to hatred (for example, violence cannot be justified by prior provocation).[1]

Building on that, faith-based and civil society actors working in the field of human rights gathered in Beirut on 28 and 29 March 2017. This resulted in the formulation of 18 commitments by which the participating religious actors have undertaken to take actions to combat hate speech that constitutes incitement to discrimination, hostility and violence. Among those actions, religious leaders have pledged to: (i) revisit religious interpretations that appear to condone or trigger hate speech; (ii) stand up for the rights of all persons belonging to minorities; (iii) publicly denounce all instances of advocacy of hatred that incites to violence, discrimination or hostility; (iv) monitor interpretations, determinations or other religious views that manifestly conflict with universal human rights norms and standards; and (v) refine the curricula, teaching materials and textbooks.[2]

It is the purpose of this chapter to concretize those actions and to sketch out other measures that could be used by religious leaders in combatting hate speech within their communities. This will be done through a commonsensical approach, which observes the various roles assumed by religious leaders, deducing the measures that they could use to combat hate speech. It is necessary to emphasize in this context that this chapter will focus on religious leaders in Muslim communities, owing to the authors' religious identity. Nevertheless, we share the Beirut participants' deep conviction that "all respective religions and beliefs share a common commitment to upholding the dignity and the equal worth of all human beings",[3] and thus we believe that the internal measures suggested in this chapter can be generalized to be used by religious leaders belonging to other religions.

Before sketching out the internal measures that could be used by religious leaders to combat hate speech in Muslim communities, it is necessary to clarify that the rights and duties in Islámic law originate in the *Qur'án* and in the authentic *Sunnah* of the Prophet of Islám (the Prophet Muḥammad).

Islámic law ('*Sharí'ah*') is rooted in the political, legal and social structures of all Islámic states and is the standard of governance in all Islámic

---

1 Annex to the Report of the UN High Commissioner for Human Rights on the Expert Workshops on the Prohibition of Incitement to National, Racial or Religious Hatred, UN Doc. A/HRC/22/17/Add.4, 11 January 2011 (https://www.legal-tools.org/doc/oymwge/).

2 OHCHR, 18 Commitments on "Faith for Rights", 29 March 2017 (https://www.legal-tools.org/doc/qp9nv2/).

3 OHCHR, Beirut Declaration on "Faith for Rights", 29 March 2017 (https://www.legal-tools.org/doc/k178m1/).

nations.[4] Often considered by both Muslims and Orientalists as the archetype of the Islámic way of life, it has been described as the core and kernel of Islám itself.[5] Other commentators, however, critique what they consider to be the over-emphasis placed on the legal foundations of the Islámic religion, and do not believe Islám was meant to be as much of a law-based religion as it has often been portrayed to be.[6] In any case, Islámic law, one of the world's recognized legal systems,[7] is a particularly instructive example of a 'sacred law' and draws such significant contrast with other legal systems that its study is imperative to adequately appreciating the full range of possible legal phenomena.[8]

Islámic law, like Roman law, used to be a 'jurist law', a product of neither legislative authority nor case law, but rather a creation of the classical jurists who elaborated on the sacred Islámic texts.[9] This changed, however, with the advent of Islámic codification in the mid-nineteenth century, transforming it into a 'statutory law' promulgated by a national territorial legislature.[10]

Islámic law has evolved over many centuries of juristic effort into a subtle, complex and highly developed reality which, not necessarily monolithic, is reflective of the pluralistic nature of human society.[11] Such complexity does not, however, make Islámic law indeterminable[12] and the diverging legal opinions contained therein might be viewed as "different manifestations of the same divine will" which form "a diversity within unity".[13] Seventy-five per cent of the legal conclusions attributed to the four Sunní schools of Islámic law – namely, *Ḥanafí*, *Malikí*, *Shafi'í* and *Ḥanbalí* – are identical, while the remaining

4 See Hamid Enayat, *Modern Islamic Political Thought*, University of Texas Press, 1982; Albert Hourani, *Arabic Thought in the Liberal Age: 1798–1939*, Cambridge University Press, 1983; Wael B. Hallaq, *A History of Islamic Legal Theory: An Introduction to Sunní Úṣúl-al Fiqh*, Cambridge University Press, 1997, p. 202.

5 Joseph Schacht, *An Introduction to Islamic Law*, Clarendon Press, 1964, p. 1.

6 Mohammad Hashim Kamali, *Shari'ah Law: An Introduction*, Oneworld Publications, 2008, p. 18.

7 See René David and John Brierley, *Major Legal Systems in the World Today*, Free Press, 1978, p. 421.

8 Schacht, 1964, p. 2, see *supra* note 5.

9 Aharon Layish, "The Transformation of the *Sharí'ah* from Jurists' Law to Statutory Law", in *Die Welt des Islams*, 2004, vol. 44, no. 85, p. 86; see also Farooq A. Hassan, "The Sources of Islamic Law", in *Proceedings of the American Society of International Law Annual Meeting*, 1982, vol. 76, no. 65, p. 65.

10 *Ibid.*, p. 86.

11 Mashood A. Baderin, *International Human Rights and Islamic Law*, Oxford University Press, 2005, pp. 32–33.

12 *Ibid.*, pp 32–33.

13 *Ibid.*, p. 431, referring to Mohammad Hashim Kamali, *Principles of Islamic Jurisprudence*, Islamic Texts Society, 1991, p. 169 and Hallaq, 1997, p. 202, see *supra* note 4.

questions and variances within a single family of explainers of the *Qur'án* and the prophetic *Sunnah* are traceable to methodological differences in understanding or authenticating the primary textual evidence.[14]

Islámic law, like other legal systems, has its 'sources' ('*al-máṣádir*'); it also has its 'guiding principles' ('*al- 'úṣúl*') that dictate the nature of its 'evidence' ('*al-adillah*'); it equally employs the use of 'legal maxims' ('*al-qáwa'id al-fiqhíyyah*') and utilizes a number of underlying 'objectives' ('*al-maqáṣid*') to underpin the structure of its legal theory.[15] For example, the doctrine of *máṣlaḥah* is considered to be fundamental to the enduring realization of Islámic ideals. Directly translating to 'benefit' or 'welfare', the doctrine pursues the objectives of promotion of human welfare and prevention of harm, both in the sense of ensuring the collective well-being of the Muslim community and in the sense of protecting the human rights of its individual members.[16] Ash-Sháṭibí conceives the doctrine in three hierarchical categories; at the top, indispensable – or fundamental – benefits ('*ḍárúríyyát*'): the protection of life, religion, intellect, family and property; supplemented by necessary benefits ('*ḥajiyyat*'), those which make life tolerable but are not indispensable to the endurance of society; and finally, improvement benefits ('*taḥsiníyyat*') which ameliorate the enjoyment of life.[17]

The doctrine of *máṣlaḥah* provides the "basis of rationality and extendibility of Islamic law to changing circumstances (and also) as a fundamental principle of the universality and certainty of Islámic law".[18] As pronounced by Kamali:

> The doctrine of *maṣlaḥah* is broad enough to encompass within its fold a variety of objectives, both ideal and pragmatic, to nurture the standards of good government and to help develop the much-needed public confidence in the authority of statutory legislation in Muslim societies. The doctrine of *maṣlaḥah* can strike balance between the highly idealistic levels of expectation from the government on the part of the public and the efforts of the latter to identify more meaningfully with Islam.[19]

14 Ahmad ibn Naqib al-Misri, *Reliance of the Traveller: A Classic Manual of Islamic Sacred Law 'Umdat al-Salik*, Nuh Ha Mim Keller (ed. and trans.), Amana Publications, Ellicott City, 1994, p. vii.

15 Gavin Picken (ed.), *Islamic Law*, 4 vols., Routledge, London, 2010.

16 Baderin, 2005, pp. 42–43 see *supra* note 11.

17 See *ibid.*, p. 44.

18 Muhammad Khalid Masud, *Shatibi's Philosophy of Islamic Law*, Islamic Research Institute, Islamabad, 1995, p. viii.

19 Mohammad Hashim Kamali, "Have We Neglected the Shariah Law Doctrine of Maṣlaḥah", in *Islamic Studies*, 1988, vol. 27, no. 4, pp. 287–288.

The term 'Islámic law' encompasses the entire system of law and jurisprudence associated with the religion of Islám. It is comprised of two parts, namely, the primary sources of law (*Sharí'ah* in the strict legal sense) and the subordinate sources of law, that is, the methodology used to deduce and apply the law (Islámic jurisprudence, or '*fiqh*').[20] *Sharí'ah* translates literally to 'pathway',[21] and its original articulation and implementation denoted the road to the watering place or path leading to the water, that is, the way to the source of life.[22] It governs all public and private behaviour, as well as legal aspects.[23] The word '*Sharí'ah*' occurs once in the *Qur'án*: "Thus, We put thee On the (right) way [*sharī'atan*] Of Religion: so follow Thou that (Way) and follow not the [whimsical] desires [*hawā*] of those who know not [or 'have no knowledge']" (*Qur'án*, 45:18).[24]

Sharí'ah is derived directly from the *Qur'án* and the *Sunnah*, which are considered by Muslims to be of divine revelation and thus comprise the immutable part of Islámic law, while *fiqh* was produced from human reasoning. Zahraa discusses the sacrosanctity and exhaustiveness of the divine revelation:

> Muslim jurists throughout history have not been concerned with establishing a particular field or science or even theory – to them, the divine sources are comprehensive enough to encompass any possible human action, conduct or transaction.[25]

However, it is important to note the belief of the *Shí'ah* – in contrast to that of the *Sunní* – that divine revelation continued to be transmitted after the Prophet's death, by means of their recognized religious leaders ('*Imáms*'),[26] whose infallible pronouncements are thus considered to be part of divine revelation.[27]

---

[20] Baderin, 2005, pp. 32–34, see *supra* note 11. Some scholars use the terms Islámic law, *Sharí'ah* and *fiqh* interchangably; for example, Kamali consideres *Sharí'ah* to also include *fiqh*; see Kamali, 2008, p. 1, *supra* note 6; see also *ibid.*, pp. 287–288.

[21] Irshad Abdal-Haqq, "Islamic Law: An Overview of its Origin and Elements", in *Islamic Law and Culture*, 2002, vol. 7, no. 4, referring to Abdur Rahim, *The Principles of Islamic Jurisprudence,* Kitab Bhavan, New Delhi, 1994, p. 389.

[22] Francis Robinson, *Atlas of the Islamic World Since 1500*, Phaidon Press, Oxford, 1982, p. 320.

[23] Abdullah S. Alarefi, "Overview of Islamic Law", in *International Criminal Law Review*, 2009, vol. 9, no. 707, pp. 707–8; Schacht, 1964, pp. 1–5, see *supra* note 5.

[24] This chapter uses the English translation of the *Qur'án* by Abdullah A. Yūsuf 'Alī, Lahore, 1937, unless otherwise noted.

[25] Mahdi Zahraa, "Characteristic Features of Islamic Law: Perceptions and Misconceptions", in *Arab Law Quarterly*, 2000, vol. 15, no. 168, p. 171.

[26] Kamali, 2008, p. 88, see *supra* note 6.

[27] *Ibid.*, p. 88.

For Muslims, the *Qur'án* is the embodiment of the words of God as revealed to the Prophet Muḥammad through the angel Gabriel. It is the seminal source of Islámic law, in which all other sources are rooted.[28] However, far from being a textbook of jurisprudence, it is rather a book of guidance on all aspects of the life of every Muslim:[29] "We have sent down to thee the Book explaining All things, a Guide, a Mercy, And Glad Tidings to Muslims" (*Qur'án* 16:89).

The *Qur'án* comprises more than six thousand verses ('*ayat*').[30] There is a lack of consensus among jurists as to how many consist of legal subject-matter, with differing methods of classification employed for determining what constitutes a legal verse – estimates range from 80 up to 800 verses.[31] The legal verses are not confined to their own separate chapter ('*súráh*') but are scattered throughout the *Qur'án*, enunciated alongside verses about belief, general behaviour, the nature of existence or the history of bygone peoples. A particular judgement may occur on multiple occasions and in different styles, deepening and broadening a believer's understanding of the reiterated rule.[32]

The *Qur'án* is an indivisible whole, a guide to be accepted and followed in its entirety.[33] It was revealed incrementally over a period of 23 years, culminating with the demise of the Prophet Muḥammad in 632 CE. To properly understand its legislation, one must take into consideration the *Sunnah* as well as the circumstances and the context that existed at the time of the revelation. According to the common understanding of Muslims, the secondary source of Islámic law comprises the sayings and practices of the Prophet Muḥammad, or the *Sunnah*, collected in *ḥadíṯh*.[34] While the *Qur'án* is believed to be of manifest revelation, that is, the direct words of God conveyed to the Prophet Muḥammad through the angel Gabriel, the *Sunnah* falls into the category of internal revelation, that is, concepts inspired by God but conveyed through the Prophet Muḥammad's own words.[35]

---

[28] Alarefi, 2009, pp. 709–10, see *supra* note 23.

[29] Muhammed S. El-Awa, "Approaches to Sharí'a: A Response to NJ Coulson's A History of Islamic Law", in *Journal of Islamic Studies*, 1991, vol. 2, no. 143, p. 146.

[30] 6239 verses, M. Cherif Bassiouni, *The Shari'a and Post-Conflict Justice*, 2010, p. 15; 6235 verses, Kamali, 2008, see *supra* note 6; 6666 verses, Abdal-Haqq, 2002, p. 27, see *supra* note 21.

[31] There are 80 legal verses according to Coulson, 120 according to Bassiouni, 350 according to Kamali, 500 according to Ghazali, 800 according to Ibn al-'Árábí, while according to Shawkani any calclulation can only amount to a rough estimate.

[32] El-Awa, 1991, p.146, see *supra* note 29.

[33] Kamali, 2008, p. 22, see *supra* note 6.

[34] El-Awa, 1991, p. 153, see *supra* note 29.

[35] Kamali, 2008, p. 18, see *supra* note 6.

The *Sunnah* complements the *Qur'án* as a source for understanding the divine will, as the *Qur'án* itself explicates: "take what the Apostle [or 'Messenger'] Assigns to you, and deny Yourselves that which he Withholds from you [or 'has forbidden to you']" (*Qur'án* 59:7).

The *Qur'án* authorizes the Prophet Muḥammad to take legal decisions in response to the developments in the Muslim community and delegates to him the task of explaining the judgements of the *Qur'án*:[36]

> Judge thou between them by what God hath revealed and follow not their vain desires (*Qur'án* 5:49);
>
> But no by thy Lord they can have no (real) Faith until they make thee judge in all disputes between them and find in their souls no resistance against thy decisions but accept them with the fullest conviction [or 'complete submission'] (*Qur'án* 4:65).

Where an issue is not specifically addressed in either the *Qur'án* or the *Sunnah*, the Prophet mandated the exercise of sound reasoning to reach a judgement.[37] When appointing a judge to Yemen, the Prophet asked him:

> "According to what shalt thou judge?" He replied: "According to the Book of Allah. And if thou findest nought therein? According to the Sunnah of the Prophet of Allah. And if thou findest nought therein? Then I will exert myself to form my own judgement." [The Prophet replied] "Praise be to God Who had guided the messenger of His Prophet to that which pleases His Prophet."[38]

This concept of using reason to determine a matter of law ('*ijtihad*') is the essence of *'úṣúl al-fiqh*, a legal method of ranking the sources of law, their interaction, interpretation and application.[39] The result of this method is *fiqh*, which literally means human understanding and knowledge, developed by means of deduction in applying the prescriptions of the *Sharí'ah* in real or hypothetical cases.[40] As such, it does not command the same authority as that of the *Sharí'ah* and its employment lacks uniformity among the *Sunní* and *Shí'ah* traditions, who adopt differing scholarly and methodological approaches.[41]

In the formative period of Islámic law, the science of *'úṣúl al-fiqh* did not yet exist as a branch of intellectual endeavour in its own right and the sources

36 El-Awa, 1991, p. 147, see *supra* note 29.

37 Abdal-Haqq, 2002, p. 35, see *supra* note 21.

38 Said Ramadan, *Islamic Law Its Scope and Equity*, 2nd ed., P.R. Macmillan, London, 1970, p. 75.

39 Kamali, 1991, p. 469, see *supra* note 13.

40 Kamali, 2008, pp. 40–41, see *supra* note 6.

41 Bassiouni, 2010, p. 10, see *supra* note 30.

of Islámic law were not determinatively hierarchized.[42] With time, the *Qur'án*'s primacy over the *Sunnah* became almost universally recognized, followed next in the hierarchy by *'ijma'* and *qiyas*, the two main proofs of law attained through human reasoning.

When the *Qur'án* and the *Sunnah* do not provide an answer on an issue, learned jurists must reach a consensus of opinion ('*'ijma'*'), a practice established by the companions of the Prophet ('*aṣ-Ṣáḥabah*').[43] *'Ijma'* is a rational proof of *Sharí'ah* and, due to its binding nature, in theory it mandates absolute and universal consensus; however, in practice, it has often also been claimed for rulings reached through majority consensus.[44]

Qiyas is the application of a *Sharí'ah* value or ruling from an original case to a new case, not found in the *Qur'án*, the *Sunnah* nor a definite *'ijma'*, on the grounds that the new case has the same effective cause as the original one.[45] An example of *qiyas* is the extension of the prohibition of wine to a prohibition of any drug that causes intoxication, because the prevention of intoxication is the effective cause of the original prohibition.[46] Other methods include *is istiḥsan* ('equity' in Islámic law), *máṣlaḥah mursalah* ('considerations of public interest'), *'urf* ('custom') and *istiṣḥab* ('presumption of continuity').[47]

There are two primary classifications of interpretative methods in the contemporary Islámic legal system. The traditionalist approach adheres strictly to the original interpretations of the *Sharí'ah* enunciated in the tenth century, while evolutionists employ flexibility in their interpretation, situating the *Sharí'ah* within its current context, evolved to cater to contemporary issues of the world. Baderin has previously advocated for the expedience of the aforementioned legal doctrine of *máṣlaḥah,* as "a veritable Islamic legal doctrine for the realization of international human rights within the dispensation of Islamic law",[48] one that contains the "seeds of the future of the *Sharí'ah* and its viability as a living force in society".[49] The scope for this compatibility between Islámic law and

42 Jonathan E. Brockopp, "Competing Theories of Authority in Early Maliki Texts", in Bernard. G. Weiss (ed.), *Studies in Islamic Legal Theories*, Brill, Leiden, 2002, p. 3.

43 Abdal-Haqq, 2002, p. 55, see *supra* note 21.

44 *Ibid.*, pp. 228–29.

45 Kamali, 1991, p. 264, see *supra* note 13. The *'Ulama'* (Muslim jurists) are in unanimous agreement that the *Qur'án* and the *Sunnah* constitute the sources of the original case, but there is some disagreement as to whether *'ijma'* constitutes a valid source for *qiyas*, see Kamali, 1991, p. 268, see *supra* note 13.

46 *Ibid.*, p. 267.

47 Kamali, 1991, p. 267, see *supra* note 13.

48 Baderin, 2005, p. 43, see *supra* note 11.

49 Kamali, 1988, p. 288, see *supra* note 19.

international human rights law depends upon which interpretative approach is adopted, with the more flexible evolutionist approach undoubtedly more amenable to the harmonization of both legal traditions.[50]

Having provided a brief introduction to Islámic law, this chapter will be divided into five sections. Section 27.2. seeks to clarify the notion of 'religious leaders' in Islám to which we are referring. Section 27.3. will provide an overview of freedom of speech and its limitations in Islámic law. Section 27.4. intends to examine the source in Islámic law that obliges religious leaders to combat hate speech, and how Islámic law empowers those leaders in that respect. Based upon the role of religious leaders in their communities, Section 27.5. will sketch out internal measures and informal sanctions by which religious leaders are equipped to fight hate speech. Finally, Section 27.6. will address the various challenges that could undermine the efficacy of measures adopted by religious leaders and seeks to present solutions to those challenges.

27.2. Identifying Religious Leaders in Islám

The term 'religious leaders' in this chapter refers to persons who have some type of religious authority in the sense of – as sketched by Gudrun Krämer and Sabine Schmidtke – having the "ability (chance, power, or right) to define correct belief and practice, or orthodoxy and orthopraxy, respectively; to shape and influence the views and conduct of others accordingly; to identify, marginalize, punish or exclude deviance, heresy and apostasy and their agents and advocates"; to "define the canon of 'authoritative' texts and the legitimate methods of interpretation".[51]

In that respect, it is worth noting the difficulty in determining where religious authority lies in Islám. Unlike Christianity, there is no ordained clergy in Islám.[52] In the words of A. Kadir Yildirim, "Islam does not have a centralized hierarchical institution to establish the orthodoxy for its adherents".[53] Rather, there is a proliferation of actors who claim the right to exercise some form of religious authority.[54] While there are various terms used to refer to those actors

---

[50] Baderin, 2005, p. 44, see *supra* note 11.

[51] Gudrun Krämer and Sabine Schmidtke, "Religious Authority and Religious Authorities in Muslim Societies: A Critical Overview", in Gudrun Krämer and Sabine Schmidtke (eds.), *Speaking for Islam: Religious Authorities in Muslim Societies*, vol. 100, Brill, Social, Economic and Political Studies of the Middle East and Asia Series, 2006, pp. 1–14.

[52] Unlike Shí'ah clergy in Iran. See on that, Eric Hooglund and William Royce, "The Shi'i Clergy of Iran and the Conception of an Islamic State", in *State, Culture, and Society*, 1985, vol. 1, no. 3, pp. 102–117.

[53] A. Kadir Yildirim, "The New Guardians of Religion: Islam and Authority in the Middle East", Rice University's Baker Institute for Public Policy, March 2019, p. 9.

[54] See also Krämer and Schmidtke, 2006, p. 12, see *supra* note 51.

(for example, '*'ulama*'', '*Imám*', '*Sheikh*', '*Faqíh*'), a discussion of these terms is outside the scope of this chapter, as there is a lack of consensus on what each term denotes in terms of competence.[55]

Having said that, and building on the qualities elaborated below in Adel Maged's chapter,[56] religious leaders responsible for combatting hate speech, for the purposes of this chapter, can be grouped into two categories: the first category includes individual religious leaders and the second category includes religious leaders who act as part of a formal institution[57] or who act as part of an informal group.[58] While individual religious leaders – not affiliated to any formal or informal group[59] – do not possess as many tools for combatting hate speech as religious leaders in the second category, their inclusion in this chapter is warranted, particularly as empirical research has found that they can have similar or even more legitimacy than actors affiliated with religious institutions, thus necessitating their inclusion in the responses to hate speech.[60]

One last point needs to be addressed in the context of identifying religious leaders in Islám. It concerns the extent to which the role of women could be considered among those religious leaders charged with combatting hate speech. Women have long been excluded from the right to claim religious authority in

55 For a brief discussion of those terms and their usages, see Michele Brignone, "Religious Authorities in Islam", Fondazione Oasis, 3 March 2017.

56 See Chapter 29 of this anthology titled "The Role of Al-Azhar Alsharif in Combating Extremism and Hate Speech in Light of International Instruments".

57 A formal institution refers to either an institution vested by some type of religious authority by virtue of law, or an institution established according to the law with the objective of exercising some type of religious authority. An example for the former is the Al-Azhar institution in Egypt which is – according to Article 7 of the Egyptian Constitution – the "main authority for religious sciences, and Islamic affairs. It is responsible for preaching Islam and disseminating the religious sciences and the Arabic language in Egypt and the world" (Constitution of Egypt, 10 January 2015, Article 7 (https://www.legal-tools.org/doc/632f2f/)). An example of the latter is Muhammadyiah Ulama in Indonesia which is a non-governmental organization established with the objective of spreading the values and teachings of Islám. Another example is the Islam Presentation Committee in Kuwait, a non-governmental organization with the mandate of presenting Islám and training preachers.

58 Projects such as 'Generating Respect for Humanitarian Norms' tend also to include this wide spectrum of religious leaders in studying the role of religious leaders in inducing compliance with international humanitarian law during armed conflicts. For the project's study on religious leaders and influence, see The Generating Respect Project's web site.

59 Examples of that are Amr Khaled and Moustafa Hosny, who are Egyptian television preachers not affiliated to any specific group.

60 See Yildirim, March 2019, p. 9, see *supra* note 53; see also Nathan J. Brown, "Official Islam in the Arab World: The Contest for Religious Authority", Carnegie Endowment for International Peace, 11 May 2017. For the different types of legitimacy possessed by religious leaders, see Ioana Cismas, *Religious Actors and International Law*, Oxford University Press, 2014, pp. 55–58.

Muslim communities.[61] However, the reason behind that is not the existence in Islámic law of a prohibition to proclaim women as eligible to exercise religious authority. On the contrary, the *Qur'án* allows women to practice religious authority, reflected in *Allah*'s saying, "[t]he Believers, men And women, are [friends and] protectors, One of another: they enjoin What is just [or 'good'], and forbid What is evil" (*Qur'án*, 9:71).

Throughout history, women have held religious authority and played different roles as transmitters of the Prophet Muḥammad's sayings ('*ḥadíths*'), his traditions, and his authoritative reports of his deeds.[62] They have also been judges and scholars of Islámic jurisprudence (*fiqh*). Nevertheless, an account of all those women remains largely unknown.[63] The decline in female religious leadership owes primarily to the social perception of the role of women in Muslim societies,[64] which in turn had an impact on the understanding of the Islámic concept of *Qiwamah*, that is arguably defined as men's custodianship over women.[65] For example, according to Asma Afsaruddin,

> jurists and theologians by the fifteenth century had decided that leadership of prayer of mixed congregations was not an

61 A problem that seems to be shared by other non-Muslim religious communities. See on that Aleksandra Sandstrom, "Women Relatively Rare in Top Positions of Religious Leadership", Pew Research Centre, 2 March 2016.

62 See on that Muhammad Z. Siddiqi, *Ḥadíth Literature: Its Origins, Development & Special Features*, Islamic Texts Society, Cambridge, 1993, pp. 117–124. For a comprehensive study on the role of women in society during the Prophet Muḥammad's lifetime, see 'Abd al-Ḥalím Abú Shuqqáh, *Taḥrír al-Már'ah fí 'Áṣr ar-Risalah*, 6 vols., Dar el Qalam, 1990 (in Arabic). See also Mohammad Akram Nadwi, *Al-Muhaddithat: The Women Scholars in Islam*, Interface Publications, Oxford, 2007.

63 See on that, Roja Fazaeli, "Female Religious Authority in Muslim Majority Contexts: Past Examples and Modern State-Initiatives", in Adele Bardazzi and Alberica Bazzoni (eds.) *Gender and Authority Across Disciplines, Space and Time*, Palgrave Macmillan, Cham, 2020, pp.195–219. For a historical account for female religious authority, see also Mirjam Künkler and Devin J. Stewart, *Female Religious Authority in Shi'i Islam: Past and Present*, Edinburgh University Press, 2021.

64 See, for example, Tamer Koburtay, Tala Abuhussein and Yusuf M. Sidani, "Women Leadership, Culture, and Islam: Female Voices From Jordan", in *Journal of Business Ethics*, 2023, vol. 183, pp. 347–363. The authors noted that "understanding women's societal and leadership role is not restricted to variances in textual interpretations. The nature of early Muslim societies, and how they evolved historically, has had a significant impact on how women's role developed and changed".

65 Yusuf M. Sidani, *Muslim Women at Work: Religious Discourses in Arab Society*, Palgrave Macmillan, Cham, 2018, pp. 64–65.

> appropriate role for women and that virtuous women best exercised their virtue within the confines of their homes.[66]

The practice of religious authority by women was arguably resisted as it challenged the popular stereotype that women were subordinate to men.[67]

Recent developments have witnessed an increase in female religious leadership. This growth, as Hilary Kalmbach highlights, is "inherently linked to larger social, religious, and political changes that have impacted Muslim communities since the early twentieth century".[68] An increasing number of Muslim states have allowed the training of women in various roles of religious authority.[69] For example, the year 2006 witnessed the first class of female religious guides ('*Murshidat*') to graduate from a programme hosted by the Moroccan Ministry of Religious Affairs.[70] Much of their work would take place in mosques in the form of structured classes comprising literacy classes and *Qur'ánic* recitation classes.[71] The *Murshidat* are also empowered to conduct counseling sessions with women regarding their social and psychological needs or other religious matters.[72] They are also part of religious opinion ('*Ifta'*') committees.[73]

Albeit with challenges, women are increasingly accepted as *fatwá* givers (authentic interpreters of Islámic sources), religious educators and *imáms*.[74] In light of the foregoing, the term 'religious leaders responsible for combatting hate

[66] Asma Afsaruddin, "Literature, Scholarship, and Piety: Negotiating Gender and Authority in the Medieval Muslim World", in *Religion & Literature*, 2010, vol. 42, nos. 1–2, p. 117.

[67] Britta Frede, "Female Islamic Knowledge in Africa: A Forgotten Story", Fondazione Oasis, 30 November 2020.

[68] Hilary Kalmbach, "Introduction: Islamic Authority and the Study of Female Religious Leaders", in Masooda Bano and Hilary Kalmbach (eds.) *Women, Leadership, and Mosques: Changes in Contemporary Islamic Authority*, Brill, Leiden, 2012, p. 1.

[69] Although women were allowed to be educated in religious institutions as early as the 1950s, barriers stood in their war to becoming religious scholars or exercise some other form of religious authority. See Hilary Kalmbach, "Female Mosque Leadership and Islamic Authority in Syria and Further Afield", in *Travail, Genre et Sociétés*, 2012, vol. 27, no. 1, p. 77.

[70] Brown, 2017, p. 10, see *supra* note 60.

[71] Meriem El Haitami, "Restructuring Female Religious Authority: State-Sponsored Women Religious Guides (Murshidat) and Scholars ('Alimat) in Contemporary Morocco", in *Mediterranean Studies*, 2012, vol. 20, no. 2, p. 229.

[72] *Ibid.*, p. 229.

[73] *Ibid.*, p. 230. For examples in other countries, see the monograph in Bano and Kalmbach, 2012, see *supra* note 68.

[74] Women prayer leaders (*imáms*) however, remain rare. See Rachel Rinaldo, "How a Growing Number of Muslim Women Clerics Are Challenging Traditional Narratives", *The Conversation*, 7 June 2017. Rachel noted that "many Muslims in Indonesia and elsewhere believe that women can be prayer leaders only to all-female congregations. Women-only mosques are still unusual, as in most Muslim societies, women pray at home or in a special section of the mosque. The only place with a long tradition of Muslim women who lead prayers is China".

speech' in this chapter is to be understood to comprise not only male religious leaders but female leaders as well.

Having clarified what the term 'religious leaders' denotes in this chapter, the following section provides an overview of freedom of speech in Islám and its limitations, before turning to tackling the sources in Islám for empowering religious leaders to combat hate speech, as well as the tools and measures available to them in their fight against hate speech.

27.3. An Overview of Freedom of Speech in Islám and Its Limitations

Notably, human freedom is regarded by Islám as both a right and a gift; this formulation entails the right to practise freedom of speech. Some Muslim scholars have gone as far as to argue that individualism and free choice are primary values of the *Qur'ánic* view of mankind.[75] Muslim intellectuals commonly cite in support the *Qur'ánic* verse: "Every man's fate We have fastened On his own neck : On the Day of Judgment We shall bring out For him [or 'each person'] a scroll [or 'record'], Which he will see Spread open.".[76]

Indeed, without this specific freedom, human beings would not be able to learn, to express their views, to expose evil or wrongdoing, or to warn others of danger. One *Qur'ánic* verse even invites doubters to question the holy text via speech: "And if ye are in doubt as to what We have revealed […] then call your witnesses or helpers (if there are any) besides God if your (doubts) are true.".[77]

Yet untrammelled freedom can turn into a licence and even, at times, into an evil itself. Acknowledgement of this truth is repeated in many guises throughout the sources of the *Qur'án*, the *ḥadíths*, the *Sunnah*, in practice, and in Muslim tradition through the ages.

Hate speech constitutes an abuse of free speech and as such, it is condemned by normative Islám. From an Islámic perspective, hate speech can be understood as the rhetoric that aims to degrade the honour of other humans and distort their image, and that instigates the recipients of such rhetoric to discriminate against them and to despise or harm them morally or physically, irrespective of the method in which it is formed or the medium by which it is represented, whether through provocation, allusion, writing, drawing, or any other form.[78]

Clearly, hate speech causes offence; yet offence alone is arguably not a sufficient cause in fathoming the notion of hate speech. Some contemporary Muslim scholars amplify this point, with a warning that:

---

75 Professor Abdul S. Kassem, "The Concept of Freedom in the Quran", in *American Journal of Contemporary Research*, 2012, vol. 2, no. 4, pp. 165–173.

76 *Qur'án*, 17:13–14.

77 *Qur'án*, 2:23.

78 Ahmed Y. Al-Karalah, Khitab al-Karahiya, "Hate Speech", *Al-Ghad*, 13 December 2013.

> the context in which hate speech takes place as well as its consequences which could harm groups or individuals, become important in determining whether to regulate hate speech. Historical evidence indicates that when danger posed by hate speech is "clear and present", it may have been too late to deal with its consequences.

It is also latterly wrapped up, it can be argued, in culture wars and exacerbated by social media.[79] Turan further shows how Islám is not alone in feeling that it suffers hate speech from others, citing Catholic complaints to the European Commission on Human Rights. He reminds readers that there is a fine line between hate speech and free speech; yet, if unchecked, "hate speech can unleash violent conflict, and historically has proven its capacity to trigger genocides."[80]

An adequate understanding of the principles of *Sharí'ah* on freedom of expression inevitably brings us into contact with the conditions of human society and its vision of the types of freedom it could visualize and accept. Although it is true that Islám has not been shaped by the dictates of social reality, it has, nevertheless, taken into consideration both the reality and the potential of the society in which it came into being.[81]

27.3.1. On the Arabic Terminology of Freedom of Expression

Contemporary Muslim intellectuals – as observed by Kamali – are not consistent in the use of terminology in relation to freedom of expression. For example, while some utilize the terms of '*ḥurríyyat ar-rá'y*', literally 'freedom of opinion', and '*ḥurríyyat al-qáwl*', literally 'freedom of speech', other writers, however, have utilized alternative terminology such as '*ḥurríyyat at-tafkír*', literally 'freedom of thought', '*ḥurríyyat at-ta'bír*', literally 'freedom of expression or interpretation', and '*ḥurríyyat ar-rá'y*' and '*ḥurríyyat ar-rá'y wat-ta'bír*', which specifically means freedom of opinion and expression.[82] To summarize his point, Kamali goes on to explain how the latter phrase is more preferable:

> thought is a hidden phenomenon and a mental activity which is communicated in words, and until then, thought which has not been expressed in words, remains outside the concern of law. It is the external manifestation of thought which we refer to as ra'y (opinion). To use the phrase *hurriyyat al-ra'y wal-ta'bīr* is thus

79 Mustafa O. Turan, "Drawing the Line: Blasphemy, Hate Speech and Freedom of Expression", Muslim Political Participation and Human Rights, 17 September 2012.

80 *Ibid.*

81 Mohammad Hashim Kamali, *Freedom of Expression in Islam*, Islamic Texts Society, Cambridge, 2010, p. 15, "Preliminary Remarks".

82 *Ibid.*, p. 5.

> preferable as it leaves no doubt that the thought, idea or opinion at issue has been expressed and communicated.[83]

Moreover, Kamali provides some examples of other writers who use various terms to illustrate this topic. For example, 'Abd al-Ḥamíd Mutwallí uses *ḥurríyyat ar-rá'y* and *ḥurríyyat ar-rá'y wat-ta'bír*, while Muhammad Kamíl Laylah prefers the term *ḥurríyyat ar-rá'y*. Furthermore, 'Abd al-Waḥid Wafí uses *al-ḥurríyyah al-fikríyyah*, literally 'freedom of thought', while 'Abd al-Qádir 'Udah and Sayyid al-Sabiq tend to use the term *ḥurríyyat at-tafkír.*[84] It is common for these writers to distinguish freedom of expression from freedom of religion. In specific terms, these are '*ḥurríyyat at-tadayyun*' (literally 'freedom of religion'), '*ḥurríyyat al-'áqídah*' (literally 'freedom of belief'), and '*al-ḥurríyyah ad-díníyyah*' (specifically meaning 'religious freedom'). However, it is generally acknowledged that freedom of expression in Islám is effectively complementary to freedom of religion. It is therefore perceived as an extension and a logical consequence of the freedom of conscience and belief which the *Sharí'ah* has validated and upheld.[85]

27.3.2. Seeking a Balance

Muslim scholars have long debated how to strike the right balance between guaranteeing the right to speak freely and the duty to mind one's tongue and to cause no damage. Within this rubric, the sin of '*fitnah*' ('sedition', 'unrest', 'undermining of a rule of law') is a key element in determining how and where to impose protective limits on free speech. Likewise, there are times when the value of free speech clashes with other core Islámic values. Kamali contends that sometimes,

> expressing a true opinion or even telling the truth may fail to achieve a good purpose. The speaker is, therefore, urged to be mindful of the end result […]. *Sunnah* permits silence in regard to the truth or even allows the telling of a white lie if it would serve a higher objective, such as saving a person from imminent danger.

Thus, the greater good of preserving life and a just cause may triumph over the general requirement of truth-telling and not dissimulating ('*táqqiyah*').[86] One of the most reliable sources in *Shafi'í* jurisprudence, 'The Reliance of the Traveller', devoted a chapter to the importance of holding one's tongue in Islám.[87] According to one *ḥadíth*, the Prophet said: "Whoever believes in

83 *Ibid.*, pp. 5–6.

84 *Ibid.*, p. 6.

85 *Ibid.*, p. 6.

86 *Ibid.*, p. 68.

87 Naqib al-Misri, 1994, pp. 726–776, see *supra* note 14.

Allah and the Last Day, let him say what is good or remain silent.”.[88] In another *ḥadíth*, when the Prophet was asked “O Messenger of Allah, which of the Muslims is best?”, he said: “He who the Muslims are safe from his tongue and his hand.”.[89]

The aim of this section is to examine what Islámic law and moral precepts, as derived from the *Qur'án*, have to say on setting the right balance between free speech and its limitations; and what one can do regarding imposing legal restraints on abuse of free speech, beyond moral restraints.

Given that the focus of the present study is ‘hate speech’, one should acknowledge that the topic concerns Islámic thought in two principal ways. Firstly, there is hate speech directed against Muslims. Secondly, we see hate speech promulgated by Muslims (or people who purport to be speaking in the name of Muslims) against other Muslims, or against non-Muslim members or institutions of the societies in which they live. The focus of this section will be primarily on the second category.

27.3.3. An Overarching Legal Perspective

First, it is necessary to define what Islámic law identifies as abuses of free speech, encompassing, *inter alia*, hate speech. Islámic law and thought, as understood from its primary sources, include the tools with which to both identify, and combat hate speech. This is true even of cases where the accused may claim that he or she is speaking out ‘in defence of Islám’. Such a claim on its own does not imply veracity. Indeed, if proven false, the ‘defendant’ could be subject to further charges of ‘lying’ – another infraction of free speech. To support that charge, note the *Qur'ánic* quote: “truly God guides not one Who transgresses and lies.”.[90]

Similarly, we can read another *Qur'ánic* verse: “And cover [or ‘mix’] not Truth with falsehood nor conceal the Truth when ye know (what it is).”.[91]

Lying, similar to backbiting, is considered a grave sin; both charges are often, and rightly so, levelled against purveyors of hate speech.

Kamali has identified the following seven areas which together constitute abuse of free speech: Public Utterance of Hurtful Speech (‘*al-jáhr bil-sú' min al-qáwl*’), Slanderous Accusation (‘*Qádhf*’), Libel (‘*Iftirá'*’), Insult (‘*sabb*’ or ‘*shatm*’), Cursing (‘*la'n*’), Attribution of Disbelief to a Muslim (‘*Takfír al-muslim*’), and Sedition (‘*fitnah*’).[92] Centuries earlier, the great theologian, jurist and

---

[88] al-Bukhárí, Book 73, *ḥadíth* 70.

[89] at-Tirmidhí, Book 37, *ḥadíth* 90.

[90] *Qur'án*, 40:28.

[91] *Qur'án*, 2:42.

[92] Kamali, 1991, pp. 166–67, see *supra* note 13.

mystic, al-Ghazalí[93] listed five types of "calamities of speech" or '*afat al-lisan*'; these are lying, backbiting, acrimony, sycophancy, and unrestricted jocularity.[94]

With respect to hate speech, the most obviously relevant subject areas would appear to be *fitnah* and *takfir,* which thus warrant a more detailed discussion. Nonetheless, all the other forms of abuse have some bearing on our consideration, depending on the context.

27.3.4. On the Meaning of Slander ('*Ghíbah*') and Talebearing ('*Namímah*')

Slander (*ghíbah*) means to mention anything concerning a person that he would dislike, whether about his body, religion, everyday life, self, disposition, property, son, father, wife, turban, garment, gait, movements, smiling, dissoluteness, frowning, cheerfulness or anything else connected with him. However, quoting someone's words to another in a way that worsens relations between them is considered to be '*namímah*'. The prohibition of slander and talebearing is found in the *Qur'án* and *Sunnah. Allah* Most High says: "Nor speak ill of each other Behind their backs [or 'do not slander one another']" (*Qur'án* 49:12), and the Prophet has said: "The talebearer will not enter paradise". Though unlawful, slander is sometimes permissible for a lawful purpose. Redressing grievances and eliminating wrongdoing are but two of five forms of permissible slander.

Insult and slander accusations, two of the concepts listed by Ghazali and Kamali, appear to be inherent in hate speech. Consider the way hate preachers impugn the reputations of members of society, violate their dignity, and try to persuade others to feel the same. Putatively, Islámic speakers of hate speech can thus be accused of insult (*sabb*) against others. They may also be guilty of slanderous accusation, or *qádhf,* in that they tarnish the all-important good name of their victim. In a sense, argues Professor Kamali, *sabb* brings a double punishment: first, it is wrong in itself; second, it can bar the sinner of being a future witness.

Similarly, ridicule is condemned as a breach of free speech, as in the *Qur'ánic* quote: "O ye who believe! Let not some men Among you laugh [or 'ridicule'] at others […].".[95]

On the moral plane, the founders of two of the four major Muslim schools of jurisprudence, ash-Shaafi'í and Ibn Ḥanbal, agree that *qádhf* violates the right of a human. Thus, when hate preachers mock others, Muslims or not, they are insulting their humanity. Moreover, the tone or mode of discourse of extremist speakers would seem to exclude their words from acceptable free speech.

[93] Britannica, "Al-Ghazali" (available on Britannica's web site).

[94] Kamali, 2010, p. 122, see *supra* note 81.

[95] *Qur'án*, 49:11 – cited in Kamali, 2010, p. 118, see *supra* note 81.

Consider the *Qur'án* verse that enjoins believers to "speak fair [or 'good words'] to the people" (*Qur'án*, 2:83).

Hate preachers persistently aim to promote, or at least exploit, divisions in society. The latter may be defined as '*fitnah*' (which will be discussed later) or acrimony (*mu'amarát*), something which Ghazali condemned. Allied to these sins is their tendency of backbiting (*gh͟íbah*). Furthermore, libel (*iftirá'*) seems pertinent to hate speech too. The great commentator Ibn Taymíyyah argues that false charges against a chaste man or woman can rebound on the person who makes such charges. Further, if the accused forgives the accuser, no court can impose a punishment. He makes a striking statement of human rights, or '*ḥáq al-adamí*': "In all cases of retaliation the personal rights of the defendant and the owner, respectively, take priority (even) over the Right of God.".[96]

The prohibition of Hurtful Speech in Public (*al-jáhr bis-sú' min al-qáwl*) derives directly from the *Qur'ánic* verses 4:148–149 and constitutes one of the most far-reaching rulings on restrictions of free speech. It is worth quoting in full to capture the broad extent of its concerns and the wisdom of its advice:

> God loveth not that evil should be noised abroad in public speech [or 'public utterance of evil speech'] except where injustice hath been done [or 'by one who has been wronged']; for God is He who heareth and knoweth all things.
>
> Whether ye publish a good deed or conceal it or cover evil with pardon [or 'forgive evil'] verily God doth blot out (sins) and hath power (in the judgment of values) [or 'God is forgiving, omnipotent'].[97]

In the first sentence of the quotation above, we detect a general denunciation of public evil speech, or harsh words; with the important proviso that such speech has merit when it purports to address a wrong.

Regarding hate speech in the modern age, it is worth noting that the word '*al-jáhr*' can translate as broadcasting, which is easily adapted to the age of television, Internet and social media. The hurtful speech in question may be directed to an individual, a group, or a community at large. Hurtful speech can cover everything from finding fault in others, to promoting obscenity, to indulgent talk about misdeeds or failings. No distinction is drawn between whether the offensive words are true or false, or the end to which they are intended.[98]

---

96 Cited in Kamali, 2010, p. 175, footnote 24, see *supra* note 81.

97 *Qur'án*, 4:148–149.

98 There is one exception made: for "one who has been wronged". In such a case, justice decrees that this person must be given a hearing, no matter the possible 'offense' caused, for only that way can one fight against '*ẓulm*', a state of injustice. *Ẓulm* is also defined as wrongfully

27.3.5. Fitnah

The general term '*fitnah*' is employed at least sixty times in the *Qur'án,* and can variously include misguidance, temptation, commotion, strife, affliction and torture. In Islámic juridical terms, it tends to imply 'seditious speech which attacks the legitimacy of a lawful government'. It can also imply denying the faithful the ability to practice their faith.[99]

Some may contend that such an apparent contradiction is problematic. One might argue, by contrast, that it shows the flexibility of Islámic religious practice. In the first instance, the interpretation offers tools to fend off *fitnah*-inducing radicalism, sometimes by errant Muslims; and in the second instance, it can be employed to protect Muslim citizens from bigoted, Islámophobic hate speech.

The opposite of *fitnah* ('tribulation') is a well-ordered society. As to what that might mean, the great Muslim philosopher al-Ghazalí suggested that psychological attitude is all-important; one should discipline oneself to promote forbearance ('*ḥilm*') and good character ('*ḥusn al-khuluq*').[100]

Moreover, the sense of *fitnah* as a necessary, even unavoidable, trial on this earth adds another layer of nuance, which puts the matter into perspective. As the *Qur'án* states: "And Know ye That your possessions And your progeny Are but a trial; And that with God With whom lies Your highest reward".[101]

Amongst other characteristics of *fitnah* is '*shirk*',[102] the false association of other deities with God, or as al-Alusí put it, aggression against and the destruction of religion. Stressing this violent aspect, which all of humanity should oppose, the *Qur'án* states that "oppression (*fitnah*) is worse than killing". One might ask whether extremists' association of a divine authority to unqualified leaders in itself constitutes *shirk*; though this is a topic for further development elsewhere.

---

depriving someone of their legal and moral rights, or taking from them for oneself, or giving to another. See Moiz Amjad, "What is "Zulm"?", Understanding Islam, 13 May 2002. Thus, as per the quotation, where *ẓulm* is proven, the question of justice takes priority over the duty to prevent evil speech. Extremist perpetrators of hate speech often claim to be combating *ẓulm* in society, whether that society is Muslim, Christian, secular or other. However, by rejecting the right of fellow Muslims to judge their claims, they surely lose the right to substantiate the assertion that they are "fighting for justice".

99 Kamali, 2010, p. 30, footnote 74, see *supra* note 81.

100 Kamali, 2010, p. 123, see *supra* note 81.

101 *Qur'án*, 8:28 and 64:15.

102 Francis E. Peters, *Islam: A Guide for Muslims and Christians,* Princeton University Press, 2003, p. 205.

Fitnah often peaks during times of war. Other commentators condemn *fitnah* as tempting weak Muslims with a superficially easy path. Perpetrators of *fitnah* need not be rebels only; even misguided rulers can be held guilty of this sign. Likewise, rampant corruption that undermines society and communities counts as *fitnah*; as do challenges to lawful governments; and actions that cloud understanding to such an extent that people can no longer advocate the truth.[103] In all of these myriad cases, *fitnah* and hate speech would appear to be close partners.

Returning to *fitnah* in history, the commentator Abu Zahrah amplified the idea that the Kharijites were not, as they claimed, exercising legitimate freedom of expression in pursuit of truth, but were jeopardizing security and threatening the community with destruction.[104] The Kharijites sinned, said subsequent commentators, because they rejected Caliph Ali's choice of arbitration in a dispute (thus flouting the advice of negotiation and peaceful resolution). Furthermore, they falsely claimed that a community could administer its own affairs; said that a major sinner was, by definition, '*kafir*'; rejected the imámate; and charged the Prophet's companions with apostacy.[105]

Conversely, the Mu'tazilí, ultra-rationalists, in the later Abbásíd period created their own form of *fitnah* by suppressing the accepted interpreters of faith. Famously, or infamously, they stressed the created nature of the *Qur'án*; in the eyes of more orthodox critics, they suggested it was man-made and not ordained by God. Again, in comparison with Muslims today, those who undermine faith in Islám from a secular perspective may also be akin to creators of *fitnah*; although the charge needs careful proving on a case-by-case basis.

Sometimes the perpetrator of alleged *fitnah* offers a patina of morality. Apparently Abú Dhárr al-Ghaffarí was right to urge people not to acquire gold and silver in excess, yet the governor of Syria expelled him in order to prevent sedition. Subsequent scholars now see al-Ghaffarí as at least partly justified. The above instance arguably illustrates how attitudes and perceptions change over time – here, in regard to the primacy of social justice – while the underlying principles of Islám remain constant.

The *ḥadíths* sagely note that *fitnah* rears its head precisely at times of leadership succession. Obedience is required, once the leader is declared by election or consensus; disobedience, in older days, was declared to be liable to a death sentence. Clearly, such attitudes sit ill with Muslims today, whether as minorities in the West, or as citizens of Muslim majority states. In the latter cases,

[103] Kamali, 2010, p. 194, footnote 85, see *supra* note 81.

[104] Kamali, 2010, p. 194, see *supra* note 81.

[105] *Ibid.*, p. 197.

we should also admit that some dictatorial leaders demand total loyalty, even at the expense of human rights. The moral point, though, seems paramount: namely that a state of order and mutual respect is preferable to social anarchy, or *fitnah*.

27.3.6. Takfír

'*Takfír*' is the category of abuse with which hate speech is most directly associated (the other being *fitnah*). The term denotes the attribution of disbelief, blasphemy or heresy to a Muslim, and is derived from the Arabic word for disbelief ('*kufr*'). Mainstream *Sunní* Islám condemns Muslims who engage in the practice of *takfír* ('excommunication'), a right they consider to be held solely by God.[106] In the Islámic faith, both the *Qur'án* and the *Sunnah* explicitly condemn this practice, and three *ḥadíths* demonstrate the Prophet's consideration of such a declaration as a sin. In one such *ḥadíth*, the Prophet cautions Muslims "not to declare a person a disbeliever for committing a sin, and not to expel him from Islam by an action".[107] Another *ḥadíth* declares that: "If a man says to his brother, 'O infidel', it redounds upon one of them".[108]

Accusations of *kufr* ('disbelief') have nevertheless been levelled for centuries by certain Muslim groups against members of their own faith. From the Khawarij in the seventh century CE through to the Iraqi insurgency led by Abú Muṣ'áb al-Zárqáwí, to the so called Islamic State of Iraq and Syria ('IS') in the twentyfirst century, *takfírism* has been the political weapon of choice.[109] IS liberally discharged it "to license a fratricidal civil war against the Iraqi *Shí'ah* community".[110] On the surface it draws comparison to the mass excommunication of individuals from the Catholic Church in the middle ages,[111] defined – in the Christian sense – as a "form of ecclesiastical censure by which a person is

[106] Mohamed Elewa Badar, Masaki Nagata and Tiphanie Tueni "The Radical Application of the Islamic Concept of Takfir", in *Arab Law Quarterly*, 2017, vol. 31, pp. 134–162, pp. 136–139; Ismail ibn Kathir, *Tafsir ibn Kathir,* vol. 3, 2nd ed., Darussalam, 2003, p. 436. According to Ibn Kathir, verse 6:108 of the *Qur'án* means that *Allah* has forbidden the Prophet Muḥammad and his followers from insulting other religions, as such insults could lead to their followers retaliating in kind.

[107] Abu Dawud, *English Translation of Sunan Abu Dawud,* Nasiruddin al-Khatab (trans.), vol. 3, Darussalam, 2008.

[108] Muhammad ibn Ismail al-Bukhari, *The Translation of Meanings of Sahih Al-Bukhari*, Dr. Muhammad Muhsin Khan (trans.), vol. 8, no. 6103, Kazi Publications Inc., Chicago, 1997, p. 77.

[109] Badar, Nagata, and Tueni, 2017, p. 135, see *supra* note 106.

[110] Shiraz Maher, *Salafi-Jihadism: The History of an Idea*, Hurst & Co. Publishers, 2016, p. 71.

[111] Felicity Hill, "Excommunication and Politics in Thirteenth Century England", unpublished doctoral thesis, University of East Anglia, 2016, p. 12.

excluded from the communion of believers, the rites or sacraments of a church, and the rights of church membership".[112]

The devastating consequences of the practice of *takfīr* have been felt across Muslim majority states, as:

> From Indonesia to Pakistan, the Levant, the Arabian Peninsula, and across North Africa, militant groups have frequently invoked the doctrine to justify mass casualty attacks against ordinary Muslims – ironically, the very constituency in whose defence they often claim to act.[113]

In the past three decades, the Arab world has witnessed countless *takfīr* campaigns and trials, based upon accusations of apostasy, blasphemy and unbelief, instigated primarily by the Islámist lobby to coincide "with their demand for the codification and implementation of Islamic law (*sharī'a*)".[114] Charges of *takfīr* can be levelled at any individual, regime, or society, regardless of their own profession of belief, on the grounds of their allegedly un-Islámic actions, resulting in their being subject to discrimination or even lawful killing.[115] The three forms of *takfīr* must be defined at the outset: (i) *takfīr* of individuals by private persons; (ii) *takfīr* of the state or democracy by private persons or Islámist parties; and (iii) *takfīr* of individuals by the state or its judicial or religious institutions.

The practice of each form is underpinned by its own ideology. In the Arab region generally, and in Tunisia particularly, different forms of *takfīr* have been utilized by different radical groups. *Takfīr* of the society, the government or democracy is mainly practiced by *salafī* jihádist movements, such *Anṣár as͟h-S͟harí'ah* in Tunisia and Libya and *Jabhat an-Nuṣráh* and *Aḥrár as͟h-S͟ham* in Syria, who follow the *Wahhabí* ideology. These jihádist groups, together with *al-Qá'idah*, renounce democracy as an un-Islámic system based upon their genuine belief that the human drafting of legislation and enforcement of law that

---

112 Britannica, "Excommunication" (available on its web site).

113 Maher, 2016, p. 83 (italic added), see *supra* note 110.

114 Roswitha Badry, "On the *Takfīr* of Arab Women's Rights Advocates in Recent Times", in Camilla Adang, Hassan Ansari, Maribel Fierro and Sabine Schmidtke (eds.), *Accusations of Unbelief in Islam*, no. 4, Brill, Leiden, 2016, p. 354.

115 Toshihiko Izutsu, *The Concept of Belief in Islamic Theology: A Semantic Analysis of Iman and Islam*, Books for Libraries, 1980, p. 11; Ibrahim Karawan, "Takfir", in John Esposito (ed.), *The Oxford Encyclopedia of the Modern Islamic World*, vol. 5, Oxford University Press, 2009, p. 311. On *takfīr* in general, see Adang *et al.*, 2016, *ibid.* On *takfīr* by contemporary extremist militant groups, see Badar, Nagata and Tueni, 2017, pp. 134–162, see *supra* note 106.

occurs within democracy is an usurpation of the role of God, as the ultimate source of power and authority, and thus amounts to *kufr* ('unbelief').[116]

27.3.7. The Prohibition of Declaring *Takfír* in the *Qur'án*

As explained in the introductory section of this chapter, the *Qur'án* is considered to be the seminal and most important source of Islámic law. The *Qur'án* is often selectively cited by IS and other groups as justification for declaring *takfír* and issuing punishments to those they deem unbelievers, even where those deemed unbelievers profess to follow the Muslim faith. Such selective citation of *Qur'ánic* verses, however, removes them from their broader contextual background and thus obscures their true meaning.

Understanding the *Qur'ánic* position on *takfír* is the crux of the issue. The term itself is not referenced in the *Qur'án*, yet it is implicitly prohibited. For example, verse 6:108 of the *Qur'án* reads as follows:

> Revile not ye those whom they call upon besides God [non-believers] lest they out of spite revile God in their ignorance. Thus have We made alluring to each people its own doings. In the end will they return to their Lord and We shall then tell them the truth of all that they did.[117]

Ibn Kat͟hír interprets verse 6:108 as *Allah* prohibiting the Prophet Muḥammad and his followers from insulting other religions, on the grounds that such insults could prompt retaliation in kind.[118] This prohibition of *takfír* is repeated in other verses, such as 4:94:

> O ye who believe! [W]hen ye go abroad in the cause of God, investigate carefully, and say not to anyone who offers you a salutation: "Thou art none of a believer!" Coveting the perishable goods of this life: with God are profits and spoils abundant. Even thus were ye yourselves before, till God conferred on you His favours: therefore carefully investigate for God is well aware of all that ye do.[119]

According to Abbas, *Allah* revealed verse 4:94 following the murder of Mirdas Ibn Nuhayk al-Fárárí by Usamah Ibn Zayd, both of whom were Muslims.[120] This verse prohibits the killing of any Muslim who has openly

[116] Joas Wagemakers, "'The *Kāfir* Religion of the West': Takfīr of Democracy and Democrats by Radical Islamists", in Adang *et al.*, 2016, pp. 329–330, see *supra* note 114.

[117] *Qur'án*, 6:108.

[118] Ibn Kathir, 2003, p. 436, see *supra* note 106.

[119] *Qur'án*, 4:94.

[120] Ibn Abbas, *Tafsīr Ibn 'Abbās*, Mokrane Guezzou (trans.), Royal Aal al-Bayt Institute for Islamic Thought, Amman, 2007, p. 98.

committed to *Allah* by reciting the *Shahadah* ('There is no god but *Allah*, Muḥammad is the Messenger of *Allah*').[121]

Many *Qur'ánic* verses mention unbelievers, yet apostasy is not defined in the *Qur'án*; rather, the Islámic definition of apostasy has been developed through human effort.[122] This is notwithstanding that, according to the *Qur'ánic* verses noted above, only God (and not man) has the right to declare *takfír*, as only God holds the right to decide whether one is a believer or not, a decision made only in the hereafter. Consequentially, *takfír* declarations made by human beings amount to a religious sin under *Sharí'ah* law.

Thus, the lack of *Qur'ánic* support for the earthly punishment of apostasy by man may be unequivocally asserted, unlike for sins or crimes such as theft or fornication, which are subject to prescribed punishments.[123] Capital punishment for turning away from Islám thus arises from human creative endeavour aimed at criminalizing a sin, which by definition, is only accountable for in the hereafter.

27.3.8. The Prohibition of Declaring *Takfír* in the *Sunnah*

The *Sunnah* is considered to be the second source of *Sharí'ah*. It consists of a compilation of narratives developed in the centuries following the Prophet's era, collectively known as *Aḥadíth* (singular is *ḥadíth*), detailing what the Prophet said, did or approved.[124] Upon his death, the Prophet could no longer directly explain the significance of any particular act or speech[125] and so *Sharí'ah* was further developed through the scholarly (re)interpretation of the *Sunnah* in order to address the new situations that inevitably arose.

In respect of *takfír*, the Prophet cautioned Muslims "not to declare a person a disbeliever for committing a sin, and not to expel him from Islam by an action".[126] The Prophet further stated that insulting a believer was "an evil

---

121 The *Shahadah* is a declaration of belief in only one God (*tawḥid*) and an acknowledgement that Muḥammad is his Messenger.

122 Various scholars have sought to define apostasy; some mediaeval scholars drew up 'apostasy lists'. See Naqib al-Misri, 1994, p. 596, see *supra* note 14; Ibn Qudama, *The Mainstay Concerning Jurisprudence (Al-Umda fi l-Fiqh - Handbook of Hanbali Fiqh)*, Muhtar Holland (trans.), Al-Baz Publishing Incorporated, Fort Lauderdale, 2010, p. 309.

123 Apostasy is referred to as *riddah* and prescribed punishments as *ḥudúd*. See Abdullah Saeed and Hassan Saeed, *Freedom of Religion*, Apostasy and Islam, Ashgate, Aldershot, 2004, pp. 69–87.

124 Wael B. Hallaq, *An Introduction to Islamic Law*, Cambridge University Press, 2009, p. 16.

125 Ibn Khaldun, *The Muqaddimah: An Introduction to History,* Franz Rosenthal (trans.), vol. 3, Princeton University Press, 1980, pp. 23–24.

126 Dawud, 2008, p. 223, see *supra* note 107.

action";[127] labelling another Muslim a *kafir* in itself constituted unbelief. The Prophet's teachings are littered throughout the *aḥadíth*, including in *Ṣáḥíḥ al-Bukhárí*,[128] *Ṣáḥíḥ Muslim*[129] and *Sunann An-Nasa'í*.[130] They elaborate not only the Prophet's prohibition of *takfír*, but also his consideration of such declarations of excommunication as a sin.

27.4. Sources and Tools for Combating Hate Speech in Islám

Islámic tradition has the tools to fight hate speech – including when such speech emanates from within the Muslim community itself. Short of punitive measures, which are often inapplicable in contemporary societies, the battle against hate speech is well served by the principles of '*ḥisbah*' ('upholding community morals') and '*náṣíḥah*' (often translated as 'advice' or 'wise counsel'). '*Máṣlaḥah*', or 'the public interest', is a third Islámic concept that can be employed in the endeavour.

27.4.1. Ḥisbah

Qur'ánic verse 3:104 instructs Muslims to command good and forbid evil ("*al-ámr bil-ma'rúf wan-nahy 'an al-munkár*") and is considered as "a cardinal *Qur'ánic* principle which lies at the root of many Islamic laws and institutions".[131] It is from this verse that the concept of *ḥisbah* is derived. According to al-Ghazalí, the definition of good ('*ma'rúf*') or evil ('*munkár*') is to be determined with reference to *Sharí'ah*, "in particular to those rules that pertain to the protection of the five values, namely, life, faith, intellect, property and lineage".[132] The *Malikí* jurist al-Qáráfí outlined the following three conditions to be observed in the implementation of *ḥisbah*, which provide basic guidance to

[127] Abu A.A.M.H. Ash-Shaibani, Huda Al-Khattab (ed.), *English Translation of Musnad Imam Ahmad bin Hanbal*, Nasiruddin Al-Khattab (trans.), vol. 3, no. 4345, Darussalam, Riyadh, 2012, p. 591.

[128] "If a man says to his brother, 'O *Káfir* (disbeliever)!' Then surely, one of them is such [that is a *káfir*]", Al-Bukhari, 1997, p. 77, see *supra* note 108.

[129] "Any man who knowingly attributes himself to someone other than his father is guilty of disbelief. Whoever claims something that does not belong to him is not one of us; let him take his place in Hell. Whoever calls a man a disbeliever *(Káfir)* or says to him: 'O enemy of Allah!' when he is not like that, it will rebound upon him". Imam Muslim, *Sahih Muslim*, Nasiruddin al-Khattab (trans.), vol. 1, no. 217, Darussalam, Riyadh, 2007, p. 158.

[130] It was narrated from "Abdur Rahman bin 'Abdullah, from his father, that the Messenger of *Allah* said: 'Defaming a Muslim is evildoing and fighting him is *kufr*'". Al-Nasa'i, *Sunan An-Nasa'I*, Nasiruddin al-Khattab (trans.), vol. 5, no. 4113, Maktaba Dar-us-Salam, Riyadh, 2007, p. 85.

[131] Kamali, 2010, p. 28, see *supra* note 81. The principle of "enjoining what is right and forbidding what is wrong" is reiterated in verse 3:110.

[132] *Ibid.*, p. 33, citing Muḥammad A.H. al-Ghazalí, *Iḥya' 'Ulúm al-Dīn*, vol. II, 2nd ed., *Dar al-Fikr*, Cairo, 1980, p. 324.

governing the activity of the '*muḥtasib*' (the person who bids good or forbids evil): (i) The *muḥtasib* must act from a position of knowledge, since an ignorant individual, unsure of his grounds, may neither enjoin good nor forbid evil; (ii) the *muḥtasib* must be reasonably sure that their attempts to prevent evil do not give rise to a greater evil; and (iii) the *muḥtasib* must act on the basis of an overwhelming probability ('*aẓ-ẓánn al-ghalib*') that the attempt to enjoin good or forbid evil will directly achieve the desired result.[133] The second element restricts the implementation of *ḥisbah* to situations where, in relation to the evil conduct (or crimes) being committed, "the *muhtasib* is in a position to prevent it, or to bring about a change to an on-going situation".[134] According to al-Qáráfí, the absence of either of the first two conditions renders the *ḥisbah* illegitimate. On the other hand, the absence of the last condition downgrades the characterization of the *ḥisbah*, from obligatory ('*wajib'* – an obligation or duty arising from the decisive injunctions of the *Qur'án* and *Sunnah*) to a mere permissibility ('*mubaḥ*').[135] "Let there arise [*waltakun*] out of you a band of people inviting [or 'calling others'] to all that is good enjoining what is right [or 'good'] and forbidding what is wrong [or 'evil']; they are the ones to attain felicity [*mufliḥūn*, or 'successful ones']."[136]

Commenting on the above verse, Kamali suggests that "[i]t is best, therefore, if the whole of the community observes *hisbah*, but it may be observed by only some members – men or women or both".[137] Kamali locates support for this interpretation in the *Qur'ánic* verse which states: "The Believers, men And women, are protectors [*awliyā*, or 'protectors and friends'], One of another: they enjoin What is just [or 'good'], and forbid What is evil" (*Qur'án*, 9:71).

Reading this verse in conjunction with other *Qur'ánic* verses, Kamali concludes:

> a successful implementation of *hisbah* requires a collective effort by the entire society. If implementing certain aspects of *hisbah* require an active role to be assigned to women alone, or through cooperation between men and women, then the *Qur'án* authorises this.[138]

Early Muslim jurists were further preoccupied by the debate as to whether *ḥisbah* is a collective duty ('*fárḍ kafa'í*'), or an individual obligation ('*fárḍ*

[133] *Ibid.*, p. 28, citing Shihab al-Dín al-Qáráfí, *Kitab al-Furúq*, vol. IV, *Maṭba'at Dar Iḥya' al-Kutub al-'Árábíyyah*, Cairo, 1346 A.H., p. 255.

[134] *Ibid.*, p. 183.

[135] *Ibid.*

[136] *Qur'án*, 3:104; see also *Qur'án*, 3:110 and 22:41.

[137] Kamali, 2010, p. 30, see *supra* note 81.

[138] Kamali, 2010, p. 30, see *supra* note 81.

'ayní') of each and every Muslim. According to Ibn Kat͟hír, verse 3:104 asserts that although *ḥisbah* is incumbent on each member of the '*'Ummah*', that is, the Muslim community or society as a whole, to the extent of one's ability, the fulfilment of this task falls to a specific segment of the *'Ummah.*[139] It has been argued that *ḥisbah* becomes an individual obligation, creating a personal responsibility for the individual concerned, in just one situation: "when there is only one person in the entire community, or when a single individual witnesses evil being committed".[140] Thus in all other situations, *ḥisbah* remains a collective duty of the community as a whole.

The dual characterization of *ḥisbah* as both rights and duties is recognized in the 1981 Universal Islamic Declaration of Human Rights, under Article 4 "The Right to Justice".[141] Paragraph (c) of this provision explicitly defines *ḥisbah* as "the right and duty of every person to defend the rights of any other person and the community in general".

According to the following *ḥadít͟h* (plural *ḥadít͟hs or aḥadít͟h*), believers are encouraged to carry out *ḥisbah* to the extent of both their own ability and what their circumstances permit. The *ḥadít͟h* further outlines the (minimum of) three ways of performing *ḥisbah*:

> Whoever among you sees an evil action, let him change it with his hand (by taking action); if he cannot, then with his tongue (by speaking out); and if he cannot, then with his heart (by hating it and feeling it is wrong), and that is the weakest of faith.[142]

Clearly the *ḥadít͟h* commands physical action, and it is the literal interpretation of this part by groups such as IS which is problematic. The issue lies in the broad interpretation of what is considered 'evil', combined with jihádists' interpretation "which turns *use of the hand* into a strict ideology of hisbah applied to all spheres of life, especially public piety".[143] If 'evil' were interpreted as, for example, an attack on an innocent person, then preventing that physically would pose no problem. However, when 'evil' is interpreted as any deviation from moral rules, even when the effect of such deviation does not go beyond the person themself, then this defies the *Qur'ánic* stipulation that God should be the only judge in such matters.

---

139 Kathir, 2003, p. 233, see *supra* note 106.

140 Kamali, 2010, p. 29, see *supra* note 81.

141 Islamic Council of Europe, Universal Islamic Declaration of Human Rights, 19 September 1981 (https://www.legal-tools.org/doc/9a9cfe/).

142 Muslim, 2007, pp. 143–44, see *supra* note 129.

143 Seth H. George, "Commanding the Right Islamic Morality and Why It Matters Chaplain", in *Military Review*, 2016, vol. 96, no. 5, pp. 60–67, p. 63.

It has been argued that putting things right ('*taghíyyr*') with the hand is the prerogative of political authorities, who, it is argued, are implementing the tongue of scholars and the heart of the common people.[144] "This elitist interpretation", according to Cook and Meijer, "confirms the state's monopoly of force and the 'natural' hierarchical structure of society".[145]

As a function of the state, *ḥisbah* was instituted from the early Abbasid Caliphate, whereby the 'Caliph' or Sultán would appoint a '*muḥtasib*', that is, the chief of municipal administration and policing with three main functions: policing of markets; monitoring the state of the roads and buildings in the city; and enforcement of public morals.[146] The *muḥtasib* occupied a position between the *qáḍí* and the police[147] and generally had to be "a *faqíh* [someone with an understanding of *fiqh* (Islámic jurisprudence)], aware of the rules of Islamic law so as to know what to order and what to forbid".[148] They had the power to enforce the honouring of debts and to take such other actions that did not require formal hearings or verdicts.[149]

The term *ḥisbah* is mentioned in the *Qur'án* only in the context of a volunteer, thus it is fair to state that by making it an official religious post, the Abbásíd Caliph transformed the concept into a political tool to eliminate potential enemies and to portray himself as a defender of the faith.[150] Enforcing *ḥisbah* should not create greater mischief than the one that is to be prevented,[151] the *Qur'án* clearly states in verse 2:256 that there is no compulsion in religion, therefore enforcing Islám upon people by violent means directly contradicts this.

144 Michael Cook, *Forbidding Wrong in Islam*, Cambridge University Press, 2003, pp. 3–4 and pp. 11–12.

145 Roel Meijer, "Commanding Right and Forbidding Wrong as Principle of Social Action: The Case of the Egyptian al-Jama'a al-Islamiyya", in Roel Meijer (ed.), *Global Salafism: Islam's New Religious Movement*, Columbia University Press, 2009, p. 191, citing Cook, 2003, *ibid.*

146 Sami Zubaida, *Law and Power in the Islamic World*, I.B. Tauris, London, 2003, p. 59.

147 Knut S. Vikor, *Between God and the Sultan: A Historical Introduction to Islamic Law*, Hurst, London, 2004, p. 197.

148 Abd al-Rahmān b. Nasr al-Shayzarī, *The Book of the Islamic Market Inspector: Nihayat al-Rutba fi Talab al-Hisbah (The Utmost Authority in the Pursuit of Hisbah)*, Ross. P. Buckley (trans. and ed.), Oxford University Press, 1999, p. 28.

149 Khaldun, 1980, p. 463, see *supra* note 125.

150 Ahmed Mansour, Ahl AlQuran, "Hisbah: A Historical Overview", International Quranic Center, 7 August 2006.

151 Kamarudin bin Ahmad, "*Wilayat Al-Hisbah*; A Means to Achieve Justice and Maintain High Ethical Standards in Societies", in *Mediterranean Journal of Social Sciences*, 2015, vol. 6, pp. 201–206, p. 205.

27.4.2. The Misuse of *Ḥisbah*

There are numerous examples of states, extremist groups, and courts using *ḥisbah* to impose apostasy sentences, such as that declared by the Supreme *Sharí'ah* Court of Sudan against al-Amín Dawúd Muḥammad Ṭáhah. The point of interest here is that the litigants used *ḥisbah* as the grounds for their legal action against Ṭáhah, successfully asking the court to declare Ṭáhah's '*riddah*' ('apostasy') or to consider him as a '*murtad*' ('apostate').[152]

A similar example of the use of *ḥisbah* in a court was a 1995 Egyptian case involving Náṣr Ḥamid Abú Zayd, a lecturer of Arabic literature at Cairo University. Abú Zayd's promotion was blocked by Dr. 'Abd al-Ṣábúr Shahín, a member of the review committee, who issued a declaration of apostasy on the grounds that Zayd's work offended Islám.[153] Dr. Shahín's counsel grounded his lawsuit against *Zayd* in the concept of *ḥisbah*,[154] and the court acquiesced, acknowledging society's "direct interest in filling a *hisbah* suit".[155]

27.4.3. Náṣíḥah

Náṣíḥah is one of the key tools one could use to combat hate speech, so it seems fit to delve deeper into what this term might mean. *'Náṣíḥah'* is often translated as 'sincere advice' and 'wise counsel'. The dictionary defines the term *náṣíḥah* as "sincere advice, friendly admonition, and friendly reminder".[156] Sheikh Riyáḍ al-Ḥáq stresses a generous intention stemming from the root meanings of purity and wishing well embedded in the word *náṣíḥah*: "The idea of someone advising another is that they have the other person's best interests at heart. They wish well for them and want them to succeed".[157]

Kamali states that *náṣíḥah* is to be distinguished from reprimand (referred to as '*tawbíkh*'), in order to avoid any confusion that may be caused from their possible overlap. al-Ghazalí demonstrates that the principal difference between *náṣíḥah* and *tawbíkh* is that the former is perceived to be more confidential and courteous, whereas the latter is public and tactless.[158] To further this point, Imám ash-Shafi'í observed that when an individual advises his brother in a

[152] Mohamed A. Mahmoud, *Quest For Divinity: A Critical Examination of the Thought of Mahmud Muhammad Taha*, Syracuse University Press, New York, 2006, p. 22.

[153] Susanne Olsson, "Apostasy in Egypt: Contemporary Cases of *Hisbah*", in *The Muslim World*, 2008, vol. 98, pp. 95–115, p. 104.

[154] Hussein Ali Agrama, *Questioning Secularism: Islam, Sovereignty, and the Rule of Law in Modern Egypt*, University of Chicago Press, 2012, p. 46.

[155] Cairo Court of Appeals, Case No. 287 of Judicial Year 11, 14 June 1995 in Agrama, 2012, *ibid.*, p. 49 (https://www.legal-tools.org/doc/dcmm56/).

[156] Shaykh R. ul Haq, "The Meaning of 'Nasihah'", in *Al Kawthar Academy*, 8 December 2017.

[157] *Ibid.*

[158] Kamali, 2008, p. 34, see *supra* note 6.

confidential manner, he has provided him *náṣíḥah*. However, if he chooses to carry out the same act publicly or openly, he has ridiculed and belittled him and has therefore given him *tawbíkh*. In the words of Kamali:

> The essence of *nasīhah* in Islam is to encourage a vigilant but caring attitude on the part of the believers, who are expected to maintain and protect the moral and religious values of Islam. Thus, the individual is entitled to give sincere counsel to others when he is convinced of the essential benefit of his advice. *Nasīhah* is generally seen as an integral part of *hīsbah*, with the only proviso being that the emphasis in *nasīha* is laid on the first of its twin aspects, namely, enjoining good (*al-amr bi'l-ma'rūf*) rather than forbidding evil. In this way, *nasīhah* takes for granted the right of every individual to form an opinion or advice in which he or she sees a benefit, and the right to convey it in confidence to others, be it a fellow citizen or a government leader [...]. The centrality of *nasīhah* to the promotion of good and prevention of evil is once again confirmed in a *Hadīth* in which *nasīhah* is declared to be the essence of the religion [...]. *Nasīhah* is also the antidote of *ghībah* (backbiting), in that when Muslim observes a fault on the part of another, or a benefit that he envisages for him, the matter should be communicated between them.[159]

In context, the term *náṣíḥah* is a *Qur'ánic* concept that refers to the purpose and function of the prophethood. Therefore, it is the prophets Noah, Salid Hud and Shuʿayb who informed their people that they must provide warning, much like a sincere advisor does, as part of their mission. Further to this, the *ḥadíth* provides that *náṣíḥah* is a given right that every Muslim has which consists of, for example, responding to a greeting ('*salam*'). To exercise this right, the *ḥadíth* provides that "when you are asked for *nasihah*, then you must give it". To accommodate the right, Imám Aḥmad Ibn Ḥanbal demonstrates that *náṣíḥah* is a collective obligation (*fárḍ kafa'í*) which is required to be given even where it has not been solicited or asked for.[160]

The first of the two *ḥadíths* both begin with "the right of a Muslim" (*'háq al-Muslim'*) and so within this context, *náṣíḥah* in this *ḥadíth* is understood to embody a right that can be claimed, not necessarily an obligation that is required to be fulfilled. In relation to the involvement of *Sharí'ah* in this concept, it does not regulate the manner in which *náṣíḥah* is provided, due to its nature of concerning the good conscience and sincerity of the individual.[161] Rather than

---

[159] Kamali, 2008, pp. 34–35, see *supra* note 6.

[160] *Ibid.*, p. 34.

[161] *Ibid.*, p. 36.

providing a particular procedure in which *náṣíḥah* should be followed, the *Sunnah* advocates guidance in which the best form of *náṣíḥah* can be followed:

(a) That *náṣíḥah* must not involve exposing or exploring the privacy and personal weaknesses of people (*tatabbu' al-'áwrát*);
(b) that it is given in the best possible form, with an awareness of the suitability of the occasion, time and place;
(c) that it is founded on certainty and not on speculation, estimation, or suspicion;
(d) that it is given to the extent necessary and that excess is avoided;
(e) that it is in harmony with the guidance of the *Qur'án* and the *Sunnah.*[162]

Early Islámic history offers instances of the dangers of "rushing to judgement" in cases of public hate speech. For instance, in a liberal treatment of charges, the Caliph 'Alí accepted that someone who committed apostasy was nonetheless not *kafír*; rather, he should be given sincere advice ('*náṣíḥah*') to correct his error. This follows the *Qur'ánic* invocation that argumentation should be conducted with tolerance and courtesy[163] – lessons that might well counter those guilty of hate speech in the present, as fierce punishment may make them more rigid in their wrongful ways.

27.4.4. Máslaḥah

Dr. Muhammad Khalid Masud, director of the Appellate Division of the main *S̲harí'ah* court in Pakistan, has explored the concept of '*máṣlaḥah'* and its ethical implications in the present. He concludes that the concept has utility beyond *S̲harí'ah* rulings. In particular, he argues that in facing the broader demands of modern society, and where one finds no clear precedent from the past, including from *Sunnah* and *ḥadít̲h̲s*, we can employ intellect and analogies beyond the five key stipulations (as listed by Kamali above). He says one should consider the purpose of law and its spirit, rather than just the letter of the law. He further argues that *máṣlaḥah* and Islámic law can be "applicable and understandable not only for Muslims but also in the globalized world we live in today, especially regarding [questions of] human rights".[164] Indeed, the *Sunnah* and *ḥadít̲h̲s* repeatedly commend believers to contribute to fraternity and peace in society. One such text insists that this mode is not confined to Muslims alone. One should

---

162 *Ibid.*, p. 37.

163 *Qur'án*, 16:125.

164 "Dr. Muhammad Khalid Masud: The Concept of 'Maṣlaḥah' and its Ethical Implications", Lecture at the Research Centre for Islamic Legislation and Ethics, Doha, 2 December 2015 (available on YouTube).

aim for a world-wide brotherhood where everyone feels safe, under the principle of "promoting good and preventing evil".[165]

27.4.5. Tools in Islámic Law for Reacting to Hate Speech Against Muslims

The *Qur'án* itself contains advice on how to react to hate speech: "heed not their annoyances [or 'annoying talk]"[166] and "when ye hear the signs of God held in defiance and ridicule [or 'disbelieved in and mocked at'] ye are not to sit with them unless they turn to a different theme".[167]

Among options for non-juridical opposition to evil, Kamali notes that several *Sunní* commentators recommend the stance of "silent disapproval". For instance, the well-known Muslim jurist Aḥmad Ibn Ḥanbal advised a follower who knew the *Sunnah,* but was faced with a hostile and ignorant crowd, to speak their truth and then remain silent, rather than indulging in a "hostile exchange". Conversely, other commentators consider such a passive approach, akin to '*táqiyah*', as potentially dangerous because heresy and corruption may prevail; in such a situation, few can tell truth from falsehood.[168] As Aḥmad Ibn Ḥanbal averred, when learned persons are the ones promoting such confusion, how can the ignorant hope to find guidance?[169]

Another element to consider is the role of forgiveness when confronted by hate speech, as well as limits to the implementation of forgiveness. The virtue of forgiveness is further amplified in *Qur'ánic* verses 3:134 and 13:43. Moreover, the second part of the famous *Qur'ánic* verse 4:149 encapsulates useful guidance on this question. It reads: "Whether ye publish a good deed or conceal it or cover evil with pardon [or 'forgive evil'] verily God doth blot out (sins) and hath power (in the judgment of values) [or 'God is forgiving, omnipotent']". According to interpretation, the verse appears to enjoin upon the one who is sinned against a moral duty to forgive, but not necessarily a legal one. This comes in anticipation of the ultimate judge, God, and his cherishing of mercy. These are crucial established parameters for considering the balance between law and morality. The challenge is to identify the point where continuous forgiveness acts as an aid to evil, and not as a means of countering it.

27.5. Internal Measures and Informal Sanctions

Religious leaders can play an important role in combatting hate speech, by virtue of the multiple roles they perform in their societies. The role of religious leaders

---

[165] Kamali, 2008, pp. 169–70, see *supra* note 6.

[166] *Qur'án*, 33:48.

[167] *Qur'án*, 4:140.

[168] Kamali, 2008, p. 159, see *supra* note 6.

[169] *Ibid.*, p. 160.

does not stop at offering interpretations of Islám (*'fatwás'*), but rather they also assume other roles in administering endowments and charities, regulating mosques and prayers, training preachers, supervising Islámic education, and proposing legislations. It is the purpose of this section to sketch a number of measures that religious leaders can implement in those different roles to combat hate speech.

27.5.1. Endowments and Charity

Beginning with endowments, the idea of Islámic endowments (*'al-Wáqf'*) is that the owner (mainly of a real estate) gives up his property rights by a permanent and irrevocable legal act, so that the property can no longer be sold or transferred, but rather is repurposed for religious, educational or any other benevolent purposes. There are two kinds of Islámic endowments: the family endowment, where the beneficiary is a particular person or a family member or his descendants; and the public endowment, where the beneficiary is the public, for example, giving up a piece of land to be used for building a hospital or a school. Although originally endowments were private initiatives administered by the donor himself,[170] they are now largely administered by the state's ministry of endowments. It is here that religious leaders are engaged, as the heads of such ministries of endowments. In that respect, religious leaders should ensure that none of the members of the ministry have engaged or continue to engage in hate speech or support extremist ideology. Religious leaders, in their role within ministries of endowments, should verify that an endowment's assets are not used in inciting violence and hate speech, nor that its beneficiaries are involved or have been involved in inciting violence and hatred.

While endowments are somehow centralized by being administered through the ministry of endowments, charities, in the form of almsgiving (*'Zakah'*) and voluntary giving (*'Ṣádáqát'*), are decentralized, and are thus more prone to being used to finance extremists.[171] Given that religious leaders are key players when it comes to collecting donations and organizing charities, due to

[170] See Jamal Malik, *Islam in South Asia: A Short History*, Brill, Leiden, 2008, p. 234.

[171] Unlike the situation in the United Arab of Emirates, where the Law No. 3 for the year 2021 has banned the collection – by all means – of donations by individuals and allows only its collection by only certain organizations. For the legislation (in Arabic), see United Arab Emirates, Federal Law No. 3 of 2021 Concerning the Regulation of Fundraising Activities (authors' translation), 21 April 2021 (https://www.legal-tools.org/doc/l2jlk8/). Moving towards the centralization of the process of collecting donations, the Egyptian Ministry of Endowments adopted in 2013 a decision to ban the collection of donations through mosques to prevent the use of money collected in funding extremists. See Hind Mustafa, "Ba'd Qárár al-Áwqáf bi-man' Jam' at-Tabáru'at – Istikhdam al-Masajid fi Jam' al-Amwal li-Khidmat Fáṣíl Siyasí Intihak li-Ḥormatiha", *Ahram*, 3 September 2013. However, full centralization in that context has not yet been achieved in Egypt.

their influence in society, they are thus responsible for ensuring that donations are used for their intended charitable purposes. As such, religious leaders should actively campaign against donating to certain groups known to engage in hate speech and incitement of violence.

As a measure to emphasize the peaceful co-existence of all religions and to combat hate speech, religious leaders should also encourage making donations to non-Muslims. In 2009, Sheikh Muḥammad Ṭánṭáwí, the head of Al-Ázhár University ('Al-Azhar'), issued a *fatwá* that a Muslim is permitted to participate in building a church, and that it is incorrect to depict the building of churches as a sinful act under Islámic law.[172] During the Covid-19 pandemic, the Egyptian Dar Al-Ifta issued a *fatwá* that donations (*ṣádáqát*) are allowed to be directed at non-Muslims.[173]

27.5.2. Mosques and Prayers

Mosques can indeed constitute a fertile ground for hate speech to grow and spread if preachers (imáms) holding prayers adhere to extremist ideology. Therefore, an important measure to be implemented by religious leaders is to prevent the access of those preachers to prayers or devotional gatherings. Nevertheless, the implementation of this measure will vary depending on the degree of authority held by religious leaders in appointing and dismissing preachers in mosques. In some countries – for example, Egypt,[174] Tunisia[175] and Morocco[176] – the control and supervision of mosques is retained by the state, and represented by its Ministry of Endowments or the Ministry of Religious Affairs. This has facilitated the dismissal of imáms with extremists ideology and those who have engaged in spreading hate speech against other religious minorities.[177] Additionally, for example in Egypt, the Ministry of Endowments, in collaboration with the Al-Azhar institution, has unified topics addressed by preachers during the

[172] Issam Saliba, "Egypt: Contribution by Muslims to Build a Church Allowed in Islam", in *Library of Congress*, 26 August 2009.

[173] Egypt Today Staff, "Egypt's Dar al-Iftaa: Alms-Giving Permissible for Non-Muslims to Reduce COVID-19 Economic Impacts", *Egypt Today*, 16 May 2020. A similar *fatwá* was issued when asked whether Muslims are allowed to donate to the UN High Commissioner for Refugees ('UNHCR'). See on that, UNHCR, "Dar al-Ifta al-Missriyyah, Egypt", 2 September 2020.

[174] Mena, "Awqaf Minister in Full Control of All Mosques: Minister", *Egypt Today*, 20 June 2017.

[175] State control over mosques and the appointment of imáms have been controversial. See on that Teije Hidde Donker and Kasper Netterstrom, "The Tunisian Revolution and Governance of Religion", in *Middle East Critique*, 2017, vol. 26, pp. 137–157.

[176] Control over mosques and the appointment of imáms began in 2003 after the Casablanca terrorist attacks. Brown, 2017, p. 13, see *supra* note 60.

[177] Tarek Radwan, "Egypt's Ministry of Endowments and the Fight Against Extremism", Atlantic Council, 23 July 2015.

Friday prayer sermons as a measure to prevent hate speech.[178] When the appointment of imáms is not state-centered, for example in Nigeria,[179] or in Muslim communities in Europe,[180] religious leaders can use their influence on the public and campaign for the appointment of non-radicalized imáms as well as for the dismissal of those who have exhibited extremist ideologies.

27.5.3. Media

It is beyond any shadow of a doubt that "the misuse of traditional and social media is an enormous factor in spreading hate speech"[181] and, as a consequence, religious leaders should exert effort to combat hate speech in the media. While religious leaders have no direct control over media content or agendas, they can still play an important role in combating hate speech in the media. Using their influence on their communities, religious leaders can launch campaigns demanding the suspension of those inciting hate speech from access to mass-media. Muslim religious leaders can also take advantage of being consulted by state authorities in many instances to regulate media content. For example, in 2017, the Al-Azhar institution in Egypt exclusively authorized fifty scholars to issue religious *fatwás* in media outlets, and entrusted the oversight of such authorizations in the Egyptian Supreme Council for Media, which is responsible for monitoring the content of media outlets. In response, the Council has threatened to sue channels that do not abide by the list. This measure was adopted in response to the increase in the number of *fatwás* issued that tarnished the image of Islám. In addition to that, religious leaders can play an active role, filing lawsuits against those engaged in hate speech and incitement to violence.

The Egyptian Office of the State *Muftí* ('*Dar Al-Ifta al-Miṣríyyah*')[182] and Al-Azhar have taken the fight against extremism one step further, by establishing an observatory that has as its main objective the combatting of extremist ideology.[183] This observatory monitors, *inter alia*, hate speech and incitement to violence conducted in media outlets, be they traditional or online social

[178] Egypt, Law No. 51 of 2014, 5 June 2014 (https://www.legal-tools.org/doc/lekdze/).

[179] Ismael Saka Ismael and Abdulmumini A. Oba, "Administration of Mosques and Appointment of Imams in Nigeria: Between Islamic Law, Customs, and State Law", in *Islamabad Law Review*, 2020, vol. 4, iss. 1 and 2.

[180] See generally about imáms in Western Europe, Mohammed Hashas, Jan Jaap de Ruiter and Niels V. Vinding (eds.), *Imams in Western Europe: Developments, Transformations, and Institutional Challenges*, Amsterdam University Press, 2018.

[181] G20 Interfaith Forum Policy Brief, "A G20 Interfaith Forum Policy Brief, Countering Hate speech: Roles of Religion and Culture", 5 November 2020, p. 5.

[182] See Egypt's Dar Al-Ifta web site.

[183] See the web sites of the Dar Al-Ifta Observatory and the Al-Azhar Observatory for Combatting Extremism.

media.[184] Members of the observatory, then, condemn those statements and provide counter arguments, delegitimizing those responsible.[185] The observatory also works to document instances of hate speech and incitement to violence that could be beneficial in holding those responsible criminally liable. The establishment of observatories has been praised as an important measure in combatting extremism,[186] such as the Saudi Observatory of Etidal which was established in 2017.[187] Observatories are proactive measures that facilitate responses to hate speech and that can prevent it from escalating to violence.

27.5.4. Legislative Efforts

Religious leaders can have direct or indirect access to legislative bodies in Muslim countries. Thus, they can play an important role in presenting legislative proposals or participate in formulating proposals that aim to combat hate speech. For example, in Egypt, Al-Azhar proposed in 2017 a stand-alone piece of legislation to combat religiously-motivated hate speech. Religious leaders can also launch campaigns in support of draft legislation that aim to combat religion-based hate speech.

27.5.5. Education

Education remains one of the most important measures in combatting hate speech. Religious leaders have a key role to play in that respect, primarily on foot of their influence within their communities. Additionally, religious leaders affiliated to state religious institutions have the privilege of accessing educational systems, either directly in the case of religious schools or indirectly by contributing to decisions around the legal content of religious textbooks taught at schools falling under the umbrella of the state's ministry of education. For example, Al-Azhar in Egypt revised its learning curriculum in 2013, removing

[184] It has been reported that the Dar Al-Ifta Observatory has monitored "more than 5,500 fatwas worldwide, most of which were deemed to give incorrect or misleading opinions about the relationship between Muslims and Christians in Islám; 70% of the fatwas prohibited Muslims from dealing with non-Muslims and 20% of them strongly advised against it". See Nader A. Foutouh, "The Fight of Egypt's Dar al-Ifta Against Extremism, Islamophobia", *The Arab Weekly*, 2 February 2020.

[185] See, for example, the report issued by Dr. Sháwqí 'Allam, The Grand Mufti of Egypt, *The Ideological Battlefield: Egypt's Dar-al Iftaa Combats Radicalization*, Dar al-Iftaa in Egypt, 2018.

[186] See Dar Al-Ifta, "The UN Praises Dar al-Ifta for Its Efforts in Combating Extremism"; Dar Al-Ifta, "Japanese Ambassador in Cairo Applauds the Efforts of Al-Azhar Observatory", 14 June 2021; see also Press Trust of India, "India to Set up IT Center in Egypt's Al Azhar University", *Economic Times*, 21 December 2017.

[187] Global Center for Combatting Extremist Ideology.

content considered to incite hate and violence against Christians.[188] This revision is to be conducted every three years. Al-Azhar also focuses on Islámic education in '*Katatíb*' (places where children learn to memorize and understand the *Qur'án*).[189]

Furthermore, Al-Azhar alumni published a magazine for children entitled 'The Light' ('*an-Núr*'), with the main objective of spreading a moderate version of Islám and its moral values.[190] The Egyptian Ministry of Endowments, on its part, has initiated the International *Áwqáf* Academy to train imáms.[191] Another important measure to be implemented by religious leaders in the educational context is to dismiss those with radical ideology from accessing educational institutions as an instructor.

27.6. Challenges to the Effectiveness of Measures Adopted by Religious Leaders

The significant potential impact of measures adopted by religious leaders in combatting hate speech could nevertheless be undermined, due to several factors. The aim of this section is to identify those challenges and to suggest some thoughts on ways to increase the effectiveness of the role of religious leaders in combatting hate speech within their communities.

One of the challenges to the effectiveness of measures adopted by religious leaders is the fragmentation of the religious authority in Muslim countries. For example, in Egypt, religious authority is exercised across the *Dar Al-Ifta Al-Miṣríyyah*,[192] the Al-Azhar institution, and the Ministry of Endowments.[193] In Saudi Arabia, there is the Commission for the Promotion of Virtue and the Prevention of Vice, the Council of Senior Scholars,[194] and the Ministry of Religious Affairs. While in Morocco, there is the Ministry of Religious Affairs and the Supreme *'Ulama'* Council, the latter headed by the King. This is not to mention that official religious leaders are challenged by individual religious leaders not affiliated to any institution.

---

188 Hisham A. Hellyer, "Country Report: Egypt, in GREASE Religion, Diversity and Radicalization", in *GREASE*, November 2019.

189 Reham Mokbel, "Al-Azhar Rethinks Primary School Teaching to Encourage Moderation", *Al Monitor*, 13 July 2015.

190 The magazine is published under the auspices of Al-Azhar.

191 See on that, Ahmed Aleem, "Egypt Launches International Academy for Preachers, Imams", *Al Monitor*, 24 January 2019.

192 Dar Al-Ifta was established in 1895 and affiliated to the Ministry of Justice on 21 November 1895 by Decree No. 10. For its role, see Dar Al-Ifta, "About" (available on its web site).

193 See the web site of the Ministry of Áwqáf of Egypt.

194 It was established by Royal Decree in 1972 under King Faisal. It is vested with the right to produce official religious rulings, or *fatáwá*, within the kingdom.

The fragmentation of religious authority can be detrimental to the effectiveness of measures adopted by some religious leaders without co-operating with the others. For example, in Egypt, the measure of enlisting fifty jurists by Al-Azhar (approved by the Egyptian Supreme Council for Media) as those exclusively entitled to issue *fatwás* was challenged by the Ministry of Endowments, because not one of its members was included on the list. In response, the Ministry presented its own list of preachers who it deemed to have the exclusive authority of issuing *fatwás*.[195] This can have the effect of delegitimizing the measure taken to combat extremism in the eyes of the public, as the lists presented might be perceived as competing for religious authority, while there is no clear criteria for which persons should included on the list. Similarly, the measure of unifying sermons delivered on Fridays during prayers – implemented by the Ministry of Endowments – was rejected by Al-Azhar.[196] This has raised concerns among the public. Furthermore, it has been reported that a number of leaders explicitly rejected preachers reading the sermons from a written paper by tearing the paper down,[197] revealing the negative effect of non-co-operation between religious leaders in implementing measures in combatting hate speech.

Another factor undermining the effectiveness of measures adopted by religious leaders is public concern that those measures would impinge upon their rights, particularly their freedom of expression. For example, in Egypt, Al-Azhar's response to the opinions of Islám El Behairy, a TV host and researcher, about the need to reform the Islámic discourse within Al-Azhar itself, as well as the sources on which it relies, has been criticized for violating his freedom of expression.[198] Al-Azhar filed a law suit against El Behairy, who was then charged with blasphemy and sentenced to five years in prison (later reduced to one year upon appeal). The rising concern among the public that religious leaders seek to restrict their freedom of expression results in resisting measures adopted to combat hate speech. For example, in Egypt, Al-Azhar's proposal of legislation criminalizing hate speech against religions was rejected on the basis

[195] Karim El Taki, "Rivalry for Religious Dominance in Egypt", Carnegie Endowment for International Peace, 21 December 2017.

[196] "Al-Azhar Rejects Unified Written Friday Sermons", *Daily News*, 27 July 2016.

[197] «الخطبة المكتوبة»: أئمة «الأوقاف» يلتزمون و«الأزهريون» يرفضون.. والوزير: لن تفرق وحدتنا», *El Watan News*, 6 August 2016.

[198] Egyptian Initiative for Personal Rights, "EIPR Concerned With the Court Verdict Against Islam el-Beheiry, Demands A Suspension of Execution and Warns That the Case is But a Proof of Menace to Freedoms by Agencies Desiring to Act as Guardians to Society", press release, 29 December 2015; Ishak Ibrahim, "Obstacles to Renewing Religious Discourse in Egypt: Reasons and Results", The Tahir Institute for Middle East Policy, 31 October 2019.

that this proposal unduly restricts the freedom of expression, as protected by the Egyptian Constitution and international treaties.[199]

In that respect, religious leaders should – in the first instance – seek to educate themselves on human rights issues.[200] They should also encourage human rights education and training for imáms.[201] Religious leaders could also condition the appointment of imáms in mosques upon their receipt of human rights education. They should address the public and provide justifications for restrictions of freedom of speech in order to increase the legitimacy of measures adopted to combat hate speech and reduce resistance from within their communities to such measures, thereby increasing their effectiveness.

One of the main challenges that significantly undermines the effectiveness of measures implemented by religious leaders to combat hate speech is the involvement of the government– either explicitly or tacitly – in inciting hatred and violence against religious minorities. For example, in 2013, the Egyptian *Shí'ah* Sheikh Ḥassan Shiḥatah and three of his followers were killed in Zawyat Abú Musallam, Giza Governate. This drastic incident was reported to occur in the wake of months of incitement to hatred and violence against *Shí'ah*.[202] It has also been reported that the then-President Mohamed Morsi tacitly supported incitement against *Shí'ah* by failing to condemn the evocation of inciting speech

---

[199] For a discussion on this proposal with a professor at Al-Azhar University, see Rehab Ismail, "Al-Azhar Proposes Law Against Religious Hatred, Violence", *Egypt Today*, 25 June 2017. For a criticism of this law, see (in Arabic): "Al-Wiṣáyah ad-Díníyyah Laysat Ḥallan al-Mubadarah al-Miṣríyyah', Tuḥadhir miin Muqṭáráḥ Qánún Khiṭáb al-Káráhíyah al-Muqáddam min Mashyakhat al-Ázhár", 22 August 2022, Egyptian Initiative for Personal Rights, 22 August 2017.

[200] It has been argued that religious leaders in Egypt receive no training or continuing education once they are placed in positions of responsibility. See Brown, 2017, p. 10, *supra* note 60.

[201] Human rights training programmes have been designed for religious leaders. For example, the Organization for Security and Co-operation in Europe Office for Democratic Institutions and Human Rights organized a training for trainers of imáms and community leaders on responding to hate crimes against Muslims, see "Training for Trainers of Imams and Community Leaders on Responding to Hate Crimes Against Muslims", OSCE, 9–11 November 2013. Furthermore, Turkey has trained through the Rights Education Action Programme faith groups and religious authorities: see Amnesty International, "Human Rights Education Engaging New Target Groups", May 2010; Habib Toumi, "Qatar Imams Undergo Human Rights Training", *Gulf News*, 22 June 2011. See as well, The Imam Training Academy of the Foundation of Bangladesh (Joint Learning Initiative on Faith and Local Communities (JLIFLC), "Imam Training Academy of the Islamic Foundation of Bangladesh"); William Watkinson, "Italy to Train Muslim Imams on Country's Constitution to Improve Integration and Fight Terrorism", *International Business Times*, 1 November 2017.

[202] Human Rights Watch, "Egypt: Lynching of Shia Follows Months of Hate Speech", 27 June 2013.

against them during a conference on 'Egypt-Syria Solidarity'.[203] Furthermore, government agencies failed to take measures against those responsible for inciting hatred against *S̲hí'ah*.[204] Against this background, measures adopted by Al-Azhar – be it the mere condemnation of the killing incident or the convening of a conference including *Sunní* and *S̲hí'ah* imáms and scholars – have proved ineffective in reducing incitement to hatred and violence against *S̲hí'ah*, especially as some of its members and other members affiliated with official religious institutions – at that time – were allegedly involved in inciting hatred against *S̲hí'ah*.[205]

Another challenge to the effectiveness of measures adopted by religious leaders that warrants highlighting in this chapter is the limited outreach of those measures. Indeed, attempts of religious leaders to respond to online extremism and hate speech by issuing e-*fatwás* and online counter-narratives have been praised for reaching a wider audience. Nevertheless, moving online is arguably insufficient, because interpretations and counter-narratives provided by religious leaders are not accessible to poor people, who have neither Internet access nor the necessary equipment to access those interpretations. Given that people living in poverty are more vulnerable to extremism,[206] focusing on countering extremist ideology online is deficient, undermining the overall effectiveness of measures adopted in combatting hate speech and incitement of violence. Therefore, religious leaders should work on disseminating counter-narratives to interpretations advanced by extremists through means accessible to the various economic classes within their communities.[207]

Counter-interpretations and narratives adopted by religious leaders have also been criticized for having limited impact on extremists themselves, undermining the effectiveness of those measures in reducing hate speech. It has been argued, for example, that the terrorist group *Da'is̲h̲*/IS does not browse *fatwá*

---

[203] Ryan J. Suto, "Former President Morsi's Legal Liability for Incitement to Violence", Atlantic Council, 7 October 2013.

[204] Amnesty International, "Egypt: President Morsi Must Send Clear Message Against Attacks on Shí'ah Muslims", 24 June 2013.

[205] It has been reported that the Under Secretary of the Egyptian Ministry of Endowments incited violence against *S̲hí'ah*. See Egyptian Initiative for Personal Rights, "State's Islam and Forbidden Diversity: Shia and the Crisis of Religious Freedoms in Egypt, 2011–2016, Analytical Report", June 2016.

[206] See on that, Corinne Graff, "Poverty, Development, and Violent Extremism in Weak States", in Susan E. Rice *et al.* (eds.), *Confronting Poverty: Weak States and U.S. National Security*, Brookings Institution Press, 2010, pp. 42–89.

[207] The Al-Azhar institution in Egypt has, for example, installed 'Fatwá Kiosks' in underground metro stations to offer religious advice to commuters. See on that, "Azhar Opens Fatwá Kiosks in Cairo Metro Station to Counter Terrorism", *Ahram Online*, 20 July 2017.

and counter-interpretations put forward by the Al-Azhar Observatory for Combatting Extremism.[208] And while the dismissal of imáms with extremist ideology, or their suspension from access to media outlets, can have a deterrent effect, it still can be counter-productive in combatting hate speech. In that respect, it is recommended for religious leaders to establish rehabilitation programmes for members of their group who have engaged in hate speech or who have shown extremist tendencies. The importance of rehabilitation programmes is becoming widely recognized in the context of combatting terrorism and extremism.[209] This is reflected in the resolution adopted by the UN Human Rights Council on the effects of terrorism on the enjoyment of all human rights, where the Council urged:

> States to adopt rehabilitation and reintegration strategies for returning foreign terrorist fighters […] and to adopt a com- prehensive approach that includes the development of national centers for counsel and deradicalization […] and in this regard welcomes the role of the Mohammed bin Naif Counseling and Care Centre in countering terrorist ideologies and activities.[210]

Rehabilitation programmes in the context of counterterrorism are a tool for the deradicalization of terrorists and extremists in the sense "of divorcing a person, voluntarily or otherwise, from their extreme views".[211] It is acknowledged that religious leaders play a key role in those programmes, particularly in counselling, which is a process of "reeducat[ing] violent extremists and extremist sympathizers through intensive religious debates" with the objective of encouraging extremists to "to renounce 'terrorist ideologies,' particularly the doctrine of *Takfir*".[212] Religious leaders play a key role in raising support among the pubic for rehabilitation programmes, thus "serving as a nexus between the rehabilitation program and the local community".[213] This is of paramount significance to helping communities reconcile with the rehabilitated persons and to

208 See Reham Mokbel, "Al Azhar Goes Online to Fight Extremism", *Al Monitor*, 26 June 2015.

209 For case studies of rehabilitation programmes in different countries, see the Report of the International Peace Institute: Ellie B. Hearne and Nur Laiq, "A New Approach? Deradicalization Programs and Counterterrorism", International Peace Institute, June 2010, p. 2; Lorenzo Vidino (ed.), *Deradicalization in the Mediterranean: Comparing Challenges and Approaches,* Ledizioni-LediPublishing, Milano, 2018; Angel Rabasa *et al.* (eds.), *Deradicalizing Islamist Extremists*, RAND Corporation, 2010.

210 UN Human Rights Council, Effects of Terrorism on the Enjoyment of All Human Rights, A/HRC/31/L.13/Rev.1, 23 March 2016 (https://www.legal-tools.org/doc/cs5gla/).

211 See Hearne and Laiq, 2010, p. 2, *supra* note 209.

212 See Christopher Boucek, "Saudi Arabia's 'Soft' Counterterrorism Strategy: Prevention, Rehabilitation, and Aftercare", in *Carnegie Papers*, 2008, no. 97, p.11.

213 See Andrew Mcdonnel, "A Community Approach to Jihadis' Rehabilitation in Tunisia", Carnegie Endowment for International Peace, 27 September 2018.

avoid the latter's marginalization and limitation of opportunities, which can drive them back to extremism and which make them more vulnerable to recruitment by terrorists.

Similarly, religious leaders should establish rehabilitation programmes to deradicalize imáms and others engaged in religion-based hate speech. They should also build support for those programmes, so that rehabilitated persons will not themselves encounter hate speech from within their communities.

27.7. Conclusion

While the international community increasingly stresses the role of religious leaders in combatting hate speech that constitutes incitement to discrimination, hostility or violence, religious leaders under Islámic law are obliged to act against hate speech. As previously discussed, the source of this obligation lies in the Islámic concept of *ḥisbah*. In this regard, the pure *ḥadíth* states that:

> Whoever amongst you sees an evil, he must change it with his hand. If he is not able to do so, then with his tongue. And if he is not able to do so, then with his heart, and that is the weakest form of faith.[214]

This *ḥadíth* offers not only a timeless moral compass but also a call to action in the battle against evil – in this case, against hate speech.

"Change with his hand [...] then with his tongue" entails that religious leaders should use the tools available to them – through the different roles they assume in their communities – to combat hate speech. This chapter has attempted to sketch out a number of measures that could be used in that context. Besides interpretations (*fatwás*) and naming and shaming, those measures may include denial of access to mosques; inability to serve on boards or in other capacities in humanitarian or educational institutions of the community; inability to lead prayer or other forms of communal worship; denial of the right to make financial contributions to (certain) funds of the community; and suspension of access to mass-media.

Nevertheless, hate speech is not confined to Muslim communities, but is a common challenge to all communities. As previously stressed, the present authors share the Beirut participants' deep conviction that "all respective religions and beliefs share a common commitment to upholding the dignity and the equal worth of all human beings".[215] Thus, religious leaders in non-Muslim communities share a similar responsibility in combatting hate speech within their communities.

---

214 "Forty Ḥadíth of an-Nawawi, Ḥadíth 34, 40 Ḥadíth an-Nawawi" (available on the *Sunnah.com.fl* web site).

215 OHCHR, 2017, see *supra* note 3.

Given that the role of religious leaders in non-Muslim and Muslim communities is relatively similar – as both assume roles in administering endowments and charities,[216] regulating places of worship, training preachers, supervising religious education, proposing legislations and broadcasting religious content – this chapter concludes by expressing the hope that measures sketched above may be generalized and adapted to be applied by religious leaders in non-Muslim communities as well, albeit with consideration of variances between different religions.

216 See on that, Gabriel Baer and Miriam Hoexter, "The Muslim Waqf and Similar Institutions in Other Civilizations", in Michael Borgolte (ed.), *Stiftungen in Christentum, Judentum und Islam vor der Moderne*, Akademie Verlag, Berlin, 2009, pp. 257–280; Julia R. Lieberman and Michal Jan Rozbicki (eds.), *Charity in Jewish, Christian, and Islamic Traditions*, Lexington Books, 2017.

28

Religion as a Legal Resource: Religious or Belief Leaders and the Countering of 'Hateful Speech'

Nazila Ghanea[*]

Having long been involved in assessing the relationships between freedom of religion or belief, freedom of expression and minority rights from a human rights law perspective, the challenge of examining this topic from the standpoint of the role of religious or belief leaders in this sphere was certainly an interesting and very welcome one.

28.1. Religion as Grounds and as Response

The topic of religion, education and human rights is very broad ranging. There is the question of education about human rights in the formal education system and in informal education. The role of religious or belief leaders could be implicated in either of these depending on their national standing in the education system. Then there is the question of religious education in schools and how that can best respect the rights of minorities and those of different religions and beliefs, and the question of opt-outs from school religious education classes. There is also the topic of the right to education itself.

Separately to that, there have been efforts over the years to develop soft law standards regarding the role of religious leaders in advancing and securing international human rights law. These have tended to focus on atrocity crimes and interfaith understanding.

---

[*] Dr. **Nazila Ghanea** is Professor of International Human Rights Law at the University of Oxford and the United Nations ('UN') Special Rapporteur on Freedom of Religion or Belief. She is also the Director of Human Rights Programmes and is a Fellow of Kellogg College (B.A. Keele, M.A. Leeds, Ph.D. Keele and M.A. Oxon). She is the Deputy Chair of the Board of Trustees of the Geneva-based Universal Rights Group, and serves on the United Kingdom Foreign Secretary's Advisory Group on Human Rights. Her publications include *Freedom of Religion or Belief: An International Law Commentary* and a number of other monographs, edited collections, journal articles and UN publications. This chapter originates from the presentation at the Florence conference addressing "The Role of Education Within Religion and Belief Communities", CILRAP Film, 9 April 2022, Florence (https://www.cilrap.org/cilrap-film/220409-ghanea/), which was discussed in the conference section on 'Internal Measures Available to Religious Leaders'.

In this chapter, we are considering quite a specific angle on this subject matter – the question of education as a tool in the hands of religious leaders and for the specific purpose of intervening to diminish hateful speech.[1]

The hypothesis behind considering education as an internal measure available to religious leaders is, indeed, a sound one. Since hateful speech and violence – even acts of terrorism – may have had the speeches of religious or belief leaders as their trigger, sometimes allegedly in the name of God, this gives rise to the question of whether we can retrace our steps. Essentially, can religious or belief leaders help prevent or reduce hateful expression and violence by their own members, in the name of their faith?

From a legal point of view, and for our purposes, whether hateful speech and violence is grounded in religion or just perpetuated in the name of religion is not the most pertinent question. In both instances, religion is the resource which perpetuates hateful speech. It is for the same reason that the late Asma Jahangir, former UN Special Rapporteur on freedom of religion or belief, would utilize the term 'violence in the name of religion'.[2] This term is agnostic on the question of whether such violence actually stems from religion or not, that is something for theologians and religious studies experts to ponder rather than lawyers. The caution in some domestic legal systems to ensure that courts do not engage themselves in determining theological questions also provides our cue. In so far as international human rights law is concerned it is clear that, "[v]iolence in the name of religion cannot be accepted" and the relevant authorities should take "all necessary and appropriate action"[3] to combat it.

---

1 I have fully adopted this terminology from the Centre for International and Public Law of Brunel University conference and e-book title in order to allow consistency in this study. The standard used in Article 20 of the International Covenant on Civil and Political Rights, 19 December 1966 ('ICCPR') (https://www.legal-tools.org/doc/2838f3/) is "advocacy of national, racial or religious hatred that constitutes incitement to discrimination, hostility or violence" and of the 16/18 resolution is "combating intolerance, negative stereotyping and stigmatisation of, and discrimination, incitement to violence, and violence against persons based on religion or belief", see Combating Intolerance, Negative Stereotyping and Stigmatization of, and Discrimination, Incitement to Violence and Violence Against, Persons Based On Religion Or Belief, UN Doc. A/HRC/RES/16/18, 11 April 2011 ('HRC Resolution 16/18') (https://www.legal-tools.org/doc/0a86d2/). See also, Marc Limon, Nazila Ghanea, and Hilary Power, "Combating Global Religious Intolerance: The Implementation of Human Rights Council Resolution 16/18", in *Universal Rights Group*, 2014.

2 For example, this language can be found in: Report of the Special Rapporteur on Freedom of Religion or Belief, Asma Jahangir: Addendum, Mission to the Republic of Serbia, Including Visit to Kosovo, UN Doc. A/HRC/13/40/Add.3, 28 December 2009 (https://www.legal-tools.org/doc/sksonf/).

3 *Ibid.*, para. 62.

Regardless of whether religion is the source of hateful speech or merely instrumentalized to perpetuate it, we are concerned with exploring whether the 'resource' of religion can not only be inoculated against utility in this manner, but can even serve as the basis of countering hateful speech.

28.2. Education and Human Rights

The right to education is upheld in numerous human rights law instruments including the International Covenant on Economic, Social and Cultural Rights ('ICESCR').[4] Its Article 13(1) upholds that the right to education is for "everyone" and that it "shall be directed at the full development of the human personality and the sense of its dignity". It is clear that hateful speech stunts the development of the human personality and sense of dignity of both the victim and indeed the perpetrator(s).

Article 13(1), though, goes further. Education is to "strengthen the respect for human rights and fundamental freedoms" and "enable all persons to participate effectively in a free society, promote understanding, tolerance and friendship among all nations and all racial, ethnic or religious groups, and further [...] the maintenance of peace". In addressing the countering of hateful speech through education, it is important to be mindful of these wider objectives – not only of halting hateful speech, but positively nurturing the full development of human personality and dignity, their equal and effective participation, the respect of all for the rights and freedoms of others and advancing peace.

The question of whether the education we are concerned with here, involving religious or belief leaders, is within the formal education system or in informal education is not pertinent to the fact that Article 13(1) applies. General Comment No. 13, which is the interpretative statement of the body with oversight over the realisation of the ICESCR, notes that "States parties agree that all education, whether public or private, formal or non-formal, shall be directed towards the aims and objectives identified in article 13(1)".[5] This need to uphold Article 13(1) objectives is reiterated on a number of occasions in the General Comment. This is important to note since, in *most* instances, religious or belief leaders have a role in private and non-formal educational sectors rather than the public and formal.

---

[4] ICESCR, UN Doc. A/RES/21/2200, 16 December 1966 (https://www.legal-tools.org/doc/06b87e/).

[5] Committee on Economic, Social and Cultural Rights ('CESCR'), Implementation of the ICESCR, General Comment No. 13 (Twenty-first Session, 1999): The Right to Education (Article 13 of the Covenant), UN Doc. E/C.12/1999/10, 8 December 1999, para. 4 ('General Comment No. 13') (https://www.legal-tools.org/doc/918c95/).

The emphasis on non-discrimination in the provision of education is also repeated a number of times in the General Comment.[6] Clearly, hate speech is outrightly antithetical to this. The soft law instrument, the Abidjan Guiding Principles, detail the non-discrimination obligation in its overarching principle 1, that "States must respect, protect, and fulfil the right to education of everyone within their jurisdiction in accordance with the rights to equality and non-discrimination".[7] This requires regular monitoring of compliance, with all human rights principles, whether by public or private educational institutions.[8] The Abidjan Guiding Principles outline that "[t]he obligation to prohibit all forms of discrimination includes direct and indirect discrimination, harassment and denial of reasonable accommodation, as well as multiple, intersectional, associative, and perceptive discrimination".[9]

Alongside these principles and objectives lies the right of parents and legal guardians to "ensure the religious and moral education of their children in conformity with their own convictions".[10] This is a right that is upheld not only in Article 13(3) of ICESCR, but also Article 18(4) of the ICCPR and Article 14(2) of the Convention on the Rights of the Child ('CRC').[11] This does not, however, bring about any change to the need to uphold the principles upheld in Article 13(1). All educational institutions are to uphold these regardless of whether they are state-run or otherwise.[12]

The above serve to underscore that the educational role of religious leaders needs to be in full compliance with human rights, and therefore non-discriminatory, and upholding the principles and objectives of education which go beyond that. Their role in countering hateful speech fits under that call to desist from allowing discrimination or anything that undermines dignity and rights in education, but could also proactively go beyond to seek to alter environments within which hateful speech can take root.

28.3. Turning Things Around

28.3.1. The Actors

This approach of bringing one of the actors or resources who may sometimes prove the source of human rights challenges, or a potential obstacle in the

6 *Ibid.*, see especially para. 6(b)(i).

7 "The Ten Overarching Principles", in *The Abidjan Principles*, 21 March 2019, Overarching Principle 1.

8 *Ibid.*, p. 10, Overarching Principle 8.

9 *Ibid.*, p. 13, Article 24.

10 ICESCR, para. 13(3), see *supra* note 4.

11 CRC, UN Doc. A/RES/44/25, 20 November 1989 (https://www.legal-tools.org/doc/f48f9e/).

12 General Comment No. 13, see especially para. 13(4), see *supra* note 5.

advancement of human rights, on board has emerged in recent years as an international human rights law approach. It has particularly gained traction over the past decade.

I have observed elsewhere[13] how women's rights norms largely neglected reference to religion until 2014, on the occasion of the thirty-fifth anniversary of the Convention on the Elimination of all Forms of Discrimination Against Women ('CEDAW') and the twenty-fifth anniversary of the CRC. Finally, in the joint General Recommendation No. 31 of the CEDAW Committee and General Comment No. 18 of the CRC Committee on Harmful Practices, it is stated that harmful practices "are deeply rooted in societal attitudes according to which women and girls are regarded as inferior to men and boys […]", in practices "that often involve violence or coercion […]", that have "often been justified by involving socio-cultural and religious customs and values". Harmful practices "are often associated with serious forms of violence or are themselves a form of violence against women and children".[14]

Embedded deep in the document, we find the following:

> One of the primary challenges in the elimination of harmful practices relates to the lack of awareness or capacity of relevant professionals, including front-line professionals, to adequately understand, identify and respond to incidents of or the risks of harmful practices. A comprehensive, holistic and effective approach to capacity-building should aim to engage influential leaders, such as traditional and religious leaders, and as many relevant professional groups as possible […] at all levels. They need to be provided with accurate information about the practice and applicable human rights norms and standards with a view to promoting a change in attitudes and behaviours of their group and the wider community.[15]

In this instance, and after so many decades, religious leaders have been referenced along with a wide array of actors, each serving as possible actors in addressing the scourge of harmful practices against women and girls. They are not singled out for a particular role nor consulted on their own sense of their best contribution, but as one of many first responders to harmful practices. It offered a breakthrough in this field, even though it reveals only a rather surface

13 Nazila Ghanea, "Women and Religious Freedom: Synergies and Opportunities", United Sates Commission on International Religious Freedom, July 2017.

14 Committee on the Rights of the Child, Joint General Recommendation/General Comment No. 31 of the Committee on the Elimination of Discrimination Against Women and No. 18 of the Committee on the Rights of the Child on Harmful Practices, UN Doc. CEDAW/C/GC/31-CRC/C/GC/18, 4 November 2014, paras. 5–6 (https://www.legal-tools.org/doc/f02030/).

15 *Ibid.*, para. 69.

encounter between religious leaders and matters relating to international human rights law.

The effort to bring religious and belief leaders and actors on board to address the challenge of hateful speech has a longer track record and is discussed more fully in other chapters of this collection. They will, however, be sketched below, as they are so foundational to our concern.

In 2011 the UN Human Rights Council adopted Resolution 16/18 as a consensual and practical resolution focused on combatting religious intolerance.[16] Subsequently, the 'Istanbul Process'[17] was set up as a "dedicated mechanisms for follow-up on the implementation of the action plan set out in Human Rights Council Resolution 16/18",[18] in short to take stock of state actions in advancing the resolution's action plan. The Special Adviser of the UN Secretary-General on the Prevention of Genocide shepherded the Fez Plan of Action for religious leaders and actors to prevent incitement to violence that could lead to atrocity crimes[19] and the High-Level Symposium on the fifth anniversary of the Fez Plan of Action in 2022. The Rabat Plan of Action[20] addressed the Prohibition of Advocacy of National, Racial or Religious Hatred that Constitutes Incitement to Discrimination, Hostility or Violence. The Faith for Rights initiative drew inspiration from that and adopted its 18 Commitments in March 2017[21] complemented previous developments, but articulated the voice and role of faith-based actors in advancing human rights more broadly. The Rabat+5 Symposium in December 2017 then focused on the human rights responsibilities of faith actors and, in particular, religious leaders.[22] These instruments have been

---

16 HRC Resolution 16/18, see *supra* note 1. See also discussion in Limon, Ghanea and Power, 2014, *supra* note 1.

17 About the Istanbul Process, see its web site. For past Istanbul Process meetings, see the reports by Universal Rights Group, "Combatting Religious Intolerance (Resolution 16/18)" (available on its web site).

18 It is also noted that the Istanbul Process follows up on HRC Resolution 16/18, see *supra* note 1.

19 UN Office on Genocide Prevention and the Responsibility to Protect, "Plan of Action for Religious Leaders and Actors to Prevent Incitement to Violence that Could Lead to Atrocity Crimes", 14 July 2017 (https://www.legal-tools.org/doc/8723g7/).

20 Report of the UN High Commissioner for Human Rights on the Expert Workshops on the Prohibition of Incitement to National, Racial or Religious Hatred, UN Doc. A/HRC/22/17/Add.4, 11 January 2013 (https://www.legal-tools.org/doc/oymwge/).

21 UN High Commissioner for Human Rights, "The Beirut Declaration and Its 18 Commitments on Faith of Rights: Report and Outlook", 7 March 2022 ('The Beirut Declaration and its 18 Commitments on Faith of Rights, Report').

22 UN High Commissioner for Human Rights, "Concept Note of the Rabat+5 Symposium on the Follow-up to The Rabat Plan of Action", 6 December 2017.

foundational to a range of other civil society trainings, processes and initiatives around the world.

Bringing together the elements of religious leaders as actors and religious communities as targets, therefore, we now need to turn to the resource that is within reach of religious leaders in seeing to influence the alleged followers, and that is religious texts as resource.

28.3.2. The Resource

We turn to religious leaders, and the internal religious resources and measures available to them, for several reasons. On the one hand, we do so in recognition of the power and potency, energy and determination of religion, and on the other, due to its potential for harm – whether violence, hateful speech or other violations of human rights – if not channelled positively.

The 1981 UN Declaration on the Elimination of All Forms of Intolerance and of Discrimination Based on Religion or Belief ('1981 Declaration') speaks to the potential for harm from the abuse of religion in its Preamble:

> Considering that the disregard and infringement of human rights and fundamental freedoms, in particular of the right to freedom of thought, conscience, religion or whatever belief, have brought, directly or indirectly, wars and great suffering to mankind, especially where they serve as a means of foreign interference in the internal affairs of other States and amount to kindling hatred between peoples and nations.[23]

Even the leadership of one of the world's religions has given recognition to this potential for harm, positing very starkly:

> Tragically, organized religion, whose very reason for being entails service to the cause of brotherhood and peace, behaves all too frequently as one of the most formidable obstacles in the path [...].[24]

On the other hand, the same 1981 Declaration also recognizes the power and vitality of religion or belief.[25] The Preamble of the 1981 Declaration also recognizes:

> Considering that religion or belief, for anyone who professes either, is one of the fundamental elements in his conception of life and that freedom of religion or belief should be fully respected and guaranteed,

[23] 1981 Declaration, UN Doc. A/RES/36/55, 25 November 1981, Preambular para. 3 (https://www.legal-tools.org/doc/hexdsg/).

[24] Universal House of Justice, "To the World's Religious Leaders", in *Bahá'í Library*, April 2002.

[25] It should be noted that international human rights law norms uphold freedom of 'thought, conscience, religion or whatever belief' and that this is abbreviated as 'religion or belief'.

> Considering that it is essential to promote understanding, tolerance and respect in matters relating to freedom of religion or belief and to ensure that the use of religion or belief for ends inconsistent with the Charter, other relevant instruments of the United Nations and the purposes and principles of the present Declaration is inadmissible,
>
> Convinced that freedom of religion or belief should also contribute to the attainment of the goals of world peace, social justice and friendship among peoples and to the elimination of ideologies or practices of colonialism and racial discrimination.[26]

What can be deduced from the 1981 Declaration is that we invest hope in religious leaders in dual recognition of the power of religion to inspire and recognition of the extent to which hateful expression and violence can be perpetuated in the name of religion.

The potential to inspire to positively advance human rights can also be traced to the fact that the norms of religion or belief oftentimes go beyond legal standards regarding respect for the dignity of others, empathy, and the need to avoid hurt to others. At its best, religion activates an innate reservoir of transformative and spiritual resources in each of us, allowing us to reach a higher purpose of elevation, of beauty and of love.

It is interesting that the most prominent recognition of the importance of the spiritual aspects of the human is captured in the CRC. Article 17 of the CRC refers to the "social, spiritual and moral well-being and physical and mental health"[27] of the child, to the "cultural and spiritual development"[28] of the child, to "the right of every child to a standard of living adequate for the child's physical, mental, spiritual, moral and social development",[29] and to the protection of the child from economic exploitation or work that could be "harmful to the child's health or physical, mental, spiritual, moral or social development".[30]

Suggesting that religion's activation potential should merely be of service in seeking to counter hateful expression and call for an end to violence is doing it a disservice. It could potentially do so much more. Spiritual values promoting our common dignity, understanding and love for all regardless of any belonging or characteristics, and forgiveness have the potential to change attitudes and behaviours, and give rise to a moral self-vigilance and care which could stem

---

26 1981 Declaration, Preambular para. 6, see *supra* note 23.

27 CRC, para. 17, see *supra* note 11.

28 *Ibid.*, para. 23.3.

29 *Ibid.*, para. 27.1.

30 *Ibid.*, para. 32.1.

hateful attitudes and expression. Standards of expected behaviour here would not be limited to legal obligations or standards of the state, but would go beyond that.

UN experts, such as Arcot Krishnaswami, recognized this in as early as 1960:

> Truly great religions and beliefs are based upon ethical tenets such as the duty to widen the bounds of good-neighbourliness and the obligation to meet human need in the broadest sense. The precept that one should love one's neighbour as oneself was part of the faith of Christianity even before it had been organized as a Church. The same idea permeates Judaism and Islam, as well as the various branches of Buddhism, Confucianism and Hinduism, and it may also be found in the teachings of many non-religious beliefs.
>
> While most religions and beliefs are imbued with a sense of the oneness of mankind, history probably records more instances of man's inhumanity to man than examples of good-neighbourliness and the desire to satisfy the needs of the less fortunately placed. Not infrequently, horrors and excesses have been committed in the name of religion or belief [...]. However, it must be stressed that such manifestations of intolerance by organized religions or beliefs were usually the result of traditions, practices and interpretations built up around them; often the followers of a religion or belief considered it to be the sole repository of truth and felt therefore that their duty was to combat other religions or beliefs.[31]

Fifty-six years later, the same stance motivated the adoption of the Beirut Declaration under the auspices of Faith for Rights. The Faith for Rights framework "provides space for a cross-disciplinary reflection and action on the deep, and mutually enriching, connections between religions and human rights"[32] with the objective of contributing to peaceful societies of respect, equality, and diversity. It points out the positive potential of faith and rights in that,

> [i]ndividual and communal expression of religions or beliefs thrive and flourish in environments where human rights are protected. Similarly, human rights can benefit from deeply rooted ethical and spiritual foundations provided by religions or beliefs. Rather than focusing on theological and doctrinal divides, the Beirut Declaration favours the identification of common ground among all

[31] Arcot Krishnaswami, "Study of Discrimination in the Matter of Religious Rights and Practices", UN Doc. E/CN.4/Sub.2/200/Rev.1, 1960, Introduction (https://www.legal-tools.org/doc/fitlrl/).

[32] The Beirut Declaration and Its 18 Commitments on Faith of Rights, Report, p. 5, see *supra* note 21.

> religions and beliefs to uphold the dignity and equal worth of all human beings.[33]

28.4. Educational Resource: The Appeal of Religious Leaders to Religion and Belief Communities

Can religious leaders build on such positively focused and uniting endeavours in their educative role in countering hateful speech? The focus on religious leaders in addressing education is in assuming their directive role, or at least influential role, regarding the pattern of transmission and compliance with religious norms, and their leadership role in promoting alignment with these profound spiritual standards. The educative role of religious leaders within religion or belief communities, is considered a key lever of potential influence.

We are investing hope in these leaders to augment, supplement and extend the tools in our existing toolbox in addressing hateful expression through an education which has a wider appeal, reach and even power than the law and the state. We are hoping to reach religious leaders in order to fast-track our impact into religious or belief communities, and recognition of the influence of their voice on the 'hearts and minds' of the faithful and the dominance of the traction of their interpretation of religious and belief texts and norms. We are counting, also, on their own positive example in speaking out against "intolerance, including advocacy of religious hatred that constitutes incitement to discrimination, hostility or violence".[34]

The importance of this has been highlighted in the UN General Assembly and Human Rights Council's Resolution 16/18. The Resolution calls on states to take actions to foster a domestic environment of religious tolerance, peace and respect, by, *inter alia*:

> Encouraging the creation of collaborative networks to build mutual understanding, promoting dialogue and inspiring constructive action towards shared policy goals and the pursuit of tangible outcomes, such as servicing projects in the fields of education, health, conflict prevention, employment, integration and media education;[35] […]

---

[33] *Ibid.*, p. 5.

[34] Resolution Adopted by the Human Rights Council on 1 April 2022: Combatting Intolerance, Negative Stereotyping and Stigmatization of, and Discrimination, Incitement to Violence and Violence Against, Persons Based on Religion or Belief, UN Doc. A/HRC/RES/49/31, 13 April 2022, para. 7(e) (https://www.legal-tools.org/doc/jbgoyo/).

[35] *Ibid.*, para. 7(a).

> Encouraging the efforts of leaders to discuss within their communities the causes of discrimination, and evolving strategies to counter those causes.[36]

This is of contemporary times. But it has its antecedents. Turning to the observations of former Special Rapporteur on freedom of religion or belief, Abdolfattah Amor, it can be noted that he observed that, "many […] identify themselves in both racial and religious terms and, in many cases, the division between race and religion is by no means watertight. Indeed, discrimination is often aggravated where multiple identities are involved";[37] and that the "main victims of inter- and intrareligious extremism are minorities, on the one hand, and women on the other".[38] Amor would sometimes refer to violence in the name of religion as "pseudo-religious extremism".[39]

Amor insisted that "education and interreligious dialogue are vital pillars of the strategy to prevent […] religious extremism […] and […] pseudo-religious discrimination".[40] In addressing education, he drew attention to school curricula and textbooks, the need for it to permeate a range of disciplines including history, and the importance of reviewing teaching methods and improving teacher training.[41] He stated that "[i]nteractive participation and renewed effort [would be required] on the part of the main religious actors" to counter otherness and "to bear witness to the vital role of interreligious dialogue as a factor in preventing conflict".[42]

Under his mandate he also shepherded the adoption of the Final Document of the International Consultative Conference on School Education in relation to Freedom of Religion or Belief, Tolerance and Non-discrimination in Madrid ('Madrid Final Document') from 23–25 November 2001, on the twentieth anniversary of the 1981 Declaration.[43] Religious leaders and communities are conspicuous in their absence from all the calls in this document. It is perhaps telling to note that this conference was held some ten weeks after the 9/11 attacks when the world was still in shock and the very holding of the conference has to be deemed a success under those conditions. Though religious leaders

---

36 *Ibid.*, para. 7(d).

37 UN Economic and Social Council, Civil and Political Rights, Including Religious Tolerance, UN Doc. E/CN.4/2003/66, 15 January 2003, para. 135 (https://www.legal-tools.org/doc/kf6zal/).

38 *Ibid.*, para. 136.

39 *Ibid.*, para. 138.

40 *Ibid.*, para. 141.

41 *Ibid.*, para. 142.

42 *Ibid.*, para. 144.

43 Madrid Final Document, in Civil and Political Rights, Including Religious Tolerance, UN Doc. E/CN.4/2002/73, 14 March 2002, Appendix (https://www.legal-tools.org/doc/o0746a/).

were absent, the Madrid Final Document notes the fact that "in many countries students gain knowledge, including in the field of freedom of religion or belief, through the mass media outside educational establishments". It therefore calls for "appropriate and constructive" use of traditional and new educational technology, the Internet, in co-operation with media institutions, NGOs and others, to "combat the propagation of intolerant and discriminatory stereotypes".[44] The elaborate and rich Toledo Guiding Principles on Teaching about Religions or Beliefs in Public Schools[45] also focuses on school education and remains silent on religious leaders.

In 2010, some nine years after Amor's initiative at Madrid, Special Rapporteur Heiner Bielefeldt's report focused on school education in the field of religion or belief, yet its ideas can be adapted and adopted by religious leaders. He called on school authorities to, *inter alia*, provide "voluntary opportunities for meetings and exchanges with their counterparts of different religious or beliefs";[46] "exchanges of teachers and students and facilitating educational study abroad";[47] "[s]trengthening a non-discriminatory perspective in education and of knowledge in relation to freedom of religion or belief at the appropriate levels";[48] a focus on the equal rights and protection of the rights of women, girls and those who may be vulnerable;[49] evaluating all curricula, teaching and teaching methods and teacher-training; and taking measures against intolerance and discrimination.[50]

28.5. Problematizing Our Understandings

28.5.1. The Nexus Between Religious Leaders and Education

However, our outreach to the educational approach of religious leaders may have been a somewhat blunt and undiscerning at times, assuming authority and influence to be highly centralized in the hands of few religious leaders who are both on board with and able to bring about transformative and impactful educational changes with regard to hateful expression and calls for violence by all of their members.

---

44 *Ibid.*

45 Organization for Security and Co-operation in Europe, Office for Democratic Institutions and Human Rights, "Toledo Guiding Principles on Teaching About Religions and Beliefs in Public Schools", 2007.

46 Report of the Special Rapporteur on Freedom of Religion or Belief, Heiner Bielefeldt, UN Doc. A/HRC/16/53, 15 December 2010, para. 61(a) (https://www.legal-tools.org/doc/pjfrc0/).

47 *Ibid.*, para. 61(b).

48 *Ibid.*, para. 61(c).

49 *Ibid.*, para. 61(d).

50 *Ibid.*, para. 61(a).

We have not adequately sought to consider a clear prioritisation in the religious leaders we are trying to reach, their reach and impact on members, or to seek to ascertain the (other) changemakers in the educational sphere within their communities.

Let us turn to some questions as to the complexities that go unexplored in such an approach. This approach sidesteps instances where religion is deeply entangled with state educational curricula and perpetuating hateful expression and violence. This gives rise to the question of whether we are only seeking to address informal education and not formal education? What about where the (state) religious education is a stigmatizing, discriminatory or selective one? Or where publicly funded education is implicated in religious education that is imbued with hateful speech? What about when such education is not sufficiently regulated by the state in the case of some private schools, and counter to international standards and the Abidjan Principles in this regard? Even were we to only consider informal education, what of religious structures that are less hierarchical and more decentralized? Are we mindful of those religious channels and structures, and are we nuancing our outreach in accordance with them? Are we seeking to influence education within the family? If so, how? And are we cognisant of the gender dimensions of such an endeavour and the need for inclusion?

In short, it is suggested that our broad-brush rhetorical concern with religious leaders and education has stalled and we need to be pursuing far more sophisticated and discerning projects at the grassroots that are tailored to the realities on the ground, and very mindful of the questions raised above.

28.5.2. Religion or Belief Communities

Our understanding of religious or belief communities to date has been somewhat out of sync with international human rights law. We are perhaps envisaging stable, cohesive, accessible and uniform communities who are directed, or at least highly and readily influenced by, a limited number of religious leaders. But is that really so?

Are the followers of the religious or belief communities so limited, stable and loyal? Whether or not we are seeking to address harmful practices against women and girls or hateful speech, the target in question is the community membership. 'Membership' itself can both be contested and may be tenuous. Was the Boston attacker in May 2022 a Christian, and was the *Charlie Hebdo* bomber in January 2015 a Muslim? Certainly, both have vigorously been denied as believers, as they flouted fundamental Christian and Muslim beliefs of brotherhood, compassion, mercy and love. Since it is not for us to determine the believers, perhaps it is more accurate for us to replace 'member' with 'alleged followers', but what are the exact parameters of this, and are our assumptions about discrete groups falling into line under particular religious leaders correct?

There is a far greater openness in the understanding of persons belonging to religious or belief 'minorities' in international human rights law – persons who, in turn, often gather as 'communities', whether religious or otherwise.

This minority rights understanding[51] is based on the person's willingness to continue characteristics, the level of their engagement, their participation, and their solidarity with others. In those discussions, we are alert to the need to include belief communities, hence we need to factor in the contours of freedom of thought, conscience and religion.

Sociological data and studies of trends in religion are the most informative regarding religious and belief landscapes around the world or, more accurately, religion or belief belonging. Both in international human rights law terms, and in terms of assessing the chances of direct impact of religious leaders on those engaging in hateful speech and violence within communities, we need to bore down upon obedience as well as belonging.

Research regarding trends in religion suggest that there is a stark trend away from previous forms of religiosity in many parts of the world towards more flat structures and less institutionalized or organized groupings of worship. We need to keep in touch with these trends and realities and adjust our methods accordingly.

28.5.3. Which 'Religious Leaders'

In line with the above, our understanding of religious leaders to date has been a hierarchical and somewhat narrow one. This means we are, at best, working through the most traditional of channels, in some instances, to bring about the most ambitious of objectives, which is to address the hatred and profound polarisation of our times which serve as fodder to conflicts worldwide.

The challenge of this has been that, essentially, we are likely to either be preaching to the converted or reaching to leaders who have a vested interest in not addressing hateful expression and calls for violence, and therefore impervious to our appeal.

This hierarchical and conservative approach has been counterintuitive, not only because it runs the serious risk of being counterproductive, but also because it runs against the grain of human rights perspectives on the matter.

[51] For a discussion and analysis of religious or belief minorities and international human rights norms pertaining to them, see Nazila Ghanea, "Are Religious Minorities Really Minorities?", in *Oxford Journal of Law and Religion*, 2012, vol. 1, no. 1, pp. 57–79.

Where do religious leaders 'fit' into international human rights law norms and standards? On the one hand, they appear in our understanding of manifestation of freedom of religion or belief and, on the other, in discussions around registration of religion or belief communities and 'religious autonomy'. Article 6 of the 1981 Declaration states that the right to freedom of thought, conscience, religion or belief shall include, *inter alia*, the freedom "[t]o teach a religion or belief in places suitable for these purposes"[52] and "[t]o train, appoint, elect or designate by succession appropriate leaders called for by the requirements and standards of any religion or belief".[53]

We have tended towards a hierarchical and conservative approach in that our focus has primarily been on inviting the international leaders to elite conferences to make formal statements or to come to agree joint statements. We have been at this formal level of individual or co-ordinated statements since 1893 and the first World Parliament of Religions! Efforts are being made and we are becoming more conscious of its limitations, and the need for innovation here, but there is still a long way to go.

The Faith for Rights initiative is somewhat different because its stated aim is to provide:

> space for a cross-disciplinary reflection and action on the deep, and mutually enriching, connections between religions and human rights. The objective is to foster the development of peaceful societies, which uphold human dignity and equality for all and where diversity is not just tolerated but fully respected and celebrated.[54]

Those that sign up to it are not religious leaders as such, but "faith-based and civil society actors in the field of human rights".[55] This is a double-edged sword. It is liberating and emancipating, but risks being marginalized until such a time that it is adopted into the mainstream.

Human rights actors and criminal lawyers are not the gatekeepers for assessing, weighting and evaluating religion or belief leaders and representatives. If we single out those that are likely to have the 'biggest problems' in relation to hateful speech and violence, we would be playing into stereotypes and discrimination. Therefore, how are we to proceed? Completely in a 'blind' manner; or with an 'open to all' policy that risks attracting the like-minded? We seem to go in circles here, never progressing to a more purposeful approach. If a research project were to assess our invitation list for key events for religious leaders or

52 1981 Declaration, para. 6(e), see *supra* note 23.

53 *Ibid.*, para. 6(g).

54 The Beirut Declaration and Its 18 Commitments on Faith of Rights, Report, see *supra* note 21.

55 *Ibid.*, opening para. 1.

representatives on addressing hate speech and incitement over the last 15 years and plotted that against an objective assessment of reach and risk, that may well be helpful, but it would certainly be criticized.

At the very least, we should look beyond the most hierarchical and conservative perspectives of who are the religious leaders of religion or belief communities, because it risks either reaching the converted or the most hard-to-get on board as they may have vested interests in allowing hateful expression and calls for violence to continue.

28.5.4. Religious Landscapes

Entanglement of state in religion and religion in state complicates the scene. As a Pew Research Center survey outlines regarding their methodology, the distinction between state restrictions and societal restrictions in the arena of freedom of religion or belief or other human rights is an important one to maintain.

Religious leaders can straddle both. They may be in government leadership, serving in the government apparatus, in the opposition, employed as civil servants and paid by the state, appointed by the state or independent of state. In relation to hateful expression and calls for violence, therefore, have we been cognisant of who, along this spectrum, we are referring to as 'religious leaders'? Is it only the latter – those that are fully independent of the state? If so, why are we engaging the others and why are we being unclear in our appeal? If we are referring to those who are entangled in the state apparatus to a greater or lesser extent, then our reference points should at least also include international legal obligations that the state is party to.

28.6. What Is Our Theory of Change?

What is not clear in the various standards to date is our theory of change. How is sustainable change to be brought about? We need the educational resources that counter hateful expression and calls for violence and transform towards positive respect for all regardless of any belonging or characteristics. We need to be mindful of the on-the-ground reality of religion or belief communities as they exist in the contexts we hope to reach. We need access to religious leaders who have promoted hate to date, but who have now become persuaded to stem the tide of hateful speech. We also need religious leaders in reach who are independent and determined to stamp out any intolerance in their communities and seek to turn that around into tolerance and understanding, and can do so without counter efforts by the state.

In our approaches so far, we seem to have been reliant on appeals to the positive power of religion. We have also had a lot of trust in our convening power and opportunities for encounter, outweighing any appeal and benefit from continuing in perpetuating, or at least not addressing, hateful expression and calls for violence by community members. We have likely been over-reliant on the crafting of numerous interfaith commitments, declarations and proclamations for providing the rhetoric that we believed would bring about and sustain change in society at large. Nevertheless, we have seen little evidence of the outreach within the respective communities of even those who had been crafting and drafting those declarations. Although interfaith dialogue can create networks of impetus and accountability for stemming the tide of hateful expression and calls for violence, it is not the mere episodic rhetoric of agreement that is going to achieve that potential.

Let us turn to the power invested in religion to inspire. The international governing body of the Bahá'ís of the world, the Universal House of Justice, observes:

> Religion, as we are all aware, reaches to the roots of motivation. When it has been faithful to the spirit and example of the transcendent Figures who gave the world its great belief systems, it has awakened in whole populations capacities to love, to forgive, to create, to dare greatly, to overcome prejudice, to sacrifice for the common good and to discipline the impulses of animal instinct. Unquestionably, the seminal force in the civilizing of human nature has been the influence of the succession of these Manifestations of the Divine that extends back to the dawn of recorded history. […] As the course of civilization demonstrates, religion is […] capable of profoundly influencing the structure of social relationships […]. [Religion has held up] a vision of potentialities as yet unrealized.[56]

28.7. Summary

Whilst the efforts in this arena to date, and the recognition of the importance of these actors, is welcome, much work remains to be done.

In relation to the international human rights law efforts, we need to admit that human rights actors are neither fully conversant with the tools, powers and potential of religion or belief, nor do they have free reign to squarely address them. The reluctance to even factor in religious communities and religion was some six decades long in the international human rights law arena. It has only started to be addressed fairly recently: Camden, 16/18, Rabat, Istanbul Process, Rabat+5, Beirut and the resulting Faith for Rights.

These initiatives need to become more serious about their reach, which actors they prioritize, who they appeal to, and the theory of change they are working with.

---

[56] Universal House of Justice, April 2002, see *supra* note 24.

The challenge of addressing hateful expression and violence is an ambitious and urgent one, and our initiatives need to keep developing and deepening, in order to hope to keep in step with the challenge at hand.

In pulling the threads together, we may propose that initiatives should recognize education as one of the most powerful tools we have for sustainably addressing prejudices and intolerance which are at the root of hateful speech and violence. And religious and belief leaders and communities are the actors that are closest shapers of attitudes of what may be perpetuated in the name of religion or belief.

We should widen our understanding of who religious and belief 'leaders' and 'shapers' are – and reach beyond the high leadership to those most active in the educational arena, those most accessible through various media, those most referenced by the younger generations. In doing so we should be alert to women in this role and local actors. We should also be mindful of intrareligious diversities and tendencies. We should seek to be up to date with trends of religiosity, belief and non-belief to seek out religious and belief 'influencers' too. We also need to be cognisant of data on numbers, power and influence over hate speech and violence, but we cannot exclusively focus on that as in the realm of influencing spiritual ideas, numbers and power are not the defining criteria. Any perpetuation of hateful speech reaches beyond the obvious impact on the targets and weakens the foundations of society as a whole, including its impact on the perpetrators themselves.

29

The Role of Al-Ázhár Ash-Sharíf in Combating Extremism and Hate Speech in Light of International Instruments

Adel Maged*

> Call thou to the way of thy God with wisdom and good admonition, and argue with them in the better way. Surely thy God knows very well those who have gone astray from His path, and He knows very well those who are rightly guided.[1]

29.1. Introduction

As the above verse of the *Qur'án* stipulates, Islámic discourse is based on dialogue and tolerance. Religious hatred, as illustrated in Chapter 16 above, is prohibited by Islám. That chapter tackles extremism and hate speech from a theological perspective. In this chapter I will investigate the role of Islámic religious scholars and leaders in combating these concepts, in light of the applicable international standards, with an institutional approach. I will attempt to address

---

* **Adel Maged** is Judge and Vice President of the Egyptian Court of Cassation (Criminal Chambers). He was appointed Public Prosecutor in 1987, and served as a Judge at the Courts of First Instance, Chief Prosecutor at the Criminal Division of the Court of Cassation, Judge at the Egyptian Court of Appeals, and was for several years on secondment to the Ministry of Justice of the United Arab Emirates as a Legal Advisor on International Law and Treaties. He is also a lecturer at National Centre for Judicial Studies and the Faculty of *Sharí'ah* and Law, Al-Ázhár Ash-Sharíf University in Cairo, and a founding member of the research group 'Islám, Law and Modernity' at Durham Law School. He has advised the International Criminal Court's Office of the Prosecutor and the Arab League of States on international criminal law issues. His publications include books and articles, in Arabic and English, on international criminal law, Islámic law, justice reform, transitional justice, combating extremism, terrorism and combating migrant smuggling and human trafficking. He holds a Bachelor of Law from Alexandria University; an LL.M. on Internationalization of Crime and Criminal Justice from Utrecht University; and a Diploma on International Law and Organization for Development from the Institute of Social Studies, The Hague. The author thanks Morten Bergsmo for his conceptual input, Ms. Medha Damojipurapu for her profound review and valuable comments, and Ms. Rawan Maged for her research assistance. For an audio-visual recording of Judge Maged's statement to CILRAP's conference in Florence in April 2022 on the topic of this anthology, please see https://www.cilrap.org/cilrap-film/220409-maged/.

1 The *Qur'án*, 16:125.

the major role that is undertaken by religious institutions in confronting forms of unethical behaviour.

Undoubtedly, extremism and hate speech constitute forms of unethical behaviour which pose grave danger to the security and stability of society. Therefore, the vital role performed by religious institutions in this field has been emphasized in international instruments on the confrontation of extremism and terrorism. It is recognized that the binding force of international instruments varies depending on the nature of the instrument in question and on whether it is a United Nations ('UN') Security Council resolution, an international treaty or a resolution of the UN General Assembly or one of its affiliated organs.[2]

In this chapter, I will try to prove that religion, despite its misuse by fanatics and extremists, is one of the most successful tools to combat extremist ideology and hate speech, if adequately utilized and presented – an approach that is quite relevant to the 'renewal of the religious discourse' initiative, advocated by the political leadership in Egypt and adopted by Al-Ázhár Ash-Sharíf ('Al-Azhar') as a religious institution through the renewal of religious thought as declared by the Grand Imam on many occasions. This will be expounded below.

The reader will notice that adopting a holistic approach is a common feature in my writings on combating extremism and terrorism, albeit predominantly addressing the matter from a legal perspective due to my specialization. Undoubtedly, I am convinced that legal-penal intervention is effective against fanaticism, radicalization and extremism only if they take the form of an antisocial behaviour which harms a protected social interest. Therefore, criminal law alone falls short against these reprehensible forms of behaviour, especially extremism, which can be of varying degrees. Criminal law is relevant only when a person commits an act amounting to criminal behaviour as prescribed by the law. Typically, this only takes place during the advanced stages of extremism. However, in the earlier stages, related to the formation of extremist ideologies, religious institutions have a major and decisive role to play, as underlined by several chapters in this volume. This is particularly true if drivers of extremism are based on religious misconceptions, which is the main topic of the research

---

2 For information about the legal value of international instruments and resolutions cited herein, see Adel Maged, "Mass'úlíyyat ad-Dúwal 'an al-Isa'ah ila al-Adían wal-Rumúz ad-Díníyyah" (The Responsibility of States for Defamation of Religion and Religious Figures), in *Strategic Studies Series (The Emirates Centre for Strategic Studies and Research)*, 2007, no. 125, pp. 35–46; see also Rabab A. Es-Sayíed, "Al-Bina' al-Ma'rifí wal-'Amn al-Fikrí", Ḥurríyyat al-'Áqídah bayn al-Ḥáẓr wal-Ibaḥah fí Dú' Mashrú' Qánún Mukafaḥat al-Karáḥíah wal-'Unff b-Ism ad-Dín al-Muqáddam min Al-Ázhár Ash-Sharíf, 12–13 December 2017, Third International Scientific Conference of the Faculty of Islamic and Arabic Studies for Girls, Cairo, pp. 43–46.

presented in this chapter. As the author himself witnessed many violent events driven by religious hatred in Egypt, reference to the drivers of violent extremism advocated by extremist groups as well as the reaction of the national institutions to it, fall within the scope of this chapter.

It is in light of the above that the UN has stressed in many international instruments the role of religious institutions in confronting perverted ideology, hate speech and violent extremism. This role is to be performed by correcting religious misconceptions and spreading a culture of tolerance.

The central role of religious scholars and leaders in implementing these preventive policies is acknowledged by the UN. According to the UN, this pivotal role is mainly based on confronting vicious thoughts by presenting what it referred to as 'counter-narratives'. Falling into the category of preventive policies and measures, 'counter-narrative' refers to the rhetoric used by religious institutions and other related entities to refute 'perverted ideology', confront 'hate speech', and combat 'violent extremism'.

Undoubtedly, having these goals achieved helps to encircle perverted ideologies and undermine hate speech which supports the State's efforts to dismantle extremist networks and establish security and stability in society.

I believe that it has become a patriotic duty for the country's scholars, experts and researchers to contribute to efforts to renew religious discourse by making available relevant knowledge and instructing people about the correct teachings of Islám. This is true especially when it comes to phenomena that took innocent lives of civilians or army and police personnel, that is, extremism conducive to terrorism. For this contribution to be effective, national values and traditions should be maintained, religious principles should be upheld, and the above-mentioned contribution should be made by knowledgeable scholars, each in their field of specialty.

Teleological jurisprudence related to the concept of 'renewal of religious discourse' falls outside the scope of this chapter as it is a highly specialized discipline in the Islámic context. As described by the Grand Imám, this discipline is exclusively mastered by people who are well-versed and qualified in religious knowledge and jurisprudence,[3] the first among them being Al-Azhar scholars. Hence, I will refer occasionally to the importance of the renewal of religious discourse and the development of research methodologies and techniques in the face of extremism and hate speech to accommodate applicable international standards and achieve a comprehensive confrontation approach that tackles

3 "Speech of the Grand Imam, Professor Ahmed Al-Ṭayyeb", Final Statement, Al-Azhar International Conference on Renovation of Islámic Thought, Cairo, 27–28 January 2020.

these phenomena.[4] To add dynamism to this study, I will support it with religious leaders' opinions on the topics that it addresses.

I have selected the present topic as it reflects my appreciation of religious institutions' major role in negating perverted ideologies and combating hate speech. The proper administration of this role requires a comprehensive multidisciplinary approach.

The main purpose of the present chapter is to help Al-Azhar's scholars to discharge their mission in renewing religious discourse in order to pave the way to combat extremism and hate speech. The chapter is specifically tailored for religious scholars and leaders who act as part of a formal institution, that is, the Al-Azhar (including men and women). But the study may also help other individual religious leaders to comprehend how they can contribute to the fight against extremism and hate speech.

Further, this chapter aims to help scholars in Al-Azhar and researchers in Islámic studies concerned with confronting perverted religious ideology, extremism and terrorism to understand the legal aspects of this conduct and familiarize themselves with the applicable international standards. To this end, the chapter explains how such conduct is addressed by international instruments, it defines relevant terminology and illustrates the applicable legal framework. The ultimate goal is to clarify necessary countermeasures and the active role that can be performed by the clergy to put those measures into practice, ensuring that different forms and phases of perverted ideology and extremism are comprehensively treated and confronted.

Additionally, my chapter seeks to highlight Al-Azhar's preventive role against behaviour conducive to extremism, for example, hate speech, by providing advice and guidance to those who have already been caught up in this ideology. It also provides a commentary on Al-Azhar's statements and declarations focusing mainly on rejecting violence and calling for tolerance. In Chapter 16 of the present anthology, I addressed the ethical approach of Islámic *Sharí'ah* towards hate speech. In this chapter, I will discuss how tolerance, as a component of the required religious discourse, is a principal value in Islám.

I discuss the role of religious institutions in combating extremism and hate speech highlighted in relevant international instruments, shedding light on the main tasks and obligations of religious institutions in response to perverted ideology, extremism and hate speech in light of the relevant international instruments, with an in-depth examination of the concept of 'counter-narrative'

---

[4] For a judicial opinion on the importance of '*ijtihad* and renovation in response to contemporary issues and changing situations, see Egypt, Supreme Constitutional Court, *Case No. 29 of Judicial Year 11*, Judgment, Technical Office 6, Volume 1, 26 March 1994, p. 231 ('Case No. 29 of Judicial Year 11') (https://www.legal-tools.org/doc/ufhjfh/).

contained therein. I emphasize Al-Azhar's efforts in response to the challenges of extremism and hate speech through its sober, moderate discourse.

Before I delve into the role of religious institutions and leader in combating extremism and confronting hate speech, it is important to examine how international instruments address these phenomena.

29.2. Confronting Extremism and Hate Speech in International Instruments

According to Article 4 of the International Convention on the Elimination of All Forms of Racial Discrimination, States Parties condemn all propaganda and organizations which are based on ideas or theories of superiority of one race or group of persons of one colour or ethnic origin, or which attempt to justify or promote racial hatred and discrimination in any form, and undertake to adopt immediate and positive measures designed to eradicate all incitement to, or acts of, such discrimination.[5]

Article 20 of the International Covenant on Civil and Political Rights requires States to draft necessary laws to prohibit any advocacy of national, racial or religious hatred that constitutes incitement to discrimination, hostility or violence. It also stresses that incitement to any form of discrimination which would undermine the concept of citizenship, violates provisions of Article 7 of the Universal Declaration of Human Rights, whether as to religion or race.[6]

Events which have recently occurred throughout the world confirm that hate speech is a serious issue and can result in tragedies and massacres. One such event took place in Christchurch, New Zealand, in 2019, when a gunman attacked people praying at two mosques in the city, claiming the lives of more than fifty Muslims. As I see it, this event was the result of a racist narrative that has been spreading hatred against Muslims for years, distorting their image and demonizing them in the Western collective mind. As a result of racist narratives against Muslims, there have been racist statements or attacks against Muslim individuals or Islámic institutions. For example, attempts were made to burn mosques and to smear walls of mosques with blood or with racist drawings. Attacks were carried out in the street against Muslim women wearing *ḥijab*. These attacks have been on the rise in recent years, especially following terrorist

---

5 International Convention on the Elimination of All Forms of Racial Discrimination, 21 December 1965 (https://www.legal-tools.org/doc/43a925/)

6 International Covenant on Civil and Political Rights, 16 December 1966 (https://www.legal-tools.org/doc/2838f3/); Universal Declaration of Human Rights, 10 December 1948 (https://www.legal-tools.org/doc/de5d83/).

attacks and the noteworthy activity of far-right parties and groups in a number of Western countries.[7]

In general, the UN opposes hate speech, regardless of the form of incitement it implies (discrimination, hostility or violence).[8] Therefore, the international community was keen to develop a work plan against all forms and manifestations of hate speech – the Rabat Plan of Action on the Prohibition of Advocacy of National, Racial or Religious Hatred that Constitutes Incitement to Discrimination, Hostility or Violence ('Rabat Plan').[9] As such, this plan deals with all calls for hatred on equal footing, regardless of their reference, be it racist or religious.

Further, on 18 June 2019, in response to the alarming trend of rising hate speech around the world, the UN launched the UN Strategy and Plan of Action on Hate Speech. The Strategy embodies the firm commitment by the UN to step up co-ordinated action to tackle hate speech both at the global and national levels.

The danger of hate speech is exacerbated when it is expressed by political or religious leaders or influential figures in general in society, such as celebrities or athletes. Given the gravity of hate speech issued by figures influencing target groups, the Rabat Plan calls upon political and religious leaders to act firmly and promptly against all forms of intolerance, discriminatory stereotyping and hate speech. Therefore, the UN made the following recommended in a milestone declaration:

> politicians and other leadership figures in society should refrain from making statements which encourage or promote racism or intolerance against individuals on the basis of protected characteristics, including race, nationality or ethnicity.[10]

---

7 See *Qirá'ah fí at-Tanawúl al-I'lamí li-Bá'ḍat-Taṣríḥát al-'Unṣuríyyah ḍidḍ al-Islám fí Álmányá, Waḥdat Ráṣd al-Lughah al-Álmáníyyáh*, German Language Monitoring Unit, Al-Azhar Observatory, 27 May 2019.

8 See Report of the Special Rapporteur on Freedom of Religion or Belief, Heiner Bielefeldt, Addendum: Mission to Jordan, UN Doc. A/HRC/25/58/Add.2, 27 January 2014 ('Report of the Special Rapporteur on Freedom of Religion or Belief, 27 January 2014') (https://www.legal-tools.org/doc/qniu9w/).

9 OHCHR, Rabat Plan, UN Doc. A/HRC/22/17.Add.4, Annex, Appendix, 5 October 2012 (https://www.legal-tools.org/doc/jh1be1/).

10 See Recommendation (h) in the UN Special Rapporteur on Freedom of Opinion and Expression, the Organization for Security and Co-operation in Europe Representative on Freedom of the Media, the Organization of American States Special Rapporteur on Freedom of Expression and Special Rapporteur of the African Commission on Human Rights and Peoples on Freedom of Expression and Access to Information, "Joint Declaration on Freedom of Expression and Combating Violent Extremism", May 2015 (https://www.legal-tools.org/doc/ae7oa2/).

It should be noted that the UN Security Council Resolution 2354 of 2017 urged member States to adopt counter-narratives against violent extremism and called on them to follow several guidelines (measures) to reach this goal.[11] The term 'counter-narrative' is used by the UN to refer to nationally-drafted narratives, in partnership with relevant institutions, in order to counter the rhetoric of incitement to commit acts of terrorism motivated by extremism and intolerance, usually promoting hatred and violence. The counter-narrative is considered by the UN as part of a comprehensive approach which responds to the threats of terrorism and violent extremism as and when conducive to terrorism.[12]

From a religious approach, the basic objectives of 'counter-narratives' are to:

- counter perverted ideologies;
- unmask extremists' reality, reveal the weaknesses of their underlying value system and refute their statements and allegations and expose their and delusions; and
- correct religious misconceptions.

The counter-narrative measures can be successful only if they are adopted by competent religious institutions and implemented by qualified religious leaders.

29.3. Role of Religious Institutions and Leaders in Relevant International Instruments

The role of religious institutions and leaders in confronting extremism and terrorism is based on the theme of protection and prevention mentioned above and highlighted in relevant international and regional instruments. These instruments contain explicit reference to the role of religious institutions and leaders in combating discrimination, extremism and hate speech by addressing the root causes conducive to violent extremism and terrorism.[13] This role was highlighted by several instruments such as the UN Global Counter-Terrorism Strategy, the UN Plan of Action to Prevent Violent Extremism and the Comprehensive International Framework to Counter Terrorist Narratives, which also provided several recommendations to prevent extremism potentially conducive to

[11] UNSC Resolution 2354 (2017), UN Doc. S/RES/2354 (2017), 24 May 2017 (https://www.legal-tools.org/doc/9ae36f/).

[12] See Comprehensive International Framework to Counter Terrorist-Narratives, UN Doc. S/2017/375, 28 April 2017, Item 15 ('Comprehensive International Framework to Counter Terrorist-Narratives') (https://www.legal-tools.org/doc/43nh0x/).

[13] See, for example, Malabo Declaration, Fourth Africa-Arab Summit, Malabo, Equatorial Guinea, AAS/Decl.1(IV) S- 033/ (16/11) /08- D (0523), 23 November 2016, Preambular para. VIII (https://www.legal-tools.org/doc/hj4w3g/).

violence and, accordingly, to terrorism. They mainly recommended examining and addressing factors conducive to extremism which are overlapping and intertwining and take no specific rigid pattern. Rather, they change from one group to another, from one country to another and probably from one person to another, and therefore, national peculiarities should be considered while drafting counter-extremism strategies, work plans and programmes.

The author seeks to highlight that any person involved in the implementation of the measures and recommendations contained in the above-mentioned instruments – concerning the protection from and prevention of dangers of extremism and terrorism – must have access to all other international instruments related to combating discrimination and incitement to hatred, such as the

1. International Covenant on Economic, Social and Cultural Rights;
2. International Covenant on Civil and Political Rights;
3. International Convention on the Elimination of All Forms of Racial Discrimination;
4. Convention on the Elimination of all Forms of Discrimination Against Women;
5. Convention against Torture and Other Cruel, Inhuman or Degrading Treatment or Punishment;
6. Convention on the Rights of the Child and its two Optional Protocols; and
7. Convention on the Rights of Persons with Disabilities.

In addition, access to reports of the Special Rapporteur on Contemporary Forms of Racism, Racial Discrimination and Xenophobia, and the Special Rapporteur on Freedom of Religion or Belief, as well as relevant UN resolutions and action plans, must also be referred to.

Further, UN Security Council Resolution 2354 (2017), supported by the Egyptian Ministry of Foreign Affairs and which contains several effective measures to combat violent extremism conducive to terrorism, should also guide and inform the drafting of any policies, strategies, work plans, initiatives or national programmes in the confrontation of extremism and hate speech, given the binding nature of Security Council resolutions. The UN document titled 'Comprehensive International Framework to Counter Violent Extremism' also contains important recommendations in this regard.

Major international instruments which highlight the role of religious institutions and leaders in combating extremism and violence include the United Nations Development Program 'Toolkit for Design, Monitoring and Evaluation of Programs that Focus on Preventing Violent Extremism' of 2018.

As far as combating religion-based hate speech is concerned, the UN calls upon States, whenever they take measures to prevent or combat hate, to fully respect freedom of religion or belief, freedom of expression and other mutually reinforcing rights to freedom.[14]

The author introduces a personal perspective, deriving mainly from international instruments examined herein, that any serious efforts to combat extremism conducive to violence and terrorism must seek to:

- eliminate discrimination in all its forms and manifestations;
- address the root factors conducive to extremism, such as unemployment, poverty, marginalization, exclusion, corruption and human rights violations;[15]
- tackle ideologies leading to intolerance and extremism;
- develop counter-extremism and -hate speech narratives;
- promote concepts of citizenship and nation State; and
- spread a culture of tolerance.

It goes without saying that the role of religious institutions in combating extremism and hate speech is crucial, as this endeavour will only succeed if conducted by qualified religious leaders. In Chapter 27 of the present anthology, Professor Mohamed Badar defines the term 'religious leaders' and distinguishes between formal and informal leaders. In this chapter, I will attempt to specify the required qualifications of religious leaders, emphasizing the role of those who are affiliated with Al-Azhar and its institutions.

29.4. Focus of International Instruments on the Concept of 'Counter-Narrative'

Any observer of international instruments which address combating extremism and hate speech will notice that their focus is on the notion of 'alternative narratives' or 'counter-narratives' as preventive measures against extremism and hate speech. Conspicuously, the international community is interested in developing preventive measures against extremism and hate speech. Religious institutions play a major role in propagating alternative narratives. UN Security Council Resolution 2178 (2014)[16] highlighted the importance of efforts "to develop non-violent alternative avenues to decrease the risk of radicalization to

[14] See Report of the Special Rapporteur on Freedom of Religion or Belief, 27 January 2014, para. 61, see *supra* note 8.

[15] For more details on aspects related to confronting root factors leading to violent extremism, see UNDP, "Preventing Violent Extremism through Inclusive Development and the Promotion of Tolerance and Respect for Diversity", 1 July 2016, p. 5 (https://www.legal-tools.org/doc/guylbf/).

[16] UNSC Resolution 2178 (2014), UN Doc. S/RES/2178 (2014), 24 September 2014 (https://www.legal-tools.org/doc/009656/).

terrorism" and to "promote peaceful alternatives to violent narratives espoused by foreign terrorist fighters". The role of religious institutions is undoubtedly evident in achieving these goals.

In the same vein, the UN states that combating violent extremism requires collective efforts, "including the prevention of radicalization, recruitment and mobilization of individuals into terrorist groups, and becoming foreign terrorist fighters".[17] This requires the preparation of religious, educational and cultural initiatives which are carefully examined to confront extremism, potentially conducive to violent extremism and therefore to terrorism.

It should be noted that the comprehensive international framework to counter terrorist narratives consists of three core elements:

1. legal and law enforcement measures in accordance with obligations applicable under international law, including international human rights law and relevant Security Council resolutions meant to implement General Assembly resolutions;
2. the establishment of public–private partnerships; and
3. the development of counter-narratives.

The role of religious institutions in combating extremism and hate speech is highlighted in the third pillar of the comprehensive international framework through the development of counter-narratives on hate speech and violence.

In this regard, operative paragraph 2 of UN Security Council Resolution 2354 (2017) adopted several essential measures to combat 'violent extremism' which the author believes should be introduced to the reader, including the following points:

> (f) Efforts to counter terrorist narratives can benefit through engagement with a wide range of actors, including youth, families, women, religious, cultural, and education leaders, and other concerned groups of civil society;
>
> (g) States should consider supporting the efforts aimed at raising public awareness regarding counter terrorist narratives through education and media, including through dedicated educational programs to pre-empt youth acceptance of terrorist narratives;
>
> (h) The importance of promoting enhanced dialogue and broadened understanding among societies;
>
> (i) States should consider engaging, where appropriate, with religious authorities and community leaders, that have relevant

[17] See UN Secretary-General, Plan of Action to Prevent Violent Extremism, UN Doc. A/70/674, 24 December 2015, para. 5 (https://www.legal-tools.org/doc/ui69e3/).

> expertise in crafting and delivering effective counter-narratives, in countering narratives used by terrorists and their supporters;
>
> (j) Counter-narratives should aim not only to rebut terrorists' messages, but also to amplify positive narratives, to provide credible alternatives and address issues of concern to vulnerable audiences who are subject to terrorist narratives;
>
> (k) Counter-narratives should take into account the gender dimension, and narratives should be developed that address specific concerns and vulnerabilities of both men and women;
>
> (l) Continued research into the drivers of terrorism and violent extremism is necessary in order to develop more focused counter-narrative programmes [...].[18]

The author believes that religious leaders should be aware of the content of this resolution and other international instruments which address the concept of 'counter-narrative'. The notion of 'renewal of religious discourse', which was encouraged by the political leadership and developed by the religious institutions in Egypt, is perhaps consistent with the notion of 'counter-narrative' frequently advocated for by UN instruments. According to the Counter-Terrorism Committee's proposal for a comprehensive international framework to counter terrorist narratives:

> Counter-narrative campaigns fall conceptually within the broader category of counter-incitement and common vulnerabilities and exposures strategies of States that aim to address factors that may lead to terrorism and violent extremism as and when conducive to terrorism. They tackle the motivations that lead certain vulnerable people to consider joining terrorist groups, in part by addressing issues such as feelings of alienation, discrimination, lack of economic opportunity and anger over unresolved conflict.[19]

Having highlighted the main international instruments which indicate the importance of measures preventing the risk of extremism and countering hate speech, and having stressed the vital role of religious institutions in this regard, this chapter will now explore the critical role undertaken by Al-Azhar in achieving these goals.

29.5. Al-Azhar's Role in Combating Extremism and Hate Speech

When the role of national institutions in combating discrimination, extremism and hate speech is addressed, these institutions are clustered into two main groups. The first comprises national institutions mandated by the legislature or

[18] UNSC Resolution 2354 (2017), see *supra* note 11.

[19] See Comprehensive International Framework to Counter Terrorist-Narratives, para. 17, *supra* note 12.

relevant statutory mandate to combat extremism and hate speech, such as the Supreme Council for Combating Terrorism and Extremism ('Council') and the National Council for Human Rights in Egypt. The second group comprises national institutions and bodies contributing to the fulfilment of these goals using the process of drafting counter-extremism and -hate speech narratives, such as Al-Azhar.

29.5.1. Reflections on Al-Azhar's Functions

Al-Azhar is recognized as the key authority for the Muslim world in terms of religious doctrine and teachings and Islámic affairs. As such, it assumes the responsibility of delivering the message of Islám (*Da'úah*) and the dissemination of religious awareness and the basics of Arabic language in Egypt and throughout the world, as the language of the *Qur'án*.[20] In fact, the tasks assigned to Al-Azhar and its institutions, pursuant to Law No. 103 of 1961 on the Reorganization of Al-Azhar Institutions, include the preparation of its specialized scholars to undertake this vital role in confronting extremism and hate speech. To this end, Al-Azhar is the competent authority to preserve, study, interpret and disseminate Islámic heritage; to demonstrate the tolerant nature of Islám; to ensure security, tranquillity and peace of mind for all people in this life and in the hereafter; to revive the Arab nation's civilization and academic and intellectual heritage; and to serve the society in its national and humanitarian goals and spiritual values. Al-Azhar is the ultimate authority in all matters related to Islámic affairs, doctrine, heritage and modern intellectual jurisprudence. Its scholars are entrusted to advance religious knowledge, establish linkages between belief and behaviour, and contribute to the enablement of all factors conducive to activity, production, increment, providing a good example and *Da'úah* for the path of Allah with wisdom and good exhortation.[21]

This vital role has been consolidated by provisions of Article 4(4) of Law No. 25 of 2018 on the Establishment of the Supreme Council for Combating

[20] Constitution of Egypt, 10 January 2015, Article 7, reads as follows (https://www.legal-tools.org/doc/632f2f/):

> Al-Azhar is an independent academic Islámic institution, with exclusive competence over its own affairs. It is the main authority for religious knowledge and Islámic affairs. It assumes the responsibility of delivering the message of Islám (*Da`wah*) and the dissemination of religious knowledge and Arabic in Egypt and throughout the world. The State shall provide enough financial allocations to achieve its purposes.

[21] See Egypt, Law No. 103 of 1961 on the Reorganization of Al-Azhar Institutions, Article (2) as amended by Law No. 13 of 2012 ('Law No. 103 of 1961') (https://www.legal-tools.org/doc/k3xsko/).

Terrorism and Extremism.[22] Article 4(4) enumerates the Council's terms of reference, stating that the Council is mandated, *inter alia,* to: "Coordinate with religious institutions and security and media entities to enable moderate religious discourse; and disseminate the proper concepts of religion in the society against all forms of extremist narrative". Undoubtedly, having the Grand Imám on the Council's board helps Al-Azhar to perform an effective role in confronting extremism and hate speech.

In the sections below, I will highlight Al-Azhar's role in combating extremism and hate speech, in line with its mandated functions, and stress the importance of maximizing Al-Azhar's role in combating these phenomena. I will also address Al-Azhar's role in implementing the concept of 'counter-narrative', given that Al-Azhar's role in confronting extremism and hate speech and implementing the concept of 'counter-narratives' is closely related to the dissemination of a culture of tolerance.

29.5.2. Maximizing Al-Ázhár's Role in Confronting Extremism and Hate Speech

I have already pointed out that the comprehensive fight against terrorism must include countering extremist ideology to enable the elimination of the roots of terrorism. Therefore, specialized religious scholars are unanimously convinced that a close link exists between extremism, violence and terrorism and that their role should focus on confronting intolerance, radicalization and extremism, and naturally hate speech, which is used as a modality to promote extremism and perpetrate violence. Those who are already caught into the trap of radicalization and *ghulú*[23] may build their arguments upon strong justifications for the commission of violence.[24] In reference to the link between extremism and terrorism, many scholars stress that extremism should not always be seen as exclusively religious or exclusively Islámic,[25] as some allege. In fact, other forms of extremism exist, potentially conducive to violence and terrorism, the most dangerous of which is racist extremism. From the author's point of view, this opinion constitutes a central perception that should receive attention by Muslim scholars in their internally and externally addressed narratives.

According to the preponderant jurisprudence, in order to succeed in combating *ghulú* and religious extremism, factors which drive a person to adopt a

[22] Egypt, Law No. 25 of 2018 on the Establishment of the Supreme Council for Combating Terrorism and Extremism, 24 April 2018 ('Law No. 25 of 2018') (https://www.legal-tools.org/doc/o0x16s/).

[23] For a detailed understanding of the term '*ghulú*', see Chapter 16 of the present anthology.

[24] See Moḥíuddín "'Afífí Aḥmad: fí: al-Ghulú wat-Taṭárruff", in *Al-Ghulú wat-Taṭárruff*, Islamic Research Academy, Research Academy Series, 47th Year, Book II, 2015, p. 6.

[25] See Muḥammad Samak, "Fí at-Taṭárruff wal-Iirhab", in *ibid.*, p. 36.

perverted ideology potentially conducive to extremism must be identified.[26] One of the main reasons for religious extremism is the misunderstanding of texts in a manner that may be conducive to radicalization,[27] because embracing misleading ideas and distorted interpretations of religion leads to the disruption of society[28] together with the associated intolerance which is conducive to violence.[29] Accordingly, religious extremism is usually attributed to fanaticism for ideologies rooted in misinterpretations of religious texts. This fanaticism usually arises from *ghulú* in understanding and interpreting religious concepts, which is usually supported by the radical religious narrative.

The risk of religious extremism is even higher when it is based on *takfír* of the other. Writes a renowned authority in Islámic jurisprudence: "This confused *takfiri* ideology, which renders legitimacy to the killing of individuals without any judgment or ruling of the *Sharí'ah*".[30] It was admitted by another authority that "those who adopt a *takfiri* ideological approach will most probably use violence in practice".[31] Therefore, Al-Azhar believes that conceptual religious difference, if associated with ideological deviation and religious extremism, will inevitably lead to conflict and wars.[32]

The determination of causes for extremism should be followed by a phase of response and confrontation, by labelling and calling out destructive teachings and doctrines so that people can be aware of them, listing suspicions raised by people of *ghulú* and extremism and providing decisive responses to them.[33] Therefore, some religious scholars unanimously agree as follows:

---

26 See Aḥmad K. Shárqáwí, "Dáwr Al-Ázhár fí Múajahat al-Ghulú wat-Taṭárruff", in *ibid.*, pp. 57–58.

27 See former Grand Imám of Al-Azhar, Jad al-Ḥáq 'Alí Jad al-Ḥáq, "At-Taṭárruff ad-Díní wa-Ab'aduh: Amníyyann ... wa-Siyasíyyann ... wa-Jtima'íyyann", in *Jama'at Anṣár al-Sunnah al-Muḥammaddiyyah* (Religious Extremism and Its Dimensions), no. 8, pp. 33–34.

28 See *ibid.*, pp. 53.

29 For an in-depth analysis of the religious extremism phenomenon, see former Grand Imám of Al-Azhar Jad al-Ḥáq 'Alí Jad al-Ḥáq, *Bayan Lil-Nas min Al-Ázhár Ash-Sharíf* (A Statement by Al-Azhar to the People), Part One, Al-Márṣád Al-Sharíf Press, 1988, pp. 23–28.

30 According to preponderant jurisprudence, a person may be labelled as '*kafir*' only by the judiciary; judgment of the person's implications of being *kafir* in the hereafter shall be left to the justice of Allah; see, for example, Muḥammad S.A. al-Musayyár, *Qáḍíyyat at-Takfír fí al-Fikr al-I'lamí*, 1st ed., Dár aṭ-Ṭibá'ah *Al-Muḥammaddíyyah*, 1996, pp. 48–50.

31 Jalal-ud-Dín M. Ṣáliḥ, *Intellectual Terrorism: Its Forms and Practices*, Centre for Studies and Research, Naif Arab University for Security Sciences, 2008, p. 162.

32 See Al-Ḥáq, 1988, p. 28, *supra* note 29.

33 Ibráhím Ráshid al-Muraíkhí, "Dawr al-'ulama' wal-Mú'asasat ad-Díníyyah fí *Múajahat* al-Ghulú wat-Taṭárruff", in *Múajahat al-Ghulú wat-Taṭárruff*, Islamic Research Academy, 2015, p. 81.

> It has become imperative to confront suspicious ideologies using an appropriate and disciplined thought which avoids complacency, slander, insult, bickering, hatred, falsehood and fight. They consider extremist ideologies and the resulting ideological and material terrorism as an illness. According to some contemporary jurists, the treatment for this illness is to have people learn the truth and have in-depth knowledge of and aspiration for it so that the truth becomes likeable and preferable by them; have them learn and get acquainted with justice until they have obeyed it; to disclose the falsehood in terms of its ugliness, iniquity and misdeeds; and highlight how it caused people to live in misery and societies to be ruined.[34]

To best enable Al-Azhar to assume its desired role, the Mufti of Ukraine believes that:

> Al-Azhar's role should be activated and developed; its work mechanisms should be modernized, its capacity should be scaled up, and its narrative should be rationalized. With this, Al-Azhar will become an inclusive platform and a unified authority for schools of jurisprudence of *ahl al-Sunnah wa'l-jamá'ah* (those who adhere to the Sunnah traditions and unite in following it, generally the *Sunnís*) as well as for academic coordination between institutions of *fatwa.* This will highly affect the relationships among the peoples of Islámic countries on the one hand, and their relationship with other cultures and countries on the other hand. This would contribute to reduce the emergence of organizations and movements which politicize religion and dare to falsely claim to be the global or regional authority and spokespersons of Muslim peoples.[35]

An observer of Al-Azhar's efforts in this field will notice that it has always been keen to protect the national fabric against sectarian strife, whether fabricated or real, as well as from all forms and manifestations of racist calls and generally from any threat to the integrity of the country, the solidarity of its people, and the unity of its territory.[36] Many researchers are of the view that the

34 "Dawr Al-Ázhár fí Múajahat al-Ghulú wat-Taṭárruff", p. 56, see *supra* note 26.

35 See Aḥmad Tamím, the Mufti of Ukraine, "Makháṭir at-Taṭárruff wa-Dawr al-Márji'íyyat ad-Díníyyah fí Múajahatih", in *Al-Ghulú wat-Taṭárruff*, by a Group of Scholars, Islamic Research Academy, Research Academy Series, 47th Year, Book II, 2015, p. 111 (footnote omitted).

36 See, for example, "Al-Azhar Document to Renounce Violence", February 2013, para. 9.

role of Al-Azhar and Dar al-Ifta[37] in combating extremism and hate speech has recently increased in relevance.

The author believes that Al-Azhar is already undertaking the role envisaged by the Mufti of Ukraine. To maximize the impact of this role, it is important, in terms of combating extremism and hate speech, to develop clear strategies and programmes against extremism and hate speech, involving strategic goals to be achieved through carefully developed plans of action and effective initiatives sponsored by Al-Azhar's reverend scholars under a reform, development and renewal approach.

The Al-Azhar performs this role through its distinguished scholars, who are cognizant of the fact that they are revered by the public who trusts their knowledge, follows their sayings, and implements their teachings. The public looks at them as the guardians of the moderate message and methods of Islám, stemming from the provisions of *Sharí'ah*.[38] They are, as the Mufti of Ukraine believes, "the first frontline and the strongest defense line; should they collapse, the road would be clear for extremists whose goals will be easily attainable".[39]

Al-Azhar's scholars and other specialized researchers should fulfil their lofty goals in confronting extremist ideologies and hate speech, guided by newly developed international provisions and the standards listed herein. For this purpose, they should highlight *Sharí'ah* provisions in order to renew the classical religious discourse and develop a counter-narrative against extremism and hate speech, and address the emerging issues brought about by these phenomena. This process should be carried out within, and never beyond, the framework of the overall tenets of *Sharí'ah*, in line with its well-established regulations, adhering to its methods of inference of practical teachings and to the rules governing its branches. It should take place in a manner that ensures the achievement of the major purposes of *Sharí'ah*, that is, the protection of sound religious practice, life, sanity, offspring and property.[40]

Scholars entrusted with the implementation of counter-narrative strategies should fulfil the following requirements:

- academic eligibility;
- devoutness and piety;

---

37 Dar al-Ifta al-Miṣríyyah (Egypt) is considered among the pioneering foundations for *fatwas* in the Islámic world. More information about its role and function is available on its official web site.

38 "Dawr Al-Ázhár fí Múajahat al-Ghulú wat-Taṭárruff", p. 56, see *supra* note 26.

39 See "Makháṭir at-Taṭárruff wa-Dawr al-Márji'íyyat ad-Díníyyah fí Múajahatih", 2015, pp. 111–112, see *supra* note 35.

40 See Case No. 29 of Judicial Year 11, p. 231, *supra* note 4.

- moderation and wisdom in handling religious matters;
- patience in discussion and debate;
- fairness;
- in-depth research experience;
- awareness of people's realities, conditions and circumstances and *nawazil* (latest problematic questions of religion);
- renewing knowledge; and
- disassociation with any approaches based on '*ghulú*' and extremism,[41] while adhering to Al-Azhar's moderate approach in its knowledge and conduct, reflecting the approach of *ahl al-Sunnah wal-jama'ah*; a method which has been accepted by the Muslim *'ummah* in both the principles of religion and the branches of the four schools of jurisprudence.[42]

These qualifications would enable Al-Azhar scholars and leaders to perform their vital role in providing people with guidance to pursue a rational religious path by fortifying them with the proper religious thought, protecting them from destructive misguided ideas and teaching them to establish the meanings of 'good' by themselves. This effort should contribute to the consolidation of the foundations of moderate thought and to the fight against perverted ideologies. The above-mentioned requirements should be fulfilled by those undertaking this major role.

In this regard, a viewpoint was offered by an educational psychologist who noted that, in recognition of the importance of *Da'úah* in Britain, the preachers' role is no longer perceived as exclusively leading Muslims in prayer and other religious rituals. Rather, the perception has evolved to include the public sphere. Therefore, a righteous Imám in Britain is the one who has the ability to integrate into society, contributes to the development of voluntarism and shares activities and services with others of different religions.[43]

This requires, as explained above, competent religious scholars able to practice *Da'úah* and preach Islámic tradition with a moderate and wise approach in handling religious matters. In his renowned interpretation of the *Qur'án*, Imám Ibn Kathir commented on verse 125 of *Súrát* Al-Naḥl, mentioned above. He asserted that Allah commands his Messenger to call for his path and debate

41 See "Dawr al-'Ulama' wal-Mú'asasat ad-Díníyyah", p. 78, *supra* note 33.

42 See Law No. 103 of 1961, Article 32 *bis*(b), para. 7, *supra* note 21.

43 Muḥammad I. Muḥammad, "Al-Ma'aíyyr al-Biríṭáníyyah li-Jawdit A'immat al-Masajid li-Múajahat al-Taṭárruff wal-Irhab", in *Shabakat Día' lil-Mú'tamarát wad-Dirásat*, 27 May 2017.

with people only with wisdom and kind words ('excellent admonition').[44] This instruction is very important for scholars and religious leaders who are engaged in the propagation of Islámic teachings and in the defense of its principles. They should always undertake their duties in a manner characterized by 'wisdom' and 'excellent admonition'. 'Wisdom' implies that one should use discretion during teaching and peaching Islámic traditions. 'Excellent admonition' implies that Islámic clerks should not confine themselves merely to arguments in condemning evils and deviations, but should try to convince the other of their repugnance that lies embedded in the human nature. This naturally supports their endeavours in combating extremism and religious hatred. Admonition should be administered in such a manner as to show sincere concern for the welfare of the addressee. 'Best manner' implies that one should use kind words and methods in his *Da'úah* and preaching, show noble character, give reasonable and appealing arguments, and refrain from indulging in polemics, argumentation and controversies.[45]

As already explained, a comprehensive countering of perverted ideology, extremism and terrorism requires carefully planned religious, educational and cultural initiatives to confront extremism potentially conducive to violent extremism and terrorism. The decision to establish the Council reflects the main pillars related to the confrontation of extremism (which are co-implemented by the Council and the religious institutions), including:

- co-ordination with religious institutions and security services to enable moderate and balanced religious discourse and disseminate correct religious concepts in society against all forms of extremism;
- determining core elements of improvement that should be included in curricula at all educational levels, supporting the tolerance and acceptance of others and the rejection of violence and extremism.

It should be noted that the first pillar is fully consistent with international standards for combating extremism, violent extremism and hate speech, as it gives due consideration to the role of religious institutions in drafting a moderate

---

[44] Imám Ibn Kathir, *Tafsír al-Qur'án al-'Aẓím* (Interpretation of the Noble Qur'án), Al-Maktabah Al-'Áṣríyyah, Beirut, 2006, p. 721.

[45] Imám al-Qurṭubí, *Al-Jami' li-Aḥkam, al-Qur'án*, vol. 5, Dar al-Ḥadíth, Cairo, 2007, p. 543; *Ibid.*, p. 44; Abú-al-A'la al-Mawdúdí, "The Meaning of the *Qur'án* in English" (available on the *English Tafsir* web site); Saheeh International, *The Qur'án: English Meanings*, Abul-Qasim Publishing House, 1997; "Sayyid Abú-al-A'lá al-Maúdúdiyy – Tafhiyym al-Qur'án – The Meaning of the Qur'án" (available on the *English Tafsir* web site); Muhammad Taqi-ud-Din Al-Hilali and Muhammad Muhsin Khan, *The Noble Qur'an: The English Translation of the Meanings and Commentary (Arabic)*, King Fahd Complex For the Printing of the Holy Qur'an, Medina, 1998.

and balanced religious discourse that falls under the concept of 'counter-narrative'.

29.5.3. Al-Ázhár's Role in Implementing the 'Counter-Narrative'

As mentioned earlier, international instruments in the field of combating violent extremism and terrorism focus on the importance of drafting a counter-narrative in response to the extremist narrative employed by terrorists to recruit followers and supporters. Therefore, it is necessary to engage religious leaders who have the appropriate experience in drafting and introducing an effective counter-narrative in response to radical and terrorist narratives. The Rabat Plan on prohibiting advocacy of national, racial or religious hatred that constitutes incitement to discrimination, hostility or violence has already stressed the need for an 'alternative narrative' in response to extremist forms of hate speech.[46]

In light of the relevant international instruments, basic objectives of the 'counter-narratives' may be stated as follows: (i) combating perverted ideologies; (ii) combating hateful and terrorist narratives; and (iii) spreading a culture of tolerance and acceptance of the other. The author believes that drafting such a narrative is not an easy task, as it requires extensive knowledge of the phenomena in question, obtained by conducting research and studies to determine the nature and dimensions of the extremist, hateful and terrorist narratives and the nature of the 'counter-narratives' needed in response. Moreover, the process involves the identification of the addressees and the content of this narrative – a process which should be guided by the national peculiarities which are reflective of the basic interests of the country and consistent with the prevailing values and traditions. Combating perverted ideologies and hate speech should come at the centre of the counter-narrative. As such, the resulting counter-narrative will be in harmony with reality, sensitive to events and circumstances, and recognize the latest *nawazel* (plural of *nazilah*; *nazilah* is a new occurrence that requires a new *Sharí'ah* ruling).

The desired counter-narrative should interact with the social and political context at the national level and the prevailing international standards. It should also consider the psychological and intellectual characteristics of target individuals and contribute to the construction of the religious architecture of citizens, so that it becomes an element of improvement rather than of sabotage and destruction, moderation rather than *ghulú* and patience rather than haste.[47]

Since the Arab region suffers from the spread of *takfír* terrorist groups, the desired counter-narrative must take into account the domestic conditions and

---

46 Rabat Plan, see *supra* note 9.

47 See Ṣaliḥ bin Ghanim al-Sudlan, *Asbab al-Irhab wal-'Unff wat-Taṭárruff*, Majallat al-'Amn wal-Ḥayah, no. 286, Naif Arab University for Security Sciences (NAUSS), 2006, p. 57.

must address the existing challenges. Therefore, it is imperative to examine the architecture and the nature of extremist groups and terrorist organizations[48] which promote narratives of extremism, hatred and terrorism, especially those using intense violence to achieve their goals, regardless of the labels attributed to them, be it '*takfír*' or 'armed terrorist' groups.[49]

Al-Azhar undoubtedly has a leading position among religious institutions which have the capacity to draft such a 'counter-narrative', especially when extremism is attributed to ideological deviation or faith defects caused by narratives of radicalization and hate.

Al-Azhar's role in confronting extremism and hate speech is carried out through its vital message of "developing a good moderate Islámic thought" in response to crises in the Islámic arena.[50] Therefore, the Grand Imám reiterated his call to adopt this moderate approach in thought, belief and deeds and in the implementation of the provisions of the *Qur'án* and the Prophet's *Sunnah*.[51] Besides the established principles in the *Qur'án*, Al-Azhar scholars are of the opinion that concrete guidelines on confronting extremism and radicalization do exist in prophetic discourse. They consider it the most important pillar of educating individuals on the basis of the moderation of Islám, due to its authentic values, sublime meanings and divine directives. [52] This is due to the merciful and compassionate approach of the prophetic discourse, which find its spirit in the Prophet's characteristics.[53]

In order to trigger Al-Azhar's functions as specified in the Constitution of Egypt and Law No. 103 of 1961, in light of the international instruments cited herein, the author believes that the counter-narrative assumed by Al-Azhar and its institutions through its moderate discourse should fulfil the following criteria:

---

48 This usually takes place by being familiarized with the architecture, cohesion and types of internal and external communications of these groups as well social and behavioural roles within a single group.

49 See Adel Majed and Rawan Majed, "Huqúq al-Insan wa-Múajabahat al-Jama'at al-Irhabíyyah al-Musallaḥah" (Human Rights and Confronting Armed Terrorist Groups), in *Journal of Studies in Human Rights*, May 2018, no. 1, p. 21.

50 Na'ím Ḥassan, "Dáwr al-'Ulama' wal-Mú'asasat ad-Díníyyah", in *Múajahat al-Ghulú wat-Taṭárruff*, p. 103, see *supra* note 33.

51 Grand Imám of Al-Azhar, Professor Ahmed Al-Ṭayyeb, Al-Azhar International Conference on Confronting Extremism and Terrorism, *Khuṭúrat at-Takfír* (Danger of Takfír), *Taṣḥíḥ al-Mafahím* (Correcting Concepts), vol. 1, Islámic Research Academy Publications, Cairo, 2017, p. 110.

52 See Heba Ibrahim, "Al-Khitáb al-Nabawí fí Múajahat al-Ghulú wat-Taṭárruff" (The Prophetic Discourse in the Face of al-Ghulú and Extremism), in *The Scientific Journal, Faculty of Fundamentals of Religion and Da'wah in Zagazig-Al-Azhar University*, 1st ed., vol. 33, no. 1, 2021, p. 911.

53 *Ibid.*, p. 916.

- tackling stray narratives, destructive practices[54] and ideologies conducive to intolerance, fanaticism and ideological radicalization;
- analysing the perverted ideologies and explaining their levels and dimensions;
- refuting statements, allegations and arguments promoted by terrorist and extremist groups and exposing their disguises and covers;
- correcting religious misconceptions;
- fortifying the society by spreading the correct understanding of the moderate and balanced Islám;
- disseminating a culture of tolerance and acceptance of the other.

Numerous studies and statements have already been issued by Al-Azhar and its institutions, identifying the sources and underlying principles of destructive practices and refuting allegations promoted by extremists and terrorists. Moreover, they also provided an analysis of the relevant ideological intellectual arguments promoted by the extremists and deconstruct them, on the basis of *Sharí'ah*, practical and academic terms to expose them as misleading, and address them with the proper understanding of religion.[55]

It should be noted that the Al-Azhar Observatory for Combating Extremism ('Observatory') performs a vital role in combating extremism, terrorism and hate speech, as highlighted in international instruments. It monitors, collect data, analyses, and rectifies messages, ideologies and hate speech broadcast by extremist groups on the Internet and social media. For this purpose, the Observatory adopts a moderate and balanced narrative which refutes and responds to perverted ideologies. As such, it has managed to deconstruct ideological arguments set forth by extremist groups based on *Sharí'ah*. The Observatory has also clarified practical and academic terms using critical thinking and knowledge. Accordingly, the Observatory was able to reveal the dangers of extremist groups' ideological references, the corruption of their underlying foundations, and their dangerous role in damaging and destabilizing the social fabric using their destructive methods.[56]

---

[54] For information about what is meant by 'destructive approaches', see "Dawr al-'Ulama' wal-Mú'sasat ad-Díníyyah", p. 79, see *supra* note 33.

[55] Muḥammad S. al-Ḥaddad, "Mú'alajat aṣ-Ṣuḥuff al-Islamíyyah al-Miṣríyyah li-Qáḍáya al-Irhab", Ph.D. thesis in Media, Department of Journalism, Faculty of Media, Islamic University of North America, 2019, p. 168.

[56] Muḥammad J. Aḥmad, "Sardiyyat at-Tamkín fí Khitáb al-Jama'at al-Mutaṭárrifah" (Empowerment Narrative in Speech of Extremist Groups), in *Islamic Military Coalition to Combat Terrorism*, 23 January 2020 (available on the Coalition's web site).

As for the pivotal role of correcting religious misconceptions, Al-Azhar and its scholars have always been disseminating accurate knowledge based on conclusive *Sharí'ah* evidence and clear textual proofs.[57] It is not an easy task as it requires in-depth understanding of jurisprudence and awareness of society's issues and concerns, including the causes and treatments of such issues. Moreover, rectifying misconceptions requires scholars to be fully neutral in explaining the issues in question so that they are consistent with logic and based on objective and sound academic foundations, to be welcomed in the readers' minds and hearts,[58] bearing in mind that Al-Azhar is the haven to be resorted to for rectifying misconceptions, and the protector of their culture, heritage and the moderation of *Sharí'ah*.

It goes without saying that a comprehensive framework for combating extremist religious ideologies and hate speech is currently a priority of the Egyptian State through the mechanism of 'renewing religious discourse'. In this regard, the State endeavours to refine religious discourse in consultation with religious leaders, in furtherance of the spirit of dialogue, tolerance and the avoidance of extremism.

According to specialists of Egypt's National Council for Human Rights,

> religious discourse undoubtedly needs to be developed and modernized following centuries of evolution of Islámic countries, in which rulers' violations were often justified, relations between holders of different monotheistic religions were developed, political thought was developed and the concept of citizenship, national state and international co-operation was well established.[59]

Al-Azhar and its institutions exert efforts towards the renewal of religion using their up-to-date jurisprudence and thought, as stipulated in Law No. 103 of 1961, recognizing that mechanisms for renewing religious discourse can never be in conflict with the established facts of Islám or necessarily known matters of religion.

The religious discourse adopted by Al-Azhar is simple, moderate and well-balanced, all of which are features of *Sharí'ah*. Enumerating the features of Al-Azhar's moderate discourse, the Grand Imám states that "Al-Azhar has exerted and will continue to exert a consistent effort to draft a conscious and

---

57 See Muḥammad Yússif (General Secretary of the Supreme Scientific Council in the Kingdom of Morocco), "Muhimmat al-'Ulama' fí Mukafaḥat al-Ghulú wal-Irhab", in *Al-Ghulú wat-Taṭárruff*, p. 121, see *supra* note 24.

58 See al-Ḥaddad, 2019, pp. 77–78, *supra* note 55.

59 Cairo Declaration on "The Role of Awareness Institutions in Confronting Violent Extremism and Incitement to Hate", 17 July 2017, Item (III) on the role and responsibility of "the clergy" against violent extremism.

rational religious discourse based on *Qur'án*, the Prophet's *Sunnah*, and the jurisprudence accepted by the (Islámic) nation".[60] This confirms that Al-Azhar is implementing the counter-narrative envisaged in international instruments using its long-standing 'moderate narrative' which is being renewed presently.

To enable the achievement of Al-Azhar's lofty goals, scholars who confront perverted ideologies and extremism must familiarize themselves with the nature of the perverted mindsets they are dealing with, a process described by some scholars and specialists as "the intellectual anatomy of the extremist mindset".[61] In this process, a distinction should be made between the essence and nature of perverted ideologies which cause the problem, and the psychological state which drives the person in question to adopt those ideologies.

Introducing a personal viewpoint based on his readings in various disciplines (security, political, legal, social, psychological and religious), the author believes that for scholars to succeed in confronting extremism and hate speech, they must follow the steps listed below.

Step one: determine the form and type of extremism they are addressing, and whether it is based on religious, racial, ethnic, racist, social or political origins or on a combination thereof. In case of religion-based extremism, the underlying values and beliefs of the religion in question should be understood.

Step two: identify the content and nature of the perverted ideologies used to influence the concerned persons.

Step three: recognize means and methods used to attract a person to adopt these perverted ideologies, including, naturally, hate speech.

Step four: diagnose push, pull, personal and psychological factors which result in the adoption of such ideologies.

Step five: determine the phase in which the person is with regard to the adoption perverted ideologies – whether the person is in the initial phases of imbibing perverted ideologies, or has moved to the phases of fanaticism and radicalization, or has already been infected with the illness of extremism.

Step six: determine the system of values, ideas and perceptions controlling the person's mindset in the phase under diagnosis.

Step seven: on one hand, determine the nature of religious discourse required to confront the essence of those perverted ideologies and false values, and on the other hand, select necessary measures to address the state of

[60] Grand Imám of Al-Azhar, Professor Ahmed Al-Ṭayyeb, Al-Azhar International Conference on Confronting Extremism and Terrorism, 2017, p. 110, see *supra* note 51.

[61] "Al-Tashríḥ al-Thaqáfí li-'Áqlíyyat al-Mutaṭárriff" (The Intellectual Anatomy of the Extremist Mindset), 11th Cultural Salon, Ṭabah Research and Development Consulting Foundation (available on Tabah Foundation's web site).

extremism that afflicts the person or group concerned. The purpose of this is to refute perverted ideologies, to reveal the weaknesses of their underlying system of values and then to confront and refute allegations made by persons or groups promoting them. And finally, to correct misconceptions among those who have adopted and embraced such ideologies, and among the public as a precautionary measure, by enlightening people of the tolerant nature of Islám and promoting a culture of coexistence.

29.5.4. Importance of Al-Ázhár's Role in Promoting the Culture of Tolerance

Tolerance is a basic principle of Islám and the cornerstone of various verses of the *Qur'án*. It is a religious and moral duty and is viewed as a prerequisite for coexistence. Clear elicitation of tolerance is expressed in primary sources of Islámic *Sharí'ah*.[62] In various verses of the *Qur'án,* God calls his believers to enter a peaceful state.[63] For the *Qur'án*, peace is the ultimate goal, and if there is to be peace, there must first be tolerance.[64] On the basis of this concept, many verses of the *Qur'án* recognize diversity and variations. Accordingly, these qualities must not only be expected but tolerated. The Prophet's *Sunnah* and Islámic heritage are also rich in providing numerous examples of Islám's tolerance towards the other, and the Prophet (ﷺ) actively promoted peace, tolerance and compassion for all non-Muslim minorities. Reliable *ḥadíth* reports affirm that tolerance is a core value of Islám. It was narrated that Má 'qil Ibn Yasár reported that the Messenger of Allah (ﷺ) said: "the best of faith is patience and tolerance".[65] To stress that mutual relations among people should be based on tolerance, Ibn Abbas (a companion of the Prophet) reported that Prophet Muhammad (ﷺ) said: "Be tolerant and you will receive tolerance".[66]

A Saudi prominent scholar attributes the phenomenon of extremism to the lack of role models who provide sound advice and to the absence of proper

---

62 For a comprehensive view on the sources of Islámic *Sharí'ah*, see Adel Maged, "*Sharí'ah* Sources and Reflections on Integrity", in Morten Bergsmo and Viviane E. Dittrich (eds.), *Integrity in International Justice*, Torkel Opsahl Academic EPublisher, Brussels, 2020, pp. 93–150 (https://www.toaep.org/nas-pdf/4-bergsmo-dittrich/).

63 See, for example, the *Qur'án*, 2:204.

64 Mustafa Köylü, "Peace Education: An Islámic Approach", in *Journal of Peace Education*, 2004, vol. 1, no. 1, pp. 59–76.

65 Imám al-Ṭábárání, *Makarim al-Akhláq* (Noble Morals), Muhammad Abd Elkader Ahmad Atta (ed.), 1st edition, Dar al-Kutub al-'Ilmíyyah, Beirut, 1989, "Section on Patience", pp. 322–323.

66 Imám al-Albaní, *Al-Jami' al-Ṣághír*, *ḥadíth* no. 981, vol. 1, Alpha Publishing and Art Production House, 2008; Zohair Al-Shaweesh (ed.), 1st ed., Islámic Office Publisher, Beirut, 1988, vol. 16, p. 229.

education guiding individuals to follow good morals and to avoid reprehensible behaviour.[67] Religious institutions play a role in educating young people, providing a good example, spreading the principles of love and tolerance and rejecting violence and extremism. Therefore, the Plan of Action to Prevent Violent Extremism calls to engage religious leaders in providing a platform for intra-faith and inter-faith dialogue and discussions, in order to promote tolerance and understanding between local communities and voice their rejection of the doctrine of violence by emphasizing the peaceful and humanitarian values inherent in their theologies.[68] As affirmed by the UN Strategy and Plan of Action on Hate Speech, religious leaders responsible for developing and implementing counter-hate speech strategies should be mindful of the international standards and values that promote intercultural, interfaith, interreligious dialogue and mutual understanding.

Most notably, the Al-Azhar has recently dedicated its efforts to the consolidation of relevant provisions of the *Sunnah* by upholding the values of brotherhood, tolerance, pluralism, citizenship, equality and acceptance of the other. This is consistent with the declaration made by the Grand Imám and His Holiness Pope Francis in the Document on Human Fraternity for World Peace and Living Together. The Document was issued in the form of a flagship historic statement in which Al-Azhar and the Catholic Church stressed that:

> Religions must never incite war, hateful attitudes, hostility and extremism, nor must they incite violence or the shedding of blood. These tragic realities are the consequence of a deviation from religious teachings. They result from a political manipulation of religions and from interpretations made by religious groups who, in the course of history, have taken advantage of the power of religious sentiment in the hearts of men and women in order to make them act in a way that has nothing to do with the truth of religion. This is done for the purpose of achieving objectives that are political, economic, worldly and short-sighted.[69]

It follows that Islám calls for co-existence between Muslims and non-Muslims. In this context, the Grand Imam states that:

> According to the Glorious *Qur'án*, there are three interrelated facts regarding Islam's view of humanity: the first fact is that it is out of Allah's Will that people are created different in religion, creed,

[67] See al-Sudlan, 2006, p. 57, see *supra* note 47.

[68] Plan of Action to Prevent Violent Extremism, para. 49 (e), see *supra* note 17.

[69] See His Holiness Pope Francis and the Grand Imám of Al-Azhar Ahmad Al-Ṭayyeb, "A Document on Human Fraternity for World Peace and Living Together", Apostolic Journey of His Holiness Pope Francis to the United Arab Emirates (3–5 February 2019), 4 February 2019 ('Document on Human Fraternity') (https://www.legal-tools.org/doc/dxyrbx/).

> colour, language and gender. Such differences never change or vanish. The second fact comes as a consequence of the first which is that it is inevitable that the relationship between different [groups] and nations be based on '*ta'āruf*' (mutual co-operation). The *Qur'án* declares this clearly in *súrah Al-Hujarāt*. The third fact that brings together the aforementioned two facts is the right to freedom of belief as safeguarded by Islám. Accordingly, Islám sets rules and regulations for Muslims when dealing with non-Muslims in order to preserve the mutual relationships and respect among followers of divine religions, non-divine religions and even among all people, even if they do not believe in any religion, as long as they do not belittle religions.[70]

The foregoing has established that tolerance is Islám's cardinal principle and that Islámic *Sharí'ah* upholds the principles of coexistence. In order to put into practice these tenets, Al-Azhar employs its vital mission to consolidate the philosophy of coexistence, disseminate a jurisprudence of peaceful coexistence among nations, revive the approach of dialogue and respect the beliefs of others. The ultimate goal is to consolidate and strengthen the moderate understanding of the teachings of Islám in the modern era. Undoubtedly, these lofty purposes contribute to undermining discriminatory policies and hate speech.

The Al-Azhar has been keen to reject violence and protect the national fabric in Egypt and other Islámic nations from all forms and manifestations of racist calls, and generally from all threats to the nation's integrity, the solidarity of its people, and the unity of its territory. The Al-Azhar has issued many documents and statements investigating causes of extremism and revealing its various dimensions. In the Document on Human Fraternity, the Al-Azhar and the Catholic Church stressed the following:

> History shows that religious extremism, national extremism and also intolerance have produced in the world, be it in the East or West, what might be referred to as signs of a "third world war being fought piecemeal". In several parts of the world and in many tragic circumstances these signs have begun to be painfully apparent, as in those situations where the precise number of victims, widows and orphans is unknown.[71]

This important document acknowledges that policies of extremism and division and hateful ideological tendencies are dangerous for the concept of human fraternity. It calls upon all concerned to avoid using religions to incite

[70] Ahmad Al-Ṭayyeb, *Islam First*, 1st ed., Dar al-Quds al-'Árábí, Cairo, 2019, pp. 10–11.

[71] Document on Human Fraternity, see *supra* note 69.

hatred, violence, extremism and blind fanaticism, and to refrain from using the name of Allah to justify acts of murder, exile, terrorism and oppression.

The Grand Imám has frequently stressed in interviews the importance of disseminating the jurisprudence of peaceful coexistence among nations, reviving the dialogue methodology and the respect for the beliefs of others. This is done to consolidate and strengthen the moderate understanding of the teachings of Islám in the modern era. In fact, this approach reflects the preventive measures adopted by the UN in response to the threat of hate speech, extremism and terrorism.

29.6. Conclusion

Experience has shown, as illustrated in various international instruments, that countering perverted ideologies, extremism and hate speech requires all State institutions to join forces, and scholars, experts and researchers in related disciplines to examine and analyse the phenomena in question, especially in the case of patterns of thoughts and forms of behaviour, in order to identify the drivers and the factors which may lead a person to extremism. In general, successful measures to combat extremism and confront hate speech require identifying the root causes, drivers and conditions conducive to hate speech.

The next step is to address these drivers and factors by developing general policies on the prevention techniques and control measures, which usually result in the development of strategies and work plans identifying responsibilities and tasks, where religious institutions are assigned a critical role. Initiatives that aim to prevent and combat religious extremism must address ideologies that drive a person into extremism by monitoring and evaluating the structure of values, ideas and perceptions which shape the person's attitudes and behaviours. Meanwhile, social, cultural, economic, political and legal interventions against perverted or extremist ideologies should be provided for.

The chapter also stresses that the moderate interpretation of religious texts will ensure that all forms of extremism and racism are reduced. The role of religious institutions and their leaders is highly relevant in this regard, in terms of spreading moderate religious thought by developing a moderate counter-narrative in response to narratives of radicalization and hatred, tackling perverted ideologies using wisdom and good advice, treating the extremist mindset and seeking to correct misconceptions.

It is necessary for the proposed religious discourse to be contextualized on a case-by-case basis. For example, the narrative required to prevent extremism or to deal with a person vulnerable to extremism is different, in terms of content and objectives, from the narrative needed to treat a person who is already an extremist.

It has been demonstrated, through the international instruments reviewed in the present chapter, that the international community realizes that an effective way to counter violent extremism should not be exclusively based on the 'security' pillar. Rather, it calls for a counter-narrative in response to the extremism and hate speech rhetoric employed by extremist groups and terrorist organizations. Moreover, the international community advocates for the promotion of the concept of tolerance to confront extremist ideology. This is an essential role which has been undertaken by the Al-Azhar, using its lofty message which aims to consolidate the philosophy of coexistence, spread a jurisprudence of peaceful coexistence among nations, revive the approach to dialogue, and ensure respect for the beliefs of others.

This chapter has shown the important role of the religious leaders in countering perverted ideologies, extremism and hate speech, due to their unique positions of authority, credibility, institutional resources, and ties with communities. In this context, the chapter emphasizes the vital role of Al-Azhar and its religious figures in this process.

The author has asserted that the Al-Azhar is and must remain the guardian which protects the nation's thought from extremism and radicalization. Its mandate is specified in Law No. 103 of 1961 and Law No. 25 of 2018. Accordingly, the Al-Azhar and its specialized scholars are well-qualified to perform this vital role. In this regard, the Al-Azhar is an enabling factor for moderate religious discourse, it spreads reasonable religious concepts in society, and advocates against all forms of extremist narratives. This mission is undertaken by its venerable scholars who have a responsibility, under *Sharí'ah*, to guard religious ordinances and protect the nation's values.

This chapter has shown that the Al-Azhar's leaders have recommended in several conferences and academic fora that it is necessary to issue a comprehensive law on countering perverted ideologies, extremism and hate speech. Supported by specialists, some of the Al-Azhar's scholars have endeavoured to draft a proposed law on 'Combating Hate and Violence in the Name of Religion'. The purpose of this law would be to reduce manifestations of hate and intolerance promoted by extremist groups and movements, and to stress the values of citizenship and coexistence among the nation's people. The author believes that this draft law should be discussed in further seminars and fora, to ensure that international standards presented are met and that the resulting law is consistent with the principles enshrined in the Egyptian Constitution and the rule of law.

As to the criminal aspects of the phenomena, this chapter has shown that criminal law cannot be invoked when perverted ideologies are still at the stage of *genesis* and are evolving into extremism. It can be invoked only when an extremist person demonstrates verbal or actual external behaviour that is legally criminalized. Therefore, any law issued in the field of countering extremism and hate speech must pay attention to protective and preventive measures, in addition to the penal measures prescribed for criminalized behaviour.

I hope that the present chapter will serve as a resource and reference guide for the clergy and researchers in the field of countering extremism and hate, to support their role in addressing hate speech narratives and promote the values of tolerance, non-discrimination and pluralism. Hopefully, it will help them to develop the counter-narrative called for by international instruments and adopted by the Al-Azhar in its 'moderate narrative'. Lastly, the hope is also that the ideas and modalities presented in this chapter will assist religious scholars and leaders in their endeavours to renew religious discourse by incorporating concepts and principles established by international conventions in the field of combating extremism and hate speech.

29.6.1. Recommendations

1. Efforts against extremism and hate speech should be undertaken from a comprehensive and specialized perspective which involves relevant institutions, most notably the Al-Azhar, especially when extremism is based on religious grounds.
2. Religious leaders should be engaged in identifying the problems and their solutions from the beginning, rather than engaging them only in the context of solutions already devised by others, in a way that could make them feel that they are being used rather than consulted. This will give them an opportunity to intervene in the early stages of radicalization.
3. To determine the nature of the content of religious discourse necessary to counter perverted ideologies and extremism, the impactful social, cultural, political and economic conditions should be understood together with the nature of ideologies that contribute to the formation of an extremist's mindset and affect his intellectual configuration. It is important to understand the process which begins with the adoption of perverted ideologies, develops into fanaticism for these ideologies, and eventually evolves to radicalization conducive to extremism and then to violent extremism, in turn potentially conducive to terrorism.
4. The desired religious discourse should be based on a specialized academic jurisprudence and methodology which distinguishes between countering an ideology and addressing the psychological conditions of the targeted individuals. This process should focus on monitoring, analysing and refuting extremist ideologies and hate speech, and exposing the statements, allegations, arguments and disguises of terrorist and extremist groups. In parallel,

religious misconceptions should be corrected and proper understanding of moderate Islám should be disseminated.

5. To facilitate the desired religious discourse, international mechanisms in force against ideological deviation, extremism and hate speech should be mastered. In this regard, the standards established by international instruments should be investigated and new terminology and concepts contained therein should be probed, such as 'violent extremism' and 'counter-narrative'. This would contribute to the renewal of religious discourse in line with the latest international developments and standards.
6. Those mandated to deliver the mission of countering extremism and hate speech should be made more aware of the existing legal frameworks applicable to conduct associated with extremism, violence and terrorism.
7. Consideration should be given to having a diverse religious discourse against extremism and hate speech, including preventive, curative and rehabilitative aspects, in line with the diversity of the target groups.
8. It is proposed to conduct a specialized academic study, jointly between the Al-Azhar and the Egyptian National Center for Social and Criminal Research, to identify the causes and the drivers of religious extremism in society. The course of study should address the underlying perverted ideologies and the nature of hate speech employed by extremist groups to attract young people and other vulnerable groups to adopt these ideologies. The study should also define the resulting impact on the evolution of persons into radicalization and extremism, while proposing the best academic and integrated methods to address these destructive phenomena.
9. Consideration should be given to the promulgation of a comprehensive law on countering extremism and hate speech in Egypt, as was the case in several Arab and Western countries. The law should be informed and guided by the draft law on 'Combating Hate and Violence in the Name of Religion' proposed by the Al-Azhar. The resulting law should be of a general and neutral nature, to ensure that it does not violate the governing principles enshrined in the Egyptian Constitution.

30

Reflections on the Potential of Social Media to Assist Religious Actors Who Seek to Prevent or Reduce Hate Speech

Peter J. Stern*

30.1. Introduction

I am grateful for having the opportunity to contribute to this anthology and to present at the conference on 'Religion, Hateful Expression and Violence' in Florence on 8–9 April 2022, organized by the Centre for International Law Research and Policy ('CILRAP') and partners. I found the presentations at the conference to be very stimulating and informative.[1] As a lawyer by training, I joined Facebook (now Meta) almost nine years ago, seeking an opportunity to engage directly with issues of corporate social responsibility and user trust. At Facebook, I am part of the Content Policy team, which creates the Community Standards,[2] the rules governing what people are allowed to share on our technologies, for example, Facebook and Instagram. The Content Policy team also develops standards for advertisements[3] for certain feed ranking algorithms[4] and for a wide range of commerce products, like Fundraiser. Additionally, I was involved in the creation of the Facebook Oversight Board, which has emerged as a successful effort for bringing transparency and accountability to our technologies.[5]

---

* **Peter J. Stern** is Director of the Content Policy Stakeholder Engagement ('Content Policy team') at Meta in Menlo Park, California. He leads a stakeholder engagement team that builds relationships with non-governmental organizations ('NGOs'), academics and other thought leaders to incorporate external feedback into Meta's content policy development process. Prior to joining Facebook in 2014, he was a partner at the San Francisco law firm Morrison & Foerster LLP, where he specialized in international litigation and spent 11 years in its Tokyo office. He holds a B.A., *summa cum laude*, from Amherst College and an M.A. (History) and J.D. from the University of California, Berkeley. He was a Law Clerk to Judge John T. Noonan, Jr., United States Court of Appeals for the Ninth Circuit (1993–1994). For an audio-visual recording of Peter J. Stern's statement to CILRAP's conference in Florence in April 2022 on the topic of this anthology, please see https://www.cilrap.org/cilrap-film/220409-stern/.

1 The audio-visual recordings of the CILRAP conference are available at https://www.cilrap.org/events/220408-09-florence/.

2 Meta, "Facebook Community Standards – Transparency Center" (available on its web site).

3 Meta, "Advertising Policies" (available on its web site).

4 Meta, "Types of Content We Demote", 17 June 2022 (available on its web site).

5 Information on the Facebook Oversight Board is available on its web site.

Within the Content Policy team, my role is to run a stakeholder engagement function.[6] This involves developing relationships with non-governmental organizations ('NGOs'), academics and other thought leaders around the world to provide information on our content policies and to gather feedback on how people feel we should change our policies. The notion of stakeholder engagement itself is hardly new, but we think that it is very important – and novel – that a major technology company would seek to build engagement into its policy-making process.

Every time we consider a change to our policies, the Content Policy team develops a stakeholder engagement strategy. The team then seeks input from dozens (often hundreds) of experts and others affected by the potential change, focusing on those who may be the most vulnerable. Members of the Content Policy team speak frequently with members of religious (and atheist) communities. These opinions help shape our policies.

With this as background, the present chapter will reflect on the potential of social media to assist religious actors who seek to prevent or reduce hate speech. Having thought extensively about both the benefits and the potential harms of social media, I will address this subject at three levels:

(i) the first way for religious actors to prevent or reduce hate speech is to encourage members of their communities to report hate speech, so social media platforms like Facebook can address it. This may be called a *defensive* strategy, that is, addressing the bad. I will explain our rules on hate speech and how they are enforced later on in this chapter;

(ii) I will analyse an *offensive strategy* and explain how religious actors can prevent or reduce hate speech by *increasing positive speech* about religion and tolerance, pushing back on hate and drowning out intolerance. This will involve describing the growing field of *counter-speech*; and

(iii) I will reflect on an ambitious and extremely important theme, that is, how can religious actors use social media *to build interfaith understanding and tolerance*? Facebook has devoted thought to this topic and I would like to offer some initial reflections in this chapter.

---

6 Meta, "The Principles That Guide Meta's Stakeholder Engagement", 26 January 2022 (available on its web site).

30.2. Assisting Religious Leaders in Preventing or Reducing Hate Speech

30.2.1. Removing Hate Speech on Facebook

Facebook believes that people use their voice and connect more freely when they do not feel attacked on the basis of who they are. That is why we do not allow hate speech on our technologies such as Facebook and Instagram. Hate speech creates an environment of intimidation and exclusion and, in some cases, may promote offline violence.

There is no universally accepted definition of 'hate speech'. Nonetheless, after reviewing numerous legal models and in consultation with experts (including human rights experts), Facebook has developed and enforces a ban on hate speech. Let me briefly explain what 'hate speech'[7] means as far as Facebook is concerned and how we implement our rules against hate speech.

We define hate speech as a *direct attack against people* on the basis of what we call '*protected characteristics*'. Pertinently, protected characteristics include *race*, *ethnicity*, *religious affiliation* and *caste* under Facebook's policies, which define an 'attack' as violent or dehumanizing speech, harmful stereotypes, statements of inferiority, expressions of contempt, disgust or dismissal, cursing, and calls for exclusion or segregation. Facebook also prohibits the use of harmful stereotypes, which it defines as dehumanizing comparisons that have historically been used to attack, intimidate or exclude specific groups and that are often linked with offline violence.

Almost every piece of content appearing on Facebook or Instagram – every post, comment, page, group and event – can be reported to us for review under our policies. We maintain a system of reviewers (currently around 15,000 individuals) who are trained in our policies. One of those policies is hate speech. We also make extensive use of automation to flag potential hate speech and send it to reviewers. Currently, over 95 per cent of the hate speech on which action has been taken is identified by our systems before actually being reported by anyone.[8]

Zero tolerance does not mean zero instances, however, and there will always be examples of things that our systems may miss, as well as things we may take down by mistake. Facebook continuously faces a challenge to cover the necessary languages and understand the changing trends and patterns by which people express themselves online, sometimes with hateful animus. However, we

[7] Meta, "Facebook Community Standards – Hate Speech" (available on its website).

[8] For data from the recent reporting period (that is, the first quarter of 2023), see Meta Transparency Center, "Community Standards Enforcement Report – Hate Speech" (available on its web site).

are making progress. The latest figures published by Facebook show that the amount of hate speech people actually see on Facebook – what is termed 'prevalence' – has declined significantly since we first started publishing these figures a few years ago. Now, for every 10,000 content views on Facebook, just two or three would contain hate speech that violates our policies.[9]

We have found that many people do not know how to report content on our platforms; in some cases, they do not even know that Facebook has rules regulating content posted on its platforms. Therefore, a part of what religious actors can do to help deal with the problem of online hate speech is to report, and encourage others to report, content for us to review under our policies. In the past, Facebook has worked with religious NGOs to prepare manuals on how to report content. We welcome contact with religious leaders to build out such approaches.

30.2.2. Embracing Counter-Speech

As I suggested at the outset of the chapter, there are additional, more positive ways for religious actors to address the problem of hate speech. Another element of the solution is to encourage *counter-speech.*[10] It is important to understand what exactly is meant by the term 'counter-speech'. One expert has defined counter-speech as, "[a]ny direct response to hateful or harmful speech which seeks to undermine – that is, diminish – it".[11]

Nadine Strosser, former President of the American Civil Liberties Union, captured the notion of counter-speech more expansively when she stated that:

> In recent years, we have witnessed a remarkable and bipartisan outpouring of speech and peaceful demonstrations that have denounced hateful ideologies while celebrating our nation's renewed commitments to equality, inclusivity, and intergroup harmony.[12]

Counter-speech seeks to harness the power of social media for good – through engagement, virality and collective action – all directed *against* hateful speech, not countering hate with hate, but rather lifting up, showing support, adding balance, asserting facts and restoring a tone of civility and tolerance. Counter-speech has the advantage of relying on the power of individual users' voices and not requiring intervention from any online platform other than the use of the platform itself. Counter-speech may take many forms. Of greatest

---

9 *Ibid.*

10 Facebook, "Counterspeech" (available on its web site).

11 Cathy Buerger, "The Anti-Hate Brigade: How a Group of Thousands Responds Collectively to Online Vitriol", *Dangerous Speech Project*, 14 December 2020 (available on its web site).

12 Nadine Strossen, "Counterspeech in Response to Changing Notions of Free Speech", in *Human Rights Magazine*, 2018, vol. 43, no. 4.

relevance is collective efforts, often co-ordinated by local organizations, to identify hateful speech and to direct people to speak out against it – by posting *positive* comments and encouraging further discussion on those positive themes. Some examples of this are provided later in the present chapter.

Like many aspects of online behaviour, the serious study of counter-speech is a work in progress. My observations in the present chapter rely not only on work done by Facebook, but also on research from an influential United States-based NGO called 'The Dangerous Speech Project'.[13] Most counter-speech does not seek to change the minds of those who express hateful views. That is difficult. More often, counter-speech is directed at what some have called the 'moveable middle' – shaping the public discourse for good, steering it in a more positive direction, making the victims of hate speech feel that they are not alone and empowering those who speak out against hate. Internet users take cues from each other. The presence of supportive peers motivates people to speak out against hate.

Research and experience have identified important features of successful online counter-speech, including tone (positive is better than negative), format (pictures and humour help), and also the source (counter-speech is more credible, and therefore more effective, when it comes from known sources who are identified with the community and who have social standing and moral authority). In the case of counter-speech directed against radical extremism, for example, former adherents of radical ideologies have substantial credibility.

Although counter-speech may sound simple, it is not. However, over the past few years, there have been important examples of the success of counter-speech, as noted below. Facebook hopes to see many more such positive examples of counter-speech.

The success of counter-speech can be discerned by reflecting on some cases in which counter-speech has been used as a strategy to combat hate speech. Perhaps the best studied organization devoted to counter-speech is a group called 'I am here' (in English), based in Sweden.[14] It is a grassroots organization which has over 70,000 members in Sweden and an additional 150,000 around the world. The group operates in Facebook groups, and members share links to hateful comments (for example, in the comments section of newspapers) on issues like immigration and encourage each other to post positive comments. Because there are so many members, these positive comments crowd out the negative comments and become visible in place of the hateful comments. Some

13 Cathy Buerger, "Counterspeech: A Literature Review", *Dangerous Speech Project*, 16 June 2021 (available on its web site).

14 Information on the organization 'I Am Here' is available on its web site.

observers have credited 'I am here' with shaping – for the better – popular discourse around immigration in Sweden.[15]

Another example from Europe is the Online Civil Courage Initiative ('OCCI').[16] Launched in 2016, OCCI is a Europe-wide initiative of the Institute for Strategic Dialogue, in partnership with Facebook. The OCCI Counter-speech Labs help NGOs design and deliver their own counter-speech campaigns. This organization brings together regional activist groups and pairs them with content creators and marketing agencies to improve the work of counter-speech campaigners. The OCCI is engaged with over 100 anti-hate and anti-extremism organizations and has reached over 3.5 million people on its Facebook page. Planning a counter-speech campaign requires a strategy: Who is the audience? What is the core message of the campaign? Who will be the messenger or voice of the campaign? The OCCI seeks to help local groups pursue effective strategies.

Finally, an example from Southeast Asia is The Resiliency Initiative.[17] It is a partnership between Facebook and the Asia Foundation which aims to promote tolerance, strengthen inter-faith and inter-ethnic understanding, and counter violent extremism by helping to build resilient communities across Asia. The Resiliency Initiative helps civil society organizations develop localized positive narrative campaigns online. These campaigns aim to counter intolerance and discrimination, focusing primarily, but not solely, on areas or groups affected by violent conflict. In 2020, the Resiliency Initiative reached a range of activists working with marginalized communities from over 60 organizations across 10 countries in Asia (Indonesia, Thailand, Philippines, Malaysia, Pakistan, Sri Lanka, Maldives, Bangladesh, Nepal and India). As the project grows, so will its geographic scope.

Counter-speech faces hurdles wherever it appears. However, embracing counter-speech is another important response mechanism through which religious actors can prevent or reduce hate speech.

30.2.3. Promoting Inter-Faith Dialogue

Third and finally, I would like to address what seems to be the most ambitious goal for the use of social media to prevent or reduce hate speech –building inter-faith dialogue.

I am not an expert in building such a dialogue. However, Facebook has a team devoted to what we call 'faith partnerships'.[18] This team seeks to advance

[15] Buerger, 14 December 2020, see *supra* note 11.

[16] Facebook, "Counterspeech: The Online Civil Courage Initiative" (available on its web site).

[17] Facebook, "Counterspeech: Resiliency Initiative" (available on its web site).

[18] Meta, "Faith" (available on its website).

Facebook's goal of making its platforms known as trusted spaces for communities, creators and individuals of faith and spirituality to experience and nourish their connections, goals and initiatives, based on our core values, which are: (i) *Social impact*: we enable people and their houses of worship and faith-based communities to grow their online presence and achieve their mission and community goals; (ii) *Diversity*: we develop resources that can be used by people of any faith community to create their online presence and foster meaningful connections with their community; (iii) *Responsibility*: we seek to make Facebook a safe and empowering place for people of all faiths and spirituality; and (iv) *Innovation*: we develop tools and features that support the unique needs of people of faith and their houses of worship and faith-based communities for fostering their online communities (this has been a huge focus for us during the Covid-19 pandemic).

Based on conversations with my colleagues in the Faith Partnerships team and insights gained from a number of stakeholders in religious communities, I would like to offer a few thoughts about social media and inter-faith dialogue. First, however, I would like to frame the issue with two observations. The first is that, promoting inter-faith dialogue online is not *that* different from promoting such dialogue offline. Many of the building blocks we may be familiar with in traditional settings (exposure to and knowledge of the other, religious literacy, tolerance and pluralism) are not fundamentally dissimilar online. Therefore, when we talk about promoting interfaith dialogue online, what is being referred to is the power of social media, if used well, to improve and enhance familiar paths to change: to humanize people and create empathy.

The second observation is that, as a number of people have told me, just as religion is both the most local and the most global way people organize their lives, social media is very effective at *uniting the local and the global*. This is an insight that seems to me to be powerful in thinking about the capacity of social media to promote religious dialogue.

In light of these observations, it is important to reflect on what religious actors can do to further such dialogue. I suggest that social media has a role to play for members of organized religions in sharing with others an understanding of their *own* faith. That is, one way to use social media to enhance dialogue is to make use of its extraordinary power to aid *discovery*, *connection* and *learning* between faiths. One of Facebook's core values is 'voice'. We pride ourselves on making it possible for people to share their voice, and also for others to hear voices they would not otherwise encounter. This has special relevance in a religious setting. For example, we have documented how the Hindu America Foundation in the United States found inaccurate information about Hinduism in textbooks and used Facebook to respond by creating visually engaging educational toolkits that could readily be shared online. These educational materials cover information about Hindu concepts, philosophy and inspirational figures.[19]

We have also seen Buddhist groups spread information about Buddhist practices such as meditation. One such group called 'BuddhaGang', based in the United States, with more than 14,000 followers on its Facebook page, seeks to provide an accessible, culturally modern form of faith. During the Covid-19 pandemic, it found a large audience on Facebook.[20]

The American Jewish Committee ('AJC') runs a Facebook page in Arabic, 'AJC Arabic', with more than 650,000 followers. Through this page, AJC provides information about religion and holidays and positive developments touching on the relations between Muslims and Jews.[21]

Some of these efforts are explicitly inter-faith, like the 'Sisterhood of Salaam Shalom', which has a Facebook page with more than 9,000 followers, which it uses to build trust, respect and relationships between Muslim and Jewish women and teenage girls. This group's web site states:

> Together we commit to stand up for one another, educate one another about our faith and cultural practices, engage in social action, and work to end acts of hate for all human beings.[22]

We have also worked closely with 'Faiths4Vaccines', an initiative that seeks to increase opportunities for faith-based institutions, particularly houses of worship, to engage and support the United States government in its efforts to increase vaccination rates through the advancement of equitable vaccine distribution and the combatting of vaccine hesitancy.[23]

In each of these cases, social media enhances opportunities to build understanding across faiths by doing better what inter-faith groups have sought to do previously.

Finally, I suggest that social media has the capacity for religious actors to *support each other in moments of crisis*, offering empathy and affirming our common humanity. These moments are powerful and offer the potential to build important connections. There are numerous such examples that may be mentioned. For example, Facebook has close relations with the Elijah Interfaith Institute, a multinational organization dedicated to fostering peace between diverse faith communities of the world through inter-faith dialogue, education,

[19] Meta, "Building Cultural Literacy Through Social Media: Dr. Shireen Bhalla, Hindu American Foundation" (available on its web site).

[20] Meta, "Modern Faith: Steven Barker, Leader, BuddhaGang" (available on its web site).

[21] Information on the Arabic Jewish Committee is available on its Facebook page.

[22] Information on the Sisterhood of Salaam Shalom is available on its Facebook page.

[23] Information on Faiths4Vaccines is available on its web site.

research and dissemination.[24] During the Covid-19 pandemic, the Institute used Facebook to promote 'Coronaspection', a series of video interviews with religious leaders worldwide, sharing wisdom and spiritual advice in the face of a global crisis. Following the mass shooting at the Tree of Life synagogue in Pittsburg, Pennsylvania in 2018, the AJC launched '#showupforshabat', which according to the AJC became the largest ever expression of solidarity with the American Jewish community. This effort was driven by widespread engagement on social media, with more than 250 million people engaging with the 'show up' hashtag.

30.3. Conclusions

If you visit Facebook's offices, you may see signs on the wall saying: "Social media's history is not yet written". Among other things, that is an admonition for those of us working in the field to maximize its potential for good.

Today, the online and the offline worlds are increasingly interdependent and complementary. I hope that through my observations in the present chapter, I have been able to suggest: first, how social media can be an online tool to connect us for good in the real world; and second, how social media can amplify and lift up the good that happens offline so that many more millions of people are able to share and experience it together.

[24] Information on the Elijah Faith Institute is available on its web site.

31

Translational and Terminological Sensitizing of Muslim Religious Leaders of Al-Ázhár in the Combat Against Hate Speech

Fathi M.A. Ahmed*

31.1. Introduction

Nine years have passed since the establishment of '*Da'ish*', previously named the Islamic State in Iraq and Syria ('ISIS'), the Islamic State in Iraq and the Levant ('ISIL') and the Islamic State ('IS') among other names. Although it is alleged to have been militarily defeated, its extremist ideology is reportedly still spreading virally, not only in the Arab world, but also in the whole world. *Da'ish*, the discourse of which is the focus of this chapter, has also lured significant numbers of recruits through online propaganda material, including videos and magazines, produced in and translated into English, French, German, Spanish, Turkish, Swahili and a variety of other languages. The group presents its ideology in specific language templates and uses certain terminologies. For this

* **Fathi M.A. Ahmed**, pronounced as *Fatḥí Muḥammad 'Abderrá'oúf Aḥmad*, is one of the leading Arabic-English-Arabic translators in the fields of international law and organization. He has, *inter alia*, translated several books by the late M. Cherif Bassiouni into Arabic and has multiple publications on translation-related matters. He holds a Master's degree in translation studies from the University of London and did his undergraduate studies at Helwan University (both *summa cum laude*), followed by diploma studies in translation at the American University of Cairo which hired him to teach legal and United Nations ('UN') translation. He has also taught at Ain Sham University in Cairo where he co-developed legal, UN and other translation courses. Having passed several international competitive language examinations, he has provided translation, terminology and editing services to the UN Secretariat (New York, Geneva, Vienna and Nairobi), several UN specialized agencies (including the World Health Organization, the International Atomic Energy Agency and the UN Environment Programme), the International Criminal Court ('ICC') Office of the Prosecutor, International Committee of the Red Cross, International Center for Asset Recovery of the Basel Institute on Governance, Bahrani Independent Commission of Inquiry and the Siracusa International Institute for Criminal Justice and Human Rights. He is the Centre for International Law Research and Policy's ('CILRAP') Arabic Translation Team Leader, who revised and project-managed the Arabic translation of the Lexsitus Commentary on Law of the International Criminal Court the comprises the ICC Statute and Rules of Procedure and Evidence, among other projects. For an audio-visual recording of his statement to CILRAP's conference in Florence in April 2022 on the topic of this anthology, please see https://www.cilrap.org/cilrap-film/220409-ahmed/.

purpose, it either takes on translating specific verses of the *Holy Qur'án* ('*Qur'án*') and Prophet Muḥammad's *ḥadíths* (that is, sayings) or selectively picks out an existing translation that best reflects its unorthodox interpretation of the *Sharí'ah* law.

Although the root causes of violent extremism are complex, multifaceted and intertwined, strategies to combat hate speech, as a driver of extremism, concentrate on the subject-matter rather than the language. Language is the means through which hate speech is expressed and is countered.

According to the UN Development Programme's Conceptual Framework for Preventing Violent Extremism, strategies for preventing violent extremism should include, "working with faith-based organizations and religious leaders to counter the abuse of religion by violent extremists".[1]

In November 2020, the author delivered a lecture at Al-Ázhár Ash-Sharíf ('Al-Azhar'),[2] namely, Al-Azhar's Observatory for Combating Extremism ('Observatory'), one of the most prominent entities engaged in combating extremist discourse in 13 languages, on how to best use translation and terminology in drafting counter-narratives.[3] The lecture aimed at helping the Observatory fine-tune its commendable efforts in this critical domain. The recommendations and the best practices that were shared included: giving preference to writing than to translation; giving preference to affirmative than to negative language forms; being concise in drafting; using challenging rather than self-proclaimed names of extremist organization; avoiding euphemism in quoting from and responding to hate speech; using internationally agreed terminologies and gender-inclusive language for a universally harmonized response; using cautious language as appropriate; using fact-based rather than rhetorical language; highlighting wrong translations of the *Qur'án* or *Sharí'ah* terminology; and co-operating with social media platforms and providing them with relevant, smartly-drafted and updated keywords for identifying, reviewing and removing, if appropriate, hate speech content without compromising freedom of expression.

---

1 UN Development Programme, "Preventing Violent Extremism Through Promoting Inclusive Development, Tolerance and Respect for Diversity: A Development Response to Addressing Radicalization and Violent Extremism", 1 July 2016, pp. 30–31 ('Preventing Violent Extremism Through Promoting Inclusive Development, Tolerance and Respect for Diversity') (https://www.legal-tools.org/doc/guylbf/).

2 Often written *Al-Azhar Al-Sharif* as an official name.

3 "Al-Azhar Observatory for Combating Extremism Organizes a Lecture on the Impact of Terminological and Translational Accuracy in Promoting Counter Extremism Activities", *Al-Azhar Observatory for Combating Extremism*, 22 November 2020 ('Al-Azhar Observatory for Combating Extremism Organizes a Lecture') (in Arabic). For a valuable discussion of and more information on the role of Al-Azhar Al-Sharif in combating extremism and hate speech in light of international instruments, see Chapter 29 of this anthology.

The lessons learned from this experience are making advice problem-centred rather than content-centred; giving advice an experience shared rather than a lesson taught; involving religious leaders in discussion, giving religious leaders the impression that they lead the discussion; and giving sensitive advice in the form of a thought to reflect on or a question to answer.

This chapter addresses how to draft stronger, more relevant and more effective counter-speech and how to approach religious leaders. It aims at providing a set of criteria to be used in drafting counter-speech from a translational, terminological and more generally a linguistic point of view. It gives concrete examples of more effective language that ought to be used in combating extremism and shows how it can promote a universally harmonized response. It also shows the lessons learned from the experience mentioned above.

31.2. Definitions

For the purposes of this chapter, the following terms are defined as follows:

- *Hate speech* is:

  > any kind of communication in speech, writing or behaviour, that attacks or uses pejorative or discriminatory language with reference to a person or a group on the basis of who they are, in other words, based on their religion, ethnicity, nationality, race, colour, descent, gender or other identity factor.[4]

- *Counter-speech* is any kind of communication in speech, writing or behaviour that presents an alternative to hate speech and that responds to it by refuting its narratives.
- *Faith-based organization* is:

  > [an] organization that derives inspiration and guidance for its activities from the teachings and principles of the faith or from a particular interpretation or school of thought within that faith.[5]

- *Religious leader* is a man or a woman who is formally or informally affiliated to a faith-based organization and who plays an influential role on his or her community, followers and/or supporters and/or on the wider society.

[4] UN Office on Genocide Prevention and the Responsibility to Protect, United Nations Strategy and Plan of Action on Hate Speech, 31 May 2019, p. 2 (https://www.legal-tools.org/doc/5rrb5b/). Although it acknowledges that there is no international legal definition of hate speech, the UN defines hate speech as shown.

[5] Gerard Clarke and Michael Jennings (eds.), *Development, Civil Society and Faith-Based Organizations: Bridging the Sacred and the Secular*, Palgrave Macmillan, London, 2008, p. 107.

31.3. Working with Religious Leaders to Counter Hate Speech

Over the past two decades, the international community has sought to address violent extremism primarily within the context of security-based counter-terrorism measures adopted in response to the threat posed by al-Qá'idah and its affiliated groups. However, with the emergence of a new generation of groups, there is a growing international consensus that such counter-terrorism measures have not been sufficient to prevent the spread of violent extremism. Violent extremism encompasses a wider category of manifestations and there is a risk that a conflation of the two terms may lead to the justification of an overly broad application of counter-terrorism measures, including against forms of conduct that should not qualify as terrorist acts.[6]

In his Plan of Action to Prevent Violent Extremism, the UN Secretary-General noted that,

> Faith and community leaders are critical in mentoring vulnerable followers so as to enable them to reject violent ideologies and in providing opportunities for intra- and interfaith dialogue and discussion as a means of promoting tolerance, understanding and reconciliation between communities.[7]

He adds that,

> [t]here is a need to take a more comprehensive approach which encompasses not only ongoing, essential security-based counter-terrorism measures, but also systematic preventive measures which directly address the drivers of violent extremism that have given rise to the emergence of these new and more virulent groups.[8]

According to the UN Development Programme's conceptual framework for Preventing Violent Extremism Through Promoting Inclusive Development, Tolerance and Respect for Diversity, global, regional and national strategies for preventing violent extremism should include, among others, "working with faith-based organizations and religious leaders to counter the abuse of religion by violent extremists".[9]

On 12 October 2015, the United Nations Human Rights Council ('UNHRC'):

---

6 UN Secretary-General, Plan of Action to Prevent Violent Extremism, UN Doc. A/70/674, 24 December 2015, para. 4 (https://www.legal-tools.org/doc/ui69e3/).

7 *Ibid.*, para. 36.

8 *Ibid.*

9 Preventing Violent Extremism Through Promoting Inclusive Development, Tolerance and Respect for Diversity, 2016, see *supra* note 1.

> [Underscored] that preventing and countering violent extremism requires a whole-of-society approach, involving government, civil society, local and religious leaders and the private sector, and acknowledging that the active participation of civil society is a key factor in governmental efforts to protect human rights and fundamental freedoms while preventing and countering violent extremism.[10]

Faith matters to people. Spiritual faith is the driver for action for many of them. In many parts of the world, faith-based organizations and religious leaders are influential in both the political and social spheres and have a broad following in their societies. Their presence in local communities, coupled with their capacity to deliver critical services, allow them to mobilize grassroots support, earn the trust of vulnerable groups and influence cultural norms – all of which make them vital stakeholders in development. With their involvement in local communities and their standing as moral leaders, many faith-based organizations and religious leaders command the respect of local and national authorities, which can make them valuable peace mediators in tense environments.[11]

Religion is a source of motivation and inspiration for the vast majority of people around the world, who act in a spirit of generosity and kindness. Strategies to combat violent extremism must be rooted in a nuanced understanding of the role of religion, ideology and identity and its impact on individuals, communities and institutions. It is also important to counter the growing narrative that it is religion *per se* that is the cause of violence; manipulation of religious politics and fanatical ideas is the challenge. Religious leaders therefore bear a particular responsibility to help prevent violent extremism. 'Intra-faith' and 'interfaith' dialogues at the regional and global levels can promote a counter-narrative to violent extremism and also develop more concrete measures at the local and community levels that could be implemented through networks of religious organizations and institutions. Regional context needs to be taken into account.[12]

On 2 July 2021, the UN Security Council:

> [Urged] all Member States and the United Nations to unite against terrorism and violent extremism as and when conducive to terrorism, encourages the efforts of relevant actors, including religious leaders of all faiths, to discuss within their communities the drivers of terrorism and violent extremism conducive to terrorism and to

[10] UNHRC, Resolution 30/15 on Human Rights and Preventing and Countering Violent Extremism, UN Doc. A/HRC/RES/30/15, 12 October 2015 (https://www.legal-tools.org/doc/bf95de/).

[11] UN Development Programme, "Guidelines on Engaging with Faith-Based Organizations and Religious Leaders", October 2014.

[12] Preventing Violent Extremism Through Promoting Inclusive Development, Tolerance and Respect for Diversity, 2016, pp. 31–32, see *supra* note 1.

> evolve strategies to address them, and underlines that Member States, regional organizations, non-governmental organizations, religious bodies and the media have an important role to play in promoting tolerance and facilitating understanding, inclusive dialogue and respect for religious and cultural diversity and human rights.[13]

Working with religious leaders can be complex for many reasons including the fact that many of them do not have an inclusive perspective. Furthermore, different interpretations of sources of religion can make working with those leaders even more complex. Faith actors are not the same even in any given local community. All religious leaders need to be engaged in dialogue on countering hate speech as a driver of extremism. Religious leaders left behind can be a source resentment which may trigger hate speech.[14]

31.4. Case Study

In November 2020, the author delivered a lecture[15] at Al-Azhar,[16] or the Observatory,[17] on how to best use translation and terminology in drafting counter-narratives. The lecture aimed at helping the Observatory foster and fine-tune its commendable efforts in this critical domain. Following are the recommendations given and best practices shared. They should apply to all situations of giving specialist advice to religious leaders *mutatis mutandis*.

Responders to hate speech are advised to:

31.4.1. Give Preference to Writing Than to Translation

Translation is an imperfect reflection of any original text. In order to avoid the problems and pitfalls of translation and not to have something lost in translation, preference should be given to writing than to translation, if possible and appropriate. It would be more effective and relevant to write in 13 different languages, taking into account the specificities of each culture as reflected by its language than to write a master text in Arabic, for example, and then translate it into those languages. An outline can still be used showing the overall idea of the body of responders, who should then adapt it to the respective languages they use in their

---

13 UNHRC, Resolution No. 75/291 on the United Nations Global Counter-Terrorism Strategy: Seventh Review, UN Doc. A/RES/75/291, 2 July 2021, para. 13 (https://www.legal-tools.org/doc/ww6q5g/).

14 For an informative and in-depth discussion of how responsible religious leaders should react to hate speech in their communities, see Chapter 27 of this anthology.

15 Al-Azhar Observatory for Combating Extremism Organizes a Lecture, 2020, see *supra* note 3.

16 For more information on Al-Azhar, see its web site (in Arabic but partially available in other languages).

17 For more information on the Observatory, see its web site.

response. A hate speech message originated in Africa, for example, should be responded to in a way that is unique to the African context.

31.4.2. Give Preference to Affirmative Than to Negative Language Forms

Affirmative language sounds stronger and firmer than negative language. Sounding defensive is always a weaker form of expression. For example, when a religious leader says that 'Islám *does not* promote hate for non-Muslims', it simply means that he or she has this idea at the back of his or her mind and that he or she is now trying to refute it. While this may be the case in some situations, it should not be the general practice in writing or speaking in the context of counter-speech.

31.4.3. Write and Speak Concisely

In addition to clarity and coherence, and unlike in the context of preaching, conciseness should be observed in counter-speech in particular. Conciseness denotes solid ideas and stronger beliefs, whereas lengthy language denotes weak argument and the speaker's or writer's need to cover up his or her weak argument. According to Joseph M. Williams, a good practice is to delete: (i) useless adjectives and adverbs; (ii) words that mean little or nothing, that repeat the meaning of other words and that are implied by other words; and (iii) to replace phrases with words.[18]

31.4.4. Use Challenging Rather Than Self-Proclaimed Names of Extremist Organizations

Having expanded into Syria in 2013, *Da'ish* adopted the name: (الدولة الإسلامية في العراق و الشام). The group's name was translated as the *Islamic State in Iraq and Ash-Sham*,[19] the *Islamic State in Iraq and Syria* (both abbreviated as 'ISIS') or the *Islamic State in Iraq and the Levant* (abbreviated as 'ISIL'). In June 2014, the group declared the creation a so-called '*caliphate*' and shortened its name to *Islamic State* (abbreviated as 'IS') to reflect its expansionist ambitions. However, *Da'ish* has been widely used by the group's Arabic-speaking detractors when referring to it, because this name is considered derogatory. It resembles the Arabic words '*da'is*' (داعس), that means one who crushes, or tramples down, something underfoot. Thus, the latter name has been used as a way of challenging the legitimacy of the group due to the negative connotations of the word in Arabic. The group's supporters object to its use.[20] Within areas under its control, *Da'ish*

---

18 Joseph M. Williams, *Style: Ten Lessons in Clarity and Grace*, 8th ed., Longman, London, 2005, p. 122.

19 '*Ash-Sham*' is the Arabic name for the Levant or Greater Syria.

20 Faisal Irshaid, "Isis, Isil, IS or Daesh? One Group, Many Names", *BBC News*, 2 December 2015.

punished the use of this name by flogging[21] or cutting out the tongue.[22] In December 2015, United Kingdom ('UK') Prime Minister, David Cameron, addressed the UK Parliament mentioning that "this evil death cult is neither a true representation of Islam, nor is it a state" and announced that "it is time to join our key ally France, the Arab League, and other members of the international community in using as frequently as possible the terminology Daesh rather than ISIL".[23]

Da'ish is currently used at the UN as a preferred name to refer to the group. In an internal circular, the UN Secretariat mentioned that, as of July 2021, *Da'ish* will be the preferred term for ISIL and should be used in all documents originating in the Secretariat.[24]

Following the names self-proclaimed by terrorist organization is a form of acknowledgment of their claims. Therefore, the author's recommendation is to use the names that best challenge such organizations' ambitions and legitimacy. *Da'ish* should be the name given to this group in order to terminologically confirm that it is no more than a terrorist organization. Furthermore, this would be in line with the author's recommendation in Section 31.4.6.

31.4.5. Avoid Euphemism in Quoting from and Responding to Hate Speech

According to Merriam-Webster's Online Dictionary, euphemism is "the substitution of an agreeable or inoffensive expression for one that may offend or suggest something unpleasant".[25] Euphemisms may be used to mask profanity or refer to topics some consider taboo such as disability, sex, excretion or death in a polite way.[26] It is a general rule to use euphemism and be politically correct. However, hate speech content should be refuted openly and directly. For example, when post or tweet on social medial refers to a moderate Muslim leader, such as the Grand Imám of Al-Azhar,[27] offensively as sheep, which is an

---

21 Rania Abouzeid, "Syria's Uprising Within an Uprising, European Council on Foreign Relations", *European Council on Foreign Affairs*, 16 January 2014.

22 Maria Vultaggio, "ISIL, ISIS, Islamic State, Daesh: What's The Difference?", *International Business Times*, 16 November 2015.

23 Office of the Prime Minister of the United Kingdom, "PM's Opening Statement to Commons Debate on Military Action in Syria", 2 December 2015.

24 UN Secretariat, "Internal Circular to UN Language Staff dated 2 July 2021", 2 July 2021 (on file with the author).

25 "Euphemism", in *Merriam-Webster's Dictionary*.

26 "Euphemism", in *Online Etymology Dictionary*.

27 For more information about the current Grand Imám of Al-Azhar, see the web site of Al-Imám aṭ-Ṭáyyib (in Arabic).

offensive reference in Arabic, it is recommended to quote the offensive expression as is and expose it explicitly.

31.4.6. Use Internationally Agreed Terminologies and Gender-Inclusive Language for a Universally Harmonized Response

Religious leaders are advised to be aware of and use internationally agreed terminologies, such as hate speech, extremist ideologies, extremist narratives and the like terminologies. A universally harmonized response requires a harmonized lexicon. They are also invited to add to this lexicon.

In addition, it was recommended to translate these terminologies using the functional rather than purely linguistic equivalents. This also applies to international humanitarian law and international criminal law terminologies. Take, for example, the crime of aggression. The crime is expressly mentioned in the *Qur'án*. In the second chapter of the *Qur'án*, God commands Muslims as follows:

وَقَٰتِلُواْ فِى سَبِيلِ ٱللَّهِ ٱلَّذِينَ يُقَٰتِلُونَكُمْ وَلَا تَعْتَدُوٓاْ إِنَّ ٱللَّهَ لَا يُحِبُّ ٱلْمُعْتَدِينَ [البقرة:190]

Pickthall's English translation of the verse reads:

> Fight in the way of Allah against those who fight against you, but begin not hostilities. Lo! Allah loveth not aggressors [The *Qur'án*, 2:190].[28]

Arberry's English translation of the verse reads:

> And fight in the way of God with those; who fight with you, but aggress not: God loves not the aggressors [The *Qur'án*, 2:190].[29,30]

Regarding gender-inclusive language, attention was drawn to the fact that Arabic is a gender-inclusive language by nature. However, it has a unique system of gender. It uses what seems to be masculine gender when gender-neutrality is meant.[31] This is the reason why it is commonly misunderstood. Inadequate translations of the *Qur'án* from Arabic language into other languages may well promote this wrong understanding, leading to exclusion of and possibly bias against women. Any *Qur'ánic* verse about men is about men and women alike unless it is specifically about women or about men.

---

28 Mohammed M. Pickthall, *The Meaning of The Glorious Koran: An Explanatory Translation*, 2nd ed., George Allen & Unwin, London, 1948, p. 48.

29 Arthur J. Arberry, *The Koran Interpreted: A Translation*, Oxford University Press, London, 1964, p. 1.

30 For an in-depth discussion of the crime of aggression in the *Qur'án*, see, Tallyn Gray (ed.), *Islam and International Criminal Law and Justice*, Torkel Opsahl Academic EPublisher ('TOAEP'), Brussels, 2018, pp. 87–99 (https://www.toaep.org/nas-pdf/2-gray/).

31 See, for example, Fatima B. Said, "Masculine and Feminine Words of the Noble Qur'án: A Descriptive Analytical Study", Master's dissertation, Al-Haj Al-Khedr University, 2008.

Following is an example of a *Qur'ánic* verse where the word '*rijal*' (رجال), which literally means *men*, is used. The context of the verse is the condition of people in Paradise. The verse reads:

[...] وَعَلَى الْأَعْرَافِ رِجَالٌ يَعْرِفُونَ كُلًّا بِسِيمَاهُم [...] [الأعراف:46]

In Ibn Kat͟hír's commentary on the *Qur'án*,[32] reference to what is literally *men* is in fact to *people* of Paradise. In addition, two modern commentaries by Al-Azhar,[33] and Ḥijazí,[34] introduced by the current Imám of Al-Azhar, interpret the word '*rijal*' as *people*.

A modern English translation by Mufti Taqi Usmani, that reflects this understanding, reads:

> And on A'ráf (the Heights), there shall be people who recognize each group through their signs [The *Qur'án*, 7:46].[35]

Another translation by Sarwar, that reflects this understanding, reads:

> There will be people on the heights who know everyone by their faces and who will say to the people of Paradise, "Peace be upon you [The *Qur'án*, 7:46].[36]

Unfortunately, seven out of 13 different translations of the *Qur'án*, reviewed by the author for the purposes of this chapter, literally render what seems to be *men* as *men*.[37]

In addition, it was recommended to use universally accepted standards for transliterating Arabic names into English and other languages in order to avoid potential confusion or incrimination of innocents, including by using the spelling of names used in the UN Consolidated List of Individuals and Entities Subject to Measures Imposed by the Security Council,[38] among other credible sources.

---

32 Ibn Kat͟hír, *Tafsír Al-Qur'án 'Al-'Áẓím (Commentary on the Great Qur'án)*, Ibn Ḥazm Publishing House, Beirut, 2000, p. 315.

33 A Committee of Scholars, *At-Tafsír Al-Wásiṭ Lil-Qur'án Al-Karím (Semi-Abridged Commentary on the Noble Qur'án)*, Islamic Research Academy of Al-Azhar Al-S͟hareef, Cairo, 1997, pp. 1428–1429.

34 Muḥammad M. Ḥijazí, *At-Tafsír Al-Wáḍiḥ (Self-Explanatory Commentary (on the Qur'án))*, Muslim Council of Elders, Cairo, 2019, pp. 759/1–761/1.

35 Mufti Taqi Usmani, *The Noble Quran*, Maktaba Ma'ariful Quran, Karachi, 2016, p.15.

36 Muhammad Sarwar, *The Holy Quran*, Islamic Seminary, New Jersey, 2001, p. 62.

37 Out of 13 translations published on the Quran Explorer's web site, six translations *explicitly* reflect this gender-inclusive understanding. They are one out of five for English, one out of one for French, one out of two for Spanish, one out of one for Turkish, two out of three for Urdu and one out of one for German.

38 UN Security Council, "United Nations Security Council Consolidated List".

31.4.7. Use Cautious Language as Appropriate

Cautious language, also referred to as hedging language, is used to convey how certain you are of the opinions or arguments you are using in your writing or speaking, especially when writing an argument. It is important to be cautious or tentative in your claims unless they are proved without any doubt. According to Andy Gillett, examples of hedging language include using: (i) introductory verbs: for example, seem, tend, look like, appear to be, think, believe, doubt, be sure, indicate, suggest; (ii) certain lexical verbs: for example, believe, assume, suggest; (iii) certain modal verbs: for example, will, must, would, may, might, could; (iv) adverbs of frequency: for example, often, sometimes, usually; (v) modal adverbs: for example, certainly, definitely, clearly, probably, possibly, perhaps, conceivably; (vi) modal adjectives: for example, certain, definite, clear, probable, possible; (vii) modal nouns: for example, assumption, possibility, probability; (viii) 'that' clauses: for example, 'It could be the case that', 'It might be suggested that', 'There is every hope that'; (ix) to-clause plus adjective: for example, 'It may be possible to obtain', 'It is important to develop', 'It is useful to study'.[39] Therefore, in news stories, for instance, until someone is irrevocably convicted of a crime, he or she should always be referred to as alleged perpetrator, suspect or accused, as the case may be, but not perpetrator or actor. Showing respect to facts is a value added to counter-speech. It is also a way to gain credibility and show how accurate, precise and honest responders are.

31.4.8. Use Fact-Based Rather Than Rhetorical Language

A rhetorical device is a technique that an author or speaker uses to convey to the listener or reader a meaning with the goal of persuading them towards considering a topic from a perspective, using language designed to encourage or provoke an emotional display of a given perspective or action. Rhetorical devices evoke an emotional response in the audience through use of language, but that is not their primary purpose. Rather, by doing so, they seek to make a position or argument more compelling than it would otherwise be.[40] Rhetorical language is commonly used by religious leaders in preaching. However, when it comes to responding to hate speech and refuting perverse ideologies, it is advised to rely more largely on fact-based statements. A well-drafted fact-based statement will include specific quotations, times, events, numbers and so on. A rhetorically drafted statement will include none of the items mentioned and will rely on too general wordings. An example of a fact-based statement is, 'Dealing justly with

[39] Andy Gillett, "Features of Academic Writing: Hedging" (available on the Using English for Academic Purposes' web site).

[40] Timothy Crews-Anderson, *Critical Thinking and Informal Logic*, Humanities-Ebooks, London, 2010, p. 40.

non-Muslims is instructed in the *Qur'án* twelve times as in the following verses. The contexts of revelation were as follows'. An example of a rhetorical language statement is, 'Those who deny the injunction to deal justly with non-Muslims are just liars'.

31.4.9. Highlight and Correct Wrong Translations of the *Qur'án* and *Sharí'ah* Terminology

There are hundreds of different translations of the *Qur'án*. Translation of the *Qur'án* is particularly challenging due to many reasons including the fact that all languages exist *sui generis*, that is, not exemplified or unclassifiable in reference to one another and each offering a new version of life or a new window on the world. Arabic, the original language of the *Qur'án* and *Sharí'ah*, is particularly unique. It has its own features and characteristics such as parsing, duality, inter-sentence connectors and diacritical markers. It is the only language in which the *Qur'án* is positively believed to be fully understood.[41]

Al-Ghussain argues that:

> [through] translation, translators become transmitters of different civilizations. Inevitably to some extent, any translation will reflect the translator's own mental and cultural outlook, despite the best of impartial intentions. Every translator has her/his own beliefs, knowledge and attitudes.[42]

The opening chapter of the *Qur'án* (Al-fatiḥah) is recited by a Muslim at least 17 times a day. It is a summary of the teachings of the *Qur'án*. Therefore, a translation of this chapter is essential for practicing as well as understanding Islám. The last verses of that chapter read:

ٱهْدِنَا ٱلصِّرَٰطَ ٱلْمُسْتَقِيمَ (ٱهْدِنَا ٱلصِّرَٰطَ ٱلْمُسْتَقِيمَ (٦) صِرَٰطَ ٱلَّذِينَ أَنْعَمْتَ عَلَيْهِمْ غَيْرِ
ٱلْمَغْضُوبِ عَلَيْهِمْ وَلَا ٱلضَّآلِّينَ (٧) [الفاتحة:6-7]

The verses make a reference to two categories of people. According to Yusuf Ali's widely acceptable translation of the *Qur'án*, the verses read:

> Show us the straight way. The way of those on whom Thou hast bestowed Thy Grace, Those whose (portion) is not wrath and who go not astray [The *Qur'án*, 1:6–7].[43]

---

[41] Muhammad Abdul-Fattah A. Taghian, *Translating Qur'ānic Mutashābihāt: A Linguistic Approach*, LAP Lambert Academic Publishing, London, 2014, p. 10.

[42] Reem A.A.L. Al-Ghussain, "Areas of Cultural and Linguistic Difficulty in English-Arabic Translation", unpublished Ph.D. Thesis, University of Durham, 2003, p. 15.

[43] Abdullah Y. Ali, *The Holy Qur'an: Text, Translation and Commentary*, Tahrike Tarsile Qur'án, 1998, p. 4.

In addition, according to Arberry's translation of the *Qur'án*, the verses read:

> Guide us in the straight path,
> the path of those whom Thou hast blessed,
> not of those against whom Thou art wrathful,
> nor of those who are astray [The *Qur'án*, 1:6–7].[44]

Also, according to Assami and others, often referred to as 'Ṣaḥeeḥ International',[45] the verses read:

> The path of those upon whom You have bestowed favor, not of those who have evoked [Your] anger or of those who are astray [The *Qur'án*, 1:6–7].[46]

However, few other translations depart from this orthodox understanding, as reflected by the above translation, not to mention the exact wording of the Arabic text. Furthermore, a review of several commentaries on the *Qur'án*, including three commentaries by Al-Azhar Islamic Research Academy;[47] by *Qur'án* and Prophetic Tradition Commission of the Supreme Council of Islamic Affairs of Egypt;[48] by Eissa, an Al-Azhar Scholar,[49] introduced by a prominent Al-Azhar scholar, Muḥammad Mitwallí a<u>sh</u>-<u>Sh</u>á'ráwí; and by Ḥijazí,[50] introduced by the current Imám of Al-Azhar, shows that those two categories of people are: those who have ignored the right path and those who are already away from the right path unknowingly and because of unwarranted confusion. Therefore, the above translations reflect the understanding of Al-Azhar of these verses.

On the other hand, a translation by Al-Hilali and Khan, that is among the most widely read translations in the world and is mostly misused by ultraconservatives, extremists and promoters of hate speech reads:

> Guide us to the Straight Way. The Way of those on whom You have bestowed Your Grace, not (the way) of those who earned Your

---

44 Arberry, 1964, see *supra* note 29.

45 This English translation is frequently used by the Observatory.

46 Ṣaḥeeḥ International, *The Qur'an: English Meanings*, Emily Assami, Mary Kennedy and Amatullah Bantley (trans.), Abdul-Qasim Publishing House, Jeddah, 1997, p. 1.

47 A Committee of Scholars, 1997, pp. 22–23, see *supra* note 33.

48 Qur'án and Prophetic Tradition Commission of Supreme Council of Islamic Affairs, *Al-Muntakhab fí Tafsír Al-Qur'án Al-Karím (Elected Commentary on the Noble Qur'án)*, 26th ed., Dar Al-Thaqafa, Supreme Council of Islamic Affairs, Cairo, 2018, p. 1.

49 'Abdul-Jalíl 'Issa, *Taysír At-Tafasír* (An Abridged Commentary [on the Qur'án]), Muslim Council of Elders, Cairo, 2019, p. 49.

50 Ḥijazí, 2019, p. 84/1, see *supra* note 34.

> Anger (such as the Jews), nor of those who went astray (such as the Christians) [The *Qur'án*, 1:6-7].[51]

Another example is the designation of '*al-kufár*' (الكفار). It is the plural form of '*kafir*'. It shares the same root as '*takfír*' meaning "excommunication/accusation of unbelief in Islam"[52] of a Muslim by a Muslim person or a Muslim body. In extremist Islámic discourse in languages other than Arabic, reference is typically made to non-Muslims using the word '*al-kufár*' in Arabic.[53] That is to say, the word is transliterated rather than translated. As such, it only gives a strong impression that it has a meaning that is peculiar to Arabic and does not have an English equivalent. Therefore, non-Arabic speaking Muslims understand it as derogatory word used with pejorative overtone. Since it means something that is not simply *others*, it gives the impression that non-Muslims are enemies of Muslims.[54] However, this word simply means unbelievers, according to Arberry's translation[55] for instance. In a Muslim context, it means non-Muslims.[56] Furthermore, in the second chapter of the *Qur'án*,

---

51 Muhammad T. al-Hilali and Muhammad M. Khan, *Translation of the Meanings of the Noble Qur'an in the English Language*, King Fahd Complex for the Printing of the Holy Qur'án, Madinah, 1999, pp. 14–15.

52 Gray, 2018, p. xii, see *supra* note 30.

53 For a useful elaboration on the approaches of extremists to Islámic *Sharí'ah* that lead to religious hatred, see Chapter 16 of this anthology.

54 According to Muḥammad Rashíd Reḍa, *Terminologies Used by Contemporary Writers*, Majallat al-Manár, Vol. I, Cairo, 1898, pp. 17–18:

> The designation of *al-kufár* applies, as usually used by writers today, to atheists […]. Whenever we use it in our writings or speech, we mean what I have just said. We do not call believers in other religions *al-kufár*, because the designation does not apply to them in this sense. Furthermore, I hold that that it is not permissible in *Sharí'ah* to call them *al-kufár*; because the designation has become one of the ugliest insults and the most painful ways of humiliation. This act is prohibited by *Sharí'ah* as unanimously acknowledged by scholars of Islam. This argument is not at odds with the tradition of using the designation during the first eras of revelation. It was not used at the time of divine legislation for this purpose. It was rather used as one of the most courteous designations. It was devoid of any connotation of respect or offense, not to mention insult or harm, to non-Muslims, which would be otherwise be contrary to the purposes and morals of the religion. Since the situation has become different and the [language] usage has changed, followers of a religion, who believe in God, should not be called *al-kufár*.

55 Arberry, 1964, p. 664, see *supra* note 29.

56 In a recent statement by the Grand Imám of Al-Azhar, he referred to non-Muslims literally as *non-Muslims* amid a controversy aroused by an Egyptian restaurant which denied serving food to a non-fasting (non-Muslim) person during the day in the month of *Rámáḍán*, maintaining that placing restrictions on non-Muslims during *Rámáḍán* is an absurd act. See, for example, "Restrictions on Non-Muslims During Ramadan 'Absurd', Says Al-Azhar Imam", *Egypt Today*, 19 April 2022 (in English) and Abdulrahman Mohammed, "Sheikh of Al-Azhar:

reference is made to Muslim believers as those who are '*al-kufár*' of evil, meaning that they are unbelievers in evil.

The same applies to the word *ṭághút* (الطَّاغُوت), which, according to Yusuf Ali's translation, means *evil* in general. Verse no. 256 of Al-Baqarah (the Heifer) reads:

> لَا إِكْرَاهَ فِي الدِّينِ ۖ قَد تَّبَيَّنَ الرُّشْدُ مِنَ الْغَيِّ ۚ فَمَن يَكْفُرْ بِالطَّاغُوتِ وَيُؤْمِن بِاللَّهِ فَقَدِ اسْتَمْسَكَ بِالْعُرْوَةِ الْوُثْقَىٰ لَا انفِصَامَ لَهَا ۗ(البقرة-256)
>
> Let there be no compulsion in religion. Truth stands out clear from Error; whoever rejects Evil and believes in Allah hath grasped the most trustworthy hand-hold, that never breaks [The *Qur'án*, 2-256].[57]

In addition, according to Arberry's translation of the *Qur'án*, the English translation of the verse reads:

> No compulsion is there in religion. Rectitude has become clear from error. So whosoever disbelieves in idols and believes in God, has laid hold of the most firm handle, unbreaking; God is All-hearing, All-knowing [The *Qur'án*, 2:256].[58]

However, the English translation of the *Qur'án* by al-Hilali and Khan reads:

> There is no compulsion in religion. Verily, the Right Path has become distinct from the wrong path. Whoever disbelieves in *Tâghût*,[59] and believes in Allâh, then he has grasped the most trustworthy handhold that will never break. And Allâh is All-Hearer, All-Knower [The *Qur'án*, 2:256].[60]

In ultraconservative discourse, reference is made to evil, especially political tyranny and rulers in general using the word '*ṭághút*', which is transliterated but not translated, to describe opponent politicians who, in the view of extremists, do not properly apply *Sharí'ah* law. As such, the term is burdened with political connotations that best serve the ideology of extremists. However, according to Ḥijazí for example, '*ṭághút*' linguistically means exceeding limits. Technically, it refers to Satan and is ascribed to any thing or person, other than

Restricting Non-Muslims in Food and Drink During the Day in Ramadan Is Against Religion", *El Balad News*, 19 April 2022 (in Arabic).

57 *Ibid*., p. 34.

58 Arberry, 1964, p. 37, see *supra* note 29.

59 This chapter uses the transliteration '*ṭághút*', pursuant to TOAEP editorial guidelines.

60 Al-Hilali and Khan, 1999, p. 33, see *supra* note 51.

God, that is worshipped.[61] Even in old classical commentaries, such as the Commentary by Ibn Kat͟hír,[62] '*ṭághút*' is interpreted as Satan.

Therefore, responders to hate speech should have in place an informed methodology based on which they select the most credible translation that best serves their counter-speech strategy, not to mention taking this point into their consideration when translating the *Qur'án* themselves. A counter-speech content that is even very well drafted in English, for example, but uses an English translation that is not in line with the understanding of the *Qur'án* and *S͟harí'ah* by responders would be counterproductive.

Through its own translation centre, Al-Azhar is currently developing its first-ever translation of the *Qur'án* into English, French and Swahili languages. It plans to translate it into 27 other languages.[63] A translation by Al-Azhar, reflecting its orthodox understanding of the *Qur'án* would be an excellent value added to the global understanding of Islám and would be a step forward in promoting the multilingualism of Al-Azhar's response to hate speech.

31.4.10. Co-operate with and Provide Training to Social Media Platforms

According to the Italian Institute for International Political Studies, the conflicts in Syria and Iraq have attracted over 40,000 foreign fighters, who have travelled to these countries to join the ranks of *Da'ish* and other armed groups.

Although accurate figures are not available, it is estimated that at least 5,000 jihádist foreign fighters came from Europe. Over 1,500 have already returned home, while at least 1,000 might still be in Syria and Iraq. These jihádist travellers include not only male adults, often with combat experience, but also women and children, with different backgrounds and motivations.[64]

According to *Da'ish* Youth Recruitment Strategy by the Observatory, the group holistically and effectively uses social media platforms, such as YouTube, Facebook, Twitter, Instagram, Telegram among other platforms to communicate with and recruit its supporters to join its ranks and/or to disseminate its message including by tweeting and retweeting, to gather intelligence and to co-ordinate the group's response to the voices expressed in defiance to its activities and aims. The Observatory is of the view that using social media by the group is due to its popularity among young people who can be easily deceived while seeking more freedom from traditional ways of thinking. The Observatory also notes that the

61 Ḥijazí, 2019, p. 240/1, see *supra* note 34.

62 Ibn Kat͟hír, 2000, p. 322, see *supra* note 32.

63 Shaima A. Hadi, "Al-Azhar Translation Centre Coordinator: The Centre Plans to Translate the Noble Qur'án into 30 Languages", *Al-Ahram News Portal*, 2 April 2018.

64 Francesco Marone, "Tackling the Foreign Fighter Threat in Europe", *Italian Institute for International Political Studies*, 9 January 2020.

group uses highly influential videos, in addition to other videos in which it shows how powerful it has become, trying, through using very eloquent language, to persuade young people to join it. It also uses the power of images which includes decontextualized *Qur'ánic* verses and *ḥadíths* translated into a variety of languages in a bid to legitimize its acts of killing and other heinous acts. It also uses infographics to show the numbers of its suicide operations and training sessions. In addition, the group uses surveys to assess and direct public opinion. It also uses private chats for more recruitments. The group created an Android-based application to publish its news. In an effort to create a new generation that supports its ideology, it developed a mobile application asking children if they wish to attack tourist attractions such as the Statue of Liberty. Children were given points if their answers were yes. In 2017, it had 30 to 40 channels on Telegram. It also created videos in sign language. In order to reach the biggest number of social media users, the group uses hashtags very effectively including irrelevant hashtags to show, including to accidental viewer, their wide presence and power. In 2014, for example, they used #Brazil2014 to gain more views of their tweets.[65]

An example of the initiatives to combat online hate speech is the Joint Statement of European Union ('EU') Ministers for Justice and Home Affairs and Representatives of EU Institutions on the Terrorist Attacks in Brussels on 22 March 2016, dated 24 March 2016, which underlines that:

> the [European] Commission will intensify work with [information technology] companies, notably in the EU Internet Forum, to counter terrorist propaganda and to develop by June 2016 a code of conduct against hate speech online.[66]

According to The EU Code of Conduct on Countering Illegal Hate Speech Online,

> the [information technology ('IT')] Companies [are] to encourage the provision of notices and flagging of content that promotes incitement to violence and hateful conduct at scale by experts, particularly via partnerships with [civil society organizations ('CSOs')], by providing clear information on individual company Rules and Community Guidelines and rules on the reporting and notification processes. The IT Companies [are] to endeavour to strengthen partnerships with CSOs by widening the geographical spread of such partnerships and, where appropriate, to provide

65 Al-Azhar Observatory for Combating Extremism, *Da'esh Youth Recruitment Strategy*, Cairo, 2017, pp. 30–35.

66 Council of the EU, Joint Statement of EU Ministers for Justice and Home Affairs and Representatives of EU Institutions on the Terrorist Attacks in Brussels on 22 March 2016, 24 March 2016, No. 158/16.

> support and training to enable CSO partners to fulfil the role of a "trusted reporter" or equivalent, with due respect to the need of maintaining their independence and credibility. […]
>
> The IT Companies [are] to provide regular training to their staff on current societal developments and to exchange views on the potential for further improvement.[67]

In practice, the algorithms and human interventions recently used by social media platforms to identify, review and remove hate speech content have proven to be inadequate. Another good reason for this is that those platforms inadequately trained persons to review the potentially harmful content. Most recently, social media platforms have been widely criticized for failure to remove offensive hate speech content while removing normal everyday content instead.

Therefore, it was recommended to co-operate with social media platforms by providing them with smartly drafted and updated keywords for alerting their systems. Training of human reviewers on how to do this critical job without compromising freedom of expression was also highly recommended. Engagement should also include exchanging views on the potential for further improvement. For example, a simple quotation of the *Qur'án* should not be censored unless it is accompanied with a perversive interpretation or a specific hate speech content directed at a religion, ethnicity, nationality, race, colour, descent, gender or any other identity factor. Also, Arabic expressions, such as *Állâhu Akbár* (الله أكبر), which means '*God is greater*', although unfortunately linked to use by suicide bombers and extremists, should not be censored *per se*, simply because this is a Muslim everyday expression. It does not have any violence-related meaning or connotation.

31.5. Lessons Learned

For a specialist advice to religious leaders responding to hate speech to be effective and productive, leaders should be approached very carefully and delicately. In a nutshell, the following rules are recommend:

1. Trust building and showing respect for faith should be the first steps to take.
2. Finding a common ground, on countering hate speech in this context, should follow.

---

[67] European Commission, "Code of Conduct on Countering Illegal Hate Speech Online", 30 June 2016, pp. 2–3 (https://www.legal-tools.org/doc/i7l80r/).

3. Advice should be relevant and problem-centred rather than content-centred. This means that examples given should reflect the real-life challenges.[68]
4. Advice should be given as an experience shared rather than a lesson taught.
5. Religious leaders should be involved in discussion, giving them the impression that they lead it and are not just listeners or learners. The advisor should still have control on the discussion. In in this regard, elicitation, as a presentation technique, can be used.

Some sensitive advice should be shared as a thought to reflect on or a question to answer in order to open the door for a discussion without any provocation or defensiveness.[69]

68 The author used examples from the website of the Observatory in preparation for the lecture delivered at the Florence conference on 9 April 2022.

69 For example, gender-inclusive language was addressed, in the context of showing religious leaders a world trend, asking them if this could be accommodated without prejudice to religious rules. Examples of Arabic language being gender-inclusive by nature were shown.

INDEX

A

C

D

E

F

I

J

K

P

Q

R

S

Ṣ

S

V

W

X

Y

Z

TOAEP TEAM

OTHER VOLUMES IN THE *PUBLICATION SERIES*

Morten Bergsmo, Mads Harlem and Nobuo Hayashi (editors):
Importing Core International Crimes into National Law
Torkel Opsahl Academic EPublisher
Oslo, 2010
FICHL Publication Series No. 1 (Second Edition, 2010)
ISBN: 978-82-93081-00-5

Nobuo Hayashi (editor):
National Military Manuals on the Law of Armed Conflict
Torkel Opsahl Academic EPublisher
Oslo, 2010
FICHL Publication Series No. 2 (Second Edition, 2010)
ISBN: 978-82-93081-02-9

Morten Bergsmo, Kjetil Helvig, Ilia Utmelidze and Gorana Žagovec:
The Backlog of Core International Crimes Case Files in Bosnia and Herzegovina
Torkel Opsahl Academic EPublisher
Oslo, 2010
FICHL Publication Series No. 3 (Second Edition, 2010)
ISBN: 978-82-93081-04-3

Morten Bergsmo (editor):
Criteria for Prioritizing and Selecting Core International Crimes Cases
Torkel Opsahl Academic EPublisher
Oslo, 2010
FICHL Publication Series No. 4 (Second Edition, 2010)
ISBN: 978-82-93081-06-7

Morten Bergsmo and Pablo Kalmanovitz (editors):
Law in Peace Negotiations
Torkel Opsahl Academic EPublisher
Oslo, 2010
FICHL Publication Series No. 5 (Second Edition, 2010)
ISBN: 978-82-93081-08-1

Morten Bergsmo, César Rodríguez Garavito, Pablo Kalmanovitz and Maria Paula Saffon (editors):
Distributive Justice in Transitions
Torkel Opsahl Academic EPublisher
Oslo, 2010
FICHL Publication Series No. 6 (2010)
ISBN: 978-82-93081-12-8

Morten Bergsmo, César Rodriguez-Garavito, Pablo Kalmanovitz and Maria Paula Saffon (editors):
Justicia Distributiva en Sociedades en Transición
Torkel Opsahl Academic EPublisher
Oslo, 2012
FICHL Publication Series No. 6 (2012)
ISBN: 978-82-93081-10-4

Morten Bergsmo (editor):
Complementarity and the Exercise of Universal Jurisdiction for Core International Crimes
Torkel Opsahl Academic EPublisher
Oslo, 2010
FICHL Publication Series No. 7 (2010)
ISBN: 978-82-93081-14-2

Morten Bergsmo (editor):
Active Complementarity: Legal Information Transfer
Torkel Opsahl Academic EPublisher
Oslo, 2011
FICHL Publication Series No. 8 (2011)
ISBN print: 978-82-93081-56-2
ISBN e-book: 978-82-93081-55-5

Morten Bergsmo (editor):
Abbreviated Criminal Procedures for Core International Crimes
Torkel Opsahl Academic EPublisher
Brussels, 2017
FICHL Publication Series No. 9 (2017)
ISBN print: 978-82-93081-20-3
ISBN e-book: 978-82-8348-104-4

Sam Muller, Stavros Zouridis, Morly Frishman and Laura Kistemaker (editors):
The Law of the Future and the Future of Law
Torkel Opsahl Academic EPublisher
Oslo, 2010
FICHL Publication Series No. 11 (2011)
ISBN: 978-82-93081-27-2

Morten Bergsmo, Alf Butenschøn Skre and Elisabeth J. Wood (editors):
Understanding and Proving International Sex Crimes
Torkel Opsahl Academic EPublisher
Beijing, 2012
FICHL Publication Series No. 12 (2012)
ISBN: 978-82-93081-29-6

Morten Bergsmo (editor):
Thematic Prosecution of International Sex Crimes
Torkel Opsahl Academic EPublisher
Brussels, 2018
Publication Series No. 13 (Second Edition, 2018)
ISBN print: 978-82-8348-025-2
ISBN e-book: 978-82-8348-024-5

Terje Einarsen:
The Concept of Universal Crimes in International Law
Torkel Opsahl Academic EPublisher
Oslo, 2012
FICHL Publication Series No. 14 (2012)
ISBN: 978-82-93081-33-3

莫滕·伯格斯默 凌岩(主编):
国家主权与国际刑法
Torkel Opsahl Academic EPublisher
Beijing, 2012
FICHL Publication Series No. 15 (2012)
ISBN: 978-82-93081-58-6

Morten Bergsmo and LING Yan (editors):
State Sovereignty and International Criminal Law
Torkel Opsahl Academic EPublisher
Beijing, 2012
FICHL Publication Series No. 15 (2012)
ISBN: 978-82-93081-35-7

Morten Bergsmo and CHEAH Wui Ling (editors):
Old Evidence and Core International Crimes
Torkel Opsahl Academic EPublisher
Beijing, 2012
FICHL Publication Series No. 16 (2012)
ISBN: 978-82-93081-60-9

YI Ping:
戦争と平和の間——発足期日本国際法学における「正しい戦争」の観念とその帰結
Torkel Opsahl Academic EPublisher
Beijing, 2013
FICHL Publication Series No. 17 (2013)
ISBN: 978-82-93081-66-1

Morten Bergsmo and SONG Tianying (editors):
On the Proposed Crimes Against Humanity Convention
Torkel Opsahl Academic EPublisher
Brussels, 2014
FICHL Publication Series No. 18 (2014)
ISBN: 978-82-93081-96-8

Morten Bergsmo and Carsten Stahn (editors):
Quality Control in Fact-Finding
Torkel Opsahl Academic EPublisher
Brussels, 2020
Publication Series No. 19 (Second Edition, 2020)
ISBN print: 978-82-8348-135-8
ISBN e-book: 978-82-8348-136-5

Morten Bergsmo, CHEAH Wui Ling and YI Ping (editors):
Historical Origins of International Criminal Law: Volume 1
Torkel Opsahl Academic EPublisher
Brussels, 2014
FICHL Publication Series No. 20 (2014)
ISBN: 978-82-93081-11-1

Morten Bergsmo, CHEAH Wui Ling and YI Ping (editors):
Historical Origins of International Criminal Law: Volume 2
Torkel Opsahl Academic EPublisher
Brussels, 2014
FICHL Publication Series No. 21 (2014)
ISBN: 978-82-93081-13-5

Morten Bergsmo, CHEAH Wui Ling, SONG Tianying and YI Ping (editors):
Historical Origins of International Criminal Law: Volume 3
Torkel Opsahl Academic EPublisher
Brussels, 2015
FICHL Publication Series No. 22 (2015)
ISBN print: 978-82-8348-015-3
ISBN e-book: 978-82-8348-014-6

Morten Bergsmo, CHEAH Wui Ling, SONG Tianying and YI Ping (editors):
Historical Origins of International Criminal Law: Volume 4
Torkel Opsahl Academic EPublisher
Brussels, 2015
FICHL Publication Series No. 23 (2015)
ISBN print: 978-82-8348-017-7
ISBN e-book: 978-82-8348-016-0

Morten Bergsmo, Klaus Rackwitz and SONG Tianying (editors):
Historical Origins of International Criminal Law: Volume 5
Torkel Opsahl Academic EPublisher
Brussels, 2017
FICHL Publication Series No. 24 (2017)
ISBN print: 978-82-8348-106-8
ISBN e-book: 978-82-8348-107-5

Morten Bergsmo and SONG Tianying (editors):
Military Self-Interest in Accountability for Core International Crimes
Torkel Opsahl Academic EPublisher
Brussels, 2015
FICHL Publication Series No. 25 (2015)
ISBN print: 978-82-93081-61-6
ISBN e-book: 978-82-93081-81-4

Wolfgang Kaleck:
Double Standards: International Criminal Law and the West
Torkel Opsahl Academic EPublisher
Brussels, 2015
FICHL Publication Series No. 26 (2015)
ISBN print: 978-82-93081-67-8
ISBN e-book: 978-82-93081-83-8

LIU Daqun and ZHANG Binxin (editors):
Historical War Crimes Trials in Asia
Torkel Opsahl Academic EPublisher
Brussels, 2016
FICHL Publication Series No. 27 (2015)
ISBN print: 978-82-8348-055-9
ISBN e-book: 978-82-8348-056-6

Morten Bergsmo, Mark Klamberg, Kjersti Lohne and Christopher B. Mahony (editors):
Power in International Criminal Justice
Torkel Opsahl Academic EPublisher
Brussels, 2020
Publication Series No. 28 (2020)
ISBN print: 978-82-8348-113-6
ISBN e-book: 978-82-8348-114-3

Mark Klamberg (editor):
Commentary on the Law of the International Criminal Court
Torkel Opsahl Academic EPublisher
Brussels, 2017
FICHL Publication Series No. 29 (2017)
ISBN print: 978-82-8348-100-6
ISBN e-book: 978-82-8348-101-3

Stian Nordengen Christensen:
Counterfactual History and Bosnia-Herzegovina
Torkel Opsahl Academic EPublisher
Brussels, 2018
Publication Series No. 30 (2018)
ISBN print: 978-82-8348-102-0
ISBN e-book: 978-82-8348-103-7

Stian Nordengen Christensen:
Possibilities and Impossibilities in a Contradictory Global Order
Torkel Opsahl Academic EPublisher
Brussels, 2018
Publication Series No. 31 (2018)
ISBN print: 978-82-8348-104-4
ISBN e-book: 978-82-8348-105-1

Morten Bergsmo and Carsten Stahn (editors):
Quality Control in Preliminary Examination: Volume 1
Torkel Opsahl Academic EPublisher
Brussels, 2018
Publication Series No. 32 (2018)
ISBN print: 978-82-8348-123-5
ISBN e-book: 978-82-8348-124-2

Morten Bergsmo and Carsten Stahn (editors):
Quality Control in Preliminary Examination: Volume 2
Torkel Opsahl Academic EPublisher
Brussels, 2018
Publication Series No. 33 (2018)
ISBN print: 978-82-8348-111-2
ISBN e-book: 978-82-8348-112-9

Morten Bergsmo and Emiliano J. Buis (editors):
Philosophical Foundations of International Criminal Law: Correlating Thinkers
Torkel Opsahl Academic EPublisher
Brussels, 2018
Publication Series No. 34 (2018)
ISBN print: 978-82-8348-117-4
ISBN e-book: 978-82-8348-118-1

Morten Bergsmo and Emiliano J. Buis (editors):
Philosophical Foundations of International Criminal Law: Foundational Concepts
Torkel Opsahl Academic EPublisher
Brussels, 2019
Publication Series No. 35 (2019)
ISBN print: 978-82-8348-119-8
ISBN e-book: 978-82-8348-120-4

Morten Bergsmo, Emiliano J. Buis and SONG Tianying (editors):
Philosophical Foundations of International Criminal Law: Legally-Protected Interests
Torkel Opsahl Academic EPublisher
Brussels, 2022
Publication Series No. 36 (2022)
ISBN print: 978-82-8348-121-1
ISBN e-book: 978-82-8348-122-8

Terje Einarsen and Joseph Rikhof:
A Theory of Punishable Participation in Universal Crimes
Torkel Opsahl Academic EPublisher
Brussels, 2018
Publication Series No. 37 (2018)
ISBN print: 978-82-8348-127-3
ISBN e-book: 978-82-8348-128-0

Xabier Agirre Aranburu, Morten Bergsmo, Simon De Smet and Carsten Stahn (editors):
Quality Control in Criminal Investigation
Torkel Opsahl Academic EPublisher
Brussels, 2020
Publication Series No. 38 (2020)
ISBN print: 978-82-8348-129-7
ISBN e-book: 978-82-8348-130-3

Morten Bergsmo, Wolfgang Kaleck and Kyaw Yin Hlaing (editors):
Colonial Wrongs and Access to International Law
Torkel Opsahl Academic EPublisher
Brussels, 2020
Publication Series No. 40 (2020)
ISBN print: 978-82-8348-133-4
ISBN e-book: 978-82-8348-134-1

Morten Bergsmo and Kishan Manocha (editors):
Religion, Hateful Expression and Violence
Torkel Opsahl Academic EPublisher
Brussels, 2023
Publication Series No. 41 (2023)
ISBN print: 978-82-8348-141-9
ISBN e-book: 978-82-8348-142-6

All volumes are freely available online at http://www.toaep.org/ps/. For printed copies, see http://www.toaep.org/about/distribution/. For reviews of earlier books in this Series in academic journals and yearbooks, see http://www.toaep.org/reviews/.

www.ingramcontent.com/pod-product-compliance
Lightning Source LLC
Chambersburg PA
CBHW051542260926
51849CB00011B/514/J